MW01198739

EXPERIENCING LAW SERIES™

EXPERIENCING TRUSTS AND ESTATES

SECOND EDITION

Deborah S. Gordon
Associate Professor of Law
Drexel University Thomas R. Kline School of Law

Karen J. Sneddon
Professor of Law
Mercer University School of Law

Carla Spivack
Professor of Law
Oklahoma City University School of Law

Allison Anna Tait
Professor of Law
University of Richmond School of Law

Alfred L. Brophy
Judge John J. Parker Distinguished Professor of Law

WEST
ACADEMIC
PUBLISHING

© 2017 LEG, Inc. d/b/a West Academic
© 2021 LEG, Inc. d/b/a West Academic
    444 Cedar Street, Suite 700
    St. Paul, MN 55101
    1-877-888-1330
West, West Academic Publishing, and West Academic are trademarks of West Publishing Corporation, used under license.

Printed in the United States of America

ISBN: 978-1-64708-370-0

Summary of Contents

Table of Contents

Table of Cases

The principal cases are in bold type.

EXPERIENCING TRUSTS AND ESTATES

SECOND EDITION

CHAPTER 1

The Drama of Intergenerational Wealth Transfer

CHAPTER LEARNING OUTCOMES

Following your work with the material in this chapter, you should be able to do the following:

- Describe the individuals, entities, and institutions involved in inheritance

- List the commonly used estate planning documents

- Define basic vocabulary related to inheritance

- Distinguish between probate succession and nonprobate succession

- Identify the textbook themes

> "All the world's a stage,
> And all the men and women merely players;
> They have their exits and their entrances. . ."
> —*As You Like It*, William Shakespeare

A. Introduction: Setting the Stage

If all the world is indeed a stage, the purpose of this textbook is to introduce readers to one particular play that recurs on that stage—the drama of intergenerational wealth transfer. It will also introduce the players in that drama. Wealth transfer at death is a universal experience, even though what people transfer varies tremendously in economic value and personal meaning, and even though people rely on a range of mechanisms (including default rules) to make the transfers.

All families, regardless of their wealth or status, have a unique range of resources that they wish to pass down from one generation to another. These resources may be economically valuable, such as a family business, a family home, or even family furniture that has been cherished and preserved through the years. Families also pass down objects that have primarily sentimental value, such as recipes, holiday decorations, and photo albums. In all these cases, inheritance is important because it creates bonds among family members. Passing down special books, jewelry, or any other collectibles from a parent to a child creates a shared space of ownership and memory. Likewise, as we will see, leaving a child out of a will or estate plan may send strong signals and say something about family dynamics. Wealth transfer is also important because it is the way in which families as a whole create intergenerational identity as well as a sense of family belonging. Items that transfer from one generation to the

People acquire and dispose of a variety of assets during their lifetime. These Sèvres vases, manufactured around 1750, were owned by the Rothschilds, the Countess of Carnarvon, and the Walters Family in Baltimore. They currently are on display in the Walters Art Museum, Baltimore.

next through inheritance are building blocks for families as the items shape stories, memories, and traditions to build a sense of "family identity." Inheritance helps families to define, and maintain, their special identity, and this identity is communicated not only among family members but also to the world at large.

Widening the stage, we will see how inheritance rules shape the social landscape of wealth and inequality. While it is true that all families have some form of resources and unique legacies to pass on, some families have vast and valuable assets that they pass down, allowing them to consolidate family wealth, privilege, and status. As one report has stated: "The historical wealth advantage . . . is transferred to the next generation as they inherit wealth of previous generations and use that wealth to provide themselves and their children with access to education, capital for entrepreneurship, and opportunities to build more wealth."[1] In other words, wealth flows down the generations in families, and accumulates along the way, creating and recreating inequality. At the end of this book, we will circle back to this issue when we discuss taxation. We will ask, to what extent governments should use taxes to divert some of the wealth that

1   Mariko Chang, *Lifting as We Climb*, INSIGHT CTR. COMMUNITY ECON. DEV. (2010), available at https://static1.squarespace.com/static/5c50b84131d4df5265e7392d/t/5c5c7801ec212d4fd499ba39/1549563907681/Lifting_As_We_Climb_InsightCCED_2010.pdf.

flows through families to the rest of society—estate and gift taxes, inheritance taxes, and wealth taxes.

High-net-worth families consolidate their wealth through inheritance while middle- and low-wealth families pass down much smaller amounts of wealth and sometimes just debt. The Forbes billionaires list and "Richest 400" lists provide a window into this link between wealth and inheritance. In 2019, seven of the twenty wealthiest members of the Forbes 400 made the list solely on the basis of their inherited wealth, and many were members of the same family. These families strategically transferred wealth from one generation to the next through a complicated system of trusts, charitable foundations, and corporate entities. That same Forbes billionaire list evidences a gender wealth gap, showing that out of 2,153 billionaires, only 244 (11%) were

Issues of race, gender, and class will be explored throughout this textbook. ©AndyDavey, first published in The Sun (London), 2010.

women. There is also a well-documented racial wealth gap. White families are significantly more likely to inherit than their black counterparts and "28 % of whites received bequests, compared to just 7.7 % of black families."[2] Even among those families receiving inheritances, black families receive less: "Blacks received 8 cents of inheritance for every dollar inherited by whites."[3] Black families, as a result, hold less wealth than white families do even in the upper echelons of wealth: "The 99th percentile black family is worth a mere $1,574,000 while the 99th percentile white family is worth over 12 million dollars."[4] Similar studies have found that, "while Latinx workers are more likely to hold full-time jobs than white workers, their median wealth is only 14.6% of the typical white family's wealth."[5] Not surprisingly, the starkest measure of the wealth gap involves women who are Black, Indigenous and People of Color (BIPOC). While there is most certainly a gender wealth gap—such that overall in 2013 single women held only 32 cents of wealth for every dollar of wealth owned by

[2]   Cedric Herring & Loren Henderson, Wealth Inequality in Black and White: Cultural and Structural Sources of the Racial Wealth Gap, 8 RACE & SOC. PROBS. 4 (2016).

[3]   Id.

[4]   William Darity Jr. et al., What We Get Wrong About Closing the Racial Wealth Gap, INSIGHT CTR. COMMUNITY ECON. DEV. 2 (2018), available at https://socialequity.duke.edu/sites/socialequity.duke.edu/files/site-images/FINAL%20COMPLETE%20REPORT_.pdf.

[5]   https://www.americanprogress.org/press/release/2018/12/05/461651/release-latinx-wealth-gap-latinx-families-work-hold-less-one-sixth-wealth-white-families/.

a single man[6]—the numbers for BIPOC women are even more uneven. According to a 2015 report, "the median wealth of White single women was $15,640. Yet, the median wealth for single Black women and Latina women was $200 and $100 respectively, about one cent for every dollar of White women's wealth."[7] These wealth gaps are important to consider as we explore who gets to play what role onstage in our wealth transfer production and how we might revise the script to not only include but also benefit an expanded set of players.

The main goal of this textbook is to introduce you to the rules of intergenerational wealth transfer and to apply them to various wealth transfer scenarios. We will explore all the different modes of transfer, most particularly wills and trusts, and we will ask questions about what the consequences of our current legal framework for wealth transfer are—as well as what outcomes we would like to see. This chapter provides an overview of the players in our drama, the various settings that serve as a backdrop to wealth transfer, and the tools and scripts that our players use. In **Part B**, we introduce you to the players involved in wealth transfer: lawyers, clients, judges, and courts. You will also learn about the people who are left out of the play and overlooked by the traditional legal narrative. **Part C** explores the tools of wealth transfer and provides an overview of what documents people use for planning—from healthcare directives to wills and trusts; which institutions, both public and private, govern transfers; and where these processes take place—in family homes, probate courts, and bank offices. **Part D** then provides a roadmap for the book and explains in greater detail what the chapters to come discuss and the approach we have taken to assessing your understanding and opinions on these issues. In this part we also explain, as authors, our personal and collective approach to the material and some of the key themes that have motivated us in putting together these materials.

B. The Players on the Stage

1. The Lawyers

Estate planning lawyers play many roles. Of course, they help clients with planning for wealth transfer upon death, by drafting their wills and trusts, as well as with end-of-life planning, such as **living wills**,[8] **advance directives**, and

---

[6]   https://inequality.org/racial-wealth-divide-snapshot-women/.

[7]   https://inequality.org/racial-wealth-divide-snapshot-women/.

[8]   Bolded terms are defined in the Glossary.

health care proxies, and planning for loss of capacity with **powers of attorney.** As an estate planning attorney, you might have other roles as well, such as:

- You might find yourself advising an executor or trustee about that fiduciary's duties under a will or a trust and, in fact, you might find yourself serving in one of those roles

- You might advise someone who was left out of a will, or who received less than expected, and wants to challenge the will's validity

- You might have as a client a bank or life insurance company with questions about the rights and duties associated with an account or about paying out death benefits

- You might serve as an advisor to a state legislature investigating whether to adopt a Uniform Act or change the state's succession laws

- Your client might hold a power of attorney or a health care proxy and have questions about duties under the instrument

- You might advise a family business about transferring ownership from one generation to the next or outside the family altogether

- You might work for a charity, trust company, bank, or other organization or entity to help guide benefactors or clients to plan in a way that benefits the organization in addition to the individuals

- You might help a client who stands to inherit under a will about the consequences of accepting or refusing to accept (**disclaiming**) the gift: taxes, eligibility for government benefits, etc.

2.   The Clients

Estate planning clients often—but not always—fall into certain categories. For example, there is the category of the young married couple with young children. Each category—or grouping—requires you to address particular issues in its estate plan (for example, a couple with minor children needs to plan for their children in case something happens to both of them). Indeed, many estate planning attorneys have different intake questionnaires for each group, based on the needs that type of client is likely to have.

Here are some common categories:

- Young, single professional
- Married couple without children
- Married couple with young children
- Married couple with adult children
- Older married couple with grandchildren
- Widow or widower
- Unmarried cohabitants without children
- Unmarried cohabitants with children
- Older, never married cohabitants
- Divorced, not remarried individuals

The above categories are different, but each one is pretty straightforward. Below are some more complicated, but not unusual, situations you may encounter:

- A client who wants to disinherit one of her children, a daughter, because she is gay and is in a committed relationship with another woman

- A client who has three children and two grandchildren but wants to leave his entire estate to the National Wildlife Foundation; he says his children are doing fine and can take care of themselves and their own families

- A client who is in a second marriage, with a child of that marriage, and also has a child from a former marriage; she wants to leave part of her estate to the child from the former marriage, but her current spouse wants everything to go to the child they have together

- A client who is old and a bit cranky, sometimes wanders off topic, and tells stories from the past; he does know what he owns, however, and to whom he wants to leave it

- A client who is a very rushed single parent without much money

- A client who is a self-made millionaire, has built many businesses from the ground up, and wants her kids to work for a living; she wants to leave her estate to the local University Theater Department

- A client who is REALLY uncomfortable talking about death

- A client who has two children, a son, who is a doctor and makes a half a million a year, and a daughter, who works part time as a librarian; the client wants to leave the bulk of his estate to the daughter, who needs it more, and he has already explained this plan to the son, who is okay with the plan and seems to understand why the client wants to do it this way

- And, sooner or later, you'll have the client who wants to disinherit her kids and leave her estate to someone to care for her twelve cats

ASSESSMENTS

1. Imagine you work for an estate planning law firm that is redesigning its client intake questionnaire. Write a memo to your supervisor listing some of the primary concerns and issues of the people in each of the above "common" categories.

2. Pick one of the more complicated categories listed above and roleplay a meeting where you counsel that client. As you prepare for and conduct the client meeting, consider what additional considerations you might want to cover, including:

- Would you recommend any additional measures or documents besides the basic will/trust/power of attorney advance directive?

- Would you advise the client to take any action on their own to make sure their wishes were carried out smoothly?

- In your role as holistic counselor, what advice other than strictly legal advice might you offer the client, if any?

3. The Judges

Generally, a judge who deals with the disposition of a decedent's estate is a **Probate Court Judge** (although probate courts go under a variety of names in different states, such as **Orphans' Courts**, **Chancery Courts**, or **Surrogate's Courts**). Probate judges are generally selected by the same process as other state judges—they can be elected or appointed, depending on the state. Usually, a probate judge must have a law degree, but some states do not require it. Despite this, probate judges often deal with many other issues besides wills and decedent's estates: in some states, this court's jurisdiction includes adoption, competency hearings, appointment of guardians and conservators, and sometimes family matters—divorce, child support, visitation—as well.

Probate judges have different duties depending on the nature of the probate. In cases where there is a will, everyone involved gets along, and no one contests the will, the judge's role generally consists of signing orders to move the probate process along its various stages.[9] In cases where there is a will, but some beneficiaries or heirs contest it, or have other disputes with each other or with the executor, the judge will be more involved. The judge may make rulings about disputed issues and decide whether to allow various kinds of evidence. Where the decedent did not leave a will—died **intestate**—the probate judge must appoint a personal representative (called an **administrator**) who will be in charge of gathering the estate assets, paying debts, and distributing the remaining property to the heirs. Once there is a personal representative, the judge's role is minimal, mostly the same as it would be in cases of an uncontested will.

4. Who Is Missing from the Stage?

Many people who would benefit from receiving estate planning services do not receive them. Over half the population dies intestate, and that percentage is greater in minority communities. As we will see, the laws that govern **intestate succession** (the distribution of property of people who die without wills) are far from perfect, and often fail to carry out what decedents would have wanted. For most people, working with an estate planning attorney will more accurately carry out their wishes and benefit those they want to benefit.

Intestacy laws fail to acknowledge all categories of people who might be a decedent's intended beneficiaries. Intestacy laws are based on what some have criticized as outdated notions of family—notions that family is defined solely by ties of blood, marriage, or formal adoption. This approach ignores the many ties people form today that fall outside of these categories. For example, 40% of children today are born to unwed parents, and large numbers are being raised by couples who live together without formal marriage. But there are more hurdles to inheriting from an unmarried parent than from one who was legally married to the biological mother. And, about half the couples living together are unmarried. Yet when one of these partners dies without a will, intestacy usually does not allow the survivor to inherit any of the estate. Nor do intestacy laws include foster children or stepchildren who are not formally adopted. Given the

---

[9]   Some jurisdictions do not require a judge's involvement at all if a will is not contested; probate is commenced by filing with the Registry of Wills and overseen by an elected official.

number of blended families, these gaps leave out many intended beneficiaries whom the decedent may have treated like biological children.

And then there is the requirement that a child be formally adopted to inherit under intestacy. For communities with less access to law and lawyers, informal adoption is more the norm. Moreover, many Black and other minority communities have long-standing traditions of informal adoption—a custom arising from slavery, when children whose enslaved parents were sold were taken in and cared for by other adults. Here, intestacy laws fail to recognize a parent-child relationship with all the emotional attachment of any other and do so in a way that disadvantages minority communities in particular. Throughout the book, we'll consider under what circumstances the laws need to be updated, expanded, or adapted to reflect modern relationships and modern forms of property.

Given the inadequacy of intestacy, why do so many people fail to do estate planning? There are many reasons: fear of death, concerns about cost, reluctance to deal with lawyers, lack of awareness, and good old procrastination. Another theme we will return to in this book is how estate planning attorneys can better reach out to these people in general, and underserved communities in particular, to encourage estate planning and make it accessible and affordable.

Sometimes people do recognize the importance of estate planning but do it on their own without legal advice. Someone like this might draft her own will, for example, or use a preprinted will form or online will drafting package. Unfortunately, these methods often fail to carry out the property owner's intent or fail entirely and cause the estate to wind up in intestacy anyway. For one thing, homemade wills often fail because they do not have the requisite execution formalities (witnesses, etc.) which in many states are still quite strict. People who cannot afford—or think they cannot afford—estate planning advice can fall into this category. The laws requiring very specific and detailed execution formalities leave out those who cannot pay an attorney to get them right.

As the course progresses, the theme of who is left out will keep resurfacing. There are many career possibilities in finding ways to include omitted groups in the estate planning process, and this inclusion can also help more people's wishes to be carried out and more intended beneficiaries to receive their shares.

C. Different Documents and Different Procedures

The clients who seek the assistance of lawyers in this area will have varied goals and needs that encompass, but are broader than, planning for property transfer at death. It may be helpful to think of these needs in these three categories:

- Property management during life
- Care of self in medical matters
- Transmission of property at death

Each of these categories may require a variety of documents, all of which an attorney may need to draft, interpret, or file.

1. Property Management

Although an individual may equate estate planning with transmission of property upon the property owner's death, a significant part of the practice involves property management during the property owner's lifetime. Property management may require the creation, interpretation, or filing of the following documents:

- Lifetime **trusts** (including **revocable trusts** and **irrevocable trusts**, often to make gifts or hold life insurance)
- Financial power of attorney (both **durable powers of attorney** and **springing powers of attorney**)
- Deeds (such as joint tenancy with right of survivorship)
- Multi-party bank accounts (including true joint accounts and convenience accounts)
- Partnership agreements
- Beneficiary designation forms (including beneficiary designation forms for life insurance policies and retirement plans)
- Business entity formation and governance documents
- Gift agreements
- Charitable gift agreements and **private foundations**
- Marital agreements (premarital agreements, marital agreements, and divorce settlements)
- Contracts for personal services
- Tax returns (such as individual income tax returns, **fiduciary income tax returns**, **gift tax returns**, **estate tax returns**, and entity tax returns)

- Other tax-related documentation (such as **Crummey letters**)

2.   Care of Self

Moreover, planning in this area is not restricted to decisions related to property. They also include making decisions about care in the event an individual is unable to participate in the decision-making process. The following documents may be created, interpreted, or filed:

- Advance directives (including a living will and a health care power of attorney)

- Guardianship proceeding materials and related documents (such as reports from the guardian ad litem)

3.   Transmission of Property at Death

A significant aspect of planning does, of course, involve the transmission of property upon the death of the property owner. As we'll see throughout this book, tensions can arise when balancing the competing interests of the wishes of the individual property owner, the needs of the survivors, and goals of the community. The transmission of property upon death includes the creation, interpretation, and filing of the following documents:

- Wills (which may include testamentary trusts), **codicils**, and will revocations

- Deeds (particularly the **TOD Deed**)

- Contracts (including life insurance contracts and retirement accounts)

- Multi-party bank accounts (specifically payable-on-death accounts, transferable-on-death accounts, and joint accounts)

- Revocable trusts

- Probate petitions and related probate proceedings (such as interrogatories of attesting witnesses)

- Objections (also called **caveats**) to the probate proceedings

- **Accountings** by fiduciaries

Some of the documents created to transmit property upon the death of the property owner will have lifetime property management benefits too. They all, however, provide for a mechanism to transfer property upon the death of the property owner. To understand the legal instruments and processes under which property is transferred upon death, you need to understand the nature of the property interests. Specifically, you need to grasp the distinction between **probate property** and **nonprobate property**, which can help you understand the different ways in which the court may (or may not) become involved in facilitating the transmission of these property interests.

The following subsections take you through what happens when an individual dies. The purpose of this discussion is to illustrate the role of the documents created, interpreted, and filed, and the procedures, specifically probate succession versus nonprobate succession, that are foundational to the work in all later chapters.

a. *What to Do When Someone Dies*

As we'll discuss in the next chapter, a significant portion of an estate planner's work focuses on death and dying. Although we all have had personal experiences with a loved one's death, we do not necessarily recognize all the legal aspects of death. After an individual dies, a legal pronouncement of death is required. If the individual dies in a medical setting, the medical staff or hospital administrators arrange for the legal pronouncement. If the individual dies in a non-medical setting, the police should be contacted. Possible organ donation is then explored, as informed by the individual's choices on a driver's license or an advance directive. Family members must make decisions involving the final disposition of the individual's remains, keeping in mind wishes the person may have expressed in the advance directive or in other ways. The individual, for example, may have contracted with a funeral home or expressed preferences to loved ones. If the person never expressed any preferences, the traditional choices are burial, cremation, or full-body donation. But, as we discuss later in the book, today there are increasingly creative and eco-friendly options for disposal of remains.

The family should promptly notify the individual's loved ones, as well as the individual's employer and the Social Security Office. Someone should also arrange for care of the individual's dependents and pets. It's also important that the family secure the person's property by collecting personal effects from the hospital and ensuring that the home is locked. Then, the survivors need to arrange the memorial service, arrange to have an obituary written, and buy a headstone, if necessary.

After the survivors address the immediate matters surrounding a loved one's death, attention turns to handling the transfer of the individual's many and varied property interests. An initial step is to order multiple copies of the death certificate. Arranging for all necessary transfers requires approximately 5–10. The funeral director can obtain the copies, as can a family member, from the local records office, such as city hall. Then, the loved ones can begin the procedures for transferring the individual's property.

The individual who has died is known as the **decedent**, and we use that term throughout the textbook. A decedent may express wishes about the transfer of the decedent's property by creating some of the legal instruments described above. Alternatively, the decedent may have never created a valid legal instrument (a will, trust, beneficiary designation, or otherwise) expressing his or her wishes. To understand the procedure or procedures in that case, it's necessary to understand the probate process and the nonprobate process, which we discuss below.

b.   *Probate Administration and Key Probate Vocabulary*

Two categories of property go through the probate process. When the decedent dies owning **probate property**, which is property transferred by the terms of a valid testamentary instrument (i.e., a **will** or **codicil**), **probate succession** occurs. The procedure for the transfer of probate property is called **probate administration, probate proceeding,** or **probate process**. The procedure is typically referred to as just "**probate**." When someone dies without a will but owning property that cannot be transferred by the terms of a governing instrument (like a deed or life insurance policy), this property also passes through probate. This is called **intestate succession.** We first explain probate succession and then intestate succession. Notice that a person could leave both property passing by will and property that passes by intestate succession because it was left out of the will.

The decedent's loved ones need to determine whether the decedent ever created a valid will. If so, there will be probate succession. A decedent who dies with a valid will is the **testator** (that is, a person who left a testament). In general, the will is a writing (in very rare instances, it could be an oral communication) that is signed by the testator and appropriately witnessed. The will leaves instructions for what should happen with the testator's property. Traditionally, we would speak of real property as having been **devised** and personal property **bequeathed**, although few distinguish between these terms nowadays. The will designates the decedent's **beneficiaries**. When the decedent dies with a valid will, the property that the will governs is referred to as the **testate estate**, the **probate estate**, or simply the **estate**.

Language Note: Historically, gendered suffixes distinguished female from male actors. So, for example, a woman who made a will was a "testatrix" while a man who made a will was a "testator" and a female executor was referred to as an "executrix." Our language and law have evolved, and that gendered language has fallen out of use. *See Reed v. Reed,* 404 U.S. 71, 76–77 (1971) (invalidating on Equal Protection grounds an Idaho statute that preferred men over women as estate fiduciaries). Accordingly, all cases in the text have been edited to use the term testator, executor, administrator, without distinction as to gender. *Reed v. Reed* was the first sex discrimination case that Ruth Bader Ginsburg briefed to the Supreme Court; she called it her "grandmother case." Her role in this case began her decades long series of cases that piece by piece dismantled sex discrimination under the law. *Reed* provided the basis for, among others, the decision in *United States v. Virginia,* which struck down the Virginia Military Academy's male only admissions policy.

Ruth Bader Ginsburg and Allen Derr argued on behalf of Sally Reed to challenge the Idaho law that preferred male personal representatives over female representatives in the case of *Reed v. Reed,* 404 U.S. 71 (1971). Sixteen lawyers refused Reed's case before she found Derr. The Sally Reed Memorial is in Boise, Idaho.

A will also typically names an **executor** (sometimes called a **personal representative**) to handle probate. The executor may be an individual, several individuals, or an institution with fiduciary powers, such as a trust company. The executor continues, at least for a time, the legal existence of the decedent. The executor has a series of duties. The duties primarily require the executor to do the following:

- Collect and inventory the assets of the estate
- Give notice to creditors of the estate and permit them to file claims against the estate
- Pay creditors
- Distribute estate assets

In addition to the duties above, the executor also manages the estate while probate is pending. This means that the executor must safeguard and maintain the probate property during the proceedings. For instance, the executor should ensure that property insurance premiums and property taxes are paid. The executor is also responsible for filing the individual's last income tax return and notifying credit reporting agencies.

The core functions of the probate process go hand-in-hand with the executor's duties. Specifically, the probate proceedings do the following:

- Provide evidence of transfer of title
- Satisfy (and protect) creditors by providing a procedure for paying debts
- Collect assets and distribute the remainder to persons or institutions after creditors are paid
- Resolve conflicts among heirs and beneficiaries

When a decedent dies without a will, that person is said to have died **intestate** (and the person is sometimes actually called the **intestate**). **Intestate succession**, rather than testate succession, occurs. The property may be referred to as the **intestate estate**. The property may also be referred to as the probate estate or the estate, even in intestacy. **Intestate succession statutes** in the state of the decedent's domicile at the time of the decedent's death determine the identity of the decedent's intestate **heirs**. The state statute also determines who should be appointed to **administer** the estate (and that person is the **administrator** rather than the executor). The term "probate" typically refers only to probate succession proceedings. Intestate succession proceedings are called **administration**, although many people commonly refer to administration as probate even when the procedures deal with intestate succession. An administrator's duties are much the same as those of an executor.

The case that follows helps to illustrate the expectations that probate courts have for an executor.

In re Estate of Walter[10]

191 A.3d 873 (Pa. Super. Ct. 2018)

STEVENS, J.

Lynn M. Walter, former Executor for the estate of Carryl Walter, appeals from the order entered by the Court of Common Pleas of Cumberland County sustaining objections to her accounting upon a finding of improper distributions and misappropriation of funds. We affirm.

PROCEDURAL HISTORY

A Decree of Probate and a Grant of Letters Testamentary were entered on May 19, 2011, in the Cumberland County Office of Register of Wills and Clerk of the Orphans' Court for Decedent's Will executed on November 12, 2010. The Commonwealth, acting as parens patriae because the will named charities as beneficiaries, filed a petition to void gifts allegedly made pursuant to the Will.

In June 2015, the Executor was removed.

FACTS

This case arises out of the embezzlement of Estate funds by the now-former Estate attorney, while under the fiduciary eyes of the now-former Executor. Carryl Walter died testate on May 11, 2011; Decedent left major assets of cash, a gold and silver coin collection in a safe deposit box, and a mobile home. Executor is Decedent's ex-daughter-in-law who is a former payroll supervisor with the Harrisburg School District.

In the Will, bequests were given to Executor, $50,000.00; to Executor's daughter, $20,000; to Executor's son, $20,000.00; with a specific gift of the coin collection to the National Military Family Association.

The coin collection was removed from a safe deposit box and sold for $92,314.00. Executor set up a separate Estate bank account for the coin proceeds to send to the charity per good accounting practice, but instead the

---

[10]　　All cases have been edited by the textbook authors to be more conducive to the learning goals of the text. Full versions of the cases are available on electronic research databases.

funds were transferred to Attorney's account allegedly at the charity's request, and Attorney subsequently embezzled those funds. Executor was told by Attorney that the charity had sent an email requesting cash in lieu of coin delivery, but she never saw any documentation to that effect. Attorney also embezzled various funds from the Estate, including directly from the Estate's bank savings accounts, totaling $32,623.36. Attorney has been permitted by Executor to be the lone signatory of such accounts.

DISCUSSION

When reviewing a decree entered by the Orphans' Court, this Court must determine whether the record is free from legal error and the court's factual findings are supported by the evidence.

Our Supreme Court has recognized that "[w]here a fiduciary acts upon the advice of counsel, such fact is 'a factor to be considered in determining good faith, but is not a blanket of immunity in all circumstances.' " *In re Lohm's Estate*, 440 Pa. 268, 269 A.2d 451, 455 (1970). The initial choice of counsel must have been prudent under all the circumstances then existing, and the subsequent decision to rely upon this counsel must also have been a reasonably wise and prudent choice.

Executor argues the Orphans' Court failed to give appropriate weight to the undisputed fact that her choice of Attorney was prudent under all circumstances then existing. Neither the Commonwealth nor Appellee (the present Administrator of Decedent's Estate) disputes that the appointment of Attorney, which was consistent with the directive of Decedent's Will, was reasonable. They do contest, however, Executor's suggestion that this factor carries enough weight to offset her subsequent pattern of inattention to the depletion of estate assets over the course of years.

The Orphans' Court acknowledged a prudent person in Executor's position may not have discovered all Attorney's actions that gave rise to the objections filed in this matter—Attorney's avarice and gambling addiction were unforeseeable causes of early estate dissipation. Attorney's protracted pattern of embezzlement, however, was discoverable with the exercise of due diligence, such that Executor was not discharged from her fiduciary accountabilities to protect and preserve the estate in this respect. We agree.

We also find the record belies Executor's contention that the weight of the evidence tipped in favor of finding that she made good faith efforts to act with prudence and wisdom in administering the estate only to be derailed by Attorney's skillful deception. Indeed, the instances of Executor's administrative breakdowns, which ranged from recurring failures of due diligence to benefitting herself to the detriment of other beneficiaries, were many.

"One's appointment as an estate executor confers an honor and trust and, commensurately, the duty to oversee the administration with competence to avoid compromising the probity of the estate. At a minimum, this requires one to investigate estate transactions to determine their soundness prior to approval." *Matter of Estate of Frey*, 693 A.2d 1349, 1353 (Pa. Super. Ct. 1997).

Rather than investigate three separate bank notices advising overdraft fees had been assessed on checking and savings accounts holding estate assets, Executor simply relied upon Attorney's unsubstantiated assurances that the notices were of no concern, which enabled Attorney to steal from the estate for years. A prudent executor with experience as a professional bookkeeper would have investigated and ascertained the reasons for the serial overdraft notices. Executor's failure to bequeath Decedent's valuable gold and silver coin collection to the National Military Family Association, as the Will specifically directed, was another example of Executor's unreasonable administration of the estate. Instead of carrying out the Will's bequest in this regard, Executor opted to believe Attorney's false claim that the charity preferred cash instead of the coins, and she agreed to convert the estate's interest in the coins to $92,314.00 cash and to place the funds in Attorney's account on the pretense that he would distribute them to the charity.

Never did Executor verify with the charity that it had made this request or investigate if it was within her powers to deviate from the Will's specific bequest. Nor, for that matter, did she ask Attorney to provide documentary proof that the charity received all income from the coin sale. Instead, Executor uncritically agreed with Attorney's plan to liquidate a unique and valuable estate asset and place the cash into his account, over which she would have no supervisory powers. Clearly, this was another in a series of unreasonable and imprudent decisions inconsistent with Executor's fiduciary duties to the estate and its intended beneficiaries.

More was due from Executor than strict adherence to the estate attorney's advice. We discern no abuse of discretion in the Orphans' Court's findings and conclusions.

ASSESSMENT

Your client's cousin has just asked if the client would be willing to serve as executor of the cousin's estate. Advise the client, either in writing or a face-to-face meeting, about what the client will need to do as executor.

c. Nonprobate Proceedings and Key Nonprobate Vocabulary

The decedent may have died owning no probate property, yet the decedent may still have property interests that require transfer upon death. In that instance, the decedent probably owned property that is classified as **nonprobate property**. Nonprobate property is property that passes upon the property owner's death by a legal instrument that is *not* a will or a codicil. The nonprobate property is controlled by a **nonprobate device**, also called a **will substitute**. The nonprobate device may be a contract, a deed, a multi-party bank account, or a trust instrument. Each of these devices has its own procedures that allow the **designated beneficiary** to receive the property. The nonprobate device may designate the **primary beneficiary** and may designate a **contingent beneficiary**, also called an alternate beneficiary.

The process typically involves the submission of completed paperwork and the decedent's death certificate to the financial institution, plan administrator, or trustee who manages the property. The transfer of property interests via nonprobate devices is called **nonprobate succession**. Today, substantial amounts of property are passed via nonprobate succession. Typically, the transfer of nonprobate property is outside of the supervision of the probate court. When disputes arise, however, such as to who is the properly designated beneficiary, parties may seek resolution in the probate court. To what extent the nonprobate property may be subject to the decedent's debts or creditor claims is a topic in Chapter 13.

d. Summary of Probate Proceeding Mechanics

While this course is largely about the law of wills and trusts, rather than probate procedure, it is helpful to have some familiarity with the mechanics of the probate proceedings. Even lawyers who focus on the drafting and creating of the documents often engage in this aspect of court proceedings. As noted above, each jurisdiction has its own unique probate system, with considerable variation among (and sometimes even within) states. Early probate courts in the United States exercised equity jurisdiction. Modern counterparts of equity courts are chancery, surrogate, and orphan's courts. In other jurisdictions, a judge within a court of broader jurisdiction has responsibility for probate cases because of that judge's expertise or interest. And still other states have full-time probate judges or even separate probate courts. In 2012, a joint task force studied probate proceedings around the country and appointed a 15-member commission that ultimately promulgated national standards in an effort to reform and improve "the administration, operations, and performance" of courts exercising probate jurisdiction; these standards, which are "intended to promote uniformity, consistency, and improvement in the operation of probate courts" were adopted by the National College of Probate Court Judges and various court and bar associations. Primarily an aspirational document, these standards also describe the evolution of, and challenges faced by, probate courts. *See* Revised National Probate Court Standards (2013).

Probate proceedings are generally held in the state and county where the decedent died domiciled. If the decedent owned property in another state, an **ancillary probate** (that is, a probate in that state) might be necessary (and an **ancillary executor** or **ancillary administrator** appointed). Procedures vary from state to state. States typically have two types of probate proceedings: **solemn form** and **common form**. Although the two forms have much in common, the solemn form requires notification to all heirs with the common form requiring no notification. For that reason, the common form probate procedures do not become binding until a longer period has elapsed from the initial filings. The state court system often has a manual that documents the basic procedures for estate administration in that jurisdiction. This manual is typically posted on the probate court's website. Standard forms are also made available on the website.

Typically, the probate process begins with the named executor filing for **letters testamentary** in the county where the decedent was domiciled. Commencing the probate process usually involves filing a petition along with a death certificate and the original will. In Philadelphia, for example, probate of a testate estate begins at the Register of Wills, which "maintains records of wills, inventory of estates, and other miscellaneous documents" and serves as "agent for the Commonwealth of Pennsylvania for filing and payment of Inheritance Taxes." *About the Register of Wills*, https://secureprod.phila.gov/row/. The named executor provides the Register of Wills with the original executed will, a "Petition for Grant of Letters," the decedent's death certificate, something called an "Estate Information Sheet, and the probate filing fee. This fee is determined based on the size of the estate. Once before the Register, the executor takes an oath to "faithfully discharge the duties of the office." In the case of people who die without wills or when the executor is unable to serve with no successor nominated in the decedent's will, the process begins with the filing of a petition for letters of administration by a person authorized to serve as "administrator" of the decedent's estate. In Pennsylvania, administrators include, in the following order, those entitled to the residuary estate under the will, surviving spouse, intestate heirs, decedent's principal creditors at the time of death, other fit persons, a nominee appointed by the Register, and others. *See* 20 PA. CONN. STAT. § 3155(b).

Following the issuance of letters testamentary—or letters of administration for intestate estates—the executor (or administrator) then provides notice to creditors and other interested parties, collects assets, pays creditors, files an estate inventory, and distributes the property. Many states have a "small estates" statute, which has an expedited probate process. *See, e.g.,* 20 PA. CONN. STAT. § 3102 (estates under $50,000). Even for estates that the law does not classify as "small estates," probate often is a short and expeditious process. In other instances, the probate process becomes complicated and requires a significant amount of time to resolve. There may be a challenge by disappointed family members (or former family members) to a will. There may be challenges to the executor's (or administrator's) handling of the estate or the distribution of property.

ASSESSMENT

Toni Terrell died owning a house in joint tenancy with Toni's spouse, Shon (who survives by at least 120 hours) worth $450,000; a life insurance policy naming Shon as beneficiary, worth $500,000; a bank account owned in joint tenancy with Shon, with balance of $25,000; an IRA payable to Shon, with balance of $175,000; a 401K pension payable to Toni's two children in equal shares, worth $800,000; a mutual fund account payable in equal shares to Toni's two children, worth $250,000; tangible personal property worth $50,000; and a car titled in Toni's name only, worth $25,000. Toni also owned a summer house with two siblings as tenants-in-common, which the three of them inherited from their parents about a decade ago. The house is worth $300,000.

Toni's valid will has the following provision:

ARTICLE II: I devise and bequeath all my property to my spouse, Shon. If Shon does not survive me, I devise and bequeath all my property, in equal shares, to my children, Ella and Elroy; provided, however, that if either of my children does not survive me, I direct my executor to distribute the predeceased child's share, per stirpes, to that child's living descendants.

What is the size of Toni's **probate** estate?

To answer this question, it is helpful to separate each piece of property, identify how it passes, and identify its value. We can then add up all the probate property to see the size of the probate estate:

Item of Property	Value—Probate	Value—Nonprobate
• House		450
• Life Insurance		500
• Bank Account		250
• IRA		175
• 401K		900
• Mutual Fund		250
• Tangible Personal Property	50	
• Car	25	
• Summer House	100	
	Total: 175	**Total:** 2 425,000

NOTES

1. Car title poses a special issue. While cars that are owned by decedents at the time of death are part of their probate estates, states statutes typically provide for them to pass without the need to open a probate proceeding. For instance, North Carolina provides by statute that a person who is entitled to inherit a car from a decedent (that is, someone who is the beneficiary under the will or is an intestate heir) can petition the DMV to transfer title without having to go through probate if probate is otherwise unnecessary and the creditors have either been satisfied or the estate is small enough that the creditors are not entitled to be paid. N.C. GEN. STAT. § 20–77(b).

2. Why is the size of the probate estate relevant? One important reason is to know whether probate (or administration) is even necessary. It may be that there is nothing to probate—or so little that it can be handled through a non-judicial small estate administration statute that allows the surviving spouse (or sometimes other heirs) to receive the property without notice to creditors (because the size of the estate is small enough that creditors are not entitled to any piece of it). Or maybe the creditors have already been satisfied. Another reason we care about the size of the probate estate is that some property that

passes outside of probate—typically property owned in joint tenancy and the proceeds of life insurance policies—is not reachable by creditors. And yet another reason we might care is because in some states the surviving spouse is entitled to an "elective share" of just the probate estate.

Often, probate is unnecessary. Probate is, however, necessary for Toni (above), at least to change the title to the summer house Toni owns jointly with Toni's siblings.

3.   Although the size of Toni's *probate* estate is small, the size of Toni's gross estate, which might be used for federal or state estate tax purposes, is substantially larger. Tax obligations apply to any property over which the decedent had control at the time of death, so includes probate and nonprobate property. What is Toni's gross estate for estate tax purposes?

D. The Play and Its Producers

Now that you understand the idea of intergenerational wealth transfer, including the players, documents, and processes involved, it seems appropriate to discuss how this textbook unfolds and the motivating interests and concerns of its authors, the so-called producers of this play.

Rather than taking an exclusively litigation-focused or backward-looking approach to this topic, as many of your law school textbooks do, this book takes a more layered approach, looking also at how to plan more thoughtfully and avoid problems beforehand that can lead to litigation. We use cases, uniform laws, and statutes to teach the laws of wealth transfer and to investigate who benefits from existing rules and how, what, or whom these rules leave out, and even disadvantage. We also ask you to think about how the law and estate planning might change to include a wider range of people, their interests, and their concerns.

The textbook also strives to be student- and learning-centered: each chapter begins with a series of learning goals, and we provide many opportunities to practice skills that will reinforce those goals throughout the chapter. We also end each chapter (other than this one) with one or more comprehensive assessments. The diversity of activities and assignments will help you develop the technical expertise, drafting skills, interpersonal skills, and sensitivity to clients' competing interests that a trusts and estates lawyer can expect to need. To that end, you will find problems, questions, and hypotheticals, as you would in most textbooks. You also will find drafting, advising, and roleplaying scenarios that require you to synthesize the (often-picky) rules and then use them in a practical context. Finally, we have included "critical reading" notes throughout; these notes highlight practice tips, unique uses of language, and connections to other areas of law (or to other topics in the book). As you read the book, complete the assessments, and master the learning goals, consider how each chapter looks forward to plan for a client's transfer of wealth and looks backward to analyze and learn from prior planning challenges, mistakes, and successes.

All the authors write critical trusts and estates scholarship. We share a commitment to thinking about how gender, race, sexuality, class, and age factor into the study of trusts and estates, and wealth transfer law more generally. We have, therefore, assembled these materials in such a way as to not only teach you the relevant legal frameworks but also to point out the gaps, biases, oversights, and omissions that characterize wealth transfer law and that produce various forms of inequality. Finally, we believe that the study of any area of law, but this area of law in particular, must be taught and learned in a recursive manner; while the chapters are, by necessity, organized in the sequence described below, they build on each other, looking back and forward for connections. The goal is for you to acquire a nuanced understanding of how the law of intergenerational wealth transfer intersects with care of property, care of family, and care of self during life, at death, and with society as a whole.

The chapters are organized as follows:

- Chapter 1. The Drama of Intergenerational Wealth Transfer

- Chapter 2. Planning for Incapacity and the Physical Act of Death

- Chapter 3. Donative Freedom and the Lawyer-Client Relationship in Inheritance Law

- Chapter 4. Intestacy

- Chapter 5. Wills I: Execution

- Chapter 6. Wills II: Challenges

- Chapter 7. Wills III: Sequential Wills and Other Documents

- Chapter 8. Wills IV: Drafting and Interpretation

- Chapter 9. Private Trusts I: Who, What, and Why?

- Chapter 10. Private Trusts II: Fiduciary Duties

- Chapter 11. Private Trusts III: Asset Protection Trusts

- Chapter 12. Private Trusts IV: Modification and Trustee Removal

- Chapter 13. Will Substitutes and Other Non-Testamentary Forms of Inheritance

- Chapter 14. Spousal Protections and the Elective Share

- Chapter 15. Charitable Trusts

- Chapter 16. The Taxation of Trusts and Estates and Gratuitous Transfers: An Overview

E. Conclusion and Takeaways

We hope you enjoy the opportunities this book offers to explore this topic in depth, including opportunities to think about creative and meaningful approaches you might take in your professional life as an attorney and in your personal life too, as you navigate your own and your family's decision-making. As you progress through the book, you should consider the following:

- What policy goals are being advanced by each rule you encounter?

- What assumptions underlie the reasoning supporting each rule?

- How do you balance the different interests at play (donor/ beneficiary; present/future; fairness/efficiency)?

- Whose interests should take priority, and whose interests are not taken into account?

- What is the attorney's role in each aspect of inheritance law?

Test Your Knowledge

To assess your understanding of the material in this chapter, click here to take a quiz.

CHAPTER 2

Planning for Incapacity and the Physical Act of Death

CHAPTER LEARNING OUTCOMES

Following your work with the material in this chapter, you should be able to do the following:

- Identify the primary documents used to plan for incapacity, including living wills, health care powers of attorney, and financial powers of attorney

- Distinguish between living wills and health care powers of attorney

- Locate model living wills, health care powers of attorney, and financial powers of attorney for any jurisdiction

- Evaluate the key provisions of typical advance directives and how to modify them to serve client needs and preferences

- Identify the consequences of failing to have a plan in place to deal with incapacity

- Explain the duties of an agent acting under a financial power of attorney and the lawyer representing that agent

- Distinguish mandatory from nonmandatory provisions in a financial power of attorney

- Apply the survivorship rules that govern in the case of simultaneous death

- Draft a survivorship clause to use in a governing document

A. Introduction

Trusts and Estates, as you learned in the last chapter, is a course about planning for the transmission of property from one generation to another. Much of what we will study involves how to make that transition as smooth as possible. Sometimes the transfer will take place during life, in the form of an inter vivos gift. Often, though, the transmission will take place at death. One way a transfer at death takes place is through what is called the "probate process," that is, with court supervision. Increasingly often, these days, that transmission will happen outside of probate, through use of **will substitutes** (like living trusts, retirement accounts, joint bank accounts, and other devices discussed below). There is a period leading up to these transfers, however, where people who are still alive may no longer be capable of caring for themselves or their property. We therefore begin the course with a discussion about planning for incompetency and the physical act of death.

Part B covers planning for health care, including the right of individuals to control end-of-life decision-making. This section introduces some documents that individuals use to plan for incompetency: the **advance directive** for health care decision-making (popularly known as a "**living will**"); and the **durable power of attorney for health care decision-making** (sometimes called a **health care proxy**). These documents are a common part of any comprehensive estate plan, so we will discuss how they are useful, how to find the statutory forms for your jurisdiction, and how to think about markups your clients might make to them. This section also covers how health care decision-making takes place in the absence of these planning documents.

Part C moves from care of self to care of property, including a discussion of a document known as a **durable financial power of attorney**. This document gives the agent the power to make decisions regarding financial matters—such as the purchase or sale of real property, withdrawals from bank accounts, sometimes even creation and modification of trusts and wills. The agent sometimes has the power to make financial decisions while the principal is still competent; and the agent also has the power when the principal is incompetent. Durable financial powers of attorney are popular devices because they are flexible and inexpensive and, unlike **guardianship**, do not typically involve on-going court supervision. Unfortunately, the benefit of flexibility and minimal supervision comes at a cost: the potential for abuse by agents. The section has two cases that explore the limits of financial powers of attorney. The first involves the limits on an agent's power to make gifts to him or herself. The second is a cautionary tale of a lawyer who was suspended for two years for assisting a client with using a durable power of attorney to drain assets from another client.

Part D discusses the physical act of death. It focuses on the meaning of "**survivorship**" in a case where it is difficult to tell the order of death.

B. The Right to Control End-of-Life Health Care Decision-Making

This section focuses on health care decision-making, starting with *Cruzan v. Missouri Department of Health*, the U.S. Supreme Court case that established the right of individuals to control health care decision-making about prolonging life. Nancy Cruzan did not put her wishes into writing. As you read the case, consider how the result would have been different had Cruzan executed a living will or health care power of attorney.

Cruzan v. Director, Missouri Department of Health

497 U.S. 261 (1990)

REHNQUIST, C. J., delivered the opinion of the Court.

Petitioner Nancy Beth Cruzan was rendered incompetent as a result of severe injuries sustained during an automobile accident. Co-petitioners Lester and Joyce Cruzan, Nancy's parents and co-guardians, sought a court order directing the withdrawal of their daughter's artificial feeding and hydration equipment after it became apparent that she had virtually no chance of recovering her cognitive faculties. The Supreme Court of Missouri held that because there was no clear and convincing evidence of Nancy's desire to have life-sustaining treatment withdrawn under such circumstances, her parents lacked authority to effectuate such a request. We granted certiorari, and now affirm.

On the night of January 11, 1983, Nancy Cruzan lost control of her car as she traveled down Elm Road in Jasper County, Missouri. The vehicle overturned, and Cruzan was discovered lying face down in a ditch without detectable respiratory or cardiac function. Paramedics were able to restore her breathing and heartbeat at the accident site, and she was transported to a hospital in an unconscious state. An attending neurosurgeon diagnosed her as having sustained probable cerebral contusions compounded by significant anoxia (lack of oxygen). The Missouri trial court in this case found that permanent brain damage generally results after 6 minutes in an anoxic state; it was estimated that Cruzan was deprived of oxygen from 12 to 14 minutes. She remained in a coma for approximately three weeks and then progressed to an unconscious state in which she was able to orally ingest some nutrition. In order to ease feeding and further the recovery, surgeons implanted a gastrostomy feeding and hydration tube in Cruzan with the consent of her then husband. Subsequent rehabilitative efforts proved unavailing. She now lies in a Missouri state hospital in what is commonly referred to as a persistent vegetative state: generally, a condition in which a person exhibits motor reflexes but evinces no indications of significant cognitive function. The State of Missouri is bearing the cost of her care.

The State Supreme Court, adopting much of the trial court's findings, described Nancy Cruzan's medical condition as follows:

> (1) Her respiration and circulation are not artificially maintained and are within the normal limits of a thirty-year-old female; (2) she is oblivious to her environment except for reflexive responses to sound and perhaps painful stimuli; (3) she suffered anoxia of the brain resulting in a massive enlargement of the ventricles filling with cerebrospinal fluid in the area where the brain has degenerated and [her] cerebral cortical atrophy is irreversible, permanent, progressive and ongoing; (4) her highest cognitive brain function is exhibited by her grimacing perhaps in recognition of ordinarily painful stimuli, indicating the experience of pain and apparent response to sound; (5) she is a spastic quadriplegic; (6) her four extremities are contracted with irreversible muscular and tendon damage to all extremities; (7) she has no cognitive or reflexive ability to swallow food or water to maintain her daily essential needs and she will never recover her ability to swallow sufficient [sic] to satisfy her needs. In sum, Nancy is diagnosed as in a persistent vegetative state. She is not dead. She is not terminally ill. Medical experts testified that she could live another thirty years.

Cruzan v. Harmon, 760 S.W.2d 408, 411 (Mo. 1989) (en banc). In observing that Cruzan was not dead, the court referred to the following Missouri statute:

> For all legal purposes, the occurrence of human death shall be determined in accordance with the usual and customary standards of medical practice, provided that death shall not be determined to have occurred unless the following minimal conditions have been met:
>
> > (1) When respiration and circulation are not artificially maintained, there is an irreversible cessation of spontaneous respiration and circulation; or
> >
> > (2) When respiration and circulation are artificially maintained, and there is total and irreversible cessation of all brain function, including the brain stem and that such determination is made by a licensed physician.

MO. REV. STAT. § 194.005 (1986). Since Cruzan's respiration and circulation were not being artificially maintained, she obviously fit within the first proviso of the statute.

After it had become apparent that Nancy Cruzan had virtually no chance of regaining her mental faculties, her parents asked hospital employees to terminate the artificial nutrition and hydration procedures. All agree that such a removal would cause her death. The employees refused to honor the request without court approval. The parents then sought and received authorization from the state trial court for termination. The court found that a person in Nancy's condition had a fundamental right under the State and Federal Constitutions to refuse or direct the withdrawal of "death prolonging procedures." The court also found that Nancy's "expressed thoughts at age twenty-five in somewhat serious conversation with a housemate friend that if sick or injured she would not wish to continue her life unless she could live at least halfway normally suggests that given her present condition she would not wish to continue on with her nutrition and hydration."

The Supreme Court of Missouri reversed by a divided vote. The court recognized a right to refuse treatment embodied in the common-law doctrine of informed consent, but expressed skepticism about the application of that doctrine in the circumstances of this case. The court also declined to read a broad right of privacy into the State Constitution which would "support the right of a person to refuse medical treatment in every circumstance," and expressed doubt as to whether such a right existed under the United States Constitution. It then decided that the Missouri Living Will statute, MO. REV. STAT. § 459.010 et seq. (1986), embodied a state policy strongly favoring the preservation of life. The court found that Cruzan's statements to her roommate regarding her desire to live or die under certain conditions were "unreliable for the purpose of determining her intent," "and thus insufficient to support the co-guardians['] claim to exercise substituted judgment on Nancy's behalf." It rejected the argument that Cruzan's parents were entitled to order the termination of her medical treatment, concluding that "no person can assume that choice for an incompetent in the absence of the formalities required under Missouri's Living Will statutes or the clear and convincing, inherently reliable evidence absent here."

We granted certiorari to consider the question whether Cruzan has a right under the United States Constitution which would require the hospital to withdraw life-sustaining treatment from her under these circumstances.

At common law the logical corollary of the doctrine of informed consent is that the patient generally possesses the right not to consent, that is, to refuse treatment. Until about 15 years ago and the seminal decision in *In re Quinlan*, 70 N.J. 10, 355 A.2d 647 (1976), the number of right-to-refuse-treatment decisions was relatively few. Most of the earlier cases involved patients who refused medical treatment forbidden by their religious beliefs, thus implicating First Amendment rights as well as common-law rights of self-determination. More recently, however, with the advance of medical technology capable of sustaining life well past the point where natural forces would have brought certain death in earlier times, cases involving the right to refuse life-sustaining treatment have burgeoned.

As these cases demonstrate, the common-law doctrine of informed consent is viewed as generally encompassing the right of a competent individual to refuse medical treatment. Beyond that, these cases demonstrate both similarity and diversity in their approaches to decision of what all agree is a perplexing question with unusually strong moral and ethical overtones. State courts have available to them for decision a number of sources—state constitutions, statutes, and common law—which are not available to us. In this Court, the question is simply and starkly whether the United States Constitution prohibits Missouri from choosing the rule of decision which it did. This is the first case in which we have been squarely presented with the issue whether the United States Constitution grants what is in common parlance referred to as a "right to die." The Fourteenth Amendment provides that no State shall "deprive any person of life, liberty, or property, without due process of law." The principle that a competent person has a constitutionally protected liberty interest in refusing unwanted medical treatment may be inferred from our prior decisions. In *Jacobson v. Massachusetts*, 197 U.S. 11 (1905), for instance, the Court balanced an individual's liberty interest in declining an unwanted smallpox vaccine against the State's interest in preventing disease.

Just this Term, we recognized that prisoners possess "a significant liberty interest in avoiding the unwanted administration of antipsychotic drugs under the Due Process Clause of the Fourteenth Amendment." Still other cases support the recognition of a general liberty interest in refusing medical treatment. But determining that a person has a "liberty interest" under the Due Process Clause does not end the inquiry; "whether respondent's constitutional rights have been violated must be determined by balancing his liberty interests against the relevant state interests."

Petitioners insist that under the general holdings of our cases, the forced administration of life-sustaining medical treatment, and even of artificially delivered food and water essential to life, would implicate a competent person's liberty interest. Although we think the logic of the cases discussed above would embrace such a liberty interest, the dramatic consequences involved in refusal of such treatment would inform the inquiry as to whether the deprivation of that interest is constitutionally permissible. But for purposes of this case, we assume that the United States Constitution would grant a competent person a constitutionally protected right to refuse lifesaving hydration and nutrition.

Petitioners go on to assert that an incompetent person should possess the same right in this respect as is possessed by a competent person. The difficulty with petitioners' claim is that in a sense it begs the question: An incompetent person is not able to make an informed and voluntary choice to exercise a hypothetical right to refuse treatment or any other right. Such a "right" must be exercised for her, if at all, by some sort of surrogate. Here, Missouri has in effect recognized that under certain circumstances a surrogate may act for the patient in electing to have hydration and nutrition withdrawn in such a way as to cause death, but it has established a procedural safeguard to assure that the action of the surrogate conforms as best it may to the wishes expressed by the patient while competent. Missouri requires that evidence of the incompetent's wishes as to the withdrawal of treatment be proved by clear and convincing evidence. The question, then, is whether the United States Constitution forbids the establishment of this procedural requirement by the State. We hold that it does not.

Whether or not Missouri's clear and convincing evidence requirement comports with the United States Constitution depends in part on what interests the State may properly seek to protect in this situation. Missouri relies on its interest in the protection and preservation of human life, and there can be no gainsaying this interest. As a general matter, the States—indeed, all civilized nations—demonstrate their commitment to life by treating homicide as a serious crime. Moreover, the majority of States in this country have laws imposing criminal penalties on one who assists another to commit suicide. We do not think a State is required to remain neutral in the face of an informed and voluntary decision by a physically able adult to starve to death.

But in the context presented here, a State has more particular interests at stake. The choice between life and death is a deeply personal decision of obvious and overwhelming finality. We believe Missouri may legitimately seek to safeguard the personal element of this choice through the imposition of heightened evidentiary requirements. It cannot be disputed that the Due Process Clause protects an interest in life as well as an interest in refusing life-sustaining medical treatment. Not all incompetent patients will have loved ones available to serve as surrogate decision makers. And even where family members are present, "there will, of course, be some unfortunate situations in which family members will not act to protect a patient." A State is entitled to guard against potential abuses in such situations. Similarly, a State is entitled to consider that a judicial proceeding to make a determination regarding an incompetent's wishes may very well not be an adversarial one, with the added guarantee of accurate fact-finding that the adversary process brings with it. Finally, we think a State may properly decline to make judgments about the "quality" of life that a particular individual may enjoy, and simply assert an unqualified interest in the preservation of human life to be weighed against the constitutionally protected interests of the individual.

In our view, Missouri has permissibly sought to advance these interests through the adoption of a "clear and convincing" standard of proof to govern such proceedings. "The function of a standard of proof, as that concept is embodied in the Due Process Clause and in the realm of fact-finding, is to 'instruct the factfinder concerning the degree of confidence our society thinks he should have in the correctness of factual conclusions for a particular type of adjudication.' "

We think it self-evident that the interests at stake in the instant proceedings are more substantial, both on an individual and societal level, than those involved in a run-of-the-mill civil dispute. But not only does the standard of proof reflect the importance of a particular adjudication, it also serves as "a societal judgment about how the risk of error should be distributed between the litigants." The more stringent the burden of proof a party must bear, the more that party bears the risk of an erroneous decision. We believe that Missouri may permissibly place an increased risk of an erroneous decision on those seeking to terminate an incompetent individual's life-sustaining treatment. An erroneous decision not to terminate results in a maintenance of the status quo; the possibility of subsequent developments such as advancements in medical science, the discovery of new evidence regarding the patient's intent, changes in the law, or simply the unexpected death of the patient despite the administration of life-sustaining treatment at least create the potential that a wrong decision will eventually be corrected or its impact mitigated. An erroneous decision to withdraw life-sustaining treatment, however, is not susceptible of correction.

In sum, we conclude that a State may apply a clear and convincing evidence standard in proceedings where a guardian seeks to discontinue nutrition and hydration of a person diagnosed to be in a persistent vegetative state. The Supreme Court of Missouri held that in this case the testimony adduced at trial did not amount to clear and convincing proof of the patient's desire to have hydration and nutrition withdrawn. In so doing, it reversed a decision of the Missouri trial court which had found that the evidence "suggested" Nancy Cruzan would not have desired to continue such measures, but which had not adopted the standard of "clear and convincing evidence" enunciated by the Supreme Court. The testimony adduced at trial consisted primarily of Nancy Cruzan's statements made to a housemate about a year before her accident that she would not want to live should she face life as a "vegetable," and other observations to the same effect. The observations did not deal in terms with withdrawal of medical treatment or of hydration and nutrition. We cannot say that the Supreme Court of Missouri committed constitutional error in reaching the conclusion that it did.

The judgment of the Supreme Court of Missouri is Affirmed.

JUSTICE O'CONNOR, *concurring:*   — *giving pwr to other is enough*

I agree that a protected liberty interest in refusing unwanted medical treatment may be inferred from our prior decisions and that the refusal of artificially delivered food and water is encompassed within that liberty interest. I write separately to emphasize that the Court does not today decide the issue whether a State must also give effect to the decisions of a surrogate decision maker. Few individuals provide explicit oral or written instructions regarding their intent to refuse medical treatment should they become incompetent. States which decline to consider any evidence other than such instructions may frequently fail to honor a patient's intent. Such failures might be avoided if the State considered an equally probative source of evidence: the patient's appointment of a proxy to make health care decisions on her behalf. Delegating the authority to make medical decisions to a family member or friend is becoming a common method of planning for the future. Several States have recognized the practical wisdom of such a procedure by enacting durable power of attorney statutes that specifically authorize an individual to appoint a surrogate to make medical treatment decisions. Some state courts have suggested that an agent appointed pursuant to a general durable power of attorney statute would also be empowered to make health care decisions on behalf of the patient. Other States allow an individual to designate a proxy to carry out the intent of a living will. These procedures for surrogate decision-making, which appear to be rapidly gaining in acceptance, may be a valuable additional safeguard of the patient's interest in directing his medical care.

Today's decision, holding only that the Constitution permits a State to require clear and convincing evidence of Nancy Cruzan's desire to have artificial hydration and nutrition withdrawn, does not preclude a future determination that the Constitution requires the States to implement the decisions of a patient's duly appointed surrogate. Nor does it prevent States from developing other approaches for protecting an incompetent individual's liberty interest in refusing medical treatment. As is evident from the Court's survey of state court decisions, no national consensus has yet emerged on the best solution for this difficult and sensitive problem.

NOTES

1.   *Cruzan* stands for the proposition that a patient has a liberty interest in choosing to terminate life support. But, oddly, Nancy Cruzan's selection of termination was not proven by clear and convincing evidence, which is the standard that Missouri requires, because there was nothing in writing about Cruzan's desires. The various courts had to rely on testimony from family members and friends because no written evidence of Cruzan's intentions existed. Over a vigorous dissent, the Missouri Supreme Court concluded there was not clear and convincing evidence of Cruzan's desire for termination of life support. Thus, though the case established the right to termination if there is sufficient evidence of the individual's wishes, Cruzan did not meet that standard. At a subsequent hearing, the family produced more evidence and ultimately obtained a probate court order to have feeding tubes removed. Cruzan died soon thereafter, on December 26, 1990.

2.   *Cruzan* established that a state could require clear and convincing evidence of a patient's desire to terminate life support. In the wake of that decision, most states have adopted statutes that permit termination upon a showing of clear and convincing evidence. Such evidence may come in the form of an advance directive commonly known as a "living will." In a living will, the patient gives instructions regarding her wishes for the provision of extraordinary care in case she is incapacitated. A sample living will, based on FLA. STAT. § 765.303, appears in the Appendix.

3.   The most famous instance of a court acting to terminate life support based on the oral testimony of family members is the Terri Schiavo case, which gripped the country in the spring of 2005. On February 25, 1990, Theresa Marie Schiavo (Terri), age 27, suffered a cardiac arrest resulting from a potassium imbalance.

Her husband, Michael, called 911, and Terri was rushed to the hospital; she never regained consciousness. Terri lived in nursing homes in a persistent vegetative state, fed and hydrated by tubes. Brain scans in mid-1996 showed that much of Terri's cerebral cortex had deteriorated and had been replaced by spinal fluid, and testimony established that medicine could not cure her condition. Terri had not put her wishes in writing, and her husband and parents disagreed about what decision Terri would have made if she were able to assess her own condition and make her own decision. Michael, whom the court appointed as Terri's guardian, filed a petition to authorize the termination of life-prolonging procedures under the relevant Florida statute and the constitutional guidelines enunciated in *In re Guardianship of Browning*, 568 So. 2d 4 (Fla. 1990), and Terri's parents, the Schindlers, objected. The trial court granted Michael's petition, and the Florida Supreme Court affirmed, explaining its decision in quite moving language:

> The testimony in this case establishes that Theresa was very young and very healthy when this tragedy struck. Like many young people without children, she had not prepared a will, much less a living will. She had been raised in the Catholic faith, but did not regularly attend mass or have a religious advisor who could assist the court in weighing her religious attitudes about life-support methods. Her statements to her friends and family about the dying process were few and they were oral. Nevertheless, those statements, along with other evidence about Theresa, gave the trial court a sufficient basis to make this decision for her.

> In the final analysis, the difficult question that faced the trial court was whether Theresa Marie Schindler Schiavo, not after a few weeks in a coma, but after ten years in a persistent vegetative state that has robbed her of most of her cerebrum and all but the most instinctive of neurological functions, with no hope of a medical cure but with sufficient money and strength of body to live indefinitely, would choose to continue the constant nursing care and the supporting tubes in hopes that a miracle would somehow recreate her missing brain tissue, or whether she would wish to permit a natural death process to take its course and for her family members and loved ones to be free to continue their lives. After due consideration, we conclude that the trial judge had clear and convincing evidence to answer this question as he did.

In re Guardianship of Schiavo, 780 So. 2d 177 (Fla. 2001). Terri's parents continued to challenge Michael's efforts to have Terri's feeding and hydration discontinued. These events came to a focal point in 2004 and 2005, as the Florida legislature passed an act that would give Governor Jeb Bush the power to enjoin the discontinuation of Terri's life support. Michael challenged this statute, and the Florida Supreme Court ultimately struck it down. *See Bush v. Schiavo,* 885 So. 2d 321 (Fla. 2004).

4.   One complication hovering over the *Schiavo* case involved money. As Terri's intestate heir, Michael stood to take any money the estate received from an earlier malpractice action that Michael had filed on Terri's behalf. The Florida Supreme Court explained that if Michael divorced Terri, "in order to have a more normal family life, the fund remaining at the end of Theresa's life would presumably go to her parents." Although there was some suspicion that the parties were acting based on their own "monetary self-interest," all courts to consider the issue found no evidence that this was so. In dicta, the appellate court wrote: "If anything is undeniable in this case, it is that Theresa would never wish for this money to drive a wedge between the people she loves. We have no jurisdiction over the disposition of this money, but hopefully these parties will consider Theresa's desires and her memory when a decision about the money is ultimately required." Notwithstanding this finding, money made the *Schiavo* parties suspicious of each other's motives and exacerbated an already difficult situation. This situation is not unique; money may be a hidden motivation in healthcare decision-making.

5.   Living wills are statements about treatment preferences and therefore may be incomplete or static. As a result, they are criticized for being inflexible. Justice O'Connor's *Cruzan* dissent recognizes a second approach to termination of treatment: appointment of a health care agent acting pursuant to a durable power of attorney. The idea behind a durable power of attorney is that once the principal executes it, the "agent," who is also known as an attorney-in-fact, can stand in the shoes of the principal. In the case of a durable power of attorney for health care, the agent can make decisions for the principal, even if the principal is incompetent. This is valuable for all sorts of decisions regarding treatment and care of an incompetent person, not just end-of-life decisions. In many states, the health care agent may decide, independent of any wishes expressed by the principal to others during her life, so long as the durable power of attorney permits termination of treatment. A sample durable health care power of attorney, based on N.C. GEN. STAT. § 32A–25.1, appears in the Appendix.

6.   If the patient has no living will and no durable power of attorney, then the court typically appoints a proxy to make health care decisions. Often, the order of priority mirrors the hierarchy of intestacy. For example, the Florida Statute that applied in the *Schiavo* case and resulted in Michael's appointment as guardian has the following order of priority:

1.   A previously appointed guardian, if there is one

2.   The patient's spouse

3.   An adult child of the patient, or if the patient has more than one adult child, a majority of the adult children who are reasonably available for consultation

4.   A parent of the patient

5.   The adult sibling of the patient or, if the patient has more than one sibling, a majority of the adult siblings who are reasonably available for consultation

6.   An adult relative of the patient who has exhibited special care and concern for the patient and who has maintained regular contact with the patient and who is familiar with the patient's activities, health, and religious or moral beliefs

7.   A close friend of the patient

8.   A clinical social worker licensed. If the social worker decides to withhold or withdraw life-prolonging procedures, that decision is reviewed by the provider's bioethics committee

FLA. STAT. § 765.401. The statute also provides that the proxy's decision to withhold or withdraw life-prolonging procedures must be supported by "clear and convincing evidence that the decision would have been the one the patient would have chosen had the patient been competent." If there is not sufficient evidence of, or, if there is no indication of, what the patient would have chosen, then the decision must be made in the patient's "best interest." Michael provided evidence that termination of life support was in keeping with Terri's wishes. If there had been no evidence that Terri had wanted termination, there is a possibility that Michael could have obtained termination by arguing that the "patient's best interest" was "that proposed treatments are to be withheld." What would be the basis for this argument? Are there any concerns with this standard?

7.　A related issue that has garnered much attention in the past few years is the emergence of "death with dignity" or "physician-assisted death" laws. Many people relate the "death-with-dignity" movement to Brittany Maynard, who

Brittany Maynard, who was diagnosed with terminal brain cancer, became an advocate for the death-with-dignity movement.

spoke candidly in 2016 about her choice to end her life, after being diagnosed with terminal brain cancer. Maynard's desire to control her destiny conflicted with the laws of her home state, so Maynard moved to Oregon to take advantage of that state's Death with Dignity statute, OR. REV. STAT. §§ 127.800 to 127.897). Today, ten states, including California, Colorado, District of Columbia, Hawaii, Montana, Maine, New Jersey, Oregon, Vermont, and Washington, allow medical aid in dying. This topic will come up again in connection with the slayer rule, covered in Chapter 4, which prevents a person who intentionally kills someone from inheriting.

ASSESSMENTS

1.　A common criticism of living wills is that they do not cover a sufficient range of health care situations. Read the Florida living will form document in the Appendix and answer the following questions:

[handwritten note in margin: Surogat or end stage / yes you die]

a.　What would happen to a patient who is hospitalized with a serious but not terminal condition?

b.　If a patient is on a ventilator and has mild dementia, would the Florida form support removal of the ventilator? *[handwritten: Must be incapacitated]*

c.　How would you decide whether someone is "terminally ill" for the purposes of the Florida form? *[handwritten: 2 dr's agree]*

d.　Who do you think is involved in creating these form documents and how frequently do you think they are updated? *[handwritten: Past cases & Drs]*

For a discussion of these issues, see *David Orentlicher, The Limitations of Legislation,* 53 MD. L. REV. 1255 (1993).

2.　One of the reasons behind statutory forms is that legislatures are trying to make legal documents more accessible to modest income individuals. The forms also help to standardize and presumably improve the documents. Read the North Carolina document for health care decisions in the Appendix and answer the following questions:

a. Is the North Carolina form clear enough that lay people can adequately understand and fill it out? *probably not all will understand*

b. The form presumes that the agent may terminate nutrition and hydration unless the principal provides otherwise. Is this the right default provision? *Yes 2 birds one stone*

c. The form presumes that the agent may *not* donate organs unless the principal provides otherwise. Is this the right default provision? Does it contradict the hydration/nutrition default? *Yes it contradicts*

d. Might a principal want to give several people the power to make decisions collectively? How could that be done with this form? *A, B, & C positions*

C. Control of Financial Decision-Making

In addition to a power of attorney for health care decision-making, many people execute powers of attorney for financial matters. The first case below, *Estate of Ferrara*, examines whether an agent, acting under a New York statutory short form durable financial power of attorney, exceeds his power when he makes significant gifts to himself that are inconsistent with the principal's testamentary planning. The second case, *In re Winthrop*, involves a disciplinary proceeding for an attorney who drafted a financial power of attorney for an elderly client, Corinne Rice, at the request of a second client, who was appointed agent and ended up misappropriating funds from the principal, arguably with the attorney's knowledge and help. As you read these cases, pay attention to why a person might execute a financial power of attorney and what the agent promises to do under such a document.

In the Matter of the Estate of George J. Ferrara, Deceased

852 N.E.2d 138 (N.Y. 2006)

READ, J.

Article 5, title 15 of the General Obligations Law prescribes what a statutory short form power of attorney must contain, specifies the powers that the form may authorize, and defines their scope. On this appeal, we hold that an agent acting under color of a statutory short form power of attorney that contains additional language augmenting the gift-giving authority must make gifts pursuant to these enhanced powers in the principal's best interest.

I.

On June 10, 1999, decedent George J. Ferrara, a retired stock-broker residing in Florida, executed a will "mak[ing] no provision . . . for any family member . . . or for any individual person" because it was his "intention to leave [his] entire residuary estate to charity." Accordingly, he bequeathed his estate to a sole beneficiary, the Salvation Army, "to be held, in perpetuity, in a separate endowment fund to be named the 'GEORGE J. FERRARA MEMORIAL FUND' with the annual net income therefrom to be used by the Salvation Army to further its charitable purposes in the greater Daytona Beach, Florida area." On August 16, 1999, decedent executed a codicil naming the Florida attorney who had drafted his will and codicil as his executor, and otherwise "ratif[ied], confirm[ed] and republish [ed][his] said Will of June 10, 1999." Decedent was single and had no children. His closest relatives included his brother, John, and John's children.

According to John's son, Dominick, after decedent was hospitalized in Florida in December 1999, Dominick and his father "were called to assist." Dominick traveled to Florida to visit decedent, who

> told [him] he wanted to move to New York to be near his family and asked [him] to obtain Powers of Attorney for his signature so that [he] could attend to [decedent's] affairs. At [decedent's] direction [Dominick] went to a local stationery store and obtained several Powers of Attorney which [he] filled out in [his] own words and gave to [decedent] for his review and signature. [Decedent] reviewed them and signed all of them before a Notary Public.

Decedent traveled to New York and was admitted to an assisted living facility. He was thin, malnourished, and weak, and was suffering from an array of serious chronic maladies. On January 25, 2000, 10 days later, decedent signed multiple originals of a "Durable General Power of Attorney: New York Statutory Short Form," appointing John and Dominick as his attorneys-in-fact, and allowing either of them to act separately,

> IN [HIS] NAME, PLACE AND STEAD in any way which [he][him]self could do, if [he] were personally present, with respect to the following matters [listed in lettered subdivisions (A) through (O)] as each of them is defined in Title 15 of Article 5 of the New York

General Obligations Law to the extent that [he was] permitted by law to act through an agent.

Subdivision (M) specified "making gifts to my spouse, children and more remote descendants, and parents, not to exceed in the aggregate $10,000 to each of such persons in any year." Decedent authorized his attorneys-in-fact to carry out all of the matters listed in subdivisions (A) through (O). Critically, decedent also initialed a typewritten addition to the form, which stated that "[t]his Power of Attorney shall enable the Attorneys in Fact to make gifts without limitation in amount to John Ferrara and/or Dominick Ferrara."

Dominick insists that this provision authorizing him to make unlimited gifts to himself was added "[i]n furtherance of [decedent's] wishes," because decedent repeatedly told him in December 1999 and January 2000 that he "wanted [Dominick Ferrara] to have all of [decedent's] assets to do with as [he] pleased." When asked if he and decedent had discussed making gifts to other family members, Dominick replied that they had not. Dominick acknowledges that decedent made no memorandum or note to this effect, and only once expressed these donative intentions in the presence of anyone else—Dominick's wife. Dominick sought out an attorney in New York City "to discuss [his] Uncle's wishes," and this attorney provided him with the power of attorney that decedent ultimately executed.

Decedent's condition deteriorated. He was admitted to the hospital on January 29, 2000, and never left. Decedent died on February 12, 2000, approximately three weeks after executing the power of attorney. During those three weeks, Dominick transferred about $820,000 of decedent's assets to himself, including the IBM stock and about $300,000 in cash. After decedent's death, he filed a 1999 federal income tax return for decedent and collected a refund in the amount of roughly $9,500.

The Salvation Army found out about decedent's will after a doctor in Florida, learning of decedent's death, contacted decedent's Florida attorney to inquire about an unpaid bill. Claiming that Dominick had stonewalled every effort to obtain relevant information, the Salvation Army subsequently commenced a proceeding against Dominick and others. The Ferrara respondents moved to dismiss the turnover proceeding on the ground that, prior to decedent's death, Dominick had properly transferred substantially all of decedent's assets to himself pursuant to the power of attorney. The Surrogate denied the motion.

The Surrogate dismissed the petition on March 31, 2004. He first determined that decedent was competent to execute the power of attorney, and that it was properly signed and notarized. The Surrogate noted that there was at one time "a presumption of impropriety due to the appearance of impropriety and self-dealing" when an attorney-in-fact made self-gifts. He opined, however, that amendments to article 5, title 15 of the General Obligations Law, effective January 1, 1997, had eliminated this presumption. Thus, "when a post-January 1, 1997 power of attorney specifically and expressly authorizes gifting by the agent to himself, the presumption of impropriety no longer applies and the burden of proving the validity of the gift is no longer on the agent." As a result, "the burden of proving the invalidity of the gift is on [the Salvation Army]," and here, the Salvation Army "failed to demonstrate that the transfers pursuant to the power of attorney [were] invalid."

The Appellate Division affirmed. We now reverse.

II.

Section 5–1501 of the General Obligations Law sets out the forms creating a durable and nondurable statutory short form power of attorney. By these forms, the principal appoints an attorney-in-fact to act "IN [HIS] NAME, PLACE AND STEAD" with respect to any or all of 15 categories of matters listed in lettered subdivisions (A) through (O) "as each of them is defined in Title 15 of Article 5 of the New York General Obligations Law." In 1996 the Legislature amended section 5–1501(1) to add lettered subdivision (M), authorizing the attorney-in-fact to "mak[e] gifts to [the principal's] spouse, children and more remote descendants, and parents, not to exceed in the aggregate $10,000 to each of such persons in any year." Section 5–1502M construes this gift-giving authority,

> to mean that the principal authorizes the agent . . . [t]o make gifts . . . either outright or to a trust for the sole benefit of one or more of [the specified] persons . . . only for purposes which the agent reasonably deems to be in the best interest of the principal, specifically including minimization of income, estate, inheritance, generation-skipping transfer or gift taxes.

Such gifts may not exceed $10,000 "unless the statutory short form power of attorney contains additional language pursuant to section 5–1503 of the general obligations law authorizing gifts in excess of said amount or gifts to other beneficiaries." Section 5–1503(2), in turn, permits "additional language" that "[s]upplements one or more of the [enumerated] powers ... by specifically listing additional powers of the agent."

Thus, section 5–1502M unambiguously imposes a duty on the attorney-in-fact to exercise gift-giving authority in the best interest of the principal. Nothing in section 5–1502M indicates that the best interest requirement is waived when additional language increases the gift amount or expands the potential beneficiaries pursuant to section 5–1503. The Ferrara respondents argue that because section 5–1503(2) does not also contain a best interest requirement, an attorney-in-fact has no obligation to act in the principal's best interest unless the additional language explicitly so directs. But section 5–1503(2) states that the "additional language" may "[s]*upplement* one or more of the powers enumerated in one or more of the constructional sections" (emphasis added). The Legislature intended section 5–1503 to function as a means to customize the statutory short form power of attorney, not as an escape hatch from the statute's protections.

The Legislature sought to empower individuals to appoint an attorney-in-fact to make annual gifts consistent with financial, estate or tax planning techniques and objectives—not to create gift-giving authority generally, and certainly not to supplant a will.

The best interest requirement is consistent with the fiduciary duties that courts have historically imposed on attorneys-in-fact. Because "[t]he relationship of an attorney-in-fact to his principal is that of agent and principal ..., the attorney-in-fact must act in the utmost good faith and undivided loyalty toward the principal, and must act in accordance with the highest principles of morality, fidelity, loyalty and fair dealing." *Semmler v. Naples*, 166 A.D.2d 751, 752 (3d Dept. 1990).

In short, whether the gift-giving power in a statutory short form power of attorney is limited to the authority spelled out in lettered subdivision (M) section 5–1501(1), or augmented by additional language in conformity with section 5–1503, the best interest requirement remains. Thus, Dominick was only authorized to make gifts to himself insofar as these gifts were in decedent's best interest, interpreted by section 5–1502M as gifts to carry out the principal's financial, estate or tax plans. Here, Dominick consistently testified that he made the self-gifts "[i]n furtherance of [decedent's] wishes" to give him "all of his assets to do with as [Dominick] pleased." The term "best interest" does not include such unqualified generosity to the holder of a power of attorney, especially where the gift virtually impoverishes a donor whose estate plan, shown by a recent will, contradicts any desire to benefit the recipient of the gift.

Accordingly, the order of the Appellate Division should be reversed, without costs, and the matter remitted to Surrogate's Court for further proceedings in accordance with this opinion.

In re Winthrop

848 N.E.2d 961 (Ill. 2006)

FITZGERALD, J.

The Administrator filed a complaint against respondent, Peter Deforest Winthrop, charging him with violations of the Illinois Rules of Professional Conduct. Respondent asks this court to uphold the finding of the Hearing Board dismissing all charges against him or, in the alternative, to impose a sanction of reprimand or censure.

BACKGROUND

Respondent was charged with professional misconduct resulting from his representation of Corrine Rice, a 92-year-old woman for whom he drafted a will and a power of attorney. In 2000, respondent met Farouq Nobani and represented him on some traffic matters. In July 2001, Nobani contacted respondent about preparing a will for Rice, an elderly woman who resided in his condominium complex. Respondent first visited Rice sometime in July 2001 and learned that Rice was never married, had no children, and was an only child. Respondent also learned that Rice owned her condominium, had two bank accounts, and intended for her neighbor, Fardous Hassan, to be the beneficiary and executor of her will.

Approximately one week after this meeting, respondent returned to Rice's apartment with a draft of the will. Rice informed respondent that she also wanted to appoint someone to handle her financial affairs, as it was becoming inconvenient for her. Respondent testified that he advised Rice to create a trust, possibly with Northern Trust Bank. He explained that the bank would pay her bills. According to respondent, Rice questioned whether there would be a yearly and/or monthly fee for this service, and when told that a fee would be involved, suggested that Nobani be appointed to manage her finances. Respondent stated that he "gleaned" from his conversation with Rice that she wanted Nobani to have unfettered discretion over all of her financial affairs. Respondent drafted a power of attorney pursuant to Rice's requests. Nobani refused to serve unless language was added to the document protecting him from liability. Accordingly, respondent added a paragraph to the power of attorney which stated: "I, Farouq

Nobani, agree to this power of attorney, and hereby promise to do my very best, but under no conditions do I guarantee the outcome of any matter."

After Rice agreed to the power of attorney, respondent advised her that it had to be signed and notarized. A bank officer who helped Rice with her banking, Virginia Paluch, notarized Rice's will and power of attorney. Paluch testified that she was "uncomfortable" with the documents and the circumstances under which they were signed. Rice's behavior was out of the ordinary: she came to the bank at night; she appeared to be dressed in clothing that belonged to someone else; and she was much less independent than she had been. Paluch was concerned about the legitimacy of the documents because respondent and Nobani wanted to withdraw funds immediately for payment of personal fees he and Nobani had incurred in assisting Rice. Paluch denied their request.

Respondent and Nobani returned to the bank on Saturday, August 4, 2001, and spoke to bank manager JoAnne Reiser. Reiser told respondent she would not honor Rice's power of attorney because it was not the Illinois statutory property power form. Respondent and Nobani proceeded to Advance Bank, where Rice held other accounts. While at the second bank, Nobani used the power of attorney to close a certificate of deposit account held by Rice. Nobani directed the bank to issue a cashier's check in his name for the remaining balance on the account, which was approximately $87,000. Although respondent was present for a majority of Nobani's conversations, he testified that he did not know Nobani was closing the account and did not know that Nobani asked for the cashier's check to be issued in his name although respondent sat next to Nobani as the transaction was occurring.

Nobani opened an account at United Trust and Federal Savings Bank and proceeded to write checks from the account for his own personal use. He paid off a car loan of $11,545.99 and wrote checks to "Cash" for large sums.[2]

Reiser contacted the Oak Lawn police department and PLOWS Council on Aging (PLOWS). Detective Christopher Parker went to Rice's home and reported his observations. He stated that Rice lived an "eccentric" life. She slept on two folding chairs in her kitchen. Her kitchen counters were covered with collectable items, and both bedrooms, as well as the bathroom, were filled, floor to ceiling, with her belongings. He added that Rice was confused and agitated. Rice repeatedly stated that she was tired of people asking her about her money

---

[2]   As of August 17, 2001, the balance of Rice's funds in Nobani's account was $2,313.60. Nobani returned the entire sum of Rice's funds pursuant to a probate court order. He was criminally charged, but not convicted. Nobani did not testify in respondent's hearing.

and that she just wanted to be left alone. Jessica O'Leary, a caseworker employed by PLOWS, visited Rice to conduct a well-being and safety check. She discussed the power of attorney with Rice. At first, Rice did not remember signing it; she then said that signing it was a mistake. Rice stated that she did not want the power of attorney and could handle her own finances. O'Leary thus presented Rice with a revocation of her power of attorney and Rice signed it. O'Leary opined that Rice was suffering from dementia and stated that Rice was confused, agitated, and disoriented as to place and time. Nevertheless, she felt that Rice knew what she was signing when she signed the revocation document.

PLOWS was seeking to freeze Rice's accounts and a hearing was scheduled the following day in probate court. The PLOWS attorney stated that she received a call from respondent prior to the hearing on these motions. Respondent stated that he represented Nobani. He then asked the PLOWS attorney why she was bringing a petition to freeze Rice's accounts when "[t]hey [the banks] didn't give us any money anyway." The PLOWS attorney testified that respondent did not reveal that Nobani had already withdrawn funds from the bank. The probate court entered an order for PLOWS to provide necessary assistance to Rice, for Rice's accounts to be frozen, and ultimately determined that Rice was incapable of making personal and financial decisions and appointed the office of the public guardian as plenary guardian of her person and estate.

Next, the Hearing Board concluded that the evidence presented at the hearing was insufficient to establish that respondent had knowledge of, or was compliant with, Nobani's misconduct and recommended that the charges against respondent be dismissed.

Appeal was taken to the Review Board, which found that "the circumstances of Rice's mental state required "special care" to protect her interests." The Review Board also concluded that respondent breached his fiduciary duty when he did not attempt to protect Rice's interests when Nobani withdrew a large sum of her money from Advance Bank. The Review Board found that respondent engaged in a conflict of interest by representing Rice when his representation was materially limited by his own interests and his responsibilities to Nobani, and that the evidence showed that respondent tried to protect Nobani's interests over Rice's by drafting the overly broad power of attorney. After reaching these findings, the Review Board imposed sanctions on respondent.

Respondent sought leave to file exceptions to this court asserting that the Review Board improperly reversed the Hearing Board's findings, and alternatively arguing that the sanction imposed by the Review Board was unduly harsh.

ANALYSIS

I.   Breach of Fiduciary Duty

The issue of whether the drafting of Rice's power of attorney amounted to a breach of fiduciary duty hinges on a legal determination of the breadth of the document. If the document provided the same legal protection to Rice that she would have been afforded under the statutory version, we cannot say that respondent breached his duty of care.

A comparison of the power of attorney in question to the Illinois statutory property power of attorney demonstrates that the power of attorney drafted by respondent was not overly broad. Nobani was given full power and authority to sign Rice's name to affidavits, drafts, and checks; to withdraw money on her behalf from any financial instruments or accounts; to dispose of and use all accounts and real property; to dispose of and use all of Rice's monies; and to handle her financial affairs as he saw fit. The statutory property power form provides the same powers. Thus, we cannot conclude that respondent breached his fiduciary duty on this basis. As the plain language of the statute makes clear, agents are required to exercise due care if they choose to act and will be held liable for negligent conduct. The language added by respondent to Rice's power of attorney did not relieve Nobani from his responsibility to act with due care, nor did it relieve him from liability in the event of negligence. Respondent's inartfully drafted clause did nothing more than assuage Nobani's anxiety. Thus, we cannot say that respondent breached his fiduciary duty to his client, Rice, in adding this language to the power of attorney. In light of these facts, we cannot find that the Hearing Board erred in concluding that the evidence was insufficient to support the charge against respondent.

We are compelled to note that respondent's testimony with respect to the events which occurred at Advance Bank at the time Nobani withdrew the money in question is suspicious. Respondent's version of events is difficult to believe when he states that he sat in a cubicle with Nobani and the bank manager and, yet, did not have any knowledge of the content of their conversation. That being said, Nobani acted within the authority that was granted to him by the power of attorney because, under that document, Nobani was permitted to withdraw funds and handle Rice's finances as he saw fit. Respondent did not have a fiduciary duty to protect Rice from Nobani's conduct when Nobani's conduct was authorized by the power of attorney Rice had executed. Accordingly, while we do not condone respondent's conduct, we cannot say that it rises to the level of a breach of fiduciary duty warranting discipline.

II. Conflict of Interest

Rule 1.7(b) provides: "A lawyer shall not represent a client if the representation of that client may be materially limited by the lawyer's responsibilities to another client or to a third person, or by the lawyer's own interests." In considering whether respondent represented Rice under a conflict of interest, we are mindful that, while the circumstances of respondent's representation of Rice may arouse suspicion, "suspicious circumstances, standing alone, are not sufficient to warrant discipline." *In re Lane*, 127 Ill. 2d 90, 111, 535 N.E.2d 866 (1989). The facts demonstrate that Nobani and his wife contacted respondent to prepare a will for Rice, an elderly woman in their apartment complex whom they recently befriended. The decision to contact respondent was not random—Nobani and respondent had an ongoing business relationship. In the course of discussing the will, respondent agreed to draft a power of attorney for Rice. Respondent testified that the power of attorney was Rice's idea and was drafted at her behest. There is no evidence suggesting that respondent influenced Rice's decision or that he assisted Nobani in exerting influence over Rice. Once the power of attorney was executed, Nobani withdrew a large amount of money from Rice's bank account and then misappropriated the funds for his own use. There is no evidence that respondent participated in or benefitted from the misappropriation.

We cannot ignore the fact that respondent's conduct with respect to Rice and Nobani was suspicious, and at the very least, demonstrated extremely poor judgment. However, we cannot say the Hearing Board's judgment was so unreasonable as to be against the manifest weight of the evidence.

III. False Statement of Material Fact to a Third Person

Rule 4.1(a) provides: "In the course of representing a client a lawyer shall not: (a) make a statement of material fact or law to a third person which statement the lawyer knows or reasonably should know is false." The evidence presented to the Hearing Board demonstrated, clearly and convincingly, that respondent made a false statement of fact. The PLOWS attorney testified that respondent stated that Nobani was denied access to Rice's funds and that respondent specifically asked her why she was bringing a petition to freeze Rice's accounts when "[t]hey [the banks] didn't give us any money anyway." Respondent provided no evidence which impeached these statements. Furthermore, the evidence presented demonstrated that respondent had to know that his statement was false, as he was physically present when Nobani closed Rice's bank account at Advance Bank, watched Nobani receive a cashier's check, and by his own admission, asked Nobani what he intended to do with the money. Respondent's false statement was material, because preventing Nobani from accessing Rice's funds was one of the primary purposes of the probate hearing. Providing the court with information that could have aided in protecting Rice's assets should have been respondent's main concern as Rice's attorney.

NOTES

1.   A durable power of attorney offers a simple alternative to guardianship. It is called "durable" because the document's powers continue to be legally valid even when the principal becomes incapacitated. But note that the power of attorney, whether durable or not, is not valid after the principal's death. The power of attorney thus operates only during the principal's lifetime. As the above two cases make clear, the simplicity of this document comes at the cost of increasing the agent's ability to abuse the power. Estate planners realize that there are substantial problems of abuse of the power by an agent. *See* E. Thomas Shilling, *Report on ACTEC Elder Law Committee Questionnaire on Possible Abuse of Financial Durable Power of Attorney*, 21 AM. C. TR. & ESTATE COUNSEL NOTES 247 (1995); Linda S. Whitton, *Durable Powers as an Alternative to Guardianship: Lessons We Have Learned*, 37 STETSON L. REV. 7 (2007); Jane A. Black, Note, *The Not-So-Golden Years: Power of Attorney, Elder Abuse, and Why Our Laws Are Failing a Vulnerable Population*, 82 ST. JOHN'S L. REV. 289 (2008).

2.   A sample model durable financial power of attorney, based on ALA. CODE § 26–1A–301, appears in the Appendix. The American College of Trusts and Estates ("**ACTEC**"), a nonprofit association of lawyers experienced in estate matters, has compiled a 50-state survey of powers of attorney as of 2019, which is available at https://www.actec.org/assets/1/6/Douglass_Powers_of_Attorney_Survey.pdf. Many of the form powers, including the Alabama example in the Appendix, have some form of the following provision:

> An agent that is not my ancestor, spouse, or descendant MAY NOT use my property to benefit the agent or a person to whom the agent owes an obligation of support unless I have included authority in the Special Instructions.

That direction is designed to limit an agent's use of the principal's money for the agent's benefit. Even without this provision, such a gift would violate the agent's duty of loyalty.

3.   A durable power of attorney may, and often does, permit an agent to give the agent a gift of the principal's property. This power is often to permit tax-advantageous planning. *See In re Estate of Lambur*, 397 S.W.3d 54 (Mo. App. 2013). Sometimes, even if the durable power of attorney permits such gifts, the gifts are successfully challenged. One basis for challenge is undue influence, a topic that will appear later in this book. *See In re Guardianship of Mowrer*, 979 P.2d 156 (Mont. 1999). Another basis appears in *Ferrara*, where the gift to the agent, although authorized in the power of attorney, undermined the principal's estate plan and therefore was not in the principal's best interest.

4.   Winthrop did not use the Illinois statutory financial power of attorney, and the non-standard form caused the bank officer to become suspicious. Obviously, those suspicions were well-founded, but are there circumstances in which it makes sense to customize a statutory form? One reason Winthrop did not use the statutory form may be that he wanted to absolve Nobani of liability for violation of fiduciary duties but, under Illinois law, those duties are not waivable. 755 ILL. COMP. STAT. 45/3–4. The **Uniform Probate Code ("UPC")**, in its provisions addressing durable powers of attorney, acknowledges that many agents are family members and that they will have conflicts of interest between their duties as fiduciaries and their choices on behalf of the principal. The UPC has a default provision that "an agent who acts with care, competence and diligence for the best interest of the principal is not liable solely because the agent also benefits from the act or has conflicting interests." UPC § 5B–114(d). The UPC also allows a principal to include a clause exonerating the agent. UPC § 5B–115.

5.   When the bank officer in *Winthrop* became suspicious, she refused to honor the power of attorney. It is worth asking whether all bank officers would be this vigilant. In most jurisdictions when third parties honor durable powers of attorney in good faith, they have no liability to the principal. *See, e.g.*, TEX. PROB. CODE ANN. § 487. This removal of liability may make it more likely that third parties will not police durable powers of attorney closely. Some of the reforms of durable powers of attorney are aimed at getting more oversight of the actions of agents. For instance, North Carolina requires that agents file durable powers of attorney with a court when the principal becomes incompetent. N.C. GEN. STAT. § 32A–9. Fortunately, in *Winthrop*, the bank officer was vigilant enough to limit the misuse of the durable power.

But what if this had not been a case of misuse of the power? Banks frequently refuse to honor powers of attorney for reasons as simple as a missing middle initial in the agent's name or that it was executed more than five years earlier. *See* Paul Sullivan, *Wealth Matters: Power of Attorney is Not Always a Solution,* N.Y. TIMES Aug. 22, 2014. What steps can be taken to compel a third party to accept a durable power of attorney? In fact, third party non-acceptance of a durable power of attorney is a problem. William M. McGovern, *Trusts, Custodianships, and Durable Powers of Attorney,* 27 REAL PROPERTY PROBATE & TRUST 1, 39 (1992). Some states have statutes that permit an agent to seek a court order to compel acceptance. *See* CAL. PROB. CODE § 4541(f).

6.   Durable powers of attorney are widely accessible and often filled out without an attorney's advice. That can lead to liability on the part of the person or entity that provided the form. For instance, in *DeBoer v. Sr. Bridges of Sparks Fam. Hosp.,* 282 P.3d 727 (Nev. 2012), a nursing home provided a form to a vulnerable individual as part of her discharge from the home. The form named a caregiver as agent. The Nevada Supreme Court allowed a negligence suit to go forward against the nursing home on the theory that the nursing home had a duty to its patient and that the form had facilitated the caregiver's misappropriation of the patient's assets.

7.   One suggestion for limiting abuse of a durable power of attorney is using a "springing power." The springing power of attorney takes effect only upon the principal's incapacity (rather than upon signing). A person or group of people, often a physician or family members, must certify that the principal has lost capacity before the power "springs" into use. How difficult do you think it would be to get this certification? For a discussion of springing powers of attorney, see John C. Craft, *Preventing Exploitation and Preserving Autonomy: Making Springing Powers of Attorney the Standard,* U. BALT. L. REV. 407 (2015). For a discussion of how these documents affect autonomy and vulnerability of people as they age, see Mary F. Radford, *What If Granny Wants to Gamble? Balancing Autonomy and Vulnerability in the Golden Years,* 45 ACTEC L.J. 221 (2020).

8.   For further discussion of durable powers of attorney and problems with them regarding abuse by agents and third parties, as well as potential reforms, see Carolyn L. Dessin, *Acting As Agent Under a Financial Durable Power of Attorney,* 75 NEB. L. REV. 574 (1996) and Karen E. Boxx, *The Durable Power of Attorney's Place in the Family of Fiduciary Relationships,* 36 GA. L. REV. 1 (2001). There is a growing literature on abuse of durable powers of attorney and on how such issues are going to occur more frequently as the population ages. *See* Nina Kohn, *Elder Empowerment as a Strategy for Curbing the Hidden Abuses of Durable Powers of Attorney,* 59 RUTGERS L. REV. 1 (2006); Ben Chen, *Elder Financial Abuse: Fiduciary Law and Economics,* 34 NOTRE DAME J.L. ETHICS & PUB. POL'Y 307 (2020).

ASSESSMENTS

1. Read the Alabama statutory form durable power of attorney set forth in the Appendix and answer the following questions:

    a. What are some advantages of using a financial power of attorney? In other words, why would someone opt to sign this document?

    b. What powers in the Alabama form are mandatory for the agent and what powers can the principal waive?

    c. Does the Alabama power of attorney allow an agent to change the principal's estate plan? What might be a reason to limit this authority?

    d. Do you think a lay person filling out the Alabama form would realize that it applies only to financial matters and not health care? How?

    e. What improvements would you suggest for making the Alabama form more user-friendly?

2. The UPC's section on durable powers of attorney, § 5B–114, provides that some of the duties of agents are **mandatory**. That is, they cannot be waived. According to UPC § 5B–114(a), the agent must:

    (1) Act in accordance with the principal's reasonable expectations to the extent actually known by the agent, and otherwise in the principal's best interest

    (2) Act in good faith

    (3) Act only within the scope of authority granted in the power of attorney

    However, the UPC makes several other duties **waivable**. That is, that the agent must follow *unless* the power of attorney waives them. According to UPC § 5B–114(b), the power of attorney may waive the duties to:

    (1) Act loyally for the principal's benefit

    (2) Act so as not to create a conflict of interest that impairs the agent's ability to act impartially in the principal's best interest

    (3) Act with care, competence, and diligence normally exercised by agents in similar circumstances

(4)   Keep record of all receipts, disbursements, and transactions made on behalf of the principal

(5)   Cooperate with a person that has authority to make health-care decisions for the principal to carry out the principal's reasonable expectations to the extent actually known by the agent and, otherwise, act on the principal's best interest

(6)   Attempt to preserve the principal's estate plan

Imagine that you represent George Ferrara. Write a short letter to him explaining which, if any, of these duties he should consider waiving and explain why. This letter should use legally accurate but client accessible language.

D. The Physical Act of Death and Defining Survivorship

One of the questions that this introductory material on planning for self raises is when does the physical fact of death occur? The order of death matters when there are simultaneous or nearly simultaneous deaths within families. Order of death for a married couple may be important because it can determine which spouse's estate controls the distribution of property. The following famous but perhaps not carefully reasoned case, *Janus v. Tarasewicz*, arose out of the still unsolved crime of Tylenol poisoning which led to the tragic deaths of two newly married spouses within a short time of one another. The issue was whether the wife had survived long enough to avoid the application of the Illinois simultaneous death act and thus allow her father to take her entire estate (including her husband's life insurance policy that listed the wife as a primary beneficiary and the husband's mother as a secondary beneficiary). If the couple died simultaneously, on the other hand, the husband's mother would have taken the proceeds of her son's life insurance policy. As you read the case, see if you agree with the court's fine parsing of how the evidence fits within the applicable survivorship statute.

Janus v. Tarasewicz

482 N.E.2d 418 (Ill. App. 1985)

O'CONNOR, J.

This non-jury declaratory judgment action arose out of the death of a husband and wife, Stanley and Theresa Janus, who died after ingesting Tylenol capsules which had been laced with cyanide by an unknown perpetrator prior to its sale in stores. Stanley Janus was pronounced dead shortly after he was admitted to the hospital. However, Theresa Janus was placed on life support systems for almost two days before being pronounced dead. Claiming that there was no sufficient evidence that Theresa Janus survived her husband, plaintiff Alojza Janus, Stanley's mother, brought this action for the proceeds of Stanley's $100,000 life insurance policy which named Theresa as the primary beneficiary and plaintiff as the contingent beneficiary. Defendant Metropolitan Life Insurance Company paid the proceeds to defendant Jan Tarasewicz, Theresa's father and the administrator of her estate. The trial court found sufficient evidence that Theresa survived Stanley Janus. We affirm.

The facts of this case are particularly poignant and complex. Stanley and Theresa Janus had recently returned from their honeymoon when, on the evening of September 29, 1982, they gathered with other family members to mourn the death of Stanley's brother, Adam Janus, who had died earlier that day from what was later determined to be cyanide-laced Tylenol capsules. While the family was at Adam's home, Stanley and Theresa Janus unknowingly took some of the contaminated Tylenol. Soon afterwards, Stanley collapsed on the kitchen floor.

Theresa was still standing when Diane O'Sullivan, a registered nurse and a neighbor of Adam Janus, was called to the scene. Stanley's pulse was weak so she began cardiopulmonary resuscitation (CPR) on him. Within minutes, Theresa Janus began having seizures. After paramedic teams began arriving, Ms. O'Sullivan went into the living room to assist with Theresa. While she was working on Theresa, Ms. O'Sullivan could hear Stanley's "heavy and labored breathing." She believed that both Stanley and Theresa died before they were taken to the ambulance, but she could not tell who died first.

Ronald Mahon, a paramedic for the Arlington Heights Fire Department, arrived at approximately 5:45 p.m. He saw Theresa faint and go into a seizure. Her pupils did not respond to light, but she was breathing on her own during the time that he worked on her. Mahon also assisted with Stanley, giving him drugs to stimulate heart contractions. Mahon later prepared the paramedic's report on Stanley. One entry in the report shows that at 18:00 hours Stanley had "zero blood pressure, zero pulse, and zero respiration." However, Mahon stated that the times in the report were merely approximations. He was able to say that Stanley was in the ambulance en route to the hospital when his vital signs disappeared.

When paramedic Robert Lockhart arrived at 5:55 p.m., both victims were unconscious with non-reactive pupils. Theresa's seizures had ceased but she was in a decerebrate posture in which her arms and legs were rigidly extended, and her arms were rotated inward toward her body, thus, indicating severe neurological dysfunction. At that time, she was breathing only four or five times a minute and, shortly thereafter, she stopped breathing on her own altogether. Lockhart intubated them both by placing tubes down their tracheae to keep their air passages open. Prior to being taken to the ambulance, they were put on "ambu-bags" which is a form of artificial respiration whereby the paramedic respirates the patient by squeezing a bag. Neither Stanley nor Theresa showed any signs of being able to breathe on their own while they were being transported to Northwest Community Hospital in Arlington Heights, Illinois. However, Lockhart stated that when Theresa was turned over to the hospital personnel, she had a palpable pulse and blood pressure.

The medical director of the intensive care unit at the hospital, Dr. Thomas Kim, examined them when they arrived in the emergency room at approximately 6:30 p.m. Stanley had no blood pressure or pulse. An electrocardiogram detected electrical activity in Stanley Janus' heart but there was no synchronization between his heart's electrical activity and its pumping activity. A temporary pacemaker was inserted in an unsuccessful attempt to resuscitate him. Because he never developed spontaneous blood pressure, pulse or signs of respiration, Stanley Janus was pronounced dead at 8:15 p.m. on September 29, 1982.

Like Stanley, Theresa Janus showed no visible vital signs when she was admitted to the emergency room. However, hospital personnel were able to get her heart beating on its own again, so they did not insert a pacemaker. They were also able to establish a measurable, though unsatisfactory, blood pressure. Theresa was taken off the "ambu-bag" and put on a mechanical respirator. In Dr. Kim's opinion, Theresa was in a deep coma with "very unstable vital signs" when she was moved to the intensive care unit at 9:30 p.m. on September 29, 1982.

While Theresa was in the intensive care unit, numerous entries in her hospital records indicated that she had fixed and dilated pupils. However, one entry made at 2:32 a.m. on September 30, 1982, indicated that a nurse apparently detected a minimal reaction to light in Theresa's right pupil but not in her left pupil.

On September 30, 1982, various tests were performed to assess Theresa's brain function. These tests included an electroencephalogram (EEG) to measure electrical activity in her brain and a cerebral blood flow test to determine whether there was any blood circulating in her brain. In addition, Theresa exhibited no gag or cord reflexes, no response to pain or other external stimuli. As a result of these tests, Theresa Janus was diagnosed as having sustained total brain death, her life support systems then were terminated, and she was pronounced dead at 1:15 p.m. on October 1, 1982.

Death certificates were issued for Stanley and Theresa Janus more than three weeks later by a medical examiner's physician who never examined them. The certificates listed Stanley Janus' date of death as September 29, 1982, and Theresa Janus' date of death as October 1, 1982. Concluding that Theresa survived Stanley, the Metropolitan Life Insurance Company paid the proceeds of Stanley's life insurance policy to the administrator of Theresa's estate.

On January 6, 1983, plaintiff brought the instant declaratory judgment action against the insurance company and the administrators of Stanley and Theresa's estates, claiming the proceeds of the insurance policy as the contingent beneficiary of the policy. Also, the administrator of Stanley's estate filed a counterclaim against Theresa's estate seeking a declaration as to the disposition of the assets of Stanley's estate.

During the trial, the court heard the testimony of Ms. O'Sullivan, the paramedics, and Dr. Kim. There was also testimony that, while Theresa was in the intensive care unit, members of Theresa's family requested that termination of her life support system be delayed until the arrival of her brother who was serving in the military. However, Theresa's family denied making such a request.

In addition, Dr. Kenneth Vatz, a neurologist on the hospital staff, was called as an expert witness by plaintiff. Although he never actually examined Theresa, he had originally read her EEG as part of hospital routine. Without having seen her other hospital records, his initial evaluation of her EEG was that it showed some minimal electrical activity of living brain cells in the frontal portion of Theresa's brain. After reading her records and reviewing the EEG, however, he stated that the electrical activity measured by the EEG was "very likely" the result of interference from surrounding equipment in the intensive care unit. He concluded that Theresa was brain dead at the time of her admission to the hospital, but he could not give an opinion as to who died first.

The trial court also heard an evidence deposition of Dr. Joseph George Hanley, a neurosurgeon who testified as an expert witness on behalf of the defendants. Based on his examination of their records, Dr. Hanley concluded that Stanley Janus died on September 29, 1982. He further concluded that Theresa Janus did not die until her vital signs disappeared on October 1, 1982. His conclusion that she did not die prior to that time was based on: (1) the observations by hospital personnel that Theresa Janus had spontaneous pulse and blood pressure which did not have to be artificially maintained; (2) the instance when Theresa Janus' right pupil allegedly reacted to light; and (3) Theresa's EEG which showed some brain function and which, in his opinion, could not have resulted from outside interference.

At the conclusion of the trial, the court held that the evidence was sufficient to show that Theresa survived Stanley, but the court was not prepared to say by how long she survived him. Plaintiff and the administrator of Stanley's estate appeal. In essence, their main contention is that there is not sufficient evidence to prove that both victims did not suffer brain death prior to their arrival at the hospital on September 29, 1982.

Dual standards for determining when legal death occurs in Illinois were set forth in the case of *In Re Haymer*, 115 Ill. App. 3d 349 (1983). There, the court determined that a comatose child attached to a mechanical life support system was legally dead on the date he was medically determined to have sustained total brain death, rather than on the date that his heart stopped functioning. The court stated that in most instances death could be determined in accordance with the common law standard which is based upon the irreversibly cessation of circulatory and respiratory functions. *Id.* at 355. If these functions are artificially maintained, a brain death standard of death could be used if a person has sustained irreversible cessation of total brain function. In a footnote, the court stated that widely accepted characteristics of brain death include: (1) unreceptivity and unresponsivity to intensely painful stimuli; (2) no spontaneous movement or breathing for at least one hour; (3) no blinking, no swallowing, and fixed and dilated pupils; (4) flat EEG's taken twice with at least a 24-hour intervening period; and (5) absence of drug intoxication or hyperthermia. *Id.* at 354 n. 9; *see* Report of the Ad. Hoc Committee of the Harvard Medical School to Examine the Definition of Brain Death: A Definition of Irreversible Coma, 205 J.A.M.A. 337 (1968); *Lovato v. District Court*, 601 P.2d 1072, 1076–77 (Colo. 1979); *see also* Report of the Medical Consultants on the Diagnosis of Death to the President's Commission for the Study of Ethical Problems in Medicine and Biomedical and Behavioral Research, 246 J.A.M.A. 2184 (proposing other criteria.) However, the court refused to establish criteria for determining brain death because it noted that the advent of new research and technologies would continue to change the tests used for determining cessation of brain function. 115 Ill. App. 3d at 354 n. 9. Instead, the court merely required that the diagnosis of death under either standard must be made in accordance with "the usual and customary standards of medical practice." *Id.* at 355.

Even though *Haymer* was decided after the deaths of Stanley and Theresa, we find that the trial court properly applied the *Haymer* standards under the general rule that a civil case is governed by the law as it exists when judgment is rendered, not when the facts underlying the case occur. The application of *Haymer* is not unfair since the treating physicians made brain death diagnoses at the time of the deaths, and the parties presented evidence at trial regarding brain death.

Regardless of which standard of death is applied, survivorship is a fact which must be proven by a preponderance of the evidence by the party whose claim depends on survivorship. *In Re Estate of Moran*, 77 Ill. 2d 147, 150 (1979). The operative provisions of the Illinois version of the Uniform Simultaneous Death Act provides in pertinent part:

> If the title to property or its devolution depends upon the priority of death and there is no sufficient evidence that the persons have died otherwise than simultaneously and there is no other provision in the will, trust agreement, deed, contract of insurance or other governing instrument for distribution of the property different from the provisions of this Section:
>
> (a)   The property of each person shall be disposed of as if he had survived. . . .
>
> (d)   If the insured and the beneficiary of a policy of life or accident insurance have so died, the proceeds of the policy shall be distributed as if the insured had survived the beneficiary.

ILL. REV. STAT. 1981, ch. 110½, par. 3–1.

In cases where the question of survivorship is determined by the testimony of lay witnesses, the burden of sufficient evidence may be met by evidence of a positive sign of life in one body and the absence of any such sign in the other. *In Re Estate of Lowrance*, 66 Ill. App. 3d 159, 162 (1978); *Prudential Insurance Co. v. Spain*, 339 Ill. App. 476 (1950). In cases such as the instant case where the death process is monitored by medical professionals, their testimony as to "the usual and customary standards of medical practice" will be highly relevant when considering what constitutes a positive sign of life and what constitutes a criteria for determining death. *See In Re Haymer*, 115 Ill. App. 3d 349. Although the use of sophisticated medical technology can also make it difficult to determine when death occurs, the context of this case does not require a determination as to the exact moment at which the decedents died. Rather, the trial court's task was to determine whether there was sufficient evidence that Theresa Janus survived her husband. Our task on review of this factually disputed case is to determine whether the trial court's finding was against the manifest weight of the evidence.

See Fransen Construction Co. v. Industrial Commission, 384 Ill. 616, 628–29 (1943); *In Re Estate of Adams*, 348 Ill. App. 115, 121 (1952). We hold that it was not.

In the case at bar, both victims arrived at the hospital with artificial respirators and no obvious vital signs. There is no dispute among the treating physicians and expert witnesses that Stanley Janus died in both a cardiopulmonary sense and a brain death sense when his vital signs disappeared en route to the hospital and were never reestablished. He was pronounced dead at 8:15 p.m. on September 29, 1982, only after intensive procedures such as electro-shock, medication, and the insertion of a pacemaker failed to resuscitate him.

In contrast, these intensive procedures were not necessary with Theresa Janus because hospital personnel were able to reestablish a spontaneous blood pressure and pulse which did not have to be artificially maintained by a pacemaker or medication. Once spontaneous circulation was restored in the emergency room, Theresa was put on a mechanical respirator and transferred to the intensive care unit. Clearly, efforts to preserve Theresa Janus' life continued after more intensive efforts on Stanley's behalf had failed.

It is argued that the significance of Theresa Janus' cardiopulmonary functions, as a sign of life, was rendered ambiguous by the use of artificial respiration. In particular, reliance is placed upon expert testimony that a person can be brain dead and still have a spontaneous pulse and blood pressure which is indirectly maintained by artificial respiration. The fact remains, however, that Dr. Kim, an intensive care specialist who treated Theresa, testified that her condition in the emergency room did not warrant a diagnosis of brain death. In his opinion, Theresa Janus did not suffer irreversible brain death until much later, when extensive treatment failed to preserve her brain function and vital signs. This diagnosis was confirmed by a consulting neurologist after a battery of tests were performed to assess her brain function. Dr. Kim denied that these examinations were made merely to see if brain death had already occurred. At trial, only Dr. Vatz disagreed with their finding, but even he admitted that the diagnosis and tests performed on Theresa Janus were in keeping with the usual and customary standards of medical practice.

There was also other evidence presented at trial which indicated that Theresa Janus was not brain dead on September 29, 1982. Theresa's EEG, taken on September 30, 1982, was not flat but rather it showed some delta waves of extremely low amplitude. Dr. Hanley concluded that Theresa's EEG taken on September 30 exhibited brain activity. Dr. Vatz disagreed. Since the trier of fact determines the credibility of expert witnesses and the weight to be given to their testimony, the trial court in this case could have reasonably given greater weight to Dr. Hanley's opinion than to Dr. Vatz'. In addition, there is evidence that Theresa's pupil reacted to light on one occasion. It is argued that this evidence merely represents the subjective impression of a hospital staff member which is not corroborated by any other instance where Theresa's pupils reacted to light. However, this argument goes to the weight of this evidence and not to its admissibility. While these additional pieces of neurological data were by no means conclusive, they were competent evidence which tended to support the trial court's finding, and which also tended to disprove the contention that these tests merely verified that brain death had already taken place.

In support of the contention that Theresa Janus did not survive Stanley Janus, evidence was presented which showed that only Theresa Janus suffered seizures and exhibited a decerebrate posture shortly after ingesting the poisoned Tylenol. However, evidence that persons with these symptoms tend to die very quickly does not prove that Theresa Janus did not in fact survive Stanley Janus. Moreover, the evidence introduced is similar in nature to medical presumptions of survivorship based on decedents' health or physical condition which are considered too speculative to prove or disprove survivorship. *See In Re Estate of Moran*, 77 Ill. 2d 147, 153 (1979). Similarly, we find no support for the allegation that the hospital kept Theresa Janus on a mechanical respirator because her family requested that termination of her life support systems be delayed until the arrival of her brother, particularly since members of Theresa's family denied making such a request.

In conclusion, we believe that the record clearly established that the treating physicians' diagnoses of death with respect to Stanley and Theresa Janus were made in accordance with "the usual and customary standards of medical practice." Stanley Janus was diagnosed as having sustained irreversible cessation of circulatory and respiratory functions on September 29, 1982. These same physicians concluded that Theresa Janus' condition on that date did not warrant a diagnosis of death and, therefore, they continued their efforts to preserve her life. Their conclusion that Theresa Janus did not die until October 1, 1982, was based on various factors including the restoration of certain of her vital signs as well as other neurological evidence. The trial court found that these facts and circumstances constituted sufficient evidence that Theresa Janus survived her husband. It was not necessary to determine the exact moment at which Theresa died or by how long she survived him, and the trial court properly declined to do so. Viewing the record in its entirety, we cannot say that the trial court's finding of sufficient evidence of Theresa's survivorship was against the manifest weight of the evidence.

Because of our disposition of this case, we need not and do not consider whether the date of death listed on the victims' death certificates should be considered "facts" which constitute *prima facie* evidence of the date of their deaths. *See* ILL. REV. STAT.1981, ch. 111½, par. 73–25; *People v. Fiddler*, 45 Ill. 2d 181, 184–86 (1970).

Accordingly, there being sufficient evidence that Theresa Janus survived Stanley Janus, the judgment of the circuit court of Cook County is affirmed.

NOTES

1.   The Tylenol murders were a flashpoint for fear when they happened in 1982 in Chicago. Cyanide-laced pills killed seven people, including the Janus family members. The murders were never solved and if you want to learn more about them, there are a number of good podcasts. *See* Stuff You Should Know, *The Tylenol Murders* (May 28, 2019); My Favorite Murder, Episode 43 "In Arrears" (Nov. 17, 2016). The Tylenol murders also changed the way that pharmaceutical companies produced and packaged pills, bringing us tamper-resistant packaging and the caplet. *See* Clyde Haberman, *How an Unsolved Mystery Changed the Way We Take Pills*, N.Y. TIMES (Sept. 16, 2018); Howard Markel, *How the Tylenol murders of 1982 changed the way we consume medication*, PBS NewsHour, Sep 29, 2014.

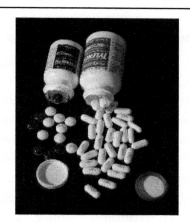

The (unsolved) Tylenol murders led Johnson & Johnson to redesign their product packaging and implement changes to improve product safety.

2.   The Illinois Simultaneous Death Act that applied in *Janus* required the court to determine whether there was "no sufficient evidence" of survival. Was the court correct that there was "sufficient" evidence that Theresa survived Stanley? Do you see any problems with this statute? The current (1991) version of the Uniform Simultaneous Death Act ("USDA") differs from the Illinois statute in that it requires "clear and convincing evidence" of survival for at least "120 hours" as follows:

> Except as otherwise provided . . . , where the title to property, the devolution of property, the right to elect an interest in property, or any other right or benefit depends upon an individual's survivorship of the death of another individual, an individual who is not established by clear and convincing evidence to have survived the other individual by at least 120 hours is deemed to have predeceased.

The UPC likewise uses 120 hours, providing that "an individual who is not established by clear and convincing evidence to have survived an event, including the death of another individual, is deemed to have predeceased the event." UPC § 2–702; *see also* UPC § 2–104. This rule applies to testate and intestate estates, to property passing under a will or any other governing document, and to jointly held property. How would *Janus* have been decided if the USDA or UPC applied? Do you think that 120 hours is too long (or too short)? Why might an estate planner include a provision requiring that a survivor live longer than 120 hours (or five days)? What would the purpose of a three-month, for example, survivorship provision be?

3.   Of course, sickness, aging, and death involve issues that extend far beyond considering how to define survivorship. Death underlies all that a trusts and estates lawyer does, and we will discuss throughout the course the psychological and emotional components of death and dying that every member of an estate planning team should consider. *See* Steve Leimberg, *Death and Dying—What Every Financial Service Professional Needs to Know,* http://www.naepc.org/events/ newsletter/5/2020. One way that people cope with dying is to write what is called an "ethical will." An ethical will is not considered a legal document but is a non-testamentary writing "intended to pass along values and beliefs to succeeding generations." Zoe M. Hicks, *Is Your (Ethical) Will in Order,* 33 ACTEC J. 154, 162 (2007). Ethical wills originated in ancient times when Jews, who were not allowed to own land, used ethical wills "to bequeath to their friends and family the wealth they did have, which included family histories, religious traditions, and spiritual practices." Cindy E. Faulkner, *Happily Ever After: An Ethical Will May be a Step on that Journey,* 12 T.M. COOLEY J. PRAC. & CLINICAL LAW 451, 451 (2010). These documents often relate family history, tell personal stories, or transmit the writer's values to future generations. *Id.* For more on ethical wills, and how to write them, see BARRY K. BAINES, M.D., ETHICAL WILLS: PUTTING YOUR VALUES ON PAPER (2d ed. 2006)

4.   One planning question that people face concerns burial and disposal of remains. The health care power of attorney in the Appendix, for example, has an organ donation provision; many people decide to become organ donors by checking a box on their drivers' license applications. People also choose quite a variety of ways to dispose of their remains, from traditional burial and cremation, to preservation in remembrance jewelry, tattoos, even fireworks, to the expanding market for ecofriendly or "green" burials.

Caitlin Doughty's book, *Will My Cat Eat My Eyeballs,* answers many of the questions people have about what happens to bodies after they die and what burial processes are like.

For a discussion of burial and funeral practices, see Victoria J. Haneman, *Funeral Poverty*, 55 U. RICH. L. REV. 387 (2021).

5.   Decisions about the disposition of remains also entail, for many people, decisions about financing and budgets. The average cost of a funeral ranges from $8,000 to $15,000 depending on where you live (see https://www.funeralwise.com/plan/costs/). This is a large expense for many people, as Victoria Haneman describes in her article, *Funeral Poverty*:

> [P]utting the deceased to rest carries (often-unexpected) funerary expenses for cremations, funerals, burials, and/or memorials. In 2019, the median cost of an adult funeral with viewing and burial exceeded $9,000. This number is particularly stark given that four out of ten Americans would have difficulty covering an unexpected $400 expense, and 12% would be unable to pay the unexpected $400 by any means. Although there are ways in which the consumer may mitigate cost, planning for a funeral or burial is expensive and complicated, and the consumer is frequently inexperienced and vulnerable.

Why are funeral costs so high? One answer, provided by Jessica Mitford in her classic 1963 book, THE AMERICAN WAY OF DEATH, is that funeral homes pad their bills with unnecessary expenses, inducing "vulnerable families . . . to pay for a luxury satin-lined casket and more roses in their funeral wreaths" at a time when the families are not equipped to make good financial decisions. To read more about Jessica Mitford, see David Robson, *The woman who forced us to look death in the face*, BBC https:// www.bbc.com/future/article/20160721- how-jessica-mitford-changed-our-ideas- about-death. Because of high costs, there are many companies that offer pre-paid funeral plans on installment. Many of these, however, are fraudulent schemes that lead to financially ruinous results for vulnerable individuals. See https://www. acfeinsights.com/acfe-insights/2017/5/12/funeral-fraud-scamming-the-dearly-departed.

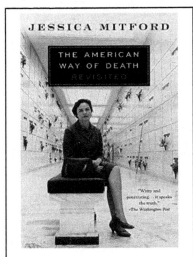

Jessica Mitford has been referred to as "the woman who forced us to look death in the face."

6.   Based on these kinds of critiques about burial planning and practices, a new generation of funeral professionals is attempting to make funeral planning more transparent, accessible, and financially affordable. In the U.K. Beyond.com has advertised affordable pricing for funeral services, but many of their ads have been rejected by the supervisory Ad Council as insensitive. *See* https://www.nytimes.com/2018/08/01/world/europe/uk-beyond-funeral-ads.html.

Beyond.com is an example of a company working to make funeral planning more accessible and affordable.

ASSESSMENTS

1.   Corey and Delta were recently married when they died while hiking in the mountains. Both died after falling from a forty-foot cliff. Search and rescue found the couple six days after they were due to arrive back at their basecamp.

An autopsy revealed that there was carbon monoxide in Corey's bloodstream and dirt underneath Corey's fingernails. Delta's skull was crushed, and there was no carbon monoxide in Delta's bloodstream. Corey's sole heir is Corey's mother, Mary. Delta's sole heir is Delta's father, Frederick. Corey's will left everything to Delta, and Delta's will left everything to Corey. Neither will named contingent beneficiaries or had a survivorship provision. At death, Corey owned tangible personal property and a life insurance policy payable to his estate. Delta owned a bank account in Delta's sole name. How should the executors distribute Corey and Delta's property if the UPC applies?

2.   Draft a provision to include in your married clients' mirror wills to address the case of simultaneous death. Consider whether you need to define the term "simultaneous death" and how you should direct the disposition of property in the event of simultaneous death.

3.   Play the role of an estate planning lawyer who is counseling a new client about an estate plan. You can either videotape yourself doing this counseling or pair up with a classmate who should play your client. The client has two children. (Christopher is ten years old, and Erin is four years old.) Your client's spouse has died, and your client has no plans to remarry. The conversation has now progressed to the advance directive. Explain to the client the document and the circumstances under which it would be used. Help your client decide whether she/he would like to execute the advance directive and who should be named to act as her/his agent.

E. Conclusion and Takeaways

Planning for incapacity, and for the physical act of death, is essential to the "care of self" component of this course. Nearly every estate planning lawyer will include incapacity documents—both financial and health-related—in a basic estate plan, so it is important to understand what these documents do and say. We will turn next to theories underlying wealth transfer, including donative freedom and the right to transmit property on death. We will ask if there are restrictions on this important right and, if not, whether there should be. The next chapter will also explore professional responsibility concerns that arise frequently and are unique to a practice that involves representing multiple parties who are part of the same family but often do not share the same interests.

CHAPTER 2 COMPREHENSIVE ASSESSMENTS

1.   **ADVANCE DIRECTIVE REVIEW AND CLIENT LETTER.** Find the statutory living will, health care power of attorney (or any equivalent advance

directives), and financial power of attorney for your jurisdiction. The jurisdiction may be the state in which you currently reside or any other state that interests you. Review the forms and answer the following questions:

a. Does your jurisdiction have separate forms for a living will and a health care power of attorney? What might be the reason for combining these documents? When were these forms last updated?

b. How do the provisions of your jurisdiction's living will differ from the Florida form that appears in the Appendix? How would you modify your jurisdiction's model living will to fit your own preferences?

c. How do the provisions of your jurisdiction's health care power of attorney form differ from the North Carolina form that appears in the Appendix? How would you modify your jurisdiction's health care power to fit your own preferences? Who would you choose to serve as your attorney(s)-in-fact?

d. How do the provisions of your jurisdiction's financial power of attorney form differ from the Alabama form that appears in the Appendix? How would you modify your jurisdiction's durable financial power to fit your own preferences?

Choose one of the above model documents and write a letter to a client explaining the document's purpose, any changes you would recommend to the model form to serve that client's purpose, and your reasons for these changes.

2. **DRAFT AN ETHICAL WILL.** Draft your own ethical will in the form of a letter to a particular loved one in which you share messages, advice, or lessons learned during your life.

Test Your Knowledge

To assess your understanding of the material in this chapter, click here to take a quiz.

CHAPTER 3

Donative Freedom and the Lawyer-Client Relationship in Inheritance Law

CHAPTER LEARNING OUTCOMES

Following your work with the material in this chapter, you should be able to do the following:

- Explain the right to transmit property at death, including limits on that right

- Identify the unique challenges impacting the lawyer-client relationship in a trusts and estates practice, and strategies to address those challenges

- Describe what is involved in meeting new estate planning clients, including the role of the initial meeting and intake questionnaire

- Locate resources to help with client engagement letters

- Recite the privity rule for malpractice liability

- Apply malpractice rules to errors in drafting and executing estate planning documents

A. Introduction

Now that we have some basic grounding in how individuals plan for incapacity and death, we will return to the topic of intergenerational wealth transfer. This chapter examines the policy issues at stake in a system that allows virtually unfettered donative freedom by individual property owners. **Donative freedom** is the property owner's right to give away property, during life or at death, as the owner desires, including determining who receives it; the form in which that person receives it; and whether someone else has the power to make these choices once the owner has died. **Part B** provides a short history of a property owner's right to transmit property at death, which you may recognize from your first-year Property course as one of the metaphorical "sticks" in an individual's bundle of property rights.

Part C turns to the limits on donative freedom. The first case you will read involves a gift conditioned on a beneficiary's making a certain marital choice. The second involves a racially restricted charitable trust that was established in a 1911 will and challenged in the 1960s. These cases illustrate a tension— between the "**dead hand**" control of the dead owner's wishes and the living beneficiaries' interests.

Following this discussion of donative freedom, **Part D** turns to the lawyer-client relationship. This part explores the professional responsibility obligations and unique challenges for an estate planning lawyer, including a discussion of best practices and potential malpractice liability. Notice that these two issues may overlap: if a client wants to make a bequest that pushes the limits of testamentary freedom, how should the lawyer respond?

B. The Right to Transmit Property by Will

A property owner's "right" to dispose of property by will was formally recognized in a pair of cases involving the Indian Land Consolidation Act ("ILCA"). *See Babbit v. Youpee*, 519 U.S. 234 (1997); *Hodel v. Irving*, 481 U.S. 704 (1987). The ILCA provision at issue sought to address the "extreme fractionation problem" arising from multiple owners of tribal land allotments; it provided that certain small interests in Indian lands **escheated** to the tribe on the landowner's death. The U.S. Supreme Court held that this provision effected a taking of private property without just compensation, reasoning that "the right to pass on property—to one's family in particular—has been part of the Anglo-American legal system since feudal times" and "[s]uch a complete abrogation of the rights of descent and devise could not be upheld." *Hodel*, 481 U.S. at 716. Congress amended the ILCA, and the *Youpee* case rejected the revised provision and reaffirmed the Court's earlier holding.

These cases have come to stand for the proposition that there is a quasi-constitutional right to pass on property at death. This argument has a distinguished lineage. In 1906, the Wisconsin Supreme Court discussed extensively the precedent for the constitutional right—indeed, it said, "natural" right—to pass on property in *Nunnemacher v. State*, 108 N.W. 627 (Wis. 1906). The court, nevertheless, upheld an unusual Wisconsin inheritance tax, which increased in degree as testators left property to remote relatives. *See also* Jack Stark, *A History of The Wisconsin Inheritance Tax*, 88 MARQ. L. REV. 947 (2005).

NOTES

1.   Although the right to dispose of one's wealth and assets by will is treated as a historical and deeply entrenched right by the U.S. Supreme Court in both *Hodel* and *Youpee*, it is worth remembering that the right to devise property by will was not a legal right or tradition in English law. In the context of feudalism, land could not be devised by the owner and instead descended automatically to the owner's eldest son through primogeniture. Primogeniture was designed to avoid the exact problem that plagues the court in *Hodel* and *Youpee*—the fractionalization of land. For more on primogeniture and the customs of forced heirship, see Carole Shammas, *English Inheritance Law and Its Transfer to the Colonies*, THE AMERICAN JOURNAL OF LEGAL HISTORY, Vol. 31, No. 2 (Apr.1987), pp. 145–163. Of course, feudal landholders found ways around the law, but the law itself

Primogeniture was the English system of succession where a family's land passed to the eldest son. The Allen Brothers (Portrait of James and John Lee Allen), circa 1790, Kimbell Art Museum, Fort Worth, Texas.

did not allow the choice of heir until 1540. One interesting feature of the passage of land was that all of the fixtures of the house constituted part of the real property and passed with it; the owner could not devise these things separately from the land itself. Fixtures included certain items of furniture, and ancestral armor. Remember that Hamlet's father's ghost appears fully dressed in armor in Act One, Scene One, of the play, "armed . . . so like the King / That was and is the question of these wars." Carla Spivack argues, in *The Woman Will Be Out: A New Look at the Law in Shakespeare's Hamlet*, 20 YALE J.L. & HUMAN. 31 (2008), that the Ghost's armor signals a theme in the play of anxiety over the very fact that ancestral land could be given, sold, or wagered away, instead of being bound to stay in the family down the generations. What, you may ask, happened to the land if there was no son, but there was a daughter? Authorities conflicted. At least one, the author of THE LAWES RESOLUTION OF WOMENS RIGHTS, a legal manual for women published in 1632, asserted that a daughter who was a direct descendant was to be preferred over a "transversal" male—like a nephew. One aristocrat, Lady Anne Clifford, based her claim to her ancestral lands on this authority and spent decades in court fighting for possession, which she eventually attained. *See* Carla Spivack, *Law, Land, Identity: The Case of Lady Anne Clifford*, 87 CHI.-KENT L. REV. 393 (2012).

2.   It is also worth remembering that the right to donative freedom, characterized by the U.S. Supreme Court as such a strong right in *Hodel* and *Youpee*, has also always been available primarily to elite white men. Married women had, historically, very limited abilities to draft wills and bequeath property because of their disability under coverture. Similarly, enslaved people were legally barred from both owning property and making wills. The right to dispose of one's assets, then, was not a longstanding right for everyone. And these disabilities have been a significant factor in creating the wealth gaps discussed in Chapter 1.

C. The Right to Restrict Property by Will

While property owners thus have a recognized right to *transmit* property at death, there is no corresponding right to *receive* property. In fact, a property owner can disinherit anyone from receiving property (except, in all but one state, the testator's spouse); indeed, a phrase that appears repeatedly in inheritance cases is that the testator's "intent" is paramount. The next case, *Shapira v. Union National Bank*, raises questions about permissible public policy limits on testamentary freedom. It involves a son's challenge to his father's will because the father conditioned receipt of property on the son's marrying someone of the same religion. As you read the case, consider the reasons for prioritizing the property owner's intent and what, if any, limits should constrain what testators may do with their property.

Shapira v. Union National Bank

315 N.E.2d 825 (Ohio Misc. 1974)

HENDERSON, J.

This is an action for a declaratory judgment and the construction of the will of David Shapira, M.D., who died April 13, 1973, a resident of this county. By agreement of the parties, the case has been submitted upon the pleadings and the exhibit.

The portions of the will in controversy are as follows:

> Item VIII. All the rest, residue and remainder of my estate, real and personal, of every kind and description and wheresoever situated, which I may own or have the right to dispose of at the time of my

decease, I give, devise and bequeath to my three (3) beloved children, to wit: Ruth Shapira Aharoni, of Tel Aviv, Israel, or wherever she may reside at the time of my death; to my son Daniel Jacob Shapira, and to my son Mark Benjamin Simon Shapira in equal shares, with the following qualifications:

(b)   My son Daniel Jacob Shapira should receive his share of the bequest only, if he is married at the time of my death to a Jewish girl whose both parents were Jewish. In the event that at the time of my death he is not married to a Jewish girl whose both parents were Jewish, then his share of this bequest should be kept by my executor for a period of not longer than seven (7) years and if my said son Daniel Jacob gets married within the seven year period to a Jewish girl whose both parents were Jewish, my executor is hereby instructed to turn over his share of my bequest to him. In the event, however, that my said son Daniel Jacob is unmarried within the seven (7) years after my death to a Jewish girl whose both parents were Jewish, or if he is married to a non Jewish girl, then his share of my estate, as provided in item 8 above should go to The State of Israel, absolutely.

The provision for the testator's other son Mark, is conditioned substantially similarly. Daniel Jacob Shapira, the plaintiff, alleges that the condition upon his inheritance is unconstitutional, contrary to public policy and unenforceable because of its unreasonableness, and that he should be given his bequest free of the restriction. Daniel is 21 years of age, unmarried and a student at Youngstown State University.

CONSTITUTIONALITY

Plaintiff's argument that the condition in question violates constitutional safeguards is based upon the premise that the right to marry is protected by the Fourteenth Amendment to the Constitution of the United States. *Meyer v. Nebraska*, 262 U.S. 390 (1923); *Skinner v. Oklahoma*, 316 U.S. 535 (1942); *Loving v. Virginia*, 388 U.S. 1 (1967). In *Loving v. Virginia*, the court held unconstitutional as violative of the Equal Protection and Due Process Clauses of the Fourteenth Amendment an antimiscegenation statute under which a black person and a white person were convicted for marrying. In its opinion the United States Supreme Court made the following statements:

Marriage is one of the 'basic civil rights of man,' fundamental to our very existence and survival. The Fourteenth Amendment requires that the freedom of choice to marry not be restricted by invidious racial discriminations. Under our Constitution, the freedom to marry, or not marry, a person of another race resides with the individual and cannot be infringed by the State.

From the foregoing, it appears clear, as plaintiff contends, that the right to marry is constitutionally protected from restrictive state legislative action. Plaintiff submits, then, that under the doctrine of *Shelley v. Kraemer*, 334 U.S. 1 (1948), the constitutional protection of the Fourteenth Amendment is extended from direct state legislative action to the enforcement by state judicial proceedings of private provisions restricting the right to marry. Plaintiff contends that a judgment of this court upholding the condition restricting marriage would, under *Shelley v. Kraemer*, constitute state action prohibited by the Fourteenth Amendment as much as a state statute.

In *Shelley v. Kraemer* the United States Supreme Court held that the action of the states to which the Fourteenth Amendment has reference includes action of state courts and state judicial officials. Prior to this decision the court had invalidated city ordinances which denied blacks the right to live in white neighborhoods. In *Shelley v. Kraemer* owners of neighboring properties sought to enjoin blacks from occupying properties which they had bought, but which were subjected to privately executed restrictions against use or occupation by any persons except those of the Caucasian race. Chief Justice Vinson noted, in the course of his opinion: 'These are cases in which the purposes of the agreements were secured only by judicial enforcement by state courts of the restrictive terms of the agreements.'

In the case at bar, this court is not being asked to enforce any restriction upon Daniel Jacob Shapira's constitutional right to marry. Rather, this court is being asked to enforce the testator's restriction upon his son's inheritance. If the facts and circumstances of this case were such that the aid of this court were sought to enjoin Daniel's marrying a non-Jewish girl, then the doctrine of *Shelley v. Kraemer* would be applicable, but not, it is believed, upon the facts as they are.

Counsel for plaintiff asserts, however, that his position with respect to the applicability of *Shelley v. Kraemer* to this case is fortified by two later decisions of the United States Supreme Court: *Evans v. Newton*, 382 U.S. 296 (1966), and *Pennsylvania v. Board of Directors of City Trusts of the City of Philadelphia*, 353 U.S. 230 (1957).

Evans v. Newton involved land willed in trust to the mayor and city council of Macon, Georgia, as a park for white people only, and to be controlled by a white board of managers. To avoid the city's having to enforce racial segregation in the park, the city officials resigned as trustees and private individuals were installed. The court held that such successor trustees, even though private individuals, became agencies or instrumentalities of the state and subject to the Fourteenth Amendment by reason of their exercising powers or carrying on functions governmental in nature. The following comment of Justice Douglas seems revealing: 'If a testator wanted to leave a school or center for the use of one race only and in no way implicated the State in the supervision, control, or management of that facility, we assume arguendo that no constitutional difficulty would be encountered.' 382 U.S. at 300.

The case of *Pennsylvania v. Board*, as the full title, above, suggests, is a case in which money was left by will to the city of Philadelphia in trust for a college to admit poor white male orphans. The court held that the board which operated the college was an agency of the state of Pennsylvania, and that, therefore, its refusal to admit the plaintiffs because they were negroes was discrimination by the state forbidden by the Fourteenth Amendment.

So, in neither *Evans v. Newton* nor *Pennsylvania v. Board* was the doctrine of the earlier *Shelley v. Kraemer* applied or extended. Both of them involved restrictive actions by state governing agencies, in one case with respect to a park, in the other case with respect to a college. Although both the park and the college were founded upon testamentary gifts, the state action struck down by the court was not the judicial completion of the gifts, but rather the subsequent enforcement of the racial restrictions by the public management.

Basically, the right to receive property by will is a creature of the law and is not a natural right or one guaranteed or protected by either the Ohio or the United States constitution. It is a fundamental rule of law in Ohio that a testator may legally entirely disinherit his children. This would seem to demonstrate that, from a constitutional standpoint, a testator may restrict a child's inheritance. The court concludes, therefore, that the upholding and enforcement of the provisions of Dr. Shapira's will conditioning the bequests to his sons upon their marrying Jewish girls does not offend the Constitution of Ohio or of the United States.

PUBLIC POLICY

The condition that Daniel's share should be 'turned over to him if he should marry a Jewish girl whose both parents were Jewish' constitutes a partial restraint upon marriage. If the condition were that the beneficiary not marry anyone, the restraint would be general or total, and, at least in the case of a first marriage, would be held to be contrary to public policy and void. A partial restraint of marriage which imposes only reasonable restrictions is valid, and not contrary to public policy: The great weight of authority in the United States is that gifts conditioned upon the beneficiary's marrying within a particular religious class or faith are reasonable.

Plaintiff contends, however, that in Ohio a condition such as the one in this case is void as against the public policy of this state. In Ohio, as elsewhere, a testator may not attach a condition to a gift which is in violation of public policy. There can be no question about the soundness of plaintiff's position that the public policy of Ohio favors freedom of religion and that it is guaranteed by Section 7, Article I of the Ohio Constitution, providing that 'all men have a natural and indefeasible right to worship Almighty God according to the dictates of their own conscience.' Plaintiff's position that the free choice of religious practice cannot be circumscribed or controlled by contract is substantiated by *Hackett v. Hackett* (C.A. Lucas 1958), 150 N.E.2d 431. This case held that a covenant in a separation agreement, incorporated in a divorce decree, that the mother would rear a daughter in the Roman Catholic faith was unenforceable. However, the controversial condition in the case at bar is a partial restraint upon marriage and not a covenant to restrain the freedom of religious practice; and, of course, this court is not being asked to hold the plaintiff in contempt for failing to marry a Jewish girl of Jewish parentage.

Counsel contends that if 'Dr. David Shapira, during his life, had tried to impose upon his son those restrictions set out in his Will he would have violated the public policy of Ohio as shown in *Hackett v. Hackett*. The public policy is equally violated by the restrictions Dr. Shapira has placed on his son by his Will.' This would be true, by analogy, if Dr. Shapira, in his lifetime, had tried to force his son to marry a Jewish girl as the condition of a completed gift. But it is not true that if Dr. Shapira had agreed to make his son an inter-vivos gift if he married a Jewish girl within seven years, that his son could have forced him to make the gift free of the condition.

It is noted, furthermore, in this connection, that the courts of Pennsylvania distinguish between testamentary gifts conditioned upon the religious faith of the beneficiary and those conditioned upon marriage to persons of a particular religious faith. In *In re Clayton's Estate*, 13 Pa. D. & C. 413, the court upheld a gift of a life estate conditioned upon the beneficiary's not marrying a woman of the Catholic faith. In its opinion the court distinguishes the earlier case of *Drace v. Klinedinst*, 118 A. 907 (Pa. 1922), in which a life estate willed to grandchildren, provided they remained faithful to a particular religion, was held to violate the public policy of Pennsylvania. In *Clayton's Estate*, the court said that the condition concerning marriage did not affect the faith of the beneficiary, and that the condition, operating only on the choice of a wife, was too remote to be regarded as coercive of religious faith.

Plaintiff's counsel also cites *Maddox v. Maddox*, 52 Va. (11 Grattain's) 804 (1854). The testator in this case willed a remainder to his niece if she remain a member of the Society of Friends. When the niece arrived at a marriageable age there were but five or six unmarried men of the society in the neighborhood in which she lived. She married a non-member and thus lost her own membership. The court held the condition to be an unreasonable restraint upon marriage and void. While the court considered the testamentary condition to be a restraint upon marriage, it was primarily one in restraint of religious faith. The court said that with the small number of eligible bachelors in the area the condition would have operated as a virtual prohibition of the niece's marrying, and that she could not be expected to 'go abroad' in search of a helpmate or to be subjected to the chance of being sought after by a stranger.

In arguing for the applicability of the *Maddox v. Maddox* test of reasonableness to the case at bar, counsel for the plaintiff asserts that the number of eligible Jewish females in this county would be an extremely small minority of the total population especially as compared with the comparatively much greater number in New York, whence have come many of the cases comprising the weight of authority upholding the validity of such clauses. There are no census figures in evidence. While this court could probably take judicial notice of the fact that the Jewish community is a minor, though important segment of our total local population, nevertheless the court is by no means justified in judicial knowledge that there is an insufficient number of eligible young ladies of Jewish parentage in this area from which Daniel would have a reasonable latitude of choice. And of course, Daniel is not at all confined in his choice to residents of this county, which is a very different circumstance in this day of travel by plane and freeway and communication by telephone, from the horse and buggy days of the 1854 *Maddox v. Maddox* decision. Consequently, the decision does not appear to be an appropriate yardstick of reasonableness under modern living conditions.

Plaintiff's counsel contends that the Shapira will falls within the principle of *Fineman v. Central National Bank*, 175 N.E.2d 837 (Ohio 1961), holding that the public policy of Ohio does not countenance a bequest or device conditioned on the beneficiary's obtaining a separation or divorce from his wife. Counsel argues that the Shapira condition would encourage the beneficiary to marry a qualified girl just to receive the bequest, and then to divorce her afterward. This possibility seems too remote to be a pertinent application of the policy against bequests conditioned upon divorce.

Finally, counsel urges that the Shapira condition tends to pressure Daniel, by the reward of money, to marry within seven years without opportunity for mature reflection and jeopardizes his college education. It seems to the court, on the contrary, that the seven-year time limit would be a most reasonable grace period, and one which would give the son ample opportunity for exhaustive reflection and fulfillment of the condition without constraint or oppression. Daniel is no more being 'blackmailed into a marriage by immediate financial gain,' as suggested by counsel, than would be the beneficiary of a living gift or conveyance upon consideration of a future marriage-an arrangement which has long been sanctioned by the courts of this state. *Thompson v. Thompson*, 17 Ohio St. 649 (1867).

In the opinion of this court, the provision made by the testator for the benefit of the State of Israel upon breach or failure of the condition is significant for two reasons. First, it distinguishes this case from *Maddox v. Maddox*. Second, and of greater importance, it demonstrates the depth of the testator's conviction. His purpose was not merely a negative one designed to punish his son for not carrying out his wishes. His unmistakable testamentary plan was that his possessions be used to encourage the preservation of the Jewish faith and blood, hopefully through his sons, but, if not, then through the State of Israel. Whether this judgment was wise is not for this court to determine. But it is the duty of this court to honor the testator's intention within the limitations of law and of public policy. The prerogative granted to a testator by the laws of this state to dispose of his estate according to his conscience is entitled to as much judicial protection and enforcement as the prerogative of a beneficiary to receive an inheritance.

It is the conclusion of this court that public policy should not and does not preclude the fulfillment of Dr. Shapira's purpose, and that in accordance with the weight of authority in this country, the conditions contained in his will are reasonable restrictions upon marriage, and valid.

NOTES

1. *Shapira* involves conflicts among competing policy interests. The testator imposed on his son a condition that the son marry within the Jewish faith before reaching age 27 to qualify to receive property from the testamentary trust, and the court upheld the condition. This case might appear, at first glance, to be a relic of its time and location, but the question of how far the right to donative

freedom should extend continues to arise. *See, e.g., In re Estate of Max Feinberg*, 19
N.E.2d 888 (Ill. 2009); *In re Estate of Jameson*, No. A-2154-14T4 (N.J. Super. Ct.
App. Div. Aug. 12, 2016) (explaining that the testator's motivation for
disinheritance not relevant, even if based on religion).

2.   If some limits on donative freedom are permissible as a public policy
matter, what types are they? For example, what if a testator requires that a
descendant marry someone of the same race, rather than religion, to receive
property? What if a testator requires that a descendant, who is homosexual,
marry someone of the opposite gender? Does your view change if the conditions
of inheritance appear as "incentives" to encourage or reward "positive"
behavior, such as achieving career success, reaching an educational milestone,
or having children? Consider the trust established by a retired Harvard
psychology professor, Truman Lee Kelley, which had an elaborate set of
instructions and a point system for distributions on his sons' marriages and the
birth of their children. The "eugenics trust" would award $400 for every point
the sons and their spouses scored above the average population on their
marriage and $500 for every point on the birth of a child. *See* Paul A. Lombardo,
When Harvard Said No to Eugenics: The J. Ewing Mears Bequest, 1927, 57 BIOLOGY
AND MEDICINE 374, 388 (2014); *The Fitter, The Richer: Prof's Will Sets up Fitness
Test for Sons*, SPOKESMAN REVIEW (May 12, 1961).

ASSESSMENT

Identify at least three justifications for allowing unrestricted testamentary
freedom and at least three justifications for limiting such freedom. In
formulating these reasons, consider various perspectives, such as the property
owner's, the property owner's family members, and society in general.

The following case arose from the 1911 will of Senator Augustus O. Bacon
of Macon, Georgia. He left property for creation of a segregated park along with
the explicit statement that the park should not be integrated. In 1963, when it
became apparent to some of the trustees—all of whom had to be white under
the provisions of Bacon's will—that the city of Macon was not enforcing the
racial restriction, the trustees sued, joined by some of Bacon's heirs. The case
went up to the U.S. Supreme Court *twice* before the property was returned to
Bacon's relatives. *See Evans v. Newton*, 382 U.S. 296 (1966) (concluding that
Baconsfield park could not be operated on a segregated basis); *Evans v. Abney*,
396 U.S. 435 (1970) (upholding reversion). In the opinion reproduced below,
the Georgia Supreme Court had to decide whether to modify the discriminatory

gift to allow the property to benefit everyone or to have the property revert to the testator's family. You will see references to the doctrine of **"cy pres,"** which we discuss in greater detail in Chapter 15 on charitable trusts. Cy pres allows a court to modify a trust when a charitable purpose "becomes unlawful, impracticable, impossible to achieve, or wasteful."

Baconsfield Park in Macon, Georgia was a racially segregated park established in the 1911 will of Senator Augustus O. Bacon. Image shows ponds in Baconsfield Park, Macon, Georgia. (1930).

Evans v. Abney

165 S.E.2d 160 (Ga. 1968)

MOBLEY, J.

This appeal is from an order of Bibb Superior Court which held that a trust created by Senator A. O. Bacon in his will dated March 28, 1911, providing for a park in the City of Macon, to be called Baconsfield, for the benefit of "white women, white girls, white boys and white children of the City of Macon," had failed and the property would revert by operation of law to the heirs at law of Senator Bacon.

The litigation was commenced in May, 1963, when Charles E. Newton and others, as members of the Board of Managers of Baconsfield, brought a petition against the City of Macon, as trustee under the will of Senator Bacon, and others, as successor trustees, asserting that the City of Macon was failing and refusing to enforce the provisions of the will with respect to the exclusive use of Baconsfield, and praying that the city be removed as a trustee. Reverend E. S. Evans and others, Negro residents of the City of Macon, filed an intervention, contending that the restriction in the trust limiting the use of the park to white women and children was illegal, and praying that the general charitable purpose of the testator be effectuated by refusing to appoint private persons as trustees. The heirs at law of Senator Bacon also intervened, praying that, if the relief sought by the original petitioners not be granted, the property revert to the heirs. The City of Macon in its answer alleged that it could not legally enforce segregation. The city later amended its answer, alleging that it had by resolution resigned as trustee under the will, and praying that its resignation be accepted by the court. The superior court accepted this resignation by the City of Macon and appointed new trustees. On appeal by the Negro intervenors from this judgment, this court affirmed the judgment of the trial court.

> **Language Note:** The *Evans* case uses the word "Negro" to refer to the intervenors. We have left the original language intact, even though the word is not appropriate in modern usage, to reflect one aspect of the case's history and vernacular. It is worth pausing to recognize this use of language, though, because "legal language is uniquely powerful" and can become "entrenched because of the necessarily iterative nature of the legal process." Lucy Jewel, Elizabeth Berenguer, and Terri A. McMurtry-Chubb, *Gut Renovations: Using Critical and Comparative Rhetoric to Remodel How the Law Addresses Privilege and Power*, 23 HARV. LATINX L. REV. 205, 214–15 (2020).

The Supreme Court of the United States granted *writ of certiorari* and reversed the judgment of this court, holding in part:

> Under the circumstances of this case, we cannot but conclude that the public character of this park requires that it be treated as a public institution subject to the command of the Fourteenth Amendment, regardless of who now has title under state law. We may fairly assume that had the Georgia courts been of the view that even in private hands the park may not be operated for the public on a segregated basis, the resignation would not have been approved and private trustees appointed. We put the matter that way because on this record we cannot say that the transfer of title *per se* disentangled the park from segregation under the municipal regime that long controlled it.

Evans v. Newton, 382 U.S. 296.

The judgment of the Supreme Court of the United States was made the judgment of this court. On remand, the Superior Court of Bibb County entered a summary judgment decreeing as follows:

> The relief prayed by Reverend E. S. Evans and other Negro intervenors is denied. Under the decision of the United States Supreme Court the essential purpose of the trust creating Baconsfield in Senator Bacon's will has become impossible of performance, and the trust has failed and is terminated. There is no general charitable purpose expressed in the will. It is clear that the testator sought to benefit a certain group of people, white women and children of Macon, and the language of the will clearly indicates that the limitation to this class of persons was an essential and indispensable part of the testator's plan for Baconsfield. There has been no dedication of Baconsfield as a park for the use of the general public. There is nothing in the record to support the contention that the Bacon heirs are estopped from claiming a reversion to them. The property has reverted by operation of law to these heirs.

On appeal, the intervenors urge that the doctrine of *cy pres* should be applied to Senator Bacon's will, and that the nearest effectuation of the intention of Senator Bacon would be to operate the park for the benefit of all citizens of the City of Macon. The doctrine of *cy pres* is expressed by Code § 108–202 as follows:

> When a valid charitable bequest is incapable for some reason of execution in the exact manner provided by the testator, donor, or founder, a court of equity will carry it into effect in such a way as will as nearly as possible effectuate his intention.

Senator Bacon in the provision of his will creating Baconsfield was specific in listing the persons for whose benefit the trust was created, the beneficiaries being "the white women, white girls, white boys and white children of the City of Macon." He empowered the board of managers to exercise their discretion in also admitting "white men of the City of Macon, and white persons of other communities." He left no doubt as to his wish that the park be operated on a segregated basis.

It is contended that, in obedience to the mandate of the United States Supreme Court, the City of Macon should be ordered re-instated as trustee of Baconsfield and directed to operate the park on a non-segregated basis. The opinion of the Supreme Court of the United States held that the park could not be operated for the public on a segregated basis and generally reversed the judgment of this court affirming the judgment accepting the resignation of the City of Macon as trustee and appointing new trustees. The United States Supreme Court did not decide the question of whether the trust would terminate because of the inability of the trustees to effectuate the testator's purpose in creating the trust.

The intervenors urge that they have been denied designated constitutional rights by the judgment of the Superior Court of Bibb County holding that the trust has failed and the property has reverted to Senator Bacon's estate by operation of law. We recognize the rule announced in *Shelley v. Kraemer*, 334 U.S. 1, that it is a violation of the equal protection clause of the Fourteenth Amendment of the United States Constitution for a state court to enforce a private agreement to exclude persons of a designated race or color from the use or occupancy of real estate for residential purposes. That case has no application to the facts of the present case.

Senator Bacon by his will selected a group of people, the white women and children of the City of Macon, to be the objects of his bounty in providing them with a recreational area. The intervenors were never objects of his bounty, and they never acquired any rights in the recreational area. They have not been deprived of their right to inherit, because they were given no inheritance.

The action of the trial court in declaring that the trust has failed, and that, under the laws of Georgia, the property has reverted to Senator Bacon's heirs, is not action by a state court enforcing racially discriminatory provisions. The original action by the Board of Managers of Baconsfield seeking to have the trust executed in accordance with the purpose of the testator has been defeated. It then was incumbent on the trial court to determine what disposition should be made of the property. The court correctly held that the property reverted to the heirs at law of Senator Bacon.

NOTES

1.   *Evans* raises the question of racially restricted testamentary provisions. Looking at the language of Bacon's will, do you think the court's determination was correct? Should the testator's preference matter in a case like this one, where the gift is charitable and where it continues to take effect long after it was created? Should public policy concerns limit racial restrictions in wills and trusts?

2.   The Baconsfield litigation centered on state action. Recall that the *Shapira* court based its holding, at least in part, on an assertion that validating the

discriminatory trust provision at issue was not state action, and therefore not barred under equal protection. In fact, *Shapira* cites to and distinguishes *Evans v. Newton*. Are the two rulings consistent? Should courts look more broadly to public policy considerations to remove discriminatory provisions in all testamentary gifts?

42 U.S.C. § 1982, codifying the Civil Rights Act of 1866, provides that:

> All citizens of the United States shall have the same right, in every State and Territory, as is enjoyed by white citizens thereof to inherit, purchase, lease, sell, hold, and convey real and personal property.

In *Jones v. Alfred H. Mayer Co.*, the U.S. Supreme Court held that § 1982 "bars all racial discrimination, private as well as public, in the sale or rental of property, and that the statute, thus construed, is a valid exercise of the power of Congress to enforce the Thirteenth Amendment." 392 U.S. 409, 410 (1968). Based on the language of § 1982 and *Mayer*, does § 1982 protect a potential beneficiary from being rejected as a beneficiary of property, whether by inheritance or other form of transfer, because of race? One scholar argues that this is indeed the case. *See* Frances Wagman Roisman, *The Impact of the Civil Rights Act of 1866 on Racially Discriminatory Donative Transfers*, 53 ALA. L. REV. 463, 467 (2002).

3.   Race appears in unexpected ways in wills and trusts. Before the Civil War, humans were often the property passed on in wills in the states where slavery was legal. Sometimes, on the other hand, a will freed the testator's slaves. One early case of testamentary emancipation came in *Pleasants v. Pleasants*, 6 Va. (2 Call) 319 (1800), where the testator had promised freedom to the slaves he owned if that became possible. When the Virginia legislature passed a general emancipation statute—that allowed owners to free their slaves—the executor went to free them. Yet, Pleasant's heirs claimed that the promise of emancipation in the future was a violation of the rule against perpetuities. The will was upheld in a model of a flexible approach to the rule. Southern legislatures and courts increasingly restricted such testamentary emancipation, however. *See, e.g., Cleland v. Waters*, 16 Ga. 496, 514 (1854); *Maddox v. Maddox's Admin.*, 52 Va. (11 Grattan) 804 (1854). One case that received a lot of attention arose in Mississippi. It involved a testator who left his plantation to his son (who was also the child of the testator's slave). The testator had taken the son and his mother to Ohio and emancipated them but made the mistake of returning with them to Mississippi. The testator's white heirs sued and had the emancipation invalidated on that ground that it was done in Ohio rather than Mississippi. The testator's family, to whom he had wanted to leave his property, were returned to slavery. *Hinds v. Brazealle*, 3 Miss. (2 How.) 837 (1838). Harriett Beecher Stowe

turned that sad case into a vignette in her 1856 anti-slavery novel *Dred: A Tale of the Great Dismal Swamp*. Much more frequently wills provided for the devise of humans to a surviving spouse or to the testator's issue. *See, e.g.,* Stephen D. Davis & Alfred L. Brophy, *"The most solemn act of my life": Family, Property, Will, and Trust in the Antebellum South*, 62 ALA. L. REV. 757 (2011) (discussing appearance of slaves in pre-Civil War wills).

ASSESSMENTS

1.   Esmeralda died at age 65, leaving her property in a testamentary trust for her two daughters, Isabela and Janelle. The trust provides that when a daughter reaches age 35, she would receive her trust property outright so long as she is married to someone who follows the religion of Islam. At Esmeralda's death, Janelle is 37, married to a Muslim man, and the mother of three children. Isabela, however, is 30 and unmarried. Isabela sues to declare the trust invalid. Is she likely to succeed?

2.   You represent Maria Vega, who has been named the executor of the estate of Avi Ellis, a world-renowned musician. Vega was a lifelong friend of Ellis. Although Vega does not have a close relationship with Ellis's children, Vega is aware that Ellis supported the children and that the children continue to have financial need. Ellis's will directs the executor to destroy, on the musician's death, any compositions that have not been recorded or released. All other property passes to Ellis's children. Write a letter to the children that uses legally accurate but client-accessible language to explain how you will treat the provision in Ellis's will.

D. The Client-Lawyer Relationship in Inheritance Matters

This part addresses the unique role of the lawyer in a trusts and estates practice. One of the realities of serving as a trusts and estates lawyer is that it often means representing people in challenging circumstances, including:

- Clients who are elderly, ill, or dying

- Clients who have just suffered the death of a loved one

- Clients who seek some form of joint representation but have divergent goals

The lawyer may very well have questions about who the client is, whether the client has capacity, and whether the lawyer has any other family members as clients already (or whether several family members are seeking representation together). The lawyer also must elicit quite personal information from the client to represent the client properly.

1.   Clients with Diminished Capacity

Trusts and estates lawyers frequently face a special set of questions about how to represent clients with diminishing or diminished capacity. Chapter 2 used *In re Winthrop*, 848 N.E.2d 961 (Ill. 2006), to raise some of the problems with abuse of elderly clients in the context of durable powers of attorney; this problem will appear again in Chapter 6 with will challenges, where contestants commonly assert that the testator lacked capacity and was subject to undue influence. Here, the question involves the lawyer's obligations when the potential client is alive but appears to have some form of diminished capacity, either because of advanced age or infirmity. The *Model Rules of Professional Conduct* frame the attorney's duties regarding representation of people with diminished capacity in Section 1.14 as follows:

Rule 1.14 Client with Diminished Capacity

(a)   When a client's capacity to make adequately considered decisions in connection with a representation is diminished, whether because of minority, mental disability or for some other reason, the lawyer shall, as far as reasonably possible, maintain a normal client-lawyer relationship with the client.

(b)   When the lawyer reasonably believes that the client has diminished capacity, is at risk of substantial physical, financial or other harm unless action is taken and cannot adequately act in the client's own interest, the lawyer may take reasonably necessary protective action, including consulting with individuals or entities that have the ability to take action to protect the client and, in appropriate cases, seeking the appointment of a guardian *ad litem*, conservator or guardian.

(c)   Information relating to the representation of a client with diminished capacity is protected by Rule 1.6. When taking protective action pursuant to paragraph (b), the lawyer is impliedly authorized under Rule 1.6(a) to reveal information about the client, but only to the extent reasonably necessary to protect the client's interests.

ACTEC publishes its own set of commentaries on the *Model Rules* and explains the test of "testamentary capacity" as follows:

Testamentary Capacity. If the testamentary capacity of a client is uncertain, the lawyer should exercise particular caution in assisting the client to modify his or her estate plan. The lawyer generally should not prepare a will, trust agreement or other dispositive instrument for a client who the lawyer reasonably believes lacks the requisite capacity. On the other hand, because of the importance of testamentary freedom, the lawyer may properly assist clients whose testamentary capacity appears to be borderline. In any such case the lawyer should take steps to preserve evidence regarding the client's testamentary capacity. In cases involving clients of doubtful testamentary capacity, the lawyer should consider, if available, procedures for obtaining court supervision of the proposed estate plan, including substituted judgment proceedings.

ACTEC COMMENT. ON MODEL RULES OF PRO. CONDUCT 132 (4th ed. 2006). The *Model Rules* require lawyers to continue to follow the wishes of clients, even if they have diminished capacity. *See, e.g.,* South Dakota Ethics Opinion 2007–3 (requiring that lawyer follow wishes of client to keep will secret from family members) (discussed in ANNOTATIONS TO ACTEC MODEL RULES COMMENTARIES, 2005–09, at 12).

NOTES

1.   ACTEC also publishes a checklist of issues a lawyer should consider before accepting the representation of any client involved in an inheritance matter. A copy of the checklist can be found in the Appendix. The first item on the checklist is, not surprisingly, to ascertain whether the client has capacity. How should a lawyer go about doing so? What type of "tests" would allow a lawyer to make this judgment? How often does the lawyer need to revisit this question during the course of representation?

2.   When a lawyer drafts a will or trust for a client who is subsequently shown to lack capacity, the typical remedy includes denying probate to the will or invalidating the trust. *See, e.g., Taylor v. Shipley,* 2005 Mich. App. LEXIS 2301. When a lawyer fails to take adequate precautions for a client who lacks capacity, the client's estate may have a cause of action. *See, e.g., Thiel v. Miller,* 164 S.W.3d 76 (Mo. App. 2005) (supporting malpractice liability against attorney who failed to prepare a durable power of attorney that would have permitted a family member to alter a trust to reduce the estate tax); *see also* Kerry R. Peck, *Estate Planning/ Elder Law Ethical Issues in Representing Elderly Clients with Diminished Capacity,* http://www.isba.org/ibj/2011/11/ethicalissuesinrepresentingelderlyc.

There are also cases where lawyers take overt action to defraud clients who lack capacity. *See, e.g., In re Cofield*, 937 So. 2d 330 (La. 2006) (disbarring attorney who drafted irrevocable trust for client with diminished capacity that appointed attorney as trustee). And there are other cases where lawyers are not benefitting personally from fraud but are acting without consulting clients who seem to lack capacity. In *Disciplinary Counsel v. Taylor*, 899 N.E.2d 955 (Ohio 2008), for instance, a lawyer revised a will for a client who lacked capacity and had it executed without telling the client that her husband had died; the will omitted a daughter whom the now-deceased husband had thought was stealing from the couple.

2. Representing Clients Jointly

Trusts and estates lawyers often are asked to represent multiple clients who may have different needs and objectives. Frequently, for example, a married couple will seek estate planning advice as joint clients. Joint engagements can pose problems where one spouse says something to the lawyer that the spouse does not want the other spouse to know. The lawyer is in the unenviable position of having confidential information that, perhaps, the other spouse needs to know for the purposes of that spouse's own estate planning, potentially leading to a conflict between the duty to maintain client confidences and the duty to keep another client informed. A model engagement letter for a married couple, part of ACTEC's sample engagement letters, appears in the Appendix, as do several provisions of the *Model Rules* that are particularly important to joint engagements. These rules include: Rule 1.2, prohibiting a lawyer from doing anything that furthers fraud by a client; Rule 1.4, requiring a lawyer to keep clients informed; Rule 1.6, requiring a lawyer to maintain client confidences; and Rule 1.7, dealing with conflicts of interest.

The following cases involve different forms of joint representation: representation of married couples; and representation of different generations in the same family. *A v. B* involves a law firm that discovers information about one spouse that will affect the estate planning of the other spouse. *Hotz v. Minyard* involves a lawyer that misleads a client's daughter about estate planning the firm did for her father. As you read these cases, consider what the lawyers could have done to reduce the likelihood that litigation would ensue.

A. v. B.

726 A.2d 924 (N.J. 1999)

POLLOCK, J.

This appeal presents the issue whether a law firm may disclose confidential information of one co-client to another co-client. Specifically, in this paternity action, the mother's former law firm, which contemporaneously represented the father and his wife in planning their estates, seeks to disclose to the wife the existence of the father's illegitimate child.

A law firm, Hill Wallack (described variously as "the law firm" or "the firm"), jointly represented the husband and wife in drafting wills in which they devised their respective estates to each other. The devises created the possibility that the other spouse's issue, whether legitimate or illegitimate, ultimately would acquire the decedent's property.

Unbeknown to Hill Wallack and the wife, the husband recently had fathered an illegitimate child. Before the execution of the wills, the child's mother retained Hill Wallack to institute this paternity action against the husband. Because of a clerical error, the firm's computer check did not reveal the conflict of interest inherent in its representation of the mother against the

> **Language Note:** The *A. v. B.* court uses the term "illegitimate" to refer to the child who was born outside of the marriage. The current vernacular, which you will see used in the UPC and the Uniform Parentage Act, is the term "non-marital child." Chapter 4 discusses the rights of non-marital children to inherit property through intestacy.

husband. On learning of the conflict, the firm withdrew from representation of the mother in the paternity action. Now, the firm wishes to disclose to the wife the fact that the husband has an illegitimate child. To prevent Hill Wallack from making that disclosure, the husband joined the firm as a third-party defendant in the paternity action.

In the Family Part, the husband, represented by new counsel, Fox, Rothschild, O'Brien & Frankel ("Fox Rothschild"), requested restraints against Hill Wallack to prevent the firm from disclosing to his wife the existence of the child. The Family Part denied the requested restraints. The Appellate Division reversed and remanded.

Hill Wallack then filed motions in this Court seeking leave to appeal, to present oral argument, and to accelerate the appeal.

I.

Although the record is both informal and attenuated, the parties agree substantially on the relevant facts. Because the Family Part has sealed the record, we refer to the parties without identifying them by their proper names. So viewed, the record supports the following factual statement.

In October 1997, the husband and wife retained Hill Wallack, a firm of approximately sixty lawyers, to assist them with planning their estates. On the commencement of the joint representation, the husband and wife each signed a letter captioned "Waiver of Conflict of Interest." In explaining the possible conflicts of interest, the letter recited that the effect of a testamentary transfer by one spouse to the other would permit the transferee to dispose of the property as he or she desired. The firm's letter also explained that information provided by one spouse could become available to the other. Although the letter did not contain an express waiver of the confidentiality of any such information, each spouse consented to and waived any conflicts arising from the firm's joint representation.

Unfortunately, the clerk who opened the firm's estate planning file misspelled the clients' surname. The misspelled name was entered in the computer program that the firm uses to discover possible conflicts of interest. The firm then prepared **reciprocal wills** and related documents with the names of the husband and wife correctly spelled.

In January 1998, before the husband and wife executed the estate planning documents, the mother coincidentally retained Hill Wallack to pursue a paternity claim against the husband. This time, when making its computer search for conflicts of interest, Hill Wallack spelled the husband's name correctly. Accordingly, the computer search did not reveal the existence of the firm's joint representation of the husband and wife. As a result, the estate planning department did not know that the family law department had instituted a paternity action for the mother. Similarly, the family law department did not know that the estate planning department was preparing estate plans for the husband and wife.

A lawyer from the firm's family law department wrote to the husband about the mother's paternity claim. The husband neither objected to the firm's representation of the mother nor alerted the firm to the conflict of interest. Instead, he retained Fox Rothschild to represent him in the paternity action. After initially denying paternity, he agreed to voluntary DNA testing, which revealed that he is the father. Negotiations over child support failed, and the mother instituted the present action.

After the mother filed the paternity action, the husband and wife executed their wills at the Hill Wallack office. The parties agree that in their wills, the husband and wife leave their respective residuary estates to each other. If the other spouse does not survive, the contingent beneficiaries are the testator's issue. The wife's will leaves her residuary estate to her husband, creating the possibility that her property ultimately may pass to his issue. Under N.J.S.A. 3B:1–23, the term "issue" includes both legitimate and illegitimate children. When the wife executed her will, therefore, she did not know that the husband's illegitimate child ultimately may inherit her property.

The conflict of interest surfaced when Fox Rothschild, in response to Hill Wallack's request for disclosure of the husband's assets, informed the firm that it already possessed the requested information. Hill Wallack promptly informed the mother that it unknowingly was representing both the husband and the wife in an unrelated matter.

Hill Wallack immediately withdrew from representing the mother in the paternity action. It also instructed the estate planning department not to disclose any information about the husband's assets to the member of the firm who had been representing the mother. The firm then wrote to the husband stating that it believed it had an ethical obligation to disclose to the wife the existence, but not the identity, of his illegitimate child. Additionally, the firm stated that it was obligated to inform the wife "that her current estate plan may devise a portion of her assets through her spouse to that child." The firm suggested that the husband so inform his wife and stated that if he did not do so, it would. Because of the restraints imposed by the Appellate Division, however, the firm has not disclosed the information to the wife.

II.

This appeal concerns the conflict between two fundamental obligations of lawyers: the duty of confidentiality, *Rules of Professional Conduct* (RPC) 1.6(a), and the duty to inform clients of material facts, RPC 1.4(b). The conflict arises from a law firm's joint representation of two clients whose interests initially were, but no longer are, compatible.

Crucial to the attorney-client relationship is the attorney's obligation not to reveal confidential information learned in the course of representation. Thus, RPC 1.6(a) states that "[a] lawyer shall not reveal information relating to representation of a client unless the client consents after consultation, except for disclosures that are impliedly authorized in order to carry out the representation." Generally, "the principle of attorney-client confidentiality imposes a sacred trust on the attorney not to disclose the client's confidential communication." *State v. Land*, 73 N.J. 24, 30, 372 A.2d 297 (1977).

A lawyer's obligation to communicate to one client all information needed to make an informed decision qualifies the firm's duty to maintain the confidentiality of a co-client's information. RPC 1.4(b), which reflects a lawyer's duty to keep clients informed, requires that "[a] lawyer shall explain a matter to the extent reasonably necessary to permit the client to make informed decisions regarding the representation." In limited situations, moreover, an attorney is permitted or required to disclose confidential information. Hill Wallack argues that RPC 1.6 mandates, or at least permits, the firm to disclose to the wife the existence of the husband's illegitimate child. RPC 1.6(b)(1) requires that a lawyer disclose "information relating to representation of a client" to the proper authorities if the lawyer "reasonably believes" that such disclosure is necessary to prevent the client "from committing a criminal, illegal or fraudulent act that the lawyer reasonably believes is likely to result in death or substantial bodily harm or substantial injury to the financial interest or property of another." Despite Hill Wallack's claim that RPC 1.6(b) applies, the facts do not justify mandatory disclosure. The possible inheritance of the wife's estate by the husband's illegitimate child is too remote to constitute "substantial injury to the financial interest or property of another" within the meaning of RPC 1.6(b).

By comparison, in limited circumstances RPC 1.6(c) permits a lawyer to disclose a confidential communication. RPC 1.6(c) permits, but does not require, a lawyer to reveal confidential information to the extent the lawyer reasonably believes necessary "to rectify the consequences of a client's criminal, illegal or fraudulent act in furtherance of which the lawyer's services had been used." RPC 1.6(c)(1). Although RPC 1.6(c) does not define a "fraudulent act," the term takes on meaning from our construction of the word "fraud," found in the analogous "crime or fraud" exception to the attorney-client privilege. *See* N.J.R.E. 504(2)(a) (excepting from attorney-client privilege "a communication in the course of legal service sought or obtained in the aid of the commission of a crime or fraud"). When construing the "crime or fraud" exception to the attorney-client privilege, "our courts have generally given the term 'fraud' an expansive reading." *Fellerman v. Bradley*, 99 N.J. 493, 503–04, 493 A.2d 1239 (1985).

We likewise construe broadly the term "fraudulent act" within the meaning of RPC 1.6(c). So construed, the husband's deliberate omission of the existence of his illegitimate child constitutes a fraud on his wife. When discussing their respective estates with the firm, the husband and wife reasonably could expect that each would disclose information material to the distribution of their estates, including the existence of children who are contingent residuary beneficiaries. The husband breached that duty. Under the reciprocal wills, the existence of the husband's illegitimate child could affect the distribution of the wife's estate, if she predeceased him. Additionally, the husband's child support payments and other financial responsibilities owed to the illegitimate child could deplete that part of his estate that otherwise would pass to his wife.

From another perspective, it would be "fundamentally unfair" for the husband to reap the "joint planning advantages of access to information and certainty of outcome," while denying those same advantages to his wife. Teresa S. Collett, *Disclosure, Discretion, or Deception: The Estate Planner's Ethical Dilemma from a Unilateral Confidence*, 28 REAL PROP. PROB. TR. J. 683, 743 (1994). In effect, the husband has used the law firm's services to defraud his wife in the preparation of her estate.

Under RPC 1.6, the facts support disclosure to the wife. The law firm did not learn of the husband's illegitimate child in a confidential communication from him. Indeed, he concealed that information from both his wife and the firm. The law firm learned about the husband's child through its representation of the mother in her paternity action against the husband. Accordingly, the husband's expectation of nondisclosure of the information may be less than if he had communicated the information to the firm in confidence.

In addition, the husband and wife signed letters captioned "Waiver of Conflict of Interest." These letters acknowledge that information provided by one client could become available to the other. The letters, however, stop short of explicitly authorizing the firm to disclose one spouse's confidential information to the other. Even in the absence of any such explicit authorization, the spirit of the letters supports the firm's decision to disclose to the wife the existence of the husband's illegitimate child.

Neither our research nor that of counsel has revealed a dispositive judicial decision from this or any other jurisdiction on the issue of disclosure of confidential information about one client to a co-client. Persuasive secondary authority, however, supports the conclusion that the firm may disclose to the wife the existence of the husband's child.

The forthcoming *Restatement (Third) of The Law Governing Lawyers* § 112 comment l (Proposed Final Draft No. 1, 1996) ("the *Restatement*") suggests, for example, that if the attorney and the co-clients have reached a prior, explicit agreement concerning the sharing of confidential information, that agreement controls whether the attorney should disclose the confidential information of one co-client to another. An attorney, on commencing joint representation of co-clients, should agree explicitly with the clients on the sharing of confidential information. In such a "disclosure agreement," the co-clients can agree that any confidential information concerning one co-client, whether obtained from a co-client himself or herself or from another source, will be shared with the other co-client. Similarly, the co-clients can agree that unilateral confidences or other confidential information will be kept confidential by the attorney. Such a prior agreement will clarify the expectations of the clients and the lawyer and diminish the need for future litigation.

In the absence of an agreement to share confidential information with co-clients, the *Restatement* reposes the resolution of the lawyer's competing duties within the lawyer's discretion:

> [T]he lawyer, after consideration of all relevant circumstances, has the . . . discretion to inform the affected co-client of the specific communication if, in the lawyer's reasonable judgment, the immediacy and magnitude of the risk to the affected co-client outweigh the interest of the communicating client in continued secrecy.

Restatement (Third) of The Law Governing Lawyers, supra, § 112 comment l.

Additionally, the *Restatement* advises that the lawyer, when withdrawing from representation of the co-clients, may inform the affected co-client that the attorney has learned of information adversely affecting that client's interests that the communicating co-client refuses to permit the lawyer to disclose. In the context of estate planning, the *Restatement* also suggests that a lawyer's disclosure of confidential information communicated by one spouse is appropriate only if the other spouse's failure to learn of the information would be materially detrimental to that other spouse or frustrate the spouse's intended testamentary arrangement. *Id.* § 112 comment l, illustrations 2, 3. The *Restatement* provides two analogous illustrations in which a lawyer has been jointly retained by a husband and wife to prepare reciprocal wills. The first illustration states:

> Lawyer has been retained by Husband and Wife to prepare wills pursuant to an arrangement under which each spouse agrees to leave most of their property to the other. Shortly after the wills are executed, Husband (unknown to Wife) asks Lawyer to prepare an *inter vivos* trust for an illegitimate child whose existence Husband has kept secret from Wife for many years and about whom Husband had not previously

informed Lawyer. Husband states that Wife would be distraught at learning of Husband's infidelity and of Husband's years of silence and that disclosure of the information could destroy their marriage. Husband directs Lawyer not to inform Wife. The *inter vivos* trust that Husband proposes to create would not materially affect Wife's own estate plan or her expected receipt of property under Husband's will, because Husband proposes to use property designated in Husband's will for a personally favored charity. In view of the lack of material effect on Wife, Lawyer may assist Husband to establish and fund the *inter vivos* trust and refrain from disclosing Husband's information to Wife.

Id. § 112 comment l, illustration 2.

In authorizing non-disclosure, the *Restatement* explains that an attorney should refrain from disclosing the existence of the illegitimate child to the wife because the trust "would not materially affect Wife's own estate plan or her expected receipt of property under Husband's will." *Ibid.*

The other illustration states:

Same facts as [the prior Illustration], except that Husband's proposed *inter vivos* trust would significantly deplete Husband's estate, to Wife's material detriment and in frustration of the Spouses' intended testamentary arrangements. If Husband will neither inform Wife nor permit Lawyer to do so, Lawyer must withdraw from representing both Husband and Wife. In the light of all relevant circumstances, Lawyer may exercise discretion whether to inform Wife either that circumstances, which Lawyer has been asked not to reveal, indicate that she should revoke her recent will or to inform Wife of some or all the details of the information that Husband has recently provided so that Wife may protect her interests. Alternatively, Lawyer may inform Wife only that Lawyer is withdrawing because Husband will not permit disclosure of information that Lawyer has learned from Husband.

Id. § 112 comment l, illustration 3.

Because the money placed in the trust would be deducted from the portion of the husband's estate left to his wife, the *Restatement* concludes that the lawyer may exercise discretion to inform the wife of the husband's plans.

Similarly, the American College of Trust and Estate Counsel (ACTEC) also favors a discretionary rule. The ACTEC suggests that the lawyer first attempt to convince the client to inform the co-client. *Id.* When urging the client to disclose the information, the lawyer should remind the client of the implicit understanding that all information will be shared by both clients. The lawyer also should explain to the client the potential legal consequences of non-disclosure, including invalidation of the wills. *Id.* Furthermore, the lawyer may mention that failure to communicate the information could subject the lawyer to a malpractice claim or disciplinary action. *Id.*

The ACTEC reasons that if unsuccessful in persuading the client to disclose the information, the lawyer should consider several factors in deciding whether to reveal the confidential information to the co-client, including: (1) duties of impartiality and loyalty to the clients; (2) any express or implied agreement among the lawyer and the joint clients that information communicated by either client to the lawyer regarding the subject of the representation would be shared with the other client; (3) the reasonable expectations of the clients; and (4) the nature of the confidence and the harm that may result if the confidence is, or is not, disclosed. *Id.* at 68–69. The Section of Real Property, Probate and Trust Law of the American Bar Association, in a report prepared by its Special Study Committee on Professional Responsibility, reached a similar conclusion.

The Professional Ethics Committees of New York and Florida, however, have concluded that disclosure to a co-client is prohibited. New York State Bar Ass'n Comm. on Professional Ethics, Op. 555 (1984); Florida State Bar Ass'n Comm. on Professional Ethics, Op. 95–4 (1997).

The Florida Ethics Committee addressed the following situation:

Lawyer has represented Husband and Wife for many years in a range of personal matters, including estate planning. Husband and Wife have substantial individual assets, and they also own substantial jointly-held property. Recently, Lawyer prepared new updated wills that Husband and Wife signed. Like their previous wills, their new wills primarily benefit the survivor of them for his or her life, with beneficial disposition at the death of the survivor being made equally to their children. * * *

Several months after the execution of the new wills, Husband confers separately with Lawyer. Husband reveals to Lawyer that he has just executed a codicil prepared by another law firm) that makes substantial beneficial disposition to a woman with whom Husband has been having an extra-marital relationship.

Florida State Bar Ass'n Comm. on Professional Ethics, Op. 95–4, *supra.*

Reasoning that the lawyer's duty of confidentiality takes precedence over the duty to communicate all relevant information to a client, the Florida Ethics Committee concluded that the lawyer did not have discretion to reveal the information. In support of that conclusion, the Florida committee reasoned that joint clients do not necessarily expect that everything relating to the joint representation communicated by one co-client will be shared with the other co-client.

"Surprising me—that's your life's work."

A lawyer who jointly represents spouses in estate planning should establish, at the beginning of the representation, how "confidential" information will be treated.

In several material respects, however, the present appeal differs from the Florida example. First, the Florida rule, unlike RPC 1.6(c), does not except disclosure needed "to rectify the consequences of a client's fraudulent act in the furtherance of which the lawyer's services had been used." Second, Hill Wallack learned of the husband's paternity from a third party, not from the husband himself. Third, the husband and wife signed an agreement suggesting their intent to share all information with each other.

Because Hill Wallack wishes to make the disclosure, we need not reach the issue whether the lawyer's obligation to disclose is discretionary or mandatory. In conclusion, Hill Wallack may inform the wife of the existence of the husband's illegitimate child.

The judgment of the Appellate Division is reversed, and the matter is remanded to the Family Part.

Hotz v. Minyard

403 S.E.2d 634 (S.C. 1991)

GREGORY, C.J.

This appeal is from an order granting respondents summary judgment on several causes of action. We reverse in part and affirm in part.

Respondent Minyard (Tommy) and appellant (Judy) are brother and sister. Their father, Mr. Minyard, owns two automobile dealerships, Judson T. Minyard, Inc. (Greenville Dealership), and Minyard Waidner, Inc. (Anderson Dealership). Tommy has been the dealer in charge of the Greenville Dealership since 1977. Judy worked for her father at the Anderson Dealership beginning in 1983; she was also a vice-president and minority shareholder. In 1985, Mr. Minyard signed a contract with General Motors designating Judy the successor dealer of the Anderson Dealership.

Respondent Dobson is a South Carolina lawyer practicing in Greenville . Dobson did legal work for the Minyard family and its various businesses for many years. On October 24, 1984, Mr. Minyard came to Dobson's office to execute a will with his wife, his secretary, and Tommy in attendance. At this meeting he signed a will which left Tommy the Greenville Dealership, gave other family members bequests totaling $250,000.00, and divided the remainder of his estate equally between Tommy and a trust for Judy after his wife's death. All present at the meeting were given copies of this will. Later that afternoon, however, Mr. Minyard returned to Dobson's office and signed a second will containing the same provisions as the first except that it gave the real estate upon which the Greenville dealership was located to Tommy outright. Mr. Minyard instructed Dobson not to disclose the existence of the second will. He specifically directed that Judy not be told about it.

In January 1985, Judy called Dobson requesting a copy of the will her father had signed at the morning meeting on October 24, 1984. At Mr. Minyard's direction, or at least with his express permission, Dobson showed Judy the first will and discussed it with her in detail.

Judy testified she had the impression from her discussion with Dobson that under her father's will she would receive the Anderson Dealership and would share equally with her brother in her father's estate. According to Dobson, however, he merely explained Mr. Minyard's intent to provide for Judy as he had for Tommy when and if she became capable of handling a dealership. Dobson made a notation to this effect on the copy of the will he discussed with Judy. Judy claimed she was led to believe the handwritten notes were part of her father's will.

In any event, Judy claims Dobson told her the will she was shown was in actuality her father's last will and testament. Although Dobson denies ever making this express statement, he admits he never told her the will he discussed with her had been revoked.

In January 1986, Mr. Minyard was admitted to the hospital for various health problems. In April 1986, he suffered a massive stroke. Although the date of the onset of his mental incompetence is disputed, it is uncontested he is now mentally incompetent.

Judy and Tommy agreed that while their father was ill, Judy would attend to his daily care and Tommy would temporarily run the Anderson Dealership until Judy returned. During this time, Tommy began making changes at the Anderson Dealership. Judy questioned the wisdom of her brother's financial dealings. When she sought to return to the Anderson Dealership as successor dealer, Tommy refused to relinquish control. Eventually, in August 1986, he terminated Judy from the dealership's payroll.

Judy consulted a law firm concerning her problems with her brother's operation of the Anderson Dealership. As a result, on November 15, 1986, Mr. Minyard executed a codicil removing Judy and her children as beneficiaries under his will. Judy was immediately advised of this development by letter.

In March 1987, Judy met with Tommy, her mother, and Dobson at Law Firm's office. She was told if she discharged her attorneys and dropped her plans for a lawsuit, she would be restored under her father's will and could work at the Greenville Dealership with significant fringe benefits. Judy testified she understood restoration under the will meant she would inherit the Anderson Dealership and receive half her father's estate, including the real estate, as she understood from her 1985 meeting with Dobson. Judy discharged her attorneys and moved to Greenville. Eventually, however, Tommy terminated her position at the Greenville Dealership.

As a result of the above actions by Tommy and Dobson, Judy commenced this suit alleging various causes of action. We address only the trial judge's ruling on the cause of action against Dobson for breach of fiduciary duty.

ANALYSIS

Judy's complaint alleges Dobson breached his fiduciary duty to her by misrepresenting her father's will in January 1985. As a result, in March 1987 she believed she would regain the Anderson Dealership if she refrained from pursuing her claim against her brother. This delay gave Tommy additional time in control of the Anderson Dealership during which he depleted its assets.

The trial judge granted Dobson summary judgment on the ground Dobson owed Judy no fiduciary duty because he was acting as Mr. Minyard's attorney and not as Judy's attorney in connection with her father's will. We disagree.

We find the evidence indicates a factual issue whether Dobson breached a fiduciary duty to Judy when she went to his office seeking legal advice about the effect of her father's will. Law Firm had prepared Judy's tax returns for approximately twenty years until September 1985 and had prepared a will for her she signed only one week earlier. Judy testified she consulted Dobson personally in 1984 or 1985 about a suspected misappropriation of funds at one of the dealerships and as late as 1986 regarding her problems with her brother. She claimed she trusted Dobson because of her dealings with him over the years as her lawyer and accountant.

A fiduciary relationship exists when one has a special confidence in another so that the latter, in equity and good conscience, is bound to act in good faith. An attorney/client relationship is by nature a fiduciary one. Although Dobson represented Mr. Minyard and not Judy regarding her father's will, Dobson did have an ongoing attorney/client relationship with Judy and there is evidence she had "a special confidence" in him. While Dobson had no duty to disclose the existence of the second will against his client's (Mr. Minyard's) wishes, he owed Judy the duty to deal with her in good faith and not actively misrepresent the first will. We find there is a factual issue presented whether Dobson breached a fiduciary duty to Judy. We conclude summary judgment was improperly granted Dobson on this cause of action.

NOTES

1.   It is common for spouses and other family members to seek some form of joint representation in estate planning matters because there are many efficiencies that come from this form of representation. For example, the lawyer will assess a single fee, and many of the same background facts will apply. Apart from confidential information that the parties do not want to share, can you think of other potential conflicts that might arise? Should an attorney agree to undertake joint representation?

2.   One important way to guard against inter-spousal conflicts and resulting problems is to have an engagement letter that authorizes the lawyer to disclose confidences to either spouse. In cases where a lawyer is representing a married couple in estate planning, ACTEC's model engagement letter includes the following statement:

> It is common for a husband and wife to employ the same lawyer to assist them in planning their estates. You have taken this approach by asking me to represent both of you in your planning. It is important that you understand that, because I will be representing both of you,

you are considered my client, collectively. Ethical considerations prohibit me from agreeing with either of you to withhold information from the other. Accordingly, in agreeing to this form of representation, each of you is authorizing me to disclose to the other any matters related to the representation that one of you might discuss with me or that I might acquire from any other source. In this representation, I will not give legal advice to either of you or make any changes in any of your estate planning documents without your mutual knowledge and consent. Of course, anything either of you discusses with me is privileged from disclosure to third parties, except (a) with your consent, (b) for communication with other advisors, or (c) as otherwise required or permitted by law or the rules governing professional conduct.

The entire suggested letter deals with other situations as well, including how a lawyer will handle conflicts of interest that arise.

3.   Should the presumption be that it is ethical to represent couples jointly— or not? Carla Spivack argues that this presumption is highly problematic, given the many vehicles available today to disinherit a spouse, and the continuing statistical lower economic status of women. *See* Carla Spivack, *Twenty-First Century Trusts and Ethics: Estate Planning for Couples,* 53 CREIGHTON L. REV. 683, 684 (2020) (asking whether "given the economic inequality between men and women, and between primary caregivers and primary wage-earners in today's American family, can a couple—same or opposite sex—ever be assumed to be non-adverse in estate planning?").

ASSESSMENTS

1.   What, if anything, did the Hill Wallack firm do correctly in the *A v. B* matter? Write a short memo to the head of the Hill Wallack firm identifying at least three actions, statements, or documents to evidence the firm's correct conduct. Complete the memo by making at least two suggestions for what the firm should do differently moving forward.

2.   Draft an engagement letter from Dobson to Judy Minyard setting forth the scope of the firm's work in connection with drafting Judy's will. You might refer to the engagement letter in the Appendix or others on the ACTEC website.

3.   Create, in narrative form, the background story of two clients who arrive at your office for estate planning advice. These two clients may be married, related by blood, or in some less formal but significant relationship. You may

base the narrative on real people or make it up entirely. Then conduct a roleplay where you use the client checklist in the Appendix to explain and define the scope of your representation to your imagined joint clients.

3. Liability for Legal Malpractice

Trusts and estates lawyers may face claims regarding their representation of clients some years after their active representation of those clients has ceased, largely because drafting problems or problems in client counseling may remain unknown for a long time. These claims are especially complicated when the client is deceased, as is true in both cases set forth below. The first, *Simpson v. Calivas*, involves a malpractice action filed by a disappointed child of the testator and an attorney who argues that his duties ran only to the client and not to third parties (the "**privity defense**"). The second case, *Sisson v. Jankowski*, rejects a disappointed relative's claim that the attorney committed malpractice by delaying the will's execution. Although both cases are about malpractice liability, they also provide cautionary tales about how easy it is for attorneys to make mistakes that undermine testator intent.

Simpson v. Calivas

650 A.2d 318 (N.H. 1994)

HORTON, J.

The plaintiff, Robert H. Simpson, Jr., appeals from a directed verdict, grant of summary judgment, and dismissal of his claims against the lawyer who drafted his father's will. The plaintiff's action, sounding in both negligence and breach of contract, alleged that the defendant, Christopher Calivas, failed to draft a will which incorporated the actual intent of Robert H. Simpson, Sr. to leave all his land to the plaintiff in fee simple. The trial court dismissed the action, ruling that under New Hampshire law an attorney who drafts a will owes no duty to intended beneficiaries. We reverse and remand.

In March 1984, Robert H. Simpson, Sr. (Robert Sr.) executed a will that had been drafted by the defendant. The will left all real estate to the plaintiff except for a life estate in "our *homestead* located at Piscataqua Road, Dover, New Hampshire" (emphasis added), which was left to

> **Connection Note:** In Chapter 8, we will discuss how courts address drafting errors and ambiguities in the context of will interpretation, including the type of evidence that is admissible to resolve any ambiguities.

Robert Sr.'s second wife, Roberta C. Simpson (stepmother). After Robert Sr.'s death in September 1985, the plaintiff and his stepmother filed a joint petition in the Strafford County Probate Court seeking a determination, essentially, of whether the term "homestead" referred to all the decedent's real property on Piscataqua Road (including a house, over one hundred acres of land, and buildings used in the family business), or only to the house (and, perhaps, limited surrounding acreage). The probate court found the term "homestead" ambiguous, and in order to aid construction, admitted some extrinsic evidence of the testator's surrounding circumstances, including evidence showing a close relationship between Robert Sr. and plaintiff's stepmother. The probate court, however, did not admit notes taken by the defendant during consultations with Robert Sr. that read: "House to wife as a life estate remainder to son, Robert H. Simpson, Jr. . . . Remaining land . . . to son Robert A. [sic] Simpson, Jr." The probate court construed the will to provide Roberta with a life estate in all the real property. After losing the will construction action—then two years after his father's death—the plaintiff negotiated with his stepmother to buy out her life estate in all the real property for $400,000.

The plaintiff then brought this malpractice action. At trial, the plaintiff presented evidence, including the defendant's notes and testimony of some of Robert Sr.'s friends and acquaintances, to show that Robert Sr. had intended that his son take the buildings used in the family business and the bulk of the land in fee simple. The trial court directed a verdict on the reasoning that the plaintiff had failed to introduce any evidence of intent that conflicted with the terms of the will as construed.

We reverse and remand.

I. Duty to Intended Beneficiaries

In order to recover for negligence, a plaintiff must show that "there exists a duty, whose breach by the defendant causes the injury for which the plaintiff seeks to recover." *Goodwin v. James*, 595 A.2d 504, 507 (N.H. 1991). The critical issue, for purposes of this appeal, is whether an attorney who drafts a testator's will owes a duty of reasonable care to intended beneficiaries. We hold that there is such a duty.

As a general principle, "the concept of 'duty' . . . arises out of a relation between the parties and the protection against reasonably foreseeable harm." *Morvay v. Hanover Insurance Co.*, 506 A.2d 333, 334 (N.H. 1986). The existence of a contract between parties may constitute a relation sufficient to impose a duty to exercise reasonable care, but in general, "the scope of such a duty is limited to those in privity of contract with each other." *Robinson v. Colebrook Savings Bank*, 254 A.2d 837, 839 (N.H. 1969). The privity rule is not ironclad, though, and we have been willing to recognize exceptions particularly where, as here, the risk to persons not in privity is apparent. *Id.* In *Morvay*, for example, we held that investigators hired by an insurance company to investigate the cause of a fire owed a duty to the insureds to perform their investigation with due care despite the absence of privity. Accordingly, the insureds stated a cause of action by alleging that the investigators negligently concluded that the fire was set, thereby prompting the insurance company to deny coverage. *Morvay*, 506 A.2d at 335; *see also Spherex, Inc. v. Alexander Grant & Co.*, 451 A.2d 1308 (N.H. 1982) (accountants may be liable in negligence to those who reasonably rely on their work despite lack of privity); *Robinson*, 254 A.2d at 837 (bank owes duty to beneficiary of account with survivorship feature set up by depositor).

Because this issue is one of first impression, we look for guidance to other jurisdictions. The overwhelming majority of courts that have considered this issue have found that a duty runs from an attorney to an intended beneficiary of a will. R. Mallen & J. Smith, LEGAL MALPRACTICE 3d. § 26.4, at 595 (1989 & Supp.1992); *see, e.g., Stowe v. Smith*, 441 A.2d 81 (Conn. 1981); *Needham v. Hamilton*, 459 A.2d 1060 (D.C. 1983); *Ogle v. Fuiten*, 466 N.E.2d 224 (Ill. 1984); *Hale v. Groce*, 744 P.2d 1289 (Or. 1987). A theme common to these cases, similar to a theme of cases in which we have recognized exceptions to the privity rule, is an emphasis on the foreseeability of injury to the intended beneficiary. As the California Supreme Court explained in reaffirming the duty owed by an attorney to an intended beneficiary:

> When an attorney undertakes to fulfil the testamentary instructions of his client, he realistically and in fact assumes a relationship not only with the client but also with the client's intended beneficiaries. The attorney's actions and omissions will affect the success of the client's testamentary scheme; and thus the possibility of thwarting the testator's wishes immediately becomes foreseeable. Equally foreseeable is the possibility of injury to an intended beneficiary. In some ways, the beneficiary's interests loom greater than those of the client. After the latter's death, a failure in his testamentary scheme works no practical effect except to deprive his intended beneficiaries of the intended bequests.

Heyer v. Flaig, 70 Cal. 2d 223 (1969). We agree that although there is no privity between a drafting attorney and an intended beneficiary, the obvious foreseeability of injury to the beneficiary demands an exception to the privity rule.

Reversed and remanded.

Sisson v. Jankowski

809 A.2d 1265 (N.H. 2002)

BROCK, C.J.

The United States District Court for the District of New Hampshire (McAuliffe, J.) has certified the following question of law:

> Whether, under New Hampshire law and the facts as pled in plaintiff's verified complaint, an attorney's negligent failure to arrange for his or her client's timely execution of a will and/or an attorney's failure to provide reasonable professional advice with respect to the client's testamentary options (*e.g.*, the ability to cure a draft will's lack of a contingent beneficiary clause by simply inserting a hand-written provision), which failure proximately caused the client to die intestate, gives rise to a viable common law claim against that attorney by an intended beneficiary of the unexecuted will.

For the reasons stated below, we answer the certified question in the negative.

Because this question arose in the context of a motion to dismiss and absent a copy of the plaintiff's complaint, we assume the truth of the factual allegations recited by the court in its certification order, and construe all inferences in the light most favorable to the plaintiff.

In December 1998, the decedent, Dr. Warren Sisson, retained the defendants, Attorney Jankowski and her law firm, Wiggin & Nourie, P.A., to prepare his will and other estate planning documents. According to the plaintiff, Thomas K. Sisson, the decedent informed Attorney Jankowski that he was suffering from cancer, did not want to die intestate, and, therefore, wished to prepare a will that would pass his entire estate to the plaintiff, his brother. The decedent told Attorney Jankowski that he was particularly interested in ensuring that none of his estate pass to his other brother, from whom he was estranged.

Attorney Jankowski prepared a will and other estate planning documents and, in mid-January 1999, mailed them to the decedent for his review and execution. The decedent was injured in mid-January, however, and, therefore, did not receive the documents until January 22, 1999, when a neighbor delivered them to him at a nursing home. Three days later, the plaintiff contacted Attorney

Jankowski to tell her that the decedent wanted to finalize his estate planning documents quickly because of his deteriorating condition.

On February 1, 1999, Attorney Jankowski and two other law firm employees visited the decedent in the nursing home to witness his execution of the estate planning documents. The decedent executed all of the documents except his will. After Attorney Jankowski asked him whether the will should include provisions for a contingent beneficiary, the decedent expressed his desire to insert such a clause, thereby providing that his estate would pass to a charity in the event the plaintiff predeceased him.

According to the plaintiff, the decedent's testamentary intent was clear as of the end of the February 1, 1999 meeting: the unexecuted will accurately expressed his intent to pass his entire estate to the plaintiff. Nevertheless, rather than modifying the will immediately to include a hand-written contingent beneficiary clause, modifying it at her office and returning later that day for the decedent's signature, or advising the decedent to execute the will as drafted to avoid the risk of dying intestate and later drafting a codicil, Attorney Jankowski left without obtaining the decedent's signature to the will.

Three days later, Attorney Jankowski returned with the revised will. The decedent did not execute it, however, because Attorney Jankowski did not believe he was competent to do so. She left without securing his signature and told him to contact her when he was ready to sign the will.

The decedent died intestate on February 16, 1999. His estate did not pass entirely to the plaintiff as he had intended, but instead was divided among the plaintiff, the decedent's estranged brother, and the children of a third (deceased) brother. The plaintiff brought legal malpractice claims against the defendants, alleging that they owed him a duty of care because he was the intended beneficiary of their relationship with the decedent.

For the purposes of this certified question, there is no dispute as to the decedent's testamentary intent: he wanted to avoid dying intestate and to have his entire estate pass to the plaintiff. Nor does the plaintiff claim that the defendants frustrated the decedent's intent by negligently preparing his will. Rather, the plaintiff asserts that the defendants were negligent because they failed to have the decedent execute his will promptly and to advise him on February 1 of the risk of dying intestate if he did not execute the draft presented at that meeting.

The narrow question before us is whether the defendants owed the plaintiff a duty of care to ensure that the decedent executed his will promptly. Whether a duty exists is a question of law. A duty generally arises out of a relationship between the parties. While a contract may supply the relationship, ordinarily the scope of the duty is limited to those in privity of contract with one another. We have, in limited circumstances, recognized exceptions to the privity requirement where necessary to protect against reasonably foreseeable harm.

Ultimately, whether to impose a duty of care "rests on a judicial determination that the social importance of protecting the plaintiff's interest outweighs the importance of immunizing the defendant from extended liability."

In *Simpson v. Calivas*, 650 A.2d 318 (N.H. 1994), we recognized an exception to the privity requirement with respect to a will beneficiary and held that an attorney who drafts a testator's will owes a duty to the beneficiaries to draft the will non-negligently. In *Simpson*, a testator's son sued the attorney who drafted his father's will, alleging that the will failed to incorporate his father's actual intent. The will left all real estate to the plaintiff, except for a life estate in "our homestead," which was left to the plaintiff's stepmother. *Id.* The probate litigation concerned whether "our homestead" referred to all of the decedent's real property, including a house, over one hundred acres of land and buildings used in the family business, or only to the house, and perhaps limited surrounding acreage. The plaintiff argued that the decedent intended to leave him the buildings used in the family business and the bulk of the surrounding land in fee simple. The plaintiff lost the will construction action, and then brought a malpractice action against the drafting attorney, arguing that the decedent's will did not accurately reflect his intent.

We held that the son could maintain a contract action against the attorney, as a third-party beneficiary of the contract between the attorney and his father, and a tort action, under a negligence theory. With respect to the negligence claim, we concluded that, "although there is no privity between a drafting attorney and an intended beneficiary, the obvious foreseeability of injury to the beneficiary demands an exception to the privity rule."

Simpson is consistent with the prevailing rule that a will beneficiary may bring a negligence action against an attorney who failed to draft the will in conformity with the testator's wishes. *See generally* R. Mallen & J. Smith, LEGAL MALPRACTICE § 32.4, at 735 (5th ed.2000); *Stowe v. Smith*, 441 A.2d 81 (Conn. 1981); *Lucas v. Hamm*, 364 P.2d 685, 688–89 (Cal. 1961), *cert. denied*, 368 U.S. 987 (1962); *Succession of Killingsworth*, 292 So.2d 536, 542 (La. 1973); *Hare v. Miller, Canfield, Paddock & Stone*, 743 So. 2d 551 (Fla. Dist. Ct. App. 1999).

Simpson is not dispositive of the certified question, however. The duty in *Simpson* was to draft the will non-negligently, while the alleged duty here is to ensure that the will is executed promptly. Courts in several jurisdictions have declined to impose a duty of care where the alleged negligence concerns the failure to have the will executed promptly. *See Krawczyk v. Stingle*, 543 A.2d 733 (Conn. 1988); *Miller v. Mooney*, 725 N.E.2d 545 (Mass. 2000); *Charia v. Hulse*, 619 So. 2d 1099 (La. Ct. App.1993); *Radovich v. Locke-Paddon*, 41 Cal. Rptr. 2d 573 (1995); *Babcock v. Malone*, 760 So. 2d 1056, 1056–57 (Fla. Dist. Ct. App. 2000). The majority of courts confronting this issue have concluded that imposing liability to prospective beneficiaries under these circumstances would interfere with an attorney's obligation of undivided loyalty to his or her client, the testator or testatrix.

In *Krawczyk*, 543 A.2d at 733–34, for instance, the decedent had met with his attorney approximately ten days before he died and informed her that he was soon to have open heart surgery and wanted to arrange for the disposition of his assets without going through probate. Accordingly, he directed the attorney to prepare two trust documents for his execution. *Id.* at 734. Completion of the trust documents was delayed, and by the time they were ready for execution, the decedent was too ill to see his attorney. He died without signing them. *Id.*

The Connecticut Supreme Court concluded that imposing liability to third parties for negligent delay in executing estate planning documents would contravene a lawyer's duty of undivided loyalty to the client. *Id.* at 736. As the court explained:

> Imposition of liability would create an incentive for an attorney to exert pressure on a client to complete and execute estate planning documents summarily. Fear of liability to potential third party beneficiaries would contravene the attorney's primary responsibility to ensure that the proposed estate plan effectuates the client's wishes and that the client understands the available options and the legal and practical implications of whatever course of action is ultimately chosen. These potential conflicts of interest are especially significant in the context of the final disposition of a client's estate, where the testator's testamentary capacity and the absence of undue influence are often central issues.

Id.

Both parties cite compelling policy considerations to support their arguments. The plaintiff asserts that there is a strong public interest in ensuring that testators dispose of their property by will and that recognizing a duty of an attorney "to arrange for the timely execution of a will" will promote this public interest. He further argues that "[t]he risk that an intended beneficiary will be deprived of a substantial legacy due to delay in execution of testamentary documents" requires the court to recognize the duty he espouses. The defendants counter that recognizing a duty to third parties for the failure to arrange for the timely execution of a will potentially would undermine the attorney's ethical duty of undivided loyalty to the client.

After weighing the policy considerations, we conclude that the potential for conflict between the interests of a prospective beneficiary and a testator militates against recognizing a duty of care. "It is the potential for conflict that is determinative, not the existence of an actual conflict." *Miller*, 725 N.E.2d at 550. Whereas a testator and the beneficiary of a will have a mutual interest in ensuring that an attorney drafts the will non-negligently, a prospective beneficiary may be interested in the will's prompt execution, while the testator or testatrix may be interested in having sufficient time to consider and understand his or her estate planning options. As the Massachusetts Supreme Judicial Court recognized:

> Confronting a last will and testament can produce complex psychological demands on a client that may require considerable periods of reflection. An attorney frequently prepares multiple drafts of a will before the client is reconciled to the result. The most simple distributive provisions may be the most difficult for the client to accept.

Id. at 551.

Creating a duty, even under the unfortunate circumstances of this case, could compromise the attorney's duty of undivided loyalty to the client and impose an untenable burden upon the attorney-client relationship. To avoid potential liability, attorneys might be forced to pressure their clients to execute their wills summarily, without sufficiently reflecting upon their estate planning options.

On balance, we conclude that the risk of interfering with the attorney's duty of undivided loyalty to the client exceeds the risk of harm to the prospective beneficiary. For these reasons, we join the majority of courts that have considered this issue and hold that an attorney does not owe a duty of care to a prospective will beneficiary to have the will executed promptly. Accordingly, we answer the certified question in the negative.

NOTES

1.   Most jurisdictions have, like New Hampshire, rejected the privity defense for attorney malpractice. *See* RESTATEMENT 3RD LAW GOVERNING LAWYERS § 51 (allowing malpractice suits when testators' intent is proven by clear and convincing evidence); *Wood v. Hollingsworth*, 603 S.E.2d 388 (N.C. 2004) (rejecting privity defense by an attorney who was never engaged as an attorney by a victim of a car accident). Why might a jurisdiction retain the privity defense? Is it convincing to argue that the client was not injured because there was no loss to the estate? *See* Martin Begleiter, *First Let's Sue All the Lawyers—What Will We Get*, 51 HAST. L.J. 3254 (2000).

Planning Note: A good trusts and estates lawyer would prefer not to appear in a law school textbook! In fact, one of the challenges of teaching trusts and estates is to remind you that, as interesting as the family disputes may be to read, the ultimate goal is to have a completely uneventful estate or trust experience, so that property passes without incident to the intended recipients. Part of achieving that result is careful planning, with full knowledge of the client's family circumstances, the client's goals, and the law's impact on each. As you read further about mistakes and failures that arise at different stages of estate planning and administration, think about whether better planning by the lawyers (and clients) might have helped avoid the resulting problems.

2. Jurisdictions that allow suits without privity sometimes limit standing to the executor rather than including disappointed beneficiaries. *See Schneider v. Finmann*, 933 N.E.2d 718 (N.Y. 2010); *Smith v. O'Donnell*, 288 S.W.3d 417 (Tex. 2009). Others require that the existing estate planning documents actually name that intended beneficiary. *See, e.g., Chang v. Lederman*, 172 Cal. App. 4th 67 (2009) (limiting liability of drafting attorney who refused to update will to provide for new spouse absent a psychiatric evaluation, because the new spouse was not an intended beneficiary on estate documents); *Charfoos v. Schultz*, 2009 Mich. App. LEXIS 2313 (dismissing suit against drafting attorney by children because they did not appear as beneficiaries in the will).

3.   *Sisson* found no liability for the failure to execute an estate plan, and other courts have agreed. In *Rydde v. Morris*, 675 S.E.2d 431 (S.C. 2009), for example, a South Carolina court rejected a claim by prospective beneficiaries that the attorney failed to execute a will for her client. The client first told the lawyer whom she wanted as beneficiaries on September 22, 2005. The client then became incapacitated on September 28, before the lawyer prepared the will. The

client died on October 3, 2005. The court might have relied on the short time between when the client approached her and the client's death, but instead it concluded more broadly that the lawyer did not owe a duty to a non-client, prospective beneficiary.

4.   Another common area of malpractice liability is the failure to provide adequate estate tax advice. In *Schneider v. Finmann*, 933 N.E.2d 718 (N.Y. 2010), for example, the court held that a personal representative of an estate may maintain a legal malpractice claim for pecuniary losses to an estate caused by an attorney's estate tax planning advice. The *Schneider* court reasoned that even in jurisdictions that allow strict privity as a bar against claims by disappointed beneficiaries, the personal representative of an estate should be able to sue because "the attorney estate planner surely knows that minimizing the tax burden of the estate is one of the central tasks entrusted to the professional." *See also Security Bank & Trust Co. v. Larkin, Hoffman, Daly & Lindgren*, 897 N.W.2d 821 (Minn. Ct. App. 2017) (finding executor to have standing to sue estate planning lawyer for malpractice for failing to consider application of the generation-skipping transfer tax, resulting in GST tax liability of over $1.6 million).

E. Conclusion and Takeaways

This chapter covers some fundamental concepts underlying everything else you will study in this course, including: an owner's right to give away property, during life or at death ("donative freedom), as balanced against the right, if any, to receive that property. It also discusses the unique challenges of serving as a lawyer in an inheritance practice. We now turn to the system that governs when a property owner declines or forgets to take advantage of this right to choose how property passes. The intestacy laws, which vary significantly from state to state, provide a default system for anyone who dies without an estate plan in place. As we consider these default rules—this state-imposed system of inheritance—we will discuss not only how the rules work but also who they benefit, who they omit, and what theories underlie these choices.

CHAPTER 3 COMPREHENSIVE ASSESSMENTS

1.   **DRAFT A CLIENT LETTER.** You have just finished an introductory meeting with a new estate planning client. Write a letter to that client that follows up on this meeting and does the following:

   a.   Restates your understanding of the client's estate planning goals, as discussed in the meeting;

b. Encloses a follow-up estate planning questionnaire to gather further information about the client. A model questionnaire appears in the Appendix.

The letter should explain any parts of the questionnaire that are not self-evident, including what an executor does and why it is important to know how property is titled.

2. **DONATIVE FREEDOM REVIEW.** You are a law student surfing the internet and come across the following question, from Ted, in a popular blog:

> My Grandmother (Gigi) died in March 2020, leaving an estate of a million dollars. Gigi had the belief that only women should be inheriting as they "need/deserve a leg up." She grew up in a very misogynistic home that favored sons to an extreme, then ended up in an abusive marriage to a husband who was much older than she, where she had no agency until husband died. Gigi had two sons, me and my brother Ben. I have two-year-old twins: a son, Sam, and a daughter, Dee. Ben has an eight-year-old daughter, Deb. Gigi set up a trust to benefit Dee and Deb, naming me (Ted) and Ben as trustee of each granddaughter's trust. Gigi made no provisions for Sam.
>
> While the most fair situation would be to pool the trust funds and split it in 3, I can't control that. But in our household, we're in a situation where one of my children is getting HALF A MILLION and the other is getting absolutely nothing, on gender alone. This feels horrible as a parent, and technically I can stop it. I want to forcibly split my daughter's trust in two, which would give both a quarter million. This would be more fair. We have friends and family that are on both sides of the issue, and I honestly don't know what to do.

Write a blogpost responding to Ted.

Test Your Knowledge

To assess your understanding of the material in this chapter, click here to take a quiz.

CHAPTER 4

Intestacy

CHAPTER LEARNING OUTCOMES

Following your work with the material in this chapter, you should be able to do the following:

- Define intestacy, heirs, spouse, and descendants

- Explain the different between intestate succession and testate succession, and identify types of property that pass each way

- Identify the hierarchy of heirs

- Assess the connections between family law and succession

- Explain the applicability of voluntary bars and involuntary bars to succession

- Allocate probate property by applying the principles of intestate succession

- Explain and apply the three methods of representation

- Calculate shares based upon the hierarchy of heirs and eligibility of heirs

- Identify the demographic groups the intestacy laws leave out

A. Introduction

Dying may be a universal experience; will-making is not. Trusts and estates is indeed a course about planning for the orderly transmission of property. Part of that planning process is how to handle situations in which the property owner does not construct a complete or legally enforceable plan. In the United States, approximately 60% to 70% of all individuals die without a leaving a valid will that completely disposes of their probate property. *See generally* Caryl A. Yzenbaard, *Intestate Property Distribution at Death in the United States*, 8 MODERN STUDIES IN PROPERTY LAW 177 (2015); Alyssa A. DiRusso, *Testacy and Intestacy: The Dynamics of Wills and Demographic Status*, 23 QUINNIPIAC PROB. L.J. 35 (2009).

Older and wealthy individuals are more likely to have valid wills than younger and less affluent people. Yet, a number of individuals with a wide range of property interests, a variety of relationships, and extensive experience with the law still do not create valid wills. The reasons for not having a will are many, including the reluctance to plan for death, inertia, privacy concerns, the desire not to discuss family issues especially if it is a blended family, and the thought that one does not have enough assets to justify a will. Many people from a variety of backgrounds will die without a valid will despite the benefits of will-making. For example, when the musician Prince died on April 21, 2016, he died intestate. During his life, Prince supported a number of organizations, friends, and family members. He left behind significant assets, including copyrights to his famous music catalog. Yet, he died without a valid will to express his wishes.[1]

Prince died without a valid will, which means that he died intestate. Prince on stage at Coachella (2008).

Moreover, people choose to interact with law in different ways. Alyssa DiRusso has written: "Testacy and intestacy offer descriptive symbolism beyond their function. Testacy and intestacy are not just two parallel paths for property distribution at death, but two distinct methods of interacting with the law and being defined by it. Whether one is testate and intestate is the law's final characterization of an individual, and casts his interaction with the legal system as either passive vessel or active leader." Whatever the reason, a backup or default plan for the distribution of such estates is necessary for the orderly transmission of probate property.

Every jurisdiction has a statute that defines who will take and what share of the decedent's probate property that individual will take when a decedent dies **intestate**. These statues, often known as the statutes of descent and distribution, contain provisions relating to the disposition and administration of intestate

---

[1]   The court proceedings are available at https://www.mncourts.gov/InReTheEstateofPrinceRogers Nelson.aspx.

estates.[2] The process whereby probate property is passed via intestacy is called **intestate succession**.

> **Intestate succession** may occur for one of the following four reasons:
>
> - The decedent did not create a valid will
>
> - The decedent created a valid will that did not dispose of all the decedent's probate property, resulting in what is known as partial intestacy
>
> - The decedent created a valid will but later validly revoked the will
>
> - The decedent created what purported to be a valid will but was not ultimately admitted to probate following the decedent's death

The intestacy statute provides the default distributions, that is, who gets what share of the decedent's property. The individuals who receive property via intestate succession are referred to as **heirs**. The statute provides a hierarchy of heirs that prioritizes certain familial relationships over others. In addition, the intestate statute contains default administrative terms. In other words, where the decedent does not specify the beneficiaries, determine how to allocate shares of property, or define legal terms of art, the intestacy statute supplies the information. Additionally, the intestacy statutes may determine who has standing to challenge a will, define terms used in a will, and offer the rules for providing a share for an **omitted spouse** or **omitted child**. Indeed, the identification of an "heir" under intestacy statutes may provide the basis for individuals to receive benefits outside of the probate systems, such as receiving benefits in accordance with the Social Security Act.

Language Note: Notice how we do not use the gendered term "heiress." As shared in Chapter 1, this book avoids use of gendered terms. Consider what the term "heiress" means. How would you describe an "heiress"? Is there a masculine equivalent term?

---

[2]   Historically, separate statutes governed the disposition of real property and the disposition of personal property. Some states, like Kentucky and North Carolina, still follow this practice, though most jurisdictions now have a combined statute for real and personal property.

Intestacy statutes are supposed to reflect the presumed intent of most individuals. This presumed intent may be supported by examining records of testate succession to evaluate preferences testators have expressed. Intestacy laws may also reflect the values of a particular legislature: for example, the protection of family members. Intestacy statutes may also reflect commonly accepted social norms. The law takes on an expressive function, which conveys implicit state approval of certain relationships and implicit state disapproval of other relationships. As intestacy statutes are not frequently updated, some statutes may reflect a limited or antiquated conception of family or what most individuals would prefer. To that end, intestacy statutes may be considered a "one-size fits some" default statutory scheme.

A person's legally recognized relationship to the decedent determines whether that person receives property under an intestacy statute. That person may, however, ultimately be ineligible to receive the property. For one thing, as discussed in Chapter 2, the individual needs to **survive** the decedent to inherit the probate. In limited circumstances, the behavior of an individual may affect that individual's ability to inherit. Such circumstances include involuntary bars and voluntary bars, which we discuss later in this chapter.

Intestacy statutes establish a hierarchy of **heirs**. In all intestacy statutes, the heirs have a legally recognized familial relationship with the decedent. To qualify as an heir, an individual will need to establish that familial relationship. Because the determination of who is an heir does not occur until the decedent's death, during the decedent's life, the individual has **heirs apparent**.

Part B of this chapter discusses the family member who receives the greatest protection in most intestacy statutes: the surviving spouse. It discusses the definition of a spouse and then explains the spouse's share. **Part C** discusses the decedent's **descendants** (e.g., children, grandchildren, great-grandchildren), focusing on all the different ways that families are created. In many cases, intestacy law reflects the traditional nuclear family and does not protect committed but unmarried partners, stepchildren, foster children, or others in less formal relationships. There are also some dramatic differences between modern statutes, like the newest version of the UPC, and more traditional statutes in the size of the share that different family members receive.

Part D focuses on other potential heirs in this hierarchy, including **ancestors** (e.g., parents, grandparents), who typically receive a share only if none of the decedent's descendants survive, and **collateral kindred** (e.g., siblings, nieces, nephews, aunts, uncles, cousins), who share in an estate only if there are no descendants or ancestors. It also discusses what happens if none of these relatives survive.

Part E addresses different schemes of **representation**, which apply when multiple heirs are eligible to receive the decedent's probate property. **Part F** discusses actions, behaviors, or even documents that may prohibit an heir from inheriting by operating as a bar to inheritance.

B.   The Share of the Surviving Spouse

1.   Defining the Spouse

Today, all jurisdictions' intestacy statutes give the surviving **spouse** the greatest priority. In fact, the UPC provides that a surviving spouse receives the entire intestate estate, even if the decedent is survived by parents and descendants, so long as the descendants are children of both the decedent and the surviving spouse and neither has any other descendants:

UPC § 2–102 Share of Spouse

The intestate share of a decedent's surviving spouse is:

(1)   The entire estate if:

(A)   no descendant or parent of the decedent survives the decedent; or

(B)   all of the decedent's surviving descendants are also descendants of the surviving spouse and there is no other descendant of the surviving spouse who survives the decedent;

(2)   the first [$300,000], plus three-fourths of any balance of the intestate estate, if no descendant of the decedent survives the decedent, but a parent of the decedent survives the decedent; *[P's - no Ds]*

(3)   the first [$225,000], plus one-half of any balance of the intestate estate, if all of the decedent's surviving descendants are also descendants of the surviving spouse and the surviving spouse has one or more surviving descendants who are not descendants of the decedent; *[Wife has own 0 kids and 0 kids]*

(4)   the first [$150,000], plus one-half of any balance of the intestate estate, if one or more of the decedent's surviving descendants are not descendants of the surviving spouse. *[0 his non wife kids]*

Historically, the law favored blood relatives over the surviving spouse on the theory that the surviving spouse was a "stranger" to the decedent's bloodline. Modern intestacy statutes presume that decedents wish to favor the individual with whom the decedent voluntarily created a legal relationship. Such preference may facilitate the continued economic health of the family by having a head of the household receive the property. How does the law define the surviving spouse? An initial definition is: A surviving spouse is an individual who was validly married to the decedent at the time of death. The duration of the marriage or the happiness of the spouses is not relevant for identifying the surviving spouse for purposes of intestacy. Rather, the focus is whether the marriage was validly entered into and not dissolved at the time of the decedent's death. UPC § 2–802.

Let's consider the following case, *In re Estate of Gardiner*, 42 P.3d 120 (Kan. 2002), to explore how conceptualizations of marriage, which is a legal, political, social, and economic relationship, may change over time. This case raises the question of whether another definition or a more flexible definition of "spouse" should be used for purposes of succession.

In re Estate of Gardiner

42 P.3d 120 (Kan. 2002)

ALLEGRUCCI, J.

J'Noel Gardiner appealed from the district court's entry of summary judgment in favor of Joseph M. Gardiner, III, (Joe) in the probate proceeding of Marshall G. Gardiner. The district court had concluded that the marriage between Joe's father, Marshall, and J'Noel, a post-operative male-to-female transsexual, was void under Kansas law.

The Court of Appeals reversed and remanded for the district court's determination whether J'Noel was male or female at the time the marriage license was issued. The Court of Appeals directed the district court to consider a number of factors in addition to chromosomes. Joe's petition for review of the decision of the Court of Appeals was granted by this court.

J'Noel was born in Green Bay, Wisconsin. J'Noel's original birth certificate indicates J'Noel was born a male. The record shows that after sex reassignment surgery, J'Noel's birth certificate was amended in Wisconsin, pursuant to Wisconsin statutes, to state that she was female. Marshall was a businessman in northeast Kansas who had accumulated some wealth. He had one son, Joe, from whom he was estranged. Marshall's wife had died some time before he met J'Noel. There is no evidence that Marshall was not competent. Indeed, both Marshall and J'Noel possessed intelligence and real-world experience. J'Noel had a Ph.D. in finance and was a teacher at Park College.

J'Noel met Marshall while on the faculty at Park College in May 1998. Marshall was a donor to the school. After the third or fourth date, J'Noel testified that Marshall brought up marriage. Sometime in July 1998, Marshall was told about J'Noel's prior history as a male. 'Noel Ball and Marshall Gardiner were married in Kansas in September 1998. Marshall died intestate in August 1999.

This legal journey started with Joe filing a petition for letters of administration, alleging that J'Noel had waived any rights to Marshall's estate. J'Noel filed an objection and asked that letters of administration be issued to her. The court then appointed a special administrator. Joe amended his petition, alleging that he was the sole heir in that the marriage between J'Noel and Marshall was void since J'Noel was born a man. J'Noel argues that she is a biological female and was at the time of her marriage to Marshall. There is no dispute that J'Noel is a post-operative transsexual, which is defined as a person who has undergone medical and surgical procedures to alter "external sexual characteristics so that they resemble those of the opposite sex." STEDMAN'S MED. DICT. 1841 (26th ed. 1995).

The sole issue for review is whether the district court erroneously entered summary judgment in favor of Joe on the ground that J'Noel's marriage to Marshall was void.

On the question of validity of the marriage of a post-operative transsexual, there are two distinct "lines" of cases. One judges validity of the marriage according to the sexual classification assigned to the transsexual at birth. The other views medical and surgical procedures as a means of unifying a divided sexual identity and determines the transsexual's sexual classification for the purpose of marriage at the time of marriage. The essential difference between the two approaches is the latter's crediting a mental component, as well as an anatomical component, to each person's sexual identity.

In his petition for review, Joe complained that the Court of Appeals failed to "ask the fundamental question of whether a person can actually change sex within the context of K.S.A. 23–101." On the issue of the validity of the marriage, Joe's principal arguments were that the Court of Appeals failed to give K.S.A.2001 Supp. 23–101 its plain and unambiguous meaning and that the Court of Appeals' opinion improperly usurps the legislature's policy-making role. K.S.A.2001 Supp. 23–101 provides:

> The marriage contract is to be considered in law as a civil contract between two parties who are of opposite sex. All other marriages are declared to be contrary to the public policy of this state and are void. The consent of the parties is essential. The marriage ceremony may be regarded either as a civil ceremony or as a religious sacrament, but the marriage relation shall only be entered into, maintained or abrogated as provided by law.

Joe's principal argument is that the statutory phrase is plain and unambiguous. His statements of the issue and his position, however, go beyond the statutory phrase to pin down the time when the two parties are of opposite sex. The plain and unambiguous meaning of K.S.A.2001 Supp. 23–101, according to Joe, is that a valid marriage must be between two persons who are of opposite sex at the time of birth.

Joe's fallback argument is that the legislature's intent was to uphold "traditional marriage," interpreting K.S.A.2001 Supp. 23–101 so that it invalidates a marriage between persons who are not of the opposite sex; *i.e.,* a biological male and a biological female.

The Court of Appeals found deficiency in the district court's entry of summary judgment. Supplying some of what the district court omitted, the Court of Appeals included in its opinion a review of some scientific literature. As courts typically do, the Court of Appeals also turned to a law journal article that reported on scientific matters relevant to legal issues. The Court of Appeals quoted extensively from Julie E. Greenberg, *Defining Male and Female: Intersexuality and the Collision between Law and Biology,* 41 ARIZ. L. REV. 265, 278–92 (1992). Greenberg's thesis is that sexual identification is not simply a matter of anatomy, as demonstrated by a number of intersex conditions—chromosomal sex disorders, gonadal sex disorders, internal organ anomalies, external organ anomalies, hormonal disorders, gender identity disorder, and unintentioned amputation. The Court of Appeals rejected the district court's sex-at-birth-answers-the-question rationale in part, at least, because the Court of Appeals opined that there are a number of factors that make sexual identification at birth less than certain.

We disagree with the decision reached by the Court of Appeals. We view the issue in this appeal to be one of law and not fact. The resolution of this issue involves the interpretation of K.S.A.2001 Supp. 23–101. The interpretation of a statute is a question of law, and this court has unlimited appellate review.

The fundamental rule of statutory construction is that the intent of the legislature governs. In determining legislative intent, courts are not limited to consideration of the language used in the statute, but may look to the historical background of the enactment, the circumstances attending its passage, the purpose to be accomplished, and the effect the statute may have under the various constructions suggested. Words in common usage are to be given their natural and ordinary meaning. When a statute is plain and unambiguous, the court must give effect to the intention of the legislature as expressed, rather than determine what the law should or should not be.

The words "sex," "male," and "female" are words in common usage and understood by the general population. BLACK'S LAW DICTIONARY, 1375 (6th ed.1999) defines "sex" as "[t]he sum of the peculiarities of structure and function that distinguish a male from a female organism; the character of being male or female." WEBSTER'S NEW TWENTIETH CENTURY DICTIONARY (2d ed.1970) states the initial definition of sex as "either of the two divisions of organisms distinguished as male or female; males or females (especially men or women) collectively." "Male" is defined as "designating or of the sex that fertilizes the ovum and begets offspring: opposed to *female*." "Female" is defined as "designating or of the sex that produces ova and bears offspring: opposed to *male*." [Emphasis added.] According to BLACK'S LAW DICTIONARY, 972 (6th ed.1999) a marriage "is the legal status, condition, or relation of one man and one woman united in law for life, or until divorced, for the discharge to each other and the community of the duties legally incumbent on those whose association is founded on the distinction of sex."

The words "sex," "male," and "female" in everyday understanding do not encompass transsexuals. The plain, ordinary meaning of "persons of the opposite sex" contemplates a biological man and a biological woman and not persons who are experiencing gender dysphoria. A male-to-female post-operative transsexual does not fit the definition of a female. The male organs have been removed, but the ability to "produce ova and bear offspring" does not and never did exist. There is no womb, cervix, or ovaries, nor is there any change in his chromosomes. J'Noel does not fit the common meaning of female.

That interpretation of K.S.A.2001 Supp. 23–101 is supported by the legislative history of the statute. That legislative history is set out in the Court of Appeals decision. The Court of Appeals then noted:

The legislative history contains discussions about gays and lesbians, but nowhere is there any testimony that specifically states that marriage should be prohibited by two parties if one is a post-operative male-to-female or female-to-male transsexual. Thus, the question remains: Was J'Noel a female at the time the license was issued for the purpose of the statute?

We do not agree that the question remains. We view the legislative silence to indicate that transsexuals are not included. If the legislature intended to include transsexuals, it could have been a simple matter to have done so. We apply the rules of statutory construction to ascertain the legislative intent as expressed in the statute. We do not read into a statute something that does not come within the wording of the statute.

As we have previously noted, the legislature clearly viewed "opposite sex" in the narrow traditional sense. The legislature has declared that the public policy of this state is to recognize only the traditional marriage between "two parties who are of the opposite sex," and all other marriages are against public policy and void. We cannot ignore what the legislature has declared to be the public policy of this state. Our responsibility is to interpret K.S.A.2001 Supp. 23–101 and not to rewrite it. That is for the legislature to do if it so desires. If the legislature wishes to change public policy, it is free to do so; we are not. To conclude that J'Noel is of the opposite sex of Marshall would require that we rewrite K.S.A. 2001 Supp. 23–101.

Finally, we recognize that J'Noel has traveled a long and difficult road. We are not blind to the stress and pain experienced by one who is born a male but perceives oneself as a female. We recognize that there are people who do not fit neatly into the commonly recognized category of male or female, and to many life becomes an ordeal. However, the validity of J'Noel's marriage to Marshall is a question of public policy to be addressed by the legislature and not by this court.

The Court of Appeals is affirmed in part and reversed in part; the district court is affirmed.

NOTES

1.   The Kansas statutes referenced in *Gardiner* were repealed in 2011. States may regulate entry and exit from marriage, so long as those regulations are consistent with the U.S. Constitution. States will thus continue to differ about who may enter into marriage and what circumstances will support a dissolution

proceeding. For instance, states have different age requirements when someone below the age of 18 may marry with the consent of a **guardian**. States will also have different degrees of prohibited kinship. Subject to constitutional limits, a state may define who may marry and who is qualified to perform the marriage ceremony. For example, Kentucky adults may marry unless their kinship by consanguinity is closer than second cousins; or if a person has been adjudged mentally disabled; or if there is a husband and a wife living from whom the person entering the marriage has not been divorced. *See* KY. R.S. §§ 402–010—402.030. A minor may marry if a parent or judge has given proper consent.

2.   Marriage recognized in one state will, in general, be recognized in another state. Thus, if a couple lawfully married in state A and later moved to state B where one party died, the surviving individual will be a surviving spouse in state B. Following the decision in *Obergefell v. Hodges*, 576 U.S. 644 (2015), all states must recognize and permit same sex marriages. Questions can arise, however, as to individuals in **registered domestic partnerships**. Those registered as domestic partners before *Obergefell* may not be considered surviving spouses unless they marry. At least that is the conclusion of the New Jersey Tax Court in its unpublished opinion, *Jiwungkul v. Director, Division of Taxation*, 2016 WL 2996871 (Tax Ct. N.J.). The decedent and his surviving partner were registered domestic partners in New Jersey, but they had not entered either a civil union or a marriage. As a result, the survivor was not entitled to be viewed as a surviving spouse for calculation of the New Jersey estate tax. A few states explicitly grant inheritance rights to individuals who have registered as domestic partners or who have entered civil unions.[3]

3.   A few states also recognize inheritance rights in a "**common law spouse**."[4] Common law marriages, or informal marriages, occur when a couple does not procure a license or participate in a solemnization proceeding (that is a formal marriage ceremony) but there exists no bar to entering into a marriage, the couple had the intent to be married, and the couple held themselves out as married. Merely residing in the same household is not sufficient to establish a common law marriage. There must be a holding out by the couple as married,

---

[3]   Several states enacted such legislation to allow inheritance especially as between same sex partners. Now that same sex marriages are permitted, however, the civil union may not be recognized for inheritance purposes if the statute is silent. The UPC has not taken a position on inheritance by those who are not spouses but rather have a civil union.

[4]   States that recognize common law marriage include Alabama, Colorado, The District of Columbia, Georgia (if created before 1/1/97), Idaho (if created before 1/1/96), Iowa, Kansas, Montana, New Hampshire (inheritance purposes only), Ohio (if created before 110/10/91), Oklahoma (maybe only if created before 11/1/98), Pennsylvania (if created before 1/1/05), Rhode Island, Texas, and Utah. *See also* RESTATEMENT 3RD OF PROPERTY § 2.2 comment f.

as well as evidence like joint bank accounts, tax returns, deeds, etc. If the common law marriage was valid where formed and the couple moves to a state that does not allow for common law marriage, the marriage may still be recognized, and property entitlements will exist for a surviving spouse pursuant to the doctrine of lex loci.

4.   Some individuals believe that they are lawfully married, but for some technical reason the marriage is not valid. The ceremony itself may have been invalid or one of the individuals may have been unable to validly enter the marriage because the individual was still married to someone else. In general, this type of "**putative spouse**" will still be able to inherit. The amount that such putative spouses may inherit varies, but, at least in some instances, the putative spouse and the "legal" spouse will equally share the spousal portion of the decedent's intestate estate. Many states will protect a putative spouse either by case law or by statute based on § 209 of the Uniform Marriage and Divorce Act, which allows such a spouse to receive an equitable share. *See also Estate of Vargas*, 36 Cal. App. 3d 714 (1974) (dividing the decedent's probate estate between his legal spouse and his putative spouse).

5.   Absent the above, inheritance rights will not be granted to the survivor of two individuals who were residing together but were unmarried (typically

As default rules, intestacy is a one-size-fits-some system of property distribution and marriage is an important factor.

referred to as "**unmarried cohabitants**" or "nonmarital partners"). Unmarried cohabitants may have built a life together over a long period of time, but they do not have the same recognized legal status as married individuals or registered domestic partners. *See generally* Raymond C. O'Brien, *Marital versus Nonmarital Entitlements*, 45 ACTEC L.J. 79 (2020). An unmarried cohabitant may have a claim on the death of a partner based on contract, even if there is no right to inherit under the intestacy statutes, but many jurisdictions require an express written contract. *See Levar v. Elkins*, 604 P.2d 602 (Alaska 1980) (evidence supported the finding of an express or an implied contract). Some commentators have called for a functional rather than status-based approach to protect unmarried but committed partners. *See, e.g.,* Mary Louise

Fellows et al., *Committed Partners and Inheritance: An Empirical Study*, 16 L. & INEQUALITY 1 (1998); E. Gary Spitko, *An Accrual/Multi-Factor Approach to Intestate Inheritance Rights for Unmarried Committed Partners*, 81 OR. L. REV. 255 (2002). Issues that have arisen, however, include evidentiary concerns (including length and nature of the relationship), efficiency concerns (including reducing the need for litigation), and fairness concerns (including how broad to permit judicial discretion).

6.   Just as the spousal relationship must be lawfully *created* to receive inheritance rights, the spousal relationship must be lawfully terminated to extinguish the inheritance rights. The spousal relationship may be terminated by divorce or annulment proceedings. Such termination will eliminate the inheritance rights unless the individuals subsequently remarry. A decree of separation usually is not sufficient. In a few states, however, a spouse who has abandoned his or her spouse is prevented from taking—even though the marriage relationship was not lawfully terminated. Most statutes do not address the issue, though. The UPC, in § 2–802, requires what the comments call "a definitive legal act to bar the surviving spouse."

ASSESSMENTS

1.   Jules and Britt lived together for twenty years. During those twenty years, they had various relationship highs and lows. They considered getting married at various points during their relationship. Jules died without a valid will. Britt asks you (a) what protections may be available and (b) what requirements need to be satisfied to receive those protections. How do you respond?

2.   Sheridan and Oakley are registered as partners in a state that permitted such registration. Later the state recognized same sex marriages, but Sheridan and Oakley did not marry. When Oakley dies, will Sheridan be entitled to the protections as a surviving spouse? Does the answer change if Sheridan and Oakley participated in a same-sex marriage ceremony before same-sex marriage was legally recognized in their state?

2.   Share of the Spouse

Just because all jurisdictions protect and prioritize a surviving spouse, the surviving spouse is not necessarily entitled to the decedent's entire intestate estate. To understand why an intestacy statute may consider different allocations of property between the surviving spouse and others, first consider how these principles work by applying them to a series of families. For each of these families, assume that the decedent died intestate.

Family A consists of two spouses who have been married to each other for twenty-five years. They have two children who were born during the marriage. Neither spouse was married before. The decedent spouse is survived by the surviving spouse and the two children. How would the decedent spouse's probate property be distributed?

The current UPC gives the entire estate to the surviving spouse to the exclusion of all others. UPC § 2–102(1). This contrasts with the original UPC, and many state statutes, which would have allocated to the surviving spouse the first $50,000 of the decedent's probate estate and one-half of the remaining probate estate. The children received the other one-half. UPC § 2–102(3) (pre-1990 version). In Georgia, the surviving spouse will split the property with the children so long as the surviving spouse inherits one-third of the probate estate. O.C.GA. § 53–2–1(c)(1). In North Carolina, the surviving spouse will receive one-third of any real property as well as $60,000 and one-third of all personal property. N.C. GEN. STAT. §§ 29–14(a)(2); 29–14(b)(2). What does the intestacy statute of your state provide? Which of these views do you prefer? Why? Note that the son was an adult whereas the daughter was a minor. Should that matter? What if both children are adults, or both minors?

Family B is a blended family. The decedent spouse was married before and has an older son from that marriage. The decedent spouse and the surviving spouse have been married for the past twenty-five years and they, together, have two children. How would the decedent spouse's probate property be distributed?

Under the current UPC, the surviving spouse will now inherit $150,000 plus one-half of the estate. The remaining one-half will be shared equally by the three children. UPC § 2–102(3). (All sums are subject to an annual cost-of-living adjustment under UPC § 1–109.) Under the original UPC, the surviving spouse inherited one-half of the estate and the three children shared the remaining one-half. In Georgia, the surviving spouse would inherit one-third of the estate and the three children share the remaining two-thirds of the estate.

Family C is also a blended family. Both the decedent spouse and the surviving spouse have one child from a prior marriage. The spouses together have two children. How would the decedent spouse's probate property be distributed?

Under the current UPC, the surviving spouse will receive $225, 0000 plus one-half of the estate. UPC § 2–102(3). The decedent spouse's children (i.e., the child from the previous relationship and the two children shared with the surviving spouse) will share the remaining one-half of the estate. The decedent spouse's stepchild (i.e., the surviving spouse's child from a previous relationship) receives nothing because she is not considered a descendant of the decedent spouse. Why does the current UPC allocate property in this manner? If the UPC's assumption is that the surviving spouse will not care for the surviving spouse's stepchild (i.e., the decedent spouse's child from a prior relationship), is that assumption accurate? Does it make sense to draw this distinction? And if it does, should the UPC protect more robustly than it does the interest of the decedent's children who are not descendants of the surviving spouse?

Under the original UPC, the surviving spouse received $50,000 and one-half of the estate. The decedent's descendants equally shared the other one-half of the estate. The decedent's stepchild receives nothing. UPC § 2–102(3) (pre-1990 version). Under Georgia law, the surviving spouse would receive one-third of the estate, and all the decedent's descendants would share the remaining two-thirds of the estate. Notice that under Georgia law, the surviving spouse and the decedent's descendants will always share the estate, regardless of whether the children are the decedent's from a prior relationship or a relationship with the surviving spouse. The decedent's stepchild, absent an adoption, would not be considered a descendant of the decedent.

Family D consists of two spouses who have no children. The decedent spouse is survived by the surviving spouse, a parent, a sister, and the sister's child (i.e., the decedent's nephew). How would the decedent spouse's estate be distributed?

Under the current UPC, the surviving spouse will inherit $300,000 and three-quarters of the estate. UPC § 2–102(2). The remaining one-fourth will pass to the decedent spouse's parent. If the parent did not survive the decedent, then the surviving spouse would inherit all the decedent spouse's probate estate. UPC § 2–102(1)(A). Notice that under no circumstance will the sister or the sister's child be an heir. Under the original UPC, the decedent spouse will inherit $50,000 and one-half of the estate. The other one-half goes to the decedent's parent. If the parent did not survive the decedent, the surviving spouse inherits all the decedent's estate. How does your state's statute allocate shares if there is a surviving spouse but no descendants? What do you prefer? Should the age of the decedent matter?

NOTES

1. It should be clear from the examples above that the amount the surviving spouse receives turns on whether or not there are children and, in particular, whether or not the children are from the marriage between the decedent and the surviving spouse or from a previous marriage of the decedent. What does this framework say about stepparents? More specifically, what assumptions are inherent in these rules about the relationship between a stepparent and

Consider what assumptions are embedded within the hierarchy of intestate succession, perhaps about wicked stepmothers? Illustration by Franz Jüttner, from Sneewittchen (Snow White), circa 1905.

stepchildren? Are these assumptions fair ones to make? What family structures can you imagine that would contradict the assumptions made by these intestate distributions?

2. You might notice that when determining the amount the surviving the spouse receives, there is no mention of the length of marriage. Full intestate rights are available to a spouse for a marriage of any length. (This approach is different from the UPC rule for the elective share, which depends on the length of the marriage, as discussed in Chapter 14.) This result also differs from a claim for spousal support that arises upon the dissolution of a marriage. The amount award for spousal support typically increases with the length of the marriage. Would it be a good idea to index the amount of the intestate share to the length of the marriage? Why or why not?

> **Connection Note:** The decedent's surviving spouse will have a number of claims against the estate. Those claims include a probate allowance, an elective share, and an intestate share. These claims may produce different amounts. Why would a spouse pursue one of these claims over another possible claim? Consider legal, economic, social, and emotional considerations.

ASSESSMENTS

1. Dale died intestate with a probate estate valued at $150,000. Dale was survived by a spouse named Sawyer and a parent named Parker. Dale had no

descendants. Who receives the estate under the current UPC? What if Dale's probate estate was $600,000?

2.   Corey received a gift of land from his mother as a 21st birthday gift. Ten years later, Corey died survived by his spouse Skyler and his mother Moira. Who receives the land under the current UPC (assuming it and the rest of Corey's estate is worth less than $300,000)? What result under the current UPC if Corey had received the gift from his mother for his 16th birthday and died the next year survived by a maternal grandmother, his father, and his mother?

3.   Evaluate each of the four families described above. For each family, evaluate the approaches taken under the current UPC and under the intestacy statute for your jurisdiction. Should another approach be taken that considers the age, need, or closeness of the relationship? Should one approach apply regardless of the family structure?

C. Defining Descendants

Although the surviving spouse receives the greatest priority in intestacy statutes, the surviving spouse does not necessarily receive the exclusive priority. Along with a surviving spouse, descendants (also known as "issue," refers to children, grandchildren, great-grandchildren, etc.) receive priority in inheritance statutes. Section 2–103 of the UPC, for example, provides that any part of the intestate estate not passing to the surviving spouse passes according to the following hierarchy:

UPC § 2–103 (b)–(j)

(b)   **[Heirs Other Than Surviving Spouse.]** Any part of the intestate estate not passing under Section 2–102 to the decedent's surviving spouse passes to the decedent's descendants or parents as provided in subsections (c) and (d). If there is no surviving spouse, the entire intestate estate passes to the decedent's descendants, parents, or other heirs as provided in subsections (c) through (j).

(c)   **[Surviving Descendant.]** If a decedent is survived by one or more descendants, any part of the intestate estate not passing to the surviving spouse passes by representation to the decedent's surviving descendants.

The different schemes of "representation," which govern how these shares are allocated, are discussed in Section E. To receive a share as a descendant, though, parentage must be established. **Parentage** refers to the establishment of a legally recognized parent-child relationship. The focus becomes one of identifying an individual's legal parents. Establishing parentage for purposes of succession will reference methods of establishing parentage originally developed within family law. Family law, however, has additional methods for establishing parentage that have yet to be translated into intestacy statutes. This section is organized based upon different descriptions of the parent-child relationships that may be recognized in intestacy statutes. Keep in mind that tensions arise as to how narrow or broad to define these parent-child relationships for purposes of intestate succession. Intestacy provides for a series of defaults, which means that a decedent could customize his or her estate planning to provide for relationships that would not otherwise be recognized in intestacy. Given the relatively low rates of testation, the relationships recognized by intestacy will have widespread impact, however.

> **Language Note:** Older cases and statutes may use the term "natural parent" instead of "legal parent." Because parentage can be establishing in a growing number of ways, the term "legal parent" is the appropriate term to use.

1. Genetic Child of the Marriage

Historically, parentage was established by marriage. A child born during the marriage is still presumed to be the child of each of the spouses and is referred to as a **marital child**. The Uniform Parentage Act § 204 provides that parentage is presumed if the child is born during the marriage (and even if the marriage may later be declared invalid) or within 300 days after the marriage ends. Although the presumption may be rebutted, it is difficult to do. *See, e.g.*, *Michael H. v. Gerald D*, 491 U.S. 110 (1989) (upholding the constitutionality of a California statute presuming conclusively that a child born during the marriage was a marital child of the spouses, even when an individual outside of the marriage asserts a claim to establish parentage). Such a child remains a child of both members of the married couple even if the parents later divorce. In addition, if partners have a child outside of marriage but later marry, the child will become a marital child.

When establishing parentage through marriage, the relationship established by marriage to an individual who already has a child will *not* automatically make the new spouse a parent of the stepchild. *See generally* Terin Barbas Cremer,

Reforming Intestate Inheritance for Stepchildren and Stepparents, 18 CARDOZO J.L. & GENDER 89 (2011). For that child to become a marital child of the new marriage, the new spouse must generally adopt the child. In some states, and under the UPC, stepchildren will inherit but only if there are no other qualified relatives and the property would otherwise escheat to the estate. UPC § 2–103(b). Some have asked whether stepchildren should receive greater priority in the hierarchy of heirs.

NOTES

1.   The extent to which the "marital presumption" applies to married same-sex couples is unclear in some instances. *See generally* Leslie Joan Harris, *Obergefell's Ambiguous Impact on Legal Parentage*, 92 CHI. KENT L. REV. 55 (2017); June Carbone & Naomi Cahn, *Marriage and the Marital Presumption Post-Obergefell*, 84 UMKC L. REV. 633 (2016). The recent case of *Pavan v. Smith*, 137 S. Ct. 2075 (2017), has cleared the way for the marital presumption to apply to same-sex couples, but there are still remaining issues that relate to the statutory variations that define the marital presumption. Consider the following statute:

1.   Marital presumption established. A person is presumed to be the parent of a child if:

A.   The person and the woman giving birth to the child are married to each other and the child is born during the marriage;

B.   The person and the woman giving birth to the child were married to each other and the child is born within 300 days after the marriage is terminated by death, annulment, divorce or declaration of invalidity or after a decree of separation; or

C.   Before the birth of the child, the person and the woman giving birth to the child married each other in apparent compliance with law, even if the attempted marriage is or could be declared invalid, and the child is born during the invalid marriage or within 300 days after its termination by death, annulment, divorce or declaration of invalidity or after a decree of separation.

2.   Equivalent status in other jurisdictions. The marital presumption in subsection 1 applies to a legal relationship that provides substantially the same rights, benefits and responsibilities as marriage and is recognized as valid in the state or jurisdiction in which it was entered.

3. Nonmarital presumption established. A person is presumed to be a parent of a child if the person resided in the same household with the child and openly held out the child as that person's own from the time the child was born or adopted and for a period of at least 2 years thereafter and assumed personal, financial or custodial responsibilities for the child.

4. Rebuttal of presumption. A presumption established under this subchapter may be rebutted only by a court determination.

ME. STAT. TIT. 19–a § 1881 (2015).

2. Consider whether the following statute extends the marital presumption to same-sex couples:

> When necessary to implement the rights, benefits, protections, and responsibilities of spouses under the laws of this State, all gender-specific terminology, such as "husband," "wife," "widow," "widower," or similar terms, shall be construed in a gender-neutral manner. This interpretation shall apply to all sources of law, including statutes, administrative rules, court decisions, common law, or any other source of law.

HAW. REV. STAT. § 572–1.8 (2013).

2. Non-Marital Child

The common law and many state statutes historically drew a distinction between marital and non-marital children. A **non-marital child** refers to a child who is born to individuals who are not married at the time of the child's birth and do not later get married. In the 1970s, the U.S. Supreme Court held that an Illinois statute basing a child's intestate succession rights on the parents' marital status violated the Fourteenth Amendment's Equal Protection Clause. *Trimble v. Gordon*, 430 U.S. 762 (1977). Subsequently, the U.S. Supreme Court struck down a Pennsylvania law that limited paternity actions to six years after a child's birth. The Court applied an intermediate level of scrutiny in that Equal Protection challenge and found that the limitation was unconstitutional. *Clark v. Jeter*,

> **Language Note:** The term "illegitimate child" is no longer used to refer to a child who is born outside of wedlock. Older cases, older statutes, and older form documents do include the term. Nonetheless, the appropriate term to use is "non-marital child."

486 U.S. 456 (1988). Thus, a child born to parents who were not legally married may still inherit.

This means that the marital status of the parents does not necessarily preclude a child's inheritance rights. Section 2–117 of the UPC provides that there is no distinction based on marital status. Where individuals are not married, the question becomes how to establish parentage. Generally, a child is presumed to have a genetic link to the child's birth mother. *See, e.g.,* N.C. GEN. STAT. § 29–19(a). Historically the lack of ability to prove paternity was an obstacle to inheritance rights for nonmarital children. With the advent of reliable genetic testing, however, things have changed, since paternity may be established through medical testing.

What becomes important is defining when the child can or must establish parentage. *Lalli v. Lalli,* 439 U.S. 259 (1978), upheld a New York statute that required paternity to be established before the putative father's death. And as recently as 2015 the California Court of Appeals re-affirmed this decision. *Britel v. Britel,* 236 Cal. App. 4th 127 (2015). In *Britel,* the non-marital child of a world-class bicyclist who was killed in a cycling accident at age 41 claimed an intestate share. The California statute at issue required "clear and convincing evidence that the father has openly held out the child as his own." A genetic test administered after the decedent's death showed that the child was the decedent's genetic child, but the decedent had repeatedly refused contact with the child and did not provide any financial support for the child during the decedent's lifetime. The court determined that the child was not an intestate heir, so the decedent's mother received the entire probate estate.

Britel v. Britel

236 Cal. App. 4th 127 (2015)

IKOLA, J.

Amine Britel died intestate in 2011. Appellant Jackie Stennett, the mother of A.S., a child born out of wedlock, petitioned to administer Amine's estate and for A.S. to be declared Amine's heir under Probate Code section 6453, subdivision (b)(2) (section 6453(b)(2)). Under section 6453(b)(2), a nonmarital child may establish that he or she is the natural child of an intestate decedent by proving the decedent "openly held out the child as his own."

The court denied Jackie's petitions. It granted the petition of respondent Mouna Britel (Amine's adult sister) to administer Amine's estate, which petition listed respondent Rhita Bhitel (Amine's mother) as Amine's surviving parent.

We affirm the court's order. In doing so, we conclude section 6453(b)(2)'s phrase, "openly held out," requires the alleged father to have made an unconcealed affirmative representation of his paternity in open view. We also conclude substantial evidence supports the court's finding Amine did not openly hold out A.S as his child. Finally, we conclude section 6453(b)(2) does not violate the state or federal equal protection rights of nonmarital children or of nonmarital children who can prove paternity using DNA tests.

FACTS

In the fall of 1999, Amine and Jackie met at Harvard Business School and developed a romantic relationship. In the early summer of 2000, they graduated. Jackie went to work in Atlanta, Georgia, while Amine moved to Newport Beach, California.

In August 2000, Jackie phoned Amine and told him she was pregnant. The next day, Amine sent Jackie an e-mail message saying he was "devastated," he would never be able to share the news with his parents, and that having a child out of wedlock was contrary to his Muslim religion and his culture and would bring him "a total shame [he would] have to bear for the rest of [his] life." Amine continued: "Please understand that I do love you but I am just not ready to be a father right now. I want us to have a child through a legitimate marriage and not outside of wedlock. We need to live together, learn about each other, and then make a commitment [sic] for life. I perceive marriage as a very serious engagement. I was devastated for the past two years as a result of a bad marriage. In all fairness, I believe I should be a part of this decision. It is important for us to meet to discuss this issue as soon as possible and find a suitable arrangement for both of us."

Later that month or possibly in early September, Jackie visited Amine in California for three or four days. She had initially planned to stay around a week, but the trip was cut short and she returned to Atlanta. Within the next few days, Amine and Jackie spoke by phone between five to 10 times. The end result was that Amine told Jackie not to contact him again and that he did not want her or the baby to be in touch with him or his family.

Amine told his best friend, Youssef Choukri, that Jackie said she was pregnant with his baby, and that his having a child out of wedlock would bring shame to his family (who were highly regarded in Morocco) and might possibly cause Amine to be disinherited. Amine initially told Choukri he was not sure whether Jackie was really pregnant, but that he had told Jackie that if she was indeed pregnant, he would like her to have an abortion.

In late 2000 or early 2001, Amine told Choukri that Jackie had had an abortion. Amine and Choukri never discussed the matter again.

At trial, Jackie testified she never told Amine she had had an abortion.

A.S. was born to Jackie in February 2001. Amine is not listed as the father on A.S.'s birth certificate. Prior to Amine's death, Jackie never sought a paternity order to determine whether Amine was A.S.'s father. Amine never provided any financial support to A.S., never met her, and never communicated with her.

For many years, Jackie comported with Amine's request that she not contact him. Then, in November 2006, Jackie sent Amine an e-mail message, which stated in part, "Per your last request I have kept my distance from you for the past six years." Jackie's e-mail message informed Amine that A.S. wanted a relationship with him.

Amine did not respond to Jackie's e-mail message, so Jackie phoned him. In the phone call, Jackie told Amine that A.S. asked about him and wanted him in her life. Amine was "terse and cold," asked Jackie not to phone him again, and made it clear he wanted nothing to do with Jackie or A.S. This phone call and Jackie's e-mail message were the only communications between Jackie and Amine from the time A.S. was born until Amine's death.

Amine was close with his family members, but never told them he had a child.

In February 2011, Amine was 41 years old, and a world class bicyclist. He was riding his bicycle in broad daylight, when he was struck and killed by a drunk, texting driver. At the time of his death, Amine was not married and had no domestic partner. He died intestate.

Jackie never sought a paternity order while Amine was alive because she wanted him "to participate when he was ready and by his own choice," and she did not "want to force his hand."

Over respondents' objection, the court admitted into evidence a DNA test showing a 99.9996 percent probability that Amine was A.S.'s father.

The court ruled: ". . . Jackie Stennett did not carry her burden of establishing by clear and convincing evidence that Amine Britel openly held out [A.S.] as his own child in accordance with [section] 6453(b)(2). . . ." The court denied Jackie's petitions for determination of heirship and for letters of administration and granted Mouna's petition for letters of administration. By doing so, the court ruled that Amine's mother Rhita is his sole heir.

DISCUSSION

At issue here is subdivision (b)(2) of section 6453. Under section 6453(b)(2), a natural parent and child relationship may be established when "[p]aternity is established by clear and convincing evidence that the father has openly held out the child as his own."

Jackie contends that even if the court correctly interpreted and applied section 6453, the statutory scheme violates the equal protection rights of nonmarital children because marital children enjoy a rebuttable presumption of a natural parent-child relationship under section 6453, subdivision (a). Amici argue the statutory scheme violates the equal protection rights of nonmarital children who can prove paternity using DNA tests.

Whether a statutory classification is unconstitutional "depends upon the character of the discrimination and its relation to legitimate legislative aims." *Matthews v. Lucas*, 427 U.S. 495, 503–04 (1976). The United States Supreme Court has generally applied an intermediate level of scrutiny to discriminatory classifications based on illegitimacy. *Clark v. Jeter*, 486 U.S. 456, 461 (1988). "To withstand intermediate scrutiny, a statutory classification must be substantially related to an important governmental objective." *Id.* Although "illegitimacy is analogous in many respects to the personal characteristics that have been held to be suspect when used as the basis of statutory differentiations," the Supreme Court has "concluded that the analogy [is] not sufficient to require 'our most exacting scrutiny.'" *Trimble v. Gordon*, 430 U.S. 762, 767 (1977).

Jackie contends the modern-day accuracy of DNA tests compels the conclusion that section 6453 violates the equal protection rights of nonmarital children. She argues DNA proof of paternity eliminates the risk of fraudulent claims and therefore section 6453 no longer serves that state interest. Even if that were true, however, section 6453 effectuates the state's important interests in carrying out an intestate decedent's likely intent and in doing so efficiently.

Jackie relies on *Clark*, and *Mills v. Habluetzel*, 456 U.S. 91 (1982), both of which involved statutes of limitation for paternity actions, not intestate succession statutes. The state interests implicated in *Clark* and *Mills* differ from the legislative purposes underlying intestacy succession laws. Paternity actions enforce "the State['s] interest in ensuring that genuine claims for child support are satisfied," *Clark*, and that a child may have a relationship with his or her father. *County of Shasta v. Caruthers*, 31 Cal. App. 4th 1838, 1841 (1995). California's intestate succession laws, in contrast, further the state's interest in carrying out the likely intent of a decedent, at the time of death, in the distribution of his or her estate. As recognized by the United States Supreme Court, state intestacy laws embody "the popular view within the jurisdiction of how a parent would have his property devolve among his children in the event of death." *Mathews*, 427 U.S. at 514–15.

Jackie also relies on *Lalli*, 439 U.S. 259, which involved intestate succession. *Lalli* identified another state interest underlying laws limiting the right of nonmarital children to inherit from putative fathers who die intestate: Unless reasonable restrictions are imposed, such inheritance can significantly disrupt the administration of estates.

Lalli involved a constitutional challenge to a New York statute that allowed a nonmarital child to inherit from an intestate father only if a court had issued a paternity decree during the father's lifetime. *Lalli*, 439 U.S. at 261–62. Drafted by a state commission of experts "in the practical problems of estate administration," *id.* at 269, the statute "was intended to soften the rigors of previous law which permitted illegitimate children to inherit only from their mothers." *Id.* at 266. "Although the overarching purpose of the proposed statute was 'to alleviate the plight of the illegitimate child,' [the commission] considered it necessary to impose the strictures of [the challenged statutory provision] in order to mitigate serious difficulties in the administration of the estates of both testate and intestate decedents." *Id.* at 269–70. The commission identified serious problems which would arise in both intestacy and will probate proceedings if nonmarital children were unconditionally entitled to notice and an opportunity to be heard. For example, " '[h]ow does one cite and serve an illegitimate of whose existence neither family nor personal representative may be aware? And of greatest concern, how [does one] achieve finality of decree in any estate when there always exists the possibility however remote of a secret illegitimate lurking in the buried past of a parent or an ancestor of a class of beneficiaries?' " *Id.* at 270.

In *Lalli*, a divided Supreme Court held the statute was "substantially related to the important state interests the statute is intended to promote" and therefore found no violation of the Equal Protection Clause. *Lalli*, 439 U.S. at 275–76 (plur. opn. of Powell, J.). Justice Powell's plurality opinion observed that the statute was intended "to ensure the accurate resolution of claims of paternity . . . to minimize the potential for disruption of estate administration," and to permit a man to defend his reputation against unjust paternity claims. *Id.* at 271.

Lalli recognized that in some cases, unfairness would result: "We do not question that there will be some illegitimate children who would be able to establish their relationship to their deceased fathers without serious disruption of the administration of estates and that, as applied to such individuals, [the statute] appears to operate unfairly. But few statutory classifications are entirely free from the criticism that they sometimes produce inequitable results. Our inquiry under the Equal Protection Clause does not focus on the abstract 'fairness' of a state law, but on whether the statute's relation to the state interests it is intended to promote is so tenuous that it lacks the rationality contemplated by the Fourteenth Amendment." *Lalli*, 439 U.S. at 272–73.

Here, section 6453, subdivision (b)(1), under which a paternity decree entered during the father's lifetime creates a natural parent-child relationship for purposes of intestate succession, is similar to (and more generous than) the New York statute upheld in *Lalli*. Section 6453 provides two additional methods by which paternity can be established, i.e., pursuant to section 6453(b)(2)'s "openly held out" standard and section 6453, subdivision (b)(3)'s "impossibility" provision. Thus, *Lalli* upheld the constitutionality of a New York statute that was "similar [to], but even more restrictive" than, section 6453. *Campbell ex rel. Campbell v. Apfel*, 177 F.3d 890, 894 (9th Cir. 1999).

As *Lalli* recognized, "the States have an interest of considerable magnitude" in "the just and orderly disposition of property at death." *Lalli*, 439 U.S. at 268. Section 6453(b)(2)'s "openly held out" standard promotes the purpose of minimizing disruption of estate administration: If a putative father has openly held out a child as his own, the child is less likely to be a " 'secret' " or " 'unknown' illegitimate [ ]" with concomitant concerns of identification and finality discussed in *Lalli*, 439 U.S. at 270. Equally important, section 6453(b)(2) carries out the decedent's likely intent at the time of death as to the distribution of his estate. Because section 6453(b)(2) is substantially related to these important state interests, it does not violate the federal or state Constitutions.

The order is affirmed.

ASSESSMENTS

1. The California statute requires a non-marital child establish paternity or have the paternity acknowledged before the father dies for the non-marital child to take an intestate share of the father's estate. What policy considerations does such a rule favor? What policy considerations does such a rule overlook?

2. In many other states, the non-marital child also may inherit from the father if paternity is proven—even after the father's death. The Uniform Parentage Act defines when a parent-child relationship exists, § 201; provides other circumstances when a person is presumed to be a parent., including residing in

the same household with the child for the first two years of the child's life, § 204; authorizes an adjudication of paternity, § 601; and allows genetic testing, including after the death of the parent if the individual seeking testing shows "good cause," § 510. The current UPC mirrors the provisions of the Uniform Parentage Act. What do you think is the appropriate approach?

3.   To what extent should the policy considerations relating to establishing parentage for purposes of family law inform rules about establishing parentage for purposes of succession?

3.   Adopted Child

Adoption is establishing parentage by legal decree. A child legally adopted by the decedent is a descendant of the decedent and inherits from and through the adoptive parent. The adoption also typically cuts off inheritance rights between the adoptive child and the adoptive child's genetic family. As a result, the child receives a fresh start in the child's adoptive family and generally does not retain inheritance rights from the child's genetic parents. Under the UPC, a child in the process of being adopted when one spouses dies is treated as adopted by the deceased spouse if the adoption is later granted to the surviving parent. In a few states, the adoptive child continues to inherit from and through the birth parent although the birth parent does not inherit from the child.

Many states and the current UPC §§ 2–118(a), 2–119(b)(2), allow for a child who is adopted by the spouse of a genetic parent to inherit from and through the genetic parents as well as from and through the adoptive parent. This so-called **stepparent exception** typically occurs when a genetic parent has died, and the surviving spouse remarries or where the rights of a genetic parent have been terminated and that genetic parent consents to the adoption. Some states have a narrower exception that applies to stepparent adoption that follows the death of the genetic parent but does not apply upon divorce of the parents. *E.g.*, OR. REV. STAT. § 112.175(2) (2016). The stepparent exception recognizes that the adoptive child may maintain a relationship with the genetic parent's family.

Many states do not distinguish between adoption of a minor and adoption of an adult regarding inheritance by either the parent or the child. The UPC does not, either, for purposes of intestate succession. It does, however, distinguish for purposes of class gifts, which is a topic we will discuss later. UPC § 2–705. *See also* Sarah Ratliff, *Adult Adoption: Intestate Succession And Class Gifts Under The Uniform Probate Code*, 105 NW. U. L. REV. 1777 (2011).

A child who has not been **formally adopted** may still inherit under the concept of an **equitable adoption**, which is also called **informal** or **virtual** adoption and recognized in approximately one-half of the jurisdictions. Typically, in equitable adoption, the child may inherit from the parent, but the parent may not inherit from the child. The traditional equitable adoption was based on either an express or implied promise to adopt. The more modern trend is to find an equitable adoption if the child was held out as a child by the alleged parent. Although jurisdictions may agree upon the need for the concept of equitable adoption, parties can find it challenging to prevail on such a claim. As you will see, the following case, *O'Neal v. Wilkes*, 439 S.E.2d 490 (1994), reveals the split over just how "formal" the equitable adoption needed to be. How do you think a more formal or less formal understanding of the doctrine of equitable adoption advances or undermines the purpose of the doctrine?

O'Neal v. Wilkes

439 S.E.2d 490 (Ga. 1994)

FLETCHER, J.

In this virtual adoption action, a jury found that appellant Hattie O'Neal had been virtually adopted by the decedent, Roswell Cook. On post-trial motions, the court granted a judgment notwithstanding the verdict to appellee Firmon Wilkes, as administrator of Cook's estate, on the ground that the paternal aunt who allegedly entered into the adoption contract with Cook had no legal authority to do so. We have reviewed the record and conclude that the court correctly determined that there was no valid contract to adopt.

O'Neal was born out of wedlock in 1949 and raised by her mother, Bessie Broughton, until her mother's death in 1957. At no time did O'Neal's biological father recognize O'Neal as his daughter, take any action to legitimize her, or provide support to her or her mother. O'Neal testified that she first met her biological father in 1970.

For four years after her mother's death, O'Neal lived in New York City with her maternal aunt, Ethel Campbell. In 1961, Ms. Campbell brought O'Neal to Savannah, Georgia, and surrendered physical custody of O'Neal to a woman identified only as Louise who was known to want a daughter. Shortly thereafter, Louise determined she could not care for O'Neal and took her to the Savannah home of Estelle Page, the sister of O'Neal's biological father. After a short time with Page, Roswell Cook and his wife came to Savannah from their Riceboro, Georgia home to pick up O'Neal. Page testified that she had heard that the Cooks wanted a daughter and after telling them about O'Neal, they came for her.

Although O'Neal was never statutorily adopted by Cook, he raised her and provided for her education and she resided with him until her marriage in 1975. While she never took the last name of Cook, he referred to her as his daughter and, later, identified her children as his grandchildren.

In November 1991, Cook died intestate. The appellee, Firmon Wilkes, was appointed as administrator of Cook's estate and refused to recognize O'Neal's asserted interest in the estate. In December 1991, O'Neal filed a petition in equity asking the court to declare a virtual adoption, thereby entitling her to the estate property she would have inherited if she were Cook's statutorily adopted child.

DISCUSSION

1.   The first essential of a contract for adoption is that it be made between persons competent to contract for the disposition of the child. A successful plaintiff must also prove:

> Some showing of an agreement between the natural and adoptive parents, performance by the natural parents of the child in giving up custody, performance by the child by living in the home of the adoptive parents, partial performance by the foster parents in taking the child into the home and treating [it] as their child, and . . . the intestacy of the foster parent.

Williams v. Murray, 236 S.E.2d 624 (Ga. 1977). The only issue on this appeal is whether the court correctly determined that Page was without authority to contract for O'Neal's adoption.

2.   O'Neal argues that Page, a paternal aunt with physical custody of her, had authority to contract for her adoption and, even if she was without such authority, any person with the legal right to contract for the adoption, be they O'Neal's biological father or maternal aunts or uncles, ratified the adoption contract by failing to object.

As a preliminary matter, we agree with O'Neal that although her biological father was living at the time the adoption contract was allegedly entered into, his consent to the contract was not necessary as he never recognized or legitimized her or provided for her support in any manner. What is less clear are the rights and obligations acquired by Page by virtue of her physical custody of O'Neal after her mother's death.

3.   The Georgia Code defines a "legal custodian" as a person to whom legal custody has been given by court order and who has the right to physical

custody of the child and to determine the nature of the care and treatment of the child and the duty to provide for the care, protection, training, and education and the physical, mental, and moral welfare of the child. OCGA § 15–11–43, Code 1933, § 24A–2901. A legal custodian does not have the right to consent to the adoption of a child, as this right is specifically retained by one with greater rights over the child, a child's parent, or guardian.

O'Neal concedes that, after her mother's death, no guardianship petition was filed by her relatives. Nor is there any evidence that any person petitioned to be appointed as her legal custodian. Accordingly, the obligation to care and provide for O'Neal, undertaken first by Campbell, and later by Page, was not a legal obligation but a familial obligation resulting in a custodial relationship properly characterized as something less than that of a legal custodian. Such a relationship carried with it no authority to contract for O'Neal's adoption. While we sympathize with O'Neal's plight, we conclude that Page had no authority to enter into the adoption contract with Cook and the contract, therefore, was invalid.

4.   Because O'Neal's relatives did not have the legal authority to enter into a contract for her adoption, their alleged ratification of the adoption contract was of no legal effect and the court did not err in granting a judgment notwithstanding the verdict in favor of the appellee.

Judgment affirmed.

SEARS-COLLINS, J., dissenting.

I disagree with the majority's holding that O'Neal's claim for equitable adoption is defeated by the fact that her paternal aunt was not a person designated by law as one having the authority to consent to O'Neal's adoption.

1.   In *Crawford v. Wilson*, 78 S.E. 30 (Ga. 1913), the doctrine of equitable or virtual adoption was recognized for the first time in Georgia. Relying on the equitable principle that "equity considers that done which ought to have been done," *id.* at 659; *see* O.C.GA. § 23–1–8, we held that

> an agreement to adopt a child, so as to constitute the child an heir at law on the death of the person adopting, performed on the part of the child, is enforceable upon the death of the person adopting the child as to property which is undisposed of by will. . . . We held that although the death of the adopting parents precluded a literal enforcement of the contract, equity would "enforce the contract by decreeing that the child is entitled to the fruits of a legal adoption."

Id. In *Crawford*, we noted that the full performance of the agreement by the child was sufficient to overcome an objection that the agreement was unenforceable because it violated the statute of frauds. *Id.* at 658. We further held that

> [w]here one takes an infant into his home upon a promise to adopt such as his own child, and the child performs all the duties growing out of the substituted relationship of parent and child, rendering years of service, companionship, and obedience to the foster parent, upon the faith that such foster parent stands in loco parentis, and that upon his death the child will sustain the legal relationship to his estate of a natural child, there is equitable reason that the child may appeal to a court of equity to consummate, so far as it may be possible, the foster parent's omission of duty in the matter of formal adoption.

Id. at 660.

Although the majority correctly states the current rule in Georgia that a contract to adopt may not be specifically enforced unless the contract was entered by a person with the legal authority to consent to the adoption of the child, Crawford did not expressly establish such a requirement, and I think the cases cited by the majority that have established this requirement are in error.

Instead, I would hold that where a child has fully performed the alleged contract over the course of many years or a lifetime and can sufficiently establish the existence of the contract to adopt, equity should enforce the contract over the objection of the adopting parents' heirs that the contract is unenforceable because the person who consented to the adoption did not have the legal authority to do so. Several reasons support this conclusion.

First, in such cases, the adopting parents and probably their heirs know of the defect in the contract and yet voice no objection to the contract while the child fully performs the contract and the adopting parents reap the benefits thereof. Under these circumstances, to hold that the contract is unenforceable after the child has performed is to permit a virtual fraud upon the child and should not be countenanced in equity. Moreover, the purpose of requiring consent by a person with the legal authority to consent to an adoption, where such a person exists, is to protect that person, the child, and the adopting parents. However, as equitable adoption cases do not arise until the death of the adopting parents, the interests of the person with the consent to adopt and of the adopting parents are not in jeopardy. On the other hand, the interests of the child are unfairly and inequitably harmed by insisting upon the requirement that a person with the consent to adopt had to have been a party to the contract.

That this legal requirement is held against the child is particularly inequitable because the child, the course of whose life is forever changed by such contracts, was unable to act to insure the validity of the contract when the contract was made.

Furthermore, where there is no person with the legal authority to consent to the adoption, such as in the present case, the only reason to insist that a person be appointed the child's legal guardian before agreeing to the contract to adopt would be for the protection of the child. Yet, by insisting upon this requirement after the adopting parents' deaths, this Court is harming the very person that the requirement would protect.

For all the foregoing reasons, equity ought to intervene on the child's behalf in these types of cases and require the performance of the contract if it is sufficiently proven. In this case, I would thus not rule against O'Neal's claim for specific performance solely on the ground that her paternal aunt did not have the authority to consent to the adoption.

2.   Moreover, basing the doctrine of equitable adoption in contract theory has come under heavy criticism, for numerous reasons. For instance, as we acknowledged in *Wilson*, the contract to adopt is not being specifically enforced as the adopting parents are dead; for equitable reasons we are merely placing the child in a position that he or she would have been in if he or she had been adopted. Furthermore, because part of the consideration for these contracts is the child's performance thereunder, the child is not merely a third-party beneficiary of a contract between the adults involved but is a party thereto. Yet, a child is usually too young to know of or understand the contract, and it is thus difficult to find a meeting of the minds between the child and the adopting parents and the child's acceptance of the contract. I agree with these criticisms and would abandon the contract basis for equitable adoption in favor of the more flexible and equitable theory advanced by the foregoing authorities. That theory focuses not on the fiction of whether there has been a contract to adopt but on the relationship between the adopting parents and the child and in particular whether the adopting parents have led the child to believe that he or she is a legally adopted member of their family.

3.   Because the majority fails to honor the maxim that "[e]quity considers that done which ought to be done," § 23–1–8, and follows a rule that fails to protect a person with superior equities, I dissent.

I am authorized to state that Justice Hunstein concurs in the result reached by this dissent.

NOTES

1. Compare the reasoning of the majority opinion and the dissenting opinion. Which opinion do you believe better reflects the purpose of the doctrine of equitable adoption?

2. The city of Riceboro, Georgia has a population of less than 1,000.[5] The population is almost 90% Black. Approximately one-third of the households would be classified as "married-couple families." Adults in Riceboro are less likely to have earned a high school diploma than the typical American adult. The median household income is almost $17,000 below the median income in the state of Georgia and almost $22,000 less than the national median income. The poverty rate is almost 20% with the state average being 16% and the national average being 14%. Geographically, Riceboro is located in Liberty County and is thirty-seven miles from the city of Savannah. The city of Savannah is located in Chatman County, which as a population of almost 300,000. In contrast, the population of Liberty County today is just over 60,000 people. Liberty County would be considered to be a predominantly rural county. How does this demographic and geographic information inform your analysis of the opinions?

3. *O'Neal* is part of the *Feminist Judgments* project. You can find a rewritten opinion and commentary in FEMINIST JUDGMENTS: REWRITTEN TRUSTS AND ESTATES OPINIONS 81–99 (eds. Deborah S Gordon, Browne C. Lewis, & Carla Spivack) (Cambridge Univ. Press 2020) (two commentaries and rewritten opinion). What would you revise about the majority opinion if you had the chance to rewrite the opinion? How would you justify the revisions?

4. Both the *O'Neal* majority and dissent refer to the absence of a "**guardian of the person**" for Hattie O'Neal, though they draw different conclusions from that absence. The majority emphasizes the person who placed Hattie O'Neal with the Cooks lacked the authority to enter into a contract for adoption. The dissent sees the requirement of a guardian as yet another legal impediment in the way of what should be a flexible equitable adoption regime. Parents of minor children often name a guardian of their children in a will. Quite frequently, the guardian of the person of minor children will also be custodian of the children's property. Naming a guardian of the person as custodian of property allows them flexibility in managing property, which subjects them to managing the property as a fiduciary. Sometimes courts will appoint a person as "guardian" of property (rather than custodian), which typically involves on-going and extensive

---

[5]   https://worldpopulationreview.com/us-cities/riceboro-ga-population. For additional statistics, see http://www.city-data.com/city/Riceboro-Georgia.html.

oversight. *See* Michael J. Higdon, *When Informal Adoption Meets Intestate Succession: The Cultural Myopia of the Equitable Adoption Doctrine*, 43 WAKE FOREST L. REV. 223 (2008).

5.   Three years after *O'Neal*, the Georgia Supreme Court declined to find equitable adoption in another case because, it held, that "[a]n essential element of a virtual adoption claim is the existence of an adoption agreement between persons who were competent to contract for the disposition of the child." *Franklin v. Gilchrist*, 491 S.E.2d 361, 362 (Ga. 1997). The court stressed the absence of evidence showing the genetic father, referred to in the case as "the natural father," agreed to the adoption and the lack of evidence to explain the failure to obtain the father's agreement. Both cases reveal how difficult it is to succeed on a claim of equitable adoption.

6.   Yet another informal relationship that arises with some degree of frequency is that of a decedent who cares for grandchildren, so has an *informal* parent-child relationship and a *formal* grandparent-child relationship. *See* Kristine S. Knaplund, *Grandparents Raising Grandchildren and the Implications for Inheritance*, 48 ARIZ. L. REV. 1 (2006). Current intestacy statutes do not take into account a grandparent raising a grandchild as a method of creating a parent-child relationship unless the grandparent has adopted the grandchild. Often the parents of the child are alive but are not caring for the child and their rights have not been terminated. These arrangements are informal; the grandchild is young and the grandparent elderly; and the grandchild has not seen his or her parents for years. If the grandparent dies intestate, it is likely that the estate will pass to the parent who is the child of the decedent, rather than to the grandchild.

ASSESSMENTS

1.   Blake and Harper are validly married. They formally adopt a child named Cary who is the genetic child of Moira and Nate. Thereafter Blake, Harper, Moira, and Nate die. From whom may Cary inherit? What if Blake's mother then died? May Cary inherit from Blake's mother? What if Cary died first? Who inherits from Cary?

2.   Rowen and Shawn are validly married. They are the genetic parents of a child named Crystal. Shawn dies. Rowen later marries Zara who adopts Crystal. Shawn's father then dies intestate.

    a.   May Crystal inherit from Shawn's father? May Crystal inherit if Zara dies intestate?

b.   What if Crystal died intestate survived only by Rowen's father? May Rowen's father take?

c.   What if Zara, who married Rowen following Shaw's death, never formally adopted Crystal? If Zara died intestate, does Crystal ever take? To what extent does the analysis change if Crystal died intestate first? Could Zara inherit from Crystal if Zara never formally adopted Crystal?

4.   Child of a De Facto Parent

De facto parentage is a functional approach to parentage, which is recognized in the Uniform Parentage Act and the Uniform Probate Code. De facto parentage recognizes that individuals, who have no established relationship via genetics or adoption, have nevertheless created a relationship that functions as a parent-child relationship. A "de facto parent" means a person who has been adjudicated to be a parent of a child under the applicable de facto parentage statute. UPC § 2–115(3). The Uniform Parentage Act outlines the requirements for the adjudicating of the claim of de facto parentage of a child, which includes commencement of a proceeding by an individual claiming to be a de facto parent when the individual is alive and when the child is under the age of 18. The individual claiming to be a de facto parent must establish by clear and convincing evidence the following: (1) the individual resided in the child's household for a significant period of time, (2) the individually consistently engaged in caretaking, (3) no financial compensation was expected, (4) the individual held out the child as the individual's child, (5) a bonded and dependent relationship with the child was established by the individual, (6) another of the child's parents fostered or supported such bond, and (7) continuing the relationship is in the child's best interests. Uniform Parentage Act § 609(d).

The 2019 revisions to the Uniform Probate Code incorporate the recognition that a parent-child relationship established by the doctrine of de facto parentage is another way to determine parentage for succession purposes, including for purposes of intestate succession and class-gifts. UPC § 2–118(b). Expanding the way in which parentage may arise recognizes that a child may have more than two parents or two sets of grandparents. By expanding these definitions, we recognize that individuals construct a variety of familial relationships. *See generally* J. Herbie DiFonzo & Ruth C. Stern, *Breaking the Mold and Picking Up the Pieces: Rights of Parenthood and Parentage in Nontraditional Families*, 51 FAM. CT. REV. 104 (Jan. 2013).

5. Foster Child

A **foster child** does not inherit from his or her foster parents unless the doctrine of equitable adoption applies. In other words, foster care is not generally a method of establishing parentage for purposes of intestate succession. An exception is California, which allows a foster child to inherit if the parent-child relationship was established during the child's minority, continued thereafter, and it can be established by clear and convincing evidence that the foster parent would have adopted the foster child but for a legal barrier. CAL. PROB. CODE § 6454.

6. Posthumously Born Children and Posthumously Conceived Children

Typically, the term **posthumous child** refers to a child who, though conceived before the death of a parent, is born after such death. Literature's most famous posthumous child was David Copperfield, who bemoaned his birth after the death of his father: "I was a posthumous child. My father's eyes had closed upon the light of this world six months, when mine opened on it. There is something strange to me, even now, in the reflection that he never saw me; and something stranger yet in the shadowy remembrance that I have of my first childish association with his white grave-stone in the churchyard." CHARLES DICKENS, DAVID COPPERFIELD 8. It is a long-standing principle that a posthumous child will take as an intestate heir.

The ability of a **posthumously conceived child** to inherit is a more recent, and more complicated, issue. A posthumously conceived child is both conceived after the decedent's death using stored genetic material and born after the decedent's death. **Assisted reproductive technologies (ART)** and gestational contracts have challenged the law to expand the methods to determine parentage. The UPC was amended in 2008 to address the issue of ART and revised in 2019 to reflect a more modern understanding of the many potential participants in reproduction. Many jurisdictions, like the original UPC, have not yet clearly addressed all issues involving ART and inheritance. The current UPC refers to the Uniform Parentage Act for the purposes of determining the parent-child relationship in both surrogacy and other ART relationships. For further examination of issues involving ART, see Raymond C. O'Brien, *Assessing Assisted Reproductive Technology*, 27 CATH. U.J.L. & TECH. 1 (2018); Deborah Zalesne, *The Intersection of Contract Law, Reproductive Technology, and the Market: Families in the Age of ART*, 51 U. RICH. L. REV. 419 (2017).

The question of the rights of a posthumously conceived child has arisen in the context of whether that child is eligible for social security survivor benefits. Eligibility for such benefits turns on whether a child is an intestate heir under the law of the state where the child was born. In *Astrue v. Capato*, the U.S. Supreme Court confirmed that state intestacy law would determine if such a child would qualify for social security benefits. Several state courts have dealt with rights regarding intestate succession of these children with varying results. The Massachusetts Supreme Judicial Court found that posthumously conceived children *can be* intestate heirs so long as the deceased parent consented to the be treated as a parent. *See Woodward v. Commissioner of Social Security*, 760 N.E.2d 257 (Mass. 2002). Other states are not so generous. Florida, the state where *Astrue* originated, does not consider posthumously conceived children to be intestate heirs.

Astrue v. Capato

566 U.S. 541 (2012)

GINSBURG, J.

Karen and Robert Capato married in 1999. Robert died of cancer less than three years later. With the help of *in vitro* fertilization, Karen gave birth to twins 18 months after her husband's death. Karen's application for Social Security survivors benefits for the twins, which the Social Security Administration (SSA) denied, prompted this litigation. The technology that made the twins' conception and birth possible, it is safe to say, was not contemplated by Congress when the relevant provisions of the Social Security Act (Act) originated (1939) or were amended to read as they now do (1965).

Karen Capato, respondent here, relies on the Act's initial definition of "child" in 42 U.S.C. § 416(e): " '[C]hild' means . . . the child or legally adopted child of an [insured] individual." Robert was an insured individual, and the twins, it is uncontested, are the biological children of Karen and Robert. That satisfies the Act's terms, and no further inquiry is in order, Karen maintains. The SSA, however, identifies subsequent provisions, §§ 416(h)(2) and (h)(3)(C), as critical, and reads them to entitle biological children to benefits only if they qualify for inheritance from the decedent under state intestacy law, or satisfy one of the statutory alternatives to that requirement.

We conclude that the SSA's reading is better attuned to the statute's text and its design to benefit primarily those supported by the deceased wage earner in his or her lifetime. And even if the SSA's longstanding interpretation is not the only reasonable one, it is at least a permissible construction that garners the Court's respect under *Chevron U. S. A. Inc. v. Natural Resources Defense Council, Inc.,* 467 U.S. 837 (1984).

I

Karen Capato married Robert Capato in May 1999. Shortly thereafter, Robert was diagnosed with esophageal cancer and was told that the chemotherapy he required might render him sterile. Because the couple wanted children, Robert, before undergoing chemotherapy, deposited his semen in a sperm bank, where it was frozen and stored. Despite Robert's aggressive treatment regime, Karen conceived naturally and gave birth to a son in August 2001. The Capatos, however, wanted their son to have a sibling.

Robert's health deteriorated in late 2001, and he died in Florida, where he and Karen then resided, in March 2002. His will, executed in Florida, named as beneficiaries the son born of his marriage to Karen and two children from a previous marriage. The will made no provision for children conceived after Robert's death, although the Capatos had told their lawyer they wanted future offspring to be placed on a par with existing children. Shortly after Robert's death, Karen began in vitro fertilization using her husband's frozen sperm. She conceived in January 2003 and gave birth to twins in September 2003, 18 months after Robert's death.

Karen Capato claimed survivors insurance benefits on behalf of the twins. The SSA denied her application, and the U.S. District Court for the District of New Jersey affirmed the agency's decision. In accord with the SSA's construction of the statute, the District Court determined that the twins would qualify for benefits only if, as § 416(h)(2)(A) specifies, they could inherit from the deceased wage earner under state intestacy law. Robert Capato died domiciled in Florida, the court found. Under that State's law, the court noted, a child born posthumously may inherit through intestate succession only if conceived during the decedent's lifetime.

The Court of Appeals for the Third Circuit reversed. Courts of Appeals have divided on the statutory interpretation question this case presents.

To resolve this case, we must decide whether the Capato twins rank as "child[ren]" under the Act's definitional provisions. Section 402(d) provides that "[e]very child (as defined in section 416(e) of this title)" of a deceased insured individual "shall be entitled to a child's insurance benefit." Section 416(e), in turn, states: "The term 'child' means (1) the child or legally adopted child of an individual, (2) a stepchild [under certain circumstances], and (3) . . . the grandchild or stepgrandchild of an individual or his spouse [who meets certain conditions]."

The word "child," we note, appears twice in § 416(e)'s opening sentence: initially in the prefatory phrase, "[t]he term 'child' means . . . ," and, immediately thereafter, in subsection (e)(1) ("child or legally adopted child"), delineating the first of three beneficiary categories. Unlike §§ 416(e)(2) and (3), which specify the circumstances under which stepchildren and grandchildren qualify for benefits, § 416(e)(1) lacks any elaboration. Compare § 416(e)(1) (referring simply to "the child . . . of an individual") with, e.g., § 416(e)(2) (applicant must have been a stepchild for at least nine months before the insured individual's death).

An applicant for child benefits who does not meet § 416(h)(2)(A)'s intestacy-law criterion may nonetheless qualify for benefits under one of several other criteria the Act prescribes. First, an applicant who "is a son or daughter" of an insured individual, but is not determined to be a "child" under the intestacy-law provision, nevertheless ranks as a "child" if the insured and the other parent went through a marriage ceremony that would have been valid but for certain legal impediments. § 416(h)(2)(B). Further, an applicant is deemed a "child" if, before death, the insured acknowledged in writing that the applicant is his or her son or daughter, or if the insured had been decreed by a court to be the father or mother of the applicant, or had been ordered to pay child support. § 416(h)(3)(C)(i). In addition, an applicant may gain "child" status upon proof that the insured individual was the applicant's parent and "was living with or contributing to the support of the applicant" when the insured individual died. § 416(h)(3)(C)(ii).

Reference to state law to determine an applicant's status as a "child" is anything but anomalous. Quite the opposite. The Act commonly refers to state law on matters of family status. For example, the Act initially defines "wife" as "the wife of an [insured] individual," if certain conditions are satisfied. § 416(b). Like § 416(e), § 416(b) is, at least in part, tautological (" 'wife' means the [insured's] wife"). One must read on, although there is no express cross-reference, to § 416(h) (rules on "[d]etermination of family status") to complete the definition. Section § 416(h)(1)(A) directs that, "for purposes of this subchapter," the law of the insured's domicile determines whether "[the] applicant and [the] insured individual were validly married," and if they were not, whether the applicant would nevertheless have "the same status" as a wife under the State's intestacy law. (Emphasis added.) The Act similarly defines the terms "widow," "husband," and "widower." *See* §§ 416(c), (f), (g), (h)(1)(A).

Indeed, as originally enacted, a single provision mandated the use of state intestacy law for "determining whether an applicant is the wife, widow, child, or parent of [an] insured individual." 42 U.S.C. § 409(m) (1940 ed.). All wife, widow, child, and parent applicants thus had to satisfy the same criterion. To be sure, children born during their parents' marriage would have readily qualified under the 1939 formulation because of their eligibility to inherit under state law. But requiring all "child" applicants to qualify under state intestacy law installed a simple test, one that ensured benefits for persons plainly within the legislators' contemplation, while avoiding congressional entanglement in the traditional state-law realm of family relations.

Just as the Act generally refers to state law to determine whether an applicant qualifies as a wife, widow, husband, widower, 42 U.S.C. § 416(h)(1) (2006 ed.), child or parent, § 416(h)(2)(A), so in several sections (§§ 416(b), (c), (e)(2), (f), (g)), the Act sets duration-of-relationship limitations. *See Weinberger v. Salfi*, 422 U.S. 749–782 (1975) (discussing § 416(e)(2)'s requirement that, as a check against deathbed marriages, a parent-stepchild relationship must exist "not less than nine months immediately preceding [insured's death]"). Time limits also qualify the statutes of several States that accord inheritance rights to posthumously conceived children. No time constraints attend the Third Circuit's ruling in this case, under which the biological child of married parents is eligible for survivors benefits, no matter the length of time between the father's death and the child's conception and birth.

We have recognized that "where state intestacy law provides that a child may take personal property from a father's estate, it may reasonably be thought that the child will more likely be dependent during the parent's life and at his death." *Matthews v. Lucas*, 427 U.S. 495, 514 (1976). Reliance on state intestacy law to determine who is a "child" thus serves the Act's driving objective. True, the intestacy criterion yields benefits to some children outside the Act's central concern. Intestacy laws in a number of States, as just noted, do provide for inheritance by posthumously conceived children, and under federal law, a child conceived shortly before her father's death may be eligible for benefits even though she never actually received her father's support. It was nonetheless Congress' prerogative to legislate for the generality of cases. It did so here by employing eligibility to inherit under state intestacy law as a workable substitute for burdensome case-by-case determinations whether the child was, in fact, dependent on her father's earnings.

Tragic circumstances—Robert Capato's death before he and his wife could raise a family—gave rise to this case. But the law Congress enacted calls for resolution of Karen Capato's application for child's insurance benefits by reference to state intestacy law. We cannot replace that reference by creating a uniform federal rule the statute's text scarcely supports.

NOTES

1.   The current UPC addresses the rights of posthumously conceived children by incorporating Article Seven of the Uniform Parentage Act. *See* § UPC 2–120. Section 708 of the Uniform Parentage Act, addressing the parental status of a deceased individual, provides that a posthumously conceived child is treated as the child of the deceased parent if the embryo was in utero no later than 36 months after the individual's death or born no later than 45 months after the individual's death. In addition, the decedent must have either signed a record giving consent for the assisted reproduction or there must be other clear and convincing evidence that decedent intended to be treated as the parent of the posthumously conceived child.

2.   States vary in their approach to posthumously conceived children. Florida, as *Astrue* points out, does not recognize posthumously conceived heirs as interstate heirs (and therefore such children are ineligible for social security survivor benefits). Consent is often critical. In California, a child conceived posthumously—using sperm extracted from his genetic father after the father passed away in a vehicle accident—was found not to be an intestate heir because the father had never consented to the removal of his sperm or its use to conceive a child. *Vernoff v. Astrue*, 568 F.3d 1102 (9th Cir. 2009). Arizona is more lenient. In 2004, the Ninth Circuit interpreted Arizona's intestacy law to dispense with the consent requirement, concluding that a posthumously conceived child born to the pre-deceased father's widow was a child for purposes of intestacy. *See Gillett-Netting v. Barnhart*, 371 F.3d 593 (9th Cir. 2004). Other states are more restrictive and will not treat posthumously conceived children as intestate heirs even if there is consent. In *Eng v. Commissioner Social Security Administration*, 930 A.2d 1180 (N.H. 2007), the New Hampshire Supreme Court concluded based on its reading of New Hampshire intestacy law that a posthumously conceived child—even where the deceased father consented in writing to the conception—is not an intestate heir of the father.

ASSESSMENTS

1.   The Capatos specifically told their lawyer that they were contemplating using ART. They also shared that, as recited in the case, "they wanted future

offspring to be placed on par with existing children." The documents produced at trial did not reflect these wishes.

    a.   Did the lawyer commit malpractice by failing to provide for posthumously conceived children?

    b.   Did the lawyer violate an aspect of the professional code of conduct? For example, Model Rule of Professional Conduct 1.1 provides as follows: "A lawyer shall provide competent representation to a client."

    c.   Formulate at least three questions that a lawyer should ask of an individual about posthumously conceived children and inheritance.

2.   Ray has hired your law firm for help with his estate planning. Ray recently ended a long-term relationship with Sara. Ray had wished to get married, but Sara did not wish to do so. Ray and Sara have a five-year-old daughter named Mohini. They have agreed to jointly raise Mohini. Ray has recently inherited a significant amount of property from his aunt. He would like to use this inheritance to create a trust for the benefit of his descendants. He has been doing some online research about trusts, and he wants the trust to have the broadest definition of descendants as possible to account for a number of circumstances that might arise. Draft a definition of "descendants" that reflects Ray's wishes.

D. Defining Other Takers

As previously mentioned, intestacy statutes create a hierarchy of heirs, including a point at which to cut off any further heirs from taking. The full UPC provision showing where the descendants and others fall within this hierarchy follows:

UPC § 2–103(b)–(j)

(b) **[Heirs Other Than Surviving Spouse.]** Any part of the intestate estate not passing under Section 2–102 to the decedent's surviving spouse passes to the decedent's descendants or parents as provided in subsections (c) and (d). If there is no surviving spouse, the entire intestate estate passes to the decedent's descendants, parents, or other heirs as provided in subsections (c) through (j).

(c) **[Surviving Descendant.]** If a decedent is survived by one or more descendants, any part of the intestate estate not passing to the surviving spouse passes by representation to the decedent's surviving descendants.

(d)   **[Surviving Parent.]** If a decedent is not survived by a descendant but is survived by one or more parents, any part of the intestate estate not passing to the surviving spouse is distributed as follows:

(1)   The intestate estate or part is divided into as many equal shares as there are:

(A)   surviving parents; and

(B)   deceased parents with one or more surviving descendants, if any, as determined under subsection (e).

(2)   One share passes to each surviving parent.

(3)   The balance of the intestate estate or part, if any, passes by representation to the surviving descendants of the decedent's deceased parents, as determined under subsection (e).

(e)   **[When Parent Survives: Computation of Shares of Surviving Descendants of Deceased Parent.]** The following rules apply under subsection (d) to determine whether a deceased parent of the decedent is treated as having a surviving descendant:

(1)   If all the surviving descendants of one or more deceased parents also are descendants of one or more surviving parents and none of those surviving parents has any other surviving descendant, those descendants are deemed to have predeceased the decedent.

(2)   If two or more deceased parents have the same surviving descendants and none of those deceased parents has any other surviving descendant, those deceased parents are deemed to be one deceased parent with surviving descendants.

(f)   **[Surviving Descendant of Deceased Parent.]** If a decedent is not survived by a descendant or parent but is survived by one or more descendants of a parent, the intestate estate passes by representation to the surviving descendants of the decedent's deceased parents.

(g)   **[Surviving Grandparent.]** If a decedent is not survived by a descendant, parent, or descendant of a parent but is survived by one or more grandparents, the intestate estate is distributed as follows:

(1)   The intestate estate is divided into as many equal shares as there are:

(A)   surviving grandparents; and

(B) deceased grandparents with one or more surviving descendants, if any, as determined under subsection (h).

(2) One share passes to each surviving grandparent.

(3) The balance of the intestate estate, if any, passes by representation to the surviving descendants of the decedent's deceased grandparents, as determined under subsection (h).

(h) **[When Grandparent Survives: Computation of Shares of Surviving Descendants of Deceased Grandparent.]** The following rules apply under subsection (g) to determine whether a deceased grandparent of the decedent is treated as having a surviving descendant:

(1) If all the surviving descendants of one or more deceased grandparents also are descendants of one or more surviving grandparents and none of those surviving grandparents has any other surviving descendant, those descendants are deemed to have predeceased the decedent.

(2) If two or more deceased grandparents have the same surviving descendants and none of those deceased grandparents has any other surviving descendant, those deceased grandparents are deemed to be one deceased grandparent with surviving descendants.

(i) **[Surviving Descendant of Deceased Grandparent.]** If a decedent is not survived by a descendant, parent, descendant of a parent, or grandparent but is survived by one or more descendants of a grandparent, the intestate estate passes by representation to the surviving descendants of the decedent's deceased grandparents.

(j) **[Surviving Descendant of Deceased Spouse.]** If a decedent is not survived by a descendant, parent, descendant of a parent, grandparent, or descendant of a grandparent but is survived by one or more descendants of one or more deceased spouses, the intestate estate passes by representation to the surviving descendants of the deceased spouse or spouses.

----

1. Defining Ancestors and Collateral Kindred

Although the spouse and descendants will receive the highest priority, the decedent's ancestors (parents and grandparents) and collateral kindred (siblings, nieces, nephews, aunts, uncles, and cousins) may, in the absence of lineal descendants, be heirs.

Under the original and the current UPC, the surviving parent or parent(s) receive the entire estate if the decedent had no surviving spouse and no descendants. The current UPC also provides some protection for parents if the decedent was not survived by descendants but was survived by a spouse. In such case the spouse would receive the first $300,000 of the decedent's intestate estate and, to the extent any property is left, the spouse would divide the remaining estate as follows: three-quarters of the estate to the spouse and one-quarter of the estate to the parent(s). Under the original UPC, the share passing to parents was even more generous; the surviving parent or parents would receive $50,000 plus one-half of the estate and the spouse the other one-half.

Typically, intestacy statutes do not take into account the circumstances under which the decedent obtained the probate property. Some states, however, specifically address property that the decedent inherited from his or her ancestors. This property is referred to as ancestral property and draws upon the civil law tradition of treating "patrimony" distinct from the decedent's other probate property. Civil law legal systems generally have limitations on the decedent's ability to transfer patrimony outside of the familial line. Even jurisdictions that have limited if any connection to civil law traditions may treated ancestral property different from the decedent's other probate property. For example, in Kentucky, if an individual dies intestate, without issue, owning real property that had been the *inter vivos* gift of either parent, then the giving parent, if living, will inherit such real property to the exclusion of all others. KEN. REV. STAT. § 391.020. How does treating ancestral property different correspond to the goals of intestacy statutes?

Parents inherit to the exclusion of their descendants (the decedent's siblings, for example) and more remote ancestors and their descendants (aunts, uncles, and cousins). If no parents survive the decedent, the property passes to other heirs. Remember, that intestacy statutes do not equally share the decedent's property among all the decedent's surviving family. When the decedent is not survived by descendants, spouse, or parents, the next category of heirs are the descendants of the decedent's parents (e.g., the decedent's siblings, nieces, and nephews). If there are no surviving collateral relatives who are descended from parents, the next category are the decedent's grandparents and the grandparents' descendants (e.g., the decedent's aunts, uncles, and cousins).

Siblings may be of the whole blood or of the **half-blood**. A sibling (or other relative) is a half-blood who shares one but not both relatives with another. Thus, if spouses have two children (whether genetic or adopted) the two children are full blooded siblings. They share the same two parents. If, however, one of the spouses had a third child, by a prior marriage, the three children share only one parent. The current UPC and most jurisdictions treat individuals of the full and half-blood equally. Some jurisdictions provide that collaterals of the half-blood shall inherit only half as much as those of the whole blood. Mississippi, MISS. CODE ANN. § 91–1–5, provides that if within the class to inherit there are members of the full blood and of the half-blood, the full blood members take to the exclusion of the half-blood members. Which view do you prefer?

One way of visualizing the hierarchy for the ancestors and the collateral kindred is the **Table of Consanguinity** (or relationship based on blood[6]). The decedent ("person") is at the far left in the top box, and beneath the decedent running down the left column are children, grandchildren, great grandchildren. You will also note a number in each box that notes how far removed each individual is from the decedent. Thus, from the decedent to a child is one step; to a grandchild is two steps and to a great grandchild it is three steps. This is called the degree of kinship. If there are no descendants, we then go to the first parentela or first degree of relationship (or first line collaterals) which would be parents, then siblings, nieces, and nephews, etc. Only if there are no heirs in this relationship will we go to the second parentela.

More about determining how shares pass to collateral relatives is discussed in the context of allocating shares in Section C.

---

[6]   Relationships based upon marriage are relationships based upon affinity.

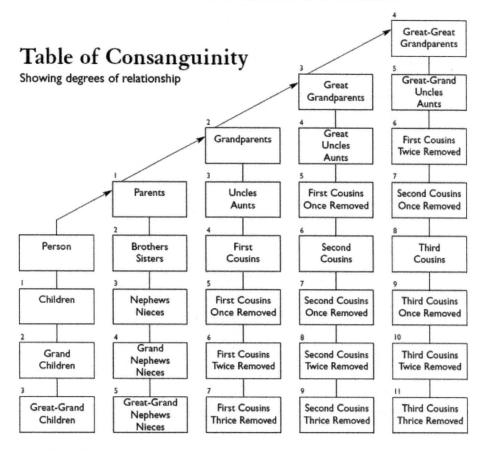

Table of Consanguinity
Showing degrees of relationship

				Great-Great Grandparents (4)
			Great Grandparents (3)	Great-Grand Uncles Aunts (5)
		Grandparents (2)	Great Uncles Aunts (4)	First Cousins Twice Removed (6)
	Parents (1)	Uncles Aunts (3)	First Cousins Once Removed (5)	Second Cousins Once Removed (7)
Person	Brothers Sisters (2)	First Cousins (4)	Second Cousins (6)	Third Cousins (8)
Children (1)	Nephews Nieces (3)	First Cousins Once Removed (5)	Second Cousins Once Removed (7)	Third Cousins Once Removed (9)
Grand Children (2)	Grand Nephews Nieces (4)	First Cousins Twice Removed (6)	Second Cousins Twice Removed (8)	Third Cousins Twice Removed (10)
Great-Grand Children (3)	Great-Grand Nephews Nieces (5)	First Cousins Thrice Removed (7)	Second Cousins Thrice Removed (9)	Third Cousins Thrice Removed (11)

2. No Heirs

The intestacy statutes do not allow for judicial discretion in determining who is a decedent's heirs. The status-based approach does not provide for the consideration of individual facts and circumstances. If no eligible heir exists within the relevant hierarchy, then the decedent's intestate estate **escheats** to the state.

A question as to how far to extend the hierarchy of heirs is appropriate to consider. Many jurisdictions are "trimming the family tree" to eliminate the so-called "laughing heirs" (heirs so remote they did not know the decedent, and whose only reaction to the person's death is

> **Policy Note:** The issue of escheat raises the question of whether the law should provide other mechanisms for determining a decedent's probable intent. For example, should close friends be able to assert a claim if the only other option is escheat? What about an organization that the decedent supported during the decedent's lifetime? What does escheat say about what relationships the law values?

to laugh their way to the bank). The UPC, for example, does not go further than grandparents and their descendants. If a decedent is not survived by a spouse, descendants, parents, parents' descendants, grandparents, or grandparents' descendants, any remaining property will pass to "descendants of deceased spouses" (stepchildren). UPC § 2–106(g). If there are no stepchildren, the decedent's property will pass to the state. UPC § 2–105.

While we are thinking about groups of people the intestacy laws leave out, we should also think about intestacy default laws for real property and how they omit—or disadvantage—different groups of people. As you learned in Property, the default form of real property ownership is tenancy in common. Because people with lower incomes are more likely to die intestate, the real property of people in this demographic group is disproportionately likely to pass to tenants in common. One author has called tenancy in common the most unstable form of real property ownership in the common law: any one tenant may petition a court for the sale of the property, and courts tend to grant these petitions *See* Thomas Mitchell, *Reforming Property Law to Address Devastating Land Loss*, 66 ALA. L. REV. 1 (2014). This structure gives one tenant power over the fate of the property, even if that person lives far away and has no connection to it. This default rule has had a disproportionate effect on so-called "heirs property," land that has descended over time to multiple heirs all over the country, and has caused significant land loss in particular to Black landowners. *See* Thomas W. Mitchell, *From Reconstruction to Deconstruction: Undermining Black Landownership, Political Independence, and Community through Partition Sales of Tenancies in Common*, 95 NW. U. L. REV. 505, 507 (2001) (calling "partition sales of black-owned land held under tenancies in common" the main cause of "involuntary black land loss in recent times"). Thomas Mitchell led the Uniform Law Commission's drafting of the Uniform Partition of Heirs Property Act (2010), which has now been adopted in 14 states—states as diverse as Texas and New York. The Act places some limits on the sale of heirs property by a minority owner or owners.

Another real property consequence of intestacy is that heirs often fail to go through the formal process of probate, simply remaining on the land or in the house. One or two generations later, the deceased owner's name remains on the deed which, in turn, makes it impossible for the current owners—who did in fact inherit the land or house through intestacy—to prove their legal title. This inability has serious consequences: because of this title defect, the owners cannot qualify for loans on the property. It also disqualifies these owners from getting Federal disaster aid to rebuild, as many discovered after Hurricane Katrina struck New Orleans in 2005. The title defect may also mean that the owners will be unable to sell their homes. *See* Heather K. Way, *Informal Homeownership in the United States and the Law*, 29 ST. LOUIS U. PUB. L. REV. 113, 157 (2009) (noting that "Informal homeowners with co-tenant interests face numerous difficulties in not only improving their homes but also selling their homes on the market").

Finally, consider Indian land fractionation, the subject of the *Hodel* case we discussed in Chapter 3. Native Americans have higher than average intestacy rates, leading to more and more heirs at each generation sharing smaller and smaller fractions of land plots. Partition sales are not an option because of the trust status of much Native land, so the property continues to fractionate. Justice O'Connor pointed in *Hodel* to a 40-acre tract of Indian Trust land that "produces $1,080 in income annually. It is valued at $8,000. It has 439 owners, one-third of whom receive less than $.05 in annual rent and two-thirds of whom receive less than $1." *Hodel v. Irving*, 481 U.S. 704, 713 (1987). Efforts to address the problem of Indian Land fractionation and intestacy include the American Indian Probate Reform Act of 2004, and American Indian Wills Clinics like the one at Oklahoma City University School of Law.

A Recluse and Some Laughing Heirs. Huguette Clark was the heir to a copper mining fortune. She was born in 1906, the youngest daughter of Montana senator and industrialist William A. Clark and his second wife Anna Clark. Clark spent her early life in Paris before relocating with her family to New York City, where she lived the rest of her life—until the age of 104. She was briefly married in the 1920s, but quickly divorced and had no children. Her sister died young, in 1919, and her mother died in 1963. She was an artist and a collector, and she owned multi-million-dollar properties in California, Connecticut, and New York. As she got older, however, she worried about living alone

A self-portrait by Huguette Clark in the 1950s or 1960s in her New York apartment on Fifth Avenue. Photo courtesy of Estate of Huguette Clark from EmptyMansionsBook.com.

and her health, so she spent the last twenty years of her life—in quite good health—in Beth Israel Medical Center in New York, being taken care of by a private nurse in a private room. When Clark died, her closest relatives were descendants from her father's first marriage, most of whom she had never met. These relatives, eager to get a part of her $300 million estate—contested Clark's will and in particular her gifts to her longtime caretaker. You'll learn more about this contest in Chapter 6. Ultimately, the parties reached a settlement, but one wonders if these distant relatives did in fact laugh all the way to the bank. For more on Huguette Clark, read Meryl Gordon's THE PHANTOM OF FIFTH AVENUE (2014) or Bill Dedman and Paul Clark Newell, Jr., EMPTY MANSIONS: THE MYSTERIOUS LIFE OF HUGUETTE CLARK AND THE SPENDING OF A GREAT AMERICAN FORTUNE (2013).

3. Other Uses for Intestacy Definitions

Intestacy statutes establish not just dispositive defaults, but also administrative defaults. For example, the rules relating to defining a spouse or descendants in intestacy can apply to circumstances in which these terms appear, but are not defined, in various legal instruments. For example, a will or a trust instrument often includes gifts to an individual's "children" or "descendants." This is referred to as a **class gift**. The members of the class proportionally share

> **Connection Note:** Keep in mind that intestacy statutes are "gap fillers." The rules may be used to interpret and supplement the provisions of wills, trusts, and will substitutes.

the property. An individual must qualify as a member of the class to be eligible to share the property. The will or trust instrument typically includes a definition of such terms in the instrument's definitions section. Not all legal instruments will define terms that are used within the instrument. This is not good drafting.

Generally, if the legal instrument does not include a definition, then the definition from the applicable state intestacy statute will be used. That rule applies to a variety of terms, including the use of class designations such as "descendants." Applying the definition from intestacy statutes to a legal instrument raises concerns about whether the definition from intestacy accurately reflects the intent of the individual who created the legal instrument. Most decedents have limited, if any, knowledge of intestacy statutes. In addition, the definitions in intestacy will evolve over time. Whether the definition should be referenced based upon current intestacy statutes or intestacy statutes in effect at the time the instrument was created is a point for consideration. Issues arise as to whether adopted children, non-marital children, a child born by assisted reproduction, or a gestational child should be included in a class gift when that class gift is in a legal document not made by the legal parent. In other words, when a legal device created by a nonparent, such as the decedent's grandparent, creates a gift to the decedent's "descendants," should the decedent's adopted children, non-marital children, and child born using ART be included? We will take up these issues later when we discuss interpretation of wills and trusts.

ASSESSMENT

Heirs qualify by having a particular status which does not depend on the emotional nature of quality of the relationship the individual may or may not have, as the case may be, with the decedent. Should methods for establishing intestacy rights (determining parentage, for example) move from a status-based approach to a functional-based approach? Should organizations or people or even animals that have a relationship with the decedent receive recognition in intestacy, given the relatively low rates at which people opt out of these default rules? What are the problems with this approach and what are the benefits?

E. Calculating Shares

Intestacy statutes could be considered as having a goal of making a "fair distribution" of the decedent's probate property in the absence of the decedent's wishes being expressed. What is "fair" not only refers to identifying those individuals who should receive the decedent's probate property but also what is a "fair" share of that property when multiple family members survive the decedent.

Intestacy statutes theoretically could divide the property equally among all eligible heirs, but they take a different approach. Instead, they aim for a "fair" allocation of property that reflects the presumed intent of the decedent to benefit more those closest to him or her on the family tree. This allocation requires an understanding of three different schemes of "representation." It also may require taking into account property **advanced** to an heir during life. As you read this material, consider what you believe would a "fair distribution."

Intestate succession relies upon familial relationships and seeks to treat branches of the family tree fairly in a manner that replicates the presumed intent of most decedents.

1. Shares of Descendants

A surviving spouse and descendants will inherit to the exclusion of all others under intestacy statutes. This is true even if the decedent has supported a parent or a sibling. Intestacy focuses on the status, not the needs of the heirs or the habits of the decedent.

If the decedent has no surviving spouse, the descendants will inherit all the decedent's probate property in intestacy. So what happens if the decedent is survived by both children and grandchildren? How should the property be allocated into "fair" shares? Although dividing the property equally among all surviving descendants would be an appropriate method, intestacy statutes use a concept called representation. Representation refers to allocating shares between and among a multi-generational class of heirs. Consider the following family tree.

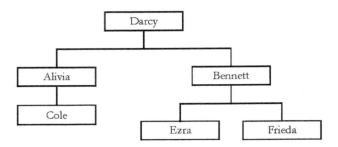

If Darcy is survived by Alivia and Bennett, the two children of Darcy will divide Darcy's intestate estate. But what if Bennett does not survive Darcy? Does Alivia, the sole surviving child, inherit all of Darcy's property? What about Bennett's children Ezra and Frieda? Should Ezra and Frieda now receive their parent's share? The law's resolution of this property allocation is representation. Bennett's children Ezra and Frieda will "represent" their deceased parent. In other words, Ezra and Frieda will stand in Bennett's shoes to receive the share that Bennett would have received if Bennett had survived Darcy. Although the idea of representation seems relatively straightforward, a surviving descendant will represent a predeceased ancestor, things can be complicated. Jurisdictions will have one of three methods of representation used as a default rule, though individuals may create a legal instrument that adopts another method of representation.

We will use an example to work through these three methods and will use fractions as the property is divided and then sub-divided. Following this example will be problems for you to work with that provide you with dollar amounts to allocate as appropriate.

Consider the following family of Wyn, who dies intestate. You should draw a family tree to use for this family. Wyn has four children, named Ava, Bryan, Carmen, and Dallas. Ava has two children, Etta, and Fergus. Etta has one child, Jade. Fergus has two children, Kayla, and Lilly. Bryan has one child Gavin, who

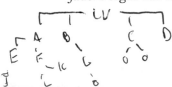

has one child Melinda. Carmen has two children Hudson and Isabel. Isabel does not have children, but Hudson has a child Nate. Dallas has no children or grandchildren.

If Wyn is survived by all four children (Ava, Bryan, Carmen, and Dallas), each child will take one-quarter of Wyn's intestate estate. None of Wyn's grandchildren or great-grandchildren will take because each has an ancestor (i.e., parent or grandparent) who inherits a share of Wyn's estate. The presumption is that any individual who inherited a share would ultimately pass that inheritance, or what remains of that inheritance, to that individual's descendants.

"One day son, 60 percent of this will be yours."

CartoonStock.com

Representation aims to produce a fair division of property among a multi-generational class.

What if Wyn is not survived by all the children? How should Wyn's intestate estate be divided now? Representation provides a method to allocate and distribute Wyn's property among the multi-generational heirs, that is Wyn's children and grandchildren.

There are three commonly used methods of representation. These methods apply to any multi-generational distributions, whether that is descendants, siblings/nieces/nephews, or aunts/uncles, cousins. Representation responds to two questions. First, how many shares should be allocated? Second, what happens to a share that is allocated to an individual who does not survive the decedent?

This section explains the three methods of representation. Following each explanation is an example of how the shares would be allocated using the method of representation. Following this section is a series of additional problems in the Assessments to help you work with the three methods of representation.

a. *Strict per Stirpes*

The oldest method of representation is **strict per stirpes**, also referred to as English per stirpes. The decedent's property is distributed based on bloodlines, also called "roots" or "stocks."

Under strict per stirpes, the property is divided into shares at the generational level closest to the decedent—even if everyone at that generational level predeceases the decedent. For our example, this level will be the child's level. The question as to the number of shares depends upon (1) how many children survive the decedent and (2) how many children did not survive the decedent but nevertheless have a descendant who does survive the decedent. If a child predeceases the decedent and that child has no surviving descendants, no share is allocated to that family line. That family line becomes a "dead branch" on the family tree and no longer counts for purposes of representation.

Once the number of shares at the initial generational level is set, then the shares are distributed. Each child who survives the decedent takes a share. For shares that are allocated for a predeceased child who has descendants who survive the decedent, that share is passed along the predeceased child's family line. In other words, the predeceased child's share passes along the bloodline to his or her own children.

To apply **strict per stirpes**, let's work with the following facts. None of Wyn's children survive Wyn. Ava, Bryan, and Carmen have one or more descendants who do survive Wyn. Dallas does not have any children or grandchildren who survive Wyn. This means that Wyn's property will be divided into three shares. One share is allocated for each of the three predeceased children who has at least one descendant who survives Wyn. Because Dallas neither survives Wyn nor has any descendants who survive Wyn, no share is allocated to Dallas. Ava's one-third share will pass to Ava's two children and be split equally between them. Bryan's one-third share will pass to his child. Carmen's one-third share will pass to her two children and be divided between them.

Strict per stirpes has what is referred to as a vertical distribution. It does not matter how many grandchildren or great grandchildren the decedent had. Keep in mind that distribution does not necessarily treat all individuals at the same generational level in the same way. For example, Ava's children Etta and Fergus and Carmen's children Hudson and Isabel will each take one-sixth of Wyn's intestate estate. That is because Etta and Fergus split Ava's one-third share. Hudson and Isabel split Carmen's one-third share. In contrast, Gavin takes a one-third share because Gavin is the sole child of Bryan, so Gavin inherits Bryan's entire one-third share.

Let's continue to work with strict per stirpes but now assume that no child and no grandchild survives Wyn. Wyn is survived only by the great-grandchildren, Jade, Kayla, Lilly, Melinda, and Nate. How will Wyn's property be distributed?

Wyn's property will still be divided into three shares. One share is allocated for Ava, Bryan, and Carmen because, although they do not survive Wyn, each predeceased child has at least one descendant who does survive Wyn. Dallas neither survives Wyn nor has a descendant who survives Wyn. Ava's one-third share will still be split into two shares. Jade will inherit her mother Etta's share. This means that Jade takes all of Etta's one-half of Ava's one-third of Wyn's estate, and thus takes one-sixth of Wyn's estate. Kayla and Lilly will split their father Fergus's share. Each will thus receive one-half of Fergus's share, which was one-sixth. Thus, Kayla and Lilly take one-twelfth of Wyn's estate. Bryan's one-third share passes through his son Gavin to his granddaughter Melinda who thus inherits one-third of Wyn's estate. For Carmen's one-third share, Nate, like Melinda, inherits the entire one-third share. Because Isabel does not have a descendant who survives Carmen, Isabel becomes a dead branch and no longer counts for purposes of representation. Carmen's entire one-third share passes along Hudson's family line to Nate. In other words, descendants at the same generational level receive significantly different shares of the estate.

b.   *Modern per Stirpes*

Many jurisdictions and the original UPC adopted the representation method known as **modern per stirpes**, which alleviates some of the disparities described above. Using modern per stirpes, the initial division of the decedent's property is made at the generational level closest to the decedent in which there is one or more individuals who survive the decedent. The property then passes along the family bloodlines. So as long as at least one individual at the level closest to the decedent survives (that is the child level in our fact pattern), strict per stirpes and modern per stirpes will produce the same result. If, on the other hand, no individual at the level closest to the decedent survives, then the results under strict per stirpes and modern per stirpes will differ.

For example, let's assume that Wyn is not survived by any children, but Wyn is survived by all of the grandchildren and great-grandchildren identified above. How would Wyn's property be distributed under modern stirpes?

The initial division of property will be made at the grandchild's level. Because none of the children survive Wyn, the grandchild's level is the generational level closest to the decedent in which there is one or more individuals who survive the decedent. A share is allocated for (1) each grandchild who survives Wyn and (2) each grandchild who does not survive Wyn but has at least one descendant who does survive Wyn. This means that Wyn's intestate estate here is divided into 5 shares with each grandchild taking a $1/5$ share of

Wyn's estate. Remember that none of Wyn's great-grandchildren would take a share because each has a parent who inherits a share.

Let's change the facts. Wyn is now survived only by Etta, Jade, Kayla, Lilly, Melinda, and Nate.

The initial division will occur at the generational level closest to the decedent in which there is a survivor. None of Wyn's children survive Wyn, but one grandchild does survive Wyn. Because Etta survives Wyn, Wyn's property is divided into four shares. One share is allocated for the grandchild Etta who survives Wyn, and one share is allocated for each predeceased grandchild who has a descendant who survives Wyn, that is Fergus, Gavin, and Hudson. Because Isabel neither survives Wyn nor has a descendant who survives Wyn, no share is allocated for Isabel. Etta takes her one-quarter share of Wyn's estate. Fergus's one-quarter share is divided between his children Kayla and Lilly with each taking one-eighth of Wyn's estate. Gavin's one-quarter share passes in its entirety to Melinda. Hudson's one-quarter share passes in its entirety to Nate.

c. *Per Capita at Each Generation*

The current UPC and a handful of jurisdictions have adopted a third method of representation called per capita at each generation.

UPC § 2–106. Representation

(b) **[Decedent's Descendants.]** If, under Section 2–103(a)(1), a decedent's intestate estate or a part thereof passes "by representation" to the decedent's descendants, the estate or part thereof is divided into as many equal shares as there are (i) surviving descendants in the generation nearest to the decedent which contains one or more surviving descendants and (ii) deceased descendants in the same generation who left surviving descendants, if any. Each surviving descendant in the nearest generation is allocated one share. The remaining shares, if any, are combined and then divided in the same manner among the surviving descendants of the deceased descendants as if the surviving descendants who were allocated a share and their surviving descendants had predeceased the decedent.

As with modern per stirpes, the initial division of property for the per capita at each generation (or UPC) method is made at the generational level closest to the decedent in which there is an individual who survives the decedent. What happens next may produce a result that differs from the modern per stripes method; with per capita at each generation, any shares that are not distributed at the generational level of the initial division no longer automatically pass along the bloodlines. Instead, the undistributed property is combined or, as it is frequently described, repooled. That repooled amount is then divided equally among the next generation of eligible takers. Per capita at each generation aims to bring horizontal equality so that eligible members of the same generational level inherit the same amount.

Let's apply per capita at each generation with the following facts. Assume that Wyn is survived only by Gavin, Isabel, Jade, Kayla, Lilly, Melinda, and Nate. How should Wyn's property be distributed?

The initial division of property will be made at the grandchildren's level because that is the generational level closest to the decedent Wyn is which there is an individual who survives Wyn. In fact, two individuals, Gavin and Isabel, survive Wyn. The property is thus divided into 5 shares. Gavin takes one-fifth of Wyn's property. Isabel takes one-fifth of Wyn's property. Unlike what happens with strict per stirpes or modern per stirpes, the shares that were allocated for Etta, Fergus, and Hudson are not passed along their family bloodlines. Instead, these three one-fifth shares are combined. This repooled three-fifths share of Wyn's property will be divided equally among the great-grandchildren who are eligible to receive the property. That means that Jade, Kayla, Lily, and Nate each receives one-quarter of the three-fifths of Wyn's estate. Each then takes three-twentieths ($^3/_{20}$) of Wyn's estate. Notice that Melinda does not take any share under these facts, even though she is a surviving great-grandchild. That is because her father Gavin has already inherited a share of Wyn's estate. You see this allocation of shares in the chart below with a comparison as to how the shares would have been allocated using strict per stirpes, modern per stirpes, and per capita at each generation.

Potential Heir	Share Under Strict Per Stirpes	Share Under Modern Per Stirpes	Share Under Per Capita at Each Generation
Ava	0 Ava does not survive Wyn.	0 Ava does not survive Wyn.	0 Ava does not survive Wyn.

Etta	0 Etta does not survive Wyn.	0 Etta does not survive Wyn.	0 Etta does not survive Wyn.
Jade	$1/6$ Jade receives Etta's $1/2$ share of Ava's $1/3$ share.	$1/5$ Jade receives Etta's 1/5 share.	$3/20$ Jade receives $1/3$ of the repooled $3/5$ share.
Fergus	0 Fergus does not survive Wyn.	0 Fergus does not survive Wyn.	0 Fergus does not survive Wyn.
Kayla	$1/12$ Kayla receives $1/2$ of Fergus' $1/2$ of Ava's $1/3$ share.	$1/10$ Kayla receives $1/2$ of Fergus' $1/5$ share.	$3/20$ Kayla receives $1/3$ of the repooled $3/5$ share.
Lilly	$1/12$ Lilly receives $1/2$ of Fergus' $1/2$ of Ava's $1/3$ share.	$1/10$ Lilly receives $1/2$ of Fergus' $1/5$ share.	$3/20$ Lilly receives $1/3$ of the repooled $3/5$ share.
Bryan	0 Bryan does not survive Wyn.	0 Bryan does not survive Wyn.	0 Bryan does not survive Wyn.
Gavin	$1/3$ Gavin receives Bryan's 1/3 share.	$1/5$ Wyn's estate is divided into five shares, at the grandchild's level.	$1/5$ Wyn's estate is divided into five shares, at the grandchild's level.
Melinda	0 Melinda's parent Gavin receives a share.	0 Melinda's parent Gavin receives a share.	0 Melinda's parent Gavin receives a share.

Carmen	0 Carmen does not survive Wyn.	0 Carmen does not survive Wyn.	0 Carmen does not survive Wyn.
Hudson	0 Hudson does not survive Wyn.	0 Hudson does not survive Wyn.	0 Hudson does not survive Wyn.
Nate	$1/6$ Nate receives Hudson's ½ share of Carmen's $1/3$ share.	$1/5$ Nate receives Hudson's $1/5$ share.	$3/20$ Nate receives $1/3$ of the repooled $3/5$ share
Isabel	$1/6$ Isabel receives ½ of Carmen's 1/3 share.	$1/5$ Wyn's estate is divided into five shares, at the grandchild's level.	$1/5$ Wyn's estate is divided into five shares, at the grandchild's level.
Dallas	0 Dallas does not survive Wyn.	0 Dallas does not survive Wyn.	0 Dallas does not survive Wyn.

The information in the chart shows that the method of representation can produce different results.

As you work through representation problems, remember the following tips:

1.   DIAGRAM THE FAMILY TREE.

Identify the familial relationship between the decedent and the potential heirs. Make sure that each heir is placed on the proper family line and in the proper generational level.

2.   VERIFY ELIGIBILITY OF EACH POTENTIAL HEIR.

To inherit property via intestacy, the heir needs to be eligible. Eligibility includes, but is not limited to, survivorship and other definitional rules (like stepchildren do not take but adopted children do). Remember that if an ancestor is living, that individual's descendants do not take. Remember too that you do not count any bloodline that has no surviving issue.

3. UNLESS OTHERWISE PROVIDED, PERFORM THE CALCULATION FOR EACH OF THE THREE METHODS OF REPRESENTATION.

The governing instrument or applicable state intestacy statute may determine which method of representation is applicable. If the method is not clear, run the calculation for each method to determine what differences may be produced under each method.

4. TALLY THE TOTAL AMOUNT OF THE PROPERTY OR SHARES ALLOCATED.

You can't allocate more probate property than the decedent owned. Don't forget to double check your math!

ASSESSMENTS

1.   Which method of representation do you think is the fairest? Which method of representation do you believe that most people would prefer? Why?

2.   Stan's two children, Ari and Beverly, predeceased Stan. Ari had three children named Cara, Dave, and Errol. Dave had one child named Hilda. Beverly had two children named Finn and Gavin. Finn had two children named Isla and Jaylin. Stan died on April 5. Two days later, Dave and Finn were in a car accident and died instantly. Stan did not create a Will. Her probate property is valued at $600,000.

   a.   Who will inherit Stan's property? Identify specific individuals and specific dollar amounts each individual will inherit.

   b.   Does it make a difference which method of representation is used? Explain.

3.   Penny Ryan was a member of a large and close family. Her grandparents Claire and Eli were getting ready to celebrate their 65th wedding anniversary. The last major family event was five years ago when Penny's brother Andon married his long-time partner Baylor. Penny was happy to plan family events. Penny lived on fifteen acres of property called Holly Brook Farm with her two children and their dog named Nolan. Holly Brook Farm was located outside of the city limits. Penny rented the property for different events, such as weddings, parties, and corporate retreats. Four nights a week, Penny ran a vegan "farm to table" restaurant on the property.

When planning the anniversary event for her grandparents, Penny was surprised to learn that her grandfather Eli had actually been married before he met her grandmother Claire. Eli met Claire and instantly "fell in love" fifty-two years ago. He divorced his first spouse named Maureen following the birth of Eli and Maureen's son named Oscar. Claire and Eli then married. Eli maintained a close relationship with Oscar, and Eli was pleased that Penny invited Oscar to attend the 50th wedding anniversary.

Claire and Eli had three children named Lucie, Gene, and Rob. Lucie and Gene had died years ago in a plane accident. But Claire and Eli were happy to have a number of grandchildren and great-grandchildren to visit. Lucie had two children named Penny and Andon. Penny had two children named Zoe and Clyde. Andon and Baylor had two children named Darcy and Emerson. Gene had one child named Waylin, and Waylin had one child named Hillary. Rob had three children named Jade, Sierra, and Faye. Jade had one child named Tate. Faye had one child named Kai.

Following the anniversary celebration on March 31, 2019, a multi-car traffic accident occurred. Andon, Faye, Sierra, and Waylin died at the scene. Claire and Rob were transported to the local hospital. Claire died en route to the hospital. Rob died the following day following complications from an emergency surgery.

a. Following Claire's death, assume that no will is admitted to probate. Claire's probate property is valued at $825,000. How would Claire's estate be distributed? Identify the potential heirs and exact dollar amount each heir would receive.

b. When distributing Claire's probate property, does it make a difference what method of representation is used? Explain your response.

2. Shares of Siblings and Their Descendants

If the decedent dies intestate and has no surviving spouse, no descendants, and no surviving parents, the estate will be shared by the decedent's **siblings** (the decedent's brothers and sisters). In general, the siblings will share equally if they are all alive. If, on the other hand, a deceased sibling leaves living issue, the sibling's descendants (e.g., the decedent's nieces, nephews, grandnieces, and grandnephews) will take by representation. The representation system probably will be the same as employed for decedent's descendants (i.e., either strict per stirpes, modified per stirpes, or per capita at each generation). Remember that although jurisdictions may establish the default method of representation to be used, individuals may opt-out of this default method by defining which method of representation should be used in their valid will, will substitute, or trust.

ASSESSMENT

Declan's parents Pedro and Yvonne had four children. The siblings are Anya, Britt, Cole, and Declan. After their parents' death, the siblings began to celebrate all family events together. Declan never had any children, but Anya had two children named Elena and Felix. Felix had one child named Irwin. Britt had one child named Gareth. Cole had one child named Hugo. Hugo had two children named Jenna and Kristi.

Assume that Declan dies intestate with a probate estate valued at $100,000. Using the family described above, apply the three methods of representation. Does it make a difference which method is used? Explain.

3.   Advancements

An individual, typically a parent, may have given property to a child during the parent's lifetime. These funds may be a gift, a loan, or an **advancement** against the child's inheritance. These funds are then not part of the estate when the parent dies.

If the gift was an *inter vivos* gift, the child received the funds outright. The child then need not repay the amount. The child will receive his or her full share of the parent's intestate estate.

If, on the other hand, the funds were a loan, then the child must repay the loan. If the child has not repaid the loan during the parent's lifetime, the child is liable for reimbursement to the estate. The child, however, is still entitled to inherit his or her intestate share. The current and original UPC provides that a debt owed to a decedent is not charged against the intestate share of any individual except the debtor. If the debtor fails to survive the decedent, the debt is not taken into account when computing the intestate share of the debtor's descendants.

If it was an **advancement**, the child need not repay the funds to the estate; however, the child's intestate share will be reduced. The traditional view of the common law was that any lifetime gift to a child was presumed to be an advancement. The rationale was that the decedent was presumed to want to treat all children equally. Thus, the burden was placed on the child to prove that the transfer was intended as an absolute gift rather than an advancement.

The current UPC reverses the presumption of the common law. UPC § 2–109. All lifetime transfers to a child or other heir are presumed to be gifts. For the lifetime transfer to be viewed as an advancement, the UPC requires a writing by the decedent that was drafted contemporaneously with the transfer and indicates that the gift was intended as an advancement or that the gift is to be considered in the distribution of the decedent's estate. Alternatively, if the donor did not make the contemporaneous writing, the recipient may acknowledge in a writing at that time or later that the gift was an advancement or that is to be considered in the distribution of the decedent's estate. Note that the current UPC applies to a gift made to any heir. Most jurisdictions apply the concept of advancement only to gifts made by a parent or a grandparent to an heir.

If the money given was an advancement, a method known as a **hotchpot** is used. Under this method, the value of all advancements (determined as of the date of the gift) is added to the net intestate estate of the decedent. That sum is then distributed "on paper" according to the Statute of Descent and Distribution. The sum of money or property actually distributed to an heir will be the value so determined less any advancement. If, on the other hand, an heir received an advancement greater than the amount so determined, the heir need not participate in the estate distribution. That heir will receive no additional property and need not return any property to the estate.

ASSESSMENTS

1. Jesse has three adult children named Kennedy, Rory, and Tatum. Jesse gave Kennedy $60,000 for the purchase of a house. Rory needed funds to attend law school. Jesse gave Rory $30,000. Jesse then died intestate with a net estate of $600,000.

    a. How should Jesse's estate be distributed?

    b. What if Jesse's net estate totaled only $150,000? What if the net estate totaled on $60,000?

    c. What if Kennedy predeceased Jesse but was survived by a spouse and a minor child?

2. Assume that a parent named Oakley has two children named Adrian and Brooklyn. Oakley wishes to give Adrian the sum of $50,000 to help with expenses as Adrian is currently between jobs. Oakley wants the $50,000 to be considered an advancement on Adrian's inheritance. Advise Oakley on what specific steps to take to memorialize this intent.

F. Eligibility of Heirs

The hierarchy of heirs is based upon the legally recognized relationship the individual has with the decedent. Intestacy is thus status based. Nonetheless, an heir may lose his or her eligibility due to some action or behavior by the heir or someone else. For example, an heir may engage in misconduct, sign an agreement to change the estate's distribution, or disclaim the property. There also may be a document, like a negative will or contract regarding inheritance, that changes the default rules of intestacy.

1. Survivorship

An individual must not only have the recognized relationship to the decedent to inherit the intestate property, the individual must also survive the decedent. The Uniform Simultaneous Death Act, which we studied in Chapter 2, requires that the person inheriting from a decedent survive the decedent by at least one hundred and twenty hours (5 days). All states have adopted this act or a similar act. What is the rationale behind requiring proof of survivorship? A will can alter the period required for survivorship. It could reduce the period of survivorship to fewer than 120 hours, but when wills speak to the issue of survivorship, they frequently require more than 120 hours.

2. Bars to Inheritance

In limited circumstances, the heir's behavior or actions may prevent the individual from receiving an intestate share. There are two kinds of bars: (1) involuntary; and (2) voluntary. To the extent that a jurisdiction recognizes these bars to inheritance, they apply both to intestate and testate succession.

a. *Involuntary Bars*

Involuntary bars arise due to the heir's behavior or actions. These bars are supported on various policy grounds. First, these bars represent the decedent's presumed intent in the case of an heir behaving in one of these ways. Second, these bars reflect societal disapproval of certain actions. Third, these bars serve as a deterrent for behavior that society considers problematic. Although these involuntary bars may appear to be default rules, most states do not permit individuals to opt out of their application. Such an approach reflects the multiple policy considerations supporting their application.

This section addresses the following three involuntary bars: (a) abandonment, (b) killing, and (c) abuse. As you read this section, consider whether additional grounds to bar inheritance may be appropriate.

i.   Abandonment

Abandonment may be an involuntary bar for succession. The current UPC provides that a parent whose parental rights have been terminated may not inherit from that child. UPC § 2–114. Nor may a parent inherit from the child if the child died prior to reaching the age of majority and there is clear and convincing evidence that immediately before the death of the child, the parental rights could have been terminated on the basis of nonsupport, abandonment, abuse or neglect. UPC § 2–114. Some states have variations of this rule, providing that a parent may not inherit if the parent "willfully abandoned the care and maintenance" of the child. *E.g.,* KY. REV. STAT. § 391.033. UPC § 2–804 does not bar a surviving spouse from inheriting based on abandonment.

Consider both the goals of intestacy and the challenge of proving abandonment. Should abandonment be a basis for non-inheritance? Should a surviving spouse be treated differently from a surviving descendant?

ii.   Killing

All states, primarily now by statute but also by case law, provide that one who has killed the decedent may not inherit. This bar operates in intestate succession, testate succession, and nonprobate succession. This prohibition is typically referred to as a **slayer rule**, or a **slayer statute** if the rule has been statutory enacted. The law varies concerning what is required to bar the individual's ability to inherit. In general, a conviction is required, and the killer is treated as having predeceased the victim. The UPC for instance, provides that those who kill someone else intentionally and feloniously are barred from inheriting from their victim. UPC § 2–803. Jurisdictions are not consistent on whether this bar extends to all types and degrees of manslaughter.

UPC § 2–803(b). Effect of Homicide on Intestate Succession, Wills, Trusts, Joint Assets, Life Insurance, and Beneficiary Designations

(b)   [Forfeiture of Statutory Benefits.] An individual who feloniously and intentionally kills the decedent forfeits all benefits under this [article] with respect to the decedent's estate, including an intestate share, an elective share, an omitted spouse's or child's share, a homestead allowance, exempt property, and a family allowance. If the decedent died intestate, the decedent's intestate estate passes as if the killer disclaimed his [or her] intestate share.

When the issue of such a bar initially arose, many states needed to resolve the issue without reliance on a statute. In the following case, *Mahoney v. Grainger,* an individual named Charlotte Mahoney killed her husband. As you will see, the Vermont court said that the probate statute had to be followed; the probate court had no authority to deviate from the statute. The court, however, suggested that the decedent's parents could use a constructive trust to capture the property that Charlotte Mahoney inherited from her husband. This means that Charlotte, who was the heir with the greatest priority under the state intestacy statute, was effectively barred from inheriting her husband's intestate estate. We are going to be dealing again with constructive trust; the key feature of this remedy is that there must be a finding of some tortious action, which then triggers the imposition of a "constructive trust."

In re Estate of Mahoney

220 A.2d 475 (Vt. 1966)

SMITH, J.

The decedent, Howard Mahoney, died intestate on May 6, 1961, of gunshot wounds. His wife, Charlotte Mahoney, the appellant here, was tried for the murder of Howard Mahoney in the Addison County Court and was convicted by jury of the crime of manslaughter in March, 1962. She is presently serving a sentence of not less than 12 nor more than 15 years at the Women's Reformatory in Rutland.

Howard Mahoney left no issue and was survived by his wife and his father and mother. His father, Mark Mahoney, was appointed administrator of his estate which at the present time amounts to $3,885.89. After due notice and hearing, the Probate Court for the District of Franklin entered a judgment order decreeing the residue of the Estate of Howard Mahoney, in equal shares, to the father and mother of the decedent. An appeal from the judgment order and decree has been taken here by the appellant widow. The question submitted is whether a widow convicted of manslaughter in connection with the death of her husband may inherit from his estate.

The general rules of descent provide that if a decedent is married and leaves no issue, his surviving spouse shall be entitled to the whole of decedent's estate if it does not exceed $8,000. 14 V.S.A. § 551(2). Only if the decedent leaves no surviving spouse or issue does the estate descend in equal shares to the surviving father and mother. 14 V.S.A. § 551(3). There is no statutory provision in Vermont regulating the descent and distribution of property from the decedent to the slayer. The question presented is one of first impression in this jurisdiction.

In a number of jurisdictions, statutes have been enacted which in certain instances, at least, prevent a person who has killed another from taking by descent or distribution from the person he has killed.

Courts in those states that have no statute preventing a slayer from taking by descent or distribution from the estate of his victim, have followed three separate and different lines of decision.

(1)   The legal title passed to the slayer and may be retained by him in spite of his crime. The reasoning for so deciding is that devolution of the property of a decedent is controlled entirely by the statutes of descent and distribution; further, that denial of the inheritance to the slayer because of his crime would be imposing an additional punishment for his crime not provided by statute, and would violate the constitutional provision against corruption of blood.

(2)   The legal title will not pass to the slayer because of the equitable principle that no one should be permitted to profit by his own fraud, or take advantage and profit as a result of his own wrong or crime. Decisions so holding have been criticized as judicially engrafting an exception on the statute of descent and distribution and being "unwarranted judicial legislation."

(3)   The legal title passes to the slayer but equity holds him to be a constructive trustee for the heirs or next of kin of the decedent. This disposition of the question presented avoids a judicial engrafting on the statutory laws of descent and distribution, for title passes to the slayer. But because of the unconscionable mode by which the property is acquired by the slayer, equity treats him as a constructive trustee and compels him to convey the property to the heirs or next of kin of the deceased.

The reasoning behind the adoption of this doctrine was well expressed by Mr. Justice Cardozo in his lecture on "The Nature of the Judicial Process." "Consistency was preserved, logic received its tribute, by holding that the legal title passed, but it was subject to a constructive trust. A constructive trust is nothing but 'the formula through which the conscience of equity finds expression.' Property is acquired in such circumstances that the holder of legal title may not in good conscience retain the beneficial interest. Equity, to express its disapproval of his conduct, converts him into a trustee." *See* 4 SCOTT ON TRUSTS (2d ed. 1956) § 402.

The New Hampshire court was confronted with the same problem of the rights to the benefits of an estate by one who had slain the decedent, in the absence of a statute on the subject. *Kelley v. State*, 196 A.2d 68. Speaking for an unanimous court, Chief Justice Kenison said: "But, even in the absence of statute, a court applying common law techniques can reach a sensible solution by charging the spouse, heir or legatee as a constructive trustee of the property where equity and justice demand it." *Kelley v. State*, at 69, 70. We approve of the doctrine so expressed.

However, the principle that one should not profit by his own wrong must not be extended to every case where a killer acquires property from his victim as a result of the killing. One who has killed while insane is not chargeable as a constructive trustee, or if the slayer had a vested interest in the property, it is property to which he would have been entitled if no slaying had occurred. The principle to be applied is that the slayer should not be permitted to improve his position by the killing, but should not be compelled to surrender property to which he would have been entitled if there had been no killing. The doctrine of constructive trust is involved to prevent the slayer from profiting from his crime, but not as an added criminal penalty.

The appellant here was, as we have noted, convicted of manslaughter and not of murder. She calls to our attention that while the Restatement of Restitution, approves the application of the constructive trust doctrine where a devisee or legatee murders the testator, that such rules are not applicable where the slayer was guilty of manslaughter. RESTATEMENT OF RESTITUTION, § 187, comment e.

The cases generally have not followed this limitation of the rule but hold that the line should not be drawn between murder and manslaughter, but between voluntary and involuntary manslaughter.

We think that this is the proper rule to follow. Voluntary manslaughter is an intentional and unlawful killing, with a real design and purpose to kill, even if such killing be the result of sudden passion or great provocation. Involuntary manslaughter is caused by an unlawful act, but not accompanied with any intention to take life. It is the intent to kill, which when accomplished, leads to the profit of the slayer that brings into play the constructive trust to prevent the unjust enrichment of the slayer by reason of his intentional killing.

In Vermont, an indictment for murder can result in a jury conviction on either voluntary or involuntary manslaughter. The legislature has provided the sentences that may be passed upon a person convicted of manslaughter, but provides no definition of that offense, nor any statutory distinction between voluntary and involuntary manslaughter.

The cause now before us is here on a direct appeal from the probate court. Findings of fact were made below from which it appears that the judgment of the probate court decreeing the estate of Howard Mahoney to his parents, rather than to his widow, was based upon a finding of the felonious killing of her husband by Mrs. Mahoney. However, the appellees here have asked us to affirm the decree below by imposing a constructive trust on the estate in the hands of the widow.

But the Probate Court did not decree the estate to the widow, and then make her a constructive trustee of such estate for the benefit of the parents. The judgment below decreed the estate directly to the parents, which was in direct contravention of the statutes of descent and distribution. The Probate Court was bound to follow the statutes of descent and distribution and its decree was in error and must be reversed.

The Probate Court was without jurisdiction to impose a constructive trust on the estate in the hands of the appellant, even if it had attempted to do so. Probate courts are courts of special and limited jurisdiction given by statute and do not proceed according to common law. While probate courts possess a portion of equitable powers independent of statute, such powers do not extend to the establishment of purely equitable rights and claims. The claim of the parents here to the Estate of Howard Mahoney is equitable in its origin, and in the extent of the rights in the estate claimed. The equity powers conferred upon the probate court do not extend to the establishment of purely equitable claims and equitable rights.

However, the jurisdiction of the court of chancery may be invoked in probate matters in aid of the probate court when the powers of that court are inadequate, and it appears that the probate court cannot reasonably and adequately handle the question. The jurisdiction of the chancery court in so acting on probate matters is special and limited only to aiding the probate court.

The Probate Court, in making its decree, used the record of the conviction of the appellant for manslaughter for its determination that the appellant had feloniously killed her husband. If the jurisdiction of the court of chancery is invoked by the appellees here it will be for the determination of that court, upon proof, to determine whether the appellant willfully killed her late husband, as it will upon all other equitable considerations that may be offered in evidence, upon charging the appellant with a constructive trust. "The fact that he is convicted of murder in a criminal case does not dispense with the necessity of proof of the murder in a proceedings in equity to charge him as a constructive trustee." RESTATEMENT OF RESTITUTION, § 187, comment d.

The jurisdiction over charging the appellant with a constructive trust on the estate of Howard Mahoney lies in the court of chancery, and not in the probate court.

Decree reversed and cause remanded, with directions that the proceedings herein be stayed for sixty days to give the Administrator of the Estate of Howard Mahoney an opportunity to apply to the Franklin County Court of Chancery for relief. If application is so made, proceedings herein shall be stayed pending the final determination thereof. If application is not so made, the Probate Court for the District of Franklin shall assign to Charlotte Mahoney, surviving wife, the right and interest in and to the estate of her deceased husband which the Vermont Statutes confer.

NOTES

1.   Charlotte Mahoney represented herself *pro se*. To what extent, if any, do you think that influenced the adjudication of this case?

2.   When reading cases, whether in law school or in practice, it is important to consider what additional facts or circumstances may be missing from the opinion. Carla Spivack has recovered the facts of *Mahoney* in her article *Killers Shouldn't Inherit From Their Victims—Or Should They?*, 48 GEORGIA L. REV. 145, 166–68, 226 (2013). Below are excerpts from the article.

> Charlotte Mahoney shot her husband twice with a rifle and was convicted of manslaughter, whereupon the slain husband's relatives brought suit to bar her under equity from succeeding to his intestate estate.

> This opinion exemplifies, as do many of these cases, a total lack of interest in the context or details of the crime—in what Richard Posner calls "the rebarbative character of reality." In this sense, it exemplifies what I am criticizing about Slayer-Rule cases overall: their lack of interest in or concern for the origins and context—the "reality"—of the killing. The terse summary in Mahoney is so intent on repressing whatever reality existed in that case that it creates a gap where the actual deed should appear; there is no act between "Howard Mahoney[ ] died . . . of gunshot wounds" and "Charlotte Mahoney . . . was tried for the murder . . . and was convicted" connecting the two events. The narrative structure presents them as completely separate and unrelated, connected only by syntax. Such a gap raises, rather than suppresses, the key question: why did she shoot him?

I suspected that Charlotte Mahoney's killing of her husband might have been related to spousal abuse. Considerable digging in the archives revealed support for my intuition. As it turns out, Charlotte Mahoney was the first woman to be tried for murder in Vermont in fifty years and her case generated considerable press: the archives of the Burlington Free Press and other local papers contain over twenty articles about her trial. They reveal signs that she suffered abuse at the hands of her husband, and that her killing of him was a result of that abuse. She testified that, on the day of the murder, they had been having an argument in front of the house: she had tried to get into a car that her husband was getting ready to drive and he slammed the window shut on her hand several times before rolling it down and punching her in the face. Getting out of the car, he chased her into the house, shouting that "he would kill her if he got her," and if she ever tried to leave him, he would kill her. She testified that he then slapped her face and pulled her by the arm. She locked herself in the bedroom, but he entered it through another door, carrying his rifle. She testified that, as she tried to escape the house through the front door, he "made a pass" at her with the butt of the gun, causing her to fall. Her dog jumped him, the gun went off, and he fell "in a sitting position on the floor." From this position, he cursed her and picked up the gun. She ran for help. When she returned, he was dead.

Some of the evidence in these accounts of abuse does not require a trained eye to detect: the physical assaults are explicit, as are the state doctor's finding of bruises on Charlotte Mahoney's neck and jaw. There are also more subtle signs, including the husband's reported threat to kill her if she ever tried to leave him, a threat typical of spousal-abuse situations. Other evidence adduced at trial gives rise to the same inference of abuse: one witness stated that the couple seemed "more concerned about each other than normal"—a phrase hinting at the surveillance and control associated with abuse. Of course, we will never know for sure what went on in the Mahoneys' marriage, but the evidence is sufficient to raise a serious question about the presence of abuse as a significant factor in this case. In any event, a jury of seven women and five men convicted Charlotte of manslaughter, and the court sentenced her to twelve to fifteen years in the Reformatory for Women in Rutland.

Now, reflect upon court's opinion. Do you now have a different view of the opinion? Spivack's conclusion is as follows:

> Legal, moral, and policy considerations demand reassessment and reformulation of the interacting laws of homicide and inheritance. It is time to face the real circumstances in which Slayer-Rule killings occur and to acknowledge and remedy the injustices resulting from applying these Rules to those individuals (usually women and children) that society and law have trapped in regimes of terror or without help for mental illness. For example, in consequence of losing her probate action, Charlotte Mahoney lost about $3,000, the exact amount that it would have taken to pay the remaining mortgage on her house. As a result, she emerged from prison homeless. If indeed she was a battered spouse, her case offers an illustration not just of Slayer Rules, but of their need for reform.

Spivack also makes the compelling point that much of the violence that occurs within families—violence that would bar one family member from inheriting another's wealth—is the result of patterns and cycles of family violence and intra-family abuse—whether spousal abuse or child abuse. Accepting that premise, what changes in the way we think of the slayer rule?

3.   Vermont now has a slayer statute.

VT. STAT. ANN. § 322. Unlawful Killing Affecting Inheritance

Notwithstanding sections 311 through 314 of this title or provisions otherwise made, in any case in which an individual is entitled to inherit or receive property under the last will of a decedent, or otherwise, such individual's share in the decedent's estate shall be forfeited and shall pass to the remaining heirs or beneficiaries of the decedent if the individual intentionally and unlawfully kills the decedent. In any proceedings to contest the right of an individual to inherit or receive property under a will or otherwise, the record of that individual's conviction of intentionally and unlawfully killing the decedent shall be admissible in evidence and shall conclusively establish that such individual did intentionally and unlawfully kill the decedent.

4.   What limits should be placed on the slayer rule? For example, should the slayer rule apply to situations where an individual aids another in dying? *E.g.*, Ryan Konsdorf & Scott Alden Prulhiere, *Killing Your Chances of Inheriting: The Problem with the Application of the Slayer Statute to Cases of Assisted Suicide*, 39 ACTEC L.J. 399 (2013); Jeffrey G. Sherman, *Mercy Killing and the Right to Inherit*, 61 U.

CIN. L. REV. 803 (1993). Is there a potential for abuse if the slayer rule were not to apply in that situation?

5.   A constructive trust is a remedial trust that may apply to prevent unjust enrichment. When it would be inequitable for an heir or beneficiary to inherit property, such as the case of fraud, the constructive trust is a mechanism that would redirect such inheritance. Before jurisdictions codified the slayer rule in slayer statutes, courts could use the constructive trust. For further discussions of the constructive trust, see Chapter 6 and Chapter 9.

iii.   Abuse

Recently states have begun to provide that abuse, whether financial, physical, or psychological, should operate as an involuntary bar on inheritance. The UPC so far has not specifically addressed this issue. Under the 2008 revisions of the UPC, however, a parent is now barred from inheriting from a child if parental rights were terminated and the parent-child relationship was not judicially re-established, or the child dies before age 18 and immediately before death the parental rights could have been terminated. A few states now include a provision that a person may not inherit if that person has been convicted of the abuse, neglect, or exploitation of an elder. Should conviction for elder abuse prevent inheritance? *See generally* Linda K. Kisabeth, *Slayer Statutes and Elder Abuse: Good Intentions, Right Results? Does Michigan's Amended Slayer Statute Do Enough to Protect the Elderly*, 26 QUINNIPIAC PROB. L J 373 (2013). Consider to what extent behavior by an individual should serve as an involuntary bar to inheritance. What evidence of that behavior should the law require before applying the bar?

ASSESSMENTS

1.   Anya and Jacob married forty years ago. Anya left Jacob thirty-five years ago and moved to another jurisdiction. Neither Anya nor Jacob instituted any dissolution proceeding. Jacob died intestate and was survived by his brother Luis and by Anya. Who is entitled to Jacob's estate under the current UPC? Would your response depend on the reasons motivating Anya's decision to leave or the decision not to seek any dissolution proceeding?

2.   Norman was convicted of the murder of his spouse Alma. Alma died intestate survived by Norman, their two adult children, and her mother Gwen. What additional information do you need before determining who will inherit Alma's estate?

b. *Voluntary Bars*

Although otherwise eligible to receive property via intestacy, an individual can decline to receive the property. This may be done for a variety of reasons including disinterest in the property to be inherited, the cost of receiving the share, the wish for another to inherit the property, or the concern that creditors of the heir may attached the property. These voluntary bars are one method of post-mortem estate planning. The heirs alter the system of intestate succession, testate succession, nonprobate succession, or some combination thereof. This alteration may be done by private agreement or disclaimer. One important difference between the two is that a person who disclaims cannot otherwise dictate who will receive the estate property.

i. Private Agreement

The UPC allows for competent heirs to agree among themselves to alter their interests or shares under the intestacy law or under the will of the decedent, subject to the rights of creditors and the taxing authority. UPC § 3–912. The UPC refers to a written agreement "executed by all who are affected"; however, a letter may be sufficient, and some states do not even require a writing.

In many jurisdictions, administration of an intestate estate or testate estate also may be dispensed with it if there are no debts owed by the estate, all persons beneficially entitled to the estate have agreed in writing that there should be no administration, and either there are no claims due the estate, or a trustee is designated to deal with such claims. If a person is under a disability, consent may be given by a guardian, curator, or conservator.

If private individuals can alter their interests in the decedent's estate, the question arises as to whether a court also has authority to rearrange the distribution of the decedent's estate. If a person dies intestate, the intestacy statute applies mechanically. The courts have no judicial discretion to alter the distribution. Such mechanical application is considered to be efficient and produce consistent, predictable results. Whether such mechanical application, as we have raised throughout this chapter, is fair is another matter.

Should a court consider the needs of the heirs and make adjustments if the heir has a number of resources? Or if another heir, who does not have the highest priority in the intestate hierarchy, has a greater need? Should the court consider not just the closeness of the relationship as measured by the table of consanguinity but the emotional closeness of the relationship? Many jurisdictions outside of the United States have a mechanism that allows a court to alter the intestate, and even testate shares, to provide for certain persons related to or dependent on the decedent. These are typically referred to as "Family Maintenance Statutes" and provide for judicial discretion in reallocating the decedent's property to those who were dependent upon the decedent, regardless of what estate planning documents the decedent has properly executed. *See* Caryl Yzenbaard, *Intestate Property Distribution at Death in the United States*, 8 MODERN STUDIES IN PROPERTY LAW 177 (2015) (advocating such proposal when there is need or when consideration of justice require). Should such Family Maintenance Statutes be adopted in the United States? What would be gained by such adoption? What may be lost or jeopardized?

ii.   Disclaimer

Disclaimers are a common way to rearrange the disposition of a decedent's estate. Traditionally, an heir could not renounce an interest in intestacy but a beneficiary under a will could disclaim. Most, if not all states today allow both an heir and a beneficiary to prevent title from coming to him or to her through the execution of a valid **disclaimer**. The most common reasons to disclaim are to avoid taxes, to keep property from creditors, or to avoid having to manage the property. An heir or a devisee may have other reasons to disclaim, such as the wish for an alternate beneficiary or heir to inherit the property.

When the heir or beneficiary is seeking to prevent creditors from reaching the property, issues may arise. In general, the disclaimant is treated as having predeceased the decedent, so the relation-back theory means a creditor cannot reach the property. This is true unless the disclaimer was to avoid a federal tax lien, to qualify for public assistance or Medicaid benefits, and perhaps to avoid inclusion in a bankruptcy estate. *See Drye v. United States*, 528 U.S. 49 (1999) (tax lien) and *Troy v. Hart*, 697 A.2d 113 (Md. App. 1997) (Medicaid). *Compare Jones v. Atchison (In re Atchison)* 101 B.R. 556 (Bankr. S.D. Ill., 1989) (pre-petition disclaimer was effective) with *William v. Chenoweth (In re Chenoweth)*, 132 B.R. 161 (Bankr. S.D. Ill., 1991) (post-petition violated U.S. C. § 549.). Thus, it matters if the disclaimer was made prior to or after the filing of the bankruptcy proceeding.

Most statutes, including the UPC, require a signed writing that typically must be given to the personal representative of the estate. UPC §§ 2–1105, 2–1112. There are strict timing rules for disclaimers that vary by jurisdiction. The original UPC required the disclaimer to be made within six months of death. The current UPC has no time limit, but many states provide that that disclaimer must be made within nine months of death (or nine months from when the transfer was made). Finally, a disclaimer will not be effective if the property was accepted in any form. Once a disclaimer is made, the decision is irrevocable.

Drye v. United States

528 U.S. 49 (1999)

GINSBURG, J.

The relevant facts are not in dispute. On August 3, 1994, Irma Deliah Drye died intestate, leaving an estate worth approximately $233,000, of which $158,000 was personalty and $75,000 was realty located in Pulaski County, Arkansas. Petitioner Rohn F. Drye, Jr., her son, was sole heir to the estate under Arkansas law. On the date of his mother's death, Drye was insolvent and owed the Government approximately $325,000, representing assessments for tax deficiencies in years 1988, 1989, and 1990. The Internal Revenue Service (IRS or Service) had made assessments against Drye in November 1990 and May 1991 and had valid tax liens against all of Drye's "property and rights to property" pursuant to 26 U.S.C. § 6321.

Drye petitioned the Pulaski County Probate Court for appointment as administrator of his mother's estate and was so appointed on August 17, 1994. Almost six months later, on February 4, 1995, Drye filed in the Probate Court and land records of Pulaski County a written disclaimer of all interests in his mother's estate. Two days later, Drye resigned as administrator of the estate.

Under Arkansas law, an heir may disavow his inheritance by filing a written disclaimer no later than nine months after the death of the decedent. The disclaimer creates the legal fiction that the disclaimant predeceased the decedent; consequently, the disclaimant's share of the estate passes to the person next in line to receive that share. The disavowing heir's creditors, Arkansas law provides, may not reach property thus disclaimed. In the case at hand, Drye's disclaimer caused the estate to pass to his daughter, Theresa Drye, who succeeded her father as administrator and promptly established the Drye Family 1995 Trust (Trust).

On March 10, 1995, the Probate Court declared valid Drye's disclaimer of all interest in his mother's estate and accordingly ordered final distribution of the estate to Theresa Drye. Theresa Drye then used the estate's proceeds to fund the Trust, of which she and, during their lifetimes, her parents are the beneficiaries. Under the Trust's terms, distributions are at the discretion of the trustee, Drye's counsel Daniel M. Traylor, and may be made only for the health, maintenance, and support of the beneficiaries. The Trust is spendthrift, and under state law, its assets are therefore shielded from creditors seeking to satisfy the debts of the Trust's beneficiaries.

Also in 1995, the IRS and Drye began negotiations regarding Drye's tax liabilities. During the course of the negotiations, Drye revealed to the Service his beneficial interest in the Trust. Thereafter, on April 11, 1996, the IRS filed with the Pulaski County Circuit Clerk and Recorder a notice of federal tax lien against the Trust as Drye's nominee. The Service also served a notice of levy on accounts held in the Trust's name by an investment bank and notified the Trust of the levy.

B

On May 1, 1996, the Trust filed a wrongful levy action against the United States. On cross-motions for summary judgment, the District Court ruled in the Government's favor. The United States Court of Appeals for the Eighth Circuit affirmed the District Court's judgment. *Drye Family 1995 Trust* v. *United States*, 152 F.3d 892 (1998).

II

Under the relevant provisions of the Internal Revenue Code, to satisfy a tax deficiency, the Government may impose a lien on any "property" or "rights to property" belonging to the taxpayer. Section 6321 provides: "If any person liable to pay any tax neglects or refuses to pay the same after demand, the amount . . . shall be a lien in favor of the United States upon all property and rights to property, whether real or personal, belonging to such person." 26 U.S.C. § 6321. The language "is broad and reveals on its face that Congress meant to reach every interest in property that a taxpayer might have."

Section 6334(a) of the Code is corroborative. That provision lists property exempt from levy. Inheritances or devises disclaimed under state law are not included in § 6334(a)'s catalog of property exempt from levy.

Just as "exempt status under state law does not bind the federal collector," *Mitchell*, 403 U.S., at 204, so federal tax law "is not struck blind by a disclaimer," *United States* v. *Irvine*, 511 U.S. 224, 240 (1994). Thus, in *Mitchell*, the Court held that, although a wife's renunciation of a marital interest was treated as retroactive under state law, that state-law disclaimer did not determine the wife's liability for federal tax on her share of the community income realized before the renunciation. *See* 403 U.S. at 204 (right to renounce does not indicate that taxpayer never had a right to property).

IV

The Eighth Circuit, with fidelity to the relevant Code provisions and our case law, determined first what rights state law accorded Drye in his mother's estate. It is beyond debate, the Court of Appeals observed, that under Arkansas law Drye had, at his mother's death, a valuable, transferable, legally protected right to the property at issue.

Drye emphasizes his undoubted right under Arkansas law to disclaim the inheritance, a right that is indeed personal and not marketable.

The disclaiming heir or devisee, in contrast, does not restore the status quo, for the decedent cannot be revived. Thus, the heir inevitably exercises dominion over the property. He determines who will receive the property—himself if he does not disclaim, a known other if he does. This power to channel the estate's assets warrants the conclusion that Drye held "property" or a "righ[t] to property" subject to the Government's liens.

In sum, in determining whether a federal taxpayer's state-law rights constitute "property" or "rights to property," "[t]he important consideration is the breadth of the control the [taxpayer] could exercise over the property." *Morgan*, 309 U.S., at 83. Drye had the unqualified right to receive the entire value of his mother's estate (less administrative expenses) or to channel that value to his daughter. The control rein he held under state law, we hold, rendered the inheritance "property" or "rights to property" belonging to him within the meaning of § 6321, and hence subject to the federal tax liens that sparked this controversy.

For the reasons stated, the judgment of the Court of Appeals for the Eighth Circuit is

Affirmed.

NOTE

In general, if property has been disclaimed the property passes as if the disclaimant had died immediately before the time of distribution. UPC § 2–1106(b)(3)(B). Note that only the "disclaimed interest" passes. UPC § 2–1106(b)(3)(C).

ASSESSMENTS

1.   Dave died intestate. He was survived by his spouse Jan and their two adult children named Sidney and Harper. Sidney has a minor child named Cameron.

Harper has one child named Julianna who is about to attend college. Sidney and Harper have discussed allowing Jan to inherit Dave's entire intestate estate. What issues should they consider? What actions might they consider taking?

2.   Darla died intestate. Darla had two children named Addison and Bailey. Addison and Addison's four children all survived Darla. Bailey did not survive Darla, but Bailey's child named Sage did survive Darla. If Addison properly executes a valid disclaimer, how should Darla's property be distributed? What does UPC § 2–1106(b)(3)(C) provide?

3.   Dana executed a valid will that, in its entirety, provides as follows: "I expressly disinherit my sister Alice and my sister Betty." Dana is survived by Dana's three sisters named Alice, Betty, and Carol. Dana is also survived by Alice's child named Errol. Who inherits Dana's probate property?

4.   Trudi's uncle Marvin died intestate last month. Trudi and her brother Kelvin will be the heirs, but Trudi is unsure whether she wants to inherit her share of Marvin's property. Trudi knows that her brother has some pressing financial concerns. Trudi is in a profession with higher earning potential than Kelvin. Trudi also knows that Kelvin has recently incurred some medical bills. Trudi has two teenage children who will be soon attending college. Kelvin has one adult child. Trudi hires your law firm for advice.

    a.   Write an email to Trudi about the potential use, value, and consequences of (i) a private agreement and (ii) a disclaimer. Use legally accurate and client-accessible language.

    b.   What additional facts would you wish to gather to help Trudi evaluate her options?

    c.   Assume that after appropriate consideration Trudi decides to disclaim her interest in her uncle's intestate estate. Trudi wishes her interest to pass to her two children. Draft an appropriate disclaimer for Trudi to sign.

3.   Negative Will

A provision in a will that an heir is to receive no property under intestacy traditionally had no legal effect. The only way to make sure such an heir did not take under intestacy was for the decedent to effectively devise the entire estate to other persons. If the decedent died totally or

> **Practice Note:** A negative will is relevant to intestate succession because a negative will essentially disinherits an intestate heir with the decedent's property being distributed to the decedent's other intestate heirs.

partially intestate, the heir would still inherit, so long as the heir was eligible. Section 2–101(b) of the current UPC, adopted in a few jurisdictions, provides that such a statement of disinheritance is effective, even if the will does not provide any disposition of property. In that circumstance, the heir is treated as predeceasing the decedent. Such a will is called a **negative will**. Unless specifically provided in the terms of the negative will, the heir's surviving descendants retain their eligibility to inherit as heirs.

4. Contracts Regarding Inheritance

Contracts may expand, modify, or extinguish an individual's ability to inherit property. This section explores the most common types of contracts relating to succession.

a. *Transfer of an Expectancy*

Until the decedent dies, a would-be heir has an expectancy of an inheritance. The would-be heir must survive the decedent, the heir must receive priority under intestacy statutes, and the heir's ability must not be barred. Furthermore, if the decedent makes a valid will that otherwise disposes of the property or the property is sold or given away during the owner's lifetime, no property would be available to be disposed of via intestacy. Nevertheless, such an heir might agree to release that expectancy to the decedent during the decedent's lifetime or might agree to transfer the expectancy to a third person by way of an assignment. A release or transfer like this typically will be enforced. An assignment of an expectancy is often enforced in a court of equity, though not in a court of law, provided there was adequate consideration. A few jurisdictions will not enforce an assignment under any circumstances.

b. *Marital Agreements*

The parties to a marriage may agree either before or after marriage to alter their inheritance rights at the time of death. This altering may be a complete waiver of any rights, an expansion of inheritance rights, or otherwise a modification. If the agreement is created before the parties marry, the agreement is described as a premarital, prenuptial, or ante-nuptial agreement. If the agreement is created during the marriage when no

> **Connection Note:** Notice that a divorced spouse is not eligible to receive an intestate share. Revocation upon divorce statutes, discussed in Chapters 13 and 14, will revoke nominations and gifts to a former spouse in testamentary instructions and non-testamentary instruments.

dissolution proceeding is contemplated, the agreement is described as a marital or post-nuptial agreement. A divorce settlement agreement, created during the marriage but when the parties are contemplating divorce, is subject to separate rules.

Premarital and marital agreements are discussed later in the book in connection with spousal rights, but it is useful to mention them here because they provide an opt-out from the default rules of intestacy. The usual requirements are that the agreement be in writing and signed, that there is consideration, that the agreement was freely entered into by the parties and, in most states, that there has been full disclosure of assets.

c.   Other Contracts

In addition to transfers of expectancies and marital agreements, individuals may create a contract to make a will, a contract not to make a will (and thus die intestate), a contract not to revoke a will, or a contract to revoke a will. If a party to a valid contract dies and at the time of the death the contract has been breached, the contract beneficiary may have a cause of action for contract damages, a court may impose a constructive trust to prevent unjust enrichment, or the court may award the remedy of specific performance. To have a valid contract, many jurisdictions require a signed writing. UPC § 2–514. Absent a writing, a

"AN ORAL CONTRACT IS NOT WORTH THE PAPER IT'S WRITTEN ON."

CartoonStock.com

Contracts can play an important role in inheritance.

contract beneficiary still may be entitled to restitution of the value of services rendered the decedent by way of quantum meruit.

A contract to make a will often arises in the context of marital agreements discussed above, in the context of a divorce agreement, or as part of an agreement to care for another individual.

Finally, there may be a contract not to revoke a will. This type of contract often is an agreement between a married couple, each of whom has children from a prior marriage, to leave the estate to the survivor but, on the surviving spouse's death, to have the remainder divided equally among their joint issue. The couple may execute mutual wills (often called reciprocal or mirror-image wills) in which each signs a separate will devising all to the survivor and then to the issue of both of them. Or they may execute only one will which is signed by both spouses, known as a joint will. When the first spouse dies, the will is probated, and it is probated again on the death of the second spouse. Most jurisdictions do not find the execution of these wills by themselves raise a presumption of a contract not to revoke the will. Instead, any contract must be proven by clear and convincing evidence. We discuss these contracts in greater detail in Chapter 8 in the context of will interpretation and construction.

G. Conclusion and Takeaways

The freedom of disposition includes the ability to refrain from exercising that freedom. Thus, the law needs to provide a back-up or series of default rules relating to disposition of probate property and various administrative rules. The goal of intestate succession statutes is to facilitate the efficient transmission of probate property in the absence of disposition in the decedent's valid will. Intestacy statutes are based upon the presumed intent of most decedents, but the statutes also express assumptions about norms. This raises the question as to how often intestacy statutes should be evaluated and revised. Should they, for example, be evaluated once every generation to confirm their continued relevance? More often?

To opt out of intestacy, an individual needs to create a valid will that disposes of all probate property. As we will see in the next four chapters, creation of such a testamentary instrument may not be as simple as it seems.

CHAPTER 4 COMPREHENSIVE ASSESSMENTS

1. **DEVELOP A COMMUNITY PRESENTATION.** You have been invited to speak at a community gathering about estate planning. Although you don't know exactly who will attend the presentation, you do know that the attendees will have a variety of property interests and a variety of family relationships. As part of your presentation, develop presentation slides and an accompanying script that highlight what information an individual needs to understand about intestacy. You may use either the UPC or a jurisdiction's intestacy statutes of your choice in the presentation. Make sure to use language that is substantively accurate but is accessible to nonlawyers. Minimize use of jargon. Use graphics or images to complement the text.

The content of the presentation must do the following:

- define intestacy

- describe of the purpose of intestacy

- share at least three hypotheticals to demonstrate the parameters, the limitations, the benefits, and the deficiencies of intestacy statutes

- showcase three takeaways from the presentation.

2. **REPRESENTATION REVIEW.** Dylan's family gathered to celebrate his 100th birthday. His two children Jayne and Gail died years before, but Dylan was fortunate to have a number of grandchildren and great-grandchildren attend the party. Jayne had two children named Martha and Noelle. Martha had two children named Clare and Portia. Noelle had one child named Ajax. Gail had four children, Rob, Liam, Etta, and Henri. Liam had one child named Sam, and Rob had one child named Isla. During the previous year, the family had gathered for the funerals of Martha and Henri.

When Rob drove Dylan home from the birthday party, their car was involved in a traffic accident. Dylan died at the scene. Rob was rushed to the hospital and died three days later. No will was found upon Dylan's death.

A.   Assume that Dylan's probate property is valued at $600,000. How should his probate property be distributed? Identify the potential heirs and exact dollar amount each heir would receive. Define and apply all relevant terms.

B.   Does it make a difference what model of representation is used? Explain your response.

3. **DESIGN A MODEL INTESTATE SUCCESSION ACT.** This assignment has two components. First, draft a Model Intestate Succession Act that identifies the potential heirs, outlines the hierarchy, and describes the apportionment of shares. Second, write a brief explanation/commentary of your intent and decisions that reflect the purpose of intestate succession, the nature of property, and the realities of familial relationships.

Below are some suggestions to help you develop and write the model act and accompanying explanation.

- Identify the potential categories of heirs, considering how relationships and family patterns have and are continuing to change. You may include a definitions section in your model act.

- Consider eligibility (i.e., what qualifications or bars are appropriate), priority (i.e., hierarchy), and shares (i.e., whether the individual would receive fractions or percentages of the property).

- Recognize the tension between efficiency and fairness as you determine the role of presumptions and the type of evidence that may be presented by potential heirs.

While you may draw inspiration from existing intestacy statutes, the model act should reflect your own thinking. In other words, do not simply copy one country/state's intestate succession statute(s) in its entirety. Instead, create a model act that that reflects your thoughts on the purpose of intestate succession and how a model act could reflect modern/developing family patterns.

Test Your Knowledge

To assess your understanding of the material in this chapter, click here to take a quiz.

CHAPTER 5

Wills I: Execution

CHAPTER LEARNING OUTCOMES

Following your work with the material in this chapter, you should be able to do the following:

- Assess by reference to the language and surrounding circumstances whether a document shows testamentary intent

- Describe and evaluate the requirements for testamentary capacity

- Identify the formalities required for will execution

- Design an execution ceremony for a successful will execution

- Recognize how to satisfy the purposes of will formalities when circumstances interfere with literal compliance

- Explain the value and pitfalls associated with online wills

- Assess the validity of a purported will based on state law

A. Introduction

Now that you have some familiarity with how default rules work when a person dies intestate, we are going to dive into the heart of the estate planning process by looking at the most basic of testamentary documents: the will. A will is a written document by which an individual (the "testator") sets out that person's wishes for disposition of probate property at death and appoints a fiduciary (known as an "executor" or "personal representative") to oversee the probate process. But not every written document qualifies as a will. Much of this chapter discusses the requirements for a valid will, including intent, capacity, and formalities.

Part B addresses the first requirement for a valid will: that the testator have **testamentary intent**, meaning that the document in question is intended as a will. **Part C** discusses **testamentary capacity** or the **mental capacity** for creating a will, which you will see is quite low.

Will execution is a rule-bound process and has traditionally required a number of safeguards to prevent fraud and protect the intent and last wishes of the decedent. **Part D** discusses will formalities. The key formalities have not changed much over time and include: 1) a written document; 2) the decedent's signature; and 3) witnessing (also called **attestation**). **Part E** discusses levels of compliance with the formalities of will execution and introduces the concepts of harmless error and substantial compliance, which may apply if the formalities are not satisfied.

B. Testamentary Intent

In Property, you learned about the elements of donor intent: intent to relinquish all rights to something, delivery, and acceptance. A gift would occur, for example, if someone takes off her watch, hands it to you, and says, "Here, take this watch—I know you like it and I'd like you to have it. It's all yours." Testamentary intent is different: it requires a showing that the testator was not only thinking about the distribution of her possessions at her death, but also meant for the writing in question to act as a will (as opposed to being just a set of notes or a first draft). Traditional will language is meant to convey this type of intent. Here is a very traditional example:

> In the name of God, amen/Known by all men present, I, MARLA CHIN, residing in Bibb County, Georgia, being of sound and disposing mind, considering the uncertainty of this frail and transitory life, do now hereby declare, make, and publish this as my Last Will and Testament, hereby revoking all prior Wills and Codicils by me heretobefore made.

Although no magic words are necessarily required to establish intent, phrasing such as "I declare this to be my will" or "I intend to make the following testamentary gift" help establish testamentary intent.

Sometimes, however, people don't use the formal language and yet they create a document that looks as if it was meant to express testamentary intent. Without the formal language for expressing testamentary intent, it can sometimes be hard to be sure: was the person truly contemplating death? Did that person intend for the document in question to be a will? Or was there something else going on? If so, what? That was the dilemma in the following case.

In re the Estate of Charles Kuralt

15 P.3d 931 (Mont. 2000)

TRIEWEILER, J.

Elizabeth Shannon, longtime personal companion of the deceased, Charles Kuralt, challenged the testamentary disposition of Kuralt's real and personal property in the District Court for the Fifth Judicial District in Madison County. The District Court initially granted partial summary judgment in favor of the Estate and Shannon appealed. This Court reversed the District Court and remanded for a determination of disputed issues of material fact. Following an evidentiary hearing, the District Court found that Kuralt executed a valid holographic codicil which expressed his testamentary intent to transfer the Madison County property to Shannon. The Estate now appeals from the order and judgment of the District Court. We affirm the District Court's order and judgment.

The parties present the following issue on appeal: Did the District Court err when it found that the June 18, 1997 letter expressed a present testamentary intent to transfer property in Madison County?

FACTUAL BACKGROUND

Most of the relevant facts were previously before this Court. *See In re Estate of Kuralt (Kuralt I)*, 981 P.2d 771 (Mont. 1999). To summarize, Charles Kuralt and Elizabeth Shannon maintained a long-term and intimate personal relationship. Kuralt and Shannon desired to keep their relationship secret, and were so successful in doing so that even though Kuralt's wife, Petie, knew that Kuralt owned property in Montana, she was unaware, prior to Kuralt's untimely death, of his relationship with Shannon.

Over the nearly 30-year course of their relationship, Kuralt and Shannon saw each other regularly and maintained contact by phone and mail. Kuralt was the primary source of financial support for Shannon and established close, personal relationships with Shannon's three children. Kuralt provided financial support for a joint business venture managed by Shannon and transferred a home in Ireland to Shannon as a gift.

In 1985, Kuralt purchased a 20-acre parcel of property along the Big Hole River in Madison County, near Twin Bridges, Montana. Kuralt and Shannon constructed a cabin on this 20-acre parcel. In 1987, Kuralt purchased two additional parcels along the Big Hole which adjoined the original 20-acre parcel. These two additional parcels, one upstream and one downstream of the cabin, created a parcel of approximately 90 acres and are the primary subject of this appeal.

On May 3, 1989, Kuralt executed a holographic will which stated as follows:

May 3, 1989

In the event of my death, I bequeath to Patricia Elizabeth Shannon all my interest in land, buildings, furnishings and personal belongings on Burma Road, Twin Bridges, Montana.

Charles Kuralt

34 Bank St.

New York, N.Y. 10014

Although Kuralt mailed a copy of this holographic will to Shannon, he subsequently executed a formal will on May 4, 1994, in New York City. This Last Will and Testament, prepared with the assistance of counsel, does not specifically mention any of the real property owned by Kuralt. The beneficiaries of Kuralt's Last Will and Testament were his wife, Petie, and the Kuralts' two children. Neither Shannon nor her children are named as beneficiaries in Kuralt's formal will. Shannon had no knowledge of the formal will until the commencement of these proceedings.

On April 9, 1997, Kuralt deeded his interest in the original 20-acre parcel with the cabin to Shannon. The transaction was disguised as a sale. However, Kuralt supplied the "purchase" price for the 20-acre parcel to Shannon prior to the transfer. After the deed to the 20-acre parcel was filed, Shannon sent Kuralt, at his request, a blank buy-sell real estate form so that the remaining 90 acres along the Big Hole could be conveyed to Shannon in a similar manner. Apparently, it was again Kuralt's intention to provide the purchase price. The second transaction was to take place in September 1997 when Shannon, her son, and Kuralt agreed to meet at the Montana cabin.

Kuralt, however, became suddenly ill and entered a New York hospital on June 18, 1997. On that same date, Kuralt wrote the letter to Shannon which is now at the center of the current dispute:

June 18, 1997

Dear Pat—

Something is terribly wrong with me and they can't figure out what. After cat-scans and a variety of cardiograms, they agree it's not lung cancer or heart trouble or blood clot. So, they're putting me in the hospital today to concentrate on infectious diseases. I am getting worse, barely able to get out of bed, but still have high hopes for recovery. . . if only I can get a diagnosis! Curiouser and curiouser! I'll keep you informed. I'll have the lawyer visit the hospital to be sure you inherit the rest of the place in MT. if it comes to that.

I send love to you & [your youngest daughter,] Shannon. Hope things are better there!

Love,

C.

Enclosed with this letter were two checks made payable to Shannon, one for $8000 and the other for $9000. Kuralt did not seek the assistance of an attorney to devise the remaining 90 acres of Big Hole land to Shannon. Therefore, when Kuralt died unexpectedly, Shannon sought to probate the letter of June 18, 1997, as a valid holographic codicil to Kuralt's formal 1994 will.

The Estate opposed Shannon's Petition for Ancillary Probate based on its contention that the June 18, 1997 letter expressed only a future intent to make a will. The District Court granted partial summary judgment for the Estate on May 26, 1998. Shannon appealed from the District Court order which granted partial summary judgment to the Estate. This Court, in *Kuralt I*, reversed the District Court and remanded the case for trial in order to resolve disputed issues of material fact. Following an abbreviated evidentiary hearing, the District Court issued its Findings and Order. The District Court held that the June 18, 1997 letter was a valid holographic codicil to Kuralt's formal will of May 4, 1994 and accordingly entered judgment in favor of Shannon.

> **Connection Note:** Kuralt had a series of wills, some of which he drafted and at least one of which a lawyer drafted. The 1994 attorney-drafted will provided that all of Kuralt's property would pass to his wife and children and likely contained a clause expressly revoking all prior wills. This meant that Kuralt's 1989 will no longer took effect. The question posed to the court was whether the 1997 letter was an effective amendment ("codicil") to the 1994 will, specifying how the Montana land would pass on Kuralt's death. In Chapter 7, we will discuss multiple wills, including when a later will or codicil revokes or modifies an existing will.

The Estate now appeals from that order and judgment.

DISCUSSION

Did the District Court err when it found that the June 18, 1997 letter expressed a present testamentary intent to transfer property in Madison County?

The argument on appeal, while clothed as a legal argument, addresses factual findings made by the District Court. However, if the factual findings of the District Court are supported by substantial credible evidence and are not otherwise clearly erroneous, they will not be reversed by this Court.

The record supports the District Court's finding that the June 18, 1997 letter expressed Kuralt's intent to affect a posthumous transfer of his Montana property to Shannon. Kuralt and Shannon enjoyed a long, close personal relationship which continued up to the last letter Kuralt wrote Shannon on June 18, 1997, in which he enclosed checks to her in the amounts of $8000 and $9000. Likewise, Kuralt and Shannon's children had a long, family-like relationship which included significant financial support.

The District Court focused on the last few months of Kuralt's life to find that the letter demonstrated his testamentary intent. The conveyance of the 20-acre parcel for no real consideration and extrinsic evidence that Kuralt intended to convey the remainder of the Montana property to Shannon in a similar fashion provides substantial factual support for the District Court's determination that Kuralt intended that Shannon have the rest of the Montana property.

The June 18, 1997 letter expressed Kuralt's desire that Shannon inherit the remainder of the Montana property. That Kuralt wrote the letter in extremis is supported by the fact that he died two weeks later. Although Kuralt intended to transfer the remaining land to Shannon, he was reluctant to consult a lawyer to formalize his intent because he wanted to keep their relationship secret. Finally, the use of the term "inherit" underlined by Kuralt reflected his intention to make a posthumous disposition of the property. Therefore, the District Court's findings are supported by substantial evidence and are not clearly erroneous. Accordingly, we conclude that the District Court did not err when it found that the letter dated June 18, 1997 expressed a present testamentary intent to transfer property in Madison County to Patricia Shannon.

June 18 1997

Dear Pat —

Something is terribly wrong with me and they can't figure out what. After cat-scans and a variety of cardiograms, they agree it's not lung cancer or heart trouble or blood clot. So they're putting me in the hospital today to concentrate on infectious diseases. I am getting worse, barely able to get out of bed, but still have high hopes for recovery ... if only I can get a diagnosis! Curiouser & curiouser! I'll keep you informed.

I'll have the lawyer visit the hospital to be sure you inherit the rest of the place in MT. if it comes to that.

I send love to you & Shannon. Hope things are better there!

Love,

C.

EXHIBIT
21

Letter from Charles Kuralt to Pat Shannon, written from his hospital bed.

NOTE

Tombstones of Charles Bishop Kuralt and Petie Baird Kuralt at the Old Chapel Hill Cemetery in Chapel Hill, North Carolina.

Charles Kuralt was an American journalist who was most well-known for "On the Road" segments on *The CBS Evening News* and as the first anchor of *CBS News Sunday Morning*, a position he held for fifteen years. Kuralt hit the road in a motor home beginning in 1967 with a small crew, taking the back roads in search of small towns and interesting people. He wore out six motor homes and won two Peabody awards before he was through. It was on one of these trips that he met Patricia Shannon. As one author wrote:

> They vacationed together, celebrated Christmases together, camped, hiked and picnicked together. Kuralt put her oldest daughter through law school and helped put her son through college. He bought her a cottage in Ireland. Over the years, he sent her enough money that she didn't have to work; the checks came monthly, $5,000 here, $8,000 there, well over half a million dollars. Even as Kuralt and Shannon drifted apart (he refused to leave his wife), he continued sending money and notes of affection.

See Paige Williams, *A Double Life on the Road*, The Washington Post, June 1, 1998.

ASSESSMENTS

1.   What language in Kuralt's letter and what surrounding circumstances seem to indicate Kuralt's testamentary intent—or lack thereof? Can you think of any other reason Kuralt might have written Shannon the letter other than wanting to make her a testamentary bequest? Do you think the *Kuralt* case was correctly decided? Why or why not?

2.   The following are examples of writings in which testamentary intent was contested. Evaluate each excerpt and the surrounding circumstances shared below. Identify the language in the writing that may or may not demonstrate testamentary intent and assess whether each one indicates that the writer intended the writing to be a will disposing of property at death.

   a.   'The Kimmel Bro. and Family We are all well as you can expect for the time of the Year. I received your kind & welcome letter from Geo & Irvin all OK glad you poot your Pork down in Pickle it is the true way to keep meet every piece gets the same, now always poot it down that way & you will not miss it & you will have good pork fore smoking you can keep it from butchern to butchern the hole year-round. Boys, I won't agree with you about the open winter I think we are gone to have one of the hardest. Plenty of snow & Verry cold verry cold! I dont want to see it this way but it will will come see to the old sow & take her away when the time comes well I cant say if I will come over yet. I will wright in my next letter it may be to ruff we will see in the next letter if I come I have some very valuable papers I want you to keep fore me so if enny thing hapens all the scock money in the 3 Bank liberty lones Post office stamps and my home on Horner St goes to George Darl & Irvin Kepp this letter lock it up it may help you out. Earl sent after his Christmas Tree & Trimmings I sent them he is in the Post office in Phila working.

'Will clost your Truly,

Father.'

This letter was mailed by the decedent at Johnstown, Pa., on the morning of its date, Monday, December 12, 1921, to two of his children, George and Irvin; the envelope was addressed to them at their residence in Glencoe, Pa. Kimmel died suddenly on the afternoon of the same day. *In re Kimmel's Estate*, 123 A. 405, 405 (Pa. 1924).

b.   In *Estate of Perez*, 155 S.W.3d 599 (Tex. App. 2004), the testator wrote: "because I am sick and waiting for a heart surgery, and providing ahead of any emergency, I make the following disposition to be fulfilled in case my death occurs during the surgery."

The testator survived the surgery but died six months later.

c.   "Karen Greenwood . . . has all legal rights to my estate in the case of my untimely or timely death." *In re Estate of Silverman*, 2019 Tex. App. LEXIS 4579.

d.   "I am going on a journey and I may not ever return. And if I do not, this is my last bequest." *Eaton v. Brown*, 193 U.S. 411 (1904).

e.   LOUISVILLE, January 14, 1859:

"If any accident should happen to me that I die from home, my wife, J A. L., shall have every thing I possess," etc.

The decedent died at home. *Likefield v. Likefield,* 82 Ky 589 (1885).

    f.   "Dated this day,

        August 22, 1998

        If anything should happen to me on this trip to Rapid City. Everything I own is to go to Ann, Sheldon, and McKensey and Bradley Sheridan. Inculding [sic] rest of money from Bert and the land.

        Leslie Mary Martin

        405 S. Lincoln St

        Groton, So. Dak"

In re Estate of Martin, 635 N.W.2d 473, 477 (S.D. 2001)

    g.   "STATE OF MISSISSIPPI, MONROE COUNTY:

        For the love and affection that I have for my wife, Harriet N. Sartor, I give unto her all my property, real and personal, during her widowhood; and if she marries it is all to go back to my niece, Sally Sartor, and she is to pay Coleman, my brother's children-namely, Elizabeth, Selina, Daniel, and Medora—one thousand dollars apiece, commencing to pay one year from the time she receives the property, Elizabeth hers first, and Selina next, and so on until she pays all four of them, which will be twelve months apart from the first, second, and so on.

        Given under my hand and seal, this April 4th, 1857"

Sartor v. Sartor, 39 Miss. 760 (1861).

    h.   Found in decedent Tai kin Wong's office after he committed suicide: envelopes decorated with stickers that said, "You're Special" and "I love You," a handwritten note which read "All Tai-Kin Wong's—Xi Xhao, my best half." *Estate of Wong,* 40 Cal. App. 4th 1198, 1201 (1995).

3.   Imagine you are visiting your Aunt Julia, and she says to you, "I want you to have my Ming vase when I die. I'll keep it for you until then but consider it yours." Does her statement suffice to indicate testamentary intent?

4.   Without using standard phrases like "last will and testament" or using the language in the introduction in Section B1, draft an introductory paragraph for a will that shows testamentary intent.

C. Testamentary Capacity

Now we move on to testamentary *capacity*, which is different from testamentary intent. Testamentary capacity refers to the testator's ability to "be capable of knowing and understanding in a general way." A typical definition of testamentary capacity requires that the testator know:

(1) The nature and extent of his or her property

(2) The natural objects of his or her bounty

(3) The disposition that he or she is making of that property and

(4) Must be capable of understanding how these elements relate

RESTATEMENT (THIRD) OF PROPERTY: WILLS AND OTHER DONATIVE TRANSFERS § 8.1(b) (2003).

A person can be eccentric and even confused or disoriented and still have the capacity to execute a valid will. Problems arise when it becomes difficult to tell whether a testator is simply eccentric or whether the testator is unable to form a rational and orderly desire about the disposition of her property. All that is necessary for capacity is what is called a "lucid moment"—a brief time when the testator has the requisite capacity even if she appears not to have it most of the time. As you read the next case, keep this in mind, and identify these lucid moments.

Wilson v. Lane

614 S.E.2d 88 (Ga. 2005)

FLETCHER, C. J.

After Executrix Katherine Lane offered Jewel Jones Greer's 1997 last will and testament for probate, Floyd Wilson filed a caveat, challenging Greer's testamentary capacity. A Jasper County Superior Court jury found that Greer lacked testamentary capacity at the time she executed her will, but the trial court granted Lane's motion for judgment notwithstanding the verdict. Wilson appeals. Because we agree that there was no evidence to show that Greer lacked testamentary capacity, we affirm.

A person is mentally capable to make a will if she "has sufficient intellect to enable [her] to have a decided and rational desire as to the disposition of [her] property." In this case, the propounders introduced evidence that the will in question distributed Greer's property equally to seventeen beneficiaries, sixteen of whom are blood-relatives to Greer. The only non-relative beneficiary is Katherine Lane, who spent much of her time caring for Greer before her death in 2000. The drafting attorney testified that in his opinion, at the time the 1997 will was signed, Greer was mentally competent, and that she emphatically selected every beneficiary named in the will. Numerous other friends and acquaintances also testified that Greer had a clear mind at the time the will was signed.

Thus, the propounders established a presumption that Greer possessed testamentary capacity.

The caveators challenged Greer's capacity by showing that she was eccentric, aged, and peculiar in the last years of her life. They presented testimony that she had an irrational fear of flooding in her house, that she had trouble dressing and bathing herself, and that she unnecessarily called the fire department to report a non-existent fire. But "[t]he law does not withhold from the aged, the feeble, the weak-minded, the capricious, the notionate, the right to make a will, provided such person has a decided and rational desire as to the disposition of his property." Although perhaps persuasive to a jury, "eccentric habits and absurd beliefs do not establish testamentary incapacity." All that is required to sustain the will is proof that Greer was capable of forming a certain rational desire with respect to the disposition of her assets.

In addition to Greer's eccentric habits, the caveators also introduced evidence of a guardianship petition filed for Greer a few months after the will was executed, the testimony of an expert witness, and a letter written by Greer's physician. None of that evidence, however, was sufficient to deprive Greer of her right to make a valid will, as none of it showed that she was incapable of forming a rational desire as to the disposition of her property.

The expert admitted that he had never examined Greer, and that his testimony was based solely on a cursory review of some of Greer's medical files. Further, he was equivocal in his testimony, stating only that "it appears that she was in some form of the early to middle stages of a dementia of the Alzheimer's type." Regardless of the stigma associated with the term "Alzheimer's," however, that testimony does not show how Greer would have been unable to form a rational desire regarding the disposition of her assets. Indeed, the expert offered no explanation of how her supposed condition would affect her competency to make a valid will.

The testimony of Greer's physician also failed to show how she lacked testamentary capacity. In 1996, the physician wrote a letter stating that Greer "was legally blind and suffered from senile dementia." But the doctor testified that he was "not sure whether she had senile dementia at the time or not, even though I wrote that." He stated further that he only wrote the letter to try and assist Greer in obtaining help with her telephone bill because she had been having trouble with her eyes. In any event, a vague reference to "senile dementia" cannot eliminate testamentary capacity. If it could, it would undermine societal confidence in the validity and sanctity of our testamentary system.

Finally, as the dissent points out, Lane filed a guardianship petition in 1998, after the will was executed, proclaiming that Greer was no longer capable of managing her own affairs alone. According to the testimony, however, the petition was filed solely in order to satisfy the Department of Family and Children Service's concerns regarding Greer's ability to continue living on her own, and thus to allow Greer to remain in her home. Even if Greer's inability to live alone existed at the time the will was executed, which was not proven by any evidence, that fact bears no relation to her ability to form a rational desire regarding the disposition of her assets.

Similarly, in this case, no testimony, expert or otherwise, was offered to establish that at the time the will was executed, Greer suffered from a form of dementia sufficient in form or extent to render her unable to form a decided and rational desire regarding the disposition of her assets. Notwithstanding the dissent's attempt to piece together "the totality of the evidence," none of the evidence, either alone or in combination, provided any proof that Greer lacked testamentary capacity, as that term is defined in this State. At most, there was evidence that Greer was an eccentric woman whose mental health declined towards the end of her life. Accordingly, the evidence demanded a verdict upholding the validity of the will, and the trial court was correct to reverse the jury's contrary verdict.

Judgment affirmed.

CARLEY, J., *dissenting*.

I agree that the evidence in this case would have authorized a finding that Ms. Greer possessed the requisite testamentary capacity when she executed a will in September of 1997. However, the jury found that she lacked such capacity, and we must decide whether the evidence supports that finding.

The fact that Ms. Greer was elderly, sickly, eccentric or forgetful does not authorize a finding that she lacked the necessary testamentary capacity to make a valid will. However, evidence that, as the result of her age or health, her mental condition had deteriorated to the extent that she was unable to form a decided and rational desire regarding the disposition of her property will authorize a finding that the instrument she executed is invalid.

Here, the Caveators presented expert medical opinion testimony showing that, at the time Ms. Greer executed the will, "she was in some form of the early to middle stages of a dementia of the Alzheimer's type." A year earlier, her own physician had expressed his belief that she exhibited "senile dementia." In January of 1998, a petition was filed which alleged that Ms. Greer was an "incapacitated" adult and sought the appointment of a guardian. This petition for guardianship was supported by the affidavit of her doctor, who stated his opinion that she had "dementia-Alzheimer's type," that she suffered from "poor memory, poor judgment, [was] difficult to reason with," and that she was "incapacitated on a permanent basis." It was only four months between the time she signed the instrument tendered for admission into probate and the petition alleging that she was "permanently incapacitated" due to "dementia" based upon Alzheimer's disease.

In addition to the expert medical opinion evidence showing that Ms. Greer suffered from dementia attributable to Alzheimer's disease shortly before, during and shortly after the time she executed the will, the Caveators introduced evidence which was indicative of the extent to which her mental acuity had been impaired. She had an irrational fear that her home was being flooded. She even refused to get into the bathtub, and insisted on sponge baths. Visitors to her home

> couldn't flush the commode, couldn't really run the water in her kitchen sink. [S]he had a phobia of water and when you went to [visit her] you dare not go in the commode, use the bathroom, you didn't cut on the water to get a drink of water or anything so you just had to sit.

There was additional evidence showing that in mid-December of 1997, only three months after executing the will, Ms. Greer was disoriented as to time and, believing that it was March, she was unaware that Christmas was imminent. She did not know her own social security number. She had a list of first names and telephone numbers, but could not provide last names for any of those on that list. As the majority notes, she called the fire department to report a non-existent fire.

"[A] court must allow the issue of testamentary capacity to go to the jury when there is a genuine conflict in the evidence regarding the testator's state of mind." While no single element of the Caveators' proof, standing alone, might otherwise be a sufficient predicate for invalidating Ms. Greer's will, when the totality of the evidence as to her mental condition during the relevant time period is considered, a jury certainly would be authorized to find that she suffered from serious dementia. If the evidence supports such a finding, then the jury was authorized to return a verdict holding that she lacked the requisite testamentary capacity.

NOTES

1.   Why is the threshold for testamentary capacity so low? Executing a contract, for example, requires a higher level of capacity. The only legally binding agreement that requires a lower level of capacity than executing a will is marriage. Do these different levels of capacity make sense? In a later chapter, we will discuss non-testamentary instruments like trusts and POD designations. When we do so, we will return to the issue of levels of capacity and see that they are not consistent for all testamentary transfers. What is the connection between the lower levels of capacity required for testation and marriage and our view of the importance of the choices underlying those two institutions?

2.   In Chapter 3, we discussed the role of an attorney faced with a client whose capacity may be called into question and quoted an ACTEC commentary advising as follows:

> The lawyer generally should not prepare a will, trust agreement or other dispositive instrument for a client who the lawyer reasonably believes lacks the requisite capacity. On the other hand, because of the importance of testamentary freedom, the lawyer may properly assist clients whose testamentary capacity appears to be borderline. In any such case the lawyer should take *steps* to preserve evidence regarding the client's testamentary capacity.

ACTEC COMMENT. ON MODEL RULES OF PRO. CONDUCT 132 (4th ed. 2006) (emphasis added). What steps might those be?

3.   Keeping in mind that burden of proof can make or break a case, what should the burden of proof be in wills cases where capacity is at issue? Should the proponent or the contestant start out with the burden of proof? Your answer probably depends on what you worry about more: invalid wills being admitted

to probate, or valid wills being denied probate, which would result in the testator's estate passing under the intestacy statutes.

4. Testamentary capacity has both an age requirement and a mental capacity requirement. A person must be 18 to execute a valid will. Why? Minors can own property (property can be held in trust for them, for example), so does this age requirement make sense? Although it seems intuitively appealing, see Marc Glover, *Rethinking the Testamentary Capacity of Minors*, 79 MINN. L. REV. 69 (2014) (arguing that minors should be deemed to have testamentary capacity). Note that emancipated minors—children whom a court has decreed free from parental control and no longer the financial responsibility of their parents—can execute valid wills even if they are under 18.

5. How does mental health affect testamentary capacity? What about powerful psychotropic medication or extreme use of alcohol or drugs? Can someone who commits suicide have testamentary capacity, or is such a person per se lacking capacity? *See, e.g., Estate of Richard Doe*, 10 CONN. PROB. L.J. 212 (1995).

Britney Spears has become the center of controversy over her judicial attempts to undo her conservatorship. The #FreeBritney movement supports her. Britney Spears performing on the National Mall, 2003.

6. As we have seen, the capacity required for wills is very low: even someone with dementia who has "lucid moments" can execute a valid will. What about someone a court has put into a **conservatorship**? The fact of a conservatorship alone is not indication that the conservatee lacks testamentary capacity, *see Smith v. Osborn (In re Estate of Anderson)*, 671 P.2d 165 (Utah 1983), especially given how long some conservatorships may last. Sometimes judges issue protective orders based on predictions about a conservatee's testamentary capacity in the future. *See* Ralph C. Brashier, *Conservatorships, Capacity, and Crystal Balls*, 87 TEMP. L. REV. 1, 46 (2014). Does this type of order seem problematic?

7. Notions of testamentary capacity have changed over time. Historically, a married woman lacked testamentary capacity under the common law because whatever she owned became the property of her husband. And of course,

enslaved people had no legal capacity to make wills or contracts of any kind—but they could be given away as property in wills: the decedent in *Sartor*, discussed in the Assessments in Part B, listed in the property he left to his wife "twelve negroes." For a long time, wills leaving a decedent's estate to a same sex-partner were challenged—successfully—on the grounds of capacity. Does this suggest that capacity is defined to some extent by the social norms/biases of the time? The role of social norms in validating wills is something to think about in the next chapter on will challenges: are will challenges more likely to succeed if the will subverts those norms?

8.   What is the difference between eccentricity and incapacity? The line between these two categories shifts according to social and cultural norms: as we will see in Chapter 6 when we discuss will contests, a court invalidated the will of a woman who left her estate to an organization that worked for women's rights on the ground that the testator must have been mentally deranged to make such a disposition.

9.   How should we factor drug and alcohol use into capacity assessment? The painter Thomas Kinkade whose estate totaled sixty-six million dollars at death wrote two purported holographic wills leaving ten million dollars and some property to his girlfriend, despite having a formally executed will leaving his assets to his estranged wife. A handwriting expert testified that the notes were either written by someone with Parkinson's Disease (which there is no evidence that Kinkade had) or someone who was "three sheets to the wind." Danielle and Andy Mayoras, *Did Artist Thomas Kinkade Change His Will While Drunk?* Forbes, Jul 9, 2012.

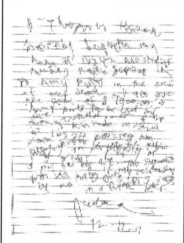

The artist, Thomas Kinkade, wrote a holographic will in December, 2011, 4 months before his death from an accidental overdose.

ASSESSMENTS

1.   You are preparing for a meeting with a new client who, you have learned, has "borderline" capacity, per the definition in the ACTEC commentary above. Review the client intake questionnaire in the Appendix to prepare for your meeting. Then outline your plan for assessing the client's family situation, assets, and natural objects of the client's bounty.

2.   Imagine now that you have drafted the will for the client described above and are preparing to have the client execute the will. Write a memo to your supervisor outlining the steps you plan to take to preserve the evidence that the client had capacity at the time the client executed the will. Bear in mind that this memorialization of capacity may be used as evidence in a future will contest.

D. Will Execution and Formalities

Assuming a testator has testamentary intent and capacity, the document that is being offered for probate also must comply with various formality requirements. The most common are that the will must be in writing, signed, and attested by two or more disinterested individuals who witness the testator sign the document as his or her will in the presence of the testator and the presence of each other.

These requirements have a long historical pedigree. The Statute of Frauds, adopted in England in 1677, required that any will disposing of real property be in writing and signed by the testator in the presence of three witnesses. A little over two centuries later, in 1837, the English Parliament enacted the Wills Act, which required similar formalities for all wills, whether they were disposing of real or personal property. The modern rules are not all that different, although new technologies are starting to test the limits of these rules.

1.   Will Formalities and the UPC

The UPC prescribes the following formalities for wills:

UPC § 2–502 Execution; Witnessed or Notarized Wills

(a)   [Witnessed or Notarized Wills.] Except as otherwise provided in subsection (b) and in Sections 2–503 [on substantial compliance], 2–506 [on wills executed in other jurisdictions], and 2–513 [on tangible personal property devised via separate writing], a will must be:

(1)   in writing;

(2)   signed by the testator or in the testator's name by some other individual in the testator's conscious presence and by the testator's direction; and

(3)   either:

(A)   signed by at least two individuals, each of whom signed within a reasonable time after the individual witnessed either the signing of the will as described in paragraph (2) or the testator's acknowledgment of that signature or acknowledgement of the will; or

(B) acknowledged by the testator before a notary public or other individual authorized by law to take acknowledgements.

———————

The following sections break down these elements.

a. *In Writing*

Generally, a "writing" means any form of writing, whether by hand or machine. The following forms of writing have been found to satisfy the writing requirement:

- A will "written" on a Samsung Galaxy (*In re Estate of Javier Castro*, No. 2013ES00140 (Lorain Cnty. Ohio Ct. Com. Pl. June 19, 2013))

- A will scratched with a nail on the fender of a tractor (*In re Harris Estate* (13 July 1948), Kerrobert, SK 1902 (Surr. Ct.))

- A will written on a 14"x14" piece of wood, shown below

This is the will of Marilyn Rhodeback, who not only drafted her will on the piece of wood; over time, she amended it, dated it, and had her sisters sign it.

Marilyn died on April 7 in Johnstown, Ohio, and the will was probated at the Licking County Courthouse. The court found it to be a valid holographic will. All wills must be kept on file in the courthouse, but the wooden "document" won't fit in the regular file drawers. So, the courthouse made a copy of the will for the file and is keeping the original in the vault.[1]

The holographic will of Marilyn Rhodeback, drafted on a piece of wood.

———————

[1]   https://curtissesq.typepad.com/matthew_curtiss_esq/2010/09/johnstown-womans-will-recorded-on-wood-newarkadvocatecom-the-newark-advocate.html.

b. *Signed by the Testator*

The signature requirement is intended to provide evidence of finality, distinguishing a will from mere notes or a draft. In other words, it helps confirm testamentary intent. A testator need not sign with her legal name, however, if most people know the testator by some other name, such as a nickname. Signing a will as "Mother" or "Father" may be valid, for example, as it was in the *Kimmel* case that appears in the Assessments in Part B. The testator may even sign with any kind of cross or notation indicating a signature as long as the mark is made by the testator. *See In re Estate of McCabe*, 274 Cal. Rptr. 43 (App. 1990) (testator's X sufficed); *Taylor v. Holt*, 134 S.W. 3d 830 (Tenn. App. 2003) (typewritten signature).

> **Practice Note:** Estate planning attorneys usually have a testator sign (or initial) every page of the will, in addition to the last. That way, it is easy to tell that all the pages are intended to be part of a single document. Other ways to tell include sewing the pages together and using a formal binding. We will discuss this topic of "integration" in Chapter 7.

Notice that the testator may also direct someone else to sign for her if she is physically incapable of signing. This must be done in the testator's "**conscious presence**." The UPC adopts the "conscious presence" test instead of the traditional "**line-of-sight**" test for proxy signing, and it eliminates the need for witnesses to sign in the testator's presence at all. But note that the traditional "line-of-sight" test still the law in some jurisdictions, like the one in the *Stevens v. Casdorph* case below, and many jurisdictions still require the witnesses to sign in the presence of the testator.

What does "conscious presence" mean? Basically, it means that the testator is aware of the act of signing, even if the person who is signing is not visible at that very moment the signing is performed. One case has explained that the test is satisfied when the witnesses "are so near at hand that they are within the range of any of [the testator's] senses, so that he knows what is going on." *In re Demaris' Estate*, 110 P.2d 571, 585 (Or. 1941). A witness signing in a room adjacent to the one the testator is in has been held valid. *In re Estate of Politowicz*, 304 A.2d 569, 571–72 (N.J. Super. Ct. App. Div. 1973). Under either the conscious presence or line-of-sight test, can a witness sign while on the phone with the testator? *See Kirkeby v. Covenant House*, 970 P.2d 241 (Or. Ct. App. 1998).

What challenges will technology pose for these requirements? Consider, for example, an execution ceremony where the testator and witnesses are connected via videophone or Zoom? This would seem to pass the "line-of-sight" test. Does it fail the "conscious presence" test? What consideration, if any, should be given to physical proximity to the testator and the witnesses' awareness of the physical surroundings of the testator?

c. Acknowledgement

Notice that the UPC does not require the witnesses to witness the testator actually sign the will; they may also witness the testator either acknowledge the will or acknowledge the signature on it. So, what are the witnesses actually witnessing—that is, what are they attesting *to*? They don't read the will or know what it says. Even if the witnesses don't know the testator, they are not required to see any identification. All that the witnesses are attesting to is the fact that the testator has told them that the will is hers.

If all they attest to is seeing the testator sign the will, acknowledge the signature on the will, or just acknowledge the will, how do they know the will represents the testator's true intent? How do they know the signed will is the will the testator thinks it is?

A witness must be competent to testify about the will's execution. At common law, an **interested witness** was not competent to testify. An interested witness is an individual who is identified as a beneficiary or nominated to serve as a fiduciary in the terms of the purported will. Because the witness has an interest in the will, the witnesses has a stake in the outcome of the proceedings determining the validity of that will. Thus, the witness's testimony may not be impartial and independent. Some states have continued to require that witnesses be disinterested or have placed significant limitations on the use of interested witnesses. *E.g.*, N.Y. E.P.T.L. § 3–3.2. Other states have removed the requirement that witnesses be disinterested. UPC § 505(b), for example, provides as follows: "The signing of a will by an interested witness does not invalidate the will or any provision of it." Consider why the UPC and some states would remove the requirement that a witness must be disinterested. Who benefits from the removal of this formal requirement?

Even if the state requires or encourages the use of disinterested witnesses, an interested witness may still be able to receive at least a portion of the testamentary gift or accept the nomination. An interested witness may still receive the full testamentary gift or accept the nomination if the individual is a **supernumerary witness**. States require two witnesses be able to testify about the will execution. A supernumerary witness is thus a third (or even fourth!) individual who signed as an attesting witness but is not needed to testify about the will execution. An interested may also receive all or a portion of the testamentary gift if the state has a **purging statute**. A purging statute would remove or "purge" the witness of the interest that he or she would otherwise receive under the terms of the purported will. If the interested witness loses his or her interest (that is the testamentary gift), the witness no longer has an interest in the purported will and can thus testify impartially to the events of the will execution. Some purging statutes remove only a part of the testamentary gift. These statutes purge what is referred to as the interested witness's "extra benefit." The extra benefit refers to a testamentary gift in excess of what the interested witness would have received if the decedent had died intestate. *E.g.*, N.Y. E.P.T.L. § 3–3.2(3). The interested witness thus can receive up to his or her intestate share and still testify about the will's execution.

> **Practice Note:** Even if the state does not require witnesses to be disinterested, the best practice is to avoid having interested witnesses. The use of an interested witness may be a "suspicious circumstances" for purposes of an undue influence challenge or support a claim of fraud. Having disinterested witness can be one way to minimize the likelihood of a successful will contest.

Notice that such a statutory formulation would prevent the interested witness who is not an intestate heir from receiving any testamentary gift. What competing policy considerations is such a statute attempting to balance?

2.   Why Have Formalities?

Will formalities derive from and are justified by the unique circumstances surrounding will executions. They serve several functions:

- Because many testators are elderly or infirm, formalities help counter a testator's potential vulnerability by serving a **protective function**: during the ceremony, the testator is asked whether she knows she is signing her will

- Formalities also serve a **cautionary or ritual function**, impressing upon a testator the seriousness of the occasion and that her actions and statements have important consequences

- Moreover, the primary and best witness—the testator—is necessarily absent when the will takes effect; formalities therefore serve an **evidentiary function** by creating a record of the free will and intent of the testator to which witnesses can testify

- Finally, these formalities serve a **channeling function**; by putting the testator's wishes into standardized forms and testamentary language which are immediately recognizable and understandable to professionals

An excellent and informative article on the purposes of formalities is Ashbel G. Gulliver & Catherine J. Tilson, *Classification of Gratuitous Transfers*, 51 YALE L.J. 1 (1941).

What are the pros and cons of requiring strict formalities for a will to be valid? As discussed above, the formalities may provide protections for the testator and confirm the testator's intent. But what about people who can't afford, or don't get, legal assistance and therefore fail to follow these rules? The people in that position are statistically likely to be lower income and members of minority groups. While about 60 percent of the population overall dies intestate, over 70 percent of Black Americans do. Does requiring compliance with the formalities mean denying probate to wills just because the testator could not afford a lawyer? On the other hand, how much can the law loosen up the formalities without risking fraud?

In the following case, the testator was trying to follow the rules. Nonetheless, the court denied probate. What do you think of the court's reasons? What does the reasoning indicate about the roles of witnesses in will execution? Do you prefer the reasoning of the majority or the dissent? This case falls into the category of "Don't let this Happen to You—Or Your Client!"

Stevens v. Casdorph

508 S.E.2d 610 (W. Va. 1998)

PER CURIUM.

The plaintiffs below and appellants herein Janet Sue Lanham Stevens, Peggy Lanham Salisbury, Betty Jean Bayes, and Patricia Miller Moyers (hereinafter collectively referred to as the "Stevenses") appeal a summary judgment ruling for the defendants by the Circuit Court of Kanawha County. The Stevenses instituted this action against Patricia Eileen Casdorph and Paul Douglas Casdorph, individually and as executor of the estate of Homer Haskell Miller, defendants below and appellees herein (hereinafter referred to as "Casdorphs"), for the purpose of challenging the will of Homer Haskell Miller. The circuit court granted the Casdorphs' cross-motion for summary judgment. On appeal, this Court is asked to reverse the trial court's ruling. Following a review of the parties' arguments, the record, and the pertinent authorities, we reverse the decision of the Circuit Court of Kanawha County.

FACTUAL BACKGROUND

On May 28, 1996, the Casdorphs took Mr. Homer Haskell Miller to Shawnee Bank in Dunbar, West Virginia, so that he could execute his will. Once at the bank, Mr. Miller asked Debra Pauley, a bank employee and public notary, to witness the execution of his will. After Mr. Miller signed the will, Ms. Pauley took the will to two other bank employees, Judith Waldron and Reba McGinn, for the purpose of having each of them sign the will as witnesses. Both Ms. Waldron and Ms. McGinn signed the will. However, Ms. Waldron and Ms. McGinn testified during their depositions that they did not actually see Mr. Miller place his signature on the will. Further, it is undisputed that Mr. Miller did not accompany Ms. Pauley to the separate work areas of Ms. Waldron and Ms. McGinn.

Mr. Miller died on July 28, 1996. The last will and testament of Mr. Miller, which named Mr. Paul Casdorph as executor, left the bulk of his estate to the Casdorphs. The Stevenses, nieces of Mr. Miller, filed the instant action to set aside the will. The Stevenses asserted in their complaint that Mr. Miller's will was not executed according to the requirements set forth in W. Va. Code § 41–1–3 (1995). After some discovery, all parties moved for summary judgment. The circuit court denied the Stevenses' motion for summary judgment, but granted the Casdorphs' cross motion for summary judgment. From this ruling, the Stevenses appeal to this Court.

DISCUSSION

The Stevenses' contention is simple. They argue that all evidence indicates that Mr. Miller's will was not properly executed. Therefore, the will should be voided. The procedural requirements at issue are contained in W. Va. Code § 41–1–3 (1997). The statute reads:

> No will shall be valid unless it be in writing and signed by the testator, or by some other person in his presence and by his direction, in such manner as to make it manifest that the name is intended as a signature; and moreover, unless it be wholly in the handwriting of the testator, *the signature shall be made or the will acknowledged by him in the presence of at least two competent witnesses, present at the same time; and such witnesses shall subscribe the will in the presence of the testator, and of each other,* but no form of attestation shall be necessary. (Emphasis added.)

The relevant requirements of the above statute call for a testator to sign his/her will or acknowledge such will in the presence of at least two witnesses at the same time, and such witnesses must sign the will in the presence of the testator and each other. In the instant proceeding the Stevenses assert, and the evidence supports, that Ms. McGinn and Ms. Waldron did not actually witness Mr. Miller signing his will. Mr. Miller made no acknowledgment of his signature on the will to either Ms. McGinn or Ms. Waldron. Likewise, Mr. Miller did not observe Ms. McGinn and Ms. Waldron sign his will as witnesses. Additionally, neither Ms. McGinn nor Ms. Waldron acknowledged to Mr. Miller that their signatures were on the will. It is also undisputed that Ms. McGinn and Ms. Waldron did not actually witness each other sign the will, nor did they acknowledge to each other that they had signed Mr. Miller's will. Despite the evidentiary lack of compliance with W. Va. Code § 41–1–3, the Casdorphs argue that there was substantial compliance with the statute's requirements, insofar as everyone involved with the will knew what was occurring. The trial court found that there was substantial compliance with the statute because everyone knew why Mr. Miller was at the bank. The trial court further concluded there was no evidence of fraud, coercion or undue influence. Based upon the foregoing, the trial court concluded that the will should not be voided even though the technical aspects of W. Va. Code § 41–1–3 were not followed.

Our analysis begins by noting that "[t]he law favors testacy over intestacy." However, testamentary intent and a written instrument, executed in the manner provided by W. Va. Code § 41–1–3, existing concurrently, are essential to the creation of a valid will." Mere intent by a testator to execute a written will is insufficient. The actual execution of a written will must also comply with the dictates of W. Va. Code § 41–1–3. The Casdorphs seek to have this Court establish an exception to the technical requirements of the statute. In *Wade v. Wade*, 195 S.E. 339 (W. Va. 1938), this Court permitted a narrow exception to the stringent requirements of the W. Va. Code § 41–1–3. This narrow exception is embodied in syllabus point 1 of *Wade*:

> Where a testator acknowledges a will and his signature thereto in the presence of two competent witnesses, one of whom then subscribes his name, the other or first witness, having already subscribed the will in the presence of the testator but out of the presence of the second witness, may acknowledge his signature in the presence of the testator and the second witness, and such acknowledgment, if there be no indicia of fraud or misunderstanding in the proceeding, will be deemed a signing by the first witness within the requirement of Code,

41–1–3, that the witnesses must subscribe their names in the presence of the testator and of each other.

Wade stands for the proposition that if a witness acknowledges his/her signature on a will in the physical presence of the other subscribing witness and the testator, then the will is properly witnessed within the terms of W. Va. Code § 41–1–3. In this case, none of the parties signed or acknowledged their signatures in the presence of each other. This case meets neither the narrow exception of Wade nor the specific provisions of W. Va. Code § 41–1–3.

CONCLUSION

In view of the foregoing, we grant the relief sought in this appeal and reverse the circuit court's order granting the Casdorphs' cross-motion for summary judgment.

WORKMAN, J., *dissenting*:

The majority once more takes a very technocratic approach to the law, slavishly worshiping form over substance. In so doing, they not only create a harsh and inequitable result wholly contrary to the indisputable intent of Mr. Homer Haskell Miller, but also a rule of law that is against the spirit and intent of our whole body of law relating to the making of wills.

There is absolutely no claim of incapacity or fraud or undue influence, nor any allegation by any party that Mr. Miller did not consciously, intentionally, and with full legal capacity convey his property as specified in his will. The challenge to the will is based solely upon the allegation that Mr. Miller did not comply with the requirement of West Virginia Code 41–1–31 that the signature shall be made or the will acknowledged by the testator in the presence of at least two competent witnesses, present at the same time. The lower court, in its very thorough findings of fact, indicated that Mr. Miller had been transported to the bank by his nephew Mr. Casdorph and the nephew's wife. Mr. Miller, disabled and confined to a wheelchair, was a shareholder in the Shawnee Bank in Dunbar, West Virginia, with whom all those present were personally familiar. When Mr. Miller executed his will in the bank lobby, the typed will was placed on Ms. Pauley's desk, and Mr. Miller instructed Ms. Pauley that he wished to have his will signed, witnessed, and acknowledged. After Mr. Miller's signature had been placed upon the will with Ms. Pauley watching, Ms. Pauley walked the will over to the tellers' area in the same small lobby of the bank. Ms. Pauley explained that Mr. Miller wanted Ms. Waldron to sign the will as a witness. The same process was used to obtain the signature of Ms. McGinn. Sitting in his wheelchair, Mr. Miller did not move from Ms. Pauley's desk during the process of obtaining the witness signatures. The lower court concluded that the will was valid and that Ms. Waldron and Ms. McGinn signed and acknowledged the will "in the presence" of Mr. Miller.

In *Wade*, we addressed the validity of a will challenged for such technicalities and observed that "a narrow, rigid construction of the statute should not be allowed to stand in the way of right and justice, or be permitted to defeat a testator's disposition of his property." 195 S.E. at 340–341. We upheld the validity of the challenged will in *Wade*, noting that "each case must rest on its own facts and circumstances to which the court must look to determine whether there was a subscribing by the witnesses in the presence of the testator; that substantial compliance with the statute is all that is required." *Id.* at 340. A contrary result, we emphasized, "would be based on illiberal and inflexible construction of the statute, giving preeminence to letter and not to spirit, and resulting in the thwarting of the intentions of testators even under circumstances where no possibility of fraud or impropriety exists." *Id.* at 341.

The majority's conclusion is precisely what was envisioned and forewarned in 1938 by the drafters of the *Wade* opinion: illiberal and inflexible construction, giving preeminence to the letter of the law and ignoring the spirit of the entire body of testamentary law, resulting in the thwarting of Mr. Miller's unequivocal wishes.

The majority strains the logical definition of "in the presence" as used in the operative statute. The legal concept of "presence" in this context encompasses far more than simply watching the signing of the will, which is the technical, narrow interpretation of the word apparently relied upon by the majority. Where the attestation of the will by the witnesses occurred within the same room as the testator, there is, at the very minimum, prima facie evidence that the attestation occurred within the "presence" of the testator.

The majority embraces the line of least resistance. The easy, most convenient answer is to say that the formal, technical requirements have not been met and that the will is therefore invalid. End of inquiry. Yet that result is patently absurd. That manner of statutory application is inconsistent with the underlying purposes of the statute. Where a statute is enacted to protect and sanctify the execution of a will to prevent substitution or fraud, this Court's application of that statute should further such underlying policy, not impede it. When, in our efforts to strictly apply legislative language, we abandon common sense and reason in favor of technicalities, we are the ones committing the injustice.

NOTES

1.   Does *Casdorph* stand for the proposition that the attorney should always supervise the execution ceremony? Would you feel it necessary to do so for your clients? Under what circumstances may you decide that you do not need to supervise the execution ceremony?

2.   The "writing" requirement has been challenged by some unique factual circumstances that question what it means to put intent into a fixed form and have it witnessed. *See In re Estate of Reed*, 672 P.2d 829 (Wyo. 1983) (video is not a writing); *see also* Gerry W. Beyer & Claire G. Hargrove, *Digital Wills: Has the Time Come for Wills to Join the Digital Revolution?*, 33 OHIO N.U. L. REV. 865 (2007); Joseph Karl Grant, *Shattering and Moving Beyond the Gutenberg Paradigm: The Dawn of the Electronic Will*, 42 U. MICH. J.L. REFORM 105 (2008). We discuss electronic wills later in the chapter.

3.   Many will defects involve how the execution ceremony is conducted and, especially, the "presence" of witnesses. As *Stevens* makes clear, the traditional rule is that the testator and witnesses must be together for a will to be valid. Some courts have recognized a "line of vision" test that asks whether the testator was capable of seeing the witnesses sign. *See McCormick v. Jeffers*, 281 S.E. 2d 666 (Ga. 2006). What is the UPC's requirement for witnesses? Is anything lost by allowing witnesses to sign later? Must they still see the testator sign or acknowledge her signature?

4.   The UPC also recognizes as valid wills that are not witnessed but are notarized. UPC § 2–502(a)(3)(B) ("acknowledged by the testator before a notary public or other individual authorized by law to take acknowledgements"). Should every will be signed by a notary? Very few states have adopted this notary provision. Why might they be reluctant to do so? One issue with recognizing notarized wills is that immigrants from civil law countries may understand the role and abilities of the notary very differently. Notaries in civil law countries are legally trained and give advice about many legal issues, including estate planning; they must give the parties legal advice regarding the implications of the transaction to be notarized. Might this difference cause a person with a civil law background to think she had a valid American will when she did not? For discussion of notarized wills, see Anne-Marie Rhodes, *Notarized Wills*, 27 QUINNIPIAC PROB. L.J. 419 (2014).

5.   As many scholars have critiqued formalism in wills as have defended it, although the movement against strict formalism keeps gaining ground. One of the first critics was John Langbein, *Substantial Compliance with the Wills Act*, 88

HARV. L. REV. 489, 489 (1975), arguing that a "finding of a formal defect should lead not to automatic invalidity, but to a further inquiry: does the noncomplying document express the decedent's testamentary intent, and does its form sufficiently approximate Wills Act formality to enable the court to conclude that it serves the purposes of the Wills Act?" Such critiques led to the relaxation of some formalities, as we will discuss in the next section. One frequent charge is that requiring strict compliance with formalities disadvantages people who lack access to legal services. Peter T. Wendel, *Wills Act Compliance and the Harmless Error Approach: Flawed Narrative Equals Flawed Analysis?*, 95 OR. L. REV. 337 (2017). In the end, it may come down to whether you worry more about valid wills being denied probate or invalid wills being probated. Which do you think is the greater concern?

ASSESSMENTS

1.   You receive an email from a long-time client who is leaving for a vacation at the end of the week. The client has executed two wills under your supervision over the past ten years. In the email, your client tells you that she wants to execute the new will that you drafted for her last week before she leaves for vacation but does not have the time to come into your office. She requests that you email the document to her so she can print it out and sign it. Draft a reply. Make sure to explain your response and to give any specific instructions that may be necessary. You also should indicate if your firm has any policy in place to address this type of request.

2.   The COVID-19 pandemic is causing your state legislature to reconsider its will and execution formalities given the difficulties of in-person meetings. Draft a model statute to cover the writing requirement and other will formalities that will govern during the pandemic. Then write a brief commentary that explains your provisions, addresses the need for these provisions and the risks of allowing socially distant will executions, and describes any limitations that you have put in place to address those risks. For reference, you might wish to consult Nevada's video will statute, NEV. REV. STAT. § 133.085.

3.   You have been asked to teach a Continuing Legal Education class on will execution ceremonies for new practitioners. Design materials that include the design and layout of the room, the roles of the participants, where you would seat everyone, what is on the table, what you would say, what the testator would say, and how you would organize the various steps of the attestation.

3.   Self-Proving Affidavits

In addition to the witnesses' signatures on the will itself, many states also offer a further level of attestation called a "Self-Proving Affidavit." Below is the Minnesota statutory version:

MINNESOTA SELF-PROVING AFFIDAVIT

I, _____, the Testator, sign my name to this instrument this _____ day of _____, 20_____, and being first duly sworn, do hereby declare to the undersigned authority that I sign and execute this instrument as my Will and that I sign it willingly (or willingly direct another to sign for me), that I execute it as my free and voluntary act for the purposes therein expressed, and that I am 18 years of age or older, of sound mind, and under no constraint or undue influence.

Testator's Signature _____

We, _____ and _____, the witnesses, sign our names to this instrument, being first duly sworn, and do hereby declare to the undersigned authority that the Testator signs and executes this instrument as the Testator's Will and that the Testator signs it willingly (or willingly directs another to sign for the Testator), and that each of us, in the presence and hearing of the Testator, hereby signs this Will as witness to the Testator's signing, and that to the best of our knowledge the Testator is 18 years of age of older, of sound mind, and under no constraint or undue influence.

Witness's Signature _____

Witness's Signature _____

State of _____

County of _____

NOTARY ACKNOWLEDGMENT

Subscribed, sworn to, and acknowledged before me by _____, the Testator, and subscribed and sworn to before me by _____, and _____, witnesses, this _____ day of _____, 20_____.

Notary Signature _____

Official Capacity of Officer _____

ASSESSMENT

Read the Minnesota self-proving affidavit (above) and prepare a short memo describing what this affidavit adds to the standard witness attestation.

4.   Holographic Wills and Preprinted Forms

Some states allow for **holographic wills**, which are handwritten wills signed and dated by the testator. Historically, in England, holographic wills were valid with respect to both personal and real property until the time of the Statute of Frauds in 1677 and for the disposition of personal property until 1837. In the United States, these wills were allowed in frontier states where legal services were scarce but have become less common as access to formal will-making has become more common. Nevertheless, as the legal historian R.H. Helmholz has pointed out, the holographic will is no "merely historical curiosity" and that holographs "have had an inherent capacity for coming back to life even when reformers think they have killed it." *See* R.H. Helmholz, *The Origin of Holographic Wills in English Law*, 15 J. LEGAL HIST. 97 (1994). Holographic wills, time and again, prove useful in allowing testators to express their final wishes in extreme circumstances, when unexpected accidents occur, and in the context of military service. Moreover, holographs facilitate law's preference for testacy over intestacy.

Although the holographs we have seen so far, in cases like *Kuralt*, are completely handwritten, a proliferation of online will forms that people can fill in and print out have tested the limits of what constitutes a holographic will. Originally, holographic wills had to be entirely in the testator's handwriting. This so-called "first generation" of holographs gave way to a rule that allowed a holograph to include some typewritten portions so long as, if those portions were disregarded, the handwritten portions set forth the testator's wishes. As the *Gonzales* case below makes clear, however, even that rule does not work for preprinted forms. The online documents that are now so readily available are mostly printed, with the testator's handwriting filling in specific gifts and a signature. Technically, these wills require the same formalities—witnesses—as attested wills, but often people fail to recognize this requirement and do not get them witnessed. The result is invalid wills which people really intended to be valid and which express their intent. So, wills law has made provisions for such forms by allowing them (under the right conditions) to be probated as holographic wills, while still trying to protect the testator from fraud, duress, and undue influence.

The UPC provision for holographs, discussed in *Gonzales*, is an example of the most liberal approach, allowing the typewritten words to provide evidence of the testator's intent:

UPC § 2–502

(b) [Holographic Wills.] A will that does not comply with subsection (a) [will formalities] is valid as a holographic will, whether or not witnessed, if the signature and material portions of the document are in the testator's handwriting.

(c) [Extrinsic Evidence.] Intent that a document constitute the testator's will can be established by extrinsic evidence, including, for holographic wills, portions of the document that are not in the testator's handwriting.

Estate of Fermin A. Gonzales

855 A.2d 1146 (Me. 2004)

ALEXANDER, J.

Todd and Alison Gurney appeal from a judgment of the York County Probate Court (Nadeau, J.), finding that the will of Fermin Gonzalez was a valid holographic will. The Gurneys contend that material provisions of the will were not handwritten, and therefore it was not a valid holographic will. We affirm the Probate Court's judgment.

I.   CASE HISTORY

In August of 2001, Fermin Gonzalez visited his brother, Joseph, and Joseph's wife, Elizabeth. Gonzalez was planning to fly to Florida, and he wanted to prepare his will before he left. Gonzalez showed Elizabeth and Joseph two copies of a preprinted will form. On the first copy of the form, Gonzalez had handwritten his testamentary wishes. Elizabeth testified that he had already filled out the form by the time she saw it, but that she did see him sign the document. The document, with italics indicating handwriting, reads as follows:

> **BE IT KNOWN** that I, *Fermin Arlnaldo Gonzalez*, a resident of *Lot 5 35 Russell Rd. W. Newfield*, County of *York*, in the State of *Maine*, being of sound mind, do make and declare this to be my Last Will and Testament expressly revoking all my prior Wills and Codicils at any time made.

III. BEQUESTS

I direct that after payment of all my just debts my property be bequeathed in the manner following:

That the property on lot #5 AKA 35 Russell Rd. W. Newfield ME. the house, cabin and barn.

All the contents of my personal property including my 1993 Mercury Capri Convertible my 1971 Ford P.Up along with all jewelry gold I.D. braclet, [sic] stainless stell [sic] Rolex submariner all power tools including my 1999 white self prop. lawn mower/tractor. My horse a paint quarter horse Blossom become the property of my three daughters, Kerry Ann Gonzalez, Tara Maureen Gonzalez Grenon Kristin Julia Gonzalez. Each holding an equal right + share and should they decide to sell all of the above that 10,000 (Ten Thousand of the proceeds after the sale of all of the above be given to my former wife Maureen T. Gonzalez Philp and 10,000 Ten Thousand Dollars be given to my mother Sol Amalia Gonzalez

I also wish that should my daughters decide to sell, liquidate all of the aforementioned that my brothers Joseph Ramon and Walter be given the first rights to purchase any or all of property. Including personal items. Also order that my dog "Magnolia" a Jack Russell Terrier female be given to Mrs. Elizabeth M. Vail of 7 Winfield Court N.H. along with $5,000 dollars for the care of said animal. I also wish that Thomas Francis Lynch Jr. of 68 Perry St. E. Weymouth MA. see to my proper dress and grooming in my Marine Corps dress blue uniform w/saber upon preparation for my wake and funeral. It is also my wish that the following persons be excluded from any and all access to my funeral arrangement. They are Maureen T. Philp, my former wife, Colleen T. Cunningham, David P. Murphy, Janet Francis Hickey and James F. Foley Sr.

This document was signed by Gonzalez, but not by any witnesses. Additionally, several phone numbers and other notes appear to be written in the margins of the document.

Gonzalez also presented Elizabeth and Joseph with a blank copy of the form. Elizabeth testified that Gonzalez was planning to copy the information neatly onto the blank form, and that he asked Elizabeth, Joseph, and his mother to sign the blank form as witnesses. They signed the blank document.

Gonzalez became ill suddenly and died on August 22, 2001. Three of Gonzalez's daughters, Kerry Gonzalez, Tara Gonzalez Grenon, and Kristin Gonzalez petitioned to probate the will. Todd and Alison Gurney, who are also Gonzalez's children, moved for a summary judgment, arguing that the will was not a valid holographic will.

After trial, the Probate Court denied the motion, and found that the will was a valid holographic will. The court reasoned that:

> [T]he hand written language of the decedent independently evidences his intent, when he completed his will, to include the printed language on the form he utilized to create his will, so as to give the will greater clarity. . . . Although the preponderance of the evidence confirms that the bare handwritings contained on the will at least marginally created a testamentary instrument, the decedent's insertion of the hand-written material or material provisions in the blank spaces implicitly adopted and incorporated the printed text on the form and converted the form into a more clear will. It would appear illogical to conclude that the handwritings did not fulfill that apparent purpose. The circumstantial evidence presented at trial, corroborates that the decedent's material handwriting, supported by his very signature which he would not likely have affixed if he had believed there was no immediate need to do so, evidenced that the printed portions of the document, together with his handwriting, constituted his will.

II. DISCUSSION

The document that Gonzalez signed does not qualify as a will under 18–A M.R.S.A. § 2–502 (1998), because it was not signed by any witnesses. Therefore, in order to be allowed or admitted to probate, the document must qualify as a holographic will under 18–A M.R.S.A. § 2–503 (1998). A holographic will is one where "the signature and the material provisions are in the handwriting of the testator." 18–A M.R.S.A. § 2–503. The comment from the Uniform Probate Code helps to explain the meaning of the statutory language:

> By requiring only the "material provisions" to be in the testator's handwriting (rather than requiring, as some existing statutes do, that the will be "entirely" in the testator's handwriting) a holograph may be valid even though immaterial parts such as date or introductory wording be printed or stamped. A valid holograph might even be executed on some printed will forms if the printed portion could be eliminated and the handwritten portion could evidence the testator's will.

Unif. Probate Code § 2–503 comment (1998).

The Gurneys argue that Gonzalez did not execute a valid holographic will because a material provision of the will-evidence of testamentary intent-appears in the preprinted portion of the document and was not handwritten. They maintain that the handwritten words are a list of what Gonzalez wanted to do with his property, but the handwritten words do not indicate that the conveyances were testamentary in nature.

We have not yet addressed the impact that preprinted will forms have on holographic wills. Most jurisdictions have dealt with this issue in one of two ways.

Some courts have looked to the preprinted language in order to determine the context of the handwritten words. In *Estate of Muder*, 765 P.2d 997, 1000 (Ariz. 1988), the Supreme Court of Arizona held that a person who handwrote his wishes on a preprinted will form had effectuated a valid holographic will because the person's testamentary intent was clear. The court stated:

> We hold that a testator who uses a preprinted form, and in his own handwriting fills in the blanks by designating his beneficiaries and apportioning his estate among them and signs it, has created a valid holographic will. Such handwritten provisions may draw testamentary context from both the printed and the handwritten language on the form. We see no need to ignore the preprinted words when the testator clearly did not, and the statute does not require us to do so.

Other courts have ignored all of the preprinted words, and determined whether the handwritten words, taken alone, fulfill the requirements of a holographic will.

We agree with the Supreme Court of Arizona and hold that printed portions of a will form can be incorporated into a holographic will where the trial court finds a testamentary intent, considering all of the evidence in the case. The Probate Court, after reviewing the document and hearing the evidence, explicitly found such an incorporation into the holographic will in this case: "[T]he hand-written material . . . implicitly adopted and incorporated the printed text on the form and converted the form into a more clear will."

The Uniform Probate Code comment states that "a holograph may be valid even though immaterial parts such as date or introductory wording be printed or stamped." Unif. Probate Code § 2–503 comment (1998). The printed words in Gonzalez's will: "BE IT KNOWN that I ___, a resident of ___, County of ___, in the State of _____, being of sound mind, do make and declare this to be my Last Will and Testament expressly revoking all my prior Wills and Codicils at any time made" and "I direct that after payment of all my just debts my property be bequeathed in the manner following" are introductory phrases and may be preprinted. When filled in by the testator's handwriting, as here, they can become a valid statement of testamentary intent in a holographic will.

We have long subscribed to the principle "that the right of testamentary disposition is considered to be of great importance." . . . This principle has resulted in a "well-known policy of the courts to uphold wills and not destroy them." This policy must particularly hold true in the realm of holographic wills.

Because we read 18–A M.R.S.A. § 2–503 and its comments in light of this policy, Gonzalez's handwritten words may be read in the context of the preprinted words, and the Probate Court could properly find that the document is a valid holographic will.

The entry is: Judgment affirmed.

NOTES

1.   Holographic wills are often thought to be problematic. But just how problematic are they? Stephen Clowney set out to test whether holographic wills are more prone to errors that traditional wills. He surveyed wills probated in Pittsburgh, Pennsylvania, and found they were rarely the subject of will contests. *See* Stephen Clowney, *In Their Own Hand: An Analysis of Holographic Wills and Homemade Willmaking*, 43 REAL PROP. TR. & EST. L.J. 27 (2008). Clowney concluded that "an indispensable tool for testators who are either unwilling or unable to commission a traditional will. Homemade testaments provide a low-cost alternative to intestacy, improve the overall quantity of will-making, function as a safety-net for testators who fall suddenly ill, and rarely result in litigation." Should more states allow holographic wills? What is lost when no witnesses are part of the execution ceremony?

2.   Statistics show that the likelihood of a testator having a will is directly related to the testator's income level. Permitting the probate of holographic wills helps to make sure that a testator's wishes are implemented as opposed to the default rules of intestacy. *See* Bridget J. Crawford & Anthony C. Infanti, *A Critical Research Agenda for Wills, Trusts, and Estates*, 49 REAL PROP. TR. & EST. L.J. 317 (2014). Does enabling more people from lower brackets of wealth and income to die testate provide a means for addressing wealth equality? If so, how?

3.   It's one thing to have a formally valid will, but that doesn't mean that the instrument's language will convey the testator's intent in a way that those probating the will can understand it. As we will see in Chapter 8, lawyers use many terms of art and drafting conventions in preparing wills to make the testator's wishes comprehensible to everyone professionally involved in the

probate process. How much good does it do to accept holographic wills as a valid form of will when the legal services required for accurate drafting are still lacking?

5. Electronic or Recorded Wills

Given that people spend more time these days on their phones than they do in live interactions with other people, isn't it about time that it was possible to have a valid electronic will? Some legislatures, as well as the Uniform Law Commission, think so too. As of 2019, legislatures in Arizona, California, the District of Columbia, Florida, Indiana, New Hampshire, Texas, and Virginia have considered bills authorizing electronic execution of wills. Arizona, Indiana, and Florida have adopted electronic wills laws, and Nevada has revised its existing electronic wills statute.

The Uniform Electronic Wills Act reads as follows:

SECTION 5. EXECUTION OF ELECTRONIC WILL.

(a)   [An] electronic will must be:

(1)   a record that is readable as text at the time of signing under paragraph (2);

(2)   signed by:

(A)   the testator; or

(B)   another individual in the testator's name, in the testator's physical presence, and by the testator's direction; and

(3)   [either:

(A)] signed in the physical [or electronic] presence of the testator by at least two individuals[, each of whom is a resident of a state and physically located in a state at the time of signing and] within a reasonable time after witnessing:

[(A)] [(i)] the signing of the electronic will under paragraph (2); or

[(B)] [(ii)] the testator's acknowledgment of the signing of the electronic will under paragraph (2) or acknowledgement of the will[; or

   (B)   acknowledged by the testator before and in the physical [or electronic] presence of a notary public or other individual authorized by law to notarize records electronically].

(b)   Intent of a testator that the record under subsection (a)(1) be the testator's electronic will may be established by extrinsic evidence.

As you can see, the Act keeps the traditional formalities of writing, signature, and attestation but adapts them to the electronic form. Notice that it requires that the will exist in the electronic equivalent of text when it is electronically signed, thus precluding audio and video wills, unless they are transcribed into text prior to the testator's signature.

Utah adopted the Uniform Act in 2020, making it the first state to do so. But COVID-19 has prompted widespread emergency measures to allow people to execute wills while staying safe—and many practitioners have been ingenious about designing socially distanced execution ceremonies. Between March 26 and April 9, 2020, Connecticut, Illinois, Kansas, Michigan, New York, and Tennessee issued Executive Orders that temporarily allow people to witness wills by appearing with audio-video technology rather than in person. Colorado and North Dakota—which are the only jurisdictions that allow notaries to serve as substitutes for witnesses in attesting to wills—have authorized remote notarization. On April 10, the District of Columbia Mayor approved a bill that authorized both remote witnessing and electronic wills during periods in which the Mayor has declared a public health emergency.

NOTES

1.   We tend to think of electronic wills as expanding access and increasing convenience—but does the use of these technologies also leave out groups like the elderly who are often not as "tech savvy" as younger people? How does it affect those in low income or rural communities without internet access?

2.   A number of states considering electronic wills are also using electronic notaries public and software like DocuSign to help execute the wills and provide additional validation above and beyond the two witnesses. Are there concerns about these kinds of electronic platforms for notarization? What would you think about Blockchain Wills? Bridget Crawford writes that: "In conjunction with the E-Wills Act's embrace of new technologies, blockchain wills can provide evidence that the purposes of wills formalities are met, or that the decedent signed the document with the intention that it serve as her will. It is

no understatement to say that blockchain also has the potential to transform all of legal practice." *See* Bridget Crawford, *Blockchain Wills*, 95 IND. L.J. 735 (2020).

3. What concerns you most about electronic wills? The potential for fraud? Problems with storage? Issues around revocation? One scholar has noted that "dangers are lurking" in the world of electronic wills, including the deterioration of electronic records, the evanescence of these businesses (most of which are startups), and the risk of hacking. Adam J. Hirsch, *Technology Adrift: In Search of A Role for Electronic Wills*, 61 B.C. L. REV. 827, 862 (2020). Another scholar notes that disputes over e-wills are intensely time-consuming," and encourages states to consider the costs to the court systems and the parties involved before adopting electronic wills. David Horton, *Tomorrow's Inheritance: The Frontiers of Estate Planning Formalism*, 58 B.C. L. REV. 539, 575 (2017).

ASSESSMENT

Evaluate how the following fact pattern, which arose in a state that had not adopted the Uniform Electronic Wills Act, would have been decided under the Act:

> Shortly before his death by suicide, Duane Horton (a 21-year-old man) handwrote a journal entry stating that a document titled "Last Note" was on his phone. The journal entry provided instructions for accessing the note, and he left the journal and phone in his room. The Last Note included apologies and personal comments relating to his suicide as well as directions relating to his property. Mr. Horton typed his name at the end of the document.

In re Estate of Horton, 925 N.W. 2d 207 (Mich. 2018).

E. Loosening Formalities?

As you saw in some cases like *Stevens v. Casdorph*, strict compliance with the formalities may sometimes act to undermine testator intent and invalidate a will that accurately represented what the testator wanted. The doctrines of **"harmless error"** and **"substantial compliance"** both allow for the probate of wills that do not strictly meet the formality requirements but nonetheless comply enough to alleviate concerns about fraud, duress, undue influence and lack of capacity.

The substantial compliance doctrine allows a non-conforming will to be admitted to probate, notwithstanding certain defects in execution (such as having one witness instead of two) if there is clear and convincing evidence that the purposes of will formalities have been satisfied. The dissent in *Stevens* discusses this doctrine, although it has not gained wide adoption.

Harmless error, which has been codified in the UPC, allows a nonconforming document to be admitted to probate if there is clear and convincing evidence that the decedent intended the document to be his or her will.

UPC § 2–503 Harmless Error

Although a document or writing added upon a document was not executed in compliance with § 2–502, the document or writing is treated as if it had been executed in compliance with that section if the proponent of the document or writing establishes by clear and convincing evidence that the decedent intended the document or writing to constitute:

(1)   the decedent's will,

(2)   a partial or complete revocation of the will,

(3)   an addition to or an alteration of the will, or

(4)   a partial or complete revival of his [or her] formerly revoked will or of a formerly revoked portion of the will.

The aim of relaxing the rigor of strict compliance is to allow for the probate of wills that may be defective in execution but that carry no concern about fraud. The question is how much should formalities be relaxed—that is to say, what amount of compliance with the wills formalities is "just right"? The case below offers an example of how a court would apply Harmless Error. As you read it, consider all the ways that the court evaluated whether the document—a birthday card—was testamentary.

In the Matter of the Estate of Ronald Wiltfong

148 P.3d 465 (Col. Ct. App. 2006)

BERNARD, J.

In this formal testacy probate proceeding, Randall Rex (proponent), the proponent of a document alleged to be a will, appeals the trial court's order finding decedent, Ronald Wiltfong, died intestate. We reverse and remand for further proceedings.

I.   Background

The following facts are undisputed. Proponent and decedent were domestic partners for twenty years until decedent's death. They lived together and intermingled most of their finances.

On proponent's birthday in 2003, proponent and decedent celebrated with two friends. In the presence of the friends, decedent gave proponent a birthday card containing a typed letter decedent had signed. The letter expressed decedent's wish that if anything should ever happen to him, everything he owned should go to proponent. The letter also stated that proponent, their pets, and an aunt were his only family, and "everyone else is dead to me." Decedent told proponent and the friends the letter represented his wishes.

Decedent died from a heart attack the following year.

Proponent filed a petition to have the letter admitted to probate as decedent's will. Margaret Tovrea (contestant), the mother of decedent's three nephews who would be decedent's heirs if he died intestate, objected to the petition.

The trial court ruled the letter was not a will because it did not meet the requirements of § 15–11–503(2), C.R.S.2006, and therefore the nephews would take decedent's estate by intestate succession. This appeal followed.

Proponent contends the trial court erred in concluding decedent did not intend the letter to be his will. We conclude that further proceedings are necessary to resolve this question.

II.   General Principles

We apply the following general principles regarding testacy proceedings, execution of wills, holographic wills, standard of review, and burden of proof.

A.   Formal Testacy Proceedings

Formal testacy proceedings to determine whether a decedent left a valid will are governed by statute. Section 15–12–401, et seq., C.R.S.2006. In contested cases, proponents of a will have the burden of presenting prima facie evidence to show the will was duly executed. Once such evidence is presented, those contesting a will's validity have the burden of proving by a preponderance of the evidence lack of testamentary capacity, undue influence, fraud, or the like.

B.   Execution of Wills

The underlying purposes of the Colorado Probate Code (Code) are to simplify and clarify the law concerning the affairs of decedents; to discover and make effective the intent of decedents in distributing their property; and to promote a speedy and efficient system for settling estates of decedents and distributing their property to their successors. The Code is to be liberally construed and applied to promote these purposes. Section 15–10–102, C.R.S.2006.

As relevant here, § 15–11–502(1), C.R.S.2006, establishes three requirements for a will: (1) it must be in writing; (2) it must bear the testator's signature or be signed in the testator's name; and (3) it must also bear the signatures of at least two persons who witnessed either the testator's signature or the testator's acknowledgment of the signature. There is no need to publish the document as the testator's will or to have witnesses sign the document in the presence of the testator or the other witnesses. *In re Estate of Royal*, 826 P.2d, 1236 (Colo.1992).

Although these three formalities represent a reduction over time in the number of formalities surrounding the execution of wills, compare § 15–3–502, C.R.S.1963, with § 15–11–502(1), they "require strict adherence in order to prevent fraud because statutes governing execution are designed to safeguard and protect the decedent's estate." *Royal*, 826 P.2d at 1238.

C.   Holographic Wills

Section 15–11–502(2), C.R.S.2006, provides that handwritten wills may also be valid: "A will that does not comply with subsection (1) of this section is valid as a holographic will, whether or not witnessed, if the signature and material portions of the document are in the testator's handwriting."

Proof of a decedent's intent that a document serve as a holographic will can be established by extrinsic evidence, including parts of the document that are not in the decedent's handwriting. Section 15–11–502(3), C.R.S.2006. Holographic wills are viewed as valid even if "immaterial parts such as date or introductory wording are printed, typed, or stamped" or if printed will forms are used and the "material portions of the document are handwritten." Uniform Probate Code § 2–502 cmt. subsec. (b).

Here, the trial court found the letter was not a holographic will. Neither party disputes this finding on appeal.

D.   Harmless Error

While scrupulous adherence to the formalities associated with executing wills serves the important purpose of preventing fraud, it can also "defeat intention . . . [or] work unjust enrichment." *Restatement (Third) of Property: Wills &*

Other Donative Transfers § 3.3 cmt. b (1999). To address this concern, among others, the Code was amended in 1994 to align Colorado's law with extensive changes suggested by the Uniform Probate Code. *In re Estate of Sky Dancer*, 13 P.3d 1231 (Colo. App.2000).

One of these changes was affected by § 15–11–503(1), C.R.S.2006. This statute governs how potential donative documents are treated when they have not been executed pursuant to the three requirements established by § 15–11–502(1). Sections 15–11–503(1) states:

> Although a document, or writing added upon a document, was not executed in compliance with section 15–11–502, the document or writing is treated as if it had been executed in compliance with that section if the proponent of the document or writing establishes by clear and convincing evidence that the decedent intended the document or writing to constitute:
>
> (a)   The decedent's will.

The purpose of adding § 15–11–503(1) was to provide a mechanism for the application of harmless error analysis when a probate court considers whether the formal requirements of executing a will have been met. Applying a harmless error standard in these circumstances supports the purposes of the Code and follows the general trend of the Uniform Probate Code extending the principle of harmless error to probate transfers.

Thus, the question is whether a defect is harmless in light of the statutory purposes, not in light of the satisfaction of each statutory formality, viewed in isolation. To achieve those purposes, the issue is whether the evidence of the conduct proves the decedent intended the document to be a will. Restatement, *supra*, § 3.3 cmt. b.

Certain errors cannot be excused as harmless, like the failure of a proponent to produce a document. Other errors are difficult, although not impossible, to excuse as harmless, like the absence of a signature on a document. Restatement, *supra*, § 3.3 cmt. b. In this regard, § 15–11–503(2) reads: "Subsection (1) of this section shall apply only if the document is signed or acknowledged by the decedent as his or her will."

Adopted in 2001, Colo. Sess. Laws 2001, ch. 249 at 887, § 15–11–503(2) was designed to limit the harmless error concept to minor flaws in the execution of wills. Thus, § 15–11–503(2) establishes the condition precedent that a document be "signed or acknowledged by the decedent as his or her will" before a court may move to the next step and decide whether there is clear and convincing evidence the decedent intended the document to be a will.

The kinds of errors viewed as harmless in Colorado are technical drafting mistakes that frustrate the testator's intent.

E.   Burden of Proof Under § 15–11–503

Under § 15–11–503, a proponent of a document must show, by clear and convincing evidence, the decedent intended the document to be a will. This enhanced burden is "appropriate to the seriousness of the issue." Uniform Probate Code § 2–503 cmt. Clear and convincing evidence is stronger than a mere preponderance; it is highly probable evidence free from serious or substantial doubt. The greater the deviation from the requirements of due execution established by § 15–11–502, the heavier the burden on the document's proponent to prove, by clear and convincing evidence, that the instrument establishes the decedent's intent.

III.   "Signed or Acknowledged by the Decedent as His or Her Will"

Proponent contends the trial court erred in interpreting § 15–11–503(2) to require a document to be both signed and acknowledged by a decedent as his or her will. We agree.

Statutory interpretation is a question of law we review de novo. When interpreting a statute, our task is to give effect to the legislature's intent. We look first to the language of the statute, giving words and phrases their plain and ordinary meaning, and we interpret the statute in a way that best effectuates the purpose of the legislative scheme. The trial court found decedent signed the letter, but did not acknowledge the letter as his will. The court ruled the phrase "signed or acknowledged" must be read in the conjunctive and therefore, the letter could not be admitted to probate. We conclude the court's interpretation was erroneous.

The term "or" in a statute is presumed to be used in the disjunctive sense unless the legislative intent is clearly contrary. *People v. McCoy*, 821 P.2d 873 (Colo.App.1991). Here, there is no indication the General Assembly intended a document to be both signed and acknowledged to satisfy § 15–11–503(2).

Hence, the trial court erred in interpreting § 15–11–503(2) to require a document to be both signed and acknowledged by a decedent.

IV. Conclusion

In this case, the court found decedent's letter did not satisfy the formal requirements of a will pursuant to § 15–11–502(1) and that it was not a holographic will pursuant to § 15–11–502(2). We agree.

Thus, it was appropriate to determine whether the letter was a writing intended as a will under § 15–11–503. However, the trial court erroneously interpreted § 15–11–503(2) by holding decedent had to sign and acknowledge the letter as a will, even though decedent "stated his intent" in the letter.

In support of this ruling, the trial court added, "[T]he Legislature intends that a person has to say 'this is my will.' " However, § 15–11–503 does not require a decedent to announce, "This is my will." The trial court's interpretation added a restriction not present in the statute. Because this legal error affected the trial court's decision, the order must be reversed and the case remanded for a new hearing.

On remand, the court should determine whether the defects in decedent's letter were technical drafting mistakes that should not be allowed to frustrate decedent's testamentary intent and, thus, harmless error under § 15–11–503(1) and (2). Under a proper formulation of the harmless error analysis, once a court determines a decedent has signed or acknowledged a document as a will, as the trial court did here, the issue becomes whether the proponent can establish by clear and convincing evidence the decedent intended the document to be a will.

This proof may take the form of extrinsic evidence, such as decedent's statements to others about the letter. The language of the letter is also relevant evidence, including, for example, whether the letter disposes of all decedent's property and whether the letter identifies a beneficiary.

Affirmed.

NOTE

The Electronic Wills Act allows for harmless error:

SECTION 6. HARMLESS ERROR.

A record readable as text that is not executed in compliance with Section 5(a) is deemed to comply with Section 5(a) if the proponent of the record establishes by clear and convincing evidence that the decedent intended the record to be:

(1) the decedent's will;

(2) a partial or complete revocation of the decedent's will;

(3) an addition to or modification of the decedent's will; or

(4) a partial or complete revival of a formerly revoked will or part of a will.

ASSESSMENTS

1. Vasil and Hellen, his wife, retained a lawyer to draw their wills and wished to leave their property to each other. By mistake Hellen signed the will which had been prepared for her husband, and Vasil signed the will which had been prepared for his wife. The lawyer who drew up the will and the lawyer's secretary signed both wills as witnesses. The wills were kept by Vasil and Hellen. Hellen died first, but her will was never offered for probate. When Vasil died, the residuary legatee (Hellen's brother) offered Hellen's will—which had been signed by Vasil—for probate. Vasil's intestate heirs argued that the court could not probate the will because it did not satisfy the requirement that it had signed by the testator. What arguments would you make in favor of probating the will using substantial compliance and harmless error?

2. What are the limits of the harmless error doctrine? Do you think the doctrine of harmless error should apply to the following scenario, taken from a case:

Louise Macool went to Calloway's law office with the intent of changing her will. Toward that end, she gave Calloway a handwritten note that read as follows:

get the same as the family *Macool* gets

Niece

Mary Rescigno [indicating address] If any thing happen[s] to Mary Rescigno [,] her share goes to he[r] daughter Angela Rescigno. If anything happen[s] to her it goes to her 2 children. 1. Nikos Stylon 2. Jade Stylon

Niece + Godchild LeNora Distasio [indicating address] if anything happe[ns] to [her] it goes back in the pot

I [would] like to have the house to be left in the family Macool.

I [would] like to have.

1. Mike Macool [indicating address]

2.   Merle Caroffi [indicating address]

3.   Bill Macool [indicating address]

Take

After discussing the matter with Louise and using her handwritten notes as a guide, the attorney "dictated the entire will while she was there." Either later that afternoon or the next morning, his secretary typed a draft version of Louise's will, with the word "Rough" handwritten on the top left corner of the document. Louise left Calloway's office with the intention of having lunch nearby. Calloway expected Louise to make an appointment to review the draft will sometime after he had reviewed it. Sadly, Louise died approximately one hour after her meeting with Calloway. She thus never had the opportunity to see the draft will.

Should the harmless error doctrine be applied to recognize the unsigned document drafted by the attorney as Louise's will? What risks are raised by applying the harmless error doctrine in such a situation?

F. Conclusion and Takeaways

A will is a written document by which an individual shares wishes for disposition of probate property at death and nominates a fiduciary to oversee the probate process. Yet, as we have seen in this chapter, not every written document will qualify as a valid will. Because the validity of the will is determined upon the death of the testator, the wills act formalities seek to protect freedom of disposition by ensuring that if a written document is validly created, it will be respected after the testator's death. Too rigid an interpretation of these formalities, however, may frustrate the freedom of disposition. Other ways that freedom of disposition are challenged include undue influence on the testator, fraud, duress, insane delusion, and tortious interference with an expectancy. The next chapter examines these grounds for will contests and ways to avoid such challenges.

CHAPTER 5 COMPREHENSIVE ASSESSMENTS

1.   **CREATE A "HOW TO" MANUAL.** In the age of COVID-19 or any other public health crisis, how can a lawyer comply with wills formalities? Create guidelines for an execution ceremony that does so while keeping everyone safe. That means everyone must be at least six feet apart, wear masks, and not touch anything with bare hands. Be specific as you create these guidelines using a "how-to" format.

2.   **REVIEW AND MODIFY FORM DOCUMENTS.** Go to an online will website of your choice and answer enough questions so that you get a draft of your will.[2] Once you have the draft, access its execution section. (Alternative, read the Wisconsin Model Will in the Appendix.) Do the execution instructions contain sufficient detail to ensure that a layperson would execute the will in compliance with the legal will execution requirements for your state? What modifications, if any, would you suggest?

Test Your Knowledge

To assess your understanding of the material in this chapter, click here to take a quiz.

---

[2]   The following website allows for free access: https://www.lawdepot.com/contracts/last-will-and-testament-usa/preview.aspx?loc=USOK&.

CHAPTER 6

Wills II: Challenges

CHAPTER LEARNING OUTCOMES

Following your work with the material in this chapter, you should be able to do the following:

- Identify situations when a client's testamentary capacity, nature of the bequests, or some other aspect of the estate plan or will execution might invite will challenges

- Apply the framework for an undue influence challenge, including recognizing how and when the burden of proof shifts

- Explain the types of fraud and how they differ from duress in will challenges

- Assess "insane delusion" and articulate examples of how insane delusion might be raised in a will challenge

- Define tortious interference with an expectancy and describe how it differs from other will challenges

- Design measures to prevent successful challenges to a will

- Evaluate the merits and predict the outcome in a challenge to a will under the available doctrines

A. Introduction

Someone who is unhappy with a will's distribution of an estate may object to the probate of the will on several grounds. Allowing will challenges (known as will "**contests**") arguably helps protect the decedent's intent: if a will contestant has evidence that the will was the product of undue influence, fraud, or duress, or that the testator lacked capacity, then the will fails to express the testator's true intent and should be denied probate. Thus, the doctrines described in this chapter can serve to protect testamentary disposition. They can be a double-edged sword, however. As we will see, will contests can sometimes undermine testamentary freedom by having wills denied probate because their plans of distribution fail to conform to social norms and arouse a court or a jury's disapproval. For example, many people believe that it is unnatural to leave one's family out of the will and leave the bulk of an estate to someone else, and there is some evidence that juries are sympathetic to disinherited family members who challenge such wills.

The person who challenges a will is usually called the "**contestant**" (and sometimes the "**caveator**") and the person who asserts the will's validity is the "**proponent.**" A contestant can object to the probate of a will on the grounds that it fails to satisfy one of the requirements of will validity discussed in Chapter 5—that is, the will was not validly executed, or the testator lacked capacity, either general capacity or testamentary capacity.

This chapter also covers other grounds for will challenges. **Part B** discusses the doctrine of **undue influence** and what it means to claim that someone exerted an inappropriate amount of influence over a testator. We will see that these claims are often inflected with notions about who the "right" beneficiaries are and what relationships are appropriate—in other words, social norms become very important.

Part C takes up challenges based on **fraud, duress,** and **insane delusion. Part D** introduces the claim of **tortious interference with an expectancy** or inheritance. You will notice that in many of the cases, the contestants challenge the will on a number of these grounds. This makes sense because if, for example, a testator lacks capacity, that person might be more susceptible to undue influence or fraud. **Part E** discusses what happens when a will contest is successful, some of the most common scenarios that produce will contests, and how you might think about proactively preventing these situations.

B. Undue Influence

The doctrine of undue influence refers to a situation where someone exerted so much inappropriate influence over the testator that the resulting will expressed the influencer's intent and not the testator's. What makes this doctrine difficult is the fact that people influence each other all the time, especially family members—in particular, married couples. How much is too much; when does the influence become a reason to deny a will probate?

The RESTATEMENT (THIRD) OF PROPERTY: WILLS AND OTHER DONATIVE TRANSFERS, § 8.3(b) (2003) provides: "A donative transfer is procured by undue influence if the wrongdoer exerted such influence over the donor that it[:] overcame the donor's free will and caused the donor to make a donative transfer that the donor would not otherwise have made. . . ."

The elements of undue influence are:

- The testator must be a person susceptible to the influence

- The alleged influencer must have had an opportunity to exert undue influence upon the testator

- The alleged influencer must have a disposition to exert undue influence

- There must be a testamentary plan or bequest resulting from the influence

So often, these cases tell vastly conflicting stories: the beneficiary accused of the influence is a friend or relative who has helped an elderly or infirm testator when no one else would and thus quite rightly benefits from the testator's gratitude and therefore bounty; alternatively, the beneficiary is an overreaching opportunist who helped the weakened testator not because she was generous but rather because she wanted to receive property. Deciding between these two versions often hinges on who bears the burden of proof.

1.   A Classic Case of Undue Influence

The case below is a kind of "classic" undue influence case.

Moriarty v. Moriarty

150 N.E.3d 616 (Ct. App. Ind. 2020)

CRONE, J.

Mary Eve Kassen Moriarty (Eve) appeals the trial court's order entering judgment in favor of Catherine C. Moriarty (Cathy) and Paula A. Bowers (Paula) (collectively Daughters) on their claim to reject the probate of the purported last will and testament of William J. Moriarty (the Purported Will) on the basis of lack of testamentary capacity and/or undue influence and on their claim of tortious interference with inheritance. Eve contends that the trial court's legal conclusions are clearly erroneous. Finding no error, we affirm.

Facts and Procedural History

The unchallenged findings of fact show that William and Doreen Moriarty are Daughters' parents. On April 1, 2016, Doreen died. William and Doreen had been married for fifty-eight years.

The Moriarty family was a "closely knit, loving family." William was a devoted husband and father. Cathy and Paula had close relationships with both parents, although at times Paula and William would disagree. Paula has two children, Nicholas and Jackson, who both had loving relationships with William and Doreen. Based on numerous specific statements by William over many years, Paula and Cathy each expected to inherit one-half of William's assets. In addition, William discussed his intention that everything he and Doreen owned would be split between Cathy and Paula with Doreen's sister, Elaine Suurendonk, who had significant interaction with the Moriarty family over several decades.

Dr. Edward Fry is a cardiologist who treated both Doreen and William. Doreen was his patient from 2007 until her death. In April 2015, William became Dr. Fry's patient when William was hospitalized and diagnosed with congestive heart failure (CHF). At an appointment in May 2016, William reported to Dr. Fry that he had been under a great deal of stress due to the prolonged and complex illness of his wife who had recently passed away.

Eve, who had met William at Holy Spirit Parish when Doreen was still living, began dating him within weeks after Doreen died. Cathy learned about Eve in an email from William but did not realize that they were dating. William never mentioned Eve by name to Paula or invited Paula to meet Eve. Paula noticed a change in her relationship with William when he stopped calling, emailing, and otherwise communicating with her after Father's Day 2016. William had never stopped communicating with Paula before. Cathy did not understand why William suddenly stopped communicating with Paula. In June 2016, William did not want Cathy to visit him in Indianapolis, and she thought that was very strange. In August 2016, Cathy visited William, and he told her that he was engaged to be engaged, but she did not understand what he meant.

On October 25, 2016, Eve married William. This was Eve's fourth marriage. William's daughters, grandsons, sister, sister-in-law, and longtime close friends were not invited to the wedding. Sometime before the wedding, "Cathy found out that Eve planned to marry William," but Paula was not informed about the wedding, and she was shocked to learn that William married Eve so soon after Doreen's death. Although Suurendonk had maintained regular contact with William following Doreen's death, he did not tell her that he was going to be married, and she was surprised to learn that William had married Eve so soon after Doreen's death. William's longtime friend Danial Kocher, who maintained regular contact with William, was not informed that William was going to marry Eve and was shocked to learn that William married Eve. Eve never invited Paula or Cathy to her home, did not invite them to William's surprise birthday party, and did not meet Paula until the day before William died.

After Eve married William, Paula and Cathy were not permitted to participate in William's medical care as they had previously with William and with Doreen." "Dr. Fry viewed this as a significant change from the family dynamic over the previous nine years. Eve was present at the office visit when William told Dr. Fry that he did not want Paula and Cathy involved in his medical care." "During the course of Dr. Fry's treatment of William, Dr. Fry diagnosed William with anxiety and depression, and Dr. Fry's medical records reference symptoms of anxiety and depression nine times from April 2016 through William's death in May 2017."

On November 17, 2016, William and Eve closed on the purchase of a home on Glen Ridge Circle (Glen Ridge House) for $412,620.11. The Glen Ridge House was paid for by wire transfer from an account owned solely by William, which had been funded by the sale of his prior home and a money market account owned solely by him. The amount of money William spent on the Glen Ridge House was out of character for him.

A patient with CHF, like William, would become physically reliant on others for assistance with activities of daily living. In March 2017, Eve fired William's home healthcare service provider, the same provider who had served Doreen. William said nothing, which was out of character for him.

On March 20, 2017, William signed a request to surrender his Prudential life insurance policy. Eve initially testified that she had not seen the request before William died, but she admitted to writing everything on it except William's signature. The policy's surrender value of $11,591.80 was deposited into an account, which was owned jointly by William and Eve.

On April 6, 2017, William executed the Purported Will. The Purported Will directs all tangible personal property and the entire residue of William's estate to be distributed to Eve if she survives him and nominates Eve to serve as personal representative of his estate. The Purported Will also provides that if Eve does not survive William, then the personal property and residue of his estate are to be distributed to Daughters, per stirpes. The Purported Will included a self-proving clause.

The Purported Will was prepared by attorney Greg Cagnassola. Eve had been a client of Cagnassola for eight to ten years. Cagnassola departed significantly from his ordinary practices when meeting with and preparing an estate plan for William. Other than dropping off a draft of the Purported Will at William's house, Cagnassola did not have in-person interaction with William until the signing of the Purported Will at William's house. Eve was home when the Purported Will was signed. Eve prepared the check that William signed to pay for the preparation of the Purported Will. Also on April 6, William signed a general durable power of attorney naming Eve as his attorney-in-fact and a healthcare power of attorney naming Eve as his healthcare power of attorney, both effective immediately. Eve never signed a will or trust naming William as a beneficiary. Eve never named William as her healthcare power of attorney or healthcare representative or attorney-in-fact.

In April 2017, although he was no longer driving, William owned a 2015 Lincoln MKX truck that was paid for and had low mileage. Eve leased an Acura, which had a net amount of $4860.38 due to the dealership. On April 27, 2017, William and Eve traded in their cars and purchased a 2017 Lexus RX 350 for $62,973.01. The net amount due to purchase the Lexus, after credit for the value of William's truck and the amount due on Eve's Acura were applied, was $44,533.39. A check for $40,000 was written from a bank account owned solely by William. It was out of character for William to trade in his truck and to spend that amount of money on a new car.

On May 7, 2017, William died. On May 22, 2017, Daughters filed a verified petition for supervised administration of William's estate. The following day, Eve filed a petition for probate of the Purported Will without court supervision. Ultimately, the two causes were consolidated, and a special administrator was appointed.

In September 2017, Daughters initiated the underlying action by filing a verified complaint alleging that the Purported Will was invalid because William was of unsound mind when he executed it and/or the Purported Will was a product of undue influence and alleging that Eve tortiously interfered with their inheritance. Prior to trial, Daughters requested that the trial court issue findings and conclusions thereon pursuant to Indiana Trial Rule 52(A).

Trial Court Findings

The trial court found that Eve exercised undue influence over William and based that finding upon all of the evidence and specifically upon (a) Eve's marriage to William less than seven months after Doreen died, (b) Eve's involvement in the grief ministry at Holy Spirit in which William was a participant, (c) the Purported Will and non-probate transfers representing a dramatic shift in William's intent regarding the passing of his estate less than six months after the wedding and only one month before his death, (d) the testimony of Eve that she contributed at least $232,500 in physical cash to William toward the purchase of the Glen Ridge House and the Lexus, which this Court found not credible, (e) the involvement by Eve in the procurement of and payment for the Purported Will, (f) the involvement of Eve in the surrendering of William's Prudential life insurance policy, (g) the purchase of the Lexus only ten days before William's death when William was no longer driving, (h) the lack of any effort by Eve to form relationships with Paula, Cathy, and William's other family and long-time friends, (i) Eve's firing of William's longtime medical caregiver, (j) William's significant reliance on Eve, (k) the wedding occurring without any of William's family or long-time friends attending or even being invited, (*l*) Eve inheriting virtually all of William's assets to the exclusion of his daughters and grandsons, and (m) Eve's demeanor in court, which consisted of a flat affect during emotional testimony of Paula and Cathy about their father's last hours and during Eve's own testimony, which leaves this factfinder with no confidence that Eve married William because she loved him and with the conclusion that Eve planned to take all of William's money all along.

<u>Conclusions of Law</u>

Based on the evidence, including reasonable inferences the Court draws from the facts and circumstances and further based on the findings above, the Court concludes that: William was susceptible to undue influence, Eve exercised undue influence over William at the time he executed the Purported Will, and the Purported Will was a product of Eve's exercise of undue influence over William. These findings apply to the inter vivos transfers as well as to the execution of the Purported Will.

Affirmed.

NOTES

1. The burden of proof in undue influence cases is critical. Generally, the burden lies with the person seeking to challenge the will to create a presumption of undue influence. This is done by showing that both a **"confidential" relationship** between the alleged influencer and the decedent existed and that there were also one or more **suspicious circumstances** present. In some jurisdictions, however, the mere fact that the alleged influencer had a "confidential relationship" with the testator raises the presumption of undue influence, which the proponent must then rebut. A "confidential relationship" is one in which one person relies on and trusts another to make decisions and do what is best for that person. A confidential relationship may also be one the law defines as fiduciary, such as a relationship with one's attorney, but the term encompasses more than that. It can refer a relationship in which an individual

relies upon the judgment of another, such as a doctor or religious leader. It can also refer to an informal personal relationship between friends or neighbors—or family members. The next section explores the concept of "confidential relationship" in greater detail.

2.   In many jurisdictions, a confidential relationship must be accompanied by "suspicious circumstances" to trigger the presumption of undue influence. The RESTATEMENT (THIRD) OF PROPERTY provides a list of considerations to determine whether circumstances were suspicious:

- The extent to which the donor was in a weakened condition, physically, mentally, or both, and therefore susceptible to undue influence

- The extent to which the alleged wrongdoer participated in the preparation or procurement of the will or will substitute

- Whether the donor received independent advice from disinterested advisors in preparing the will or will substitute

- Whether the will was prepared in secrecy or in haste

- Whether the donor's attitude toward others had changed by reason of his or her relationship with the alleged wrongdoer

- Whether there is a decided discrepancy between a new and previous wills

- Whether there was a continuity of purpose indicating a settled intent in the disposition of his or her property

- Whether the disposition of the property is such that a reasonable person would regard it as unnatural, unjust, or unfair, for example, whether the disposition abruptly and without apparent reason disinherited a faithful and deserving family member

3.   Notice that the daughters in *Moriarty* contested the will on three grounds: lack of capacity; undue influence; and tortious interference with an expectancy. As you will see, most will contests allege more than one ground because all the grounds are related. Once the contestant has asserted lack of capacity, for example, an inference of undue influence might seem to follow logically.

4.   What was the lawyer's role in *Moriarty*? The court notes that the lawyer departed from his usual practice in not having any "in-person interaction with William until the signing of the Purported Will at William's house." Why do you think he failed to follow his normal procedure for interviewing estate planning

clients? Is there ever a reason for a lawyer to do so? Should lawyers face liability for enabling the exercise of undue influence in this way?

5.   The situation in *Moriarty* is a common one in undue influence cases: a younger (usually) wife marries an older man, who leaves her a large portion of his estate, infuriating his children from a former marriage. The most famous example of this scenario is probably that of Anna Nicole Smith, a model and actress, who married oil billionaire J. Howard Marshall when he was 86 and she was 26. When Marshall died and left Smith a large portion of his estate, it led to a famous legal battle which went on for years and even made its way at one point to the U.S. Supreme Court. *Marshall v. Marshall*, 547 U.S. 293 (2006). We will discuss that case further in connection with tortious interference with inheritance claims.

ASSESSMENTS

1.   Imagine you are the estate planning lawyer in *Moriarty* and you receive a call from Eve about drafting a will for William, her very ill husband. Roleplay your response to Eve's request.

2.   Now imagine you are the trial lawyer for Eve, the defendant in the *Moriarty* case. Once the will contestant has created the presumption of undue influence, the burden shifts to the alleged influencer to disprove it. Consider what facts you will draw upon to rebut the presumption that Eve unduly influenced William and then craft a short opening statement to the court that uses these specific facts to rebut the presumption of undue influence.

2.   Undue Influence, Confidential Relationship, and Burden of Proof

As you read the next case, think about the nature of the confidential relationship and how it came about. Does it make sense for the existence of such a relationship to shift the burden of proving the absence of undue influence to the will proponent? In considering this question, focus on the difficulty of disproving undue influence.

Estate of Lakatosh

656 A.2d 1378 (Pa. Super. Ct. 1995)

CIRILLO, J.

This is an appeal from an order of the Court of Common Pleas of Northampton County denying Roger Jacob's post-trial exceptions. We affirm.

This matter involves the finances of an elderly woman, Rose K. Lakatosh (Rose), and the scurrilous motives and actions of a man, Roger Jacobs (Roger), who sought to take advantage of the confidential relationship he developed with Rose so as to siphon money from her for his own benefit. On August 10, 1990, Donald F. Spry, II, Guardian of the Estate of Rose K. Lakatosh, deceased, filed a Petition for an Accounting and Imposition of a Constructive Trust on Roger Jacobs. On March 3, 1993, Spry filed a petition seeking revocation of Rose's last will and testament, dated November 11, 1988, on grounds of undue influence.

Rose was a woman in her early to mid seventies in March of 1988 when Roger Jacobs came into her life. Roger introduced himself to Rose by delivering his business card to her at her home in Northampton, Pennsylvania, after which he began to perform odd jobs for Rose. At the time Roger came to know Rose, Rose had no contact with any of her family members except for an occasional visit from her sister, Margaret Berg. Roger had an active relationship with Rose from the spring of 1988 until June of 1990, when a fire partially destroyed Rose's home.

Roger had much contact with Rose after they first met in March of 1988. Roger lived just a few miles from Rose and visited her at least once a day and sometimes as often as two or three times a day. Roger assisted Rose around her house and drove Rose to various appointments and took her on various errands. These facts suggest that this elderly woman came to depend on Roger as the only person with whom she really had substantial contact. As subsequently discussed at greater length, we agree with the trial court that Roger gained the confidence of Rose. This determination is also supported by Rose's conduct.

In March of 1988, Rose expressed her concern to Roger about a slander lawsuit which had been filed against her by her nephew, Dean Berg. Roger responded to Rose's concerns by contacting his second cousin, Attorney Richard Jacobs, who agreed to be Rose's attorney. Also, in June 1988, Rose told Roger that she owned some stock and asked Roger to contact Janney Montgomery Scott ("JMS"), a financial investment company, to check on her investments. On several occasions between June of 1988 and November of 1988, Roger took Rose to meet with a representative of JMS to review various stock certificates. Roger was present at these meetings and also actively participated in these meetings.

In the summer of 1988, Roger suggested to Rose that she execute a power of attorney so that she would have someone to care for her should she need it. On November 11, 1988, Rose executed a power of attorney making Roger her attorney-in-fact. On that same date, Rose executed a new will which left all of her estate to Roger, except for a $1,000.00 gift to her church. Both the will and the power of attorney were prepared by Attorney Richard Jacobs and, at that time, he concluded, after conferring with Rose about her will, that she was of sound mind and capable of disposing of her assets. Three days later, however, after the execution of the will, Attorney Jacobs prepared a petition to have Rose evaluated in order to determine if she was competent to assist her counsel in the defense of the slander action. The petition supposedly was Attorney Jacobs' response to Rose's inability to provide information for discovery requests in July of 1988, as well as Rose's inability to remember things and grasp the value of her stocks or realize their worth in the fall of 1988. In addition, in an answer to a motion for sanctions in the slander action, Attorney Jacobs requested the court not to issue sanctions until Rose could be evaluated to determine her mental capacity to assist her counsel in the defense of the action.

Although Roger was not present in Attorney Jacob's office at the time the will and the power of attorney were executed, Rose informed Roger of the new will and its provisions on the very same day that it was executed.

Prior to the trial concerning the petition for the imposition of a constructive trust brought by Petitioner Spry, Spry also filed a petition to revoke Rose's will dated November 11, 1988 based on undue influence. The trial court granted Spry's request to revoke the will. We must now determine, in view of the aforementioned facts, whether the trial court committed error or abused its discretion in its application of the law when it found that Rose's will should be revoked.

Spry maintains that the will must be revoked because Roger failed to carry his burden of proving the absence of undue influence surrounding Rose's execution of the November 11th will.

When the proponent of a will proves that the formalities of execution have been followed, a contestant who claims that there has been undue influence has the burden of proof. The burden may be shifted so as to require the proponent to disprove undue influence. To do so, the contestant must prove by clear and convincing evidence that there was a confidential relationship, that the person enjoying such relationship received the bulk of the estate, and that the decedent's intellect was weakened.

Initially, it must be ascertained whether a confidential relationship existed between Roger Jacobs and Rose Lakatosh. A confidential relationship exists "whenever one person has reposed a special confidence in another to the extent that the parties do not deal with each other on equal terms, either because of an overmastering dominance on one side, or weakness, dependence or justifiable trust, on the other.

The existence of a power of attorney given by one person to another is a clear indication that a confidential relationship exists between the parties.

The trial court properly concluded that the testimony at trial indicated that a confidential relationship existed between Rose and Roger. The facts illustrate that from the time Roger came to know Rose he developed a close relationship with her which included her confiding in him about her legal problems as well as her financial affairs. Since Rose had very little contact with other individuals, she became dependent upon Roger's assistance in her everyday life. Roger developed a confidential relationship with Rose since he occupied a position towards Rose as an advisor, counselor and confidant, and inspired Rose's confidence that he would act in good faith for her interests. Such a finding is especially true here as Roger spent a great deal of time with Rose and assisted in her care. Also, all of this occurred even before Rose made Roger her power of attorney which, in and of itself, is sufficient for a finding that a confidential relationship existed. Furthermore, Roger admitted, both in his answer to Spry's petition and in his brief on appeal, that he had gained the confidence of Rose.

Next, Spry, as contestant of the will, needed to prove that the person enjoying the confidential relationship received the bulk of the estate. On November 1, 1988, the date of the will's execution, the value of Rose's estate amounted to $268,672.11. Since Roger was to receive all of Rose's estate, except for the $1,000.00 gift to her church, it is without question that Roger was to receive the bulk of Rose's estate.

Lastly, it must be ascertained whether Rose suffered from a weakened intellect at the time the will was executed.

Although Roger testified that Rose was in good physical and mental health on the day the will was executed and that he had no difficulty communicating with her, he also testified that, around the time of the will's execution, Rose had trouble remembering things and had no understanding of her estate or assets. Significantly, it was Roger himself who suggested that Rose execute a power of attorney so that someone could help her if it was necessary. According to Roger's testimony, he was concerned with Rose's susceptibility to being taken advantage of, and it was this concern which sparked the idea for the power of attorney.

Moreover, the representations made by Attorney Jacobs in the pleadings and correspondence in the slander suit questioning Rose's competence and ability to understand her estate also indicate that her intellect was weakened at the time the will was executed.

Further, an audio tape, which had been made of a conversation between Rose and Attorney Jacobs on the day the will was executed, also evidences the notion that Rose suffered from a weakened intellect at the time. Attorney Jacobs testified at trial that, because Roger was to receive the bulk of Rose's estate and was not her blood relative, he thought it wise to make the tape as evidence of the will's validity, should it be challenged. Instead of reinforcing the integrity of the will, the audio tape supports the proposition that Rose suffered from a weakened intellect.

The audio tape revealed that Rose was easily distracted and clearly had difficulty remaining focused on the issue of the will. Also, as pointed out by the trial court, even though Attorney Jacobs repeatedly attempted to re-direct Rose's attention to the issue of the will, she could not remain focused or coherent. Rose made several comments on the tape which indicate that she had a weakened intellect and that she was somewhat out of touch with reality. Specifically, Rose referred to Roger as "an angel of mercy" who "saved her life" because, before she met him, she had been "so low in hell." Rose also repeatedly claimed that her nephew, Dean Berg, threatened to rob and kill her and that he was persecuting and torturing her.

Finally, proof of Rose's weakened intellect can be seen in the state in which she was living. That is, she was an elderly woman; helpless and unable to prevent the consumption of her assets by Roger during the period before and after the execution of her will, from September 1988 to June 1990, when she finally had Roger's power of attorney revoked. Also, Rose was living in filth in the spring of 1990, with her bills not having been paid, and, after a house fire, it was discovered that her house was in shambles with trash throughout and dead cats found in her freezer and bathtub.

Consequently, we conclude that the trial court's findings rest on legally competent evidence and the trial court did not commit error or abuse its discretion in finding that Rose's will should be revoked because Roger failed to carry his burden of proving the absence of undue influence.

NOTES

1.   Because the court found Rose Lakatosh's will to be the product of undue influence, her probate estate passed by intestacy to relatives with whom she had no contact. Does that seem fair, given that those relatives had left Rose to live

in squalor, making her vulnerable to someone like Jacobs? Is that what she would have wanted? Does it matter that, at one point, Rose described Jacobs to the lawyer who drafted the will, as an "angel of mercy" who lifted her up when she had been "so low in hell"?

2.   Notice how the audio recording, intended to prove Rose's capacity, had exactly the opposite effect. Why did it backfire? What does this suggest about the use of recordings as evidence of capacity?

3.   Courts hesitate to let a confidential relationship between spouses trigger a presumption of undue influence, even when evidence suggests that one spouse used influence to cause a disposition in the spouse's favor. *See, e.g., In re Estate of Glogovsek*, 618 N.E.2d 1231, 1237 (Ill. Ct. App. 1993) (observing "that the use of the presumption of undue influence must be applied with caution as to marital relationships, because of the unique relationship between spouses and the importance of marriages in our society").

4.   What about caretakers? Caretakers provide valuable assistance, and yet may be controlling access to or the activities of the testator. When the reclusive Huguette Clark, whom we read about in Chapter 4, died in 2011, she left thirty million dollars to the nurse, Hadassah Peri, who had taken care of Clark for twenty years. Clark's will specifically stated that she wanted nothing to go to her relatives, who were not a part of her life in any significant way, and most of whom she had not seen since 1957. But these relatives contested the will arguing, among other things, undue influence by Peri. When everyone finally settled, Peri did not receive anything; in fact, Peri even had to return some money that Clark had given her while Clark was alive. As NBC News reported, the attorney general's office determined that "the gifts to a caregiver were excessive and presumed to be the product of undue influence." Is this a fair presumption?

5.   Certain states have gone so far as to enact statutes providing that any gifts to caretakers are presumed to be the product of undue influence. An excerpt of the California statute follows:

Californian Probate Code 21350

(a)   A provision of an instrument making a donative transfer to any of the following persons is presumed to be the product of fraud or undue influence:

* * *

(3)   A care custodian of a transferor who is a dependent adult, but only if the instrument was executed during the period in which the

care custodian provided services to the transferor, or within 90 days before or after that period.

Under an earlier version of this statute, a court invalidated a bequest from an elderly widow to the young couple who had cared for her in her final months. As the court itself described it,

> Foley did decedent's grocery shopping, prepared some meals for her and occasionally attended to her personal needs, including helping to change the diapers she wore. Foley also made decedent's bed and assisted her with bathing. He applied topical medications to decedent's body, sometimes with Erman's assistance. Erman prepared meals for decedent, spent every day with her, assisted her in getting to and from the bathroom, helped her into bed, fixed her hair, cleaned her bedroom and did her laundry. . . . washed [her] face and hands . . . administered oral medications to decedent . . . helped decedent apply ointments to a rash that had developed in her intimate areas. Erman also cared for decedent's wounds, applying salves and antibiotics to sores on her legs and thereafter bandaging those areas.

Bernard v. Foley, 139 P.3d 1196, 1202 (Cal. 2006).

Certainly, financial abuse of the elderly by caregivers happens, but there are also cases in which the caregiver was a generous and hardworking employee and friend to the decedent.

ASSESSMENT

Draft a narrower version of the California statute quoted above that could protect the vulnerable from exploitation by caregivers while also allowing for bequests which were in fact voluntary expressions of gratitude for care.

3.   Undue Influence: Valid Challenge or Social Punishment?

As mentioned above, stereotyping and bias may play a role in undue influence cases, precisely because the cause of action is elusive and hard to pin down. Largely based on inference because the influence happens, by definition, in private, undue influence has served as a vehicle for channeling estates to socially approved recipients and for punishing socially unacceptable relationships. As you read the cases in this section, consider the role, if any, played by gender, age, race, and disability in the majority and dissenting opinions.

In re Last Will and Testament of Fannie Traylor Moses

227 So. 2d 829 (Miss. 1963)

SMITH, J.

Mrs. Fannie Traylor Moses died on February 6, 1967. An instrument, dated December 23, 1957 and purporting to be her last will and testament, was duly admitted to probate in the Chancery Court. Thereafter, on February 14, 1967, appellant, Clarence H. Holland, an attorney at law, not related to Mrs. Moses, filed a petition in that court tendering for probate in solemn form, as the true last will and testament of Mrs. Moses, a document dated May 26, 1964, under the terms of which he would take virtually her entire estate. This document contained a clause revoking former wills and Holland's petition prayed that the earlier probate of the 1957 will be set aside.

> **Connection Note:** In the next chapter, we will discuss the interplay among sequential wills, like the 1957, 1961, and 1964 wills referred to in the *Moses* case. For now, just remember to start by analyzing the most recent will to see if it is valid. If it fails, you analyze the earlier will(s).

The beneficiaries under the 1957 will responded to Holland's petition, denied that the document tendered by him was Mrs. Moses' will, and asserted, among other things, that it was (1) the product of Holland's undue influence upon her, (2) that at the time of its signing, Mrs. Moses lacked testamentary capacity, and, (3) that the 1957 will was Mrs. Moses' true last will and testament and its probate should be confirmed. Respondents prayed that Holland's apparent ownership of an interest in certain real estate had been procured by undue influence and that it should be cancelled as a cloud upon the title of Mrs. Moses, the true owner.

After hearing and considering a great deal of evidence, oral and documentary, together with briefs of counsel, the chancellor, in a carefully considered opinion, found that (1) the 1964 document, tendered for probate by Holland, was the product of undue influence and was not entitled to be admitted to probate, (2) the earlier probate of the 1957 will should be confirmed and, (3) Mrs. Moses had been the true owner of the interest claimed by Holland in the real estate and his claim of ownership should be cancelled as a cloud upon the title of Mrs. Moses.

Holland's appeal is from the decree entered denying probate to the 1964 document and cancelling his claim to an undivided one-half interest in the real estate.

Appellant's chief argument is addressed to the proposition that even if Holland, as Mrs. Moses' attorney, occupied a continuing fiduciary relationship with respect to her on May 26, 1964, (the date of the will's execution) the presumption of undue influence was overcome because, in making the will, Mrs. Moses had the independent advice and counsel of one entirely devoted to her interests.

A brief summary of facts found by the chancellor and upon which he based his conclusion that the presumption was not overcome, follows:

Mrs. Moses died at the age of 57 years, leaving an estate valued at $125,000. She had lost three husbands in less than 20 years. Throughout the latter years of her life her health became seriously impaired. She suffered from serious heart trouble and cancer had required the surgical removal of one of her breasts. For 6 or 7 years preceding her death she was an alcoholic.

On several occasions Mrs. Moses had declared her intention of making an elder sister her testamentary beneficiary. She had once lived with this sister and was grateful for the many kindnesses shown her. Mrs. Moses' will of December 23, 1957 did, in fact, bequeath the bulk of her estate to this sister.

The exact date on which Holland entered Mrs. Moses' life is unclear. There is a suggestion that she had met him as early as 1951. Their personal relationship became what the chancellor, somewhat inaccurately, characterized, as one of 'dubious' morality. The record, however, leaves no doubt as to its nature. Soon after the death of Mrs. Moses' last husband, Holland, although 15 years her junior, began seeing Mrs. Moses with marked regularity, there having been testimony to the effect that he attended her almost daily. Holland was an attorney and, in that capacity, represented Mrs. Moses. She declared that he was not only her attorney but her 'boyfriend' as well. During the period in which the evidence shows that Holland was Mrs. Moses' attorney, she executed a document purporting to be her will. This instrument was drawn by an attorney with whom Holland was then associated and shared offices. It was typed by a secretary who served both Holland and the associate. It was witnessed by Holland's associate and their secretary.

In addition to other testamentary dispositions, this document undertook to bequeath to Holland 'my wedding ring, my diamond solitaire ring and my three gold bracelets containing twenty-five (25) pearls each.' In it Holland is referred to as 'my good friend.' The validity of this document is not an issue in the present case.

After Mrs. Moses died, the 1964 will was brought forward by another attorney, also an associate of Holland, who said that it had been entrusted to him by Mrs. Moses for safekeeping. He distinguished his relation with Holland from that of a partner, saying that he and Holland only occupied offices together and shared facilities and expenses in the practice of law. He also stated that he saw Mrs. Moses on an 'average' of once a week, most often in the company of Holland.

Throughout this period, Mrs. Moses was a frequent visitor at Holland's office, and there is ample evidence to support the chancellor's finding that there existed a continuing fiduciary relationship between Mrs. Moses and Holland, as her attorney.

In May 1962, Holland and the husband of Holland's cousin, one Gibson, had contracted to buy 480 acres of land for $36,000. Mrs. Moses was not originally a party to the contract. Gibson paid $5,000 in earnest money but testified that he did not know where it had come from and assumed that it came from Mrs. Moses. At the time, Mrs. Moses had annuity contracts on which she obtained $31,341.11, which were deposited in a bank account called 'Cedar Hills Ranch.' She gave Holland authority to check on this account and her personal account. About this time, Gibson disappeared from the land transaction. At closing, the persons present, in addition to the grantors and their agents and attorney, were Mrs. Moses and Holland, her attorney. Mrs. Moses had no other counsel. Holland issued a check on the Cedar Hills Ranch account (in which only Mrs. Moses had any money) for the $31,000 balance. Although none of the consideration was paid by Holland, the deed from the owners purported to convey the land to Holland and Mrs. Moses in equal shares, as tenants in common. The next day, Holland issued another check on the Cedar Hills Ranch account (in which he still had deposited no money) for $835.00 purportedly in payment for a tractor. This check was issued by Holland to his brother. Eight days later Holland drew another check on this account for $2,100.00 purportedly for an undisclosed number of cattle. This check was issued to Holland's father.

The evidence supports the chancellor's finding that the confidential or fiduciary relationship which existed between Mrs. Moses and Holland, her attorney, was a subsisting and continuing relationship, having begun before the making by Mrs. Moses of the will of August 22, 1961, under the terms of which her jewelry had been bequeathed to Holland. Moreover, its effect was enhanced by the fact that throughout this period, Holland was in almost daily attendance upon Mrs. Moses on terms of the utmost intimacy. There was strong evidence that this aging woman, seriously ill, disfigured by surgery, and hopelessly addicted to alcoholic excesses, was completely bemused by the constant and amorous attentions of Holland, a man 15 years her junior. There was testimony too indicating that she entertained the pathetic hope that he might marry her. Although the evidence was not without conflict, it was sufficient to support the finding that the relationship existed on May 26, 1964, the date of the will tendered for probate by Holland.

Moreover, the chancellor was correct in his conclusion of law that such relationship gave rise to a presumption of undue influence which could be overcome only by evidence that, in making the 1964 will, Mrs. Moses had acted upon the independent advice and counsel of one entirely devoted to her interest.

Appellant takes the position that there was undisputed evidence that Mrs. Moses did, in fact, have such advice and counsel. He relies upon the testimony of the attorney in whose office that document was prepared to support his assertion. This attorney was and is a reputable and respected member of the bar, who had no prior connection with Holland and no knowledge of Mrs. Moses' relationship with him. He had never seen nor represented Mrs. Moses previously and never represented her afterward. He was acquainted with Holland and was aware that Holland was a lawyer.

A brief summary of his testimony, with respect to the writing of the will, follows:

Mrs. Moses had telephoned him for an appointment and had come alone to his office on March 31, 1964. She was not intoxicated and, in his opinion, knew what she was doing. He asked her about her property and 'marital background.' He did this in order, he said, to advise her as to possible renunciation by a husband. She was also asked if she had children in order to determine whether she wished to 'pretermit them.' As she had neither husband nor children this subject was pursued no further. He asked as to the values of various items of property in order to consider possible tax problems. He told her it would be better if she had more accurate descriptions of the several items of real and personal property comprising her estate. No further 'advice or counsel' was given her.

On some later date, Mrs. Moses sent in (the attorney did not think she came personally and in any event he did not see her), some tax receipts for purposes of supplying property descriptions. He prepared the will and mailed a draft to her. Upon receiving it, she telephoned that he had made a mistake in the devise of certain realty, in that he had provided that a relatively low valued property should go to Holland rather than a substantially more valuable property which she said she wanted Holland to have. He rewrote the will, making this change, and mailed it to her, as revised, on May 21, 1964. On the one occasion when he saw Mrs. Moses, there were no questions and no discussion of any kind as to Holland being preferred to the exclusion of her blood relatives. Nor was there any inquiry or discussion as to a possible client-attorney relationship with Holland. The attorney-draftsman wrote the will according to Mrs. Moses' instructions and said that he had 'no interest in' how she disposed of her property. He testified 'I try to draw the will to suit their purposes and if she wanted to leave him everything she had, that was her business as far as I was concerned. I was trying to represent her in putting on paper in her will her desires, and it didn't matter to me to whom she left it. I couldn't have cared less.'

When Mrs. Moses returned to the office to execute the will, the attorney was not there, and it was witnessed by two secretaries. One of these secretaries, coincidentally, had written and witnessed the 1961 will when working for Holland and his associate.

The attorney's testimony supports the chancellor's finding that there was no discussion of her relationship with Holland, nor as to who her legal heirs might be, nor as to their relationship to her, after it was discovered that she had neither a husband nor children.

It is clear from his own testimony that, in writing the will, the attorney-draftsman, did no more than write down, according to the forms of law, what Mrs. Moses told him. There was no meaningful independent advice or counsel touching upon the area in question and it is manifest that the role of the attorney in writing the will, as it relates to the present issue, was little more than that of scrivener. The chancellor was justified in holding that this did not meet the burden nor overcome the presumption.

Meek v. Perry, 36 Miss. 190 (1858), is perhaps the leading case. It involved a will by a ward leaving a substantial amount of her property to her guardian. The Court held that the presumption of invalidity applies to transactions between persons in confidential relations. The Court will not permit them to stand, unless the circumstances demonstrate the fullest deliberation on the part of the testator and the most abundant good faith on the part of the beneficiary. Hence the law presumes the existence of undue influence, and such dealings are prima facie void, and will be so held 'unless the guardian show by clearest proof' that he took no advantage over the testator, and the act was a result of his own volition and upon the fullest deliberation.

Where there is no presumption of undue influence, the burden of proof rests upon the proponents throughout and never shifts to the contestants, both on undue influence and mental incapacity. Undue influence is an intangible thing, which only rarely is susceptible of direct or positive proof. As was stated in *Jamison v. Jamison*, 51 So. 130 (Miss. 1909), 'the only positive and affirmative proof required is of facts and circumstances from which the undue influence may be reasonably inferred.'

The able and respected attorney who prepared the will upon data furnished him, testified that, in his opinion, the testator was mentally competent, and the instrument reflected testator's independent purpose. However, the record indicates that the witness had not conferred with Mr. Alder about the will prior to its drafting. Moreover, his testimony does not negate the presumption of undue influence resulting from prior actions by the principal beneficiary who was in the confidential relation.

'The difficulty in proving undue influence is also enhanced by the fact, universally recognized, that he who seeks to use undue influence does so in privacy. He seldom uses brute force or open threats to terrorize his intended victim, and if he *does* he is careful that no witnesses are about to take note of and testify to the fact. He observes, too, the same precautions if he seeks by cajolery, flattery, or other methods to obtain power and control over the will of another, and direct it improperly to the accomplishment of the purpose which he desires. Subscribing witnesses are called to attest the execution of wills, and testify as to the testamentary capacity of the testator, and the circumstances attending the immediate execution of the instrument.

We do not think that the testimony of the attorney who attested the will, as to his observations at that particular time, can suffice to rebut the already existing presumption.

In *Croft*, this Court quoted the rule as stated in 57 Am. Jur. Wills sections 389, 390 as follows:

> [A]lthough the mere existence of confidential relations between a testator and a beneficiary under his will does not raise a presumption that the beneficiary exercised undue influence over the testator, as it does with gifts inter vivos, such consequence follows where the beneficiary 'has been actively concerned in some way with the preparation or execution of the will, or where the relationship is coupled with some suspicious circumstances, such as mental infirmity of the testator;'

Holland, of course, did not personally participate in the actual preparation or execution of the will. If he had, under the circumstances in evidence, unquestionably the will could not stand. It may be assumed that Holland, as a lawyer, knew this.

Undue influence operates upon the will as well as upon the mind. It is not dependent upon a lack of testamentary capacity. The chancellor's finding that the will was the product of Holland's undue influence is not inconsistent with his conclusion that 'Her mind was capable of understanding the essential matters necessary to the execution of her will on May 26, 1964, at the time of such execution.' A weak or infirm mind may, of course, be more easily over persuaded. In the case under review, Mrs. Moses was in ill health, she was an alcoholic, and was an aging woman infatuated with a young lover, 15 years her junior, who was also her lawyer. If this combination of circumstances cannot be said to support the view that Mrs. Moses suffered from a 'weakness or infirmity' of mind, vis-a-vis Holland, it was hardly calculated to enhance her power of will where he was concerned. Circumstances in evidence, both antecedent and subsequent to the making of the will, tend to accord with that conclusion.

The sexual morality of the personal relationship is not an issue. However, the intimate nature of this relationship is relevant to the present inquiry to the extent that its existence, under the circumstances, warranted an inference of undue influence, extending and augmenting that which flowed from the attorney-client relationship.

In 94 C.J.S. WILLS § 263 (1956) it is stated:

> The mere existence of illicit, improper, unlawful, or meretricious relations between the testator and the beneficiary or the beneficiary's mother is insufficient of itself to prove fraud or undue influence, although the existence of such relations is an important fact to be considered by the jury along with other evidence of undue influence, giving to other circumstances a significance which they might not otherwise have; and much less evidence will be required to establish undue influence on the part of one holding wrongful and meretricious relations with the testator.

In *Croft* and *Taylor*, the beneficiary was present at or participated at some stage or in some way in the preparation or execution of the will. The rule laid down in *Croft*, would have little, if any, practical worth, if, under circumstances such as those established in this case, it could be nullified by a mere showing that the beneficiary was not physically present when the will was prepared and executed. There is no sound reason supporting the view that a testator, whose will has become subservient to the undue influence of another, is purged of the effects of that influence merely because the desired testamentary document is prepared by an attorney who knows nothing of the antecedent circumstances.

Viewed in the light of the above rules, it cannot be said that chancellor was manifestly wrong in finding that Holland occupied a dual fiduciary relationship with respect to Mrs. Moses, which gave rise to a presumption of undue influence in the production of the 1964 will, nor that he was manifestly wrong in finding that this presumption was not overcome by 'clearest proof' that in making and executing the will Mrs. Moses acted upon her 'own volition and upon the fullest deliberation,' or upon independent advice and counsel of one wholly devoted to her interest.

Petition for rehearing sustained, original opinion withdrawn, and decree of chancery court affirmed.

ROBERTSON, J. *dissenting*:

I am unable to agree with the majority of the Court that Mrs. Moses should not be allowed to dispose of her property as she so clearly intended.

No matter what the form of the instrument, if it represented the free, voluntary and knowledgeable act of the testator or testatrix it is a good will, and the directions of the will should be followed. We said in *Gillis v. Smith*, 75 So. 451, 453 (Miss. 1917):

> A man of sound mind may execute a will or a deed from any sort of motive satisfactory to him, whether that motive be love, affection, gratitude, partiality, prejudice, or even a whim or caprice.

Mrs. Fannie T. Moses was 54 years of age when she executed her last will and testament on May 26, 1964, leaving most of her considerable estate to Clarence H. Holland, her good friend, but a man fifteen years her junior. She had been married three times, and each of these marriages was dissolved by the death of her husband. Holland's friendship with Mrs. Moses dated back to the days of her second husband, Robert L. Dickson. He was also a friend of her third husband, Walter Moses.

She was the active manager of commercial property in the heart of Jackson, four apartment buildings containing ten rental units, and a 480-acre farm until the day of her death. All of the witnesses conceded that she was a good businesswoman, maintaining and repairing her properties with promptness and dispatch, and paying her bills promptly so that she would get the cash discount.

She was a strong personality and pursued her own course, even though her manner of living did at times embarrass her sisters and estranged her from them.

The chancellor found that she was of sound and disposing mind and memory on May 26, 1964, when she executed her last will and testament, and I think he was correct in this finding.

The chancellor found that there was a confidential relationship between Mrs. Moses and Holland, who had acted as her attorney in the past, and who was, in addition, a close and intimate friend, and that because of this relationship and some suspicious circumstances a presumption of undue influence arose.

There is no proof in this voluminous record that Holland ever did or said anything to Mrs. Moses about devising her property to anybody, much less him. It is conceded that in the absence of the presumption of undue influence that there is no basis to support a finding that Holland exercised undue influence over Mrs. Moses. This being true, the first question to be decided is whether the presumption of undue influence arises under the circumstances of this case.

It is my opinion that the presumption did not arise. The fact, alone, that a confidential relationship existed between Holland and Mrs. Moses is not sufficient to give rise to the presumption of undue influence in a will case.

It was not contended in this case that Holland was in any way actively concerned with the preparation or execution of the will. Appellees rely solely upon the finding of the chancellor that there were suspicious circumstances. However, the suspicious circumstances listed by the chancellor in his opinion had nothing whatsoever to do with the preparation or execution of the will. These were remote antecedent circumstances having to do with the meretricious relationship of the parties, and the fact that at times Mrs. Moses drank to excess and could be termed an alcoholic, but there is no proof in this long record that her use of alcohol affected her will power or her ability to look after her extensive real estate holdings. It is common knowledge that many persons who could be termed alcoholics, own, operate and manage large business enterprises with success. The fact that she chose to leave most of her property to the man she loved in preference to her sisters and brother is not such an unnatural disposition of her property as to render it invalid.

In this case, there were no suspicious circumstances surrounding the preparation or execution of the will, and in my opinion the chancellor was wrong in so holding. However, even if it be conceded that the presumption of undue influence did arise, this presumption was overcome by clear and convincing evidence of good faith, full knowledge and independent consent and advice.

When she got ready to make her will she called Honorable Dan H. Shell for an appointment. Shell did not know her, although he remembered that he had handled a land transaction for her third husband, Walter Moses, some years before. Shell had been in the active practice of law in Jackson since 1945; he was an experienced attorney with a large and varied practice. She came alone to his office on March 31, 1964, and advised him that she wanted him to prepare a will for her. Mr. Shell testified that she was alert, intelligent and rational, and knew exactly what she was doing.

He advised her that he needed specific legal descriptions of her various properties. She got this information and brought it to his office. He prepared the first draft of the will and mailed it to her on May 1, 1964. Shell testified:

> Then she called me in just a few days and pointed out that the will was not correct, that the property which I had described as being devised to Robert Miller was not the right tract of land and it should have been another piece of property that I had incorrectly devised to Clarence Holland and it should have been devised to Robert Miller, and the tract I had devised to Robert Miller should have been devised to Clarence Holland.

The majority was indeed hard put to find fault with his actions on behalf of his client. He ascertained that Mrs. Moses was competent to make a will; he satisfied himself that she was acting of her own free will and accord, and that she was disposing of her property exactly as she wished and intended. No more is required.

There is not one iota of testimony in this voluminous record that Clarence Holland even knew of this will, much less that he participated in the preparation or execution of it. The evidence is all to the contrary. The evidence is undisputed that she executed her last will after the fullest deliberation, with full knowledge of what she was doing, and with the independent consent and advice of an experienced and competent attorney whose sole purpose was to advise with her and prepare her will exactly as she wanted it.

What else could she have done? She met all the tests that this Court and other courts have carefully outlined and delineated. The majority opinion says that this still was not enough, that there were 'suspicious circumstances' and 'antecedent agencies', but even these were not connected in any shape, form or fashion with the preparation or execution of her will. They had to do with her love life and her drinking habits and propensities.

I think that the judgment of the lower court should be reversed, and the last will and testament of Fannie T. Moses executed on May 26, 1964, admitted to probate in solemn form.

NOTES

1. Why did the court think Moses was susceptible to Holland's undue influence? Were stereotypes about women at work in its reasoning? One author found that of the cases in her jurisdiction over a ten-year time period, 60 percent of the wills of female testators were overturned for undue influence, while only 30 percent of the wills of male testators were invalidated for that reason. Veena K. Murthy, *Undue Influence and Gender Stereotypes: Legal Doctrine or Indoctrination?*, 4 CARDOZO WOMEN'S L.J. 105, 112 (1997). Murthy found, further, that all the cases in which a woman left her estate to a romantic partner found undue influence, while the court failed to find undue influence in any of the cases in which a male testator left his estate to a female lover. *Id.* at 113.

2. Why does the court characterize Fannie Moses' hope that Holland might marry her as "pathetic"? In FEMINIST JUDGMENTS: REWRITTEN TRUSTS AND ESTATES OPINIONS 62 (eds. Deborah S Gordon, Browne C. Lewis, & Carla Spivack) (Cambridge Univ. Press 2020), Julia Belian rewrites the *Estate of Moses* opinion to read, "perhaps Holland entertained the pathetic hope that *she* would marry *him*." Is there evidence in the case that Moses wished to marry Holland?

3. Would *Moses* have come differently if the couple had been married? What if the man, Holland, had been the older party? What if the sexes of the parties had been reversed?

4. One scenario often giving rise to undue influence challenges before *Obergefell v. Hodges* was that of one partner in a same-sex relationship leaving a will benefitting the other partner. Before the U.S. Supreme Court legalized same-sex marriage in 2016, this was one way partners in same sex couples could leave their estates to each other. But these bequests often gave rise to will contests by disappointed relatives, who could rely on court biases against same-sex relationships to overturn these wills.

One famous instance was the case of the will of Robert Kaufmann, heir to the Kay Jewelers fortune. Robert met Walter Weiss in 1959, and the two lived together for ten years before Robert's unexpected death in 1959. Over the years, Robert drafted and redrafted wills which left more and more of his estate to Walter. After his death, Robert's family challenged his will, claiming that it was the product of Walter's undue influence. Perhaps anticipating trouble, Robert had attached a letter to the will explaining why he had left Walter his estate. The letter explained the disposition to Walter in the following terms:

> I am eternally grateful to my dearest friend—best pal, Walter A. Weiss. What could be more wonderful than a fruitful, contented life and who more deserving of gratitude now, in the form of an inheritance, than the person who helped most in securing that life? I cannot believe my family could be anything else but glad and happy for my own comfortable self-determination and contentment and equally grateful to the friend who made it possible.

In re Kaufmann's Will, 20 A.D.2d 464, 474 (N.Y. App. Div. 1964), aff'd, 205 N.E.2d 864 (1965).

Instead of reading this letter as proof of Robert's sincere intent to benefit Walter, however, the court took it as proof of exactly the opposite, as proof of the power of Walter's influence over Robert. It ruled that the will was indeed the product of undue influence. Given this response to evidence intended to rebut undue influence, how can a will proponent accused of undue influence overcome such a charge?

5.   Ray Madoff writes: "[T]he undue influence doctrine denies freedom of testation for people who deviate from judicially imposed testamentary norms-in particular, the norm that people should provide for their families." *See* Ray D. Madoff, *Unmasking Undue Influence*, 81 MINN. L. REV. 571, 576 (1997). Is undue influence just another form of family protection that law offers at death? And, if so, is this a good thing?

6.   Carla Spivack argues that the doctrine of undue influence in wills law should be abolished:

> The unsatisfactory doctrine of undue influence challenges us to decide what we, as a society, care about. . . . If we value testamentary freedom over protecting families, let courts give it effect. If we care about the elderly, let us institute measures that will protect them more effectively than a doctrine that acts only after a testator's death. Whatever our social priorities, the conclusion is clear: the doctrine of undue influence must be abandoned.

See Carla Spivack, *Why the Testamentary Doctrine of Undue Influence Should Be Abolished*, 58 U. KAN. L. REV. 245 (2010). Do you agree? Are there other, satisfactory mechanisms for protecting the elderly? For protecting testator intent? What new measure could we imagine to replace undue influence?

7.   Can an organization, say, a religious one, exert undue influence? For centuries, English law contained "mortmain" laws that restricted testamentary gifts to corporations (in effect, the Church) out of worry that people's "deathbed fears" would cause them to leave too much land in the Church's hands. A.H. Oosterhoff, *The Law of Mortmain: An Historical and Comparative Review*, 27 U. TORONTO L.J. 257, 267 (1977). Most American states have abandoned such laws, but in *Can Religious Influence Ever Be "Undue" Influence?*, 73 BROOK. L. REV. 579, 583 (2008), Jeffrey G. Sherman, argues for a legal presumption that the "relationships between a testator and her religious or spiritual advisor are per se 'confidential relationships' for purposes of litigating any will contest." Do you agree? Can exhortations from the pulpit—or warnings that God will punish those who do not make donations—constitute undue influence? *See Roberts-Douglas v. Meares*, 624 A.2d 405 (D.C. 1992). Some courts have held that a spiritual advisor can unduly influence a congregant, even if the gift is left to the entity and not to the advisor. *See Olsen v. Corporation of New Melleray*, 60 N.W.2d 832 (Iowa 1953); *see also Estate of Maheras*, 897 P.2d 268 (Okla. 1995) ("Whether the person exerting the overbearing influence actually benefits personally under the will's terms is immaterial.").

In the following case, consider the role of race in shaping the undue influence claim.

Dees v. Metts

17 So. 2d 137 (Ala. 1944)

HORNE, J.

This cause was originally assigned to Mr. Justice BOULDIN. Upon consideration of his opinion by the Court in Division consultation, the writer prepared the following opinion in dissent thereto. And upon further consideration of the cause by the whole Court, the conclusion reached by this dissenting opinion met the approval of the majority and here controls the result.

The unnumbered jury instruction, given at the request of contestants, and forming the basis of the fourth assignment of error below, reads as follows:

> The court charges the jury that if the consideration in the deed is so extremely inadequate as to satisfy the conscience of the jury that there must have been imposition, or undue influence, which in the opinion of the jury amounted to oppression, the jury should return a verdict for the contestant.

The deed recited the consideration as follows: "That for and in consideration of 1 and 00/100ths dollars to the undersigned grantor J.B. Watts in hand paid by Nazarine Parker the receipt whereof is acknowledged."

The principle attempted to be brought forward by this jury instruction could have reference only to a transaction regarding bargain and sale—a vendor and purchaser. But it has no application whatever to the deed here in question. There was no bargain and sale. Confessedly, it was a deed of gift, and nothing more.

The action of the trial court in giving this instruction cannot be sustained. To do so would be to permit the application of legal principles to a given case which are entirely foreign thereto. We must assume that the jury gave some consideration to this instruction. They had it with them in the jury room. Doubtless they had also with them the deed. So considered, they are told by this charge that if they view the consideration of $1 as extremely inadequate, this may be considered as indicating undue influence amounting to oppression, justifying a verdict for the contestants.

Looking at it from a practical standpoint, it would appear that would be the only practical construction of the jury instruction. The undisputed evidence was that the real estate described in the deed was worth from $2,000 to $2,500. The jury was bound to know, therefore, that the expressed consideration of $1, as found in the deed, was "extremely inadequate." As a consequence, in practical effect it appears the jury instruction amounted to affirmative instructions in favor of the contestants, so far as the deed is concerned.

> **Language Note**: As noted with both *Evans* (in Chapter 3) and as you will see with *Girard College* (in Chapter 15), the *Dees* court uses the word "Negro." We have left the original language intact, even though the word is not appropriate in modern usage, to reflect this aspect of the case's history and vernacular.

Mr. Lee, a reputable attorney, testified concerning the preparation of this deed for Ben Watts. His evidence was to the effect that he had known Watts for a period of 25 years. Watts had consulted him previously about his will, and Lee had advised Watts that it was quite sufficient to carry out his wishes; i.e., giving his property to Nazarine Parker. Several months later, and a few months before he died, Watts called upon him again, and asked if he could legally convey his lands to Nazarine Parker reserving the use of his lands during his lifetime, and stating that he anticipated his people might try to break his will; and that "he wanted to do everything possible to make sure that his will would be carried out." Lee advised him such a deed could be made reserving a life estate; and he prepared the deed for him. He further testified that Watts "was absolutely of sound mind, and there was no question about him understanding the nature of the business he was transacting. * * * He was determined and wanted to see that none of his people got any of his money. He stated that this Negro had helped him and taken care of him, and he wanted her to have the property." Lee further stated that Nazarine Parker was not in his office at the time the deed was prepared; that in fact he had never seen her during Ben Watts' lifetime. "I never saw her to know who she was. I do not know where Nazarine Parker is today."

J.B. Barnett had been in the banking business close to 39 years, and had been acquainted with Ben Watts during most of that time. Watts did his banking with the bank in which Barnett was interested. Barnett testified that Watts was a man of sound mind, "a man of special keenness, and in my judgment he was a man of strong determination. He was not easily persuaded. He was very determined in his ideas."

Reference is made to some of the testimony as found in the record merely to demonstrate there was abundant proof upon which the jury could rest a finding the deed was executed free from any undue influence. Yet, as I think the jury were bound to construe the instruction. I am fully persuaded inescapable error was committed in the giving of this jury instruction.

But my disagreement goes beyond this point and to the very essence of the case. Coming to a consideration of the will, I am unable to find sufficient proof in the record to justify its invalidity. I am, of course, in full accord with all that is said in Mr. Justice Bouldin's opinion concerning the policy of our State, as found in our Constitution and statute, intended to safeguard the racial integrity of white peoples as well as the racial integrity of Negro peoples. I freely admit, also, that a universal public opinion prevalent in both races recognizes at least two grades of depravity in matters of illicit relationship. It is reprehensible enough for a white man to live in adultery with a white woman, thus defying the laws of both God and man, but it is more so, and a much lower grade of depravity, for a white man to live in adultery with a Negro woman.

Fortunately, the cases of such depravity are very rare. The contest of the will of one Ryal Noble, found reported in *Allen v. Scruggs*, 67 So. 301 (Ala.), furnishes a disgraceful example. The opinion discloses that Noble was a white man coming from an entirely respectable family of people; that soon after the War between the States he began a meretricious association with Kit Allen, a Negro woman who lived on his plantation, and during many years he had his residence in a building nearby to that occupied by her. There were five children born, and to these children he willed his property. At the execution of the will the woman, Kit Allen, was present. The case was very ably presented to this court, and quite an elaborate discussion of the facts and the applicable principles of the law are to be found in the opinion. The will had been lost. The proof satisfied the court that, nevertheless, it had existed, and that it expressed the fixed will of the testator. The result was that the ruling of the probate judge was reversed, and one here rendered admitting the will to probate.

For such meretricious conduct our laws are more severe, the punishment more extreme. Yet it appears that organized society—the law—took no step to interfere, and the guilty parties left unmolested. One thing, however, is clear, and that is—however reprehensible the conduct and however deservedly severe the punishment, the law forfeits no right to ownership of property of either of the guilty parties, nor challenges the right of free disposal thereof.

It is the settled law of this State that illicit relationship is not sufficient per se to warrant a conclusion of undue influence. And no presumption of undue influence arises merely from the fact that a man who is of sound mind makes a will in favor of his mistress, or in favor of one with whom his relations have been meretricious.

The existence of confidential relations between the testator and the beneficiary under the will must be "coupled with activity on the part of the latter in and about the preparation or execution of the will, such as the initiation of proceedings for the preparation of the instrument, or participation in such preparation, employing the draughtsman, selecting the witnesses, excluding persons from the presence of the testator at or about the time of the execution, concealing the making of the will after it was made, and the like." This, as the opinion points out, will raise up the presumption of undue influence and cast upon the beneficiary the burden of showing it was not induced by coercion or fraud on his part, directly or indirectly; but no such presumption can be predicated alone on confidential relations.

Of course, all the cases recognize that undue influence must be sufficient to destroy the free agency of the testator. In *Dunlap v. Robinson*, 28 Ala. 100, speaking to the matter of undue influence in connection with the contest of a will made largely to the children of the alleged mistress, to whom it appears, however, a life estate was reserved as to a portion of the property, the Court observed: "Undue influence, as that term is understood in this connection, must be such as, in some measure, destroys the free agency of the testator, and prevents the exercise of that discretion which the law requires a party should possess as essential to a valid testamentary disposition of his property. It is not enough that by the testator's own improper conduct he has brought about a condition of things, over which, at the time of making his will, he had no control to change or remedy, but which, as a moral inducement, operated upon his mind, influencing him to make a disposition of his property which, under other circumstances, he might not have made."

It must be such influence as dominates the grantor's will and coerces it to serve the will of another in the act of conveying. And in this connection the court considers the matter of dominant party. In the instant case testator was of the "dominant race." And the dictates of common sense tell us that this unlawful relationship must have been initiated by Watts himself, and the proof is abundant that he in fact was a man of determined will.

Mr. Dees, who wrote the will, had known Watts since 1920. Watts came into the bank and informed him he wanted to make a will; "that he wanted some white man to represent him to act as executor of the will, and he wanted me to do it and represent him." The witness then continues: "and he said 'I want you to draw up a will and I want to fix it up this morning. * * * I want to leave what I have for this Negro woman that has been taking care of me all the time. You know how white people are about Negroes, and I want to be sure this thing is handled right because I want her to have what I've got. All my own people have ever done for me was to borrow money and never pay it back. I want to see that she gets it, and I want to see that some white man sees that she does get it.' "

Dees was named executor without bond, and propounded the will for probate. He testifies: "From my relations with him and from what I was able to observe, I would say that Ben Watts was a man of very sound mind. He was a man of strong determination. I would not think he could be easily swayed from his judgment." He further added that Watts "was a successful man."

Dr. Smith, a practicing physician since 1912, had known Watts for years. He thought he was a "man of absolutely sound mind." Another merchant; the post office clerk; the sheriff of the County; Mr. Lee, the attorney; Mr. Salter of the newspaper business, who had considerable dealing with him and saw him frequently; and others engaged in business in Monroeville, testified to like effect. Some of the witnesses also indicate that Watts made some contributions in aid of the support of his people, but to what extent it is not at all clear.

The only evidence offered by contestants seeking to impeach the testimony of these business men of Monroeville had relation to Watts' conduct at the home of his mother. If this testimony is to be given its full credence, he acted most shamefully in the abusive language used. His conduct would appear clearly to have been the result of resentment on his part for their attempted interference. Indeed, he had at last built a smaller house for himself near the larger house where Nazarine Parker lived.

But all this considered, it is clear enough from the proof that Ben Watts was a man of perfectly sound mind and one of strong will power. Indeed, the original opinion holds nothing to the contrary.

The record shows that his prejudice towards his relatives was largely the result of his resentment of their criticism of his conduct, but in no event did any such prejudice as here shown serve a purpose to reflect upon his testamentary capacity. 28 R.C.L. p. 104–108. And the same may be said as to display of violent temper as above indicated. 28 R.C.L. p. 89. But this question need be pursued no further, as we have observed the opinion in no manner questions his testamentary capacity, and as I view it, is rested solely upon the ground of undue influence.

The courts are not concerned with the matter to whom this property goes, but we should be greatly concerned lest we destroy the right of free disposal of property, which is inherent in its ownership. However sinful Ben Watts may have been, and however disgraceful his conduct, if he was of sound mind and not unduly influenced, the courts are bound to give respect to his wishes.

I am fully persuaded the record discloses no valid reason in law why the determined will of Ben Watts should not be upheld by the courts.

Reversed and Remanded.

BOULDIN, J., *dissenting*.

Prevention of race amalgamation, safeguarding the racial integrity of white peoples and the racial integrity of negro peoples, is the fixed public policy of Alabama. It is written into our Constitution in these words: "The legislature shall never pass any law to authorize or legalize any marriage between any white person and a negro, or descendant of a negro." Article IV, § 102, Constitution of 1901.

It finds legislative expression in our miscegenation statute, which reads: "If any white person and any negro, or the descendant any negro intermarry, or live in adultery or fornication with each other, each of them shall, on conviction, be imprisoned in the penitentiary for not less than two nor more than seven years." Title 14, § 360, Code of 1940.

We are now confronted with a case involving the validity of a will made by a white man bequeathing his entire estate to a negro woman with whom he was living in a state of adultery or fornication, followed by a deed of gift conveying to her his real estate, reserving its use and enjoyment during his life.

After his death the alleged will was offered for probate by the executor therein named. A contest was instituted by next of kin of decedent on the grounds of undue influence and mental incapacity. The cause was transferred to the circuit court for trial.

A bill in equity was also filed in the circuit court to cancel the deed upon like grounds. By agreement the cases were consolidated and the issues submitted to a jury who found both instruments invalid.

Among the questions here presented is whether there was evidence of undue influence presenting a jury question; and, if so, whether a new trial should have been granted because of the great weight of the evidence on that issue.

The evidence disclosed that decedent and beneficiary were living together in a state of adultery or fornication at the time the will was executed and for many years prior thereto; that the same illicit and criminal relation continued to the time of making the deed, some two years after making the will, and continued to the death of decedent, some five months after making the deed. This evidence was not controverted, and is not challenged on appeal.

Further evidence disclosed they lived together in the residence owned by decedent which, with some acreage connected therewith, was covered by both will and deed, and constituted the greater portion of decedent's estate.

Other evidence was to the effect that decedent kept up a day-time connection with his family, taking his mid-day meal at the family residence in the same neighborhood; that he had, without cause, long conceived an intense dislike for his kindred, including a brother, a sister and an aged mother, all of whom pre-deceased him; that he was abusive and menacing in his manner, speaking to and of his people in contemptuous terms, with most opprobrious epithets, etc.

Nevada Nelson, testifying as an intimate neighbor having full knowledge of their illicit relation, said: "She would tell him what she wanted and he would give her what she asked for. She told me that he had willed her every damn thing he had, and that she was going to get it."

Dill Brooks testified she cooked for them and, among other things, said: "She just called him good names, she never did say anything ugly to him. I never heard him refuse her any request she made, nor ask for anything that he would refuse. He always shelled it out to her."

Proponent's evidence, in substance, disclosed a fixed purpose of the decedent to will his property to the negro woman, who, he said, had helped him and taken care of him all the time; disclosed he was apprehensive of a contest of the will, wanted a white man as executor to see that the devisee got the property; that the deed was executed on his insistence as an additional muniment of title in case the will was defeated. Nazarine was not present when either instrument was executed.

There are special elements in the peculiar confidential relations existent between the parties.

The man, in such case, gets his consent to a way of life made a continuous felony by the laws of his state, a higher offense than in case of such relation between persons of the same race. He faces a loss of respect on the part of friends and neighbors of his own race, the better element of both races; is probably ostracized to a degree by the social laws of his community; sacrifices his own self-respect; humiliates his family, his blood relatives. All this in a special and peculiar measure in cases of this sort.

The inspiration and objective of his ugly, intimidating attitude toward his kindred, without any evidence of good reason therefor, was for the solution of the jury in the light of all the circumstances. There was some evidence of efforts on their part to change his way of living. Whether his fixed purpose to give the property to his paramour as insistently declaimed to the draftsman of both instruments was the expression of his own will, or a mere echo of her will, was a jury question. Proof of illicit relations is not alone sufficient to show undue influence in will cases. Evidence of such relations is admissible in connection with other evidence tending to show undue influence.

The evidence supported a finding of both instruments invalid on the ground of undue influence. Indeed, under the evidence, and the law of undue influence in will cases, and the law relating to gifts inter vivos, the jury could not well have found the will invalid and the deed valid and effective.

I, therefore, dissent.

NOTES

1.   Both the majority and the dissent express the same disapproval of the testator's relationship with the beneficiary. How do you think they reach opposite legal conclusions?

2.   Why do you think the testator drew up the deed to Kit reserving a life estate for himself instead of just leaving his property in his will?

3.   The intersection of slavery and testation in the Antebellum South is multifaceted. *See* Alfred L. Brophy & Douglas Thie, *Land, Slaves, and Bonds: Trust and Probate in the Pre-Civil War Shenandoah Valley*, 119 W. VA. L. REV. 345, 346 (2016) (showing the varying use of wills and trusts both to leave property to and emancipate enslaved people, and to bequeath them as property to others); *see also* Bernie D. Jones, *"Righteous Fathers," "Vulnerable Old Men," and "Degraded Creatures": Southern Justices on Miscegenation in the Antebellum Will Contest*, 40 TULSA L. REV. 699 (2005).

4.   George Wythe was a famous judge in Colonial Virginia. He had signed the Declaration of Independence and later ruled "that the free and equal clause created a general presumption of freedom for all persons," a ruling that the Virginia Supreme Court overruled in 1806. Robert J. Reinstein, *Completing the Constitution: The Declaration of Independence, Bill of Rights and Fourteenth Amendment*, 66 TEMP. L. REV. 361, 410 (1993). In 1806, Wythe wrote codicils to his will that made Michael Brown, his 15-year-old freed slave, the beneficiary of an educational trust and appointed President Jefferson as Brown's guardian. Wythe's grandnephew, George Sweeney, who was next in line for the inheritance, murdered Wythe and Brown. On his deathbed, Wythe accused Sweeney of the crime and disinherited him. At Sweeney's murder trial, the chief prosecution witness, whom Wythe had freed from slavery, was not allowed to testify because Virginia law prohibited the introduction of testimony by blacks against whites. The murderer of the judge who attempted to end slavery was acquitted by the operation of Virginia's slave code. WILLIAM CLARKIN, SERENE PATRIOT: A LIFE OF GEORGE WYTHE 208–19 (1970); Julian P. Boyd, *The Murder of George Wythe*, 12 WM. & MARY. Q. 513–42 (1955).

5.   The lawyer identified only as Mr. Lee in the *Dees* case is Amasa Coleman Lee, the father of novelist Harper Lee. Mr. Lee served as the model for Atticus Finch in Lee's 1960 novel *To Kill a Mockingbird*. Max Cassady, a lawyer from

Harper Lee became famous when she published *To Kill a Mockingbird* in 1960. Harper Lee, pictured circa 1962.

Fairhope, Alabama, has investigated the case and written an extensive article about it, which makes the very reasonable argument that that Ben Watts served as the model for Dolphus Raymond in *To Kill a Mockingbird*. Cassady quotes extensively the trial testimony that included charges by Watts's intestate heirs that he had lived with Parker since around 1920 and that mental illness ran in his family; Watts's business associates, on the other hand, said he was capable of making his will and also was trustworthy. *See* Max Cassady, *Harper Lee's Dolphus Raymond inspired by father's client*, LAGNIAPPE WEEKLY (July 8, 2015).[1] Harper Lee fans may recognize an additional irony related to allegations of misconduct in connection with the publishing in 2015 of Lee's novel *Go Set a Watchman*. The circumstances are described in a New York Times article as follows:

> After publishing her beloved novel, "To Kill a Mockingbird" in 1960, she not only never published another book; for most of that time she insisted she never would. Until now, that is, when she's 89, a frail, hearing- and sight-impaired stroke victim living in a nursing home. Perhaps just as important, her sister Alice, Lee's longtime protector, passed away last November. Her new protector, Tonja Carter, who had worked in Alice Lee's law office, is the one who brought the "new novel" to HarperCollins's attention, claiming, conveniently, to have found it shortly before Alice died.

Joe Nocera, *The Harper Lee 'Go Set a Watchman' Fraud*, N.Y. TIMES (July 14, 2015).[2] Undue influence by Lee's publisher? You decide.

ASSESSMENT

Read the following fact pattern and assess the strength of the cousins' claim that the will described below should fail because the testator lacked testamentary capacity and/or the will was the product of undue influence:

> Upon her death in 1989, eighty-six-year-old Pearl Rose left her Great Danes to a local kennel, a $5000 bequest to her church, and a rental property she owned to the family who had rented it for years. The rest, residue, and remainder of her estate she gave to sixty-two-year-old Lewis Everett Peck, who was not a relative. He was an acquaintance of Pearl Rose who said that he had agreed to care for her on the condition that he would inherit her estate when she died. Pearl's estate consisted of land worth approximately $20 million, including a large 17th century home and 947 acres of land that surrounded it. Pearl's relatives assert that she was mentally ill, as well as physically incapacitated. Pearl had no children, and she was a widow. She had no siblings. However, 44 cousins—many of whom

---

1   Available at: http://lagniappemobile.com/harper-lees-dolphus-raymond-inspired-fathers-client/.

2   Available at https://www.nytimes.com/2015/07/25/opinion/joe-nocera-the-watchman-fraud.html.

had never met her or had not seen her for years—filed an objection to the probate of her will, alleging lack of testamentary capacity and undue influence.

Lewis Peck says that he began talking with Pearl at Town Council meetings and trading political information since he was a Republican town council member, and she was active in the Democratic Party. He denies that he traded information with her in an attempt to take advantage of her. In 1978, they began discussing an arrangement where he would care for her when she became ill. Lewis Peck also claims that they agreed that if he took care of her and that she did not die in a nursing home, that he would be the sole beneficiary of her will.

Two years later, in 1980, Pearl signed a will to that effect. The will provided that:

> Failure to provide for any of my relatives or heirs-at-law has not been by accident or mistake, but intentional, since I have provided for them during my lifetime.

Pearl's lawyer, John Lynch, has stated that Pearl was a person who intended to do exactly what she did, and that was to exclude her relatives from the will. He said she had had a will since she was twenty-five years old.

In 1982, Pearl was hospitalized for a broken hip. The cousins claim that during this hospitalization, her medical records indicated that she suffered from hallucinations and severe depression. They also claim that Pearl's mental state had been deteriorating for years, and that she lived in absolute filth, with dogs and goats roaming around the house. The house had no electricity or bathrooms despite her vast wealth. There was an outhouse in the yard. They claimed that she was known to eat decayed food, sat in a chair for days, and urinated and drank from the same jar.

In 1986, Pearl fell again and was partially paralyzed, requiring daily care. At that point, Lewis Peck moved her into his house. He claims that he bathed her, took care of her, and fed her by hand. She remained at his house until she died in 1989.

Based upon your assessment, predict how a court would resolve the cousins' challenges to Pearl Rose's will.

C. Duress, Fraud, and Insane Delusion

Although most will challenges involve claims of undue influence or lack of capacity, there are some other grounds for contest too. This section briefly describes traditional challenges like duress, fraud, and insane delusion.

1. Duress

Duress arises when physical coercion is used to exert influence. Duress is defined as follows: "A donative transfer is procured by duress if the wrongdoer threatened to perform or did perform a wrongful act that coerced the donor into making [or failing to make] a donative transfer that the donor would not otherwise have made." RESTATEMENT (THIRD) PROPERTY: WILLS AND OTHER DONATIVE TRANSFERS § 8.3(c) (2003).

Duress need not involve someone holding a gun to someone else's head: imagine an elderly parent dependent on a son to take her to doctor's appointments or pick up medicine. If the son threatens to stop helping the parent unless she leaves him her estate, this could be duress. Or imagine a testator on an oxygen tank whose daughter manipulates the controls while asking the testator to execute a will favoring her.

In one of the more bizarre cases in the history of will contests, Mary Sheldon Lyon executed a will in 1943 leaving her estate to Father Divine, a charismatic and controversial religious (some said cult) leader. When Lyon died in 1946, her heirs challenged the will, claiming that she had wanted to change her will to benefit them, but that Father Divine had had her killed before she could do so, by arranging to have her operated on by a surgeon working for him.

Father Divine was a source of great controversy both for his financial dealings and his civil rights work. Mother and Father Divine, circa 1953.

Lyon was an active member of Father Divine's congregation, as seen in this picture. Is there anything in the picture that suggests why a court was willing to invalidate her will? It's worth noting in thinking about this case that Father Divine, whose full self-given name was Reverend Major Jealous Divine, advocated for racial equality and called for members of lynch mobs to be charged with murder. For more about Father Divine's life and times, *see* JILL WATTS, GOD, HARLEM, U.S.A.: THE FATHER DIVINE STORY (1992); ROBERT

WEISBROT, FATHER DIVINE AND THE STRUGGLE FOR RACIAL EQUALITY (1983).

2. Fraud

Fraud is the same in wills law as it is in contracts. The elements of fraud include:

- A deliberate misrepresentation

- Made with the intent to induce the disposition

- Resulting in the testator making a disposition she otherwise would not have made

In a case of fraud, the testator freely makes a new estate plan, but does so as a result of having been misled.

Fraud in the wills context comes in two varieties: fraud in the inducement and fraud in the execution. **Fraud in the inducement** involves a misrepresentation that causes the testator to execute or revoke a will, to refrain from executing or revoking a will, or to include particular provisions in the wrongdoer's favor. For example, Rosario intentionally tells Teresa that her daughter has died, causing Teresa to revise her will to omit the daughter and benefit Rosario. In a case of undue influence, in contrast, the testator makes a new estate plan because of influence that overcomes the testator's free will.

Fraud in the execution involves a misrepresentation about the character or contents of the instrument signed by the testator, which does not in fact carry out the testator's intent. For example: Beth intentionally tells Tomas that he is signing a school permission slip that actually is a will leaving everything to Beth.

Brooke Astor was a famed philanthropist and fixture on the New York social circuit. Brooke Astor in 2002 in her duplex on Park Avenue.

Another, famous example of a will contest involves the estate of Brooke Astor, a New York philanthropist with an estate worth hundreds of millions of dollars. When Astor died in 2007 at age 105, authorities in New York charged her son, Anthony Marshall, with fraud, embezzlement, and forgery with regard to codicils to her will that dramatically increased Marshall's inheritance. Marshall was tried in criminal court, an unusual venue for such a proceeding, found guilty, and sentenced to three years in prison.

> **Connection Note:** Note that fraud is not the same as mistake: a testator could make a provision in a will as a result of a genuine mistake of law or fact and, under some circumstances, the court might reform the will to conform to the testator's true intent. *See* RESTATE (THIRD) OF PROP.: WILLS AND OTHER DONATIVE TRANSFERS § 12.1, cmt. G (2003). For example, a mistake of fact would occur if a testator disinherited a child because she mistakenly believed that child had become addicted to drugs. A mistake of law might be a testator leaving her estate to her children because she thought the law required her to do so.

3. Insane Delusion

Insane delusion arises when the testator:

- Suffers from a belief contrary to reality

- Refuses to change that belief even when confronted with evidence to the contrary, and

- Disposition is the result of that belief

Notice that a testator could have a delusion—or many—and still have a perfectly valid will as long as the insane beliefs did not actually cause the dispositions in the will. And while a will contestant would likely allege incapacity in combination with insane delusion, they are not the same thing. It might seem likely that someone who has an insane delusion probably lacks capacity, but this is not necessarily the case. A testator could suffer from insane delusion and still have testamentary capacity—that is, know what his estate was and who his family members were. In such a case, the will would be valid as long as the delusion did not cause the bequest in the will.

NOTES

1. Like undue influence, the doctrine of insane delusion has received a lot of criticism for its subjectivity and lack of scientific basis. *See, e.g.,* Bradley E.S. Fogel, *The Completely Insane Law of Partial Insanity: The Impact of Monomania on Testamentary Capacity,* 42 REAL PROP. PROB. & TR. J. 67, 93 (2007) Kevin Bannardo, *The Madness of Insane Delusion,* 69 ARIZ. L. REV. 601 (2018); Joshua C. Tate, *Personal Reality: Delusion in Law and Science,* 49 CONN. L. REV. 891 (2017); Patricia R. Champine, *A Sanist Will?* 46 NY L. SCH. L. REV. 547 (2002/3).

2.   Think about how subjective the assessment of insanity/insane delusion is: in 1947, the New Jersey Supreme Court denied probate to Louisa Strittmater's will because she had left her estate to the National Woman's Party, a group that advocated for women's suffrage. The Court ruled that her passionate feminism was a form of insanity and threw out her will as the product of insane delusion. *In re Strittmater's Will*, 53 A.2d 205 (N.J. 1947). Strittmater had been active in this Party for many years and was a vocal feminist. On the other hand, she had no contact with the relatives who contested the will. Nonetheless, by invalidating the will, the court gave her estate to these family members from whom she had been estranged. The *Strittmater* court used medical language and norms of the day to find that the testator was mentally disturbed, noting:

**The American Weekly,
November 24, 1946**

Her disease seems to have become well developed by 1936. In August of that year she wrote, "It remains for feministic organizations like the National Wom[a]n's Party, to make exposure of women's 'protectors' and 'lovers' for what their vicious and contemptible selves are." She had been a member of the Wom[a]n's Party for eleven years at that time, but the evidence does not show that she had taken great interest in it. I think it was her paranoic condition, especially her insane delusions about the male, that led her to leave her estate to the National Women's Party.

Id. at 205–06.

For analyses of the way courts used medical science and social norming to invalidate bequests that fall outside socially acceptable boundaries, see Pamela R. Champine, *My Will Be Done: Accommodating the Erring and the Atypical Testator*, 80 NEB. L. REV. 387, 447–52 (2001); Adam Hirsch, *Testation and the Mind*, 74 WASH. & LEE L. REV. 285, 326–38 (2017).

3.   For a look at the uses of insane delusion to shape notions of the moral self in American history, see Susanna Blumenthal, *The Deviance of the Will: Policing the Bounds of Testamentary Freedom in Nineteenth Century America*, 119 HARV. L. REV. 959 (2006). In the article, Blumenthal tells the following story:

By all accounts, George Moore was a dissolute bachelor who most likely drank himself to death. In his last years, Moore's drunkenness was "nearly without intermission" so that he was almost entirely confined to his bed. In early March 1822, a physician "candidly apprised him that his case was a hopeless one, and advised him to arrange his temporal affairs and think of eternity." Days before his death, Moore executed a will disinheriting his three brothers and leaving much of his estate to his female slave, with whom he had lived "in a state of concubinage."

Moore's disappointed heirs challenged his will on three grounds: testamentary incapacity, undue influence, and fraud. At trial, they presented testimony that Moore had contracted a severe fever some twenty-five years earlier, during which time he "conceived an antipathy against his brothers"; he became convinced that they "designed to destroy or injure him, although they attended him constantly in his illness." The fever eventually subsided, but Moore was never entirely divested of this "unnatural and unfounded aversion." His brothers contended that Moore's devisees took advantage of his deranged state of mind and encouraged his malicious disposition toward his natural heirs. To counter this testimony, the will's proponents called witnesses who maintained Moore was in his right mind when the disputed document was made, possessing more than sufficient intellect to competently dispose of his estate.

The trial court denied the will probate, and this judgment was affirmed on appeal. In so ruling, Kentucky's highest court did not deny the credibility of the proponents' witnesses. In fact, the opinion indicated that the court would have had no hesitation admitting the will to record but for two critical pieces of evidence offered by the contestants. First, Moore's female slave apparently "possessed considerable influence over him," particularly in his declining years. Second, he manifested great hostility toward his unoffending brothers long after his fever passed. The court viewed this "groundless" disaffection as definitive proof of the testator's "derangement in one department of his mind." Accordingly, Moore could not be "accounted a free agent in making his will, so far as his relatives [were] concerned, although free as to the rest of the world."

Id. at 960–61.

Although the grounds for the will challenge were testamentary incapacity, undue influence, and fraud, the court ended up finding a "derangement," which sounds more like insane delusion. Did George's hatred of his brothers, even if there was no apparent basis for it, amount to an insane delusion? Could there have been other reasons the court denied the will probate?

D. Tortious Interference with Inheritance: Necessary Remedy or Litigation Breeder?

In 27 states, a person seeking to invalidate a will or gift can also sue in tort. The RESTATEMENT (SECOND) OF TORTS § 774B (1977) provides that "One who by fraud, duress or other tortious means intentionally prevents another from receiving from a third person an inheritance or gift that he would otherwise have received is subject to liability to the other for loss of the inheritance or gift." By inheritance the Restatement means "any devise or bequest that would otherwise have been made under a testamentary instrument or any property that would have passed to the plaintiff by intestate succession." *Id.*, cmt. b. Tortious interference with inheritance is a controversial doctrine because its boundaries are unclear, and it threatens to re-open litigation of issues that maybe should have been settled in probate.

> **Connection Note:** While law school courses are necessarily divided into different subject areas, practice areas are far more likely to overlap. Tortious interference in probate disputes is one example of such an overlap, but there are many more. For example, tort-related claims, which may result in the awarding of damages for mental anguish, may be raised in connection with a contract dispute. Can you think of other overlaps?

Plaintiffs have also successfully asserted tortious interference with an inheritance where third parties have encouraged testators (1) to revise their wills or trusts, (2) to retitle property, or (3) to change payable on death contracts to eliminate heirs—or have interfered with the execution of a will that would leave property to an heir. The first case below is a continuation of the first undue influence decision in this chapter, *Moriarty v. Moriarty*, here addressing the claim of tortious interference as an additional basis on which to invalidate transfers to the surviving spouse. The next case, *Schilling v. Herrera*, involves a caretaker whose actions deprived a testator's family member the opportunity to challenge the will.

Moriarty v. Moriarty

150 N.E.3d 616 (Ct. App. Ind. 2020)

CRONE, J.

The trial court also entered judgment in favor of Daughters on their claim for tortious interference with inheritance.

Tortious interference with an inheritance occurs when "[o]ne who by fraud or other tortious means intentionally prevents another from receiving from a third person an inheritance or gift that he would otherwise have received is subject to liability to others for the loss of the inheritance or gift." *Minton v. Sackett*, 671 N.E.2d 160, 162 (Ind. Ct. App. 1996) (adopting RESTATEMENT (SECOND) OF TORTS § 774B (1979)). This action is prohibited "where the remedy of a will contest is available and would provide the injured party with adequate relief." *Id.*

According to Eve, the trial court properly relied on *Minton* but failed to apply the clear and convincing evidence standard to the joint accounts, citing *Womack v. Womack*, 622 N.E.2d 481 (Ind. 1993). Specifically, Eve directs us to the following language: "the party challenging the survivor's right to the proceeds of the joint account must show by clear and convincing evidence that the decedent did not intend the survivor to receive the proceeds of the account without the benefit of a presumption of undue influence." *Id.* at 483; *see also* IND. CODE § 32–17–11–18 ("Sums remaining on deposit at the death of a party to a joint account belong to the surviving party or parties as against the estate of the decedent unless there is clear and convincing evidence of a different intention at the time the account is created.").

Although the trial court did not specifically cite *Womack* or Section 32–17–11–18, it indisputably applied the clear and convincing standard to the joint accounts in finding: "The Court concludes that [Daughters] have by clear and convincing evidence established that William did not intend for Eve to inherit the value of the Joint Accounts." We find no error on this basis.

Schilling v. Herrera

952 So. 2d 1231 (Fla. Dist. Ct. App. 2007)

ROTHENBERG, J.

The plaintiff, Edward A. Schilling ("Mr. Schilling"), appeals from an order granting the defendant Maria Herrera's ("Ms. Herrera") motion to dismiss the amended complaint with prejudice based on the trial court's finding that the amended complaint fails to state a cause of action and that Mr. Schilling is barred from filing to action because he failed to exhaust his probate remedies. We disagree as to both findings and, therefore, reverse and remand for further proceedings.

PROCEDURAL HISTORY

Mr. Schilling, the decedent's brother, sued Ms. Herrera, the decedent's caretaker, for intentional interference with an expectancy of inheritance. Ms. Herrera moved to dismiss the complaint, arguing that Mr. Schilling failed to state a cause of action and that he was barred from filing his claim because he failed to exhaust his probate remedies. The trial court granted the motion to dismiss without prejudice.

Thereafter, Mr. Schilling filed an amended complaint asserting the same cause of action against Ms. Herrera. The amended complaint alleges that in December 1996, Mignonne Helen Schilling (the decedent) executed her Last Will and Testament, naming her brother and only heir-at-law, Mr. Schilling, as her personal representative and sole beneficiary, and in May 1997, she executed a Durable Power of Attorney, naming Mr. Schilling as her attorney-in-fact. In December 1999, the decedent was diagnosed with renal disease, resulting in several hospitalizations. During this period, Mr. Schilling, who resides in New Jersey, traveled to Florida to assist the decedent. In January 2000, the decedent executed a Power of Attorney for Health Care, naming Mr. Schilling as her attorney-in-fact for health care decisions.

On January 12, 2001, when the decedent was once again hospitalized, Mr. Schilling traveled to Florida to make arrangements for the decedent's care. After being released from the hospital, the decedent was admitted to a rehabilitation hospital, then to a health care center, and then to the Clairidge House for rehabilitation. While at the Clairidge House, Ms. Herrera became involved in the decedent's care, and when the decedent was discharged from the Clairidge House on December 16, 2001, Ms. Herrera notified Mr. Schilling.

After being discharged from the Clairidge House, the decedent returned to her apartment, and Ms. Herrera began to care for her on an "occasional, as needed basis." In 2003, when the decedent's condition worsened and she was in need of additional care, Ms. Herrera converted her garage into a bedroom, and the decedent moved in. The decedent paid Ms. Herrera rent and for her services as caregiver.

When Mr. Schilling spoke to Ms. Herrera over the phone, Ms. Herrera complained that she was not getting paid enough to take care of the decedent, and on April 10, 2003, Mr. Schilling sent Ms. Herrera money. While living in the converted garage, the decedent became completely dependent on Ms. Herrera. In September 2003, without Mr. Schilling's knowledge, Ms. Herrera convinced the decedent to prepare and execute a new Power of Attorney, naming Ms. Herrera as attorney-in-fact, and to execute a new Last Will and Testament naming Ms. Herrera as personal representative and sole beneficiary of the decedent's estate.

Mr. Schilling visited the decedent in March of 2004. On August 6, 2004, the decedent died at Ms. Herrera's home.

On August 24, 2004, Ms. Herrera filed her Petition for Administration. On December 2, 2004, following the expiration of the creditor's period, Ms. Herrera petitioned for discharge of probate. On December 6, 2004, after the expiration of the creditor's period and after Ms. Herrera had petitioned the probate court for discharge of probate, Ms. Herrera notified Mr. Schilling for the first time that the decedent, his sister, had passed away on August 6, 2004. Shortly thereafter, in late December 2004, the Final Order of Discharge was entered by the probate court. Mr. Schilling alleges that prior to being notified of his sister's death on

> **Practice Note:** Ordinarily, Mr. Schilling, as an intestate heir and beneficiary under a prior will, would receive notice of the probate of his sister's will. An anomaly in the Florida probate procedure meant that he was not notified until after the probate was complete.

December 6, 2004, he attempted to contact the decedent through Ms. Herrera, but Ms. Herrera did not return his calls until the conclusion of probate proceedings and did not inform him of his sister's death, thereby depriving him of both the knowledge of the decedent's death and the opportunity of contesting the probate proceedings. Mr. Schilling further alleges that prior to the decedent's death, Ms. Herrera regularly did not immediately return his phone calls, and that Ms. Herrera's "intentional silence was part of a calculated scheme to prevent [Mr.] Schilling from contesting the Estate of Decedent, and was intended to induce [Mr.] Schilling to refrain from acting in his interests to contest the probate proceedings in a timely fashion, as [Mr.] Schilling was used to long delays in contact with [Ms.] Herrera, and did not suspect that the delay was intended to fraudulently induce [Mr.] Schilling to refrain from acting on his own behalf." Finally, Mr. Schilling alleges that he expected to inherit the decedent's estate because he was the decedent's only heir-at-law and because he was named as the sole beneficiary in the 1996 will; Ms. Herrera's fraudulent actions prevented him from receiving the decedent's estate, which he was entitled to;

and but for Ms. Herrera's action of procuring the will naming her as sole beneficiary, he would have received the benefit of the estate.

After Mr. Schilling filed his amended complaint, Ms. Herrera filed a renewed motion to dismiss, arguing the same issues that she had raised in her previous motion to dismiss. The trial court granted the motion to dismiss with prejudice, finding that Ms. Herrera had no duty to notify Mr. Schilling of the decedent's death as Mr. Schilling did not hire Ms. Herrera to care for the decedent, and therefore, there was "no special relationship giving rise to a proactive responsibility to provide information." The trial court also found that Mr. Schilling was barred from filing a claim for intentional interference with an expectancy of inheritance because he failed to exhaust his probate remedies.

LEGAL ANALYSIS

To state a cause of action for intentional interference with an expectancy of inheritance, the complaint must allege the following elements: (1) the existence of an expectancy; (2) intentional interference with the expectancy through tortious conduct; (3) causation; and (4) damages. *Claveloux v. Bacotti*, 778 So. 2d 399, 400 (Fla. 2d DCA 2001)(citing *Whalen v. Prosser*, 719 So. 2d 2, 5 (Fla. 2d DCA 1998)). The court in *Whalen* clearly explained that the purpose behind this tort is to protect the testator, not the beneficiary:

> Interference with an expectancy is an unusual tort because the beneficiary is authorized to sue to recover damages primarily to protect the testator's interest rather than the disappointed beneficiary's expectations. The fraud, duress, undue influence, or other independent tortious conduct required for this tort is directed at the testator. The beneficiary is not directly defrauded or unduly influenced; the testator is. Thus, the common law court has created this cause of action not primarily to protect the beneficiary's inchoate rights, but to protect the deceased testator's former right to dispose of property freely and without improper interference. In a sense, the beneficiary's action is derivative of the testator's rights.

Whalen, 719 So. 2d at 6.

In essence, the amended complaint alleges that Mr. Schilling was named as the sole beneficiary in the decedent's last will and testament; that based on this last will and testament, he expected to inherit the decedent's estate upon her death; that Ms. Herrera intentionally interfered with his expectancy of inheritance by "convincing" the decedent, while she was ill and completely dependent on Ms. Herrera, to execute a new last will and testament naming Ms.

Herrera as the sole beneficiary; and that Ms. Herrera's "fraudulent actions" and "undue influence" prevented Mr. Schilling from inheriting the decedent's estate. Based on these well-pled allegations, we conclude that the amended complaint states a cause of action for intentional interference with an expectancy of inheritance. Therefore, the trial court erred, as a matter of law, in dismissing the amended complaint on that basis.

Mr. Schilling also contends that the trial court erred in finding that he was barred from filing a claim for intentional interference with an expectancy of inheritance as he failed to exhaust his probate remedies. We agree.

The decision was appealed to a federal district court, and the federal court determined it would be better for the Florida Supreme Court to decide the issue, certifying the following question to the Florida Supreme Court:

The Florida Supreme Court stated that "[t]he rule is that if adequate relief is available in a probate proceeding, then that remedy must be exhausted before a tortious interference claim may be pursued." *Id.* at 218. The Court, however, stated that an exception to this general rule is that "[i]f the defendant's fraud is not discovered until after probate, plaintiff is allowed to bring a later action for damages since relief in probate was impossible." *Id.* at 219.

A review of the amended complaint reflects that Mr. Schilling has alleged two separate frauds. The first alleged fraud stems from Ms. Herrera's undue influence over the deceased in procuring the will, whereas the second alleged fraud stems from Ms. Herrera's actions in preventing Mr. Schilling from contesting the will in probate court. We acknowledge that if only the first type of fraud was involved, Mr. Schilling's collateral attack of the will would be barred. However, a subsequent action for intentional interference with an expectancy of inheritance may be permitted where "the circumstances surrounding the tortious conduct effectively preclude adequate relief in the probate court." *Id.*

In the instant case, we must accept the facts alleged by Mr. Schilling as true. He alleges in the amended complaint that when the decedent began to live in Ms. Herrera's home, pursuant to powers of attorney executed by the decedent, Mr. Schilling was the decedent's attorney-in-fact; throughout the decedent's numerous illnesses, Mr. Schilling made decisions regarding the decedent's care; Mr. Schilling traveled to Miami on numerous occasions to visit the decedent, whose condition progressively worsened; Mr. Schilling stayed in contact with Ms. Herrera while the decedent was living in her home; Mr. Schilling relied on Ms. Herrera to obtain information regarding the decedent; Mr. Schilling sent money to Ms. Herrera to pay for the decedent's care; after the decedent passed away, Mr. Schilling called Ms. Herrera numerous times, but she would not return his calls; and Ms. Herrera did not inform Mr. Schilling of his sister's death until after she petitioned for discharge of probate. As the facts in the amended complaint sufficiently allege that Mr. Schilling was prevented from contesting the will in the probate court due to Ms. Herrera's fraudulent conduct, we find that the trial court erred in finding that Mr. Schilling's claim for intentional interference with an expectancy of inheritance was barred.

Accordingly, we reverse the order dismissing Mr. Schilling's amended complaint, and remand for further proceedings.

NOTES

1.   Some scholars argue that tortious interference with inheritance offers a parallel legal regime for addressing issues of testamentary freedom, and that tort law is not as well-designed as the law of probate to address such issues:

> [I]nheritance law has developed a host of specialized doctrines and procedures to deal with these difficulties. There is thus little reason to suppose that tort concepts and procedures, which have developed primarily to deal with less subtle forms of injurious misconduct, will help courts better distinguish a bona fide claim of wrongful interference from a strike suit by a disappointed expectant beneficiary. Because the interference-with-inheritance tort changes the rules under which inheritance disputes are litigated and offers different remedies than inheritance law, recognition of the tort is in truth recognition of a rival legal regime for addressing these same problems. The tort allows a disappointed expectant beneficiary to choose his preferred rules of procedure and potential remedies—the specialized rules of inheritance law, or the general civil litigation rules of tort law.

John C.P. Goldberg & Robert H. Sitkoff, *Torts and Estates: Remedying Wrongful Interference with Inheritance*, 65 STAN. L. REV. 335, 338 (2013).

There remain good reasons, however, to allow the tort, because sometimes it is difficult to assert the fraud claim in probate. One reason, for example, is that probate has already closed or the claims are being asserted against people who are not parties to the probate procedure, although Goldberg and Sitkoff argue that in a case like *Schilling*, for example, the brother could have petitioned to reopen the probate proceeding. There are cases with even more extreme facts. In *Allen v. Hall*, 974 P.2d 199 (Oregon 1999), for example, the plaintiffs alleged that beneficiaries of a testator's will admitted the testator to a hospital and then used a durable power to attorney to terminate his life support before he could update his will. *See* Diane Klein, *"Go West, Disappointed Heir": Tortious Interference with Expectation of Inheritance—A Survey with Analysis of State Approaches in the Pacific States*, 13 LEWIS & CLARK L. REV. 209 (2009).

2.   The main doctrinal difference among the states that have adopted tortious interference with inheritance is whether they require a plaintiff to exhaust probate remedies—that is, will contests—before suing in tort. Most states do require such exhaustion. As the Florida Supreme Court explained, "[c]ases which allow the action for tortious interference with a testamentary expectancy are predicated on the inadequacy of probate remedies." *Dewitt v. Duce*, 408 So. 2d 216, 217 (Fla. 1981). On the other hand, probate court does not always offer a remedy; the same court noted "[p]robate can strike from the will something that is in it as a result of fraud but cannot add to the will a provision that is not there nor can the probate court bring into being a will which the testator was prevented from making and executing by fraud." *Id.*

3.   The most famous case of tortious interference with an expectancy is *Marshall v. Marshall*, 547 U.S. 293 (2006). The case, which we mentioned in the context of undue influence, involved a claim by Anna Nicole Smith against her stepson, J. Pierce Marshall. Ms. Smith claimed that her stepson had wrongfully encouraged his father (Smith's husband) to leave Smith out of his estate plans. This became an issue in the federal courts when Smith was in bankruptcy in California and claimed as an asset her tortious interference claim. The U.S. Supreme

Anna Nicole Smith on the red carpet for 2005 MTV Video Music Awards. Photo: Toby Forage

Court concluded that the bankruptcy court could adjudicate these claims, thereby cutting back on the long-standing "probate exception" to federal jurisdiction. That "probate exception" had been invoked at various times so that federal courts could avoid adjudication of probate disputes. Why might a federal court refuse to adjudicate probate claims? *See* Judith Resnik, *"Naturally" Without Gender: Women, Jurisdiction, and the Federal Courts*, 66 N.Y.U. L. REV. 1682 (1991).

ASSESSMENT

Frieda spends a lot more time with her grandmother, Elke, than does her sister, Marie. One day when Frieda and Elke are talking, Frieda told Elke a funny story about Marie getting drunk at a birthday party a few months earlier. Frieda loves her sister and did not mean to cause trouble between her and their grandmother, but Elke immediately got it into her head that Marie was becoming an alcoholic and angrily revoked the bequest to Marie in her will and replaced it with a nasty note in the margin about not leaving her money to a "drunk." Shortly thereafter, Elke dies. Marie finds the will and demands to know what happened, so Frieda tells her. Marie sues Frieda for fraud and tortious interference. Frieda is very upset; she never meant to cause Elke to cut Marie out of her will. What advice do you give Frieda?

E. What Happens if a Will Is Denied Probate and How to Avoid Will Challenges

If a will is found invalid for any of the reasons discussed in this chapter, what happens to the probate estate? The answer to this question will depend on whether there was an earlier valid will, as in *Moses*, and even on whether the later will that was invalidated disposed of the entire estate or was simply an amendment (or codicil) dealing with only part of the estate. The next chapter discusses these issues in detail. In essence, though, if a prior will exists, that will can be probated. If there is no earlier valid will, the estate—or the challenged bequest—will pass under the state's s intestacy laws. Thus, will contestants likely assume they will do better either under intestacy laws or under an earlier will than they will under the will they are contesting.

How can estate planning attorneys prepare themselves for, and so hopefully avoid, will contests? The scenarios most likely to foretell a future will contest include but are not limited to the following:

- A blended family (a second or third marriage with children from either spouse's prior marriage)

- An elderly person who is forgetful, has early stages of dementia or Alzheimer's, but whom you believe has testamentary capacity

- Unequal bequests to people on the same generational line (i.e., siblings)

- A history of family discord

- One or more siblings bringing a parent in to execute a will when other siblings are not present

Protective planning can be structural—so built into the estate planning itself. For example, some testators write a letter of wishes to accompany and explain an estate plan. We saw this type of planning in the *Kaufmann* case. Other testators may include expressive language in the document itself. *See* Deborah S. Gordon, *Reflecting on the Language of Death*, 34 SEATTLE U. L. REV. 379, 384 (2011) (surveying undue influence case law and arguing that "directly infusing wills with individualized, expressive, and what some might call 'extra' language' better insulates them against challenges."). Another structural mechanism is a clause inserted in the will that disinherits anyone who tries to challenge the will. These are called **forfeiture clauses**, **in terrorem clauses**, or **no-contest clauses**. A typical no-contest clause reads as follows:

> In the event that any person shall contest this Will or attempt to establish that he or she is entitled to any portion of my estate or to any right as an heir, other than as herein provided, I hereby give and bequeath unto any such person the sum of one dollar.

Karen J. Sneddon, *Voice, Strength, and No-Contest Clauses*, 2019 WIS. L. REV. 239, 262 (2019); *see Lipper v. Weslow*, 369 S.W.2d 698 (Tex. Civ. App. 1963). A couple of caveats are in order regarding these clauses: first, it's important that the will actually leave a large enough bequest to make it risky for the person to challenge it; second, many states (and the UPC) will decline to enforce such clauses if there is probable cause for contesting a will. UPC 2–517. Why do you think this is?

Protective planning also can take the form of conduct before, during, or after the will execution. We have already discussed the video or audiotaping of a will execution ceremony. Because that type of recording can, as it did in *Lakatosh*, highlight infirmities of the testator, estate planning attorneys might instead write a memo to their files memorializing that the testator was able to answer questions and otherwise show capacity. Choosing good witnesses, too, can help shore up a will's validity. Many experienced estate planning attorneys will meet with families to discuss estate plans planning while everyone in the family—testators and beneficiaries—are alive to answer (and ask) questions.

Another suggestion for preventing will challenges has been the idea of "ante-mortem" probate. Four states (North Dakota, Ohio, Arkansas, and Alaska) have enacted statutes that permit testators, if they choose, to have a court declare their wills valid while they are alive. *See, e.g.,* ARK. CODE ANN. § 28–40–201, *et seq.*; ALASKA STAT. ANN. § 13.12.530, *et seq.*; N.D. CENT. CODE ANN. § 30.1–08.1–01, *et seq.* What do you think of this idea? Would you choose to take part in such a proceeding? Would your parents/grandparents?

Even if your state does not offer this kind of proceeding, there are other prophylactic measurers you can take on your own. Once you have determined that your client has testamentary capacity and is making dispositions free of fraud, duress, and undue influence, consider what extra measures you might take to prevent a future contest.

ASSESSMENTS

1.   Your client is Brenda, who is in her second marriage. Brenda has two children from her first marriage who are adults and professionally successful. Her current husband, Mario, on the other hand, is a carpenter who loves to work with his hands and makes beautiful furniture pieces but does not earn much money. Brenda is a retired doctor who has a considerable estate. Mario has a daughter, Alina, Brenda's stepdaughter, who is disabled and not able to work. Over the time she's been married to Mario, Brenda has become very close with Alina and wants to leave her a significant amount in her will. She also wants to leave Mario, if he survives her, the bulk of her estate. She is afraid her children from her first marriage will contest the will. What grounds would you anticipate as the basis for a possible challenge to Brenda's will, and what measures would you recommend she take now to avoid such a challenge?

2.   Look back at the problem about Pearl Rose in the assessments after the Undue Influence section. What measures would you have advised Pearl to take at the time she executed her will to try to prevent the lawsuit by her cousins?

3.   Your clients Jaleessa and Akhil have come to you to do their estate plan, but they are worried. They have four children who are all adults, married, and have children of their own. Sadly, the children do not all get along. They seem to have split into factions, and the parents are positive that, no matter how fairly they treat everyone, there will be fights over the estate after they are gone. In particular, the parents have a collection of art and, though they will try to make sure each child gets the pieces he or she is especially attached to, they know the kids will still be unhappy. They really don't want litigation over their estate. What measures can you take now to reassure them?

F. Conclusion and Takeaways

Wills are open to challenges on the basis of formalities and lack of testamentary capacity but, as we can see from this chapter, are also subject to challenges on the basis of undue influence, fraud, duress, and insane delusion. All these challenges operate on the assumption that someone has undermined the testator's intent and that the resulting will is therefore invalid. Undue influence is the most common and also the most malleable claim; it often involves caretakers or someone else who is not a close family member— someone who is in a "confidential" relationship with the testator. This chapter also explains the claim of tortious interference with an inheritance. Estate planning attorneys can and should take measures to prevent a will challenge, especially in circumstances where challenges are most common. If a will fails for any reason, what happens next depends on what other documents exist. The next chapter takes up the topic of multiple and sequential wills.

CHAPTER 6 COMPREHENSIVE ASSESSMENTS

1. **CREATE A "BEST PRACTICES" MANUAL.** Your firm has asked you to draft a practice manual on how to anticipate and defuse a will contest. Draft something concise and direct—use lists and bullet points—that someone can glance at quickly to know what to do before, during, and after the will execution.

2. **DRAFT A SIMPLE WILL.** Your client, Tessa Thompson, is a thirty-eight-year-old web-designer. From her client intake questionnaire, you learn that Tessa is unmarried but has been in a committed relationship with another professional woman, Alexis Wechsler, for several years. Tessa's elderly parents are in their late 70s. They are still alive and married to each other. Tessa has a brother, Mark, who is a few years older, is married, and has two daughters.

Tessa owns a townhouse worth approximately $350,000; it has a mortgage with approximately $200,000 outstanding. Tess also has a 401K retirement account with approximately $150,000 and a life insurance policy for $400,000, a bank account with approximately $25,000 in it, and a car worth $8,000. Tessa's tangible personal property also includes a number of gourmet cooking utensils, worth several thousand dollars, china and silver she inherited from her grandmother, and athletic equipment, including kayaks and camping gear. Tessa would like to make sure that her parents have adequate assets to live comfortably and also wants to leave the condominium, car, and cooking utensils, to her partner, Alexis. Finally, Tessa wants her two beloved nieces to receive the china, silverware, and athletic equipment. She would also like to provide for them in other ways, if that's possible.

Draft a very simple will for Tessa. Chapter 8 will go into detail about how to draft for specific issues that arise in making bequests; for the moment, just try drafting simple bequests for Tessa's beneficiaries and the other standard parts of a will for her.

You should include the following components in the following order, which are standard provisions in any will:

a. **Exordium, or Introduction:** This is the opening paragraph of the will that sets out testamentary intent, the name and a few other details (age, residence) of the testator, members of the testator's family, and the revocation of all previous wills.

b. **Specific Devises:** These are the specific items of tangible personal property the testator wishes to leave individuals.

c. **General Devises:** These are gifts of money, usually stated in amounts.

d. **Residuary Devise:** This section bequeaths what remains of the estate after the specific and general devises have been taken out.

e. **Appointment of Executor:** This section appoints the estate fiduciary.

f. **Signature:** Draw up a signature block with the appropriate number of lines for witnesses.

You may want to refer to documents in the Appendix for models of any of these provisions.

Test Your Knowledge

To assess your understanding of the material in this chapter, click here to take a quiz.

CHAPTER 7

Wills III: Sequential Wills and Other Documents

CHAPTER LEARNING OUTCOMES

Following your work with the material in this chapter, you should be able to do the following:

- Determine which, in a sequence of wills, is operative

- Describe how a will is effectively revoked, including revocation by act, by writing, and by inconsistency

- Explain how a will is effectively revived and assess whether a will has been revived in a given fact pattern

- Apply formalities doctrines to written will revocations

- Evaluate the legal effects of republishing a will by codicil

- Analyze and apply the doctrines of incorporation by reference, integration, and acts of independent significance

- Devise and draft estate planning options for tangible personal property

A. Introduction

Once a will satisfies the basic requirements for validity (testamentary intent, testamentary capacity, compliance with formalities), the will is admitted to probate in the vast majority of cases. Sometimes, though, a testator has executed one or more instruments purporting to be wills, and this can raise the question of which testamentary instrument should be operative. For example, suppose a testator thinks she revoked a will but did not in fact comply with the requirements for doing so? Or executes Will One, then executes Will Two. Normally, Will Two would revoke Will One, either in whole or in part. But what if Will Two is invalid for some reason (insufficient attestation, for example)? Or what if the testator tore up Will Two? Should the person's property pass by intestacy, or should we use one of the existing wills? This chapter discusses the timeline of acts that can follow the execution of the original will: revocation, revival, and documents or acts that are outside of the formal will but can become part of it if they satisfy certain requirements.

Part B addresses the topic of **will revocation** (by physical act, operation of law, and a subsequent writing). *Thompson v. Royall*, although an old case, is useful because demonstrates the different ways that wills can be revoked—both effectively and ineffectively. *Estate of Stoker* is a more recent (but quite memorable) case which shows how the harmless error and will revocation doctrines interact. **Part C** discusses codicils (or will amendments) and how they affect prior and subsequent wills. **Part D** addresses the topic of **reviving** a revoked will. **Part E** discusses ineffective revocation and the doctrine of **dependent relative revocation**. **Part F** focuses on papers or acts that exist or occur outside the will but are somehow made a part of it, focusing on doctrines known as "incorporation by reference" and "acts of independent significance."

B. Will Revocation

As complicated (and picky) as will formalities rules may seem, the requirements for executing a valid will are pretty straightforward when applied to a single testamentary document. Often, however, a testator's wishes change, and the testator either tries to destroy an existing will or make a new one, leaving survivors with the problem of deciding which will, if any, governs. A testator can revoke a will by a "revocatory act" upon the will or by a "subsequent writing" that revokes the prior will either expressly or by implication. The cases that follow, *Thompson* and *Stoker*, involve various, sometimes ineffective attempts to revoke testamentary instruments by the above methods. As you read the cases, pay attention to which revocations were effective and why.

Thompson v. Royall

175 S.E. 748 (Va. 1934)

HUDGINS, J.

The only question presented by this record, is whether the will of Mrs. M. Lou Bowen Kroll had been revoked shortly before her death.

On September 4, 1932, Mrs. Kroll signed a will, typewritten on five sheets of paper; the signature appeared on the last page duly attested by three subscribing witnesses. Mr. Brittain, the executor named in the will, was given the instrument for safe-keeping. A codicil typed on the top third of one paper dated September 15, 1932 was signed by the testator in the presence of two witnesses. This instrument was given to Judge Coulling, the attorney who prepared both documents.

On September 19, 1932, at the request of Mrs. Kroll, Judge Coulling and Mr. Brittain took the will and the codicil to her home where she told her attorney, in the presence of Mr. Brittain and another, to destroy both. But instead of destroying the papers, she decided to retain them as memoranda to be used in the event she decided to execute a new will. Upon the back of the manuscript cover, which was fastened to the five sheets, in the handwriting of Judge Coulling, signed by Mrs. Kroll, there is the following notation:

> **Language Note:** This case uses the gendered term "testatrix" to refer to Mrs. Kroll, the maker of this will. The editors have replaced that term with the term "testator" to reflect the modern vernacular.

> This will null and void and to be only held by H. P. Brittain, instead of being destroyed, as a memorandum for another will if I desire to make same. This 19 Sept 1932.
>
> M. LOU BOWEN KROLL.

The same notation was made on the back of the sheet on which the codicil was written, except that the name, Judge Coulling, was substituted for Mr. Brittain; this was likewise signed by Mrs. Kroll.

Mrs. Kroll died on October 2, 1932, leaving an estate valued at approximately $200,000. The will and codicil were offered for probate. All the interested parties including the heirs at law were convened, and the jury found that the instruments dated September 4th and 15, 1932, were the last will and testament of Mrs. Kroll. From an order sustaining the verdict and probating the will this writ of error was allowed.

For more than one hundred years, the means by which a duly executed will may be revoked have been prescribed by statute. These requirements are found in section 5233 of the 1919 Code. The pertinent parts read:

> No will or codicil, or any part thereof, shall be revoked, unless * * * by a subsequent will or codicil, or by some writing declaring an intention to revoke the same, and executed in the manner in which a will is required to be executed, or by the testator, or some person in his presence and by his direction, cutting, tearing, burning, obliterating, canceling, or destroying the same, or the signature thereto, with the intent to revoke.

The notations, dated September 19, 1932 are not wholly in the handwriting of the testator, nor are her signatures thereto attached attested by subscribing witnesses; hence under the statute they are ineffectual as "some writing declaring an intention to revoke." The faces of the two instruments bear no physical evidence of any cutting, tearing, burning, obliterating, canceling, or destroying. The only contention made by appellants is that the notation written in the presence, and with the approval, of Mrs. Kroll, on the back of the manuscript cover and on the back of the sheet containing the codicil constitute "canceling" within the meaning of the statute.

Both parties concede that to effect revocation of a duly executed will, in any of the methods prescribed by statute, two things are necessary: (1) The doing of one of the acts specified, (2) accompanied by the intent to revoke. Proof of either, without proof of the other, is insufficient.

The proof established the intention to revoke. The entire controversy is confined to the acts used in carrying out that purpose. The testator revoked her will by written memoranda, admittedly ineffectual as revocations by subsequent writings, but appellants contend the memoranda, in the handwriting of another, and testator's signatures, are sufficient to effect revocation by cancellation. To support this contention, appellants cite authorities which hold that the modern definition of cancellation includes, "any act which would destroy, revoke, recall, do away with, overrule, render null and void, the instrument."

Most of the authorities were dealing with the cancellation of simple contracts, or other instruments that require little or no formality in execution. However, *Warner v. Warner's Estate*, 37 Vt. 356, applies this extended meaning of "canceling" to the revocation of wills. In this case, proof of the intent and the act were a notation on the same page below the signature of the testator, reading: "This will is hereby cancelled and annulled. In full this the 15th day of March in the year 1859," and written lengthwise on the back of the fourth page upon which no part of the written will appeared, were these words, "Cancelled and is null and void. (Signed) I. Warner." This was sufficient to revoke the will under a statute similar to the one here.

In *Evans' Appeal*, 58 Pa. 238, the Pennsylvania court approved the reasoning of the Vermont court in *Warner's Estate*, but the force of the opinion is weakened when the facts are considered. There were lines drawn through two of the three signatures of the testator appearing in the *Evans* will, and the paper on which material parts of the will were written was torn in four places. It therefore appeared on the face of the instrument that there was a sufficient defacement to bring it within the meaning of both obliteration and cancellation.

The construction of the statute in *Warner's Estate* has been criticized and the courts in the majority of the states in construing similar statutes have refused to follow the reasoning in that case. The above, and other authorities hold that revocation of a will by cancellation within the meaning of the statute, contemplates marks or lines across the written parts of the instrument, a physical defacement, or some mutilation of the writing itself with the intent to revoke. If written words are used for the purpose, they must be so placed as to physically affect the written portion of the will, not merely on blank parts of the paper on which the will is written. If the writing intended to be the act of cancelling, does not mutilate, or erase, or deface, or otherwise physically come in contact with any part of written words of the will, it cannot be given any greater weight than a similar writing on a separate sheet of paper, which identifies the will referred to. If a will may be revoked by writing on the back, separable from the will, it may be done by a writing not on the will. This the statute forbids.

The learned trial judge, A.C. Buchanan, in his written opinion, pertinently stated:

> The statute prescribes certain ways of executing a will, and it must be so executed in order to be valid, regardless of how clear and specific the intent. It also provides certain ways of revoking and it must be done so in order to a valid revocation, regardless of intent.

The attempted revocation is ineffectual, because testator intended to revoke her will by subsequent writings not executed as required by statute, and because it does not physically obliterate, mutilate, deface, or cancel any written parts of the will.

For the reasons stated, the judgment of the trial court is affirmed.

In re Estate of Stoker

122 Cal. Rptr. 3d 529 (App. 2011)

GILBERT, J.

At one time the Probate Code appeared to refute the dictum, "Nothing endures but change." Not anymore. Destiny Gularte, Donald Karotick and Robert Rodriguez (appellants) appeal a judgment that denied a petition to probate a 1997 will and a trust of Steven Wayne Stoker (decedent), and granted the petition of Danine Pradia and Darrin Stoker (respondents) to probate decedent's 2005 will. We conclude that the trial court did not err by ruling that the 2005 will was valid, and substantial evidence supports that decedent had revoked the 1997 will and trust. We affirm.

FACTS

On May 22, 1997, decedent executed a will and nominated Gularte to be the executor of his estate. In article two of the will, he listed Karotick and Gularte as the beneficiaries of gifts of personal property. In article three, he stated, "I give the residue of my estate to the trustee of the 1997 Steven Wayne Stoker Revocable Trust, created under the declaration of trust executed on the same date as, but immediately before, the execution of this will." Gularte was listed as the successor trustee of that trust. Decedent died on February 27, 2008.

On March 17, 2008, Gularte filed a petition to probate the will and requested that she be appointed the executor. On March 18, Gularte served a notice to decedent's children (respondents) that pursuant to sections 16061.7 and 16061.8, they had 120 days to bring an action to contest the trust. On March 25, Pradia filed an objection to Gularte's petition to probate the 1997 will and claimed that her father had executed a more recent will. She objected to Gularte being appointed executor. She said, "Gularte is the former girlfriend of my father. My father and [Gularte's] relationship ended in an angry moment in 2001, about 7 years ago. My father told me in November 2007 that he was afraid of [Gularte] and thought she was coming into his home and taking things."

On April 28, respondents filed a petition to probate a handwritten will signed by their father on August 28, 2005. The will provides,

> To Whom It May Concern: [¶] I, Steve Stoker revoke my 1997 trust as of August 28, 2005. Destiny Gularte and Judy Stoker to get nothing. Everything is to go to my kids Darin [sic] and Danene [sic] Stoker. Darin [sic] and Danene [sic] are to have power of attorney over everything I own.

The will contained no witnesses' signatures.

Decedent's friend, Anne Marie Meier, testified that one night in 2005, decedent was discussing "estate planning," and he asked Meier to "get a piece of paper and a pen." He then dictated the terms of the 2005 will. Meier wrote that document in her handwriting "word for word" from decedent's dictation. She handed it to him, "he looked at it and he signed it." Decedent told Meier that this was his last will and testament. In front of the witnesses, he urinated on a copy of the 1997 will and then burned it. Homer Johns, a friend of decedent's, testified that he saw decedent sign the 2005 will.

The trial court found that respondents "established that the 2005 document was created at Decedent Stoker's direction and that he signed it," and that there was clear and convincing evidence that the 2005 will "evinces Decedent Stoker's intent." The court ruled that "[s]ince the 2005 will has been accepted for probate by this Court, the 1997 will has been revoked by law."

DISCUSSION

The Validity of the 2005 Will

Appellants claim that the will does not meet the requirements for a "[f]ormal [w]itnessed [w]ill," and therefore the trial court erred by admitting it to probate. A will must be signed by the testator and at least two witnesses. Here the 2005 will is signed by decedent, but it contains no witnesses' signatures. Two witnesses, however, saw decedent sign it, and they testified in court to verify that this will was genuine.

Respondents note that the Probate Code contains a provision that allows wills that are defective in form to be admitted to probate if they are consistent with the testator's intent. Section 6110(c)(2) provides, "If a will was not executed in compliance with paragraph (1), the will shall be treated as if it was executed in compliance with that paragraph if the proponent of the will establishes by clear and convincing evidence that, at the time the testator signed the will, the testator intended the will to constitute the testator's will." Here the trial court found that the 2005 document constituted decedent's last will.

Additionally, where the statute is inclusive, containing no limiting or qualifying language to exclude persons from its scope, the words the legislators used should control. Here the statutory language is clear and broad and applies to wills that are "in writing" and signed by the testator. Consequently, handwritten non-holographic wills are not excluded from the scope of this statute. The 2005 document is a written will signed by decedent.

Moreover, the broad and remedial goal of this provision is to give preference to the testator's intent instead of invalidating wills because of procedural deficiencies or mistakes. Including the 2005 will within the purview of this statute is consistent with that purpose.

Substantial Evidence

The 2005 document is certainly not a model will. But "[n]o particular words are necessary to show a testamentary intent . . . " as long as the record demonstrates that the decedent intended the document to be his last will and testament. Here decedent's testamentary intent is evident. The document provides that all of decedent's property will go to his children, that the 1997 trust is revoked, that Gularte will receive "nothing," and that his children will have power of attorney "over everything."

Even if the document is ambiguous, the trial court properly admitted extrinsic evidence. That evidence confirmed decedent's testamentary intent. Meier testified that decedent told her the document was "my last will and testament," and "[t]hese are my wishes." Johns testified that decedent told him that the will represented "his final wishes."

Lastly, a will may be revoked where the testator executes a subsequent inconsistent will or where he or she burns or destroys the will. The 2005 will expressly and unequivocally revoked the 1997 trust. The statement in the will that his children were to receive all his property was an express revocation of the earlier 1997 will, which purported to give this property to others. In addition, Gretchen Landry testified that in 2001 decedent took his copy of the 1997 will, urinated on it and then burned it. Decedent's actions lead to the compelling conclusion he intended to revoke the 1997 will.

NOTES

1.   *Thompson v. Royall* requires a revocatory act to touch the writing on the will. The UPC revocation provision, reproduced below, is explicit that "A burning, teaching, or canceling is a 'revocatory act on the will,' whether or not the burn, tear, or cancellation touched any of the words on the will." While the UPC is an expansion of the holding in cases like *Thompson*, it is consistent—as the *Thompson* court acknowledged—with some earlier cases, like *Warner v. Warner's Estate*, 37 Vt. 356 (1864). Consider whether the *Thompson* case would have turned out differently had UPC § 2–507, reproduced below, applied instead of the Virginia statute.

UPC § 2–507 Revocation by Writing or By Act

(a)   A will or any part thereof is revoked:

(1)   by executing a subsequent will that revokes the previous will or part expressly or by inconsistency; or

(2)   by performing a revocatory act on the will, if the testator performed the act with the intent and for the purpose of revoking the will or part or if another individual performed the act in the testator's conscious presence and by the testator's direction. For purposes of this paragraph, "revocatory act on the

will" includes burning, tearing, canceling, obliterating, or destroying the will or any part of it. A burning, tearing, or canceling is a "revocatory act on the will," whether or not the burn, tear, or cancellation touched any of the words on the will.

----

2.   A will, as you know, can also be revoked by a subsequent writing that was executed with the appropriate formalities. Why wasn't Mrs. Kroll's will revoked by writing?

3.   What curative doctrine allowed the *Stoker* court to find that the decedent had revoked his will by writing? Was the will also effectively revoked by physical act? Why or why not? Does the same curative doctrine apply to both kinds of revocation? Should it?

3.   In many jurisdictions, a will may also be **partially** revoked by a physical act. Consider along those lines the will of Gonzella Byrne Stockhart, pictured below and probated in Dallas County, Alabama. The testator cut out all the language listing the devisees and what they would take. She died with a will—that named an executor—but her entire estate was distributed according to the rules of intestacy. *See Board of Trustees of the University of Alabama v. Calhoun*, 514 So. 2d 895 (Ala. 1987). What do you think would have happened if Stockhart had cut out her signature too? If the jurisdiction did not allow partial revocation, do you think Stockhart's act would have revoked the will?

The testator of this will, Gonzella Byrne Stockhart, cut out all the language listing the devisees and what property they would take. The will was admitted to probate, but all property passed by the rules of intestacy.

C. Codicils and Will Revocation by Inconsistent Writing

The cases in Part B show that revocation of a will requires both *intent* and a revocatory *act* (either a writing or cancellation of some sort). Both cases also involve testators who want to revoke the prior testamentary documents completely and are explicit about their intent to revoke those prior documents. In other words, the intent exists, even though the acts (writing or cancellation) may be deficient. The more complicated question is what happens if there are a series of documents and the later ones are inconsistent with the earlier ones? For example, what if the subsequent testamentary instrument is a simple amendment that names a new executor? How does that amendment—or "codicil"—affect the terms of the earlier will, if the later document does not mention the earlier one? That's where the rest of UPC § 2–507, and the various presumptions about revocation, come in.

Note that it is **not** important what the later document is called—will or codicil. In fact, the definition of a will "includes codicil and any testamentary instrument that merely appoints an executor, revokes or revises another will, nominates a guardian, or expressly excludes or limits the right of an individual or class to succeed to property of the decedent." UPC § 1–201(57). Rather, it is important to determine if the later document "makes a complete disposition," meaning that it disposes of the residue of the testator's estate with language like "everything else I own" or "the rest of my property."

The UPC provides the following presumptions:

UPC § 2–507 Revocation by Writing or by Act

(b)   If a subsequent will does not expressly revoke a previous will, the execution of the subsequent will wholly revokes the previous will by inconsistency if the testator intended the subsequent will to replace rather than supplement the previous will.

(c)   The testator is presumed to have intended a subsequent will to replace rather than supplement a previous will if the subsequent will makes a complete disposition of the testator's estate. If this presumption arises and is not rebutted by clear and convincing evidence, the previous will is revoked; only the subsequent will is operative on the testator's death.

(d)   The testator is presumed to have intended a subsequent will to supplement rather than replace a previous will if the subsequent will does not make a complete disposition of the testator's estate. If this presumption arises and is not rebutted by clear and convincing evidence, the subsequent will revokes the previous will only to the extent the subsequent will is inconsistent with the previous will; each will is fully operative on the testator's death to the extent they are not inconsistent.

As you can see, if a later document—a will or codicil—is silent about how it affects an earlier document, UPC § 2–507(b) instructs us to look at the testator's intent. § 2–507(c) presumes an intention to *replace* the earlier will if the later document "makes a complete disposition" or, in other words, contains a residuary clause like "everything else I own" or "the rest of my property." If the later document simply changes a bequest or adds a devise or changes the executor, the later document is presumed to be a supplement and not a revocation. § 2–507(d). Of course, these presumptions can be rebutted by clear and convincing evidence that the testator intended a different result.

ASSESSMENTS

1.   While backpacking across Australia, Hamid met and fell in love with Miguel. They returned home and decided to move in together. A few weeks later, Hamid executed a valid will that read, "All to my best friend and companion Miguel." After some time passed, Hamid and Miguel's relationship grew stale. While Miguel was out of town, Hamid wrote another document, which he validly executed, stating, "My car to my brother Bryan, my television to my sister Lydia, and $5,000 to my tennis partner Bridget." Hamid died shortly thereafter. How will Hamid's probate estate be distributed?

2.   Draft a codicil to the Will of Katherine Hepburn, which you can find in the Appendix. Assume for the purposes of this exercise that Hepburn has had a falling out with Erik A. Hanson and no longer wishes to name him as a fiduciary or to provide him with any beneficial interest in her estate. Leslie Q. Perry will take Hanson's place as executor and trustee. Any gifts currently going to Hanson should be deleted. Draft a codicil that accomplishes these goals and be prepared to conduct an execution ceremony that will make the codicil effective.

D. Will Revival

If a testator revokes will 1 and subsequently revokes will 2, the question arises as to what becomes of will 1—is it **revived** or does it stay revoked, so that it must be re-executed? For an analysis of will revival, see Adam J. Hirsch, *Waking the Dead: An Empirical Analysis of Revival of Wills*, 53 U.C. DAVIS L. REV. 2269 (2020).

The UPC revival provision, § 2–509 reproduced below, imposes rebuttable presumptions for when a revoked will is revived. The presumptions depend on the method of revocation: act or writing. As with § 2–507, the presumptions also depend on what is being revoked—a document that "wholly revoked" a previous will (a will) or a document that "partly revoked" a previous will (a codicil):

UPC § 2–509 Revival of a Revoked Will

(a)   If a subsequent will that wholly revoked a previous will is thereafter revoked by a revocatory act under Section 2–507(a)(2), the previous will remains revoked unless it is revived. The previous will is revived if it is evident from the circumstances of the revocation of the subsequent will or from the testator's contemporary or subsequent declarations that the testator intended the previous will to take effect as executed.

(b)   If a subsequent will that partly revoked a previous will is thereafter revoked by a revocatory act under Section 2–507(a)(2), a revoked part of the previous will is revived unless it is evident from the circumstances of the revocation of the subsequent will or from the testator's contemporary or subsequent declarations that the testator did not intend the revoked part to take effect as executed.

(c)   If a subsequent will that revoked a previous will in whole or in part is thereafter revoked by another, later will, the previous will remains revoked in whole or in part, unless it or its revoked part is revived. The previous will or its revoked part is revived to the extent it appears from the terms of the later will that the testator intended the previous will to take effect.

To understand how these revival rules work, consider the following examples:

Case 1. Twyla dies in 2018. Twyla's intestate heirs are her children, Amelie and Edwina. Found in Twyla's nightstand are the following documents, all duly executed:

- A 2003 document that devises all of Twyla's property to The American Red Cross, for its charitable uses and purposes

- A 2010 document that devises all Twyla's property to Philabundence, for its charitable uses and purposes

- A document executed in 2012 reading "I revoke my 2010 will"

Assuming no other evidence, who takes Twyla's property under UPC § 2–509, the Red Cross, Philabundence, or her children?

The 2012 document is a written revocation, so § 2–509(c) applies. Because nothing in that document calls for revival, the presumption is that the earlier wills are not revived. Accordingly, Twyla dies without a will, and Amelie and Edwina will inherit through intestacy.

> **Case 2.** Assume Twyla executed the 2003 and 2010 documents but, instead of executing the 2012 document, Twyla tears the 2010 will into 100 pieces. Who takes Twyla's property?

In Case 2, § 2–509(a) would apply because the 2010 document wholly revoked the 2003 document, and Twyla revoked the later will by physical act. The 2003 will is **not** revived unless there is some evidence that Twyla intended the revival, so, as with Case 1, the children will take Twyla's property. If, instead, Twyla calls the director of Philabundence and says, "I do not like the way you are spending donors' money—I'm tearing up my will because I prefer that the Red Cross inherit my estate," and Twyla then tears the 2010 will into 100 pieces, the result would be different. Twyla's physical destruction of the 2010 will and her "contemporaneous declaration" that she wants the Red Cross to inherit is likely sufficient to revive the 2003 will.

> **Case 3.** Assume Twyla executed the 2003 document devising all her property to the Red Cross. In 2010, she executed a document devising her car to her friend, Basil. In 2012, Twyla tears the 2010 document into 100 pieces. Who takes Twyla's property?

In Case 3, § 2–509(b) would apply because the 2010 document **partly revoked** the 2003 document, and Twyla revoked the later will (actually a codicil) by act. The presumption is that the 2003 will is therefore revived, absent evidence to the contrary. The Red Cross will take Twyla's property.

Do the presumptions in the UPC revival statute make sense?

> **Practice Note:** The concepts of revocation and revival can be confusing. Here are some practical ways to approach a problem that has multiple wills and documents:
>
> - Identify all of the potential testamentary documents
>
> - Order the documents based upon date from most recent to oldest
>
> - Classify the documents as wills (complete dispositions) or codicils (partial dispositions)
>
> - Working from the newest to the oldest, evaluate the validity of each document

> • Resolve any inconsistencies or conflicts, recognizing the role of the wills act formalities, the principles of revocation, and the concept of revival

ASSESSMENT

Adebisi and Rashad had been best friends for over 15 years. One day in 2017 they decided to make their wills. Adebisi wrote and properly executed a valid will, which read, "Everything to my best friend Rashad." At the same time, Rashad wrote and properly executed a valid will, which read, "Everything to my best friend Adebisi." Two years later in 2019, Adebisi and Rashad decided to write new wills to devise additional specific property. Adebisi's valid 2019 will read in full, "My boat to Rashad, and my gold earrings to Stella." Rashad's valid 2019 will read, "My car to my beloved Adebisi and my watch to Stella." Last month Adebisi and Rashad's friendship began to wane. Adebisi posted on her Facebook page, "Rashad is getting on my last nerve; I don't know how much more of this nonsense I can take." Rashad responded by messaging Adebisi directly, as follows: "Airing our business on social media is the exact reason why this friendship is over." In response, Adebisi tore her 2017 will into confetti-sized pieces. At the same time, Rashad took out his 2019 will, lit a match, and turned the document to ash. If Adebisi dies on January 20, 2020, who inherits her property? If, instead, Rashad dies on January 20, 2020, who inherits his property?

E. Dependent Relative Revocation

The common law doctrine of dependent relative revocation (or DRR) applies when a testator executes a new will revoking a formerly valid will, but the new will turns out to be invalid for some reason. In the case below, the new will(s) were all invalid because they were products of undue influence. But those new wills included a beneficiary who would not inherit under intestacy. DRR allowed the court to re-establish the older, valid but revoked, will, reasoning that the revocation of the older will "depended" on the new will being valid. The rationale is that the testator would prefer the older will to intestacy. As you read the *Murphy* case, consider if and when it makes sense to apply this law of "second best."

In re Estate of Virginia E. Murphy

184 So. 3d 1221 (Fla. Dist. Ct. App. 2016)

LUCAS, J.

At the age of 107, Virginia E. Murphy passed away, leaving behind an estate worth nearly twelve million dollars, a series of wills, a phalanx of potential heirs, and extensive litigation. Following a trial, appeal, and remand from this court, the probate court entered an order in which it concluded that the vast majority of Mrs. Murphy's estate should pass through intestacy. For the reasons explained below, we are compelled to reverse the probate court's order because it failed to apply the presumption of dependent relative revocation to Mrs. Murphy's last will.

I.

Born in 1899, Virginia Murphy died on September 6, 2006, after more than a decade of declining health and acuity. Her parents and husband predeceased her, and she had no children or siblings. In the years before her passing, Mrs. Murphy executed a number of wills prepared by her longtime attorney, Jack S. Carey, including her last will and testament dated February 2, 1994 ("1994 will"). When Mrs. Murphy died, Mr. Carey filed a Petition for Administration submitting the 1994 will to probate. The 1994 will named Mr. Carey as personal representative of Mrs. Murphy's estate; and it purported to leave the bulk of that estate to Mr. Carey, Gloria DuBois (Mr. Carey's legal assistant), and George Tornwall (Mrs. Murphy's accountant, who died the year before Mrs. Murphy passed away).

Upon learning of the probate proceedings, Mrs. Murphy's second cousin, Jacqueline "Jackie" Rocke, a devisee under one of Mrs. Murphy's prior wills, filed an objection to the residuary devises in the 1994 will. In her objection, Ms. Rocke alleged undue influence on the part of Mr. Carey and Ms. DuBois over Mrs. Murphy.

We briefly summarize the testamentary schemes set forth in the last six of Mrs. Murphy's wills that were admitted into evidence, as they are all pertinent to this appeal:

May 10, 1989, Will ("1989 Will")

This will included a specific bequest to Ms. Rocke in the amount of $150,000 and specific bequests to Mr. Tornwall, Mr. Carey, and Ms. DuBois in the amount of $50,000 each and devised the entire residuary of the estate to Northwestern University's medical school.

June 11, 1991, Will ("1991 Will")

This will contained specific bequests to the Northwestern University medical school in the amount of $500,000, Ms. Rocke in the amount of $400,000, and Mr. Tornwall, Mr. Carey, and Ms. DuBois in the amount of $100,000 each, with the residuary of the estate divided in equal fourths between Ms. Rocke, Mr. Tornwall, Mr. Carey, and Ms. DuBois.

February 4, 1992, Will ("February 1992 Will")

This will, nearly identical to the 1991 will, also contained specific bequests to Northwestern University's medical school in the amount of $500,000, Ms. Rocke in the amount of $400,000, and Mr. Tornwall, Mr. Carey, and Ms. DuBois in the amount of $100,000 each, while the residuary of the estate was divided in equal fourths between Ms. Rocke, Mr. Tornwall, Mr. Carey, and Ms. DuBois. Ms. Rocke argued below and on appeal that this will's residuary devises (excluding Mr. Carey, Mr. Tornwall, and Ms. DuBois's devises) should have been the controlling testamentary scheme for probate of the residuary estate.

August 25, 1992, Will ("August 1992 Will")

This will included specific bequests to the medical school of Northwestern University in the amount of $500,000, Ms. Rocke in the amount of $400,000, and Mr. Tornwall, Mr. Carey, and Ms. DuBois in the amount of $100,000 each, but the residuary of the estate was now divided into equal thirds between Mr. Tornwall, Mr. Carey, and Ms. DuBois.

January 29, 1993, Will ("1993 Will")

The 1993 will contained specific bequests to Northwestern University's medical school in the amount of $500,000, Ms. Rocke in the amount of $400,000, Ms. DuBois in the amount of $150,000, and Mr. Tornwall and Mr. Carey in the amount of $100,000 each. The residuary of the estate was devised in equal thirds between Mr. Tornwall, Mr. Carey, and Ms. DuBois.

1994 Will

This will, like the 1993 will, included specific bequests to Northwestern University's medical school in the amount of $500,000, Ms. Rocke in the amount of $400,000, Ms. DuBois in the amount of $150,000, and Mr. Tornwall and Mr. Carey in the amount of $100,000 each. The residuary of the estate was again devised in equal thirds between Mr. Tornwall, Mr. Carey, and Ms. DuBois.

In addition to these testamentary documents, the probate court also considered the testimony of Mr. Carey, Ms. DuBois, Ms. Rocke, and other witnesses who had been involved with Mrs. Murphy's estate planning. By nearly all accounts, Mrs. Murphy maintained few personal relationships in the final decades of her life; she never knew anyone in her extended family other than Ms. Rocke, with whom she had enjoyed a close, social relationship since the early 1960s. Over time, Mr. Carey and Ms. DuBois built their own relationship with Mrs. Murphy (Ms. DuBois would eventually manage Mrs. Murphy's day-to-day finances for several years) founded upon Mr. Carey's service as her counsel. While Mrs. Murphy's health and mental awareness diminished, Mr. Carey and Ms. DuBois' share of the estate grew under the wills Mr. Carey drafted.

After the conclusion of the trial, on August 1, 2008, the probate court entered its Order, which included thorough and detailed findings that Mr. Carey and Ms. DuBois had, in fact, exerted undue influence through their confidential, fiduciary, and personal relationships with Ms. Murphy in order to become residuary devisees of her estate. The probate court further concluded that the residuary devises in the 1994 will were void but that "[t]he remainder of the provisions of the will are valid and shall control the disposition of the assets specifically devised." The court then admitted the 1994 will to probate, excluding its residuary devises, and ordered that "the rest, residue and remainder [of the estate] shall pass by the laws of intestate succession" as a lapsed gift.

Implicit in the probate court's determination was that the 1994 will's revocation clause, revoking all of Mrs. Murphy's prior wills, remained valid, so that the vast majority of Mrs. Murphy's estate would now pass to her intestate heirs who were, as yet, still unknown. Suffice it to say, none of the litigants were particularly satisfied with that result.

II.

We begin by examining the legal construct at the heart of this appeal, the doctrine of dependent relative revocation. Founded in the common law of early eighteenth century England, the doctrine was first adopted by the Florida Supreme Court, which explained:

> This doctrine has been stated and reiterated by many courts since it was first expounded in 1717, but stated simply it means that where [a] testator makes a new will revoking a former valid one, and it later appears that the new one is invalid, the old will may be re-established on the ground that the revocation was dependent upon the validity of the new one, [the] testator preferring the old will to intestacy.

Stewart v. Johnson, 194 So. 869, 870 (1940). Grounded in the axiom of probate law that intestacy should be avoided whenever possible, the doctrine of dependent relative revocation, our court has observed, is "a rule of presumed intention" that creates a rebuttable presumption that the testator would have preferred to have a prior will effectuated over statutory intestacy. The presumption's application hinges on whether "the provisions of the present invalid will are sufficiently similar to the former will." In cases of undue influence, if a prior will is sufficiently similar to an invalidated will then the presumption arises but may be rebutted by evidence that "the revocation clause was not invalidated by undue influence and that it was not intended by the decedent to be conditional on the validity of the testamentary provisions" of the will.

Comparing Mrs. Murphy's wills in the appropriately broad light, and in the light of all the evidence, we find there were sufficient similarities between Mrs. Murphy's 1994 will and her prior wills to support the application of the doctrine of dependent relative revocation to the 1994 will. We discern several contours of similarity that were unrefuted in the record.

First, Mrs. Murphy's execution of six wills over a period of five years evidences a sustained concern about the disposition of her property upon her death. Mrs. Murphy prized her right to dictate how her property should be divided, and she exercised that right, repeatedly, in the final years of her life. No one seriously disputes that she preferred testacy over intestacy. And that is, of course, the very foundation for the doctrine of dependent relative revocation's application.

Moreover, the testamentary documents themselves evince an overall pattern of similarity. Each of Mrs. Murphy's wills employed a similar testamentary scheme in which Mrs. Murphy made numerous specific bequests to charities and caregivers while limiting the division of the residuary of her estate to a few devisees. Although their respective proportions varied from will to will, the identities of the devisees and beneficiaries within the six wills, overall, remained fairly constant. Once the effect of Mr. Carey and Ms. DuBois' undue influence is properly taken into account, there is only one change between the six wills' residuary clauses that did not involve Mr. Carey or Ms. DuBois' illicit gain over the residuary estate: the change between the 1989 will and the 1991 will, which exchanged Northwestern University's medical school and Ms. Rocke's respective positions as a specific beneficiary and a residuary devisee. For her part, Ms. Rocke appeared repeatedly throughout Mrs. Murphy's wills, either as a residuary devisee, a designee of a specific bequest, or both.

Finally, the extrinsic evidence proffered before the probate court further demonstrated the appropriateness of applying the presumption in this case.

With the exception of four individuals, including Ms. Rocke, none of the forty-eight intestate heirs ultimately identified in the Final Order Determining Beneficiaries were mentioned within any of Mrs. Murphy's six wills. In contrast to the close relationship she had with Ms. Rocke, it appears Mrs. Murphy never knew her intestate heirs, and they never knew her. The intestate heirs' ancestral ties to Mrs. Murphy apparently remained forgotten until this litigation (and an heir search firm) brought them to light. Intestacy, in this case, would usurp the repeated testamentary dispositions of Mrs. Murphy's property throughout her wills, dispositions that were invariably tied to individuals she cared about or charities and institutions which she supported.

Stripping the undue influence that spanned the residuary devises of Mrs. Murphy's last six wills leaves two alternative residuary devises that remained untainted: the medical school of Northwestern University or Ms. Rocke. Northwestern University would receive the entire residuary of Mrs. Murphy's estate under the express provision of the 1989 will. Ms. Rocke would stand to receive all of the residuary estate by operation of law under the February 1992 will as the only remaining residuary devisee in that will. See § 732.5165 (establishing that any part of a will procured by undue influence is void, "but the remainder of the will not so procured shall be valid if it is not invalid for other reasons"). The question then becomes which devise from which will should determine the disposition of the residuary estate.

From our review of the evidence proffered below, the February 1992 will's residuary clause, which includes the last untainted residuary disposition Mrs. Murphy made, controls the disposition of her residuary estate. Although it is true Mr. Carey and Ms. DuBois procured part of the February 1992 will's residuary clause through their illicit efforts, the probate court made no finding—as, indeed, no one has ever argued—that Ms. Rocke was, in any way, associated with that exertion of undue influence over Mrs. Murphy. The February 1992 will would remain perfectly intelligible and true to Mrs. Murphy's repeated indications of preferring testacy over intestacy had the probate court excised Mr. Carey and Ms. DuBois' devises and left Ms. Rocke's to stand. The court must honor the last uninfluenced residuary devise Mrs. Murphy made: to her cousin, Jackie Rocke.

In conclusion, we hold that in cases of undue influence over a testator, the presumption from the doctrine of dependent relative revocation requires only a showing of broad similarity between a decedent's testamentary instruments. We further hold that a probate court may consider any admissible extrinsic evidence when measuring similarity for purposes of the doctrine's application. When the doctrine's presumption arises, the burden of proof then shifts to the opponent of the presumption to show that the testator held an independent, unaffected intention to revoke the otherwise affected will.

Having clarified the doctrine's application, we find that the presumption under the doctrine was established here and was not rebutted. The probate court erred and should have admitted the February 1992 will to probate with Ms. Rocke receiving the residuary of the estate as the last remaining devisee. Accordingly, we reverse the order of the probate court and remand with directions to enter an order consistent with this opinion.

NOTES

1.   The doctrine of revival applies when a testator has revoked a later will that itself revoked an earlier will. DRR, on the other hand, applies when a will revoking a prior will is itself invalid.

> **Connection Note:** Can you think of any other "intent-effectuating" doctrines that we have studied so far? We might think of a rule that revokes a will on divorce or a slayer rule as "intent-effectuating." We will see many more of these doctrines in the next chapter, when we discuss gap filling rules like ademption and lapse. Because so much of inheritance law is about trying to discern the decedent's intent in the absence of a clear indication in the governing document, "intent effectuating" doctrines exist throughout the textbook.

2.   DRR is another intent-effectuating doctrine in that it recognizes that adherence to formalities rules may not always engender a result that is consistent with the testator's wishes. In the *Murphy* case, if the court had taken a strict formalistic approach, who would have benefited? Do you think it was clear from the facts that such a disposition was inconsistent with the testator's intent?

3.   DRR applies when a will revocation is based on a mistaken understanding of fact or law. If the mistake is one of fact rather than law, the mistaken fact must be recited in the revoking instrument itself for DRR to apply. Because today's curative doctrines, like harmless error, may provide a way to admit to probate the better will (meaning the will that more closely effectuates the testator's intent), the doctrine of DRR is applied less frequently. For jurisdictions that still apply strict compliance rules, however, DRR can be valuable to effectuate intent. For a discussion of DRR and partial intestacy, see Richard F. Storrow, *What's Wrong with Partial Intestacy?*, 100 MARQ. L. REV. 1387 (2017).

ASSESSMENTS

1.   In 2014, Shakira executed a valid will leaving her poster collection to Ravi, her grandmother's violin to Li, and all the rest of her property to her closest friends, Melinda and Ola. In 2017, Shakira revisited her estate planning and executed a new will. The 2017 will expressly revoked the 2014 will and left Shakira's poster collection to Ravi, her grandmother's violin to Jack, and all the rest of her property to Melinda and Ola. Shakira signed and dated the will, and her friend Jack witnessed it. Shakira then tore up the 2014 will. All the devisees in the 2014 and 2017 wills were Shakira's friends. When Shakira died, her nieces (Shakira's sole heirs at law) filed a petition alleging that Shakira died intestate because the 2017 will was not executed in accordance with the jurisdiction's formalities requirements. In a jurisdiction that does not recognize harmless error, who will inherit Shakira's property?

2.   Clause Five of Jai's valid typewritten will provides: "I bequeath the sum of $5000 to my friend, Faizel." Two years later, Jai takes the will, grabs a pen, crosses out the "$5000," and writes above it "$10,000." In a state that does not recognize partial revocation by physical act, how much money will Faizel receive from Jai's estate?

F.   What Papers or Events Comprise the Will?

The cases in this section involve wills that refer to documents or events that are **extrinsic** to the will, lack the requisite formalities to make them testamentary in their own right, but nevertheless change the will's meaning and effect. As you read through the cases and learn about the doctrines, consider whether these doctrines adequately satisfy the purposes underlying the formalities doctrines, as discussed in Chapter 5.

1.   Incorporation by Reference and Republication by Codicil

The two cases that follow analyze whether informal documents (a typewritten letter and what appears to be a part of a will) are "**incorporated by reference**" into the respective duly executed wills. You will see that one of the requirements for an unattested or informal document to be "incorporated" into a will is that the document exist before the will is executed. If a testator executes a codicil that changes some part of the will and reaffirms the rest of its terms, even if that codicil makes no mention of the extrinsic document, this **republication** can help satisfy the timing requirement.

Simon v. Grayson

102 P.2d 1081 (Cal. 1940)

WASTE, J.

The question presented for determination upon this appeal involves the construction and effect to be given a provision in a will purporting to incorporate a letter by reference. Respondent's claim to certain of the estate's funds is based upon the terms of the letter. The appellants, who are residuary legatees under the will, contend that the attempted incorporation by reference was ineffectual. The facts, which were presented to the trial court upon an agreed statement, are as follows:

S. M. Seeligsohn died in 1935. His safe deposit box was found to contain, among other things, a will and codicil and a letter addressed to his executors. The will, which was dated March 25, 1932, contained a provision in paragraph four, leaving $6,000 to his executors "to be paid by them in certain amounts to certain persons as shall be directed by me in a letter that will be found in my effects and which said letter will be addressed to Martin E. Simon and Arthur W. Green (the executors) and will be dated March 25, 1932." Paragraph four also provided that any one having an interest in the will "shall not inquire into the application of said moneys" and that the executors "shall not be accountable to any person whomsoever for the payment and/or application of said sum . . . this provision . . . is in no sense a trust."

The letter found in the testator's safe deposit box was dated July 3, 1933, and stated: "In paragraph VIII of my will I have left you $6,000—to be paid to the persons named in a letter and this letter is also mentioned in said paragraph. I direct that after my death you shall pay said $6,000 as follows: To Mrs. Esther Cohn, 1755 Van Ness Ave. San Francisco, Calif. the sum of $4,000—. . . If any of the said persons cannot be found by you within six months after my death, or if any of the said persons shall predecease me, the sum directed to be paid to such persons . . . shall be paid by you to my heirs as described in paragraph IX of my said Will. . . ." This letter was written, dated, and signed entirely in the handwriting of the testator. No letter dated March 25, 1932, was found among his effects.

The codicil to the will was executed November 25, 1933. It made no changes in paragraph IV of the will and contained no reference to the letter, but recited, "Except as expressly modified by this Codicil, by Will of March 25th 1932 shall remain in full force and effect."

Esther Cohn's whereabouts was known to the testator's executors immediately following his death, but she herself died a week later. Respondent, as her executor, claimed the $4,000 mentioned in the letter. This claim was challenged by appellants, residuary legatees under Seeligsohn's will, and his executors brought suit interpleading the disputants. From the agreed facts the trial court drew conclusions of law and rendered judgment in favor of the respondent.

The chief question is whether the letter was effectually incorporated by reference into the will.

It is settled law in this state that a testator may incorporate an extrinsic document into his will, provided the document is in existence at the time and provided, further, that the reference to it in the will clearly identifies it, or renders it capable of identification by extrinsic proof. An attempt to incorporate a future document is ineffectual, because a testator cannot be permitted to create for himself the power to dispose of his property without complying with the formalities required in making a will.

In the case at bar the letter presumably was not in existence when the will was executed, for the letter bore a date subsequent to the date of the will. However, the letter was in existence at the time the codicil to the will was executed. The respondent points out that under the law the execution of a codicil has the effect of republishing the will which it modifies and argues from this that Seeligsohn's letter was an "existing document" within the incorporation rule. The only authorities cited by the parties on this point are several English decisions. These cases hold that although an informal document is not in existence when the will referring to it is executed, a later republication of the will by codicil will satisfy the "existing document" rule and will incorporate it by reference provided the testamentary instruments sufficiently identify it. The principle of republication thus applied is unquestionably sound. In revising his scheme of testamentary disposition by codicil a testator presumably reviews and reaffirms those portions of his will which remain unaffected. In substance, the will is re-executed as of that time.

Therefore, the testator's execution of the codicil in the present case must be taken as confirming the incorporation of the letter then in existence, provided the letter can be satisfactorily identified as the one referred to in the will. And this is true, notwithstanding the codicil made no reference to the letter and recited that the will should remain in full force "except as expressly modified by this codicil", for the letter, if properly incorporated, would be an integral part of the republished will.

We are also of the opinion that the trial court did not err in concluding that the letter found with the will was the letter referred to in the will. Conceding the contrary force of the discrepancy in dates, the evidence of identity was, nevertheless, sufficient to overcome the effect of that factor. The controlling authorities in this state do not require that the informal document be identified with exact precision; it is enough that the descriptive words and extrinsic circumstances combine to produce a reasonable certainty that the document in question is the one referred to by the testator in his will. Here the letter was found in the safe deposit box with the will. It was addressed to the executors, as the will stated it would be. No other letter was found. Moreover, the letter is conceded to have been written by the testator, and its terms conform unmistakably to the letter described in the will. It identifies itself as the letter mentioned in the will and deals with the identical subject matter referred to in that portion of the will. All these circumstances leave no doubt that the letter of July 3, 1933, is the one that the testator intended to incorporate in paragraph four of his will. The judgment is affirmed.

Estate of Norton

410 S.E.2d 484 (N.C. 1991)

MEYER, J.

Propounder Teab Norton sought to have a paper writing probated as the last will and testament of his father, Lawrence Norton, who died on 15 January 1987. The writing is a document consisting of a legal cover sheet and eight sheets of paper. The first page of the document following the legal cover is entitled "Last Will and Testament of Lawrence Norton." Its first paragraph provides:

> I, Lawrence Norton, of Scotland County, North Carolina, do hereby revoke all wills and codicils heretofore made by me, and do hereby make, publish, and declare this my last will and testament in manner and form as follows . . . .

The dispositions conclude at the bottom of the sixth page, in mid-sentence of a description of a real property devise. These first six pages are stapled to the flap of the legal cover sheet. The pages do not bear the signatures of any witnesses or a notary public, nor a date, but in the lower right-hand side of each of the six pages is the testator's signature.

The seventh page of the document is entitled "Codicil to Last Will and Testament of Lawrence Norton." It states:

> I, Lawrence Norton, of Scotland County, North Carolina, do hereby will, devise, and bequeath to my son, Alton Norton, the following tract of land with the stipulation that it is not to be sold for a period of ten (10) years . . . .

After the property description comes the following language:

> In Testimony Whereof, I, the said Lawrence Norton, have signed this typewritten page and the following Certificate of Self-Proven Codicil to my Will which together constitutes this Codicil to my Last Will and Testament and do hereunto set my hand and seal this 17th day of September, 1984.

Beneath this paragraph, decedent's mark and the signatures of two witnesses appear. Self-proving language, the signatures of a notary and two witnesses, and decedent's mark are found on the final page. These last two pages are stapled together, and the second page is stapled to the cover sheet, adhering the codicil to the six aforementioned pages. The envelope containing these pages has printed on it "Will" and then the typewritten words "Of Lawrence Norton and Codicil to Will of Lawrence Norton."

Propounder's evidence showed the following. On 17 September 1984, decedent had Ms. Blanche Blackwelder type the two-page document entitled "Codicil to the Last Will and Testament of Lawrence Norton." That same day, Blackwelder and a co-worker witnessed the notary public guiding the decedent's hand to make his mark on the document. Decedent had suffered a stroke and needed assistance.

Dorinda Wells, decedent's granddaughter, testified that in September 1984 she had accompanied decedent to Blackwelder's "to have something typed up requesting that Alton Norton would receive the pond." Decedent later asked Wells to "staple the ones that he received from Ms. Blanch[e] [Blackwelder] to the copy of his will" and said that "they had to be attached to the will if they were to be any good." Wells complied with the request and testified that the document at issue was the same as the one she stapled together.

Shirley Stone, former legal secretary for attorney Walter Cashwell, testified that she knew decedent as a regular client of Cashwell. She testified that she typed the "Last Will and Testament of Lawrence Norton," that the six pages were the same ones she had typed, and that the signature at the bottom of each of the six pages was that of decedent. Further, Stone testified that she had prepared a number of different wills for the deceased but that she did not remember when she had prepared the other wills relative to the six-page document at issue.

Clerk Whitfield Gibson testified that soon after decedent's death he inventoried decedent's safe-deposit box at First Union Bank. Therein was a brown envelope with no writing on it, inside of which was a white envelope designated "Will of Lawrence Norton and Codicil to the Will of Lawrence Norton" that contained the eight-page document propounded as decedent's last will and testament. Clerk Gibson also found another writing within the brown envelope, a two-page document in a white legal cover designated "Codicil to Will of Lawrence Norton." This document was properly executed 14 February 1975 and begins midsentence. No reference to a specific will or other paper writing is made in the document.

The trial court submitted the following issues to the jury:

Issue #1

Was the two-page paper writing dated September 17, 1984, executed by Lawrence Norton a valid last will and testament or a valid codicil to a last will and testament?

Issue #2

Were the first six (6) pages incorporated by reference by Lawrence Norton into the paper writing dated September 17, 1984 so as to constitute one document?

Issue #3

Is the eight-page document and every part thereof the Last Will and Testament of Lawrence Norton?

The jury found in favor of the propounder on each of the issues. Respondents moved for judgment notwithstanding the verdict as to issues two and three. The trial court granted this motion and entered judgment in favor of respondents.

On appeal, the Court of Appeals unanimously affirmed the trial court. The court concluded that the first six typewritten pages propounded as decedent's last will and testament, although designated as such, do not constitute a legally valid will because of the lack of witness signatures. Further the two-page codicil fails to adequately identify the attached six pages so as to effectuate a valid incorporation by reference. Propounder's claims on appeal were denied.

We conclude that the Court of Appeals did not err, and we affirm.

The documents at issue in this case are susceptible of numerous potential interpretations. The six-page document may possibly be conceived as a validly attested will. *See* N.C.G.S. § 31–3.3 (1984). However, we agree with the Court of Appeals that the stapled pages at issue here cannot constitute a legally valid will. Although decedent's signature on each page suggests that these six pages may have been part of an attested will, the lack of witnesses' signatures vitiates this. The question, therefore, turns on whether the properly executed 1984 codicil gives life to the six pages through incorporation by reference.

N.C.G.S. § 31–5.8 provides in pertinent part: "No will or any part thereof, which shall be in any manner revoked, can be revived otherwise than by a reexecution thereof, or by the execution of another will in which the revoked will or part thereof is incorporated by reference." Here, there is no evidence that the six pages were reexecuted.

The requirements for an incorporation by reference were articulated by this Court in *Watson v. Hinson*, 162 N.C. 72, 77 S.E. 1089 (1913). Applied here, those requirements are whether there is: (1) reliable evidence that the six pages were in existence at the time of the codicil and (2) a "clear and distinct" reference in the codicil itself, or otherwise, such as to provide "full assurance" that the six pages were intended to be incorporated in the testamentary wishes of decedent.

Sufficient evidence exists to satisfy the first *Watson* requirement that the extrinsic document be in existence at the time of the creation of the codicil. Stone testified that she had typed the six-page document. Further, she testified that the signature contained on the pages was that of decedent. Given that the document was typed before 1977 and that decedent's signature was on the pages at least before 17 September 1984, the propounder offered sufficient evidence to satisfy the first prong of the *Watson* test.

However, as to the second *Watson* requirement we conclude that propounder's claim fails. While decedent had the codicil stapled to the document designated as "his will" and inserted the documents in an envelope that had typed on the outside "Will of Lawrence Norton and Codicil of Lawrence Norton," there exists no reference within the codicil itself that is "in terms clear and distinct" designating the six pages as the document to be incorporated. It is critical that the extrinsic document be adequately identified so as to give "full assurance" that it was the document to be incorporated. Without adequate reference derived from the codicil itself or other evidentiary sources, a reviewing court cannot be assured that the decedent intended to incorporate the extrinsic document.

Because the two requirements of *Watson* have not been met, we are compelled to conclude that the evidence is insufficient as a matter of law to justify the jury's verdict in propounder's favor, and we therefore affirm the Court of Appeals.

MARTIN, J., *dissenting.*

I respectfully dissent.

The two-page codicil is a valid testamentary document, the Court of Appeals so held. No one has appealed from that holding. Under N.C.G.S. § 12–3(9), a codicil can be treated as a will. Therefore, documents can be incorporated by reference into a codicil. This is true whether they are attached or not. Further, N.C.G.S. § 31–5.8 provides that a will can be revived through an incorporation by reference. A duly executed codicil may incorporate a paper in the form of a will which was never properly executed as a will.

There is no argument but that the six typewritten pages were in existence at the time that the codicil was executed. No one disputes this point, and the evidence is overwhelming that the six-page document was prepared prior to 1977, and the codicil was executed in 1984.

The codicil refers to itself as a "Codicil to [Norton's] Last Will and Testament." The question is what is the will to which the testator so refers. Under the facts of this case the six pages were stapled to a lightweight cardboard legal cover together with the two-page codicil. The legal cover had the title: "Will of Lawrence Norton and Codicil to the Will of Lawrence Norton." The stapled papers were inside another legal envelope which bore the same inscription. The evidence further shows that the testator presented the two-page codicil and the six-page document to his granddaughter and asked her to staple them together. He told his granddaughter that the six pages had to be attached to the will "if they were to be any good." This could only mean that he intended the entire eight pages to be his will. The stapling of the six-page document to the duly executed codicil and the placing of them in the safety deposit box of the testator give full assurance as to the identity of the extrinsic paper being incorporated.

NOTES

1.   What are the concerns with allowing a will to incorporate another document by reference? How does the *Simon* court address these concerns? Why does the *Nelson* court reach the opposite result? Do you agree with the majority or dissent in *Nelson*?

2.   The UPC's incorporation by reference provision, § 2–510, is reproduced below:

UPC § 2–510 Incorporation by Reference

A writing in existence when a will is executed may be incorporated by reference if the language of the will manifests this intent and describes the writing sufficiently to permit its identification.

The UPC provision eliminates the requirement, applied in some common law jurisdictions, that the will *refer* to the document as being in existence at the time of the will's execution. The Comment to this section explains the requirement as being "sometimes troublesome." Does eliminating this requirement make the doctrine more or less trustworthy?

3.   A companion doctrine to incorporation by reference, called "integration," looks at what pages actually comprise the will. If, for example, a testator leaves five unnumbered pages disposing of property, integration would ask which of these pages is part of the will. Integration issues rarely occur when a will is drafted by an estate planning professional, because they use techniques, like binding or sewing, that ensure the pages are integrated.

> **Connection Note:** You may recall that Chapter 5's discussion of signatures included a practice note about having a testator sign or initial each page of a will. One reason for this recommendation is to avoid integration questions when, for example, the testator decides she wants to change a provision during execution, the lawyer reprints the page, and the replaced page is stapled to the will in the incorrect order. The signature ensures that the page is considered an integrated part of the will.

When do you think integration becomes more of an issue? What might you look for to determine which sheets comprised an integrated whole?

4.   Some jurisdictions, including the UPC, recognize as binding "separate writings" that lack will formalities and dispose solely of tangible personal property regardless of when these writings are prepared and signed. The UPC's tangible personal property provision, § 2–513, is reproduced below. Why might this type of writing be useful? What makes this type of writing trustworthy? Does it matter if the writing is a memorandum or something less formal, such as a notebook? Would it matter if the notebook's pages could be removed?

UPC § 2–513 Separate Writing Identifying Devise of Certain Types of Tangible Personal Property

Whether or not the provisions relating to holographic wills apply, a will may refer to a written statement or list to dispose of items of tangible personal property not otherwise specifically disposed of by the will, other than money. To be admissible under this section as evidence of the intended disposition, the writing must be signed by the testator and must describe the items and the devisees with reasonable certainty. The writing may be referred to as one to be in existence at the time of the testator's death; it may be prepared before or after the execution of the will; it may be altered by the testator after its preparation; and it may be a writing that has no significance apart from its effect on the dispositions made by the will.

5.   The *Simon* case illustrates the relationship between the doctrines of incorporation by reference and republication by codicil. Consider the following fact pattern, which comes from the case of *Clark v. Greenhalge*, 582 N.E.2d 949 (Mass. 1991). In 1977, Helen Nesmith executed a valid will which, among other things, named her cousin, Frederic Greenhalge, as executor and principal beneficiary of her estate. The will devised Nesmith's tangible property to Greenhalge except items she "designated by memorandum." One valuable item that Nesmith owned was a large oil painting of a farm scene signed by T.H. Hinckley, dated 1833, and valued at approximately $1800. In 1972, Nesmith, aided by Greenhalge, wrote a document called "memorandum" which listed various items of personal property but did not include the Hinckley painting. Nesmith, however, kept a plastic covered notebook in a desk drawer and periodically made entries in this notebook, which bore the title "List to be given Helen Nesmith 1979." In the notebook, there was an entry written by Nesmith that read: "Ginny Clark farm picture hanging over fireplace. Ma's room." Over the years, Nesmith expressed to her nurses her intent that she wanted her close friend and neighbor Virginia Clark to receive the Hinckley painting and, in 1980, Nesmith told Clark about the gift and that she planned to record it in a book she kept for the purpose of memorializing her wishes with respect to certain of her belongings. Nesmith executed two codicils to her 1977 will, both in 1980. The codicils amended certain specific bequests and otherwise ratified the 1977 will in all respects. When Nesmith died in 1986, Greenhalge received the notebook, distributed property as specified in the 1972 memorandum and in the notebook but kept the Hinckley painting for himself. Clark sued Greenhalge

seeking to compel him to deliver the farm scene painting to her. What should be the result and why?

**Thomas Hewes Hinckley, Landscape with Dogs, 1868,
Museum of Fine Arts, Boston.**

ASSESSMENTS

1.   On September 12, 2005, Vincent validly executed his will. This 2005 will appoints Stu as executor, provides that $10,000 in cash is to be paid to "the individuals named in a letter addressed to my executor and kept in my safe deposit box #812B at Chemical Bank & Loan," and leaves the residue of Vincent's estate to his mother. On November 6, 2007, Vincent validly executed a codicil. The codicil appoints Angela to serve as co-executor with Stu but makes no other changes. On January 7, 2008, Vincent died. The only letter in the safe deposit box was signed by Vincent and dated September 13, 2005. The letter names Bonnie and Marti to receive $5,000 each in cash. Are Bonnie and Marti entitled to the cash gifts?

2.   Ronnie owned a significant sports memorabilia collection. On May 1, 2010, Ronnie executed a will that left his tangible personal property to his executor to distribute as Ronnie provided in a separate document or documents. Ronnie then adhered "Post-its" to the bottom or back of each item of his sports memorabilia. Ronnie wrote on each Post-it with permanent marker the name of a family member and the date. Please advise Ronnie's executors how to distribute the memorabilia.

2.   Events of Independent Significance

The case below, *Dennis v. Holsapple*, involves whether "**acts of independent significance**," events that occur in everyday life, can change how a will is interpreted. The *Dennis* testator leaves the residue of her estate to "Whoever shall take good care of [her]"; pay attention to how the court determines that this phrase is a valid devise even though it depends on an event that changes the meaning of the will because it occurs after the will was executed.

Dennis v. Holsapple

148 Ind. 297 (1897)

JORDAN, J.

This was a proceeding in the lower court by the appellee, Ella Holsapple, to secure a construction of the last will of Emily J. Shull, deceased, and to obtain an order directing the appellant, the administrator, to turn over to the former certain property to which she claimed to be entitled as a devisee under the will in question. She prevailed in the action.

The will over which the controversy arose was duly executed by Emily J. Shull on April 9, 1889 and was probated in the circuit court of Washington county, Indiana, January 7, 1896. The will, omitting the attesting clause, is as follows:

> The following is the last will and testament of Emily J. Shull, of Salem, Indiana, to-wit: So far as my property which I leave at my death is concerned, I declare the following to be my desire and will: 1. Any valid debts due from me at my death shall be paid. 2. I command that my funeral at my death shall be decent and rendered in a proper manner. 3. Also I direct my executor to erect at my grave a proper monument not to cost less than seventy-five dollars ($ 75.00). 4. *Whoever shall take good care of me and maintain, nurse, clothe, and furnish me with proper medical treatment at my request, during the time of my life yet, when I shall need the same, shall have all of my property of every name, kind, and description left at my death.* 5. The person, or persons, whom shall be selected by me to earn my estate, as provided in 4th clause, shall have a written statement signed by me to that effect to entitle her, him, or them to my estate. 6. Samuel B. Voyles of Salem is nominated for my executor of this will.

(Emphasis added.)

On January 6, 1895, the testator wrote and sent the following letter to the appellee:

> Well, Ella, I am sick; . . . I have made my will, and whoever stays with me at my last hours gets everything I leave, except funeral expenses paid. I don't want your father or the Shulls to have a cent of my earnings, and want you to have everything I have after my death and funeral expenses are paid.

Ella, the appellee and granddaughter of the testator, came and remained with Mrs. Shull, waited upon, and took care of her until she died. The contention is: (1) That the will is invalid for the reason that it does not name any devisee; (2) that the testator undertook by her pretended will to reserve to herself the right or power to name the beneficiary by the written statement mentioned in the will, and which was written after the execution thereof. Appellants further insist that the person to whom Mrs. Shull attempted to bequeath her estate is not made certain by the will, and that the latter does not furnish the means by which a devisee can be identified.

For any and all of these reasons appellants insist that, under the law, the will is void and the court erred in admitting it and the letter in question in evidence, and in hearing evidence to identify appellee as the beneficiary under the will.

We concur with the contention of appellant, that a testator, under the law, is not authorized or invested with the power of reserving in his will the right to name or appoint a legatee or devisee by means of a written statement, or instrument of the character or kind as is the letter referred to in this opinion. Neither are courts permitted to receive extrinsic evidence in order to add to, vary, or change the literal meaning of the terms of a will, or to give effect to what may be supposed or presumed to have been the unexpressed intention of the testator. However, a will may be explained by such evidence—first, as to the person intended; second, the thing intended; third, the intention of the testator, as to each. Or, in other words, the law never opens the door to parol evidence in order to add to or take from such instruments, but for the legitimate purpose only of applying their terms or provisions to the objects or subjects referred to, and in order to reach a correct interpretation of such language or terms as are therein expressed. *Grimes' Executors v. Harmon*, 35 Ind. 198.

Courts entertain great respect for the will of those who are dead and it is only when the instrument violates, or is not in accord with the well settled rules of law, or is utterly uncertain, that the carrying out of the disposition of the estate thereunder is denied. An examination of the terms and provisions of the will in controversy discloses that the intent and purpose of the testator was to make at her death, the object of her bounty, the person who, should take good care of her, and provide for and administer to her wants and necessities. The will, although not skillfully drawn, made a complete disposition of all of Mrs. Shull's estate. The will did not name any particular person as devisee, nor was there anyone at the time of its execution who occupied the status, however, it so designated the person whom the testator contemplated and intended should have the estate bequeathed at her death could be clearly identified and ascertained by the aid of extraneous facts.

Appellee is the only one who claims, under the will, the property devised. The evidence conclusively shows that she occupied the status and responded to the person described, to whom Mrs. Shull intended her estate to go. Mrs. Shull left the person whom she thereby intended to become the object of her bequest to depend upon the happening of future events. This person depended upon the future volition of the testator in being chosen to perform the exacted services, and upon the consent of the latter in accepting the request, and in discharging the obligation imposed by the will; but the subsequent volition exercised by Mrs. Shull in this respect cannot be deemed in a legal sense as testamentary in its nature or character.

Judgment affirmed.

NOTES

1.   The *Dennis* court held that Mrs. Shull devised her residuary estate to a person who held a particular *status*, and it did not matter that no one occupied such status at the time of the will's execution. Is it helpful to think of the doctrine of "acts of independent significance" in this way? How would this reasoning change if instead of a person's status (like caretaker), the bequest related to an item ("the car I own at my death")? Should a gift to "the employees of my company" be valid? What about a gift of "the contents of my safety deposit box"? What about "the contents of my desk drawer"? What about "the contents of my car glove box"? What policy concerns underlie the doctrines discussed in this section?

2.   The UPC provision is set forth below:

––––––––––––

UPC § 2–512 Events of Independent Significance

A will may dispose of property by reference to acts and events that have significance apart from their effect upon the dispositions made by the will, whether they occur before or after the execution of the will or before or after the testator's death. The execution or revocation of another individual's will is such an event.

ASSESSMENT

Evaluate the validity of the following bequests:

1. "I leave $1,000 to each of my employees." ✓

2. "I leave the contents of my safety deposit box to my friend, Ο Fiona."

3. "I leave the car I own at my death to my cousin, Clyde." ✓

4. "I leave $10,000 to each of my grandchildren." ✗

5. "I leave the contents of my jewelry box to my caretaker, ✓ Shanique."

6. "I leave the contents of my car glove box to Sally M. Gibbs, of ✓ San Antonio, Texas."

7. "I leave all the paintings hanging on the walls of my home to the ✓ Barnes Institute of Merion Pennsylvania for its general charitable uses and purposes."

G. Conclusion and Takeaways

The rules governing will formalities are complicated enough when only a single document is involved. This chapter extends those rules to circumstances where there is more than one document to explore how those documents interact, and how the law chooses among conflicting documents using doctrines like revival and DRR. It also addresses other non-testamentary documents or acts that can modify the will without any formalities. The next chapter adds an additional layer to this analysis by looking at how testamentary documents are affected by the passing of time, especially when the provisions in the document do not anticipate changes or ambiguities that might arise between the will's execution and its probate.

CHAPTER 7 COMPREHENSIVE ASSESSMENTS

1.   **SEQUENTIAL WILLS AND EXTRINSIC DOCUMENTS REVIEW.** Jintao's will, validly executed on June 15, 2020, provides as follows:

> I leave my living room furniture to my friend, Min;

> I leave my watch collection to the people listed on a paper I will write;

> I leave $5000 to any charity named by my sister, Cho, in her will;

> I leave all the rest of my property to be divided equally and distributed among those of my children who survive me.

The next day, Jintao creates a document on his computer that says: "June 16, 2020. Seung gets my watches. She's the best friend anyone could imagine." Jintao prints and signs the document.

On July 17, 2020, Jintao handwrites, dates, and signs the following document: "I would like my sister, Cho, to be my executor."

On August 17, 2020, Jintao tears up the July document.

Jintao dies on September 1, 2020, survived by Min, Cho, Seung, and two children. How should Jintao's probate estate be distributed, assuming all the items bequeathed in the June 15 will still exist and there is $65,000 cash in the probate estate?

2.   **CREATE A "BEST PRACTICES" GUIDE.** Imagine you work as an associate in a firm that regularly drafts wills and codicils for clients and supervises their execution. Write a memo to your supervisor. In the memo, propose best practices for when and under what circumstances a new will (as opposed to a codicil) should be executed. Make sure to recognize the benefits and pitfalls associated with your proposed best practices. Conclude with recommendations on what to do with old wills that the testator intends no longer to apply.

Test Your Knowledge

To assess your understanding of the material in this chapter, click here to take a quiz.

CHAPTER 8

Wills IV: Drafting and Interpretation

CHAPTER LEARNING OUTCOMES

Following your work with this material in this chapter, you should be able to do the following:

- Distinguish between latent and patent ambiguities and determine when extrinsic evidence will be admitted to interpret language in a will

- Classify gifts in a will and apply the classifications to situations of lapse and abatement

- Apply lapse rules and antilapse statutes to assess the possible results of a beneficiary or class of beneficiaries dying before the testator

- Apply ademption and non-ademption rules in situations where property bequeathed in a will is gone or has changed form when the testator dies

- Apply the doctrines of satisfaction, accessions, exoneration, and abatement to property in an estate

- Describe the effect of a testator having children, marrying, or divorcing after executing a will

- Summarize the effect of joint wills and contracts not to change wills on probate and non-probate property.

- Draft dispositions in a will addressing changes in beneficiaries or property that may have occurred by the time the testator dies

A. Introduction

Once you understand the basic requirements for a valid will (testamentary capacity, compliance with formalities, and no illicit interference with donative intent), you must draft the will correctly to carry out that intent. Sometimes the language of a document is ambiguous, either on its face or as applied. A huge part of the estate planning attorney's role is to prevent these ambiguities from arising. Your job is to anticipate events that might take place between the will's execution and the client's death, to ask the client what should happen if these events occur, and then to translate the client's wishes into language that indicates to everyone involved in the process what the testator meant. If you are dealing with a will someone else drafted, you must understand the rules of will interpretation to resolve ambiguities.

Part B addresses the topic of will interpretation—what the words of the will mean—and the topic of court reformation of a will. As with will execution formalities, the law started out with rigid rules but (at least in some jurisdictions) has evolved into a more functional approach. *Mahoney v. Grainger*, for example, applies the "plain meaning" doctrine, regardless of extrinsic evidence that indicates the plain meaning contradicts the testator's intent. The remaining cases are more forgiving in their approaches to interpretation because, like with formalities, a too strict approach may end up thwarting testator intent.

Many things can happen between the time the will is executed and the time it is probated: an intended beneficiary may die; an asset devised in the will may be sold, given away, lost, or encumbered by debt; the testator may have another child; and the estate may shrink significantly in value. Often, a client will not have considered all the possibilities, and it is the estate planning attorney's job to anticipate at least the most common events, ascertain the client's wishes in such circumstances, and then draft the will in accordance with those wishes. Even in the best of circumstances, though, a client may not return to amend a will when an unanticipated circumstance arises. Alternatively, a will may have been drafted without anticipating future circumstances, either because the will is drafted by a layperson or by an attorney who lacks experience. In those cases, rules of construction apply. The balance of this chapter addresses how these rules apply to fill gaps in what might be referred to as "**stale**" wills.

Part C discusses the doctrine of lapse, which applies when a beneficiary named in a will dies before the testator. **Part D** addresses what happens when property changes form in some way between will execution and probate. **Part E** addresses what happens when the testator has a child, marries, or divorces after the will is executed. Finally, **Part F** discusses what happens when a married couple executes a **joint will** or enters into a contract not to change their reciprocal wills, and then the surviving spouse executes a new will after the first spouse dies.

B. Will Interpretation: Plain Meaning and Extrinsic Evidence

The cases in this section address a topic that shows up in many law classes and that confronts the reader of any text: how to establish the meaning of the text's language. In the area of wills and trusts, however, the fact that the main witness is *never* available when the interpretation becomes necessary makes this task ever more challenging. Whatever evidence does exist is never the "best evidence" of what the decedent wanted. Many of these cases turn on whether a court will look outside of the four corners of the document to determine the testator's intent. Traditionally, extrinsic evidence was allowed only when the ambiguity was not obvious from reading the document (a "**latent ambiguity**") and was disallowed when the ambiguity was obvious from reading the document (a "**patent ambiguity**"). Does this distinction make sense? The modern trend is to consider the quality of the extrinsic evidence rather than the type of ambiguity. As you read this trio of cases, pay attention to which approach appears more consistent with the policies of wills law as we have seen them so far.

Mahoney v. Grainger

186 N.E. 86 (Mass. 1933)

RUGG, J.

This is an appeal from a decree of a probate court denying a petition for distribution of a legacy under the will of Helen A. Sullivan among her first cousins who are contended to be her heirs at law. The residuary clause was as follows:

> All the rest and residue of my estate, both real and personal property, I give, demise and bequeath *to my heirs at law living at the time of my decease, absolutely; to be divided among them equally, share and share alike;* provided, however, that the real property which I own at my decease shall not be sold or disposed of until five (5) years after my decease, unless there is not sufficient personal property at the time of my decease to pay my specific legatees; in which case said real property may be sold. The income from said real property during said five (5) years is to be distributed among my heirs at law, as I have directed.

(Emphasis added.) The trial judge made a report of the material facts in substance as follows:

The sole heir at law of the testator at the time of her death was her maternal aunt, Frances Hawkes Greene, who is still living and who was named in the petition for probate of her will. The will was duly proved and allowed on October 8, 1931, and letters testamentary issued accordingly. The testator was a single woman about sixty-four years of age, and had been a school teacher. She always maintained her own home but her relations with her aunt who was her sole heir and with several first cousins were cordial and friendly. In her will she gave general legacies in considerable sums to two of her first cousins. About ten days before her death the testator sent for an attorney who found her sick but intelligent about the subjects of their conversation. She told the attorney she wanted to make a will. She gave him instructions as to general pecuniary legacies. In response to the questions "whom do you want to leave the rest of your property to? Who are your nearest relations?" she replied, "I've got about twenty-five first cousins . . . let them share it equally." The attorney then drafted the will and read it to the testator, and it was executed by her.

> **Language Note:** This is yet another case where the court uses the word "testatrix" rather than testator to refer to the female property owner. The court also uses the word "draftsman," which we have left in place but wanted to highlight. By the way, why do you suppose the court felt it necessary to observe that the testator was a school teacher who maintained her own home?

The trial judge ruled that statements of the testator "were admissible only in so far as they tended to give evidence of the material circumstances surrounding the testator at the time of the execution of the will: that the words heirs at law were words in common use, susceptible of application to one or many: that when applied to the special circumstances of this case that the testator had but one heir, notwithstanding the added words 'to be divided among them equally, share and share alike,' there was no latent ambiguity or equivocation in the will itself which would permit the introduction of the statements of the testator to prove her testamentary intention." Certain first cousins have appealed from the decree dismissing the petition for distribution to them.

There is no doubt as to the meaning of the words "heirs at law living at the time of my decease" as used in the will. Confessedly they refer alone to the aunt of the testator and do not include her cousins.

A will duly executed and allowed by the court must under the statute of wills be accepted as the final expression of the intent of the person executing it. The fact that it was not in conformity to the instructions given to the draftsman who prepared it or that he made a mistake does not authorize a court to reform or alter it or remold it by amendments. The will must be construed as it came from the hands of the testator. Mistakes in the drafting of the will may be of significance in some circumstances in a trial as to the due execution and allowance of the alleged testamentary instrument. Proof that the legatee actually designated was not the particular person intended by the one executing the will cannot be received to aid in the interpretation of a will. *See National Society for the Prevention of Cruelty to Children v. Scottish National Society for the Prevention of Cruelty to Children*, [1915] A.C. 207. When the instrument has been proved and allowed as a will, oral testimony as to the meaning and purpose of a testator in using language must be rigidly excluded. It is only where testamentary language is not clear in its application to facts that evidence may be introduced as to the circumstances under which the testator used that language in order to throw light upon its meaning. Where no doubt exists as to the property bequeathed or the identity of the beneficiary there is no room for extrinsic evidence; the will must stand as written.

In the case at bar there is no doubt as to the heirs at law of the testator. The aunt alone falls within that description. The cousins are excluded. The circumstance that the plural word "heirs" was used does not prevent one individual from taking the entire gift.

Decree affirmed.

Estate of Gibbs

111 N.W.2d 413 (Wis. 1961)

FAIRCHILD, J.

Decedent Gibbs left a will that included a gift to "Robert J. Krause of 4708 North 46th Street, Milwaukee, Wisconsin." Respondent, named Robert Krause, lived in Milwaukee (but not at the referenced address), was known to decedent as "Bob," and had worked in close contact with decedent for nearly twenty years. Appellant, who was named Robert J. Krause and lived at the specified address, claimed that the plain and unambiguous language of the gift meant he, and not the former employee, was its intended recipient.

Miss Krueger, who had been the Gibbs housekeeper for twenty-four years up to 1958 and was a legatee under both wills, corroborated much of respondent's testimony. She also testified that Mr. Gibbs had told her he made a will remembering various people including "the boys at the shop," referring to them as "Mike, Ed, and Bob."

Miss Pacius, a legatee under both wills, who had been Mr. Gibbs' private secretary for many years while he was in business, testified to Mr. Gibbs' expressions of high regard for respondent. Another former employee also testified to a similar effect. Of the individuals named in the wills as legatees, all except two were shown to be relatives of Mr. or Mrs. Gibbs, former employees, neighbors, friends, or children of friends.

The attorney who drew several wills for Mr. and Mrs. Gibbs produced copies of most of them. They were similar in outline to the wills admitted to probate except that Mr. Gibbs' wills executed before Mrs. Gibbs' death bequeathed his property to her if she survived. The first ones were drawn in 1953 and each contained a bequest to "Robert Krause, of Milwaukee, Wisconsin, if he survives me, one per cent (1%)." There was testimony that Mrs. Gibbs' will, executed in August 1955, contained the same language. In the 1957 wills the same bequest was made to "Robert Krause, now of 4708 North 46th Street, Milwaukee, Wisconsin." In several other instances street addresses of legatees were given for the first time in 1957. In the 1958 wills the same bequest was made to "Robert J. Krause, now of 4708 North 46th Street, Milwaukee, Wisconsin." The scrivener also produced a handwritten memorandum given to him by Mr. Gibbs for the purpose of preparing Mr. Gibbs' 1958 will, and the reference on that memorandum corresponding to the Krause bequest is "Bob, 1%." Four bequests (to Gruener, Krause, Preuschl, and Owen) appear in the same order in each of the wills and are reflected in the memorandum referred to as "Fred Gruener, Bob, Mike, and Ed." Gruener, Preuschl, and Owen were former employees of Gibbs Steel Company, as was respondent. A street address was inserted for the first time in each case in the 1957 wills and repeated in the later ones.

Prior to 1950 respondent had lived at several different locations. From 1950 until April 1960, he lived at 2325 North Sherman Boulevard. We take judicial notice that this address and 4708 North Forty-Sixth Street are in the same general section of the city of Milwaukee, and that both are a number of miles distant from the Gibbs home. We also take judicial notice that the telephone directory for Milwaukee and vicinity listed 14 subscribers by the name of Robert Krause with varying initials in October 1958, and 15 in October of 1959. The listing for appellant gives his middle initial J. as well as his street address.

The only evidence which suggests even a possibility that Mr. or Mrs. Gibbs may have known of appellant may be summarized as follows:

For a time, appellant had a second job as a part-time taxi driver, and he recalled an elderly lady who was his passenger on a lengthy taxi trip in June 1955. He did not recall where he picked her up. He had driven her across the city, waiting for her while she visited in a hospital, and then driven her back across the city. The place where he let her out, however, was not her home. He did not recall that she had given him her name, but she had inquired as to his. They had conversed about the illness of appellant's wife and his working at an extra job in order to make ends meet. She had expressed sympathy and approval of his efforts. Presumably when he was notified that his name appeared in the Gibbs wills as legatee, he endeavored to find an explanation of his good fortune and concluded that the lady in question must have been Mrs. Gibbs. The 1955 taxi ride, however, could not explain the gift to Robert Krause in the 1953 wills, and it is clear that the same legatee was intended in the Krause bequests in all the wills.

Propriety of considering extrinsic evidence.

As stated above, the county court could reach no other conclusion upon consideration of the extrinsic evidence than that Mr. and Mrs. Gibbs intended to designate respondent as their legatee. The difficult question is whether the court could properly consider such evidence in determining testamentary intent.

Under rules as to construction of a will, unless there is ambiguity in the text of the will read in the light of surrounding circumstances, extrinsic evidence is inadmissible for the purpose of determining intent.

A latent ambiguity exists where the language of the will, though clear on its face, is susceptible of more than one meaning, when applied to the extrinsic facts to which it refers. There are two classes of latent ambiguity. One, where there are two or more persons or things exactly measuring up to the description in the will; the other where no person or thing exactly answers the declarations and descriptions of the will, but two or more persons or things answer the description imperfectly. Extrinsic evidence must be resorted to under these circumstances to identify which of the parties, unspecified with particularity in the will, was intended by the testator.

Had the probated wills used the language of the 1953 wills "To Robert Krause of Milwaukee," such terms would have described both appellant and respondent, as well as a number of other people. Upon such ambiguity of the first type above mentioned becoming apparent, extrinsic evidence would be admissible in order to determine which Robert Krause Mr. and Mrs. Gibbs had in mind as their legatee.

Had the will said "To my former employee, Robert J. Krause of 4708 North 46th Street," neither appellant nor respondent would have exactly fulfilled the terms. Latent ambiguity of the second type would thus have appeared, and again extrinsic evidence would be admissible to determine what individual testators had in mind.

The terms of the bequest exactly fit appellant and no one else. There is no ambiguity.

Under the circumstances before us, can a court properly consider evidence showing that some of the words were used by mistake and should be stricken or disregarded? It is traditional doctrine that wills must not be reformed even in the case of demonstrable mistake. This doctrine doubtless rests upon policy reasons. The courts deem it wise to avoid entertaining claims of disappointed persons who may be able to make very plausible claims of mistake after the testator is no longer able to refute them.

Although the courts subscribe to an inflexible rule against reformation of a will, it seems that they have often strained a point in matters of identification of property or beneficiaries in order to reach a desired result by way of construction. In *Will of Stack*, where the will devised "Block 64," the court included part of block 175 in the provision to conform to the unexpressed intent of the testator. In *Will of Boeck* where the will devised the "northeast quarter of the northwest quarter" of a section, which was not owned by the testator, the court held such provision passed the southeast quarter of the northwest quarter, to conform to the misexpressed intent of the testator. In *Moseley v. Goodman* where testator bequeathed property to "Mrs. Moseley," the court denied the claim of Mrs. Lenoir Moseley to the gift and held that Mrs. Trimble had been intended by the testator. Mrs. Trimble was known to the testator by the nickname "Mrs. Moseley."

We conclude that details of identification, particularly such matters as middle initials, street addresses, and the like, which are highly susceptible to mistake, particularly in metropolitan areas, should not be accorded such sanctity as to frustrate an otherwise clearly demonstrable intent. Where such details of identification are involved, courts should receive evidence tending to show that a mistake has been made and should disregard the details when the proof establishes to the highest degree of certainty that a mistake was, in fact, made.

We therefore consider that the county court properly disregarded the middle initial and street address and determined that respondent was the Robert Krause whom testators had in mind.

In re Estate of Cole

621 N.W.2d 816 (Minn. App. 2001)

CRIPPEN, J.

The will of decedent Ruth N. Cole states a bequest to her friend, appellant Veta J. Vining, in "the sum of two hundred thousand dollars ($25,000)." Appellant disputes the trial court's determination to consider testimony of the will's scrivener that explains the contradictory language of the will. We affirm.

FACTS

Rule N. Cole executed a will on July 1, 1999 and died testate on July 8, 1999. Respondent personal representative petitioned the court for a construction of the will to find that appellant's bequest was for $25,000. After appellant contested the construction, the personal representative moved for summary judgment, basing the motion principally upon the affidavit and file notes of the scrivener, attorney Robert C. Black, III. Black's affidavit explains that he used his computer to "copy and paste" another paragraph of the will bequeathing "two hundred thousand dollars ($200,000.00)" to another individual and changed the name to Veta Vining. Black then changed the numerals to $25,000, the amount chosen by his client, but failed to change the words indicating the amount to "twenty-five thousand dollars." Appellant offered no evidence to contradict Black's affidavit or file notes and did not request the opportunity to cross-examine Mr. Black.

The trial court classified the bequest as patently ambiguous because the inconsistency appears on the face of the instrument. Referring to historic precedents for admitting direct evidence of intention for latent but not patent ambiguities, the court concluded that the distinction serves no useful purpose. The court then undertook the task of assessing the credibility of the evidence and found that the scrivener's testimony was reliable, that no genuine issue of material fact remained for further litigation, and that the bequest to appellant Vining must be construed as "the sum of twenty-five thousand dollars ($25,000)."

ISSUE

Did the trial court properly consider direct evidence of a testator's intention in resolving contradictory provisions of a will?

ANALYSIS

The history of the construction of wills and other instruments has been shaped by two overriding rules. First, the court is to avoid doing any violence to the words employed in the instrument and to distrust the reliability of looking to sources outside the instrument for information about its meaning; second, the court is to effectuate the testator's intent. Thus, the common-law use of outside sources was suspect and only grudgingly permitted. At the end of the seventeenth century, although courts of equity freely considered extrinsic evidence, including direct evidence of intent—because judges "could distinguish what weight and stress ought to be laid on such evidence"—common-law courts would not allow evidence of intent because "it [was] not safe to admit a jury to try the intent of the testator."

To avoid declaring bequests void for uncertainty, courts began to consider evidence of the testator's intent with respect to so-called equivocations, often referred to as latent ambiguities, which involve instruments that describe a person or thing in terms equally applicable to more than one when the surrounding circumstances are taken into account. *E.g.*, *Wheaton v. Pope*, 97 N.W. 1046, 1048 (Minn. 1904) (stating the rule that extrinsic evidence may be used to remove a latent ambiguity that arises because the will " 'names a person as the object of a gift, or a thing as the subject of it, and there are two persons or things that answer such name or description' " (quoting *Patch v. White*, 117 U.S. 210, 217 (1886)). Courts also created exceptions permitting direct evidence of the testator's intent in certain other circumstances. *E.g.*, *In re Estate of Wunsch*, 225 N.W. 109, 110 (Minn. 1929) (finding admissible the attorney's testimony about the testator's intent because "it is settled that oral testimony is competent to prove intentional pretermission" (citation omitted)); *Wheaton*, 97 N.W. at 1049 (allowing scrivener's testimony about the testator's intent and instructions to clear up an ambiguity that arose because of an inaccurate metes and bounds description). *See generally* 9 John Henry Wigmore, EVIDENCE IN TRIALS AT COMMON LAW §§ 2474–2477 (James H. Chadbourn rev. 1981) (noting exceptions for erroneous description, "rebutting an equity," and the *falsa demonstratio non nocet* principle).

Notwithstanding the developments for admission of evidence showing the testator's intentions, some authorities continue to state that no direct evidence of intent should be considered when construing patent ambiguities, *i.e.*, those contradictions appearing on the face of the instrument.

We are satisfied that the trial court correctly denigrated the usefulness of a distinction between patent and latent ambiguities for determining what type of extrinsic evidence should be considered when construing ambiguous or contradictory provisions. Because it is reasonable for the Minnesota judiciary to weigh evidence of the testator's declarations of intent, the basis for the patent/latent distinction appears outmoded. Moreover, we appreciate, in general, the frustration scriveners encounter in trying to express perfectly their client's wishes, which frequently creates ambiguities, such that justice requires consideration of extrinsic evidence to determine intent.

Subject to prospective limitations, none of which bears on the immediate case, the scrivener's testimony may be employed to resolve contradictory provisions in the will. The first limitation is that surrounding circumstances should be examined first, and direct evidence of the testator's intention should be considered only if the ambiguity or contradiction persists. Second, extrinsic evidence is to be used to determine what the testator meant by the words used, not to determine an intent that cannot be found in the words employed in the instrument. *In re Estate of Smith*, 580 P.2d 754, 757 (Ariz. Ct. App. 1978) (stating the general rule that extrinsic evidence is "not admissible to show what the testator intended to say, but rather to show what he intended by what he did say" and allowing "the statement of the attorney who drew up the will" to show what the testator meant by the words "money and coin collection").

In this case, the trial court construed what the testator meant by the words she used, and the surrounding circumstances as posed by appellant permit only speculation regarding the desires of the testator. Nothing in the history of Minnesota case law suggests cause for blinding the courts to evidence of the testator's intention in cases where the will contains contradictory language.

NOTES

1.   What are the different approaches to will interpretation taken in this trio of cases? What is an example of a patent ambiguity in the cases? What is an example of a latent ambiguity? Is the distinction between patent ambiguity and latent ambiguity meaningful? How do these courts' approaches to extrinsic evidence reinforce or undermine the policies we have studied so far about will doctrine and drafting?

2.   Why does the *Mahoney* court refuse to look at evidence of the testator's intent? Do you agree that there was no ambiguity in Helen Sullivan's will? Where might the court have found ambiguity, had the court wanted to, in order to better effectuate testator intent?

3.   In cases where there is an ambiguity that does not appear on the face of the document (a "latent" ambiguity) courts typically allow extrinsic evidence, as the *Gibbs* court explains. There might be **equivocation**, where several people or objects fit a description in the will. (Such as "my cousin Ophelia," when I have two cousins named Ophelia.) Or it might be **misdescription**, where no person or object fits the description. One example of the latter is the will of Maria F. McCalla, who left property in trust for—in addition to an African American hospital in Savannah—"the Seventh Georgia Regiment of Georgia." The Seventh Georgia was a famous regiment during the Civil War; but by the time she died in 1905, the regiment was long gone. There was, however, an association of the survivors of the Seventh Regiment. Extrinsic evidence was permitted to show that the survivors' association was the intended beneficiary of one-fifth of her testamentary trust. *Association of Survivors of Seventh Ga. Regiment v. Larner*, 3 F.2d 201 (Ct. App. D.C. 1925).

4.   In *Cole,* the ambiguity was patent—you could tell by reading the will that something was amiss (ambiguous), for the will said, "two hundred thousand dollars" *and* $25,000. Both obviously could not be correct. Traditionally no extrinsic evidence would be permitted for this type of ambiguity. (The rationale for this rule was that errors on the face of the will should have been picked up at the execution stage, or before.) The *Cole* court rejects the distinction and allows extrinsic evidence regardless of whether the ambiguity is latent or patent. Are there concerns with allowing extrinsic evidence whenever a mistake occurs? What if there was no ambiguity at all—there was just an error by the scrivener, who was willing to testify to the error? Would there be relief under the rationale of *Cole* in that case?

> **Connection Note:** You may recall Chapter 3's discussion of malpractice liability for attorney drafting errors. Leaving aside the privity rule, which still applies in various jurisdictions, requiring a beneficiary to sue the attorney for damages may not be a good solution. Can you think of reasons why?

5.   What is the difference between interpretation of a will, the reformation of a will, and the construction of a will? Why do you think courts have historically been so unwilling to reform wills? The following UPC provision was added in

2008. Is reformation even necessary if courts are willing to look at extrinsic evidence to aid interpretation?

UPC § 2–805 Reformation to Correct Mistakes

The court may reform the terms of a governing instrument, even if unambiguous, to conform the terms to the transferor's intention if it is proved by clear and convincing evidence what the transferor's intention was and that the terms of the governing instrument were affected by a mistake of fact or law, whether in expression or inducement.

ASSESSMENTS

1.   Which of the following provisions from Taahira's will are patent ambiguities and which are latent ambiguities?

  a.   "My house to my aunt, Siya Dhar." Taahira has two aunts: Diya Dhar and Siya Shar.

  b.   "The sum of five thousand dollars ($50,000) to my brother, Raj."

  c.   "My boat to my friend, Amelia Bane; my bike to my friend, Amelia Kris, and my diamond ring to my friend Amelia."

  d.   "My blue Tesla to Mary." Taahira has a blue Volkswagen and a silver Tesla.

2.   Identify the ambiguities in the following bequest and redraft it to be clear and unambiguous: "I direct my executor to divide my furniture equally among my nieces and nephews."

3.   Imagine you are an associate at the firm that represented Ruth N. Cole. Prepare a "best practices" memo addressed to Robert C. Black setting forth the steps your department will take in the future to avoid the drafting error that arose in Cole's will.

C. Lapse

This section explores the doctrine of **lapse**, which applies when a beneficiary named in a will predeceases the testator. In such a circumstance, the beneficiary's gift is said to lapse—that is, fail—unless the jurisdiction's **antilapse** statute provides a substitute gift to the predeceased beneficiary's descendants. Although nearly every state has an antilapse statute, those statutes apply to differing classes of beneficiaries. Here is an example of a typical antilapse statute from Connecticut:

> **Death of devisee or legatee.** When a devisee or legatee, being a child, stepchild, grandchild, brother or sister of the testator, dies before him, and no provision has been made in the will for such contingency, the issue of such devisee or legatee shall take the estate so devised or bequeathed.

CONN. GEN. STAT. ANN. § 45a–441. As you can see, if a Connecticut testator left a bequest to her brother, and that brother predeceased her, the law would provide that the gift would go instead to the brother's children, if he had any. On the other hand, if the testator left a gift to a cousin who died before the testator, the antilapse statute would not apply, and the gift would fail. If a beneficiary does not fall within the scope of the applicable antilapse statute, such as a friend or more remote blood relative, common law lapse rules govern. Accordingly, the first thing to do when a lapse problem arises is to read the language of the will to see if the testator intended the property to pass to an alternative beneficiary and, if not, to read the applicable antilapse statute to see if it covers the predeceased beneficiary. The antilapse statute does not prevent the lapse from occurring. If applicable, the antilapse statute simply redirects the lapsed gift to another individual or group of individuals. If antilapse statutes do not apply, the common law rules of lapse will govern.

Under the common law rule of lapse, how the doctrine applies depends on how the gifts are classified: as **specific** ("my car," "my jewelry," or "my stock in Kodak"); **general** ("10,000 dollars" or "20% of the value of my estate); **demonstrative** ("10,000 dollars, to be paid from sale of my Netflix stock"); or **residuary** ("everything else I own" or "the residue of my estate"). If a specific, general, or demonstrative gift lapses, the lapsed gift falls into the residue. If a residuary gift lapses, however, there are two possible results. A majority of jurisdictions provide that the lapsed portion of the residue passes to the remaining residuary beneficiaries. Other jurisdictions apply a **"no residue of a residue"** rule, meaning that the lapsed portion of the residue passes to the testator's heirs at law (that is, by intestacy).

As with most gap-filling rules, a careful draftsperson can always anticipate the eventuality and draft around it. Before reading the *Kehler* case, which raises the precise question of whether Emerson Kehler's will anticipated what would happen if one of his siblings predeceased him, it might be helpful to look at some examples of how lapse rules work. Consider the following:

> **Case 1.** Assume Terrence executes a will leaving one-half of his estate to his daughter, Anya, and one half of his estate to his son, Balboa. Balboa predeceases Terrence, leaving a son Chinue. If the jurisdiction has an antilapse statute like UPC § 2–603, how will Terrence's estate be distributed?

In Case 1, § 2–603(b) provides that a "substitute gift" is created in Balboa's surviving descendants, so Chinue would take Balboa's share.

> **Case 2.** Assume the same facts, except that Terrence's will leaves his estate, in equal shares, to his friends Dinah and Eliezer. (Assume the same children and grandchild, including that Balboa is predeceased.) If Eliezer dies before Terrence, how will Terrence's estate be distributed?

In Case 2, § 2–603 does not apply because the deceased beneficiary is a friend. Accordingly, if the jurisdiction follows the majority rule, Eliezer's death means that Dinah will inherit the entire residue. If, however, the jurisdiction follows the "no residue of a residue" approach, Dinah will receive half of the residue and Anya and Chinue will receive the other half. What would happen if the residuary beneficiaries were Terrence's heirs at law but were not covered by the antilapse statute?

> **Case 3.** Assume Terrence's will instead leaves his car to his daughter, Anya, $10,000 to his son, Balboa, and the residue of his estate to be divided into equal shares and distributed to his children. If, on Terrence's death, Balboa is predeceased (again survived by Chinue) and the UPC applies, how will Terrence's estate be distributed?

In Case 3, § 2–603 does not distinguish among different types of gifts. It also applies to so-called "class gifts" where, instead of naming the beneficiaries as in Case 1, the testator simply leaves the gift to my children. Here, Chinue would take the $10,000 left to Balboa and also Balboa's share of the residue. The rationale behind antilapse statutes is that the testator is presumed to intend that a gift to a relative who is related in a close enough degree pass to that relative's bloodline and not to someone else. If the common law applied to Case 3, the general gift of $10,000 would lapse and be treated as part of the residue.

As you read the following case, consider what you think Emerson Kehler, the testator, intended to have happen to the property held in his estate if a beneficiary predeceased him.

Estate of Kehler

411 A.2d 748 (Pa. 1979)

ROBERTS, J.

Testator, Emerson Kehler, died in April of 1975. By paragraph THIRD of his will, he disposed of the residue of his estate:

> All the rest, residue and remainder of my estate, real, personal and mixed, of whatsoever nature and wheresoever situated, I give, devise and bequeath unto my brother, RALPH KEHLER, of Reading, Pennsylvania, and my sisters, VIOLA WELKER, of Lavelle, Pennsylvania, ADA SHARTEL, of Reading, Pennsylvania, and GERTRUDE KRAPF, of Stroudsburg, Pennsylvania, and to the survivor or survivors of them, equally, share and share alike, to have and to hold unto themselves, their heirs and assigns forever.

Ralph Kehler predeceased testator, but Ralph Kehler's daughter, appellant Ethel Chupp, survived testator.

At issue on this appeal is whether appellant may take the share of the residue her father Ralph Kehler would have received had he survived testator. Appellant takes the position that testator's intent concerning the disposition of the bequest to a predeceased sibling is ambiguous. She maintains, therefore, that the relevant "antilapse" statute, 20 PA. C.S. § 2514(9), applies. Section 2514(9) provides:

Rules of interpretation

In the absence of a contrary intent appearing therein, wills shall be construed as to real and personal estate in accordance with the following rules:

* * *

(9) **Lapsed and void devises and legacies; substitution of issue.** A devise or bequest to a child or other issue of the testator or to his brother or sister or to a child of his brother or sister whether designated by name or as one of a class shall not lapse if the beneficiary shall fail to survive the testator and shall leave issue surviving the testator but shall pass to such surviving issue who shall take *per stirpes* the share which their deceased ancestor would have taken had he survived the testator: Provided, That such a devise or bequest to a brother or sister or to the child of a brother or sister shall

lapse to the extent to which it will pass to the testator's spouse or issue as a part of the residuary estate or under the intestate laws.

The Orphans' Court disagreed. It concluded that the language of testator's will, particularly "and to the survivor or survivors of them," manifests testator's "contrary intent" within the meaning of section 2514 to limit takers to those named siblings who are living at testator's death, thus precluding operation of subsection (9). We agree with appellant that the court misinterpreted testator's will.

This Court has not yet held that a testator must expressly provide for a possible lapse to manifest "contrary intent" overcoming operation of the antilapse statute. *See Corbett Estate*, 241 A.2d 524, 527 n.7 (Pa. 1968). Surely, however, a "contrary intent" must appear with reasonable certainty. See *id.* at 527–28. *Accord, Sykes Estate*, 383 A.2d 920, 921 (Pa. 1978).

Testator's will here permits no such certainty. In paragraph THIRD of his will, Testator fails to make an express statement concerning his intended disposition of residue in the event a named beneficiary predeceases him. Instead, he merely states his desire to leave the residue to his named siblings "and to the survivor or survivors of them." By contrast, in other paragraphs of his will, testator expressly provides for the possibility of lapse. In paragraph FIRST, in which testator gives his nephew Emerson Asher Shoemaker a monetary gift, testator provides: "I give and bequeath the sum of One Thousand ($1,000.00) Dollars, unto my nephew, EMERSON ASHER SHOEMAKER, of Reading, Pennsylvania, should he survive me, but if he predeceases me, then this paragraph of my Will shall be null and void and of no effect." In Paragraph SECOND, testator employs the identical language manifesting an intent to provide a lapse in another bequest of $1,000 to another nephew, Larry Welker. There, testator again stated "if he predeceases me, then this paragraph of my Will shall be null and void and of no effect."

Testator's careful use of express language directing a lapse of these bequests in his will raises considerable doubt that he intended a lapse in paragraph THIRD, where no such language is used. It cannot now be said with the requisite reasonable certainty that testator intended a lapse of residuary bequests under paragraph THIRD. In accordance with the Legislature's directive contained in 20 PA. C.S. § 2514(9), it must be presumed that testator did not intend his bequest to Ralph Kehler to lapse. By way of the same statute, appellant may share in the residuary estate. Decree vacated and case remanded for proceedings consistent with this opinion. Each party pays own costs.

LARSEN, J., *dissenting.*

I dissent. I believe the testator clearly expressed his intention in Paragraph Third to distribute the residue of his estate to the survivor or survivors of the four named siblings. It is not surprising that testator used different language in the first and second paragraphs as those paragraphs mentioned only one individual each—each paragraph was a specific monetary legacy to a specific individual.

The majority observes the testator "merely states his desire to leave the residue to his named siblings 'and to the survivor or survivors of them.' " I agree with this observation, but contrary to the majority, I would affirm the Orphans' Court because of this "merely stated" expression of intent and would affirm the distribution of the estate in accordance with his intent.

NOTES

1.   Almost every state has an antilapse statute, but the provisions differ. The Pennsylvania statute, discussed in *Kehler*, only applies when the beneficiary is "a child or other issue of the testator or . . . his brother or sister or . . . a child of his brother or sister." Why would a remedial statute be limited in this way? In contrast, Georgia's antilapse statute applies to all beneficiaries. O.C. GA. § 53–4–64. The UPC's antilapse statute, § 2–603, provides in relevant part as follows:

UPC § 2–603 Antilapse; Deceased Devisee; Class Gifts

(b) [Substitute Gift.] If a devisee fails to survive the testator and is a grandparent, a descendant of a grandparent, or a stepchild of either the testator or the donor of a power of appointment exercised by the testator's will, the following apply:

(1) Except as provided in paragraph (4), if the devise is not in the form of a class gift and the deceased devisee leaves surviving descendants, a substitute gift is created in the devisee's surviving descendants. They take by representation the property to which the devisee would have been entitled had the devisee survived the testator.

(2) Except as provided in paragraph (4), if the devise is in the form of a class gift, other than a devise to "issue," "descendants," "heirs of the body," "heirs," "next of kin," "relatives," or "family," or a class described by language of similar import, a substitute gift is created in the surviving descendants of any deceased devisee. The property to which the devisees

would have been entitled had all of them survived the testator passes to the surviving devisees and the surviving descendants of the deceased devisees. Each surviving devisee takes the share to which he [or she] would have been entitled had the deceased devisees survived the testator. Each deceased devisee's surviving descendants who are substituted for the deceased devisee take by representation the share to which the deceased devisee would have been entitled had the deceased devisee survived the testator. For the purposes of this paragraph, "deceased devisee" means a class member who failed to survive the testator and left one or more surviving descendants.

(3)   For the purposes of Section 2–601, words of survivorship, such as in a devise to an individual "if he survives me," or in a devise to "my surviving children," are not, in the absence of additional evidence, a sufficient indication of an intent contrary to the application of this section.

––––––––––

2.   Because a testator can exhibit intent that a gift *not* pass to a deceased recipient's heirs, questions often arise as to whether language of survivorship (such as "if he survives me" or "to my surviving children") is enough to bar application of the antilapse statute. Do you agree that the language in *Kehler's* will did not address the issue of lapsed gifts? *See also Estate of Harper*, 975 A.2d 1155 (Pa. Super. Ct. 2009). Because of a concern that survivorship language is boilerplate and does not, in fact, represent the testator's intent, some antilapse statutes expressly provide that "mere" language of survivorship does not override the antilapse statute. *See* UPC § 2–603(b)(3). Do you agree with the UPC's approach?

3.   It is important to remember that the antilapse rules are default rules and therefore can be avoided through common drafting practices. Most attorney drafted wills are much more specific and usually include language requiring beneficiaries to survive, specifying alternative gifts, and otherwise opting out of antilapse statutes. Lapse rules can sometimes have unintended consequences, so it is always preferable to ask what the testator wants to have happen in the event a beneficiary does not survive and then draft for that contingency.

4.   One common form of gift is a "class gift," which is a gift that applies to a category or class of people, such as "my siblings" or "my children." Without an antilapse statute, only those members of

> **Connection Note:** You will see a more extensive discussion of class gifts in connection with trusts in Chapter 9.

the class (in other words, the siblings who survive the testator) share in the gift. Most antilapse statutes apply to class gifts, so that descendants of a predeceased class member share that deceased beneficiary's portion. *See* UPC § 2–603(b)(2).

5.   Antilapse rules exist to carry out the decedent's intent. The assumption is that the average testator would want a gift to a close relative to pass to that person's heirs if the relative predeceased the testator. Do you think this is a fair assumption?

ASSESSMENTS

1.   Phoebe died testate. Her will directs her executor to distribute the residue of Phoebe's estate one-half to Phoebe's friend Bertha and one-half to her friend Bernard. Bernard predeceased Phoebe. Phoebe's only intestate heirs are her two surviving children, Dorothy and Lizzie. How should Phoebe's probate estate be distributed under the UPC?

2.   Assume you are in a jurisdiction that applies the UPC. Draft a will provision that makes a specific gift, a general gift, and a residuary gift. For all three, including language that opts out of the antilapse statute.

D. Changes to Property

This section looks at what happens when a testator executes a will and then some change occurs to the property gifted in the will. It is part of your job to draft for such changes, but you may face a will drafted by a layperson or an inexperienced attorney that lacks direction in the document. In such cases, the court applies "gap filling" rules that are designed to approximate the decedent's intent—so called "intent effectuating" rules. The first case, *YIVO Institute for Jewish Research v. Zeleski*, covers the doctrine of **satisfaction** (also called **ademption by satisfaction**), which applies to a gift that a testator makes during life to "satisfy" a testamentary bequest (so resembles **advancement** in the intestacy context). The next topic, also mentioned in *YIVO* but addressed more directly in *Estate of Anton*, is **ademption** (also called **ademption by extinction**), which applies when a testator's will contains a gift of a specific item that is no longer in the estate when the testator dies. Three other topics discussed in the notes cover: when property that is in the estate has produced additional property (**accretions and accessions**); when property in the estate is insufficient to make all of the gifts (**abatement**); and when property in the estate has debt associated with it (**exoneration**).

YIVO Inst. for Jewish Research v. Zaleski

874 A.2d 411 (Md. 2004)

GREENE, J.

In this case we are asked to revise the Maryland law of ademption by satisfaction and require that a testator's intention to adeem a legacy can be proven only by a writing made contemporaneous with an *inter vivos* gift. Petitioner, in its attempt to persuade us to change the law, relies in part on the assertion that the doctrine of ademption conflicts with the Maryland Code, the Restatement (Third) of Property, and the Uniform Probate Code. For reasons to follow in this opinion, we decline the invitation to rewrite the law of ademption and affirm the judgment of the intermediate appellate court.

Background

Dr. Karski was a hero of the Polish underground during World War II. He reported to Allied powers on the events transpiring in Poland until he was captured by the Nazis. During his confinement he was tortured and suffered greatly. After attempting suicide to avoid disclosures that could have endangered the underground movement, Dr. Karski was taken to a Nazi-controlled hospital in critical condition. He was rescued from the hospital by members of the underground movement. Several lives were lost during the rescue effort.

After the war, Dr. Karski emigrated to the United States and settled in Chevy Chase, Maryland. Dr. Karski remained committed to Polish culture until his death, developing ties with several Polish organizations, including The Kosciusko Foundation ("Foundation") and The American Center of Polish Culture ("Center"). He spent much of his life attempting to mend the relationship between Jewish and non-Jewish Poles which had been fractured by events occurring in Poland during WW II. Following the death of his wife, Dr. Karski developed a plan to memorialize both of them by creating an award to acknowledge Jewish authors of Polish origin. In 1992, Dr. Karski entered into an agreement with YIVO to establish an endowment fund to provide an annual award of $5,000 to authors whose works focused on or otherwise described contributions to Polish culture and Polish science by Poles of Jewish origin. Dr. Karski formalized his pledge in a letter dated November 25, 1992 ("Letter Agreement"). The Letter Agreement provided, in pertinent part:

> The endowment will consist of a gift of $100,000.00 in cash to be made by me to YIVO in my will, or in cash and/or marketable securities of the same total market value during my lifetime.

A second letter, identical to the November 25, 1992, letter, was signed February 25, 1993. It is unclear from the record, however, why the second letter was executed.

On October 25, 1993, eight months after writing the second Letter Agreement, Dr. Karski executed his will. Article SECOND of the will provides:

> I hereby give and bequeath to YIVO—Institute for Jewish Research (tax exempt organization Dr. Lucjan Dobroszycki and Dr. Ludwik Seidenman)—all my shares of Northern States Power (N.St.Pw.) of which 400 share certificates are located in Riggs National Bank, Friendship Branch (4249 block of Wisconsin Avenue), Safe Deposit Box 240, and the rest approximately 1,780 shares, is held by Northern States Power as automatic reinvestment. All these shares (approximately 2,180) should be transferred (not sold) to YIVO.

At the time the will was executed, Northern States Power Company shares had a value of about $100,000. At the time of Dr. Karski's death the shares were worth $113, 527.64.

In addition, pursuant to the Third Clause of the will, stock in two other utilities, New York State Gas & Electric and Ohio Edison, was left to the Washington Performing Arts Society ("WPAS"). Most of the remaining estate was bequeathed in equal shares to the Foundation, the Center, three of Dr. Karski's elderly relatives in Poland, and Zofia, a woman who had helped rescue him from the hands of the Nazis.

During the period November 28, 1995, to January 22, 1996, Dr. Karski made a series of lifetime gifts of utility stocks to YIVO consisting of 1,809 shares of New York State Electric & Gas Corporation, 2,300 shares of Ohio Edison Company, and cash. The value of these stock gifts totaled $99,997.69. On February 7, 1996, Dr. Karski made a further gift of $2.31, bringing the total value of the gifts to YIVO to exactly $100,000. Dr. Karski did not amend his will to reflect the *inter vivos* transfer of utility stock and cash to YIVO.

Dr. Karski died on July 12, 2000. At that time, the shares of Northern States Power Company remained an asset of his estate. Paul Zaleski, who qualified as personal representative, denied YIVO's request for payment of the bequest on the basis that Dr. Karski's earlier gift satisfied the legacy. As a result, YIVO filed a Petition for Order Directing Distribution of Specific Bequest.

The Orphans' Court conducted an evidentiary hearing and rendered an oral opinion finding that Dr. Karski intended for his lifetime gifts to YIVO to satisfy the legacy under the will. Following the entry of final judgment, YIVO appealed to the Court of Special Appeals which affirmed the judgment of the Orphans' Court. We granted YIVO's petition for a writ of certiorari.

Discussion

At the outset, we find it important to determine the precise meaning of "ademption." BLACK'S LAW DICTIONARY defines "ademption" as "the destruction or extinction of a testamentary gift by reason of a bequeathed asset's ceasing to be a part of the estate at the time of the testator's death."

There are two distinct types of ademption. The first occurs when "the unique property that is the subject of the specific bequest has been sold, given away, or destroyed, or is not otherwise in existence at the time of the testator's death." BLACK'S LAW DICTIONARY 42 (8th ed., 2004). This is referred to as ademption by extinction. Ademption by extinction results because of "the doing of some act with regard to the subject-matter which interferes with the operation of the will."

By comparison the other type of ademption occurs when the testator, while alive, has already given something of value to the beneficiary in lieu of the legacy. BLACK'S LAW DICTIONARY 42 (8th ed. 2004). This is known as ademption by satisfaction. The doctrine of ademption by satisfaction "refers to the situation in which the testator gives in his lifetime to a legatee what he had left him in his will."

In the case before us there is no claim of ademption by extinction. The question here is whether there was an ademption by satisfaction. Under the doctrine of ademption by satisfaction, the intent of the testator is "relevant to determine whether the testator's actions regarding the legatee amounts to a withdrawal of the gift from the operation of the will." The law is established in this State that, "when a testator in his lifetime pays to a legatee the amount of money given by the will, and such payment is intended to be in satisfaction of the legacy, the legacy is thereby adeemed." Therefore, if a testator intended that an *inter vivos* gift should abrogate the legacy, the legacy is adeemed either in whole or in part; but if a testator intended that the legatee should receive both the testamentary gift and the *inter vivos* benefit, the legacy is not adeemed.

Petitioner argues that a subsequent writing is necessary to show a clear intention of satisfaction. YIVO relies upon revisions to Maryland's law in 1968 concerning advancements and intestate estates which resulted from the Governor's Commission to Review the Testamentary Law of Maryland ("The Henderson Commission"). The Henderson Commission recommended, and the Maryland Code now reflects, that for an *inter vivos* gift to be treated as an advancement, there must be written evidence of such an intent. Petitioner posits that there is no reason to "maintain standards for ademption of a legacy by satisfaction that differ from those applicable to advancement of an intestate share."

In our view, principles governing advancement and intestate shares do not help resolve the issues in this case. In the present case, the decedent did not die intestate, he died with a will. The laws of intestate succession concern disposition of property by operation of law under circumstances where the decedent failed to declare his or her intention with regard to the disposition of his or her property at the time of death. The law of ademption by satisfaction, however, is concerned with the intention of the testator at the time the *inter vivos* gift was made.

In addition, petitioner contends we should adopt the view of 1 *Restatement (Third) of the Law of Property (Wills and Other Donative Transfers)* § 5.4 (1999) (hereinafter, "*Restatement*") and the Uniform Probate Code § 2–609. Section 5.4 of the *Restatement* provides:

> An *inter vivos* gift made by a testator to a devisee or to a member of the devisee's family adeems the devise by satisfaction, in whole or in part, if the testator indicated in a contemporaneous writing, or if the devisee acknowledged in writing, that the gift was so to operate.

Under the UPC, § 2–609 Ademption by Satisfaction, the required evidence of intent can take one of three forms:

> (i) a statement in the will itself providing for deduction of the gift or any future gifts, (ii) a written statement of the testator in a contemporaneous writing indicating that the gift is in full or partial satisfaction of the devise, or (iii) a written statement of the devisee acknowledging that the gift is in full partial satisfaction of the devise.

Maryland, however, has neither expressly adopted the *Restatement* § 5.4 nor the UPC. Both provisions require a writing to prove that an *inter vivos* gift operates as an ademption by satisfaction. We are not persuaded, however, to adopt either view. We are guided by the long-standing rule that the intention of the testator at the time of the *inter vivos* gift is the heart of ademption by satisfaction.

The doctrine of ademption by satisfaction is an intent-effecting doctrine. The doctrine operates to prevent the legatee from receiving a double gift against the testator's wishes. The question is one wholly of intention, and the burden is upon those who assert that the *inter vivos* gift was intended to satisfy the legacy. There are, however, certain circumstances where the intent to adeem will be presumed. For example, "the rule is that if the bequests are for a particular purpose, a subsequent gift to the legatee by the testator in his lifetime for the same purpose operates as a satisfaction of the legacy to the amount of the gift." The rule, however, is subject to the qualification that the *inter vivos* gift must not be substantially different in kind from the legacy. Additionally, it is well established that "if a testator has given a legacy in order to accomplish a certain purpose, and he subsequently accomplishes that purpose himself, the legacy is presumed to be adeemed."

In reaching its conclusion that Dr. Karski's lifetime gifts of $100,000 to YIVO were given to adeem the legacy of approximately $100,000, the Orphans' Court first needed to determine the purpose of the legacy in the will. The Court deemed it reasonable in assessing the purpose of the legacy to look to the facts surrounding it, the commitment Dr. Karski made to YIVO, and the Letter Agreement. In this context, the Court found, as a matter of fact, that the purpose of the legacy was to fulfill or otherwise provide security for the commitment that Dr. Karski made to YIVO. Petitioner claims no specific purpose was attached to the bequest. We disagree. Despite the fact that no specific purpose is explicitly stated in Dr. Karski's Will, the Orphans' Court was correct in its conclusion because it arrived at its findings after it considered the bequest in the context of Dr. Karski's relationship with YIVO. Dr. Karski had no continuing charitable relationship with YIVO. We hold that the Orphans' Court did not abuse its discretion in concluding, as it did, the purpose of the legacy.

Once it was determined that the purpose of the legacy was security, the Orphans' Court could properly find, based upon the evidence in the record, that the lifetime gifts had a purpose identical to that of the legacy. Dr. Karski gave the lifetime gifts to secure his promise in the Letter Agreement to provide a bequest of $100,000 to YIVO. This finding of a same purpose operates as a satisfaction of the legacy, unless the lifetime gift was substantially different in kind. Dr. Karski bequeathed shares of Northern States Power to YIVO. At the time Dr. Karski drafted his will these shares were worth approximately $100,000. Dr. Karski's lifetime gift to YIVO consisted of shares of New York State Gas & Electric, shares of Ohio Edison, and cash in the amount of $2.31, thus bringing the total value of the gifts to $100,000. While the stock given to YIVO during Dr. Karski's life were shares from a different company than that named in the will, we agree with the Orphans' Court and the intermediate appellate court that there was no evidence that the stock in the legacy had any particular significance. Dr. Karski's own Letter Agreement referred to "cash and/or marketable securities," evidencing that Dr. Karski treated the shares as equivalent to cash. The Orphans' Court correctly found that Dr. Karski intended that the different company shares and the cash were identical to one another. Thus, the shares were not substantially different in kind.

Having established that the *inter vivos* gifts to YIVO were the same in purpose and in kind as the bequest to YIVO in Dr. Karski's Will, the Orphans' Court found a presumption of ademption. Where a presumption of ademption arises "it is one of fact and not of law and may be rebutted by competent evidence." The petitioner did not offer any competent evidence to rebut the presumption of ademption and, absent such evidence, the Orphans' Court was correct to find that it was Dr. Karski's intention to adeem the legacy with his lifetime gifts to YIVO. Accordingly, the bequest to YIVO was satisfied and, as such, YIVO is not entitled to an additional gift.

NOTES

1.   *YIVO* involves charities fighting about whether a bequest was **"adeemed by satisfaction"** as a result of lifetime gifts made by the testator. What does the court mean when it states that, "ademption by satisfaction is an intent-effecting doctrine"? What are some other "intent-effecting" (or "intent-effectuating doctrines") that you have seen? Why does the court distinguish the satisfaction rules for intestate and testate estates? Do you agree? What would have happened if Maryland applied the UPC rule, which appears below?

UPC § 2–609 Ademption by Satisfaction

(a)   Property a testator gave in his [or her] lifetime to a person is treated as a satisfaction of a devise in whole or in part, only if (i) the will provides for deduction of the gift, (ii) the testator declared in a contemporaneous writing that the gift is in satisfaction of the devise or that its value is to be deducted from the value of the devise, or (iii) the devisee acknowledged in writing that the gift is in satisfaction of the devise or that its value is to be deducted from the value of the devise.

------

2.   In a portion of the *YIVO* opinion not included above, the court affirmed the Orphans' Court's admission into evidence of testimony by Dr. Hanna-Kaya Ploss, Executive Director of the American Center of Polish Culture and a friend of Dr. Karski's, regarding statements made by Dr. Karski in 1998 and the years preceding his death. Specifically, Dr. Ploss testified that,

I don't know what was in that will, but Dr. Karski was not a compulsive man who would pound on something over and over, but from time to time he said, "You know, maybe I should change my will just in case the YIVO Institute will come and ask once more for the money when I already have given it to them," and then he always answered his own question, "No. They are much too decent to do such [a] thing. No."

* * *

He was absolutely sure they will not come a second time and ask for the money when I have already given it to them, that is something that sticks in my mind, "I have already given them the money."

How do you think Dr. Ploss's testimony affected the *YIVO* outcome?

ASSESSMENTS

1. Imagine you represent Dr. Karski in his estate planning. Re-draft Dr. Karski's letter agreement and will to clarify his intention regarding any lifetime gifts to YIVO.

2. Why do you think the *YIVO* court goes into such detail about Dr. Karski's past? Does that information help resolve the issue before the court, or might there be some other reason?

———

Gifts can also adeem by extinction, which means the gifted property is no longer in the estate at the testator's death because it was sold, lost, or destroyed—or maybe it just vanished. What happens then depends on whether the jurisdiction follows an **identity approach** or an **intent approach**. As you read the following case, think about which approach the court settles on and why it might be a good one.

In re Estate of Anton

731 N.W.2d 19 (Iowa 2007)

APPEL, J.

In this case, we consider whether the sale of certain property by an attorney-in-fact prior to the death of the testator resulted in ademption of a specific property bequest. The district court found that under the facts and circumstances presented, the bequest was adeemed. The court of appeals affirmed. For the reason set forth below, we reverse.

FACTUAL BACKGROUND.

In 1972, the testator, Hestor Mary Lewis Anton (Mary), married Herbert Anton, the father of Gretchen Coy. It was the second marriage for both Herbert and Mary. During this marriage, Gretchen, Mary's stepdaughter, deeded a piece of real property to her stepmother and father. Herbert and Mary built a duplex on the property. After the death of Herbert in 1976, Mary became the sole owner of the duplex property.

In 1981, Mary executed a will. In the will, she bequeathed half of her interest in the duplex to Gretchen. The remaining half interest was bequeathed to her biological son, Robert Lewis. Mary bequeathed the remainder of her estate to Robert and her daughter, Nancy Ezarski.

In 1986, Mary was involved in a serious automobile accident. After the accident, she lived in a series of nursing homes. For a short period of time, she lived in a nursing home called Riverside. Thereafter, she moved to Green Hills Health Center in Ames, where she had a private suite. Among other things, Mary suffered from Huntington's Chorea, a malady that impacts the nervous system.

Shortly after the accident, Mary executed a durable power of attorney authorizing her daughter Nancy to manage her financial affairs. The power of attorney took effect immediately. The document was a "durable" power of attorney: it explicitly stated that it would remain in full force and effect until Mary's death and would be unaffected by any mental or physical disability that might occur after its execution.

From 1986 until Mary's death on December 2, 2003, Nancy handled her mother's financial affairs. There is no evidence in the record indicating that Nancy did anything improper in connection with Mary's assets.

On Memorial Day 1998, Nancy and her mother discussed selling the family residence to provide her mother with necessary support. After this conversation, staff at the nursing home advised Nancy that she should not discuss financial matters with her mother as it would exacerbate her condition and cause distress. As a result of this input from nursing home staff, Nancy and her mother had no further discussions regarding her financial affairs.

Nancy, acting as attorney-in-fact, began selling her mother's assets in order to pay her ongoing living expenses. Mary was generally aware her assets were being sold off to pay for her expenses. Her only concern was that she would have enough money to continue living at Green Hills. There was, however, no evidence that Mary was ever aware that the duplex was sold.

By 2003, the only asset remaining in Mary's estate was the duplex. The combined income from that asset and from Mary's husband's trust was insufficient to meet her ongoing expenses. At this point, Nancy listed the duplex property for sale. Nancy then received a call from Gretchen's son, who informed Nancy of the terms of Mary's will and told her she could not sell the duplex.

In light of the phone call from Gretchen's son, Nancy took the duplex off the market and contacted an attorney, who issued an opinion stating that Nancy had the power and authority to sell the duplex. The attorney also advised, however, that the trustee of the Harold R. Lewis Trust had the discretion to distribute the principal of the trust to Mary for her health, well-being, and maintenance. Nancy then contacted the trust officer at First National Bank to inquire about obtaining a loan from the trust. She was informed that the bank preferred that all of Mary's assets be sold prior to invading the trust's principal. As a result, Nancy believed she had no other choice but to sell the property, which was accomplished on August 28, 2003.

The evidence in the record regarding Mary's capacity at the time of the sale is thin. Nurses' notes indicate that on April 16, 2003, Mary had "periods of confusion." A social service progress note dated October 9, 2003, six weeks after the sale, makes reference to "advanced dementia." At trial, Nancy testified that her mother was "not incompetent" at the time of the duplex's sale. The net proceeds of the duplex's sale were $133,263. Nancy began to pay Mary's living expenses out of the proceeds. At the time of Mary's death, the remaining balance was $104,317.38.

PRIOR PROCEEDINGS.

After Mary's death, Gretchen filed a claim with the estate, asserting that she was entitled to $72,625 because of the specific bequest of the duplex in Mary's 1986 will. Nancy, acting as executor of the estate, disallowed the claim. Gretchen then proceeded to file a claim in probate court.

The estate moved for summary judgment. The estate argued that at the time of the duplex's conveyance, Mary was not under a guardianship of any kind. The estate further asserted that all other assets previously held by Mary had been liquidated, and that the trustee of the Harold R. Lewis Trust had refused to advance funds from the trust's principal to pay for Mary's expenses as long as there were other assets that could be liquidated. As a result, the estate argued that the specific bequest of the duplex had been adeemed by extinction because it was no longer in the estate.

Gretchen countered the motion for summary judgment by asserting that there was a question of fact regarding Mary's intention in connection with the sale of the duplex. Gretchen cited the conversation she had with Nancy in June 2003, in which Nancy indicated that Mary "sleeps almost all the time." Gretchen argued that the only clear evidence of Mary's intent was the original will. Gretchen asserted that at no time did Mary ever indicate to her an intention to alter the terms of her will. Based on this evidence, Gretchen urged the court to deny the estate's motion for summary judgment.

On March 29, 2005, the district court denied the estate's motion for summary judgment. The court noted that the summary judgment record shows little, if anything, about whether Mary was consulted about the sale of the duplex and whether she was able to understand her financial circumstances. The court found that there was a genuine issue of material fact as to the mental state of Mary at the time of the duplex's sale and her involvement, if any, in the decision leading up to the sale.

The matter came to trial on August 10, 2005. On August 25, 2005, the district court entered an order denying Gretchen's claim. The district court reasoned that the power of attorney was not affected even if Mary was disabled or incompetent at the time of the sale of the duplex. The district court found that given the choice, Mary's intent was clear and established: she preferred to sell the assets and remain cared for in the nursing home. As a result, the district court held that the specific bequest in Mary's will was adeemed by Nancy's sale of the duplex.

The court of appeals affirmed, noting that Nancy had power of attorney which was unaffected by any mental disability that Mary may have had at the time the duplex was sold. The court of appeals adopted the trial court's finding that the sale of the duplex was clearly a part of the testator's intent and plan, which had been implemented over the course of several years. As a result, the property was adeemed by its sale. We granted further review.

LEGAL BACKGROUND.

What happens when a testator makes a specific bequest of property in a validly executed will, but the property is missing from the estate at the time of death? The doctrine of ademption by extinction has been developed to address some of the difficulties that arise under these circumstances. Ademption generally means "a taking away," and, in the context of the law of wills, refers to the removal or elimination of a specific bequest prior to the time of death. Joseph Warren, *The History of Ademption*, 25 IOWA L. REV. 290, 292 (1940).

In the early twentieth century, this court adopted the identity theory of ademption. Under the identity rule, if specifically bequeathed property was not found in the estate at the time of death, the bequest was adeemed. This has court routinely applied the identity rule. *In re Estate of Bernhard*, 112 N.W. 86 (Iowa 1907); *In re Estate of Keeler*, 282 N.W. 362 (Iowa 1938); *In re Estate of Sprague*, 57 N.W.2d 212 (Iowa 1953). Beginning in the 1960s, however, this court began to depart from the rigid application of the identity theory in all settings.

For example, in *In re Estate of Bierstedt*, 119 N.W.2d 234 (Iowa 1963), this court considered whether the sale by a guardian of specifically bequeathed real estate without the knowledge and consent of an incompetent testator caused ademption by extinction under the identity rule. In *Bierstedt*, the court rejected application of a "rigid identity rule" and applied what it called a "modified intention" approach. The court noted that the order establishing the guardianship demonstrated that Bierstedt was incompetent at the time the land was sold, thereby creating a presumption of lack of testamentary capacity. As a result, because the testator did not have the testamentary capacity to, in effect, work a change in the will, the sale could not be considered to manifest an intention on the part of the testator to modify the will. Therefore, no ademption occurred. The court expressly noted, however, that the rulings in *Keeler*, *Sprague*, and *Bernhard*, where competent testators themselves had sold or otherwise disposed of specific devises and bequests, "are sound and we adhere to them." *Id.* at 238.

Similarly, in *In re Estate of Wolfe*, 208 N.W.2d 923 (Iowa 1973), this court considered whether the destruction of property which was the subject of a specific bequest, contemporaneous with the death of the testator, worked an ademption. In *Wolfe*, the testator had specifically bequeathed his automobile, a 1969 Buick Electra, to his brother. The testator was killed in an automobile accident in which his automobile was a total loss. Insurance proceeds that included the value of the auto were paid to the estate. The brother claimed he was entitled to the proceeds. In holding for the brother and against the estate, the court rejected the identity rule and emphasized that the intent of the testator is paramount in determining whether an ademption has occurred. *Id.* at 924. As a result, the court reasoned that where property is missing from the estate because of some act or event involuntary as to the testator, there is no ademption. *Id.*

In summary, our cases hold that the identity rule will not be rigidly applied in all cases. Under what the court has called the "modified intention theory," the identity rule will not be applied to cases where specifically devised property is removed from the estate through an act that is involuntary as to the testator. This includes cases where the property is sold by a guardian, or conservator, or is destroyed contemporaneously with the death of the testator. Until now, however, we have not had occasion to consider whether ademption occurs when specifically devised property is sold by an attorney-in-fact.

ANALYSIS.

Although the identity rule has been subject to substantial criticism and has been abandoned or substantially altered in the Uniform Probate Code and the Restatement (Third) of Property, neither party questioned its continued vitality. Instead, the parties have focused on whether Mary was competent at the time of sale and whether the rule in *Bierstedt* should be extended to cases involving attorneys-in-fact. In this posture, we do not examine the continued vitality of the identity rule, but simply apply the principles established in our case law to the facts of this case. For the reasons expressed below, we hold that the sale of the duplex by an attorney-in-fact under the circumstances presented did not result in ademption of the bequest.

A.   Effect of Sale if Mary was Incompetent at Time of Sale.

If Mary was incompetent at the time of sale of the duplex, the act would clearly be involuntary as to her. The question then arises whether the rule in *Bierstedt* should be extended to cases involving the sale of specifically devised property by an attorney-in-fact or whether the extension should be rejected.

The rationale of *Bierstedt* is that ademption does not occur when specifically devised property is sold as a result of acts that are involuntary to the testator. The rationale of our cases is that ademption occurs where a testator had knowledge of a transaction involving a specific devise, realizes the effect of the transaction on his or her estate plan, and has an opportunity to revise the will. Where these elements are not present, no ademption occurs. The focus of analysis is on the testator and whether the testator has made a deliberate decision not to revise the will, and not on the nature of the agency causing the involuntary act.

The district court held that if, in fact, Mary was disabled or incompetent at the time of the sale of the duplex, Iowa Code section 633.705(1) would cause the specific bequest of the duplex to fail as a result of ademption because the act of the attorney-in-fact would have the same force and effect as the act of the testator.

We do not agree. The purpose of Iowa Code section 633.705(1) is to change the common law rule that the mental disability of the principal terminated the agency relationship. Under section 633.705(1), "acts" of the agent are binding on third persons, including heirs. Here, the agent has not acted to cause an ademption, but only to cause the sale of property. This act—namely the sale of the property—is indeed binding on third parties, including heirs. The statute, however, is silent on the issue of who is entitled to the proceeds of the sale where the principal has made a specific bequest in a will and where identifiable proceeds are found in the estate.

B.   *Effect of Sale if Mary was Competent at Time of Sale.*

In the alternative, assuming that Mary was competent at the time of the duplex's sale, the question arises as to whether an ademption should occur based, not upon the act of the attorney-in-fact in selling the property, but upon the intent of the testator expressed prior to the sale. Specifically, the estate claims that Mary knew that her assets would need to be sold for her support and specifically approved of the sale of her residence by her attorney-in-fact. There appears to have been no specific discussion, however, of the sale of the duplex at any time. Further, it is conceded that Mary had no knowledge of the actual sale of the duplex over five years later. Nancy simply sold it without telling her mother in order to avoid aggravating her condition.

We do not question the wisdom of Nancy's decision to sell the property without consulting Mary. Our only concern is the legal consequences that flow from it. This case thus raises the question of what result should occur where the principal is competent, but the attorney-in-fact sells a specific devise without the knowledge of the testator.

If Mary was aware of the transaction, was aware of the impact the transaction had on her estate plan, and did not change her will, ademption would, of course, occur under the identity theory. Here, however, Mary only had a general knowledge that assets may need to be sold for her support at some time in the future. This is simply not the same as contemporaneous knowledge that an asset that is subject to a specific devise has, in fact, been removed from the estate. Most ordinary persons would not run down to the lawyer's office to change their will in light of a remote future contingency that has not been specifically discussed and which may or may not occur in the future. An expression of intent in the indefinite future to sell assets for support is not sufficient to cause ademption under our "modified intention theory" where the testator is not aware that the specific action has taken place.

It is true that Nancy did not sell the duplex until all other sources of revenue had been exhausted for her mother's support. It may well be that, under the circumstances, her mother would have assented to the sale of the duplex in 2003 had she been asked. But under our cases, the relevant issue is not whether Mary would have assented to the sale had she been asked, but rather whether Mary had the opportunity to change her will once she knew that the duplex was no longer part of her estate. Under the record here, she simply did not have that opportunity.

There remains a question of remedy. Gretchen seeks to recover $72,625, or half the proceeds realized upon the sale of the duplex. Some courts have held that where ademption does not occur, the devisee is entitled to the entire value notwithstanding the fact that the proceeds may have been used for the care of the testator. We have considered the issue, however, and have held that in cases where specific devises are removed from the estate as a result of an involuntary act, the devisee is entitled only to the proceeds which have not been expended on the support of the testator. *Stake v. Cole*, 133 N.W.2d 714, 717 (Iowa 1965). As a result, Gretchen is entitled to $52,158.69.

CONCLUSION

For the reasons expressed above, we hold that under the facts and circumstances of this case, the sale of the duplex did not cause ademption to the extent that there were specifically identifiable proceeds in the estate at the time of death.

NOTES

1. The traditional approach to ademption by extinction was called the "identity approach"; if the property was no longer in the estate, the gift failed even if that property had been replaced. The UPC takes a different approach based on "intent," which allows for the beneficiary to receive the replacement value or replacement property of the adeemed gift under certain circumstances. The UPC's provision on ademption is reproduced below:

UPC § 2–606 Nonademption of Specific Devises

(a) A specific devisee has a right to specifically devised property in the testator's estate at the testator's death and to: . . .

(3) any proceeds unpaid at death on fire or casualty insurance on or other recovery for injury to the property; . . .

(5) any real property or tangible personal property owned by the testator at death which the testator acquired as a replacement for specifically devised real property or tangible personal property; and

(6) if not covered by (the above) paragraphs . . ., a pecuniary devise equal to the value as of its date of disposition of other specifically devised property disposed of during the testator's lifetime but only to the extent it is established that ademption would be inconsistent with the testator's manifested plan of distribution or that at the time the will was made, the date of disposition or otherwise, the testator did not intend ademption of the devise.

Estate of Anton describes Iowa's "modified intention" approach to ademption. What are the benefits to an intent approach? Are there any downsides?

2. In *Estate of Anton*, the daughter uses a durable financial power of attorney to address her mother's financial needs. But even the daughter's proper use of the power of an attorney has an impact on the mother's estate plan. What is the impact? Should the daughter have done anything differently? What about the mother (or her estate planning lawyer)?

3. In addition to property not being in the estate when the will is probated, property gifted in a will also may generate more property between the time a will is executed and when it takes effect. These increases are generally known as accretions and, when the property involves securities, accessions. For example, consider a gift of "100 shares of Widget Co. stock." What happens if the Widget Co. declares a stock dividend; does that dividend pass with the gift or is it considered part of the residue? What if, instead, the dividend is declared in cash? What if, instead, the gift was "*my* 100 shares of Widget Co. stock"? Traditionally, the rules differed depending on whether the gift of securities was characterized as specific or general, which resulted in disagreements over how to characterize gifts. The issue of **accessions**, increases as a result of ownership of securities, is now addressed in UPC § 2–605 and does not depend on the type of gift but rather what type of property resulted from it:

UPC § 2–605 Increase in Securities; Accessions

(a) If a testator executes a will that devises securities and the testator then owned securities that meet the description in the will, the devise includes additional securities owned by the testator at death to the extent the additional securities were acquired by the testator after the will was executed as a result of the testator's ownership of the described securities . . .

(b) Distributions in cash before death with respect to a described security are not part of the devise.

---

4. Another "gap filling" rule applies to gifts of property that have some form of lien or mortgage associated with that property. The question is whether the property passes *subject to* that debt or free of it. If a jurisdiction **exonerates** (pays off) the debt, that payment can have a significant effect on what the residuary beneficiary (often the person who is intended to get the bulk of the estate) actually receives. Wills often are silent on this topic, although many contain a general directive to pay the testator's debts. If you were the devisee of a home that was valued at $300,000 but subject to a $100,000 mortgage, and the testator's will instructed the executor to pay all of the testator's "just debts," what would you argue?

> **Connection Note:** Exoneration rules took on particular significance during the burst of the real estate bubble in 2007. Many estates were forced into insolvency because there were insufficient funds to pay off liens associated with the real property in the estate.

5. Most jurisdictions follow the "non-exoneration of liens" doctrine, as in UPC § 2–607 reproduced below:

UPC § 2–607 Nonexoneration

A specific devise passes subject to any mortgage interest existing at the date of death, without right of exoneration, regardless of a general directive in the will to pay debts.

---

6. Another issue that may arise over the passing of time is what happens if a testator dies without adequate assets to make all the gifts set forth in the will? This is the question of **abatement**, and you may have noticed that this problem arises in the *Anton* case. Traditionally, assets **abate** in the following order:

residuary devises abate first; then general devises; and finally specific devises. (Demonstrative devises are treated as specific up to the value of the property sold and then are treated as general.) Within each category, gifts abate proportionally. The UPC provision follows this order:

UPC § 3–902 Abatement

(a)   [S]hares of distributees abate, without any preference or priority as between real and personal property, in the following order:(i) property not disposed of by the will; (ii) residuary devises; (iii) general devises; (iv) specific devises. For purposes of abatement, a general devise charged on any specific property or fund is a specific devise to the extent of the value of the property on which it is charged, and upon the failure or insufficiency of the property on which it is charged, a general devise to the extent of the failure or insufficiency. Abatement within each classification is in proportion to the amounts of property each of the beneficiaries would have received, if full distribution of the property had been made in accordance with the terms of the will. Distributions in cash before death with respect to a described security are not part of the devise.

7.   Do you see any flaws with this default order of abatement? Having the residuary gift abate first often undermines the testator's intent that the person or people named in the residue receive the bulk of the estate. A draftsperson, in consultation with the testator, can always vary this order of abatement. Should courts have discretion to alter the order of abatement in all circumstances?

ASSESSMENTS

1.   Tully gifts to her daughter "my home at 120 Bennetts Farm Road, Ridgefield, CT" (worth $500,000 at the time the will was drafted) and to her son "the residue of my estate" (valued at $500,000 when the will was drafted). If Tully sold her Connecticut home and purchased a replacement property, also worth $500,000, in Palm Beach, how would her probate estate be distributed under the traditional identity approach to ademption? What would be the result under UPC § 2–606?

2.   Ira's will provides as follows:

I devise my first edition volume of LITTLE WOMEN to my sister, Julie.

I devise $30,000 each to my children, Noah, Eli, and Rosie.

I devise $30,000 to my daughter, Daisy, and I direct that my 2012 Jeep be sold to satisfy this bequest.

I devise the residue of my estate to my spouse, Olive.

At Ira's death, Ira's probate estate consists of the book (valued at $10,000), the 2012 Jeep (also valued at $10,000) and $75,000 in cash. Ira has debts of $20,000. Distribute the assets.

3.   Tara owns a home worth $500K (with a $400K mortgage), a car worth $50K (with a $25K loan), and cash ($425K). She leaves her brother her home, her sister her car, and her mother the residue. How should Tara's estate be distributed if the jurisdiction exonerates the liens on the car and home? What would be the result under UPC § 2–606?

4.   Your firm regularly transmits copies of executed estate planning documents to clients with a cover letter explaining that the engagement is complete. Draft a paragraph in that letter that explains when and how often the clients should review the documents to ensure that they continue to function as intended. Are there any professional ethics concerns with attorneys putting the decision on when to revisit documents in the client's hands?

E. Changes to a Will by Operation of Law

Another way that will provisions may be affected over time is when events occur after the will is executed that change the testator's status and relationships. For example, after the will execution, a testator may have or adopt one or more children , marry, or divorce and die without changing the will that was in place before these events.

1. Omitted or Pretermitted Children

Estate of Glomset

547 P.2d 951 (Okla. 1976)

BARNES, J.

On October 16, 1972, the deceased, John Larson Glomset, Sr. ("John Sr."), and the Appellant, Margie V. Glomset ("Margie"), made and signed joint and reciprocal wills leaving each other all of the other's property in case of death of the other, except in the case of a common disaster, in which instance the whole of the estate was to go to John Larson Glomset, Jr. ("John Jr."), the son of the deceased. The deceased's 40-year-old daughter, Carolyn Gay Ghan ("Carolyn"), was not named in the will.

On October 15, 1973, John Sr., died, and on October 17, 1973, his will was filed for probate. The will was admitted to probate, but the question of whether Carolyn was a pretermitted heir was reserved. On February 7, 1974, a hearing was held in which Carolyn's motion for a declaratory judgment that she was a pretermitted heir, as defined by Title 84 O.S. § 132, and entitled to share in her father's estate, was sustained. The Trial Court found:

> The Court finds, from a complete reading of the will that the Contestant was omitted therefrom, and that said will provides for her in no manner whatsoever. The Court finds that a complete reading of the will discloses no intent to intentionally not provide for said Contestant. No intention to disinherit Contestant affirmatively appears from the four corners of the will. The Court, therefore, finds that Contestant was unintentionally omitted from deceased's said will, and is, therefore, entitled to have the same share in the estate of the decedent as if decedent had died intestate, all as provided in 84 O.S. § 132.

Margie disputes the Trial Court's finding that Appellee is a pretermitted heir. Title 84 O.S. § 132 provides as follows:

> When any testator omits to provide in his will for any of his children, or for the issue of any deceased child *unless it appears that such omission was intentional,* such child, or the issue of such child, must have the same share in the estate of the testator, as if he had died intestate, and succeeds thereto as provided for in preceding section.

(Emphasis added.) There was no dispute concerning the fact that Carolyn was a daughter of the deceased. The only question for our determination is whether deceased's omission of Carolyn appears to have been intentional.

We must first determine if the intent of the deceased must be determined from the will itself or if extrinsic evidence is admissible. In deciding if extrinsic evidence is admissible, we must determine whether or not an intention to disinherit Carolyn affirmatively appeared from the four corners of the will. We have previously held that if there are no uncertainties appearing on the face of the will, extrinsic evidence is not admissible. *See O'Neill v. Cox*, 270 P.2d 663 (Okla. 1954), and *Dilks v. Carson*, 168 P.2d 1020 (Okla. 1946).

There are no uncertainties on the face of the will in this case. The testator admittedly failed to mention his daughter, Carolyn, and also failed to indicate any reason for his failure to mention her. Thus, if we are to follow previous decisions of this Court interpreting 84 O.S. § 132, we must find that Carolyn is a pretermitted heir and entitled to inherit her proportionate share of her deceased father's estate.

Margie has failed to set forth a compelling reason why the interpretation of 84 O.S. § 132 should be changed at this time to permit introduction of extrinsic evidence to show intent of the testator where no ambiguity appears on the face of the will.

HODGES, J. *(dissenting)*.

The majority opinion holds the will is unambiguous on its face and, therefore, extrinsic evidence is inadmissible to determine the intention of the testator. I believe this perpetuates a misinterpretation of the applicable statute, 84 O.S. 1971 § 132.

It is generally recognized that pretermitted heir statutes are not intended to limit a testator's power to dispose of his property by will, or to require him to bestow any part of his estate on any child or descendant. The purpose of the statute is to protect such heirs against omission due to unintentional oversight, forgetfulness, or mistake. Two broad general classifications of such statutes are recognized:

(1) The "Massachusetts-type" statutes, which are usually considered to emphasize the intention of the testator as the material factor in determining whether a child or descendant is disinherited; and

(2) "Missouri-type" statutes which omit reference to intention and provide for a total or partial revocation of the will if a child is not named or provided for therein.

Our statute, a "Massachusetts-type" statute, was adopted from the Dakotas. Under comparable statutes, the majority of jurisdictions have consistently held that extrinsic evidence was admissible to prove that the testator intended to disinherit an omitted child. The pretermitted heir statute raises the presumption that children are not intentionally omitted from a will. However, the presumption is rebuttable by extrinsic evidence and parol testimony. The purpose and legislative intent of the statute is to protect children unintentionally omitted from the will. It is not to be construed to alter the testamentary intent of the testator by including children he intentionally excluded from his estate. I would therefore overrule all cases in conflict with the traditional interpretation of the pretermitted heir statute.

Assuming arguendo, the majority view of our pretermitted heir statute is correct, I further believe the will is ambiguous on its face, and that the testator's intention to disinherit appears from the will itself. The statute which guides our interpretation of intention, 84 O.S. 1971 152[6] permits introduction of extrinsic evidence to show the circumstances under which the will was executed. This court has held that the question of the intention to omit may be drawn from inference of the language as well as the face of the will, and that the drawing of such inference is not only within the power of the court, but is the duty of the court:

> In determining whether the omission of a child is intentional or not, no set form of words, indicating testator's intention to omit such child, is requisite. The will is to be taken as a whole; and if it appears from the entire instrument that testator intended to omit such child, the statute does not apply. * * * It is not necessary that testator should name his child, or even refer, in terms, to the fact that it is his child.

Extrinsic evidence should have been admissible because, by omitting the daughter from the will she thereby is entitled to her statutory share, while the son who was mentioned in the will receives nothing. Thus, on the face of the will an uncertainty is created, and extrinsic evidence should be allowed. The extrinsic evidence which was offered, but rejected by the trial court, definitely shows the testator intentionally omitted the daughter. She would not visit her father or even allow her child to visit him. They had not seen each other for some time because of their stained relationship.

I believe a construction which permits a child not mentioned in the will to participate in the distribution of the estate while the other child who is mentioned and designated the contingent beneficiary takes nothing, is a tortured interpretation of the will and the Oklahoma Statutes regarding testamentary intent, and reaches a result totally unintended and uncontemplated by the testator or the statute.

I, therefore, respectfully dissent.

---

6   84 O.S. 1971 § 152 provides:

In case of uncertainty, arising upon the face of a will, as to the application of any of its provisions, the testator's intention is to be ascertained from the words of the will, taking into view the circumstances under which it was made, exclusive of his oral declarations.

NOTE

The *Glomset* dissent describes the two types of statutes that govern whether a child was intentionally omitted from a will. The "Massachusetts" type statute looks to testator intent. What evidence might show that a testator intended to disinherit a child, other than explicit disinheritance language in a will? The UPC addresses omitted children in § 2–302, reproduced below:

UPC § 2–302 Omitted Child

(a)   [Parent-Child Relationship Established After Execution of Will.] Except as provided in subsection (b), if a testator becomes a parent of a child after the execution of the testator's will and fails to provide in the will for the chill, the omitted child receives a share in the estate as follows:

(1)   If the testator had no child living when the testator executed the will, an omitted after-born or after-adopted child receives a share in the estate equal in value to that which the child would have received had the testator died intestate, unless the will devised all or substantially all of the estate to another parent of the omitted child and that parent survives the testator and is entitled to take under the will.

(2)   If the testator had one or more children living when the testator executed the will, and the will devised property or an interest in property to one or more of the then-living children, the omitted child is entitled to share in the testator's estate as follows:

(A)   The portion of the testator's estate in which the omitted child is entitled to share is limited to devises made to the testator's then-living children under the will.

(B)   The omitted child is entitled to receive the share of the testator's estate, as limited in subparagraph (A), that the child would have received had the testator included all omitted children with the children to whom devises were made under the will and had given an equal share of the estate to each child.

(C)   To the extent feasible, the interest granted an omitted child under this section must be of the same character, whether equitable or legal, present or future, as that devised to the testator's then-living children under the will.

(D)   In the satisfaction of a share provided by this paragraph, devises to the testator's children who were living when the will was executed abate ratably. In abating the devises of the then-living children, the court shall preserve to the maximum extent possible the character of the testamentary plan adopted by the testator.

(b)   [Intentional Omission of Child; Provision for Child Outside Will.] Neither subsection (a)(1) nor subsection (a)(2) applies if:

(1)   it appears from the will that the omission was intentional; or

(2)   the testator provided for the omitted child by transfer outside the will and the intent that the transfer be in lieu of a testamentary provision is shown by the testator's statements or is reasonably inferred from the amount of the transfer or other evidence.

----

2.   Marriage

As to marriages that occur after a will is executed, again there are several approaches. Some statutes provide that a subsequent marriage revokes a pre-existing will, so the decedent dies intestate; sometimes beneficiaries are allowed to rebut this presumption. Other statutes presume that a failure to update the will is intentional and require the spouse to elect against the decedent's estate. UPC § 2–301, reproduced below in relevant part, reflects a third approach; this statute assumes that the premarital will reflects the testator's intent to the extent the will benefits the testator's issue (children and descendants) but presumes that gifts to anyone else are negated upon marriage. Does the UPC allow evidence to rebut this presumption?

UPC § 2–301 Entitlement of Spouse; Premarital Will

(a)   If a testator's surviving spouse married the testator after the testator executed the testator's will, the surviving spouse is entitled to receive, as an intestate share, no less than the value of the share of the estate the spouse would have received if the testator had died intestate as to that portion of the testator's estate, if any, that neither is devised to a child of the testator who was born before the testator married the surviving spouse and who is not a child of the surviving spouse nor is devised to a descendant of such a child or passes under Sections 2–603 or 2–604 to such a child or to a descendant of such a child, unless:

(1)   it appears from the will or other evidence that the will was made in contemplation of the testator's marriage to the surviving spouse;

(2)   the will expresses the intention that it is to be effective notwithstanding any subsequent marriage; or

(3)   the testator provided for the spouse by transfer outside the will and the intent that the transfer be in lieu of a testamentary provision is shown by the testator's statements or is reasonably inferred from the amount of the transfer or other evidence.

---

3.   Divorce

The flip side of marriages that occur after the execution of a will are divorces that occur after the execution of a will. Divorce automatically revokes provisions in a will that benefit a former spouse, although whether this rule applies to non-probate documents, like life insurance, varies tremendously. Responsible matrimonial lawyers will make sure that their clients visit an estate planning lawyer during or immediately following divorce to update all planning documents, including any that name the former spouse as a fiduciary. Of course, it is always an option to continue to benefit a former spouse so long as the language doing so is clear. We deal with this topic in depth in Chapter 13, when we discuss the revocation (or not) of governing instruments in the wake of divorce. *See* UPC § 2–804.

> **Connection Note:** As you saw in Chapter 4 in connection with intestacy rules, spouses have priority over other beneficiaries. The rights of spouses (present or former) who are omitted, intentionally or unintentionally, from a testator's estate plan are discussed in detail in Chapter 14.

ASSESSMENTS

1.   How would UPC § 2–302 have addressed Carolyn Gay Khan's disinheritance by her father? How would UPC § 2–302 apply if Carolyn were born after her father's will was executed, and the testator had no other children at that time? What if Carolyn were born after her father executed the will, and Glomset's son John Jr. was living at that time?

2.   Ana operated a successful restaurant. Ana's will provided that her spouse Luis would receive half of her estate, while the other half would go to "my employees." Four years after the will was executed, Ana and Luis had a child,

Juan. Luis and Ana divorced, and Ana died several years later. At the time of her death, Ana's restaurant had four employees. If the UPC applies, who is entitled to a share in Ana's estate? Assume, instead, that Ana amended her will when Juan was born to leave one-third of her estate to Luis, one-third to Juan, and the final one-third to her employees. If Ana and Luis have another child, Daniela, and then divorce, but Ana never updates her will, how will her estate be distributed on her death, assuming she is survived by Luis, Juan, Daniela, and her four employees?

3.   Your client Brad wants to leave his wife and one of his children out of his will. His reasons are that he has amply provided for his wife by making her the contingent beneficiary of his multi-million-dollar stock portfolio, and the child he wants to leave out is a surgeon who makes a large income, and whom Brad has already gifted the down payment on a house. His other child, a daughter, is an artist who makes very little money, and Brad wants to make sure she has enough money, so he is leaving her a large gift in his will. What would you draft in the will to avoid future litigation over these intentional omissions?

F.   Agreements Not to Change Wills

This section addresses promises not to change wills, which may stem from good intentions but are almost always a short-cut to litigation. Often, there is a question about whether joint wills create a contract in the first place. In the case below, however, there is no question about the existence of the contract. Instead, the *Ernest* court struggles with how to balance the interests of the surviving spouse and the decedent spouse in probate and non-probate assets.

Ernest v. Chumley

936 N.E.2d 602 (Ill. App. Ct. 2010)

STEIGMANN, J.

Plaintiffs, Deborah D. Ernest and John P. Sonneborn (the "Children"), appeal from the trial court's August 2009 order denying, in part, their complaint to construe a will. The Children argue that the court erred by finding that the mutual will executed by defendant, Dorothy L. Chumley, f/k/a Dorothy L. Sonneborn, and their since-deceased father, Robert A. Sonneborn, was not enforceable during Dorothy's lifetime. We affirm and remand with directions.

I. BACKGROUND

A. The Undisputed Facts

In October 1989, Robert and Dorothy married, each having had two children from a previous marriage.

In August 2000, Robert and Dorothy each executed mutual wills that, with the exception of references to name and gender, contained identical reciprocal clauses. In particular, Dorothy's mutual will stated, in pertinent part, the following:

ARTICLE II

In the event my husband, ROBERT A. SONNEBORN, shall survive me for a period of at least [30] days, I give him the rest, residue[,] and remainder of my estate, of whatever nature and wheresoever located. Should my said husband so survive me, I expressly make no provision for any of my children.

* * *

ARTICLE IV

Since my husband and I each have children from a prior marriage, it is our intent that upon the death of the survivor of us, that my estate or his estate, as the case may be, be divided one-half to my children and one-half to his children designated as beneficiaries in Article III. Accordingly, it is further our intent that upon the death of the first of us, the terms of the will of the surviving spouse shall become irrevocable.

In April 2003, Robert died, owning assets in joint tenancy with Dorothy valued at approximately $200,244, which included their home and several bank accounts. Two months after Robert's death, Dorothy executed a new will that bequeathed her entire estate to her biological children.

In December 2004, Dorothy married Thomas Chumley. The following month, Dorothy executed another will, in which she bequeathed her entire estate to (1) Thomas and, should he predecease her, then to (2) her biological children and Thomas's two children in equal shares. In February 2006, Dorothy sold the home she had shared with Robert, depositing the net proceeds of approximately $103,901 into a revocable trust account that she had held in joint tenancy with Robert but now held solely in her name. One week later, Dorothy withdrew $96,951 from the trust account and deposited various sums totaling the withdrawal amount into three separate certificates of deposit that she held in joint tenancy with Thomas.

B.   Procedural History

In October 2004—two months before Dorothy married Thomas—the Children filed a complaint to construe the will, requesting that the trial court (1) find Dorothy's August 2000 mutual will irrevocable, (2) order Dorothy to itemize the assets she owned with Robert immediately before his death, and (3) impose a constructive trust, prohibiting (a) Dorothy from making gratuitous transfers of those assets and (b) Thomas's or Dorothy's future spouses from making any statutory claims on the itemized assets.

At a December 2008 bench trial, Dorothy testified that her understanding of her August 2000 mutual will was that (1) upon Robert's death, she could use the remaining estate for her comfort, support, maintenance, and welfare during her lifetime; (2) upon her death, her estate, if any, would be divided equally among their four children; and (3) if Robert had survived her, her children would not have been entitled to control Robert's estate. Dorothy acknowledged that her June 2003 will, which left her entire estate to her biological children, was contrary to her intent as stated in her August 2000 mutual will.

Following the presentation of evidence and argument, the trial court permitted the parties to file additional briefs in support of their respective positions. In August 2009, the court entered the following ruling:

> As agreed by the parties, the facts are basically not in dispute. The issues revolve around the intent of the parties and whether Dorothy's will became irrevocable upon Robert's death. Based on the wills themselves and Dorothy's trial testimony, the court finds her will became irrevocable on Robert's death.

> Moreover, the court finds all the property of the survivor at the time of his or her death was subject to the testamentary scheme regardless of how obtained. The wills appear to give the survivor the unfettered right to use the property as each saw fit. There is absolutely no restriction in the wills on the use by the survivor. The Children are asking this court to do something not provided for in the wills.

> The court finds the contract is not enforceable against Dorothy during her lifetime as the will is not specific as to how Dorothy is to use her property during her life.

> The relief requested by [the Children] is denied.

This appeal followed.

II. THE APPLICABILITY OF DOROTHY'S MUTUAL WILL DURING HER LIFETIME

A. The Legal Implications of Mutual Wills

Mutual wills are the separate instruments of two or more testators that contain reciprocal terms such that each testator disposes of his or her respective property to the other. *In re Estate of Erickson*, 841 N.E.2d 1104, 1106 (Ill. App. 2006). In contrast, a joint will is a single instrument that contains the wills of two or more persons, and may be considered mutual if it contains reciprocal provisions. *Id.* In the case of mutual and reciprocal wills, "a judicial presumption arises in favor of the existence of the contract from the existence of the mutual wills themselves." *In re Estate of Aimone*, 590 N.E.2d 94, 98 (Ill. App. 1992). A contract embodied in a mutual will becomes irrevocable as to the survivor upon the death of the first testator. *Freese v. Freese*, 364 N.E.2d 983, 985 (Ill. App. 1977).

B. The Children's Claim That Dorothy's Mutual Will Implicitly Restricted Her Use of Certain Assets During Her Lifetime

The Children argue that they are entitled to (1) an accounting and (2) the imposition of a constructive trust upon the assets owned by Robert at his death. Specifically, the Children contend that although the contract embodied by Robert's and Dorothy's mutual wills did not explicitly restrict Dorothy's use of the assets at issue during her lifetime, it implicitly restricted Dorothy from (1) executing new wills, (2) selling the home she shared with Robert, and (3) transferring money into a joint account with Thomas. Thus, the narrow question before this court is whether Robert's and Dorothy's mutual wills implied restrictions upon Dorothy's use of the assets during her lifetime. With one exception, we conclude that they did not. That exception is that we conclude that Dorothy's transfer of funds from the sale of her home into three certificates of deposit that she held in joint tenancy with Thomas violated the terms of the irrevocable contract created by the execution of her joint and mutual will.

In support of their contention that the mutual wills implied restrictions upon Dorothy's use of the assets during her lifetime, the Children cite *Moline National Bank v. Flemming*, 414 N.E.2d 936 (Ill. 1980). In *Flemming*, Eva and her husband, Albert, executed an irrevocable joint and mutual will (1) giving the surviving spouse possession of the entirety of the other spouse's property in fee simple upon either spouse's death and (2) bequeathing the remaining estate to

Eva's biological son and his heirs upon the surviving spouse's death. In March 1973, Eva died and, after her death Albert created several trusts and joint accounts for an individual other than Eva's son. In January 1979, Albert died, and the executor sued to recover all accounts not benefitting Eva's son as estate assets. In concluding that Albert acted beyond his authority, the appellate court stated the following:

> Where an agreement as to mutual wills does not define the survivor's power over the property, but merely provides as to the disposition of the property at his death, the survivor may use not only the income but reasonable portions of the principal, for his support and for ordinary expenditures, and he may change the form of the property by reinvestment and the like * * * .

Id. at 941. This case, and the others cited by the Children, involve a surviving spouse's attempt to evade the will's disposition of assets after that surviving spouse's death and not during life, so do not offer the Children any support.

Here, the Children premise their argument that Robert's and Dorothy's respective mutual wills implicitly restricted Dorothy's use of the bequeathed assets during her lifetime on (1) Dorothy's attempts to make a purported testamentary transfer that was contrary to her irrevocable August 2000 mutual will and (2) the clause bequeathing them each a one-quarter interest in Dorothy's estate upon Dorothy's death. However, the Children ignore that (1) "[a] clause in a will purporting to bequeath property to someone is testamentary and has no effect until the death of the testator" (*In re Estate of Lowry*, 418 N.E.2d 10, 14 (Ill. App. 1981)) and (2) we construe the plain language of the will—that is, we do not infer provisions the testator might have made had he or she thought of a particular contingency. *Larison v. Record*, 512 N.E.2d 1251, 1253 (Ill. 1987).

In this case, the plain, unambiguous language of Robert's and Dorothy's respective August 2000 mutual wills shows, in pertinent part, that (1) upon Robert's April 2003 death, (a) Dorothy was immediately entitled to the entirety of Robert's assets without restriction, (b) the Children were not entitled to any of Robert's assets, (c) Dorothy's mutual will became irrevocable, and (2) upon Dorothy's death, the Children would each be entitled to a one-quarter interest in Dorothy's estate. If Robert and Dorothy intended to place restrictions on Dorothy's use of the bequeathed assets during her lifetime, they could have easily expressed their intent to do so in their mutual wills. They did not, and we decline to infer otherwise. However, our analysis does not end here.

Dorothy was still bound by the expressed intent of the underlying irrevocable contract created by her mutual will. Specifically, that upon Dorothy's death, the Children would each inherit one-quarter of her remaining estate. Although assets held in joint tenancy do not pass under a joint and mutual will, they can be the subject of a contractual agreement contained within a joint and mutual will and a court, under the appropriate circumstances, can enforce the agreement by limiting the surviving spouse's disposition of property. Although not immediately entitled to possession until the death of the surviving spouse, third-party beneficiaries of a joint and mutual will are entitled to enforcement of the underlying contract.

In this case, the record shows that Robert and Dorothy expressly bequeathed the entirety of their respective estates to the surviving spouse—in this case Dorothy—intending to leave the residue of that estate, however much that estate might be at the time of her death, to Robert's and Dorothy's biological children in equal shares. The record also shows that after Robert's death, Dorothy deposited a substantial portion of the funds she received from the sale of the home she previously owned with Robert into three separate certificates of deposit, which she held in joint tenancy with Thomas. However, in so doing, Dorothy effectively breached the expressed intent of her irrevocable contract by removing those funds from her estate by operation of law.

Accordingly, we remand to the trial court with directions that it enter an order mandating that Dorothy (1) terminate Thomas's interest in the aforementioned certificates of deposit and (2) refrain from taking any future action that is inconsistent with the Children's future interest in her estate except expenditures made for her own support.

For the reasons stated, we affirm the trial court's judgment and remand with direction.

NOTES

1.   Although the *Ernest* case raises some very difficult questions about how to balance the respective interests of this blended family, the one question it does not raise is whether there was a contract in the first place. Often, parties rely on the existence of a joint or mutual will to argue that there was an agreement not to change that document. What evidence should a court consider in deciding whether there was an agreement in the first place? Why does the relevant UPC provision, reproduced below, not presume such a contract when parties execute a joint will or mutual wills?

UPC § 2–514 Contracts Concerning Succession

A contract to make a will or devise, or not to revoke a will or devise, or to die intestate, if executed after the effective date of this [article], may be established only by (i) provisions of a will stating material provisions of the contract, (ii) an express reference in a will to a contract and extrinsic evidence proving the terms of the contract, or (iii) a writing signed by the decedent evidencing the contract. The execution of a joint will or mutual wills does not create a presumption of a contract not to revoke the will or wills.

2.   Think back to the Probate Property Worksheet from Chapter 1. Was the *Ernest* court correct in finding the parties' agreement not to change the will to apply to the jointly held real estate? What would have been the result if Robert's will contained a provision leaving his real estate to Deborah and John on his death? We will revisit these issues in Chapter 13 when we discuss nonprobate assets.

3.   If Dorothy and Robert had come to you while drafting their wills, what would you have advised them to do to avoid litigation in the future?

G. Conclusion and Takeaways

In a 2006 article for The New Yorker magazine, Janet Malcom wrote, "Wills are uncanny and electric documents. They lie dormant for years and then spring to life when their author dies, as if death were rain." And yet, during this period of dormancy, the testator's life goes on. As the cases and problems in this chapter illustrate, a more accurate view of an estate plan is that it is dynamic. Reviewing the plan periodically, to make sure the provisions still work, is a best practice, even if the plan is prepared by the most careful of draftspersons. We move now from our study of wills to another type of instrument, a trust, which also exists over time, even for multiple generations, raising many of the same tensions between the creator's intent and flexibility in the face of changing circumstances.

CHAPTER 8 COMPREHENSIVE ASSESSMENTS

1.   **MULTIPLE WILLS AND INTERPRETATION REVIEW.** This exercise asks you to review the will of Arnie Collins who died on April 23, 2020. Arnie had two children: Samantha, who passed away during a car accident on June 6, 2005, and Brian, who is still living. Samantha had one son, John. John has two children,

Carly and Kevin. Brian has three children, Alyssa, Lucy, and Michelle. Alyssa has one daughter, Kristina. Arnie executed a will on February 15, 1963, leaving everything "to my spouse, Barbara Collins, but if she predeceases me, then to my children, Samantha and Brian, to share and share alike." Arnie decided to update his will following the births of his grandchildren.

Arnie executed a second will on September 22, 2005, which states, in relevant part:

> I, ARNIE COLLINS, being of sound mind and body so hereby declare this to be my LAST WILL AND TESTAMENT, revoking all previous wills.
>
> TO JOHN, my only grandson, I leave my father's watch.
>
> TO ALYSSA, my granddaughter, I leave my mother's pearl earrings.
>
> TO LUCY, my granddaughter, I leave my signed Broadway Playbill collection.
>
> TO MICHELLE, my granddaughter, I leave my mother's emerald necklace.
>
> TO MY GREAT-GRANDCHILDREN, I leave $10,000 each.
>
> The rest, residue, and remainder I leave to my spouse, Barbara Collins, but if she predeceases me, I leave the residue to my children, Samantha and Brian, to share and share alike.

In August of 2019, Michelle undergoes a gender transformation and legally changes her name to Michael. On November 7, 2019, Arnie executes a document titled: CODICIL TO MY LAST WILL AND TESTAMENT in which he leaves a $10,000 donation to his church and reaffirms his will dated September 22, 2005. Barbara dies on January 15, 2020, and Arnie dies on April 1, 2020. Arnie's father's watch is valued at $10,000; his mother's pearl earrings are valued at $500; his Playbill collection is valued at $200; and his mother's emerald necklace is valued at $6,000. Arnie has $60,000 in cash and debts in the amount of $50,000.

As Arnie's family was sorting through his belongings, they found a copy of the 2005 LAST WILL AND TESTAMENT in a desk drawer. Stapled to the back was a handwritten note that says: "I still wish for my grandson, Michael, formerly my granddaughter Michelle, to be considered a beneficiary under my will."

Arnie's death caused some strife within the family, including disagreements about who receives what under the will. Brian claims he receives the entire residuary estate since his sister, Samantha, is dead; Samantha's son John disagrees. Alyssa and Lucy argue that Michael should not receive the emerald necklace because he is not mentioned anywhere in the will. Michael argues he should still take the gift since the note indicates his grandfather's wish not to disinherit him. The family has come to you to see if you can provide guidance on how the estate should be distributed. Please write a memo to the clients discussing the most likely distribution of Arnie's estate. Make sure to address each provision in the will and all property owned by the decedent.

2.   **DRAFT A WILL.** Your client, Ellen, tells you she wants to dispose of her assets as follows:

- Her Phillipe Patek watch to her niece Enid.

- Her pearl necklace to her best friend Nicola.

- Her stamp collection to her nephew Adam.

- Her stock in a new startup called Magic Dolls, now worth about $300,000, to Alan and Elisa, to pay for their children's education. Magic Dolls is about to go public and start trading on the Stock Exchange.

- Her Victorian home where she now lives to her sister and brother. There is no mortgage on it at the moment.

- $50,000 to her friend Nicola to care for Ellen's Great Dane, Hamlet, if she passes away before he does.

Imagine you have asked Ellen about the possible changes in property and beneficiaries that may occur before the will is probated. Make up any reasonable answers you want. Now draft the above provisions, accounting for the possible changes you discussed with her.

Test Your Knowledge

To assess your understanding of the material in this chapter, click here to take a quiz.

CHAPTER 9

Private Trusts I: Who, What, and Why?

CHAPTER LEARNING OUTCOMES

Following your work with this material in this chapter, you should be able to do the following:

- Advise clients in a variety of scenarios what kind of trusts would be appropriate for their estate planning needs and goals

- Analyze whether a disposition is a transfer to a trust, a present gift, or an attempted testamentary transfer

- Evaluate whether property was transferred to a trust or whether the trust failed for lack of a res

- Assess whether an attempted trust fails for lack of any of the necessary components of a trust

- Assess whether a trust is an appropriate part of a particular client's estate plan, based on the client's specific situation

- Draft deeds of trust and declarations of trust placing property into trusts

- Create an estate plan that uses trusts appropriately given a set of facts

A. Introduction

A **trust** is a way to give property to one person (the **trustee**) to manage for and distribute to another person (the **beneficiary**). Such a form of ownership might help clients in the following situations, although this list is not exclusive:

- A client who wishes to provide for minor children in case of his or her unexpected death.

- A client who wants to provide for a mentally disabled child who may not be able handle money without some kind of supervision.

- A client who wants to provide for a disabled child in a way that allows for the child to receive government assistance over and above the trust assets.

- A client who wants to provide for a child who has a drug or alcohol problem and likely cannot responsibly handle money.

- A client who is older and concerned about managing a business or assets in case of future incapacity.

- A client who wants to pass on assets to a child in a way that will encourage some kind of behavior, such as finishing college, getting a job, quitting smoking, etc.

Trusts are an extremely flexible from of property ownership and have a vast variety of uses. What all these situations have in common is that someone other than the beneficiary holds and manages the money. This chapter focuses on what a trust is and how, in its many different forms, a trust can help clients.

Part B explains what a trust is, who the parties to the trust are, and a trust's material components. This Part also details the numerous kinds of trusts that exist, some of which we will explore more fully in subsequent chapters—like charitable trusts and revocable trusts as nonprobate devices—and some which are beyond the scope of this book—like business or real estate trusts.

Part C focuses on the important role of the trustee, who has a fiduciary duty to the beneficiary, although those duties are discussed in far greater detail in Chapter 10. **Part D** explains the property requirement for the creation of trusts, and **Part E** provides more detail about the basic requirements for creating a valid trust. **Part F** introduces the concept of class gifts and explains how class gifts operate in a trust.

> **Connection Note:** This chapter is generally limited to a discussion of private trusts in the estate planning context, but trusts are also extremely common and useful in all sorts of business and investment arrangements: if you have a pension plan at work, it is all part of a giant trust governed by Federal law. And charitable trusts, discussed in Chapter 15, are a multi-billion-dollar business in the United States today.

Finally, **Part G** explores how long private trusts may last, the application of the Rule Against Perpetuities to private trusts, and reforms to the Rule Against Perpetuities that have been reshaping the trust industry.

B. What Is a Trust?

1. Trust Vocabulary and History

As explained, a trust allows a property owner, generally described as the **donor** or the **settlor**, to give assets—often money or stock, but it can also be real or personal property as well—to, in effect, two people: one who manages and distributes the assets, and the other who receives the benefit of the assets.

To understand this concept of split ownership, it may be helpful to go back to your Property course. There, you learned that the common law conceives of ownership as a bundle of sticks: the right to use, transfer, exclude, and destroy (the last is often limited by public policy). In a trust, these sticks are divided between two people, the trustee and the beneficiary. The trustee has the sticks associated with legal title, such as the right to manage the assets and distribute them to the beneficiary. The beneficiary retains the right to use the assets and enjoy the assets for her own benefit. Conversely, the trustee may not use the assets in the trust for her own benefit, as doing so would constitute self-dealing and violate one of the trustee's fiduciary duties.

> **Language Note:** In addition to the terms "donor" and "settlor," the person who sets up a trust may be called the "grantor" or even the "trustor." Why do you think there are so many different words for this role? As you will see, there are also many different words for the trust property and for revocable trusts (but there's only one word for a trustee).

The three-way relationship is a triangle. Notice that any of the three positions can be occupied by more than one person. For example, there can be co-trustees, multiple beneficiaries, and more than one settlor. What is required

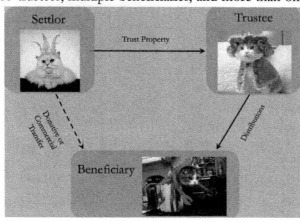

for a valid trust is that there be at least one beneficiary who is not also a trustee (although this is not true with a revocable inter vivos trust or new forms of asset protection trusts). This is generally true because the trustee must owe a duty to someone who has the ability to enforce that duty. Without that crucial separation—someone to whom the duty is owed and a trustee who owes the duty—there is no trust. In that case, the assets are owned in fee.

The advantages of a trust are that the donor can benefit someone without giving that person direct access to funds they may not be well equipped to handle. A trust also allows a donor to plan ahead for the donor's own incapacity. As we will see in Chapter 11, another advantage of this arrangement is that it can provide **asset protection** and shield the beneficiary from creditors and their claims against the trust assets.

A waqf is a kind of trust allowed by Islamic law. Calligraphy of Alfiqh (Islamic word).

Historically, trust settlors have been well versed in these advantages and eager to make use of them. People generally trace the history of the trust to the middle ages and feudalism, but in fact it goes back further. There were trusts under Roman law and the Muslim jurist Al Kassaf wrote a Treatise on Trusts around the same time the Danes were pillaging England. And can it not be said, based on Genesis, that in the Christian story God left the world in trust to humans?

Trusts were used extensively in the Middle Ages in England, mostly as a way to avoid taxes—then called "feudal incidents." (Trusts serve this function today as well, a fascinating topic that we will discuss briefly in Chapter 11, when we discuss the asset protection function of private trusts.) Trusts became recognized in the Chancery Courts (the courts of equity) during the Crusades: when Knights went off to the Holy Land, they often deeded their lands to a friend who would manage the lands while the owners were away and presumably give them back upon the owners' return. If this seems like a bad idea, that's because it was: When the friend refused to redeed the property, the knight had to seek a remedy in equity, because he had no legal one. He had signed the land

Danes invading England. From "Miscellany on the life of St. Edmund," 12th century. Pierpont Morgan Library, New York.

over by deed. The Chancery Courts recognized the truth of the arrangement that had been made and often ordered the lands returned as an equitable remedy.

Historical Note: Though Chancery began as a place to find justice denied by the law courts, by the mid-nineteenth century, it had become an object of disdain and ridicule for its interminable, costly, and inefficient processes. Chancery's impenetrable bureaucracy is one of the themes of Charles Dickens' 1853 novel BLEAK HOUSE.

The Court of Chancery during the reign of George I by Benjamin Ferrers (1725)

The Franciscan order, sworn to poverty, also used trusts. St. Francis had owned nothing, lived on donated food and clothes, and ordered his followers to do the same. This way of life turned out to be fairly unpleasant, so the Franciscans turned to trusts as a means of having beneficial use of property without actually having legal title. The legal loophole of divided ownership was also useful for married women and allowed them to own property while they were under the disability of coverture since they had equitable and not legal ownership. Trusts were, from this perspective, the first form of married women's property.

Established in the 13th century by St. Francis of Assisi, the Franciscans have long been an important monastic community.

2. Kinds of Trusts

There are a number of different kinds of trusts, and each serves a specific purpose. All of them, however, share the common triangular structure and operate in largely similar ways. They also all invoke the performance of fiduciary duties, covered in Chapter 10. Depending on your jurisdiction, the law governing trusts consists of the **Uniform Trust Code** ("UTC"), common law, and the Restatement (Third) of the Law of Trusts.

Below we categorize private trusts into revocable trusts and irrevocable trusts. Notice that under each heading, there is more than one kind of trust. As you read through the descriptions, think of the value and utility of these different kinds of trust. We also briefly discuss charitable trusts and business trusts to distinguish them from the private trusts we focus on here.

a. *Revocable or Living Trusts*

A revocable trust, also called a **living trust** or **inter vivos trust**, can be revoked or amended by the settlor at any time. A revocable trust is a will substitute, and we discuss the special characteristics of revocable trusts in greater detail in Chapter 13 in connection with other will substitutes.

A well-drafted trust should state whether it is revocable or irrevocable; if it is revocable, it should also specify the procedure for revoking it. For example, such a provision might read: "This trust may be revoked at any time by written notice to the Trustee." If the settlor wishes to revoke the trust, the settlor can email (or snail mail) the trustee to state that the trust is revoked.

But what if the trust instrument fails to indicate whether the trust is revocable or irrevocable? Under the common law, trusts were presumed to be irrevocable, but UTC § 602(a) reverses that presumption and provides that trusts are presumed revocable unless the trust instrument "expressly provides that the trust is irrevocable." The assumption is that a settlor would more likely intend to retain the power to revoke the trust. This is also a safer assumption, because it rejects the possibility that the settlor would permanently give away or encumber assets he or she might need later on.

Having property in a revocable trust makes no difference to a person's daily life. The settlor usually is the trustee and the beneficiary. The trust will provide for a successor trustee under certain conditions—such as the settlor's future incapacity—and names some future beneficiary. As long as the settlor is alive and competent, however, all activities and transactions go on as before. You might wonder why, then, a settlor would establish and fund this type of trust.

Revocable trusts are appropriate in the following situations, or any combination of these situations:

- An older person worried about possible future incapacity might use a revocable trust to appoint a trustee who could step in to manage the settlor's affairs if the settlor were ever determined to be incapacitated. The revocable trust can be more efficient than a power of attorney because the trust language can give the trustee broad authority, while a power of attorney requires that each exercise of authority must be itemized. For example, if a client owns a business or real property, the trust instrument can allow a trustee to do whatever is necessary to manage the business or property because the trustee has legal title to that property. Moreover, the trustee's power lasts past death, as opposed to power-of-attorney authority, which ends at the death of the principal.

> **Connection Note:** As we discussed in Chapter 1, the probate process involves paying creditors, clearing title, and distributing property to the appropriate beneficiaries. The probate court supervises the process. When property is held in a revocable trust, the trustee handles these actions consistent with the trust terms without the need for judicial oversight.

- Someone who wishes to avoid probate because he or she lives in a state where the probate process is particularly expensive, slow, or cumbersome. It might also be a good idea if the client owns real property in another state: real property requires probate in the state where it is located, but if it is in a trust, **ancillary probate** is not necessary.

- Parents with small children who want to plan for the possibility that something might happen to both of them. Having property in a revocable trust with a successor trustee who will also take care of the children can make the process much easier. Other options, like appointing a guardian or a conservator, requires more court supervision.

b. Irrevocable Trusts

Irrevocable trusts arise in three ways. First, irrevocable trusts often are drafted by lawyers as a form of tax planning, which we will discuss in Chapter 16, when we discuss taxes.

Second, any **testamentary trust**—that is, a trust created by a will—is irrevocable (which, if you think about it, makes sense because the settlor/testator is dead in the case of a testamentary trust). Testamentary trusts are created by will and come into existence only at the testator's death. You can see examples of testamentary trusts in the Wills of Katharine Hepburn, Elvis Presley, and Whitney Houston, all of which are in the Appendix. Related to the testamentary trust is the "pour over" trust, which is essentially a stand-alone trust that receives assets that the will "pours into" at the testator's death. Typical language in a will creating this type of trust might be: "I give the residue of my estate to the trustee of the XYZ trust, according to the terms of the XYZ Trust Instrument, created 10/10/2020." If the will pours over into a trust, the *existence* of the trust will become part of the probate file and available to the public; the trust instrument, itself, however, is not. Michael Jackson's will, in the Appendix, is an example of this type of plan. The will simply serves to pour the estate, or the assets, into the trust. Pour-over trusts (including how they are funded and the uses that they can serve in estate planning) are discussed further in Chapter 13 on will substitutes.

> **Language Note:** The term "pour over" is sometimes used to refer to the will ("pour over will"), sometimes to the trust ("pour over trust"), and sometimes to the entire plan (the will and trust together). Regardless of how the word is used, the result is the same.

Third, a revocable trust becomes irrevocable upon the settlor's death (by the same logic by which a testamentary trust is irrevocable).

Putting all or some of a person's property into a trust involves redeeding real property and transferring the rest by, for example, retitling bank accounts or drafting a deed of transfer for personal property. The Appendix also contains a form of deed to make this type of transfer.

c.   *Charitable Trusts*

Charitable trusts in the United States today contain enormous amounts of assets and are a significant area of legal and tax practice. This book covers them in Chapter 15. For the moment, here are four key differences between charitable trusts and the private trusts we are discussing in this chapter:

- Unlike private trusts, charitable trusts do not have identifiable beneficiaries. They benefit groups of people (students in need of food assistance, for example) or charitable purposes (art appreciation, for example).

- Charitable trusts receive specific tax exemptions. These are discussed in Chapter 16.

- Because they have no identifiable beneficiaries to enforce their terms, charitable trusts are overseen by the Attorney General of the state in which they operate.

- Charitable trusts last forever, whereas there are rules about how long private trusts can last. We discuss those rules at the end of this chapter when we take up the Rule Against Perpetuities.

d.   Business and Real Estate Trusts

This textbook does not cover business trusts because they are not a form of inheritance law, but it's worth mentioning them in passing because they play a large role in business and finance. Like a private trust, a business trust has trustees who hold legal title and beneficiaries who have beneficial title. Unlike private trusts, however, the trustees of a private trusts use the trust assets to manage a business, and each beneficiary has a certificate of ownership in a certain percentage of the business. These certificates are freely transferrable.

e.   Other Types of "Trusts"

So far, we have been discussing what we might call "intentional" private trusts, that is, trusts that an estate planning lawyer sets up for a client. There are other types of trusts that you would never intentionally create, but which may arise by operation of law. In general, these trusts can arise when someone made a drafting error in a will, when someone acquired property though fraud, or when a trust fails. These are not actual trusts; they are legal fictions that exist to fix a problem or remedy a fraud and are sometimes referred to as **remedial trusts**. The two most important things to remember about these types of trusts are:

- They are not trusts; and

- A lawyer would never create any of these on purpose!

i.   Constructive Trust (Think Fraud)

A court can impose a **constructive trust** on property someone has acquired through fraud. It is a legal fiction that the person who committed fraud now owns the property in trust for the real owner. Creating this legal fiction allows a court to transfer ownership form one person to another. It is necessary because courts generally aren't allowed to take away people's property and give it to the rightful owner. But once they create the legal fiction that it is actually being held in trust *for* the rightful owner. *Mahoney*, the slayer case in Chapter 4, discussed the constructive trust as a potential remedy. You will also see this remedy proposed in future chapters, and you may have encountered constructive trusts in other areas of the law too.

ii.   Resulting Trust (Assets with Nowhere to Go)

A **resulting trust** arises through faulty drafting and the failure to think ahead: this trust-by-operation-of-law happens when a trust fulfills its purpose and there are still funds remaining in the trust. For example, Ali creates a trust to pay your law school tuition, and you graduate. If the trust fails to provide for a further purpose, a resulting trust will arise. In effect, this means that the remaining funds will return to Ali, the settlor, and be considered Ali's property in fee or be distributed through Ali's estate if he is dead.

iii.   Merger (Two Become One)

This is a situation that arises when a drafter fails to think ahead. Merger occurs when the Trustee and sole beneficiary become the same person. For example, Annelise creates a trust for her son with herself and her son as co-trustees (this works because there is one trustee who is not also a beneficiary.) But then Annelise dies. Now the only trustee and the only beneficiary are one person. This leads to merger, and the trust property will become the son's in fee. Note that this merger would not occur if the trust also provided for the son's descendants (even if he had no descendants when Annelise died).

NOTES

1.   Although wills have a long history as a wealth transfer tool, trusts do as well and have allowed trust settlors, both historically and currently, to avoid probate, keep assets secure from taxation, and ensure continual management of property. For more on the history of trusts, see JOHN BAKER, AN INTRODUCTION TO ENGLISH LEGAL HISTORY (1971) and JOHN LANGBEIN & RENEE LETTOW LERNER, HISTORY OF THE COMMON LAW: THE DEVELOPMENT OF ANGLO-AMERICAN LEGAL INSTITUTIONS (2009).

2.   Frederic W. Maitland, a leading legal scholar and historian, asserted that: "Of all the exploits of Equity the largest and the most important is the invention and development of the Trust. . . . This perhaps forms the most distinctive

achievement of English lawyers. It seems to us almost essential to civilization, and yet there is nothing quite like it in foreign law." While the trust certainly has played an important role in Anglo-American law, it is not unique to this domain. Islamic law has also provided for a trust-like vehicle, known as "Waqf." According to some Islamic scholars, a valid Waqf should be settled for a "pious purpose," which includes providing for one's family. If you're a fan of mystery novels, you might like Sujata Massey's first novel, *The Widows of Malabar*, which features a woman lawyer in 1920s Bombay taking a case that involves three widows who want to give their dower to a waqf (and, of course, a murder).

3.   Business trusts, while they may sound modern, have deep historical roots. Eric Chaffee writes:

> Pinpointing the first business trust is impossible, especially considering that the term "business" is notoriously difficult to define. With that said, the popularization of business trusts corresponds with the popularization of passive investing in business entities in the 1600s. . . . Because incorporating could be an onerous process, business trusts became an alternative method of seeking capital that sidestepped the legal requirements of forming a corporation.

Eric Chafee, *A Theory of the Business Trust*, 88 U. CIN. L. REV. 797, 808 (2020). Business trusts, like religious order trusts and trusts for married women may have been popular because they "sidestepped" common law rules. Trusts were not, historically, recognized at common law and have always been associated with equity. Currently, many businesses choose to organize as business trusts and "business trusts continue to be used regularly for pension plans, mutual funds, and asset securitization." *See id.* at 978. An appealing feature of business trusts is that they are not subject to the same regulatory regime as corporations and partnerships. *See, e.g.,* Lee-Ford Tritt & Ryan Scott Teschner, *Re-Imagining the Business Trust as a Sustainable Business Form*, 97 WASH. U. L. REV. 1 (2019) (arguing that "[d]ue to business trusts' structure and flexibility, they are an ideal vehicle for sustainable businesses"); John H. Langbein, *The Secret Life of the Trust: The Trust as an Instrument of Commerce*, 107 YALE L.J. 165 (1997). For a comparative perspective on business trusts, see Steven L. Schwarcz, *Commercial Trusts as Business Organizations: An Invitation to Comparatists*, 13 DUKE J. COMP. & INT'L L. 321 (2003).

4.   **Real estate investment trusts** (REITs) are a much more recent innovation and are a specialized kind of trust. REITs were established in 1960 under the Eisenhower administration to provide investors with the opportunity to invest in income-producing real estate through the purchase of securities. The

REIT, modeled after a mutual fund, is a company that pools the capital of multiple investors to purchase, operate, or finance income-generating real estate. In this way, individual investors earn dividends from real estate investments—without having to buy, manage, or finance any properties themselves.

5.   Private trusts are a popular way for individuals to own real estate, especially if they do not want to divulge their identities. The New York Times in 2015 found that, in the prestigious Time Warner Center just on the edge of Central Park, "a majority of owners have taken steps to keep their identities hidden, registering condos in trusts, limited liability companies or other entities that shield their names." *See* Louise Story and Stephanie Saul, *Stream of Foreign Wealth*, N.Y. TIMES, Feb. 7, 2015.[1] In 2019, the New York state legislature enacted a law mandating "[e]very buyer's name . . . be publicly available under New York's Freedom of Information Law." Why do you think purchasers would like to remain anonymous, and what benefits will the new law bring?

ASSESSMENTS

1.   Read the will of Whitney Houston in the Appendix and answer the following questions:

   a.   Who are the beneficiaries of the testamentary trusts in this will?

   b.   When are the beneficiaries entitled to payments from the trust?

   c.   How long do the trusts last?

   d.   What happens to the trust property when the trust ends?

2.   Now read the sample revocable trust in the Appendix and answer the following questions:

   a.   Who are the trust beneficiaries during the settlor's (trustor's) life?

   b.   Who are the trust beneficiaries after the settlor dies?

   c.   Are there sub-trusts that get established after the settlor's death? What are they? How do they differ from each other?

   d.   When are the beneficiaries entitled to payments from the trusts?

   e.   How long do the trusts last?

   f.   What happens to the trust property when the trust ends?

---

[1]   Available at: https://www.nytimes.com/2015/02/08/nyregion/stream-of-foreign-wealth-flows-to-time-warner-condos.html.

3.   Your client is a single young professional, Yvonne. She rents her apartment, is starting to save for retirement with a 401(k), owns a car and has a bank account with about $5000 and a savings account with about $10,000. She comes to you for estate planning: she's heard that it's never too soon to start. She just wants to leave everything to her older sister, but she's also heard talk about trusts as part of an estate plan. Among other things, she asks you whether you think she should have a trust as part of her plan. What do you answer?

C. Who Are the People Involved in a Trust?

1. The Settlor

As noted above, the settlor is also called the trustor (an antiquated term less in use today), or the grantor (a term often used in the tax context), or the donor. The settlor is the person who transfers legal title of the assets to the trustee to be held in trust.

2. The Trustee

The trustee is the person who has legal title to the trust assets and manages them for the benefit of the beneficiary. The trustee has a fiduciary duty to the beneficiary and can be sued for breach of this duty. We will discuss the trustee's fiduciary duty in the next chapter in detail, but the central concept here is that fiduciary law bars a trustee from using the trust assets for her personal benefit. That benefit is reserved for the beneficiary.

A trustee can be a person or an institution, such as a bank or a corporation, and a trust can have more than one trustee. In any of these instances, the fiduciary duty applies. If, for some reason, the settlor fails to appoint a trustee, a court will do so. (You, as drafting attorney, will of course, make sure the settlor appoints one and also includes a mechanism to appoint future trustees; the failure to appoint a trustee is a mistake made by a layperson, and the kind that ends up in casebooks.) Thus, the saying "A trust will not fail for lack of a trustee." Although the trustee is an essential element of a trust, if the purpose and the beneficiaries are clear, a court can easily appoint someone to administer the trust.

3. The Beneficiary

The beneficiary has equitable title to the trust property. This means she may use it for her benefit and enjoyment according to the terms of the trust. A trust may have more than one beneficiary and may have present and future beneficiaries. For example, Mahmoud may leave money in trust for his surviving spouse for her use as long as she lives with the remainder to go to Mahmoud's children upon the spouse's death. Or Ellen could fund a trust to pay for her three grandchildren's college education.

4.   The Trust Protector

The role of trustee is as old as the hills, but more recently some settlors have been appointing trust protectors as well. The **trust protector** may exercise certain specified powers over the trust and the trustee. Most commonly, the trust protector is given the power to remove and replace trustees as a form of oversight. A trust protector also may have the power to add beneficiaries or terminate a trust.

You might consider a trust protector advisable as a way to keep an eye on the trustee, or to add flexibility to a trust that is intended to last for many generations. What remains unresolved, however, is the extent to which the trust protector is responsible for monitoring a trustee. In other words, can a beneficiary sue a trust protector for failing to remove and replace a trustee and recover losses from the protector that result from the trustee's breach of duty? *See In re Robert T. McClean Irrevocable Trust*, 418 S.W.3d 482 (Mo. Ct. App. 2013).

NOTES

1.   John Langbein has written about the transformation of the role of trustee: "Trustees of old were unpaid amateurs, that is, family and community statesmen who lent their names and honor to a conveyancing dodge. Writing in the last years of the 19th century, the great legal scholar Frederic W. Maitland could still observe that '[a]lmost every well-to-do-man was a trustee.' " *See* John H. Langbein, *Rise of the Management Trust*, 143 TR. & EST. 52 (2004). There may still be stereotypical ideas of trusteeship: who trustees are; what they look like; and what kind of background they have. What associations do you have with trustees and with trusts, more generally? We will take up this question again in the next chapter.

2.   Picking a trustee is one of the most important decisions that a trust settlor makes. One wealth manager has called the trustee-beneficiary relationship, alternately, "an arranged marriage" and a relationship of "mentoring." Which type of relationship more accurately characterizes the trustee-beneficiary relationship? Why?

This same wealth professional says that "the grantor of a trust will be well advised to consider the potential trustee's ability to mentor the beneficiaries. . . as the highest qualification among all of the things that a trustee must do." *See*

JAMES E. HUGHES, JR., FAMILY WEALTH: KEEPING IT IN THE FAMILY—HOW FAMILY MEMBERS AND THEIR ADVISERS PRESERVE HUMAN, INTELLECTUAL, AND FINANCIAL ASSETS FOR GENERATIONS (1997). Why would mentorship be important or even applicable?

3.   The author of an article in Forbes, entitled *Trust Protectors—What They Are and Why Probably Every Trust Should Have*,[2] argues (unsurprisingly) that all trusts should have a trust protector to guard against trustee abuse and corruption. He writes:

> The concept of the Protector was largely unknown in the U.S. and nearly always confined to offshore trusts thought the 1990s. Then, determined to get in on the booming trust business, the states of Alaska, Delaware and Nevada all adopted legislation that created advantages that were (they argued, and have argued since) similar to those found in offshore trusts. . . . From there, the concept of the Protector literally exploded to where today many common types of trusts routinely have provisions for a Protector—which they should. It is difficult to image the type of trust that should not have a Protector.

Fiduciary duty is meant to protect beneficiaries from trustee malfeasance and abuse. Does the rise of the trust protector mean that fiduciary duty is no longer enough to regulate trustee behavior? What abuses might fiduciary duty miss? Keep this in mind when you read about fiduciary duties in the next chapter.

ASSESSMENTS

1.   Your law firm has been asked to publish a blog post on the qualities and qualifications a settlor would want to look for in a trustee. Make a list of these qualities and explain why each is important.

2.   Return to the trusts in Whitney Houston's will and the sample revocable trust and answer the following questions:

    a.   Who are the trustees?

    b.   What happens if a trustee can no longer serve?

3.   Your clients are a young married couple, Maria and Giuseppe, who have two small children, ages five and seven. Their estate planning goals are pretty straightforward: they want the other to inherit if one of them dies, and, if

---

[2]   See https://www.forbes.com/sites/jayadkisson/2012/08/25/trust-protectors-what-they-are-and-why-probably-every-trust-should-have-one/#598e1fc75abc.

something happens to both of them, they want their estate to pass to Maria's sister, Elisa, who has agreed to take of the children. Draft a letter with your recommendations.

D. What Goes into a Trust?

In addition to people, a trust must have property, called a **res** or a **corpus**. This property can consist of anything—money, stock, a house, land, a grandfather clock, a Rolex watch. There is no minimum amount, but the trust must contain some kind of property to have legal existence. There may be problems down the road if the trust assets are not income producing (like the grandfather clock or the Rolex)

> **Practice Note:** To ensure that a trust is funded, some lawyers paperclip a small amount of cash (a five- or ten-dollar bill), and a "funding schedule" referencing that amount, to the end of every executed trust instrument.

and may have to be sold if the trustee needs to make distributions to the beneficiaries. Nevertheless, a trust can be created with any kind of property.

NOTES

1. Does the requirement that a trust have a corpus amount to another formality that thwarts the intent of settlors who lack legal advice? *See* Jane B. Baron, *The Trust Res and Donative Intent*, 61 TUL. L. REV. 45, 84 (1986) (arguing that the requirement is often intent defeating and that "[i]f the intent to create a trust and the objects of that intent are clear, and if the court can carry out that intent in accordance with some objective standard, then the trust should be upheld, even where the donor has failed to specify or segregate trust property").

2. Is a gestational carrier of a fetus a trustee with the intended parents as beneficiaries? Kevin Yamamoto & Shelby A.D. Moore, *A Trust Analysis of a Gestational Carrier's Right to Abortion*, 70 FORDHAM L. REV. 93, 96 (2001). Also, can fetuses be beneficiaries? The answer is generally "no," but that hasn't stopped some much-discussed attempts:

> Sofia Vergara's ex-fiancé is continuing his legal battle for the right to implant their two embryos, which were created when the couple was still together in 2013, in a surrogate. Nick Loeb first sued Vergara in 2014 in his home state of California, where the embryos remain frozen at a clinic in Beverly Hills. The issue gained national attention, and shortly thereafter Loeb penned an opinion piece for the New York Times titled, *"Sofia Vergara's Ex-Fiancé: Our Frozen Embryos Have a Right*

to Live" in 2015. Later that year, the judge was set to dismiss their case, when Loeb himself dropped it. . . . Later, he established a trust for the embryos (which he has named Emma and Isabella) in Louisiana, and had that trust sue Vergara in the state, according to NOLA.com, which also reports that embryos have some rights under Louisiana law.

Sam Reed, *Sofia Vergara's Complicated Legal Battle, Explained,* Instyle.com (June 29, 2018).

3.   Can the environment and natural resources be the corpus of a trust? The Code of Justinian states:

> By the law of nature these things are common to all mankind-the air, running water, the sea, and consequently the shores of the sea. No one, therefore, is forbidden to approach the seashore. All water in the state is protected by the public trust doctrine re, provided that he respects habitations, monuments, and buildings, which are not, like the sea, subject only to the law of nations. . . . All rivers and ports are public; hence the right of fishing in a port, or in rivers, is common to all men. . . The public use of the seashore, too, is part of the law of nations, as is that of the sea itself."

J. Inst. 2.1.1.

All water in the state of Alaska is protected by the public trust doctrine. In 1970, Joseph Sax argued for an extended public trust doctrine that would encompass environmental protection. Joseph L. Sax, *The Public Trust Doctrine in Natural Resource Law: Effective Judicial Intervention,* 68 MICH. L. REV. 471, 539 (1970). And the California public trust doctrine provides that the state, in its capacity as a sovereign, "owns all of its navigable waterways and the lands lying beneath them as a trustee of the public trust for the benefit of the people." *Nat'l Audubon Soc'y v. Superior Court,* 33 Cal. 3d 419, 434 (Cal. 1983) (internal quotation marks and citation omitted).

4.   What if the trustee can benefit herself and the beneficiary at the same time? We will discuss this issue in the next chapter, but start thinking about it: what if the trustee could, say, buy property from the trust at a fair price, and then use it to start her own business? Should the law allow such a transaction? On the one hand, it seems pointless to prevent the trustee from engaging in a transaction which would benefit the trust (and hence the beneficiary), but, on the other hand, does that create a slippery slope, requiring too much fact-finding and lead

to more litigation? Would it help if the trustee were allowed to engage in this conduct but only if the beneficiary were notified and consented?

ASSESSMENT

In 2019, Ivor set up a trust for his son, Ivan, who, being five, was in a low tax bracket. The corpus of the trust is to be the profits Ivor makes in stock trading in 2020. Does the trust have a valid res?

E. How to Create a Trust?

1. Basic Trust Requirements:

A trust has the following basic requirements:

1. The trust must have valid, legal purpose

2. The settlor must be competent

3. The trust must have a trustee (but, as indicated above, not really)

4. The settlor must intend to create a trust

5. The settlor must name at least one identifiable beneficiary

6. The settlor must transfer property into the trust

Accordingly, any professional who is creating a trust and wants to ensure its validity must satisfy each of these requirements. As you read the requirements, some of which we have already discussed, think about which are the most onerous and how they relate to the requirements for will validity.

2. Valid Legal Purpose

A valid purpose just means the trust must have a reason to exist, for the trustee to hold and manage the assets for another person. A common trust purpose is to pay for someone's education or to support a surviving spouse. The trust cannot have an illegal purpose or encourage illegal behavior. For example, a trust set up to fund the creation and sale of bootleg movie videos would be invalid. Of course, the limits of this rule are not always clear: what if a trust were funded to support minor children of people who commit serious crimes and serve jail sentences?

Trusts also cannot violate public policy, but again, the parameters can be fuzzy. For example, if the above trust for children of people who are in prison is deemed to support lawbreaking, it might arguably subvert public policy.

Courts rarely invalidate trusts on public policy grounds, although there are some limits, including:

- Incentivizing someone to change their religion

- Incentivizing divorce

- Rewarding someone for not marrying

- Rewarding family members for not being in contract with each other

As discussed in Chapter 3, trust restrictions on marriage are the subject of disagreement. A comment in the Restatement (Third) of Trusts states that limits on the freedom to divorce or marry are void for public policy. RESTATEMENT (THIRD) TRUSTS, Comments to Paragraph 29. But, as we saw in the context of testamentary freedom, at least one court has upheld such limitations.

3. The Settlor Must Be Competent

The different types of trusts require different levels of capacity. We have discussed the capacity requirements for valid will execution; not surprisingly, a testamentary trust requires the same capacity as a will.

The standard for creating an irrevocable trust is higher than that for a will or a testamentary trust. This makes sense: an irrevocable trust usually means a permanent loss of some assets, so it is important that the Settlor of such a trust understand not only the nature of her property and the natural objects of her bounty, but also the effect creating the trust will have on her future financial security, including that the irrevocable trust may deplete the resources she might need to care for herself or others.

What about a revocable trust? Notice that this kind of trust has a testamentary function (thus, the name "will substitute"), and does not cause the settlor to lose access to any of the assets during life. Therefore, the revocable trust requires the same capacity as does the execution of a will.

4. The Trustee

A competently drafted trust instrument will name a trustee or trustees (and will contain provisions for removing and replacing the trustee without necessity of court intervention). As noted, a trust will not fail for lack of a trustee, but a court will be involved if no trustee is named.

5. Intent

The issue of intent primarily arises at the "back" or litigation end of trust practice. When an estate planning attorney drafts a trust for a client, the attorney uses the word "trust" to show that the intent is clear, as in "I give 10,000 dollars in trust to the trustee of the Education Trust."

You may, however, encounter an instrument that is not clear as to what the person intended. Sometimes determining whether a draftsperson intended a trust can be very confusing, because a non-lawyer might or might not use the word "trust" to reflect the technical legal meaning. It therefore can be hard to distinguish among:

- A gift

- An attempted testamentary transfer

- A promise to make a gift in the future

- The creation of a life estate with a remainder to the beneficiary

- A declaration of trust

The following case raises the question of the intent of a person who signed an instrument called a "declaration of trust" but otherwise did not act as if a trust existed. As you read *Palozie v. Palozie*, consider what facts the court relies on to determine the property owner's intent.

Palozie v. Palozie

927 A.2d 903 (Conn. 2007)

BORDEN, J.

The plaintiff, Donald L. Palozie, appeals from the judgment of the trial court affirming the judgment of the Probate Court denying the plaintiff's application for title and right of possession to a twenty-three-acre parcel of land situated on Crane Road in Ellington (Crane Road property). The plaintiff claims that the trial court improperly concluded that a declaration of trust executed by the plaintiff's deceased mother, Sophie H. Palozie (decedent), was invalid and unenforceable because the decedent had not manifested an unequivocal intent to create a trust and to impose upon herself the enforceable duties of a trustee. We affirm the judgment of the trial court.

After conducting a trial on the merits of the plaintiff's application, the trial court found the following facts. "On February 23, 1988, the decedent asked her grandson David Palozie, who is also the plaintiff's son, to visit her. It was

David's birthday, and he did go to the decedent's home with his wife Susan. While there the decedent asked David and his wife, Susan, to witness her signature on a document and they did so. The document is entitled '[d]eclaration of [t]rust.' At the time David did not know what the document purported to be, nor was there any evidence that Susan did either. The signature of the settlor appears to be that of the decedent, and it has not been shown otherwise.

At the same time the decedent asked David and Susan Palozie to witness a second document purporting to be a quitclaim deed to the Crane Road property, again with the witnesses having no knowledge of what the document was. The quitclaim deed purports to convey to herself as trustee under the terms of the declaration of trust, the Crane Road property. The quitclaim deed was not acknowledged and neither it nor the declaration of trust were recorded on the land records.

No one, other than the decedent was aware of the nature of these documents. Apparently, she kept them in either a small metal box or a suitcase in her home. The decedent died, in her home on March 13, 1991, intestate.

Family members, including the plaintiff and the decedent's daughter, Gaye Reyes, gathered at the house. They retrieved a small metal box and a suitcase. The contents of the metal box were briefly examined and then taken by the plaintiff to the house trailer in which he lived, which was located on the property. [The decedent lived separately in a house on the same property.]

Gaye Reyes was appointed administrator of the estate and filed an inventory on March 24, 1992, which included the Crane Road property as an asset of the estate. Gaye was removed as administrator approximately ten years later because the administration of the estate was not proceeding timely. Two of the decedent's grandchildren, Richard Palozie and Joanne Palozie-Weems, were appointed as successor coadministrators in June 2002. In January 2003, they filed an application to sell the real estate in question. The plaintiff objected to the

> **Language Note:** Even though this case is recent (decided in 2007), it's interesting to note that the original opinion contains the gendered suffix "administratrix."

proposed sale claiming, for the first time since the decedent's death in 1991, that he, and not the decedent's estate, held legal title to the property by virtue of the purported trust.

On the basis of the foregoing facts, the trial court concluded that the plaintiff had failed to prove, by clear and satisfactory evidence, that the decedent had "adequately manifest[ed] an intention to create a trust and to accept the enforceable duties of trustee. The trial court observed that the decedent had not informed "[t]he witnesses to the '[d]eclaration of [t]rust' . . . what the instrument was," and had "kept the document under her total control during her lifetime with no obligation to the supposed beneficiaries." "The likelihood is that the decedent wished to retain total control of the property during her lifetime for her own benefit, and not as a trustee for the plaintiff and, therefore, the trust instrument was a poorly designed effort to establish a testamentary document, rather than a trust with the requirements that would entail." In arriving at this determination, the trial court found it noteworthy that: (1) "there was evidence that the decedent and the plaintiff were not always without conflict in their relationship," as reflected by a family violence protective order issued against the plaintiff on behalf of the decedent in 1990; and (2) the quitclaim deed "was never recorded, nor was it properly acknowledged as required by General Statutes § 47–5." Accordingly, the trial court determined that the declaration of trust was void and unenforceable and, therefore, rendered judgment in favor of the defendants. This appeal followed.

The following additional facts are relevant to our resolution of the present appeal. The declaration of trust provides in relevant part:

> "Whereas I, Sophie H. Palozie, of the Town of Ellington, County of Tolland, State of Connecticut, am the owner of certain real property located at (and known as) 315 Crane Road in the Town of Ellington, State of Connecticut, NOW THEREFORE, KNOW ALL MEN BY THESE PRESENTS, that I do hereby acknowledge and declare that I hold and will hold said real property and all my right, title and interest in and to said property and all furniture, fixtures and personal property situated therein on the date of my death, IN TRUST being of sound mind to wit I make this my last private verbal act [f]or the use and benefit of Donald L. Palozie, Trustee under declaration of trust February 23, 1988, but if such beneficiary be not surviving, for the use and benefit of Gaye M. Reyes."

The instrument further provides:

> "Upon my death, unless the beneficiaries shall predecease me or unless we all shall die as a result of a common accident or disaster, my successor trustee is hereby directed forthwith to transfer said property and all my right, title and interest in and to said property unto the beneficiary absolutely and thereby terminate this trust."

The plaintiff claims that the trial court improperly found that the decedent had not manifested an intent to create a trust, or to impose upon herself the enforceable duties of a trustee, based on her failure to communicate her intent and on her exclusive retention and control of the trust instrument and quitclaim deed during her lifetime. We disagree and, accordingly, we affirm the judgment of the trial court.

One owning property can create an enforceable trust by a declaration that he holds the property as trustee for the benefit of another person." "No trust, however, is created unless the settlor presently and unequivocally manifests an intention to impose upon himself enforceable duties of a trust nature. If what has been done falls short of showing the complete establishment of a fiduciary relationship, as where the intent to become a trustee is doubtful because what was said or done is as compatible with an intent to make a future gift as with an intent to hold the legal title to property for the exclusive benefit of another, the proof fails to show more than a promise without consideration."

To determine whether the decedent manifested an intent to create a trust and to impose upon herself the enforceable duties of a trustee, we begin with the language of the trust instrument. This is because "where the manifestation of the settlor's intention is integrated in a writing, that is, if a written instrument is adopted by the settlor as the complete expression of the settlor's intention, extrinsic evidence is not admissible to contradict or vary the terms of the instrument in the absence of fraud, duress, undue influence, mistake, or other ground for reformation or rescission." 1 RESTATEMENT (THIRD), § at 21, comment (a), p. 322.

Although the instrument plainly states that the decedent intended to hold the Crane Road property in trust, it also contains the following language, "being of sound mind to wit I make this my last private verbal act," which imports ambiguity into the trust instrument. Of particular significance for purposes of our analysis is the decedent's characterization of it as her last act. In light of this language, it is unclear whether the decedent intended to create a presently enforceable trust, with all of the rights, duties and responsibilities that such a trust entails, or whether she intended to execute a testamentary document, which would become effective and enforceable only after her death.

Although communication of intent to create a trust and delivery of the trust instrument are "not essential to the existence of a trust [they are] of great importance in determining the real intent of the alleged declarant." 90 C.J.S., TRUSTS § 66, p. 192 (2002). This is because a settlor's failure to communicate his or her intent and to deliver the trust instrument "is some indication of the absence of a final and definitive intention to create a trust." 1 A. Scott, W. Fratcher & M. Ascher, THE LAW OF TRUSTS, § at 4.2.2, p. 189.

In the present case, it is undisputed that the decedent informed neither the beneficiaries of the trust nor anyone else that she had intended to hold the Crane Road property in trust. Additionally, it is undisputed that she never delivered the trust instrument or the quitclaim deed to the beneficiaries or any other third party, and that she never recorded the trust instrument or the quitclaim deed on the town land records. These undisputed facts amply support the trial court's finding that the decedent had not arrived at a final and definitive intention to create a trust and to impose upon herself the enforceable duties of a trustee.

The plaintiff claims, however, that the trial court's factual finding was clearly erroneous because "different uncontested evidence clearly shows the decedent's intention to create a trust and to impose upon herself the duties of a trustee." In support of this claim, the plaintiff points out that the decedent acted in a manner consistent with the interests of the beneficiaries during her lifetime by preserving the trust instrument and quitclaim deed and by maintaining the Crane Road property. We reject this claim because the trier of fact "is not required to draw only those inferences consistent with one view of the evidence, but may draw whatever inferences from the evidence or facts established by the evidence it deems to be reasonable and logical." *PSE Consulting, Inc. v. Frank Mercede & Sons, Inc.*, 838 A.2d 135 (Conn. 2004). The trial court reasonably and logically found that the decedent had not manifested an unequivocal intent to create a trust or to impose upon herself the enforceable duties of a trustee.

The judgment is affirmed.

NOTE

In a number of cases, the testator expresses a "wish," "hope," or "recommendation" that property be used in a particular manner by the beneficiary. The problem is that the language is **precatory** rather than mandatory. Discussing the question of precatory language and gendered uses of language, Alyssa DiRusso has written:

> The law of precatory language in wills is complicated and unpredictable.... Although people are more likely to choose precatory language when they do not intend to create a legally binding trust, their desire to bind or not bind is not the only factor that determines the language they choose. The language we use is determined both by socialization and biological factors and varies

greatly based on sex. Specifically, men and women tend to choose different words, sometimes without full regard to the legal implications of the words chosen.

Alyssa DiRusso, *He Says, She Asks: Sex, Language, and the Law of Precatory Words in Wills*, 22 WIS. WOMEN'S L.J. 1 (2010).

Do you agree that gendered language might lead to uneven results for men and women in the creation of trusts? And do you think that gendered language might be a problem elsewhere?

ASSESSMENTS

For each of the following, assess whether the language in these instruments creates a valid trust:

1.   The June 4, 1995 will of Homer Oehlers provides in relevant part:

> If there are any assets left in the Life Trust not used to support my wife, I instruct James A. Pabilonia to distribute all remaining assets as he will determine at that time. No specified instructions for distribution of all remaining assets are implied or suggest [sic] in this my last will and testament.

The July 8, 1995 codicil provides:

> Upon my passing, for all my worldly goods and resources not designated in my will, I, Homer C. Oehlers of Lebanon, CT, instruct Mr. James A. Pabilonia, Willimantic, CT. as Sole Trustee for a Trust he is to establish for the exclusive benefit of my wife Mrs. Colina Oehlers as sole beneficiary except for any and all trust expenses. Upon my wife's passing if there are any assets remaining, the trust shall distribute these assets at the trustee's sole discretion.

Estate of Homer Oehlers, Late of Lebanon Court of Probate, District of Lebanon, District Number 071, 14 QUINNIPIAC PROB. L.J. 195, 198 (1999).

2.   The will of attorney A.H. Lumpkin gives the estate to the testator's wife "absolutely, for and during her natural life, to have the use and benefit thereof during her said natural life," and gives the remainder to the testator's lodge. It names independent executors and provides that, "to the end that [they] shall have full power and authority to handle and settle my said estate without the necessity of court orders, I hereby confer upon them all such powers as are given to Trustees under and by virtue of the provisions of the Texas Trust Act."

Perfect Union Lodge No. 10 v. Interfirst Bank of San Antonio, 748 S.W.2d 218 (Tex. 1988).

3.   The will of Stanley Hope McReynolds provides as follows:

> The purpose of this Trust is to provide for the support and welfare of my father, Charles R. McReynolds. (b) The Trustee shall pay over the net income to the said Charles R. McReynolds or so much thereof as should be required to provide adequately for his care, welfare and support in convenient intervals, and shall use such amounts of principal as shall be required in his discretion to provide for any emergency, illness or insufficient income for the benefit of my father.

> (c) Upon the death of my father, Charles R. McReynolds, the Trustee may, out of such funds remaining pay the funeral expenses and last illness and related expenses of my father and shall distribute the remainder of the assets to Rev. Herbert W. Armstrong, Box 111, Pasadena, California 91123 and I request that said legatee shall use the money so received by him in the promotion and furtherance of his Radio Ministry and the spreading of the Gospel as he may see fit, and the Trust shall terminate.

The trust beneficiary, Charles R. McReynolds, and the remainderman, Herbert W. Armstrong (Reverend Armstrong), died prior to the death of Stanley Hope McReynolds. There was no provision for the disposition of the trust property in the event both beneficiaries of the trust predeceased the testator.

Estate of McReynolds, 800 S.W.2d 798, 799 (Mo. Ct. App. 1990).

4.   The will of Marilyn Linder provides as follows:

> Paragraph F: My house and all real property shall go to Margaret Woods, as the guardian of and with whom my beloved dog, Lolli, and my beloved cat, Purrah, actually live and are pampered as indoor members of the family.

> Paragraph G: After distribution as directed above, 100% (one hundred per cent) of all my money, bonds, certificates of deposit, treasury direct account, savings account, checking account(s), money market accounts, zero municipal investment trusts, etc. shall go to Margaret Woods, as the guardian of and with whom my beloved dog, Lolli, and my beloved cat, Purrah, actually reside and are pampered as indoor [emphasis in original] members of the family to cover the costs

of veterinary bills, food, toys, and all manner of luxurious comforts to which they are accustomed. Specifics related to their care and the location of all my wealth can be found in my safe deposit box at People's Bank, Rte 111. Monroe, CT.

Paragraph H: Under no [emphasis in original] circumstances shall Emelia (Millie) Conkling or any member of her family become a successor guardian for my dog, Lolli, or my cat, Purrah.

In Re: The Estate of Marilyn Linder, 31 QUINNIPIAC PROB. L.J. 29, 30–31 (2017).

6. Identifiable Beneficiary

The trust structure requires that the beneficiary or beneficiaries be able to hold the trustee accountable for exercising the trustee's fiduciary duty. Therefore, a valid trust must have at least one identifiable beneficiary, or this aspect of the trust relationship is nonexistent. Beneficiaries like "my friends" would be invalid. On the other hand, a provision reading "To my friends Aimee, Becca, and Carlos" would be valid, because it identifies specific people.

7. Property

As noted above, a trust must be funded to be valid. How does someone go about putting property into a trust? This depends on the kind of property being transferred.

- Real property must be deeded (or redeeded) to the trustee of the trust: "To Bill Jones, as Trustee of the ABC Trust."

- Bank accounts, stock accounts, securities accounts and the like must be retitled in name of the trustee: The owner of the account is listed as "Bill Jones, Trustee of the ABC Trust."

- Personal property should be listed on a schedule attached to an instrument transferring it to the trustee: "I hereby transfer this property/items listed on Schedule A attached to Bill Jones, Trustee of the ABC Trust."

A person can transfer property to someone else in trust and can also transfer property to herself as trustee, as in *Palozie.* The latter transfer is called a **Declaration of Trust**.

One notable exception to the rule that a trust must be funded applies to a pour-over trust. As discussed above, sometimes a will has a clause that pours over assets into a trust. When it comes time to probate the will, it turns out that the trust was never funded. This might happen because the decedent never got around to funding it. This can happen even if an attorney drafted the will: sometimes a client may decide to save money by transferring property into the trust on her own and then simply forget to do so. This happens enough that the Uniform Law Commission drafted a statutory exception to the rule that a trust must be funded to be valid. The "Uniform Testamentary Additions to Trust Act" (or UTATA), is a standalone act but also appears as UPC § 2–511:

Uniform Testamentary Additions to Trusts Act (1991)

(a)   A will may validly devise property to the trustee of a trust established or to be established (i) during the testator's lifetime by the testator, by the testator and some other person, or by some other person, including a funded or unfunded life insurance trust, although the trustor has reserved any or all rights of ownership of the insurance contracts, or (ii) at the testator's death by the testator's devise to the trustee, if the trust is identified in the testator's will and its terms are set forth in a written instrument, other than a will, executed before, concurrently with, or after the execution of the testator's will or in another individual's will if that other individual has predeceased the testator, regardless of the existence, size, or character of the corpus of the trust. The devise is not invalid because the trust is amendable or revocable, or because the trust was amended after the execution of the will or the testator's death.

ASSESSMENTS

1.   Three days before his death C. P. Craft penned a lengthy personal letter to Mrs. Iva Rippstein. The letter was not written in terms of his anticipated early death; in fact, Craft spoke in the letter of his plans to go to the Mayo Clinic at a later date. The portion of the letter at issue reads as follows:

> 'Used most of yesterday and day before to 'round up' my financial affairs, and to be sure I knew just where I stood before I made the statement that I would send you $200.00 cash the first week of each month for the next 5 years, also to send you $200.00 cash for Sept. 1960 and thereafter send that amount in cash the first week of the following months of 1960, October, November and December.'; opposite which in the margin there was written:

> 'I have stricken out the words 'provided I live that long' and hereby and herewith bind my estate to make the $200.00 monthly payments provided for on this Page One of this letter of 9–17–60.'

Mrs. Rippstein argued that the letter created a trust for her benefit with instructions to pay her $200 per month out of the assets of his estate. If you were the judge who heard the case, what would you decide? *See Unthank v. Rippstein*, 386 S.W.2d 134 (Tex. 1964).

2.   Angela deeds her house to her daughter, Tricia, so she can qualify for a low-interest loan program for people with limited assets. Once she receives the loan, she asks Tricia to deed the house back to her, saying, "You know, like we agreed." Tricia, however, enjoys living in the house with her three children, and refuses. Angela sues. What result?

3.   Prepare a presentation for your local PTA about how trusts should be part of an estate plan for people with minor children. Be creative: use PowerPoint, or any other media or visual aids you think would engage people, get your points across, and explain how trusts work. Highlight both the legal consequences and the practical consequences of creating a trust relationship.

F. Class Gifts

Often the settlor of a trust wishes to benefit a group of people—children or grandchildren, for example, or all descendants. These gifts are called class gifts, and they are quite common. A class gift provides for the proportional division of property among all qualified members of a class. The issue then becomes who qualifies for class membership. The general rule is a class closes at the testator's death, unless the will or trust document specifies otherwise. For example, a document that provides a gift to "all my grandchildren now living" would have the class close on the date the document was executed.

Class gifts raise interesting questions in light of modern reproductive technology: does a class gift to "my grandchildren" or "my issue" include children conceived after the death of the parent, who was a child of the settlor? The following case involves a claim by two children, conceived after their father passed away, to take a share of a trust set up by their grandfather. The grandfather's grandchildren were the residuary beneficiaries of the trust.

In re Martin B.

17 Misc. 3d 198 (N.Y. Misc. 2007)

ROTH, SURR.

This uncontested application for advice and direction in connection with seven trust agreements executed on December 31, 1969 by Martin B. (the grantor) illustrates one of the new challenges that the law of trusts must address as a result of advances in biotechnology. Specifically, the novel question posed is whether, for these instruments, the terms "issue" and "descendants" include children conceived by means of in vitro fertilization with the cryopreserved semen of the grantor's son who had died several years prior to such conception.

The relevant facts are briefly stated. Grantor (who was a life income beneficiary of the trusts) died on July 9, 2001, survived by his wife Abigail and their son Lindsay (who has two adult children), but predeceased by his son James, who died of Hodgkin's lymphoma on January 13, 2001. James, however, after learning of his illness, deposited a sample of his semen at a laboratory with instructions that it be cryopreserved and that, in the event of his death, it be held subject to the directions of his wife Nancy. Although at his death James had no children, three years later Nancy underwent in vitro fertilization with his cryopreserved semen and gave birth on October 15, 2004 to a boy (James Mitchell). Almost two years later, on August 14, 2006, after using the same procedure, she gave birth to another boy (Warren). It is undisputed that these infants, although conceived after the death of James, are the products of his semen.

Although the trust instruments addressed in this proceeding are not entirely identical, for present purposes the differences among them are in all but one respect immaterial. The only relevant difference is that one is expressly governed by the law of New York while the others are governed by the law of the District of Columbia. As a practical matter, however, such difference is not material since neither jurisdiction provides any statutory authority or judicial comment on the question before the court.

All seven instruments give the trustees discretion to sprinkle principal to, and among, grantor's "issue" during Abigail's life. The instruments also provide that at Abigail's death the principal is to be distributed as she directs under her special testamentary power to appoint to grantor's "issue" or "descendants" (or to certain other "eligible" appointees). In the absence of such exercise, the principal is to be distributed to or for the benefit of "issue" surviving at the time of such disposition (James's issue, in the case of certain trusts, and grantor's issue, in the case of certain other trusts). The trustees have brought this proceeding because under such instruments they are authorized to sprinkle principal to decedent's "issue" and "descendants" and thus need to know whether James's children qualify as members of such classes.

The question thus raised is whether the two infant boys are "descendants" and "issue" for purposes of such provisions although they were conceived several years after the death of James.

Although the particular question presented here arises from recent scientific advances in biotechnology, this is not the first time that the Surrogate's Court has been called upon to consider an issue involving a child conceived through artificial means.

Over three decades ago, Surrogate Nathan R. Sobel addressed one of the earliest legal problems created by the use of artificial insemination as a technique for human reproduction. *Matter of Anonymous*, 74 Misc. 2d 99. In that case, the petitioner sought to adopt a child that his wife had conceived, during her prior marriage, through artificial insemination with the sperm of a third-party donor (heterologous insemination). The question before Surrogate Sobel was whether the former husband had standing to object to the adoption. In the course of his analysis, the learned Surrogate predicted that artificial insemination would become increasingly common and would inevitably also complicate the legal landscape in areas other than adoption. Indeed, he specifically forecast that, as a result of such technological advances, "[legal] issues . . . will multiply [in relation to matters such as] intestate succession and will construction." Surrogate Sobel noted, however, that there was at that point a dearth of statutory or decisional guidance on questions such as the one before him.

The following year New York enacted Domestic Relations Law § 73, which recognized the status of a child born to a married couple as a result of heterologous artificial insemination provided that both spouses consented in writing to the procedure to be performed by a physician. Such statute reflected the evolution of the state's public policy toward eliminating the distinction between marital and nonmarital children in determining family rights. Thus, where a husband executes a written consent (or even in some instances where he has expressed oral consent) to artificial insemination the child is treated as his natural child for all purposes despite the absence of a biological connection between the two.

Surrogate Sobel's predictions in *Anonymous* proved to be prophetic. Some 30 years later, the novel issues generated by scientific developments in the area of assisted human reproduction are perplexing legislators and legal scholars.

Decisions and enactments from earlier times—when human reproduction was in all cases a natural and uniform process—do not fit the needs of this more complex era. These new issues, however, are being discussed and in some jurisdictions have been the subject of legislation or judicial decisions. But, as will be discussed below, neither New York nor the District of Columbia, the governing jurisdictions, has a statute directly considering the rights of post-conceived children. In this case legislative action has not kept pace with the progress of science. In the absence of binding authority, courts must turn to less immediate sources for a reflection of the public's evolving attitude toward assisted reproduction—including statutes in other jurisdictions, model codes, scholarly discussions and Restatements of the law.

We turn first to the laws of the governing jurisdictions. At present, the right of a posthumous child to inherit in intestacy (EPTL 4–1.1[c] [in intestacy]), or as an after-born child under a will (EPTL 5–3.2 [under a will]), is limited to a child conceived during the decedent's lifetime. Indeed, a recent amendment to section 5–3.2 (L 2006, ch 249, eff July 26, 2006) was specifically intended to make it clear that a post-conceived child is excluded from sharing in the parent's estate as an "after-born" (absent some provision in the will to the contrary [EPTL 5–3.2 (b)]). Such limitation was intended to ensure certainty in identifying persons interested in an estate and finality in its distribution.

It, however, is by its terms applicable only to wills and to "after-borns" who are children of the testators themselves and not children of third parties. Moreover, the concerns related to winding up a decedent's estate differ from those related to identifying whether a class disposition to a grantor's issue includes a child conceived after the father's death but before the disposition became effective.

With respect to future interests, both the District of Columbia and New York have statutes which ostensibly bear upon the status of a post-conceived child. In the District of Columbia Code Annotated, the one statutory reference to posthumous children appears in section 42–704, which in relevant part provides that "[w]here a future estate shall be limited to heirs, or issue, or children, posthumous children shall be entitled to take in the same manner as if living at the death of their parent. . . ." New York has a very similar statute, which provides in relevant part that, "[w]here a future estate is limited to children, distributees, heirs or issue, posthumous children are entitled to take in the same manner as if living at the death of their ancestors." EPTL 6–5.7 [a]. In addition, EPTL 2–1.3 (a) (2) provides that a posthumous child may share as a member of a class if such child was conceived before the disposition became effective.

Each of the above statutes read literally would allow post-conceived children—who are indisputably "posthumous"—to claim benefits as biological offspring. But such statutes were enacted long before anyone anticipated that children could be conceived after the death of the biological parent. In other words, the respective legislatures presumably contemplated that such provisions would apply only to children en ventre sa mere.

We turn now to the jurisdictions in which the inheritance rights of a post-conceived child have been directly addressed by the legislatures—namely Louisiana, California and Florida—and to the seven states that have adopted, in part, the Uniform Parentage Act (2000, as amended in 2002)—namely, Delaware, North Dakota, Oklahoma, Texas, Utah, Washington and Wyoming. Although we are concerned here with a male donor, the legislation also covers the use of a woman's eggs. Uniform Parentage Act § 707.

In Louisiana, a post-conceived child may inherit from his or her father if the father consented in writing to his wife's use of his semen and the child was born within three years of the father's death. However, it is noted parenthetically that the statute also allows a person adversely affected to challenge paternity within one year of such child's birth. La. Rev. Stat. Ann. § 9:391.1.

In order for a post-conceived child to inherit in the State of California, the parent must have consented in writing to the posthumous use of genetic material and designated a person to control its use. Such designee must be given written notice of the designation and the child must have been conceived within two years of decedent's death. Cal. Prob. Code § 249.5.

Florida, by contrast, requires a written agreement by the couple and the treating physician for the disposition of their eggs or semen in the event of divorce or death. A post-conceived child may inherit only if the parent explicitly provided for such child under his or her will. Fla. Stat. Ann. 742.17.

Under the Uniform Parentage Act, a man who provides semen, or consents to assisted reproduction by a woman as provided under section 704, with the intent to become a father, is the parent of the child who is born as a result. Under section 704 of the Uniform Parentage Act, both the man and the woman must consent in writing to the recognition of the man as the father. The Uniform Parentage Act has also addressed the situation where the potential parent dies before the act of assisted reproduction has been performed. In such situation, decedent is the parent of the child if decedent agreed to the use of assisted reproduction after his death.

On a related question, the courts of three states have held that a post-conceived child is entitled to benefits under the Social Security Act: Massachusetts, *Woodward v Commissioner of Social Sec*, 760 N.E.2d 257 (Mass.);

New Jersey, *In re Estate of Kolacy*, 753 A.2d 1257 (Super. Ct. Ch. Div. 2000); and Arizona, *Gillett-Netting v Barnhart*, 371 F.3d 593 (9th Cir. 2004). All three courts concluded that post-conceived children qualified for such benefits.

As can clearly be seen from all the above, the legislatures and the courts have tried to balance competing interests. On the one hand, certainty and finality are critical to the public interests in the orderly administration of estates. On the other hand, the human desire to have children, albeit by biotechnology, deserves respect, as do the rights of the children born as a result of such scientific advances. To achieve such balance, the statutes, for example, require written consent to the use of genetic material after death and establish a cutoff date by which the child must be conceived. It is noted parenthetically that in this regard an affidavit has been submitted here stating that all of James's cryopreserved sperm has been destroyed, thereby closing the class of his children.

Finally, we turn to the instruments presently before the court. Although it cannot be said that in 1969 the grantor contemplated that his "issue" or "descendants" would include children who were conceived after his son's death, the absence of specific intent should not necessarily preclude a determination that such children are members of the class of issue. Indeed, it is noted that the Restatement (Third) of Property suggests that

> [u]nless the language or circumstances indicate that the transferor had
> a different intention, a child of assisted reproduction [be] treated for
> class-gift purposes as a child of a person who consented to function
> as a parent to the child and who functioned in that capacity or was
> prevented from doing so by an event such as death or incapacity.

The rationale of the Restatement, *Matter of Anonymous* and section 73 of the Domestic Relations Law should be applied here, namely, if an individual considers a child to be his or her own, society through its laws should do so as well. It is noted that a similar rationale was endorsed by our state's highest Court with respect to the beneficial interests of adopted children. Accordingly, in the instant case, these post-conceived infants should be treated as part of their father's family for all purposes. Simply put, where a governing instrument is silent, children born of this new biotechnology with the consent of their parent are entitled to the same rights "for all purposes as those of a natural child."

Although James probably assumed that any children born as a result of the use of his preserved semen would share in his family's trusts, his intention is not controlling here. For purposes of determining the beneficiaries of these trusts, the controlling factor is the grantor's intent as gleaned from a reading of the trust agreements. Such instruments provide that, upon the death of the grantor's wife, the trust fund would benefit his sons and their families equally. In view of such overall dispositive scheme, a sympathetic reading of these instruments warrants the conclusion that the grantor intended all members of his bloodline to receive their share.

Based upon all of the foregoing, it is concluded that James Mitchell and Warren are "issue" and "descendants" for all purposes of these trusts.

As can be seen from all of the above, there is a need for comprehensive legislation to resolve the issues raised by advances in biotechnology. Accordingly, copies of this decision are being sent to the respective chairs of the Judiciary Committees of the New York State Senate and Assembly.

NOTE

Although *In re Martin B.* does not discuss UPC § 2–120, (Child Conceived by Assisted Reproduction Other than Child Born to Gestational Carrier), or UPC § 2–705, (Class Gifts Construed to Accord with Intestate Succession; Exceptions), those statutes produce the same result as the court reached in *In re Martin B.*

Connection Note: Although UPC § 2–120 is technically an intestacy statute, remember that one purpose of intestacy law is to provide help with interpreting and drafting testamentary instruments.

As to UPC § 2–120(f), which is reproduced below, the father in *In re Martin B.* evidenced intent to be treated as the father of the posthumously conceived child.

UPC § 2–120 Child Conceived by Assisted Reproduction Other than Child Born to Gestational Carrier

(f) [Parent-Child Relationship with Another.] Except as otherwise provided in subsections (g), (i), and (j), and unless a parent-child relationship is established under subsection (d) or (e), a parent-child relationship exists between a child of assisted reproduction and an individual other than the birth mother who consented to assisted reproduction by the birth mother with intent to be treated as the other parent of the child. Consent to assisted reproduction by the birth mother with intent to be treated as the other parent of the child is established if the individual:

(1) before or after the child's birth, signed a record that, considering all the facts and circumstances, evidences the individual's consent; or

(2) in the absence of a signed record under paragraph (1):

(A) functioned as a parent of the child no later than two years after the child's birth;

(B) intended to function as a parent of the child no later than two years after the child's birth but was prevented from carrying out that intent by death, incapacity, or other circumstances; or

(C) intended to be treated as a parent of a posthumously conceived child, if that intent is established by clear and convincing evidence.

Once we establish that the posthumously conceived child should be treated as the child of the deceased father, there is a question whether the child (or children in the case of *In re Martin B.*) are entitled to take under the trust. Here UPC § 2–705 is useful in helping us decide who are takers of the class gift. Note, in particular, that the right to take does not turn on the date of the father's death. The right to take turns on the date of the grandmother's death (when her life estate ends and she either appoints among the settlor's issue and a limited set of other possible appointees or—in default of her appointment—the property is distributed to the settlor's issue). Therefore, UPC § 2–705 does not exclude the posthumously conceived children from the class even though the last child was not born until more than five years (45 months) after the father passed away.

UPC § 2–705 Class Gifts Construed to Accord with Intestate Succession

(g) [Class-Closing Rules.] The following rules apply for purposes of the class-closing rules:

(1) A child in utero at a particular time is treated as living at that time if the child lives 120 hours after birth.

(2) If a child of assisted reproduction or a gestational child is conceived posthumously and the distribution date is the deceased parent's death, the child is treated as living on the distribution date if the child lives 120 hours after birth and was in utero not later than 36 months after the deceased parent's death or born not later than 45 months after the deceased parent's death.

(3) An individual who is in the process of being adopted when the class closes is treated as adopted when the class closes if the adoption is subsequently granted.

The comments to UPC § 2–705 have an illustration based on *In re Martin B*:

> G created a revocable inter vivos trust shortly before his death. The trustee was directed to pay the income to G for life, then "to pay the income to my wife, W, for life, then to distribute the trust principal by representation to my descendants who survive W." When G died, G and W had no children. Shortly before G's death and after being diagnosed with leukemia, G feared that he would be rendered infertile by the disease or by the treatment for the disease, so he left frozen sperm at a sperm bank. G consented to be the parent of the child within the meaning of Section 2–120(f). After G's death, W decided to become inseminated with G's frozen sperm so that she could have his child. The child, X, was born five years after G's death. W raised X. Upon W's death many years later, X was a grown adult. X is entitled to receive the trust principal, because a parent-child relationship between G and X existed under Section 2–120(f) and X was living on the distribution date.

ASSESSMENTS

1.   You are representing a client named Logan who has three adult children and five grandchildren. In accordance with Logan's wishes, the draft will contains separate share testamentary trusts for each of Logan's children with a predeceased child's share to be held in trust for the child's children. Logan's strong wish is that the names of Logan's children and grandchildren be used in the will. Logan wants to be sure that Logan's descendants realized they were specifically remembered. Logan has expressed the wish to avoid using class designations in the will.

    a.   Share with Logan the benefits and risks of using individual names in testamentary instruments and trusts, rather than using class designations. Provide Logan with at least two hypotheticals that illustrate the benefits and the risks.

    b.   Propose to Logan a way to draft the will provisions so that both the individual names and class designations are used in the will. State which specific provisions and what language could be used to reflect Logan's wishes and the benefits related to the use of class designations.

2.   You are working with a new client named Oswin. Fifteen years ago, Oswin executed a pour-over will and revocable trust. Oswin has hired your law firm to review the documents and to determine whether the documents need to be changed in any way. From the client intake questionnaire, you know that Oswin has two adult children, one of whom has two sons. Oswin has three nephews, one of whom has three daughters. The pour over will directs that all of Oswin's property be added to the revocable trust. The revocable trust, which was funded at the time the trust was created, includes two general gifts. One general gift directs that $100,000 is to be divided "in equal shares between my then living nephews," and the other general direct gift directs that $100,000 is to be divided "in equal shares among my then living grandnieces." The balance of the property will be held in a continuing trust for "my grandsons." Upon the death of the last then living grandson, the trust property is to be distributed to "my then living issue per stirpes." Write a memo for the client file that includes the following information:

a.   Describes the potential consequences of the gender-based class designations;

b.   Identifies what questions you will ask Oswin at the next client meeting; and

c.   Outlines relevant drafting considerations you may wish to share with Oswin.

G. How Long Can a Private Trust Last?

Now that you understand how a trust is created, it is also important to understand how long one can last. With wills, this is never a question or a problem. A will is a document that effects a one-time transfer and is operative only as long as the probate process is ongoing. Trusts, on the other hand, have often been referred to as "gifts across time" because they are operative over a span of years, often decades. Trusts are not just a guiding document but a form of property ownership that provides ongoing management for as long as the law permits. Without any limiting rules, a trust could in theory last forever, passing down assets from one generation to the next. And this is where the **Rule Against Perpetuities** comes into the story.

The Rule Against Perpetuities does not create an exact limit in years on a private trust. Rather, it requires that all interests vest or fail within a certain timeframe (called the perpetuities period). In so doing, the Rule Against Perpetuities effectively limits how long private trusts can last—circumscribing their existence to a period of around ninety years.

The rule, which came into being in English law in the seventeenth century, serves an important function, which is to force interests to vest after a certain, specified amount of time. Put another way, the purpose of the rule is to ensure the alienability of property and to curb dead-hand control. The rule, over time, has gained a bad reputation because of its archaic formulation, the absurdity of some of the related assumptions, and the supposed difficulty of calculation. Nevertheless, the policy function that it serves—reducing dead-hand control—remains as relevant and important as ever.

> **Connection Note:** In our discussion of intestacy and wills, we have already seen doctrines that balance between the "dead-hand" of the property owner and the interests of live beneficiaries. We will continue to encounter this tension as we discuss trusts, nonprobate instruments, and tax laws.

In this Part, we will learn about the common law rule, how it works, and what changes have occurred over time because of law reform. We will also, in the last section, discuss the related trend across states to repeal or abolish the Rule Against Perpetuities. This approach is one favored by states seeking to attract trust business and by trust companies themselves, eager to attract clients by marketing "**perpetual**" or "**dynasty**" trusts.

1. Common Law Rule

The common law rule is thought to have originated in 1682 in the Duke of Norfolk's Case. The case involved the Earl of Arundel's estate and his sons vying

Portrait of Henry Howard, 6th Duke of Norfolk (1628–1684). This portrait was once part of the Lenthall collection and is now owned by the Tate Gallery.

for control. Because his eldest son was mentally incapacitated, the Earl created a plan in which some of his property would pass to his eldest son and then to his second son while other property, namely the Barony of Grostock, would pass to his second son, but then to his fourth son. The Earl died and all went according to plan, except when the first son died and the second son assumed the title and the properties that had belonged to the first son, the second son was unwilling to give up the properties he had initially inherited in association with the Barony of Grostock, which were supposed to go to the fourth son.

The fourth son consequently brought a bill to enforce his claim to the Barony against his brother, the second son (who had brought about the restoration of the title "Duke of Norfolk," giving name to the case). The second son argued that the fourth son's executory interest was a perpetuity and therefore void. The Lord Chancellor, ruling on the case, disagreed and concluded that the fourth son's interest would vest within the span of a lifetime. Nevertheless, the Chancellor recognized the importance of an interest vesting within a certain time period and stated that a future interest was only good if it would vest or fail during or at the end of a life in being.

After the Duke of Norfolk's Case, courts continued to use this rule and refine it. The rule also traveled and became a feature of American law as well. Most famously, the rule gained new wording (as well as a new advocate) when John Chipman Gray, a Harvard Law professor, stated the rule in his treatise. Gray wrote: "No interest is good unless it must vest, if at all, not later than twenty-one years after some life in being at the creation of the interest." This formulation is still what most law students learn in Property class.

Identifying the "life in being" and determining whether a future interest violates the Rule is often frustrating for students. What is important is to remember that the Rule only applies to contingent interests and is a safeguard against uncertainties in vesting.

Here are two examples; note the difference and why one violates the Rule, and the other doesn't.

Case 1. Rainbowacre to Adrian for life, then to Ben if Ben goes to the planet Saturn.

- Adrian has a life estate (vested interest)

- Ben has a contingent remainder in fee simple (contingent on Ben's going to the planet Saturn)

- Grantor has a reversion in fee simple

- Ben's contingent remainder is valid since the event must occur, if it does occur, during Ben's lifetime.

Case 2. Rainbowacre to Adrian for life, then to Ben if any person goes to the planet Saturn.

- Unlike in Case 1, the event that would cause Ben's contingent remainder to vest might occur beyond 21 years after the death of Adrian and Ben (the only persons relevant to vesting)

- Ben dies, and his contingent remainder is transmitted to his heirs or devisees and on to their heirs or devisees

- More than 21 years later—it could be well into the twenty-second century—someone makes it to the planet Saturn

- The contingent interest would consequently vest more than 21 years after the relevant lives in being are dead.

Students and, well, most people who deal with the Rule Against Perpetuities also find frustrating the cast of characters that come along with the rule. This cast of characters represents assumptions that must be made in conjunction with the application of the rule. Here is a sampling:

- The fertile octogenarian (one must assume that a woman can give birth at any age)

- The unborn widow (one must consider the possibility of remarriage at any age)

- The slothful executor (one must assume an estate could be tied up for more than 21 years after the death of everyone alive at the death of the testator)

These scenarios and "magical creatures" have sometimes led to the invalidation of trust interests and have often caused consternation. Accordingly, the Rule against Perpetuities may indeed be one of the least understood and least liked of legal rules, and most law students remember it only as a source of confusion in studying for the bar exam.

2. Savings Clauses, Reformation, and the Uniform Rules

Because of the sometimes bizarre and byzantine rules and assumptions associated with the Rule Against Perpetuities, reformers have sought to simplify the rule just as estate planners have sought to avoid it.

a. *Savings Clauses*

To avoid any problems or unintended mistakes due to the Rule against Perpetuities, estate planners have routinely included "savings" clauses when drafting trust documents. Here is an example:

> Notwithstanding any other provisions in this instrument, any trust created hereunder shall terminate, if it has not previously terminated, 21 years after the death of the survivor of the beneficiaries of the trust living at the date this instrument becomes effective. In case of such termination, the then remaining principal and undistributed income of the trust shall be distributed to the then income beneficiaries in the same proportions as they were, at the time of termination, entitled to receive the income.

Perpetuities savings clauses are incredibly common because, in the past, problems with trusts that violated the rule were frequent and judicial invalidation of these trusts resulted in many malpractice claims.

b. *Reform (or Cy Pres)*

Some states began to move away from the strict application of the Rule Against Perpetuities by allowing for reformation (or **cy pres**) doctrine, either by statute or judicial decision. In these states, courts may modify a trust that violates the Rule Against Perpetuities in order to carry out the testator's intention within the perpetuities period. (Remember, this is not an issue for charitable trusts, which are not subject to the Rule.)

c. *The Uniform Statutory Rule Against Perpetuities (USRAP)*

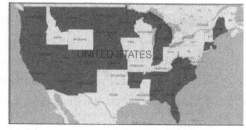

Another approach that states have adopted is the "wait-and-see" approach, which has been also embraced by uniform law. Pennsylvania was the first state to adopt this approach, and "wait-and-see" became the basis for the Uniform Statutory Rule Against Perpetuities in 1986. As of 2020, thirty-one states had adopted the USRAP.

This version of the Rule simplifies the formula by allowing courts to see what might happen with a contingent interest rather than invalidating such an interest because of what might happen. The USRAP drafters have remarked in the Act's comments: "Since the chains of events that make such interests invalid are so unlikely to happen, it was rather natural to propose that the criterion be shifted from possible post-creation events to actual post-creation events." The other innovation of this framework is that the waiting period is always ninety years, meant to approximate the common law "life in being plus twenty-one years" without forcing the calculations. Basically, then, courts wait ninety years to see whether an interest vests or not, and no interest is invalidated before that point. At the ninety-year mark, if the interest fails to vest, then the court has the power to reform the trust terms.

3. The Repeal of the Rule Against Perpetuities

Legal reformers have generally embraced the USRAP approach, but some states have gone even further and have abolished the Rule Against Perpetuities altogether. Repeal efforts have been led less by the desire for increased simplicity and rule reform and more by the desire of both states and trust companies to compete effectively for lucrative trust business. Changes in the tax code in 1986 propelled a number of states to repeal the Rule Against Perpetuities in order to allow for "perpetual" or "dynasty" trusts. Some states, like South Dakota, had repealed the rule even earlier, attempting to draw trust business to the state. This excerpt tells a little bit of the South Dakota story:

> Outsiders tend to know South Dakota for two things: Mount Rushmore, which is carved with the faces of four US presidents; and Laura Ingalls Wilder, who moved to the state as a girl and wrote the Little House on the Prairie series of children's books. But its biggest impact on the world comes from a lesser-known fact: it was ground

zero for the earthquake of financial deregulation that has rocked the world's economy. . . .

In 1983, [then Governor Janklow] abolished the Rule Against Perpetuities and, from that moment on, property placed in trust in South Dakota would stay there for ever. A rule created by English judges after centuries of consideration was erased by a law of just 19 words. Aristocracy was back in the game. . . .

A decade ago, South Dakotan trust companies held $57.3bn in assets. By the end of 2020, that total will have risen to $355.2bn. Those hundreds of billions of dollars are being regulated by a state with a population smaller than Norfolk, a part-time legislature heavily lobbied by trust lawyers, and an administration committed to welcoming as much of the world's money as it can. US politicians like to boast that their country is the best place in the world to get rich, but South Dakota has become something else: the best place in the world to stay rich.

Oliver Bullough, *The great American tax haven: why the super-rich love South Dakota*, THE GUARDIAN, Nov. 14, 2019.

When Delaware repealed the Rule Against Perpetuities in 1986, the state legislature explicitly stated the reason was to compete with other states, like South Dakota, who had already repealed the rule and were therefore able to attract trust business. The bill's synopsis stated:

Several states . . . have abolished altogether their rules against perpetuities, which has given those jurisdictions a competitive advantage over Delaware in attracting assets held in trusts created for estate planning purposes. . . .The multi-million dollar capital commitments to these irrevocable trusts . . . will result in the formation of a substantial capital base in the innovative jurisdictions that have abolished the rule against perpetuities. . . Delaware's repeal of the rule against perpetuities for personal property held in trust will demonstrate Delaware's continued vigilance in maintaining its role as a leading jurisdiction for the formation of capital and the conduct of trust business.

See ROBERT H. SITKOFF & JESSE DUKEMINIER, WILLS, TRUSTS, AND ESTATES, 10TH EDITION at 908 (2017)

As of 2020, thirty-four states have either repealed the Rule Against Perpetuities or, like Virginia, allow perpetual trusts for personal property on an opt-in basis while still maintaining the default rule of USRAP. Many of the same states that have fully repealed the Rule Against Perpetuities combine this trust feature with new forms of asset protection (which we will discuss in Chapter 11) and decanting (also discussed in Chapter 12) in order to market highly specialized and attractive trust forms to high-wealth clients.

NOTES

1.   In many ways, the benefits and the detriments of perpetual trusts are the same. What is a benefit to the trust settlor may be a detriment to future beneficiaries and even to the larger community. Perpetual trusts grew in popularity because they allowed trust settlors to take advantage of a loophole in the generation-skipping transfer (or "GST") tax. This loophole provides a tax exemption, and the perpetual trust compounds the tax avoidance potential. To read more about tax avoidance and perpetual trusts, see Mary Louise Fellows, *Why the Generation-Skipping Transfer Tax Sparked Perpetual Trusts*, 27 CARDOZO L. REV. 2511 (2005–2006); Max Schanzenbach & Robert Sitkoff, *Perpetuities or Taxes—Explaining the Rise of the Perpetual Trust*, 27 CARDOZO L. REV. 2465 (2005–2006); and Lawrence Waggoner, *Effectively Curbing the GST Exemption for Perpetual Trusts*, TAX NOTES, Vol. 135, No. 10, June 2012.

2.   Another objection that arises with perpetual trusts is a policy problem related to dead-hand control, a problem some call "first-generation monopoly." Philosophers from Adam Smith to Thomas Jefferson all held the strong belief that every generation possessed a right to exert control over the property around them and they supported the limits established by a perpetuities period. Thomas Jefferson famously said: "I suppose to be self-evident, 'that the earth belongs in usufruct to the living': that the dead have neither powers nor rights over it." What do you see as the problems with allowing increased amounts of dead-hand control? For more on this question, see Jesse Dukeminier & James Krier, *The Rise of the Perpetual Trust*, 50 UCLA L. REV. 1303 (2002–2003).

3.   How do perpetual trusts square with some state constitutions? Robert Sitkoff and Steven Horowitz write:

> [L]ittle-noticed provisions in the constitutions of nine states, including in five that purport to allow perpetual (or effectively perpetual) trusts, proscribe "perpetuities." The North Carolina provision, which dates back to 1776, is illustrative: "Perpetuities and monopolies are contrary to the genius of a free state and shall not be allowed."

Steven J. Horowitz & Robert H. Sitkoff, *Unconstitutional Perpetual Trusts*, 67 VAND. L. REV. 1769, 1772 (2014). They ask, "Is a statute that authorizes perpetual (or effectively perpetual) trusts constitutional in a state with such a provision? Should a court in a state with such a provision give effect to another state's?" *Id.* How would you respond to these questions? For one answer, see *Brown Bros. Harriman Trust Co. v. Benson*, 688 S.E.2d 752 (N.C. App. 2010) (upholding a perpetual trust statute).

ASSESSMENT

Imagine that your state legislature is debating repeal of the Rule Against Perpetuities (maybe they already did). Imagine the constituent groups—who is advocating for repeal and who, if anyone, is countering those arguments? Consider the viewpoint of the trust industry, the business community, the legal community, and the general citizenry. For each group, write down why the members of this group are either in favor of or against the repeal.

H. Conclusion and Takeaways

A trust is always a tripartite arrangement between a settlor, a trustee, and a beneficiary. The settlor funds the trust; the trustee manages the property in the trust, and distributes the assets to the beneficiary as the trust instrument directs; and the beneficiary receives income from the trust and/or enjoys and uses the trust property. A trust must be funded at the time of creation or funded at the time of death if it is a testamentary trust. Trusts can be revocable or irrevocable, or a trust can be charitable. Traditionally, trust duration was limited by the Rule Against Perpetuities. Recently, some jurisdictions have modified or abolished the rule, allowing trusts to last longer—sometimes far longer—than before. Now that you understand what a trust is and how (and why) it is created, the next chapter turns to the heart of the trust: fiduciary duties.

CHAPTER 9 COMPREHENSIVE ASSESSMENTS

1. **PREPARE A COUNSELING PLAN.** Luis and Elena come to you for estate planning. They are in their 30s and have two children who are four and ten. Their goals for estate planning are straightforward: they want each to inherit from the other, and, if something happens to both of them, they want to provide for their children. Luis's brother is an investment banker, who is married and has one young child. Elena's sister is an elementary school teacher, married, with no children. Both of these siblings would be willing to take care of Elena and

Luis's children if Elena and Luis were both to die. Prepare a counseling plan for them, addressing the following:

a.   Do you recommend a trust as part of the plan? If not, why not? If so, when should it come into existence and how should it be structured? Would the trust take effect on the first death or only on the death of the survivor? Would it be a single "pot" trust for both children, separate trusts for each, or a single trust that breaks into separate trusts when each child reaches a certain age?

b.   What roles should Luis's brother and Elena's sister play in the event something happens to both Luis and Elena?

2.   **DRAFT AN ADVICE COLUMN.** Here is a letter asking for advice from *The Moneyist*, an MSN personal finance columnist:

> My mother plans to leave her house, which is paid in full, equally to me and my sister. This has already been addressed with her will. However, she ultimately wants it to go to her grandchildren. I have one child and my sister has two children. As it stands now, my sister and I will each inherit 50% of the house, meaning my child will inherit my half and my sister's kids will get her half. My daughter is 12 years of age, and my sister's kids are aged 16 and 19. We know our mom's intention is for the kids to equally have part of the home. Does that sound fair to you? When the house passes to us, what do we need to do so that the kids each get one-third of the house? My husband and I have an estate plan, but my sister and her husband do not.

Draft a response using what you have learned in this chapter and giving advice to the author about how she can best resolve this situation with her sister.

Test Your Knowledge

To assess your understanding of the material in this chapter, click here to take a quiz.

CHAPTER 10

Private Trusts II: Fiduciary Duties

CHAPTER LEARNING OUTCOMES

Following your work with the material in this chapter, you should be able to do the following:

- Develop criteria for the selection of a trustee or trustees based on the nature of the trust, the intent of the settlor, and the identity of the beneficiaries

- Explain to a potential trustee the nature of the trustee's fiduciary duties and the conduct the trustee should follow to satisfy these duties

- Explain to a potential trustee the nature of her duty to inform the beneficiaries about the trust, including the information she is required to transmit, which beneficiaries must be informed, and how often information must be provided

- Explain to a potential trustee and a settlor the use and limitations of exculpatory clauses in trusts

- Analyze the facts of a particular case to determine whether the trustee has breached any duties and describe what defenses might be available

- Describe the remedies that are available for a breach of any of the duties and predict under what circumstances a court might order them

A. Introduction

Now that we've established what a trust is, this chapter and the next discuss the people who are central to its ongoing operation: the trustee (this chapter) and the beneficiary (the next chapter). Each of these positions in the trust triangle has its own set of laws. In the case of the trustee, the laws mainly address the trustee's duties to the beneficiary; the laws relevant to the beneficiary mainly address the beneficiary's (and the beneficiary's creditors') rights to the trust assets.

The trustee plays the central role in the trust relationship. One author has described the role as "serving as the primary ongoing link between the dead and the living."[1] As this author goes on to observe, "the trustee wields significant power over the trust and its beneficiaries. The trustee's decision-making and relationship with those beneficiaries determine whether a trust functions smoothly or is beset by conflict. The identity of whomever is appointed to serve in this role is thus a critical decision to any property owner who is considering using a trust vehicle."[2] Many myths surround the figure of the trustee: is he the grey-haired older male mentor of myth and story, or the stingy scrooge, also of myth and story? Or does the trustee take on some other form? As we proceed, it's worth thinking about our own preconceptions about this figure, and to remember that, above all, the trustee is only human, and bound by laws. This is true even if the official trustee is an institution, such as a bank.

The trustee's duty to the beneficiary is a fiduciary one. This means that the trustee must always act, in dealing with the trust assets, in the interests of the beneficiaries and the trust and never in the trustee's own interest. This duty consists of a series of rules that govern the trustee's interaction with the beneficiaries and the trust: **the duty of obedience to the settlor's intent**, the **duty of loyalty to the beneficiaries**, the **duty of prudence**, the **duty of impartiality**, and the **duty to inform and report**. In this chapter, we will examine each of these duties in turn.

You, as an attorney, will deal with the trustee at both ends of the process. For example, at the estate planning stage, you may advise the settlor about the choice of the trustee or trustees; although the prior chapter started you thinking about these choices, the fiduciary duties described in this chapter and the distribution provisions described in the next may cause you to rethink how you choose a trustee. As an estate planning lawyer, you also will draft instructions to the trustee about to distribute and manage the assets of the trust. From the litigation angle, you may review an accounting or trust to determine if a trustee has breached any duties. Over the past two decades, drafters and lawmakers have imported increasing flexibility into the laws of fiduciary duty, making some of the rules waivable by the settlor, and creating exceptions to the trustee's duty to act solely in the trust's interest and never in her own. Part of your job as attorney is to advise clients about the wisdom of such waivers in their own instruments

---

[1]   Deborah S. Gordon, *Engendering Trust*, 2019 WIS. L. REV. 213, 229 (2019).

[2]   *Id.*

of trust. You may also find yourself advising a trustee about her duties under specific trust provisions, or a beneficiary about what she can demand from the trustee.

Before breaking down the trustee's duties, **Part B** explains how a trustee can accept and resign a trusteeship. **Part C** then explores in depth the fiduciary duties that govern a trustee's actions as they relate to all the various facets of trust administration, including investment and distribution. Finally, in **Part D**, we take up the question of **exculpatory clauses** and examine to what extent a trustee can be exculpated from following the rules of fiduciary duty.

B. Acceptance and Resignation of Trusteeship

A person who is nominated as trustee is under no obligation to serve as trustee and may decline the nomination. Because a trustee is subject to the myriad obligations of fiduciary duty and exposed to liability for breaching these obligations, the designated trustee must make some sign of affirmative acceptance. Once a person has accepted a trusteeship, there is then a procedure that the person must follow in order to resign. Below are the UTC rules for acceptance and resignation.

UTC § 701 Accepting or Declining Trusteeship

(a)   Except as otherwise provided in subsection (c), a person designated as trustee accepts the trusteeship:

(1)   by substantially complying with a method of acceptance provided in the terms of the trust; or

(2)   if the terms of the trust do not provide a method or the method provided in the terms is not expressly made exclusive, by accepting delivery of the trust property, exercising powers or performing duties as trustee, or otherwise indicating acceptance of the trusteeship.

(b)   A person designated as trustee who has not yet accepted the trusteeship may reject the trusteeship. A designated trustee who does not accept the trusteeship within a reasonable time after knowing of the designation is deemed to have rejected the trusteeship.

(c)   A person designated as trustee, without accepting the trusteeship, may:

(1)　act to preserve the trust property if, within a reasonable time after acting, the person sends a rejection of the trusteeship to the settlor or, if the settlor is dead or lacks capacity, to a qualified beneficiary; and

(2)　inspect or investigate trust property to determine potential liability under environmental or other law or for any other purpose.

———————

Notice that under (a)(1), the trustee may accept the role of trustee by complying with the method prescribed in the instrument. When you draft a trust for a client, the trust instrument will specify the method by which the trustee accepts the position. Usually, the trust instrument will direct that acceptance be made in a writing delivered to the settlor or the settlor's counsel. The trust may also indicate whether the method prescribed by the instrument is the exclusive way of accepting trusteeship. UTC § 701 mostly serves as a default rule for situations when an attorney did not draft the trust, and a dispute arises about whether someone accepted the role of trustee. Notice also that the person nominated for the role may decline under (2)(b).

A person can accept the role (and duties) of a trustee without a formal procedure—and sometimes without even realizing that they have accepted the role of a fiduciary. Consider the following example.

Example: A father's employer gives him a U.S. Savings Bond and tells the father the bond is for his children's college fund. The father puts the bond in a separate bank account and keeps it there. After a few years, however, the father has some financial problems and cashes the bond out to pay some bills. Did the father violate a fiduciary duty?

Answer: Yes, accepting the money and segregating it in a separate account, the father implicitly accepted the duties of a trustee and the fiduciary role attached to them. By not comingling it with his own assets, he demonstrated his understanding that the money was not his and that he had a duty to preserve it for its intended use.

———————

UTC § 705 Resignation of Trustee

(a)　A trustee may resign:

(1)　upon at least 30 days' notice to the qualified beneficiaries, the settlor, if living, and all cotrustees; or

(2)　with the approval of the court.

(b) In approving a resignation, the court may issue orders and impose conditions reasonably necessary for the protection of the trust property.

(c) Any liability of a resigning trustee or of any sureties on the trustee's bond for acts or omissions of the trustee is not discharged or affected by the trustee's resignation.

If all the beneficiaries and any living Settlor agree, the trustee may resign. If the beneficiaries do not accept her resignation, the trustee must get a court order.

ASSESSMENT

You are the trustee of the Logan Family Trust, and the eldest of the three Logan siblings. Your father made you trustee because he thought you would be best at making impartial judgments about distributions to the beneficiaries, all of his three children. You have become fed up, however, with your siblings' constant demands for money and squabbles with each other. You want to resign. Your father drew up the trust instrument himself, and it lacks any directions for a trustee on what procedure to follow when resigning. You don't think your siblings will object (they insist that they could do everything better), and your sister Belle wants to be trustee anyway.

a. Draft a letter establishing your resignation as trustee.

b. Draft a letter for your sister to sign to accept the role of trustee.

C. The Trustee's Duties

Historically, trustees were not subject to fiduciary duties. Trusts most often contained land, meaning that there were fewer opportunities for trustee mismanagement of assets, and trust law guarded against trustee abuse by severely limiting trustee powers. The modern rules take a different approach. Recognizing that trusts now hold a variety of assets, which are increasingly liquid and not land-based, trust law has chosen to empower trustees and then hold them accountable through their fiduciary duties. This approach is set forth in the RESTATEMENT (THIRD) OF TRUSTS, which states that "a trustee presumptively has comprehensive powers to manage the trust estate and otherwise to carry out the terms and purpose of the trust, but that all powers held in the capacity of trustee must be exercised, or not exercised, in accordance with the trustee's fiduciary obligations."

Now, once a nominated trustee has accepted that role, the trustee is subject to a range of fiduciary obligations and must take affirmative steps to ensure the proper administration of the trust. The requirements and obligations of fiduciary duty are designed to regulate the trustee's actions both in her relationship with the beneficiaries and also in her management of the trust assets. A trustee who is found to have breached one or more of these duties may be removed from office for cause, and the beneficiaries will be entitled to restitution. The following sections describe each duty, but you will see that they overlap.

1. Duty of Obedience

The duty of obedience refers to the trustee's duty to follow the settlor's wishes as to the disposition of the trust. In general, the trustee determines these wishes from the terms of the trust instrument, but there are other ways the settlor can communicate her intent to the trustee. A dilemma of trust drafting is the need to give the trustee direction without binding the trustee's hands in case of unanticipated developments, such as a child being born disabled, a grandchild being adopted, a descendant developing a substance abuse problem, or someone dying unexpectedly. As you can imagine, reminiscent of the sound of one hand clapping, this might be called "the Zen of trust law." It is very hard to achieve the right balance.

With respect to the duty of obedience, the UTC provides:

UTC § 801 Duty to Administer Trust

Upon acceptance of a trusteeship, the trustee shall administer the trust in good faith, in accordance with its terms and purposes and the interests of the beneficiaries, and in accordance with this [Code].

When drafting the trust instrument, the attorney should get enough specifics from the settlor about her wishes to be able to provide guidance to the trustee. For example, if the settlor wants the trustee to make distributions to pay for a beneficiary's welfare, what does "welfare" mean to the settlor? Does it mean expensive vacations, luxury homes and cars, or does it mean a decent standard of living without any frills? Other questions might include whether to consider the beneficiary's other sources of income when making a distribution, and, if there are several beneficiaries, whether the trustee should equalize the distributions to each one or instead make distributions according to each beneficiary's unique needs.

One way to balance the need for flexibility with the desire to provide clear guidance is to supplement the trust provisions with a **"letter of wishes"** to the trustee from the settlor. This is a separate document, and not legally binding, so the beneficiaries do not need to see it. A letter of wishes can elaborate for the trustee the settlor's hopes and aspirations for the use of the trust assets without binding the trustee to act in literal obedience to those wishes. In other words, it expresses the spirit of the trust rather than the law. These kinds of documents may be particularly important when the trust is a discretionary one, as we will discuss in Chapter 11.

> **Connection Note:** In many respects, the letter of wishes resembles the ethical will that we discussed in Chapter 3. Both are aspirational and not legally binding but can be quite meaningful to the writer and the recipients.

In practice, the duty of obedience arises at planning for the settlor, in the counseling and representation of trustees, and in litigation for trustees and beneficiaries. In estate planning, you will draft trust provisions that will give the trustee clear guidance as to the settlor's wishes. You also may advise trustees about their duties on an ongoing basis, including how to interpret the standards in a trust. From the litigation perspective, you may represent a beneficiary who believes that the trustee violated the duty of obedience by failing to follow the settlor's wishes or may defend the trustee against those claims by beneficiaries. Keep all these perspectives in mind while reading the material in this chapter.

ASSESSMENTS

1.   Your client, Carmella, is a well-to-do older woman who wants to set up a trust for her grandchildren's education. In anticipation of your meeting with Carmella, prepare a list of questions to ask Carmella that will help you understand and draft for her intent regarding the meaning of "education," including exactly what she would like to pay for and what expenses she might want to exclude.

2.   Now assume you represent the trustee of Carmella's trust. The trustee is seeking advice about the trust, which was drafted by a different attorney several years ago. There are three grandchildren, Kim (age 25), Aliah (age 20), and Malcolm (age 18). Malcolm is applying to college and hoping to get into an Ivy

> **Language Note:** If a court ever describes how a fiduciary should act by using the phrase "[t]he punctilio of an honor the most sensitive," you can be fairly certain that the fiduciary has breached one or more duties. This famous quotation comes from Justice (then judge) Cardozo's opinion in *Meinhard v. Salmon*, 164 N.E. 545 (N.Y. 1928).

League school but knows that he has a better shot if he doesn't indicate on his application that he needs financial support. The trust has already paid for Kim's college degree at a public university and is paying for Aliah's. Malcolm has asked the trustee to set aside enough funds to pay Ivy League tuition. Kim wants to go to medical school, Aliah has two more years of college, and she plans to go to law school. The settlor's letter of wishes states: "I want to pay for my grandchildren's education because I believe that education is the foundation for success in life." The trustee asks you what she should do. What do you advise her? Is there anything else you want to know?

2. Duty of Loyalty

One of the most fundamental rules that a trustee must follow is the duty of loyalty, which is meant to guard against the potential for divided interests. The duty of loyalty prohibits **self-dealing**, including any **conflict of interest**. This prohibition is meant to disallow any transactions in which the trustee would be on both sides of the deal. A trustee may not engage in any such activity, even one with the appearance of self-interest, and this prohibition extends not just to the trustee but also to a trustee's close family members and any representatives of the trustee.

Benjamin Cardozo was a famous jurist who was the Chief Judge of the New York Court of Appeals and an Associate Justice of the U.S. Supreme Court.

a. *Common Law Rule*

Traditionally, the law barred the trustee from any dealing with trust property that benefited the trustee personally. These transactions were strictly prohibited under the common law of trusts, even if the trustee could show that the transaction was fair and profitable for both herself and the beneficiaries.

This rule is known as the "**no further inquiry**" rule, which essentially states that once a trustee engages in some form of self-dealing, there will be "no further inquiry" into the merits and fairness of the transaction to the trust and the beneficiaries.

The case below, *In re Gleeson's Will*, involves a trustee who argued for an exception to the no further inquiry rule because the trustee's decision to continue to farm the settlor's land even after accepting the role of trustee provided a benefit to the trust. As you read the case, think about what purposes underlie the no further inquiry rule. This strict rule differentiates the trust law standard for the duty of loyalty from the corporate law standard, which allows for "self-dealing" if the transaction is fair or benefits the corporation.

In re Gleeson's Will

124 N.E.2d 624 (Ill. App. Ct. 1955)

CARROLL, J.

Mary Gleeson, who died testate on February 14, 1952, owned among other properties, 160 acres of farmland in Christian County, Illinois. By her will admitted to Probate March 29, 1952, she nominated Con Colbrook, petitioner-appellee, executor thereof. Colbrook was also appointed as trustee under the will and the residuary estate, including the aforesaid 160 acres of land, was devised to him in trust for the benefit of decedent's 3 children, Helen Black, Bernadine Gleeson, and Thomas Gleeson, an incompetent, who are respondents herein.

On March 1, 1950, the testator leased the 160 acres for the year ending March 1, 1951 to Colbrook. On March 1, 1951, she again leased the premises to Colbrook for the year ending March 1, 1952. Upon the expiration of this latter lease, Colbrook held over as tenant under the provisions thereof and farmed the land until March 1, 1953, at which time Colbrook leased the land to another tenant. While there is no written lease in evidence, the record indicates the terms thereof provided for payment to the lessor of $10 per acre cash rent and a share in the crops of $1/2$ of the corn and $2/5$ of the small grain.

Colbrook's appointment as trustee was confirmed by the Circuit Court of Christian County on April 29, 1953. On July 22, 1953, he filed his first semi-annual report, and respondents filed certain objections. We are concerned here with only one of the said objections, which is as follows:

'1. Report shows trustee was cotenant of trust real estate but fails to account for share of profits received by trustee as co-tenant which by law should be re-paid by him to trust estate.'

The record indicates no dispute as to the fact that Colbrook as trustee leased a portion of the real estate of the trust to himself as a partner of William Curtin and that Colbrook received a share of the profits realized by him and Curtin from their farming operation of said real estate. Upon a hearing the Court entered an order overruling the objection of the respondents to the report. From such order respondents have brought this appeal.

It is contended by respondents that the Circuit Court erred in overruling their objection for the reason that the law prohibits a trustee from dealing in his individual capacity with the trust and making a profit from such dealings.

The Courts of this state have consistently followed a general principle of equity that a trustee cannot deal in his individual capacity with the trust property. Colbrook recognizes the existence of this general rule but argues that, because of the existence of the peculiar circumstances under which he proceeded, the instant case must be taken to constitute one of the rare exceptions to such rule. The circumstances alluded to as peculiar are pointed out as being the facts that the death of Mrs. Gleeson occurred on February 14, 1952, only 15 days prior to the beginning of the 1952 farm year; that satisfactory farm tenants are not always available, especially on short notice; that the petitioner had in the preceding fall of 1951 sown part of the 160 acres in wheat to be harvested in 1952; that the holding over by the trustee and his partner was in the best interests of the trust; that the same was done in an open manner; that Colbrook was honest with the trust; and that it suffered no loss as a result of the transaction.

Colbrook contends that since only 15 days intervened between the death of Mrs. Gleeson and the beginning of the farm year, and that good tenant farmers might not be available at such a time, it was in the interests of the trust that he continue to hold over for the year of 1952. No showing is made that Colbrook, as trustee, tried to obtain a satisfactory tenant to replace Colbrook and Curtin on March 1, 1952. The record discloses that subsequent to the testator's death, Colbrook discussed continuance of the farming operation with two of the beneficiaries under the trust and voluntarily raised the cash rent from $6 to $10 per acre. This evidence tending to show that Colbrook was interested in continuing a tenancy under which he was leasing trust property to himself would seem to refute any contention that an effort to lease the property to anyone other than the partnership was made. The fact that the partners had sown wheat on the land in the fall of 1951 cannot be said to be a peculiar circumstance. It is not suggested that the trust would have suffered a loss if someone other than Colbrook had farmed the land in 1952 and harvested the wheat. It would appear that a satisfactory adjustment covering the matter of the wheat could have been made between the trust and the partnership without great difficulty.

The good faith and honesty of Colbrook, as trustee, or the fact that the trust sustained no loss on account of his dealings therewith, are all matters which can avail petitioner nothing so far as a justification of the course he chose to take in dealing with trust property is concerned.

We think the holding of the Court in *Johnson v. Sarver*, 113 N.E.2d 584 (Ill. App.), is applicable to the question to be decided in the instant case. Among the questions with which the Court dealt in that case was the right of trustees to lease real estate of the trust to themselves. Holding that the trustees were without power to do so, the Court had this to say:

> Counsel for appellants state that the holding of the chancellor to the effect that the trustees must refrain from self-dealing and cease to occupy their homes as tenants unduly discriminates against them, inasmuch as none of the other children were required to abandon their accustomed modes of making an independent living in order to share in the benefits of the trust. A trustee must maintain a high level of conduct and owes to those whose property he controls undivided loyalty. It is not compulsory or mandatory that any of the trustees accept the appointment made by their father. They have accepted and asked the court to instruct them as to their duties, and if they are dissatisfied with the amount of compensation or any other requirement which the court has imposed, there is a method by which they can be relieved of their duties. The chancellor properly decreed that appellants, as trustees, cannot lease the real estate involved in this trust to themselves or deal with themselves.

We think the decision in the foregoing case suggests that Colbrook, upon the death of the testatrix, instead of conferring with her beneficiaries concerning continuance of his tenancy of the trust property, should have then decided whether he chose to continue as a tenant or to act as trustee. His election was to act as trustee and as such he could not deal with himself.

This Court, therefore, reaches the conclusion that the Circuit Court erred in overruling respondent's objection to the trustee's amended first semi-annual report, and that petitioner should have been required to recast his first semi-annual report and to account therein for all monies received by him personally as a profit by virtue of his being a co-tenant of trust property during the 1952 crop year, and to pay the amount of any such profit to the trust.

Reversed and remanded.

NOTES

1. Does the outcome and the application of the no further inquiry rule in *Gleason* seem harsh? Does such a strict application of the rule to a well-meaning and honest trustee—who may also be a friend or family member and may not know the rule—discourage people from accepting the role of trustee? Would it be acceptable for a trustee to engage in a transaction with the trust if it were beneficial and fair to both the trustee and the trust? The concerns above, as well as the sense that a mutually beneficial transaction should not result in punishing a faithful trustee, led the drafters of the UTC to modify this rule, as discussed in the following section.

2. What should the remedies be for breach? The usual remedies are "disgorgement" and compensatory damages. Disgorgement means that the trustee has to return all the gain she received in the transaction. In *Gleeson*, that meant returning to the trust any profits made from farming the 160 acres. Compensatory damages, which you may recall from contract law, refers to compensating the injured party for additional losses he may have suffered because of the self-dealing.

b. Self-Dealing Under the Uniform Trust Code

In an attempt to smooth out some of the more severe edges of the common law rule, the UTC made some modifications. As you can see below, UTC § 802 allows for certain exceptions to the rule against self-dealing:

UTC § 802 Duty of Loyalty

(a) A trustee shall administer the trust solely in the interest of the beneficiaries.

(b) Subject to the rights of persons dealing with or assisting the trustee as provided in Section 1012, a sale, encumbrance, or other transaction involving the investment or management of trust property entered into by the trustee for the trustee's own personal account or which is otherwise affected by a conflict between the trustee's fiduciary and personal interests is voidable by a beneficiary affected by the transaction unless:

(1)   the transaction was authorized by the terms of the trust;

(2)   the transaction was approved by the court;

(3)   the beneficiary did not commence a judicial proceeding within the time allowed by Section 1005;

(4)   the beneficiary consented to the trustee's conduct, ratified the transaction, or released the trustee in compliance with Section 1009; or

(5)   the transaction involves a contract entered into or claim acquired by the trustee before the person became or contemplated becoming trustee.

(c)   A sale, encumbrance, or other transaction involving the investment or management of trust property is presumed to be affected by a conflict between personal and fiduciary interests if it is entered into by the trustee with:

(1)   the trustee's spouse;

(2)   the trustee's descendants, siblings, parents, or their spouses;

(3)   an agent or attorney of the trustee; or

(4)   a corporation or other person or enterprise in which the trustee, or a person who owns a significant interest in the trustee, has an interest that might affect the trustee's best judgment.

———————————

Notice that UTC § 802(b) creates some exceptions to the duty of loyalty: a self-dealing transaction is allowed if the transaction was authorized by the terms of the trust instrument, approved by a court, or authorized by the trustee. Notice also that there is a time limit on the beneficiary to file an action under this section. Section 802(c) rejects the no further inquiry rule in favor of creating a presumption, which a trustee can rebut by showing an absence of conflict.

The UTC's limitations of the rule against self-dealing and its abrogation of the no further inquiry rule is controversial and has sparked considerable debate. In support, John Langbein, one of the drafters of the UTC, argues that the rule is a relic of the eighteenth and nineteenth centuries, when trust cases were adjudicated in chancery court, which lacked authority to find facts and assess evidence. This prohibition made it difficult for a beneficiary to prove malfeasance by the trustee. Today, Langbein argues, fact-finding and extensive regulation have eliminated this need. He also asserts that the rule does actual harm in that it over-deters by preventing trustees from engaging in transactions that will benefit both the trust and its beneficiaries. Langbein urges that self-dealing transactions be evaluated, instead, on whether they are in the best interest of the trust and the beneficiaries. *See* John H. Langbein, *Questioning the Trust Law Duty of Loyalty: Sole Interest or Best Interest?*, 114 YALE L.J. 929, 944 (2005). In response, Melanie Leslie argues that the proposed "best interests" standard would impose the risk of serious harm on beneficiaries, and that the no further inquiry rule is not as problematic as Langbein suggests. Leslie notes that most beneficiaries are not in a good position to monitor the trustee's behavior, that beneficiaries cannot simply leave the relationship when they are unsatisfied, and there are no market or social forces at play to control the trustee's actions. *See* Melanie B. Leslie, *In Defense of the No Further Inquiry Rule: A Response to Professor John Langbein*, 47 WM. & MARY L. REV. 541 (2005).

UTC § 802 codifies the common law exception that a trustee can charge fees for acting as trustee. In addition to modifying the no further inquiry rule, the UTC makes other adjustments to the common law duty of loyalty:

UTC § 802 Duty of Loyalty

(f)   An investment by a trustee in securities of an investment company or investment trust to which the trustee, or its affiliate, provides services in a capacity other than as trustee is not presumed to be affected by a conflict between personal and fiduciary interests if the investment otherwise complies with the prudent investor rule of Article 9. In addition to its compensation for acting as trustee, the trustee may be compensated by the investment company or investment trust for providing those services out of fees charged to the trust. If the trustee receives compensation from the investment company or investment trust for providing investment advisory or investment management services, the trustee must at least annually notify the persons entitled under Section 813 to receive a copy of the trustee's annual report of the rate and method by which that compensation was determined.

(g)   In voting shares of stock or in exercising powers of control over similar interests in other forms of enterprise, the trustee shall act in the best interests of the beneficiaries. If the trust is the sole owner of a corporation or other form of enterprise, the trustee shall elect or appoint directors or other managers who will manage the corporation or enterprise in the best interests of the beneficiaries.

(h)   This section does not preclude the following transactions, if fair to the beneficiaries:

(1)   an agreement between a trustee and a beneficiary relating to the appointment or compensation of the trustee;

(2)   payment of reasonable compensation to the trustee;

(3)   a transaction between a trust and another trust, decedent's estate, or[conservatorship] of which the trustee is a fiduciary or in which a beneficiary has an interest;

(4)   a deposit of trust money in a regulated financial-service institution operated by the trustee; or

(5)   an advance by the trustee of money for the protection of the trust.

———————

UTC § 802(f) creates an exception to the no further inquiry rule for mutual funds: a trustee may make fees for investing in mutual funds with assets of a trust for which she is trustee. Is this a necessary change to accommodate modern investment realities, understanding that institutional trustees are much more common than they used to be, or is this modification a license for trustees to shortchange the trust and the beneficiaries?

ASSESSMENTS

1.   Your client, Hans, is a trustee for his brother's trust. The trust contains the following property: an apartment building; several office buildings; an undeveloped parcel of land in the business district of the town; and considerable assets in cash and stocks. The trust beneficiaries are Hans's adult children; Hans's brother passed away two years ago. Hans is a businessman himself and is skilled at managing property and investing. Hans also knows the children and the family very well and is in a good position to assess their needs. He comes to you for advice. He is thinking about engaging in the following transactions, but he knows about the duty of loyalty and is worried that some of them may get him into trouble. Advise Hans.

a.   Hans wants to rent out one of the suites in one of the office buildings the trust owns for his own business. He'll pay market rates, and in fact, there is a building with an empty suite that needs to be rented out.

b.   Hans wants to use some of the assets in the trust as collateral for a loan. He is sure he'll pay off the loan quickly and that there's no risk of loss to the trust.

c. Hans is engaged in negotiations with another company in town to lease some of its land for a building project. He knows that this company is eager to develop the parcel of land owned by the trust and asks you what you think of him making sure they get to develop the trust's parcel to sweeten the deal he wants to make with them. There are other bidders for the project, but Hans assures you he knows the company will pay a competitive price.

d. Hans wants to borrow money from the trust to invest in a new startup tech stock. He tells you it is a great investment. Hans has made a lot of money in the past investing in tech stock.

2. Imagine that instead of advising Hans on actions he can take as trustee for his brother's trust, you were engaged by Hans's brother to create the trust in the first instance. The brother wants to allow Hans, as trustee, to engage in any financial transactions, even if he is self-interested, so long as the trust benefits. What language would you include in the trust to authorize Hans to do so?

3. Duty of Prudence

The duty of prudence (also called the duty of care) encompasses several duties, most of which involve caring for and managing assets being held in trust. These duties range from administrative duties, such as earmarking the trust property and recordkeeping, to more substantive duties, such as distributing assets to beneficiaries and investing those assets.

The applicable section of the UTC states:

UTC § 804 Prudent Administration

A trustee shall administer the trust as a prudent person would, by considering the purposes, terms, distributional requirements, and other circumstances of the trust. In satisfying this standard, the trustee shall exercise reasonable care, skill, and caution.

In the following sections, we explain the duty to care for the trust property, the duty to inquire, and the duties associated with investment, including diversifying and allocating income and principal properly.

a. *Duty to Care for the Trust Property*

Several UTC sections deal with the duty to care for and manage the trust property, including UTC § 809, the duty to control and protect trust property; UTC § 811, the duty to enforce claims of the trust and defend against claims against the trust; and UTC § 812, the duty to compel a former trustee to transfer the trust property and to take "reasonable steps" to pursue breach claims against a former trustee. UTC § 810, which follows, sets out the duty to keep records and segregate the trust property:

UTC § 810 Recordkeeping and Identification of Trust Property

(a) A trustee shall keep adequate records of the administration of the trust.

(b) A trustee shall keep trust property separate from the trustee's own property.

(c) Except as otherwise provided in subsection (d), a trustee shall cause the trust property to be designated so that the interest of the trust, to the extent feasible, appears in records maintained by a party other than a trustee or beneficiary.

(d) If the trustee maintains records clearly indicating the respective interests, a trustee may invest as a whole the property of two or more separate trusts.

Talk about a breach of fiduciary duty: Richard the I, also known as Richard the Lionheart, went off on the Crusades and left the kingdom in the care of his younger brother, King John, who became the most hated King in English history. King John, British School, c.1618–20, Dulwich Picture Gallery.

The key requirements here are the duty to segregate the assets and to earmark them for their intended purpose. Failure to segregate the trust assets from the trustee's own property risks the attachment of the property by the trustee's creditors. Earmarking means labeling the property as intended for the use of the beneficiary. For example, this means that real property should be re-deeded in the name of the trustee: "A, as Trustee for the Children's Trust." Bank accounts and stock accounts should be similarly titled. Tangible personal property— jewelry, art—should be listed on a schedule attached to a declaration of trust.

b.   Duty to Inquire

Even a trustee who has full discretion cannot sit idly by and wait for the beneficiary to ask for distributions. As the following case shows, the trustee must make it his business to inquire as to the beneficiary's needs. As you read *Marsman v. Nasca*, pay special attention to the terms of the trust for Cappy and consider how the duty of inquiry overlaps with some of the other fiduciary duties we have discussed.

Marsman v. Nasca

573 N.E.2d 1025 (Mass. App. Ct. 1991)

DREBEN, J.

This appeal raises the following questions: Does a trustee, holding a discretionary power to pay principal for the "comfortable support and maintenance" of a beneficiary, have a duty to inquire into the financial resources of that beneficiary so as to recognize his needs? If so, what is the remedy for such failure? A Probate Court judge held that the will involved in this case imposed a duty of inquiry upon the trustee. We agree with this conclusion but disagree with the remedy imposed and accordingly vacate the judgment and remand for further proceedings.

1. Facts

Sara Wirt Marsman died in September 1971, survived by her second husband, T. Frederik Marsman (Cappy), and her daughter by her first marriage, Sally Marsman Marlette. Mr. James F. Farr, her lawyer for many years, drew her will and was the trustee thereunder.[4]

Article IIA of Sara's will provided in relevant part:

> It is my desire that my husband, T. Fred Marsman, be provided *with reasonable maintenance, comfort and support* after my death. Accordingly, if my said husband is living at the time of my death, I give to my trustees, who shall set the same aside as a separate trust fund, one-third (⅓) of the rest, residue and remainder of my estate . . .; they shall pay the net income therefrom to my said husband at least quarterly during his life; and *after having considered the various available sources of support for him,* my trustees shall, if they deem it necessary or desirable from time to time, in their sole and uncontrolled discretion, pay over to him, or use, apply and/or expend for his direct or indirect benefit such amount or amounts of the principal thereof as they shall deem advisable for his *comfortable support and maintenance.*

(Emphasis supplied). Article IIB provided:

> Whatever remains of said separate trust fund, including any accumulated income thereon on the death of my husband, shall be added to the trust fund established under Article IIC.

Article IIC established a trust for the benefit of Sally and her family. Sally was given the right to withdraw principal and, on her death, the trust was to continue for the benefit of her issue and surviving husband. The will also contained the following exculpatory clause:

> No trustee hereunder shall ever be liable except for his own willful neglect or default.

During their marriage, Sara and Cappy lived well and entertained frequently. Cappy's main interest in life centered around horses. An expert horseman, he was riding director and instructor at the Dana Hall School in

---

[4] The will provided for two trustees; however, one resigned in April, 1972, and thereafter Farr acted as sole trustee.

Wellesley until he was retired due to age in 1972. Sally, who was also a skilled rider, viewed Cappy as her mentor, and each had great affection for the other. Sara, wealthy from her prior marriage, managed the couple's financial affairs. She treated Cappy as "Lord of the Manor" and gave him money for his personal expenses, including an extensive wardrobe from one of the finest men's stores in Wellesley.

In 1956, Sara and Cappy purchased, as tenants by the entirety, the property in Wellesley which is the subject of this litigation. Although title to the property passed to Cappy by operation of law on Sara's death, Sara's will also indicated an intent to convey her interest in the property to Cappy. In the will, Cappy was also given a life estate in the household furnishings with remainder to Sally.

After Sara's death in 1971, Farr met with Cappy and Sally and held what he termed his "usual family conference" going over the provisions of the will. At the time of Sara's death, the Wellesley property was appraised at $29,000, and the principal of Cappy's trust was about $65,600.

Cappy continued to live in the Wellesley house but was forced by Sara's death and his loss of employment in 1972 to reduce his standard of living substantially. He married Margaret in March 1972, and, shortly before their marriage, asked her to read Sara's will, but they never discussed it. In 1972, Cappy took out a mortgage for $4,000, the proceeds of which were used to pay bills. Farr was aware of the transaction, as he replied to an inquiry of the mortgagee bank concerning the appraised value of the Wellesley property and the income Cappy expected to receive from Sara's trust.

In 1973, Cappy retained Farr in connection with a new will. The latter drew what he described as a simple will which left most of Cappy's property, including the house, to Margaret. The will was executed on November 7, 1973.

In February 1974, Cappy informed the trustee that business was at a standstill and that he really needed some funds, if possible. Farr replied in a letter in which he set forth the relevant portion of the will and wrote that he thought the language was "broad enough to permit a distribution of principal." Farr enclosed a check of $300. He asked Cappy to explain in writing the need for some support and why the need had arisen. The judge found that Farr, by his actions, discouraged Cappy from making any requests for principal.

Indeed, Cappy did not reduce his request to writing and never again requested principal. Farr made no investigation whatsoever of Cappy's needs or his "available sources of support" from the date of Sara's death until Cappy's admission to a nursing home in 1983 and, other than the $300 payment, made no additional distributions of principal until Cappy entered the nursing home.

By the fall of 1974, Cappy's difficulty in meeting expenses intensified.[6] Several of his checks were returned for insufficient funds, and in October 1974, in order that he might remain in the house, Sally and he agreed that she would take over the mortgage payments, the real estate taxes, insurance, and major repairs. In return, she would get the house upon Cappy's death.

Cappy and Sally went to Farr to draw up a deed. Farr was the only lawyer involved, and he billed Sally for the work. He wrote to Sally, stating his understanding of the proposed transaction, and asking, among other things, whether Margaret would have a right to live in the house if Cappy should predecease her. The answer was no. No copy of the letter to Sally was sent to Cappy. A deed was executed by Cappy on November 7, 1974, transferring the property to Sally and her husband Richard T. Marlette (Marlette) as tenants by the entirety, reserving a life estate to Cappy. No writing set forth Sally's obligations to Cappy.

Cappy was, for many years, director of Dana Hall Riding School in Weston Massachusetts. Photo: Beveridge Hall, Dana Hall School, 2012.

The judge found that there was no indication that Cappy did not understand the transaction, although, in response to a request for certain papers by Farr, Cappy sent a collection of irrelevant documents. The judge also found that Cappy clearly understood that he was preserving no rights for Margaret, and that neither Sally nor Richard nor Farr ever made any representation to Margaret that she would be able to stay in the house after Cappy's death.

Although Farr had read Sara's will to Cappy and had written to him that the will was "broad enough to permit a distribution of principal," the judge found that Farr failed to advise Cappy that the principal of his trust could be

---

6   After Sara's death, Cappy's income was limited, particularly considering the station he had enjoyed while married to Sara. In 1973, including the income from Sara's trust of $2,116, his income was $3,441; in 1974 it was $3,549, including trust income of $2,254; in 1975, $6,624, including trust income of $2,490 and social security income of $2,576. Margaret's income was also minimal; $499 in 1974, $4,084 in 1975, including social security income of $1,686. Cappy's income in 1976 was $8,464; in 1977, $8,955; in 1978, $9,681; in 1979, $10,851; in 1980, $11,261; in 1981, $12,651; in 1982, $13,870; in 1983, $12,711; in 1984, $12,500; in 1985, $12,567; in 1986, $12,558. The largest portion from 1975 on came from social security benefits.

used for the expenses of the Wellesley home. The parsimonious distribution of $300 and Farr's knowledge that the purpose of the conveyance to Sally was to enable Cappy to remain in the house, provide support for this finding. After executing the deed, Cappy expressed to Farr that he was pleased and most appreciative. Margaret testified that Cappy thought Farr was "great" and that he considered him his lawyer.

Sally and Marlette complied with their obligations under the agreement. Sally died in 1983, and Marlette became the sole owner of the property subject to Cappy's life estate. Although Margaret knew before Cappy's death that she did not have any interest in the Wellesley property, she believed that Sally would have allowed her to live in the house because of their friendship. After Cappy's death in 1987, Marlette inquired as to Margaret's plans, and, subsequently, through Farr, sent Margaret a notice to vacate the premises. Margaret brought this action in the Probate Court.

After a two-day trial, the judge held that the trustee was in breach of his duty to Cappy when he neglected to inquire as to the latter's finances. She concluded that, had Farr fulfilled his fiduciary duties, Cappy would not have conveyed the residence owned by him to Sally and Marlette. The judge ordered Marlette to convey the house to Margaret and also ordered Farr to reimburse Marlette from the remaining portion of Cappy's trust for the expenses paid by him and Sally for the upkeep of the property. If Cappy's trust proved insufficient to make such payments, Farr was to be personally liable for such expenses. Both Farr and Marlette appealed from the judgment, from the denial of their motions to amend the findings, and from their motions for a new trial. Margaret appealed from the denial of her motion for attorney's fees. As indicated earlier, we agree with the judge that Sara's will imposed a duty of inquiry on the trustee, but we disagree with the remedy and, therefore, remand for further proceedings.

2. *Breach of trust by the trustee*

Contrary to Farr's contention that it was not incumbent upon him to become familiar with Cappy's finances, Article IIA of Sara's will clearly placed such a duty upon him. In his brief, Farr claims that the will gave Cappy the right to request principal "in extraordinary circumstances" and that the trustee, "was charged by Sara to be wary should Cappy request money beyond that which he quarterly received." Nothing in the will or the record supports this narrow construction. To the contrary, the direction to the trustees was to pay Cappy such amounts "as they shall deem advisable for his comfortable support and maintenance." This language has been interpreted to set an ascertainable standard, namely to maintain the life beneficiary "in accordance with the standard of living which was normal for him before he became a beneficiary of the trust."

Even where the only direction to the trustee is that he shall "in his discretion" pay such portion of the principal as he shall "deem advisable," the discretion is not absolute. "Prudence and reasonableness, not caprice or careless good nature, much less a desire on the part of the trustee to be relieved from trouble . . . furnish the standard of conduct." That there is a duty of inquiry into the needs of the beneficiary follows from the requirement that the trustee's power "must be exercised with that soundness of judgment which follows from a due appreciation of trust responsibility."

Farr, in our view, did not meet his responsibilities either of inquiry or of distribution under the trust. The conclusion of the trial judge that, had he exercised "sound judgment," he would have made such payments to Cappy "as to allow him to continue to live in the home he had occupied for many years with the settlor" was warranted.

3.   Remedy against Marlette

The judge, concluding that, had Farr not been in breach of trust, "[C]appy would have died owning the house and thus able to devise it to his widow, the plaintiff," ordered Marlette to convey the house to Margaret. This was an inappropriate remedy in view of the judge's findings. She found that, although the relationship between Cappy and Sally was "close and loving," there was "no fiduciary relation between them" and that Sally and Marlette "were not unjustly enriched by the conveyance." She also found that "Sally and Richard Marlette expended significant monies over a long period of time in maintaining their agreement with Cappy."

Because the conveyance was supported by sufficient consideration (the agreement to pay the house expenses) and because Sally and Marlette had no notice of a breach of trust and were not themselves guilty of a breach of fiduciary duty, they cannot be charged as constructive trustees of the property. That portion of the judgment which orders Marlette to convey the property is vacated.

4.   Remainder of Cappy's trust

The amounts that should have been expended for Cappy's benefit are, however, in a different category. More than $80,000 remained in the trust for Cappy at the time of his death. As we have indicated, the trial judge properly concluded that payments of principal should have been made to Cappy from that fund in sufficient amount to enable him to keep the Wellesley property.

There is no reason for the beneficiaries of the trust under Article IIC to obtain funds which they would not have received had Farr followed the testator's direction. The remedy in such circumstances is to impress a constructive trust on the amounts which should have been distributed to Cappy but were not because of the error of the trustee. Even in cases where beneficiaries have already been paid funds by mistake, the amounts may be collected from them unless the recipients were bona fide purchasers or unless they, without notice of the improper payments, had so changed their position that it would be inequitable to make them repay. Here, the remainder of Cappy's trust has not yet been distributed, and there is no reason to depart from the usual rule of impressing a constructive trust in favor of Cappy's estate on the amounts wrongfully withheld.

> **Language Note:** This is yet another case where the court uses the term testatrix, rather than testator, to refer to Sara Marsman. (In fact, there are many more examples in this textbook, but we have pointed out just a representative few.)

That Cappy assented to the accounts is also no bar to recovery by his estate. The judge found that he was in the dark as to his rights to receive principal for the upkeep of the home. An assent may be withdrawn by a judge "if it is deemed improvident or not conducive to justice." The amounts to be paid to Cappy's estate have not been determined. On remand, the Probate Court judge is to hold such hearings as are necessary to determine the amounts which should have been paid to Cappy to enable him to retain possession of the house.

5.   *Personal liability of the trustee*

Farr raises a number of defenses against the imposition of personal liability, including the statute of limitations, the exculpatory clause in the will, and the fact that Cappy assented to the accounts of the trustee. The judge found that Farr's breach of his fiduciary duty to inquire as to Cappy's needs and his other actions in response to Cappy's request for principal, including the involvement of Sally in distributions of principal despite Sara's provision that Cappy's trust be administered separately, led Cappy to be unaware of his right to receive principal for house expenses. The breach may also be viewed as a continuing one. In these circumstances we do not consider Cappy's assent or the statute of limitations to be a bar. The judge also found that Margaret learned of Cappy's right to principal for house expenses only when she sought other counsel after his death.

The more difficult question is the effect of the exculpatory clause. As indicated in part 3 of this opinion, we consider the order to Marlette to reconvey the property an inappropriate remedy. In view of the judge's finding that, but for the trustee's breach, Cappy would have retained ownership of the house, the liability of the trustee could be considerable.

Although exculpatory clauses are not looked upon with favor and are strictly construed, such "provisions inserted in the trust instrument without any overreaching or abuse by the trustee of any fiduciary or confidential relationship to the settlor are generally held effective except as to breaches of trust 'committed in bad faith or intentionally or with reckless indifference to the interest of the beneficiary.' " The actions of Farr were not of this ilk and also do not fall within the meaning of the term used in the will, "willful neglect or default."

Farr testified that he discussed the exculpatory clause with Sara and that she wanted it included. Nevertheless, the judge, without finding that there was an overreaching or abuse of Farr's fiduciary relation with Sara, held the clause ineffective. Relying on the fact that Farr was Sara's attorney, she stated: "One cannot know at this point in time whether or not Farr specifically called this provision to Sara's attention. Given the total failure of Farr to use his judgment as to Cappy's needs, it would be unjust and unreasonable to hold him harmless by reason of the exculpatory provisions he himself drafted and inserted in this instrument."

Assuming that the judge disbelieved Farr's testimony that he and Sara discussed the clause, although such disbelief on her part is by no means clear, the conclusion that it "would be unjust and unreasonable to hold Farr harmless" is not sufficient to find the overreaching or abuse of a fiduciary relation which is required to hold the provision ineffective.[10] We note that the judge found that Sara managed all the finances of the couple, and from all that appears, was competent in financial matters.

---

[10]   The *Restatement* lists six factors which may be considered in determining whether a provision relieving the trustee from liability is ineffective on the ground that it was inserted in the trust instrument as a result of an abuse of a fiduciary relationship at the time of the trust's creation. The six factors are: "(1) whether the trustee prior to the creation of the trust had been in a fiduciary relationship to the settlor, as where the trustee had been guardian of the settlor; (2) whether the trust instrument was drawn by the trustee or by a person acting wholly or partially on his behalf; (3) whether the settlor has taken independent advice as to the provisions of the trust instrument; (4) whether the settlor is a person of experience and judgment or is a person who is unfamiliar with business affairs or is not a person of much judgment or understanding; (5) whether the insertion of the provision was due to undue influence or other improper conduct on the part of the trustee; (6) the extent and reasonableness of the provision."

There was no evidence about the preparation and execution of Sara's will except for the questions concerning the exculpatory clause addressed to Farr by his own counsel. No claim was made that the clause was the result of an abuse of confidence. The fact that the trustee drew the instrument and suggested the insertion of the exculpatory clause does not necessarily make the provision ineffective. No rule of law requires that an exculpatory clause drawn by a prospective trustee be held ineffective unless the client is advised independently.

The judge used an incorrect legal standard in invalidating the clause. While recognizing the sensitivity of such clauses, we hold that, since there was no evidence that the insertion of the clause was an abuse of Farr's fiduciary relationship with Sara at the time of the drawing of her will, the clause is effective.

NOTES

1.   James F. Farr was a well-known trusts and estates lawyer in the Boston area and author of James F. Farr & Jackson W. Wright, Jr., AN ESTATE PLANNER'S HANDBOOK (4th ed. 1979), a leading practitioner's handbook. Was Farr a good selection for trustee? Whom did he represent? Did he have any conflicts?

2.   Do you agree with the damages that the *Marsman* court awarded to Margaret? Why did the appellate court reverse the order for Marlette to transfer the house to Margaret? Do you agree with this conclusion? Can you think of other ways the court could have calculated damages here? What was the harm? Can anyone be made whole at this point?

3.   Notice that some of the problems arising in this case relate to the fact that this was a blended family. Families in which there are second and third marriages with children from an earlier marriage can create conflicts in estate planning, especially when a surviving spouse has a life interest, and the children have the remainder. Why might such a trust be appealing to a settlor?

ASSESSMENTS

1.   A bank is trustee of a trust that provides that if the income beneficiary's other income would not permit her to maintain the standard of living that she enjoyed at the date of the settlor's death, the trustee was authorized to pay as much of the principal to the beneficiary as was necessary to permit her to maintain that standard. The bank made several payments of principal to the income beneficiary without examining her bank accounts, her other sources of income, or ascertaining what kind of lifestyle she was able to maintain without

them. These payments significantly reduced the principal, and the remainder beneficiary sued. Imagine you are the judge and have the *Marsman* case as your precedent. Write a short opinion to decide the result. *Feibelman v. Worthen Nat. Bank, N.A.,* 20 F.3d 835, 836 (8th Cir. 1994).

2. You and a classmate are playing the roles of Cappy and Farr during the time that Cappy was short on funds. As you roleplay, consider the following questions:

a. For Cappy: Why didn't you just come out and ask Farr for the funds you need? Why didn't you respond to Farr's request for an itemized request? What are some of the circumstances that might prevent beneficiaries, more generally, from making affirmative requests and holding trustees accountable for distributions and how might a trustee or estate planner rectify these problems?

b. For Farr: What signs of financial distress did you overlook? Why didn't you look into Cappy's situation to see whether he needed funds? Trustees are well-known for tending toward a conservative approach in distributions. Why might a trustee prefer to be conservative rather than generous in the distribution of funds?

c. *Duty to Invest Prudently*

The most detailed and complex part of the duty of prudence is the duty to invest prudently. In fact, there is a separate act, called the UNIFORM PRUDENT INVESTOR ACT (UPIA), which is incorporated into the UTC and governs this duty.

The investment function requires that a trustee assess the trust assets and create an investment strategy suitable to support the purposes of the trust and the needs of the beneficiaries, based on the kinds of property in the trust. For example, should the trustee invest to achieve income or to increase the value of the corpus? Is there high or low risk tolerance among the beneficiaries? The three central directives of the UPIA are the duty to diversify, the duty to tailor investments to the risk tolerance of the trust, and, finally, the duty to delegate investing to professionals.

As investing philosophy has changed over the years, so has trust law. Historically, trustees were very limited in what investments they could pursue, grounded in the assumption that most investments represented too great a risk for the trust and the beneficiaries. Here is a short summary of the history:

Trust investment law "got off to a bad start." After the South Sea Bubble burst in 1720, the English Court of Chancery settled upon a list of presumptively proper investments. The list was later codified, albeit in a somewhat broader form, by statutes in England and across the United States. Reflecting the salience of default risk after the South Sea Bubble, these legal lists required risk avoidance. They tended to favor government bonds and first mortgages and to exclude investments in equity. Structurally, the legal lists were in keeping with the legal technology of the era, in which agency problems, such as between a trustee and a beneficiary, were resolved by limiting the agent's powers. In the seminal case of *Harvard College v. Amory*, 26 Mass. 446, 461 (1830), the Massachusetts Supreme Judicial Court rejected the legal list and adopted the prudent man rule. The court held that a trustee must "observe how men of prudence, discretion and intelligence manage their own affairs, not in regard to speculation, but in regard to the permanent disposition of their funds, considering the probable income, as well as the probable safety of the capital to be invested." In the mid 1900s, after the American Bankers Association sponsored a model statute codifying *Amory*, most states abrogated their legal lists in favor of the prudent man rule.

Max M. Schanzenbach & Robert H. Sitkoff, *The Prudent Investor Rule and Market Risk: An Empirical Analysis*, 14 J. EMP. LEGAL STUD. 129 (2017).

In the mid-1980s, trust law shifted from the prudent man rule to the prudent investor rule (the prudent woman never got her day in the investment office!). While the prudent man standard focused on the relative risk of each individual asset, the prudent investor standard focuses on the risk factors of the investment portfolio as a whole. In changing focus in this way, the prudent investor standard also emphasizes the duty to diversify portfolio assets as a way of managing risk, based on **modern portfolio theory**. The core concept of modern portfolio theory is that, while it is impossible to eliminate all market risk, there are certain risks (firm risk, industry risk) that can be minimized through diversification. That is to say, with a diversified portfolio, if one firm is performing poorly, the good performance of other firms will offset the losses; similarly, if one industry is in a slump and not performing well, profitable investments in other industries will compensate.

The key provisions of the UPIA, which express the modern portfolio theory of investing, follow:

UPIA § 1 Prudent Investor Rule

(a)   Except as otherwise provided in subsection (b), a trustee who invests and manages trust assets owes a duty to the beneficiaries of the trust to comply with the prudent investor rule set forth in this [Act].

(b)   The prudent investor rule, a default rule, may be expanded, restricted, eliminated, or otherwise altered by the provisions of a trust. A trustee is not liable to a beneficiary to the extent that the trustee acted in reasonable reliance on the provisions of the trust.

UPIA § 2 Standard of Care; Portfolio Strategy; Risk and Return Objectives

(a)   A trustee shall invest and manage trust assets as a prudent investor would, by considering the purposes, terms, distribution requirements, and other circumstances of the trust. In satisfying this standard, the trustee shall exercise reasonable care, skill, and caution.

(b)   A trustee's investment and management decisions respecting individual assets must be evaluated not in isolation but in the context of the trust portfolio as a whole and as a part of an overall investment strategy having risk and return objectives reasonably suited to the trust.

(c)   Among circumstances that a trustee shall consider in investing and managing trust assets are such of the following as are relevant to the trust or its beneficiaries:

(1)   general economic conditions;

(2)   the possible effect of inflation or deflation;

(3)   the expected tax consequences of investment decisions or strategies;

(4)   the role that each investment or course of action plays within the overall trust portfolio, which may include financial assets, interests in closely held enterprises, tangible and intangible personal property, and real property;

(5)   the expected total return from income and the appreciation of capital;

(6)   other resources of the beneficiaries;

(7)   needs for liquidity, regularity of income, and preservation or appreciation of capital; and

(8)   an asset's special relationship or special value, if any, to the purposes of the trust or to one or more of the beneficiaries.

(d)   A trustee shall make a reasonable effort to verify facts relevant to the investment and management of trust assets.

(e)   A trustee may invest in any kind of property or type of investment consistent with the standards of this [Act].

(f)   A trustee who has special skills or expertise, or is named trustee in reliance upon the trustee's representation that the trustee has special skills or expertise, has a duty to use those special skills or expertise.

The next case, *Estate of Janes*, was decided after New York adopted the UPIA, although the conduct in question—holding on to a high concentration of a single stock—took place when the old "prudent person" rule applied. The court nevertheless applied many of the principles that you see expressed in the statute. As you read the case, consider how investment decisions might also affect the trustee's duties of obedience and inquiry. Investment also will dictate how a trustee satisfies the duty of impartiality to different classes of beneficiaries.

In re Estate of Rodney B. Janes

681 N.E.2d 332 (N.Y. 1997)

LEVINE, J.

Former State Senator and businessman Rodney B. Janes (testator) died on May 26, 1973, survived solely by his wife, Cynthia W. Janes, who was then 72 years of age. Testator's $3,500,000 estate consisted of a $2,500,000 stock portfolio, approximately 71% of which consisted of 13,232 shares of common stock of the Eastman Kodak Company. The Kodak stock had a date-of-death value of $1,786,733, or approximately $135 per share.

Testator's 1963 will and a 1969 codicil bequeathed most of his estate to three trusts. First, the testator created a marital deduction trust consisting of approximately 50% of the estate's assets, the income of which was to be paid to Mrs. Janes for her life. In addition, it contained a generous provision for invasion of the principal for Mrs. Janes's benefit and gave her testamentary power of appointment over the remaining principal. The testator also established a charitable trust of approximately 25% of the estate's assets which directed annual distributions to selected charities. A third trust comprised the balance of the estate's assets and directed that the income therefrom be paid to Mrs. Janes for her life, with the remainder pouring over into the charitable trust upon her death.

On June 6, 1973, the testator's will and codicil were admitted to probate. Letters testamentary issued to petitioner's predecessor, Lincoln Rochester Trust Company, and Mrs. Janes, as co-executors. On July 3, 1973, letters of trusteeship issued to petitioner alone. By early August 1973, petitioner's trust and estate officers, Ellison Patterson and Richard Young had ascertained the estate's assets and the amount of cash needed for taxes, commissions, attorneys' fees, and specific bequests. In an August 9, 1973 memorandum, Patterson recommended raising the necessary cash for the foregoing administrative expenses by selling certain assets, including 800 shares of Kodak stock, and holding "the remaining issues until the trusts were funded." The memorandum did not otherwise address investment strategy in light of the evident primary objective of the testator to provide for his widow during her lifetime.

In a September 5, 1973 meeting with Patterson and Young, Mrs. Janes, who had a high school education, no business training or experience, and who had never been employed, consented to the sale of some 1,200 additional shares of Kodak stock. Although Mrs. Janes was informed at the meeting that petitioner intended to retain the balance of the Kodak shares, none of the factors that would lead to an informed investment decision was discussed. At that time, the Kodak stock traded for about $139 per share; thus, the estate's 13,232 shares of the stock were worth almost $1,840,000. The September 5 meeting was the only occasion where retention of the Kodak stock or any other investment issues were taken up with Mrs. Janes.

By the end of 1973, the price of Kodak stock had fallen to about $109 per share. One year later, it had fallen to about $63 per share and, by the end of 1977, to about $51 per share. In March 1978, the price had dropped even further, to about $40 per share. When petitioner filed its initial accounting in February 1980, the remaining 11,320 shares were worth approximately $530,000, or about $47 per share. Most of the shares were used to fund the trusts in 1986 and 1987.

In August 1981, petitioner sought judicial settlement of its account. Objections to the accounts were originally filed by Mrs. Janes in 1982, and subsequently by the Attorney-General on behalf of the charitable beneficiaries (collectively, "objectants"). In seeking to surcharge petitioner for losses incurred by the estate due to petitioner's imprudent retention of a high concentration of Kodak stock in the estate from July 1973 to February 1980, during which time the value of the stock had dropped to about one third of its date-of-death value, objectants asserted that petitioner's conduct violated, the so-called "prudent person rule" of investment.

When Mrs. Janes died in 1986, the personal representative of her estate was substituted as an objectant. Following a trial on the objections, the Surrogate found that petitioner, under the circumstances, had acted imprudently and should have divested the estate of the high concentration of Kodak stock by August 9, 1973. The court imposed a $6,080,269 surcharge against petitioner and ordered petitioner to forfeit its commissions and attorneys' fees. In calculating the amount of the surcharge, the court adopted a "lost profits" or "market index" measure of damages espoused by objectants' expert—what the proceeds of the Kodak stock would have yielded, up to the time of trial, had they been invested in petitioner's own diversified equity fund on August 9, 1973.

The Appellate Division modified solely as to damages, holding that "the Surrogate properly found petitioner liable for its negligent failure to diversify and for its inattentiveness, inaction, and lack of disclosure, but that the Surrogate adopted an improper measure of damages." *Matter of Janes,* 223 A.D.2d 20, 22. The Court rejected the Surrogate's "lost profits" or "market index" measure of damages, holding that the proper measure of damages was "the value of the capital that was lost"—the difference between the value of the stock at the time it should have been sold and its value when ultimately sold. Applying this measure, the Court reduced the surcharge to $4,065,029.

We granted petitioner and objectants leave to appeal, and now affirm.

I. *Petitioner's Liability*

Petitioner argues that New York law does not permit a fiduciary to be surcharged for imprudent management of a trust for failure to diversify in the absence of additional elements of hazard, and that it relied upon, and complied with, this rule in administering the estate. Petitioner claims that elements of hazard can be capsulized into deficiencies in the following investment quality factors: "(i) the capital structure of the company; (ii) the competency of its management; (iii) whether the company is a seasoned issuer of stock with a history of profitability; (iv) whether the company has a history of paying dividends; (v) whether the company is an industry leader; (vi) the expected future direction of the company's business; and (vii) the opinion of investment bankers and analysts who follow the company's stock." Evaluated under these criteria, petitioner asserts, the concentration of Kodak stock at issue in this case, that is, of an acknowledged "blue chip" security popular with investment advisors and many mutual funds, cannot be found an imprudent investment on August 9, 1973 as a matter of law. In our view, a fiduciary's duty of investment prudence in holding a concentration of one security may not be so rigidly limited.

New York followed the prudent person rule of investment during the period of petitioner's administration of the instant estate. This rule provides that "[a] fiduciary holding funds for investment may invest the same in such securities as would be acquired by prudent [persons] of discretion and intelligence in such matters who are seeking a reasonable income and the preservation of their capital." The prudent person rule's New York common-law antecedents can be traced to *King v. Talbot*, 40 N.Y. 76, wherein this Court stated:

> [T]he trustee is bound to employ such diligence and such prudence in the care and management [of the trust], as in general, prudent men of discretion and intelligence in such matters, employ in their own like affairs. This necessarily excludes all speculation, all investments for an uncertain and doubtful rise in the market, and, of course, *everything that does not take into view the nature and object of the trust, and the consequences of a mistake in the selection of the investment to be made. The preservation of the fund, and the procurement of a just income therefrom, are primary objects* of the creation of the trust itself, and are to be primarily regarded.

Id. at 85–86 (emphasis added). No precise formula exists for determining whether the prudent person standard has been violated in a particular situation; rather, the determination depends on an examination of the facts and circumstances of each And, while a court should not view each act or omission aided or enlightened by hindsight, a court may, nevertheless, examine the fiduciary's conduct over *the entire course of the investment* in determining whether it has acted prudently.

As the foregoing demonstrates, the very nature of the prudent person standard dictates against any absolute rule that a fiduciary's failure to diversify, in and of itself, constitutes imprudence, as well as against a rule invariably immunizing a fiduciary from its failure to diversify in the absence of some selective list of elements of hazard, such as those identified by petitioner. The inquiry is simply whether, under all the facts and circumstances of the particular case, the fiduciary violated the prudent person standard in maintaining a concentration of a particular stock in the estate's portfolio of investments.

Moreover, no court has stated that the limited elements of hazard outlined by petitioner are the only factors that may be considered in determining whether a fiduciary has acted prudently in maintaining a concentrated portfolio. Again, as commentators have noted, one of the primary virtues of the prudent person rule *"lies in its lack of specificity*, as this permits the propriety of the trustee's investment decisions to be measured in light of the business and economic circumstances existing at the time they were made." Laurino, *Investment*

Responsibility of Professional Trustees, 51 ST JOHN'S L. REV. 717, 723 (1977) (emphasis added).

Petitioner's restrictive list of hazards omits such additional factors to be considered under the prudent person rule by a trustee in weighing the propriety of any investment decision, as: "the amount of the trust estate, the situation of the beneficiaries, the trend of prices and of the cost of living, the prospect of inflation and of deflation." RESTATEMENT [SECOND] OF TRUSTS § 227, comment *e*. Other pertinent factors are the marketability of the investment and possible tax consequences (*id.* comment *o*). The trustee must weigh all of these investment factors as they affect the principal objects of the testator's or settlor's bounty, as between income beneficiaries and remainder persons, including decisions regarding "whether to apportion the investments between high-yield or high-growth securities." TURANO AND RADIGAN, NEW YORK ESTATE ADMINISTRATION ch. 14, § P, at 409 (1986).

Moreover, and especially relevant to the instant case, the various factors affecting the prudence of any particular investment must be considered in the light of the "circumstances of the trust itself rather than [merely] the integrity of the particular investment." As stated in a leading treatise:

> "The trustee should take into consideration the circumstances of the particular trust that he is administering. He should consider each investment not as an isolated transaction but in its relation to the whole of the trust estate."

3 SCOTT, TRUSTS § 227.12, at 477 (4th ed).

Thus, the elements of hazard petitioner relies upon as demonstrating that, as a matter of law, it had no duty to diversify, suffer from two major deficiencies under the prudent person rule. First, petitioner's risk elements too narrowly and strictly define the scope of a fiduciary's responsibility in making any individual investment decision, and the factors a fiduciary must consider in determining the propriety of a given investment. A second deficiency in petitioner's elements of hazard list is that all of the factors relied upon by petitioner go to the propriety of an individual investment "exclusively as though it were in its own water-tight compartment" which would encourage a fiduciary to treat each investment as an isolated transaction rather than "in its relation to the whole of the trust estate."

Contrary to petitioner's alternative attack on the decisions below, neither the Surrogate nor the Appellate Division based their respective rulings holding petitioner liable on any absolute duty of a fiduciary to diversify. Rather, those courts determined that a surcharge was appropriate because maintaining a concentration in Kodak stock, under the circumstances presented, violated certain critical obligations of a fiduciary in making investment decisions under the prudent person rule. First, petitioner failed to consider the investment in Kodak stock in relation to the entire portfolio of the estate i.e., whether the Kodak concentration itself created or added to investment risk. The objectants' experts testified that even high-quality growth stocks, such as Kodak, possess some degree of volatility because their market value is tied so closely to earnings projections. They further opined that the investment risk arising from that volatility is significantly exacerbated when a portfolio is heavily concentrated in one such growth stock.

Second, the evidence revealed that, in maintaining an investment portfolio in which Kodak represented 71% of the estate's stock holdings, and the balance was largely in other growth stocks, petitioner paid insufficient attention to the needs and interests of the testator's 72-year-old widow, the life beneficiary of three quarters of his estate, for whose comfort, support and anticipated increased medical expenses the testamentary trusts were evidently created. Testimony by petitioner's investment manager, and by the objectants' experts, disclosed that the annual yield on Kodak stock in 1973 was approximately 1.06%, and that the aggregate annual income from all estate stockholdings was $43,961, a scant 1.7% of the $2.5 million estate securities portfolio. Thus, retention of a high concentration of Kodak jeopardized the interests of the primary income beneficiary of the estate and led to the eventual need to substantially invade the principal of the marital testamentary trust.

Lastly, there was evidence in the record to support the findings below that, in managing the estate's investments, petitioner failed to exercise due care and the skill it held itself out as possessing as a corporate fiduciary. Notably, there was proof that petitioner (1) failed initially to undertake a formal analysis of the estate and establish an investment plan consistent with the testator's primary objectives; (2) failed to follow petitioner's own internal trustee review protocol during the administration of the estate, which advised special caution and attention in cases of portfolio concentration of as little as 20%; and (3) failed to conduct more than routine reviews of the Kodak holdings in this estate, without considering alternative investment choices, over a seven-year period of steady decline in the value of the stock.

Since, thus, there was evidence in the record to support the foregoing affirmed findings of imprudence on the part of petitioner, the determination of liability must be affirmed.

II. Date of Divestiture

As we have noted, in determining whether a fiduciary has acted prudently, a court may examine a fiduciary's conduct throughout the entire period during which the investment at issue was held. The court may then determine, within that period, the "reasonable time" within which divesture of the imprudently held investment should have occurred. *See Matter of Weston*, 91 N.Y. 502, 510–511. What constitutes a reasonable time will vary from case to case and is not fixed or arbitrary. The test remains "the diligence and prudence of prudent and intelligent [persons] in the management of their own affairs." *Id.* at 511.

Again, there is evidentiary support in the record for the trial court's finding, affirmed by the Appellate Division, that a prudent fiduciary would have divested the estate's stock portfolio of its high concentration of Kodak stock by August 9, 1973, thereby exhausting our review powers on this issue. Petitioner's own internal documents and correspondence, as well as the testimony of Patterson, Young, and objectants' experts, establish that by that date, petitioner had all the information a prudent investor would have needed to conclude that the percentage of Kodak stock in the estate's stock portfolio was excessive and should have been reduced significantly, particularly in light of the estate's overall investment portfolio and the financial requirements of Mrs. Janes and the charitable beneficiaries.

III. Damages

Finally, as to the calculation of the surcharge, we conclude that the Appellate Division correctly rejected the Surrogate's "lost profits" or "market index" measure of damages. Where, as here, a fiduciary's imprudence consists solely of negligent retention of assets it should have sold, the measure of damages is the value of the lost capital. In imposing liability upon a fiduciary on the basis of the capital lost, the court should determine the value of the stock on the date it should have been sold and subtract from that figure the proceeds from the sale of the stock or, if the stock is still retained by the estate, the value of the stock at the time of the accounting. Here, uncontradicted expert testimony established that application of this measure of damages resulted in a figure of $4,065,029, which includes prejudgment interest at the legal rate, compounded from August 9, 1973 to October 1, 1994. The Appellate Division did not abuse its discretion in adding to that figure prejudgment interest from October 1, 1994 through August 17, 1995, $326,302.66 previously received by petitioner for commissions and attorneys' fees, plus postjudgment interest, costs, and disbursements.

Accordingly, the order of the Appellate Division should be affirmed, without costs.

NOTES

1.   When should a trustee diversify? There is no bright-line rule but, in general, concentration of more than 5–10 percent in a single security requires some kind of explanation or documentation. Banks and trust companies usually have their own internal protocols, requiring explanatory documentation for the retention of any asset that is concentrated beyond 10 percent. Most importantly, however, the need for diversification varies according to the beneficiary's needs and risk tolerance. A surviving spouse whose sole income is her trust distribution can tolerate much less risk than a beneficiary who is young, employed, and has additional sources of income.

2.   Do you think the court came to the correct decision in *Janes*? How much foresight would the trustee have had to have to do so? At what point? What if the stock price for Kodak stock kept going up and down for several years before taking a later plunge (as it in fact did)? Should the trustee be liable for not jumping the gun? Isn't the usual investment advice to buy stock and hold it?

3.   Exceptions do exist, and diversification may not always be the right approach. A trustee is not required to diversify if, "because of special circumstances, the purposes of the trust are better served without diversifying." The exceptions, however, are relatively limited and for the most part involve family property. A trustee is not required to diversify, for example, if the trust property is a family home, family land, or family heirlooms. In these situations, a trustee may be fully justified in retaining the asset and declining to diversify the trust portfolio. But keep in mind, these kinds of assets will cost money to maintain. Who should pay for that if there are insufficient liquid assets in the trust to maintain the property? This rule about special assets is particularly important for closely-held family businesses that are in placed in trust, since the shares cannot easily be valued on the market, and the family most likely has a desire to keep the shares within the family.

4.   There is an important difference between mandatory and permissive retention of an undiversified asset. Common trust forms include a provision that permits the retention of trust property. A provision permitting retention might read as follows:

> The Trustee may retain and invest in all forms of real and personal property, including stock, common trust funds, and mutual funds of

any corporate trustee without restriction to investments authorized by law.

Permissive authorization to hold certain assets does not necessarily excuse the trustee from liability for failure to diversify if diversification is in the best interest of the trust and the beneficiaries. That is to say, the trustee may have the power to retain undiversified trust assets, but the trustee still has a fiduciary duty to invest prudently.

What if the trust terms mandate retention? In the *Pulitzer* case, which you will read more about in Chapter 12 in the context of trust modification, the court was faced with a clause mandating retention. The settlor, Joseph Pulitzer, directed that the trustee never under any circumstances sell shares of *The World*, the newspaper the settlor owned and ran. Years after Pulitzer's death, the corporation was experiencing major losses, and the trustee sought to sell the stock. What result in this conflict between settlor wishes and beneficiary rights? *See Matter of Pulitzer*, 249 N.Y.S. 87 (Sur. 1931), aff'd mem., 260 N.Y.S. 975 (App. Div. 1932).

5.   In certain circumstances, a trustee may need to **delegate** parts or all of the investment function in order to adhere to the duty of prudence. Although delegation was historically prohibited, the UTC allows (and even encourages) delegation when a trustee needs expert advice and skilled investment handling. The rules still, however, require the trustee to act diligently in overseeing the delegation:

UTC § 807 Delegation by the Trustee

(a)   A trustee may delegate duties and powers that a prudent trustee of comparable skills could properly delegate under the circumstances. The trustee shall exercise reasonable care, skill, and caution in:

     (1)   selecting an agent;

     (2)   establishing the scope and terms of the delegation, consistent with the purposes and terms of the trust; and

     (3)   periodically reviewing the agent's actions in order to monitor the agent's performance and compliance with the terms of the delegation.

(b)   In performing a delegated function, an agent owes a duty to the trust to exercise reasonable care to comply with the terms of the delegation.

(c)   A trustee who complies with subsection (a) is not liable to the beneficiaries or to the trust for an action of the agent to whom the function was delegated.

If the trustee properly selects, monitors, and reviews the conduct of the agent, the trustee will not be liable for the agent's errors.

Sometimes, if the estate is a complex one, the settlor might choose to have more than one trustee in order to have both an individual and an institutional trustee. This combination allows the settlor to select a friend or family member as trustee, based on that person's knowledge of the beneficiaries and the larger family, while placing the burden of the investment function in the hands of an institutional trustee with experience in the administrative role. To the extent more than one trustee is serving, the cotrustees usually act by a majority (unless the trust provides otherwise), "each cotrustee has a duty . . . of active, prudent participation in the performance of all aspects of the trust's administration," RESTATEMENT (THIRD) OF TRUSTS § 81 cmt. C, and liability arises when a trustee fails to take reasonable steps to prevent a cotrustee's breach of duty.

Another approach to balancing investment and other trustee functions is to name an investment director or investment advisor in the trust. What concerns might you have with splitting the fiduciary function in this way? *See Shelton v. Tamposi*, 62 A.2d 741 (N.H. 2013) (involving claim by settlor's daughter, beneficiary of a subtrust, against her brothers, whom settlor had named as "investment directors" of master trust, alleging that subtrust trustee could not properly distribute funds because investment directors would not release assets to subtrust).

ASSESSMENTS

1.   You represent the petitioner in *Janes*, a corporate fiduciary that administers a large number of trusts. Your client wants to ensure that its trust officers do not repeat the conduct that led the court to hold that the trustee had failed to follow its own institutional protocols. Prepare a summary of conduct that every trust officer should follow. Use bullet points or outline levels to make the summary user-friendly, and make sure to specify how frequently a trust officer should engage in these actions.

2.   You have a long-time client, Shirley, who enjoys speculating with her personal investments and wants her trustee to have the flexibility to do the same.

Draft a trust provision that would allow for this flexibility but adequately protect the trustee from liability.

d. Allocating, Generating, and Distributing Income and Principal

Another aspect of the duty to manage and invest prudently is the duty to allocate trust **income** and **principal** in accordance with the trust's distribution specifications; this duty also encompasses allocating costs of the trust (like fiduciary fees) proportionately to income and principal. We usually think of trust principal as the corpus or res of the trust, including any growth in its value, and trust income as anything generated by that trust corpus. For example, if a trust owns an apartment building, the building itself is the principal, and the rents are the income. More commonly today, a trust holds a diversified investment account which produces both income, in the form of dividends or interest, and principal, in the form of increased value. Traditionally, certain trust assets were classified as income for accounting purposes, and others were classified as principal.

Often, settlors give different beneficiaries rights to income and principal. We saw this in *Marsman*, where the trust for Cappy provided that he would receive all income and principal in the trustee's discretion, and Sally would receive any principal remaining on Cappy's death. The trust income was insufficient to meet Cappy's needs, and the issue was whether Farr should make additional distributions of principal. Many trusts are structured this way, with one or more lifetime beneficiaries with rights to income and possibly principal, followed by a remainder beneficiary who receives the remaining principal of the trust at the death of the life estate holder.

The trustee's investment decisions must take into account both income and principal beneficiaries, generating sufficient lifetime income but also growing the trust corpus. This duty, though, may hamper the trustee's ability to invest in accordance with modern portfolio theory. Various statutes, including The UNIFORM PRINCIPAL AND INCOME ACT, UTC, AND UPIA, allow a trustee to ignore traditional accounting categories and make allocations to trust income or principal in ways that allow for impartiality between current and future beneficiaries.

4. Duty of Impartiality

The duty of loyalty requires a trustee to act solely in the interests of the beneficiaries. There may, however, be more than one beneficiary. As indicated above, questions arise about how a trustee is supposed to balance the differing needs and demands of multiple beneficiaries. The duty of impartiality, which is codified by UTC § 803 (2000), addresses this question:

UTC § 803 Impartiality

If a trust has two or more beneficiaries, the trustee shall act impartially in investing, managing, and distributing the trust property, giving due regard to the beneficiaries' respective interests.

Remember that a trust can have successive beneficiaries ("income to Andy for life, remainder to Bernard") and multiple beneficiaries at one time ("income and principal to Andy and Bernard for their comfortable support"). In both cases, the trustee must be "impartial" in making distributions, but this requirement does not mean she must treat the beneficiaries equally. The comment to UTC § 803 states:

> The duty to act impartially does not mean that the trustee must treat the beneficiaries equally. Rather, the trustee must treat the beneficiaries equitably in light of the purposes and terms of the trust. A settlor who prefers that the trustee, when making decisions, generally favor the interests of one beneficiary over those of others should provide appropriate guidance in the terms of the trust.

When drafting trusts, it may be helpful to give the trustee guidance on how to treat the different classes of beneficiaries. For example, the settlor may want the life beneficiary to receive whatever she needs from the trust, even if that means there is little or nothing left for the remainder beneficiaries. *See Howard v. Howard*, 156 P.3d 89 (Or. App. 2007) (analyzing trust that provided, "[a]fter my death, in the event my spouse survives me, my spouse's support, comfort, companionship, enjoyment and desires shall be preferred over the rights of the remaindermen."). Or the settlor may intend the trustee to preserve a substantial corpus to distribute once the trust terminates. One way to do so, for example, is by directing the trustee to consider the life beneficiary's other sources of income before distributing any trust assets to her. The more information the trustee has about the settlor's wishes in this regard, the easier it will be her to make decisions that reflect the settlor's intent (and protect the trustee from liability).

ASSESSMENTS

1.   Your client, Sandra, comes to you because she is the remainder beneficiary of a trust her father created before his death, naming Sandra's mother as sole trustee. The trust provides for Sandra's mother for life, with remainder to Sandra at her mother's death. The trust was well-funded with several million dollars. Sandra's mother is now 77, and she has been distributing what Sandra considers to be extravagant amounts to herself since Sandra's father's death three years ago. "I don't want to begrudge my mother her standard of living," Sandra tells you, "but at this rate, she's going to use up everything in the trust before her death and there won't be anything left—I know this isn't what my father would have wanted." The trust provides no instructions on how to balance the interests of the two beneficiaries. Advise Sandra.

2.   Hart created a trust providing a life estate for the benefit of his spouse, with remainder to his children. Thornton, the trustee, comes to you for advice. Thornton has an opportunity to invest the trust's assets in a venture with a ninety percent chance of doubling but a ten percent chance of losing the assets. Thornton asks you whether it would be permissible to make the investment. What questions do you want to ask before you answer?

3.   The primary estate planning concern for Tonza Money, a 75-year-old with considerable wealth, is to assure adequate protection for her 68-year-old spouse of 18 years. At the same time, however, Tonza would like assets not needed by her spouse, at Tonza's death, to pass to her two children by a prior marriage, now aged 38 and 40.

   a.   Whom do you advise Tonza to select as trustee? Her options include: her spouse, one or both of her children, her 72-year-old sister (whose judgment she trusts and who has a great relationship with Tonza's spouse and children), the private trust department of the bank where Tonza has her accounts, the CFO of Tonza's closely held corporation (who holds a CPA), or you (her estate planning lawyer)?

   b.   What powers and limitations should Tonza include in the trust regarding investing and distributing trust income and principal?

5.   Duty to Inform and Report

Keeping beneficiaries informed about the investment performance of the trust assets and the financial status of the trust is an ongoing obligation that the trustee must fulfill. Not all beneficiaries are entitled to equal disclosure, however. UTC § 813 provides:

UTC § 813 Duty to Inform and Report

(a)   A trustee shall keep the qualified beneficiaries of the trust reasonably informed about the administration of the trust and of the material facts necessary for them to protect their interests. Unless unreasonable under the circumstances, a trustee shall promptly respond to a beneficiary's request for information related to the administration of the trust.

The definitions section of the UTC, § 103, defines a "**qualified beneficiary**" as a beneficiary who, on the date the qualification is determined:

(A)   is a distributee or permissible distributee of trust income or principal;

(B)   would be a distributee or permissible distributee of trust income or principal if the interests of the distributees described in subparagraph (A) terminated on that date; or

(C)   would be a distributee or permissible distributee of trust income or principal if the trust terminated on that date.

The basic requirements for disclosure, as set forth in UTC §§ 813(b) and (c), are that the trustee must provide an accounting: 1) upon the request of any beneficiary, 2) when there are material changes to the trust, including the creation of termination of the trust, and 3) on an annual basis, unless the trust terms state otherwise, listing "the trust property, liabilities, receipts, and disbursements, including the source and amount of the trustee's compensation, a listing of the trust assets and, if feasible, their respective market values." Whenever a beneficiary has questions or concerns about trustee management of trust assets, a request for an accounting is appropriate. An accounting may provide the beneficiary with grounds for further claims of breach of fiduciary duty.

The request for an accounting is the starting point for the following case. In 1996, on behalf of all individual Indian trust beneficiaries, Elouise Cobell, and three other named plaintiffs brought an action in equity in the U.S. District Court for the District of Columbia to compel the United States to conduct a full historical accounting of all "Individual Indian Money" ("IIM") trust funds, to correct and restate IIM account balances, to fix broken trust management systems, and to undertake other critical trust reform measures to ensure prudent trust management. Notably, since the start of the litigation, the government has spent more than five billion dollars to fix and secure broken trust management systems that previously allowed unauthorized access to IIM trust data and assets. The government's effort began in earnest after Judge Royce C. Lamberth held various federal officials, including Treasury Secretary Rubin, Interior Secretary Babbitt, and Assistant Secretary Gover, in contempt. Below is an excerpt from one of the many iterations of this case as it wound its way through the courts. As you read the case, consider the importance of full and regular accountings.

Cobell v. Babbit

91 F. Supp. 2d 1 (D.D.C. 1999), *aff'd and remanded sub nom.*
Cobell v. Norton, 240 F.3d 1081 (D.C. Cir. 2001)

LAMBERTH, J.

I.   Introduction

It would be difficult to find a more historically mismanaged federal program than the Individual Indian Money (IIM) trust. The United States, the trustee of the IIM trust, cannot say how much money is or should be in the trust. As the trustee admitted on the eve of trial, it cannot render an accurate accounting to the beneficiaries, contrary to a specific statutory mandate and the century-old obligation to do so. More specifically, as Secretary Babbitt testified, an accounting cannot be rendered for most of the 300,000-plus beneficiaries, who are now plaintiffs in this lawsuit. Generations of IIM trust beneficiaries have been born and raised with the assurance that their trustee, the United States, was acting properly with their money. Just as many generations have been denied any such proof, however. "If courts were permitted to indulge their sympathies, a case better calculated to excite them could scarcely be imagined." *Cherokee Nation v. Georgia,* 30 U.S. (5 Pet.) 1 (1831) (Marshall, C.J.).

Notwithstanding all of this, defendants, the trustee-delegates of the United States, continue to write checks on an account that they cannot balance or reconcile. The court knows of no other program in American government in which federal officials are allowed to write checks—some of which are known to be written in erroneous amounts—from unreconciled accounts—some of which are known to have incorrect balances. Such behavior certainly would not be tolerated from private sector trustees. It is fiscal and governmental irresponsibility in its purest form.

The United States' mismanagement of the IIM trust is far more inexcusable than garden-variety trust mismanagement of a typical donative trust. For the beneficiaries of this trust did not voluntarily choose to have their lands taken from them; they did not willingly relinquish pervasive control of their money to the United States. The United States imposed this trust on the Indian people. As the government concedes, the purpose of the IIM trust was to deprive plaintiffs' ancestors of their native lands and rid the nation of their tribal identity. The United States reaped the "benefit" of this imposed program long ago—sixty-five percent of what were previously tribal land holdings quickly opened up to non-Indian settlement. But the United States has refused to act in accordance with the fiduciary obligations attendant to the imposition of the trust, which are not imposed by statute.

The defendants cannot provide an accounting of plaintiffs' money, which the United States has forced into the IIM trust. This problem, which has been handed down from administration to administration of apologetic United States trustee-delegates to generation upon generation of helpless beneficiaries, continues today and is the basis for this lawsuit. It imposes far more than pecuniary costs, although those are clear and cannot be overstated. Plaintiffs' class includes some of the poorest people in this nation. Human welfare and livelihood are at stake. It is entirely possible that tens of thousands of IIM trust beneficiaries should be receiving different amounts of money—their own money—than they do today. Perhaps not. But no one can say, which is the crux of the problem.

Plaintiffs bring this lawsuit to force the government to abide by its duty to render an accurate accounting of the money currently held within the IIM trust. The component of the case currently before the court concerns the issue of whether defendants are in breach of any trust duties such that plaintiffs should be afforded some prospective relief to prevent further injury of their legal rights. Plaintiffs have stated and proved certain valid legal claims that entitle them to relief.

For the reasons stated below, the court finds that the United States government, by virtue of the actions of defendants and their predecessors, is currently in breach of certain trust duties owed to plaintiffs. The government recently has taken substantial steps toward bringing itself into compliance in several respects. Nonetheless, given the long and sorry history of the United States' trusteeship of the IIM trust, the defendants' recalcitrance toward remedying their mismanagement despite decades of congressional directives, and the consequences of allowing these enumerated breaches of trust to continue, the court will retain continuing jurisdiction over this matter. It would be an abdication of duty for this court to do anything less.

II. Findings of Fact

A. History Surrounding IIM Trust Establishment

As Chief Justice Marshall noted in 1831, the United States-Indian relationship is "perhaps unlike that of any two people in existence" and "marked by peculiar and cardinal distinctions which exist nowhere else." *Cherokee Nation*, 30 U.S. at 16. In the early 1800s, the United States pursued the policy of "removal"-i.e., the relocation of tribal communities from their homelands in the East and Midwest to remote locations in the newly acquired Louisiana Purchase territory. In 1824, the Bureau of Indian Affairs (BIA) was created to implement that removal policy. For the majority of the Nineteenth Century, the federal government entered into a series of treaties and agreements identifying the lands owned by the tribes. These treaties and agreements were frequently violated or amended to reduce Indian holdings and to open more land to non-Indian settlers. During this time period, the tribes held their land communally, so there was very little individual ownership of land. Non-Indian land, whether communally or individually owned, could be sold without the approval of the federal government.

By the late 1870s, the government had embarked upon the reservation era. This era was a particularly miserable time for the Indians because the reservation policy deprived Indians of their traditional economy and made them dependent upon the federal government. During the reservation era, the BIA became the provider of foods and goods to the tribes. Hence, by the 1870s, the government had successfully placed Native Americans in a state of coerced dependency.

After this relationship of dependency between the United States and the Indian people was forcibly established, the allotment era began. Driven by a greed for the land holdings of the tribes, Congress passed the 1887 General Allotment Act, also known as the Dawes Act. See 25 U.S.C. § 348. Through the allotment process established by the Dawes Act, a delegation of American "peace commissioners" would negotiate with the tribes for the allotment of their reservations. The tribes were compensated for their land, and each head of household was allotted some amount of property, usually in 40-, 80-, or 160-acre parcels. The "surplus" lands that were not allotted to Indian individuals were then opened to non-Indian settlement. Allotted land was held in trust by the United States for the individual Indians. Therefore, the Indians could not lease, sell, or burden their property without the approval of the federal government.

More importantly, the United States had again successfully managed to deprive the Indian people of more land, this time in return for the creation of a trust status. Between 1887 and 1934, 90 million acres—about sixty-five percent of Indian land—left Indian ownership.

The allotments were the product of the United States' effort to eradicate Indian culture. As defendant Gover testified:

> the thinking was that it was tribalism that held the Indians back; that what they needed to do was develop the sort of individualism that had been so beneficial for the United States in its expansion, and allotment was the way to do that. But the things that accompanied allotment were really even more dreadful than the allotment policy itself.

> For example, there was a system of boarding schools established, and suddenly the Indian people were subject to these mandatory education requirements imposed by the Bureau of Indian Affairs. These schools were run by the Bureau of Indian Affairs, and they would take these kids away from their families, put them in these boarding schools. They might or might not see their parents again for years, or ever. Train them in English. They forbade them their native languages. They forbade them their religions. They cut their hair, and they dressed them like non-Indian kids would be dressed, and literally tried to turn them into white people.

In 1934, another major shift in federal policy toward Indians occurred. With the enactment of the Indian Reorganization Act of 1934, the federal government reversed its assimilation policy and directed BIA to rebuild the tribal communities and government structures. *See* 25 U.S.C. § 462. This new policy ended the allotment era and authorized the Secretary of the Interior to acquire land in trust for the tribes and for individual Indians. The Reorganization Act also indefinitely extended the trust period for the allotments that had already been made, which is why the United States has a continuing duty to administer allotted Indian lands (and the funds arising from those lands) in trust today.

B.   The IIM Trust

As a result of the allotments made from 1887–1934 and the Indians Reorganization Act's indefinite extension of the resulting trust period, the United States currently holds approximately 11 million acres of plaintiffs' individual land allotments in trust. The United States itself is the trustee of the IIM trust. Congress has designated the Secretary of the Interior and the Secretary of the Treasury as the United States' trustee-delegates for certain trust management functions. Within Interior, several agencies perform some IIM trust function. These agencies include the Bureau of Indian Affairs (BIA), the Office of the Special Trustee (OST), the Office of Trust Funds Management (OTFM), the Bureau of Land Management (BLM), the Minerals Management Service (MMS), and the Office of Hearings and Appeals (OHA).

BIA generally has responsibility for trust land management and income collection. Almost any transaction involving IIM trust lands must be approved by BIA. To make these approvals, BIA maintains personnel to review the transfers of those lands and to appraise the lands in conjunction with those transactions. There are also income-producing activities on many of these lands, including grazing leases, timber leases, timber sales, oil and gas production, mineral production, and rights-of-way. Each of these activities requires the approval of BIA. These activities are the source of IIM trust funding. Given BIA's role, it logically follows that it is responsible for maintaining complete and accurate land and title records. These records, in theory, provide the basis for IIM trust payments, which are controlled by OTFM.

There are over 300,000 IIM trust accounts on Interior's system. Interior cannot provide the exact number of IIM trust accounts that should be on this system. This number could increase (assuming greater omissions than duplicates) or decrease (assuming greater duplicates than omissions). Plaintiffs contend that there should be approximately 500,000 IIM trust accounts. While the overall number of accounts is quite large, it is important to note that OTFM has identified 16,700 IIM trust accounts with a stated balance below one dollar and no activity for at least eighteen months. Of course, it is a farce to say that these accounts actually contain any given amount. Although the United States freely gives out "balances" to plaintiffs, it admits that currently these balances cannot be supported by adequate transactional documentation.

Treasury's IIM trust responsibilities include holding and investing IIM trust funds at the direction of Interior, as well as maintaining certain records related to these functions. Of course, Treasury also performs central accounting for the federal government and serves as the government's financial manager.

C.   The Indian Trust Fund Management Reform Act of 1994

By the mid-1980s there was uniform disapproval of the manner in which Interior was administering the IIM trust. In 1988, Congress began to hold oversight hearings related to the handling of government trust accounts. On April 22, 1992, the House Committee on Government Operations issued a report entitled Misplaced Trust: The Bureau of Indian Affairs' Mismanagement of the Indian Trust Fund, H.R. No. 102–499 (1992) (Pls. Ex. 1). This thoroughly documented report concluded that Interior had made no credible effort to address the problems in trust administration in a "wide range of areas" and that Interior had disobeyed many congressional directives aimed at forcing Interior to correct trust management practices and reconcile the Indian trust accounts.

In response to these criticisms, Interior, through the accounting firm Arthur Andersen, conducted a study to determine whether the IIM trust and tribal trust accounts could be reconciled simultaneously. In an initial report, Arthur Andersen concluded that, within certain parameters, the tribal accounts could be reconciled, but that the IIM trust system would pose a far more difficult task, perhaps costing over $200 million. Even that expenditure would have yielded only a "reconciliation" of approximately eighty-five percent reliability.

Based largely on the findings made in Misplaced Trust, Congress passed the Indian Trust Fund Management Reform Act. *See* Pub. L. No. 103–412 (1994) (Pls.' Ex. 1). The Act recognized and codified the trust duties of the Secretary of the Interior, as the primary trustee-delegate of the United States, toward the IIM trust. See 25 U.S.C. §§ 162a(d) & 4011 (Supp.1999).

The Secretary of the Interior is Currently in Breach of Four Statutory Trust Duties that Warrant Prospective Relief

1.   The Secretary of the Interior Has No Written Plan to Gather Missing Data

Although Interior has established numerous high-level plans and has acquired and begun to implement effective new accounting and asset management systems, it currently has no final written statement of policies and procedures for recovering missing data—as opposed to data currently retained somewhere within the bowels of Interior but not yet processed—necessary to perform an accounting. It is as though Interior believes that if the problem of missing documentation is ignored, it will simply go away or, at least, be left for another administration to handle.

2.   The Secretary of the Interior Has No Written Plan Addressing the Retention of IIM-Related Trust Documents Necessary to Render an Accounting

Interior has no finalized plan concerning the destruction of IIM-related trust documents necessary to discharge the defendants' statutory duty to render an accurate accounting. No such plan has been provided to the court, and there is no such plan in the administrative record.

3. The Secretary of the Interior Has No Written Architecture Plan

The court has declared that the Trust Fund Management Reform Act placed upon Interior the duty to establish a written plan dealing with computer and business systems architecture. Contrary to this duty, however, Interior still has no such plan. It appears that Interior recognizes the value and importance of such a plan, because an architecture plan is currently being developed.

4. The Secretary of the Interior Has No Written Plan Addressing the Staffing of Interior's Trust Management Functions

The court has declared that the Trust Fund Management Reform Act requires Interior to establish a written plan for the staffing of IIM trust management functions. Contrary to this duty, however, Interior currently has no such plan.

The Secretary of the Treasury Has Breached His Fiduciary Duty to Retain IIM-Related Trust Documents and Has No Remedial Plan to Address This Breach of Duty.

Treasury has admitted that it has treated IIM trust material the same as general records by destroying them after their age exceeded six years and seven months, without regard to the fact that the United States (through its trustee-delegates) has not rendered an accounting of plaintiffs' IIM trust money. This policy is a breach of plaintiffs' right to have retained the documents necessary to allow the United States to render an accounting.

In light of these conclusions, and to ensure that defendants diligently take steps to bring themselves into compliance with their statutory trust duties, the court will retain continuing jurisdiction over this matter for a period of five years, subject to any motion for enlargement of time that may be made, and will order as follows:

1. Beginning March 1, 2000, defendants shall file with the court and serve upon plaintiffs, quarterly status reports setting forth and explaining the steps that defendants have taken to rectify the breaches of trust declared today and to bring themselves into compliance with their statutory trust duties embodied in the Indian Trust Fund Management Reform Act of 1994 and other applicable statutes and regulations governing the IIM trust.

2. Each quarterly report shall be limited, to the greatest extent practical, to actions taken since the issuance of the preceding quarterly report. Defendants' first quarterly report, due March 1, 2000, shall encompass actions taken since June 10, 1999.

3. Defendants Secretary of the Interior and Assistant Secretary of the Interior—Indian Affairs shall file with the court and serve upon plaintiffs the revised or amended High Level Implementation Plan. The revised or amended HLIP shall be filed and served upon completion but no later than March 1, 2000.

4. Defendants shall provide any additional information required by the court to explain or supplement defendants' submissions. Plaintiffs may petition the court to order defendants to provide further information as needed if such information cannot be obtained through informal requests directly to defendants.

X. Conclusion

Although plaintiffs may be dissatisfied with the court's decision to not appoint another Special Master or Monitor at this time, plaintiffs should take great satisfaction in the stunning victory that they have achieved today on behalf of the 300,000-plus Indian beneficiaries of the IIM trust. Plaintiffs have established their entitlement to ongoing judicial review of trust reform efforts for the next five years—or longer if necessary—and a role for their own continued, close involvement in reform efforts. That is enough for today. If more becomes necessary, the court will be available. If the defendants carry out what they now say that they will do and comply with the court's order issued this date, more should not be necessary. In that case, trust reform should become a reality rather than a dream.

NOTES

1. This historic lawsuit and settlement with the government are unique. The case lasted more than sixteen years. It involved over 3,900 district court docket entries; 250 days of hearings and trials; fourteen appeals, including ten interlocutory appeals to the D.C. Circuit; and over 80 published opinions of the U.S. District Court for the District of Columbia and the U.S. Court of Appeals for the D.C. Circuit. In December 2009, the parties reached an unprecedented $3.4 billion settlement, including $1.9 billion in furtherance of trust reform and $1.5 billion in direct

President Barack Obama meets with Elouise Cobell in the Oval Office, Dec. 8, 2010. Official White House Photo by Pete Souza. Cobell was a tribal elder and activist, banker, rancher, and lead plaintiff in the groundbreaking class-action suit Cobell v. Salazar.

payments to class members. All three branches of the government approved the settlement, called the Claims Resolution Act of 2010: Congress, exercising its plenary power in relation to Indian affairs, "authorized, ratified, and confirmed" the settlement through bipartisan legislation; the President signed that legislation with an accompanying statement of support; and the district court found the settlement to be fair, reasonable, and adequate after a fairness hearing. The $3.4 billion tax-free settlement is the largest settlement with the U.S. government in American history. *See* Brooke Campbell, *Cobell Settlement Finalized After Years of Litigation: Victory at Last?*, 37 AM. INDIAN L. REV. 629, 629 (2013); Armen H. Merjian, *An Unbroken Chain of Injustice: The Dawes Act, Native American Trusts, and Cobell v. Salazar*, 46 GONZ. L. REV. 609 (2011).

2.   As we have seen in other chapters, another problem with Indian Trust land is fractionation, the process by which land is divided into fractions each time it passes to a new generation. This has resulted in many members of Indian Tribes or Nations holding tiny lots with little economic value. Part of the *Cobell* Settlement was a buyback program, whereby the government offered to buy individual plots and return them to the tribes to be consolidated. Although many individuals took advantage of the buy back, it is controversial. *See* Jered T. Davidson, *This Land Is Your Land, This Land Is My Land? Why the Cobell Settlement Will Not Resolve Indian Land Fractionation*, 35 AM. INDIAN L. REV. 575, 575, 601–602 (2011) (criticizing the buyback program for its limited time period and failure to account for those who might be unwilling to sell). *But see* Rebekah Martin, *Defending the Cobell Buy-Back Program*, 41 AM. INDIAN L. REV. 91, 91 (2016).

3.   There are two kinds of accountings that a trustee may provide: formal (judicial) and informal (nonjudicial). A judicial accounting is one that the trustee prepares with detailed accounting statements and often with the help of a lawyer, in order to ensure that the form of the accounting satisfies any local court rules. The accounting is filed with a court, the beneficiaries are notified of this filing, and the beneficiaries have a certain amount of time to respond or object to the accounting. If the beneficiaries do not object, they are subsequently barred from later bringing any claim of breach against the trustee that could have been brought in response to the accounting. (If the matter was not disclosed in the accounting, res judicata does not bar a subsequent beneficiary claim.) An informal accounting, on the other hand, is one that the trustee prepares and sends directly to the beneficiaries. Typically, the trustee will ask the beneficiaries to sign off on the informal accounting, and such an agreement may be binding (although you may recall that Farr's accounting in *Marsman* did not prevent

Cappy's surviving spouse from suing for breach). Why do you think a trustee might opt for an informal accounting?

4. Historically, at common law, a settlor could severely restrict a beneficiary's right to information, and settlors often relied on the secrecy that wealth transfers in trust provided:

> Trust law has placed such a premium on privacy that it has denied trust beneficiaries as well as the general public access to the trust instrument. To preserve trust privacy, traditional doctrines and rules have allowed a trust beneficiary to see at best the terms of the trust that the trustee deems relevant to that specific beneficiary.

See Frances H Foster, *Trust Privacy*, 93 CORNELL L. REV. 555, 566 (2008).

Some states still maintain strong privacy laws with respect to beneficiaries. South Dakota trust companies, which you will read more about in the next chapter's discussion of asset protection trusts, market the fact that South Dakota state law does not require trustees to notify beneficiaries of their trust interests, even once they reach the age of eighteen. One such South Dakota-based trust company advertises that "South Dakota is universally considered by advisors and academics to have the most comprehensive and flexible quiet trust statute in the nation, granting the settlor, trust protector, and the investment/distribution advisor the power to expand, restrict, eliminate, or modify the rights of the beneficiaries to discover information about a trust."

The UTC has moved toward increased transparency and access to information; what policy purposes are served by allowing (or disallowing) beneficiaries access to trust information? Stated differently, how much control should a trust settlor be able to exert over a beneficiary's access to information and on what grounds?

ASSESSMENT

You represent Michael Davis, who is an attorney and cotrustee of a testamentary trust established by John B. Jacob. The trust, which Michael drafted, contains the following provision:

> My Trustee shall be excused from filing any account with any court; however, my Trustee shall render an annual (or more frequent) account and may, at any other time, including at the time of the death, resignation, or removal of any Trustee, render an intermediate account of my Trustee's administration to such of the then current income beneficiaries who are of sound mind and not minors at the

time of such accounting. The written approval of such accounting by all of such income beneficiaries shall bind all persons then having or thereafter acquiring or claiming any interest in any trust and shall be a complete discharge to my Trustee with respect to all matters set forth in the account as fully and to the same extent as though the account had been judicially settled in an action or proceeding in which all persons having, acquiring, or claiming any interest were duly made parties and were duly represented.

John's surviving spouse, Harriett, is the sole beneficiary during her life and is the other cotrustee of the trust. John's son from a prior marriage, Bill, receives any remaining property on Harriett's death. Bill has asked for an accounting of the trust, and Harriett has refused. Michael asks for your advice on the following:

a.   Must Michael provide Bill with an accounting, given the trust's language and Harriett's refusal?

b.   If the answer is yes, will it be sufficient for Michael to provide Bill with bank account statements for the trust?

See Jacob v. Davis, 738 A.2d 904 (Md. Ct. Spec. App. 1999).

D. Exculpatory Clauses

A question that arises in conjunction with a trustee's fiduciary duties is whether a settlor can exculpate a trustee from breaches by inserting express terms to that effect in the trust instrument. An example of this type of clause is included in the *Marsman* case. The UTC allows for trustee exculpation, but there are limits:

UTC § 1008 Exculpation of Trustee

(a)   A term of a trust relieving a trustee of liability for breach of trust is unenforceable to the extent that it:

(1)   relieves the trustee of liability for breach of trust committed in bad faith or with reckless indifference to the purposes of the trust or the interests of the beneficiaries;

or

(2)   was inserted as the result of an abuse by the trustee of a fiduciary or confidential relationship to the settlor.

(b)   An exculpatory term drafted or caused to be drafted by the trustee is invalid as an abuse of a fiduciary or confidential relationship unless the trustee proves that the exculpatory term is fair under the circumstances and that its existence and contents were adequately communicated to the settlor.

———————

The following case was decided before Massachusetts had adopted the UTC, but it employs the Restatement standards that underlie UTC § 1008(b). Notice also that an exculpatory clause is unenforceable if it relieves the trustee of liability for bad faith or reckless indifference.

Rutanen v. Ballard

678 N.E.2d 133 (Mass. 1997)

FRIED, J.

The income beneficiaries of the Antonia Quevillon Trust commenced this action in the Probate and Family Court against the trustees of that trust for breach of their fiduciary duties to the trust in that they did not sell unproductive property of the trust. The remaindermen of the trust intervened on the side of the income beneficiaries. The judge made findings that the trustees violated their fiduciary duty and awarded damages. The trustees appealed arguing that their actions were protected by an exculpatory clause in the trust instrument, that the judge's findings of breach of trust were in error, and that the damages awarded were speculative. The Appeals Court affirmed, and we granted the defendants' application for further appellate review. We also affirm the judgment of the Probate Court.

Facts and Procedural History

In 1969, Antonia Quevillon, the settlor of the trust, consulted attorney Carl Baylis regarding the disposition of the apartment buildings she owned and operated. At that time, she was seventy years old and in poor health. She had had no prior relationship with Baylis. Baylis drafted a trust into which she transferred her property. After the death of the settlor, the trust was to provide income to her children for a period of twenty years at which point it would terminate, and the trust property was to be divided equally among the children of Marcel Quevillon, a son of the settlor.

Baylis and Estelle Ballard, daughter of the settlor and one of the income beneficiaries, were appointed cotrustees. Ballard agreed to manage the property for $50 per week. Baylis did not discuss any management fees with the settlor.

The trustees had discretion to sell the trust property. The trust also contained an exculpatory clause which stated that "[e]ach trustee shall be liable only for his own willful misconduct or omissions in bad faith."

After the settlor's death in 1971, the trust property was managed almost exclusively by Ballard until 1986, with Baylis taking little interest. The property appreciated substantially in value from $256,000 in 1971 to $1.3 million in 1986 but paid the income beneficiaries only $48,813 during that period. In 1985, the income beneficiaries met with the cotrustees to discuss the lack of income from the trust property. At that meeting, Baylis urged that the property be sold and invested in government bonds. The income beneficiaries agreed to this proposal, and the trustees began accepting offers. They received one offer of $215,000 for two of the properties and another offer, subject to the availability of financing, of $1.425 million for the other four properties. The six properties were appraised for a total of only $1.3 million.

Ballard, however, desired to own the properties herself. Baylis, knowing this, presented the offers to her and gave her an opportunity to match them, but she could not finance the purchase. She then refused to sell the property and later testified that she had not given consideration to either the income beneficiaries or the remaindermen in making that decision.

Even though Ballard refused to sell the property, Baylis forwarded purchase and sale agreements to the prospective buyers. The buyers signed the agreements and put down deposits toward the purchase price. Ballard continued to refuse to sell the property. Baylis responded by proposing that Ballard would receive the two properties for which $215,000 had been offered and would allow the other sale to proceed. Ballard agreed to this proposal, but the prospective buyer of the properties which were then going to be sold to Ballard sued the trustees, both individually and in their capacity as trustees. The trust settled the case with the buyer and paid expenses associated with the suit. Baylis prepared and filed a petition in Probate and Family Court for a license to sell the property and terminate the trust in December 1986, but Ballard withdrew her support of the sales.

The income beneficiaries sued the trustees. The trust eventually terminated, and the property was transferred to the remaindermen. At that time, the estimated value of the property was approximately $1.081 million.

The judge found that the trustees had violated their fiduciary duties, that both had acted in bad faith, that the exculpatory clause was ineffective, that the trust should not have paid all the expenses from the earlier suit over the property, and that the trustees were entitled to no fees from managing the trust. The judge awarded damages based on what the net proceeds of the sale would have been had the offers described above been accepted.

Discussion

In a case such as this where a trust is to provide income to beneficiaries for a term of years and then the trust property is to be distributed to remaindermen, the trustees are under a duty to sell the trust property when it becomes unproductive "in the absence of manifestation of intent on the part of the testator or settlor that the property be retained even if it becomes unproductive." *Springfield Safe Deposit & Trust Co. v. Wade*, 24 N.E.2d 764 (Mass. 1940). Trustees are also required to sell "under-productive property" as well—"property [that] produces an income which is substantially less than the income which would be derived if the property were sold and the proceeds were invested so as to yield the current rate of return on trust investments." RESTATEMENT (SECOND) OF TRUSTS § 240 comment b, at 594 (1959); 3A SCOTT, TRUSTS § 240 (4th ed.1988). Strict application of a rule that would require a sale whenever the income produced is lower than the current going rate, however, would interfere with the trustee's discretion granted by the settlor and might upset the settlor's preference that the property be retained at least insofar as the rate of return on the investment is not widely disparate from the return that could be had elsewhere. Thus where "the income derived is somewhat less" than the going rate, the trustee is under no obligation to sell. The duty to sell is triggered "only where the difference is so great that it is unfair to the life beneficiary to retain the property." RESTATEMENT (SECOND) OF TRUSTS § 240 comment b.

In this case, the rate of return is highly disproportionate to what could be earned elsewhere. By 1985, fourteen years into the life of the trust, the trustees had distributed only $48,813 to the income beneficiaries. The trust property was worth over $250,000 in 1971 and had increased in value to $1.3 million. By any measure, income of only slightly more than $3,000 per year is far below what would be expected on a trust corpus of this size.

Furthermore, Baylis testified that at the time of the proposed sale, the trust was nearly devoid of any cash assets. Prudential concerns do not justify retention. The properties were the only trust asset so the real estate could not be justified either as necessary for a balanced portfolio nor can the trustees argue that other assets were producing substantial income for the beneficiaries.

Second, there was evidence that the trustees, at least Baylis, were aware that property values had "peaked" and were not likely to continue rising as they had before. The offers made for the property totaled substantially more than the amount for which the properties were appraised at the time so that the trustees would have needed a reasonable expectation that the properties would have appreciated to a value more than the offer price to justify retention on this ground.

The trustees argue that the judge erred in concluding that Ballard acted in bad faith by refusing to sell the properties due to an improper motivation other than the reason Ballard gave—keeping the properties in the family to accord with what she claimed were the wishes of the settlor. Both trustees testified that Ballard wanted to own the properties rather than sell them to someone outside the family. Ballard claims that this was simply to assure that the properties remained in the family. The trustees, however, had already sold two properties to outsiders, and Ballard never offered the properties to any other family member to keep them in the family. Ballard's self-interest violates the requirement that a "trustee must exercise good faith and act solely in the interests of beneficiaries in administering the trust." *Boston Safe Deposit & Trust Co. v. Lewis*, 57 N.E.2d 638 (Mass. 1944).

Baylis asserts that, even if Ballard violated her fiduciary duty, he acted in favor of the sale and petitioned the Probate Court for instructions as to how to proceed with the sale. He argues that he therefore cannot be held liable. To fulfil his duty, a cotrustee must "participate in the administration of the trust and use reasonable care to prevent a co-trustee from committing a breach of trust or compel a co-trustee to redress a breach of trust." RESTATEMENT (SECOND) OF TRUSTS § 184 (1959). If one trustee refuses to exercise a power that the trustees are under a duty to exercise, "the other trustees are not justified in merely acquiescing in the non-existence of the power. In such a case it is their duty to apply to the court for instructions." *Id.* at § 184. The judge found that Baylis violated these principles in several ways. First, he largely abandoned his duties of administering the trust to Ballard. Second, Baylis, aware of Ballard's desire to have the properties for herself and her refusal to sell motivated by her self-interest, "never advised her . . . that her failure to sell lacked any basis, was not in the best interests of the beneficiaries, and constituted a breach of her fiduciary duties." These factual findings are uncontested. Third, while Baylis did file a petition for instructions with the Probate Court as the Restatement requires in such circumstances, he "made no attempt to pursue the petition to sell or to seek a contested hearing on the petition." Baylis's complaint, however, did not challenge Ballard's refusal at all but rather stated that Ballard had submitted her resignation to Baylis and that he had accepted it. The judge, not knowing that

Ballard was wrongfully refusing to consent, deferred judgment subject to obtaining Ballard's signature. Baylis never followed up by informing Ballard that she might be in breach of her fiduciary duty by not signing nor did he ask the judge to compel Ballard to agree to the sale. Because Baylis did not file a petition explaining to the judge that the sale would be in the best interests of the beneficiaries and that Ballard was improperly blocking the sale, he did not take the steps reasonably necessary to prevent Ballard from breaching her duty.

The trustees argue that the trial judge and the Appeals Court erred in concluding that the exculpatory clause was invalid because it was improperly inserted into the contract and it limited liability to willful misconduct or bad faith. The Restatement (Second) of Trusts § 222 (1959) states that "[t]o the extent to which a provision relieving the trustee of liability for breaches of trust is inserted in the trust instrument as the result of an abuse by the trustee of a fiduciary or confidential relationship to the settlor, such provision is ineffective." The Restatement enumerates the following six factors for determining whether such an abuse occurred: (1) whether prior to the creation of the trust, the trustee was in a fiduciary relationship to the settlor; (2) whether the trust was drawn by the trustee; (3) whether the settlor had independent advice as to the trust provisions; (4) whether the settlor is a person of experience and judgment or a person unfamiliar with business affairs; (5) whether the insertion was a product of undue influence or improper conduct by the trustee; (6) the extent and reasonableness of the provision. *Id.* at § 222 comment d, at 518.

In this case Baylis was retained as the settlor's attorney to write the trust instrument, the settlor received no independent advice, and the settlor was seventy years old, had had a stroke and was "in questionable health." On these facts, the failure of Baylis to bring the clause to the settlor's attention and explain the implications of the clause was improper and rendered the clause ineffective to protect him. *See* 3A Scott, *supra* at § 222.

Judgment affirmed.

NOTES

1.   Besides discussing the exculpatory clause with the settlor, what else could Baylis have done to protect himself from liability?

2.   Here and in cases like *Janes*, the court faults the trustee for failing to sell an asset. How much 20/20 hindsight must a trustee have in deciding whether to buy or sell property trust property? Did this court expect too much?

3. The comment to UTC § 1008(b) states that it specifically "disapproves of cases such as *Marsman v. Nasca.*" Would application of this section have changed the outcome in *Marsman*? The comment then states as follows:

> The requirements of subsection (b) are satisfied if the settlor was represented by independent counsel. If the settlor was represented by independent counsel, the settlor's attorney is considered the drafter of the instrument even if the attorney used the trustee's form. Because the settlor's attorney is an agent of the settlor, disclosure of an exculpatory term to the settlor's attorney is disclosure to the settlor.

Is this sufficient to protect an unsophisticated settlor? Why would a settlor agree to an exculpatory clause in the first place?

E. Conclusion and Takeaways

A trustee may accept or resign from the position of trustee by methods specified under the UTC or in the trust instrument. Once the trustee accepts the position, the trustee must act, or refrain from acting. consistent with the terms of the trust instrument and the trustee's fiduciary duties, including the duty of obedience to the settlor's intent, the duty of loyalty to the beneficiaries, the duty to inquire as to the beneficiaries needs, the duty to care for the trust assets and invest them prudently, the duty of impartiality, and the duty to inform and report. Keep in mind that the trust instrument may modify or expand upon many of these duties. For instance, trusts may be drafted with exculpatory clauses releasing trustees from liability for breaches of duty that fall short of bad faith or recklessness. The applicable law may also change. The UTC has been influential by, for example, transforming the no further inquiry rule into a presumption and adopting modern investing standards, which means portfolio diversification and the tailoring of risk to meet beneficiary needs. Now that we have discussed the trustee's duties to the beneficiaries, we will shift focus to explore the beneficiaries' rights (and the beneficiaries' creditors' rights) to trust assets, with a focus on why trusts can be such a valuable part of an estate plan.

CHAPTER 10 COMPREHENSIVE ASSESSMENTS

1. **DESIGN A CLIENT PRESENTATION.** Design a presentation for clients entitled "What to Know Before You Agree to Serve as Trustee." The presentation could take the form of a Power Point Presentation, a Decision Tree, an outline, a written guide, or even a graphic narrative. Whichever you choose, make sure to make it accessible to non-lawyers.

2.   **COUNSEL A CLIENT ON TRUSTEE SELECTION.** Peregrine and Glencora are in the process of creating a trust that will benefit their children. They are at the point of discussing trustee selection and are trying to decide how to go about making this decision. Please develop a list of criteria for them to consider as they make this important decision. Some questions that they might want to consider are: Should the trustee be a family member? What is the benefit of an institutional trustee? Would it be a good idea for the trustee to also be the guardian for their minor children?

3.   **FIDUCIARY DUTY REVIEW.** Mark Rothko was an internationally famous painter who died in 1970, leaving 798 paintings in his will. These paintings were

extremely valuable even while he was alive, and after his death they naturally began to grow in value. The will's fiduciaries were Bernard J. Reis, Theodoros Stamos, and Morton Levine. Reis was director of The Marlborough Gallery (Marlborough), a famous high-end art gallery in New York. Stamos was a striving artist under contract with Marlborough. Levine was an academic who had a close family relationship with Rothko and was named guardian of his son.

**Mark Rothko, 1959
(photo by James Scott).**

Within three weeks of probate, the fiduciaries contracted to sell all 798 paintings under two contracts. The first contract sold 100 paintings to a corporation named Marlborough A.G. (MAG). The second contract consigned approximately 700 paintings to Marlborough and granted Marlborough a sales commission of 40 to 50 percent for each painting. (Before Rothko's death, Marlborough had a contract with Rothko to sell his painting at a 10 percent commission.) Rothko's daughter, Kate, sought to remove the fiduciaries, enjoin the paintings' disposal, rescind the contracts, and recover damages. The trial court found that Reis and Stamos breached their fiduciary duties by entering into the contracts with conflicts of interest. The court also found that Levine breached his fiduciary duties by following Reis and Stamos with awareness of their conflicts and rejected his defense that he relied on advice of counsel to do so.

a.   If you were the appellate court, would you affirm or reverse? On what grounds? Should the no further inquiry rule apply?

b.   If you were advising Mark Rothko and he suggested these individuals as fiduciaries, what would you raise as potential concerns?

    c.   If you represented Reis, Stamos, or Levine, and they asked your advice on whether to accept this appointment, what issues would you raise?

    d.   Write a letter to Levine explaining to him his liability (and likely damages) in client-accessible language.

Test Your Knowledge

To assess your understanding of the material in this chapter, click here to take a quiz.

CHAPTER 11

Private Trusts III: Asset Protection Trusts

CHAPTER LEARNING OUTCOMES

Following your work with the material in this chapter, you should be able to do the following:

- Assess the rights of a beneficiary and creditor in a given situation

- Draft asset protection features into irrevocable trusts

- Explain the rights of non-exception creditors and explain what options they have to recover money from a trust beneficiary

- Describe the rights of exception creditors and what they must do to obtain distributions

- Identify what Domestic Asset Protection Trusts are and analyze the related policy questions

- Describe to a client what a special needs trust is and how it can help with Medicaid planning

A. Introduction

In the last chapter, we learned why **fiduciary duties** are so important in the administration of **irrevocable trusts** and how those duties work. The chapter focused on the trustee's duties to the beneficiaries. This chapter shifts focus to explore the benefits of irrevocable trusts and learn what makes them so attractive to many people not just as a wealth transfer tool but also as a wealth management vehicle. While **revocable trusts** that terminate on the death of the settlor are commonly used as **will substitutes**, irrevocable trusts (whether the trust is irrevocable from the moment of creation or becomes irrevocable at the death of the settlor) are a ubiquitous planning device for high-wealth families because of the **asset protection** they afford to the families.

In **Part B**, we begin by discussing the traditional theories on which trust law grants asset protection and how the limitation of beneficiary rights leads to a resulting limitation of creditor rights. Then, we will learn about how asset protection works in practice and how to create it through **discretionary distribution terms** and **spendthrift clauses**. We will also learn about the rights of creditors, the difference between ordinary and **"exception" creditors**, and what forms of preferential treatment exception creditors receive under either common or uniform law.

In **Part C**, we continue our inquiry into asset protection by taking a look into new trends in asset protection and the emergence of the **Domestic Asset Protection Trust**, which allows—contrary to conventional trust policy—asset protection for **self-settled trusts**, with certain conditions. From a policy perspective, questions about the asset protection that irrevocable trusts offer are some of the most interesting and controversial ones we encounter. These questions directly bear on the relationship between trust law and wealth inequality and the role of wealth transfer, more generally, in aggravating wealth gaps, including racial and gender wealth gaps. Finally, in **Part D**, we also examine a very distinctive form of the self-settled asset protection trust, the **special or supplemental needs trust**, designed to allow an individual with medical needs to qualify for governmental assistance while still retaining assets in trust.

B. Creditors' Rights and Asset Protection Trusts

Marriages have commonly been the subject of family contracts and land settlements. *The Marriage Settlement*, **William Hogarth, circa 1743.**

It will come as no surprise that high-wealth families have historically sought—and continue to seek, in the present—to protect family wealth through sophisticated and often complex planning devices, including the irrevocable trust. If you have watched even one British historical drama, you've likely encountered an entail, a trust, or some other protective form of wealth transfer that restricts what the beneficiary can do with the property while also limiting the rights of external parties to the land and other assets.

What may be a surprise is the extent to which trust law allows trust settlors to protect property and restrict the access of creditors to trust assets. These kinds of wealth protections may seem at odds with cultural notions about fair play and paying one's debts. And it may seem inequitable that the law provides mechanisms for primarily high-wealth individuals and families—families with knowledge of and access to asset protection trusts—to avoid creditors. The reason for this policy of allowing asset protection stems from the concept of donor freedom, which, at least in the United States, has prevailed over the concepts of equal obligation and financial responsibility. That is to say, the justification for asset protection is grounded in support for donor intention and donor wishes. Accordingly, courts have regularly affirmed the right of a trust settlor to restrict beneficiary rights to the trust assets to protect beneficiaries from their own worst instincts or habits. A parent who wishes to protect a child from that

Connection Note: Notice how donative freedom, which we discussed at the beginning of this textbook, influences nearly all aspects of inheritance law.

child's own financial irresponsibility can therefore create asset protective terms in a trust that thereby limit the reach of creditors.

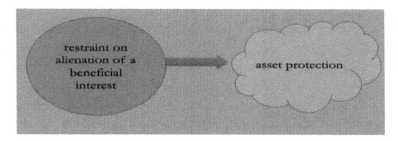

Donor intent is the theory of why we allow asset protection, from a public policy standpoint. The next question is what the operational theory of an asset protection trust is. This brings us back to the notion that restricting beneficiary rights also restricts creditor rights. Commonly, textbooks state that asset protection derives from a restraint on alienation. What does that really mean? Without any restrictions set by the donor, a beneficiary might have easy access to all the trust income and principal and might sell trust property; furthermore, the beneficiary would be able to sell an interest in the trust to satisfy debts, to raise funds, or to use it to secure a loan. A trust settlor, consequently, might want to include a provision in the trust terms that forbid a beneficiary to do any of these things. These terms act to restrain the beneficiary's ability to **alienate** trust property or an interest in the trust. These restraints on alienation create asset protection because, in the legal framework, if a beneficiary does not have a present interest in trust assets, then the trust assets cannot go to satisfy creditors. Once a beneficiary has a present interest—receives a distribution, for example— then creditors are free to pursue their claims. But not until then. Put another way, asset protection is simply based on ownership equivalence: the less control a beneficiary has over the assets, the fewer rights creditors have.

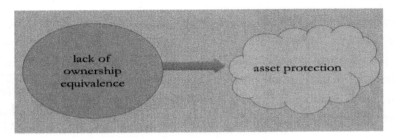

This chapter discusses three forms of asset protection trusts: discretionary trusts, spendthrift trusts, and domestic asset-protection trusts (DAPTs or self-settled asset protection trusts). For each, consider who benefits and who suffers harm by the operation of that particular trust form.

1. Discretionary Trusts

Discretionary trusts are an important tool for families whose goal is to protect wealth, and they have been used with great success for centuries. Courts affirmed the validity of these trusts in the United States around the turn of the nineteenth century on the basis of donor freedom. But how exactly do these discretionary trusts work? As we mentioned earlier, asset protection increases as beneficiary access to trust assets decreases. The simplest way of decreasing beneficiary access or rights to the trust assets is by creating trust distribution terms that are **discretionary** rather than **mandatory**. The more mandatory rights a beneficiary has to the trust assets, the less asset protection. The more that discretion to make distributions is vested in the trustee, the more asset protection exists. Accordingly, asset protection is created by crafting distribution terms that give as much discretion to the trustee as possible.

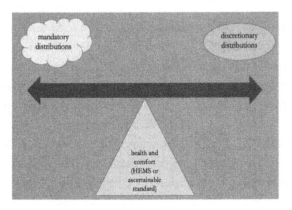

As we learned in earlier chapters, trust terms vary significantly, and the distribution terms are some of the most important in the trust document. A trust settlor might create a fully discretionary trust, in which the trustee has discretion to make distributions from both income and principal. On the other hand, income distributions may be mandatory and distributions from principal discretionary. Frequently, settlors establish **"discretionary support"** trusts that vest full discretion in the trustee but provide the guideline of support: "I leave these assets in trust to provide for the comfort and support of my spouse in the trustee's sole and absolute discretion." Does this look familiar? (Think of poor Cappy from Chapter 11). For asset protection purposes, the UTC and RESTATEMENT (THIRD) OF TRUSTS treat discretionary and discretionary support trusts the same way.[1] A particularly common form of the discretionary support trust is the discretionary trust with a "HEMS" standard—a discretionary trust that directs the trustee to make distributions for the Health, Education, Maintenance, and Support of the beneficiary. This standard is called an **ascertainable standard**, a term you will see come up frequently in the cases and in tax rules.

> **Historical Note:** William Drogo, the Ninth Duke of Manchester was born on 3 March 1877 as William Angus Drogo Montagu. He was the only son of George Montagu, 8th Duke of Manchester and Consuelo Yznaga del Valle, a Cuban American heiress. He spent much of his life abroad, evading creditors and seeking to raise money from friends, acquaintances, and anyone who seemed willing. He did marry Helena Zimmerman, the daughter a railroad president and major stockholder in Standard Oil. Nevertheless, the Duke was plagued with financial difficulties throughout his life.

What rights, then, do creditors have when trying to recover money owed from a discretionary trust beneficiary? Creditors fall into two categories: ordinary

---

[1]   For more on the collapse of discretionary and support trusts into one category, see Evelyn Ginsberg Abravanel, *Discretionary Support Trusts*, 68 IOWA L. REV. 273 (1982), and Mark Merric, Douglas Stein & Michelle Berger, *The Uniform Trust Code: A Continuum of Discretionary Trusts or a Continuum of Continuing Litigation*, 8 J. RETIREMENT PLAN. 33 (2005).

creditors and exception creditors. Ordinary creditors form the bulk of creditors. These are creditors with no special rights, and include banks, most providers of goods and services, or even friends who may have made you a loan. The most

William Montagu, 9th Duke of Manchester, circa 1910.

effective tool that ordinary creditors have is the **Hamilton order**, which a creditor must obtain from a court. The use of a Hamilton order was first authorized in the famous *Hamilton v. Drogo*, 150 N.E. 496 (N.Y. 1926) case. In that case, a New York court protected trust assets that the dowager Duchess of Manchester put in a discretionary trust for her son, William Drogo, Duke of Manchester, from creditors, concluding: "We may not interfere with the discretion which the testatrix has vested in the trustee any more than her son may do so." The creditors were out of luck. Nevertheless, the court authorized the use of what has come to be known as a Hamilton order.

With a Hamilton order, an ordinary creditor cannot compel a distribution, but the order requires that if any distributions are to be made to or for the benefit of the beneficiary, the creditor shall be paid first. The UTC follows this rule. *See* UTC § 501. The Hamilton order, consequently, saves the creditor from having to monitor whether the beneficiary receives a distribution and then from fighting with other creditors when a distribution is made. A Hamilton order also disallows the trustee from circumventing creditors by paying directly for goods and services rendered to the beneficiary; that is to say, the beneficiary cannot avoid one particular creditor and have the trustee pay others as the beneficiary wishes: "[T]he practical significance of a Hamilton order is that while the creditor may not be able to satisfy a claim by reaching a beneficiary's interest in a discretionary trust, the creditor will be able to prevent a beneficiary from receiving any benefits from the trust until the creditor's judgment is satisfied." Timothy J. Vitollo, *Uniform Trust Code Section 503: Applying Hamilton Orders to Spendthrift Interests*, 43 REAL PROP. TR. & EST. L.J. 169 (2008).

Exception creditors, as opposed to ordinary creditors, benefit from enhanced rights based on public policy rulemaking. Exception creditors can, under very limited circumstances, compel a distribution. In the past—and in states that have not adopted the UTC—common law rules have defined exception creditors to include only provisioners of necessaries (necessaries being generally limited to food, medicine, and sometimes housing). The UTC has revised which creditors are exception creditors and laid out the rules for these creditors to recover money. Providers of necessaries are no longer exception creditors in the UTC; instead, exception creditors are primarily either a child or an ex-spouse enforcing a claim for support.

UTC § 504 Discretionary Trusts; Effect of Standard

(c)   To the extent a trustee has not complied with a standard of distribution or has abused a discretion:

(1)   a distribution may be ordered by the court to satisfy a judgment or court order against the beneficiary for support or maintenance of the beneficiary's child, spouse, or former spouse; and

(2)   the court shall direct the trustee to pay to the child, spouse, or former spouse such amount as is equitable under the circumstances but not more than the amount the trustee would have been required to distribute to or for the benefit of the beneficiary had the trustee complied with the standard or not abused the discretion.

(d) This section does not limit the right of a beneficiary to maintain a judicial proceeding against a trustee for an abuse of discretion or failure to comply with a standard for distribution.

Exception creditors can, accordingly, compel a distribution, but it is not easy. In order to compel a distribution, the exception creditor (either an ex-spouse or child) must show that the trustee "has not complied with a standard of distribution or has abused a discretion." Then, after surmounting that hurdle, the amount that the exception creditor will recover is no more than what the trustee should have distributed in the first place, had the trustee complied with the applicable standard of distribution. Discretionary trusts, in this way, are extremely protective devices that enable trust settlors to dictate strong conditions and protect beneficiaries based on those conditions.

NOTES

1.   The theory upon which the discretionary trust's asset protection rests is that the beneficiary has no right to the trust assets, since all distributions are at the discretion of the trustee. Is this really true? A trust must always be for the

benefit of the beneficiary and the beneficiary always retains standing to sue the trustee to remedy a breach of trust affecting trust property that could be distributed to the beneficiary. Furthermore, even if a trustee has uncontrolled discretion over distributions, a beneficiary may also be able to compel distributions if the trustee unreasonably or abusively withheld assets from the beneficiary. How do these pieces of doctrine square with the theory of asset protection?

Practice Note: Discretionary Trusts and Divorce. Discretionary trusts play a large role in family wealth preservation and are especially useful in protecting assets at divorce. Modern courts generally consider beneficiaries of a discretionary spendthrift trust to possess nothing more than a speculative interest in the trust assets—a "mere expectancy"—because they do not have a guaranteed right to distributions from the trust. A number of states include trust interests in the marital estate at divorce only if the beneficiary has a present possessory interest or the right to withdraw trust assets. Massachusetts courts generally maintain that any interest in a discretionary trust is non-includable in the marital estate: "[A] party's beneficial interest in a discretionary trust . . . because of the peculiar nature of such a trust . . . is too remote or speculative to be so included." *D.L v. G.L,* 811 N.E.2d 1013 (Mass. App. Ct. 2004). The Colorado Supreme Court, elaborating on this rule, concluded in *In re Marriage of Jones,* 812 P.2d 1152 (Colo. 1991) that, "unlike a vested retirement plan, the beneficiary of a discretionary trust has no contractual or enforceable right to income or principal from the trust, and cannot force any action by the trustee unless the trustee performs dishonestly or does not act at all." For an interesting recent case, see *Pfannenstiehl v. Pfannenstiehl,* 475 Mass. 105, 106 (2016). The question, in that case, was whether to include the husband's trust interest in the marital estate. The trial and appellate courts included this interest because, although it was a discretionary trust with a spendthrift provision, the trust terms also included an ascertainable standard (think HEMS). In addition, both the trial and appellate courts paid particular attention to the fact that the two trustees were not impartial (one was the husband's twin brother, and one was the attorney for the husband's father and the family business), as well as the fact that

> there was a particular "pattern of distribution—substantial distributions before the divorce, then zero as the divorce loomed." The trial court judge, assessing these facts, stated that this was a case in which "the proverbial family wagons circled the family money." Nevertheless, on appeal to the Supreme Judicial Court of Massachusetts, the court concluded that "[the husband's] interest in the 2004 trust is 'so speculative as to constitute nothing more than [an] expectanc[y],' and thus that it is 'not assignable to the marital estate.' " The trust interest, the court stated, could only be considered as a factor at the point of equitable distribution. Ultimately, then, trust assets may be considered as one factor among many in a court's determination of property division or spousal support (usually under the factor of "other resources available to the individual") but are unlikely to be included as marital property, even if those assets have been the couple's sole source of income during marriage. *See Robinson v. Robinson*, 621 S.E.2d 147 (Va. Ct. App. 2005).

2.   As we have discussed, as a way of obtaining strong asset protection, many trust settlors use broad discretionary language in the distribution provisions. But are there downsides to drafting these kinds of discretionary provisions in which trustees have absolute and sole discretion? Writing about discretionary trusts and drafting problems, Edward Halbach observed:

> Too frequently trust instruments provide no guidance as to the purpose and scope of the power. Although determining and assisting in the formulation of the donor's intentions is a primary counseling function, it is apparently one of the most neglected aspects of estate planning. A poorly defined discretionary power often results.

Edward C. Halbach, Jr., *Problems of Discretion in Discretionary Trusts*, 61 COLUM L. REV. 1425 (1961). What kinds of guidance should trust settlors provide for trustees, understanding that the trustee will be called upon to implement the trust settlor's wishes? Some estate planners recommend that trust settlors write letters that document intent:

> Have the client write a memo to his trustee telling the trustee what he wants for his children. Ask the client to share some of his hopes and dreams for his children. . . . Have the client request that the terms 'health, education, support and maintenance' be interpreted in light of the client's overall intent in creating the trust.

Marjorie J. Stephens, *Incentive Trusts: Considerations, Uses and Alternatives*, Am. C. Tr. & Est. Couns. 2003 Ann. Meeting (2003). Does this seem like a good idea? What if the trust terms and the letter of intent conflict? Or what if the letter of intent expresses odd wishes that may run against the best interests of the beneficiaries?

ASSESSMENTS

1.   What would you recommend for clients creating a discretionary trust for their children to make sure that their wishes were implemented by trustees? Try making a list of questions that you would ask a client who wants to create a discretionary trust for her children.

2.   Make a list of ordinary creditors—those you think are most likely to exist for the majority of individuals. Then draft an explanation for these creditors as to their right with respect to a discretionary trust and what the benefit of a Hamilton order is for them.

2.   Spendthrift Trusts

Another mechanism for creating asset protection for an irrevocable trust is through the insertion of a spendthrift provision. Any irrevocable trust with a spendthrift provision is called a spendthrift trust. Spendthrift trusts date back in the United States to the end of the nineteenth century, when the U.S. Supreme Court affirmed their validity in *Nichols v. Eaton*, 91 U.S. 716 (1875). Mrs. Sarah Eaton established a testamentary trust for her children with the proceeds from her estate, specifying that if the bankruptcy of one of her sons would render the income "payable to some other person, then the trust . . . should immediately cease." Prescient in her planning, one son declared bankruptcy not long after the mother died and "made a general assignment of all his property to Charles A. Nichols for the benefit of his creditors." Invoking the doctrine of freedom of disposition, the Court sided with the deceased mother over the creditors, stating:

> Why a parent . . . [who] wishes to use his own property in securing the object of his affection . . . from the ills of life, the vicissitudes of fortune, and even his own improvidence, or incapacity for self-protection, should not be permitted to do so, is not readily perceived.

The decision was immediately criticized. John Chipman Gray, a vociferous critic, boldly stated: "[S]pendthrift trusts have no place in the system of the Common Law." JOHN CHIPMAN GRAY, RESTRAINTS ON THE ALIENATION OF PROPERTY, x (2d ed. 1895). Nevertheless, further support for the spendthrift trust came seven years later with *Broadway National Bank v. Adams*, 133 Mass. 170 (1882), in which the Massachusetts state supreme court affirmed the right of a donor to dispose of his property as he saw fit over the rights of creditors.

Spendthrift trusts created by third parties can, therefore, keep family wealth out of the hands of creditors with the insertion of just one small provision barring the beneficiary's alienation of the trust interest. Because they are so useful and simple to draft, spendthrift provisions are routinely inserted into trust documents—to the point that they are considered boilerplate language. In fact, spendthrift provisions are so standard that in Delaware all trusts are presumptively spendthrift. We might even wonder, given the ubiquity of these provisions, if it is not malpractice to omit such a provision. Malpractice or not, John Chipman Gray certainly lost his battle. A common spendthrift provision looks like this:

> Subject to the express grant herein of certain rights to withdraw assets and powers of appointment, neither the corpus of any trust created hereby nor the income resulting therefrom, while in the hands of any TRUSTEE hereunder, shall be subject to anticipation or assignment for consideration in any manner by any beneficiary, by sale, conveyance, transfer, assignment, encumbrance, pledge, or otherwise . . .

FAMILY ESTATE PLANNING GUIDE § 5:14 (4th ed.). And a common statute authorizing spendthrift provisions looks like this:

VA. CODE ANN. § 64.2–743 Spendthrift Provision

A.   A spendthrift provision is valid only if it restrains both voluntary and involuntary transfer of a beneficiary's interest.

B.   A term of a trust providing that the interest of a beneficiary is held subject to a "spendthrift trust," or words of similar import, is sufficient to restrain both voluntary and involuntary transfer of the beneficiary's interest.

C.   A beneficiary may not transfer an interest in a trust in violation of a valid spendthrift provision and, except as otherwise provided in this article, a creditor or assignee of the beneficiary may not reach the interest or a distribution by the trustee before its receipt by the beneficiary.

The Uniform Trust Code provision pertaining to spendthrift provisions can be found at Section 502:

UTC § 502 Spendthrift Provision

(a)   A spendthrift provision is valid only if it restrains both voluntary and involuntary transfer of a beneficiary's interest.

(b)   A term of a trust providing that the interest of a beneficiary is held subject to a "spendthrift trust," or words of similar import, is sufficient to restrain both voluntary and involuntary transfer of the beneficiary's interest.

(c)   A beneficiary may not transfer an interest in a trust in violation of a valid spendthrift provision and, except as otherwise provided in this [article], a creditor or assignee of the beneficiary may not reach the interest or a distribution by the trustee before its receipt by the beneficiary.

Once a spendthrift provision is inserted into a trust document, ordinary creditors can only reach a beneficiary's assets in trust once the trustee has made a distribution to the beneficiary. If distributions are mandatory, a creditor may have to wait until the distribution reaches the beneficiary, but the creditor is assured that there will be an opportunity to recoup at least some amount of the debt owed, if not the full amount. If distributions are discretionary, the creditor is back in the same situation we discussed previously—except this time there is no possibility of procuring a Hamilton order. In this way, spendthrift trusts are less friendly to creditors than discretionary trusts. A comment to UTC § 502 explains: "[A] creditor of the beneficiary is prohibited from attaching a protected interest and may only attempt to collect directly from the beneficiary after a payment is made." Nevertheless, under UTC § 506(b), a creditor can attach a mandatory distribution that the trustee has not made within a "reasonable time." *See* Robert T. Danforth, *Article Five of the UTC and the Future of Creditor's Rights in Trusts*, 27 CARDOZO L. REV. 2551 (2006).

Like with discretionary trusts, there are exception creditors to spendthrift trusts. The spendthrift exception creditors overlap with discretionary trust exception creditors, but spendthrift rules enlarge the category. The UTC provision follows:

UTC § 503 Exceptions to Spendthrift Provision

(a)   In this section, "child" includes any person for whom an order or judgment for child support has been entered in this or another State.

(b)   A spendthrift provision is unenforceable against:

(1)   a beneficiary's child, spouse, or former spouse who has a judgment or court order against the beneficiary for support or maintenance;

(2)   a judgment creditor who has provided services for the protection of a beneficiary's interest in the trust; and

(3)   a claim of this State or the United States to the extent a statute of this State or federal law so provides.

(c)   A claimant against which a spendthrift provision cannot be enforced may obtain from a court an order attaching present or future distributions to or for the benefit of the beneficiary. The court may limit the award to such relief as is appropriate under the circumstances.

––––––––––––

Spendthrift trusts are, in this way, more favorable to creditors than discretionary trusts. There are more exception creditors with spendthrift trusts, including the government (usually the tax authorities) and (shockingly?) the lawyer who drafted the spendthrift trust. Moreover, compelling a distribution with a spendthrift is easier than it is with a discretionary trust. The exception creditor need only show the judgment or debt claim, and the court will create an order attaching "present or future distributions."

The case that follows demonstrates the different rights that creditors have with respect to a spendthrift trust based on the trust treating income and principal differently. The case also demonstrates very vividly the explicit policy choices that are made in the selection of exception creditors, here an ex-spouse with a divorce judgment and a child with support orders.

Shelley v. Shelley

354 P.2d 282 (Or. 1960)

O'CONNELL, J.

This is an appeal from a decree of the circuit court for Multnomah county establishing the rights of the parties to the income and corpus of a trust of which the defendant, the United States National Bank of Portland (Oregon) is trustee. The trust involved in this suit was created by Hugh T. Shelley.

The pertinent parts of the trust are as follows:

'Ninth:　　All of the rest, residue, and remainder of my said estate, * * * I give, devise, and bequeath to the United States National Bank of Portland (Oregon), in trust, * * * upon the following trusts:

'(2)　I direct that, all income derived from my trust estate be paid to my wife, Gertrude R. Shelley, as long as she lives, said income to be paid to her at intervals of not less than three (3) months apart;

'(4)　If my said wife, Gertrude R. Shelley, shall predecease me, and my said son is then alive, or upon my wife's death after my death and my son being alive, it is my desire, and I direct, that, the United States National Bank of Portland (Oregon), as trustee, shall continue this estate in trust and pay all income derived therefrom to my son, Grant R. Shelley, as long as he lives, said income to be paid to him at intervals not less than three (3) months apart; Provided, Further, That when my son, Grant R. Shelley, arrives at the age of thirty (30) years, my trustee may then, or at any time thereafter, and from time to time, distribute to said son absolutely and as his own all or any part of the principal of said trust fund that it may then or from time to time thereafter deem him capable of successfully investing without the restraints of this trust; Provided, However, That such disbursements of principal of said trust so made to my son after he attains the age of thirty (30) years shall be first approved in writing by either one of my brothers-in-law, that is: Dr. Frank L. Ralston, now of Walla Walla, Washington, or Russell C. Ralston, now of Palo Alto, California, if either of them is then living, but if neither of them is then living, then my trustee is authorized to make said disbursements of principal to my son in the exercise of its sole and absolute judgment and discretion; Provided, Further, That, said trust shall continue as to all or any part of the undistributed portion of the principal thereof to and until the death of my said son.

'(5)　I further direct and authorize my trustee, from time to time (but only upon the written approval of my said wife if she be then living, otherwise in the exercise of my trustee's sole discretion) to make disbursements for the use and benefit of my son, Grant R. Shelley, or his children, in case of any emergency arising whereby unusual and extraordinary expenses are necessary for the proper support and care of my said son, or said children.

'(6) If the said Grant R. Shelley shall die, and leave surviving him children, it is my desire that, if my wife be then dead, or upon the death of my wife if she should survive said son, my trustee shall continue said trust for the benefit of said children of my son, Grant R. Shelley, and shall make periodic payments for their benefit at intervals of not less than three (3) months apart, and shall hold said estate in trust to and until the youngest child of Grant R. Shelley shall attain the age of twenty one (21) years; thereupon, said trust shall terminate, and said estate shall be distributed to the children of my son, share and share alike; If any of said children die before the youngest attains the age of twenty-one (21) years, said distributable estate shall be distributed to the surviving children, share and share alike, or, if there be only one child, to said child.

'(8) Each beneficiary hereunder is hereby restrained from alienating, anticipating, encumbering, or in any manner assigning his or her interest or estate, either in principal or income, and is without power so to do, nor shall such interest or estate be subject to his or her liabilities or obligations nor to judgment or other legal process, bankruptcy proceedings or claims of creditors or others.'

The principal question on appeal is whether the income and corpus of the Shelley trust can be reached by Grant Shelley's former wives and his children.

Grant Shelley was first married to defendant, Patricia C. Shelley. Two children were born of this marriage. Patricia divorced Grant in 1951. The decree required Grant to pay support money for the children; the decree did not call for the payment of alimony. Thereafter, Grant married the plaintiff, Betty Shelley. Two children were born of this marriage. The plaintiff obtained a divorce from Grant in August, 1958. The decree in this latter suit required the payment of both alimony and a designated monthly amount for the support of the children of that marriage.

Some time after his marriage to the plaintiff, Grant disappeared and his whereabouts was not known at the time of this suit. The defendant bank, as trustee, invested the trust assets in securities which are now held by it, together with undisbursed income from the trust estate. The plaintiff obtained an injunction restraining the defendant trustee from disbursing any of the trust assets. Patricia Shelley brought a garnishment proceeding against the trustee, by which she sought to subject the trust to the claim for support money provided for in the 1951 decree of divorce.

The trial court entered a decree subjecting the accrued income of the trust to the existing claims of the plaintiff and Patricia Shelley; subjecting future income of the trust to the periodic obligations subsequently accruing by the terms of the decrees in the divorce proceedings brought by plaintiff and Patricia Shelley; and further providing that in the event that the trust income was insufficient to satisfy such claims, the corpus of the trust was subject to invasion.

We shall first consider that part of the decree which subjects the income of the trust to the claims of plaintiff and of defendant, Patricia Shelley. The trust places no conditions upon the right of Grant Shelley to receive the trust income during his lifetime. Therefore, plaintiff and Patricia Shelley may reach such income unless the spendthrift provision of the trust precludes them from doing so.

The validity of spendthrift trusts has been established by our former cases. The question on this appeal is whether the spendthrift provision will be given effect to bar the claims of the beneficiary's children for support and the plaintiff's claim for alimony.

In *Cogswell v. Cogswell et al.*, 1946, 178 Or. 417, we held that the spendthrift provision of a trust is not effective against the claims of the beneficiary's former wife for alimony and for support of the beneficiary's child. The defendant bank concedes that the *Cogswell* case is controlling in the case at bar, but asks us to overrule it on the ground that it is inconsistent with our own cases recognizing the testator's privilege to dispose of his property as he pleases and, further, that it is inconsistent with various Oregon statutes expressing the same policy of free alienation. If we should accept the premise urged by the defendant bank, that a testator has an inviolable right to dispose of his property as he pleases subject only to legislative restriction, the conclusion is inevitable that the testator may create in a beneficiary an interest free from all claims, including those for support and alimony.

But the premise is not sound. The privilege of disposing of property is not absolute; it is hedged with various restrictions where there are policy considerations warranting the limitation. It is within the court's power to impose upon the privilege of disposing of property such restrictions as are consistent with its view of sound public policy, unless, of course, the legislature has expressed a contrary view. Our own statutes do not purport to deal with the specific question before us, that is as to whether there should be limitations on the owner's privilege to create a spendthrift trust.

We have no hesitation in declaring that public policy requires that the interest of the beneficiary of a trust should be subject to the claims for support of his children. Certainly the defendant will accept the societal postulate that parents have the obligation to support their children. If we give effect to the spendthrift provision to bar the claims for support, we have the spectacle of a man enjoying the benefits of a trust immune from claims which are justly due, while the community pays for the support of his children. We do not believe that it is sound policy to use the welfare funds of this state in support of the beneficiary's children, while he stands behind the shield of immunity created by a spendthrift trust provision. To endorse such a policy and to permit the spectacle which we have described above would be to invite disrespect for the administration of justice.

The justification for permitting a claim for alimony is, perhaps, not as clear. The adjustment of the economic interests of the parties to a divorce may depend upon a variety of factors, including the respective fault of the parties, the ability of the wife to support herself, the duration of the marriage, and other considerations. Whether alimony is to be granted and its amount are questions which are determined in light of these various interests. It is probably fair to say that the duties created by the marriage relation, at least as they are evaluated upon the termination of the marriage, are conceived of as more qualified than those arising out of the paternal relationship. On the theory that divorce terminates the husband's duty to support his former wife and that she stands in no better position than other creditors, some courts have held that the spendthrift provision insulates the beneficiary's interest in the trust from her claim.

We are of the opinion that [t]he duty of the husband to support his former wife should override the restriction called for by the spendthrift provision. The same reason advanced above for requiring the support of the beneficiary's children will, in many cases, be applicable to the claim of a divorced wife; if the beneficiary's interest cannot be reached, the state may be called upon to support her. The case of *Seidenberg v. Seidenberg*, contains an excellent review of the problem. In summary the court said:

> 'The family is the foundation of society. The duty of a married man to support and protect his wife and children is inherent in human nature. It is a part of natural law, as well as a requirement of the law of every civilized country. It is not an ordinary indebtedness, such as a contractual obligation or a judgment for damages arising out of a tort. It is a responsibility far superior to that of paying one's debts,

important as the latter obligation is. No part of a man's property or income should be exempt from meeting this liability, for he is under at least as great a duty to provide shelter, clothing, and food for his immediate family as he is to furnish them for his own person. The law should not regard with complacency any man who repudiates or ignores this obligation, which is instinctive in mankind, and should not permit him to flout it with impunity.'. . .

We hold that the beneficiary's interest in the income of the Shelley Trust is subject to the claims of the plaintiff for alimony and to the claims for the support of Grant Shelley's children as provided for under both decrees for divorce. These claims are not without limit. We adopt the view that such claimants may reach only that much of the income which the trial court deems reasonable under the circumstances, having in mind the respective needs of the husband and wife, the needs of the children, the amount of the trust income, the availability of the corpus for the various needs, and any other factors which are relevant in adjusting equitably the interests of the claimants and the beneficiary.

The question of the claimants' rights to reach the corpus of the trust involves other consideration. For the reasons heretofore stated, the beneficiary's interest in the corpus is not made immune from these claims. But, by the terms of the trust, the disbursement of the corpus is within the discretion of the trustee (or, in some instances subject to the approval of others), and, therefore, Grant Shelley's right to receive any part of the corpus does not arise until the trustee has exercised his discretion and has decided to invade the corpus. Until that time, the plaintiff and Patricia Shelley cannot reach the corpus of the trust because the beneficiary has no realizable interest in it.

NOTES

1.　In *Shelley*, the court analyzes the difference between the rights of spouses and the rights of children. This difference is something that we've encountered throughout the course, most particularly, in intestacy law and omitted relatives; we will see it again in Chapter 14 when we discuss the spousal or elective share, which is available only to spouses and not children. In general, spouses have more rights than children. Here, though, the court seems to indicate that children may have a stronger claim to recover from a trust than ex-spouses. What is the court's logic in making this suggestion and why does the court think that the interests of the custodial spouse and the children are so different? Think about whether you agree with the court and, if not, how you might revise the opinion to reflect a different understanding of marriage, the rights of minor children, and the rights of a surviving spouse. Would this change the result and how?

2.   Quoting another opinion, the *Shelley* court approves of the idea that "The duty of a married man to support and protect his wife and children is . . . not an ordinary indebtedness, such as a contractual obligation or a judgment for damages arising out of a tort." Whether to include tort creditors in the category of exception creditors is a topic that arises time and again, even though all states have already declined to do so. *See Duvall v. McGee*, 826 A.2d 416 (Md. 2003). What would be the basis for including tort creditors (think voluntary versus involuntary creditors)? In *Sligh v. First National Bank of Holmes County*, the beneficiary of two spendthrift trusts established by the beneficiary's mother was operating a motor vehicle while intoxicated and became involved in an accident with the plaintiff, leaving the plaintiff paralyzed, unable to use his legs, and with no sexual function or ability to control his bodily functions. The plaintiff alleged that the beneficiary's mother had actual knowledge that her son was an alcoholic and that she had therefore created the trusts to protect her son from the likely claims of tort creditors. Arguing his case, the plaintiff alleged that it violated public policy to uphold spendthrift provisions in cases such as his where there was gross negligence. The plaintiff went on to win a $5 million civil judgment for compensatory and punitive damages but could not recover this money because the driver had no assets apart from his trust interest. The Mississippi Supreme Court, on appeal, allowed the plaintiff to reach the money in trust concluding that spendthrift protection should not extend to judgments for "gross negligence and intentional torts." Directly on the heels of this decision, however, the Mississippi legislature enacted of the "Family Trust Preservation Act of 1998." MISS. CODE ANN. §§ 91–9–501, et seq. (1998). The act undid the state supreme court's decision, stating that a beneficiary's interest in a spendthrift trust could be neither transferred nor subjected to a money judgment until a distribution was actually made to the beneficiary. What policy objectives support such a legislative decision? Why have all states refused to consider tort creditors as exception creditors?

3.   Another question worth asking is in what other situations might we want to allow creditors to reach assets in a spendthrift trust? The Bankruptcy Code excludes any beneficial interest in trust that is not alienable "under applicable nonbankruptcy law" [that is, state law] from a debtor's bankruptcy estate, a rule that numerous cases demonstrate. *See, e.g., In re Cutter*, 398 B.R. 6 (B.A.P. 9th Cir. 2008); *In re Kent*, 396 B.R. 46 (Bankr. D. AZ. 2008). Should a beneficiary who

declares bankruptcy be able to retain trust assets in a spendthrift trust and have unchanged access to these funds after bankruptcy?

4.   John Chipman Gray, the staunch opponent of asset protection trusts, wrote:

> The general introduction of spendthrift trusts would be to form a privileged class, who could indulge in every speculation, could practice every fraud, and, provided they kept on the safe side of the criminal law, could yet roll in wealth. They would be an aristocracy, though certainly the most contemptible aristocracy with which a country was ever cursed.

JOHN CHIPMAN GRAY, RESTRAINTS ON ALIENATION OF PROPERTY § 262, at 174 (1883). Think about this statement and about what groups benefit the most from asset protection trusts. Wealth inequality in the United States is such that, from 1983–2016, the top 1% "saw their average wealth . . . rise by . . . over 15 million dollars or by 150 percent . . . , while the middle quintile showed no change and the average wealth of the poorest 40 percent fell by $15,800."[2] One economist remarked in 2019: "U.S. wealth concentration seems to have returned to levels last seen during the Roaring Twenties."[3] Similarly, the UBS Billionaires Insights report for 2018 announced that, globally, billionaires increased their wealth by $1.4 trillion or 20% and that "the past 30 years have seen far greater wealth creation than the Gilded Age of the late 19th Century."[4] How would you describe or explain the link, if any, between these trusts and wealth inequality in the United States? For more on the global growth of wealth inequality, see THOMAS PIKETTY, CAPITAL

Asset protection trusts increase wealth inequality and benefit the 1%. ©John Darkow, Cagle Cartoons, 2015

---

[2]   Edward N. Wolff, *Household Wealth Trends in the United States, 1962 to 2016: Has the Middle Class Recovered?* 13 (Nat'l Bureau of Econ. Research, Working Paper No. 24085, 2017), https://www.nber.org/papers/w24085.

[3]   Gabriel Zucman, *Global Wealth Inequality* 14 (Nat'l Bureau of Econ. Research, Working Paper No. 25462, 2019), http://www.nber.org/papers/w25462.

[4]   UBS, BILLIONAIRES REPORT 2018: NEW VISIONARIES AND THE CHINESE CENTURY 1, 24 (2018), https://www.ubs.com/global/en/wealth-management/uhnw/billionaires-report.html.

IN THE TWENTY-FIRST CENTURY (2014); and Gabriel Zucman, *Global Wealth Inequality* 14 (Nat'l Bureau of Econ. Research, Working Paper No. 25462, 2019), http://www.nber.org/papers/w25462.

5.   A comparative analysis of asset protection is trusts is interesting because it reveals that American law is an outlier in its support for these wealth preservation features. Spendthrift provisions, while they used to be common in England in the early-modern era, are no longer enforceable. See *Brandon v. Robinson*, 18 Ves. Jun. 429, 34 Eng. Rep. 379 (1811). In modern English law, courts downplay the importance of donor control and conceptualize the trust property as belonging to the beneficiaries. In civil law countries, such as France, there is nothing comparable to the asset protection trust and any such financial arrangement is against public policy.

ASSESSMENTS

1.   Burgo Fitzgerald, a compulsive gambler, borrowed $50,000 from his friend Plantagenet Palliser to pay off his gambling debts. In exchange for the loan, Burgo signed an agreement binding himself to repay Plantagenet out of the funds in a spendthrift trust created for him by his mother. Burgo went to the trustee and asked for $50,000, so he could repay Plantagenet. If you were the trustee, what response would you give to Burgo? If Plantagenet sought a court order to compel a distribution, what would the court do?

2.   Augustus Melmotte created a spendthrift trust for the benefit of his daughter, Maria. Maria accumulated over $50,000 in debt, buying antiquarian maps and Trolls paraphernalia. One of the creditors obtained a judgment against Maria and sued in an attempt to reach the trust funds. The trustee hired Phineas, a well-known lawyer, to defend the trust.

   a.   What can the creditor expect to recover? What are the best arguments that the creditor has to support his claim?

   b.   After Phineas successfully protected the trust assets, he submitted a bill for services rendered. The trustee thought that Phineas had overcharged for his services, the trustee refused to pay Phineas, and Phineas sued the trust to recover. Will Phineas prevail in his attempt to recover his fees from the trust? What if the trust, in addition to being a spendthrift trust, left distributions to the sole discretion of the trustee?

3.   In 1985, Kyle Krueger's grandmother established a trust, income to be paid quarterly to Krueger, and so much of the principal to be paid to Krueger as the

trustee determines is necessary for Krueger's maintenance, support, and education. Krueger has the right to demand payment of income more frequently, but no right to demand principal until he turns fifty (in 2016). In 1998, Krueger sexually assaulted Scheffel's minor child, videotaped the act, and then broadcast the video over the internet. Krueger's wife discovered the video, turned him in, and he was convicted of 89 counts of sexual assault and one count of simple assault. Scheffel then brought a tort suit against Krueger, and the court entered a default judgment against him for $551,286.25. Scheffel sought to enforce the tort judgment against Krueger's interest in the trust, and the trustee answered by pointing to the spendthrift clause. As Scheffel's lawyer, what arguments would you make on behalf of Scheffel in an attempt to satisfy the judgment by reaching the funds in trust? How successful do you think these arguments will be? *See Scheffel v. Krueger*, 782 A.2d 410 (N.H. 2001).

C. Domestic Asset Protection Trusts

As we've learned elsewhere in this chapter, trust law has traditionally granted asset protection benefits based on the theory of donor freedom of disposition, and the hallmark of asset protection trusts has always been that they are created by third parties, for the benefit of someone else—a child, grandchild, or some other beneficiary. The policy reason has always been clear:

> To hold otherwise would be to give unexampled opportunity to unscrupulous persons to shelter their property before engaging in speculative business enterprises, to mislead creditors into thinking that the settlor still owned the property since he appeared to be receiving its income, and thereby work a gross fraud on creditors who might place reliance on the former prosperity and financial stability of the debtor.

G.T. BOGERT, TRUSTS § 40, at 155–56 (6th ed. 1987); *see also* Henery J. Lischer, *Domestic Asset Protection Trusts: Pallbearers to Liability?*, 35 REAL PROP., PROB. AND TR. J. 479 (2000). Based on this policy logic and the idea of ownership equivalence, trusts that individuals establish for their own benefit (especially revocable trusts that act as will substitutes) never possess asset protection features. Specifically, common law rules—now codified by UTC § 505—state that individuals cannot shield assets from creditors by placing them in a trust for their own benefit. Creditors can therefore reach the maximum amount that the trustee could pay to the settlor or apply for the settlor's benefit, even if a trust is a discretionary or spendthrift trust (or both).

Now, all that is changing, and longstanding rules about asset protection for self-settled trusts are being transformed. The rules began to crumble in the 1980s when the Cook Islands amended governing law to allow for self-settled asset protection trusts in order to attract international capital. The Cayman Islands, Belize, Nevis, the Channel Islands, the Isle of Man, and other offshore jurisdictions followed suit, "and the great Offshore Boom of the 1990s came like a tidal wave."[5] This first wave of self-settled asset protection trusts were known as "Foreign Asset Protection Trusts" (FAPTs). Unwilling to cede billions of dollars in trust business to these offshore entities, American states fought back. In 1997 Alaska enacted legislation that allowed for the first Domestic Asset Protection Trusts (DAPTs). The Delaware legislature shortly followed suite, explaining that the new rules were "intended to maintain Delaware's role as the most favored domestic jurisdiction for the establishment of trusts."

Since that time, nineteen other states[6] have passed legislation authorizing DAPTs or, as Forbes has called them, "selfie" trusts. States that have already legislatively authorized the new trusts compete with one another and with offshore trust companies for business and the marketing reflects this competition. New types of asset protection trusts appear every day, playing on notions of family money and legacy building: Dynasty Trusts. Legacy Trusts. Millennium Trusts. One company offers a "Bloodline Trust." And another trust company boldly markets a "Have Your Cake and Eat It Too" Trust (HYCET Trust®). One Wyoming trust company advertises that it is "the onshore alternative for offshore trusts."[7] In a similar vein, a South Dakota company has declared that the days of offshore trusts are over: "Establishing a DAPT in a top-rated trust state like South Dakota is extremely advantageous because of the four levels of asset protection provided for in South Dakota. Off-shore asset protection has lost a lot of momentum."[8] In addition, various law practices and

---

[5]   Jay Adkisson, *A Short History of Asset Protection Trust Law*, FORBES (Jan. 26, 2015), https://www. forbes.com/sites/jayadkisson/2015/01/26/a-short-history-of-asset-protection-trustlaw/#605ecd2f3fb4 [https://perma.cc/LD83-ND5Z].

[6]   Alaska, Delaware, Connecticut. Hawaii, Indiana, Michigan, Mississippi, Missouri, Nevada, New Hampshire, Ohio, Oklahoma, Rhode Island, South Dakota, Tennessee, Utah, Virginia, West Virginia and Wyoming.

[7]   FRONTIER ADMIN. SERV., LLC., http://wyoprivatetrust.com/about-us/why-wyoming.

[8]   *Domestic Asset Protection Trust*, S.D. TR. CO., LLC, https://www.sdtrustco.com/why-south-dakota/asset-protection/.

legal commentators rank the American DAPT jurisdictions annually according to the strength of the asset protection that they offer. [9]

Exception creditors vary by state with DAPTs, and there is not yet any uniform law to provide guidelines. With states competing to be the most attractive trust-formation jurisdiction, the trend seems to be that the fewer exception creditors the better. Nevada, for example has chosen to allow for no exception creditors, which means that trust assets are protected from even ex-spouses or children with support claims. Wyoming, similarly, shields trust assets from spousal and child support claims, and Oklahoma bar spouses from access to trust assets at divorce. Other states give more weight to spousal and child support claims but doing so lowers their "ranking" and may make their jurisdiction less attractive for trust formation purposes. As several legal scholars have observed, this competition may constitute a classic example of a "race to the bottom." Stewart E. Sterk, *Asset Protection Trusts: Trust Law's Race to the Bottom*, 85 CORNELL L. REV. 1035 (2000).

These self-settled asset protection trusts do not, however, completely discard the traditional rules that govern asset protection. In all states, DAPTs must be irrevocable, thereby taking away one form of ownership and control for the settlor. In some states, the settlor cannot be the only beneficiary. W. VA. CODE § 44D–5–503b(d) ("qualified self-settled spendthrift trust means a trust if . . . at least one beneficiary other than the grantor . . .") VA. CODE ANN. § 64.2–745.2(A) ("qualified self-settled spendthrift trust means a trust if . . . at least one beneficiary other than the settlor . . ."); MO. REV. STAT. § 456.5–505(3) ("with respect to an irrevocable trust with a spendthrift provision, a spendthrift provision will prevent the settlor's creditors from satisfying claims from the trust assets except: . . . to the extent of the settlor's beneficiary interest in the trust assets, if at the time the trust become irrevocable: the settlor was the sole beneficiary of either the income or principle of the trust . . ."). Some states, like Virginia, require an independent trustee. All these requirements are acknowledgements of the core tenets of asset protection: the less ownership equivalence there is, the more asset protection. There is no getting around the fact, however, that the settlor is benefitting and perhaps even controlling the trust created from the settlor's own assets.

The following is an excerpt from a tax court case that demonstrates the protection offered by a self-settled asset protection trust as well as the

---

[9]   *See* Steve Oshins, 11th Annual Domestic Asset Protect Trust State Rankings Chart https://db78e19b-dca5-49f9-90f6-1acaf5eaa6ba.filesusr.com/ugd/b211fb_0e205011bc5f4e4cb9d6232ee68647ca.pdf.

procedures that a trust settlor needs to be aware of in order to not run afoul of fraudulent transfer rules. The petitioner in this case owed the I.R.S. money and claimed that assets in a self-settled offshore asset protection trust were not available to satisfy the amount owed. The tax court agreed.

John F. Campbell, Petitioner v. Commissioner of Internal Revenue, Respondent

T.C. Memo. 2019-4 (United States Tax Court,
Docket No. 5644-12L, February 4, 2019)

Near the end of 2002 petitioner and his family moved to St. Thomas in the U.S. Virgin Islands. During July 2002 petitioner had engaged an estate planning attorney to start the process of setting up a family trust. On April 26, 2004, petitioner established the First Aeolian Islands Trust (Trust), an irrevocable grantor trust for Federal tax purposes, in Nevis, West Indies. The duration of the trust is 99 years unless terminated earlier by the trustee. Petitioner and his family are named beneficiaries of the Trust, but he anticipates receiving no benefit from the Trust.

Petitioner funded the Trust with a $5 million contribution. At the time of the contribution petitioner's net worth was approximately $25 million. No contributions to the Trust have been made since petitioner's initial contribution in 2004. As the grantor of the Trust, petitioner is required to report on his personal tax returns any tax consequences of the Trust's activities.

Petitioner maintains no control over the trustee to make distributions or investments. Through the Trust Protector petitioner can request that the trustee be changed, but he cannot force such action. In November 2006 petitioner moved back to the United States to pursue real estate opportunities in the Gulf Coast region. He made a $27 million investment in the "GO-Zone Initiative", which resulted in a $10,490,130 net operating loss (NOL). Under the Gulf Opportunity Zone Act (GO Zone) petitioner was able to deduct that NOL against income reported on previously filed Federal tax returns. At the time of his investment, petitioner estimated that his net worth was approximately $19 million, consisting of cash and liquid investments.

Petitioner's investments in the Gulf Coast consisted of both residential and commercial real estate in Alabama, Louisiana, and Mississippi. The investments were structured through limited liability companies (LLCs) which purchased each asset. In addition to his personal cash investment, petitioner personally guaranteed all of the loans the LLCs executed to purchase the assets. Petitioner expected a 7% return on his cash investment. After making his cash investment in the GO Zone, petitioner had approximately $6.5 million remaining in liquid assets. In the summer of 2009 petitioner learned that approximately half of the residential properties owned by Slidell Property Management, LLC (Slidell), one of the LLCs that purchased property in Louisiana through the GO Zone, contained Chinese drywall. The Chinese drywall made the properties uninhabitable. The lender for the Slidell properties foreclosed on the assets in 2011. At the time of foreclosure, the outstanding balance on the loan for the Slidell assets was approximately $4.5 million. The lender sold the properties in 2011 for approximately $1.35 million.

In the RCP [reasonable collection potential] calculation respondent included, as dissipated assets, the funds petitioner had transferred to the Trust. Petitioner contributed $5 million to the Trust on April 26, 2004, 6 years before the assessment period look-back and 10 years before he made his [offer-in-compromise]. This was his only contribution to the Trust. On May 10, 2004, after making the Trust contribution, petitioner was notified that his 2001 return was under examination. Petitioner was not aware of a potential audit examination of his 2001 tax return or any increased income tax liability that might arise from the examination until after making his contribution to the Trust. Even if petitioner was aware of a potential tax liability, his net worth after making the contribution to the Trust exceeded any potential tax liability arising from the examination of his 2001 Federal tax return. During the CDP [collection due process] proceedings, petitioner demonstrated that his net worth was $19 million in 2006. This amount would have more than covered the deficiency for 2001. We find that it was an abuse of discretion for the Appeals officer to include the Trust assets as dissipated assets.

NOTES

1.   In the *Campbell* case, the court notes that "Petitioner contributed $5 million to the Trust . . . 6 years before the assessment period look-back and 10 years before he made his [offer-in-compromise]." With self-settled asset protection trusts, timing is everything. Any transfer made with knowledge of a debt or the imminent possibility of one is a possible fraudulent transfer and as such not protected by the trust terms. Fraudulent transfers may be challenged pursuant to the Uniform Fraudulent Transfer Act (amended in 2014 to become the Uniform Voidable Transactions Act), which states that transfers will be void if they were made with the intent to defraud or if "badges of fraud" are present. It is for this reason that the DAPT rankings chart includes information about the

statute of limitations for both pre-existing and future creditors as well as the fraudulent transfer standard. For more on fraudulent transfers, see Alexander Boni-Saenz & Reid Kress Weisbord, *Sham and Remedial Doctrines*, 22 TR. & TR. 850, 852 (2016).

11th Annual Domestic Asset Protection Trust State Rankings Chart

Rank	State	Statute (50% weight)	Uniform Voidable Transactions Act (12.5% weight)	Statute of Limitations (Future Creditor) (2.5% weight)	Statute of Limitations (Preexisting Creditor) (2.5% weight)	Spouse/ Child Support Exception Creditors (Spouse 3%, Alimony 1%, Child Support 1% weight)	Preexisting Torts Exception Creditors/Other Exception Creditors (5% weight)	Ease of Use – New Affidavit of Solvency required for every new transfer? (7.5% weight)	Fraudulent Transfer Standard (10% weight)	Decanting State Ranking (2.5% weight)	Total Score
1	NV	§§166.010 to 166.170	No	2 Yrs.	2 Yrs. or 0.5 Yr. Discovery	No	No	No Affidavit Required	Clear and convincing	Ranked #2	99
2	SD	§55-16-1 to 16	No	2 Yrs.	2 Yrs. or 0.5 Yr. Discovery	Divorcing Spouse; Child Support (only if indebted at time of transfer)	No	No Affidavit Required	Clear and convincing	Ranked #1	98
3	OH	Ch. 5816	No	1.5 Yrs.	1.5 Yrs. or 0.5 Yr. Discovery	Divorcing Spouse; Alimony; Child Support	No	Affidavit Required (with exceptions)	Clear and convincing	Ranked #6	85
4	MO	§456.5-505	No	4 Yrs.	4 Yrs. or 1 Yr. Discovery	Alimony; Child Support	State/U.S. to extent state/federal law provides	No Affidavit Required	Clear and convincing	Ranked #7	84.5
5	CT	Public Act No. 19-137	No	4 Yrs.	4 Yrs. or 1 Yr. Discovery	Divorcing Spouse; Alimony; Child Support (only if indebted at time of transfer)	Preexisting Torts	No Affidavit Required	Clear and convincing	None	84
6 (tie)	DE	Tit. 12 §§3570-3576	No	4 Yrs.	4 Yrs. or 1 Yr. Discovery	Divorcing Spouse; Child Support	Preexisting Torts	No Affidavit Required	Clear and convincing	Ranked #3	83.5
6 (tie)	TN	§§35-16-101 to 112	No	2 Yrs.	2 Yrs. or 0.5 Yr. Discovery	Divorcing Spouse; Alimony; Child Support	No	Affidavit Required	Clear and convincing	Ranked #4	83.5
8	AK	§34.40.110; §13.36.310	No	4 Yrs.	4 Yrs. or 1 Yr. Discovery	Divorcing Spouse	No	Affidavit Required	Clear and convincing	Ranked #8 (tie)	82.5
9	RI	§18-9.2	No	4 Yrs.	4 Yrs. or 1 Yr. Discovery	Divorcing Spouse; Alimony; Child Support	Preexisting Torts	No Affidavit Required	Clear and convincing	Ranked #14	82
10	IN	§30-4-8	No	2 Yrs.	2 Yrs. or 0.5 Yr. Discovery	Divorcing Spouse; Child Support	Property listed on app. to obtain credit – but only as to that lender	Affidavit Required	Clear and convincing	Ranked #10 (tie)	80.5
11	NH	§564-B:5-505A	No	4 Yrs.	4 Yrs. or 1 Yr. Discovery	Divorcing Spouse; Alimony; Child Support	No	No Affidavit Required	Limited clear and convincing standard	Ranked #5	79
12	WY	§§4-10-502, 504, 506(a), 510,523	No	4 Yrs.	4 Yrs. or 1 Yr. Discovery	Child Support	Property listed on app. to obtain credit – but only as to that lender	Affidavit Required	Clear and convincing	Ranked #13	78
13	MI	§§700.1041 to 700.1050	Yes	2 Yrs.	2 Yrs. or 1 Yr. Discovery	Divorcing Spouse	No	Affidavit Required (with exceptions)	Clear and convincing	Ranked #25 (tie)	75
14	MS	§§91-9-701 to 91-9-723	No	2 Yrs.	2 Yrs. or 0.5 Yr. Discovery	Divorcing Spouse; Alimony; Child Support	Preexisting Torts, State/ Criminal Restitution/ Up to $1.5MM if no $1MM Umbrella Policy	Affidavit Required	Clear and convincing	None	72.5
15	HI	§554G	No	2 Yrs.	2 Yrs. Pers. Injury; 6 Yrs. Contract	Divorcing Spouse; Alimony; Child Support	Preexisting Torts/ Certain Lenders/ Hawaii Tax	No Affidavit Required	Limited clear and convincing standard	None	72
16	UT	§25-6-502	Yes	None	2 Yrs. or 1 Yr. Discovery (also 120-day mailing/ publication action)	No	No	Affidavit Required	Missing clear and convincing standard	None	60
NR	OK	Tit. 31 §§10 to 18	No	4 Yrs.	4 Yrs. or 1 Yr. Discovery	Child Support	Must be majority Oklahoma assets	No Affidavit Required	Clear and convincing	None	NR
NR	VA	§64.2-745.1; §64.2-745.2	No	None	5 Yrs.	Child Support	Creditor who has provided services to protect trust/ U.S./city. etc	No Affidavit Required	Clear and convincing	Ranked #16 (tie)	NR
NR	WV	§44D-5-503a; §44D-5-503B	No	None	4 Yrs.	No	No	Affidavit Required	Missing clear and convincing standard	None	NR

11th Annual Domestic Asset Protection Trust State Rankings Chart created in April 2020. Original State Rankings Chart created in April 2010.
Copyright © 2010-2020 by Steve Oshins (soshins@oshins.com) / www.oshins.com / (702) 341-6000, ext. 2). All rights reserved.
The Decanting State Ranking column is based on the 7th Annual Trust Decanting State Rankings Chart (Jan. 2020) at http://www.oshins.com/state-rankings-charts.

Practitioners rank asset protection and dynasty trust states according to a number of factors. © 1997–2020 by Oshins & Associates

2. Because individual states advertise their DAPTs as having unique forms of asset protection, trust agreements generally contain provisions stating that the trust is subject exclusively to the law of the state in which it was created. Accordingly, one of the first legal issues arising with DAPTs is choice of law. In *Imo Daniel Kloiber Dynasty Trust*, 98 A.3d 924 (Del. Ch. 2014), for example, when a wife sought to reach assets in a Delaware Dynasty Trust at divorce, PNC Delaware Trust Company, along with her husband, argued that the Kentucky divorce court had no jurisdiction over the trust, claiming instead that Delaware Court of Chancery had exclusive jurisdiction based on the provision in the trust agreement. That court, however, concluded that:

When a Delaware state statute assigns exclusive jurisdiction to a particular Delaware court, the statute is allocating jurisdiction among the Delaware courts. The state is not making a claim against the world that no court outside of Delaware can exercise jurisdiction over that type of case.

[The husband] should make his arguments to the Kentucky Family Court. If the Kentucky Family Court rejects his arguments and he believes that the Kentucky Family Court has erred, then [the husband] should seek a remedy from the Kentucky Court of Appeals and, ultimately, from the Kentucky Supreme Court. Unless and until the Delaware Supreme Court instructs otherwise, this court's role does not include acting as a quasi-appellate court for interlocutory review of divorce proceedings in other jurisdictions.

Id. at 939, 953. Will DAPTs retain their utility if choice-of-law provisions fail to hold up in court? Alternately, the more states there are that authorize DAPTs, the less need there will be for trust settlors to shop among jurisdictions and create DAPTs outside of their primary state of residence. For other examples, see *Toni 1 Trust v. Wacker*, 413 P.3d 1199 (Alaska 2018) and *In re Huber*, 493 B.R. 798 (W.D. Wash. 2013).

3.   The question of bankruptcy returns with DAPTs and some of the same questions still pertain: should assets that a settlor places in a DAPT be excluded from the bankruptcy estate? For more on this question, see Michael Sjuggerud, Comment, *Defeating the Self-Settled Spendthrift Trust in Bankruptcy*, 28 FLA. ST. U. L. REV. 977 (2000) and John K. Eason, *Policy, Logic, and Persuasion in the Evolving Realm of Trust Asset Protection*, 27 CARDOZO L. REV. 2621, 2674–75 (2006).

4.   DAPTS are coming under attack in divorce court because spouses are able to create these trusts during marriage, and often they place what might be marital property in the DAPTs. An example of this is *Dahl v. Dahl*, 345 P.3d 566 (Utah 2015). Charles and Kim Dahl were married and lived in Utah for almost eighteen years before filing for divorce and beginning proceedings that the district court called a "train wreck." Charles was a cardiologist, and Kim had worked for a short time at the beginning of the marriage before becoming a stay-at-home parent and the primary caretaker of two children. In 2002, four years before Charles filed for divorce, he created the Dahl Family Irrevocable Trust in Nevada, naming himself as beneficiary, his brother C. Robert Dahl as Investment Trustee, and the Nevada State Bank as a co-trustee. Nevada was listed as place of domicile in the trust's choice of law provision. Charles funded the trust with 97% of a Utah LLC, Marlette Enterprises—a real estate

investment company that he owned and that was valued at approximately $1 million. The following year, the couple jointly transferred the deed to their primary residence to the trust.

When the marriage failed and the couple began divorce proceedings, Kim sought a share of assets in trust, claiming they were marital property. The Utah district court held that Kim had no enforceable interest in trust assets because of the choice-of-law provision and because the trust was irrevocable. On appeal, the Utah Supreme Court disagreed. The court concluded that Kim's interest in the marital home was undeniably marital property and that there was an open question as to what, if any, percentage of the real estate company was marital property. Charles admitted that at least some part of the trust assets were marital property and, consequently, the court stated: "Thus, to the extent that the Trust corpus contains marital property, Utah has a strong interest in ensuring that such property is equitably divided in the parties' divorce action." The court therefore denied enforcing the trust's choice-of-law provision and applied Utah law instead. For other examples of asset sheltering in DAPTs at divorce see, *IMO Daniel Kloiber Dynasty Trust* (mentioned in Note 1), and *Gibson v. Gibson*, 801 S.E.2d 40 (Ga. 2017). *See also* Nicholas Cofessore, *How to Hide $400 Million*, N.Y. TIMES MAGAZINE (Nov. 30, 2016), https://www.nytimes.com/2016/11/30/magazine/how-to-hide-400-million.html. To read more, generally, about DAPTs at divorce, see Allison Tait, *Trusting Marriage*, 10 U.C. IRVINE 199 (2019).

"It is certainly not unusual for couples to fight over their homes during a divorce. But the Bosarges—like many ultrawealthy people across the globe—own their homes through a complex network of

 trusts and limited liability companies. Now that they are divorcing, Mrs. Bosarge said her husband is using these complex ownership structures—over which she alleges Mr. Bosarge retains full control—to essentially eliminate her stake in the homes, and to prevent her from accessing what she said is billions in cash and other property. At issue in the case are a variety of assets held in trust in South Dakota, according to court filings and trust documents to which Mrs. Bosarge has gained access. South Dakota has become popular in recent years as a tax haven for wealthy people from all over the world." From Candace Taylor, *A High-*

Stakes Divorce Illustrates How the Rich Play Real-Estate Tug of War, WALL ST. J. (Apr. 9, 2020), https://www.wsj.com/articles/a-high-stakes-divorce-illustrates-how-the-rich-play-real-estate-tug-of-war-11586458598.

Image: In 2011, Ed Bosarge bought an apartment on the exclusive Belgrave Square and placed it in a trust.

5.   One of the first kinds of self-settled asset protection trusts was the separate estate, a special trust form available to women in both England and the United States in the seventeenth through the nineteenth centuries. The separate estate was a way for women and their families to protect wealth upon entry into marriage, when coverture rules stripped married women of most property rights. Women could create separate estate trusts for themselves before entering marriage and then enjoy the use of the assets during marriage, safe from creditors including their husbands. These trusts were an exception to coverture rules concerning property ownership within marriage because the married women were not legal owners but rather beneficial owners of the trust assets. Separate estates had a particular policy objective—what was it? And how does that policy objective differ from policy around the DAPT. For more on the separate estate, see Allison Tait, *The Beginning of the End of Coverture: A Reappraisal of the Married Woman's Separate Estate,* 26 YALE J.L. & FEMINISM 165 (2014), AMY LOUISE ERICKSON, WOMEN AND PROPERTY IN EARLY MODERN ENGLAND (1993), and SUSAN STAVES, MARRIED WOMEN'S SEPARATE PROPERTY IN ENGLAND, 1662–1833 (1990).

6.   Thinking back to our friend John Chipman Gray and his statements about spendthrift trusts creating "the most contemptible aristocracy," what changes when our attention turns to DAPTs? Do the same people and groups benefits, or can we trace a slight shift in who among the wealthy benefit from this particular trust form? Are those people who are harmed by the DAPTs the same as those harmed by other forms of asset protection trusts?

7.   There is an important and growing literature about DAPTS and the range of new asset protection trusts. For some examples, see Charles D. Fox IV & Michael J. Huft, *Asset Protection and Dynasty Trusts,* 37 REAL PROP., PROB. AND TR. J. 287 (2002); Ronald Mann, *A Fresh Look at State Asset Protection Trust Statutes,* 67 VAND. L. REV. 1741 (2014); Elena Marty-Nelson, *Offshore Asset Protection Trusts: Having Your Cake and Eating It Too,* 47 RUTGERS L. REV. 11 (1994–1995); Jay Soled & Mitchell Gans, *Asset Preservation and the Evolving Role of Trusts in the Twenty-First Century,* 72 WASH. & LEE L. REV. 257 (2015); Stewart Sterk, *Asset*

Protection Trusts: Trust Law's Race to the Bottom, 85 CORNELL L. REV. 1035 (2000); Carla Spivack, *Democracy and Trusts*, 42 ACTEC L. J. 311 (2017).

D. Special or Supplemental Needs Trusts

The special needs trust (SNT) is very specialized kind of asset protection trust. Also called a "supplemental needs" or a Medicaid trust, these congressionally authorized trusts allow individuals and families to retain assets in trust while still being able to qualify for governmental benefits when special care is needed by the beneficiary. That is to say, the assets in the special needs trust do not count when governmental agencies are qualifying the beneficiary for program eligibility, so the trust beneficiary can enjoy the use of trust assets while accessing governmental benefits. These trusts are, in this way, asset protection trusts because they protect the assets from government reach both in determining eligibility for governmental assistance programs and in payment for such programs. These trusts help clients to engage in long-term estate planning with an eye to medical expenses, assisted living costs, and any other costs associated with aging, disability, and healthcare.

For example, planning around Medicaid eligibility is very common and requires a detail-oriented approach.[10] Critical to Medicaid eligibility is a determination of the "assets available" to a Medicaid applicant. Medicaid has a five-year (60 month) look-back period at an applicant's assets, meaning that Medicaid considers as "available" all assets held by the applicant for the past 60 months (if they are not transferred for value). This rule prevents an applicant from giving away assets to family members shortly before the applicant applies for Medicaid. Though the rules vary by state, applicants are typically only eligible when their net worth does not exceed a few thousand dollars. Clients typically plan for Medicaid eligibility in several ways. Sometimes, with the look-back period in mind, they make outright gifts five years or more before they anticipate applying for Medicaid. A person who wants to employ this strategy, for instance, might give away all assets except what is needed for the next five years of living and health care expenses. One obvious problem with this approach is that the client has to agree to give up the assets—and therefore a certain amount of financial autonomy—to become eligible for Medicaid a half decade in the future. Another perhaps better option involves creating a special needs trust, either self-settled or settled by a third-party, that help protect assets by removing them from the client's pool of available assets. The following sections provide more

---

[10]   Medicaid eligibility is a rapidly changing area of the law. It is largely framed by title 42, subchapter 19, which governs "Grants To States For Medical Assistance Programs," and specifically 42 U.S. Code § 1396p, which deals with "Liens, adjustments and recoveries, and transfers of assets" for Medicaid.

detail about how both self-settled and third-party special needs trusts work before turning to questions about administering special needs trusts.

1. Self-Settled Special Needs Trusts

When it comes to asset protection, self-settled special needs trusts run into the same problems that as self-settled asset protection trusts—generally, there is very little protection without the restriction of ownership equivalence and settlor rights to the trust property. Accordingly, some settlors use "income only" Medicaid trusts, where a settlor puts property into trust with the right to receive income only; the principal, then, is distributable to people other than the settlor or the settlor's spouse. After the expiration of the look-back period, it is likely that only the income will be counted as assets available. But beware: 42 U.S.C. § 1396p(d)(3)(B)(i) is explicit that any amounts that could be paid to a Medicaid applicant are considered as available assets. Thus, if a trust provides for a settlor/beneficiary to receive mandatory distributions from income and discretionary distributions from principal, the entire income and any amount of principal that could be paid to the settlor are considered available assets. Moreover, the settlor cannot just restrict distributions during the look-back period without running into trouble. Any assets that cannot be paid to a settlor because the trust does not permit distribution during the look-back period are also considered available. 42 U.S.C. § 8 1396p(d)(3)(B)(ii). In some states, the trust corpus may also be considered part of the decedent's estate at her death and thus recoverable by Medicaid. Finally (and hopefully unsurprisingly), all of the assets in a trust are considered as available to the extent the trust is revocable.

There are two important exceptions to the rule that self-settled trusts are considered assets available for determination of Medicaid eligibility. The first exception is for trusts established at death by the decedent spouse for the benefit of the surviving spouse, as long as distributions are limited to providing for the surviving spouse's "supplemental needs." That is to say, the distribution standards cannot permit the surviving spouse to compel distributions for her general purposes, such as maintenance or health care. These supplemental needs trusts are governed by 42 U.S.C. § 1396p(d)(2)–(4), which we include below. You might notice that 42 U.S.C. § 1396p(d)(2) treats a trust set up by one spouse for another as though it was created by the beneficiary spouse. This is because law typically thinks of a married couple as one unit. There is, however, an exception in § 1396p(d)(2)(A) for these supplemental needs trusts if the spouse established the trust by will.

The second exception for self-settled trusts is a special-needs trust established by a disabled person (or a parent, grandparent, guardian, or court acting on behalf of the disable individual) using the disabled person's assets. Commonly, the trust will be formed with money received from an insurance claim, a settlement agreement, or proceeds from a judgment. Again, the trick is that the trust can provide only for supplemental needs during the beneficiary's life—that is, needs that are not covered by other governmental programs. Usually, the trust must also provide that the State will be compensated from the trust upon the beneficiary's death. More specifically, at the beneficiary's death, the state will be entitled to recover from the trust remainder the amount that the state spent on medical care. The trust, therefore, cannot be used more generally to keep property within the family. This result is different from the supplemental needs trust established by a decedent spouse via will for the surviving spouse.

42 U.S.C. § 1396p(d) Treatment of Trust Amounts

(2) (A)   For purposes of this subsection, an individual shall be considered to have established a trust if assets of the individual were used to form all or part of the corpus of the trust and if any of the following individuals established such trust other than by will:

(i)   The individual.

(ii)   The individual's spouse.

(iii)   A person, including a court or administrative body, with legal authority to act in place of or on behalf of the individual or the individual's spouse.

(iv)   A person, including any court or administrative body, acting at the direction or upon the request of the individual or the individual's spouse.

(B)   In the case of a trust the corpus of which includes assets of an individual (as determined under subparagraph (A)) and assets of any other person or persons, the provisions of this subsection shall apply to the portion of the trust attributable to the assets of the individual. . . .

(4)   This subsection shall not apply to any of the following trusts:

(A)   A trust containing the assets of an individual under age 65 who is disabled (as defined in section 1382c(a)(3) of this title) and which is established for the benefit of such individual by a parent, grandparent, legal guardian of the individual, or a court if the State will receive all amounts remaining in the trust upon the death of such individual up to an amount equal to the total medical assistance paid on behalf of the individual under a State plan under this subchapter.

(B)   A trust established in a State for the benefit of an individual if—

(i)   the trust is composed only of pension, Social Security, and other income to the individual (and accumulated income in the trust),

(ii)   the State will receive all amounts remaining in the trust upon the death of such individual up to an amount equal to the total medical assistance paid on behalf of the individual under a State plan under this subchapter; and

(iii)   the State makes medical assistance available to individuals described in section 1396a(a)(10)(A)(ii)(V) of this title, but does not make such assistance available to individuals for nursing facility services under section 1396a(a)(10)(C) of this title.

(C)   A trust containing the assets of an individual who is disabled (as defined in section 1382c(a)(3) of this title) that meets the following conditions:

(i)   The trust is established and managed by a non-profit association.

(ii)   A separate account is maintained for each beneficiary of the trust, but, for purposes of investment and management of funds, the trust pools these accounts.

(iii) Accounts in the trust are established solely for the benefit of individuals who are disabled (as defined in section 1382c(a)(3) of this title) by the parent, grandparent, or legal guardian of such individuals, by such individuals, or by a court.

(iv) To the extent that amounts remaining in the beneficiary's account upon the death of the beneficiary are not retained by the trust, the trust pays to the State from such remaining amounts in the account an amount equal to the total amount of medical assistance paid on behalf of the beneficiary under the State plan under this subchapter.

2.   Third-Party Trusts

Third parties may also establish special needs trusts for beneficiaries to help the beneficiaries qualify and maintain eligibility for Medicaid. Here, we return to the importance of carefully drafted distribution terms. While we've learned about the great utility of discretionary distribution terms in conventional circumstances, trustee discretion is very tricky for Medicaid eligibility because 42 U.S.C. § 1396p(d)(3)(B) provides that any payments that could be made under any circumstances from either the principal or income are considered resources "available" to the individual. The question often becomes whether the trust is a support or discretionary support trust—in which case whatever the beneficiary can compel are "available assets"—or something else, such as a purely discretionary trust or a supplemental needs trust. The following case demonstrates one court's approach to determining whether a trust is a discretionary, support, or supplemental needs trust.

Pikula v. Dept. of Social Services

2016 WL 1749666 (Conn. May 10, 2016)

EVELEIGH, J.

In 1989, John Pikula, the plaintiff's father, executed a will containing a testamentary trust for his two daughters: Dorothy McKee and the plaintiff, Marian Pikula (Marian). When John Pikula died in 1991, the trust became effective and the Probate Court appointed a trustee.

The testamentary language creating the trust provided as follows:

A.   Until Marian shall die, the trustee shall pay to or spend on behalf of Marian as much of the net income derived from this trust fund as the trustee may deem advisable to provide properly for Marian's maintenance and support and may incorporate any income not so distributed into the principal of the fund at the option of the trustee.

B.   I hereby authorize and empower the trustee in his sole and absolute discretion at any time and from time to time to disburse from the principal for any of the trust estates created under this will, even to the point of completely exhausting the same, such amount as he may deem advisable to provide adequately and properly for the support and maintenance of the current income beneficiaries thereof, any expenses incurred by reason of illness and disability. In determining the amount of principal to be so disbursed, the trustee shall take into consideration any other income or property which such income beneficiary may have from any other source, and the trustee's discretion shall be conclusive.

In March 2012, Marian entered a long-term care facility. At that time, she applied for financial and medical assistance under Medicaid. At the time she applied for Medicaid benefits, the trust value was approximately $169,745.91. In May 2013, the department denied Marian's application for Medicaid benefits on the ground that her assets, including the trust, exceeded the relevant asset limits.

On appeal to this court, Marian claims that the trial court improperly upheld the hearing officer's conclusion that the trust was an asset available to Marian as defined by relevant Medicaid regulations. Specifically, Marian claims that the testator intended to create a discretionary, supplemental needs trust, the assets of which should not be considered available for Medicaid purposes. The department, however, contends that the testamentary language indicates that the testator intended the trust to provide for Marian's general support, in which case it would constitute an asset available to Marian. We agree with Marian that the testator intended to create a discretionary, supplemental needs trust and, therefore, we further agree that the trust corpus and income may not be considered to be available to Marian for the purpose of determining eligibility for Medicaid benefits.

This court has stated that, "[u]nder applicable federal law, only assets actually available to a medical assistance recipient may be considered by the state in determining eligibility for public assistance programs such as [Medicaid]. A state may not, in administering the eligibility requirements of its public assistance program . . . presume the availability of assets not actually available." This principal "has served primarily to prevent the states from conjuring fictional sources of income and resources by imputing financial support from persons who have no obligation to furnish it or by overvaluing assets in a manner that attributes nonexistent resources to recipients."

To resolve the issue on appeal, we must determine whether the assets in the testamentary trust were available to the plaintiff. "For the purposes of determining eligibility for the Medicaid program, an available asset is one that is actually available to the applicant or one that the applicant has the legal right, authority or power to obtain or to have applied for the applicant's general or medical support. If the terms of a trust provide for the support of an applicant, the refusal of a trustee to make a distribution from the trust does not render the trust an unavailable asset." Gen. Stat. (Supp. 2016) § 17b–261(c). For Medicaid purposes, general support trusts are considered available because a beneficiary can compel distribution of the trust income. *See* Gen. Stat. § 52–321. In other words, the beneficiary has a "legal right . . . to obtain" the funds. *See* Gen. Stat. (Supp. 2016) § 17b–261(c). Conversely, supplemental needs trusts, in which a trustee retains unfettered discretion to withhold the income, are not considered available to the beneficiary.

In previous cases, this court identified and examined several factors that are useful in determining whether a particular testamentary trust is intended to be a general needs trust or a supplemental needs trust—namely, the amount and nature of the trustee's discretion with regards to trust income and principal, any limitations or guiding principles within which the trustee must operate, and the factual circumstances regarding the establishment of the trust, including the amount of the trust.

The language set forth previously in this opinion indicates that the trustee in the present case need only use as much income from the trust "as the trustee may deem advisable" to Marian. The testamentary language further provides that any unused income may be returned to the trust principal. Although the language in the present case indicates that the trustee may use the net income for the maintenance and support of Marian, the fact that the trustee is only required to use as much income as he "may deem advisable" to provide for such maintenance, indicates that the testator intended for the trustee to have complete discretion in determining what, if any, of the income was to be used for Marian's maintenance.

Furthermore, the fact that the trust provides that any unused income may be returned to the principal of the trust indicates that the testator did not intend to provide for the general needs of the plaintiff. The trust was only valued at approximately $169,745, therefore, it is unlikely that the income of the trust would have been significant enough to provide for Marian's maintenance at the time the testator executed his will in 1989 or when the trust was established in 1991. Furthermore, the testamentary language in the present case provides that the trustee has "sole and absolute discretion" to make disbursements from the principal of the trust. The trust further provides that the trustee's discretion "shall be conclusive as to the advisability of any such disbursement and the same shall not be questioned by anyone." Furthermore, the trust provides a release from liability for the trustee regarding any distributions of principal. On the basis of the foregoing, it is clear that no person can compel the trustee to disburse any principal to Marian. We conclude that the language regarding the discretion of the trustee in the present case is analogous to the language providing absolute and sole discretion to the trustee in previous cases.

Next, we examine whether the trust in the present case contains any limitations or guiding principles within which the trustee must operate. In the present case, the trust mentions "support" and "maintenance" in both the section providing for expenditure of the income and the section addressing disbursement of principal. Nevertheless, in each of these sections the "support" and "maintenance" language is followed or preceded by language allowing the trustee broad discretion to do so only if he deems it advisable. Nothing in the present trust mentions a standard by which the trustee shall make the expenditures or distribution. We conclude that the language in the present case provides that the trustee is required to provide only supplemental support.

We next consider the factual circumstances regarding the establishment of the trust, including the amount of the trust. In the present case, the testator had a relatively small estate. Indeed, the trust assets in the present case consisted mainly of Marian's primary residence, the testator's home. In March 2012, after the home was sold, the trust assets totaled $169,745.91. The assets of the present trust would be quickly exhausted if they were applied to the expenses related to Marian's impairment for which she has sought residential placement. Accordingly, we conclude that the factual circumstances surrounding the establishment of the trust in the present case further bolster our conclusion that it is a supplemental needs trust.

On the basis of the foregoing, we conclude that the trial court improperly dismissed the plaintiff's appeal from the decision of the hearing officer determining that the trust in the present case is a general support trust and that, therefore, the assets are available to the plaintiff. Instead, we conclude that the trust in the present case is a supplemental needs trust and that, therefore, the assets are not available to the plaintiff for the purpose of determining eligibility for Medicaid benefits. The judgment is reversed, and the case is remanded to the trial court with direction to render judgment sustaining the plaintiff's appeal.

NOTES

1.   The outcome in *Pikula* was somewhat surprising to commentators because, usually, anything that could be paid to the beneficiary is considered as an available asset, regardless of whether the trustee actually distributes funds. Courts typically look at the "could be paid" language as meaning "could be compelled" by the beneficiary. A beneficiary of a support trust, for instance, could compel payments for medical care. Similarly, a beneficiary of a discretionary support trust can often compel distribution. If these rules held, how would that have changed the outcome in this case? What would the trust terms have to look like in order to protect the trust assets from being counted as "available" to the beneficiary? Chapter 12 returns to the special needs trust in the context of trust modification.

2.   Most of the time, the assets in a wholly discretionary trust—in which the beneficiary could not compel a distribution—are not considered available assets.

Nevertheless, some states have statutes that specifically include even the assets of a wholly discretionary trust that might be paid to a beneficiary as available assets. *See, e.g.*, KAN. STAT. ANN. § 39–709(e)(3).

3.   You may be wondering whether a spendthrift trust clause in any way helps the beneficiary. The answer is no. The UTC § 503(b)(3) permits state creditors to ignore spendthrift trust provisions. The trick, then, is to have a trust where the trustee can make wholly discretionary distributions—or, at the very least, distributions limited to health care and needs that go beyond the care provided by the state.

3.   Administering the Special Needs Trust

Once a valid special needs trust exists, there are a number of administration issues, including whether trustees of a self-settled special needs trust may pay themselves to take care of the beneficiary. This issue came up in *State v. Hammans*, excerpted below. As you read the case, consider why this issue might be important.

State v. Hammans

870 N.E.2d 1071 (Ind. App. Ct. 2007)

CRONE, J.

On December 28, 1994, Nicholas Hammans was in an automobile accident. He sustained a traumatic brain injury, leaving him completely disabled and requiring twenty-four-hour supervision and care. Upon his discharge from the hospital in March of 1995, the Hammanses received the necessary training to care for him. This care included, but was not limited to, performing physical therapy, delivering medications via IV or injection, feeding him through a feeding tube, changing his tracheotomy tube, suctioning phlegm, and respiratory therapy.

On Nicholas's behalf, the Hammanses brought a lawsuit based on the accident, and the proceeds from the resulting settlement were placed in a guardianship estate supervised by the trial court. On April 17, 1996, the trial court established the Disability Trust, appointed the Hammanses as co-trustees, and funded it with $200,000 transferred from the guardianship estate. The Disability Trust was specifically set up so that Nicholas would remain eligible for Medicaid. To qualify for Medicaid in Indiana, an applicant must meet both an income eligibility test and a resources eligibility test. If either the applicant's income or the value of the applicant's resources is too high, then the applicant does not qualify for Medicaid. *Sanders v. State Family Soc. Sens. Admin.*, 696 N.E.2d 69, 71 (Ind. Ct. App. 1998). To ensure that Nicholas retained Medicaid eligibility, the Disability Trust was structured to meet the requirements of 42 U.S.C. § 1396p(d)(4)(A). This statute permits the creation of a trust, often referred to as "supplemental needs trust," "special needs trust," or "disability trust," the assets of which are excluded from determining an individual's Medicaid eligibility.

The Disability Trust provides, in relevant part:

Whereas, the Grantor, Nicholas W. Hammans, remains unconscious and is un-likely to ever be self-supporting, however, Nicholas may have a normal life expectancy;

Whereas, the projected costs of Nicholas's care and medical and rehabilitation needs over his lifetime far exceed the resources currently available to him, including all sums received in settlement of his personal injury claims; and

Whereas, medical and rehabilitation technology is advancing at a rapid rate and during Nicholas's lifetime these advances may enable him to achieve a level of restoration and rehabilitation not currently possible; and,

Whereas, at the present time Nicholas is a Medicaid recipient, and it is Nicholas's intention that this "Disability Trust" satisfy the provisions of 42 USCS § 1396p(d)(4), commonly known as the "(d)(4) exceptions," and that during the lifetime of Nicholas, the trust corpus and income will remain "unavailable," as a general resource of Nicholas under current Medicaid law; and,

Whereas, Nicholas acknowledges that in accordance with the provisions of this Trust, and in order to comply with 42 USCS § 1396p(d)(4), the State of Indiana or any other domiciliary State of Nicholas will receive all amounts remaining in the Trust upon the death of Nicholas up to an amount equal to the total medical assistance paid on behalf of Nicholas under a State Plan under 42 USCS §§ 1396 et seq.

IT IS THEREFORE AGREED UPON AS FOLLOWS:

1.   Trust Purpose. The purpose of this Trust is to protect Nicholas's long term interests and to generally provide supplemental care during his lifetime, to make available to him such restorative and

rehabilitation services that are or will become available to achieve as normal a physical and mental functioning as is possible and to increase the quality of his life after utilizing available assistance from governmental and private agencies and when such assistance or benefits are incomplete or insufficient, and not to replace assistance or benefits or to render [Nicholas] ineligible for any assistance or benefits to which he would otherwise be entitled or eligible, including Medicaid benefits.

4.   Administration of Trust During Nicholas's Lifetime.

c.   Guidelines for the Co-Trustees' Exercise of Power of Distribution. The Hammanses shall arrange for Nicholas to have services to enhance his quality of life to the greatest extent possible. Nicholas may require life-long rehabilitation services and the Trust is intended to allow Nicholas to receive such services. The expenditures that are contemplated are services provided for Nicholas's mental and physical rehabilitation, education, and training. Examples of such services include but are not limited to the following:

(7)   Expenditures for family members or other persons who provide special care or supervision to the extent of the reasonable value of services provided;

d.   Upon the death of Nicholas, the Hammanses shall terminate the Trust and distribute the entire remaining balance of the Trust estate as follows: (1) The Hammanses shall pay to the State of Indiana (or any other State that provided Medicaid benefits to Nicholas), such amount of the Trust estate which is equal to the total medical assistance paid on behalf of Nicholas under a State plan (i.e. Medicaid) under 42 USCS § 1396 . . .

On December 7, 2005, Nicholas unexpectedly died following a two-day illness. The Disability Trust had a balance of $143,860. The State's payments for Nicholas's medical care through Medicaid totaled $355,632.15.

On January 9, 2006, the Hammanses filed a verified petition seeking fees associated with the administration of the Disability Trust and compensation for the care they rendered to Nicholas and a petition to pay the Disability Trust's final attorney fees.

On March 27, 2006, the trial court issued an order authorizing payment of attorney fees of $2,500. On April 4, 2006, the trial court issued an order authorizing payment of $140,000 to the Hammanses for their administrative services as co-trustees of the Disability Trust and for personal services they provided to Nicholas. In relevant part, the order states:

The Court finds that the personal care and services provided by the Hammanses for the benefit of their disabled son from March 1995 until his death on December 7, 2005 was extraordinary and was performed with the expectation that compensation would eventually be authorized for the Hammanses prior to the death of the disabled beneficiary. The Court further finds that the Hammanses, upon receiving special training, performed all of the tasks and services specified and set forth in paragraph 4 of their petition.

10. The Court finds that from the date the disability trust was established until the death of Nicholas on December 7, 2005, Nicholas was cared for by the Hammanses in their home on a continuous "round the clock" basis, except for brief periods of hospitalization.

11. The Court finds that from the date the disability trust was established until the death of [Nicholas], the Hammanses provided and coordinated Nicholas's care for a continuous period of 3,519 days or a period of approximately 502 weeks. During this period, the Hammanses were away from Nicholas for only 2 days.

13. The Court finds that authorizing payment to the Hammanses at the rate of $15.00–$20.00 per hour is certainly a reasonable rate and a reasonable value for their services when compared to customary and usual charges of agencies providing similar services.

14. The Court finds that the care giving services rendered by the Hammanses were consistent with the purpose for which the trust was established and were consistent with the specific terms of the trust.

15. The Court finds that all care giving services and all trust administration services provided by the Hammanses were for the sole benefit of Nicholas and the Hammanses performed such services with the expectation of being compensated at a reasonable rate of compensation.

Only $1,360 remained in the Disability Trust for reimbursement to the State. On May 5, 2006, the trial court approved an additional payment of $750 for attorney fees.

Discussion and Decision

The State challenges the trial court's order awarding the Hammanses the bulk of the trust corpus for co-trustee fees and for personal services provided to Nicholas.

In furtherance of this chief purpose, paragraph 4(c) of the Disability Trust directs the co-trustees to "arrange for Nicholas to have services to enhance his quality of life to the greatest extent possible." Paragraph 4(c)(7) authorizes expenditures for family members or other persons who provide special care or supervision to the extent of the reasonable services provided. Also, paragraph 4(d)(6) grants the Hammanses all the powers set forth in Indiana Code Section 30–4–3–3, authorizing the trustee to perform every act necessary or appropriate for the purposes of the trust and providing a non-inclusive list of examples.

Given the facts of this case, we cannot say that the trial court's order authorizing payment to the Hammanses as legitimate creditors of the Disability Trust for services performed prior to the beneficiary's death was clearly erroneous.

Affirmed.

NOTE

What is at issue in *Hammans* is that the trustees—the parents of the beneficiary of the trust—pay themselves for care of their child. Their claim, which the court found reasonable, consumed pretty much all the remaining assets in the trust. The state of Kansas opposed the parents' petition because the state claimed entitlement to remaining assets in the trust. *Hammans* shows the variety of claims that can be made against a special needs trust, and it also opens up the possibility for family members to preserve some of the trust assets, despite the requirement that the remainder pass to the state. This issue arose also in *Shelf v. Wachovia Bank, NA*, 712 S.E.2d 708 (N.C. Ct. App. 2011) (questioning value of family-provided care when trust had more than one-half million dollars remaining at end of beneficiary's life and family sought compensation for services).

ASSESSMENTS

1.   Drafting special needs trusts, as you can tell by this point, is a complex job and requires great attention to statutory language in order to align perfectly with the requirements. In the Appendix, you will find sample language that New York provides by statute for a special needs trust. You might notice that the trust terms must be explicit about the settlor's intent to provide supplemental

support. (This same language appears in the trust for Nicholas in *Hammans*). You may also notice that the trustee may use both income and principal to provide that supplemental support. Imagine that Mr. Pikula came to you as a client seeking to revise the trust for Marian to avoid litigation. Write a letter to Mr. Pikula explaining how you would revise the trust terms using the model language in this statute. Be very clear on what language you would strike from the original trust and what new provisions you would incorporate.

2.   Find the statute for your state and see how it compares with the New York special needs trusts trust statute and sample language in the Appendix. What are the differences and what significance do these differences have, if any?

E. Conclusion and Takeaways

There are several ways to create protection from creditors for assets in trust. The two most common and conventional ways are through the use of discretionary distribution terms and the inclusion of a spendthrift provision. Both mechanisms diminish a beneficiary's present interest in the trust assets and consequently protect them from creditors. When and how much the creditor can recover depends on whether the creditor is an ordinary or exception creditor. Ordinary creditors can recover money primarily once the beneficiary receives a distribution, and they may obtain a Hamilton order to guarantee the priority of their claims. Exception creditors may compel a distribution under the right circumstances. Specialized forms of asset protection trusts include the self-settled asset protection trust (also called the domestic asset protection trust) and the special needs trust.

CHAPTER 11 COMPREHENSIVE ASSESSMENT

COUNSEL A TRUSTEE. Aliko, a retired businessman, created an irrevocable discretionary trust just before his death, naming his three children as beneficiaries and his younger brother, Bain, as trustee. The trust terms provide that the trustee has absolute discretion with no other guidance. The trust was funded with shares in the family's several corporate entities and produced a significant amount of income annually.

a.   Recently, the children have come to Bain with a variety of requests for distributions. Please draft a memo to Bain advising whether he should make the desired distributions and answering any related questions:

i. Charissa, Aliko's oldest daughter, is going through a messy divorce. She needs money for legal fees, and she would also like money to rent a new home while she is going through the divorce. In addition, Charissa also needs money to pay her living expenses since she has not worked outside of the home for over twenty years—since before her marriage. In Bain's last conversation with Charissa, they had also discussed whether Charissa's soon-to-be ex-spouse had a claim to Charissa's trust interest as marital property in the divorce.

ii. Dahlia, the middle daughter, has always been somewhat of a spender. She travels frequently and is a fixture on the international party circuit. She dresses in couture and spends a great deal entertaining. While her father was alive, he subsidized her lifestyle by writing checks to her and giving her gifts, always somewhat under the radar so as not to make the other sisters jealous. Now that Aliko is dead, Dahlia needs regular distributions to pay for her living expenses. She has also racked up a large amount of credit card debt that she would like to pay off before creditors begin pressing their claims.

iii. Edite, the youngest daughter, has never made any requests for distributions and has a lucrative career in finance and a tendency to save money rather than spend, like her sister Dahlia. Nevertheless, Edite has a child with significant medical needs, and she is now turning to Bain for help with these increasingly onerous bills.

b. What if, instead of giving the trustee absolute discretion, the trust terms provided that the trustee had discretion to make distributions for the health, maintenance, education, and support of the beneficiaries. Would this change your advice on any of the desired distributions?

c. How, if at all, would your advice to Bain change if Aliko left the following letter:

To My Trustee:

I thank you for taking on this sometimes-thankless job of trustee and making sure that my daughters are provided for in their lifetimes. As you know, I have put all the decision-making in your hands through a grant of absolute discretion. Nevertheless, I thought I would say a few words in case they may be helpful as you navigate the waters. I want my daughters all to live in comfort and without worry about money when it comes to emergencies and unexpected expenses. I hope that each one of them will also, however, find productive callings in life and will dedicate themselves to whatever form of work best suits in order to know the same joy and satisfaction that I found through my work.

With love and luck,

Aliko

Test Your Knowledge

To assess your understanding of the material in this chapter, click here to take a quiz.

CHAPTER 12

Private Trusts IV: Modification and Trustee Removal

CHAPTER LEARNING OUTCOMES

Following your work with the material in this chapter, you should be able to do the following:

- Explain to a beneficiary the legal mechanisms for trust modifications and what requirements must be satisfied to successfully modify trust terms

- Assess whether the Claflin doctrine, trust deviation, decanting, or trustee removal would be most helpful or appropriate in a given situation to modify a trust

- Draft a petition for trust modification

- Discuss with a client the pros and cons of decanting and explain a typical decanting statute

- Draft a petition for trustee removal

- Describe the mechanics of powers of appointment

- Evaluate the benefits associated with powers of appointment

A. Introduction

In this chapter, we shift focus to trust modification and discuss the various ways in which trustees and beneficiaries can act to modify terms of a trust when those terms have become outdated or inapt through changed circumstances. To begin the discussion, we note the continuing importance of donor intent in modification doctrine, then in **Part B**, we examine the common-law **Claflin doctrine** as well as **equitable deviation**. Both doctrines allow a trustee to petition the court for modification but require that the "material purpose" of the trust remain intact, to a certain extent.

After learning about these conventional mechanisms for modification, we will explore another trend in **Part C**, modification through **decanting**. States are adopting trust decanting statutes—there is even a Uniform Trust Decanting Act (UTDA)—that allow trustees to make certain modifications unilaterally, without judicial or beneficiary approval. **Part D** concerns trustee removal as a form of modification and examines both the grounds for trustee removal and the process for such a removal.

Part E explores the ability of trust settlors to build flexibility and modification powers into a trust by using **powers of appointment**. These special provisions give a trust beneficiary (called the **donee of the power**) the ability to direct (or appoint) property to or among a group of **permissible distributees** in a way that varies from the trust's written terms.

The materials in this chapter demonstrate the persistently tight grip of donor intent in trust law doctrine as well as ways that trust law has created to mitigate the worst effects of "dead hand" control. Ultimately, these topics lead us to think about how long donor wishes should remain dispositive as well as what, if any, additional limits we might want to place on donor conditions.

B. Trust Modification and Revocation

A revocable trust is easily modified and revoked. The same is not true for an irrevocable trust because of a policy choice that American trust law has made to uphold donor intent for the trust's duration. In general, if the settlor and the beneficiaries all agree, an irrevocable trust may be modified or terminated. If, however, the settlor is no longer living or a beneficiary objects to modification, the process is more complicated. In these cases, modification—if at all possible—requires judicial approval of proposed modifications that reflect a continuation of the donor's wishes to the extent possible. There are two doctrines available for the modification of irrevocable trusts: the material purpose (or Claflin doctrine); and deviation. Both approaches require petitioning the court.

1.   The Claflin (Material Purpose) Doctrine

The Claflin doctrine, sometimes also called the material purpose doctrine, prevents a court from modifying an irrevocable trust unless all the beneficiaries consent and all of the settlor's material purposes have been satisfied. *See Claflin v. Claflin*, 20 N.E. 454 (Mass. 1889). In *Claflin*, a father created a testamentary trust for his younger son stating: "pay the remaining one-third part thereof to my son Adelbert E. Claflin, in the manner following, viz.: Ten thousand dollars when he is of the age of twenty-one years, ten thousand dollars when he is of the age of twenty-five years, and the balance when he is of the age of thirty years." *Id.* at 455. At age twenty-five, Adelbert, not content with waiting for his money, sued to compel the trustee to terminate the trust and convey the remainder of the trust assets to him outright. The trustee refused and the parties ended up in court. Unfortunately for Adelbert, the court agreed with the trustee and remarked:

> This is not a dry trust, nor have the purposes of the trust been accomplished, if the intention of the testator is to be carried out. It cannot be said that these restrictions upon the plaintiff's possession and control of the property are altogether useless, for there is not the same danger that he will spend the property while it is in the hands of the trustees as there would be if it were in his own. The existing situation is one which the testator manifestly had in mind and made provision for. The strict execution of the trust has not become impossible; the restriction upon the plaintiff's possession and control is, we think, one that the testator had a right to make, and we see no good reason why the intention of the testator should not be carried out.

Id. at 455–56. The crux of the case and the heart of the doctrine rest on the notion that the settlor's plan should be disturbed only if the material purpose of the trust can no longer be satisfied.

What constitutes a trust's material purpose, then, becomes grounds for analysis and conflict. Over time, courts have determined that certain trust conditions are, in and of themselves, a material purpose. For example, the following limitations have traditionally prohibited a trust's early termination: (1) a spendthrift provision, (2) discretionary distribution terms, (3) language indicating that the trust is for the beneficiary's continued support, or (4) age requirements (as in the Claflin case itself).

The following case provides another example of trust beneficiaries seeking early termination of a trust. As you read the case, consider what the material purpose of the trust is and whether there would have been any circumstances in which the beneficiaries could have prevailed.

In re Estate of Brown

528 A.2d 752 (Vt. 1987)

GIBSON, J.

The trustee of a testamentary trust appeals an order of the Superior Court granting the petition of the lifetime and residual beneficiaries of the trust to terminate it and to distribute the proceeds to the life tenants. We reverse.

The primary issue raised on appeal is whether any material purpose of the trust remains to be accomplished, thus barring its termination. The appellant/trustee also raises the closely related issue of whether all beneficiaries are before the court, i.e., whether the class of beneficiaries has closed.

Andrew J. Brown died in 1977, settling his entire estate in a trust, all of which is held by the trustee under terms and conditions that are the subject of this appeal. The relevant portion of the trust instrument provides:

> The trust shall be used to provide an education, particularly a college education, for the children of my nephew, Woolson S. Brown. My Trustee is hereby directed to use the income from said trust and such part of the principal as may be necessary to accomplish this purpose. Said trust to continue for said purpose until the last child has received his or her education and the Trustee, in its discretion, has determined that the purpose hereof has been accomplished.

> At such time as this purpose has been accomplished and the Trustee has so determined the income from said trust and such part of the principal as may be necessary shall be used by said Trustee for the care, maintenance and welfare of my nephew, Woolson S. Brown and his wife, Rosemary Brown, so that they may live in the style and manner to which they are accustomed, for and during the remainder of their natural lives. Upon their demise, any remainder of said trust, together with any accumulation thereon, shall be paid to their then living children in equal shares, share and share alike.

The trustee complied with the terms of the trust by using the proceeds to pay for the education of the children of Woolson and Rosemary Brown. After he determined that the education of these children was completed, the trustee began distribution of trust income to the lifetime beneficiaries, Woolson and Rosemary.

On June 17, 1983, the lifetime beneficiaries petitioned the probate court for termination of the trust, arguing that the sole remaining purpose of the trust was to maintain their lifestyle and that distribution of the remaining assets was necessary to accomplish this purpose. The remaindermen, the children of the lifetime beneficiaries, filed consents to the proposed termination. The probate court denied the petition to terminate, and the petitioners appealed. The superior court reversed, concluding that continuation of the trust was no longer necessary because the only material purpose, the education of the children, had been accomplished. This appeal by the trustee followed.

An active trust may not be terminated, even with the consent of all the beneficiaries, if a material purpose of the settlor remains to be accomplished. As a threshold matter, we reject the trustee's argument that the trust cannot be terminated because it is both a support trust and a spendthrift trust. It is true that, were either of these forms of trust involved, termination could not be compelled by the beneficiaries because a material purpose of the settlor would remain unsatisfied. *See* RESTATEMENT (SECOND) OF TRUSTS § 337.

The trust at issue does not qualify as a support trust. A support trust is created where the trustee is directed to use trust income or principal for the benefit of an individual, but only to the extent necessary to support the individual. Here, the terms of the trust provide that, when the educational purpose of the trust has been accomplished and the trustee, in his discretion, has so determined,

> "the income . . . and such part of the principal as may be necessary shall be used by said Trustee for the care, maintenance and welfare of Rosemary and Woolson Brown so that they may live in the style and manner to which they are accustomed."

The trustee has, in fact, made the determination that the educational purpose has been accomplished and has begun to transfer the income of the trust to the lifetime beneficiaries. Because the trustee must, at the very least, pay all of the trust income to beneficiaries Rosemary and Woolson Brown, the trust cannot be characterized as a support trust.

Nor is this a spendthrift trust. "A trust in which by the terms of the trust or by statute a valid restraint on the voluntary and involuntary transfer of the interest of the beneficiary is imposed is a spendthrift trust." RESTATEMENT (SECOND) OF TRUSTS § 152(2). While no specific language is needed to create a spendthrift trust, *id.* at comment c, here the terms of the trust instrument do not manifest Andrew J. Brown's intention to create such a trust.

We find that the trust instrument at hand has two purposes. First, the trust provides for the education of the children of Woolson and Rosemary Brown. The Superior Court found that Rosemary Brown was incapable of having more children and that the chance of Woolson Brown fathering more children was remote; on this basis, the court concluded that the educational purpose of the trust had been achieved.

The settlor also intended a second purpose, however: the assurance of a life-long income for the beneficiaries through the management and discretion of the trustee. We recognize that, had the trust merely provided for successive beneficiaries, no inference could be drawn that the settlor intended to deprive the beneficiaries of the right to manage the trust property during the period of the trust. Here, however, the language of the instrument does more than create successive gifts. The settlor provided that the trustee must provide for the "care, maintenance and welfare" of the lifetime beneficiaries "so that they may live in the style and manner to which they are accustomed, for and during the remainder of their natural lives." The trustee must use all of the income and such part of the principal as is necessary for this purpose. We believe that the settlor's intention to assure a life-long income to Woolson and Rosemary Brown would be defeated if termination of the trust were allowed.

Because of our holding regarding the second and continuing material purpose of the trust, we do not reach the question of whether the trial court erred in holding that the educational purpose of the trust has been accomplished.

NOTES

1.   Why do you suppose that the Browns wanted to terminate the trust? Would they have fared better if they had a compelling reason to terminate the trust, or would the court have come to the same conclusion no matter what the reason? What if the trust terms had stated that the trust was for the purpose of providing for Rosemary's and Woolson's continuing education? Is there a distinct point when that material purpose would be fulfilled? Would Rosemary's and Woolson's statements that they no longer had any interest in continuing education be sufficient to terminate the trust?

2.   The *Brown* court noted that the trust contained no spendthrift clause or provision. Could Woolson and Rosemary have sold their interests in the trust and raised money that way?

3.   Irrevocable trusts are defined by the financial intermediation of a trustee on behalf of the beneficiary, and trust settlors often choose to transfer wealth because of this intermediation, which provides control over time. How, then, can any irrevocable trust be terminated early without explicit directions for doing so within the trust terms? Absent explicit instruction, what must a trust's terms look like in order for early termination to be a possibility?

4.   The Uniform Trust Code has implemented slight changes to the Claflin doctrine. What changes can you identify in the UTC provision that follows and are these changes for the better? Why?

UTC §411 Modification or Termination of Noncharitable Irrevocable Trust by Consent

[(a) [A noncharitable irrevocable trust may be modified or terminated upon consent of the settlor and all beneficiaries, even if the modification or termination is inconsistent with a material purpose of the trust.] [If, upon petition, the court finds that the settlor and all beneficiaries consent to the modification or termination of a noncharitable irrevocable trust, the court shall approve the modification or termination even if the modification or termination is inconsistent with a material purpose of the trust.] A settlor's power to consent to a trust's modification or termination may be exercised by an agent under a power of attorney only to the extent expressly authorized by the power of attorney or the terms of the trust; by the settlor's [conservator] with the approval of the court supervising the [conservatorship] if an agent is not so authorized; or by the settlor's [guardian] with the approval of the court supervising the [guardianship] if an agent is not so authorized and a conservator has not been appointed. . . .]

(b)   A noncharitable irrevocable trust may be terminated upon consent of all of the beneficiaries if the court concludes that continuance of the trust is not necessary to achieve any material purpose of the trust. A noncharitable irrevocable trust may be modified upon consent of all of the beneficiaries if the court concludes that modification is not inconsistent with a material purpose of the trust.

[(c) A spendthrift provision in the terms of the trust is not presumed to constitute a material purpose of the trust.]

(d)   Upon termination of a trust under subsection (a) or (b), the trustee shall distribute the trust property as agreed by the beneficiaries.

(e)   If not all of the beneficiaries consent to a proposed modification or termination of the trust under subsection (a) or (b), the modification or termination may be approved by the court if the court is satisfied that:

(1)   if all of the beneficiaries had consented, the trust could have been modified or terminated under this section; and

(2)   the interests of a beneficiary who does not consent will be adequately protected.

Ronald Chester has written: "If the trend continues toward allowing and creating long-term trusts and expanding the spendthrift limitations protecting them, the need for easier modification and termination of such trusts will increase." *See* Ronald Chester, *Modification and Termination of Trusts in the 21st Century: The Uniform Trust Code Leads a Quiet Revolution*, 35 REAL PROP., PROB. & TR. J. 697 (2001). Do the UTC reforms suffice, or should we consider other, additional reforms?

ASSESSMENTS

1.   Imagine you are the Trustee for the *Brown* trust and have been asked to justify the decision to contest the trust termination. Write a short memo setting forth your motives and obligations.

2.   Lady Mae created a valid trust in 1940 for her daughter, Gigi. The trust requires all income to be paid to Gigi and significantly limits invasion of principal, with the remainder passing to various charities on Gigi's death. The trust prohibits the trustee from making investments in corporate stock, and the trustee is required to retain the family home and surrounding property located in the hills surrounding Los Angeles as Gigi's residence. Recently, the mudslides triggered by a tropical storm destroyed the home and caused significant erosion. The trustee would like to sell the land and invest in corporate stock. In addition, due to Gigi's advanced age, her expenses have increased to the point that trust income does not provide a suitable level of care.

    a.   What is the material purpose of Lady Mae's trust?

    b.   What does the trustee need to do to modify the Lady Mae trust terms using the Claflin doctrine? Draft a short petition for modification, identifying the material purpose(s) of the trust and proposing one or more modifications in line with Lady Mae's wishes, to the extent that is possible.

c.   Can a trust have both a primary and a secondary purpose? Draft language to insert in Lady Mae's trust identifying its primary and secondary purpose.

2.   Equitable or Administrative Deviation

A second mechanism for modifying an irrevocable trust is the administrative deviation doctrine, which allows for modification based on changed circumstances. The origins of the deviation are less clear that the origins of the Claflin doctrine, but deviation has been a longstanding doctrine in maritime law dealing with commercial ships that depart from agreed upon routes. *See Hostetter v. Park*, 137 U.S. 30 (1890). Deviation, as we will see in Chapter 15, also pertains to the modification of charitable trusts.

The most famous deviation case is probably the *Pulitzer* case, involving a newspaper fortune and the idiosyncratic wishes of the founder. *See In re Pulitzer's Estate*, 249 N.Y.S. 87 (Surr. Ct. N.Y. Co. 1931). In that case, at issue were the terms of a testamentary trust created by Joseph Pulitzer restricting the sale of the newspaper stock that formed the bulk of the trust assets. Pulitzer explained:

'I further authorize and empower my Executors and Trustees . . . to sell and dispose of said stock, or any part thereof, at public or private sale, at such prices and on such terms as they may think best . . . . This power of sale, however, is limited to the said stock of the Pulitzer Publishing Company of St. Louis, and shall not be taken to authorize or empower the sale or disposition under any circumstances whatever, by the Trustees of any stock of the Press Publishing Company, publisher of 'The World' newspaper. I particularly enjoin upon my sons and my descendants the duty of preserving, perfecting and perpetuating 'The World' newspaper (to the maintenance and upbuilding of which I have sacrificed my health and strength) in the same spirit in which I have striven to create and conduct it as a public institution, from motives higher than mere gain, it having been my desire that it should be at all times conducted in a spirit of independence and with a view to inculcating high standards and public spirit among the people and their official representatives, and it is my earnest wish that said newspaper shall hereafter be conducted upon the same principles.'

The stock, however, did not fare well, and the value of the trust declined substantially. Consequently, the trustees sought to modify the sale restrictions to stem the losses and recoup some of the trust's value for the beneficiaries. The court allowed the modification, justifying it in this way:

> It has been satisfactorily established by the evidence before me that the continuance of the publication of the newspapers, which are the principal assets of the Press Publishing Company, will in all probability lead to a serious impairment or the destruction of a large part of the trust estate. The dominant purpose of Mr. Pulitzer must have been the maintenance of a fair income for his children and the ultimate reception of the unimpaired corpus by the remaindermen. Permanence of the trust and ultimate enjoyment by his grandchildren were intended. A man of his sagacity and business ability could not have intended that from mere vanity, the publication of the newspapers, with which his name and efforts had been associated, should be persisted in until the entire trust asset was destroyed or wrecked by bankruptcy or dissolution. His expectation was that his New York newspapers would flourish. Despite his optimism, he must have contemplated that they might become entirely unprofitable and their disposal would be required to avert a complete loss of the trust asset. The power of a court of equity, with its jurisdiction over trusts, to save the beneficiaries in such a situation has been repeatedly sustained in New York and other jurisdictions.
>
> The extreme circumstances in the pending case surely justify the alternative of disregarding the directions of the testator, if mandatory, and reading into the will a power of sale. . . . The trustees here find themselves in a crisis where there is no self-help available to them. . . . I accordingly hold, in this phase of the decision, that the terms of the will and codicils do not prohibit the trustees from disposing of any assets of the Press Publishing Company, that the trustees have general power and authority to act in the conveyance of the assets proposed to be sold, and that this court, in the exercise of its equitable jurisdiction, should authorize them by an appropriate direction in the decree to exercise such general authority.

As this language indicates, the court assumed that any rational settlor would want the stock sold if that person knew of the decline in value and that such a settlor would not be driven by "mere vanity." What if Pulitzer had been even more explicit in his directions and stated that the trustees were not to sell the shares even if a drastic decline in value occurred? *See* John H. Langbein,

Mandatory Rules in the Law of Trusts, 98 Nw. U. L. REV. 1105, 1118 (2004). Langbein points to the following comment to UTC § 412:

> "Although the settlor is granted considerable latitude in defining the purposes of the trust, the principle that a trust have a purpose which is for the benefit of its beneficiaries precludes unreasonable restrictions on the use of trust property. An owner's freedom to be capricious about the use of the owner's own property ends when the property is impressed with a trust for the benefit of others."

The UTC has laid out a cohesive framework for deviation. The UTC deviation doctrine allows courts to modify either the administrative or dispositive terms of a trust when faced with "circumstances not anticipated by the settlor." In addition, UTC rules permit deviation from the administrative (but not the dispositive) terms of a trust if compliance would defeat or substantially impair the accomplishment of the purposes of the trust in light of changed circumstances not anticipated by the settlor. The Uniform Trust Code rules for deviation are as follows:

UTC § 412 Modification or Termination Because of Unanticipated Circumstances or Inability to Administer Trust Effectively

(a)   The court may modify the administrative or dispositive terms of a trust or terminate the trust if, because of circumstances not anticipated by the settlor, modification or termination will further the purposes of the trust. To the extent practicable, the modification must be made in accordance with the settlor's probable intention.

(b)   The court may modify the administrative terms of a trust if continuation of the trust on its existing terms would be impracticable or wasteful or impair the trust's administration.

(c)   Upon termination of a trust under this section, the trustee shall distribute the trust property in a manner consistent with the purposes of the trust.

The following case involves a request to modify based on the Claflin doctrine and the deviation doctrine. As you read it, pay attention to the different reasons the court gives for rejecting each request.

In re Trust D Created Under Last Will and Testament of Darby

234 P.3d 793 (Kan. 2010)

GREENE, J.

In this appeal we must decide the propriety of the district court's order approving modifications to an irrevocable testamentary trust created by the Last Will and Testament of Harry Darby, deceased. Marjorie D. Alford, a daughter of Darby and a first generation beneficiary of the subject trust, was successful in achieving an order of the district court approving the modifications, but the Internal Revenue Service (IRS) is not bound by such modifications unless approved by the highest court of the state.

FACTUAL OVERVIEW

On July 15, 1986, Darby executed his last will and testament, which established several trusts for the benefit of his daughters and sister. The only trust at issue in this appeal is that denominated by his will as "Trust D," which was to be established at Darby's death by a specific bequest in the amount of $240,000 to the trustee, The Commercial National Bank of Kansas City, to be administered and distributed as follows:

> A.   The trustee shall, at convenient intervals but not less frequently than annually, pay an amount (as defined in the next sentence) each taxable year from Trust D to my daughter, MARJORIE D. ALFORD, if she is living at the time for the payment of such amount. The amount to be paid from Trust D in any taxable year as provided above may be paid in such installments during such year as the trustee deems advisable and shall be in the amount of Twelve Thousand Dollars ($12,000.00). I strongly recommend (but this recommendation shall not be deemed to be mandatory) that the payments to be made from Trust D shall be in monthly installments which shall be as nearly equal as possible. The amount to be paid shall be paid first out of the net income derived from Trust D and then out of the principal of Trust D if said net income should not be sufficient. Any excess income not needed to make the above payments shall be added to the principal of Trust D at such times as the trustee deems advisable.

> B.   Upon the death of the last to die of my daughter, MARJORIE D. ALFORD, and me, the funds then comprising Trust D, shall remain in trust, and thereafter the trustee shall continue to pay at

convenient intervals the sum of Four Thousand Dollars ($4,000.00) each to the three daughters of MARJORIE D. ALFORD, namely, DIANE CHRISTINE MUNKSGAARD, MARY CUBBINSON RESTER, and JEAN ANNE ALFORD, for their lifetime, and upon the death of each, the trustee shall pay one-third of the funds then comprising Trust D to the issue per stirpes of the decreased daughter of MARJORIE D. ALFORD."

In addition to these provisions, the will contained numerous provisions applicable to all of the trusts so created, including the following provision restricting the powers of the beneficiaries:

> J.   During the entire duration of the trust, each and every beneficiary of the trust shall be without power, voluntarily or involuntarily, to sell, mortgage, pledge, hypothecate, assign, alienate, anticipate, transfer, or convey any interest in the trust estate or the property constituting the trust estate or the income therefrom until the same is actually paid into his or her hands, and no interest of any beneficiary in, or claim to, the trust estate or any part of creditors of any beneficiary, or to judgment, levy, execution, sequestration, attachment, bankruptcy proceedings or other legal or equitable process."

In January 1987, Darby executed a codicil to his last will and testament, which increased the amount of the bequest establishing Trust D to $480,000, increased the amount of the annual distribution to Alford to $24,000, and increased the annual distributions to the second generation beneficiaries to $8,000 each. No further changes to the trust were affected by this codicil. Darby died 9 days after executing this codicil.

On July 27, 2009, Alford filed her "Petition for Modification of Testamentary Trust under the Kansas Uniform Trust Code" seeking modifications to the trust provisions in order to increase her distributions. Alford's petition alleged that her sole source of income "was her $24,000 annual distribution from Trust D" and that the "parties have determined that this annual sum is no longer sufficient to satisfy [her] basic living expenses." All of the identified qualified beneficiaries of Trust D voluntarily entered an appearance, waived notice to the hearing, and consented to the proposed modifications. No further facts were presented to the district court, and no evidentiary hearing was requested or conducted.

The district court approved the modifications, concluding in material part:

"4.   The Court is authorized, under K.S.A. § 58a–411, to modify the Trust as set forth in the Petition because all of the qualified beneficiaries of Trust D consent to such modification and such modification is not inconsistent with a material purpose of Trust D. The Court is also authorized, under K.S.A. § 58a–412, to modify the Trust as set forth in the Petition because Trust D is not providing enough income to satisfy the basic living needs of Petitioner Marjorie D. Alford, and therefore circumstances exist that were not anticipated by the settler of Trust D, and modification will further the purposes of Trust D. Finally, the Court is authorized, under K.S.A. § 58a–416, to modify the Trust as set forth in the Petition because, under the terms that presently govern the administration of Trust D, at Petitioner Marjorie D. Alford's death a significant amount of federal generation-skipping transfer tax may be unnecessarily incurred by Trust D, and therefore modification will achieve the settlor's likely tax objectives, in a manner that is not contrary to the settlor's probable intention."

DID THE DISTRICT COURT ERR IN APPROVING THE MODIFICATION INCREASING THE ANNUAL DISTRIBUTION TO ALFORD?

Alford contends on appeal that the proposed modification (Article VII, paragraph A) increasing her annual distribution amount is necessary to satisfy her basic living expenses and that this increase is consistent with Darby's "clear" intent "to ensure sufficient trust distributions to support Ms. Alford's basic needs." Alford points to no specific trust provisions to support this suggestion as to Darby's intent, but she argues that the doubling of her annual distribution in the will's codicil is indicative of Darby's intent to "properly support" Alford. Applying Kansas law, a modification of this nature may not be approved despite consent of all beneficiaries unless it "is not inconsistent with a material purpose of the trust," K.S.A. 2009 Supp. 58a–411(b), or "because of circumstances not anticipated by the settlor, modification . . . will further the purposes of the trust." K.S.A. 58a–412.

Inconsistent with a Material Purpose?

First, we disagree that the "basic support" of Alford was a "material purpose" of this trust. Darby employed no language indicating any such desire, despite the ease of inserting a clear directive to the trustee in this regard, or to permit an invasion of principal by ascertainable standards for her basic support needs. This was clearly not a support trust. *See Miller v. Kansas Dept. of S.R.S.*, 64 P.3d 395 (Kan. 2003) (support trust exists when trustee is required to inquire into the basic support needs of the beneficiary and to provide for those needs). And we are not inclined to infer a material purpose to support Alford's basic needs when the express terms fail to indicate any such purpose.

Whereas no direct or circumstantial evidence has been offered to indicate that a material purpose of the trust was to provide for Alford's basic needs, we note that a specific trust provision does substantially restrict the beneficiaries' rights and interests; this provision has been characterized as a spendthrift provision. In Kansas, a spendthrift provision is presumed to constitute a material purpose of the trust. Kansas law is in material contrast to the Uniform Trust Code, which specifically negates any such presumption. *See* UNIF. TRUST CODE, § 411(c).

For these reasons, we conclude that the proposed modification increasing Alford's annual distribution is inconsistent with material purposes of the trust and cannot be validated under K.S.A. 2009 Supp. 58a–411(b).

Circumstances not Anticipated by the Settlor?

Under K.S.A. 58a–412, the subject modification increasing Alford's annual distribution may be approved if, because of circumstances not anticipated by the settlor, it would further the purposes of the trust and can be made in accordance with the settlor's probable intention. On appeal, however, Alford does not argue that there were circumstances not anticipated by Darby; indeed, there is no evidence in the record that indicates that Darby failed to anticipate that the value of future distributions would be devalued by routine inflation. In fact, he was willing to permit principal to be invaded for purposes of the specified distributions, but he recognized that income growth alone could someday exceed that necessary for the distributions, and in this event, he directed that it be added to the principal rather than to increase the distribution to Alford.

Courts have generally been more willing to allow modification for unanticipated circumstances where there are truly unforeseen events resulting in economic hardship, the incapacity of a beneficiary, the impossibility or imprudence of a trust provision, or the diminution in value of a trust asset. *See, e.g., In re Nobbe*, 831 N.E.2d 835, 843 (Ind .App. 2005). Indeed, our appellate courts have allowed such modifications in precisely such unanticipated circumstances.

We are simply not convinced that devaluation due to normal inflation should be considered an unanticipated circumstance where the settlor has specified on two separate occasions that the distribution be measured by a fixed dollar amount. If Darby's codicil and its increase in annual distribution amount (executed only 6 months after his execution of the will) indicates an objective to provide more income for Alford's basic needs—as suggested by Alford on appeal, why would not we find in that codicil an escalator to protect against future devaluation—just like the escalator contained in the proposed modification?

In the last analysis, Darby's recognition that income might exceed the amount needed for the annual distribution, and that any such excess be added to principal rather than fund larger distributions, is antithetical to any purported failure to anticipate the normal inflationary devaluation of the specified amount. We conclude that funding an increase will inherently frustrate his intention for this growth, as well as jeopardize—or at least reduce—distributions to the second and third generation of beneficiaries. For these reasons, the proposed modification to increase Alford's annual distribution cannot be validated as an unanticipated circumstance under K.S.A. 58a–412.

In summary, we conclude that the proposed modifications to the Darby Trust D would contravene applicable Kansas law. The district court must be reversed, and this matter remanded with directions to invalidate the modifications.

NOTES

1.   In addition to modification by consent and in the case of unanticipated circumstances, the UTC allows for modification when a trust is uneconomic, UTC § 414; to correct mistakes, UTC § 415; or to achieve a tax objective, UTC § 416.

UTC § 414 Modification or Termination of Uneconomic Trust

(a)   After notice to the qualified beneficiaries, the trustee of a trust consisting of trust property having a total value less than [$50,000] may terminate the trust if the trustee concludes that the value of the trust property is insufficient to justify the cost of administration.

(b)   The court may modify or terminate a trust or remove the trustee and appoint a different trustee if it determines that the value of the trust property is insufficient to justify the cost of administration.

(c)   Upon termination of a trust under this section, the trustee shall distribute the trust property in a manner consistent with the purposes of the trust.

UTC § 415 Reformation to Correct Mistakes

The court may reform the terms of a trust, even if unambiguous, to conform the terms to the settlor's intention if it is proved by clear and convincing evidence what the settlor's intention was and that the terms of the trust were affected by a mistake of fact or law, whether in expression or inducement.

UTC § 416 Modification to Achieve Settlor's Tax Objectives

To achieve the settlor's tax objectives, the court may modify the terms of a trust in a manner that is not contrary to the settlor's probable intention. The court may provide that the modification has retroactive effect.

––––––––––

Why is the *Darby* court so resistant to a broad reading of the UTC, on all counts? Furthermore, what evidence does the court have with respect to the settlor's intent? What is the material purpose of the trust if it is not to provide for the daughter's basic needs and comfort?

2.   Returning to the topic of special needs trusts, which we discussed in chapter 11, a common scenario involves converting an irrevocable trust that is already in existence into a special needs trust. *In re Trust of Riddell*, 157 P.3d 888 (Wash. Ct. App. 2007), is a good example of this and involves a trustee's petition for a judicial modification based on changed circumstances. In *Riddell*, a grandfather created an irrevocable trust to benefit his children and grandchildren. There were two grandchildren, Donald and Nancy. Donald was a successful lawyer; Nancy suffered from schizophrenia affective disorder and bipolar disorder. At the time of the case, Nancy had been placed in a care facility and was not expected to live independently for the remainder of her life. Upon the death of Donald and Nancy's parents, the trusts were to terminate and the remainder assets to pass outright in equal shares to Donald and Nancy. The trustee—who was also Nancy's father—filed a petition to modify the trust to create a special needs trust for Nancy as opposed to her receiving the assets outright at the trust termination. "He argued that a special needs trust is necessary because, upon distribution, Nancy's trust funds would either be seized by the State of Washington to pay her extraordinary medical bills, or Nancy would manage the funds poorly due to her mental illness and lack of judgment. He argued that the modification would preserve and properly manage Nancy's

funds for her benefit." *Id.* at 489–90. The court agreed with the trustee's arguments, remarking:

> There is no question that changed circumstances have intervened to frustrate the settlors' intent. Nancy's grandparents intended that she have the funds to use as she saw fit. Not only is Nancy unable to manage the funds or to pass them to her son, but there is a great likelihood that the funds will be lost to the State for her medical care. It is clear that the settlors would have wanted a different result.

> George and Irene both died without creating a special needs trust but did not know of Nancy's mental health issues or how they might best be addressed. They clearly intended to establish a trust to provide for their grandchildren's general support, not solely for extraordinary and unanticipated medical bills.

The court consequently remanded the case to the trial court to determine the appropriate form of equitable deviation. What kinds of changed circumstances do you imagine generally lead to judicial approval for modification? Thinking about the trustee in situations like these, is it the trustee's duty to file a petition for modification? Put differently, could a trustee ever be liable for a fiduciary breach by not seeking to modify trust terms when the terms have become burdensome, inefficient, or outdated?

ASSESSMENT

Return to Lady Mae's 1940 trust for her daughter, Gigi, discussed in the prior Assessment. You will recall that the trust requires all income to be paid to Gigi, significantly limits invasion of principal, prohibits the trustee from making investments in corporate stock, and requires the trustee to retain the family home and surrounding property. The recent mudslides that destroyed the home and Gigi's advanced aged and increased expenses have already motivated the trustee to seek a trust modification using the Claflin doctrine. How does the petition change if you use deviation? Revise your petition based on the requirements and standards for deviation.

C. Trust Decanting

A new and emerging form of trust modification is the practice of "decanting," which involves a trustee pouring ("decanting") assets from one trust into another. The primary difference between the older forms of modification and decanting is that the latter allows trustees to make certain modifications without judicial or even beneficiary approval. When a trust is decanted, we speak of the original trust as the "invaded" trust and the new trust as the "appointed" trust. Initially, decanting was effectuated by trustees who had discretion to make distributions from principal "to or for the benefit of" the beneficiaries and would pay the trust corpus over into a new trust for the benefit of the same beneficiaries.

Decanting is a new trend to help trustees avoid petitioning courts for modification and is a valuable estate planning tool.

Decanting emerged as trustees saw a need for refreshed distributional and management terms. The power of decanting is recognized as a common law right in some jurisdictions if the trust permitted the trustee to make distributions from principal. *Morse v. Kraft*, 992 N.E.2d 1021 (Mass. 2013) (permitting decanting of trusts requiring impartial trustees for the decedent settlor's four children to new trusts that permitted interested trustees). Trustees saw a need to update the trust—often to have more sophisticated terms regarding distributions, such as special needs trusts for disabled beneficiaries. *In re Kroll*, 971 N.Y.S.2d 863 (N.Y. Sur. Ct. 2013) (permitting decanting into special needs trust).

As the idea grew in popularity, trust instruments themselves and then various state statutes explicitly allowed decanting, either through the use of powers of appointment that explicitly authorized the trustee (or a trust protector) to appoint the trust corpus to another trust. The New York legislature enacted the country's first decanting statute in 1992, spurred on by tax avoidance concerns brought on by the **generation-skipping transfer tax** (GST tax). If trustees could extend the duration of trusts created before a certain date, then they could take advantage of an exemption in the GST tax.

Since that time, over two dozen states have enacted decanting statutes, and they vary considerably. Some states require notice to the beneficiaries; others don't. Some states allow a trustee to remove a mandatory income interest. And some states allow the acceleration of a remainder beneficiary's interest.[1] In 2015, the Uniform Law Commissioners rolled out the Uniform Trust Decanting Act (UTDA), which authorizes decanting from an irrevocable trust where the trustee has the power to make distributions from principal. Unlike some statutes, the

---

[1]   The state rankings chart from Oshins & Associates is available at https://db78e19b-dca5-49f9-90f61acaf5eaa6ba.filesusr.com/ugd/b211fb_ad72a49164924ba58ed62863303877cb.pdf.

Uniform Trust Decanting Act does not permit the exclusion of beneficiaries. The UTDA also permits the establishment of a special needs trust even if the trustee does not have the power to make distributions from principal.

> **Example.** Oscar and Fernando, who owned and ran an elite modeling agency in California, set up a trust for their children with gifts of private company stock, providing that the trust would distribute assets to the children at the age of 35. Paulina, Oscar's sister and the trustee, decided to decant the trust. She moved the trust to Nevada and created a new, long-term trust that would last the children's lives, giving them creditor protection and saving the cost of California's top income tax rate.

This example gives you an idea of why decanting might be appealing, especially since no judicial approval is required. Some other, common reasons for decanting include:

1. Extending the trust's term

2. Converting a support trust into a discretionary trust

3. Fixing drafting errors or making ambiguous terms clear

4. Moving the trust to a state with more favorable laws

5. Adjusting powers of appointment

6. Changing trustee provisions, including removal and replacement provisions

7. Combining multiple trusts

8. Separating trusts

9. Drafting a special-needs trust

10. Qualifying the trust to own stock in an S corporation

In the following case, there was yet one more reason for decanting—to keep the trust assets out of a spouse's reach at divorce. In *Ferri v. Powell-Ferri*, the Supreme Judicial Court of Massachusetts analyzes the question of whether a trust decanting was permitted while the beneficiary was in the middle of divorce proceedings. Once again, we have a chance to see how trust interests—and here, trust decanting—work at divorce and in particular in a state without a decanting statute.

Ferri v. Powell-Ferri

72 N.E.3d 541 (Mass. 2017)

GAZIANO, J.

In this case we are asked to answer three questions certified to us by the Connecticut Supreme Court concerning the authority of a trustee to distribute (i.e., to decant) substantially all of the assets of an irrevocable trust into another trust. The questions, arising out of divorce proceedings pending in Connecticut between Nancy Powell-Ferri and her husband Paul John Ferri, Jr., the beneficiary of a Massachusetts irrevocable trust, are as follows:

"1. Under Massachusetts law, did the terms of the Paul John Ferri, Jr. Trust (1983 Trust) empower its trustees to distribute substantially all of its assets (that is, to decant) to the Declaration of Trust for Paul John Ferri, Jr. (2011 Trust)?

"2. If the answer to question 1 is 'no,' should either 75% or 100% of the assets of the 2011 Trust be returned to the 1983 Trust to restore the status quo prior to the decanting?

"3. Under Massachusetts law, should a court, in interpreting whether the 1983 Trust's settlor intended to permit decanting to another trust, consider an affidavit of the settlor, offered to establish what he intended when he created the 1983 Trust?"

Facts and Procedural History

We recite the relevant facts presented in the Connecticut Supreme Court's statement of facts for certification to this court.

The Paul John Ferri, Jr. Trust, dated June 24, 1983 (1983 Trust), was settled by Paul J. Ferri for the sole benefit of his son, Paul John Ferri, Jr. (Ferri Jr. or beneficiary), when Ferri Jr. was eighteen years old. The trust was created in Massachusetts and is governed by Massachusetts law. The 1983 Trust establishes two methods by which trust assets are distributed to the beneficiary. First, the trustee may "pay to or segregate irrevocably" trust assets for the beneficiary. Second, after the beneficiary reaches the age of thirty-five, he may request certain withdrawals of up to fixed percentages of trust assets, increasing from twenty-five per cent of the principal at age thirty-five to one hundred per cent after age forty-seven.

Ferri Jr. and Powell-Ferri were married in 1995. In October 2010, Powell-Ferri filed an action in the Connecticut Superior Court to dissolve the marriage.

See Ferri v. Powell-Ferri, 116 A.3d 297 (Conn. 2015). In March 2011, the then trustees of the 1983 Trust, Michael J. Ferri and Anthony J. Medaglia, created the Declaration of Trust for Paul John Ferri, Jr. (2011 Trust). They subsequently distributed substantially all of the assets of the 1983 Trust to themselves as trustees of the 2011 Trust.

As with the 1983 Trust, Ferri Jr. is the sole beneficiary of the 2011 Trust. The 2011 Trust is a spendthrift trust; under paragraph 1(a), the trustee exercises complete authority over whether and when to make payments to the beneficiary, if at all, and the beneficiary has no power to demand payment of trust assets. The spendthrift provision, in paragraph 4(b), bars the beneficiary from transferring or encumbering his interest and, as with similar provisions in the 1983 Trust, shields the trust from the beneficiary's creditors. The trustees decanted the 1983 Trust out of concern that Powell-Ferri would reach the assets of the 1983 Trust as a result of the divorce action. They did so without informing the beneficiary and without his consent.

At the time of the decanting, pursuant to art. II.B of the 1983 Trust, Ferri Jr. had a right to request a withdrawal of up to seventy-five per cent of the principal. During the course of this action, his vested interest matured into one hundred per cent of the assets the 1983 Trust.

Discussion

We first authorized the trustee of an irrevocable trust to decant a trust in *Morse v. Kraft*, 992 N.E.2d 1021 (Mass. 2013). In that case, we allowed the trustee to decant four subtrusts into four new subtrusts, one for each of the named beneficiaries, who had been minors when the first trust was created and who had reached the age of majority before the trust was decanted. In doing so, we relied on specific language in the trust, which did not explicitly authorize decanting, and the trustee's broad powers under that trust instrument. We declined, however, to recognize an inherent power allowing a trustee to decant irrespective of the language of the trust. Accordingly, a trustee's decanting authority turns on the facts of each case and the terms of the instrument that establishes the trust.

With these standards in mind, we turn to consideration of the questions certified by the Connecticut Supreme Court.

a.   Question 1

The term decanting ordinarily is "used to describe the distribution of [irrevocable] trust property to another trust pursuant to the trustee's discretionary authority to make distributions to, or for the benefit of, one or more beneficiaries [of the original trust]." Decanting has the effect of "amend[ing] an unamendable trust, in the sense that [the trustee] may distribute the trust property to a second trust with terms that differ from those of the original trust." The rationale underlying the authority to decant is that if a trustee has the discretionary power to distribute property to or for the benefit of the beneficiaries, the trustee likewise has the authority to distribute the property to another trust for the benefit of those same beneficiaries.

In the absence of a specific statutory provision allowing decanting, we have determined that a trustee of a Massachusetts irrevocable trust may be given the authority to decant assets in further trust through language in the trust. Here, after having examined the extremely broad authority and discretion afforded the trustees by the 1983 Trust declaration of trust, the anti-alienation provision of the 1983 Trust, the beneficiary withdrawal rights afforded under the terms of the 1983 Trust, and the settlor's affidavit, we conclude that the terms of the 1983 Trust, read as a whole, demonstrate the settlor's intent to permit decanting.

i.   Trustee's discretion.

A trustee's broad discretion to distribute the assets of an irrevocable trust may be evidence of a settlor's intent to permit decanting. States that have enacted explicit decanting provisions similarly look to a trustee's broad authority to distribute principal from the trust for the benefit of one or more of the beneficiaries when determining whether the trustee has the authority to decant. *See, e.g.*, FLA. STAT. § 736.04117.7.

The 1983 Trust contains three provisions relative to the trustee's discretion to distribute assets. Article II.A provides, "So long as [the beneficiary] is living, [the trustee] shall, from time to time, pay to or segregate irrevocably for later payment to [the beneficiary], so much of the net income and principal of this trust as [the trustee] shall deem desirable for [the beneficiary's] benefit." Article V.A states, "Wherever provision is made hereunder for payment of principal or income to a beneficiary, the same may instead be applied for his or her benefit." In addition, art. VI provides that the trustee "shall have full power to take any steps and do any acts which he may deem necessary or proper in connection with the due care, management and disposition of the property and income of the trust hereunder . . . in his discretion, without order or license of court."

The 1983 Trust also contains a number of additional provisions authorizing the trustee to distribute assets. Article II (Disposition of the Trust Property) sets forth the means by which the trustee may "dispose of the trust property" during the beneficiary's life. Article II.A states that, so long as the beneficiary is living, the trustee shall "from time to time, pay to or segregate irrevocably for later payment to [the beneficiary], as much of the net income and principal of this trust as [the trustee] shall deem desirable for [the beneficiary's] benefit."

Viewing the language of the 1983 Trust in its entirety, the trustee's extremely broad discretion is evident throughout the trust instrument. The explicit authority of the trustee of the 1983 Trust to "segregate irrevocably for later payment to" the trust beneficiary further indicates the settlor's intention to allow decanting. In common usage, to "segregate" means "to separate or set apart from others or from the general mass or main body: isolate," "to cause or force the separation of," "to separate or withdraw (as from others or from a main body)." Decanting trust assets to an irrevocable trust is one way to "segregate" assets "irrevocably."

There are, however, two sections of the trust language that might suggest, as Powell-Ferri argues, a conclusion to the contrary, and we turn next to these provisions.

ii.   Anti-alienation provision.

Article V.B of the 1983 Trust provides that "[n]either the income nor the principal of any trust hereunder shall be alienable by any beneficiary . . . and the same shall not be subject to be taken by his or her creditors by any process whatever." We have said, when confronting similar language, that this type of anti-alienation provision "evidences the settlor's intent to protect the trust income and principal from invasion by the beneficiary's creditors." It follows that if a settlor intended a trust's assets to be protected from creditors, he or she necessarily intended that the trustee have the means to protect the trust assets, consistent with his or her fiduciary duties.

iii.   Beneficiary withdrawal provisions.

Article II.B of the 1983 Trust provides that the trustee "shall pay to [the beneficiary] after he has attained the age of thirty-five (35) years such amounts of principal as he may from time to time in writing request," with explicit limitations on the percentage of the principal that may be withdrawn at different ages, up to the age of forty-seven, after which the beneficiary is entitled to withdraw one hundred per cent of the trust assets.

At the time the trustees decanted the 1983 Trust assets into the 2011 Trust, under the terms of art. II.B, the beneficiary had the right to request a withdrawal of up to seventy-five per cent of the principal of the 1983 Trust. During the pendency of this action, the beneficiary reached the age of forty-seven, and his irrevocable vested interest matured into one hundred per cent of the corpus of the trust. The beneficiary states that, throughout the life of the 1983 Trust, he has requested and received only a small percentage of the trust assets.

Powell-Ferri argues that the beneficiary's right under the 1983 Trust to request a withdrawal of a certain percentage of trust assets is wholly inconsistent with the authority to decant. She contends that decanting the 1983 trust into the 2011 spendthrift trust impaired the interests of the beneficiary to withdraw trust assets upon written request.

We do not agree, for three reasons. First, Powell-Ferri's contention runs counter to our mandate to read trust provisions consistently with the entire trust document, and in a manner that gives effect to all trust language. Second, a trustee holds "full legal title to all property of a trust and the rights of possession that go along with it." Here, at the time the trustees decanted substantially all of the 1983 Trust's assets to the 2011 Trust, the beneficiary had withdrawn only a small percentage of the assets under art. II.B. Therefore, a substantial portion of the trust assets remained in the 1983 Trust, subject to the trustee's authority and stewardship. Third, this mechanism for the beneficiary's withdrawal of trust assets does not limit the trustee's decanting authority. The two mechanisms for distribution provided under art. II are not mutually exclusive. Accordingly, reading the entirety of art. II in harmony, it provides that, unless and until all of the trust assets were distributed in response to the beneficiary's request for a withdrawal, the trustee could exercise his or her powers and obligations under the 1983 Trust, including the duty to decant if the trustee deemed decanting to be in the beneficiary's best interest.

b.   Question 3.

The third certified question asks whether, under Massachusetts law, a court should consider an affidavit by the settlor, stating his intent in establishing the 1983 Trust, in reaching a determination whether, in creating the 1983 Trust, the settlor intended to permit decanting to another trust.

The settlor's affidavit, dated July 11, 2012, states, in pertinent part:

"I intended to give to the trustee of the 1983 Trust the specific authority to do whatever he or she believed to be necessary and in the best interest of my son Paul John Ferri, Jr. with respect to the income and principal of the 1983 Trust notwithstanding any of the other provisions of the 1983 Trust. Therefore, if the trustee thought at any time that the principal and income of the 1983 Trust could be at risk, the trustee could take any action necessary to protect the principal and income of the 1983 Trust. This authority to protect assets would also extend to a situation where creditors of Paul John Ferri, Jr. may attempt to reach the assets of the 1983 Trust such as in the event of lawsuit or a divorce."

The statements in the settlor's affidavit further support the settlor's evident intention in the language of the 1983 Trust document, including the power to "segregate irrevocably" under art. II.A and the beneficiary's right to request withdrawals of trust assets at certain age milestones under art. II.B, to provide the trustee with the power to decant. Because the intent of the settlor is "paramount," and the settlor's affidavit evidences the settlor's intent at the time of execution, the settlor's affidavit should be considered.

NOTES

1.   One of the statutory requirements that differs across states is whether notice to beneficiaries of the trustee's decanting is required. Neither Nevada nor South Dakota, for example, include this requirement in their statutory language. What benefit is there to allowing this kind of privacy—or, more accurately, who benefits from this grant of privacy? States like Nevada and South Dakota give broad discretion to the trustee in decanting, even if the grant of discretion is not as broad in the original trust document. Stephanie Vara suggests that: "If the goal of United States trust law is to maintain a coherent body of law with the objective of furthering freedom of disposition, then it will be crucial for states to adopt decanting statutes like the Uniform Act, as opposed to statutes similar to the Nevada model." *See* Stephanie Vara, *Two Cheers for Decanting: A Partial Defense of Decanting Statutes as a Tool for Implementing Freedom of Disposition*, 32 QUINNIPIAC PROB. L.J. 23 (2018).

2.   Trustees have started using decanting to convert ordinary irrevocable trusts into special needs trusts. One federal district court has allowed this type of modification, over the strenuous objection of the state of Connecticut, and the Second Circuit issued a summary order affirming the District Court's preliminary injunction. *See Simonsen v. Bremby*, No. 15-cv-1399 (VAB), 2015 WL 9451031 (D. Conn. Dec. 23, 2015), *aff'd*, 679 F. App'x 57 (2d Cir. 2017). Can you imagine why a state would object to this type of conversion?

ASSESSMENTS

1.   Your state legislature is considering adopting a decanting statute, and you have been asked to present a policy statement of reasons to allow trust beneficiaries to "to extract newly available benefits that could not possibly have

influenced the trust settlor." Prepare a bullet-point list of those reasons. *See* Stewart E. Sterk, *Trust Decanting: A Critical Perspective*, 38 CARDOZO L. REV. 1993 (2017).

2.   Take a look at the UTDA and compare it with a state decanting statute of your choice, noting the differences and potential effects of those differences.

D. Trustee Removal and Replacement

Another way that beneficiaries seek to modify irrevocable trusts is through the removal of a named trustee. This type of change to the trust is not, technically speaking, a modification in the sense of we've just discussed in the previous Parts. Nevertheless, trustee removal and replacement does have the practical impact of modifying the trust by installing a new trustee and, consequently, we learn about removal in conjunction with modification.

Historically, trustees could only be removed for cause—a breach of fiduciary duty, most commonly—but now beneficiaries routinely remove trustees for much more mundane reasons, such as expense, convenience, or location. This is especially true when the trustee is an institutional one. The UTC provision with respect to trustee removal is as follows:

UTC § 706 Removal of Trustee

(a)   The settlor, a cotrustee, or a beneficiary may request the court to remove a trustee, or a trustee may be removed by the court on its own initiative.

(b)   The court may remove a trustee if:

(1)   the trustee has committed a serious breach of trust;

(2)   lack of cooperation among cotrustees substantially impairs the administration of the trust;

(3)   because of unfitness, unwillingness, or persistent failure of the trustee to administer the trust effectively, the court determines that removal of the trustee best serves the interests of the beneficiaries; or

(4)   there has been a substantial change of circumstances or removal is requested by all of the qualified beneficiaries, the court finds that removal of the trustee best serves the interests of all of the beneficiaries and is not inconsistent with a material purpose of the trust, and a suitable cotrustee or successor trustee is available.

A well-drafted trust will have broad removal and replacement provisions that make litigation unnecessary. Cases that end up in litigation have trust documents that do not provide for removal, and the trustees opposed any change in their status. As you read the following case, consider the values at stake in the removal of a trustee for purposes like convenience and how this kind of modification relates to the other forms of modification that we've read about in this chapter.

Davis v. U.S. Bank National Association

243 S.W.3d 425 (Mo. App. 2007)

SULLIVAN, J.

U.S. Bank National Association (Appellant) appeals from the trial court's summary judgment in favor of Harold A. Davis (Respondent). We affirm.

Factual and Procedural Background

On December 26, 1972, Ayers executed a Trust Indenture, pursuant to which Ayers appointed Mercantile as the Trustee and Respondent as the income beneficiary of the Trust, entitled to receive the entire net income of the Trust for life. Upon Respondent's death, the principal of the Trust is to be divided among Respondent's then living children in equal shares and distributed to each child (in trust if under the age of 21 and "outright" if 21). Respondent currently has two children, Dillon A. Davis (Son) and Marguerite S. Davis (Daughter). The Trust provides that if Respondent has no surviving children upon his death, Respondent's share of the Trust "shall pass to his or her heirs at law who are direct descendants of [Ayers]." In the event that there are no heirs at law who are direct descendants of Ayers at the time of Respondent's death, the principal passes free of trust to Lafayette College, Easton, Pennsylvania.

On May 15, 2006, Respondent filed a petition (the Petition) seeking the removal of Appellant as Trustee, the appointment of U.S. Trust Company of Delaware (UST) as successor Trustee, and an order transferring the Trust assets to UST. The Petition asserted that it was filed on behalf of all of the Qualified Beneficiaries of the Trust; that removal of Appellant as the Trustee best served the interests of all the beneficiaries of the Trust; that removal of Appellant was not inconsistent with a material purpose of the Trust; and that UST was a suitable successor Trustee, who was available and willing to serve.

On July 20, 2006, Appellant filed its Answer to the Petition, asserting that the court lacked subject matter jurisdiction to hear the dispute because

Respondent had failed to join as necessary and indispensable parties all of the Trust's beneficiaries and that the Petition failed to state a claim because Respondent could not virtually represent the other two qualified beneficiaries, Son and Daughter.

On August 23, 2006, Appellant also filed a Motion to Dismiss the Petition for failing to join necessary and indispensable parties. On August 25, 2006, Respondent filed a Motion for Summary Judgment asserting that he had satisfied all of the statutory elements for removing a trustee. On January 23, 2007, the circuit court entered its Judgment denying Appellant's Motion to Dismiss and granting Respondent's Motion for Summary Judgment. The court ordered the removal of Appellant as Trustee and appointed UST as successor Trustee of the Trust. This appeal follows.

Discussion

In 2004, the General Assembly enacted Sections 456.1–101 to 456.11–1106, effective January 1, 2005. Relevant to our discussion is Section 456.7–706.2(4), which provides for the removal of a trustee without any showing of wrongdoing by the trustee:

2.   The court may remove a trustee if:

(4)   removal is requested by all of the qualified beneficiaries and the party seeking removal establishes to the court that:

(a)   removal of the trustee best serves the interests of all of the beneficiaries;

(b)   removal of the trustee is not inconsistent with a material purpose of the trust; and

(c)   a suitable cotrustee or successor trustee is available and willing to serve.

Point I

In its first point, Appellant asserts that Respondent's failure to join all of the remainder beneficiaries of the Trust as parties to his lawsuit deprived the court of subject matter jurisdiction. This assertion is incorrect. Section 456.7–706.2(4) only requires that "qualified beneficiaries" be joined in an action to remove a trustee.

A qualified beneficiary: means a beneficiary who, on the date the beneficiary's qualification is determined:

a)   is a permissible distributee;

b)   would be a permissible distributee if the interests of the permissible distributees described in paragraph (a) of this subdivision terminated on that date; or

c)   would be a permissible distributee if the trust terminated on that date.

Section 456.1–103(20). Based on the language of this section, Respondent and Son and Daughter are the permissible distributees if Respondent's interest or the Trust terminated at the time of the filing of this suit. As such, Respondent and Son and Daughter are all of the qualified beneficiaries of the Trust. The remote remainder beneficiaries of the Trust are not qualified beneficiaries. All of the qualified beneficiaries were before the Court and therefore, all of the necessary parties were before the court.

Point II

In its second point, Appellant alleges that Respondent could not virtually represent Son and Daughter under Section 456.3–303(4). We disagree. Section 456.3–304(1) provides as follows:

Unless otherwise represented, a minor, incapacitated, or unborn individual, or a person whose identity or location is unknown and not reasonably ascertainable, may be represented by and bound by another having a substantially identical interest with respect to the particular question or dispute, but only to the extent there is no conflict of interest between the representative and the person represented with respect to a particular question or dispute.

In the instant case, Respondent and Son and Daughter have substantially identical interests which are not in conflict with regard to removing Appellant as Trustee and implementing UST as Trustee. UST is within a thirty-minute drive of Respondent and Son and Daughter's house; changing the domicile of the Trust to Delaware would avoid out of state income tax being paid on Trust income; UST has a complete understanding of Respondent and his family's unique personal financial situation; and UST will charge lower fees than Appellant.

Appellant maintains that there is an inherent conflict of interest between income beneficiaries and residual beneficiaries. However, this assertion has no basis in Missouri law.

Point III

In its third point, Appellant maintains that there remain issues of fact as to whether or not removing the Trustee is in the best interests of all of the beneficiaries. Appellant claims that it presented facts in opposition to Respondent's summary judgment motion which called into question the validity of the reduced trustee fee which Respondent claimed would be achieved by Appellant's removal and replacement with UST.

In conjunction with his motion for summary judgment, Respondent submitted the affidavit of investment advisor Daniel M. McDermott. His affidavit demonstrates how he calculated the annual savings of $10,259.55 by switching from Appellant to UST, resulting from a fee that is 23.94% lower than that being charged by Appellant, and the information on which such calculations were based. Appellant did not dispute the numbers presented by McDermott, but rather merely criticized them as hearsay and speculative.

Appellant claims that the change in trustee is inconsistent with the material purpose of the Trust as the Trust clearly did not contemplate the change but does contemplate keeping the same Trustee in the same state. Not only does this argument speculate as to what the Trust "contemplates" without any evidentiary support, but it is also irrelevant, because the statutory scheme provides for the change of Trustee as long as the terms of the Trust do not prohibit it, and the terms of the Trust in this case do not. *See* Section 456.7–706.2(4)(b).

As set forth in our discussion of Point II, Respondent presented factually supported reasons why it would be beneficial to him and Son and Daughter to remove the present Trustee in lieu of UST, and Appellant does not put any of those reasons into dispute. Nor does Appellant present us with any additional fact issues. Therefore, there are no remaining disputed factual matters into which Appellant is entitled to conduct more discovery. Additionally, Appellant presents no evidentiary support for its argument that its removal as Trustee is inconsistent with a material purpose of the trust. As such, Point III is denied.

NOTES

1. As this case implies, excessive fees are an important reason why beneficiaries seek to remove trustees. In *In re Fleet Nat. Bank's Appeal from Probate,* 837 A.2d 785 (Conn. 2004), the court supported trustee removal and replacement, commenting that there were "many . . . estates in Connecticut in which the testator . . . had selected a small hometown bank as Trustee,

recognizing both the local personnel and reasonable fees. But at the time of the death of the testator, that local bank no longer existed. The law clearly provides that in [the] event of an acquisition, the acquiring bank will succeed to the fiduciary appointments of the failed or merged bank. This leaves many beneficiaries of trust[s] . . . in the untenable position of having large out-of-state corporate trustee[s] handling their family trust, while paying fees that the . . . beneficiaries feel are very unreasonable."

2.   Does a trustee who has been removed in order to lower fees for the trust have standing to pursue an appeal in the matter? In *In re Fleet Nat. Bank's Appeal from Probate* (cited above), the court addressed that question. The court stated:

> [W]e conclude that the plaintiff has not established a protected interest, either in a representative or personal capacity, such that it has been aggrieved by the order of the Probate Court removing it as fiduciary. In the representative sense, the order of the Probate Court, terminating the plaintiff's tenure as fiduciary, was an adjudication that the plaintiff was no longer to represent the interests of the defendants with regard to the trust. Therefore, following removal as fiduciary, the plaintiff may no longer seek to assert claims on behalf of the defendants. Rather, the interests of the defendants are now represented by their current fiduciary, Putnam, and standing to appeal decrees impacting those interests is now vested solely in Putnam.

Why would corporate trustees be so invested in pursuing claims and retaining trust business? Trust management fees are an immense source of revenue for corporate trustees who charge varying amounts, calculated generally as a percentage of the value of the assets under management.[2] It's not always obvious, however, what the fee schedule is for a particular bank. One article puts it this way: "Published fee schedules offer some guidance, but since each firm includes different things, it's like comparing poodles with pigs. The kind of deal you get depends on how much money you have, the complexity of the assets, and how badly the trustee wants your business. And so much is negotiable." Amy Feldman, *Trust Costs Go Up; Get Ready to Negotiate*, BARRON'S (Feb. 28, 2015).

---

[2]   *See* https://www.thewealthadvisor.com/article/whos-charging-what-trust-services.

Who's Charging What for Trust Services							
Trust Company	State	Trust account minimum	Minimum annual fee	First $1 million	Next $2 to $3 million	$3 to $5 million	Above $5 million
ADVISORY TRUST	DE	$500,000	$3,000	0.50%	0.40%	0.30%	0.25%
Bryn Mawr Trust	DE	$1 million	$6,000	0.60%	*	0.45%	Neg.
The New Hampshire Trust Company	NH	None	$3,000	0.90%	0.55%	0.45%	0.35%
Northern Trust	IL & DE	$5 million	$20,000	0.40%	0.40%	0.40%	0.20%
RELIANCE TRUST	GA	None	$3,000	0.60%	0.35%	0.35%	0.35%
Santa Fe Trust	NM	None	$4,000	0.75%	0.75%	0.50%	0.35%
SATURNA TRUST COMPANY	NV	None	$1,000	0.50%	0.50%	0.50%	0.40%
SUMMIT TRUST COMPANY	NV	$100	$100	1.00%	0.80%	0.70%	Neg.
WEALTH ADVISORS Trust Company	SD	None	$4,000	0.50%	0.50%	0.42%	0.35%
WILMINGTON TRUST	DE	$1 million	$8,000	0.60%	0.40%	0.40%	0.25%

Trust companies charge a range of fees and compete with one another for
trust business. Credit: The Wealth Advisor (thewealthadvisor.com).

3.   One way to avoid the types of cases like the ones above is to build broad
removal and replacement powers into the trust agreement itself, so that
beneficiaries can replace trustees without court approval. The concern with such
provisions, of course, is that the beneficiaries will try to manipulate the trustee
by threatening removal. How might you combat this concern?

4.   Estate litigation frequently involves the interests of minor, unborn, or
unascertained beneficiaries. The court can appoint a guardian ad litem to protect
the interests of minor beneficiaries or the court can allow for virtual
representation, that is to say representation by a party with similar interests. The
UTC provides guidance on virtual representation in Section 304. Should the
Davis court have appointed a guardian ad litem for the children? Why or why
not?

ASSESSMENT

You work for a law firm that does estate planning work and is revising its standard trustee removal and replacement provisions to make them more flexible. The firm is concerned, however, that the beneficiaries not be able to manipulate the trustee by threatening removal. What provisions do you suggest including in the trust provisions to combat this concern? Who would have the power to remove the trustee? Would you recommend limiting who could serve as a replacement trustee? How?

E. Powers of Appointment

Powers of appointment are valuable, but often underused, estate planning tools. In general, a power of appointment is the power given by the property owner to another to choose within certain limits prescribed by the property owner who will receive certain property in the future. The power of appointment is thus both a postponement of a decision by the property owner and a delegation of that decision-making authority to another. Powers of appointment may be included in various types of trusts.

We have already seen powers of appointments in other chapters. For example, powers of appointment appear in the class gifts case, *In re Martin B*, in Chapter 9; there, the grandmother had the power to appoint among the settlor's issue (and a limited set of other people) at her death.

Before we start discussing the different types of powers, it is helpful to become familiar with the terminology unique to powers of appointment. When we talk about the creator of a power of appointment, we say that person is the **donor** of the power. The holder of the power to appoint the property is known as the **donee**. The class of people who are eligible recipients of the property subject to the power of appointment are known as the **objects** or **permissible appointees**. Those for whom the property is actually appointed are called the **appointees**. The people who take the property if the power of appointment is not exercised are known as the **takers in default**. Powers of appointment may be **general** or **limited** (also called **nongeneral** or **special**), and they may be **testamentary** or **nontestamentary**.

1. Types of Powers and Consequences

A general power of appointment is a power exercisable in favor of the holder of the power, the power holder's creditors, the power holder's estate, or the creditors of the power holder's estate. *See* RESTATEMENT (SECOND) OF PROPERTY: DONATIVE TRANSFERS § 11.4 (1986). Property over which a decedent has a generally exercisable power of appointment at death is included as part of the decedent's gross estate for estate tax purposes. Limited powers are not included in the decedent's gross estate for estate tax purposes.

A power is presently exercisable if the power holder can currently create an interest, present or future, in an object of the power. A power of appointment is not presently exercisable if exercisable only by the power holder's will or if its exercise is not effective for a specified period of time or until occurrence of some event. *See* RESTATEMENT (SECOND) OF PROPERTY: DONATIVE TRANSFERS § 11.5 (1986). Powers of appointment may be held in either a fiduciary or nonfiduciary capacity. The definition of "beneficiary" excludes powers held by a trustee but not powers held by others in a fiduciary capacity. UTC § 103.

Frequently trusts include limited powers of appointment. The next case, however, deals with a general power of appointment. It raises a question we have seen before—the rights of a family creditor to reach property held in trust. The case asks whether the ex-spouse of a holder of a general power of appointment can reach the property that the holder of the power could reach. The reason it might be plausible to reach the property is that a general power of appointment is often considered to be close to owning the property itself. Indeed, one tricky aspect to powers of appointment is that a trust need not use any magic language to create a general power of appointment. Rather, any right to withdraw property from the trust may be construed as a general power of appointment, as you will see.

Irwin Union Bank & Trust Co. v. Long

312 N.E.2d 908 (Ind. Ct. App. 1974)

LOWDERMILK, J.

On February 3, 1957, Victoria Long, appellee herein, obtained a judgment in the amount of $15,000 against Philip W. Long, which judgment emanated from a divorce decree. This action is the result of the filing by appellee of a petition in proceedings supplemental to execution on the prior judgment. Appellee sought satisfaction of that judgment by pursuing funds allegedly owed to Philip W. Long as a result of a trust set up by Laura Long, his mother.

Appellee alleged that the Irwin Union Bank and Trust Company (Union Bank) was indebted to Philip W. Long as the result of its position as trustee of the trust created by Laura Long. On April 24, 1969, the trial court ordered that any income, property, or profits, which were owed to Philip Long and not exempt from execution should be applied to the divorce judgment. Thereafter, on February 13, 1973, the trial court ordered that four percent (4%) of the trust corpus of the trust created by Laura Long which benefited Philip Long was not exempt from execution and could be levied upon by appellee and ordered a writ of execution.

The pertinent portion of the trust created by Laura Long is as follows:

ITEM V C: Withdrawal of Principal. When Philip W. Long, Jr. has attained the age of twenty-one (21) years and is not a full-time student at an educational institution as a candidate for a Bachelor of Arts or Bachelor of Sciences degree, Philip W. Long shall have the right to withdraw from principal once in any calendar year upon thirty (30) days written notice to the Trustee up to four percent (4%) of the market value of the entire trust principal on the date of such notice, which right shall not be cumulative; provided, however, that the amount distributable hereunder shall not be in excess of the market value of the assets of the trust on the date of such notice other than interests in real estate.

The primary issue raised on this appeal is whether the trial court erred in allowing execution on the 4% of the trust corpus.

Appellant contends that Philip Long's right to withdraw 4% of the trust corpus is, in fact, a general power of appointment. Union Bank further contends that since Philip Long has never exercised his right of withdrawal, pursuant to the provisions of the trust instrument, no creditors of Philip Long can reach the trust corpus. Appellant points out that if the power of appointment is unexercised, the creditors cannot force the exercise of said power and cannot reach the trust corpus in this case.

Appellee posits that the condition precedent to Philip Long's right of withdrawal has been met and therefore Philip Long has an absolute right to the present enjoyment of 4% of the trust corpus simply by making a written request to the trustee. Appellee contends that this is a vested right and is consistent with the intentions of the donor, Laura Long.

Appellee also argues that Philip has absolute control and use of the 4% of the corpus and that the bank does not have control over that portion of the corpus if Philip decides to exercise his right of withdrawal. Appellee argues that the intention of Laura Long was to give Philip not only an income interest in the trust but a fixed amount of corpus which he could use as he saw fit. Thus, Philip Long would have a right to the present enjoyment of 4% of the trust corpus. A summation of appellee's argument, as stated in her brief, is as follows: "So it is with Philip he can get it if he desires it, so why cannot Victoria get it even if Philip does not desire it?"

We have had no Indiana authority directly in point cited to us by either of the parties and a thorough research of this issue does not reveal any Indiana authority on point. Broadly speaking, a power is said to be general if it can be exercised in favor of anyone whom the donee may select. A power is defined in THOMPSON ON REAL PROPERTY, FUTURE INTERESTS, as follows:

> § 2025.   What a 'power' is. Broadly stated, a 'power' is an authority enabling one person to dispose of an interest which is vested in another. It is an authority reserved by or limited to one to do certain acts in relation to the subject matter of the gift for his own benefit or for the benefit of another. The word 'power,' as defined by the Restatement of the Law of Property, 'is an ability on the part of a person to produce a change in a given legal relation by doing or not doing a given act.' It is an authority to do some act in relation to lands, or the creation of estates therein, or of charges thereon, which the owner granting or reserving such power, might himself lawfully perform.

> Powers are either general or special. They are general when they are capable of being exercised by the donee in favor of any person, including himself, and are not restricted as to the estate or interest over which he may exercise the power, while the power is special if its exercise is restricted to particular persons, or a particular class of persons, or if it can be exercised only for certain named purposes or under certain conditions. The donee under a general power has an absolute disposing power over the estate; but where he cannot exercise the power for his own benefit during his lifetime, the power is not general."

An examination of the pertinent parts of the trust created by Laura Long indicates that the power which was given to Philip Long in Item V C falls under the definition of power of appointment, as set out above. Philip Long may exercise the power which was delegated to him by Laura Long, that being to distribute property not his own. It is obvious that Laura Long would have had the same power to dispose of her property as that given to Philip Long, had Laura Long decided to dispose of her property in such a manner.

A reading of Item V C, supra, does not disclose any direct reference to a power of appointment. However, it is not necessary that the actual words "power of appointment" be used in order to create such a power. Appellee contends that the right of withdrawal of Philip Long is a vested property right rather than a power of appointment. However, it is our opinion that such is not the case.

Contrary to the contention of appellee, it is our opinion that Philip Long has no control over the trust corpus until he exercises his power of appointment and gives notice to the trustee that he wishes to receive his 4% of the trust corpus. Until such an exercise is made, the trustee has the absolute control and benefit of the trust corpus within the terms of the trust instrument.

While not controlling as precedent, we find that the Federal Estate Tax laws are quite analogous to the case at bar. Under § 2041, Powers of Appointment, of the Internal Revenue Code, it is clear that the interest given to Philip Long under Item V C would be considered a power of appointment for estate tax purposes. A general power of appointment is defined in § 2041(b)(1) as follows:

> (1) General power of appointment. The term 'general power of appointment' means a power which is exercisable in favor of the decedent, his estate, his creditors, or the creditors of his estate.

The regulations pertinent to this issue discuss a power of appointment as it is used for estate tax purposes as follows:

> (b) Definition of 'power of appointment' (1) In general. The term 'power of appointment' includes all powers which are in substance and effect powers of appointment regardless of the nomenclature used in creating the power and regardless of local property law connotations. For example, if a trust instrument provides that the beneficiary may appropriate or consume the principal of the trust, the power to consume or appropriate is a power of appointment. 20.2041–1(b)(1)

For estate tax purposes even the failure to exercise a power of appointment may lead to tax consequences.

It is elementary that courts will seek to ascertain the intention of the testator by giving a full consideration to the entire will. The trust created in the will of Laura Long, in our opinion, has the legal effect of creating a power of appointment in Philip Long under Item V C of the trust. Philip Long has never exercised his power of appointment under the trust.

Indiana has no statute which would authorize a creditor to reach property covered by a power of appointment which is unexercised. Appellee concedes that if we find that Philip Long had merely an unexercised power of appointment then creditors are in no position to either force the exercise of the power or to reach the trust corpus. Thus, it is clear that the trial court erred when it overruled appellant's motion to set aside the writ of execution.

Reversed and remanded.

NOTES

1.   Laura Long created a trust for the benefit of her son Philip. Philip was given a noncumulative power to draw up to 4 percent of the trust principal each year. This is a general power of appointment, created to fit within the "five-or-five" rule. The "five-or-five" power is a common clause in trusts that gives the beneficiary the ability to withdraw the greater of: a) $5,000 or b) 5% of the trust's fair market value from the trust each year. The benefit of structuring trust terms and beneficiary rights in such a way is that the five-or-five power has tax benefits. Generally speaking, a general power of appointment is considered to be equivalent to ownership and therefore, for tax purposes, the donee of a general power is treated as the owner of the appointive property. One exception is for the "five-or-five" power of withdrawal. If a donee has a power to appoint property to himself, this property will not be taxed as a general power to the extent it falls within the "five-or-five" rule.

2.   Philip's former wife, Victoria, sought to reach four percent of the corpus to satisfy her divorce judgment, but the court held that Victoria couldn't reach that four percent until Philip exercised the power. Today, the trend has shifted in the opposite direction. One treatise explains: "Increasingly, . . . statutes now treat property that is subject to a general power of appointment as belonging to the donee, even if the power has never been exercised," including "for purposes of allowing the donee's creditors to reach the trust property." SCOTT AND ASCHER ON TRUSTS § 14.11.3. UTC § 505(b) would have allowed Victoria to reach Philip's trust interest to satisfy her claim.

ASSESSMENT

There are several arguments in favor of the property being safeguarded from creditor claims, including the claims of an ex-spouse. One argument—that we have seen time and time again in the context of wealth transfer—is that the donor intended to safeguard the assets from creditors and therefore the law should respect donor intention. Are there competing principles? What would you argue in favor of Victoria's rights in this situation? A second argument is that the particular power in *Long* falls with the "five-or-five" exception in the tax code, and that state trust laws regarding creditor rights should follow the federal law for taxation. Does this argument convince you? Should all creditor rights be equivalent and, of not, on what grounds should they differ?

2.   How to Exercise a Power of Appointment

To exercise a power of appointment, (1) a donee must manifest an intent to exercise the power; (2) the manner of expression must satisfy any formal requirements imposed by the donor; and (3) the appointment must be a permissible exercise of the power. The first requirement is often the one that is most vexing, because it is not always obvious whether or not the donee has exercised the power unless there is an explicit statement to that effect.

Sometimes it is quite clear when a donee does or does not exercise a power of appointment. A typical will clause might read as follows:

> All the rest, residue and remainder of my property, real and personal, of whatever nature and wherever situated (excepting, however, any property over which I have a power of appointment, because it is my intention not to exercise any power of appointment by this residuary gift in my will), I devise and bequeath to my spouse.

Sometimes, however, donees are not explicit about their exercise. For instance, holders of a testamentary power of appointment may leave a general residuary clause and make no specific reference to the power like the following provision:

> I hereby give all the rest, residue, and remainder of my property, wheresoever situated, to my brother Nico, if he survives me.

The question arises as to whether "all the rest" includes property over which the decedent has a power of appointment. It is not as clear whether the donee was exercising, or was even attempting to exercise, the power of appointment.

Donors can prevent the donee's inadvertent exercise of a power of appointment by including language in the document that created the power of appointment. The document can require that the power must be "specifically referenced" to be exercised. That language prevents the inadvertent exercise of a power of appointment by the general residuary clause in the donee's will. But what if the document creating the power of appointment does not include a specific reference requirement? In that situation, the answer turns on the following: (1) whether the power of appointment is general or specific, (2) whether there is a taker in default of appointment, (3) whether the donee used a residuary clause that refers in general terms to in the residuary devise any power of appointment the donee holds, and (4) what the instrument creating the power required in terms of exercise.

The UPC has two provisions that are relevant here, both of which are reproduced below:

UPC § 2–608 Exercise of Power of Appointment

In the absence of a requirement that a power of appointment be exercised by a reference, or by an express or specific reference, to the power, a general residuary clause in a will, or a will making general disposition of all of the testator's property, expresses an intention to exercise a power of appointment held by the testator only if (i) the power is a general power and the creating instrument does not contain a gift if the power is not exercised or (ii) the testator's will manifests an intention to include the property subject to the power.

UPC § 2–704 Power of Appointment; Meaning of Specific Reference Requirement

If a governing instrument creating a power of appointment expressly requires that the power be exercised by a reference, an express reference, or a specific reference, to the power or its source, it is presumed that the donor's intention, in requiring that the donee exercise the power by making reference to the particular power or to the creating instrument, was to prevent an inadvertent exercise of the power.

The next case, *Beals v. State Street Bank & Trust*, interprets conflicting rules in two of the great trust jurisdictions, Massachusetts and New York, and delves into whether the power at issue should be treated as a general or a specific power.

Beals v. State Street Bank & Trust Co. v. Long

326 N.E.2d 896 (Mass. 1975)

WILKINS, J.

The trustees under the will of Arthur Hunnewell filed this petition for instructions, seeking a determination of the proper distribution to be made of a portion of the trust created under the residuary clause of his will. A judge of the

Probate Court reserved decision and reported the case to the Appeals Court on the pleadings and a stipulation of facts. We transferred the case here.

Arthur Hunnewell died, a resident of Wellesley, in 1904, leaving his wife and four daughters. His will placed the residue of his property in a trust, the income of which was to be paid to his wife during her life. At the death of his wife the trust was to be divided in portions, one for each then surviving daughter and one for the then surviving issue of any deceased daughter. Mrs. Hunnewell died in 1930. One of the four daughters predeceased her mother, leaving no issue. The trust was divided, therefore, in three portions at the death of Mrs. Hunnewell. The will directed that the income of each portion held for a surviving daughter should be paid to her during her life and on her death the principal of such portion should "be paid and disposed of as she may direct and appoint by her last Will and Testament duly probated." In default of appointment, the will directed that a daughter's share should be distributed to "the persons who would be entitled to such estate under the laws then governing the distribution of intestate estates."

This petition concerns the distribution of the trust portion held for the testator's daughter Isabella H. Hunnewell, later Isabella H. Dexter (Isabella). Following the death of her mother, Isabella requested the trustees to exercise their discretionary power to make principal payments by transferring substantially all of her trust share "to the Dexter family office in Boston, there to be managed in the first instance by her husband, Mr. Gordon Dexter." This request was granted, and cash and securities were transferred to her account at the Dexter office. The Hunnewell trustees, however, retained in Isabella's share a relatively small cash balance, an undivided one-third interest in a mortgage and undivided one-third interests in various parcels of real estate in the Commonwealth, which Isabella did not want in kind and which the trustees could not sell at a reasonable price at the time. Thereafter, the trustees received payments on the mortgage and proceeds from occasional sales of portions of the real estate. From her one-third share of these receipts, the trustees made further distributions to her of $1,900 in 1937, $22,000 in 1952, and $5,000 in 1953.

In February 1944, Isabella, who was then a resident of New York, executed and caused to be filed in the registry of probate for Norfolk County an instrument which partially released her general power of appointment under the will of her father. Isabella released her power of appointment "to the extent that such power empowers me to appoint to anyone other than one or more of the . . . descendants me surviving of Arthur Hunnewell."

On December 14, 1968, Isabella, who survived her husband, died without issue, still a resident of New York, leaving a will dated May 21, 1965. Her share in the trust under her father's will then consisted of an interest in a contract to sell real estate, cash, notes and a certificate of deposit, and was valued at approximately $88,000.

Isabella did not expressly exercise her power of appointment under her father's will. The residuary clause of her will provided in effect for the distribution of all "the rest, residue and remainder of my property" to the issue per stirpes of her sister Margaret Blake, who had predeceased Isabella. The Blake issue would take one-half of Isabella's trust share, as takers in default of appointment, in all events. If, however, Isabella's will should be treated as effectively exercising her power of appointment under her father's will, the Blake issue would take the entire trust share, and the executors of the will of Isabella's sister Jane (who survived Isabella and has since died) would not receive that one-half of the trust share which would go to Jane in default of appointment.

In support of their argument that Isabella's will did not exercise the power of appointment under her father's will, the executors of Jane's estate contend that (1) Massachusetts substantive law governs all questions relating to the power of appointment, including the interpretation of Isabella's will; (2) the power should be treated as a special power of appointment because of its partial release by Isabella; and (3) because Isabella's will neither expresses nor implies any intention to exercise the power, the applicable rule of construction in this Commonwealth is that a general residuary clause does not exercise a special power of appointment.

The Blake issue, in support of their argument that the power was exercised, contends that (1) Isabella's will manifests an intention to exercise the power and that no rule of construction need be applied; (2) the law of New York should govern the question whether Isabella's will exercised the power and, if it does, by statute New York has adopted a rule that a special power of appointment is exercised by a testamentary disposition of all of the donee's property; and (3) if Massachusetts law does apply, and the will is silent on the subject of the exercise of the power, the principles underlying our rule of construction that a residuary clause exercises a general power of appointment are applicable in these circumstances.

1.   We turn first to a consideration of the question whether Isabella's will should be construed according to the law of this Commonwealth or the law of New York. There are strong, logical reasons for turning to the law of the donee's domicile at the time of death to determine whether a donee's will has exercised

a testamentary power of appointment over movables. Most courts in this country which have considered the question, however, interpret the donee's will under the law governing the administration of the trust, which is usually the law of the donor's domicile. This has long been the rule in Massachusetts. Indeed, the rule is so well established that parties have conceded the point from time to time.

If the question were before us now for the first time, we might well adopt a choice of law rule which would turn to the substantive law of the donee's domicile, for the purpose of determining whether the donee's will exercised a power of appointment. However, in a field where much depends on certainty and consistency as to the applicable rules of law, we think that we should adhere to our well-established rule. Thus, in interpreting the will of a donee to determine whether a power of appointment was exercised, we apply the substantive law of the jurisdiction whose law governs the administration of the trust.

2.   Considering the arguments of the parties, we conclude that there is no indication in Isabella's will of an intention to exercise or not to exercise the power of appointment given to her under her father's will. A detailed analysis of the various competing contentions would not add to our jurisprudence. In the absence of an intention disclosed by her will, construed in light of circumstances known to her when she executed it, we must adopt some Massachusetts rule of construction to resolve the issue before us. The question is what rule of construction. We are unaware of any decided case which, in this context, has dealt with a testamentary general power, reduced to a special power by action of the donee.

3.   We conclude that the residuary clause of Isabella's will should be presumed to have exercised the power of appointment. We reach this result by a consideration of the reasons underlying the canons of construction applicable to general and special testamentary powers of appointment. Considered in this way, we believe that a presumption of exercise is more appropriate in the circumstances of this case than a presumption of nonexercise.

When this court first decided not to extend to a special power of appointment the rule of construction that a general residuary clause executes a general testamentary power (unless a contrary intent is shown by the will), we noted significant distinctions between a general power and a special power. A general power was said to be a close approximation to a property interest, a "virtually unlimited power of disposition," while a special power of appointment lacked this quality. We observed that a layman having a general testamentary power over property might not be expected to distinguish between the appointive property and that which he owns outright, and thus "he can reasonably be presumed to regard this appointive property as his own." On the other hand, the donee of a special power would not reasonably regard such appointive property as his own: "[h]e would more likely consider himself to be, as the donor of the power intended, merely the person chosen by the donor to decide who of the possible appointees should share in the property (if the power is exclusive), and the respective shares of the appointees."

Considering the power of appointment given to Isabella and her treatment of that power during her life, the rationale for the canon of construction applicable to general powers of appointment should be applied in this case. This power was a general testamentary power at its inception. During her life, as a result of her request, Isabella had the use and enjoyment of the major portion of the property initially placed in her trust share. Prior use and enjoyment of the appointive property is a factor properly considered as weighing in favor of the exercise of a power of appointment by a will. Isabella voluntarily limited the power by selecting the possible appointees. In thus relinquishing the right to add the trust assets to her estate, she was treating the property as her own. Moreover, the gift under her residuary clause was consistent with the terms of the reduced power which she retained. In these circumstances, the partial release of a general power does not obviate the application of that rule of construction which presumes that a general residuary clause exercises a general power of appointment.

4.   A decree shall be entered determining that Isabella H. Dexter did exercise the power of appointment partially released by an instrument dated February 25, 1944, given to her by article Fourth of the will of Arthur Hunnewell.

So ordered.

NOTES

1.   Even if a donee manifests an intent to exercise a power and the manner of expression satisfies the donor's formal requirements, to be valid the appointment must be a permissible exercise of the power. In *Timmons v. Ingrahm*, yet another dispute within a blended family, the testator, Frank Sr., died in 1999, survived by his second wife, Myrtle; his two children, Frank Jr. and Jacquelyn, who were adopted during his prior marriage; and four stepchildren (Myrtle's four children from her prior marriage). Frank's will created two trusts: the Timmons Family Trust and the Timmons Marital Trust. The will gave Myrtle a

nongeneral lifetime power to appoint from the Family Trust any amount "to and among my then living lineal descendants. This limited power of appointment may be exercised by [Myrtle] even to the point of completely exhausting the entire trust corpus."

In 2007, eight years after Frank died, Myrtle purported to exercise that power by appointing to her children, Frank's stepchildren, the entire trust corpus as well as any property that would later be added to the trust "as the result of my death as a pour over from the Marital Trust." Myrtle made her intentions clear: "The effect of this exercise of this limited power of appointment shall be that the only beneficiaries of the Timmons Family Trust shall be my natural children. I understand that this exercise of limited power of appoint [sic] disinherits Frank G. Timmons, Jr. and Jacquelyn Forman." Frank Jr. and Jacquelyn argued that this purported exercise was invalid on the theory that Myrtle's children, the testator's stepchildren, did not qualify as "lineal descendants" of the testator. What result? *See Timmons v. Ingrahm*, 36 So. 3d 861 (Fla. Ct. App. 2010).

2.   Another requirement is that the exercise of power must satisfy any formal requirements imposed by the donor. For example, if the donor requires that the donee exercise the power of appointment in a will, then the donee must indeed do so. A related question that arises in this regard is what level of compliance is necessary—strict or substantial.

ASSESSMENTS

1.   Celeste and Marina executed a joint revocable trust, providing that on the death of the first spouse, the trust would become irrevocable. The survivor had the power to appoint so much or all of the trust assets as the survivor "shall appoint and direct by specific reference to this power of appointment in her last Will admitted to probate by a court of competent jurisdiction. If the power is not exercised, then the property shall be given to our children." The trust included the family home and various bank accounts. Two years after Celeste's death, Marina executed a document that purported to be an amendment to the trust. The document provided that on Marina's death, the family home would go to a friend, Tomas, who had taken care of Marina. Marina signed the document, and her lawyer notarized it.

    a.   Has Marina properly exercised the power of appointment? The answer to this question depends on whether your jurisdiction has a strict or substantial compliance rule. Look up the relevant statute in your state to find the answer.

    b.   In a strict compliance jurisdiction, what arguments can Tomas make that he should receive the family home?

2.   You have been asked to update your law firm's form file, which is a compilation of various forms and provisions that lawyers at the firm reference when drafting documents for clients. You have been given the language below to add to the form file. Using the language below do the following:

    a.   Create a descriptive heading for the provision

    b.   Describe in what document(s) and for what purpose(s) the provision may be included

    c.   Revise the language to resolve any potential drafting issues posed by the original language

[original language]

Each child of mine is to have a power of appointment over such portion of such child's trust property that remains undistributed at such child's death. Trustee shall pay such property in such proportions as that child appoints by valid Last Will and Testament so long as the Last Will and Testament specifically refers to this power of appointment. Notwithstanding the foregoing, no appointment shall be made to the child's estate, the child's creditors, or the creditors of the child's estate. If no effective power of appointment is exercised, Trustee shall pay such child's remaining trust property to that child's then surviving issue per stirpes or, if none, to my then living issue per stirpes.

3.   In which of the following cases, has the power been exercised?

    a.   Bethany's will states, "I leave my rental properties in trust for Greg for life, the remainder as Greg shall appoint by will to any one that he chooses." Greg tells Ramona he will appoint the property to her but dies intestate immediately after they speak.

    b.   Karen's will states, "I leave my real estate in trust for Jim for life, the remainder as Jim shall appoint." In his will, Jim states, "I leave my entire estate, including property over which I have an appointive power, to my friend, Jane."

    c.   Rita's will states, "I leave my entire estate in trust for Mitchell for life, the remainder as Mitchell shall appoint by will to any one of my children that he chooses." Mitchell sends a handwritten note to Rita's children telling them that he plans to leave Rita's money to them in equal parts.

d. Frances's will states, "I leave my stocks in trust for Leonard for life, the remainder as Leonard shall appoint by will." In his will, Leonard states, "I leave the residue of my estate to Lisa."

F. Conclusion and Takeaways

This chapter deals with trust modification, including trustee removal and powers of appointment. Trust modification may happen in one of three ways: the Claflin doctrine, deviation, or decanting. Claflin allows for change as long as the proposed modification is in line with the material purpose of the trust (hence why it is sometimes called the "material purpose" doctrine). Deviation allows for modification based on changed circumstances. With both Claflin and deviation, the trustee must file a petition for modification and receive judicial approval. Decanting, a relatively new trend in which states statutorily authorize trustees to make certain modifications, takes place without the trustee having to go to court. While trustee removal is not technically a modification, it may change the trust. Beneficiaries may request trustee removal and replacement not only for cause but also if the proposed change benefits the trust and is not inconsistent with the trust's material purpose. Finally, powers of appointment allow the donor to postpone the decision on who or what should ultimately be entitled to receive the donor's property by delegating that decision-making authority to someone else, thereby building flexibility and the power to modify into a trust. Now that we have covered how wills and trusts are formed, function during their existence, and can be changed, we will move to another popular form of estate planning: will substitutes.

CHAPTER 12 COMPREHENSIVE ASSESSMENTS

1. **DEVELOPING A PRESENTATION.** Imagine that you are a newly licensed attorney, and the Trusts & Estates section of your local bar association has asked your firm to create a presentation about decanting for the section's monthly meeting. Your supervising attorney has asked you to take a first stab at putting together slides and an outline for this session. Please create this set of slides and the accompanying outline and include:

a. A review of the traditional methods of trust modification and the legal framework for Claflin modification and deviation in your state.

b.   An overview of what decanting is along with several examples of how it works.

c.   How your state's decanting statute works, if there is one, or how the Uniform Trust Decanting Act works.

d.   The benefits and detriments of decanting that would be appropriate for this group of practitioners and their clients.

2.   **COUNSELING AND DRAFTING EXERCISE.** Cassandra has hired your law firm for some legal advice. Cassandra shares the following information with you:

Grayson, Cassandra's grandfather, created a trust for her when she was born. When Cassandra turned 25, she was entitled to income payable in quarterly installments and principal in such amount as the trustee, who continues to be Grayson's long-time friend and business partner, determined "in the Trustee's absolute discretion." Cassandra, who is now 36, has been receiving all of the required income distributions, and she has twice received distributions of principal. The trust property is currently valued at $2 million. The trust also contains the following provision:

Cassandra may appoint trust property to such person or persons in such portions as Cassandra shall determine appropriate.

Cassandra has recently had three conversations with individuals who are asking for her financial assistance. These conversations have motivated Cassandra's decision to visit your law firm today. Cassandra's stepchild Finley would like help with a house down payment. Cassandra's father Jeremy (Grayson's only child), who remarried following the death of Cassandra's mother, would like help with medical bills that his second wife recently incurred. Cassandra's neighbor Micah has developed "the next big idea" and would like Cassandra to invest in Micah's newly formed company.

Cassandra does not currently have liquid assets available, but she is thinking about helping with one or more of these requests.

a.   Write a letter to Cassandra that identifies and describes all the possible options she may wish to consider. Be creative in developing the options. Include the pros and cons for each identified option. Follow the formalities of a business letter (i.e., date, method of delivery, client name, client address, regarding line, closing, notation of enclosure(s), and copies). Use legally accurate and client-accessible language.

b.   Assume that Cassandra decides to exercise the power of appointment in favor of Finley for the sum of $25,000. Create a draft document for Cassandra to review that properly exercises the power of appointment. Be prepared to discuss your drafting choices.

Test Your Knowledge

To assess your understanding of the material in this chapter, click here to take a quiz.

CHAPTER 13

Will Substitutes and Other Non-Testamentary Forms of Inheritance

CHAPTER LEARNING OUTCOMES

Following your work with this material in this chapter, you should be able to do the following:

- Distinguish between wills and will substitutes

- List and describe the common types of will substitutes and explain how each one operates

- Compare and contrast the common types of will substitutes

- Describe the formalities necessary to create will substitutes

- Describe how a client can use will substitutes in an estate plan to achieve specific goals

- Explain and give examples of testamentary fragmentation

- Devise a plan to coordinate a variety of legal instruments transferring property at death

- Assess the applicability of the subsidiary law of wills to will substitutes

A. Introduction

An individual may exercise the freedom of disposition by creating an increasing variety of legal devices. As you have seen in the previous chapters on trusts, the will is not the sole legal device that can effectuate a transfer of property upon the property owner's death. Today, an increasing amount of property is transferred outside of the probate system via **nonprobate devices**. These devices, also called **will substitutes**, have some of the same functions of wills because they transfer property upon the property owner's death. Yet, these devices also take a different form from the will. These devices are contracts, deeds, and accounts. Each of these devices draws from its own traditions in contract law and property law.

As a consequence, they have their own forms and formalities. Issues arise as to whether these will substitutes, which can perform some of the same purposes as wills, should be subject to the same rules relating to the creation, revocation, interpretation, and implementation of wills.

Wills have a history that stretches back thousands of years. In contrast, will substitutes are relatively new devices. The need for will substitutes grew from the changing forms of property ownership. As forms of property ownership changed to include financial-based interests—rather than exclusive land-based interests—new legal devices to legally transfer ownership of those property interests were needed.

The development and widespread use of will substitutes has revolutionized the field of trusts and estates. In 1984, John Langbein published an influential article, "*The Nonprobate Revolution and the Future of the Law of Succession,*" in the Harvard Law Review. The article focused on the ways that people were increasingly transferring property from one generation to the next outside of probate. Some of this was through direct transfers during life, such as when parents pay for education or provide support during life, for instance, to buy a house. But then there are other nonprobate transfers at death, for instance, life insurance proceeds, beneficiary designations in bank and investment accounts and in pension plans, and in revocable trusts, which you will often hear called "living trusts." For decades, Langbein's article has stood as a guide to the ways that property passes outside of probate. It has also stood as a warning that nonprobate transfers are a parallel system to probate and the formalities required for nonprobate transfers are often different (and fewer) than those for probate transfers. One important task of the past several generations has been to unify—or at least bring into closer alignment—the requirements of probate and nonprobate transfers, such as making the will formalities look somewhat more like the lesser formalities associated with beneficiary designations in life insurance and bank and investment accounts.

Recently Melanie Leslie and Stewart Sterk returned to the nonprobate revolution and examined how the nonprobate system functions today. The beginning of their article, Melanie Leslie & Stewart Sterk, *Revisiting The Revolution: Reintegrating The Wealth Transmission System*, 56 B.C. L. REV. 61, 61–63 (2015), appears below.

Thirty years ago, in one of the most influential articles ever written about Trusts and Estates, Professor John Langbein observed and celebrated the end of what he called the "probate monopoly" and the growth of a parallel system of non-probate transfers. Langbein noted, correctly, that for many testators and beneficiaries, the opportunity to bypass the probate process would avoid wasteful expense and delay. Langbein did not ignore potential problems generated by the "nonprobate revolution," but was optimistic that those problems would be solved.

When the probate system dominated the wealth transmission process, a single document—the will—controlled most gratuitous transfers made by all but the very richest property owners. Executing a will required formalities designed to ensure that the document reflected the decedent's intent. The probate process mandated some judicial supervision of all estates, providing, at least in theory, additional protection against distributions inconsistent with the decedent's wishes.

The proliferation of mechanisms for transferring property at death outside the probate process—revocable trusts, "payable on death" ("POD") bank accounts, beneficiary designations on retirement accounts and life insurance policies—presented challenges for the legal system. Langbein identified three such challenges. First, how would the system ensure that the non-probate instruments of transfer, often prepared without formalities and without lawyer involvement, would accurately reflect the intent of the decedent? Second, how would the system coordinate distribution of a fragmented estate, in which multiple documents rather than a single will would govern the transmission of the decedent's wealth? Third, what substitutes would emerge for the protections afforded by judicial supervision of the probate estate? On this score Langbein surmised that hard cases— those that require judicial supervision—would end up in court just as they do in a system that requires judicial supervision of all cases, hard and easy.

Three decades later, it is time for reassessment. The use of revocable trusts and POD accounts has expanded, aided in many states by statutory changes. The Employee Retirement Income Security Act of 1974 (ERISA), in its infancy thirty years ago, has provoked a revolution of its own. In the course of that revolution, it has dramatically increased the dollar volume of assets likely to pass outside the probate system. For many people planning their estates, the will is now the least important document in their estate plan. This expansion in the importance of the non-probate system makes it imperative to evaluate the legal system's responses to the challenges Professor Langbein identified.

Leslie and Sterk point out a variety of problems with nonprobate transfers, such as lawyers failing to make the appropriate change to a nonprobate beneficiary designation, not knowing about all of a client's nonprobate assets, and not knowing how to implement clients' wishes with respect to those assets. As an example, Leslie and Sterk point to a California Appellate Court opinion, *McGovern v. Bigelow*, 2003 WL 22229688 (Cal. Ct. App. 2003), where a married couple went to a trust preparation service to have a trust prepared naming their children as remainder beneficiaries. The trust was intended to be irrevocable after the first settlor died, reciting as follows: "Except as otherwise provided in this Declaration, on the death of either Trustor, the designation of beneficiaries or specific gifts in the Trusts created by this Declaration shall become irrevocable and not subject to amendment or modification." The trust itself, however, did *not* say that it was irrevocable. Therefore, after the wife died in 1992, the surviving widower revoked the trust, leaving the trust property to his new partner instead of to the children. The court of appeals upheld the revocation.

> **Practice Note:** Will substitutes are used by individuals of all income levels. Coordination between and among the various legal devices is critical to modern estate planning. A client intake questionnaire should specifically ask for information about the various will substitutes the client may have created.

This chapter will identify the major types of will substitutes. **Part B** will focus on deeds. **Part C** will focus on contracts. **Part D** will focus on multi-party accounts. **Part E** will focus on one of the most powerful will substitutes, the revocable trust. In each part, this chapter will also explore how and in what circumstances owners of such property can change their beneficiaries and thus transfer property outside of the probate system. **Part F** will explore whether and under what circumstances the subsidiary law of wills should apply to will substitutes. **Part G** will assess the fragmentation that arises in estate plans and ways to coordinate planning.

As you read this chapter, consider the following questions:

- How may a property owner, alone or with the assistance of an estate planner, manage and coordinate all these legal devices given that most of these will substitutes are asset-specific?

- What role, if any, may the probate system play in nonprobate succession?

- Under what circumstances should the law of wills play a role in the creation (both in terms of form and adherence to formalities), revocation (both in terms of form and adherence to the formalities), interpretation (with use of default rules, such as the antilapse statute), and implementation (such as protections for creditors) of will substitutes?

B. Deeds

Real property deeds may function as will substitutes. Indeed, the joint tenancy with right of survivorship in real estate may be considered one of the oldest forms of will substitute. One of the newest forms of will substitutes is also a deed. That is the transfer on death deed. We describe each more fully below.

1. Joint Tenancy with Right of Survivorship in Real Estate

Joint tenancy with right of survivorship in real estate is a common form of will substitute. As discussed below, joint tenancy as a form of ownership may apply to real property or to personal property. This form of ownership has both lifetime and death time consequences. Typically, there are only two joint tenants. Upon the death of one joint tenant, that tenant's share disappears, and the remaining joint tenant owns the property outright. In other words, there is no need to devise real estate that is held in joint tenancy because it passes by operation of law. As a result, many people see the joint tenancy as a very basic building block of estate planning.

The creation of a joint tenancy with right of survivorship is a relatively simple process and is a typical form of ownership when married couples take title to real estate (sometimes called a "tenancy by the entirety" in this specific context). Often the joint tenancy is created at the time the property is acquired, but it is possible for an owner to convert ownership of the property into joint tenancy property. The creation of a joint tenancy may result in some tax consequences.

Today, the law requires an express intent to create a joint tenancy, which typically is established if the deed uses the words "joint," "jointly," "joint tenants," or "joint tenants with right of survivorship. The absence of such words, or similar words, to manifest an intent to create a joint tenancy will give rise to a presumption that the parties created a tenancy in common. This approach is a reversal of the historical common law presumption. The common law presumed that when an estate was transferred to two or more individuals, the individuals held the property as joint tenants—unless words to the contrary showed that the parties intended to hold the property as tenants in common. The common law presumption sought to ensure that the estates were not fractionalized over time, which is similar to the policy considerations supporting primogeniture. *See, e.g.*, John V. Orth, *The Perils of Joint Tenancies*, 44 REAL PROP. TR. & EST. L.J. 427 (2009); John V. Orth, *Joint Tenancy Law*, 5 GREEN BAG 2D 173 (2002). What policy considerations support the modern law reversing the common law presumption? What disadvantages accompany the modern position? Recall the discussion in Chapter 4 of the problems tenancy in common inheritance has created for Indian Trust land and for the owners of Heirs Property.

As you know, a tenancy in common does not have a right of survivorship, which means that a tenancy in common is not a will substitute. Each party to a tenancy in common can devise her share by will; if not, the share passes through intestacy.

As an interest relating to real property, the deed should be properly and promptly filed with the recorder of deeds in the county where the real property is located. Keep in mind that in many jurisdictions, deeds without consideration are valid for only a limited period of time such as two or three years. In that instance, timely filing is especially important, but recording the deed on the public land records is also motivated by the desire to provide notice to others of the interest. A sample deed for an owner to create a joint tenancy with another person is included in the Appendix.

Just as a joint tenancy can be created, a joint tenancy can be terminated. An individual may want to sever a joint tenancy, so that the individual's fractional interest in the property will pass via a will, rather than outside of probate via the deed. For example, one tenant may want someone other than the other tenant to inherit. This would require severing the joint tenancy, which creates a tenancy in common. Under some circumstances, the joint tenancy can be severed by the execution of a quitclaim deed conveying the property from two joint tenants to the same two tenants as "tenants-in-common." A person can often also sever

> **Practice Note:** The quitclaim deed can be an important tool to implement a client's estate plan. For example, an individual may use a quitclaim deed to transfer real property to a trust.

the joint tenancy by simply conveying his or her share to someone else.

2. Transfer on Death Deed

While the joint tenancy with right of survivorship deed may be one of the oldest will substitutes, a TOD deed is one of the newest. The Uniform Real Property Transfer on Death Act, which was first approved in 2009, clarifies that the **transfer on death deed** (TOD deed[1]) is nontestamentary device that nevertheless becomes effective upon the death of the property owner (i.e., the transferor). The TOD deed allows for the designation of a beneficiary to inherit the real property upon the owner's death, but unlike a joint tenancy, the beneficiary has no ownership interest in the real property during the owner's life. The owner continues to have the ability to sell the property, change the beneficiary designation, and revoke the deed. Because it is a deed and not a will, the wills act formalities are not necessary for creation or revocation of a TOD deed. Rather, it requires the proper formalities for the creation or revocation of a deed (under state law), and the deed must be properly recorded in the appropriate public land records.

Today, approximately half of the states authorize some variation of the TOD deed with more states expected to recognize the TOD deed. Some potential problems about the TOD deed, however, remain. As Danaya C. Wright and Stephanie L. Emrich have pointed out, the TOD deed does not have a third-party, such as a trustee or financial institute, involved in the process. Danaya C. Wright & Stephanie L. Emrich, *Tearing Down the Wall: How Transfer-on-Death Real-Estate Deeds Challenge the Inter Vivos/Testamentary Divide*, 78 MD. L. REV. 511, 527–28 (2019). One result is that the protections against fraud, duress, and undue influence that are present with the inclusion of a third party in other nonprobate transfers are missing from the TOD deed. As Wright and Emrich observe, states vary considerably in their approaches: for example, some states require the same will act formalities to be used to create a TOD deed. Other states do not. This split in approaches to the proper creation, which requires both the use of the proper form and the requisite mental capacity, is a common theme in this chapter. Likewise, as with most of the will substitutes, further development and clarification of which subsidiary wills rules are applicable to TOD deeds is required. For instance, should antilapse statutes apply to redirect the disposition of the property if the TOD deed designates a beneficiary who predeceased the property owner? Is the case for applying the subsidiary law of

---

[1]   On occasion, the abbreviation TODD is used. Some states use the terms "beneficiary deed," "revocable transfer-on-death deed," or even "deed-on-death."

wills to TOD deeds more or less compelling than applying the subsidiary law of wills to joint tenancies?

ASSESSMENTS

1.   Locate a deed form to create a joint tenancy. Compare that form with the example deed in the Appendix. What language is critical to create a joint tenancy? Some jurisdictions require more than the recitation of the words "joint tenancy with right of survivorship." In that instance, what specific (and perhaps additional) language should be included in the deed?

2.   What should a client understand about the role of deeds in modern estate planning? How would you explain both the lifetime consequences and deathtime consequences of deeds?

C. Contracts

Contract-based will substitutes have become increasingly popular. In general, the property is held under a contractual arrangement that results in the transfer of the property upon certain occurrences to the beneficiary designated in the contract. This section explores (1) life insurance policies and (2) retirement accounts.

1. Life Insurance Policies

Individuals may acquire a number of life insurance policies during their lifetimes. A **life insurance policy**, or more properly the proceeds from a life insurance policy, can provide additional resources to care for family members or pay debts. Another major selling point of life insurance policies is that it passes the policy proceeds outside of probate so that as soon as an insured passes away, the beneficiaries can present the death certificate to the insurance company and receive payment. Insurance companies like this approach because they can look only to their own files to know whom to pay; they generally do not need to wait for instructions from a probate court. There are, unsurprisingly, some instances where there is a controversy about who should receive the payments. For instance, there are disputes about whether the insured changed his beneficiary designation voluntarily, or whether the change was the product of undue influence or worse. *See Ex parte Estelle*, 982 So.2d 1086 (Ala. 2007) (allowing a daughter to sue her decedent father's landlord for undue influence regarding change of life insurance beneficiary from daughter to landlord). In that situation, the parties need to seek judicial resolution.

a. *Changes in Beneficiaries upon Divorce*

Beneficiary designations can become outdated if the insured does not update the beneficiary designation as the insured's circumstances change. For instance, disputes can arise when the insured failed to change beneficiary designation following a divorce. UPC § 2–804(b) allows an insurance company to provide in a "governing instrument" that an insured follow the insurance company's procedure for changing

> **Practice Note:** A qualified domestic relations order (QDRO) should address life insurance policies and retirement plans in cases of divorce.

the beneficiary designation. This requirement can lead to significant conflict between a divorced spouse, who is a beneficiary of a life insurance policy, and a new spouse (or the decedent's estate). To make matters more confusing, in some states, revocation-on-divorce rules apply to life insurance contracts, and, in others, this rule does not apply to life insurance contracts.

One of the most famous cases of this type is *Cook v. Equitable Life Assoc.*, 428 N.E.2d 110 (Ind. App. 1981), where an insured was divorced in the 1960s and then remarried and had a child. The insurance company allowed an owner to change a beneficiary designation "by written notice to the Society." In this case, however, Mr. Cook never filed that notice. In 1978, he executed a holographic will leaving all his "worldly possessions" to his second wife and their son, including "my Insurance policys (sic) with Common Welth of Ky. and Equitable Life." When he died, his former spouse was still listed as the designated beneficiary, and the insurance company wanted to pay her, rather than his new family. The insurance company said that the change of beneficiary had to be on its form and filed with the company. The court agreed and paid the insurance proceeds to the former spouse. This is a particularly dramatic case because it is clear that the insured wanted to change his beneficiary designation, but he failed to follow the proper procedure (as established by the insurance company).

More common are cases where the insured, a divorced spouse, does not leave a written record of intent. Along those lines, consider the following case of in which a beneficiary failed to make any statement about his intent regarding the life insurance after his divorce. The insured's new spouse claimed that she should have the insurance proceeds; the former spouse claimed that she was entitled to the proceeds because she was, after all, the designated beneficiary.

Allen v. Allen

589 N.E.2d 1133 (Ill. App. Ct. 1992)

Plaintiff, Carolyn Allen, appeals from the judgment of the circuit court of Lee County, finding that she had no interest in and to the proceeds of an insurance policy on the life of her deceased husband, Arnold Gene Allen, issued through his employer, Kelly-Springfield Tire Company. The court had ordered the proceeds paid to Ruth Allen, the decedent's former spouse, and her son, Timothy Allen.

The facts as adduced at the bench trial were as follows. Ruth Allen (Ruth) and Arnold Allen (Arnold) were married in 1963. In 1965 when Arnold was hired by Kelly-Springfield Tire Company (Kelly-Springfield), he named Ruth as beneficiary to the basic life insurance benefits offered by his employer as a benefit of employment. In January 1976, Ruth and Arnold were divorced. At the time they had one child, Timothy Allen (Timothy), age 10. When the divorce occurred, the basic life insurance policy was worth approximately $9,500. No optional contributory life insurance benefit plan was in effect at the time of the divorce.

The judgment for dissolution specifically found in pertinent part:

"9. The Defendant now holds life insurance policies on his life in the amount of Ten-thousand and no/hundredths dollars ($10,000)."

Additionally, the judgment ordered in pertinent part:

"G. The Defendant maintain in full force and effect all life insurance now carried by him on his life with the main beneficiary of all such insurance being Timothy S. Allen."

Arnold and Carolyn Allen (Carolyn) were married in 1976. Carolyn testified that in 1979 Arnold brought home a three-by-five card and an 8-by-10 paper with it. She filled out the card, inserting her name as beneficiary, her relationship to Arnold, and his name and social security number. Arnold then signed and dated the form. Carolyn did not make a copy of the form.

According to Carolyn, Arnold told her that he was going to take the card to work the next morning and turn it in. In the morning, the form was gone. Carolyn acknowledged that she did not accompany Arnold to work the following morning, nor did she know to whom he gave the card. Carolyn admitted that up until the time she completed the card in 1979, Ruth remained the beneficiary of Arnold's life insurance policy. Carolyn stated that she and Arnold had agreed that Timothy was to get $10,000 (of the insurance proceeds).

On June 2, 1989, Arnold died suddenly of a heart attack.

Sue Brown testified that at the time of Arnold's death she was manager of employment and safety for Kelly-Springfield. As such, she handled certain matters pertaining to employee benefits. Brown stated that it was customary for her and the union representative, Jerry Reddington, to visit a surviving spouse to explain the benefits to which the spouse was entitled.

Prior to their visit to Carolyn, Brown contacted Kelly-Springfield's home office to determine what benefits were available to Carolyn. Brown learned that in addition to the $20,000 basic life insurance available to all employees, Arnold had enrolled in the optional life insurance plan at 300% of the value of the basic plan, or $60,000. Arnold's total life insurance coverage equaled $80,000. Brown asked the home office the name of the beneficiary on file and discovered that Ruth was named as beneficiary of the insurance proceeds. Since Brown knew Ruth was not the decedent's current spouse, she asked the home office to double-check the records to make certain that no other beneficiary card was on file. The home office rechecked its files and then contacted Brown, informing her that the only beneficiary card on file named Ruth as beneficiary.

The court found that the evidence did not support Carolyn's claim that Arnold had executed a change of beneficiary on his life insurance policy. Additionally, the court found that Timothy's claim to the insurance proceeds was superior (by virtue of the dissolution judgment) to any beneficiary.

Discussion

On appeal, Carolyn contends that she is entitled to recover the life insurance proceeds subject only to a limited equitable claim in Timothy. Specifically, Carolyn asserts: (1) that the provisions of the 1976 judgment of dissolution bar Ruth from claiming any portion of the insurance proceeds; (2) that Timothy's equitable claim to the insurance proceeds is limited to payment from the basic life insurance benefit plan and to the value of the insurance at the time of the dissolution of the marriage; and (3) that under the Kelly-Springfield plan, Carolyn, as surviving spouse, is entitled to the insurance proceeds if Ruth's claim is barred.

Carolyn acknowledges that the law in Illinois is that a former spouse who is the designated beneficiary on an insurance policy is not barred from collecting the proceeds upon the death of the insured merely because they have divorced. She further concedes that a general waiver of marital property rights upon divorce does not affect the expectancy that the former spouse has in the decedent's life insurance policy as designated beneficiary. Carolyn maintains, however, that an exception or limitation exists as to the application of these principles and that the exception should be applied to the instant case. The exception exists, Carolyn asserts, if a dissolution judgment specifically addresses the entitlement to insurance proceeds. In such a case, the former spouse waives her right to claim under the beneficiary designation which still listed her as beneficiary. Because the 1976 dissolution judgment in the instant case specifically addressed life insurance, Carolyn contends that Ruth was barred from claiming any benefits payable pursuant to the beneficiary designation in effect at the time of the dissolution. Carolyn relies on two provisions of the dissolution judgment to support her position.

Paragraph 9 of the findings portion of the dissolution judgment provided:

"1.   The Defendant now holds life insurance policies on his life in the amount of Ten-thousand and no/hundredths dollars ($10,000)."

Paragraph G of the decretal portion of the judgment ordered:

"G.   The Defendant maintain in full force and effect all life insurance now carried by him with the main beneficiary of all such insurance being Timothy S. Allen."

Carolyn maintains that these provisions terminated Ruth's interest as beneficiary of any of Arnold's life insurance policies.

Conversely, we believe the provisions specifically related only to the policy in force at the time of the judgment of dissolution, *i.e.,* the basic life insurance plan. Under the terms of the dissolution judgment, Arnold was required to designate Timothy as the beneficiary of only that policy. Arnold was free to name any other person as a beneficiary of any other policy as long as such designation did not violate Timothy's equitable interest in the basic life insurance policy. We do not believe the provisions relied on by Carolyn show Ruth waived her right to take as the designated beneficiary on other insurance policies.

We conclude that the provisions of the judgment of dissolution did not bar Ruth from claiming the contributory life insurance proceeds. We conclude that Timothy was entitled to the entire proceeds of the basic life insurance policy. Carolyn is not entitled to the proceeds from the contributory life insurance. As determined earlier in this disposition, Ruth was on file with Kelly-Springfield as the designated beneficiary of that insurance, and Carolyn never proved that Arnold had executed a change in beneficiary naming her to replace Ruth. Thus, Ruth, not Carolyn, was entitled to the contributory life insurance proceeds.

Affirmed.

NOTES

1.   One lesson here is that a divorce decree should explicitly terminate the former spouse's rights to life insurance. Carolyn argued that another case, *Principal Mutual Life Insurance Co. v. Juntunen*, 545 N.E.2d 224 (Ill. App. 1989), supported her contention that a divorce decree terminated the former spouse's rights in an insurance policy. In that case, the settlement agreement provided:

> "Each of the parties hereby releases and/or waives *any* interest, beneficial or otherwise, which he or she may have acquired in or to *life insurance policy* (ies) owned by the other."

(Emphasis added.) The *Allen* court observed about Carolyn's reliance on *Principal Mutual Life* that:

> This provision differs significantly from those relied upon by Carolyn. In straightforward, express terms it bars either party from claiming life insurance proceeds from the other party's policies as well as bars any other interests the other party may have had in the policies themselves. In the instant case, no similar provision is included in the dissolution judgment. Neither paragraph 9 nor paragraph G contains a straightforward and express release of Ruth's interest in *all* insurance policies on Arnold's life. As appellees point out, the decision in *Principal Mutual Life* demonstrates the limited circumstances in which a court should find a complete waiver of a former spouse's interests in life insurance policies and does not support Carolyn's argument that paragraph 9 and paragraph G terminated any interests in Arnold's insurance policies

2.   Almost all states currently have revocation-on-divorce statutes, terminating an ex-spouse's interest not only in a will (as you learned in Chapter 8) but also in other nonprobate transfers. These statutes vary widely, however, in terms of which nonprobate transfers are included in the automatic revocation. In some jurisdictions, such as Texas, a divorce revokes a beneficiary designation in favor of a divorced spouse in a life insurance policy unless

> (1) the decree designates the insured former spouse as the beneficiary;
>
> (2) the insured re-designates the former spouse as the beneficiary after rendition of the decree; or

(3)   the former spouse is designated to receive the proceeds in trust for, on behalf of, or for the benefit of a child or a dependent of either spouse.

TEX. FAM. CODE § 9.301(a) (2006); *see also* OKLA. STAT. title 15, § 178, (A), (B)(3) (1987). In Virginia, the revocation on divorce operates to revoke all designations of the former spouse, except for trust interests. VA. CODE ANN. § 64.2–412.

3.   Kristen P. Raymond discusses the reasons that courts have been reluctant to apply automatic revocations upon divorce to life insurance contracts:

(1)   They are "fearful about the potential for the court guessing about the insured's intent when interpreting the insurance contract"

(2)   They want "to preclude the insurer from being held liable for dispensing the policy's proceeds, which, as a non-probate asset, are quickly disbursed after the policyholder's death to the wrong beneficiary"

(3)   "[T]he insurance contract derives from life insurance categorization as a non-probate asset, so courts should not play an active role in its disbursement, and considering that life insurance is a contract between two private parties, courts are bound to follow the policy terms and apply contract law principles when disputes arise"

Kristen P. Raymond, *Double Trouble—An Ex-Spouse's Life Insurance Beneficiary Status & State Automatic Revocation Upon Divorce Statutes: Who Gets What?*, 19 CONN. INS. L. J. 399, 409–11 (2013).

4.   A constructive trust may be used as a remedy to redirect the life insurance proceeds. As you recall, a constructive trust is an equitable remedial device that seeks to prevent unjust enrichment. What would a party need to present to a court for the court to impose a constructive trust?

b. Rights of Creditors of an Insured to Reach Life Insurance Proceeds

Life insurance policy proceeds may comprise a significant portion of an individual's estate. Indeed, the policy proceeds may the only liquid asset. For that reason, questions arise with some frequency about the rights of an insured's creditors to proceeds of a life insurance policy on the insured's death. New York has a statute, which is fairly typical, providing that proceeds of a life insurance policy that an insured takes out on his or his own life (for the benefit of someone

else—typically a family member) are protected against the claims of creditors of
the insured. The statute, which deals with life insurance and annuity contracts,
provides:

> (b)(1) If a policy of insurance has been or shall be effected by any
> person on his own life in favor of a third person beneficiary, or made
> payable otherwise to a third person, such third person shall be entitled
> to the proceeds and avails of such policy as against the creditors,
> personal representatives, trustees in bankruptcy and receivers in state
> and federal courts of the person effecting the insurance.

N.Y. INS. LAW § 3212 (McKinney 2000). Similarly, for instance, South Carolina,
S.C. CODE ANN. § 38–63–40(A), and Hawaii, HAWAII REV. STAT. § 431:10–
232(a), protect life insurance proceeds against creditors of the insured decedent
to the extent they are left to spouses and issue.

This approach might raise the question in your mind whether someone
who is near death might purchase a whole life insurance policy (the cost would
likely be very close to the face value of the policy) and thus protect the property
against creditors. That technique is not permitted; if done with the intent to
hinder a creditor, such a purchase would be a fraud on the creditors, which we
call a "fraudulent transfer."

2.   Retirement Accounts

Today, **retirement account** proceeds account for some of the property of
highest value for most decedents. *See generally* Stewart E. Sterk & Melanie B.
Leslie, *Accidental Inheritance: Retirement Accounts and the Hidden Law of Succession*, 89
N.Y.U. L. REV. 165 (2014). Pensions have long been a source of financial
security for many workers but the rise of the "gig economy," a labor market
where individuals perform freelance work or work in accordance with short-
term contracts, has raised the question about the future of all retirement
accounts. Many individuals in the gig economy are not accumulating savings in
retirement accounts because they may not, for example, be participating in any
employer-based retirement account.

Retirement accounts are created to provide a source of income when the
owner of the account retires. The owner of the account has the ability to
designate a beneficiary to receive any amounts remaining in the account when
the owner dies. As with any beneficiary designations, issues arise when the
beneficiary designation becomes stale.

While state probate codes frequently revoke beneficiary designations upon divorce—and the UPC provides for their revocation unless the governing instrument provides otherwise—the U.S. Supreme Court has found that these state laws are pre-empted by ERISA. Thus, as the next case explains, a beneficiary designation in a retirement plan governed by ERISA is not revoked, regardless of what the law of the decedent's domicile provides.

Egelhoff v. Egelhoff

532 U.S. 141 (2001)

THOMAS, J.

A Washington statute provides that the designation of a spouse as the beneficiary of a nonprobate asset is revoked automatically upon divorce. We are asked to decide whether the Employee Retirement Income Security Act of 1974 (ERISA), 88 Stat. 832, 29 U.S.C. § 1001 *et seq.*, preempts that statute to the extent it applies to ERISA plans. We hold that it does.

I

Petitioner Donna Rae Egelhoff was married to David A. Egelhoff. Mr. Egelhoff was employed by the Boeing Company, which provided him with a life insurance policy and a pension plan. Both plans were governed by ERISA, and Mr. Egelhoff designated his wife as the beneficiary under both. In April 1994, the Egelhoffs divorced. Just over two months later, Mr. Egelhoff died intestate following an automobile accident. At that time, Mrs. Egelhoff remained the listed beneficiary under both the life insurance policy and the pension plan. The life insurance proceeds, totaling $46,000, were paid to her.

Respondents Samantha and David Egelhoff, Mr. Egelhoff's children by a previous marriage, are his statutory heirs under state law. They sued petitioner in Washington state court to recover the life insurance proceeds. Respondents relied on a Washington statute that provides:

> If a marriage is dissolved or invalidated, a provision made prior to that event that relates to the payment or transfer at death of the decedent's interest in a nonprobate asset in favor of or granting an interest or power to the decedent's former spouse is revoked. A provision affected by this section must be interpreted, and the nonprobate asset affected passes, as if the former spouse failed to survive the decedent, having died at the time of entry of the decree of dissolution or declaration of invalidity.

Wash. Rev. Code § 11.07.010(2)(a) (1994). That statute applies to "all nonprobate assets, wherever situated, held at the time of entry by a superior court of this state of a decree of dissolution of marriage or a declaration of invalidity." § 11.07.010(1). It defines "nonprobate asset" to include "a life insurance policy, employee benefit plan, annuity or similar contract, or individual retirement account." § 11.07.010(5)(a).

Respondents argued that they were entitled to the life insurance proceeds because the Washington statute disqualified Mrs. Egelhoff as a beneficiary, and in the absence of a qualified named beneficiary, the proceeds would pass to them as Mr. Egelhoff's heirs. In a separate action, respondents also sued to recover the pension plan benefits. Respondents again argued that the Washington statute disqualified Mrs. Egelhoff as a beneficiary and they were thus entitled to the benefits under the plan.

The trial courts, concluding that both the insurance policy and the pension plan "should be administered in accordance" with ERISA, granted summary judgment to petitioner in both cases. The Washington Court of Appeals consolidated the cases and reversed. It concluded that the Washington statute was not pre-empted by ERISA. Applying the statute, it held that respondents were entitled to the proceeds of both the insurance policy and the pension plan.

The Supreme Court of Washington affirmed. Courts have disagreed about whether statutes like that of Washington are pre-empted by ERISA. To resolve the conflict, we granted certiorari.

II

ERISA's pre-emption section, 29 U.S.C. § 1144(a), states that ERISA "shall supersede any and all State laws insofar as they may now or hereafter relate to any employee benefit plan" covered by ERISA. We have observed repeatedly that this broadly worded provision is "clearly expansive." *New York State Conference of Blue Cross & Blue Shield Plans* v. *Travelers Ins. Co.,* 514 U.S. 645, 655 (1995).

We have held that a state law relates to an ERISA plan "if it has a connection with or reference to such a plan." *Shaw* v. *Delta Air Lines, Inc.,* 463 U.S. 85, 97 (1983). Petitioner focuses on the "connection with" part of this inquiry. Acknowledging that "connection with" is scarcely more restrictive than "relate to," we have cautioned against an "uncritical literalism" that would make pre-emption turn on "infinite connections." *Travelers, supra,* at 656. Instead, "to determine whether a state law has the forbidden connection, we look both to 'the objectives of the ERISA statute as a guide to the scope of the state law that

Congress understood would survive,' as well as to the nature of the effect of the state law on ERISA plans." *California Div. of Labor Standards Enforcement* v. *Dillingham Constr., N. A., Inc.,* 519 U.S. 316, 325 (1997), quoting *Travelers, supra,* at 656 (citation omitted).

Applying this framework, petitioner argues that the Washington statute has an impermissible connection with ERISA plans. We agree. The statute binds ERISA plan administrators to a particular choice of rules for determining beneficiary status. The administrators must pay benefits to the beneficiaries chosen by state law, rather than to those identified in the plan documents. The statute thus implicates an area of core ERISA concern. In particular, it runs counter to ERISA's commands that a plan shall "specify the basis on which payments are made to and from the plan," § 1102(b)(4), and that the fiduciary shall administer the plan "in accordance with the documents and instruments governing the plan," § 1104(a)(1)(D), making payments to a "beneficiary" who is "designated by a participant, or by the terms of [the] plan." § 1002(8). In other words, unlike generally applicable laws regulating "areas where ERISA has nothing to say," *Dillingham,* 519 U.S. at 330, which we have upheld notwithstanding their incidental effect on ERISA plans, this statute governs the payment of benefits, a central matter of plan administration.

The Washington statute also has a prohibited connection with ERISA plans because it interferes with nationally uniform plan administration. One of the principal goals of ERISA is to enable employers "to establish a uniform administrative scheme, which provides a set of standard procedures to guide processing of claims and disbursement of benefits." *Fort Halifax Packing Co.* v. *Coyne,* 482 U.S. 1, 9 (1987). Uniformity is impossible, however, if plans are subject to different legal obligations in different States.

The Washington statute at issue here poses precisely that threat. Plan administrators cannot make payments simply by identifying the beneficiary specified by the plan documents. Instead they must familiarize themselves with state statutes so that they can determine whether the named beneficiary's status has been "revoked" by operation of law. And in this context the burden is exacerbated by the choice-of-law problems that may confront an administrator when the employer is located in one State, the plan participant lives in another, and the participant's former spouse lives in a third. In such a situation, administrators might find that plan payments are subject to conflicting legal obligations.

To be sure, the Washington statute protects administrators from liability for making payments to the named beneficiary unless they have "actual knowledge of the dissolution or other invalidation of marriage," Wash. Rev. Code § 11.07.010(3)(a) (1994), and it permits administrators to refuse to make payments until any dispute among putative beneficiaries is resolved, § 11.07.010(3)(b). But if administrators do pay benefits, they will face the risk that a court might later find that they had "actual knowledge" of a divorce. If they instead decide to await the results of litigation before paying benefits, they will simply transfer to the beneficiaries the costs of delay and uncertainty. Requiring ERISA administrators to master the relevant laws of 50 States and to contend with litigation would undermine the congressional goal of "minimiz[ing] the administrative and financial burden[s]" on plan administrators—burdens ultimately borne by the beneficiaries. *Ingersoll-Rand Co. v. McClendon*, 498 U.S. 133, 142 (1990).

We recognize that all state laws create some potential for a lack of uniformity. But differing state regulations affecting an ERISA plan's "system for processing claims and paying benefits" impose "precisely the burden that ERISA preemption was intended to avoid." And as we have noted, the statute at issue here directly conflicts with ERISA's requirements that plans be administered, and benefits be paid, in accordance with plan documents. We conclude that the Washington statute has a "connection with" ERISA plans and is therefore pre-empted.

III

Respondents suggest several reasons why ordinary ERISA pre-emption analysis should not apply here.

Respondents emphasize that the opt-out provision makes compliance with the statute less burdensome than if it were mandatory. That is true enough, but the burden that remains is hardly trivial. It is not enough for plan administrators to opt out of this particular statute. Instead, they must maintain a familiarity with the laws of all 50 States so that they can update their plans as necessary to satisfy the opt-out requirements of other, similar statutes. They also must be attentive to changes in the interpretations of those statutes by state courts. This "tailoring of plans and employer conduct to the peculiarities of the law of each jurisdiction" is exactly the burden ERISA seeks to eliminate.

Second, respondents emphasize that the Washington statute involves both family law and probate law, areas of traditional state regulation. There is indeed a presumption against pre-emption in areas of traditional state regulation such as family law. *See, e. g., Hisquierdo v. Hisquierdo*, 439 U.S. 572, 581 (1979). But that presumption can be overcome where, as here, Congress has made clear its desire for pre-emption. Accordingly, we have not hesitated to find state family law pre-empted when it conflicts with ERISA or relates to ERISA plans. *See, e. g., Boggs v. Boggs,* 520 U.S. 833 (1997) (holding that ERISA pre-empts a state community property law permitting the testamentary transfer of an interest in a spouse's pension plan benefits).

Finally, respondents argue that if ERISA pre-empts this statute, then it also must pre-empt the various state statutes providing that a murdering heir is not entitled to receive property as a result of the killing. In the ERISA context, these "slayer" statutes could revoke the beneficiary status of someone who murdered a plan participant. Those statutes are not before us, so we do not decide the issue. We note, however, that the principle underlying the statutes—which have been adopted by nearly every State—is well established in the law and has a long historical pedigree predating ERISA. And because the statutes are more or less uniform nationwide, their interference with the aims of ERISA is at least debatable.

The judgment of the Supreme Court of Washington is reversed, and the case is remanded for further proceedings not inconsistent with this opinion.

JUSTICE BREYER, with whom JUSTICE STEVENS joins, *dissenting.*

Like Justice Scalia [whose concurrence is omitted], I believe that we should apply normal conflict pre-emption and field pre-emption principles where, as here, a state statute covers ERISA and non ERISA documents alike. Our more recent ERISA cases are consistent with this approach.

I do not agree with Justice Scalia or with the majority, however, that there is any plausible pre-emption principle that leads to a conclusion that ERISA pre-empts the statute at issue here. No one could claim that ERISA pre-empts the entire *field* of state law governing inheritance—though such matters "relate to" ERISA broadly speaking. Neither is there any direct conflict between the Washington statute and ERISA, for the one nowhere directly contradicts the other.

The Court correctly points out that ERISA requires a fiduciary to make payments to a beneficiary "in accordance with the documents and instruments governing the plan." 29 U.S.C. § 1104(a)(1)(D). But nothing in the Washington statute requires the contrary. Rather, the state statute simply sets forth a default rule for interpreting documentary silence. The statute specifies that a nonprobate asset will pass at A's death "as if" A's "former spouse" had died first—*unless the "instrument governing disposition of the nonprobate asset expressly provides otherwise."* Wash. Rev. Code § 11.07.010(2)(b)(i) (1994) (emphasis added). This state-law rule is a rule of interpretation, and it is designed to carry out, not to conflict with, the employee's likely intention as revealed in the plan documents.

There is no direct conflict or contradiction between the Washington statute and the terms of the plan documents here at issue. David Egelhoff's investment plan provides that when a "beneficiary designation" is "invalid," the "benefits will be paid" to a "surviving spouse," or "[i]f there is no surviving spouse," to the "children in equal shares." The life insurance plan is silent about what occurs when a beneficiary designation is invalid. The Washington statute fills in these gaps. Thus, the Washington statute specifies that a beneficiary designation— here "Donna R. Egelhoff wife" in the pension plan—is invalid where there is no longer any such person as Donna R. Egelhoff, wife. And the statute adds that in such instance the funds would be paid to the children, who themselves are potential pension plan beneficiaries.

The Court's "direct conflict" conclusion rests upon its claim that "administrators must pay benefits to the beneficiaries chosen by state law, rather than to those identified in the plan documents." But the Court cannot mean "identified *anywhere* in the plan documents," for the Egelhoff children were "identified" as recipients in the pension plan documents should the initial designation to "Donna R. Egelhoff wife" become invalid. And whether that initial designation became invalid upon divorce is a matter about which the plan documents are silent.

To refer to state property law to fill in that blank cannot possibly create any direct conflict with the plan documents.

The majority simply denies that there is any blank to fill in and suggests that the plan documents require the plan to pay the designated beneficiary under all circumstances. But there is nonetheless an open question, namely, whether a designation that (here explicitly) refers to a wife remains valid after divorce. The question is genuine and important (unlike the imaginary example in the majority's footnote). The plan documents themselves do not answer the question any more than they describe what is to occur in a host of other special circumstances (*e. g.,* mental incompetence, intoxication, ambiguous names, etc.). To determine whether ERISA permits state law to answer such questions requires a careful examination of the particular state law in light of ERISA's basic policies. We should not short circuit that necessary inquiry simply by announcing a "direct conflict" where none exists.

The Court also complains that the Washington statute restricts the plan's choices to "two." But it is difficult to take this complaint seriously. After all, the two choices that Washington gives the plan are (1) to comply with Washington's rule or (2) not to comply with Washington's rule. What other choices could there be? A state statute that asks a plan to choose whether it intends to comply is not a statute that directly conflicts with a plan. Quite obviously, it is possible, not " 'impossible,' " to comply with both the Washington statute and federal law.

The more serious pre-emption question is whether this state statute " 'stands as an obstacle to the accomplishment and execution of the full purposes and objectives of Congress.' " In answering that question, we must remember that petitioner has to overcome a strong presumption *against* pre-emption. That is because the Washington statute governs family property law— a "fiel[d] of traditional state regulation," where courts will not find federal preemption unless such was the " 'clear and manifest purpose of Congress,' " *Travelers*, 514 U.S. at 655 (quoting *Rice* v. *Santa Fe Elevator Corp.*, 331 U.S. 218, 230 (1947)), or the state statute does " 'major damage' to 'clear and substantial' federal interests," *Hisquierdo* v. *Hisquierdo*, 439 U.S. 572, 581 (1979) (quoting *United States* v. *Yazell*, 382 U.S. 341, 352 (1966)). No one can seriously argue that Congress has *clearly* resolved the question before us. And the only damage to federal interests that the Court identifies consists of the added administrative burden the state statute imposes upon ERISA plan administrators.

The Court claims that the Washington statute "interferes with nationally uniform plan administration" by requiring administrators to "familiarize themselves with state statutes." But administrators have to familiarize themselves with state law in any event when they answer such routine legal questions as whether amounts due are subject to garnishment, who is a "spouse," who qualifies as a "child," or when an employee is legally dead. And were that "familiarizing burden" somehow overwhelming, the plan could easily avoid it by resolving the divorce revocation issue in the plan documents themselves, stating expressly that state law does not apply. The "burden" thus reduces to a one-time requirement that would fall primarily upon the few who draft model ERISA documents, not upon the many who administer them. So meager a burden cannot justify pre-empting a state law that enjoys a presumption against pre-emption.

The Court has previously made clear that the fact that state law "impose[s] some burde[n] on the administration of ERISA plans" does not necessarily require pre-emption. *De Buono*, 520 U.S. at 815. Precisely, what is it about this statute's requirement that distinguishes it from the " 'myriad state laws' " that impose some kind of burden on ERISA plans? *De Buono*, *supra*, at 815 (quoting *Travelers*, *supra*, at 668).

Indeed, if one looks beyond administrative burden, one finds that Washington's statute poses no obstacle, but furthers ERISA's ultimate objective—developing a fair system for protecting employee benefits. The Washington statute transfers an employee's pension assets at death to those individuals whom the worker would likely have wanted to receive them. As many jurisdictions have concluded, divorced workers more often prefer that a child, rather than a divorced spouse, receive those assets. Of course, an employee can secure this result by changing a beneficiary form; but doing so requires awareness, understanding, and time. That is why Washington and many other jurisdictions have created a statutory assumption that divorce works a revocation of a designation in favor of an ex-spouse. That assumption is embodied in the Uniform Probate Code; it is consistent with human experience; and those with expertise in the matter have concluded that it "more often" serves the cause of "[j]ustice." Langbein, *The Nonprobate Revolution and the Future of the Law of Succession*, 97 HARV. L. REV. 1108, 1135 (1984).

In forbidding Washington to apply that assumption here, the Court permits a divorced wife, who *already* acquired, during the divorce proceeding, her fair share of the couple's community property, to receive in addition the benefits that the divorce court awarded to her former husband. To be more specific, Donna Egelhoff already received a business, an IRA account, and stock; David received, among other things, 100% of his pension benefits. David did not change the beneficiary designation in the pension plan or life insurance plan during the 6-month period between his divorce and his death. As a result, Donna will now receive a windfall of approximately $80,000 at the expense of David's children. The State of Washington enacted a statute to prevent precisely this kind of unfair result. But the Court, relying on an inconsequential administrative burden, concludes that Congress required it.

Finally, the logic of the Court's decision does not stop at divorce revocation laws. The Washington statute is virtually indistinguishable from other traditional state-law rules, for example, rules using presumptions to transfer assets in the case of simultaneous deaths, and rules that prohibit a husband who kills a wife from receiving benefits as a result of the wrongful death. It is particularly difficult to believe that Congress wanted to pre-empt the latter kind of statute. But how do these statutes differ from the one before us? Slayer statutes—like this statute—"gover[n] the payment of benefits, a central matter of plan administration." *Ante*, at 148. And contrary to the Court's suggestion, *ante*, at 152, slayer statutes vary from State to State in their details just like divorce revocation statutes. Indeed, the "slayer" conflict would seem more serious, not less serious, than the conflict before us, for few, if any, slayer statutes permit plans to opt out of the state property law rule.

In this case, "field pre-emption" is not at issue. There is no "direct" conflict between state and federal statutes. The state statute poses no significant obstacle to the accomplishment of any federal objective. Any effort to squeeze some additional pre-emptive force from ERISA's words (*i. e.,* "relate to") is inconsistent with the Court's recent case law. And the state statute before us is one regarding family property—a "fiel[d] of traditional state regulation," where the interpretive presumption against pre-emption is particularly strong. *Travelers*, 514 U.S. at 655. For these reasons, I disagree with the Court's conclusion. And, consequently, I dissent.

NOTES

1.   One reaction to *Egelhoff* might be the development of a state cause of action that allows post-distribution relief to the family members of a decedent whose retirement assets were distributed to an ex-spouse. The argument would be that such a state cause of action is not preempted because it does not affect plan administration but simply remedies a private injustice among the parties. This would, in essence, be a common law rule that mirrored the state probate codes. However, in 2013 the U.S. Supreme Court considered this issue in *Hillman v. Maretta*, 569 U.S. 483 (2013), a non-ERISA case involving a federal employee and a federal retirement plan. The decedent had designated his then-wife, Judy Maretta, as beneficiary of his federal pension in 1996. The decedent and Judy Maretta divorced in 1998, and the decedent remarried in 2002 but never changed his beneficiary designation. Following the decedent's death in 2008, the federal pension plan paid the proceeds to Maretta. The new spouse, Jaqueline Hillman, challenged this distribution. The parties agreed that Virginia's revocation on divorce statue was pre-empted by the laws governing the federal retirement plan. Yet, Ms. Hillman sought to use a Virginia statute that allowed recovery post-distribution of the retirement plan proceeds. The U.S. Supreme Court held that such post-distribution action was, likewise, pre-empted. One lesson of these cases is to remind clients to change their beneficiary designations after a change in marital status. This lesson is as important—if not more important—for family law practitioners as for those assisting with estate planning.

2.   The *Egelhoff* and *Hillman* cases have been heavily criticized. *See, e.g.,* John H. Langbein, *Destructive Federal Preemption of State Wealth Transfer Law in Beneficiary Designation Cases: Hillman Doubles Down on Egelhoff*, 67 VAND. L. REV. 1665 (2014). Indeed, Justice Breyer's dissent in Egelhoff notes that the logic of the majority

would preempt state-slayer statutes, which prohibit a murderer from collecting benefits from the will or life insurance of his victim. Justice Thomas responded by noting that state slayer statutes are more or less uniform from state to state and thus might survive ERISA preemption, perhaps because such rules do not interfere sufficiently with ERISA plan administration or undermine ERISA goals. Is that a convincing response? The question of ERISA preemption with the slayer rule is percolating in circuit courts and may well come before the U.S. Supreme Court one day soon. *See Laborers' Pension Fund v. Miscevic*, No. 17-2022 (7th Cir. Jan. 29, 2018).

3.   ERISA retirement plans include certain survivor protections for spouses (married for at least one year), which a plan participant cannot vary without his or her spouse's permission. For example, in a pension plan (promising a lifetime benefit), a participant's current spouse obtains an automatic survivor benefit unless the spouse waives that right in a writing either notarized or witnessed by the plan administrator. (The benefit might not be payable until the participant would have been eligible for retirement benefits and will typically be half of what the participant would have received if the participant had reached retirement age.) And in most individual account plans, including most 401(k) plans, survivor rights to the account balance belong to the surviving spouse unless the surviving spouse has waived those rights in writing, Thus, if Mr. Egelhoff had remarried before he died, his former wife would have not had rights in 401(k) plan. But here there is a caveat as well: a former spouse's rights can be preserved (or partly preserved) at divorce or separation through a qualified domestic relations order, or "QDRO," a type of state court domestic relations order that plans must accept if the order is presented to the plan and satisfies various statutory criteria. There are no ERISA statutory survivor rights for employer-provided insurance. It should also be said that a plan itself could provide for an automatic revocation of survivor rights following divorce, but few plans include such terms.

4.   Do you think a state's revocation on divorce statute, which appears neutral on its face, has an equal effect on men and women? In FEMINIST JUDGMENTS: REWRITTEN TRUSTS AND ESTATES OPINIONS 175 (eds. Deborah S Gordon, Browne C. Lewis, & Carla Spivack) (Cambridge Univ. Press 2020), Naomi Cahn rewrites the *Egelhoff* opinion to account for ERISA's role as a legislative mechanism to equalize economic differences between men and women based on social realities, including that more men had pension plans, the value of those plans was larger, and their life expectancies shorter than women's. Reaching the same preemption result, Cahn observes that if the Washington revocation-on-

divorce statute were to apply to ERISA plan benefits, it would potentially disadvantage more women in "frequency and quantity."

D. Multi-Party Accounts

Multi-party accounts are popular will substitutes. These accounts are grounded in contract law, but some of the concerns related to multi-party accounts are distinct from issues relating to contracts more broadly. Examples of such accounts include the joint account, the payable-on-death (POD) account, and the transfer-on-death (TOD) account. The property in the account is held by a financial institution, such as a bank or securities company. The owner(s) of the account may designate who has rights to access the account and what happens to the account funds upon the owner's death.

1. Joint Tenancy Bank Accounts

A **joint tenancy bank account** can serve as a will substitute. This works well, so that the surviving joint tenant can simply take a copy of the decedent joint tenant's death certificate to the bank and have the title to the account changed. As with all will substitutes, access to the property subject to the will can be accelerated compared to access to probate property—so long as no dispute arises to the property.

The title of the bank account may not represent the depositor's true intent, yet the title has legal consequences. For instance, an owner of an account might title the account as a "joint tenancy" so that a caretaker could have access to the account funds to care for the owner but not to use the funds for the caretaker's own benefit. This type of account is actually a "**convenience account**." By contrast, a joint account operates just like a joint tenancy in real estate: when one person dies, the account passes to the other person listed on the account. If the goal is easy access for a caretaker, the owner should list the caretaker as a drawer on the account but should not create a joint account. This way, the caretaker does not end up with the property at the death of the principal (and it is clear that the caretaker can only use the property for the care of the principal). It is possible to unwind a "joint tenancy" designation after an owner passes away, but it is not easy, as the next case, *Franklin v. Anna National Bank*, illustrates. In contrast to the facts of *Anna National Bank*, where the court found that the owner did not intend to give the joint tenant an interest in the account, many cases involve owners who *do* intend to convey an interest when they add a joint tenant. A joint tenant has the right to make withdrawals from a jointly owned account, but that power to withdraw leads to its own problems, as we see in the *Varela* case.

Franklin v. Anna National Bank

488 N.E.2d 1117 (Ill. App. 1986)

WELCH, J.

Plaintiff, Enola Stevens Franklin, as executor of the estate of Frank A. Whitehead, deceased, commenced this action in the circuit court of Union County against defendant Anna National Bank, alleging that the funds in a joint savings account were the property of the estate. The bank interpleaded Cora Goddard, who asserted her right to the money as the surviving joint owner. After a bench trial, the circuit court entered judgment for Mrs. Goddard. Mrs. Franklin appeals. We reverse.

Decedent died December 22, 1980. His wife Muriel Whitehead died in 1974. Mrs. Goddard was Muriel's sister. Decedent had eye surgery in May of 1978, and according to Mrs. Goddard was losing his eyesight in 1978. In April of 1978 Mrs. Goddard moved to Union County to help decedent and live with him. On April 17, 1978, Mrs. Goddard and decedent went to the bank, according to Mrs. Goddard to have his money put in both their names so she could get money when they needed it, "and he wanted me to have this money if I outlived him."

A bank employee prepared a signature card for savings account No. 3816, and Mrs. Goddard signed it. A copy of this card was in evidence at trial. The signatures of decedent and Mrs. Goddard appear on both sides of the card. It appears that Muriel Whitehead's signature was "whited out" and Mrs. Goddard's signature added. The front of the card states that one signature is required for withdrawals. The back of the card states that all funds deposited are owned by the signatories as joint tenants with right of survivorship.

Mrs. Goddard testified that she did not deposit any of the money in savings account No. 3816. She made no withdrawals, though she once took decedent to the bank so he could make a withdrawal.

Later in 1978, Mrs. Franklin began to care for decedent. In January 1979, decedent telephoned the bank, then sent Mrs. Franklin to the bank to deliver a letter to Mrs. Kedron Boyer, a bank employee. The handwritten letter, dated January 13, 1979, and signed by decedent, stated: "I Frank Whitehead wish by Bank accounts be changed to Enola Stevens joint intendency [*sic*]. Nobody go in my lock box but me." According to Mrs. Franklin, Mrs. Boyer told her to tell decedent he would have to specify what type of account he was referring to. Decedent gave Mrs. Franklin a second letter which Mrs. Franklin delivered to Mrs. Carol Williams at the bank (Mrs. Boyer was absent). This handwritten letter, dated January 13, 1979, stated: "I Frank Whitehead want Enola Stevens and me only go in my lock box. Account type Saving and Checking. In case I can't see she is to take care of my bill or sick." According to Mrs. Franklin, Mrs. Williams said she would take care of it and give the letter to Mrs. Boyer. Mrs. Franklin testified that she signed the savings passbook in the presence of decedent and Mrs. Boyer. Mrs. Franklin took her present last name on May 8, 1979.

Mrs. Boyer, Mrs. Williams, and bank president Delano Mowery all testified at trial. These witnesses explained the usual procedures for account changes. None remembered much of the circumstances surrounding the bank's receipt of the January 13, 1979, letters. According to Mr. Mowery, the bank would not remove a signature from a signature card based on a letter; the most recent signature card the bank had for savings account No. 3816 was signed by decedent and Mrs. Goddard.

Discussion

The instrument creating a joint tenancy account presumably speaks the whole truth. In order to go behind the terms of the agreement, the one claiming adversely thereto has the burden of establishing by clear and convincing evidence that a gift was not intended. The form of the agreement is not conclusive regarding the intention of the depositors between themselves. Evidence of lack of donative intent must relate back to the time of creation of the joint tenancy. The decision of the donor, made subsequent to the creation of the joint tenancy, that he did not want the proceeds to pass to the survivor, would not, in itself, be sufficient to sever the tenancy. However, it is proper to consider events occurring after creation of the joint account in determining whether the donor actually intended to transfer his interest in the account at his death to the surviving joint tenant.

There appears no serious doubt that in January of 1979, just nine months after adding Mrs. Goddard's name to savings account No. 3816, decedent attempted to remove Mrs. Goddard's name and substitute Mrs. Franklin's. The second of decedent's handwritten letters to the bank in January of 1979 indicates decedent's concern that he might lose his sight and be unable to transact his own banking business. These facts show that decedent made Mrs. Goddard (and later Mrs. Franklin) a signatory for his own convenience, in case he could not get his money, and not with intent to effect a present gift. It does not appear that Mrs. Goddard ever exercised any authority or control over the joint account. While decedent's statement that he wanted Mrs. Goddard to have the money in the account if she outlived him suggests decedent's donative intent, taken literally decedent's statement is inconsistent with intent to donate any interest during decedent's lifetime.

In the case at bar, decedent's attempts to change the account show his consistent view of the account as his own. The surrounding circumstances show decedent's concern for his health and his relatively brief use of Mrs. Goddard (and later Mrs. Franklin) to assure his access to his funds. The money in account No. 3816 should have been found to be the property of the estate.

Reversed.

Varela v. Bernachea

917 So. 2d 295 (Dist. Ct. App. Fla. 2005)

PER CURIAM.

Cristina Varela ("Varela") appeals from a Final Judgment, which declared Carlos Alberto Bernachea ("Bernachea") the sole owner of Merrill Lynch CMA account ("the CMA account"), despite the fact the account was held as a joint tenancy with a right of survivorship.

Varela and Bernachea are both Argentinean citizens who met in Buenos Aires in late 2000. They developed a romantic relationship and traveled the world together. Bernachea was an attorney in Argentina for over 30 years, but has since retired and invested in American businesses and real estate. In late 2001, at Bernachea's behest, Varela stopped working and moved into his Sunny Isles Beach condominium where the two began living together. While they were a couple, Bernachea paid all of Varela's expenses and showered her with expensive gifts. Varela claimed that she never knew Bernachea was married. Moreover, she claimed Bernachea held her out as his wife. Bernachea disputed Varela's claims and asserted that Varela knew he had a wife, yet contented herself with being his mistress.

Whatever their true arrangement, on January 4, 2002, Bernachea added Varela as a joint tenant with a right of survivorship to his Merrill Lynch CMA account. Mr. Jorge Herrera ("Herrera"), Bernachea's long-time banker, testified that he related the details of the transaction in Spanish and that Bernachea, a former practicing attorney, never stated that he did not understand the legal significance of a joint tenancy with a right of survivorship during the transaction.

As a joint owner of the account, Varela received a Visa check card for the account, which she freely used. Herrera and his assistant Ms. Zoraida Rosa ("Rosa") both testified below that they never received any instruction to restrict Varela's access to the account—be it via check or check card.

Bernachea took the position below that Varela's access to the Merrill Lynch account was restricted. Specifically, Bernachea testified that the parties maintained a separate joint account with Southtrust because Varela had check writing privileges for the Southtrust account, but lacked such privileges for the CMA account. Varela, on the other hand, testified that she and Bernachea maintained the separate Southtrust account because a Southtrust branch was conveniently located near their condominium, and they accessed the Southtrust account more frequently, largely to pay bills. Thus, the uncontested testimony established that Varela had the ability to access the CMA funds. Bernachea's testimony reflects his confusion, regarding whether Varela could only access the CMA account via her Visa check card, or could additionally access the account via conventional paper check. It was undisputed, however, that the CMA and Southtrust accounts were joint accounts and that the account funds were supplied by Bernachea.

On October 18, 2002, Bernachea suffered a heart attack in his Sunny Isles condominium. Varela called 911 and accompanied Bernachea to the hospital. While Bernachea was hospitalized, Varela stayed with him until Bernachea's daughters arrived from Argentina and barred Varela from both Bernachea's hospital room and his Sunny Isles condominium. Varela willingly vacated the apartment. On October 25, 2002, Varela visited the Merrill Lynch branch on Brickell Avenue. Once there, Varela wrote a $280,000.00 check on the CMA account and deposited it in her own name in a newly opened Merrill Lynch personal account.

A Brickell branch account executive, Mr. Daniel Diaz ("Diaz"), called the Coral Gables Merrill Lynch branch to ensure that Varela was authorized to write such a check. Diaz spoke with Herrera, who confirmed that Varela was the joint CMA owner and had the ability to write a check up to the account balance. Nevertheless, two weeks after his release from the hospital Bernachea demanded that Merrill Lynch return the $280,000.00. Merrill Lynch complied and transferred the $280,000.00 into the CMA account. Varela contested this transfer, but Merrill Lynch would not return the funds.

Bernachea subsequently sued Varela and Merrill Lynch to settle the ownership status of the CMA account. The Circuit Court entered Final Judgment for Bernachea. The court reasoned that Bernachea was the sole CMA account owner because he lacked donative intent when he added Varela as a joint account owner. Varela appeals from the Final Judgment. We reverse.

Discussion

The pertinent facts below were largely uncontested; it is the trial court's application of the factual determinations to the question of whether Bernachea overcame the presumption of a gift that is in dispute on appeal. Accordingly, this Court's review, and application of the facts to the law, is de novo.

When a joint bank account is established with the funds of one person, a gift of the funds is presumed. This presumption may be rebutted only by clear and convincing evidence to the contrary. In the instant case, the trial court erroneously found, in the absence of clear and convincing evidence, that Bernachea rebutted Varela's gift presumption.

The trial court premised its finding on Bernachea's claim that he lacked donative intent. The only evidence in support of this claim was Bernachea's own dubious testimony, claiming he misapprehended the significance of a joint tenancy, and only intended for Varela to possess "restricted" account access. However, Herrera, who the court found was a credible witness, testified that he specifically explained the details of a joint tenancy with a right of survivorship in Spanish without any questions from Bernachea, a former attorney. Thus, the court's finding that "[Bernachea] did not understand the significance of the 'joint tenancy with right of survivorship' in the English form" is inconsistent with the facts and testimony that same court found credible. Moreover, Bernachea admitted that, per his wishes, Varela had the ability to make check card purchases and write checks on the CMA account to the account balance.

Clearly, Bernachea did not rebut Varela's gift presumption when he openly admitted that he gave Varela access to their joint account via check card. Contrary to Bernachea's attempt to define a distinction, there is no principled distinction between paper checks and check cards. In fact, the check card's raison d'être is its status as a convenient replacement for paper checks. This modern reality conflicts with the trial court's holding that unfettered account access via check card, represents "restricted status." Moreover, in direct contrast to the court's conclusion, Herrera and Rosa testified that Varela's account access was never restricted. Additionally, both Merrill Lynch branches approved Varela's $280,000.00 check because she was a joint account owner with the ability to write checks up to the account balance.

The Record does not support the trial court's finding, as a matter of law, that Bernachea demonstrated an absence of donative intent. Moreover,

Bernachea failed to rebut the presumption that he intended to give Varela an equal interest in their joint bank account. Accordingly, we reverse the Final Judgment and remand with instructions to enter judgment for Varela, awarding her a one-half interest in the October 25, 2002, CMA account balance.

NOTES

1.   While *Anna National Bank* allows a family member to challenge a clear designation that an account was simply a convenience account even though it was titled a "joint tenancy," it is a mistake to have confidence that this type of challenge will succeed. Someone challenging a joint tenancy designation is swimming against the tide.

2.   What if there is an unambiguous designation that a family friend is added as a joint tenant on a bank account? Is it possible for a remainder beneficiary of a will to challenge that designation? In *Hartlove v. Md. School For Blind*, 681 A.2d 584 (Md. 1994), a charitable remainder beneficiary claimed that the account styled a "joint tenancy" was actually intended as a drawer account. The charity, the remainder beneficiary, claimed there was a breach of a fiduciary duty, as well. All of those claims were unsuccessful and the account passed to the joint tenant.

3.   What if a joint tenant—who is thus entitled to make withdrawals from an account—later is given a durable power of attorney by the joint tenant? Can the attorney-in-fact make withdrawals from the joint tenancy account? In *Schwartz v. Russ*, 734 N.W.2d 874 (Wis. 2007) a joint tenant who later obtained a POA was found to have improperly siphoned money off from a joint account.

4.   What happens to a joint tenancy when a married couple divorces? In many states, divorce severs the joint tenancy, creating a tenancy in common. *See* UPC § 2–804(b)(2). You might have noticed that § 2–804 (b) also revokes payable on death contracts on divorce, *but* that the statute has an exception "as provided by the express terms of a governing instrument." This exception is important because a lot of payable on death contracts, like insurance policies, contain an express provision that the financial institution will pay the beneficiary listed in their files. That is, divorce will *not* revoke the beneficiary designation unless there is an affirmative notification to the financial institution or insurance company. Sometimes this requirement becomes a problem for testators who try to change their beneficiary designation via will; and it also poses a problem for individuals who mistakenly believe that their beneficiary designation is revoked upon divorce.

ASSESSMENT

You are in-house counsel for a local bank and have been asked to create instructions for account owners who are seeking to open joint accounts. Make a list of the questions that you plan to include.

2. Payable on Death (POD) Accounts

One of the most common—and also easiest—probate avoidance devices is the **payable on death (POD) account**. The owner of the account designates who should receive the balance of the account upon the owner's death. Typically financial institutions have a form to designate beneficiaries that they want account owners to use. The financial institution will also have a form for the beneficiary to claim the proceeds. The beneficiary must also submit a certificate copy of the owner's death certificate.

3. Transfer on Death (TOD) Accounts

The **transfer on death (TOD) account** is another example of will substitute and is similar to a POD account. TOD accounts are often used to hold securities. The account owner has the ability to designate an individual or a group of individuals who will be entitled to receive the proceeds remaining in the account upon the owner's death. The owner must typically follow the procedure required by the financial institution to change the beneficiary designation. The beneficiaries will then follow the financial institution's procedure to claim the procedures. This, as with many will substitutes, requires the completion of paperwork and supply of a certificate death certificate.

Recall that for a beneficiary to take under a TOD or POD account, the beneficiary must survive the account owner. In Chapter 8, we discussed in the context of wills "antilapse" provisions that allow issue of a deceased beneficiary to stand in the shoes of that beneficiary *if* the decedent and the beneficiary are closely related (for example, in the case of the UPC, the beneficiary is descended from the decedent's grandparents). A will or trust can, of course, expand that rule.

In the Appendix, you can find an example of a beneficiary designation form for a TOD account with a leading financial services provider. The form has spaces for listing up to four beneficiaries and stating the percentage that each beneficiary should receive. Each beneficiary can be designated in one of four categories—"spouse, non-spouse, trust, or other entity." Observe that the beneficiary form gives these instructions:

For each beneficiary you list by name, check a beneficiary type and provide all information. A "non-spouse" is any individual who is not your spouse under federal law. As an alternative to listing each child by name, you can check "Non-Spouse" and enter "All my children" in the Name box. If you outlive the beneficiary and you want that beneficiary's share to go to his or her descendants, check "per stirpes."

Note that the form also has a space for allowing issue of any beneficiary who predeceases the account owner to take, regardless of that beneficiary's relationship to the account holder. The account owner can choose this option by checking the box listed as "per stirpes." If an account owner checks the "per stirpes" box, the issue of *any* beneficiary will take the beneficiary's share if the beneficiary predeceases the account owner. The form also provides a space for designation of "contingent beneficiaries" if all of the primary beneficiaries die before the account owner *and* either there was no "per stirpes" designation or there is no surviving issue of the primary beneficiaries.

ASSESSMENTS

1. Locate a beneficiary designation form or use the one in the Appendix. Complete the form based upon the following information. The account owner named Mel wishes to name the account owner's spouse named Raj. Mel married Raj after the death of Mel's first spouse Orion. Mel also wishes to designate Mel's child name Leigh, whose parents are Mel and Orion. Mel would like Raj and Leigh to split the account proceeds equally. Complete the form. Consider what to do to anticipate that either or both of these beneficiaries may predecease Mel. Also, consider whether Leigh's share may pass to Leigh's descendants if Leigh predeceases Mel.

2. Assume that you are working for a company and asked to review a completed beneficiary designation. The account owner named Neal listed his parent Reese as the primary beneficiary and his only sibling Ellis as a contingent beneficiary. The form provides a box labeled "per stirpes," which Neal checks. Neal's parent and sibling predecease Neal. Ellis left a valid will devising Ellis' entire estate to Ellis' spouse. Ellis' only child, who was born after the beneficiary designation form was completed, survives Neal. You are asked to determine how the $200,000 in the account should be distributed. Who receives the account proceeds? Explain your reasoning.

E. Revocable Trusts

As you know from the previous chapters, trusts can be created in various ways and serve various purposes. Trusts may arise from within the will (i.e., testamentary trusts). Trusts may also be stand-alone entities that the settlor funds during the settlor's lifetime. Trusts can facilitate ongoing management of property, segregate assets, and provide resources for beneficiaries. Another purpose for trusts is to avoid probate. People often use a specific type of trust, the **revocable trust**, to avoid probate but also to coordinate all the components of an estate plan.

Trusts, as you learned in Chapter 9, have been used for decades as devices to circumvent the process of probate. The idea is as follows. An owner of property transfers probate property into a trust. The settlor titles property in the trust. The settlor typically retains the right to control the property during the settlor's life and also retains the power to revoke the trust during the settlor's life. If, however, the settlor dies without revoking the trust, then the trust becomes irrevocable on the settlor's death, and the trust property (i.e., corpus) will be distributed according to the trust terms. The virtue of such revocable trusts, sometimes referred as "living trusts" or "revocable lifetime trusts," is that the revocable trusts allow the settlor to maintain maximum control over the property but also avoid probate. This kind of trust is, as we will discuss in detail below, a will substitute since it is an ambulatory document until the settlor's death and then, at death, functions much like a will by distributing assets outright or holding them in continued (now irrevocable) trusts.

Individuals may wish to avoid probate for a number of reasons. As discussed below, individuals may be worry that the time a court proceeding may take results in a delay in providing resources for their loved ones. An individual may worry that proceedings will be expensive and erode the value of property to be transferred to loved ones. Norman Dacey, who popularized revocable trusts as a strategy avoid probate, tapped into both of those fears.

> **Connection Note:** Many legal changes occurred because of the many popular movements in the 1960s. Remember, the first version of the Uniform Probate Code was promulgated in 1969.

Norman Dacey's 1965 book *How to Avoid Probate* scared readers with tales of an expensive, time-consuming probate process. Dacey then provided a series of pre-printed forms for consumers to fill out to put knowledge and techniques into the hands of non-lawyers. His book has forms for wills, deeds for titling real property in a trust, and of course revocable trusts to hold both real and personal property. Dacey called the revocable trust "that legal 'wonder drug.' " For the individual who changed his or her mind, the book also provided forms for revocation of trusts. At the back of *How to Avoid Probate*, the publisher, Crown Books, offered to sell other forms for a modest fee.

Dacey's book led to the popularity of revocable trusts, especially for transferring title to real property, and maybe especially for those who held real property in multiple jurisdictions. It is entirely possible that this book over-sold trusts, which can have their own substantial costs in administration.

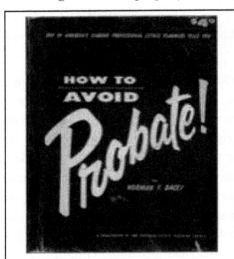

Norman Dacey's publication did much to change both nonprobate succession and probate succession.

Dacey's first-to-consumer marketing raised concerns. The trusts and estates bar reacted quite negatively to Dacey and to his ideas. A review in the Valparaiso Law Review in 1966, for instance, concluded that "the indiscriminate use of vehicle by lay [people] without professional advice will lead ultimately to heartbreak and additional costs for many families. It will take decades to measure the damage this book has done to the public, but, even then, there will be no adequate way to measure it." Delmar R. Hoeppner, *Book Review*, 1 VALPARAISO UNIV. L. REV. 197, 200 (1966). Dacey was not a lawyer; he was a financial planner based in Bridgeport, Connecticut. Dacey was successfully charged with the unlicensed practice of law in Connecticut. Dacey prevailed in a lawsuit in New York charging him with unauthorized practice of law. *New York County Lawyers' Ass'n v. Dacey*, 234 N.E.2d 459 (N.Y. 1967). That unsuccessful charge of unauthorized practice of law led to an unsuccessful suit by Dacey against the bar association. *See Norman F. Dacey and Norman F. Dacey, Doing Business As National Estate Planning Council v. New York County Lawyers' Association*, 423 F.2d 188 (2d Cir. 1970).

Dacey's book is now out of print (its most recent edition came out in 1992), and the author himself died in 1994. Its theme, however, lives on with books aimed at consumers bearing titles like GORDON MEAD BENNETT, HOW TO AVOID PROBATE BY CREATING A LIVING TRUST: A SIMPLE YET COMPLETE GUIDE (2007), and a host of computer programs, such as Quicken's Will Maker (which also creates revocable trusts). Meanwhile, a whole counter-literature has questioned the virtues of trusts. One of the more dramatic was John Huggard's 1998 book entitled LIVING TRUST, LIVING HELL in which Huggard detailed problems with living trusts, including that lay people often improperly execute them, leading to problems (like no provision for substitute fiduciaries) that land the parties in court.

As with all estate planning strategies, the strategies should be customized for the individual. One strategy does not work for everyone.

The revocable trust is both a popular and powerful will substitute. That is, at least in part, because the revocable trust is the only will substitute that could perform all the functions associated with a will. In fact, the UTC treats a revocable trust as the "functional equivalent of a will," UTC, article 6, general comments, and requires the settlor to have the same capacity as a testator. UTC § 601. It provides a general rule that unless a trust is explicitly made irrevocable that the trust is revocable. UTC § 602. The UTC also makes clear that while the trust is revocable, the settlor has complete control over it—and the trustee owes duties only to the settlor. UTC § 603(a).

While revocable trusts are a convenient way to avoid probate, they are not a good way to avoid creditors (or taxes). That's because although the assets are held in trust, the fact that the trust is revocable means that they are still functionally owned by the settlor, even at death, as the following case, *State Street Bank v. Reiser*, demonstrates. As you read the case, pay attention to how the court discusses general powers of appointment.

State Street Bank and Trust Company v. Reiser

389 N.E.2d 768 (Mass. App. Ct. 1979)

KASS, J.

State Street Bank and Trust Company (the bank) seeks to reach the assets of an inter vivos trust in order to pay a debt to the bank owed by the estate of the settlor of the trust. We conclude that the bank can do so.

Wilfred A. Dunnebier created an inter vivos trust on September 30, 1971, with power to amend or revoke the trust and the right during his lifetime to direct the disposition of principal and income. He conveyed to the trust the capital stock of five closely held corporations. Immediately following execution of this trust, Dunnebier executed a will under which he left his residuary estate to the trust he had established.

About thirteen months later Dunnebier applied to the bank for a $75,000 working capital loan. A bank officer met with Dunnebier, examined a financial statement furnished by him and visited several single-family home subdivisions which Dunnebier, or corporations he controlled, had built or were in the process of building. During their conversations, Dunnebier told the bank officer that he had controlling interests in the corporations which owned the most significant assets appearing on the financial statement. On the basis of what he saw of Dunnebier's work, recommendations from another bank, Dunnebier's borrowing history with the bank, and the general cut of Dunnebier's jib, the bank officer decided to make an unsecured loan to Dunnebier for the $75,000 he had asked for. To evidence this loan, Dunnebier, on November 1, 1972, signed a personal demand note to the order of the bank. The probate judge found that Dunnebier did not intend to defraud the bank or misrepresent his financial position by failing to call attention to the fact that he had placed the stock of his corporations in the trust.

Approximately four months after he borrowed this money Dunnebier died in an accident. His estate has insufficient assets to pay the entire indebtedness due the bank.

During the lifetime of the settlor, to be sure, the bank would have had access to the assets of the trust. When a person creates for his own benefit a trust for support or a discretionary trust, his creditors can reach the maximum amount which the trustee, under the terms of the trust, could pay to him or apply for his benefit. This is so even if the trust contains spendthrift provisions.

Under the terms of Dunnebier's trust, all the income and principal were at his disposal while he lived.

We then face the question whether Dunnebier's death broke the vital chain. His powers to amend or revoke the trust, or to direct payments from it, obviously died with him, and the remainder interests of the beneficiaries of the trust became vested. The contingencies which might defeat those remainder interests could no longer occur. In one jurisdiction, at least, it has been held that when the settlor of a revocable living trust dies, the property is no longer subject to his debts.

There has developed, however, another thread of decisions which takes cognizance of, and gives effect to, the power which a person exercises in life over property. When a person has a general power of appointment, exercisable by will or by deed, and exercises that power, any property so appointed is, in equity, considered part of his assets and becomes available to his creditors in preference to the claims of his voluntary appointees or legatees. These decisions rest on the theory that as to property which a person could appoint to himself or his executors, the property could have been devoted to the payment of debts and, therefore, creditors have an equitable right to reach that property. It taxes the imagination to invent reasons why the same analysis and policy should not apply to trust property over which the settlor retains dominion at least as great as a power of appointment. The *Restatement of Property* has, in fact, translated the doctrine applicable to powers of appointment to trusts: "When a person transfers property in trust for himself for life and reserves a general power to appoint the remainder and creates no other beneficial interests which he cannot destroy by exercising the power, the property, though the power is unexercised, can be subjected to the payment of the claims of creditors of such person and claims against his estate to whatever extent other available property is insufficient for that purpose." *Restatement of Property* § 328 (1940).

As an estate planning vehicle, the inter vivos trust has become common currency. Frequently, as Dunnebier did in the instant case, the settlor retains all the substantial incidents of ownership because access to the trust property is necessary or desirable as a matter of sound financial planning. Psychologically, the settlor thinks of the trust property as "his," as Dunnebier did when he took the bank's officer to visit the real estate owned by the corporation whose stock he had put in trust. In other circumstances, persons place property in trust in order to obtain expert management of their assets, while retaining the power to invade principal and to amend and revoke the trust. It is excessive obeisance to the form in which property is held to prevent creditors from reaching property placed in trust under such terms.

This view was adopted in *United States* v. *Ritter,* 558 F.2d 1165, 1167 (4th Cir.1977). In a concurring opinion in that case Judge Widener observed that it violates public policy for an individual to have an estate to live on, but not an estate to pay his debts with. *Id.* at 1168. The Internal Revenue Code institutionalizes the concept that a settlor of a trust who retains administrative powers, power to revoke or power to control beneficial enjoyment "owns" that trust property and provides that it shall be included in the settlor's personal estate. I.R.C. §§ 2038 and 2041.

We hold, therefore, that where a person places property in trust and reserves the right to amend and revoke, or to direct disposition of principal and income, the settlor's creditors may, following the death of the settlor, reach in satisfaction of the settlor's debts to them, to the extent not satisfied by the settlor's estate, those assets owned by the trust over which the settlor had such control at the time of his death as would have enabled the settlor to use the trust assets for his own benefit. Assets which pour over into such a trust as a consequence of the settlor's death or after the settlor's death, over which the settlor did not have control during his life, are not subject to the reach of creditors since, as to those assets, the equitable principles do not apply which place assets subject to creditors' disposal.

The judgment is reversed, and a new judgment is to enter declaring that the assets owned by the trust (Wilfred A. Dunnebier Trust, I) up to the time of Dunnebier's death can be reached and applied in satisfaction of a judgment entered in favor of the plaintiff against the estate of Dunnebier, to the extent assets of the estate are insufficient to satisfy such a judgment.

NOTES

1.   *Reiser* illustrates a problem that revocable trusts may pose for creditors of a decedent. If the decedent died owning the property, it would pass through probate and be subject to creditors' claims. But when property passes through a revocable trust, it is not listed as probate property, and creditors have a harder time chasing after the property. They have to sue the trustee, as was done in this case. On the positive side for creditors, however, because the property has not passed through probate, it is not subject to the typically short period during which creditors can make a claim against the estate.

2.   In Chapter 11, we explore issues of creditors' claims on property in irrevocable trusts, especially the difficulty that creditors have in reaching property that is in a spendthrift trust, and some of the differences that courts and legislatures draw between government and private creditors. A typical creditor is the surviving spouse pursuing a claim for the elective share. Would a surviving spouse have been able to reach the assets in Dunnebier's estate in order to satisfy the elective share claim? Why or why not? We will take up this question in Chapter 14.

3.   Because will substitutes do the functional equivalent of a will, that is, transfer property upon a property owner's death, initial thinking was the will substitutes should be executed in accordance with the wills act formalities. In other words, if will substitutes were going to function as testamentary instruments, the creation and revocation of will substitutes should comply with the requirements applicable to testamentary instruments. That view has not prevailed. Will substitutes are recognized as deeds, contracts, multi-party accounts, and trusts. Each has its own form and, consequently, its own formalities. Even though the formalities of will execution and revocation do not need apply to will substitutes, concern is raised that the protections that are connected with the wills act formalities may be lost. To change a will, for example, one of the proper methods of revocation must be used. To change a beneficiary designation of a million-dollar life insurance policy, an online form needs to be completed. While the wills act formalities may have the unintentional side effect of limiting access to will-making, the four functions of the formalities are thought to further careful decision-making that reflects the individual's testamentary intent. Concerns arise about who is actually completing the forms, who has authorized changes to the forms, and under what circumstances the forms, which are legal instruments are created. The formalities of each of these devices may provide limited, if any, protection if those forms are completed outside of the supervision of an intendent third party or completed via computer. Each will substitute does have its own form and formalities. Those often involved a third-party financial institution, though not always.

4.   No one can deny that will substitutes have revolutionized succession. Their development and use have also influenced a wide variety of succession issues. For instance, the relaxing of will formalities rules and the appeal of the harmless error rule may, at least in part, be influenced by the lack of such required formalities for will substitutes. In what other way may the rise of will substitutes influence the creation, interpretation, or implementation of wills?

5.   Another consideration to the creation of will substitutes is the requisite mental capacity. Typically, the level of capacity required to create contracts, for example, is higher than the level of capacity required to create a will. Should different mental capacity standards apply to different types of estate planning documents?

ASSESSMENTS

1.   You have been invited to present at an upcoming continuing legal education seminar. This seminar is specifically targeted for newly licensed attorneys and attorneys who have limited experience with estate planning. You have been asked to present a session titled "Revocable Trusts 101." You will be preparing a presentation (such as PowerPoint, Prezi, or Google Slides) and an accompanying handout. The content of the presentation and the handout should include the following:

- Define the revocable trust

- Identify the form and formalities

- Describe the role of the revocable trust in estate planning

- Contrast the revocable trust with both the will and other common will substitutes

- Outline the consequences to the creation of a revocable trust

2.   An examination of succession would be incomplete without an understanding of will substitutes. Will substitutes are varied and have evolved over time. To pull together your thoughts about the common forms of will substitutes, respond to the following prompts:

a.   In 100 words or less, describe the defining characteristics of will substitutes.

b.   In 200 words or less, explain what a non-lawyer needs to understand about will substitutes and their role in succession.

3.   In what way do will substitutes empower an individual to plan his or her estate? In what way does the proliferation of will substitutes create hurdles or problems?

F. Coordinating Wills and Will Substitutes, Including Applying Subsidiary Law of Wills

The subsidiary law of wills refers to the substantive-based restrictions on testamentary freedom and the rules of construction. Because these rules were housed within state probate codes, questions immediately arose as to whether these rules could be extended to will substitutes. For instance, should the slayer statute apply to the beneficiary designation of a retirement account? Does the antilapse statute apply to the beneficiary designation of a life insurance contract? As discussed above, issues of the revocation-upon-divorce statutes and

> **Language Note:** To what extent does the term "will substitute" create problems with creating, revoking, interpreting, and implementing these legal devices? Consider how a similar tension appears in the classifications of a "mortgage" and a "mortgage substitute."

creditors rights are encompassed within these concerns too. Initially, courts resolved these issues, but today many state statutes have been updated to reflect the extension of subsidiary rules to will substitutes. For example, the UPC specifically outlines which rules of construction are applicable only to wills, UPC §§ 2–601—2–609, and which ones apply to both wills and will substitutes, UPC §§ 2–701—2–711.

The *Clymer v. Mayo* case discusses a revocation-on-divorce statute's application to property held in a revocable trust. This case also shows how estate plans, including the various will substitutes, can be coordinated through careful estate planning. Because individuals create multiple will substitutes at different points during their lifetimes, issues arise about fragmentation and the lack of coordination between and among the various legal devices that transfer property upon the property owner's death. As an individual's circumstances change, the individual may remember to update a will but forget to update one or more of the will substitutes. An individual may create a will that actually transfers only a limited amount of property because the majority of the individual's property is held in one or more will substitutes. An individual may attempt to change beneficiary designations through improper means, such as executing a will. Will substitutes reflect the type of property owned and expand estate planning, but it's still important to create a unified plan.

A property owner can review beneficiary designation forms to ensure that the forms are updated and reflect a consistent choice about who or what should receive the individual's property. Another way in which an estate plan can be coordinated is with the use of pour-over wills and revocable trusts. As discussed briefly in Chapter 9, this plan is sometimes referred to as a **pour-over trust** or **pour-over plan**, deriving its name from the way the trust is funded: the will, or more specifically the residuary clause of the will, "pours over" or funnels all probate assets from the will into the trust. The term **pour over will** refers not to a form of will, such as an attested will or a holographic will, but rather to a type of provision included in the will. The following is an example:

> I give the remainder of my estate to [insert name of the Trustee], as the Trustee under the trust agreement dated [insert date] in which I am the Settlor. I direct that the remainder of my estate be added to and commingled with the trust property.

This provision adds the residue of the decedent's probate estate to the trust. The trust may not have any funds before the will is admitted to probate. This sequencing of events provides what many consider a key virtue of a "pour over" trust. The trust is funded only when it is necessary. For a great many testators, there is no need to have a trust while they are alive. But if people are worried about passing away with minor children, they may want to transfer their property to a living trust, rather than being subject to probate, which can be a cumbersome (and maybe expensive) process.

In addition, the revocable trust can receive nonprobate property if the property owner has designated the revocable trust as the beneficiary on the appropriate beneficiary forms. You may recall, for example, that the TOD beneficiary form in the Appendix lists four potential categories of beneficiaries, one being a trust. The revocable trust is the legal device that ultimately holds all of the individual's property—both probate property and nonprobate property. The terms of the revocable trust will govern the distribution of all of the decedent's property—both probate and nonprobate. As a result, the revocable trust becomes a receptacle to unify an estate plan.[2]

---

[2]   UPC § 2–511, Uniform Testamentary Additions to Trusts Act (1991), specifically validates trusts that are funded solely at death. It provides:

(a) A will may validly devise property to the trustee of a trust established or to be established (i) during the testator's lifetime by the testator, by the testator and some other person, or by some other person, including a funded or unfunded life insurance trust, although the settlor has reserved any or all rights of ownership of the insurance contracts, or (ii) at the testator's death by the testator's devise to the trustee, if the trust is identified in the testator's will and its terms are set forth in a written instrument, other than a will, executed before, concurrently with, or after the execution of the testator's will or in another individual's will if that other individual has predeceased the testator, regardless of the existence, size, or character of the corpus of the trust. The devise is not invalid because the trust is amendable or revocable, or because the trust was amended after the execution of the will or the testator's death.

Courts are increasingly willing to deal with trusts as though they are part of a unified estate plan. We see this approach in the next case, where a decedent left a will that poured over into a trust. The trust named her ex-husband as a beneficiary. In Massachusetts, as in most states, a provision in a will leaving property to a spouse is revoked upon divorce. But Massachusetts at the time did not address what happened upon divorce to a trust that left property to spouse. The *Clymer* case resolved this issue by treating the trust as though it was part of the will. Now many statutes, including the UPC, address this issue; UPC § 2–804(b)(1)(A) revokes beneficiary designations in favor of divorced spouses in wills and nonprobate transfers if they are revocable at the time of divorce.

Clymer v. Mayo

473 N.E.2d 1084 (Mass. 1985)

HENNESSEY, J.

This consolidated appeal arises out of the administration of the estate of Clara A. Mayo (decedent). We summarize the findings of the judge of the Probate and Family Court incorporating the parties' agreed statement of uncontested facts.

At the time of her death in November, 1981, the decedent, then fifty years of age, was employed by Boston University as a professor of psychology. She was married to James P. Mayo, Jr. (Mayo), from 1953 to 1978. The couple had no children. The decedent was an only child and her sole heirs at law are her parents, Joseph A. and Maria Weiss.

In 1963, the decedent executed a will designating Mayo as principal beneficiary. In 1964, she named Mayo as the beneficiary of her group annuity contract with John Hancock Mutual Life Insurance Company; and in 1965, made him the beneficiary of her Boston University retirement annuity contracts with Teachers Insurance and Annuity Association (TIAA) and College Retirement Equities Fund (CREF). As a consequence of a $300,000 gift to the couple from the Weisses in 1971, the decedent and Mayo executed new wills and indentures of trust on February 2, 1973, wherein each spouse was made the

---

(b)   Unless the testator's will provides otherwise, property devised to a trust described in subsection (a) is not held under a testamentary trust of the testator, but it becomes a part of the trust to which it is devised, and must be administered and disposed of in accordance with the provisions of the governing instrument setting forth the terms of the trust, including any amendments thereto made before or after the testator's death.

(c)   Unless the testator's will provides otherwise, a revocation or termination of the trust before the testator's death causes the devise to lapse.

other's principal beneficiary. Under the terms of the decedent's will, Mayo was to receive her personal property. The residue of her estate was to "pour over" into the inter vivos trust she created that same day.

The decedent's trust instrument named herself and John P. Hill as trustees. As the donor, the decedent retained the right to amend or revoke the trust at any time by written instrument delivered to the trustees. In the event that Mayo survived the decedent, the trust estate was to be divided into two parts. Trust A, the marital deduction trust, was to be funded with an amount "equal to fifty (50%) per cent of the value of the Donor's adjusted gross estate, for the purpose of the United States Tax Law, less an amount equal to the value of all interest in property, if any, allowable as 'marital deductions' for the purposes of such law. Mayo was the income beneficiary of Trust A and was entitled to reach the principal at his request or in the trustee's discretion. The trust instrument also gave Mayo a general power of appointment over the assets in Trust A.

The balance of the decedent's estate, excluding personal property passing to Mayo by will, or the entire estate if Mayo did not survive her, composed Trust B. Trust B provided for the payment of five initial specific bequests totaling $45,000. After those gifts were satisfied, the remaining trust assets were to be held for the benefit of Mayo for life. Upon Mayo's death, the assets in Trust B were to be held for "the benefit of the nephews and nieces of the Donor" living at the time of her death. The trustee was given discretion to spend so much of the income and principal as necessary for their comfort, support, and education. When all of these nephews and nieces reached the age of thirty, the trust was to terminate and its remaining assets were to be divided equally between Clark University and Boston University to assist in graduate education of women.

On the same day she established her trust, the decedent changed the beneficiary of her Boston University group life insurance policy from Mayo to the trustees. One month later, in March, 1973, she also executed a change in her retirement annuity contracts to designate the trustees as beneficiaries. At the time of its creation in 1973, the trust was not funded. Its future assets were to consist solely of the proceeds of these policies and the property which would pour over under the will's residuary clause. The judge found that the remaining trustee has never received any property or held any funds subsequent to the execution of the trust nor has he paid any trust taxes or filed any trust tax returns.

Mayo moved out of the marital home in 1975. In June, 1977, the decedent changed the designation of beneficiary on her Boston University life insurance policy for a second time, substituting Marianne LaFrance for the trustees. LaFrance had lived with the Mayos since 1972, and shared a close friendship with the decedent up until her death. Mayo filed for divorce on September 9, 1977, in New Hampshire. The divorce was decreed on January 3, 1978, and the court incorporated into the decree a permanent stipulation of the parties' property settlement. Under the terms of that settlement, Mayo waived any "right, title or interest" in the decedent's "securities, savings accounts, savings certificates, and retirement fund," as well as her "furniture, furnishings and art." Mayo remarried on August 28, 1978, and later executed a new will in favor of his new wife. The decedent died on November 21, 1981. Her will was allowed on November 18, 1982, and the court appointed John H. Clymer as administrator with the will annexed.

What is primarily at issue in these actions is the effect of the Mayos' divorce upon dispositions provided in the decedent's will and indenture of trust. In the first action, the court-appointed administrator of the decedent's estate petitioned for instructions with respect to the impact of the divorce on the estate's administration. The second case involved a complaint for declaratory and equitable relief filed by the Weisses. The Weisses sought a declaration that the divorce revoked all gifts to Mayo set forth in the will and indenture of trust, including the power of appointment conferred upon Mayo under the trust.

Mayo's Interest in Trust B.

The judge's decision to uphold Mayo's beneficial interest in Trust B was appealed by the Weisses, as well as by Boston University and Clark University. The judge reasoned that the decedent intended to create a life interest in Mayo when she established Trust B and failed either to revoke or to amend the trust after the couple's divorce. The appellants argue that we should extend the reach of G.L.c. 191, § 9, to revoke all Mayo's interests under the trust. General Laws c. 191, § 9 provides in relevant part:

> "If, after executing a will, the testator shall be divorced or his marriage shall be annulled, the divorce or annulment shall revoke any disposition or appointment of property made by the will to the former spouse, any provision conferring a general or special power of appointment on the former spouse, and any nomination of the former spouse, as executor, trustee, conservator or guardian, unless the will shall expressly provide otherwise. Property prevented from passing to a former spouse because of a revocation by divorce shall pass as if a former spouse had failed to survive the decedent, and other provisions conferring a power of office on the former spouse shall be interpreted as if the spouse had failed to survive the decedent."

The judge ruled that Mayo's interest in Trust B is unaffected by G.L.c. 191, § 9, because his interest in that trust is not derived from a "disposition . . . made by the will" but rather from the execution of an inter vivos trust with independent legal significance. We disagree, but in fairness we add that the judge here confronted a question of first impression in this Commonwealth.

General Laws c. 191, § 9, was amended by the Legislature in 1976 to provide in the event of divorce for the revocation of testamentary dispositions which benefit the testator's former spouse. St. 1976, c. 515, § 6. The statute automatically causes such revocations unless the testator expresses a contrary intent. In this case we must determine what effect, if any, G.L.c. 191, § 9, has on the former spouse's interest in the testator's pour-over trust.

The trust had no practical significance until the decedent's death in 1981. The decedent executed both her will and indenture of trust on February 2, 1973. She transferred no property or funds to the trust at that time. The trust was to receive its funding at the decedent's death, in part through her life insurance policy and retirement benefits, and in part through a pour-over from the will's residuary clause. Mayo, the proposed executor and sole legatee under the will, was also made the primary beneficiary of the trust with power, as to Trust A only, to reach both income and principal.

During her lifetime, the decedent retained power to amend or revoke the trust. Since the trust was unfunded, her cotrustee was subject to no duties or obligations until her death. Similarly, it was only as a result of the decedent's death that Mayo could claim any right to the trust assets. It is evident from the time and manner in which the trust was created and funded, that the decedent's will and trust were integrally related components of a single testamentary scheme. For all practical purposes the trust, like the will, "spoke" only at the decedent's death. For this reason Mayo's interest in the trust was revoked by operation of G.L.c. 191, § 9, at the same time his interest under the decedent's will was revoked.

It has reasonably been contended that in enacting G.L.c. 191, § 9, the Legislature "intended to bring the law into line with the expectations of most people. Divorce usually represents a stormy parting, where the last thing one of the parties wishes is to have an earlier will carried out giving everything to the former spouse." Young, *Probate Reform*, 18 B.B.J. 7, 11 (1974). To carry out the testator's implied intent, the law revokes "any disposition or appointment of property made by the will to the former spouse." It is indisputable that if the decedent's trust was either testamentary or incorporated by reference into her will, Mayo's beneficial interest in the trust would be revoked by operation of the statute. However, the judge stopped short of mandating the same result in this case because here the trust had "independent significance." While correct, this characterization of the trust does not end our analysis. For example, in *Sullivan* v. *Burkin*, 390 Mass. 864, 867 (1984), we ruled prospectively that the assets of a revocable trust will be considered part of the "estate of the decedent" in determining the surviving spouse's statutory share.

Treating the components of the decedent's estate plan separately, and not as parts of an interrelated whole, brings about inconsistent results. Applying c. 191, § 9, the judge correctly revoked the will provisions benefiting Mayo. As a result, the decedent's personal property—originally left to Mayo—fell into the will's residuary clause and passed to the trust. The judge then appropriately terminated Trust A for impossibility of purpose thereby denying Mayo his beneficial interest under Trust A. Yet, by upholding Mayo's interest under Trust B, the judge returned to Mayo a life interest in the same assets that composed the corpus of Trust A—both property passing by way of the decedent's will and the proceeds of her TIAA/CREF annuity contracts.

Restricting our holding to the particular facts of this case—specifically the existence of a revocable pour-over trust funded entirely at the time of the decedent's death—we conclude that G.L.c. 191, § 9, revokes Mayo's interest under Trust B.

So ordered.

ASSESSMENTS

1.   Review the client intake questionnaire in the Appendix. Identify and evaluate the questions/prompts that relate to will substitutes. What additional questions or prompts would you recommend including in the client intake questionnaire?

2.   Your law firm has re-evaluated how it handles the closing of client representations. As part of the content and enclosures related to the new disengagement letter, the assigning partner wants you to develop a table of contents for the suggested "estate planning binder." The estate planning binder will be a recommended mechanism for clients to collect and safeguard all estate planning documents and related materials. The binder would include the documents prepared by the firm, but the binder would also include other estate planning materials the client has already created, an itemization of property interests, and list of client advisors. Using the information covered in this

chapter and previous chapters, create a sample table of contents for such a binder.

G. Conclusion and Takeaways

Will substitutes have widespread acceptance. New will substitutes have developed, and even more new will substitutes may be developed in the future. Decedents are likely to have a variety of will substitutes that were created at different points in time. The types of will substitutes may take different forms, but they aim to achieve similar purposes as wills: transfer of property on death of the owner. The impact that will substitutes have had on succession cannot be overstated. How these property interests should be coordinated with other aspects of inheritance law continues to arise. In the next chapter, we explore how these will substitutes interact with a substantive limit on the freedom of disposition: spousal protections and the elective share.

CHAPTER 13 COMPREHENSIVE ASSESSMENT

CREATING A COUNSELING PLAN. Use the following information to (a) create a counseling plan and (b) a vignette. The counseling plan should reference the role that will substitutes may have in the estate plan.

A. Counseling Plan

The **counseling plan should be in the form of a memorandum**. The components of the memorandum will be the heading (i.e., to, from, date, regarding) and the information described below. Note this means that the memorandum will not include a question presented, brief answer, statement of facts, discussion, or conclusion section. You may develop any headings you determine to be appropriate. The memorandum may be no longer than 1,200 words.

In terms of content, the counseling plan **should** include the following:

- Recite the client's goals, as drawn from all of the material in the assigning email and client intake questionnaire (both included below)

- Describe intestate succession with reference to the client's family and the client's property interests using *either* the UPC or a particular state's laws

- Highlight potential legal issue(s) that may arise given the client's goals, the client's family relationships, and the client's property interests

- Outline three different potential estate plans that would reflect the client's goals, the client's family relationships, and the client's property interests with consideration given to not only different provisions in the will (such as outright gifts, fractional interests, or testamentary trusts) but also how the client may use different types of will substitutes (including but not limited to the use of revocable trusts, deeds, and multi-party accounts) to achieve the client's goals

- Reference the legal and non-legal implications for each of the three potential dispositive plans outlined

- Formulate five questions that should be posed to the client to clarify the nature of the client's family relationships and the client's property, using language appropriate for the client.

B. Vignette

The **vignette must be at least two minutes and no more than four minutes** in duration. The vignette may be "live action" or "animated."

In terms of content, the vignette **should** feature an interaction between an attorney and the client. The vignette should be based upon the client counseling plan. During the vignette, the attorney must describe one potential dispositive plan for the client to consider, referencing the client's goals, the client's family relationships, and the client's property interests. The attorney must raise and discuss the legal and non-legal implications of the choice with the client.

The tone should be professional, but you may adopt whatever level of formality you determine to be appropriate given the nature of the counseling plan and the vignette. The tone should, however, be consistent throughout.

Assigning Email:

From: seniorpartner@firm.com

To: firstyearassociate@firm.com

Subject: Help with Project / High Priority

         Attachment

Thanks for offering to help me prepare for an upcoming client meeting. As you know, we are working with a new client of the firm to draft a will and related estate planning documents.

As is our firm's practice, the client has already completed a client intake questionnaire. The client received the form via email. He completed the form on his own and dropped off the completed form at the firm's front desk.

Using the information provided by the client intake questionnaire, prepare to counsel the client on the potential options, considering the client's goals, family relationships, and property interests. Even though the client sets the goals of the representation, we want to help the client articulate his goals. In other words, do not interpret the information on the client intake questionnaire as final expressions of goals. Make sure to think about different dispositive plans that take into account different provisions in the will (that means different gifts, shares, and structures as to who gets what under what circumstances) and different nonprobate devices available.

To that end, prepare a client counseling plan. Use the client intake questionnaire to develop three different options for the client to consider. Make sure to convey the legal and non-legal implications for each option.

I'll review the counseling plan and then we'll meet with the client next at 10:00 a.m.

As always, I appreciate your willingness to help.

CONFIDENTIAL ESTATE PLANNING INTAKE FORM

This form is helpful as we assist you in meeting your estate planning goals. Please fill out as much as possible using estimated figures where information is not easily attainable and leaving blanks for those questions which are not applicable. Please feel free to write in the margins or to add other information that you think might be helpful.

A. **Background Information**

   1.   Name

                           Full legal name: *Stefan Douglas*

     _____ Mr.   _____ Mrs.   _____ Ms.   _√_ Dr.   _____ other

          Preferred name: *Stef*

2.   Home Address: *72 Bryon Lane*
                                   Macon, GA 31207

      Home Phone: *n/a*

      Business Phone: *478-301-5908*

      Cell Phone: *478-338-4978*

      E-Mail: *sdouglas@university.edu*

Where do you prefer to receive estate planning correspondence?
      home address

3.   Profession/Business: *professor—mechanical engineering*

4.   Date of Birth: *August 16, 1970*

5.   Birthplace: *Atlanta, GA*

6.   Citizenship: *USA*

B.   Family Information

Marital Status: *Brenda Holloway Douglas (d/o/b June 1, 1988—
married Feb. 3, 2020)*

Children ~~and Grandchildren~~:

1.   Name: *Micah Douglas*   Date of Birth: *3/15/1992*

      Married? Y _√_ N ___   ~~If so, name of spouse:~~ _____

      Special Considerations: *Micah is settled in his own career and
      doesn't need really anything. Shelby is Micah's spouse.
      They are expecting twins in the fall.*

2.   Name: *Robyn Douglas*   Date of Birth: *5/22/1998*

      Married? Y ___ N _√_   ~~If so, name of spouse:~~ _____

      Special Considerations: *Robbie will graduate from Georgia Tech in
      May and plans to get married within the next year or so.*

3.   Name: *Eli Douglas*   Date of Birth: *11/5/2005*

      Married? Y ___ N _√_   If so, name of spouse:

      _____

      Special Considerations: *Eli lives with us.*

4.   Name: *Darla Halloway*   Date of Birth: *3/29/2014*

Married? Y_____ N _√___   If so, name of spouse:

_____

Special Considerations: *Darla lives with us. I would like to adopt my step-daughter, but I haven't started any legal proceedings. I don't want anyone to feel rushed. Her father died three years ago.*

Other:

My uncle Casey Douglas has lived with me since the death of my sons' mother (that's my first wife) in 2009. Following her death, Casey retired so that he could take care of us—and continues to take care of the household for us. It works for everyone. Brenda appreciates not having to run the household.

My only sibling Nico Douglas lives in Chicago. I'm not really that close to him. Our father lives in Macon, and I see him every week since my mother died over a decade ago.

Brenda's mother Madge has just moved to California to live with Brenda's only sibling Leigh Reynolds. Brenda's father died when she was young.

Our dog's name is Rover.

C.   Financial Information

Approximate Annual Income

1.   Salary/commissions: **$ 131,000**

2.   ~~Interest/dividends:~~   _____

3.   ~~Bonuses:~~   _____

4.   Other income: *Brenda is a middle school language arts teacher ($48,000 per year)*

Approximate Asset Values

1.   Cash or near cash: *approximately $5,000 in a joint checking account and $10,000 in a cash management account in my name only*

2.   Investment accounts: *retirement accounts and a small stock portfolio (less than $300,000)*

3.   Home (est. FMV): **$350,000** *(outstanding mortgage—$82,000)*

4. Other real estate (est. FMV): *none—but we might buy a vacation home in Florida in the future*

5. Personal possessions (i.e., tangible items): *$10,000 (approx.)*

6. Retirement accounts: *$580,000 (me)—$165,200 (Brenda)*

7. Other: *none*

Significant Liabilities
(Mortgages, other debts, adverse legal judgments, etc.)

1. Amount and nature of liability: *car loans—$15,000 (approx.) mortgage (see above)*

2. Amount and nature of liability: *credit cards usually paid off each month*

3. ~~Amount and nature of liability:~~ _____

D. Life Insurance

Insured	*Face Value*	*Primary Beneficiary*	*Secondary Beneficiary*	*Owner*
Me	*$500,000*	*Brenda*	*estate*	*me*

E. Other Advisors

1. Accountant

   Name: *Luis Hernandez*

   Address: *871 Cherry St.*
   Macon, GA 31207

   Phone: *478-321-2930*

2. Investment Manager

   ~~Address:~~ ================

   ~~Phone:~~ ================

3. Life Insurance Agent

   Name: *Preya Patel*

   Address: *45 Riverside Dr.*
   Macon, GA 31213

   Phone: *478-420-0910*

F.   Goals

In the space below, please describe any significant concerns or questions you have about your estate planning.

I want to make sure that I don't leave a headache for my loved ones. I know that I will inherit property from my father in the future. He has already told me that he has everything planned. When his father (that is my grandfather) died, there was a huge fight over the will. My father and his brother Casey (that's the uncle who lives me) had a falling out with my aunt Juliana over the inheritance. In fact, I don't even know if Juliana is still alive. My father said that he wanted to make sure that type of fighting didn't happen over his property. I too would like to ensure that doesn't happen when I die. With the wedding and Brenda moving in, I realized that now is the time to plan.

My family is my number one concern. I want to make sure that my estate plan provides for all my family. Brenda has been such a joyful addition to the family. She adores Casey and all my sons. Micah has been a bit slow to warm up to Brenda, but I know that once everyone gets to know her like I do, they will love her.

I really appreciate your help. I look forward to talking with you soon.

Test Your Knowledge

To assess your understanding of the material in this chapter, click here to take a quiz.

CHAPTER 14

Spousal Protections and the Elective Share

CHAPTER LEARNING OUTCOMES

Following your work with this material in this chapter, you should be able to do the following:

- Explain to a client what protections a surviving spouse receives after the death of the other spouse

- Apply the different property rules in community property and separate property states to the elective share

- Identify what fraud on the elective share means and whom it mostly harms

- Compare the different approaches for determining what assets comprise the augmented estate

- Counsel clients on their rights as surviving spouses and explain whether to take the elective share or the omitted spouse's share

- Explain to a client who is choosing to take the elective share how that share will be calculated in your state

- Explain to a client the requirements for a valid and binding prenuptial agreement.

A. Introduction

Much of what we learn about wealth transfer emphasizes the importance of freedom of disposition. As we have seen, a core concept of American inheritance law is that testators have the right to leave property to whomever they like and with any restrictions they choose. The law puts very few limits on this freedom, but one important limit it does impose is the protection of surviving spouses. Surviving spouses have statutory rights to certain forms of allowance and exempt personal property after the death of the other spouse. Most importantly, the law prevents one spouse from completely disinheriting the other by either guaranteeing the surviving spouse a **forced share** in the decedent spouse's estate (in a **separate property** state) or by guaranteeing an equal share of **marital property** (in a **community property** state). In separate property states, state probate codes grant surviving spouses the statutory right to an "elective" share of the estate. It is called the "**elective share**" because the surviving spouse must elect to take this share; it is also called the "forced share" because it is forced on the estate, and the estate must pay out this share, as long as the surviving spouse meets certain requirements. The elective share has traditionally been one-third of the probate estate, based on the tradition of dower. There is no elective share available in community property states, but, in these states, the surviving spouse has an automatic right to approximately half of the couple's assets that were either earned or acquired during marriage (other than by gift or bequest).

In this chapter, we focus primarily on the elective share and separate property states (rather than community property) because the legal framework is more complex and because of recurring problems with the elective share. One major problem that has persisted over centuries is that decedents have been able to circumvent the elective share obligation by removing assets from the probate estate and transferring them through nonprobate methods, trusts in particular. Solving this problem, called **fraud on the elective share**, has vexed legal reformers and led to a variety of legal responses. More specifically, fraud on the elective share led legislators to develop the concept of the "**augmented estate**." The augmented estate, for the purposes of calculating the elective share, widens the net of the decedent's estate from just the probate estate to include the value of certain nonprobate transfers. Which nonprobate transfers are included in the augmented estate is a highly contested questions, and states vary widely in their approaches, as we will see.

Part B discusses protections the law offers to a surviving spouse as well as theories that support spousal protections. It also provides a brief history and overview of the elective share, the most important spousal protection available, and describes the basic mechanics of how the elective share works. **Part C** explains the most significant problems with the elective share and explores the different responses that state have taken to stem this kind of fraud using the "augmented estate." In particular, this part discusses the most recent UPC version of the elective share which uses a robust augmented estate that, although complicated, embraces the partnership theory of marriage. The final part, **Part D**, addresses the requirements for waiving or contracting around spousal protections, usually in a prenuptial agreement.

B. Spousal Protections

This Part explores the theoretical bases for spousal protections and provides an overview of the most common forms of protection that a surviving spouse can access. These protections are extended only to legal spouses and do not extend to nonmarital partners, individuals who are engaged but not yet married, and divorced spouses. Just as nonmarital partners have almost no rights at the termination of a marriage-like relationship during life, they have no rights at the termination of a marriage-like relationship at death. States with registered domestic partners generally extend these protections to those who qualify. Most states preserve these marital rights and spousal protections until either the filing of divorce or the actual termination of a marriage, which means that these protections are often available to a surviving spouse even if the couple was separated when one spouse died.

Conversations about spousal protections tend to be quite gendered for several reasons. When we talk about surviving spouses, we have historically assumed different-sex marriages and, in those marriages, women tend to outlive men, benefitting as they do from longer life expectancies. Moreover, spousal protections—as we will see in the material that follows—were originally put into place because married women had attenuated property rights and limited opportunities in the labor market, determined in particular by class. Married women, therefore, needed protections. Even in more modern marriages, married women are still more likely to need spousal protections when their spouses die because it is married women who, more often than not, sacrifice earning within marriage by spending more time childrearing and caretaking. As marriage changes, we will see if and how the role of gender evolves and whether the financial precarity of surviving spouses changes.

1. Why Do We Protect Spouses?

Legal systems accord rights to surviving spouse on two theories: duty of support and the idea of marriage as an economic partnership. The duty of support derives from the historical fact that husbands had a legal duty to support their wives. This duty existed because the law of coverture stripped married women of almost all their property rights and gave these rights to their husbands. Accordingly, husbands had an obligation of support. This duty of support existed during marriage and extended past the husband's death. This support for the surviving spouse manifested mainly in the dower right, about which we'll learn more in Part C.

Starting in the second half of the twentieth century, law began to reflect new ideas about the nature of marriage. The idea that marriage was an economic partnership began gaining ground because of legal reform in the realm of divorce and property distribution. This idea of economic partnership also influenced tax law and probate law, in particular the elective share. This idea of marriage as an economic partnership demonstrates an understanding that both spouses contribute to wealth creation within marriage, whether the contributions are financial or other, and that this marital wealth should be shared equally. That is to say, under an economic partnership theory, the decedent spouse must provide for the surviving spouse at death because the surviving spouse was a co-creator of the marital wealth and not because one spouse (the husband, historically) has a legal duty to financially support the other spouse (the wife).

The major practical difference between the two theories is that legal rules based on the duty of support generally entitle surviving spouses to less property than rules based on economic partnership, which generally attempt equal or equitable division. So, when you see a surviving spouse getting one-third of an estate, you know it's based on the idea of support. When you see a surviving spouse getting one half of the estate, that's partnership.

NOTES

1. As noted, nonmarital partners do not benefit from the spousal protections discussed in this chapter. What does that mean in terms of who is suffering financial harm and deprivation when a long-term relationship ends with death? Look at the demographics of marriage—who gets married and who stays married—and think about who gets left without a financial buffer. *See* Erez Aloni, *The Marital Wealth Gap*, 93 WASH. L. REV. 1 (2018); Andrew Cherlin, *Marriage Has Become a Trophy*, THE ATLANTIC (Mar. 20, 2018), https://www.theatlantic.com/family/archive/2018/03/incredible-everlasting-institution-marriage/555320/; Ralph Richard Banks, *The Racial Gap in Marriage: How the Institution Is Tied to Inequality*, THE ATLANTIC (Oct. 27, 2011), https://www.theatlantic.com/business/archive/2011/10/the-racial-gap-in-marriage-how-the-institution-is-tied-to-inequality/247324.

2. For more on the duty of support and dynamics of marriage under coverture law, see Twila L. Perry, *The "Essentials of Marriage": Reconsidering the Duty of Support and Services*, 15 YALE J.L. & FEMINISM 1 (2003). For more on marriage as an economic partnership and the changing norms of marital sharing, see Susan Gary, *Marital Partnership Theory and the Elective Share: Federal Estate Tax Law Provides a Solution*, 49 U. MIAMI L. REV. 567 (1995). And for more on the seismic shifts

in legal, cultural, and political thinking around marriage in the late twentieth century, see ALISON LEFKOVITZ, STRANGE BEDFELLOWS: MARRIAGE IN THE AGE OF WOMEN'S LIBERATION (2018).

3.   While the economic partnership theory may seem to be a more progressive frame than that of support, Laura Rosenbury has argued:

> [T]he partnership theory of marriage, while seemingly more egalitarian, may also reinforce wifely sacrifice by rewarding women for caring for their husbands and children at the possible expense of their own tangible property acquisition or other forms of individual fulfillment. The partnership theory thereby reinforces traditional gender role expectations allocating wage work to men and care work to women.

Two Ways to End a Marriage, 2005 UTAH L. REV. 1227 (2005). Economic partnership theory compensates for a specialization of labor in households but may not address the inherent structure of marriage and the ways in which it provides incentives for dependency. Are there any other theories of marriage that might help address these concerns?

2.   What Protections Are Available?

There are a variety of protections available to surviving spouses, including the elective share, and they vary quite considerably by state. Here is an overview of the most common forms of protection, which include the **homestead exemption** or **allowance**, **personal property exemptions**, the **family allowance**, and the elective share.

a.   *Homestead Exemption*

One protection for surviving spouses and minor children comes in the form of a "homestead" exemption, which generally means that the surviving spouse has some right in the marital home—although how the right works varies tremendously from state to state. In Florida, for example, the state constitution awards a surviving spouse a life interest in the family home regardless of how title is held. In other states, the homestead right is just an additional amount of allowance, like the family allowance, that represents an early distribution from the estate. A common approach is also for the homestead exemption to protect a surviving spouse's equity in the family home from creditors, up to a certain amount. In some states, like Virginia, the homestead allowance cannot be taken by the surviving spouse if that spouse is also taking elective share property; in other states the two entitlements are not mutually exclusive. Some typical statutes are KAN. STAT. ANN. § 59–401; ME. REV. STAT. ANN. TIT. 18–c, § 2–402; NEV. REV. STAT. § 146.010.

The UPC takes the allowance approach and provides for a homestead allowance, entitling a surviving spouse to $22,500 (in the latest version of the UPC). *See* UPC § 2–403. If there is no surviving spouse, minor and dependent children are entitled each to an equal portion of $22,500. The set dollar amount, the UPC drafters state, "was dictated by the desirability of having a certain level below which administration may be dispensed with or be handled summarily." In the UPC, the homestead allowance is granted to the surviving spouse in addition to any property passing to the surviving spouse through the will, intestacy, or the elective share.

b. *Exempt Personal Property*

To make sure that surviving spouses and minor children do not lose some basic forms of personal property, states allow the surviving spouse to choose a certain amount of personal property from the home. Values differ by state. Virginia, for example, authorizes a spouse to take personal property worth up to $20,000. This property is available immediately to the surviving spouse and can be used while probate administration is occurring. Furthermore, this exempt property is not subject to creditor claims. Some typical statutes can be found at ALASKA STAT. § 13.12.403; N.D. CENT. CODE § 30.1–07–01; S.C. CODE ANN. § 62–2–401.

The UPC also provides for "exempt property," which is $15,000 worth of personal property—such as "household furniture, automobiles, furnishings, appliances, and personal effects"—in excess of any security interests in such property. UPC § 2–403. Like the homestead allowance, exempt property is awarded in addition to any property that a surviving spouse is entitled to by way of elective share.

c. *Family Allowance*

A number of states offer a family allowance to support the surviving spouse and any minor children during the time of probate administration. In most states, the family allowance basically amounts to an early distribution that is then offset against final distribution. These allowances can be very helpful during probate administration when accounts might be frozen or otherwise not accessible. Some typical state statutes can be found at ALA. CODE § 43–8–112; ARIZ. REV. STAT. ANN. § 14–2404; 33 R.I. GEN. LAWS § 33–10–3.

The UPC provides for a family allowance to support "the decedent's surviving spouse and minor children whom the decedent was obligated to support and children who were in fact being supported by the decedent." UPC § 2–404. These family members are entitled to "a reasonable allowance in money out of the estate for their maintenance during the period of administration," and this allowance can be paid in either a lump sum or periodic installments. The drafters of the UPC stated in their comments: "In determining the amount of the family allowance, account should be taken of both the previous standard of living and the nature of other resources available to the family to meet current living expenses until the estate can be administered and assets distributed." However, a court order is necessary if the allowance is to exceed $2,250 a month. Usually this claim, in conjunction with the homestead allowance and the exempt property allotment, have priority over all other claims to the estate.

d. *The Spousal Elective Share*

The most important legal right and protection that a surviving spouse possesses (other than intestacy rights) after the decedent's death is the elective share. This right of the surviving spouse to a certain portion of the decedent spouse's estate has historically been an important entitlement, helping to guarantee surviving spouses a certain measure of financial stability. The elective share can be claimed by a surviving spouse if the decedent spouse dies intestate, if the elective share of the estate is larger than the intestate amount. The share can also be claimed if a surviving spouse is left out of a will or given only a token amount in the will. The elective share is also a protection against spousal disinheritance, ensuring that a surviving spouse shares in a couple's marital wealth, even against the wishes of the decedent spouse. From this perspective, the elective share is a significant policy choice and one that has enjoyed strong historical support. The intestate share, discussed in Chapter 4, and the omitted share, discussed in Chapter 8, are, on the other hand, grounded in theories of presumed intent.

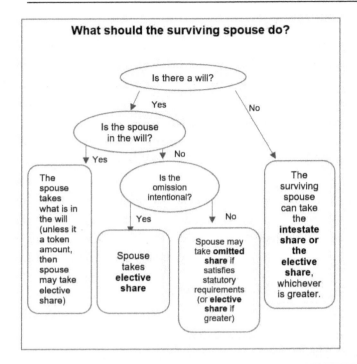

What should the surviving spouse do?

Is there a will?

— Yes → Is the spouse in the will?

— No → The surviving spouse can take the **intestate share or the elective share**, whichever is greater.

Is the spouse in the will?

— Yes → The spouse takes what is in the will (unless it a token amount, then spouse may take elective share)

— No → Is the omission intentional?

Is the omission intentional?

— Yes → Spouse takes **elective share**

— No → Spouse may take **omitted share** if satisfies statutory requirements (or **elective share** if greater)

Connection Note: Although the spousal elective share and the spousal intestate share have different justifications, a lawyer should consider how a surviving spouse will fare under each. When Steve McNair (an NFL quarterback) was murdered by a girlfriend in 2009, he left a $20 million estate, but no will. McNair had a wife and four children, two from his marriage and two nonmarital children. According to the intestacy rules in Tennessee, his domicile at death, the children were to receive the bulk (two-thirds) of the estate. The surviving spouse, Mechelle McNair, had to decide whether to receive a 33%

Steve McNair was a quarterback for the Baltimore Ravens before his untimely death in 2009.

intestate share under Tennessee law or file for a 40% elective share (which was reduced by other assets she received outside the probate estate). She chose the 40% elective share.

In terms of who benefits most from the elective share, the financial stability that the share provides is particularly important when the decedent spouse was the primary wage-earner or wealth-holder and the surviving spouse does not possess much wealth in her own right. The stability that the elective share provides is also important because the financial turmoil of a spouse's death comes, often, when the surviving spouse is older and may not be of an age to re-enter the labor market. To understand how the elective share has evolved, let's look at the history of dower.

i.   The History of Dower

The traditional method for securing a widow's financial security—or at least subsistence—after the death of her husband was dower. **Dower**, also called "the widow's share," was a property right that the bride acquired upon marriage in exchange for the loss of most of her property rights through the operation of **coverture**. The dower right vested on the husband's death and was intended to sustain a widow through her old age.

References to dower appear as far back in English history as the Magna Carta, which stated that the wife and children were entitled to their "reasonable parts," conventionally interpreted to mean one-third of the husband's real and personal property, or "probate estate." Usually, dower did not grant the widow anything more than lifetime use and enjoyment of the property, and she did not usually have the right to sell or devise the property. Janet Loengard has observed that "dower invoked conflicting sentiments" because, on the one hand, "[i]t was proper that a woman should have enough to live on and bring up her children after her husband died." On the other, dower "ran counter to the strong desire, countenanced by the family structure of feudal England, to keep landholdings undivided and in the hands of the heir." Janet S. Loengard, *Of the Gift of Her Husband: English Dower and Its Consequences in the Year 1200, in* WOMEN OF THE MEDIEVAL WORLD: ESSAYS IN HONOR OF JOHN H. MUNDY 254 (Julius Kirshner & Suzanne F. Wemple eds., Oxford 1985).

Language Note: A dowager is, historically, a widowed woman who is living on her dower, like the woman in this portrait, Dowager Queen María Cristina of Austria (painted around 1910 by Philip de László). Or think of everyone's favorite dowager, Violet Crawley, the Dowager Countess of Grantham on Downton Abbey. Dower should always be distinguished from dowry, which was a different money problem for women. Dowry was the money that a bride brought into her marriage as a gift to the husband.

Male spouses who outlived their wives also had rights to the marital estate, called **curtesy** rights. Curtesy rights granted the widower a life estate in all freehold interests held by the wife during the marriage, not just the dower portion of one third. The only requirement for a widower to receive his curtesy right was that the marriage had produced children who would inherit the property upon the widower's death (which was not a requirement for dower). In most states dower and curtesy rights have been replaced by the modern elective share right. Nevertheless, a few states still retain the traditional (some might say antiquated) and gendered rights of dower and curtesy for surviving spouses, harkening back to medieval England.

ii.   Modern Elective Share Statutes

Throughout the twentieth century, in a piecemeal fashion, states began to replace dower rights with the modern elective share statutes. These statutes eliminated the gender-based differences between dower and curtesy and provided generally a third of the probate estate to any surviving spouse, a reflection of the traditional duty of support theory. By the last decades of the twentieth century, responsive to new social norms and changes to the legal understanding of marriage, elective share statutes began to shift toward increased financial protection for surviving spouses based on the theory of economic partnership. States, however, vary dramatically in their elective share statutes, depending on the state's legal history, the influence of various lobbying groups, the composition of the legislature, and the demographics of the state's population. Consequently, while some states have embraced modern, gender-neutral and partnership-based statutes, a small number of states still retain the dower and curtesy rules. *See, e.g.*, ARK. CODE ANN § 28–11–301 et seq.; KY. REV. STAT. ANN. § 392.020), OHIO REV. CODE ANN. § 2103.02). There is only one state that has no elective share statute whatsoever—Georgia. Georgia, in place of the elective share and the family allowance, allows a surviving spouse to petition for a "year's support." An award of year's support has the highest priority under Georgia law, and takes precedence over all other creditor claims on the estate, including funeral expenses, last illness expenses, and creditor claims. This priority is helpful for surviving spouses if the estate is small or potentially insolvent.

Beginning in 1969, UPC drafters began to address ways to bolster the elective share, and the rights of the surviving spouse increased gradually in every new version of the uniform rules. By 1990, seeking to reflect the growing strength of the economic partnership theory in law—and, in particular, to equalize rights at death and divorce—the UPC drafters explicitly embraced the language of economic partnership. The drafters commented, in their revisions to the elective share, that "[t]he main purpose of the revisions is to bring elective-share law into line with the contemporary view of marriage as an economic partnership. The economic partnership theory of marriage is already implemented under the equitable distribution system applied in both the common-law." Exec. Comm. of the Nat'l Conf. Of Comm'r On Unif. State Laws, Amendments to Uniform Probate Code 1 (2008). We will discuss the UPC framework further in the next section and study the details of how the UPC operationalizes the economic partnership theory.

NOTES

1. If a surviving spouse dies without claiming a homestead allowance or exempt property out of the pre-deceased spouse's estate, may the surviving spouse's estate make those claims? *See Cater v. Coxwell,* 479 So. 2d 1181 (Ala. 1985) (concluding "[t]he surviving spouse is presented with various choices, and we see no need for or merit in requiring the homestead allowance and exempt property to vest in the surviving spouse in all cases"). In *Foiles v. Whitman,* 233 P.3d 697 (Colo. 2010) (en banc), the court came out the other way, concluding that "[n]othing in the plain language of the exempt property statute demonstrates that the General Assembly intended to limit the allowance to a living surviving spouse." For more on the homestead entitlement, see Hannah Haksgaard, *Defining "Home" Through Homestead Laws,* 33 BERKELEY J. GENDER L. & JUST. 169 (2018), and Carolyn S. Bratt, *Family Protection Under Kentucky's Inheritance Laws: Is the Family Really Protected?,* 76 KY. L.J. 387 (1987).

2. One of the only defenses that the decedent's estate can make against a surviving spouse seeking to take the elective share is that the surviving spouse abandoned the decedent prior to death. In a minority of states this is a statutory rule. See VA. CODE ANN. § 64.2–308; CONN. GEN STAT. § 45(a)–436; N.C. GEN. STAT. § 31A–1; 20 PA. CON. STAT. ANN. § 2106(a)(1). How does the defense of abandonment intersect with theories of support and partnership? What about states that cut off elective share rights at the filing of divorce?

3. Naomi Cahn points out that there are "multiple gendered dimensions of the elective share." The elective share emerged "out of an explicitly gender-based concern for protecting the dependent wife," when wives could not own property legally or when social norms prevented wives from being wage-earners

and participating in the paid labor market. Are these rationales for the elective share still relevant as gender norms change? *See* Naomi Cahn, *What's Wrong About the Elective Share "Right"?*, 53 U.C. DAVIS L. REV. 2087 (2020). Cahn also presents empirical data on who takes the elective share.

ASSESSMENTS

1.   You work as a legislative aide to a local politician who is reconsidering the state's spousal entitlements in light of the legalization of same-sex marriage. Your supervisor has asked you to draft a short, bullet-point response to the following questions:

a.   Does the legalization of same-sex marriage change the theories underlying the spousal entitlements?

b.   If marriage promotes dependency, who are the vulnerable parties in the current moment.

For help thinking through these issues, see Thomas H. Anthony & Ethel N. Laudeman, *The Demise of Dower*, 95 MICH. B.J. 34 (2016) (discussing the effects of *Obergefell v. Hodges* on Michigan's dower statute limiting benefit to widows).

2.   Who do you imagine are the spouses that take the elective share as opposed to inheriting through a will or another nonprobate transfer? What scenarios do you think are common and what kinds of family conflict lead surviving spouses to elect this option?

iii.   Community Property Rules and the Elective Share

Elective share rights turn on whether the decedent and surviving spouse lived in a community or separate property state. Although a majority of states follow a "separate" property rule, there is a small group of states—including Arizona, California, Idaho, Louisiana, Nevada, New Mexico, Texas, Washington, and Wisconsin—that follow **community property rules** to regulate property within marriage. In community property jurisdictions, marital property rights vest upon marriage rather than upon divorce. From day one of the marriage, property acquired during marriage in a community property state belongs to the "community," and each spouse owns an equal, undivided share of the property. This differs from separate property states in which marital property rights only arise at divorce. In a separate property state, spouses within an intact marriage have rights only to that which they have earned or assets titled in their name.

One major benefit of the community property system is that, because it automatically recognizes the contributions each spouse makes to the financial well-being of the marriage, there is no question that a surviving spouse will be compensated with a share of the marital wealth at both divorce and death. In separate property states, spouses are entitled to an equitable division of marital assets at divorce—and not at death. Consequently, surviving spouses in community property jurisdictions do not need an elective share, while surviving spouses in separate property jurisdictions do.

NOTES

1.   There is an additional complexity that arises from community property, relating to migration. Not all married couples spend all their married lives in a community property jurisdiction; some move to (or from) a community property jurisdiction. To address the potential problem where a couple moves from a separate property jurisdiction (where the elective share would protect the surviving spouse) to a community property jurisdiction (where the surviving spouse's protection comes in the form of property acquired during marriage), community property jurisdictions have what they call **"quasi" community property**. That is, property acquired during the marriage in a separate property jurisdiction is deemed quasi-community property. The surviving spouse then has a half-interest in the quasi-community

> **Practice Note:** An attorney who is preparing estate planning documents for married couples should always determine if they have spent any of their marriage in a community property jurisdiction to affirmatively address any migration issues.

property. *See, e.g.,* CAL. PROB. CODE § 66 (defining quasi-community property as "All personal property wherever situated, and all real property situated in this state, heretofore or hereafter acquired by a decedent while domiciled elsewhere that would have been the community property of the decedent and the surviving spouse if the decedent had been domiciled in this state at the time of its acquisition."); *id.* § 101(a) (providing that on "the death of a married person domiciled in this state, one-half of the decedent's quasi-community property belongs to the surviving spouse and the other half belongs to the decedent."). Increasingly, separate property jurisdictions are allowing couples to choose to acquire property as community property. It may very well be that in a few decades the majority of couples will elect community property even in separate property jurisdictions and, thus, largely erase the distinction between separate and community property. Then again, the process of convergence between those regimes may take much longer.

2. The elective share is only available to spouses in separate property states and not to those in community property states. What protections do spouses have in community property states that render the elective share unnecessary? *See* Joanna Grossman, *Beauty and the Billionaire: Reviewing the Anna Nicole Smith Case and the Rights of the Surviving Spouse* (Jan. 12, 2001, 4:36 PM);[1] *see also* Elizabeth Carter, *The Illusion of Equality: The Failure of the Community Property Reform to Achieve Management Equality*, 48 IND. L. REV. 853 (2014–2015).

ASSESSMENTS

1. Children's entitlements differ significantly in that there is no elective or forced share for children who are disinherited (unless you happen live in Louisiana). Please respond to the following in list form:

    a.   Five reasons why children are differently positioned than spouses

    b.   Five reasons to extend the elective share to children

    c.   Five limits you might put on a child's elective share

2. The two strongest property entitlements that spouses have are the intestate share and the elective share. They are grounded in two very different theories. Identify the primary justifications for each entitlement and discuss the difference between them rationales. Are there other wealth transfer rules that fall into either one of the two categories?

3. Develop a short fact-pattern for a married couple who presents a migration issue, as discussed above. Make sure to be specific about where the couple has have lived and for how long, what specific property the couple owns, and where, when, and how the property was acquired. Make sure to consider how the couple kept track of where the property originated and where any growth in the property took place.

C. Fraud on the Elective Share and the Augmented Estate

The first generation of elective share statutes gave an interest—often a life estate—in a one-third share of the decedent spouse's probate estate. As described above, this right was an important protection for the surviving spouse. The problem, however, was that the entitlement was easily rendered useless by

---

[1]   Available at https://www.cnn.com/2001/LAW/01/columns/fl.grossman.smith.1.12/.

the simple act of the decedent passing property outside of probate, through the type of will substitutes discussed in the previous chapter.

Any property owner could avoid the elective share simply by funding a trust because the legal rule was that there was "no dower of a trust." Historically, husbands often chose to transfer property this way in order to keep land alienable (dower was thought to be a "clog on alienations") and to mitigate what they considered to be overly generous dowers. The use of trusts was in fact so widespread that one of the goals of the Statute of Uses in 1536 was to stem their utility as a mechanism to avoid dower. Consider the following scenario and how easy it is to strip a surviving spouse of rights:

Case 1. Ambrosia, a highly successful jewelry designer is married to Ellen. The two of them have a daughter, Palatine. Ambrosia would rather leave her fortune to her daughter than her spouse, because she doesn't trust Ellen's spending habits and wants Palatine to receive a large amount of inheritance so she can carry on the family legacy. Aware of the elective share entitlement, Ambrosia transfers the bulk of her fortune into a trust. The trust gives Ellen certain rights of withdrawal during her lifetime and then transfers everything to Palatine on Ellen's death. When Ambrosia dies, there is nothing in her probate estate other than some personal property without much value. What are Ellen's rights and what, if anything, can Ellen do?

In a jurisdiction where the elective share applies only to the probate estate (a "**probate-only jurisdiction**"), Ellen would be out of luck. In the modern context, courts and legislatures have addressed this problem of fraud on the elective share in a number of ways. Early judicial attempts to address fraud on the elective share typically involved questions about the decedent's intent, how much control the decedent continued to exercise over the property, and whether the lifetime transfers were a "device or contrivance" rather than a bona fide transfer. Some jurisdictions still use these tests. Others have used multi-factor tests, taking into account factors such as the need of the surviving spouse and the relationship of the person receiving the non-probate transfer to the decedent.

Currently, however, one of the most common modes of curtailing elective share fraud is through the creation of the "augmented" estate. The idea is to "augment" the probate estate with the value of nonprobate transfers in order to capture the true wealth of the decedent. Examples of property often included in the augmented estate are the types of nonprobate transfers covered in Chapter 13, including joint tenancy property, life insurance proceeds, and revocable inter vivos trusts. The assets themselves do not necessarily go to the surviving spouse, but their value is included in the calculation of the augmented estate in order to come up with the right value—of which the spouse will then get a share. How that share is paid out to the surviving spouse depends on the asset composition of the estate, its liquidity, and, ideally, what is most mutually convenient to the estate, the other beneficiaries, and the surviving spouse.

The most notable way in which the states differ is in what assets they include in the augmented estate and therefore how they compute the decedent spouse's "estate" that is subject to the elective share. The difficult questions for states in drafting an elective share statute is deciding what to count as property for the augmented estate. Some states have enumerated lists, and other states rely on the broad concept of "ownership and control" to determine whether an asset will be included in calculating the elective share.

Delaware has a very good solution to this problem: it turns to the Internal Revenue Code. Delaware treats anything that is part of the decedent's estate for purposes of the estate tax—whether there is actually an estate tax due—as part of the "elective estate." DEL. CODE ANN. tit. 12, § 902 (elective estate defined). This approach allows Delaware to turn to the well-developed federal law to gauge what property should be included: the test is whether the decedent had enjoyment or control of the property before death. If so, the property is part of the estate. The surviving spouse is entitled to one-third of the "elective estate." *Id.* § 901 ("Right to elective share").

States also differ on what percentage of the decedent's estate a surviving spouse gets when that spouse claims the elective share. Many jurisdictions, including New York and Delaware, although they augment the probate estate, still grant the surviving spouse only one-third of the decedent's augmented estate, a trace of the dower rules. Other jurisdictions vary the size of the estate based on the duration of the marriage. In North Carolina, for example, the elective share varies from 15% of a decedent's "total net assets" for marriages that last for fewer than five years to 50% for marriages that last 15 years or longer. States that allow the possibility of a surviving spouse taking up to 50% of the estate through the elective share generally base that policy on the partnership theory.

The modern UPC relies on the concept of the marital estate to create the augmented estate, pairing it with a vesting scheme such that a surviving spouse gets an increasing amount of the decedent's (up to 50%) based on the length of the marriage. The UPC rule defines the "pot" of marital property as both the decedent's estate and the separate property of the surviving spouse. The UPC takes this approach to try to mimic property division at divorce by giving the surviving spouse a share in the total marital estate based on the length of marriage. This statutory scheme is quite complex, more so than the division of property at divorce, but it also allows for less judicial discretion.

In the following sections, we will explore the range of approaches that state courts and legislatures have taken to stemming fraud—both before the invention of the augmented estate and after. ACTEC has published a good overview of what states do.[2]

1. Illusory Transfers and Intent to Defraud

One test that courts used in the past was the **illusory transfer** test. Using this test, courts would invalidate a transfer that if it was deemed to be "illusory," which usually meant that the decedent retained some form of control over the asset, and the transfer was made with an intent to defraud the surviving spouse. The leading case with respect to illusory transfers is *Newman v. Dore*, 275 N.Y. 371 (1937), which is known as much for its salacious details as its holding. The case involved a second marriage, a pending annulment, and a husband who transferred the bulk of his estate into a revocable inter vivos trust just before his death in an attempt to defeat his spouse's elective share claim. One set of casebook authors described the problem in this way:

> [The husband's] perverted sexual habits made it impossible for [the wife] to live with him. The record never makes clear the nature of his alleged perversions although it does include a newspaper account in which he is described as having received a transplant of monkey glands by surgical operation. In the manner of a perfectly normal, red blooded octogenarian, he was highly indignant over these charges. He brought an action for annulment of the marriage, which was also pending at his death.[3]

The court recognized the problem of judging motive or intention, stating: "Motive or intent is an unsatisfactory test of the validity of a transfer of property.

---

[2]   *See* Alex S. Tanouye, *Surviving Spouse's Rights to Share in Deceased Spouse's Estate*, ACTEC (Aug. 2018), https://www.actec.org/assets/1/6/Surviving_Spouse%E2%80%99s_Rights_to_Share_in_Deceased_Spouse%E2%80%99s_Estate.pdf.

[3]   E. CLARK, L. LUSKY & A. MURPHY, CASES AND MATERIALS ON GRATUITOUS TRANSFERS 147 (3d ed.1985). *See also* John H. Langbein & Lawrence W. Waggoner, *Redesigning the Spouse's Forced Share*, 22 REAL PROP. PROB. & TR. J. 303 (1987). Monkey gland transplants were pioneered by Dr. Serge Voronoff and the transplants were thought to reverse the again process and restore virility. https://www.atlasobscura.com/articles/the-true-story-of-dr-voronoffs-plan-to-use-monkey-testicles-to-make-us-immortal. Now, monkey glands are probably best experienced as a cocktail: Colleen Graham, *Monkey Gland Cocktail*, THE SPRUCE EATS, https://www.thespruceeats.com/monkey-gland-cocktail-recipe-759322 (last updated June 30, 2019).

In most jurisdictions it has been rejected, sometimes for the reason that it would cast doubt upon the validity of all transfers made by a married man, outside of the regular course of business." *Id.* at 379. Nevertheless, the court concluded that "it would seem that the only sound test of the validity of a challenged transfer is whether it is real or illusory," and that the husband had never had any real intention of divesting himself of the property, "even when death was near." *Id.* at 379, 381.

The illusory transfer approach—because of the difficulty and subjectivity of judging motive—has been superseded in almost all instances by other doctrines and approaches, described below.

2. Multifactor Tests

Some states, moving past the illusory transfer test, have adopted a multi-factor test. The following case, *Karsenty v. Schoukroun*, deals with a surviving spouse's claim to a revocable trust established by her deceased husband; the decedent's daughter by a prior marriage was the trust beneficiary. At that time (and until 2019), Maryland was a probate-only jurisdiction (called the "net estate" there), and the state had a long history with fraud on the elective share claims. Pay particular attention, in reading the case, to what factors the court determines to be relevant and how useful those factors are.

Karsenty v. Schoukroun

959 A.2d 1147 (Md. 2008)

HARRELL, J.

We are asked in this case to decide whether an inter vivos transfer, in which a deceased spouse retained control over the transferred property during his lifetime, constitutes a per se violation of the surviving spouse's statutory, elective right to a percentage of the deceased spouse's net estate under Maryland Code § 3–203.

Sometime in 1999, Gilles met Kathleen Sexton ("Kathleen") and, by October of that year, they became engaged to be married. Kathleen had been married previously and had a child from that marriage. In the Spring of 2000, before they married, Gilles and Kathleen took out life insurance policies from Zurich Kemper. Gilles purchased a policy on his life, naming Kathleen as the beneficiary, in the amount of $200,000. Kathleen made her policy benefits payable to her estate in the amount of $200,000, with her son from her prior marriage as the beneficiary of her estate. Gilles and Kathleen were married in

Worcester County on 3 July 2000. At the time, they were 40 and 45 years old, respectively.

On 29 January 2004, Gilles learned that he had lymphoma. He underwent chemotherapy and radiation treatment between then and September 2004. He experienced little success with the conventional treatments. Gilles died on 18 October 2004. At the time of his death, Gilles was 44 years old and had been married to Kathleen for four years. Lauren, his child from a former marriage, was 14 years old when Gilles died.

This case centers on the estate planning arrangements that Gilles made in the last three to four months of his life. On 23 June 2004, Gilles prepared and executed his Last Will and Testament and a document known as the Gilles H. Schoukroun Trust (the "Trust"). In his will, Gilles named his sister, Maryse Karsenty ("Maryse"), the Personal Representative of his estate. The will provided, "I give all my tangible personal property, together with any insurance providing coverage thereon, to my wife, KATHLEEN SEXTON. . . ." Gilles bequeathed the "rest, residue and remainder" of the estate to the Trust.

With respect to the Trust, Gilles named Lauren the beneficiary. He named himself settlor and trustee during his lifetime, and he appointed Maryse trustee upon his death. In the event Maryse could not serve as trustee, Gilles named Kathleen as the alternative trustee. Clause Two of the Trust provided:

> The Settlor reserves the right to amend or terminate this trust from time to time by notice in writing delivered to the Trustee during the lifetime of the Settlor, and any amendment or termination shall be effective immediately upon delivery thereof to the Trustee, except that changes with respect to the Trustee's duties, liabilities or compensation shall not be effective without its consent. Upon the death of the Settlor, this trust shall be irrevocable and there shall be no right to alter, amend, revoke or terminate this trust or any of its provisions.

On the same day that he created the Trust, Gilles transferred into the Trust assets from three financial accounts: (1) one at E*Trade Financial, worth approximately $29,037.15; (2) one at Fidelity Investments, worth approximately $75,257.25; and (3) a second at Fidelity Investments, worth approximately $49,034.67. On 12 July 2004, Gilles named the Trust as the beneficiary of two IRA transfer-on-death ("TOD") accounts at Fidelity Investments, one worth approximately $257,863.31, the other worth approximately $14,069.51. It was clear that Fidelity managed the investments in the larger TOD account (there was no similar evidence offered as to the smaller). It appears from the record that Gilles took no distributions from either of the TOD accounts during his lifetime.

When Gilles died, Lauren became the sole beneficiary of the Trust. Kathleen received the $200,000 proceeds from Gilles's Zurich Kemper life insurance policy. In accordance with Gilles's will, Kathleen also received his 2003 Toyota Highlander, the outstanding loan balance for which he had recently paid off. The vehicle was valued at approximately $22,000.

On 2 February 2005, Gilles's will was admitted to administrative probate by the Orphans' Court in Anne Arundel County. Kathleen renounced Gilles's will and, on 17 February 2005, filed an election to take a statutory share of Gilles's estate under Section 3–203 of the Estates and Trusts Article of the Maryland Code. In short, Kathleen alleged that, despite the Trust's non-probate nature, Gilles retained lifetime dominion and control over the Trust, its assets, and the TOD accounts, of which the Trust was the beneficiary, thereby unlawfully depriving her of her statutory share of his net estate.

I.

Section 3–203 is clear and unambiguous with respect to the Trust and the TOD accounts in this case. The term "net estate," as it is used in Maryland's elective share statute, "means the property of the decedent passing by testate succession." This includes only property in which the decedent "has some interest . . . which will survive his death." Here, the Trust and the TOD accounts fall outside the definition of "net estate" because Gilles did not have any interest in either that survived his death. When Gilles created the Trust, Lauren received a vested, albeit revocable, interest therein; accordingly, Lauren became the sole beneficiary of the Trust by operation of law when Gilles died. Likewise, the TOD accounts transferred to the Trust upon Gilles's death "by reason of the contract" between him and Fidelity Investments with which the accounts were registered. Thus, by its plain language, Section 3–203 does not permit Kathleen to take a share of the Trust assets or the TOD accounts.

We must respect the "net estate" model chosen by the General Assembly. Many of our sister states, however, have taken a different approach with respect to their elective share statutes, adopting some form of the "augmented estate" concept. Although there are differences between the models adopted by the various augmented estate jurisdictions, the pith of the augmented estate concept is that a surviving spouse's elective share is calculated by including non-probate assets over which the decedent had dominion and control during her or his lifetime.

Although Kathleen urges that we decide this case, ostensibly, under the doctrine previously referred to as fraud on marital rights, what she seeks is to establish dominion and control by the decedent during his life as the sole touchstone for determining whether a non-probate asset will be included in the pool of assets that are subject to the elective share. In effect, if we were to hold that dominion and control (even absolute control) is per se fraud on marital rights, as Kathleen urges, we would be imposing, by judicial fiat, a kind of augmented estate model eschewed by the Legislature. Such a result would allow a surviving spouse to incorporate all non-probate assets, over which the decedent had control during her or his lifetime, into the elective share asset pool, regardless of the circumstances of the underlying inter vivos transfer. This we shall not endorse.

II.

The question to be determined in any case in which a surviving spouse seeks to invalidate an inter vivos transfer is whether the transfer was set up as a mere device or contrivance. If it was, the surviving spouse may have it set aside. This standard places the focus of a court's inquiry on the nature of the underlying transaction, not on the decedent's intent to defraud the surviving spouse. Determining whether an inter vivos transfer was a mere device or contrivance is indeed a question of intent; however, the intent that matters is the decedent's intent to structure a transaction by which she or he parts with ownership of the property in form, but not in substance. As we shall explain, except to the extent that it sheds light on whether a transfer was a mere device or contrivance, a decedent's intent to defraud her or his surviving spouse is not the proper focus of the analysis of the issue. While left mostly unspoken, this Court consistently has looked to the nature of the assailed inter vivos transfer, regardless of the words that were used to give a name to the doctrine under which we exercised judicial authority.

We admit that determining whether someone intended that an inter vivos transfer be a sham that changes nothing may be difficult, as it is an ethereal touchstone. There also is the complicating fact that the person whose intent matters most is deceased when the judicial inquiry typically engages itself. We believe, however, that three considerations lessen somewhat the difficulty of this analysis.

First, as a threshold matter, a surviving spouse must show that the decedent retained an interest in or otherwise continued to enjoy the transferred property. This Court has held that an inter vivos transfer in which a decedent gives up all control of the transferred property may not be invalidated by a surviving spouse as an unlawful frustration of the spouse's statutory share. This is so even if the decedent's express desire in alienating her or his property was to deprive the surviving spouse of the property. Thus, a transfer, whereby the decedent retained no interest or enjoyment at all in the transferred property, is, by its nature, not subject to later successful attack by the decedent's surviving spouse.

Second, as a guiding principle, courts should not employ their equity powers to second-guess reasonable and legitimate estate planning arrangements. For this reason, we think that a surviving spouse has a high hurdle to overcome.

Third, our case-law offers considerable guidance with respect to what factors are relevant to determining, in this context, whether a decedent intended that an inter vivos transfer be a sham. For the guidance of the trial court (and posterity), we will chronicle and elucidate those factors that we consider most relevant.

The extent of the control retained by the decedent probably is the most useful indicator when scrutinizing an inter vivos transfer. As we explained, other considerations must exist concurrently with retained control for a surviving spouse to invalidate the transfer; however, our case-law suggests that retained control is a very important factor because, in every case in which we have invalidated an inter vivos transfer, the decedent retained a significant amount of control. In the present case, Gilles retained absolute control over the Trust; however, on remand, the trial court should consider the extent to which Gilles could withdraw funds freely from the TOD accounts, especially because the TOD accounts now make up the bulk of the funds in the Trust. Funds in an IRA account may be accessible, but the ease of that accessibility (and the tax consequences) is a far cry from that of funds in a checking or savings account.

A decedent's motives are also cogent to consider. In other words, a court should consider not only whether there was collusion between the decedent and the beneficiary, but also whether the beneficiary intended to defraud the decedent or the surviving spouse.

The degree to which an inter vivos transfer deprives a surviving spouse of property that she or he would otherwise take as part of the decedent's estate is also extremely significant. Looking at the degree to which an assailed inter vivos transfer depleted the value of property available to a surviving spouse necessarily requires a court to consider also non-probate arrangements that the decedent made for the surviving spouse. A scrutinizing court also should consider as part of this factor inter vivos gifts that the decedent gave to the surviving spouse. While not the end of the inquiry, if a decedent leaves behind reasonable provisions for her or his surviving spouse, by either probate or non-probate arrangements, inter vivos gifts, or a combination thereof, it may suggest that the inter vivos transfer that the surviving spouse seeks to have set aside was complete and bona fide and should not be set aside.

Another factor that commands weight is whether the decedent actually exercised the retained control or otherwise enjoyed the property at issue, and, if so, to what extent. Simply put, use of the property suggests that the decedent did not intend really to part with ownership; conversely, failure to exercise retained powers may suggest that the decedent intended to alienate the property.

A final factor that courts should pay particular attention to is the familial relationship between the decedent and the person or persons who benefit by the challenged inter vivos transfer. This is another consideration that, until this point, we have not itemized expressly, even though it has been an apparent influence in our prior decisions. An inter vivos transfer, whereby a decedent provides for children from a previous marriage in derogation of the estate due to a surviving spouse, may be reasonable, especially if the decedent and the surviving spouse were married only a short time. Courts must be cognizant of this and view such inter vivos transfers differently than they would view a similar transaction in a single family unit. An estate planning arrangement that provides for children from a previous marriage or, for that matter, for children not born in wedlock, facially appears legitimate and, hence, may not bear the hallmarks of a mere device or contrivance. familial circumstances bear even more in favor of upholding an inter vivos transfer when the decedent was a widow or widower before marrying the surviving spouse; if that is the case, it suggests that the decedent believed that her or his children from the earlier marriage rightfully deserve the property and, hence, that the inter vivos transfer to the children was not a mere device or contrivance.

These factors are by no means an exhaustive list. We recognize that they often may overlap. As stated earlier, we are not certain what the trial court meant when it found that Gilles did not intend to defraud Kathleen. If the trial court was looking solely for fraud, it applied the wrong standard; however, we may not substitute our judgment on the facts for that of the trial court. Accordingly, we must remand this case for further proceedings not inconsistent with this opinion and, if necessary, the taking of additional evidence.

NOTES

1.   Angela Vallario, discussing the *Karsenty* case, has written: "These common law doctrines speculate as to a deceased person's motive, lack certainty, are fact specific, allow courts to do whatever they want, and can easily be resolved in favor of the side best able to litigate." Angela M. Vallario, *The Elective Share Has No Friends: Creditors Trump Spouse in the Battle Over the Revocable Trust*, 45 CAP. U. L. REV. 333 (2017). Do you think this assertion has merit? If so, who—what groups and what individuals—will benefit and who suffers harm?

2.   The *Karsenty* court emphasizes the importance of allowing decedents leeway in their estate planning when blended families are involved, stating: "An estate planning arrangement that provides for children from a previous marriage or, for that matter, for children not born in wedlock, facially appears legitimate and, hence, may not bear the hallmarks of a mere device or contrivance." Just because a transfer is a legitimate one, why should it defeat the elective share when the elective share is nothing more than a policy decision to entitle a surviving spouse to marital wealth? If the elective share is, indeed, a policy choice, why do courts look at decedent motive in any capacity?

3.   For an alternative take on this case, see the rewritten opinion in FEMINIST JUDGMENTS: REWRITTEN TRUSTS AND ESTATES OPINIONS 175 (eds. Deborah S Gordon, Browne C. Lewis, & Carla Spivack) 220–45 (Cambridge Univ. Press 2020). In the rewritten opinion, Allison Tait writing as Justice Tait unpacks the strong precedent in Maryland caselaw for a bright-line rule about control and ownership and concludes that the multi-factor test is inappropriate given the goals of Maryland's elective share, writing:

> What assets constitute the elective share and a surviving spouse's right to it is not, then, about degree of disinheritance. Nor does the amount or availability of the share turn on decedent intent. The crux of the matter is and has always been the retention of dominion and control by the decedent. This rule about dominion and control of property—the *Hays* rule—is the way our courts have navigated the competing demands of donor freedom and spousal rights. We believe that this rule, crafted early in our state's history, is the correct one for our courts to be using as they evaluate elective share cases. Consequently, we are a persuaded by and agree with Ms. Schoukroun in her interpretation and understanding of *Knell*. *Knell* returns us to the one-factor test—that of retained dominion and control—and eschews the

other tests that have haltingly and haphazardly developed around the question of the elective share.

Id. at 244–45. What would make this single-factor, bright-line approach "feminist," and what does a feminist stance toward the elective share look like?

3.   Statutory Lists

A number of jurisdictions have approached the augmented estate question by creating statutory lists, detailing what assets are included in the calculation of the net or augmented estate (and by implication which ones are not). This section illustrates the range of solutions that states have adopted in an effort to prevent fraud on the elective share—some solutions being much more robust than others. Some states take a very narrow view, completely eschewing the concept of the augmented estate but nevertheless supplementing the probate estate with one or more nonprobate transfers. This is the situation in *In re Estate of Myers*, the case in the following sub-section. Other states embrace the general idea of the augmented estate and provide broad, categorical lists but without adopting the UPC augmented estate framework (or Delaware's Internal Revenue Code approach). This is the case with states like New York, whose statute we reproduce in sub-section (b).

a.   *Narrow Statutory Lists*

The following case illustrates how the statutory approach might work in a jurisdiction that has not adopted the augmented estate, just as it illustrates some of the pitfalls of this approach.

In re Estate of Myers

825 N.W.2d 1 (Iowa 2012)

WATERMAN, J.

This appeal presents a question of first impression: whether a surviving spouse's elective share, as defined in Iowa Code section 633.238 (Supp. 2009), includes pay-on-death (POD) assets. The probate court ruled that three of Karen Myers's assets, a checking account, certificate of deposit, and an annuity, all payable on her death to her daughters, should be included in the elective share of her surviving spouse, Howard Myers. The controlling statutory language omits POD assets from the surviving spouse's elective share. Accordingly, we reverse the ruling of the probate court.

BACKGROUND FACTS AND PROCEEDINGS

Karen died on November 2, 2009, survived by her spouse, Howard. Rex Picken, Karen's brother and the executor of her estate, offered Karen's will for probate on November 20. At the time of her death, Karen owned a number of assets, either jointly or individually, which were valued at $479,989.29. Howard became the sole owner of real estate and other property he and Karen owned as joint tenants with right of survivorship. Karen left no other property to Howard in her will, aside from some household furnishings. Karen bequeathed the rest of her property to her daughters and stepson. The assets at issue in this appeal are a checking account and certificate of deposit at the First Federal Savings Bank valued at $91,085.71 and an annuity with River Resource Funds valued at $18,978.80. All three of these assets were accompanied by beneficiary designations that made them payable on death to Karen's daughters.

Howard filed for an elective share on June 30, 2010. On February 9, 2011, Howard assigned his interest in Karen's estate, including his right to an elective share, to the heirs of DeLillian Peterson, the Ramona Russell Trust, and the Helen B. Anderson Trust. Howard, a former attorney who had surrendered his law license, assigned his interest in Karen's estate to satisfy a restitution judgment against him in a criminal action. Specifically, Howard had been convicted of second- and third-degree felony theft for stealing client funds.

On May 6, the assignees filed an application to set off the surviving spouse's share. The assignees requested that the probate court determine, as an initial matter, whether the checking account, certificate of deposit, and annuity should be included in Howard's elective share. The probate court relied on our 2006 decision in *Sieh*. There, we concluded that assets in a revocable trust were to be included in the surviving spouse's elective share, even though they were not explicitly mentioned in section 633.238 at that time. In reaching that conclusion, we emphasized the fact that "the decedent had complete control over the trust assets at all times prior to his death." Similarly, the probate court emphasized that Karen retained control over the POD assets before her death and, thus, concluded that these assets, like the assets of a revocable trust, should be included in Howard's elective share. This issue has divided the trial courts of our state.

ANALYSIS

In *Sieh*, Mary Jane Sieh, the surviving spouse of Edward Sieh, argued that she should receive, as part of her elective share, assets of a revocable inter vivos trust created by Edward several years before their marriage. The beneficiaries of this trust, Edward's children, argued that the revocable trust should not be included in Mary Jane's elective share, and the probate court agreed. We reversed, emphasizing that, because Edward had full control of the assets of the inter vivos trust at the time of his death, including the power to revoke the trust, the trust assets were property possessed by the decedent during the marriage and thus subject to the spouse's statutory share under section 633.238. We reached this conclusion even though revocable trusts were not mentioned in section 633.238 at that time. We reached this conclusion by relying on the *Restatement (Third) of Property*.

The assignees understandably argue *Sieh* should be read broadly to sweep into section 633.238 property within the decedent's control at the time of her death, such as the POD assets at issue here. The probate court agreed. We reach the opposite conclusion, based on the controlling statutory language as amended after *Sieh*.

The general assembly amended section 633.238 in 2009. This amendment, effective July 1, 2009, "appl[ies] to estates of decedents and revocable trusts of settlors dying on or after" that date. 2009 Iowa Acts ch. 52, § 14(3). Karen died in November of 2009, so the statute applies as amended.

By this amendment, the legislature added "limited to" to section 633.238(1), with the result that section 633.238 now reads:

1. The elective share of the surviving spouse shall be limited to all of the following:

    a. One-third in value of all the legal or equitable estates in real property possessed by the decedent at any time during the marriage which have not been sold on execution or other judicial sale, and to which the surviving spouse has made no express written relinquishment of right.

    b. All personal property that, at the time of death, was in the hands of the decedent as the head of a family, exempt from execution.

    c. One-third of all personal property of the decedent that is not necessary for the payment of debts and charges.

    d. One-third in value of the property held in trust not necessary for the payment of debts and charges over which the decedent was a grantor and retained at the time of death the power to alter, amend, or revoke the trust, or over which the decedent waived or rescinded any such power within one year of the date of death, and to which the surviving spouse has not made any express written relinquishment.

2. The elective share described in this section shall be in lieu of any property the spouse would otherwise receive under the last will and testament of the decedent, through intestacy, or under the terms of a revocable trust.

IOWA CODE § 633.238 (Supp. 2009). The postamendment version states that "[t]he elective share of the surviving spouse shall be limited to all of the following." It is clear that the legislature, by this language, intended to limit the property that would be included in the surviving spouse's elective share to the four categories of property specifically identified in the statute. This interpretation is consistent with the general assembly's explanation accompanying the House version of the bill. Under the controlling language of the amendment, the elective share is limited to those assets specifically enumerated and cannot be judicially expanded.

The assignees make a strong public policy argument that elective share rights may be defeated by the use of POD assets if we interpret section 633.238 to omit them. The assignees' policy argument is properly directed to the legislature. The Iowa legislature chose to include revocable trusts in the elective share under section 633.238(1)(d). We conclude further legislation would be required to include POD assets in the elective share.

Based on the plain meaning of the operative statutory language as amended in 2009, we hold that only the assets specifically enumerated in section 633.238 may be included in the surviving spouse's elective share. POD accounts and annuities are not included under section 633.238. We overrule *Sieh* to the extent it is inconsistent with this opinion. Because Karen's POD assets should not be included in Howard's elective share, we reverse the ruling of the probate court and remand the case for recalculation of payments owed to the assignees.

NOTES

1. After the *Myers* decision, one Iowa estate planner wrote: "Thus, payable on death (POD), transferable on death (TOD), or any other account that has beneficiaries listed upon death could be passed on to other beneficiaries and exclude the spouse. In other words, if you want to disinherit your spouse, this is how you accomplish that result." *See* Matthew Gardner, *Iowa Spousal Elective*

Share—It Is Official Now, IOWA ESTATE PLAN (Nov. 2, 2012), http://www.iowa estateplan.com/2012/11/iowa-spousal-elective-share-it-is.html. Critics of the decision and of this approach argue that enumerated lists create a roadmap to defeat the elective share. What individuals have access to such roadmaps in their estate planning and whom does this approach favor?

2.   In states that limit the elective share right to the probate estate or something similar, as in *Myer*, courts sometimes direct the policy arguments to the state legislature. In a Wyoming case from 2011, *Poland v. Nalee*, 265 P.3d 222 (Wyo. 2011), the Supreme Court of Wyoming stated:

> [U]ntil the Wyoming legislature adopts a motive-based approach to the elective share, as well as the requirement that non-probate assets be added back to the probate estate for purposes of the elective share, the policy adopted by other states is largely irrelevant. . . . Under any circumstances this is a policy choice for the Wyoming legislature to consider, and either accept or reject.

Id. at 230.

ASSESSMENT

You represent a political group seeking to convince a resistant legislature to consider elective share reform. First, consider political groups might consider putting elective share reform on their agendas and how would they best frame the issue in order to convince a resistant legislature? Second, draft a short position paper that frames the issue and anticipates any counterarguments.

b.   *"Semi-Augmented Estate" Statutes*

Avoiding the problems of an overly constrained list, some jurisdictions, like New York, adopt a "semi-augmented" estate approach (adding in assets without explicitly adopting the UPC) and list broad categories of property that will be included when a surviving spouse takes the elective share. New York's statute, for example, includes the following "testamentary substitutes" in that state's augmented estate based on the determinative factor of "ownership and control":

N.Y. Est. Powers & Trusts Law § 5–1.1–A

(1)   Where a person dies . . . and is survived by a spouse who exercises a right of election under paragraph (a), the transactions affected by and property interests of the decedent described in clauses (A)through (H), whether benefiting the surviving spouse or any other person, shall be treated as

testamentary substitutes and the capital value thereof, as of the decedent's death, shall be included in the net estate subject to the surviving spouse's elective right:

(A)　Gifts causa mortis.

(B)　The aggregate transfers of property (including the transfer, release or relinquishment of any property interest which, but for such transfer, release or relinquishment, would come within the scope of clause (F)), other than gifts causa mortis and transfers coming within the scope of clauses (G) and (H), to or for the benefit of any person, made after August thirty-first, nineteen hundred ninety-two, and within one year of the death of the decedent, to the extent that the decedent did not receive adequate and full consideration in money or money's worth for such transfers.

(C)　Money deposited, together with all dividends or interest credited thereon, in a savings account in the name of the decedent in trust for another person, with a banking organization, savings and loan association, foreign banking corporation or organization or bank or savings and loan association organized under the laws of the United States, and remaining on deposit at the date of the decedent's death.

(D)　Money deposited together with all dividends or interest credited thereon, in the name of the decedent and another person and payable on death, pursuant to the terms of the deposit or by operation of law, to the survivor, with a banking organization, savings and loan association, foreign banking corporation or organization or bank or savings and loan association organized under the laws of the United States, and remaining on deposit at the date of the decedent's death.

(E)　Any disposition of property made by the decedent whereby property, at the date of his or her death, is held (i) by the decedent and another person as joint tenants with a right of survivorship or as tenants by the entirety where the disposition was made after August thirty-first, nineteen hundred sixty-six, or (ii) by the decedent and is payable on his or her death to a person other than the decedent or his or her estate.

(F)　Any disposition of property or contractual arrangement made by the decedent, in trust or otherwise, to the extent that the decedent (i) retained for his or her life or for any period not ascertainable without reference to his or her death or for any period which does not in fact end before his or her death the possession or enjoyment of, or the right to income from, the property except to the extent that such disposition or contractual arrangement was for an adequate consideration in money or money's worth; or (ii) at the date of his or her death retained either alone or in conjunction with any other person who does not have a substantial adverse interest, by the express provisions of the disposing instrument, a power to revoke such disposition or a power to consume, invade or dispose of the principal thereof.

(G) Any money, securities or other property payable under a thrift, savings, retirement, pension, deferred compensation, death benefit, stock bonus or profit-sharing plan, account, arrangement, system or trust, except that with respect to a plan to which subsection (a)(11) of section four hundred one of the United States Internal Revenue Code applies or a defined contribution plan to which such subsection does not apply pursuant to paragraph (B)(iii) thereof, only to the extent of fifty percent of the capital value thereof. . . .

(H) Any interest in property to the extent the passing of the principal thereof to or for the benefit of any person was subject to a presently exercisable general power of appointment, as defined in section two thousand forty-one of the United States Internal Revenue Code, held by the decedent immediately before his or her death or which the decedent, within one year of his or her death, released (except to the extent such release results from a lapse of the power which is not treated as a release pursuant to section two thousand forty-one of the United States Internal Revenue Code) or exercised in favor of any person other than himself or herself or his or her estate.

(I) A transfer of a security to a beneficiary pursuant to part 4 of article 13 of this chapter.

NOTE

Do these statutory lists for a "semi-augmented" estate run the same risks as the narrower ones? That is to say, do they also provide a roadmap for estate planners looking to help their clients defeat a spouse's elective share right?

4. Judicial Expansions of the Elective Share

In some states, the statutory rules concerning the elective share remain limited, but courts have judicially expanded the scope of the estate, allowing certain nonprobate transfers to be counted. Massachusetts is a good example of this approach. The Massachusetts elective share statute still limits the elective share to one-third of the probate estate. In *Sullivan v. Burkin*, however, the court took a more expansive view of the property subject to the elective share and expanded the property subject to the elective share. The *Sullivan* court wrapped property that passed via revocable inter vivos trust into the property subject to the elective share, discarding earlier intent-based, and illusory transfer tests and creating what the court called an "objective" test. You may recall that the *Clymer* case in Chapter 13 cited to *Sullivan* as evidence of a coordinated approach to probate and nonprobate estate planning.

Sullivan v. Burkin

460 N.E.2d 572 (Ma. 1984)

WILKINS, J.

Mary A. Sullivan, the widow of Ernest G. Sullivan, has exercised her right, under G.L.c. 191, § 15, to take a share of her husband's estate. By this action, she seeks a determination that assets held in an inter vivos trust created by her husband during the marriage should be considered as part of the estate in determining that share. A judge of the Probate Court for the county of Suffolk rejected the widow's claim and entered judgment dismissing the complaint. The widow appealed, and, on July 12, 1983, a panel of the Appeals Court reported the case to this court.

In September 1973, Ernest G. Sullivan executed a deed of trust under which he transferred real estate to himself as sole trustee. The net income of the trust was payable to him during his life and the trustee was instructed to pay to him all or such part of the principal of the trust estate as he might request in writing from time to time. He retained the right to revoke the trust at any time. On his death, the successor trustee is directed to pay the principal and any undistributed income equally to the defendants, George F. Cronin, Sr., and Harold J. Cronin, if they should survive him, which they did. There were no witnesses to the execution of the deed of trust, but the husband acknowledged his signatures before a notary public, separately, as donor and as trustee.

The husband died on April 27, 1981, while still trustee of the inter vivos trust. He left a will in which he stated that he "intentionally neglected to make any provision for my wife, Mary A. Sullivan and my grandson, Mark Sullivan." He directed that, after the payment of debts, expenses, and all estate taxes levied by reason of his death, the residue of his estate should be paid over to the trustee of the inter vivos trust. The defendants George F. Cronin, Sr., and Harold J. Cronin were named coexecutors of the will. The defendant Burkin is successor trustee of the inter vivos trust.

Although it does not appear in the record, the parties state in their briefs that Ernest G. Sullivan and Mary A. Sullivan had been separated for many years. We do know that in 1962 the wife obtained a court order providing for her temporary support. No final action was taken in that proceeding. The record provides no information about the value of any property owned by the husband at his death or about the value of any assets held in the inter vivos trust. At oral argument, we were advised that the husband owned personal property worth approximately $15,000 at his death and that the only asset in the trust was a house in Boston which was sold after the husband's death for approximately $85,000.

We are now presented with the question whether the assets of the inter vivos trust are to be considered in determining the "portion of the estate of the deceased" (G.L.c. 191, § 15) in which Mary A. Sullivan has rights.

We conclude that, in this case, we should adhere to the principles expressed in *Kerwin v. Donaghy*, 59 N.E.2d 299 (1945), that deny the surviving spouse any claim against the assets of a valid inter vivos trust created by the deceased spouse, even where the deceased spouse alone retained substantial rights and powers under the trust instrument. For the future, however, as to any inter vivos trust created or amended after the date of this opinion, we announce that the estate of a decedent, for the purposes of G.L.c. 191, § 15, shall include the value of assets held in an inter vivos trust created by the deceased spouse as to which the deceased spouse alone retained the power during his or her life to direct the disposition of those trust assets for his or her benefit, as, for example, by the exercise of a power of appointment or by revocation of the trust.

Even if the trust was not testamentary, the widow has special interests which should be recognized. Courts in this country have differed considerably in their reasoning and in their conclusions in passing on this question.

The rule of *Kerwin* is that "[t]he right of a wife to waive her husband's will, and take, with certain limitations, 'the same portion of the property of the deceased, real and personal, that she would have taken if the deceased had died intestate' (G.L. [Ter. Ed.] c. 191, § 15), does not extend to personal property that has been conveyed by the husband in his lifetime and does not form part of his estate at his death. In this Commonwealth a husband has an absolute right to dispose of any or all of his personal property in his lifetime, without the knowledge or consent of his wife, with the result that it will not form part of his estate for her to share under the statute of distributions, under his will, or by virtue of a waiver of his will. That is true even though his sole purpose was to disinherit her." In the *Kerwin* case, we applied the rule to deny a surviving spouse the right to reach assets the deceased spouse had placed in an inter vivos trust of which the settlor's daughter by a previous marriage was trustee and over whose assets he had a general power of appointment. The rule of *Kerwin* has been adhered to in this Commonwealth for almost forty years and was adumbrated even earlier. The Bar has been entitled reasonably to rely on that rule in advising clients. In the area of property law, the retroactive invalidation of an established principle is to be undertaken with great caution.

We announce for the future that, as to any inter vivos trust created or amended after the date of this opinion, we shall no longer follow the rule announced in *Kerwin*. There have been significant changes since 1945 in public policy considerations bearing on the right of one spouse to treat his or her property as he or she wishes during marriage. The interests of one spouse in the property of the other have been substantially increased upon the dissolution of a marriage by divorce. We believe that, when a marriage is terminated by the death of one spouse, the rights of the surviving spouse should not be so restricted as they are by the rule in *Kerwin*. It is neither equitable nor logical to extend to a divorced spouse greater rights in the assets of an inter vivos trust created and controlled by the other spouse than are extended to a spouse who remains married until the death of his or her spouse.

The rule we now favor would treat as part of "the estate of the deceased" for the purposes of G.L.c. 191, § 15, assets of an inter vivos trust created during the marriage by the deceased spouse over which he or she alone had a general power of appointment, exercisable by deed or by will. This objective test would involve no consideration of the motive or intention of the spouse in creating the trust. We would not need to engage in a determination of "whether the [spouse] has in good faith divested himself [or herself] of ownership of his [or her] property or has made an illusory transfer," *Newman v. Dore*, 275 N.Y. 371, 379 (1927), or with the factual question whether the spouse "intended to surrender complete dominion over the property." *Staples v. King*, 433 A.2d 407, 411 (Me. 1981). Nor would we have to participate in the rather unsatisfactory process of determining whether the inter vivos trust was, on some standard, "colorable," "fraudulent," or "illusory."

We affirm the judgment of the Probate Court dismissing the plaintiff's complaint.

NOTES

1.   The rule announced in *Sullivan*, that "assets of an inter vivos trust created during the marriage by the deceased spouse over which he or she alone had a general power of appointment," leaves open the question of what other non-probate assets satisfy this "objective" standard. Pursuing the line of logic used

by the court in *Sullivan*, what other assets should be drawn into the decedent's estate for the purposes of calculating the elective share?

2.   Almost twenty years after *Sullivan*, in *Bongaards v. Millen*, 793 N.E.2d 335 (Mass. 2003), Massachusetts revisited a question that *Sullivan* leaves open, namely what happens when the trust is created by a third party. In *Bongaards*, a mother created a trust that held real estate and stated in the trust that the daughter was to be sole lifetime beneficiary and trustee subsequent to the mother's death. After the daughter's death, the property was to be appointed among the mother's grandchildren. The court in *Bongaards* remarked that:

> Sullivan kept in the elective share "estate" property that would ordinarily have been in that "estate," refusing to give effect to a spouse's attempt to remove that property from the elective share "estate" but still retain access to it by means of a "trust." It is one thing for this court to plug loopholes to prevent a spouse's evasion of the elective share statute. It is quite another to expand the reach of the elective share statute itself and, by so doing, frustrate the intent of a third party who is a stranger to the marriage. A third party has no obligation to support someone else's spouse, and property owned by a third party has never been part of someone else's spouse's elective share "estate."

Id. at 344. If the daughter had ownership and control over the trust property during her lifetime and could have terminated the trust, taking the trust property for herself, what difference does it make that the trust was created by a third party? Whose wealth is being protected in each situation what kind of wealth does this rule favor?

The *Sullivan* holding (as applied prospectively) disallowed one spouse to keep marital wealth from the other at death. The *Bongaards* decision allows one spouse to shelter marital wealth based on the notion of third-party/donor freedom of disposition. Does this difference potentially reflect economic partnership theories as well? At divorce in a separate property state, the wife's trust interest in *Bongaards* would likely not have been subject to division as part of marital estate because it would have been a gift to the daughter and therefore separate property, even with the marriage. The doctrinal rule is that gifts from third parties are not generally part of marital wealth. Does this rule strike you as correct? In other words, should gifts be exempt from the expectation of financial partnership and sharing within marriage?

3.   In *Sullivan*, the court stated "[i]t is neither equitable nor logical to extend to a divorced spouse greater rights in the assets of an inter vivos trust created and controlled by the other spouse than are extended to a spouse who remains married until the death of his or her spouse." All states have some form of equitable division of assets at divorce but, as we've seen, states vary dramatically in the way they treat marital wealth at death. Why are the outcomes so different at death and divorce in so many states? The *Sullivan* court questions the equity of having different property outcomes at death and divorce—which spouses suffer the worst outcomes and why? For more on the difference between marriage termination at death and divorce, see Laura Rosenbury, *Two Ways to End a Marriage: Divorce or Death*, 2005 UTAH L. REV. 1227 (2005).

4.   The holding in *Sullivan* only applied prospectively; the court reasoned that: "[t]he bar has been entitled reasonably to rely on that rule in advising clients. In the area of property law, the retroactive invalidation of an established principle is to be undertaken with great caution." Whose interests are being protected by the court's refusal to apply the holding to the case at hand? Another way to look at this question is to ask what persons and groups traditionally relied on the estate planning advice, particularly with respect to navigating elective share rights?

ASSESSMENTS

1.   You are the judge in the *Sullivan*, and attorneys for the estate have raised the argument that the spouse's abandonment should bar her claim for an elective share (especially because the decedent explained his rationale for exclusion based on their separation). What is your ruling on this argument and why?

2.   Do decanting statutes offer another avenue for fraud on the elective share? As you will recall from Chapter 12, a decanting provision in a trust or a state's decanting statute allows a trustee to modify a trust by "decanting" trust assets into a new trust with different terms. Imagine you represent Eugenia, whose husband died recently. Hermann funded a trust ten years ago, naming himself as trustee and lifetime beneficiary, his brother Vernon as cotrustee, and his children from a prior marriage as remainder beneficiaries. The trust has a decanting clause. A few years before Hermann's death, Vernon exercised his authority to decant the trust into a new trust with himself as settlor, Hermann as lifetime beneficiary, and Hermann's children from a prior marriage as remainder beneficiaries. Eugenia wants to claim an elective share in the trust, relying on *Sullivan*. What do you argue? *See Ferri v. Powell-Ferri*, 476 Mass. 651

(2017) (respecting decanting and disallowing spousal access in context of equitable distribution on divorce).

5. The UPC Approach to the Augmented Estate

Beginning in 1969, drafters of the UPC began to search for ways to bolster the elective share by creating the augmented estate. The 1969 UPC was a big step forward because its purpose was not only to make sure that the surviving spouse had adequate support but also to stop fraud on the elective share. The 1969 version of the UPC gave a one-third share to the surviving spouse of the "augmented estate." UPC § 2–201(a) (1969 ed.) and defined the "augmented estate" as including, in addition to the decedent's probate estate:

> The value of property transferred during marriage, to or for the benefit of any person other than the surviving spouse, to the extent that the decedent did not receive adequate and full consideration in money or money's worth for the transfer, if the transfer is of any of the following types:
>
> i.   Any transfer under which the decedent retained at the time of his death the possession or enjoying of, or right to income from, the property
>
> ii. Any transfer to the extent that the decedent retained at the time of his death a power either alone or in conjunction with any other person, to revoke or to consume, invade or dispose of the principal for his own benefit
>
> iii. Any transfer whereby property is held at the time of decedent's death by decedent and another with right of survivorship
>
> iv. Any transfer made within two years of death of the decedent to the extent that the aggregate transfer to any one donee in either of the years exceeds $3000

The 1969 UPC also credited transfers during life to the surviving spouse, so that it wrapped non-probate provisions for the surviving spouse into the calculation. UPC § 2–202(3) (1969).

In the most recent version, promulgated in 1990 and revised in 2008, the UPC shifted its goal from providing support for the surviving spouse to reflecting an economic partnership theory of marriage, thereby giving the surviving spouse a claim of up to one half of the couple's marital wealth. In order to do this, the 1990 and 2008 versions implemented significant changes to how the augmented estate is calculated, most notably, by including the surviving spouse's wealth in the calculation and by basing the surviving spouse's share on the length of the marriage. These changes, discussed in more detail below, are substantial; whether or not they truly reflect economic partnership is an open question.

The first change in the modern version of the UPC is that it now explicitly states that the rationale for the elective share is the partnership theory of marriage, explaining that "the economic rights of each spouse are seen as deriving from an unspoken marital bargain under which the partners agree that each is to enjoy a half interest in the fruits of the marriage, i.e., in the property nominally acquired by and titled in the sole name of either partner during the marriage (other than in property acquired by gift or inheritance). A decedent who disinherits his or her surviving spouse is seen as having reneged on the bargain." UPC § 2–202 (2008 ed.) (General Comment). The drafters of the modern UPC also observed that the "economic partnership theory of marriage is already implemented under the equitable distribution system applied in both the common-law and community-property states when a marriage ends in divorce." Elective Share of the Surviving Spouse, General Comment, UPC (2008 ed.) Drawing on the logic we encountered in *Sullivan*, the drafters are attempting not only to bring the UPC into alignment with other areas of law that conceptualize marriage as a partnership but also to equalize the financial results for spouses at death and divorce.

Second, the newest version of the UPC goes through a complex computation to determine the value of the augmented estate, capturing the entire value of the couple's marital assets. UPC § 2–203. The categories of assets for inclusion are:

- The decedent's net probate estate
- The decedent's non-probate transfers to others
- The decedent's non-probate transfers to the surviving spouse
- The surviving spouse's property and non-probate transfers to others

The categories of property are further clarified by the drafters in the comments. The net probate estate is "the value of the decedent's probate estate, reduced by funeral and administration expenses, homestead allowance, family allowances, exempt property, and enforceable claims." The decedent's non-probate transfers to others include any property that was owned or "owned in substance" by the decedent immediately before death and that passed through a nonprobate mechanism. Included in this category is also any property transferred during marriage over which the decedent retained some form of control, for example a power of appointment. The decedent's nonprobate transfers to the surviving spouse are also considered. Finally, the following forms of a surviving spouse's own property are considered:

- Any interest in property held in joint tenancy with the right of survivorship interest (to the extent the interest is attributable to each joint owner—for example, half of a home counted as decedent's transfer to spouse and half as spouse's own)

- Any interest in property or accounts held in co-ownership registration with the right of survivorship equals the amount she contributed

- Any property interests that passed to the surviving spouse by reason of the decedent's death (but not including the spouse's right to homestead allowance, family allowance, exempt property, or payments under the federal Social Security system)

- Property that would have been included in the surviving spouse's nonprobate transfers to others, had the spouse been the decedent

Although it is not necessarily a simple calculation, the drafters were hoping to approximate the creation of community property (or the marital estate at divorce in a separate property state) in selecting which assets are includable in the calculation of values for the elective share. The result—the modern UPC approach—is what the drafters call partnership by approximation, "based on the theory that each spouse's fifty percent share is applied to an upwardly-trending accumulation of marital assets." Lawrence W. Waggoner, *The Uniform Probate Code's Elective Share: Time for a Reassessment*, 37 U. MICH. J.L. REFORM 1, 6 (2003). Partnership by approximation is supposed to mimic how marital property and wealth are both accumulated and valued in a community property state. The drafters chose this approach over the asset categorization approach taken in separate-property states at divorce in order to avoid the "costs and uncertainties associated with post-death classification of the couple's property to determine which is marital (community) and which is individual (separate)." *Id.* In other words, one of the complexities of a community property system is tracing how assets were owned; the UPC uses the "marital property" calculation as a surrogate for this tracing.

The third major change in the 1990 version was the introduction of a length-of-marriage factor. After the value of the augmented estate is properly calculated, that value is multiplied by the marital share percentage (based on length of marriage) and the result is known as **"the marital property portion"** of the augmented estate. That marital share is then divided in half to produce the amount of money to which the surviving spouse is entitled. Before distributions of assets, however, the statute also requires taking into account property the surviving spouse already owns. As such, the modern UPC looks to what property the surviving spouse owns in his or her own name and applies the marital property percentage to that property.

Thus, the marital property portion of the augmented estate roughly approximates community property, in that the marital share varies based on the length of marriage. It does not mirror community property because the UPC's elective share does not ask what property actually *was* acquired during marriage.

UPC § 2–203(b) [varying percentage for the marital property portion of augmented estate]:

Less than 1 year	3%
1 year but less than 2 years	6%
2 years but less than 3 years	12%
3 years but less than 4 years	18%
4 years but less than 5 years	24%
5 years but less than 6 years	30%
6 years but less than 7 years	36%
7 years but less than 8 years	42%
8 years but less than 9 years	48%
9 years but less than 10 years	54%
10 years but less than 11 years	60%
11 years but less than 12 years	68%
12 years but less than 13 years	76%
13 years but less than 14 years	84%
14 years but less than 15 years	92%
15 years or more	100%

One purpose of this new elective share statute is to increase the rights of the surviving spouse where there was a long-term marriage and the property was disproportionately titled in the name of the decedent spouse, and to decrease the rights of the surviving spouse in a long-term marriage where the property was equally titled or disproportionately titled in the surviving spouse. The drafters explain it this way: "[T]he effect is both to reward the surviving spouse who sacrificed his or her financial-earning opportunities in order to contribute so-called domestic services to the marital enterprise and to deny an additional windfall to the surviving spouse in whose name the fruits of a long-term marriage were mostly titled." Consider the following case:

> **Case 1.** Asma and Badar married in their 20s. Asma died at age 70, survived by Badar. The couple's assets are $600,000. If all marital assets are in Asma's name, Badar ends up with (typically) $1/3$ or $200,000. If marital assets are half in Asma and half in Badar's names, Badar ends up with (typically) $1/3$ Asma's probate estate (in addition to Badar's own assets of $300,000) for a total of $400,000.

Another purpose of the most recent reforms, according to the drafters, is to "deny a windfall" to a surviving spouse from a short-term marriage "because in such a marriage neither spouse is likely to have contributed much, if anything, to the acquisition of the other's wealth." Consider this case:

> **Case 2.** Envision that Badar, the surviving spouse from the previous paragraph, goes on to remarry Camilla. They are married for five years, before one spouse dies. Again, assume total assets of $600,000, with each spouse owning $300,000. The survivor is (typically) entitled to $1/3$ of decedent's property, or $100,000—and therefore ends up with a total of $400,000.

See Elective Share of the Surviving Spouse, General Comments, UPC (2008) example 2. The drafters were concerned that, in the second case, a short-term spouse would be compensated to the same degree as, or more than, a spouse in a long-term marriage, a result that the drafters sought to avoid. In addition, the drafters sought, at the termination of these second marriages at death, "to deny a windfall to the survivor's children by a prior marriage at the expense of the decedent's children by a prior marriage."

The real question, after reading all these details, is how exactly does this work? Here are several examples taken from the Notes in the UPC to demonstrate the calculations:

Fifteen-year marriage example: Percentage is 100% (see table)

- Husband's net probate estate = $300,000

- Husband's non-probate transfers to others = $100,000

- Wife's net assets and non-probate transfers to others = $200,000

- Augmented estate = $600,000 (takes into account both parties' property under § 2–203(a))

- Marital property portion = $600,000 (based on 100% being included under 2–203(b))

- Elective share amount (.5 * marital property portion) = $300,000

- Amount already satisfied = $200,000 (what wife already owns multiplied by martial property percentage); unsatisfied balance = $100,000

Elective Share of the Surviving Spouse, General Comments, UPC (2008), Example 4.

Five-year marriage example: Percentage is 30% (see table)

- Husband's net probate estate = $300,000

- Husband's non-probate transfers to others = $100,000

- W's assets and non-probate transfers to others = $200,000

- Augmented estate = $600,000

- Marital Property portion = $180,000 (augmented estate * 30% under 2–203(b))

- Elective share amount (.5 * marital property portion) = $90,000

- Amount already satisfied: $200,000 * 30% = $60,000

- Unsatisfied balance = $30,000. Surviving spouse can elect $30,000

Elective Share of the Surviving Spouse, General Comments, UPC (2008), Example 5.

The assets are the same, but the length of marriage is different, producing a significantly different result. As you can see, the UPC rewards length of marriage here—unlike with the intestate share—and the age of the marriage can make a significant difference in the value of the elective share.

NOTES

1.   In his article, *Community Property v. the Elective Share*, 72 LA. L. REV. 161, 163 (2011), Terry Turnipseed observes that: "Separate [elective] share systems can easily be defeated by the wealthy who can afford expensive counsel fees to configure assets in needless, wasteful and complex arrangements specifically designed to defeat the elective share." He therefore recommends the community property model for all states. Does the broad scope of the UPC augmented estate still leave avenues for the evasion of the elective share?

2.   As you have read, the UPC drafters chose to mimic a community property model in this version of the elective share rules rather than recreate a separate property/equitable distribution approach. Susan Gary explains that "the drafters found the discretionary aspect of equitable distribution inappropriate for an elective share statute. Under systems of equitable distribution, the court may look at subjective factors in deciding how to divide the spouses' property." What is the difficulty with using judicial discretion and subjective factors in elective share determinations? Are there other problems with the asset categorization and equitable distribution? Any benefits? *See* Susan Gary, *Marital Partnership Theory and the Elective Share: Federal Estate Tax Law Provides a Solution*, 49 U. MIAMI L. REV. 567 (1995); *see also* Raymond C. O'Brien, *Integrating Marital Property into a Spouse's Elective Share*, 59 CATH. U. L. REV. 617, 658–61 (2010); Charles H. Whitebread, *The Uniform Probate Code's Nod to the Partnership Theory of Marriage: The 1990 Elective Share Revisions*, 11 PROB. L.J. 125 (1992).

3.   To reflect economic partnership, the UPC drafters added the length-of-marriage factor. This is different from the rules for intestacy which grant the surviving spouse an automatic right to the full share, even if the marriage lasted only a day. There are a number of marital rights that turn on automatically at marriage and others that vest over time. Why the difference and which approach do you think is most appropriate?

"I married you for your money, Leonard. Where is it?"

CartoonStock.com

Money and marriage are almost impossible to separate, and marriage gives spouses many rights to marital property.

4.   The drafters, as is clear from the comments, were very concerned about "windfalls"—financial gains that are unexpected and, usually, undeserved. What kinds of stereotypes, particularly gendered ones, are invoked by these descriptions of windfalls? Karen Sneddon, writing about form books, suggests that stock characters such as "the ministering angel," the "deserving caregiver," and "the seductress" are all implicit in traditional templates. *See* Susan Chesler & Karen Sneddon, *Tales from a Form Book: Stock Stories and Transactional Documents*, 78 MONT. L. REV. 501 (2017). Do any of those characters populate the world of the elective share?

ASSESSMENTS

1.   Your client, Alix, lives in a UPC state but is still concerned that her spouse has engaged in some clandestine estate planning to evade Alix's elective share rights. Advise Alix about ways that a spouse might get around an elective share, even one that is as broad as the UPC's.

2.   You have been asked to draft a short opinion piece for *Estate Planning* magazine comparing the length-of-marriage factor in the UPC's elective share to other spousal rights that do not depend on the length of marriage (augmented estate statutes, intestate share statutes, probate-only elective shares). Discuss whether you prefer time-based entitlements or automatic vesting and the

benefits of each, including which is likely to yield the most equitable result. Make sure to discuss if one approach better maps onto theories of marriage.

D. Contracting Around Spousal Rights

Elective share rights, like the other entitlements that occur by operation of law, sometimes come into conflict or are modified by other agreements, such as prenuptial contracts, elective share waivers that occur either before or during marriage, and even other estate planning documents.

1. Prenuptial Contracts and Elective Share Waivers

If you've taken family law, you know that couples often contract around the default rules of marriage, especially with respect to property rights. These **premarital contracts** (also called prenuptial or antenuptial contracts—and **postnuptial** when executed during marriage) used to be scrutinized with skepticism by courts who doubted the ability of couples to contract with one another. Today, premarital contracts are usually rubber stamped by courts, unless they include provisions that are against public policy or deal with custody and child support.

Sometimes, as part of a marriage agreement of prenuptial contract, one spouse will ask the other to waive or limit elective share rights. This is particularly common when couples are entering later-in-life, second (or third or fourth) marriages and the spouse making the request is hoping both to leave undisturbed a complicated estate plan and to avoid conflicts between the new spouse and children from a previous marriage. When spouses make such a waiver, UPC § 2–213 governs:

UPC § 2–213 Waiver of Right to Elect and Other Rights

(1) The right of election of a surviving spouse and the rights of the surviving spouse to homestead allowance, exempt property, and family allowance, or any of them, may be waived, wholly or partially, before or after marriage, by a written contract, agreement, or waiver signed by the surviving spouse.

(2) A surviving spouse's waiver is not enforceable if the surviving spouse proves that:

   a.   he [or she] did not execute the waiver voluntarily; or

b.   the waiver was unconscionable when it was executed and, before execution of the waiver, he [or she]:

i.   was not provided a fair and reasonable disclosure of the property or financial obligations of the decedent;

ii.   did not voluntarily and expressly waive, in writing, any right to disclosure of the property or financial obligations of the decedent beyond the disclosure provided; and

iii.   did not have, or reasonably could not have had, an adequate knowledge of the property or financial obligations of the decedent.

(3)   An issue of unconscionability of a waiver is for decision by the court as a matter of law.

(4)   Unless it provides to the contrary, a waiver of "all rights," or equivalent language, in the property or estate of a present or prospective spouse or a complete property settlement entered into after or in anticipation of separation or divorce is a waiver of all rights of elective share, homestead allowance, exempt property, and family allowance by each spouse in the property of the other and a renunciation by each of all benefits that would otherwise pass to him [or her] from the other by intestate succession or by virtue of any will executed before the waiver or property settlement.

The most important factors for courts in determining whether waiver agreements are valid are voluntariness and full financial disclosure. Consequently, litigation around these waivers often turns on questions of whether there was adequate disclosure of a spouse's wealth. *See, e.g., Reece v. Elliott,* 208 S.W.3d 419 (Tenn. Ct. App. 2006). The next case, *In Re Estate of Greiff,* presents a different question, however: whether there was fraud by the party who obtained the waiver and, if so, who bears the burden of proving that the waiver is invalid.

In re Estate of Greiff

703 N.E.2d 752 (N.Y. 1998)

BELLACOSA, J.

This appeal raises the question whether the special relationship between betrothed parties, when they execute a prenuptial agreement, can warrant a shift of the burden of persuasion bearing on its legality and enforceability. A party challenging the judicial interposition of a prenuptial agreement, used to defeat a right of election, may demonstrate by a preponderance of the evidence that the premarital relationship between the contracting individuals manifested "probable" undue and unfair advantage. In these exceptional circumstances, the burden should fall on the proponent of the prenuptial agreement to show freedom from fraud, deception or undue influence.

Appellant Helen Greiff married Herman Greiff in 1988 when they were 65 and 77 years of age, respectively. They had entered into reciprocal prenuptial agreements in which each expressed the usual waiver of the statutory right of election as against the estate of the other. The husband died three months after the marriage, leaving a will that made no provision for his surviving spouse. The will left the entire estate to Mr. Greiff's children from a prior marriage. When Mrs. Greiff filed a petition seeking a statutory elective share of the estate, Mr. Greiff's children countered with the two prenuptial agreements which they claimed precluded Mrs. Greiff from exercising a right of election against her husband's estate.

A trial was held in Surrogate's Court, Kings County, on the issue of the validity and enforceability of the prenuptial agreements. The Surrogate explicitly found that the husband "was in a position of great influence and advantage" in his relationship with his wife-to-be, and that he was able to subordinate her interests, to her prejudice and detriment. The court further determined that the husband "exercised bad faith, unfair and inequitable dealings, undue influence and overreaching when he induced the petitioner to sign the proffered antenuptial agreements," particularly noting that the husband "selected and paid for" the wife's attorney. Predicated on this proof, the credibility of witnesses and the inferences it drew from all the evidence, Surrogate's Court invalidated the prenuptial agreements and granted a statutory elective share of decedent's estate to the surviving spouse.

The Appellate Division reversed, on the law, simply declaring that Mrs. Greiff had failed to establish that her execution of the prenuptial agreements was procured through her then-fiancé's fraud or overreaching. This Court granted the widow leave to appeal. We now reverse.

A party seeking to vitiate a contract on the ground of fraud bears the burden of proving the impediment attributable to the proponent seeking enforcement. Indeed, as an incentive toward the strong public policy favoring individuals ordering and deciding their own interests through contractual arrangements, including prenuptial agreements this Court has eschewed subjecting proponents of these agreements to special evidentiary or heighted burdens. Importantly, however, [prior cases do not] entirely insulate[ ] prenuptial agreements from typical contract avoidances.

This Court has held, in analogous contractual contexts, that where parties to an agreement find or place themselves in a relationship of trust and confidence at the time of execution, a special burden may be shifted to the party in whom the trust is reposed (or to the proponent of the party's interest, as in this case) to disprove fraud or overreaching. We emphasize, however, that the burden shift is neither presumptively applicable nor precluded. We eschew absolutist rubrics that might ill serve the interests of fair conflict resolution as between proponents or opponents of these kinds of ordinarily useful agreements.

This Court's role here is to clarify, harmonize and find a happy medium of views reflected in the cases. For example, *Graham* has been read as holding that prenuptial agreements were presumptively fraudulent due to the nature of the relationship between prospective spouses. *Phillips*, on the other hand, has been urged to suggest that prenuptial agreements may never be subject to burden-shifting regardless of the relationship of the parties at the time of execution and the evidence of their respective conduct.

Graham was decided in 1894 and indicated that prospective spouses stand in a relationship of confidence which necessarily casts doubt on or requires strict scrutiny concerning the validity of a prenuptial agreement. Its outdated premise, however, was that the man "naturally" had disproportionate influence over the woman he was to marry.

A century later society and law reflect a more progressive view and they now reject the inherent inequality assumption as between men and women, in favor of a fairer, realistic appreciation of cultural and economic realities. Indeed, the law starts marital partners off on an equal plane. Thus, whichever spouse contests a prenuptial agreement bears the burden to establish a fact-based, particularized inequality before a proponent of a prenuptial agreement suffers the shift in burden to disprove fraud or overreaching.

Phillips tugs in the opposite direction from *Graham*. On close and careful analysis, however, *Phillips* does not upset the balanced set of operating principles we pull together by today's decision. While holding that antenuptial agreements are not enveloped by a presumption of fraud, the Court in *Phillips* indicated that some extra leverage could arise from the "circumstances in which the agreement was proposed." This language does not turn its back entirely on *Graham*. Rather, it is generous enough to encompass the unique character of the inchoate bond between prospective spouses—a relationship by its nature permeated with trust, confidence, honesty and reliance. It allows further for a reasonable expectation that these relationships are almost universally beyond the pale of ordinary commercial transactions. Yet, the dispositive tests of legitimacy and enforceability of their prenuptial agreements need not pivot on the legalism or concept of presumptiveness. Instead, a particularized and exceptional scrutiny obtains.

This Court is satisfied that the most prudent course for the fair resolution of this case is a remittal of the case to that court for its determination.

NOTES

1. The crux of the matter with respect to how strong protections must be depends, often, on a court's view of gender inequality. Here, the court observes that, while the historical premise had been that "the man 'naturally' had disproportionate influence over the woman he was to marry," in a contemporary context, "the law starts marital partners off on an equal plane." Is this an accurate analysis in terms of how individuals enter into marriage or are there still gendered inequalities that present from the beginning of a courtship or marriage? How might any structures of power and gender change for same-sex couples? For more on prenuptial contracts and judicial paternalism, see Barbara A. Atwood, *Marital Contracts and the Meaning of Marriage*, 54 ARIZ. L. REV. 11 (2012); Elizabeth R. Carter, *Are Premarital Agreements Really Unfair: An Empirical Study of Premarital Agreements*, 48 HOFSTRA L. REV. 387 (2019).

2. Gail Frommer Brod has written that "[w]omen tend to be harmed by premarital agreements that preclude income sharing because of the gender gap in earnings. As a class, women earn less than men." She argues, therefore, that premarital contracts tend to increase gender wealth gaps. How, if this is true, would these contracts increase such a gap? Do you think that these contracts would also have an effect on the pre-existing racial wealth gaps that exist? *See* Gail Frommer Brod, *Premarital Agreements and Gender Justice*, 6 YALE J.L. & FEMINISM 229 (1994).

3. The exact number of couples that use premarital contracts, while extremely hard to pin down, is extremely low (although recent attention has been paid to millennials' use of these contracts); see Susan Shain, *The Rise of the Millennial Prenup*, N.Y. TIMES (July 6, 2018), https://www.nytimes.com/2018/07/06/smarter-living/millennial-prenup-weddings-money.html). What circumstances would make couples more or less likely to have a premarital contract? If you were advising clients, when would you recommend such an agreement?

4.   Trust companies sometimes advertise their services as an alternative to prenuptial contracts. One estate planning firm spins the trust alternative this way:

> [O]ne individual can enact premarital asset protection planning without his or her fiancé's involvement. Due to the unromantic pitfalls of negotiating a family property settlement the week of the wedding, some proactive individuals are avoiding the prenup altogether. The domestic asset protection trust is the single best alternative a single person can take to protect his or her assets from divorce.[4]

What would you tell a client who was wondering whether putting assets in trust the week before a marriage ceremony would successfully defeat any elective share claims? Would you have any concerns about fraud?

ASSESSMENT

Marianne and Connell have come to your law offices with a request for an elective share waiver. They are already married but do not have a prenuptial agreement. It is a second marriage for both, and they are beginning to plan their estates, each one seeking to benefit primarily their children from previous marriages. Marianne is general counsel at a private equity firm, and Connell runs a legal aid office. Draft a waiver of elective share for the couple and describe what steps you would advise them to take in executing the waiver.

2.   Breach of Contract and Writing Wills

The spousal elective share intersects with some of the material we have read about already, such as contracts regarding a will. The next case, *Via v. Putnam*, presents a conflict between a testator's children by previous marriage (who claimed a contractual right to property under their parents' mutual wills) and a new spouse, who claimed a share of the decedent's estate under a "pretermitted" (or omitted) spouse provision. The children argued that as third-party beneficiaries of the contract between the decedent and their mother, they deserved "creditor status," which would give them priority over the share of the pretermitted spouse; in other words, the kids would receive the entire estate. The court rejects this argument and, based on a history of protecting the surviving spouse, allows the spouse to receive a larger share (the pretermitted or

---

4   Divorce Asset Protection, https://www.assetprotectionplanners.com/strategies/divorce-2/.

intestate share) than she would have been able to take if she were restricted to a right of election.

You may recall that UPC § 2–301 also gives an intestate share to a surviving spouse when there is a will executed before marriage. But UPC § 2–301 takes out of that calculation any property devised to a child (or descendant of a child) who was born before the marriage and is not a child of the surviving spouse. In essence, the UPC takes out of the calculation property left to issue of

> **Connection Note:** Recall that Chapter 8 discusses changes to a will by operation of law, including rights of a spouse who was omitted from a premarital will.

a previous relationship (which would have had a significant effect on the results in the *Via* case). Of course, the surviving spouse can always claim an elective share, even if the entire estate was left to a child by a previous relationship.

Via v. Putnam

656 So.2d 460 (Fla. 1995)

OVERTON, J.

This case involves a dispute between a decedent's surviving spouse, who claimed a share of the decedent's estate under the pretermitted spouse statute, and the children of the decedent's first marriage, who claimed that the mutual wills executed by their parents, naming them residuary beneficiaries of their parents' estates, gave rise to a creditor's contract claim that had priority against the surviving spouse's claim against the estate.

For the reasons expressed in this opinion, we approve the decision of the district court and find that Florida has a strong public policy concerning the protection of the surviving spouse of the marriage in existence at the time of the decedent's death. This policy has been continuously expressed in the law of this state and is controlling. We agree with the district court's reasoning and conclude that the children, as third-party beneficiaries under the mutual wills of their parents, should not be given creditor status under section 733.707, Florida Statutes (1993), when their interests contravene the interests of the surviving spouse under the pretermitted spouse statute.

The record reveals the following facts. On November 15, 1985, Edgar and Joann Putnam executed mutual wills, each of which contained the following provision:

I acknowledge that this is a mutual will made at the same time as my [spouse's] Will and each of us have executed this Will with the understanding and agreement that the survivor will not change the manner in which the residuary estate is to be distributed and that neither of us as survivors will do anything to defeat the distribution schedule set forth herein, such as disposing of assets prior to death by way of trust bank accounts, trust agreements, or in any other manner.

Each will devised that spouse's entire estate to the survivor and provided that the residuary estate would go to the children upon the survivor's death. Joann Putnam died without having done anything to defeat the terms of her mutual will. Edgar Putnam later remarried and failed to execute a subsequent will to provide for his second wife, Mary Rachel Putnam (Rachel Putnam).

Upon Edgar Putnam's death, his mutual will was admitted to probate. Rachel Putnam filed both a Petition to Determine Share of Pretermitted Spouse and an Election to Take Elective Share. In response, the children filed claims against the estate alleging that, by marrying Rachel Putnam, Edgar had breached his contract not to defeat the distribution schedule set forth in his mutual will by subjecting his assets to the statutes governing homestead property, exempt property, pretermitted share, and family allowance. Rachel Putnam filed objections to the claims of the children. The children also brought independent actions in the circuit court based on breach of contract. These actions were consolidated. The trial judge, during the course of these proceedings, made the following findings. First, he found that: (a) the mutual will provision previously quoted "constituted a binding contractual agreement," of which the children are third-party beneficiaries; (b) the children properly filed a claim against the estate based upon the decedent's breach of the mutual will; and (c) the surviving spouse, Rachel Putnam, is the pretermitted spouse of Edgar Putnam. Second, the trial judge entered a summary judgment expressly finding that "Edgar J. Putnam breached his joint and mutual will that he made with Joann Putnam when he married Rachel Putnam without taking appropriate steps to protect the interests of the third-party beneficiaries under said will" and that the claims of the children "are class 7 obligations pursuant to § 733.707, Florida Probate Code." The trial judge concluded that "any pretermitted spouse share or elective share that Rachel Putnam may have is subject to the class 7 obligations of this estate."

On appeal, the district court reversed and noted that, if the children's residuary beneficiary status in the mutual wills allowed them to assert creditor status against the estate, the surviving spouse in this instance would "receive nothing except family allowance and any exempt property that may pass to her free from claims of creditors."

History of a Surviving Spouse's Rights to a Deceased Spouse's Estate

The current statutory provisions regarding the elective share were born out of the widow's right to dower at common law. At common law, the widow's right to dower consisted of "a life estate, for the term of her natural life, in one-third of all the lands and tenements of which her husband was seized in fee simple or fee tail during the coverture and of which any issue which she might have had might have been an heir." The purpose of dower was to ensure the protection and support of the decedent's widow and the nurture and education of their children. However, this right rose no higher than the husband's interest in the land; that is, the widow's right to dower attached only to real estate in which the husband had seisin or possession of legal title. In 1933, section 731.34 expanded the common law right to dower by stating that a widow's right to dower attached to all property the husband "owned," by holding legal or equitable title, at the time of his death.

The pretermitted spouse statute also had its origins in the common law principles regarding the legal effect of a marriage following the execution of a will. At common law, a man's will was automatically revoked following his marriage and the birth of issue unless provision was made in the will in contemplation of such events. Florida followed this common law rule until the enactment of the Probate Act of 1933.

The present statute, which is virtually identical to the statute enacted in 1933, reads as follows:

> When a person marries after making a will and the spouse survives the testator, the surviving spouse shall receive a share in the estate of the testator equal in value to that which the surviving spouse would have received if the testator had died intestate, unless:
>
> (1) Provision has been made for, or waived by, the spouse by prenuptial or postnuptial agreement;
>
> (2) The spouse is provided for in the will; or
>
> (3) The will discloses an intention not to make provision for the spouse.

The foregoing history indicates that Florida, by application of the common law and by statutory scheme, has always maintained a strong public policy in favor of protecting a surviving spouse of a marriage in existence at the time of a decedent's death.

The Instant Case

The children argue that they are third-party beneficiaries of the contract between the decedent and their mother and that they deserve creditor status. As creditors, they would have priority over the share of the pretermitted spouse and would receive the entire estate. Under this scheme, the second wife would receive only a family allowance, the exempt property, and a life estate in the homestead. We have previously determined that a third-party beneficiary of a mutual will does not have priority over the statutory rights of a surviving spouse. In *Tod v. Fuller*, 78 So. 2d 713, 714 (Fla. 1955), we affirmed a trial court order giving a widow's statutory right to dower priority over the claim of a third-party beneficiary under mutual wills executed by a decedent and his former spouse. This Court predicated its decision on the fact that the dower statute gave a husband freedom in the testamentary disposition of his property so long as his wife's dower rights were protected and because the second wife had no notice of the prior mutual wills executed by the husband and his first wife.

The petitioners assert that *Tod* no longer applies because it dealt with the now-abolished dower statute which entitled the surviving spouse to a share in the decedent's property free from liability for all debts of the decedent and all costs, charges, and expenses of administration under the provisions of section 731.34, Florida Statutes (1955). While it is clear that the legislature intended for the residuary beneficiaries and the surviving spouse to share the burden of the expenses of the estate after the 1974 amendment of the elective share statute, it is our view that the legislature did not intend for this modification to allow creditors' claims by third-party beneficiaries of previously executed mutual wills to take priority over the statutory rights of a pretermitted spouse and deny the pretermitted spouse any share in the decedent's estate.

We acknowledge that other jurisdictions take the view that a surviving spouse's statutory share of an estate can be subordinated to claims of third-party beneficiaries of previously executed mutual wills. These courts have advanced four different rationales for giving priority to the contract beneficiaries:

(1) The surviving spouse's marital rights attach only to property legally and equitably owned by the deceased spouse, and the will contract entered into before the marriage deprives the deceased spouse of equitable title and places it in the contract beneficiary.

(2) When the surviving testator accepts benefits under the contractual will, an equitable trust is impressed upon the property in favor of the contract beneficiaries, and the testator is entitled to only a life estate in the property with the remainder going to the beneficiaries upon the testator's death.

(3) When the surviving testator accepts benefits under the contractual will, the testator becomes estopped from making a different disposition of the property, despite any subsequent marriage.

(4) Finally, when the surviving testator breaches the will contract, the contract beneficiaries are entitled to judgment creditor status, thus giving them priority over the rights of the surviving spouse under the applicable state probate code.

It is this last theory that the trial judge adopted in ruling for the children in the instant case. Under these four theories, it makes no difference whether the surviving spouse was married to the decedent for one year or twenty-five years; the surviving spouse would be entitled to no interest in the deceased spouse's probatable estate if the third-party beneficiaries' claim consumed the estate.

In addition to the public policy underlying these statutes, the public policy surrounding the marriage relationship also suggests that the surviving spouse's claim to an elective share should be afforded priority over the claims of beneficiaries of a contract to make a will. Like the majority of other courts, we have recognized the well settled principle that contracts which discourage or restrain the right to marry are void as against public policy. We emphasize that the justification for the elective share and pretermitted spouse statutes is to protect the surviving spouse of the marriage in existence at the time of death of his or her spouse. The legislature has made these shares of a deceased spouse's estate a part of the marriage contract.

We conclude that we have no authority to judicially modify the public policy protecting a surviving spouse's interest in the deceased spouse's estate by adopting this creditor-theory approach as an exception to the pretermitted spouse statute.

Accordingly, we approve the decision of the district court of appeal in this case.

NOTES

1.   The *Via* court observes that the public policy rationales for the pretermitted spouse share and the elective share are similar. The goal is to

protect the surviving spouse even if the decedent did not intend to afford that protection. In what circumstances can a surviving spouse choose between the elective share and the pretermitted share and what will factor into the decision? In what circumstances will a surviving spouse have only the elective share option?

2.   Commenting on *Via*, Eloisa C. Rodriguez-Dod writes:

> The majority opinion superficially appears to be a feminist opinion because the court goes to great lengths, including disregarding the express language in the applicable statutes, to prioritize a surviving spouse's elective share and pretermitted share rights over claims of others to the decedent's estate. [However], by subjugating the contractual rights of the first wife, the opinion is far from feminist. In the court's desire to help one woman, Rachel, the majority silences another woman, Joann.

See FEMINIST JUDGMENTS: REWRITTEN TRUSTS AND ESTATES OPINIONS 105 (eds. Deborah S Gordon, Browne C. Lewis, & Carla Spivack) 220–45 (Cambridge Univ. Press 2020). Elena Marty-Nelson rewrote this opinion to give voice to the first wife's perspective. *Id.* at 109–22. How would you revise this opinion to take into account the first wife's position and what are the merits, if any, of this approach?

E.   Conclusion and Takeaways

This chapter discusses the protections available to surviving spouses. There are several forms of protection, including the homestead right, exempt personal property, and the family allowance; by far, though, the most robust protection is the elective (or forced) spousal share. Historically, the elective share was equal to one-third of the decedent's probate estate. In some states, this still holds true. Limiting the amount of the elective share to a percentage of the probate estate has, however, proven over time to be problematic because it is simple for a decedent to transfer wealth through nonprobate mechanisms.

In response to this problem of fraud on the elective share, legislators and the uniform law drafters have come up with some solutions, the most common being the augmented estate. Using the augmented estate approach, surviving spouses taking the elective share receive a percentage of the decedent's "augmented" estate, that is to say the probate estate augmented with certain nonprobate transfers. In general, nonprobate transfers are included in the augmented estate if the decedent retained ownership or control over the asset—

a typical example being the revocable trust. By using the augmented estate, surviving spouses are less likely to be disinherited and more likely to be compensated for their marital contributions.

CHAPTER 14 COMPREHENSIVE ASSESSMENTS

1.   **PLANNING EXERCISE.** While the cases that we read here all focus on decedent spouses and the problem of fraud on the elective share, there are in fact legitimate reasons for one spouse to not leave the bulk of her estate to her surviving spouse. Come up with and describe two to three client scenarios that fall into this category—where one spouse, your client, has a legitimate reason to not leave a large amount to the surviving spouse at death—and then list the steps or options that you would recommend your client take in order to avoid elective share or other challenges to the estate at her death.

2.   **ELECTIVE SHARE REVIEW.** Bobby and Ethel had been married 21 years when Bobby died in 2011. Bobby and Ethel had no children together, although Bobby had a son, David, and a daughter, Amanda, from a prior marriage that ended in 1988. In 1995, the couple executed "sweetheart" wills, leaving everything to the other. They were represented by a partner at White & White LLP, a boutique estate planning law firm. In 2000, Bobby began to worry about what his children would do if he should die suddenly, and he decided to change his estate plan.

Using the same attorney as he used in 1995, Bobby executed a new will giving $50,000 to Ethel and the rest of his probate estate to a revocable trust he executed on the same day. He funded that trust with $200,000 in cash and $300,000 that came from the royalties of a book he had published in 1990; the declaration of trust named Bobby as the sole trustee and beneficiary during his life, with the power to make distributions to himself as needed and the power to revoke or amend the trust at any time by providing notice to the trustee. On Bobby's death, any remaining trust property was distributed outright in equal shares to Bobby's daughter Amanda and Bobby's son David. Bobby made no other non-probate transfers.

Bobby died with the following property:

- A savings account in his name holding $150,000, all of which he earned from the publishing job he held during his marriage to Ethel

- The funded trust described above, with a date of death value of $500,000

- A home worth $300,000 (with no mortgage), held as tenants-by-the entirety with Ethel

On Bobby's death, Ethel had in her own name assets valued at $200,000, which consisted of a savings account where she deposited her monthly paychecks and 40 shares of stock she had inherited from her father when he died in 1989 (worth $40,000).

a. What are Ethel's elective share rights to Bobby's estate in a separate property jurisdiction that follows the probate-only approach to the elective share? What other protections does she have in addition to her elective share right?

b. How would your answer differ if the jurisdiction has a statute that allows a surviving spouse to elect against an "augmented" estate (like New York or Delaware)? How would your answer differ if the jurisdiction used a multi-factor test, like Maryland?

c. What are Ethel's rights to Bobby's estate in a post-2008 UPC, separate property jurisdiction?

d. How would your answer to question 3 differ if Bobby and Ethel had been married for 10 years when Bobby died?

e. Returning to the 21-year marriage, what are Ethel's rights to Bobby's estate in a community property jurisdiction?

f. If you were Bobby and Ethel's estate planning attorney, what would you tell Bobby when he asked for your help in revising his estate plan in 2000?

g. If Bobby had wished to keep his property separate from Ethel when they married in 1990, what could he have done?

Test Your Knowledge

To assess your understanding of the material in this chapter, click here to take a quiz.

CHAPTER 15

Charitable Trusts

CHAPTER LEARNING OUTCOMES

Following your work with this material in this chapter, you should be able to do the following:

- Identify the major differences between private and charitable trusts

- Categorize what charitable purposes are and be able to differentiate between a charitable purpose and private generosity

- Analyze who benefits from charitable trusts and what trustee duties change when the beneficiary is no longer ascertainable

- Explain the doctrines available for the modification of charitable trusts and gifts

- Draft a petition for cy pres modification or for modification through deviation

- Identify solutions to the problems that result from having the state attorney general be the only person with judicial standing to hold charitable institutions accountable

A. Introduction

This chapter turns to charitable trusts. These trusts are established for "**charitable**" purposes, rather than for the private purposes of the trusts we have been studying up until now. Charitable trusts have long been a favored way to simultaneously transfer wealth and engage in philanthropy and, because of the philanthropic nature of charitable trusts, they receive certain forms of preferential treatment. Charitable trusts receive preferential tax treatment, providing significant benefits for the trust settlor in that gifts made to the charitable trust are generally excludable from any form of taxation. As we will see in this chapter, there is significant interplay between charitable trusts, charitable giving, and tax law. A second form of preferential treatment is that charitable trusts are exempt from the Rule Against Perpetuities, based on the idea that they are conveying resources to a cause rather than a person.

Accordingly, we study charitable trusts because they are an important trust form, one that is quite distinctive from private trusts and serves a strong policy purpose. Through our investigation of charitable trusts, we will also see how far the reach of charitable trust law is as well as how many assets are ultimately governed by charitable trust law. Trust law, most obviously, governs all charitable trusts. This includes nonprofit organizations or private foundations that are organized as trusts, such as the Gates Foundation, which has an endowment of over $46 Billion.[1] This also includes what are called split-interest trusts, such as charitable remainder trusts, that individuals create to benefit both family members (who typically have a life interest) and a chosen charitable institution (typically receives the remainder).[2]

Trust law also, however, sets forth many of the basic rules concerning gift management, asset investment, and endowment distributions for nonprofit organizations that are organized as corporations. This means that trust law governs important administrative functions at all **nonprofit** (also call **tax-exempt**) **organizations**, the management of charitable gifts being a central one. Universities, most hospitals, churches, and museums—any organizations that are considered tax-exempt according to § 501(c)(3) of the Internal Revenue Code—are all subject to trust rules concerning gift management and modification. Take a look at this chart to see the sheer amount of assets we are talking about, just considering the ten largest university endowments.

---

[1]   *See Who We Are: Foundation Fact Sheet,* BILL & MELINDA GATES FOUND., https://www.gatesfoundation.org/Who-We-Are/General-Information/Foundation-Factsheet.

[2]   *See* Split-Interest Trusts, Filing Year 2012, INTERNAL REVENUE SERV., https://www.irs.gov/pub/irs-soi/12splitinteresttrustonesheet.pdf.

Rank	Institution	FY 2018 endowment value (in 1,000s)
1.	Harvard U.	$38,303,383
2.	U. of Texas system	$30,886,018
3.	Yale U.	$29,351,100
4.	Stanford U.	$26,464,912
5.	Princeton U.	$25,917,199
6.	Massachusetts Institute of Technology	$16,529,432
7.	U. of Pennsylvania	$13,777,441
8.	Texas A&M U. system and foundations	$13,524,947
9.	U. of Michigan (all campuses)	$11,901,760
10.	Northwestern U.	$11,087,659

University endowments rival the GDPs of many small countries.

This chapter will take up questions that are specific to charitable trusts, both large and small, and we will investigate the role these trusts play in not only transferring wealth but also serving the public. We will approach these questions through an analysis of the differences between private and charitable trusts—including purpose, beneficiaries, modification, and enforcement. In **Part B**, we will examine what constitutes a **charitable purpose**. A charitable trust must have a charitable purpose, such as education or the relief of poverty, or else it is categorized as private generosity. **Part C** explores who the beneficiaries of a charitable trust are, since a charitable trust—unlike a private trust—cannot have ascertainable beneficiaries. **Part D** explains the legal mechanisms for modifying charitable trusts, which will in part look familiar. Charitable trusts can be modified through deviation, which we learned about with private trusts; charitable trusts are also modifiable using the cy pres doctrine, which we read about at the beginning of this textbook. Modification rules are particularly important for charitable trusts because they are, as already noted, exempt from the Rule Against Perpetuities. The last part, **Part E**, addresses questions of enforcement. Because there are no ascertainable beneficiaries, the state attorney general is the traditional enforcer of fiduciary and other trust law duties. This assignment of the enforcement role to the state attorney general comes with a unique set of problems.

B. What Is a Charitable Purpose?

It is a longstanding rule that that an organization, to be considered charitable, must serve a charitable purpose. One of the first lists of charitable purposes appears in the English Statute of Charitable Uses, enacted in 1601 under Queen Elizabeth I. Some of the purposes in that Statute included: "relief of aged, impotent and poor people," "maintenance of sick and maimed soldiers and mariners, schools of learning, free schools and scholars in universities," "education and preferment of orphans," and, of course "some for marriages of poor maids." Today, UTC § 405 provides a not altogether different list of charitable purposes:

UTC § 405 Charitable Purposes

(a) A charitable trust may be created for the relief of poverty, the advancement of education or religion, the promotion of health, governmental or municipal purposes, or other purposes the achievement of which is beneficial to the community.

(b) If the terms of a charitable trust do not indicate a particular charitable purpose or beneficiary, the court may select one or more charitable purposes or beneficiaries. The selection must be consistent with the settlor's intention to the extent it can be ascertained.

(c) The settlor of a charitable trust, among others, may maintain a proceeding to enforce the trust.

Notice that § 405(a), which defines purposes, is quite broad. If a court chooses to construe the categories in the same broad manner, many trusts might potentially fall within the purview of the rule. The Virginia Supreme Court, in the *Shenandoah Valley National Bank* case that follows, had a much narrower vision of charitable purpose. While reading this case, consider first whether this trust would be valid under the UTC's definition. Then consider why providing a small amount of spending money to children at the neighborhood school, right before winter and spring holidays, is not a charitable purpose.

Shenandoah Valley National Bank v. Taylor

63 S.E.2d 786 (Va. 1951)

MILLER, J.

Charles B. Henry, a resident of Winchester, Virginia, died testate on the 23rd day of April 1949. His will dated April 21, 1949, was duly admitted to probate and the Shenandoah Valley National Bank of Winchester, the designated executor and trustee, qualified thereunder. The testator's entire estate valued at $86,000, was left as follows:

Second: All the rest, residue and remainder of my estate, real, personal, intangible and mixed, of whatsoever kind and wherever situate, I give, bequeath and devise to the Shenandoah Valley National Bank of Winchester, Virginia, in trust, to be known as the 'Charles B. Henry and Fannie Belle Henry Fund', for the following uses and purposes:

(a)   My Trustee shall invest and reinvest my trust estate, shall collect the income therefrom and shall pay the net income as follows:

(1)   On the last school day of each calendar year before Easter my Trustee shall divide the net income into as many equal parts as there are children in the first, second and third grades of the John Kerr School of the City of Winchester, and shall pay one of such equal parts to each child in such grades, to be used by such child in the furtherance of his or her obtainment of an education.

(2)   On the last school day of each calendar year before Christmas my trustee shall divide the net income into as many equal parts as there are children in the first, second and third grades of the John Kerr School of the City of Winchester, and shall pay one of such equal parts to each child in such grades, to be used by such child in the furtherance of his or her obtainment of an education.

By paragraphs (3) and (4) it is provided that the names of the children in the three grades shall be determined each year from the school records, and payment of the income to them "shall be as nearly equal in amounts as it is practicable" to arrange. Paragraph (5) provides that if the John Kerr School is ever discontinued for any reason the payments shall be made to the children of the same grades of the school or schools that take its place, and the School

Board of Winchester is to determine what school or schools are substituted for it. Under clause "Third" the trustee is given authority, power, and discretion to retain or from time to time sell and invest and reinvest the estate, or any part thereof, as it shall deem to be to the best interest of the trust.

The John Kerr School is a public school used by the local school board for primary grades and had an enrollment of 458 boys and girls so there will be that number of pupils or thereabouts who would share in the distribution of the income. The testator left no children or near relatives. Those who would be his heirs and distributees in case of intestacy were first cousins and others more remotely related. One of these next of kin filed a suit against the executor and trustee, and others challenging the validity of the provisions of the will which undertook to create a charitable trust.

The sole question presented is: does the will create a valid charitable trust? In the law of trusts there is a real and fundamental distinction between a charitable trust and one that is devoted to mere benevolence. The former is public in nature and valid; the latter is private and if offends the rule against perpetuities, it is void.

"It is quite clear that trusts which are devoted to mere benevolence or liberality, or generosity, cannot be upheld as charities. Benevolent objects include acts dictated by mere kindness, good will, or a disposition to do good. Charity in a legal sense must be distinguished from acts of liberality or benevolence. To constitute a charity the use must be public in its nature." ZOLLMAN ON CHARITIES, sec. 398, p. 268.

Appellant contends that the gift qualifies as a charitable trust under the definition in *Allaun v. First & Merchants National Bank*. It is also said that it not only meets the requirements of a charitable trust as defined in *Restatement of the Law of Trusts*, but specifically fits two of those classifications, viz.:

"(b) trusts for the advancement of education;

"(f) other purposes the accomplishment of which is beneficial to the community."

We now turn to the language of the will for from its context the testator's intent is to be derived. Its interpretation must be free from and uninfluenced by the unyielding rule against perpetuities. Yet, when the testator's intent is ascertained, if it is found to be in contravention of the rule, the will, in that particular, must be declared invalid.

Yearly on the last school day before Easter and Christmas each youthful beneficiary of the testator's generosity is to be paid an equal share of the income. In mandatory language the duty and the duty alone to make cash payments to each individual child just before Easter and Christmas is enjoined upon the trustee by the certain and explicit words that it "shall divide the net income . . . and shall pay one of such equal shares to each child in such grades."

Without more, that language and the occasions specified for payment of the funds to the children being when their minds and interests would be far removed from studies or other school activities definitely indicate that no educational purpose was in the testator's mind. It is manifest that there was no intent or belief that the funds would be put to any use other than such as youthful impulse and desire might dictate. But in each instance immediately following the above-quoted language the sentence concludes with the words or phrase "to be used by such child in the furtherance of his or her obtainment of an education." It is significant that by this latter phrase the trustee is given no power, control or discretion over the funds so received by the child. Full and complete execution of the mandate and trust imposed upon the trustee accomplishes no educational purpose. Nothing toward the advancement of education is attained by the ultimate performance by the trustee of its full duty. It merely places the income irretrievably and forever beyond the range of the trust.

In construing wills, we may not forget or disregard the experiences of life and the realities of the occasion. Nor may we assume or indulge in the belief that the testator by his injunction to the donees intended or thought that he could change childhood nature and set at naught childhood impulses and desires. We are of opinion that the testator's dominant intent appears from and is expressed in his unequivocal direction to the trustee to divide the income into as many equal parts as there are children beneficiaries and pay one share to each. This expressed purpose and intent is inconsistent with the appended direction to each child as to the use of his respective share and the latter phrase is thus ineffectual to create an educational trust. The testator's purpose and intent were, we think, to bestow upon the children gifts that would bring to them happiness on the two holidays, but that falls short of an educational trust.

If it be determined that the will fails to create a charitable trust for educational purposes (and our conclusion is that it is inoperative to create such a trust), it is earnestly insisted that the trust provided for is nevertheless charitable and valid. In this respect it is claimed that the two yearly payments to be made to the children just before Christmas and Easter produce "a desirable social effect" and are "promotive of public convenience and needs, and happiness and contentment" and thus the fund set up in the will constitutes a charitable trust. 2 BOGERT ON TRUSTS, sec. 361, p. 1090, and 3 SCOTT ON TRUSTS, sec. 368, p. 1972.

The definition of the word "charity" is relied upon to sustain this position:

The word 'charity,' as used in law, has a broader meaning and includes substantially any scheme or effort to better the condition of society or any considerable part thereof. It has been well said that any gift not inconsistent with existing laws, which is promotive of science or tends to the education, enlightening, benefit, or amelioration of the condition of mankind or the diffusion of useful knowledge, or is for the public convenience, is a charity.

Numerous cases that deal with and construe specific provisions of wills or other instruments are cited by appellant to uphold the contention that the provisions of this will, without reference to and deleting the phrase "to be used by such child in the furtherance of his or her obtainment of an education" meet the requirements of a charitable trust. Upon examination of these decisions, it will be found that where a gift results in mere financial enrichment, a trust was sustained only when the court found and concluded from the entire context of the will that the ultimate intended recipients were poor or in necessitous circumstances.

In the *Mellody* case, income from the trust fund was to be used by the trustee "to provide an annual treat or field day for the schoolchildren of Turton or as many of such children as the same will provide for." It will thus be seen that the trustee had control of and administered the income from the fund and it was devoted to a supervised annual outing for school children as such. Its intended use bore a direct relationship to their schooling and education. The court held that it was a charitable trust because it (1) tended to the advancement of education, and (2) was "for purposes beneficial to a particular section of the community." Speaking of the annual treat or field day provided for, it said:

It may well be made, and, I doubt not, often is made, the occasion for pointing out to the children those objects of the countryside and nature about which during their school hours they have read in their books, or which they have seen in the pictures displayed upon the walls of their schoolroom.

Payment to the children of their cash bequests on the two occasions specified would bring to them pleasure and happiness and no doubt cause them to remember or think of their benefactor with gratitude and thanksgiving. That was, we think, Charles B. Henry's intent. Laudable, generous and praiseworthy though it may be, it is not for the relief of the poor or needy, nor does it otherwise so benefit or advance the social interest of the community as to justify its continuance in perpetuity as a charitable trust.

Affirmed.

NOTES

1.   What if UTC § 405(a) applied to Henry's trust? As previously noted, the UTC framework is much broader than the one used by the *Shenandoah Valley* court. Think about the differences and how the decision would change using UTC rules. Consider, also, the policy purposes of having an inclusive rule rather than a narrow, exclusive one.

2.   The *Shenandoah Valley* court refers to the "unyielding rule against perpetuities." Why does Henry's trust fail to satisfy the rule and therefore fail as a private trust in this case? Once the trust fails as a private trust, what will happen to the trust corpus? Is this result preferable to distributing funds to the school children?

3.   Organizations frequently seek to demonstrate that they have a charitable purpose to qualify as tax-exempt under § 501(c)(3) of the Internal Revenue Code. Organizations want this tax status because it makes them exempt from most forms of taxation, and donors to their organizations may receive tax deductions for their gifts. For example, the Church of Scientology tried unsuccessfully for decades to be recognized as a 501(c)(3) organization until the tax authorities finally did an "astonishing turnaround" in 1993. The New York Times wrote that "[t]he landmark reversal shocked tax experts and saved the church tens of millions of dollars in taxes. More significantly, the decision was an invaluable public relations tool in Scientology's worldwide campaign for acceptance as a mainstream religion." Douglas Frantz, *Scientology's Puzzling Journey From Tax Rebel to Tax Exempt*, N.Y. TIMES (Mar. 9, 1997), https://www.nytimes.com/1997/03/09/us/scientology-s-puzzling-journey-from-tax-rebel-to-tax-exempt.html.

Other religions have had similar battles. The Temple of the Jedi Order, an organization that focuses on the "Jedi church of The Force and international ministry of the Jedi religion, Jediism, and the Jedi way of life," has received tax-exempt status in the United States but not in the United Kingdom. In ruling against them, the UK Commission stated: "The commission does not consider that the aggregate [beliefs of the Temple of the Jedi] amounts to a sufficiently

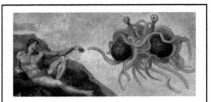

"Touched by His Noodly Appendage," a parody of Michelangelo's "Creation of Adam" has become an iconic image of the Flying Spaghetti Monster.

cogent and distinct religion." Travis Lacouter, *Jedi Denied Charitable Status in Britain (but Not in America)*, PHILANTHROPY DAILY (Dec. 29, 2016), https://www.philanthropydaily.com/jedi-denied-charitable-status-in-britain-but-not-in-america/. More recently, in 2019, the Satanic Temple was granted tax-exempt status. The Pastafarians, who lightheartedly believe that "an invisible and undetectable Flying Spaghetti Monster created the universe, probably after drinking heavily (thus explaining its many flaws)," have not had the same luck in any country. Jon Henley, *Documentary Follows Pastafarians As They Strain for Recognition*, GUARDIAN (Sept. 18, 2019), https://www.theguardian.com/world/2019/sep/18/documentary-follows-pastafarians-strain-for-recognition.

ASSESSMENTS

1.   Redraft the relevant provisions in Henry's will to make the trust a valid charitable trust. What changes did you make and why? If Henry had come to you when he first began contemplating his will, how would you have explained the charitable purposes requirement to him?

2.   Imagine your client, Leona, comes to you expressing a desire to help provide food and care for all the cats in her city. How do you advise Leona, and what options do you provide for structuring this charitable gift? Is the creation of a charitable trust the best option or are there other options that might also work? Leona also wants to help her thirteen Siamese cats along with all the other cats in the city; can her charitable trust or gift benefit her own cats?

> **Connection Note:** A charitable trust to benefit animals differs from a **"pet trust."** The latter, allowed by statute, provides funds to support the owner's pets and not animals more generally.

C.   Who Are the Beneficiaries of a Charitable Trust?

One of the major differences between private and charitable trusts is that, while private trusts must have ascertainable beneficiaries, charitable trusts cannot benefit ascertainable individuals. Charitable trusts must be for the benefit of a public, a group, a community. Sometimes the public in question is relatively easy to define, other times, less so. For instance, a charitable trust established at a college to provide scholarship aid has a relatively cognizable group of beneficiaries—all the students who benefit from the trust. A gift of art to a museum, however, may benefit a broader and less coherent public: museum goers; art lovers; residents of the city in which the museum is located.

Take what happened when Fisk University, a historically black university in Nashville, Tennessee, tried to sell two valuable paintings from its collection in order to stay afloat financially. The two paintings, one by Georgia O'Keefe and the other by Marsden Hartley, had been given to the University by Georgia O'Keefe (in her capacity as the executor of Alfred Stieglitz's estate). When the sale was proposed, the Tennessee attorney general tried to block it, arguing in his role as public representative that the paintings were meant to be located in Nashville for the benefit of the public. The proposed buyer was the Crystal Bridges museum in Bentonville, Arkansas. The appellate court, analyzing the question, stated:

> It is apparent from Alfred Stieglitz's will, the 1948 Petition Georgia O'Keeffe filed in the surrogate's court, and Ms. O'Keeffe's letters to President Johnson that followed, that the charitable intent motivating the gifts of the Stieglitz Collection and Ms. O'Keeffe's four pieces to the University was to make the Collection available to the public in Nashville and the South for the benefit of those who did not have access to comparable collections to promote the general study of art. The express language used in Alfred Stieglitz's will reveals that he desired his collection be donated to institutions to promote the study of art. The record in this case also reveals that Georgia O'Keeffe not only affirmed his expressed intent when making the gifts from his vast collection to the University and other institutions, but she also adopted her husband's charitable intent when she donated four pieces from her personal collection to the University.

> In her correspondence to President Johnson, before and after the completion of the gifts from her collection, Ms. O'Keeffe expressed her intent that the Collection, inter alia, be identified as the Stieglitz Collection (including her four pieces) and preserved, intact, for its educational study and historical value to the public. Considering the facts in the record, we have concluded that the clear intent for giving the Collection to the University was to enable the public—in Nashville and the South—to have the opportunity to study the Collection in order to promote the general study of art.

Georgia O'Keeffe Found. v. Fisk Univ., 312 S.W.3d 1, 17–18 (Tenn. Ct. App. 2010). At trial, the director of Fisk's Art Gallery added:

> "[P]art of the reasoning, as it was explained to me by older hands here, for O'Keeffe's gift to Fisk was that by giving this collection to an historically African American institution, it would assure that everyone would have access to it. And she was determined to establish a kind of niche for modernism in the south. If she were to give it to a majority institute in the south, African Americans would have been denied access to it. Fisk already had a well-established reputation as a place where races met, in Nashville."[3]

The attorney general introduced two expert witnesses trained in demography and population studies to "testify concerning the demographic profiles and characteristics of Bentonville, Arkansas, the home of the Crystal Bridges Museum, compared to Nashville and the South[.]"[4] Based on a comparison of multiple factors—including racial composition, educational levels, and household incomes—one of the expert witnesses testified that "Nashville more closely resembled the South" than Bentonville.[5] Ultimately, the parties brokered a deal whereby Fisk and Crystal Bridges would share the art on a rotational basis, allowing the University to get the much needed cash infusion and allowing Crystal Bridges to display the artwork.

In a similar vein, the following opinion involving the Hershey Trust and written by the Orphan's court in response to an emergency motion for an injunction raises the question of who is a trust beneficiary. The case was set in motion by a concern over whether the Hershey Trust was adequately diversified. Then, after the Hershey Trust appeared ready to sell its controlling interest in the Hershey Chocolate Company, the state's attorney general intervened. The theory, it seems, is that the community is an implied trust beneficiary, allowing the attorney general to request an injunction against a sale of assets that will hurt the community. If you are interested in reading the trust instrument itself, it is included in the Appendix. Other aspects of the case appear later in the chapter.

---

[3]   Brief of Intervenor-Appellee Attorney General and Reporter at 42, *In re Fisk Univ.* (Tenn. Ct. App. 2011) (No. M2010-026150COA-R3-CV), 2011 WL 2006328, at *45.

[4]   *Id.* at *2.

[5]   *Id.* at *9–10.

In re Milton Hershey School Trust

(Orphans' Court Div., Ct. of Com. Pleas, Dauphin Cty., Pa., Sept. 10, 2002)
(attached as Exhibit to 807 A.2d 324)

MORGAN, J.

The Hershey Trust Company and the Board of Managers of the Milton Hershey School (the Board of the Trust Company is also the Board of Managers) propose to sell the controlling interest in the Hershey Foods Corporation now held in trust for the School. On August 23, 2002, the Attorney General filed a Petition for an ex parte injunction against the same respondents upon which we deferred consideration until a hearing on September 3, 2002.

FINDINGS OF FACT

In 1909 Milton S. Hershey and Catherine, his wife, by deed of trust endowed for the benefit of orphan children an institution now known as the Milton Hershey School.

By his Will, Mr. Hershey gave the stock of the Hershey Trust Company to the School Trust. Accordingly, there now exists a unique arrangement for the election and composition of the Directors/ Managers. During Mr. Hershey's entire lifetime and thereafter until the 1980s the Directors/Managers all resided in Derry Township (where the community of Hershey is located) or nearby. The present membership of the Directors/Managers includes only four who live near Hershey. The Deed of Trust directs that the Milton Hershey School shall be located in Derry Township, Pennsylvania, and gives preference to children born in the Pennsylvania counties of Dauphin (where Derry Township is located) and Lebanon and Lancaster which adjoin

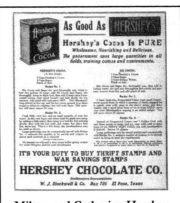

Milton and Catherine Hershey founded the school in 1909 with money they earned from their chocolate company.

Dauphin County. Moreover, in the area in close proximity to his chocolate factory he created a community, now known as Hershey, including banks, a department store, community center, hotel, sports facilities, theatre, hospital, utility companies, transportation, and homes for himself and for many of his employees. Milton Hershey's charitable interests were narrowly restricted. He was concerned for children and for his community.

Shares of Hershey Foods Corporation amounting to a controlling interest in the Corporation have comprised the corpus of the School Trust from 1918 until the present date. At the request of the present Directors/Managers, the Hershey Foods Corporation is soliciting bids for the acquisition of the Corporation which would include purchase of the shares of stock held in the School Trust representing 77% of the voting power of all outstanding shares of the Hershey Foods Corporation.

DISCUSSION

At the outset we would state that the Attorney General's Petition for a Citation raises issues of the effect on public interests of a sale by the School Trust of its controlling shares in Hershey Foods Corporation and is broad enough to also raise issues of abuse of discretion by the Directors/Managers in initiating the process.

That the Attorney General has standing in this proceeding is the law of this Commonwealth. The responsibility for public supervision of charitable trusts traditionally has been delegated to the Attorney General to be performed as an exercise of his parens patriae powers. Our Supreme Court in *In re Pruner's Estate*, 136 A.2d 107, 110 (1957), explained this interest: "[I]n every proceeding which affects a charitable trust, whether the action concerns invalidation, administration, termination or enforcement, the attorney general must be made a party of record because the public as the real party in interest in the trust is otherwise not properly represented." Property given to a charity is in a measure public property, *McKee Estate*, 108 A.2d 214 (1954), and the beneficiary of charitable trusts is the general public to whom the social and economic benefits of the trusts accrue. We conclude therefore that the Attorney General has the authority to inquire whether an exercise of a trustee's power, even if authorized under the trust instrument, is inimical to the public interest.

The Attorney General has sufficiently carried his burden of proving the potential harm that he seeks to prevent, namely, the adverse economic and social impact against the public interest if a sale of Hershey Foods Corporation takes place, particularly in its effect on employees of the Corporation and the community of Derry Township. The persuasive thrust of the testimony of Richard A. Zimmerman, a former CEO and Chairman of the Board of Hershey Foods Corporation with years of experience in mergers and acquisitions, was that a sale of the controlling interest in Hershey Foods Corporation creates a likelihood that there will be reduction in the work force and that relocations of plant operations and closing of duplicate facilities will be matters of probable immediate consideration by the acquiring company. We would add that this Court is not required to be blind and deaf to that which has been commonplace information to the public during the recent past period of numerous mergers and acquisitions of public companies.

The trust company is located in a small town built by Mr. Hershey around his manufacturing facilities and the entire fortune earned from that business by Mr. Hershey he dedicated to the School he located in that town and to its residents. The symbiotic relationship among the School, the community, and the Company is common knowledge. The business was not, during Mr. Hershey's life, is not now, nor foreseeably in financial difficulty, and the School, according to statements by officers of the Directors/Managers has ample funds in its accumulated income to carry out its purposes. The proposal by the Directors/Managers is for the sale of all of the shares of Hershey Foods Corporation. There is no suggestion of a sale of such number of shares as would still reserve control of the Corporation nor explanation why, if any need for funds exists for which a sale is necessary, it could not be met while still keeping control. The question certainly occurs as to whether an immediate premium share price obtained in losing control is a reasonable trade-off for permanently retaining it.

The Directors/Managers argue at length that the Attorney General has failed to establish that he has the required right to relief. The arguments are without merit. The Directors/Managers argue that the law of Pennsylvania establishes that the duty of a trustee is to administer the trust solely for the benefit of the beneficiaries of the trust, quoting in support the statement under Comment p. of § 1701(1) of the Restatement, Trusts, which reads, "The trustee is under a duty to the beneficiary in administering the trust not to be guided by the interest of any third person." We are familiar with these rules but do not construe them to mean that as long as the act of a trustee is an exercise of a power given in the trust instrument and purports to serve the trust, the trustee can act with impunity and without regard for adverse effects on others. We know of no case that employs the rules advanced by the Directors/Managers in the context of an Attorney General asserting his duty to see that the public interest is not harmed by an act of a trustee that may otherwise be lawful and purports to be in furtherance of the trust. Few such issues are likely to arise and rarely one with the aspects of the case before us. How many trusts enjoy holding a controlling interest in one of this nation's largest, historically profitable, and best-known corporations? The duties of a trustee and the Attorney General are concomitant in so far as assuring that the benefits of a charitable trust are delivered in accordance with the Settlor's intent; but because the socio-economic benefits of a charitable trust extend beyond the designated beneficiaries to the public itself, although ordinarily compatible with each other, the Attorney General has an added responsibility of assuring that compatibility.

We hereby Order that that pending disposition of the citation issued by the Court on August 19, 2002, and/or further order of this Court, the Board of Managers of the Milton Hershey School and the Hershey Trust Company as Trustee of the Milton S. and Catherine S. Hershey Trust shall not enter into any agreement or other understanding that would or could commit the respondents to a sale or other disposition of any or all of the shares of Hershey Foods Corporation held as corpus of the Trust

NOTES

1.   Unlike with a private trust, "[t]he trustees of an art museum, those entrusted to care for and maintain a particular community's patrimony, do not owe a fiduciary duty to a particular person but to the public as a whole." Jason R. Goldstein, *Deaccession: Not Such a Dirty Word*, 15 CARDOZO ARTS & ENT. L.J. 213, 246 (1997). What does it mean for a community or a public to have a patrimony? In the context of museums, whose patrimonies are on display and which patrimonies are privileged? See *About Us*, MUSEUM DETOX, https://www.museumdetox.org/museumdetox-about-us.

2.   Moreover, as the *Fisk* case demonstrates, defining the public is not always as simple as it sounds because the "public" can be divided and organized along numerous axes. In *Fisk,* the parties argue over which public is the public benefitting from the gift of art. Is the public something that can be geographically defined here—Tennessee, Arkansas, or, more broadly, the South? Or is the correct public defined by something else—by opportunity, access, and race? Which public would you consider to be the most relevant one in this situation? For more on this question, see Allison Tait, *Publicity Rules for Public Trusts*, 33 CARDOZO ARTS & ENT. L.J. 421 (2015).

3.   In the Hershey Trust case, there are similar questions about who the public is and who the attorney general is representing. The court remarks that "the attorney general must be made a party of record because the public as the real party in interest in the trust is otherwise not properly represented." Who is the real party in interest? The beneficiaries of the Hershey Trust? The members of the Hershey community?

To this point, Christopher Gadsden has asked, do trustees "now owe duties to the public at large? Traditionally, trustees understood that their duty was to manage prudently the assets of the trust for the benefit of the named beneficiaries or class of beneficiaries." Christopher Gadsden, *The Hershey Power Play*, TR. & EST. (Nov. 11, 2002), https://www.wealthmanagement.com/asset-protection/hershey-power-play. Gadsden worries that "the attorney general's position implies that the trustee of a charitable trust also must take into account the consequences of a trust action on all segments of the public at large. This duty potentially has no bounds. Should the trustee consider impact on the local community, the statewide population, or the nation as a whole? If a sale of the controlling interest in the company did lead to job reductions in Hershey, would additional employment opportunities be created in some other state? Must the trustee of a charitable trust prepare a form of environmental impact statement for every major action?" *Id.*

4.   The *Hershey* court also remarks that the state attorney general is exercising his parens patriae power. Historically, the parens patriae doctrine described the duty of the state to protect those who could not protect themselves. Is that really what the state attorney general is being called upon to do when representing the beneficiaries of a charitable trust? For more on the parens patriae, see Lawrence B. Custer, *The Origins of the Doctrine of Parens Patriae*, 27 EMORY L.J. 195 (1978) and Jack Ratliff, *Parens Patriae: An Overview*, 74 TUL. L. REV. 1847 (2000).

D. Expanding and Modifying Charitable Purposes

Because charitable trusts are not subject to the rule against perpetuities, modification doctrines are especially important. The purposes of a charitable trust established one hundred years ago may look much different in a modern context and require significant modification to align with modern needs and outlooks. For example, a gift given to "furnish relief" to immigrants and travelers coming to Saint Louis on their way "to settle the West" may have provided welcome aid centuries ago but has outlived its purpose in the twenty-first century. Similarly, a gift to a hospital for research on polio cannot be used in a contemporary context and needs to be modified. The ability to modify a charitable trust or gift is particularly important when a donor has placed narrow restrictions on the gift (as opposed to making the purpose quite broad or giving an unrestricted gift to an institution).

When a trust or gift needs modification, it is the job of the trustees to pursue judicial modification and there are two legal avenues available: cy pres and equitable deviation. The trustees must determine which method is more appropriate and submit a petition for modification to the court. When the trustees petition the court for modification, they must also submit a proposal for how they would like to modify the trust and how they plan to use the funds in a way that reflects and stays close to the donor's original intent (cy pres means "as near as" in old French).

1. The Cy Pres Doctrine

The doctrine of cy pres, which we first encountered in Chapter 3 with *Evans v. Abney*, is the traditional approach to modification, and it allows courts and trusts to accommodate the shifting conditions of long-lived charitable trusts and gifts under certain conditions. The Uniform Trust Code's cy pres rules provide for modification when a charitable purpose "becomes unlawful, impracticable, impossible to achieve, or wasteful."

UTC § 413 Cy Pres

(a) Except as otherwise provided in subsection (b), if a particular charitable purpose becomes unlawful, impracticable, impossible to achieve, or wasteful:

(1) the trust does not fail, in whole or in part;

(2) the trust property does not revert to the settlor or the settlor's successors in interest; and

(3) the court may apply cy pres to modify or terminate the trust by directing that the trust property be applied or distributed, in whole or in part, in a manner consistent with the settlor's charitable purposes.

We will break down each category—Impossible, impracticable, wasteful, and unlawful—in the following sub-sections.

a. *Impossible*

Impossibility is generally taken very literally by courts. That is to say, courts will grant cy pres modification requests based on impossibility when it is literally impossible to carry out the terms of the trust or gift. The following case, *Obermeyer v. Bank of America*, involves the question of how to interpret a charitable remainder trust whose residuary beneficiary, the Dental Alumni Association of Washington University in St. Louis, was no longer operating when the lifetime beneficiaries died. The case, as you will see, turns on the question of whether the donor, Dr. Kimbrough, had general or specific charitable intent. This determination controls whether the gift will be modified or will revert to the donor's estate.

Obermeyer v. Bank of America

140 S.W.3d 18 (Mo. 2004)

WOLFF, J.

Facts and Procedural History

Dr. Kimbrough was born in 1870. In 1890, he enrolled in the Missouri Dental College, which became a school at Washington University, a tax-exempt, educational institution. He was graduated from the Washington University Dental School in 1894. Dr. Kimbrough was a practicing dentist throughout his career, and he served on the faculty of the Washington University Dental School.

During his lifetime, Dr. Kimbrough made numerous gifts to Washington University. Nearly one-half of the gifts went to no specific college within the university and were unrestricted—meaning the university could use the money as it pleased. Dr. Kimbrough also named Washington University in his estate plan, which consisted of a will and trust.

Dr. Kimbrough established a trust in 1945 to provide income and principal encroachment rights for his niece and nephews during their lifetimes. He amended the trust in 1955 to provide for the distribution of the trust upon the death of his great-niece and great-nephews, Margaret Salmon Towles (Derrick), Oscar Kimbrough, and Harvey W. Salmon. Section two of the trust provided that following the death of the last of Dr. Kimbrough's niece and nephews, the trust shall be distributed as follows:

> Upon the death of the survivor of said niece and nephews and after the death of the Grantor, the property then constituting the trust estate shall be paid over and distributed free from trust unto Washington University, St. Louis, Missouri, for the exclusive use and benefit of its Dental Alumni Development Fund.

The trust did not contain a reversionary provision providing for an alternate disposition of the trust estate.

When the Dental Alumni Development Fund was created in 1954, contributions to it were unrestricted, allowing the deans of each school to use the funds for any purpose they deemed appropriate. The November 1954 edition of the Washington University Dental Journal announced the formation of the Dental Alumni Development Fund and reported that the purpose of the fund was to provide financial support for the dental school and improve the morale of the dental school's faculty. Dr. Kimbrough's gift to the Dental Alumni Development Fund in May 1954 was made before the published report on the establishment of the Fund in the November 1954 issue of the Dental Journal.

Dr. Kimbrough died in 1963, and his life beneficiaries received income until their respective deaths. Margaret Derrick, the last surviving life beneficiary, died in 2000.

Washington University stopped using the Dental Alumni Development Fund in 1965 and began using the Annual Fund as its vehicle for the donation of unrestricted gifts. The Annual Fund still exists today. In 1991, Washington University closed the dental school and merged faculty, staff, and programs into its medical school and main campus. Dental medicine continues to be a component of education at the medical school, where maxillofacial surgery, prosthodontics, cleft palate/craniofacial deformities and pediatric dentistry are taught and performed.

Louise Obermeyer and Elizabeth Salmon, Dr. Kimbrough's great, great-nieces, filed suit claiming the trust was created with specific charitable intent, making the cy pres doctrine inapplicable, and the approximately $2.8 million fund should revert to them as Dr. Kimbrough's heirs. The named defendants in this lawsuit are Bank of America, the successor corporate trustee holding the funds of Dr. Kimborough, and Washington University, which also claimed the funds. The Attorney General was joined as a necessary party.

Washington University and the Attorney General agreed with the heirs that there was a charitable trust and that it was impossible or impracticable to carry out the charitable purpose in the trust because the Dental Alumni Development Fund no longer exists. They, however, claim the trust was created with general charitable intent and that, under the cy pres doctrine, the funds should be applied to Washington University for dental-related endeavors to most nearly carry out Dr. Kimbrough's charitable intent.

The circuit court held that Dr. Kimbrough established the trust with a general charitable intent and ruled in favor of Washington University. The circuit court then applied the doctrine of cy pres and ordered the assets be used to establish and maintain one or two chairs in Dr. Kimbrough's name for research and practice in cleft palate/craniofacial deformities, or for maxillofacial surgery and prosthodontics, or both.

Cy Pres Analysis

Missouri courts hold that to apply the doctrine of cy pres, three requirements must be met. First, the trust in question must be a valid charitable trust. Second, it is or becomes impossible, impracticable, or illegal to carry out the specific terms of the trust. Finally, the settlor must have established the trust with a general charitable intent. If the settlor's intent was specific, the cy pres doctrine cannot be applied. The result would be a reversion for the settlor or the settlor's heirs.

The parties agree that a trust was created with a charitable intent and that the trust has failed because the dental school was closed, and the Dental Alumni Development Fund no longer exists. The parties maintain that the issue is whether the trust was created with general or specific charitable intent.

A general charitable intent exists where there is an intent to assist a certain general type or kind of charity. *Ramsey v. City of Brookfield*, 237 S.W.2d 143, 145 (Mo. 1951). General charitable intent "is an intent that a gift be continued within the limits of its general purpose and that shall not cease when a particular thing is accomplished. Unquestionably, when the intent is to apply the gift to a continuing problem, there is a general charitable intent." . . . . The grantor's intent is specific when the grantor intended to "aid that kind of charity only in a particular way or by a particular method or means" and further intended that, "if the particular means failed, the gift failed." *Id.*

Dr. Kimbrough's gift to Washington University for the Dental Alumni Development Fund was not for a particular task to be accomplished, but to support dental medicine at Washington University, a profession of which he was deeply proud. The trust document contained no suggestion that the gift should fail if the particular fund ceased to exist.

In determining whether the charitable intent of the grantor is specific or general, there are additional factors courts should consider.

First, courts have viewed gifts of land as "strong evidence of an absence of general charitable intent," while monetary gifts suggest general intent. *Id.* at 338. Dr. Kimbrough gave a gift of money, not real property, thus indicating general charitable intent.

The second factor is the existence of a reverter clause associated with the gift. Use of a direction for a reversion to the settlor in the case of failure indicates specific charitable intent, while the absence of a reverter clause supports general charitable intent. *Id.* Dr. Kimbrough's estate plan included reverter clauses as to the bequests for all of the individuals, which instructed the gifts to go to Washington University; however, it did not include a reverter clause as to the gift to Washington University in the will or trust.

The third relevant factor is whether the charitable gift was made in trust or outright. A gift in trust is indicative of specific charitable intent, while a gift made outright indicates general intent. *Id.* at 339. The trust provides that at the death of the survivor of the life beneficiaries, the trust is to be paid to Washington University "free from trust." Dr. Kimbrough's gift "free from trust" suggests general charitable intent.

The heirs argue that the use of the language, "for the exclusive use and benefit," requires a finding of specific charitable intent. Where the terms of a charitable trust direct a means of execution or dedicate the fund to a type of charity "forever" or "for no other purpose," or upon condition that it be applied "to no other purpose," these provisions do not necessarily demonstrate absence of a general charitable intent. *Ramsey,* 237 S.W.2d at 146. In *Ramsey,* a grant for the "sole purpose of building and equipping and maintaining a City hospital" and "no other" did "not necessarily show absence of a general charitable intent." *Id.* "Such provisions do not, ipso facto, show an intent that the trust should cease in the event of impossibility or impracticability of using the specified means." *Id.*

Dr. Kimbrough's Charitable Intent

The question remains what Dr. Kimbrough would desire if he knew that his gift could not be used by the Dental Alumni Development Fund for the continued operation and prestige of the dental school.

"[T]he accomplishment of the ultimate purpose of the testator is the matter of paramount importance and its achievement must be the object of any judicial permission to alter or deviate from the trust terms." *Reed v. Eagleton,* 384 S.W.2d 578, 586 (Mo.1964). The Court considers whether unforeseen circumstances have arisen that threaten the fulfillment of the charity and whether or not such circumstances warrant a court's exercise of its jurisdiction to enforce and protect charitable trusts. *Id.* at 585–86. In discerning the intent of the grantor, the basic equitable issue is what the settlor would desire if he or she knew that the trust could not be carried out. A court is required to consider all the surrounding circumstances evidencing the grantor's intent. To adhere too strictly to the words of the testator may result in the defeat of the testator's ultimate purpose. SCOTT ON TRUSTS, sec. 399.4, p. 535 (4th ed.1989). If the testator intended to make the property useful for charitable purposes, to render it useless for such purposes defeats the testator's intention.

The record repeatedly shows that Dr. Kimbrough loved dentistry and was very proud of his profession. Dr. Kimbrough graduated from the Washington University Dental School, taught at the Washington University Dental School, gave unrestricted gifts to Washington University, and left the remainder of his trust to Washington University, not to the dental school.

This Court agrees with the circuit court's conclusion that Dr. Kimbrough's charitable intent was to further education and dental medicine at Washington University. There is no evidence that Dr. Kimbrough wanted his gift so narrowly drawn and so inflexible that if it could not be used in a specifically named fund, it should lapse. The circuit court's decision to establish one or two chairs in Dr. Kimbrough's name for research and practice in dental fields is consistent with Dr. Kimbrough's charitable intent.

Conclusion

Cy pres literally means "as near as." Dr. Kimbrough's objective was to further dental education at Washington University. The circuit court's disposition of the gift attempts to fulfill Dr. Kimbrough's intent as near as possible because it requires Washington University to use the money for dental-related education. The fact that the Dental Alumni Development Fund and the dental school no longer exist does not frustrate that objective, as the medical school at Washington University continues to teach and practice dental medicine.

There is no evidence that Dr. Kimbrough ever contemplated that the money would go to his great, great-nieces, and he did not include a provision for the reversion of the property to his heirs in the event that the fund or dental school would cease to exist.

The general purpose of Dr. Kimbrough's gift to support educational programs and projects in dental fields at Washington University can be accomplished. While the specific fund designated by the grantor to carry out this purpose no longer exists, the circuit court's disposition of the trust assets carries out Dr. Kimbrough's intent.

The judgment of the circuit court is affirmed.

NOTES

1.   In 2003, following similar changes to the RESTATEMENT (THIRD) OF TRUSTS in 2001, the UTC shifted to a presumption of general intent, thereby eliminating most of the judicial analysis that occurred in cases like the one we just read. The problem with asking courts to distinguish between general and specific intent was clearly stated by Austin Scott in the treatise on trusts, who observed:

> [T]he trust does not fail if the testator has a more general intention to devote the property to charitable purposes. This principle is easy to state but is not always easy to apply. Indeed it is ordinarily true that the testator does not contemplate the possible failure of his particular purpose, and all that the court can do is to make a guess not as to what he intended but as to what he would have intended if he had thought about the matter.

4 Austin Wakeman Scott, The Law Of Trusts § 399.2 (3d ed. 1967).

The *Obermeyer* court posed this exact question: "The question remains what Dr. Kimbrough would desire if he knew that his gift could not be used by the Dental Alumni Development Fund for the continued operation and prestige of the dental school." Without explicit instructions or evidence regarding the donor's intent, what indicators would court have to look for in order to determine the presence of general rather than specific charitable intent? What kind of evidence would parties be forced to assemble? For more on this question, see Peter Luxton, *Cy Près and the Ghost of Things that Might Have Been*, 47 CONV. & PROP. L. 107, 116 (1983).

2.   The UTC drafters commented, in 2003 when they created the presumption of charitable intent, that this approach was appropriate because "[c]ourts are usually able to find a general charitable purpose to which to apply the property, no matter how vaguely such purpose may have been expressed by the settlor." UTC § 413(a) cmt. at 78.

There is one well-known case, however, in which the U.S. Supreme Court was called up to determine a question of general versus specific charitable intent and came down on the side of specific charitable intent. We've already encountered the case, *Evans v. Abney*, 396 U.S. 435 (1970), in Chapter 3. You will recall that the case involved willed property that Senator A.O. Bacon left in trust to his home city of Macon, Georgia for the purpose of creating a public park exclusively for the use of white people. When the city of Macon began relaxing the park restrictions on segregation in the 1960s, the park's Board of Managers sued the city to make sure that the racial restrictions were enforced. The city argued that it was unlawful and against public policy to maintain the restrictions. Ruling on the case, the Georgia Supreme Court concluded "that the sole purpose for which the trust was created has become impossible of accomplishment, and has been terminated." *Id.* at 439. The Georgia attorney general then argued that court should modify the trust through cy pres rather than terminate it. The question that then arose—and went to the U.S. Supreme Court—concerned the quality of Bacon's charitable intent. The Court remarked that "Senator Bacon could not have used language more clearly indicating his intent that the benefits of Baconsfield should be extended to white persons only, or more clearly indicating that this limitation was an essential and indispensable part of his plan for Baconsfield." *Id.* at 442. Consequently, the Court ultimately affirmed the Georgia state court in concluding that, because "racial separation was found to be an inseparable part of the testator's intent, the Georgia courts held that the State's cy pres doctrine could not be used to alter the will to permit racial integration." *Id.*

How do you think that this case would come out today using the UTC and its presumption of general charitable intent? Would the Supreme Court apply the UTC and what would be the result? For more on this case, see David S. Bogen, *Evans v. Abney: Reverting to Segregation*, 30 MD. L. REV. 226 (1970) and Grady F. Tollison, Jr., *Evans v. Abney, and Permissible Judicial Facilitation of Private Discrimination*, 42 MISS. L.J. 246 (1970).

3. The Court, in the *Evans* case, commented: "More fundamentally . . . the loss of charitable trusts such as Baconsfield is part of the price we pay for permitting deceased persons to exercise a continuing control over assets owned by them at death." 396 U.S. at 447. This comment reflects the problems with facilitating dead-hand control of property and suggests good reason for limiting the reach of dead-hand control with charitable gifts. This question will come up again in this chapter's final section when we discuss proposals to limit the power of donor conditions through doctrines like the Rule Against Perpetuities.

b. Impracticable

Impracticability constitutes a lower threshold than impossibility—compliance is not technically impossible for the trustees. "The doctrine of cy pres may also be applied, even though it is possible to carry out the particular purpose of the settlor, if to do so would not accomplish the settlor's charitable objective, or would not do so in a reasonable way." RESTATEMENT (THIRD) OF TR. § 67 cmt. c (AM. LAW. INST. 2003). The impracticability standard, in this way, recognizes that circumstances may arise in which the trust terms cannot be carried out without substantial burden to the institution or substantial impairment of the charitable purpose. At just what point gift or trust terms become impracticable, however, is a challenging question for courts.

One example is a case from Hawaii, *In re Elizabeth J.K.L. Lucas Charitable Gift*, 261 P.3d 800, 807 (Haw. Ct. App. 2011), in which a donor gifted an interest in a parcel of land to the Hawaiian Humane Society, with the restriction that the property "be used for the benefit of the public for the operation of an educational preserve for flora and fauna." The Humane Society made "numerous attempts" to use the land within the parameters established by the gift deed. The land was unsuitable for use as a public park, however, and all the Humane Society's proposals failed because they were either "physically or economically unfeasible." The Humane Society's petition for modification stated that using the gift as intended was impracticable, and the court agreed. The court concluded that cy pres was applicable "where a settlor creates a charitable trust of real property to be used for a particular purpose, but the property turns out to be unsuitable for that purpose." Consequently, the court allowed the Humane Society to enter into deals with both the State and a private partnership to sell the land and use the proceeds for environmental stewardship programming.

Another case that attracted a great deal of attention, especially in the art world, was the case of the Corcoran Gallery. The Corcoran was established in

The building that historically housed the Corcoran gallery, across the street from the White House. Washington, D.C.

1869 through a deed of trust executed by William Wilson Corcoran, a successful banker and art collector. The goal of the trust was to fund an institution in Washington D.C. that was "dedicated to Art, and used solely for the purpose of encouraging American Genius." In the following decade, the trustees also established Corcoran College, "which was integrated into the overall institution and which emphasized student access to the art collection." *Tr. of the Corcoran Gallery of Art v. District of Columbia*, 142 Daily Wash. L. Rptr. 2213, 2214 (D.C. Super. Ct. Aug. 18, 2014). In the early 2000s, the Gallery began experiencing severe financial difficulties and was struggling to meet even basic payroll obligations. In an attempt to decrease operating expenses, the Trustees had decreased staff and had deferred necessary building maintenance, but problems remained because the building's old systems were, according to the Trustees "not capable of reliably maintaining museum-level exhibit and conservation standards." *Id.* at 2221. Accordingly, the Trustees filed a cy pres petition to modify the trust conditions and close the Gallery because, they argued, maintaining the Gallery in its historical form was impracticable. Seeking a way out of this financial distress, the Trustees requested permission for the Corcoran's collection to be subsumed into the National Gallery of Art (NGA) and for the Corcoran's educational programs to be incorporated into those of the George Washington University (GWU).

Seeking to define impracticability, the court turned to contract law and commercial impracticability to gain new insights:

> In the contract context, the Court of Appeals has defined "impracticable" to mean that a party is excused from performing its obligations under a contract due to an unexpected contingency only if that contingency causes the party "extreme or unreasonable difficulty" in performing its obligations under the contract, and not if the contingency is "a mere inconvenience or unexpected difficulty."

Id. at 2218 (quoting *Island Dev. Corp. v. District of Columbia*, 933 A.2d 340, 350 (D.C. 2007). The court concluded that "a party seeking cy pres relief can establish impracticability only if it demonstrates that it would be unreasonably difficult, and that it is not viable or feasible, to carry out the current terms and conditions of the trust." *Id.* at 2219. Convinced that the Trustees were unable to find another way out of these financial problems—despite "working tirelessly . . . to come to terms with the institution's significant financial challenges and to identify creative solutions"—the court concluded that the Corcoran's circumstances were indeed impracticable. *Id.* at 2222.

NOTES

1. For more on the Corcoran Gallery controversy, see Caroline Camp, *Mr. Corcoran and the Trustees: The Corcoran Gallery of Art, a Petition for Cy Pres, and the Fate of an Institution*, CTR. FOR ART L. (Aug. 18, 2014), https://itsartlaw.org/2014/08/18/mr-corcoran-and-the-trustees-the-corcoran-gallery-of-art-a-petition-for-cy-pres-and-the-fate-of-an-institution/; Lee Rosenbaum, *Isn't There a Better Way?*, WALL ST. J. (Aug. 4, 2014), https://www.wsj.com/articles/a-possible-dismantling-1407191181; William Corcoran's Deed of Trust, (May 18,

1869)   http://www.corcoran.org/sites/default/files/CorcoranDeedofTrust.pdf.

2.   In the Corcoran decision, the court draws a comparison between contract and trust law. Is this a useful comparison or are the legal domains too different? That is to say, what are the differences between charitable organizations and for-profit companies and how should we consider these differences in crafting a standard for impracticability? For more on this see Allison Tait, *Keeping Promises and Meeting Needs: Public Charities at a Crossroads*, 102 MINN. L. REV.1789 (2017).

3.   One of the questions in the case involved deaccessioning—or the sale of art. In the *Corcoran* case, a group called Save the Corcoran intervened to block the cy pres petition, arguing that the Corcoran could raise funds through a major deaccessioning effort (as well as increased fundraising). The intervenors proposed that the Gallery sell more than 17,000 pieces from the collection, and that the funds from these sales could bridge the budgetary gap. Had the Trustees done this, however, the Gallery would have faced sanctions from the American Association of Museum Directors (AAMD), whose rules prohibit spending any money raised from deaccessioning on operating costs. Does it make sense to prohibit museums from selling art to keep the lights on? Which institutions suffer the most from these rules and in what ways do the rules shape the institutional landscape? For more on the topic, see Brian L. Frye, *Against Deaccessioning Rules*, 53 CREIGHTON L. REV. 461 (2019–2020).

Fairy tales come in all varieties. ©2/27/03 compasspoint. Tales from the nonprofit galaxy, by Miriam Engelberg.

ASSESSMENT

In 2008, the New York Board of Regents considered enacting a new rule, called the "desperation deaccessioning" rule, that would have permitted museums to sell items in its collections to another museum for the purpose of obtaining funds to pay outstanding debt, but only in cases of extreme financial distress. The proposal was heavily criticized as being too far out of alignment with industry rules and quickly abandoned. Write a short Op-ed piece discussing whether global phenomena, like public health pandemics, should be a basis to reconsider the possibility of "desperation deaccessioning" to provide support for charitable institutions that are suffering financially.

c. *Wasteful*

The category of wasteful was added to the UTC rules with respect to cy pres in 2000 and to the RESTATEMENT (THIRD) OF TRUSTS in 2003. § 67 of the RESTATEMENT says that cy pres may be appropriate when it "becomes wasteful to apply all of the property to the designated purpose," clarifying "wasteful" means that the funds far exceed what is necessary. UTC § 412(b), as revised, states, "the court may modify an administrative term if continuation of the trust on its existing terms would be impracticable, wasteful, or impair the trust's administration." The UTC revision therefore "expands the ability of the court to apply cy pres." David M. English, *The Uniform Trust Code (200) and its Application to Ohio*, 30 CAP. U. L. REV. 1, 18 (2002). UTC § 414(a) also sets forth for efficiency reasons expedited procedures for reforming small charitable trusts; a trustee may modify or terminate a trust with assets valued at less than $50,000 "if the trustee concludes that the value of the trust property is insufficient to justify the cost of administration." Generally, then, wasteful means that there is either too much or too little money in the trust for the assets to be used efficiently.

These modifications were the very direct result of a great legal battle in San Francisco over the Buck Trust, a charitable trust that had significant surplus income and ran the risk of wasteful management. Beryl Buck established the Beryl Buck Foundation Trust by bequest in 1975. Buck's will directed that the trust "shall always be held and used for exclusively non-profit charitable, religious or educational purposes in providing care for the needy in Marin County, California, and for other non-profit charitable, religious or educational purposes in that county." *Estate of Buck*, 35 Cal. Rptr. 2d 442, 443 (Ct. App. 1994). At the time of Buck's death, the assets—in the form of Belridge Oil stock—were worth approximately ten million dollars. Four years later, Shell Oil bought Belridge at the same time that oil prices soared and the trust assets, almost overnight, became worth almost 300 million dollars. Ronald Hayes Malone, Mary K. McEachron, & Jay M. Cutler, *The Buck Trust Trial—A Litigator's Perspective*, 21 U.S.F. L. REV. 585, 590 (1987). Faced with this unexpected and dramatic increase in trust assets, the distribution committee deliberated about how to disburse funds in light of trust terms requiring that the spendable income be used in Marin County, a county with "one of the highest per capita incomes in the country and relatively few charitable needs." *Id.* Ultimately, the committee, in 1984, "resolved that it was 'impracticable and inexpedient to continue to expend all of the income from the Buck Trust solely within Marin County' and authorized the filing of a petition to modify the geographic restriction of Beryl Buck's Trust." *Id.* at 591.

The Foundation's cy pres petition requested authorization to "spend an unspecified portion of Buck Trust income outside of Marin County in the four other Bay Area counties preferentially served by the Foundation." *Id.* At trial, the Foundation argued that modification of the gift conditions was appropriate "on the basis of unanticipated changed circumstances, or 'surprise,' and 'inefficiency.' " *Id.* at 609. The opposing parties countered that there were no legal grounds on which to grant cy pres and that Buck's intention had clearly been to limit expenditures to Marin County regardless of the value of the trust. On August 15, 1986, the court entered a judgment denying the cy pres petition, concluding that the Foundation had not proved that it was impossible, illegal, or impracticable, to spend the trust income as directed in the trust terms. The court concluded that "[n]either inefficiency nor ineffective philanthropy constitutes impracticability, nor does either concept constitute an appropriate standard for the application of cy pres." *Id.* at 636.

John Simon captured the hyperbolic discourse around the case, remarking that the Foundation's cy pres request "was characterized as a threat to the sanctity of wills and the health of philanthropy, and as an offense against capitalism, the American way of life, and God." John G. Simon, *American Philanthropy and the Buck Trust*, 21 U.S.F. L. REV. 641, 641 (1987). The six-month trial produced nearly 15,000 pages of trial transcript and over 2000 trial exhibits; because of the publicity surrounding the case, as well as the investment of resources in litigating it, the Buck Trust case was called the "Superbowl of Probate." *See* Ronald Hayes Malone, Mary K. McEachron, & Jay M. Cutler, *The Buck Trust Trial—A Litigator's Perspective*, 21 U.S.F. L. REV. 585, 637 (1987). More than just a sensationalistic event in the world of Bay Area nonprofits, however, the case—and severe dissatisfaction with the outcome—led reformers to advocate for the inclusion of wastefulness as a criterion for the application of cy pres.

NOTES

1.   Marin County is an extremely "affluent enclave of high real estate and rental costs," that is also "is home to the largest inequities between racial groups of any county in California." Liam Dillon, *Marin County Has Long Resisted Growth in the Name of Environmentalism. But High Housing Costs and Segregation Persist*, L.A. TIMES (Jan. 7, 2018, 12:05 AM);[6] *see also* RACE COUNTS, https://www.racecounts.org/. One of Marin's most famous residents, George Lucas, who built his Skywalker Ranch there, tried to sell some of his land to a developer for the purposes of creating affordable housing. The community response was one of alarm and residents accused him of "inciting class warfare." Norimitsu Onishi, *Lucas and Rich Neighbors Agree to Disagree: Part II*, N.Y. TIMES (May 21, 2012).[7] Faced with a denial of your cy pres petition, what kinds of distributions could the Buck Trust trustees make with the goal of spending money on the "needy" of Marin County, as directed by the trust terms?

2.   In the Buck Trust case, the wasteful conditions resulted from a chance sale and unforeseen market forces. Sometimes wasteful conditions are the result of the trustees' successful investment decisions. In some ways, the Hershey Trust is such an example. We have already read about the Hershey Trust and the state attorney general exerting his parens patriae authority. Milton Hershey left a controlling interest in his chocolate company to the trust and, as the fortunes of the company grew, so did the size of the Hershey Trust. In fact, the trust grew so much that they had trouble spending money. They had to expand the school's mission from educating orphan boys from the surrounding counties to orphan boys (and now orphan girls) from around the state, to now children from the state who need the school, regardless of whether they are orphaned.

d.   Unlawful

One area that has generated substantial litigation and controversy around charitable trusts, particularly from the 1940s through the 1970s, involves racial and gender discrimination. As laws and public policy have changed around ideas of equality and race and gender equity, charitable trusts created with

---

[6]   Available at https://www.latimes.com/politics/la-pol-ca-marin-county-affordable-housing-20170107-story.html.

[7]   Available at https://www.nytimes.com/2012/05/22/us/george-lucas-retreats-from-battle-with-neighbors.html.

discriminatory restrictions have come under scrutiny amidst calls for change and modification. The first below deals with the so-called Girard College in Philadelphia, so-called because it is really a high school established pursuant to the will of merchant and financier Stephen Girard who died in the 1830s. Mr.

> **Language Note:** As noted with both *Evans* (in Chapter 3) and *Dees* (in Chapter 6), *Girard College* uses the word "Negro." We have left the original language intact, even though the word is not appropriate in modern usage, to reflect this aspect of the case's history and vernacular.

Girard, an orphan who came to Philadelphia during the American Revolution and made his fortune, left some of that fortune to establish a school for orphaned white boys. In the 1950s, in the wake of *Brown v. Board of Education*, two fatherless Black boys, neither of whom were yet ten years old, sought admissions to Girard College and were denied on the basis of race. They took their case from the Orphan's Court in Philadelphia all the way to the U.S. Supreme Court. It is the Pennsylvania Supreme Court decision in that challenge that we present here. You will see that the issue became how to respond once it was clear that the City of Philadelphia as trustee could not discriminate. Pay special attention to Justice Musmanno's dissent and what it says about donative intent.

In re Girard College Trusteeship

138 A.2d 844 (Pa. 1958)

JONES, C.J.

When this matter was here before, we affirmed the action of the Orphans' Court of Philadelphia County denying admission to Girard College to William Ashe Foust and Robert Felder, poor male Negro orphans, for the reason that the will of Stephen Girard, the founder and endower of the College, expressly restricts admission to "poor male white orphans": see *Girard Will Case*, 127 A.2d 287 (Pa.). Although the institution is referred to as a College, the testator himself aptly termed it an "Orphan Establishment" in one of two codicils which, with the decedent's will, were probated shortly after his death in 1831.

The will nominated and appointed as trustee of the charity the Mayor, Aldermen, and Citizens of Philadelphia, the then corporate title of the City, which duly entered upon its trust duties. But, for years, the College has been administered by the Board of Directors of City Trusts of Philadelphia, a statutory body empowered to accept and execute charitable trusts bequeathed to the City of Philadelphia, as trustee. For the proper administration of the trusts committed to it, the Board of City Trusts is accountable to the Orphans' Court of Philadelphia County. That court, deeming the Board of City Trusts to be like any other trustee which is a creature of statute and authorized to accept and administer private trusts, held by its decrees, which we affirmed, that the Board of City Trusts was bound to abide faithfully by the restrictions which Girard's will imposes on admissions to the College.

However, the Supreme Court of the United States reversed our judgment of affirmance and remanded the cause for further proceedings not inconsistent with that Court's opinion which held that the Board of City Trusts is an agency of the State of Pennsylvania and that, even though the Board was acting as a trustee, its refusal to admit Foust and Felder to the College because they were Negroes was discrimination by the State which is forbidden by the Fourteenth Amendment, citing *Brown v. Board of Education*, 347 U.S. 483: *see Pennsylvania v. Board of Trusts*, 353 U.S. 230. In obedience to the Supreme Court's mandate, we vacated the decrees of the Orphans' Court and remanded the cause to that court "for further proceedings not inconsistent with the opinion of the Supreme Court of the United States."

The Orphans' Court, construing the Supreme Court's opinion to mean no more than that the Board of City Trusts was constitutionally incapable of administering Girard College in accordance with the testamentary requirements of its founder, entered decrees removing the Board as trustee of Girard College and substituting for that purpose thirteen private citizens none of whom holds any public office or otherwise exercises any governmental power under the Commonwealth of Pennsylvania or any of its political or municipal subdivisions. It is these decrees which are now before us for review on the separate appeals of Foust, Felder, the Commonwealth of Pennsylvania and the City of Philadelphia (the State and City having voluntarily become parties to the proceedings). Simply stated, the question for decision is whether the action of the Orphans' Court is inconsistent with the opinion of the Supreme Court of the United States.

It is the appellants' contention that the Supreme Court's mandate required the Orphans' Court to order the Board of City Trusts to admit Foust and Felder to Girard College forthwith. With that, we cannot agree. Had the Supreme Court so intended, it would have said so just as it did in *Sweatt v. Painter*, 339 U.S. 629 (1950), where there was involved a state-supported University's denial of admission to a Negro because of his race. The order of reversal in the *Sweatt* case also included a remand of the cause for further proceedings not inconsistent with the Supreme Court's opinion but, immediately preceding, and as a part of the order of reversal, there is the specific ruling by the Court that "the Fourteenth Amendment requires that petitioner be admitted to the University of Texas Law School." The mandate in the instant case contains no such directive.

The appellants' effort to make a "segregation" issue out of Stephen Girard's private charity, merely because of the inability of the Board of City Trusts, as trustee, to comply with the donor's express directions, serves only to confuse and obscure the real issue involved as to the right of a private individual to bequeath his property for a lawful charitable use and have his testamentary disposition judicially respected and enforced. In *Holdship v. Patterson*, 7 Watts 547, 551 (1838), Mr. Chief Justice GIBSON pertinently stated that a testamentary benefactor "has an individual right of property in the execution of the trust, and to deprive him of it would be a fraud on his generosity. To appropriate a gift to a purpose or person not intended, would be an evasion of the donor's private dominion." As lately as *Borsch Estate*, 362 Pa. 581, 586, 67 A.2d 119 (1949), we recognized, as constitutionally safe-guarded, the right of a benefactor to have enforced the limitations and restrictions affixed to his testamentary gift. The exercise of that right is but one of the manifestations of the right of private property which is fundamental to our social, economic and political order and whose preservation unimpaired is as vital to our Negro citizens as it is to their white brethren.

As we read the Supreme Court's opinion, what it holds, and all that it was presumably intended to hold, in view of what was then before the Court, is that the Board of City Trusts, being a State agency, is incapable of administering Girard College in strict compliance with the founder's prescribed racial restriction on admissions without being guilty of a violation of the Fourteenth Amendment. However, the Supreme Court did not say that there is any Constitutional or other legal barrier to the removal of the Board of City Trusts as trustee of Girard College in order that the Orphanage can be administered in accordance with all of the testator's express directions including the qualifications for admission to the student body. On the other hand, there is high authority for such procedure where a trustee is either unable or fails or refuses to administer a trust in accordance with the lawful directions of the settlor.

The inability of the Board of City Trusts to apply constitutionally the racial criterion prescribed by the testator for admissions to Girard College affects the trustee and not the trust. As the opinion for the Orphans' Court so well states,

"It is a universally accepted rule of law that the disqualification or incompetency of a trustee shall not be permitted to defeat the purposes of a charitable trust, nor to impeach its validity, nor to derogate from its enforcement the trustee must be fitted to the trust and not the trust to the trustee." It necessarily followed, therefore, that the course to be pursued in order that the trust may continue to be fully effectuated in accordance with the benefactor's intent was not to obliterate by judicial fiat an express term of his will which, as a private individual, he had a legal right to impose (*see City of Philadelphia v. Girard's Heirs*, 45 Pa. 9, 26) but for the court, which has jurisdiction of the trust and its fiduciary, to appoint substitute trustees capable of carrying out the testator's lawful prescriptions. And, that is precisely what the Orphans' Court has done.

The appellants argue that because the substituted trustees will continue to restrict admissions to Girard College to poor male orphans of a particular race, whom Girard by his will specified as alone eligible for admission, the action of the Orphans' Court will deny the present applicants of a different race the equal protection of the laws guaranteed them by the Fourteenth Amendment. In aid of this argument, the appellants unwarrantedly charge that the Orphans' Court's exercise of its judicial power in the premises was "for the sole purpose of excluding Negroes from Girard College" and that the action "was taken solely in order to enable the school to remain segregated." The Orphans' Court did not act to exclude Negroes from Girard College. None had ever been admitted. What the Orphans' Court did was to refuse to admit the Negro applicants because they did not qualify for admission under the terms of Girard's will. And, to speak of Girard College as remaining "segregated" as a result of the Orphans' Court action is to use a term whose present-day stigmatizing connotation has no proper place in this case.

The decrees are affirmed at the cost of the Commonwealth of Pennsylvania and the City of Philadelphia.

MUSMANNO, J., *dissenting.*

In May 1777, Stephen Girard of Bordeaux, France, landed in Philadelphia where he took up permanent residence and entered into business. Success smiled on his various commercial enterprises and, as ship owner, banker, and merchant, he accumulated an amount of wealth that made his name one to be conjured with on the American Rialto. As he climbed the ladder of financial achievement, he held aloft at all times the flag of gratitude for the opportunities afforded him in the New World. He became a citizen of the United States and was elected a member of the Philadelphia "City Councils."

In 1830, having reached that age when a good man contemplates how the shadow of his life may still be helpful to the living after he will have departed, he went into consultation with a scrivener, his conscience, his sense of appreciation and undying spirit of patriotism. From the conference emerged his last will and testament which, when probated in 1831, shone as a lyrical paean to Philadelphia which he loved with a devotion akin to that which Cincinnatus is reputed to have borne toward Rome. Girard revealed through this last writing that he could not do too much for the City which had been a foster mother to him. He left her funds with which to lay out new streets, pave and widen others, remove wooden houses, cleanse the docks on the Delaware, and supply water for various sections of the City. He provided for a competent police force, a division of the City into "watch districts," and in general made available facilities to "improve the city property, and the general appearance of the city itself; and, in effect diminish the burden of taxation, now most oppressive especially on those, who are the least able to bear it."

The will of Julius Caesar, dramatically proclaimed to the populace by Marc Antony, which gave to every Roman citizen the sum of 75 drachmas and to the general citizens the right to breathe fresh air in his "private arbours and orchards," was a rather paltry posthumous gift in comparison to what Girard gave to Philadelphia.

Girard was generous to public charitable institutions as the Philadelphia Hospital, the Pennsylvania Institution for the Deaf and Dumb, the Orphan Asylum of Philadelphia, and various other organizations for relief of the poor and the distressed.

He bestowed a legacy on the public schools of Philadelphia. He bequeathed $300,000 to the Commonwealth of Pennsylvania for internal improvements by canal investigation. He left some modest sums to relatives, friends, and servants, but the mass of his estate was dedicated to the public welfare. Thus, he said:

> "And whereas, together with the object just adverted to, I have
> sincerely at heart the welfare of the city of Philadelphia, and, as a part
> of it, am desirous to improve the neighborhood of the river Delaware,
> so that the health of the citizens may be promoted and preserved, and
> that the eastern part of the city may be made to correspond better
> with the interior: Now, I do give devise and bequeath all the residue
> and remainder of my real and personal estate of every sort and kind
> and wheresoever situate . . . unto 'The Mayor, Aldermen and citizens
> of Philadelphia' their successors and assigns in trust to and for the

several uses intents and purposes hereinafter mentioned and declared of and concerning the same."

Of this residue in trust he allocated two million dollars for the establishment of a college for "poor white male orphans." This college later became known as the Girard College and is the subject of the instant litigation.

The fact of the matter is that no trustee, no matter how appointed, may practice in the Girard College a discrimination which is forbidden by the Fourteenth Amendment. The Girard College, because of the nature of its origin, its legislative history, its councilmanic management, its municipal control and subservience to governmental supervision is as much a public institution as the University of Pennsylvania and is, therefore, bound by the decision of the Supreme Court of the United States in *Brown v. Board of Education*, 347 U.S. 483.

It is no answer to this statement to say that the Girard College had its genesis in private funds. The Commonwealth of Pennsylvania was once a private grant and the Island of Manhattan once belonged to a private tribe of Indians. Land and institutions may become public through purchase, through dedication, and through use. Girard College is public because Girard so planted it and because its whole growth has been accomplished in the orchard of governmental care.

A reading of the will should be enough in itself to convince the mind that Girard brought into play every possible trumpet of the English language to proclaim that his whole fortune was to be devoted to the public welfare irrevocably. With the exception of a few small bequests, long ago satisfied, Girard's entire estate is now in the hands of the City of Philadelphia. Girard was so determined to prevent his estate from falling into the classification of a private institution that he declared that if the City of Philadelphia failed to carry out the provisions of his will, his estate would pass to the Commonwealth of Pennsylvania, and if the State violated his wishes, the United States would become the final beneficiary. Is it not evident, then, that the action of the Orphans' Court, in turning the Girard estate over to private individuals, strikes at the very jugular vein of Girard's expressed intentions?

Does pinning a badge of private trustee on six heretofore declared public trustees remove the so-called incompetency of which the Orphans' Court speaks? The Majority says that "on the basis of the compelling testamentary evidence Girard college is a private charity capable of being lawfully administered by private trustees." But as I stated before, how can this Court or the Orphans' Court remove the City as trustee when the will makes the City the trustee? Of course, if the City were incapable, incompetent, or unwilling to act as trustee, the Orphans' Court might then, under the rule that a trust will not fail for want of a trustee, appoint another trustee. But the City is capable, it is competent, it is willing to act as trustee. Why then should it be removed when the removal runs counter to the wishes of the testator? The provision in the Girard will that the college be limited to male white orphans is no stronger a provision than that the City should administer and care for the estate. The City of Philadelphia is the tabernacle of the Girard Estate, it is the ark of the covenant. The whole history of the legislation, maintenance, direction of Girard College and the litigation over the estate is permeated with Philadelphia. Girard College is as much a part of Philadelphia as Benjamin Franklin is indelibly a part of Philadelphia's history.

It could never have been Girard's intention that, with an amendment to the United States Constitution, all his plans should go awry. He could never have intended that when the United States Constitution went in one direction, his college should go in another. He was interested in founding a college for poor male children. He said "white male orphans" because the times and the law would not have permitted a collective school for free children and slave children. That was the whole sum and substance of his statement. The language of the whole will demonstrates this, Girard's whole life proves it.

I would admit William Ashe Foust and Robert Felder to Girard College.

NOTES

1. After this opinion there were protests about integration and then another lawsuit, this time in federal court. The Eastern District of Pennsylvania first held that discrimination—even among a private actor—violated state law. That opinion was reversed because the issue should have been decided on federal law. *Commonwealth of Pennsylvania v. Brown*, 373 F.2d 771 (3d Cir. 1967). Shortly afterward the court found that such discrimination violated federal law. *Commonwealth of Pennsylvania v. Brown*, 392 F. 2d 120 (3rd Cir. 1968). Girard College was, thus, integrated in 1968.

2. Mr. Girard was also skeptical of religion and banned the teaching of religion at his school. That decision led to litigation in the United States Supreme Court, over whether this kind of irreligious charity could be permitted. Supreme Court Justice Joseph Story held that it could. *Vidal v. Girard's Executors*, 43 U.S. 127 (1841). And therein lies a very exciting story about the expansion of charitable purpose in the nineteenth century. But that is a story for another time. *See, e.g.*, ROBERT FERGUSON, READING THE EARLY REPUBLIC 234–53 (2009).

Al Brophy has a slightly different take on Story's goal in *Reason and Sentiment: The Moral Worlds and Modes of Reasoning of Antebellum Jurists*, 79 B.U. L. REV. 1161, 1190–91 (1999) (interpreting *Vidal v. Girard's Executors*, 43 U.S. 127 (1841), as illustrating common law's reverence for vested rights and reason as opposed to religious sentiments).

ASSESSMENT

The majority opinion in *Girard College* states, "[T]he right of private property . . . is fundamental to our social, economic and political order and [its] preservation unimpaired is as vital to our Negro citizens as it is to their white brethren." Consider the accuracy and equity of this statement, which takes as equivalent the property rights of black and white citizens. Prepare a short blogpost that evaluates this statement against a backdrop of significant racial wealth gaps and a troubled history of black citizens being dispossessed of property rights in the conventional and historical "economic and political order."

2.   Deviation

A second method of modification for charitable trusts, in addition to cy pres, is deviation. The UTC provides:

UTC § 412 Modification or Termination Because of Unanticipated Circumstances or Inability to Administer Trust Effectively

(a)   The court may modify the administrative or dispositive terms of a trust or terminate the trust if, because of circumstances not anticipated by the settlor, modification or termination will further the purposes of the trust. To the extent practicable, the modification must be made in accordance with the settlor's probable intention.

(b)   The court may modify the administrative terms of a trust if continuation of the trust on its existing terms would be impracticable or wasteful or impair the trust's administration.

(c)   Upon termination of a trust under this section, the trustee shall distribute the trust property in a manner consistent with the purposes of the trust.

What deviation provides that cy pres does not is the factor of "unanticipated circumstances." Trustees can, therefore, petition for modification if changes in circumstances render the fulfillment of trust terms difficult or impossible (and, in fact, fiduciary duty may demand that a trustee file such a petition). While this factor is implicit in a cy pres analysis, the deviation doctrine makes it explicit.

One of the most sensationalistic and controversial cases of modification based on deviation was the long-standing litigation involving the Barnes Foundation, a world-class art collection assembled by scientist and philanthropist Albert C. Barnes. Barnes, who lived in Lower Merion just outside of Philadelphia, collected primarily French Impressionist and Post-Impressionist pieces, but owned "about two thousand works in all, by artists ranging from El Greco and Rubens to Miró and Modigliani." *See* John Nivala, *Droit Patrimoine: The Barnes Collection, the Public Interest, and Protecting Our Cultural Inheritance*, 55 RUTGERS L. REV. 477, 477–78 (2003). As Barry Munitz, the president of the J. Paul Getty Trust, remarked "[t]here are some of the most spectacular paintings that the world has ever seen." Jeffrey Toobin, *Battle for the Barnes*, NEW YORKER, Jan. 21, 2002, at 34.

Aside from the quality of the collection, however, the Barnes collection may be most well-known for the restrictions placed on the artwork. The 1946 bylaws to the trust indenture drafted by Barnes, an adamant populist, stated that "plain people, that is, men and women who gain their livelihood by daily toil in shops, factories, schools, stores and similar places, shall have free access to the art gallery and the arboretum upon those days when the gallery and the arboretum are to be open to the public." Barnes insisted that the "purpose of this gift is democratic and educational in the true meaning of those words, and special privileges are forbidden." Accordingly, Barnes prohibited any "society functions commonly designated receptions, tea parties, dinners, banquets, dances, musicales or similar affairs." Barnes also prohibited the sale or loan of any of the artworks and specified that "[a]ll paintings shall remain in exactly the places they are at the time of the death of Donor and his said wife."

Over the years, the Foundation trustees bemoaned their restricted ability to charge admissions fees, loan out artwork, fundraise with a small board, and bring in larger audiences because of the out-of-the-way location. Consequently, in 2003, the trustees filed a petition to modify the trust terms through deviation in order to restructure the Foundation Board and relocate the collection from Lower Merion to Philadelphia. Specifically, the Foundation trustees requested that the court "remove restrictions in the current [indenture, charter, and bylaws] that prevent relocation of the Foundation's main gallery from the Merion facility to Philadelphia." *See* Second Amended Petition of the Barnes Foundation to

Amend its Charter and Bylaws at 9, *In re Barnes Found.*, No 58,788 (Pa. Ct. of Com. Pleas Oct. 21, 2003). They further requested that the court "remove some of the conditions and stipulations set forth in the present Indenture that restrict the Foundation. The Foundation will therefore have the flexibility in the future to manage its affairs in accordance with its best professional and business judgment."

The court granted the Foundation's requests for deviation based on the Foundation's financial circumstances. The court stated, "that the provision in Dr. Barnes' indenture mandating that the gallery be maintained in Merion was not sacrosanct, and could yield under the 'doctrine of deviation,' " provided that the proposed solution "represented the least drastic modification of the indenture that would accomplish the donor's desired ends." *In re Barnes Foundation*, No. 58,788, 2004 WL 2903655, at *1 (Pa. Ct. Com. Pl. Dec. 13, 2004). Opposition to the petition as well as

The Barnes collection in its new home, near the Philadelphia Museum of Art. Photo courtesy of Visit Philadelphia.

the resulting decision was immediate and overwhelming. The Board of Commissioners of Lower Merion Township passed a resolution stating that the Barnes Foundation was "part of the fabric, character and culture of Lower Merion Township" and any change in location was "in direct contravention of the intent and purpose of Albert Barnes." Lower Merion Board of Commissioners, Resolution of the Board of Commissioners of the Township of Lower Merion.[8] Similarly, critics called the proposed move of the collection from Merion to Philadelphia "death by disembowelment" and an "act of cultural vandalism." Robin Pogrebin, *A Move Done, Barnes Leader Makes Another*, N.Y. TIMES, Dec. 28, 2013, at C1. The collection finally opened to the public in its new location in 2012. All the paintings were placed in the same arrangements as in their previous home, and the New York Times art critic raved that "Barnes's exuberant vision of art as a relatively egalitarian aggregate of the fine, the decorative and the functional comes across more clearly, justifying its

---

[8]   Available at http://www.barnesfriends.org/downlload/legal_LowerMerionResolution.pdf.

perpetuation with a new force." Roberta Smith, *A Museum, Reborn, Remains True to Its Old Self, Only Better*, N.Y. TIMES, May 17, 2012, at A1.

NOTES

1.　　Moving the Barnes was considered by many to be a purely political act and one that would have been all the more outrageous to Barnes because of his abject hatred of the elite Philadelphia art scene and the society members who populated it. A documentary, called "The Art of the Steal," provides more about Barnes as a collector and the politics around the move of his collection.

2.　　A number of other art collections have encountered problems with similar restrictions placed on them, including the Isabella Stewart Gardener Museum in

Portrait of Isabella Stewart
Gardner (1840–1924) by John
Singer Sargent, 1888. Isabella
Stewart Gardner Museum,
Boston, MA.

Boston and the Peggy Guggenheim Collection in Venice. The Gardener museum represents the collecting efforts of its namesake, who traveled extensively and spent years carefully curating the collection in her home, the site of the museum. In accordance with Gardner's will, the collection is to be maintained in perpetuity exactly as she had arranged it. This requirement has produced an odd result because the collection was the target of a major art heist and lost over a dozen valuable works. The paintings have never been recovered and, because of the gift conditions, the empty frames remain in their original location, reminders of the loss. For more on the theft, see ULRICH BOSER, THE GARDNER HEIST: THE TRUE STORY OF THE WORLD'S LARGEST UNSOLVED ART THEFT (2009), and the documentary "Stolen," produced by the museum itself.

3.　　One question that these cases bring up is just how long donor wishes should prevail, particularly when the wishes are burdensome to the trust or charitable institution or reflect outdated modes of operation. We encountered this question with Senator Bacon and his segregated park. We also encountered this issue in our discussions about private dynasty trusts and the problems that arise in conjunction with the repeal of the rule against perpetuities. The central question persists: should donor restrictions be able to control in perpetuity? One proposal has been to think about applying some version of the rule against perpetuities to charitable trusts. *See* Alex M. Johnson, Jr., *Limiting Dead Hand Control of Charitable Trusts: Expanding the Use of the Cy Pres Doctrine*, 21 U. HAW. L. REV. 353, 353 (1999). Consider the benefits and detriments of such a proposal.

4. In the Barnes case, the trustees requested that they be able to better use their "best professional and business judgment." This sounds like a request to be aligned with corporate law practices and to benefit from the business judgment rule. Often, trustees of nonprofit corporations argue that they should be beholden to corporate rules as opposed to trust law rules, based on being formed as a corporate entity rather than a trust. What difference would this make to the trustees and what might the implications be of using corporate rather than trust rules to regulate trustee decision making? *See Dennis v. Buffalo Fine Arts Acad.*, 836 N.Y.S.2d 498 (Sup. Ct. 2007) and *Commonwealth ex rel Bowyer v. Sweet Briar Inst.*, No. 150619, 2015 WL 3646914 (Va. June 9, 2015).

ASSESSMENTS

1. Controversies abound over confederate monuments and other monuments to historical figures who supported systems of enslavement and white supremacy. Many of these monuments were gifts to localities from organizations that coalesced to fundraise for the monuments (organizations like the Daughters of the Confederacy) or from wealthy individuals. In their attempts to remove these monuments, cities have sometimes run into legal battles. In Richmond, VA, an attempt by the Governor to remove the Robert E. Lee monument ran into a roadblock when an heir of man who gifted land to the state for the purposes of erecting the monument requested an injunction,

A confederate monument, transformed after Black Lives Matter (BLM) protests in 2020. Robert E. Lee monument, Richmond, VA.

stopping the removal. In his request for an injunction, the heir referred to language in the deed signed by his family and the state saying the Virginia "will hold said statue and pedestal and circle of ground perpetually sacred to the monumental purpose to which they have been devoted and that she will faithfully guard it and affectionately protect it."

Write a memo to the Governor advising on how to treat this situation. Include the following:

    a.   How to seek modification of any gift restrictions that may be implicit in the deed

    b.   What steps the Governor should take to modify the restrictions including the best legal approach.

Attach to your memo either a proposed cy pres petition for modification or a proposed petition for deviation (or maybe try both!).

2.   You work in the development office at a University and are responsible for fundraising from major donors. You have a donor who is interested in making an endowed gift to the institution but wants to place a number of restrictive conditions on the gift. Write a letter to the donor explaining some of the possible long-term consequences of the restrictions and any related advice to the donor on how to accomplish the stated goals.

3.   In the Fisk case you read about earlier in this chapter, the resolution involved representatives from Fisk University and the purchasing museum, Crystal Bridges, brokering a deal allowing the two institutions to share the artwork on a rotating basis. In pairs or groups, roleplay this negotiation and see how it comes out. What details are important and what compromises are necessary?

E. The Problems of Charitable Trust Enforcement

As we learned with respect to private trusts, beneficiaries are responsible for holding trustees accountable and enforcing trustee compliance with fiduciary duties. If a trustee of a private trust mismanages the trust funds or fails to distribute them properly, the beneficiaries can bring a claim and hold the trustee financially accountable.

With charitable trusts, there are no ascertainable beneficiaries to hold the trustees accountable and so the state attorney general is tasked with representing the beneficiary public and enforcing the trust. Standing is also accorded to individuals with "a special interest in the enforcement of the trust." RESTATEMENT (THIRD) OF TRUSTS § 94(2). To have this kind of "special interest standing," a person must demonstrate entitlement to a particular benefit under the trust, one that is not available to the public at large. As you will see, there are problems associated with charitable trust enforcement and especially with the limitations on standing.

1.   Enforcement and the Attorney General

Critics and commentators usually raise two considerations concerning state attorneys general and their ability to effectively enforce trust terms. One problem commonly discussed is the lack of resources available for the oversight of charitable trusts at the state level:

> In some states, several assistant attorneys general form a charitable division of the attorney general's office. . . . In other states, however, one assistant attorney general supervises the nonprofit sector as only one part of his or her assignment . . . . and many states do not list any attorneys specifically assigned to charitable matters. . . . The worst abuses receive attention, but many problems probably go undetected or unaddressed.

Susan N. Gary, *Regulating the Management of Charities: Trust Law, Corporate Law, and Tax Law*, 21 U. HAW. L. REV. 593, 622–24 (1999).

The second concern raised about enforcement by state attorneys general is the political nature of the office. To demonstrate this point, we return once again to the Hershey Trust litigation. We've looked at how the state attorney general stepped into the controversy, invoking his parens patriae authority of behalf of an unclear public. What was also notable about the state attorney general's participation was his change in direction and attitude based on political popularity.

Here's the whole story. In 2002, the Hershey Foods Corporation "began soliciting bids for the acquisition of the Corporation which would include purchase of the shares of stock held in the School Trust representing 77% of the voting power of all outstanding shares of the Hershey Foods Corporation." *In re Milton Hershey School Trust*, 807 A.2d 324 (Pa. Commw. Ct. 2002). The news broke in a *Wall Street Journal* story that laid out possible plans for the sale and also reported: "People familiar with the matter say that Pennsylvania Attorney General Mike Fisher's office, while not advocating a sale of the company, has urged the Hershey trust to diversify."[9] The article also reported that a spokesman for the office "declined to comment on whether anyone there had talked to the Hershey School Trust about diversifying." But that "Mark Pacella, the chief deputy attorney general charged with overseeing charitable trusts, said . . . current market conditions have underlined 'the age-old proposition that diversification is almost always a hallmark of prudent portfolio management.' "

---

[9]   Shelly Branch, Sarah Ellison, & Gordon Fairclough, *Hersey Foods Is Considering a Plan to Put Itself Up for Sale*, https://www.wsj.com/articles/SB1027561165960914640 (last updated July 25, 2020 6:59 AM).

After the news became public that Hershey was trying to sell shares, however, an enormous resistance campaign sprang up in the community:

> Hershey residents and workers received the news grimly indeed. With "tears in his eyes" the Company CEO Richard Lenny broke the news to the Company's employees at a 9 A.M. meeting. Lenny also recorded a statement, which was broadcast on the internet every half hour, to the effect that he "disagreed with the trust's actions" and that he had offered the Trust alternative means to diversify. The next day, Friday, July 26, a local newspaper reported that "Hershey residents questioned why the trust would need to sell Hershey Foods, wondered how the sale would affect the village, and asked if a sale would be consistent with Milton Hershey's vision of social responsibility." . . . As part of a grassroots "Derail the Sale" campaign, a public rally against the sale was held on Friday, August 2. Residents began displaying yard signs with slogans such as "The Hershey Trust—An Oxymoron" and "Don't Shut Down Chocolate Town."

Jonathan Klick & Robert H. Sitkoff, *Agency Costs, Charitable Trusts, and Corporate Control: Evidence from Hershey's Kiss-Off*, 108 COLUM. L. REV. 749, 769–70 (2008).

Hershey community members then turned to the state attorney general—who was also the Republican candidate for governor in the upcoming November election—to remove the trustees and block the sale. Which he then did. Realizing that the sale of the Hershey Trust company might result in the loss of many jobs in the state and create massive dissatisfaction among Hershey employees—and voters—the state attorney general pursued the injunction to stop diversification. The Orphan's Court issued a preliminary injunction, and the Trustees appealed. On appeal, the state attorney general:

> [C]onceded that the Trust was "imprudently" undiversified "and that it would be 'desirable' for the Trust to diversify its holdings," but he also argued that "there was no testimony that it needs to do so immediately, within the next few days or weeks." By contrast, "the current employees of Hershey Foods would be worse off under an acquisition than they are now," and the sale of the Company "would seriously impair, if not destroy, the symbiotic relationship which has existed for many decades among the company, the School and its Trust, and the other institutions which together carry on Milton Hershey's unique vision."

Id. at 773–74.

Ultimately, the appellate court upheld the injunction and, even after the injunction expired, the Trustees resolved not to pursue any sale. And shortly thereafter, the state attorney general lost his gubernatorial election—despite his claim that he had saved over 6,000 Hershey jobs. The biggest losers, however, may have been the Hershey shareholders. As Jonathan Klick and Robert Sitkoff write, "the Attorney General forced the Trust to retain an asset that was worth $850 million more on the open market than in the hands of the trustees. . . . The $850 million in Trust assets destroyed translates roughly into $67,000 per resident of Hershey, or $62,000 per employee of the Company—plus the Trust's exposure to uncompensated risk was continued." *Id.* at 815–16.

NOTES

1.   After the Hershey sale fiasco, on November 6, 2002, the Governor signed an amendment to the Pennsylvania prudent investor statute. The amendment requires the trustees of a charitable trust, "in making investment and management decisions," to consider "the special relationship of [a trust asset] and its economic impact as a principal business enterprise on the community." The 2002 amendment put the burden on the trustee petitioning for sale to "prove by clear and convincing evidence" that the sale "is necessary to maintain the economic viability of the corporation and [to] prevent a significant diminution of trust assets or to avoid an impairment of the charitable purpose of the trust." How does this align with the prudent investor rules that we discussed in Chapter 10? Thinking about Sitkoff's and Kick's economic analysis, who benefits from this amendment?

2.   Dissenting in the appellate court's decision to uphold the injunction, Judge Pellegrini stated:

> The majority affirms the trial court's order, dismisses the Trust's application for a stay and directs the trial court to rule on the merits of the controversy. The decree is not in accordance with law because nowhere in the PEFC is there any authority for the Attorney General to essentially act as co-trustee or co-manager of the Trust and be part of the process leading up to a decision by the Trustees to take a certain action. The only power the court is given is to restrain a sale, not to foreclose the Trustees from reaching an agreement to be approved, let alone what the trial court did here by foreclosing any meaningful negotiation that will lead to an understanding that can be brought to the court for approval. Moreover, there is no basis in the law, either statutory or case, giving the Attorney General a right to become "fully

involved" in the decision-making of the Trust; he is neither a co-manager nor co-Trustee of the Trust. Once the Trustees exercise the discretion given to them and reach an agreement, only then can the Attorney General take action to challenge the agreement by arguing it violates the terms of the Trust. Until an agreement is negotiated, terms made final, and covenants known, it is impossible to know what or if there would be negative effects from any sale. If that is not the law, then the Attorney General, under his understanding of his parens patriae powers, can become fully involved in the decision-making of any charitable institution in this Commonwealth.

Is Judge Pellegrini correct that the Attorney General can only enforce the express terms of the trust? And if so, where in the trust might we find terms that allows an injunction because it will injure the community? Put differently, what is the basis for implying the community as a beneficiary and what are the boundaries of that implication? It is not difficult to suggest, in this particular case, that the state attorney general may have usurped trustee authority in an attempt to gain favor with voters.

2. Solutions to the Enforcement Problem

Because of these dissatisfactions with charitable trust enforcement, courts and reformers have looked to bring in new parties as trust enforcers and to craft new solutions. One of the most common suggestions is to enlarge donor standing; other solutions include the use of tax rules to discipline charitable trusts or creating charitable commissions.

a. *Enlarging Donor Standing*

There is an increasing sense among those in the nonprofit community that donors and their estates should have some rights to challenge the administration of charitable trusts (how extensive those rights should be is another question). One of the leading cases that supports donor standing, over a vigorous dissent, is a New York case from 2001, *Smithers v. St. Luke's-Roosevelt Hospital Center*, 723 N.Y.S.2d 426 (App. Div. 2001). The *Smithers* case raises the question of whether the trust should be answerable to the donor, while also asking how much the trust and those overseeing it—like the attorney general—should be free to deviate from the trust purposes.

In *Smithers*, Adele Smithers, who was the widow of R. Brinkley Smithers, sought standing to enforce the terms of a $10 million gift (given in installments) that her husband had made to St. Luke's-Roosevelt Hospital Center with the intention that the gift be used to establish an alcoholism treatment center. With $1 million from the first installment of the Gift, the Hospital purchased a building at 56 East 93rd Street in Manhattan to house the rehabilitation program, and in 1973 the Smithers Alcoholism Treatment and Training Center opened there. In addition, the Hospital agreed to use the gift to expand its treatment of alcoholism to include "rehabilitation in a free-standing, controlled, uplifting and non-hospital environment," that is, a "therapeutic community" removed from the hospital setting.

Over the years, there were conflicts between Smithers and the Hospital concerning the use of some of the funds. Nevertheless, Smithers completed the gift before dying. Approximately a year after Smithers' death, the Hospital announced plans to move the Smithers Center into a hospital ward and sell the East 93rd Street building, claiming that it had to sell the building to be operationally profitable. Adele Smithers, at this point, requested accountings from the Hospital and discovered that the Hospital had been "misappropriating monies from the Endowment Fund since before Smithers's death, transferring such monies to its general fund where they were used for purposes unrelated to the Smithers Center. Mrs. Smithers notified the Attorney General, who investigated the Hospital's plan to sell the building and discovered that the Hospital had transferred restricted assets from the Smithers Endowment Fund to its general fund."

Adele Smithers subsequently commenced a suit to "enforce the conditions of the Gift" and to enjoin the Hospital from selling the building and relocating the Smithers Center without court approval. She also sought a "return of all income lost on the funds misappropriated by the Hospital from the Gift funds, for imposition of a constructive trust, for an accounting, and for a judicial declaration concerning the terms and conditions under which the Gift fund is to be administered." The big question for the court was whether Adele Smithers had standing to pursue these claims.

Ultimately, the court decided that she did have standing, despite the traditional rule according exclusive standing to the state attorney general. The court remarked:

> Adele Smithers brought the claim as the court-appointed special administrator of the estate of her late husband to enforce his rights under his agreement with the Hospital through specific performance of that agreement. Therefore, the general rule barring beneficiaries from suing charitable corporations has no application to Mrs. Smithers. Moreover, the desire to prevent vexatious litigation by

"irresponsible parties who do not have a tangible stake in the matter and have not conducted appropriate investigations" has no application to Mrs. Smithers either. Without possibility of pecuniary gain for himself or herself, only a plaintiff with a genuine interest in enforcing the terms of a gift will trouble to investigate and bring this type of action. Indeed, it was Mrs. Smithers's accountants who discovered and informed the Attorney General of the Hospital's misdirection of Gift funds, and it was only after Mrs. Smithers brought her suit that the Attorney General acted to prevent the Hospital from diverting the entire proceeds of the sale of the building away from the Gift fund and into its general fund.

Based on these facts, the court stated that: "The donor of a charitable gift is in a better position than the Attorney General to be vigilant and, if he or she is so inclined, to enforce his or her own intent. Moreover, the circumstances of this case demonstrate the need for co-existent standing for the Attorney General and the donor. We conclude that the distinct but related interests of the donor and the Attorney General are best served by continuing to accord standing to donors to enforce the terms of their own gifts concurrent with the Attorney General's standing to enforce such gifts on behalf of the beneficiaries thereof."

NOTES

1.   The building that Smithers donated to the Hospital sits 56 East 93rd Street on the Upper East Side in Manhattan. It was constructed in the English Regency style in 1931. The mansion currently houses the Spence School's Lower School. Spence is an all-girls private school founded by Clara Spence in 1892. Spence's exterior served as a backdrop in many Gossip Girl episodes, and provided the inspiration for Constance Willard, the girls school that the characters attend (when they are not sitting on the Met steps).

Loew Goadby House, now the Spence School, on National Register of Historic Places at 56 East 93rd Street In New York City.

2. Allowing donor standing does raise the possibility that there will be significant costs to the donee, including a possible decrease in the donee's ability to use gifted assets as the donee wishes. When donor restrictions inhibit the donee's ability to use a gift, David Yermack, in *Donor Governance and Financial Management in Prominent US Art Museums*, 41 J. CULTURAL ECON. 215, 216 (2017), has called this phenomenon "donor governance":

> Restricted donations represent a form of corporate governance, because they constrain the opportunities for nonprofit managers to expropriate resources. I call this practice "donor governance." The rationale for this type of donor control increases when other forms of governance are weak and information asymmetry between donors and managers is high.

Governance in the charitable trust context is a function supposedly reserved for trustees. Should trustees not be the ones to make these kinds of operational decisions about how to manage assets and not donors? One argument in favor of donor governance is that the ability to restrict gifts and know that the restrictions will be honored is a spur to charitable giving. That is to say, if donors thought their wishes might not always be respected, they might be less inclined to make charitable gifts. Do you think this is true?

3   UTC § 405(c) provides that "[t]he settlor of a charitable trust, among others, may maintain a proceeding to enforce the trust." THE RESTATEMENT

(THIRD) OF TRUSTS, § 94, aligns with this position, stating: "A suit for the enforcement of a charitable trust may be maintained only by the Attorney General or other appropriate public officer or by a co-trustee or successor trustee, by a settlor, or by another person who has a special interest in the enforcement of the trust." Some states that have not adopted the UTC, like New York, have enlarged donor standing judicially.

Joshua Tate has pointed out that, "[i]n a departure from traditional law, section 405(c) grants standing to '[t]he settlor of a charitable trust, among others,' . . . . The UTC provision thus presents an obvious ambiguity: who are the 'others' contemplated by the uniform act?" Joshua C. Tate, *Should Charitable Trust Enforcement Rights Be Assignable*, 85 CHI. KENT L. REV. 1045, 1046 (2010). Tate presses on this question by further asking: "Should enforcement rights be granted to the settlor's personal representative, the settlor's heirs, or both? And . . . should the settlor be permitted to assign her enforcement rights to a third party?" *Id.* at 1048. How would you answer these questions and what factors would you take into consideration?

4.　　Donors are not generally granted standing in order to "recognize the completeness of the gift for public purposes." This lack of standing has driven donors to other forms of "self-help" in order to see the terms of a gift enforced, including the drafting of "contracts . . . specifying charities' performance obligations and donors' enforcement rights." Evelyn Brody, *From the Dead Hand to The Living Dead: The Conundrum of Charitable-Donor Standing* 41 GA. L. REV. 1183 (2007).

ASSESSMENT

A client of yours would like to make a major gift to a university. She very much wants to give funds to start an interdisciplinary program in Southeast Asian studies, but she is somewhat nervous because she doesn't want the gift funds to be used for general operating expenses. What would you advise her to do? Would you advise that she execute a contract and what would you suggest that she in include in such a contract?

b.　Using the Tax Code

Another mechanism for regulating charitable institutions is the tax code. Occasionally the IRS steps in and acts as guardian by policing whether a charitable trust is fulfilling its charitable—and therefore tax exempt—purpose.

Probably the single most famous example of this policing by the IRS arose in Hawaii's Bishop trust, which funds the Kamehameha School. The Bishop trust was created in the late nineteenth century by Princess Bernice Pauahi, daughter of King Kamehameha, and funded with 375,000 acres of ancestral lands of the royal Kamehameha family. The Kamehameha Trust is now one of the largest charitable trusts in the world, with an endowment valued at $12.1 billion, as of June 2019. The will left the direction of the Kamehameha Trust in the hands of five trustees, to be appointed by the justices of the Supreme Court of Hawaii. The trustees were to erect two schools, one for boys and one for girls, and to oversee not only the running of the school but also the provision of support to "orphans, and others in indigent circumstances, giving the preference to Hawaiians of pure or part aboriginal blood." You can see the princess's will in the Appendix.

Controversy arose in the late 1990s when it became public knowledge that trustees positions had become plum political assignments and that the trustees were paying themselves annual compensation approaching $1 million each. Underscoring the political ties between the Kamehameha Trust and government leaders, trustees of the school included a president of the senate, speaker of the house, chief justice of the supreme court, and the governor's closest associate. In 1997, four prominent elders of the native Hawaiian community together with Randall Roth of the University of Hawaii Law School published the essay "Broken Trust." The essay's authors uncovered the corruption of the trustees and accused them of multiple forms of fiduciary breach. The authors called out for public inquiry and, in response, the state attorney general opened an investigation.

In a special master's report, filed in August 1998, Colbert Matsumoto reported a number of instances of financial mismanagement, including insufficient financial disclosure in annual reports, inconsistent documentation of investment and management decisions, inappropriate treatment of accumulate income, and trustee conflicts of loyalty.[10] It was discovered that trustees received private benefits—a core prohibition in IRS rules for charitable trusts; one trustee went to an adult club in Las Vegas and charged thousands of dollars to the trust. When caught, he paid the money back—but was then given a bonus in that amount by the trust. Another trustee negotiated with the trust for the sale of some of its property to one of the trustee's clients.

Because of all these violations, the IRS finally entered the fray and revoked the Trust's charitable tax exemption—doing so retroactively. The IRS made it a condition of any reconsideration that the trustees in place at the time be

---

[10] For more of the report, see http://archives.starbulletin.com/98/08/07/news/masters2/masters2.html.

removed and replaced, which they were. New procedures were also put in place for the appointment of trustees, just as new governance rules were quickly drafted and approved. Ultimately the IRS restored the Trust's tax-exempt status. The IRS's actions, however, highlighted how fast the pace of change could be when tax exemption status was at stake and what an effective disciplinary mechanism withdrawal of the status was. In 2006, Randall Roth published BROKEN TRUST: GREED, MISMANAGEMENT & POLITICAL MANIPULATION AT AMERICA'S LARGEST CHARITABLE TRUST (2006), which was an instant bestseller.[11]

NOTES

1.   There has been no shortage of litigation surrounding the Kamehameha Trust. In addition to all the controversy over trustee corruption the trustees also found themselves in court over the provision in the princess's will "giving the preference to Hawaiians of pure or part aboriginal blood." For more on this litigation, see *Doe v. Kamehameha Schools*, 470 F.3d 827, 831 (9th Cir. 2006).

2.   Private charitable trusts, if they do not accept public donations, are subject to the rules for private foundations. A family, or private, foundation is defined by § 501(c)(3) of the Internal Revenue Code, which provides for two types of charitable organizations: public charities and private foundations. All organizations are presumed to be private foundations unless they prove they are a public charity by satisfying the IRS "public support" test, requiring an organization to receive at least one-third of its annual support from the general public through ongoing fundraising efforts. The main requirement of private foundations is that they distribute 5% of the fair market value of their assets each year. I.R.C. § 4942 (2018).

Private foundations faced criticism in the past for perceived abuses with foundation money going toward family expenses. *See* John R. Labovitz, *The Impact of the Private Foundation Provisions of the Tax Reform Act of 1969: Early Empirical Measurements*, 3 J. LEGAL STUD. 63, 65 (1974). Even after these reforms, however, some commentators still criticize private foundations as being generators of wealth inequality and acting as "private investment company[ies]" that use only a small part of their "excess cash flow for charitable purposes." *See* F. B. Heron Found., *New Frontiers in Mission-Related Investing* 1 (2004), https://

---

[11]   For a look at the source documents for the book, see *Selected Sources and Background Documents*, BROKEN TRUST BOOK WEBSITE, https://brokentrustbook.com/sources.html.

community-wealth.org/sites/clone.community-wealth.org/files/downloads/
report-heron.pdf.

3.   Andrew Carnegie, the steel industrialist and major philanthropist, believed
that the rich should spend all their money during their lifetimes, leaving nothing
after death. He famously said, in his 1889 essay entitled *The Gospel of Wealth*: "The
man who dies thus rich dies disgraced." He did not quite reach his goal of
spending all his wealth while alive—he ultimately endowed the Carnegie
Corporation with what remained of his fortune—but during his lifetime he
funded an enormous number of public projects, in particular the construction
of libraries around the country. Today, other philanthropists take seriously
Carnegie's call to spend down charitable trusts as a way of avoiding the problems
associated with an overabundance of dead-hand control. Bill and Melinda Gates,
founders of the Gates Foundation (currently the largest charitable trust in
existence), have projected that the Foundation will spend down all its assets and
terminate within twenty years of Bill's and Melinda's death. See *Who We Are:
Foundation Trust*, BILL & MELINDA GATES FOUND., https://www.
gatesfoundation.org/Who-We-Are/General-Information/Financials/
Foundation-Trust.

F.   Conclusion and Takeaways

This Chapter introduces charitable trusts and explains the differences
between private and charitable trusts. The main differences are in 1) who can be
a beneficiary 2) modes of modification and 3) power of enforcement. In
addition, charitable trusts differ from private trusts because they are not subject
to the Rule Against Perpetuities and they receive special tax treatment. Another
difference that we've seen is that the duties of the trustee shift once the
beneficiary is not an ascertainable individual or set of individuals. All of these
differences are grounded in the idea that charitable trusts benefit the public and
serve a charitable purpose. Despite these differences, charitable trusts—like
private trusts—raise questions about the extent to which we want to and should
allow donors to exert dead-hand control.

CHAPTER 15 COMPREHENSIVE ASSESSMENT

CHARITABLE TRUST REVIEW.

Answer the questions that follow based on this fact pattern.

Sweet Briar College opened its doors in 1906, founded with a bequest from
Indiana Fletcher Williams, a wealthy Virginia woman. Williams left all her
"plantation and a tract of land known as Sweet Briar Plantation" for the

purposes of forming "a school or seminary for the education of white girls and young women" in memory of her deceased daughter, Daisy.[12]

Without warning in March 2015, Sweet Briar College's Board of Directors announced that the college would be closing its doors at the end of the academic year because of financial difficulties. Sweet Briar's President stated that the school was in financial distress and could no longer afford to keep the school open. In an effort to control expenses, the college had previously suspended all retirement contributions on behalf of employees for five months, the president worked for two weeks without pay, and a small number of administrative and support staff positions were eliminated. None of these efforts had solved the problem.

At the time that the Sweet Briar Board announced the closing, the college's endowment was valued at approximately eighty-five million dollars. According to Standard and Poor's, however, only about one-fourth of the endowment funds were unrestricted and the donor-restricted funds could not be used for general operations or as needed by college leadership. One month after announcing the closure, college administrators sent letters to living donors requesting permission to use restricted

Postcard, **Partial view of Sweet Briar College for Women**, circa 1903–1945, Boston Public Library.

endowed funds for "general charitable purposes . . . including costs that the Sweet Briar Board . . . determines are necessary and proper to effect the closure of the college and winding up of its affairs."

A group of outraged alumnae quickly mobilized and procured the help and support of Amherst County Attorney, Ellen Bowyer, who brought a lawsuit in the name of the Commonwealth of Virginia, taking the privilege and role usually allocated to the state attorney general. *See Commonwealth of Virginia, ex rel. Ellen Bowyer, in her official capacity as County Attorney for the County of Amherst, Virginia v. Sweet Briar Institute. Commonwealth ex rel Bowyer v. Sweet Briar Inst.,* No. 150619, 2015 WL 3646914 (Va. June 9, 2015). Bowyer and the group requested an injunction to prevent the college from using any donor funds to close the school and, in their suit, claimed that the College had violated the Virginia Charitable

---

[12]   To take a look at her will, see https://archive.org/details/willofindianafle00unse.

Solicitations Act as well as the UTC by using charitable funds for the purpose of closing the College.

a. Did Ellen Bowyer have standing to bring the lawsuit in her capacity as a county attorney? The Virginia attorney general said no but declined to bring any legal action against Sweet Briar. Should Bowyer have been granted standing, or are there any other parties who should have been accorded standing to hold the College accountable in the absence of the attorney general's participation? Please list which parties, if any, you think should have had standing in this matter and why the parties have standing.

b. Lifting restrictions on potentially three-fourths of the endowment—upward of sixty million dollars—could have helped the College navigate its financial straits. If you were Sweet Briar's legal counsel, what steps could you have taken to modify conditions on the restricted endowed gifts? What facts would be the basis for a cy pres petition and what modifications would you request? Draft a cy pres petition for modification of gift restrictions. What details would change if you were to draft a petition for equitable deviation instead of a cy pres petition? What facts would you highlight for deviation and what arguments would you make?

c. If the College had closed, what could have been done with the grounds, the buildings, and the remainder of the endowment funds not used in closing the school? As counsel for the College, what would you recommend be done and what modifications would need to be obtained in order to wind down the College and divest the College of all its assets? What kinds of proposals would you suggest for new use of these assets?

d. In the lawsuit that Bowyer brought, she argued that the Sweet Briar Board was a trustee of a charitable trust and was acting in violation of its fiduciary duties under the UTC. The Board argued that the College was not a trustee because the institution had been formed as a nonprofit corporation. The question for the Supreme Court of Virginia was whether the College could be both a nonprofit corporate entity and a trustee as well, subject to trust law. Imagine that you are clerking for one of the judges deciding this case. Based on what you know about charitable institutions and trust law, how would you advise a judge hearing this case? Draft a brief memo explaining your opinion and stating why the College should (or should not) be subject to trust law.

Epilogue: For the court decision, see *Commonwealth ex rel. Bowyer v. Sweet Briar Inst.*, No. 150619, 2015 Va. LEXIS 22, at *3–4 (June 9, 2015) (unpublished). Before litigation could get too far, the parties reached a settlement and an infusion of cash from alumnae allowed Sweet Briar to keep its doors open. As part of the settlement, the state attorney general agreed to lift restrictions on sixteen million dollars in the college's endowment fund. For a detailed exploration of the case, see William H. Hurd, et al., *The Will to Prevail: Inside the Legal Battle to Save Sweet Briar*, 51 U. RICH. L. REV. 227 (2016).

Test Your Knowledge

To assess your understanding of the material in this chapter, click here to take a quiz.

CHAPTER 16

The Taxation of Trusts and Estates and Gratuitous Transfers: An Overview

CHAPTER LEARNING OUTCOMES

Following your work with the material in this chapter, you should be able to do the following:

- Determine, based on a variety of scenarios, whether a particular person's estate will be subject to taxation

- Calculate a person's gross estate, net estate, and taxable estate based on a list of the person's assets

- Assess whether the generation skipping transfer tax will apply to a given transfer

- Determine whether income tax will apply to a given transfer

- Make arguments on both sides of the debate about taxing wealth transfers, take a position, and be able to support it

A. Introduction and Background

Any time there is wealth transfer, there is potential taxation. These taxes can be a large source of income for the government, and people disagree about whether it is best to keep these taxes low and leave most of this money in private hands or shift the money to the government for spending on the general welfare—a form of wealth redistribution. Wealth transfer taxes raise other questions as well:

- How progressive should our tax system be? In other words, to what extent should people with more wealth pay higher taxes at a higher rate than people with less wealth?

- Should taxation play a role in reducing wealth concentration at the top of the scale? The media often reports that the wealthiest 1% of U.S. residents—about 3.29 million people—hold 42.5% of our national wealth, while the remaining 325.7 million people share the remaining 57.5%. This is a greater discrepancy than any other country in the developed world. Is this a problem? If so, are increased taxes on the wealthy the solution?

- Is the estate tax really a tax on dead people, as the popular name, the "Death Tax" implies?

- Are the various forms of "tax planning" available to wealthy estates—valuation discounts, estate freezes, Crummey Trusts—legitimate or should the taxation of wealth be more straightforward, based on market value?

- Does the step-up in basis that allows beneficiaries to sell an inherited asset and calculate profits based on the basis on the decedent's day of death make sense? Is it fair? Is it good tax policy?

What you think about the questions above will color your reactions to the cases and doctrine in this chapter. In fact, this chapter may provoke more controversy than any chapter yet.

Let's also remember, however, that advising clients about estate planning is advising them about its potential tax consequences. Unsurprisingly, people generally don't wish their estates, or their beneficiaries, to pay more in taxes than they absolutely have to. Part of your job is to make sure they don't.

To advise clients adequately about the tax consequences of an estate plan requires a separate course in wealth transfer taxation; this chapter can only cover some crucial basics. The goal of this chapter is to make sure you understand the basics of the federal tax on gratuitous transfers (gifts) whether at life or at death, and that you recognize the red flags—situations where your client can get into trouble with taxes. When these more complicated situations arise, you need to stop and find someone with tax expertise—or, by then, maybe you will have acquired it yourself.

As this book goes to press, we have a new President of the United States. Part of President Biden's platform contains proposed changes to fundamental aspects of estate and gift tax law. This chapter explains these cornerstone principles of estate and gift tax as they are now and indicates changes the new administration has proposed. The online component of this chapter will follow changes in estate and gift tax as they occur—or do not occur—over the next four years.

In **Part B**, we set out arguments for and against the estate tax, as well as its basic mechanics: who pays it, how it is calculated, and what it means to have a unified transfer tax system. The tax, which is a federal tax, is imposed on the donor or the donor's estate. The unified credit means that a person can give away a certain amount during life and at death (combined) before that person incurs taxes. In 2021, this amount, indexed for inflation, is $11.7 million. Married couples can combine this credit and can thus give away $22.8 million through a combination of lifetime gifts and transfers on death. If you're thinking this means that estate tax doesn't apply to you, you are probably correct: the federal estate tax applies to only 0.1 percent of Americans.

Part C addresses the tax on generation-skipping transfers. If someone leaves property to their children, and their children leave it to their children, and so on, there will be impositions of federal estate and gift tax on each transfer to the next generation. But if that person puts all her assets in a trust and makes the beneficiaries her lineal descendants over many generations, there will only be a transfer tax for the initial transfer of assets to the trust but no further transfer taxes until the trust terminates. To control this type of maneuvering, Congress enacted a tax on so-called generation-skipping trusts. (Yes, the Rule against Perpetuities would put some limits on this strategy but remember that some states have eliminated the RAP.)

Part D deals with income tax. It's important not to ignore income tax when doing estate tax planning. First, gifts can have income tax consequences to donees as well as donors, which we will discuss. Second, trusts and estates can earn income and often must pay income tax. (Michael Jackson's estate has earned over $2 billion since his death.) And finally, we will consider a special kind of income, income in respect of a decedent (IRD), which is income owned by but not yet taxed to the decedent—for example, unpaid salary, bonuses, commissions, or royalties. **Part F** addresses how state estate and inheritance taxes factor into the equation.

B. The Federal Transfer Taxes: Policies and Mechanics

1. A Century of the Federal Estate Tax

Although the federal government levied an estate tax at certain points in the nineteenth century in order to finance military operations and war, such as the Spanish-American War in 1898, it was not until the passage of the 1916 Revenue Act that a permanent estate tax came into being. At the time of its enactment, the estate tax exclusion amount was $50,000 and the highest tax rate was 10%. Since that time, the estate tax exclusion amount has fluctuated, as have the tax rates, but the estate tax has been a consistently fraught political issue. In general, proponents of the tax argue that it is a form of progressive taxation that enables wealth redistribution and reduces wealth inequality. Opponents object to the idea of a "death tax" that allegedly hurts small business owners. There are other arguments as well—compare the following policy briefs in defense of, and against, the estate tax:

Paul L. Caron, The One Hundredth Anniversary of the Federal Estate Tax: It's Time to Renew Our Vows

57 B.C. L. REV. 823, 823–27 (2016).

[The] initial reasons for our commitment to the estate tax—to raise revenue during a time of war, enhance the progressivity of the tax system, and curb concentrations of wealth—are even more compelling today than they were in 1916. This Article argues that we should rededicate ourselves to the vibrant estate tax of our youth. . . .

[This article] charts the reduced progressivity of America's tax system and increased income inequality while the estate tax has been largely defanged. [It next] documents the nation's growing wealth inequality and proposes reforms to restore the estate tax to its rightful role in helping to curb excessive concentrations of wealth. The Article concludes that a revitalized estate tax provides a surer path to raising revenue, enhancing tax progressivity, and checking wealth concentration than more fundamental tax reform ideas that are unlikely to emerge from the political gridlock in Washington, D.C.

I.   Raising Revenue

. . . Along with Joseph Bankman, this author recently argued that "the federal budget imbalance, caused by the failure of both political parties to raise the tax revenues needed to fund the nation's spending priorities, is unsustainable and threatens our nation's future." Updated economic data paint an equally bleak fiscal picture.[32]

[O]ver the past fifty years, federal spending has averaged 20.1% of gross domestic product ("GDP") while federal revenues have averaged 17.4% of GDP. This 2.7 percentage point gap between spending and revenues has produced $18.2 trillion of federal debt held by the public. This constitutes 74% of GDP—the highest in our history, except for a brief period (1944–1950) around World War II, and double the percentage at the end of 2008.

---

[32]   Paul L. Caron & James Repetti, *Occupy the Tax Code: Using the Estate Tax to Reduce Inequality and Spur Economic Growth*, 40 PEPP. L. REV. 1255, 1257–59 (2013).

Absent structural changes in the nation's spending and tax laws, the fiscal future is even bleaker: the latest Congressional Budget Office projections state that the spending/revenue shortfall will grow from 2.4 percentage points in 2015 (20.6% spending, 18.2% revenues) to 3.5 percentage points in 2021–2025 (21.7% spending, 18.2% revenues), increasing the public debt to 77% of GDP. Moreover, the CBO's projections almost certainly understate the fiscal crisis facing the nation.

The evisceration of the estate tax has thus occurred at a time of acute need for additional federal revenues. Indeed, it is especially ironic that a tax born out of fiscal demands during times of war has withered while the nation confronts radical Islamic terrorism and other threats around the world.

In its current state, the estate tax is projected to raise less than $250 billion over the 2016–2025 period. Of course, that is not an insignificant sum. But restoring the estate tax's historic role in the federal tax system would increase that number to $500 billion to $1 trillion. Such a restoration is necessary not only to help reverse the erosion in our revenue base but also to help reverse the lost progressivity in the tax system and the increased concentrations of wealth that have occurred over the past several decades.

II.   Enhancing the Progressivity of the Tax System

James Repetti and this author recently chronicled the growing income inequality in America. That article noted that "[t]he adverse effects of inequality are especially pernicious because they persist across generations." It also reviewed the numerous studies that unanimously conclude that inequality retards economic growth. Updated data show worsening inequality.

Saez reports that the top 1% has captured a majority of the income gains over the past twenty-two years. Over the entire period, 55% of the income gains went to the top 1%, who experienced 80% income growth (compared to 10.8% income growth of the bottom 99%). During the Clinton economic expansion (1993–2000), 45% of the income gains went to the top 1%, who experienced 98.7% income growth (compared to 20.3% of the bottom 99%). During the Bush economic expansion (2002–2007), 65% of the income gains went to the top 1%, who experienced 61.8% income growth (compared to 6.8% income growth of the bottom 99%). During the Obama economic expansion (2009–2014), 58% of the income gains went to the top 1%, who experienced 27.1% income growth (compared to 4.3% income growth of the bottom 99%).

To be sure, during the two economic recessions in this period (2000–2002 and 2007–2009), 57% and 49%, respectively, of the income losses were borne by the top 1%, who experienced 30.8% and 36.3% income losses of the bottom 99%). But the outsized share of the income gains the top 1% enjoyed during the predominant expansionary economy of the past twenty-two years more than made up for the similarly outsized share of losses borne by the top 1% during the briefer recessionary periods.

The weakening of the estate tax thus has coincided with historic reductions in the progressivity of the tax system. Indeed, Piketty and Saez have fingered the decline in the estate tax as one of two primary causes of the reduced progressivity of the tax system since 1960. The recent legislative changes to raise income taxes on high-income Americans have begun to redistribute some of the tax burden. There is, of course, much more that could (and should) be done on the income tax front to restore progressivity to the tax system, whether in the form of broad structural changes or reform targeted at the top of the income scale, such as modifications in the tax treatment of private equity returns.

But whatever the fate of the income tax reform battle, revitalization of the estate tax needs to be on the front lines of the broader tax reform war. There is compelling evidence that the estate tax is more efficient than the income tax because it has a less harmful effect on savings. With the nation mired in the slowest post-recession recovery since the 1930s, the estate tax should be enlisted to begin to put our fiscal house in order and stem the growth of income inequality in America.

III. Curbing Concentrations of Wealth

Wealth is even more concentrated than income at the high end, in the United States and around the world. Repetti and the present author previously argued that the estate tax is more effective than commonly thought in breaking up dynastic wealth and proposed five reforms to shore up the estate tax: (1) disallow minority discounts in certain circumstances; (2) maintain parity between the unified credit exemption amounts for the estate and gift taxes; (3) return to the $3.5 million exemption, increase the maximum rate to 45%, and limit the generation-skipping transfer tax exemption to transfers occurring within fifty years; (4) restrict the ability of gifts made in trust to qualify for the gift tax annual exclusion; and (5) impose a lifetime cap on the amount that can be contributed to a grantor-retained annuity trust. To more directly address growing concentrations of wealth at the high end, the author proposes adding a sixth reform: returning to the graduated estate tax rate tables in force for most of our history, with higher rates applied to amounts in excess of the exemption amount (an inflation-adjusted $5 million under current law or the $3.5 million exemption reform).

For most of its existence, the estate tax deployed multiple rate brackets, with top rates as high as 77% applied to estates over $150 million in inflation-adjusted terms. Due to the 2010 Act's retention of the existing tax rate schedule despite the increase in the exemption amount, only the first $1 million of a taxable estate is taxed at the graduated rate tables at an effective rate of approximately 35%, with amounts in excess of $1 million taxed at the 40% rate. We should replace our virtually flat estate tax with a graduated one, with higher rates applied to larger estates.

One possibility is the Responsible Estate Tax Act introduced by U.S. Senator Bernie Sanders. Senator Sanders's bill also returns to the $3.5 million exemption and increases the rate to 45% on taxable estates in excess of this amount. He introduces two additional brackets—50% on amounts between $10 million and $50 million, and 55% on amounts in excess of $50 million—as well as a 10% surtax on amounts in excess of $500 million.

CONCLUSION

As we prepare to celebrate the one-hundredth anniversary of the estate tax, we should remember why we first embraced it. After test driving taxes on the transfers of wealth at death during three times of war in our early history, we took the plunge during World War I to raise revenue, enhance tax progressivity, and check wealth concentration. Yet we have dithered and allowed our attention to the estate tax to stray over the past few decades. Not surprisingly, we now face unprecedented fiscal and equality challenges. Perhaps we should try to breathe new life into a tried and true tax.

Why Do We Have a Death Tax?

John Goodman (Forbes) (2015)

Not all taxation is theft. But one tax that comes about as close as possible to being theft is the estate tax. After all, dead people aren't getting any more services from government. I suppose there are a few people who are buried in pauper's graves at county expense. But those are not the ones whose estates are being confiscated.

I have never understood the logic behind seizing a part of the estates of the recently departed. If there is a valid argument for doing so, why doesn't it apply with equal force to the estates of the living?

The House of Representatives voted by a large margin the other day to abolish the estate tax. In doing so they took a very popular step.

Yet although the estate tax is one of the most hated taxes by the general public, it has long been a favorite of government. Kelly Phillips Erb reminds us that the first federal estate tax was imposed in 1797 to help fund a war against France. It was resurrected again in the Civil War, then in the Spanish-American War and it became a more or less a permanent fixture with the advent of World War I. War and estate taxation seem to go hand in hand.

By the way, it's not just the federal government . . . [some] states . . . impose estate and inheritance taxes. . . .

I suspect the reason governments like the tax is that estates don't have very powerful protectors and defenders. If the government tried to seize estates from the living, the owners would certainly resist. But after death, ownership tends to be dispersed and in many cases unresolved. So estates are a relatively easy target for the tax collectors.

President Obama says the estate tax is tax on the rich and he wants to increase the take. If he were in Economics 101, his assessment of the incidence of the tax would merit a failing grade. The burden of the estate tax doesn't fall on dead people. It falls on the heirs—some of whom may be rich and some of whom may not be. If the goal is to tax the rich, then we should be taxing heirs, based on their total income, not the deceased.

Aren't the children of rich people also rich?

Although it is somewhat dated, one of the best treatments of the estate tax is a study Bruce Bartlett did for the National Center for Policy Analysis. One of the findings: very little of the wealth of wealthy people comes from inheritance. There are exceptions of course. The Walton children are examples. But for the most part, inheritance has a tiny impact on the distribution of income in the United States.

Harvard economist Greg Mankiw has this to say about intergenerational wealth transfers:

> The correlation between the lifetime earnings of successive generations is around 0.4 or 0.5. Even adding in inheritances, the figure increases to only about 0.7. This is nowhere near a perfect correlation. And the correlation is far smaller when we look at the link between grandparents and grandchildren, and probably smaller still if we consider nephews, nieces, and other possible heirs.

How easy is it to avoid the tax?

There are a lot of loopholes and the larger the estate, the more likely that they have been exploited. As a result, the very wealthy get taxed at a lower rate than the so-so wealthy. Bartlett writes:

> So effective are [the] methods of avoiding estate taxes that it has been argued that the estate tax essentially is a voluntary tax. In the words of economist George Cooper: 'The fact that any substantial amount of tax is now being collected can be attributed only to taxpayer indifference to avoidance opportunities or a lack of aggressiveness on the part of estate planners in exploiting the loopholes that exist.' Economists Henry Aaron and Alicia Munnell put it even more bluntly. In their view, estate taxes aren't even taxes at all, but 'penalties imposed on those who neglect to plan ahead or who retain unskilled estate planners.'

By the way, it was the unfairness of tax avoidance opportunities that persuaded Sweden (often referred to as a "socialist" country) to abolish the estate tax about a decade ago. Austria, Canada, Hong Kong, India, Israel, New Zealand, Norway, Russia and Singapore are some other countries that have abolished their estate or inheritance taxes.

Who would benefit from a repeal of the estate tax?

Mankiw argues that we would all benefit. Here's why:

The estate tax is a tax on capital. As such, one would naturally expect it to discourage capital accumulation. Now, put this together with the fact that a smaller capital stock reduces productivity and labor income throughout the economy and the implication is clear: the repeal of the estate tax would stimulate growth and raise incomes for everyone, even those who never receive a bequest.

Wouldn't the government lose revenue if the estate tax were abolished?

Currently the federal government gets less than 2 percent of its income from the estate tax. Even though the sum seems paltry, wouldn't this revenue be lost if the estate tax were abolished? Mankiw writes:

> The estate tax encourages people to take avoidance actions, such as making gifts to their children. Since their children are almost always in lower tax brackets, these gifts reduce income tax collections. Repealing the estate tax would remove the incentive for such gifts and would thereby boost income tax revenues.

And, as noted, revenue that the government did not collect from the death tax would largely remain in the productive private capital market, boost incomes and (therefore) produce additional taxes on those incomes. In fact, Mankiw speculates that the government might not lose any revenue at all from the abolition of the tax.

The main bone of contention is the exemption level for the estate tax. As noted below, under current law, a decedent can transfer 11.7 million free of tax, and married couples can transfer double that amount, 23.16 million. The Tax Cuts and Jobs Act of 2017 (TCJA) doubled the exemption from prior levels, but it provided for the enhanced exemption amount to automatically sunset at the end of 2025. This is the highest the exemption amount has ever been, and Joe Biden will likely support a speeded-up sunset and a lowering of the exemption amount. In 2026, the exemption amount could return to its previous level of 5 million per person (adjusted for inflation).

NOTES

1.   Repeal of the estate tax would protect whose rights, the decedent or the heirs? If the latter, what moral claim do the heirs have to receive all of the decedent's wealth? Is the argument stronger if the decedent dies with a will than without a will?

**King Lear might have avoided taxation
if not tragic consequences.**

2.   To some extent, a person with wealth has three choices: consume the wealth, transfer it to others, or give it to charity. Does a transfer tax put too heavy a finger on the consumption side of the scale? What does Caron mean

when he suggests that a more effective estate tax would have a smaller effect on savings than raising income tax levels on the wealthy?

3.   One of Goodman's objections to the transfer tax is that the regime contains so many loopholes that most people who would otherwise be subject to it don't actually pay it because they can afford the sophisticated advice necessary to avoid it. Indeed, many wealth and tax planning websites advertise their services by stating that "paying taxes is a choice." Is the existence of loopholes that allow the wealthy to avoid paying wealth transfer taxes a fair objection to the tax itself?

4.   If a wealth transfer tax includes a deduction for bequests to charity (our system does), would the elimination of the transfer tax result in less charitable giving? Should we be concerned about that result?

5.   Is it unfair that some people receive large inheritances? Milton Freedman, the Nobel winning economist, has argued that it is no more unfair than some people being born with superior intelligence, or athletic prowess, or musical talent, or physical attractiveness. Is it right to tax one type of endowment (inheriting wealth) but not the others? Is this a logical analogy? And does an estate tax go against the very human desire to provide for the welfare and support of one's children?

6.   Goodman argues that a tax on wealth transfers is undesirable because it is a tax on capital and capital investment, which fuels economic growth. Is Goodman's argument really an argument against an estate tax, or is it more of an argument that we should have a less expensive government and/or that we should look for our revenues primarily from people who are not wealthy?

7.   Objection to the federal tax on wealth transfers is nothing new, but its most successful manifestation, which lead to the elimination of the estate tax (but only for one year), began as an orchestrated campaign by a handful of wealthy individuals and think tanks in the 1990s. The story is chronicled and analyzed in a wonderfully readable political and social history by two law professors, Michael Graetz and Ian Shapiro, *Death by a Thousand Cuts: The Fight Over Taxing Inherited Wealth*. Two strategies used by the repeal advocates were rebranding the debate as one over the "death tax" rather than the "estate" or "inheritance" tax and Congressional testimony focused on the estate tax's effect on small family farms. In 2001, David Cay Johnston, a Pulitzer Prize winning reporter, published a story in the New York Times on the estate tax and small family farms, titled *Focus on Family Farms Masks Estate Tax Confusion*. The text of the article follows:

WELLSBURG, Iowa—Harlyn Riekena worried that his success would cost him when he died. Thirty-seven years ago he quit teaching to farm and over the years bought more and more of the rich black soil here in central Iowa. Now he and his wife, Karen, own 950 gently rolling acres planted in soybeans and corn.

The farmland alone is worth more than $2.5 million, and so Mr. Riekena, 61, fretted that estate taxes would take a big chunk of his three grown daughters' inheritance.

That might seem a reasonable assumption, what with all the talk in Washington about the need to repeal the estate tax to save the family farm. "To keep farms in the family, we are going to get rid of the death tax," President Bush vowed a month ago; he and many others have made the point repeatedly.

But in fact the Riekenas will owe nothing in estate taxes. Almost no working farmers do, according to data from an Internal Revenue Service analysis of 1999 returns that has not yet been published.

Neil Harl, an Iowa State University economist whose tax advice has made him a household name among Midwest farmers, said he had searched far and wide but had never found a farm lost because of estate taxes. "It's a myth," he said.

Even one of the leading advocates for repeal of estate taxes, the American Farm Bureau Federation, said it could not cite a single example of a farm lost because of estate taxes.

The estate tax does, of course, have a bite. But the reality of that bite is different from the mythology, in which family farmers have become icons for the campaign to abolish the tax. In fact, the overwhelming majority of beneficiaries are the heirs of people who made their fortunes through their businesses and investments in securities and real estate.

The effort to end the estate tax—which critics call the death tax—gained ground when the House of Representatives voted Wednesday to reduce the tax and then abolish it in 2011. The bill faces an uncertain fate in the Senate.

The estate tax is central in the debate over taxes, not only because the sums involved are huge but also because to both sides it is a touchstone of national values. To those seeking to abolish it, the estate tax is a penalty for success, an abomination that blocks the deeply human desire to leave a life's work as a legacy for the children. It is also a complicated burden that enriches the lawyers, accountants and life insurance companies that help people reduce their tax bills.

To its supporters, on the other hand, the estate tax is a symbol of American equality, a mechanism to democratize society and to encourage economic success based on merit rather than birthright.

Yet for all the passion in the debate, the estate tax does not always seem broadly understood.

While 17 percent of Americans in a recent Gallup survey think they will owe estate taxes, in fact only the richest 2 percent of Americans do. That amounted to 49,870 Americans in 1999. And nearly half the estate tax is paid by the 3,000 or so people who each year leave taxable estates of more than $5 million. [Note: today only the richest .1% of Americans are subject to the estate tax.]

2. The Mechanics of the Estate Tax

Understanding the policy debate surrounding the estate tax is one crucial part of learning about the tax. Another important piece of the puzzle is understanding how the estate tax works.

a. *To Whom Does the Estate Tax Not Apply?*

- Someone who is married at the time of death and leaves all property to his or her spouse, since there is an unlimited marital deduction

- A decedent whose net estate is less than $11.7 million in 2021 (an amount that is indexed to the cost of living) (but see Update above)

- A surviving spouse who can use the unused exclusion of the spouse who died first (assuming appropriate elections were made by the estate of the first spouse)

As the above makes clear, even modestly effective estate-tax planning means that a couple will not be subject to the estate tax if their collective taxable estate is less than $23.4 million. This means that not only are few couples subject to the estate tax, the vast majority of individuals and married couples who you might encounter as clients will have estate planning goals other than tax minimization. Nevertheless, in an estate planning practice geared toward high-wealth clients, tax minimization will be paramount.

Connection Note: The Estate Tax and Being Unmarried

Because transfers between married spouses are tax-free transers and because one spouse can give or "port" her exemption to a surviving spouse at death, marriage becomes an important factor in tax planning. Here are two examples of how marital status makes a big difference—and examples of various forms of marital discrimination.

In 2013, U.S. Supreme Court decided *United States v. Windsor*, 570 U.S. 744 (2013), a case in which a surviving spouse (Edie Windsor) had to pay $363,053 in estate tax because the federal government did not recognize her marriage to Thea Spyer. The two women had been married in Ontario in 2007 but the Defense of Marriage Act (DOMA) prohibited recognition of this marriage. Had they been a different-sex couple, the estate would have passed from Thea to Edie tax-free. Windsor did, however, prevail, arguing that her obligation to pay the estate tax was an unconstitutional form of discrimination against same-sex couples.

One year later, actor Phillip Seymour Hoffman died with a will leaving his 35-million-dollar estate to his longtime companion and mother of the couple's three children. But because they were not married, she owed about $12 million of that in taxes. If they had been married, of course, it would have passed to her tax-free. Unlike Thea and Edie, Hoffman and his partner were legally able to

Edie Windsor, plaintiff in *United States v. Windsor*, at the DC Pride Parade in 2017.

marry and therefore, according to law, failed to avail themselves of the marital benefit. We might nevertheless ask ourselves whether this kind of privileging of married couples constitutes a form of marital-status discrimination. That is to say, why should the government provide special benefits to married couples that are unavailable to unmarried couples?

b. How Is the Estate Tax Calculated?

Estate taxes, in their simplest form, are pretty easy to calculate:

- Identify the property in the estate (the "gross estate") and value it

- Take available deductions, which produces the net estate

- Calculate the tax

- Subtract a credit from the tax

The remaining amount is the taxable amount from which the estate tax is calculated.

We will see in later sections that there is a tax on inter vivos gifts over a certain annual limit, which is coordinated with the estate tax.

c. Gross Estate—What Is in It?

Section 2033 of the Internal Revenue Code defines the gross estate as "as the value at the time of his death of all property, real or personal, tangible or intangible, wherever situated." In other words, the gross estate is everything you own. The definition is broad and non-specific, and has been interpreted by courts quite broadly. But certain types of property raise challenging issues—both conceptual and practical—and in some cases Congress has legislated specific rules for particular property interests, as described below.

But before we consider what is in the gross estate for federal estate tax purposes, we might ask what the relationship is between the gross estate and a decedent's probate estate. The short answer is that whatever relationship exists is largely coincidental. The probate estate, as we have seen, comprises the property

> **Connection Note:** This is why the current UPC uses the tax concept of the gross estate as the augmented estate for spousal share purposes, as we discussed in Chapter 14. It is a much better accounting of property the decedent had been able to benefit from than the probate estate.

of the decedent that passes to beneficiaries under a will or, if no will, through the laws of intestacy. Often individuals try to avoid the costs and inconvenience of probate through the use of trusts or insurance or joint ownership of property. Although these assets are not part of the "probate" estate, they will often be included in the gross estate. (Generally, though, everything in the probate estate is part of the gross estate.)

i.   Life Insurance

Insurance on the life of the decedent is included in the decedent's gross estate if it is paid to the executor of the estate or if the decedent retained any of the incidents of ownership of the insurance policy. Thus, estate planning for a person who might be subject to the estate tax often involves the creation of an insurance policy that is owned by a beneficiary and whose premiums are paid for by annual exempt gifts to the beneficiary. The investment component of the policy grows and neither the principal, the investment growth, nor any actual death benefits, are included in the decedent's estate. Moreover, the payments to the beneficiary are typically exempt from income tax.

What are the incidents of ownership, whose retention by the decedent will result in the inclusion of a life insurance policy in the gross estate? Basically, any significant right, such as the right to change beneficiaries, to cancel the policy, to transfer the policy, to use the cash value of the policy as collateral for a loan, are "incidents of ownership" that can result in the value of the insurance being included in the decedent's gross estate.

ii.   Powers of Appointment

As we are sure you recall from Chapter 12, a power of appointment is a power to dispose of another's property. The property to which a power of appointment applies is included in the estate of the power's holder if the power of appointment is a general power. For this purpose, a power is a general power if it is exercisable in favor of the holder, the holder's estate, or creditors of the holder or the holder's estate.

iii.   Interests in Trusts and Other Lifetime Transfers

Certain lifetime transfers of property, typically transfers that involve the creation of or use of a trust, are included in the gross estate when the decedent has retained interests in the transferred property. Three sections of the Internal Revenue Code enforce this approach: § 2036 provides that the gross estate includes transferred property in which the decedent retained enjoyment or control of the property during her life; § 2037 provides that the gross estate includes property if the transferee's right to the property is conditioned upon surviving the decedent; and § 2038 provides that the gross estate includes property that was transferred during life subject to the transferor's power to revoke.

iv.   Lifetime Gifts

Certain gifts made within three years of death are included in the gross estate. The gifts that are covered by this section include revocable transfers, transfers with retained life estates, and transfer of life insurance policies on the decedent's life. (Before 1981, when the gift tax and estate tax were unified, the category of gifts ratcheted back to the estate was broader.)

v.   Joint Interests

Section 2040 of the Internal Revenue Code provides that certain jointly-held property is included in the joint estate. The rules differ, depending on whether the property is held by husband and wife. If a married couple holds joint property with rights of survivorship, one half of the property is included in the gross estate of the first joint tenant to die. If unmarried persons hold property jointly with rights of survivorship, the entire property will be included in the gross estate of the first person to die, unless and to the extent that the estate can prove that the surviving joint tenant supplied some or all of the consideration used to purchase the property.

ASSESSMENT

You have been hired by the executor of Milo's estate to list the assets and calculate the value of his estate. Milo died intestate. He gives you the following list:

- A house, owned in tenancy by the entirety with his husband, Jack, worth $500,000

- A revocable trust, funded with one million dollars, with Milo and Jack as current beneficiaries, and Jack as future beneficiary

- A retirement account containing $450,000 with Jack as the beneficiary

- A life insurance policy owned by Milo's sister and payable to her in the amount of $250,000

- A testamentary power of appointment Milo had which allowed him to devise $500,000 to any of his nieces and nephews

- A bank account containing $50,000

- A stock trading account containing $300,000 titled in Milo's and Jack's names

The executor also tells you that two years ago, Milo funded a trust with $50,000 to pay for his nieces' and nephews' college educations.

Which items and what amounts will be in Milo's taxable estate? Will he be subject to the federal estate tax?

d. Valuing the Estate

After we determine what property is included in a decedent's gross estate for federal tax purposes, § 2031 requires that the gross estate includes the "fair market value" of that property. Some types of property—primarily publicly traded securities—have easily ascertained values, but for other types of property, where there is no published market value, valuation can be a difficult factual question. When valuation matters reach court, the courtroom can become a gladiatorial arena for expert witnesses whose estimates can differ by millions and even tens of millions of dollars.

Making things somewhat more complicated, § 2032 of the Internal Revenue Code permits the use of an "alternate valuation date," which is the date six months after the death of the decedent. If the estate elects the alternate valuation, the valuation controls for all purposes, not just for the determination of the value of the gross estate.

i. Standard for Valuation

What is the standard for valuing property when an asset is not publicly traded? Treasury regulations provide that fair market value is the price at which the property would change hands between a willing buyer and a willing seller, neither being under any compulsion to buy or to sell and both having reasonable knowledge of relevant facts. The fair market value of a particular item of property includible in the decedent's gross estate is not to be determined by a forced sale price. Nor is the fair market value of an item of property to be determined by the sale price of the item in a market other than that in which such item is most commonly sold to the public, taking into account the location of the item wherever appropriate. Thus, in the case of an item of property includible in the decedent's gross estate, which is generally obtained by the public in the retail market, the fair market value of such an item of property is the price at which the item or a comparable item would be sold at retail. Treas. Reg. § 20.2031–(b). How much does this standard clarify? Consider, for example, how you would go about valuing artwork or stock in a closely held corporation.

ii.   Entity Ownership and Minority and Other Discounts

Investments in stocks and other securities are of course a major part of most taxable estates. The price of a publicly traded security is readily determinable, but public markets are not available for securities in some entities. In such cases, § 2031 of the Internal Revenue Code provides an obvious but not very helpful approach to valuation: "In the case of stock and securities of a corporation the value of which, by reason of their not being listed on an exchange and by reason of the absence of sales thereof, cannot be determined with reference to bid and asked prices or with reference to sales prices, the value thereof shall be determined by taking into consideration the value of stock or securities of corporations engaged in the same or a similar line of business which are listed on an exchange."

We might think that the value of an estate's equity interest in an entity (whether a corporation, partnership, or limited liability company) is simply the value of the underlying enterprise, multiplied by the estate's percentage ownership in the enterprise. This turns out not necessarily to be the case. First, there are sometimes different categories of owners (in a corporation, for example, there may be more than one class of stock, with different rights with respect to profits, residual value, and voting), and these categories may have different values.

Second, the standard for valuing an equity interest is the price that a "willing and knowledgeable" buyer and seller would negotiate for the interest. The problem with this standard is that, in the case of family-run businesses, there is no "willing and knowledgeable buyer" out there. So the question becomes, how to value these businesses for tax purposes? Over time courts have agreed to use a system of discounts, called "valuation discounts," to these interests based on their lack of marketability and lack of control. These discounts apply to minority shares in family businesses on the grounds that (1) a minority shareholder in a family business is at the mercy of majority shareholder decisions that may disadvantage him and (2) cannot sell his shares on the open market if he is dissatisfied. Therefore, the logic goes, these shares are worth less than the minority shares of a publicly traded corporation, and the tax valuation should reflect this lack of control and lack of marketability. This logic obviously offers the opportunity to reduce the value of a decedent's estate by claiming these discounted values.

The following case offers an example of the use of such discounts. As you read it, consider whether the facts of this case justify the discounts.

Kimbell v. United States

371 F.3d 257 (5th Cir. 2004)

DAVIS, C.J.:

In this estate tax case, David A. Kimbell, the executor of the estate of his mother Ruth A. Kimbell, appeals the judgment of the district court denying his request for a refund of estate taxes and interest paid by the estate.

Ruth A. Kimbell ("Mrs. Kimbell" or the "Decedent") died testate on March 25, 1998. She was 96 years old. In the years prior to her death, the Decedent transferred a large portion of her estate in a series of transactions to three entities. In 1991, Mrs. Kimbell created the R.A. Kimbell Living Trust (the "Trust"), which was a revocable living trust administered by Mrs. Kimbell and her son as co-trustees. In January 1998, the Trust, David Kimbell, and his wife formed a limited liability company, the R.A. Kimbell Management Co., L.L.C. (the "LLC"). The Trust contributed $20,000 for a 50% interest. David Kimbell and his wife each contributed $10,000 for 25% interests each. David Kimbell was the sole manager of the LLC.

Later in January 1998, the Trust and the LLC formed the R.A. Kimbell Property Co., Ltd., a limited partnership under Texas law (the "Partnership").

> **Practice Note:** Note that the estate in *Kimbell* went ahead and paid the tax assessed even though it planned to dispute the tax. This is common—and smart—practice: you can always get a refund if you win, but you don't want to withhold taxes and pay penalties and interest on top of them if you end up losing.

The Trust contributed approximately $2.5 million in cash, oil and gas working interests and royalty interests, securities, notes and other assets for a 99% pro-rata limited partner interest. The oil and gas properties were a continuation of an oil and gas business that the Decedent's late husband had founded in the 1920s. The LLC contributed approximately $25,000 in cash for a 1% pro-rata general partner interest. As a result of these transfers, Mrs. Kimbell, through the Trust and the LLC, owned 99.5% of the Partnership. David Kimbell managed Mrs. Kimbell's business interest before and after the creation of the LLC and the Partnership. Not all of Mrs. Kimbell's assets were conveyed to the LLC and the Partnership. She retained over $450,000 in assets outside of the LLC and the Partnership for her personal expenses. The primary focus of this appeal is on this transfer from the LLC and the Trust to the Partnership.

Under the stated terms of the Partnership Agreement, the purposes of the Partnership were to:

increase Family wealth; establish a method by which annual gifts can be made without fractionalizing Family Assets; continue the ownership and collective operation of Family Assets and restrict the right of non-Family members to acquire interests in Family Assets; provide protection to Family Assets from claims of future creditors against Family members; prevent transfer of a Family member's interest in the Partnership as a result of a failed marriage; provide flexibility and continuity in business planning for the Family not available through trusts, corporations or other business entities; facilitate the administration and reduce the cost associated with the disability or probate of the estate of Family members; promote the Family's knowledge of and communication about Family Assets; provide resolution of any disputes which may arise among the Family in order to preserve Family harmony and avoid the expense and problems of litigation; and consolidate fractional interests in Family Assets.

The estate filed its federal estate tax return in December 1998. At the time of Mrs. Kimbell's death, the value of the Partnership assets was approximately $2.4 million. On the return, the estate claimed a 49% discount on the value of Mrs. Kimbell's interest in the Partnership and her interest in the LLC for lack of control and lack of marketability of the partnership interest. It reported her 99% interest in the Partnership as having a fair market value of approximately $1.2 million and her 50% interest in the LLC as having a fair market value of approximately $17,000.

The IRS audited the estate. It found that the value of the assets transferred to the Partnership and the LLC, rather than Mrs. Kimbell's interest in these entities, was includible in the gross estate at its full value and increased the tax due accordingly. The estate paid the additional tax and then filed for a refund, claiming that the IRS overvalued Mrs. Kimbell's interests in the Partnership and the LLC.

The district court found that the IRS correctly included the full value of the assets Mrs. Kimbell transferred to the Partnership and the LLC in the estate and granted partial summary judgment to the government. The estate appeals.

Whether the assets Mrs. Kimbell transferred to the Partnership must be recaptured into her estate at full value for estate tax purposes depends on the application of Internal Revenue Code § 2036(a). Internal Revenue Code § 2036(a) provides:

> (a)   General rule. The value of the gross estate shall include the value of all property to the extent of any interest therein of which the decedent has at any time made a transfer (except in case of a bona fide sale for an adequate and full consideration in money or money's worth), by trust or otherwise, under which he has retained for his life or for any period not ascertainable without reference to his death or for any period which does not in fact end before his death.

The statute recognizes that some assets transferred prior to death must be recaptured into the estate. By recapturing these transfers into the estate, this section of the code prevents the circumvention of federal estate tax by the use of inter vivos transactions which do not remove the lifetime enjoyment of property purportedly transferred by a decedent.

A transfer will escape the reach of § 2036(a) if it is a bona fide sale for adequate and full consideration for money or money's worth. The district court found that Mrs. Kimbell's transfer of assets to the Partnership did not qualify for this exception. The district court stated that the "applicability of the [bona fide sale] exception rests on two requirements: (1) a bona fide sale, meaning an arm's length transaction, and (2) adequate and full consideration." The court defined an arm's length transaction as one involving "two parties who are not related or not on close terms."

Because Mrs. Kimbell, or at least family members, were present on both sides of the transfer to the Partnership, the district court found that the transfer was not at arm's length and therefore not a "bona fide sale."

It is also clear that whether a transaction was made for adequate and full consideration is an objective inquiry. Addressing the government's argument that transactions between family members should be necessarily treated differently for estate tax purposes, this court stated:

> [t]he present transfer tax scheme eschews subjective intent determinations in favor of the objective requirements of the statute. Therefore, section 2036(a) permits the conclusion that a split-interest transfer was testamentary when, and if, the objective requirement that the transfer be for an adequate and full consideration is not met. Section 2036(a) does not, however, permit a perceived testamentary intent, ipse dixit, to determine what amount constitutes an adequate and full consideration.

According to Treasury Regulations, a transaction is a bona fide sale if it is made in good faith. When examining a transaction to determine if it is "real, actual, genuine and not feigned," we are again constrained to objective factors. As stated previously, Congress eliminated the decedent's subjective intent from direct consideration. A transaction motivated solely by tax planning with no business or corporate purpose is nothing more than a contrivance without substance that is rightly ignored for purposes of the tax computation. However, tax planning motives do not prevent a sale from being "bona fide" if the transaction is otherwise real, actual or genuine.

In *Church v. United States*, a mother and her children formed a Texas limited partnership to consolidate their undivided interests in a family ranch. The mother and the children were limited partners and a limited liability company was the general partner. All parties contributed their undivided interests in the ranch to the partnership. The mother also contributed approximately $1 million in securities to finance ranch operations and the purchase of interests in the ranch owned by non-partners. Each partner received a pro-rata interest in the partnership. Under these circumstances, the court found that the character of the assets transferred to the partnership changed dramatically:

> Prior to its formation ... [the several family members] owned undivided interests in the Ranch, with each interest carrying the right to use and enjoy the property, or force partition or possible sale. The Partnership eliminated these individual rights and placed ownership of a majority of the Ranch in a Partnership that was not controlled by any single person.

The district court found that the exchange of a limited partnership interest for the assets Mrs. Kimbell transferred to the Partnership was not a bona fide sale for adequate and full consideration. It concluded that Mrs. Kimbell's contribution of more than 99% of the assets into the Partnership to be managed (as they were before the transfer) by her son was nothing more than a recycling of value and the interest in the Partnership Mrs. Kimbell received was not a transfer of consideration. The government adopted that position and argues in addition that it is inconsistent for the estate to assert, on one hand, that the value of Mrs. Kimbell's interest in the Partnership is worth only 50% of the assets she transferred (as discounted for lack of control and marketability), and on the other hand claim that the Partnership interest Mrs. Kimbell received in exchange for the assets transferred was adequate and full consideration for the transfer.

The Tax Court has expressly rejected the argument that a discounted valuation of a pro rata partnership interest precludes a finding that the interest is adequate consideration for the assets transferred.

We would only add to the Tax Court's rejection of the government's inconsistency argument that it is a classic mixing of apples and oranges: The government is attempting to equate the venerable "willing buyer-willing seller" test of fair market value (which applies when calculating gift or estate tax) with the proper test for adequate and full consideration under § 2036(a). This conflation misses the mark: The business decision to exchange cash or other assets for a transfer-restricted, non-managerial interest in a limited partnership involves financial considerations other than the purchaser's ability to turn right around and sell the newly acquired limited partnership interest for 100 cents on the dollar. Investors who acquire such interests do so with the expectation of realizing benefits such as management expertise, security and preservation of assets, capital appreciation and avoidance of personal liability. Thus there is nothing inconsistent in acknowledging, on the one hand, that the investor's dollars have acquired a limited partnership interest at arm's length for adequate and full consideration and, on the other hand, that the asset thus acquired has a present fair market value, i.e., immediate sale potential, of substantially less than the dollars just paid—a classic informed trade-off.

As this principle applies to wholly unrelated buyers and sellers of interests in limited partnerships, it must be equally true of buyers and sellers of such interests who happen to be related by blood or affinity, unless (1) the evidence demonstrates the absence of good faith, i.e., a sham transaction motivated solely by tax avoidance, or (2) Congress or the courts are ready to change long-held positions and establish a per se rule that related parties can never enter into arms-length transactions for adequate and full consideration—positions that none has shown any inclination to assume. Certainly, close scrutiny must be applied when the parties are related, but close scrutiny is not synonymous with automatic proscription or impossibility vel non.

The proper focus therefore on whether a transfer to a partnership is for adequate and full consideration is: (1) whether the interests credited to each of the partners was proportionate to the fair market value of the assets each partner contributed to the partnership, (2) whether the assets contributed by each partner to the partnership were properly credited to the respective capital accounts of the partners, and (3) whether on termination or dissolution of the partnership the partners were entitled to distributions from the partnership in amounts equal to their respective capital accounts. The answer to each of these questions in this case is yes. Mrs. Kimbell received a partnership interest that was proportionate to the assets she contributed to the Partnership. There is no question raised as to whether her partnership account was properly credited with the assets she contributed. Also, on termination and liquidation of the Partnership, the Partnership Agreement requires distribution to the Partners according to their capital account balances.

Accordingly, we conclude that this transaction was for adequate and full consideration. The district court's concern that Mrs. Kimbell's transfer of assets to the partnership in exchange for a pro-rata partnership interest is a mere paper transaction resulting in "recycling of value" is better addressed under the "bona fide sale" prong of this exception.

The District Court's analysis ignored record evidence in support of the estate's position that the transaction was entered into for substantial business and other non-tax reasons.

Our review of the record reveals that the taxpayer established the following objective facts (uncontroverted by the government) that would support their position that the transfer to the Partnership was a bona fide sale:

(1)   Mrs. Kimbell retained sufficient assets outside the Partnership for her own support and there was no commingling of Partnership and her personal assets. *See Estate of Stangi*, 85 T.C.M. at 1338–39; *Estate of Harper*, 83 T.C.M. at 1650.

(2)   Partnership formalities were satisfied, and the assets contributed to the Partnership were actually assigned to the Partnership.

(3)   The assets contributed to the Partnership included working interests in oil and gas properties which do require active management. A working interest in an oil and gas lease is a cost-bearing operating interest in the property.

(4)   David Kimbell and Michael Elyea advanced several credible and unchallenged non-tax business reasons for the formation of the Partnership that could not be accomplished via Mrs. Kimbell's Trust.

Michael Elyea, Mrs. Kimbell's business advisor, testified as follows regarding the business strategy for forming the Partnership. He stated that he and Mrs. Kimbell first discussed placing the assets in a limited partnership around the same time the living trust was formed in the early 1990s. Although some business strategies were accomplished by the trust, others were not. Specifically, a living trust did not provide legal protection from creditors as a limited partnership would. That protection was viewed as essential by Mr. Elyea and Mrs. Kimbell because she was investing as a working interest owner in oil and gas properties and could be personally liable for any environmental issues that arose in the operation of those properties. Mr. Elyea also stated that Mrs. Kimbell wanted the oil and gas operations to continue beyond her lifetime and they felt that by putting the assets in a limited partnership, they could keep the pool of capital together in one entity that would be enhanced over time rather than subdivided by distributions to subsequent generations. Keeping the assets in one pool, under one management would reduce administrative costs by keeping all accounting functions together. The partnership would also avoid costs of recording transfers of oil and gas properties as the property was passed from generation to generation. Mrs. Kimbell wanted to keep the asset in an entity that would preserve the property as separate property of her descendants. The family had faced that issue during the divorce of one of Mrs. Kimbell's grandsons. The partnership also served the purpose of setting up the management of the assets if something should happen to her son, which was a concern as he had experienced some heart problems and had undergone a serious surgery. The partnership agreement provided that all disputes be resolved through mediation or arbitration to avoid interfamily litigation if disputes should arise. This statement of reasons is supported by the recitation of purposes in the formation documents of the Partnership (which the government and the district court selectively excerpt) and the deposition testimony of Mrs. Kimbell's son. More to the point, the stated reasons for the formation of the Partnership are confirmed by objective facts, many of which relate to the rights and responsibilities associated with investments in oil and gas investments.

The government contends that one fact pointing toward a conclusion that Mrs. Kimbell's transfer to the Partnership was not a bona fide sale is the de minimis contribution to the partnership made by the other partners. Mrs. Kimbell's son and his wife contributed approximately $20,000 of the $2.4 million in assets in the Partnership. This argument amounts to a restatement of the government's recycling of value argument and does not justify treating the transaction as a sham. In addition, we know of no principle of partnership law that would require the minority partner to own a minimum percentage interest in the partnership for the entity to be legitimate and its transfers bona fide. The government also points out that the management of the Partnership assets did not change as a result of the transaction. Prior to the formation of the Partnership, David Kimbell managed Mrs. Kimbell's assets in the Trust. He continued to manage the assets once they were transferred to the Partnership. However, the important fact is that David Kimbell contributed his management expertise to the Partnership after its formation. Given the business reasons established above for the change in business form, the fact that David Kimbell performed the same services for the assets in the Trust is irrelevant.

We conclude that the district court erred in granting the government's motion for summary judgment and denying the taxpayer's motion for summary judgment on the issue of whether Mrs. Kimbell's transfer to the Partnership was a bona fide sale for full and adequate consideration so as to remove the transaction from the application of § 2036. First, as stated previously, the pro rata Partnership interest Mrs. Kimbell received was adequate and full consideration for the assets she transferred to the Partnership. Second, there is no contention that the transfer did not actually take place. The assets were formally assigned to the Partnership and Mrs. Kimbell was actually credited with a pro rata partnership interest. There is no evidence that partnership formalities were ignored or that Mrs. Kimbell used Partnership assets for personal expenses. Finally, applying the heightened scrutiny applicable to transactions between family members, we are satisfied that the taxpayer has established through objective evidence recited above that the transaction was not a disguised gift or sham transaction. The government raised no material issues of fact to counter the taxpayer's evidence that the Partnership was entered into for substantial business reasons.

Accordingly, we vacate the district court's judgment granting the government's motion for summary judgment and denying the taxpayer's motion for summary judgment because we conclude on this summary judgment record that the transfer to the Partnership qualifies as a bona fide sale for adequate and full consideration so as to remove the assets transferred to the Partnership from the estate of Mrs. Kimbell.

NOTES

1.   John F. Coverdale has crafted this metaphor for the regime of valuation discounts used in the *Kimball* case:

> Imagine a primitive society in which people store gold nuggets in bags. Neither buyers nor sellers of nuggets care what color the bags are because the value of the nuggets is set solely by their weight and purity. The only time anyone cares about the color of the bag is at death, because for purposes of the estate tax, the government assigns nuggets stored in red bags a much lower value than nuggets stored in any other color bag. This means that decedents who have stored their

nuggets in red bags will owe substantially less tax than those who have used any other color.

John F. Coverdale, *Of Red Bags and Family Limited Partnerships: Reforming the Estate and Gift Tax Valuation Rules to Achieve Horizontal Equity*, 51 U. LOUISVILLE L. REV. 239, 239 (2013).

Is Coverdale's metaphor accurate? Or is there more to the system of family partnership discounts than just putting your shares in a red bag?

2. The lack of control and lack of marketability discounts are based on the assumption that their holder may suffer at the hands of majority shareholders who make decisions that disadvantage them and over which they have no control. Based on what we learn about the Kimball family, does this seem like a legitimate concern in their case?

> **Possible Update:** In August 2016, Treasury issued proposed revisions to the regime of valuation discounts that would have limited them in some cases. The proposed regulations met with considerable opposition from various lobbying groups, and after Donald Trump won the November election, Treasury withdrew them. Under President Biden, it may seek to re-issue them, and they may meet with more success.

3. The IRS has agreed that the details of family dynamics are not relevant to the inquiry into the legitimacy of minority discounts in a particular case. Do you agree?

4. On February 3, 2017, the Kimbell family made a public offering of the company that was the subject of the above case. The IPO brought them $90 million. Does this outcome raise any concerns about the assumptions the court relied on in making its decision?

iii. Special Use Valuation

There have been concerns that the estate tax might force the sale of small family-owned businesses and farms to pay the tax. Section 2032A of the Internal Revenue Code tries to mitigate this problem by permitting an executor to value certain real property used in a small business or for farming at its "current-use value" rather than fair market value. The maximum reduction in the value of such property was initially set at $750,000, with adjustments for inflation. In 2020, the amount is $1.16 million.

Property is eligible for the special-use valuation if (i) at least 50% of the value of the gross estate consists of farm or closely-held business property; (ii) at least 25% of the value of the gross estate is comprised of farm or closely-held business property; and (iii) the property was used for a qualified use by the decedent or a member of his family for five of the eight years prior to the decedent's death.

There is also a special provision in the Internal Revenue Code that permits certain estates holding a closely-held business to pay the estate tax in installments using favorable interest rates. The installment period can extend for 15 years. An estate is eligible if the value of the decedent's interest in a closely-held business exceeds 35 percent of the gross estate.

e. Deductions and Taxable Estate

The gross estate is reduced by certain deductions, the most important of which are below.

i. State Estate Taxes

Section 2058 of the Internal Revenue Code provides a deduction for any state taxes imposed on property included in the gross estate. This might include, for example, a state inheritance tax, a state estate tax, or a succession tax. The Tax Cuts and Jobs Act capped the deductible amount at $10,000.

ii. Charitable Gifts and Certain Split-Interest Trusts

Section 2055 provides an unlimited charitable deduction for any gifts made to charitable organizations.[1] The deduction differs from the charitable deduction in the income tax area in two significant ways: there is no percentage limitation on the amount of the deduction; and contributions to foreign charities are deductible. Gifts of future interests in property generally do not qualify for a transfer tax deduction, but they can qualify for an income tax deduction, and a lifetime gift of that property removes it from the estate. Thus, some wealthy individuals will create a charitable remainder trust using appreciated property; if properly structured, this form of "split-interest" trust can provide an immediate income tax deduction equal to the present value of the remainder interest, with lifetime payments made to a related beneficiary. The mirror image of the charitable remainder trust, known as charitable lead trust, provides payments to a charity for a period of time, with the remainder paid to heirs. Such a gift can be structured to provide a transfer tax deduction equal to the present value of the charitable lead gift.

---

[1]   Section 2522 provides a parallel deduction for the gift tax.

Jacqueline Kennedy Onassis structured her will with an approach toward charity and her heirs that, given the outlook for interest rates, is back in style. Through her will, Onassis left behind a sizeable inheritance for her children while incorporating an innovative estate planning tool aimed at meeting her philanthropic goals. Her will included a little known technique at the time—called a Charitable Lead Trust (CLT)— to provide a long-term benefit

Jacqueline Kennedy Onassis, then First Lady, during a trip to India in 1962. John F. Kennedy Presidential Library and Museum.

to charity and her family, while minimizing her estate tax liability. Best employed while interest rates are low, the CLT is even more attractive today than when Onassis's plan was conceived. A CLT is known as a "split-interest trust" because it provides a stream of cash flow for one set of charitable beneficiaries for a fixed term, with the remainder going to a second set of beneficiaries, usually family members. It can be established during the donor's lifetime or at death, with a goal of minimizing gift or estate tax. For example, a donor could establish a CLT today for a 10-year term. During the period, the CLT would pay an annual annuity to a charity. At the end of the 10 years, any assets remaining in the trust would pass to the donor's heirs.

Several wealthy families have used CLTs, including the heirs of Sam Walton, founder of Wal-Mart. They have deployed the structure to transfer more than $9 billion with minimum taxation. The Waltons are not alone. U.S. families in 2012 held nearly $24 billion in CLTs, according to IRS data.[2]

iii. Spousal Deduction

Section 2056 provides an unlimited marital deduction for transfers to a spouse who is a United States citizen.[3] No marital deduction, however, is generally permitted for a transfer to a spouse who is not a United States citizen. (Consider why this is true.) But property transferred to a qualified domestic trust

---

[2]   From: https://www.brownadvisory.com/us/back-fashion-jackie-onassis-trust.

[3]   Section 2523 provides a parallel deduction for the gift tax.

for the benefit of a surviving spouse who is a foreign national does qualify for the marital deduction. On the death of the surviving spouse, the trust pays the estate tax calculated as if the trust property was taxed to the transferor spouse's estate.

Until 2010, when President Obama signed into law the Tax Relief, Unemployment Insurance Reauthorization, and Job Creation Act of 2010 ("2010 Tax Act"), each spouse had his or her own credit against the estate tax, which resulted in strategies, including lifetime transfers, so that the exemption of each spouse was fully utilized at that person's death. Starting in 2010, however, a surviving spouse could utilize the unused portion of her spouse's credit. This "portability" is discussed below.

f. Tax Rates, the Unified Credit, and Estate Planning for Married Couples

Estate and gift tax rates begin at 18% and ultimately rise to 40% of the gross estate.[4] But each taxpayer receives a credit against the estate and gift taxes.[5] As of 2021, the credit amount created an exclusion amount of $11.7 million. The credit is a unified credit for both the gift tax and the estate tax. To calculate the estate tax, all taxable gifts (those not deductible and above the annual gift exclusion amount, discussed below) are added to the gross estate. The estate tax is then calculated and then reduced by the credit amount. Until 2010, the credit was personal to the taxpayer and could not be transferred to a spouse. But Congress modified this in the 2010 Tax Act, so that the executor of an estate of a surviving spouse can now use the unused credit of the spouse who died first. (The first-to-die spouse's executor must make an election to enable this.) We will return to portability at the end of this section.

Two types of trusts are often used in estate planning for married couples, sometimes in combination. The first is a family trust, which will leave an amount at least equal to the exemption amount, for the benefit of family members, which is intended to utilize the exemption amount. Such a trust is desirable if the decedent does not want to leave assets outright to beneficiaries other than the spouse.

The second trust is intended to qualify as "qualified terminable interest property," and is referred to as a QTIP-trust. A QTIP Trust must meet the following conditions:

---

4   Internal Revenue Code § 2001(c).

5   Internal Revenue Code § 2010.

(i)   it must pass from the decedent; and

(ii)   the surviving spouse must be able to receive *all* the income from the property, payable annually or at more frequent intervals, and no person may have a power to appoint any part of the property to any person other than the surviving spouse.

The QTIP trust is a way to ensure that the remainder will go to the grantor's children, usually from a prior marriage, after the death of the surviving spouse. The transfer to the QTIP will qualify for the marital deduction.

A will can provide that a QTIP trust will be funded with an estate's assets in excess of the decedent's exemption amount, which can be useful in times when the estate tax rules are constantly in flux.

> **Connection Note:** Many of the cases you read in the trust chapters describe plans with "marital" and "family" or "credit shelter" trusts.

NOTE

Does the fact that the surviving spouse in an opposite-sex marriage is statistically likely to be female shed a different light on the QTIP Trust? Wendy Gerzog has written that the QTIP Trust is

> rooted in the prejudices and stereotypes of the 1960s and can only be explained as a gender-biased, paternalistic, and degrading treatment of women. The QTIP's current income distribution requirement is merely an illusion given to the widow to pretend that an income interest is as valuable as ownership of the underlying property. The QTIP "current beneficial enjoyment" requirement has no logical explanation except as a "bone" being tossed to the obsequious surviving spouse.

She also points out that it makes no sense to allow the marital deduction for property that the surviving spouse will never own outright. *See* Wendy C. Gerzog, *The Marital Deduction Qtip Provisions: Illogical and Degrading to Women*, 5 UCLA WOMEN'S L.J. 301, 305 (1995). Do you agree?

3.   The Gift Tax

Section 2501 of the Internal Revenue Code imposes a transfer tax on lifetime gifts. If the Code did not do so, a person could minimize or avoid the estate tax by making gifts prior to death.

a. Mechanics of Gift Tax

Calculating the gift tax proceeds with the following steps:

1. The donor first calculates the amount of the gift, which is the gift's fair market value.

2. Apply any available deductions. The donor has certain deductions, primarily an unlimited marital deduction and a charitable deduction, which parallel the deductions under the estate tax.

3. Apply any available annual exclusion. There is an annual per-donee exclusion, which is described in the following section.

4. The gift (after deductions and in excess of the annual exclusion) is subject to the same tax schedule that applies to estate taxation.[6]

5. Add the amount of the gift to gifts from prior years.

6. Decide if you want to pay the gift tax now or add the gift amount to your estate tax exclusion amount.

Payments of tuition and medical expenses paid directly to providers or educational institutions are generally not subject to the gift tax.

b. Annual Exclusion and Crummey Trusts

The Internal Revenue Code provides an annual per-donee exclusion from the gift tax. The exclusion, which is indexed to inflation, is $15,000 per donee for 2021. In the case of a gift by a member of a married couple, the exclusion can be doubled if the taxpayer's spouse joins the gift. To be eligible for the exclusion, however, a gift must be of a present interest, which Treasury regulations define as an unrestricted right to the immediate use, possession, or enjoyment of the property or the income from it. Under § 2053 of the Internal Revenue Code, a gift in trust to a minor is eligible for the exclusion if all income is currently distributed and the corpus is paid to the beneficiary at age 21.

In some cases, however, a donor wants to establish a trust that does not currently distribute income and/or that will not pay the trust corpus to the beneficiary on her 21st birthday. The IRS will generally not contest the application of the annual exclusion to gifts in such trusts if the beneficiary has the power to demand immediate possession of the trust property within a window period. Such trusts are often referred to as "Crummey" trusts, named

---

6   Internal Revenue Code § 2001(c).

for a case involving such a trust when the Court ruled in favor of the taxpayer. The IRS, however, will police such trusts to ensure that the beneficiary's power is actual rather than illusory, so careful administration of these trusts is key. The power will be considered meaningful if the window period is at least thirty days; the beneficiary has actual notice of the right (which is usually made in a letter to the beneficiary, called a "**Crummey letter**"); and there is no agreement or understanding that the withdrawal right will not be exercised.

c. *Estate Freeze*

An estate freeze is a planning device in which the owner of property that is expected to appreciate in value makes a partial gift of the property while retaining current income and in the case of a business, where estate freezes are most commonly used, control. For example, an owner of a corporation may cause a recapitalization, in which common shares are exchanged for new common stock and preferred stock. The preferred stock will pay preferred dividends, provide voting control, and have liquidation rights that entitle the owner to the value of the corporation as of the time of the recapitalization. The common stock's most important feature is that it will entitle the holder to residual value beyond the rights of the preferred stock. The owner then makes a gift of the common stock, which will typically have a low value, to his children, while retaining control of the business and assuring himself current dividends. The Internal Revenue Code includes a number of anti-abuse rules, which if violated, can result in the entire value of the transferred property being included in the decedent's estate.[7]

NOTE

As noted above, a valid Crummey Trust must give the beneficiary a window of time to demand distribution of the trust property. How often do you think the beneficiary of a Crummey Trust exercises this withdrawal right? In the original case that gave this trust its name, two of the beneficiaries were 15 and 11 years old. The Commissioner of Internal Revenue challenged the applicability of the annual exclusion to the transfers in trust for the minor children, arguing that since the minors were not likely to exercise their withdrawal powers, a transfer of a present interest had not occurred. The court, however, held that the power to demand distribution of the trust funds and the legal capability of exercising that power were the sole factors for the purpose of characterizing the transfer as that of a present interest. The court declined to assess the likelihood of the

---

[7]   The anti-abuse rules are found in Internal Revenue Code §§ 2701–04.

beneficiary actually exercising withdrawal rights, saying that it was not relevant in determining the type of interest transferred. It reasoned that such a test would be too "arbitrary" when conducted by the Service. *See Crummey v. Comm'r*, 397 F.2d 82 (9th Cir. 1968). For criticism of these trusts as "loopholes" that contravene the purposes and policies of the estate and gift tax, *see* Dora Arash, *Crummey Trusts: An Exploitation of the Annual Exclusion*, 21 PEPP. L. REV. 83, 99 (1993).

C. Tax on Generation Skipping Transfers

Until 1976, a common planning strategy for people with significant wealth was to create a multi-generational trust in which income would be paid to the donor's children (second generation) during their lives, with the corpus paid to the donor's grandchildren (third generation) on the death of the second generation. This would avoid the inclusion of the trust property in the estates of the second generation. Thus, a single estate tax would be paid by the donor's estate rather than two estate taxes (one by the donor's estate and one by the estates of the second generation).

As part of the Tax Reform Act of 1976, Congress addressed this practice by creating a new transfer tax for gifts that "skip" a generation. The generation skipping transfer ("GST") tax has since been modified, particularly by the Tax Reform Act of 1986, which expanded the scope of the tax and improved its technical operation. The GST tax parallels the estate and gift tax, but the tax is generally imposed at the time of the transfer to the third generation (the donor's grandchildren).[8] The tax is imposed only over an exemption amount, which matches the exemption amount for the estate and gift tax. (Note, though, that the GST tax exclusion is in addition to the exemption amount for the estate and gift tax.)

The tax is generally imposed when a generation-skipping transfer actually occurs (which can be years after a multigenerational transfer into a trust formally occurs). The statute defines three such events:

1. A direct skip: A direct skip is a transfer to a "skip" person, someone who is in the second or later generation from the transferor a grandchild or great grandchild of the donor). A skip person can also be a trust benefiting only skip persons. Note that

---

[8] The Internal Revenue Code provides rules for determining generations; the rules include age distinctions when objects of the donor's bounty are not family members.

a direct gift to a grandchild of the donor would be a gift to a skip person, and so a "direct skip."

2.   A taxable termination: this occurs when there is a termination of an interest in trust property through death, lapses of time, release of a power, or other event, unless immediately after the termination a non-skip person retains an interest in the property.

3.   A taxable distribution: this is a trust distribution to a skip person (other than a direct skip or a taxable termination).

The tax on a generation-skipping transfer is a flat tax equal to the maximum estate and gift tax rate, currently 40 percent, multiplied by a fraction called the "inclusion ratio." The inclusion ratio reflects the donor's decision on how to allocate the exemption amount among gifts. For example, if a donor makes a $1,000,000 gift and allocates $1,000,000 of the exemption amount to the gift, the exclusion ratio would be zero and the tax would be $400,000 multiplied by 0, so no tax would be owed. If the donor allocated $500,000 of the exemption to the transfer, the exclusion ratio would be .5 and the tax would be $400,000 multiplied by .5, or $200,000. What should a donor consider when allocating the exemption amount among multiple gifts?

> **Update:** President Biden's Tax proposals include cutting the exclusions amount for Generation-skipping transfers.

How Can I Limit My GST Tax?

- Create a Wyoming Dynasty Trust for the benefit of future generations. All or a portion of a settlor's GST exemption can be allocated to assets transferred to the trust. Note that a settlor's spouse may also participate in funding a dynasty trust, resulting in a doubling of the amount exempted from GST tax.

- In many states, trust law requires that a trust terminate at some specified future date, typically 21 years after the last to die of certain identified beneficiaries. This is commonly referred to as the "rule against perpetuities." A Wyoming Dynasty Trust, however, can last up to 1,000 years, with the result being that the growth of the assets in a properly structured trust can be shielded from gift, estate, and GST tax for up to 1,000 years.

- Accordingly, a trust established in Wyoming and meeting certain other requirements could remain active for 1,000 years. As long as the trust remains in place, the assets of the trust avoid federal transfer tax. The longer the Dynasty Trust lasts, the more generations of federal taxation it escapes, resulting in tremendous growth potential for the Wyoming Dynasty Trust assets.

Trust companies market trusts that will limit the generation skipping tax (GST).

Connection Note: In Chapter 9, we learned about the rule against perpetuities and the move in a number of states to repeal the rule in order to attract new trust business by marketing "dynasty" or "perpetual" trusts. This race to repeal is often connected to the 1986 tax rules and the establishment of the generation-skipping tax—or, more precisely, to the exemption:

> Enactment of the GST tax therefore gave state perpetuities law renewed salience among estate planners. The longer a transfer-tax-exempt trust could be extended, the more generations could benefit from the trust fund free from transfer taxes. In a state that has abolished the Rule, successive generations can benefit from the trust fund, free from subsequent federal wealth transfer taxation, forever. On this view, the movement to abolish the Rule is perhaps more precisely described as a race between the states to allow donors to exploit a loophole in the federal transfer taxes.

Max M. Schanzenbach & Robert H. Sitkoff, *Perpetuities or Taxes? Explaining the Rise of the Perpetual Trust*, 27 CARDOZO LAW REVIEW, 2465, 2477 (2006). In practical terms, look at the benefits to the settlor and the settlor's family this way: "If a dynasty trust of roughly $1 million was established today . . . it would be worth $867.7 million after four generations, assuming that it grew 7 percent a year and nothing was spent. By contrast, it would be worth $35.6 million if the property was given outright to future generations and was subject each time to an estate tax of up to 55 percent." Carole Gould, *Shifting Rules Add Luster to Trusts*, N.Y. TIMES, Oct. 29, 2000.

D. Income Tax Considerations

This section covers the five income tax principles of the Internal Revenue Code most relevant to transfers of family wealth:

- The exclusion of gifts from income

- The exclusion of life insurance proceeds from income

- The calculation of the basis of gifts

- The taxation of the income of trusts and estates

- The deduction for income in respect of a decedent

1. Gifts Are Not Income

Lifetime gifts may be taxed to the donor, as discussed above, but are not taxed to the donee. This may seem odd, since other kinds of income are taxed to the person who receives the income—but Congress passed the gift tax as a backstop to the estate tax. Its purpose is to prevent people from depleting their estates with tax-free lifetime gifts. This is why the tax falls on the donor.

2. Life Insurance Proceeds Are Not Income

Life insurance is often an important component of estate planning. We have already noted that life insurance owned by a beneficiary is generally excluded from the decedent's gross estate. But § 101(a) of the Internal Revenue Code generally excludes from income the proceeds of a life insurance policy paid by reason of the death of the insured. Thus, good tax planning should probably include life insurance.

3. Basis and Recognition of Gain

A person's gain on the sale or taxable transfer of an asset is the value received less the amount the person invested in the item—generally, what the person paid for it. This initial investment amount is referred to as the "basis."

> **Example:** Ari purchases a rare coin for $1,000. Ari's basis—his investment—is $1,000. If Ari later sells the coin for $1,500, Ari is recovering his $1,000 investment and $500 in profit. The $500 profit is gain, and this is taxable. (Yes, this is capital gains tax, and the tax rate depends on how long the buyer holds the asset before selling it.)

A person's gain does not incur tax until the person has a "realization event," i.e., the person has disposed of the property in a transaction. The most common realization event is a sale of the property, but many non-cash transfers—for instance, property swaps—are also taxable occasions. But certain property transfers are not realization events, including gifts, either during lifetime or at death. This makes sense, because the donor gained no profit from the gift.

But just because a gift transaction doesn't incur tax, doesn't meant that the property gifted didn't increase in value. This increase in value that occurs between the time the donor acquires the property and the time she gifts it to the donee is called "built in gain." So when is this built-in gain taxed? As discussed below, in the case of lifetime gifts, when the donee disposes of the property in a taxable transaction. In the case of gifts at death, generally never.

a. Carryover Basis for Inter Vivos Gifts

In the case of lifetime gifts, the built-in gain is taxed when the recipient of the gift sells it. But how do we calculate the gain—or put another way, what is the basis if the donee disposes of the gift in a taxable transaction? Section 1015 of the Internal Revenue Code provides that the donee steps into the basis of the donor.

Example: Mari gives her daughter Delia stock that Mari purchased for $25 five years ago. Neither Mari nor Delia has gain at the time of the gift. If Delia later sells the stock for $40, Delia has $15 of taxable gain at the time of the sale. Note that Mari would have had the same gain if she had kept the stock and sold it herself. This is why we say, Delia steps into the shoes (that is, basis) of Mari.

b. Step up in Basis at Death

But the situation is different at death. From the standpoint of generational transfers and tax planning, the most valuable of all the provisions in our tax law is Internal Revenue Code § 1014, which provides that a recipient of property transferred at death—whether through will, intestate succession, or non-probate mechanism—takes a basis equal to the fair market value **as of the date of the decedent's death**. This special provision is called the step-up in basis.

Why is this step-up valuable? Consider the following:

Example: Joe's parents bought their house in 1970 for $50,000. When both Joe's parents had passed away, in 2005, the house was worth $300,000. Joe inherited the house and sold it in 2007 for $325,000. If Joe had to pay taxes on the profit based on the 1970 basis, he would owe taxes on $270,000. As it was, however, he only owed taxes on $25,000 of profit.

Now consider this real-life example: Herman Lay founded Lay's Potato Chips in 1932. He invested $100. His stake in Lay's increased in value and ultimately Lay's merged with Frito, forming Frito-Lay Corporation. Herman Lay was the largest shareholder in Frito-Lay, which was later acquired by PepsiCo, Inc. After the acquisition, Herman Lay owned 15% of the stock of PepsiCo. Because the merger of Lay and Frito, and the

Herman Lay's most popular
product and the source
of his fortune.

subsequent acquisition of Frito-Lay by PepsiCo were tax-free transactions, Herman Lay's basis in his PepsiCo stock was $100. If he had sold the stock while he was living, Herman Lay would have incurred considerable tax because he would have had to calculate the profit based on his original $100 basis. But he didn't sell it, and when he died his heirs received the PepsiCo stock with their basis "stepped up" to fair market value as of the date of Mr. Lay's death. They could now turn around and sell the stock without recognizing the gain that appreciated during Mr. Lay's life.

As illustrated by Mr. Lay's story, death is a wonderful income-tax avoidance device. And in 1976, Congress decided that the step-up in basis was inconsistent with an income tax and repealed it, effective 1980. In its place, the heirs would receive a carry-over basis. But intense lobbying followed the repeal. The lobbyists contended that determining the original basis for property purchased decades earlier would be difficult, although certainly no more difficult than it would be if the decedent had sold the property shortly before death. In any event, Congress was persuaded, and it repealed the repeal of step-upped basis before the repeal became effective. In 2010, the year in which the estate tax was repealed, step-up basis was also repealed. In 2011, they were both back.

> **Update:** One of President Biden's tax proposals is to tax the unrealized gain at the time of transfer to the beneficiary—regardless of whether that person sells it. We'll see how that goes.

4. Income in Respect of a Decedent

Consider this problem: a decedent's estate includes an interest in an individual retirement account worth $10,000,000, resulting in an estate tax of 40%. The retirement account later distributes the $10,000,000 to the decedent's descendants, who now must pay income tax on the distribution, for step-up in basis does not apply to IRD items. The total tax burden may seem confiscatory, since the full value was taxed for both transfer and income tax purposes. Section 691(c) of the Internal Revenue Code partly mitigates the "double" tax by providing an income tax deduction for the portion of estate tax attributable to the IRD. The most common types of IRD are retirement and IRA accounts and accounts receivable.

5. Income Taxation of Trusts and Estates

Trusts and estates are subject to a complex income taxation regime, which generally attempts to subject trust income to taxation at either the entity or beneficiary level (although in one type of trust, the "Intentionally Defective Grantor Trust," the grantor retains important aspects of control, trust income is taxed to the grantor—see below). This basic approach to taxation is achieved by providing the trust with a deduction for amounts deemed to be distributed to beneficiaries and imposing income tax on beneficiaries who are deemed to have received a distribution.

The trust or estate calculates its income in the same manner as an individual, with some significant differences. Like an individual, the trust receives a personal exemption, but the exemption is $600 for an estate and either $300 or $100 for a trust (depending on whether the trust is a simple or complex trust, terms that we will consider below). The rules for the charitable contribution deduction allowable to a trust or estate are different from those applicable to individuals.[9] In some cases, an estate must choose whether to deduct an item from the gross estate or current income. And the rules for deducting an operating loss are different for individuals and trusts. And trusts and estates receive a deduction for most distributions (and deemed distributions) to beneficiaries.

Trusts and estates pay tax at the highest marginal tax rates applicable to individuals, and also pay the 3.8% surtax on investment income imposed by the Affordable Care Act. The top rates and the investment-income surtax apply to income over $12,150, which is considerably more compressed than the graduated rate structure or thresholds applicable to individuals. For the purpose of tax rates, multiple trusts created to minimize income to which the top rates apply are aggregated and taxed as a single trust.

Trusts must use a calendar year for tax purposes, but estates can select a fiscal year.

---

[9]   For example, an individual's charitable contribution deduction is limited to 50% of the individual's adjusted gross income and nondeductible contributions are carried forward to future tax years. A trust or estate is not subject to the limitation but there are no carryovers for years in which the trust's contributions exceed the trust's applicable income. A trust or estate must allocate its contribution between taxable and exempt income for the year, with the portion allocated to exempt income non-deductible. (Gifts made from principal are not deductible for income tax purposes.) And a trust can in certain situations take a deduction for contributions that will not be made until the following year, and estates are allowed a deduction for amounts that are permanently set aside for distributions to charitable organizations, while individuals receive a deduction only in the year amounts are actually paid to a charitable organization.) Trusts and estates are allowed to deduct contributions to foreign charities, while individuals generally can only deduct contributions to domestic charitable organizations.

Different types of trusts are subject to different income tax rules. Here, we provide an overview of the main categories of trusts and the income tax rules that apply to them.

a.   Simple Trusts

A "simple trust" is a trust whose terms require (i) that all income be currently distributed, and (ii) that no amounts be paid, permanently set aside, or used in a way that will result in a deductible charitable contribution.[10] A trust does not qualify as a simple trust in any year in which it distributes more than the trust's income. Note that for these purposes, income does not refer to taxable income, but to income under the trust instrument and governing state trust law defining income and principal. Surprisingly, the definitions of income and principal can vary according to state law and the trust instrument, but this topic is beyond the purview of this book.

A simple trust is taxed on its income (see above). It receives a deduction against its income for the amounts required to be distributed. The trust beneficiaries for whom the trust instrument requires distributions pay income taxes on the amounts they receive. The trust takes a deduction equal to the distributions, regardless of whether the amounts are actually distributed.

b.   Complex Trusts (and Estates)

If a trust is not a simple trust it is a complex trust; estates are always treated as complex trusts. A complex trust receives a deduction equal to amounts required to be distributed (whether actually distributed or not) and other amounts properly distributed to beneficiaries under the governing trust instrument. To help with timing issues, a trust can elect to include amounts distributed during the first 65 days of one year as distributed in the prior year.

c.   Intentionally Defective Grantor Trusts (IDGTs)

An IDGT is a trust whose income is taxed to the grantor, but whose assets are removed from the grantor's estate for estate tax purposes. Technically, it is an irrevocable trust which nonetheless is drafted to leave one of the following key aspects of control in the grantor's hands: the power to revoke the trust, to direct payment of income or trust corpus without the consent of an adverse party, to retain significant administrative powers, or to retain more than a 5% reversionary interest. Because of these features, the grantor is considered the owner of the trust assets for income tax purposes but not for estate tax purposes.

---

[10]   Internal Revenue Code § 651(a).

Grantor trusts can be a helpful estate planning tool depending on the client's situation. For example, often an individual's tax rate is lower than that of a trust (which is the highest rate), so the fact that an IDGT's income can be taxed to the grantor, rather than to the trust, can save taxes. Meanwhile, the assets in the trust are not part of the grantor's estate for tax purposes, potentially saving estate tax. And, because the grantor is paying the income tax on the assets—whether or not the income is distributed—it preserves the growth of these assets for the next generation.

If the above scenario ever changes so that it is no longer beneficial—or feasible—for the grantor to pay the income tax, the grantor can change the trust into a simple irrevocable trust at any time.

E. State Estate and Inheritance Tax

In addition to the federal transfer taxes, six states have an inheritance tax and twelve plus the District of Columbia levy an estate tax. Maryland taxes both the estate and inheritance. This is a dramatic drop from the year 2001, when virtually all states imposed at least one of the above taxes. Why the decline in such taxes among states? Almost certainly the decline was related to the repeal of a credit against the federal estate tax for state inheritance and/or state estate taxes. The credit, which reduced the federal estate tax bill dollar for dollar for taxes paid to the state, allowed the state to, in effect, appropriate tax dollars otherwise destined for the federal government. (There were some limits on the size of the credit.)

A state estate tax, like the Federal estate tax, is imposed on the taxable estate of a decedent who is a resident in the state. (Note that a decedent who is not a state resident but owns property in a state with an estate tax may also be subject to the tax.) State-level estate taxes generally track important aspects of the federal estate tax, although the exemption amounts may be lower, and the maximum rate imposed by any state (Washington) is 20%.

Does Your State Have an Estate or Inheritance Tax?

State Estate & Inheritance Tax Rates & Exemptions in 2020

Most states have neither an estate nor an inheritance tax.

A state inheritance tax is imposed on bequests rather than the estate itself. Six states currently impose an inheritance tax, including two (Maryland and New Jersey) that also impose a separate estate tax.[11] All of the inheritance taxes exempt bequests to spouses; three fully exempt bequests to lineal descendants. Some states impose different tax rates (or have different exemption amounts) depending on the relationship of the decedent to the person or organization receiving the inheritance. No inheritance tax applies to transfers to charitable organizations.

> **Update:** Like many other tax-related issues, treatment of state inheritance and estate taxes may change under the Biden Administration.

You can deduct state inheritance and estate taxes, although the rules limiting the deduction's use are complex. Moreover, the 2016 Tax Cuts and Jobs Act capped the amount subject to the deduction.

---

[11] The estate tax liability, however, in both New Jersey and Maryland can be credited against the inheritance tax, so effectively the tax is the greater of the inheritance tax and the estate tax in those two states.

F. Conclusion and Takeaways

A comprehensive exploration of the wealth transfer tax system requires more than one chapter. The goal of this chapter has been to provide you a basic understanding of the fundamentals of the wealth transfer tax system and to highlight red flags—situations where your client can get into trouble with taxes. When these more complicated situations arise, you need to stop and find someone with tax expertise—or, by then, maybe you will have acquired it yourself. Remember, wealth transfer at death is a universal experience, but wealth transfer taxes will be paid by only a few individuals.

As you may have found this one of the more controversial chapters in the book, we also found it challenging to write. On the one hand, our goal here, as throughout the book, is to help you acquire the knowledge and skills to offer clients practical help in dealing with their estate planning issues. On the other, many aspects of the wealth transfer tax system disadvantage lower income and minority communities, an issue we are also concerned with throughout this book. For example, as this chapter has shown, anyone who can afford legal advice, can significantly reduce—if not eliminate—the wealth transfer tax. So, while it is your job to use the law to achieve your client's tax minimizing goals, you also may want to think about efforts you could join to redistribute the advantages of tax advice.

Some additional takeaways of this chapter include:

- The exemption amount for the estate tax is $11.7 million as of January 1, 2021, which means that very few people will need to worry about—or try to plan around—the tax. But as this book goes to print, we are on the cusp of a new administration, and this exemption amount may well revert to a lower number in the near future. The online update section will keep you apprised of, and explain, any changes.

- The exemption amount includes both testamentary transfers and lifetime gifts. But the reality is that only very large lifetime gifts are traced or taxed.

- The estate tax is calculated by adding up the value of everything the decedent owns at death, reducing it by the available deductions, and applying the tax to any amount over the exemption amount.

- Spouses can transfer an unlimited amount to each other without tax consequences.

- There are ways to reduce the value of a decedent's taxable estate by using valuation discounts and special use valuations.

- Some states have estate or inheritance taxes; Maryland has both.

- The income tax intersects with the estate tax in the following ways: calculation of the basis of gifts; taxation of the income of trusts and estates; and the deduction for income in respect of a decedent.

- The step-up basis applies when calculating taxes on the sale of an inherited asset.

CHAPTER 16 COMPREHENSIVE ASSESSMENTS

1.   **DEVELOPING A CLE SEMINAR.** You have been asked by a senior partner at your firm to develop a thirty-minute CLE presentation that has been given the title "Death Tax 101." The CLE is specifically designed for new estate planning attorneys who will primarily be focusing on estates that are less than $5 million dollars. Your goal is to do the following:

- Explain the policy considerations relating to the taxation of gratuitous wealth transfers.

- Summarize the misconceptions that both lawyers and non-lawyers have about the taxation of gratuitous wealth transfers.

- Describe the facts that should be gathered to determine whether tax liability may incur.

- Caution when a lawyer with tax expertise should be consulted.

Develop both a dynamic visual presentation and a meaningful one-page handout that could be distributed to the attendees. When developing the materials, use language that is appropriate for the audience.

2.   **PLANNING EXERCISE.** Your client, Muhammad Abdel, is worth about $50 million. He wants your advice about estate planning. His main goals are to minimize taxes for his estate and provide for his children and grandchildren. He also tells you that he is now married to his second wife, who has two children from a prior marriage. Muhammad plans to leave his stepchildren generous gifts in his estate plan, but he wants to make sure the bulk of his estate to his biological children and grandchildren. His property consists of several

companies of which he owns the controlling shares, some office buildings he rents out, and some investments in businesses that consist of minority shares. Without dealing with any numbers, draft a letter to Muhammad suggesting some tax planning strategies for him to achieve his goals.

3. **ETHICS/COUNSELING EXERCISE.** Your task is to prepare a Best Practices Memo for your firm about the following scenario: A well-to-do heterosexual couple seeks joint representation in estate planning. The husband tells you privately, however, that he wants to set up a QTIP Trust, leaving his wife, if she survives him, a life estate, and reserving the remainder for his children from a former marriage. Throughout the marriage, the husband has been the main breadwinner as a senior executive at a major company. The wife played the role of hostess of the many parties the husband's job required him to have at his house, and she furthered his career by socializing with and getting to know his co-workers and clients, but she never worked or had a career of her own. Does the firm face any ethical dilemmas in counseling this couple jointly? Why or why not? If it does, what should its policy be in addressing them? How should the attorney present the QTIP concept to the wife? What kind of communication would be best to have with the couple about this estate planning device?

Test Your Knowledge

To assess your understanding of the material in this chapter, click here to take a quiz.

GLOSSARY

Abatement (abate): The property in the probate estate is insufficient to pay all of the testamentary gifts in full. Traditionally, assets abate in the following order: residuary devises abate first; then general devises; and finally specific devises. Demonstrative devises are treated as specific up to the value of the property sold and then are treated as general. Within each category, gifts abate proportionally.

Accessions: Where a testamentary gift is made of securities, the gift will include additional securities owned by the testator at the time of death to the extent those additional securities were acquired after the will's execution as a result of the testator's ownership of the securities described in the will.

Accounting: A statement prepared by a fiduciary, such as a personal representative or a trustee, that describes the actions undertaken. How the property was managed, what expenses were paid, what profits were made, and what distributions were authorized will be detailed. The accounting may be informal, where the fiduciary shares the accounting with the beneficiaries for objections and consent. The accounting may be formal, where the fiduciary shares the account with the beneficiaries and the appropriate court for review.

Acknowledged: To take ownership of or admit as genuine (such as the signature to a will).

ACTEC (American College of Trusts and Estates Counsel): American College of Trusts and Estates Counsel (ACTEC) is a national organization of lawyers, judges, and professors who are experts in trusts and estates.

Acts (or Events) of Independent Significance: Everyday life events that can change how the terms of a will are interpreted.

Ademption (adeem): The extinguishing of a testamentary gift because the property has either already been given as a lifetime gift (which is ademption by satisfaction) or the property is not in the decedent's probate estate (which is ademption by extinction).

Administration: The process that involves the collection of the decedent's assets, the payment of the decedent's creditors, and the distribution of the decedent's assets to the appropriate entities or individuals. Administration may also be called probate administration, the probate process, or probate proceedings.

Administration, Ancillary: A secondary probate proceeding that typically occurs because the decedent owned real property in a county that is the not the decedent's domicile at the date of death, which is the location of the primary administration.

Administrator: The party appointed by the court to manage the decedent's probate estate where the party was not nominated to serve in the terms of the decedent's valid will. The administrator is a fiduciary.

Adoption, Equitable: Also called virtual adoption or informal adoption, equitable adoption refers to a legal fiction whereby parentage is established through either an express or implied promise to adopt. Adoption proceedings, however, had not been undertaken.

Adoption, Formal: Also called legal adoption, formal adoption refers to creating parentage by legal decree.

Adoption, Informal or Virtual: Also called equitable adoption.

Advance directive: A legal instrument that shares the wishes of an individual (called a declarant) as to health care decisions relating to treatment preferences and the designation of a proxy to make health care decisions. An advance directive is typically a combination of a "living will," which shares end-of-life care decisions, and a medical power of attorney, which designates another to participate in the health care decisions on behalf of the declarant.

Advancement: A lifetime gift that is intended to reduce or eliminate an heir's intestate share.

Alienate: The ability to transfer ownership of an interest. Alienate typically refers to a trust beneficiary's ability to transfer part or all of the beneficiary's equitable interest in the trust.

Ancestor: An individual from whom someone descends. A parent, a grandparent, and a great-grandparent are examples of ancestors.

Antilapse Statute: An antilapse statute is a statute that redirects a lapsed testamentary gift if the will does not otherwise redirect the gift and if the conditions established in the antilapse statute are satisfied. In general, an antilapse statute will apply to gifts to a deceased descendant of the decedent, but statutory variations occur.

Appointees, power of appointment: The people or entities who receive property subject to a power of appointment. The people or entities who are eligible recipients of the property subject to the power of appointment are known as the objects or permissible appointees. Those for whom the property is actually appointed are called the appointees. The people or entities who take the property if the power of appointment is not exercised are known as the takers in default.

Artificial reproductive technology (ART): Also called assisted reproductive technologies, refers to a range of medical treatments and procedures involving human genetic material that allow for reproduction without sexual intercourse.

Ascertainable standard: A standard commonly used in discretionary trusts to provide broad guidance as to the appropriate distribution. The most common ascertainable standard used is for the Health, Education, Maintenance, and Support (HEMS) of the trust beneficiary.

Asset protection trust (APT): The terms of the trust limit the ability of creditors to access the trust property.

Attestation: Refers to the witnessing of a formal (aka attested) will.

Augmented estate: Used for purposes of calculating the elective share, the augmented estate includes the decedent's probate estate and the value of certain nonprobate transfers. What probate transfers are included in the augmented estate vary by state statute.

Beneficiary: The person, class, or entity who receives property via a will or will substitute.

Beneficiary, Contingent: An alternate beneficiary, who may be a person, class, or entity, specified in the terms of the will or will substitute who is entitled to receive the property if the primary beneficiary is unable (or ineligible) to receive the property.

Beneficiary, Income: A trust beneficiary who is entitled to receive a portion of the trust income if the conditions specified in the trust are established.

Beneficiary, Primary: The person, class, or entity who are entitled to receive property as specified under the terms of the will or will substitutes. The primary beneficiary will need to be eligible to receive the property, such as surviving the decedent.

Beneficiary, Principal: A trust beneficiary who is entitled to receive a portion of the trust principal if the conditions specified in the trust are established.

Beneficiary designation: The identification of a person, class, or entity to receive property via a will substitute. The beneficiary designation is completed in accordance with the requirements of the particular will substitute and generally does not require compliance with the wills act formalities.

Bequeath: Today, commonly used as a synonym for give in the context of wills, bequeath historically refers to a testamentary gift of personal property. Devise was historically used to refer to a testamentary gift of real property. Wills may use the language "give, bequeath, and devise."

Bequest: A legacy received via the terms of a will.

Caveat, Caveator: Also called a contest, a caveat is an objection to a will submitted to a probate court. The party that files the caveat is called a caveator, also called a contestant.

Chancery court: Today, a chancery court is one of the many names for the specialized state court that deals with the decedent's estate. The general name is the probate court, but states use names such as Orphans' Courts, Surrogate's Courts, or Chancery Courts.

Charitable trust: In contrast to a private trust, a trust established to support a charitable entity or a charitable purpose.

Claflin doctrine: Also called the material purpose doctrine, the Claflin doctrine prevents a court from modifying an irrevocable trust unless all the beneficiaries consent and all of the settlor's material purposes have been satisfied. The name is derived from the *Claflin* case.

Class gift: A gift in a will, will substitute, or trust that provides for the proportional division of property among all qualified members of a class. The terms of the legal instrument may provide the qualification for class membership or the default rules of intestacy, such as the definition of children, may be used to determine qualification for class membership.

Codicil: A testamentary instrument that is a written amendment or modification to an existing will. The codicil must be created using the appropriate wills act formalities.

Collateral: Property pledged to secure a loan on more favorable terms. In inheritance, the term collateral can describe collateral kindred. Collateral kindred are neither ancestors nor descendants. Thus, the term "collateral kindred" refers to siblings, aunts, uncles, nieces, nephews, and cousins.

Common law spouse: An individual who was a party to an informal marriage, also called a common law marriage. A common law marriage occurs when a couple does not procure a license or participate in a solemnization proceeding (that is a formal marriage ceremony) but there exists no bar to entering into a marriage, the couple had the intent to be married, and the couple held themselves out as married. Merely residing in the same household is not sufficient to establish a common law marriage. There must be a holding out by the couple as married, as well as evidence like joint bank accounts, tax returns, deeds, etc. If the common law marriage was valid where formed and the couple moves to a state that does not allow for common law marriage, the marriage may still be recognized, and property entitlements will exist for a surviving spouse pursuant to the doctrine of lex loci.

Community property: Property acquired in a community property state during marriage through the efforts of either married party. Each spouse owns an equal, undivided share of the community property at the moment of acquisition, regardless of the property's title.

Consanguinity, Table of: A graphical depiction, which may be in the form of a table or chart, that indicates the degrees of kinships based upon blood.

Conscious presence: One of the two ways of measuring presence for purposes of will execution. In general, the parties are within the same general physical vicinity and are aware of the act(s) of signing through any of the senses, whether or not the individual who is signing is visible at the moment that signing is performed. The UPC has adopted the conscious presence test instead of the traditional line-of-sight test for proxy signing, and the UPC eliminates the need for witnesses to sign in the testator's presence at all.

Conservator: An individual appointed by a court of relevant jurisdiction who is authorized to handle the property of another.

Construction: Today, a synonym for the interpretation of the terms of a will. Interpretation refers to the determination of the meaning of the words, and construction refers to the drawing of conclusions when the direct expression is incomplete, ambiguous, or silent. Intent is often described as the "touchstone" of construction.

Constructive trust: A remedial trust that permits a court to direct transfer of property ownership from one who has acquired the property through unjust means, such as fraud, to another.

Contest, Contestant: Also called a caveat, a contest is an objection to a will submitted to a probate court. The party who files the contest is called a contestant, also called a caveator.

Convenience account: Also called an agency account, a convenience account is a form of multi-party account that permits one party to withdraw funds for the purposes of the party who has created the account (often called the depositor). Upon the death of the depositor, the account proceeds are not automatically transferred to the other party designed on the account. Instead, the account proceeds are typically included in the depositor's probate estate.

Corpus: Also called res or trust property, the asset to be managed by the trustee in accordance with the terms of the trust and the trustee's fiduciary duties.

Crummey letter: Named after the case *Crummey v. Commission of Internal Revenue*, a crummy letter, also called a crummy notice, informs a trust beneficiary that the beneficiary has the ability to withdraw particular trust property during a specified time period.

Curtesy: Historically, one of the ways in which a surviving spouse was protected following the death of the decedent spouse. Curtesy rights granted the widower a life estate in all freehold interests held by the wife during the marriage, not just the dower portion of one third. The only requirement for a widower to receive his curtesy right was that the marriage had produced children who would inherit the property upon the widower's death (which was not a requirement for dower). In most states dower and curtesy rights have been replaced by the modern elective share.

Cy pres: Which means "as near as" in old French, provide a mechanism to modify charitable trusts if the charitable purpose becomes unlawful, impracticable, impossible to achieve, or wasteful and the terms of the trust have not anticipated such contingency.

De facto child, parent: De facto parentage, which is recognized in the Uniform Parentage Act and the UPC, is a functional approach to establishing parentage. De facto parentage recognizes that individuals, who have no established relationship via genetics or adoption, have nevertheless created a relationship that functions as a parent-child relationship. A "de facto parent" means a person who has been adjudicated to be a parent of a child under the applicable de facto parentage statute.

Dead hand: Refers to the policy consideration that permits the wishes of a decedent to control future events. Dead hand is sometimes raised as a policy consideration to limit the freedom of disposition.

Decanting: Decanting is a new and emerging form of trust modification that involves a trustee pouring, or decanting, assets from one trust into another trust.

Decedent: The generic name to refer to a deceased property owner.

Declaration of Trust: A legal instrument that can be used to create a valid trust.

Demonstrative gift: A type of testamentary gift where a general gift is directed to be paid from an identified account or asset.

Descendant: Also called issue, refers to a decedent's children, grandchildren, great grandchildren, etc.

Deviation, administrative or equitable: A mechanism for modifying the terms of an irrevocable trust in light of changed circumstances. Originally applied only to modify administrative terms of the trust, deviation may be applied to any trust term and requires an interested party to petition the court and show a change of circumstances that was unanticipated by the trust settlor.

Devise: Today, commonly used as a synonym for give in the context of wills, bequeath historically refers to a testamentary gift of personal property. Devise was historically used to refer to a testamentary gift of real property. Wills may use the language "give, bequeath, and devise."

Devisee: Describes a will beneficiary who receives a gift of real property.

Disclaim, disclaimer: A voluntary bar of inheritance where the identified beneficiary or heir declines to receive the property.

Discretionary distribution terms: Trust terms that permit the trustee discretion as to the distribution of income, principal, or both to and among the trust beneficiaries.

Domestic Asset Protection Trust: Also called DAPTs, these trusts provide asset protection for self-settled asset protection trusts.

Donative Freedom: A policy consideration that permits property owners to direct the disposition of their property as the property owners determine to be appropriate. The degree to which this donative freedom may be limited is another policy consideration.

Donee, power of appointment: The holder of the power to appoint the property.

Donor: The generic term to refer to an individual property owner who may be creating a power of appointment, a will, a trust, or a lifetime gift.

Donor, power of appointment: The person who creates a power of appointment.

Dower: Historically, one of the ways in which a surviving spouse was protected following the death of the decedent spouse. Also called "the widow's share," dower was a property right that the bride acquired upon marriage in exchange for the loss of most of her property rights through the operation of coverture. The dower right vested on the husband's death and was intended to sustain a widow through her old age. In most states dower, like curtesy rights, has been replaced by the modern elective share.

Duress: A ground for a will contest where another exerts influence on the testator by physical coercion.

Dynasty Trust: Also called perpetual trust, a private express trust that has no durational limitation and is typically established for the benefit of the settlor's descendants.

Elective share: Also called a forced share, the elective share is one of the main ways in which a surviving spouse in a separate property jurisdiction is protected following the death of the decedent spouse. Statutory variations exist.

ERISA (Employee Retirement Income Security Act): A federal law that governs certain retirement plans and insurance policies. One of ERISA's key provisions for inheritance is the pre-emption provision.

Escheat: A reversionary interest that directs the decedent's intestate estate be awarded to the state if the decedent dies with no eligible intestate heirs.

Estate: The generic name to refer to the decedent's assets. An estate may be divided into a probate estate and a nonprobate estate.

Exception creditors: Creditors who take priority over ordinary creditors and may, under the right circumstances, compel a distribution from a trustee to satisfy a debt. Common exception creditors are ex-spouses with support orders, children with support orders, or the federal government.

Executor: A person or institution nominated within the terms of a valid will and appointed by a testator to carry out the terms of the testator's will.

Exoneration: A doctrine stating that encumbrances (i.e., a mortgage) of a property conveyed by a will are discharged with funds from the originating estate, not from the property itself. That is to say, if a jurisdiction's rules exonerate the debt, that debt will be paid before the beneficiary receives the previously encumbered property. In non-exoneration jurisdictions, a specific devise passes subject to any mortgage interest existing at the date of death.

Family allowance: An allowance (usually a lump sum) that goes to a surviving spouse and/or children at a decedent's death.

Fiduciary: A person or organization that acts on behalf of another person or persons, with a duty to observe certain duties. Being a fiduciary requires being bound both legally and ethically to act in the other person's best interests according to standards of loyalty, prudence, and good faith. Trustees and executors are both fiduciaries (as are attorneys).

Fiduciary income tax return: The Internal Revenue Service requires all fiduciaries to file Form 1041 and pay any applicable taxes before transferring the trust or estate's assets to the decedent's heirs.

Forced share: A term used interchangeably with the elective share.

Foster child: A child who lives with and is taken care of by parents that are neither biologically nor legally connected to the child.

Fraud: Wrongful or criminal deception intended to result in financial or personal gain.

Fraud in the execution: A type of fraud that involves a misrepresentation about the character or contents of the instrument signed by the testator, which does not in fact carry out the testator's intent. For example: Beth intentionally tells Tomas that he is signing a school permission slip that actually is a will leaving everything to Beth.

Fraud in the inducement: A type of fraud involving a misrepresentation that causes the testator to execute or revoke a will, to refrain from executing or revoking a will, or to include particular provisions in the wrongdoer's favor. For example, Rosario intentionally tells Teresa that her daughter has died, causing Teresa to revise her will to omit the daughter and benefit Rosario.

Fraud on the elective share: When a decedent spouse intentionally attempts to strip the surviving spouse of elective share rights to property by transferring property through nonprobate mechanisms not subject to elective share inclusion.

Generation skipping transfer (GST) tax: A tax enacted as part of the 1986 tax reforms meant to ensure that wealth transfers are taxed at every generation. The exemption to this tax and the use of trusts to maximize it, however, have been considered as main motivators of the creation of dynasty trusts and the competition between states to offer them.

Gift tax return: The form that a donor must fill out and submit if the donor gave gifts during the year totaling more than the annual exclusion amount. The federal gift tax return is Form 709.

Grantor: A term used, particularly in tax, to indicate the settlor of a trust.

Guardian: A person lawfully invested with the power, and charged with the corresponding obligation, to manage the property and rights of a person considered incapable of administering her own affairs.

Guardian of the Person: A person appointed by a court to make personal decisions for a minor child or incapacitated adult, including decisions about day-to-day living arrangements, health care, education, and other matters related to the incapacitated person's comfort and well-being.

Half-blood: Relatives that only share one common ancestor with the deceased, whereas whole-blood relations share two. For example, half brothers or sisters would only share one parent with the deceased whereas whole brothers and sisters would share both parents.

Hamilton order: A court order that a creditor can obtain that requires a trustee to pay the creditor before the beneficiary if and when the trustee makes a distribution.

Health care proxy: A document through which an individual invests an agent with the legal authority to make healthcare decisions on behalf of the individual, when that person is incapable of making and executing the healthcare decisions stipulated in the proxy.

Heir: The person legally entitled to a decedent's property at the decedent's death.

Heir apparent: A person who is first in an order of succession and cannot be displaced from inheriting by the birth of another person. An heir presumptive, by contrast, is someone who is first in line to inherit a title but who can be displaced by the birth of a more eligible heir.

HEMS (Health Education Maintenance and Support): A distribution standard often found in irrevocable trusts. This standard is often referenced in the tax rules.

Holographic wills: Wills that are handwritten and executed without satisfying the legal requirements of a traditional will.

Homestead allowance: An allowance designated for a surviving spouse. The shape and substance of this allowance varies greatly by state.

Homestead exemption: An exemption for surviving spouses, generally designed to allow the surviving spouse to stay in the marital home for some amount of time after the decedent's death.

Hotchpot: The blending of various properties in order to achieve equal division among beneficiaries or heirs. There may be cash, securities, personal belongings, and even real estate which are part of the residue of an estate to be given to "my children, share and share alike." To make such distribution possible, all of the items are put in the hotchpot and then divided after any advancements are accounted for.

Illusory transfer test: A test used by some states to determine whether a transfer was intended to defraud a surviving spouse of elective share rights.

Insane delusion: A legal term of art that indicates the decedent was motivated by a persistent, irrational belief and that belief led the decedent to make a provision in her estate plan that she otherwise would not have made, had it not been for the delusive thinking.

Intestate: The status of dying without a will or other wealth transfer plan.

Intestate succession: Succession that occurs according to state default rules because there is no other plan to distribute the decedent's estate.

Irrevocable trust: A trust that cannot be revoked by the settlor once it is created, although it can potentially be modified under the right conditions. Irrevocable trusts provide continuing management for trust assets.

Issue: A person's lineal descendants, which means all genetic as well as legally adopted descendants of a person. Issue is a narrower category than heirs.

Joint tenancy bank account: An account in which the assets belong jointly to two people. There are two primary types of joint tenancy accounts are those with rights of survivorship (JTROS) and those without rights of survivorship (often called a tenancy-in-common account).

Joint tenancy with right of survivorship (JTROS): A mode of ownership that allows a decedent's share in personal property (such as bank account) or real property to transfer automatically and outside of the probate process to the surviving owner/tenant at the decedent's death.

Joint will: A single will that is signed by two (or more) people, merging their individual wills into a single, combined last will and testament. Joint wills are most commonly used with spouses and they typically provide that all the couple's assets will go to the surviving spouse on the death of the first spouse.

Latent ambiguity: An uncertainty that does not appear on the face of a will but rather arises when extrinsic evidence suggests more than one way of interpretation. The other type of ambiguity is a patent ambiguity.

Letter of wishes: A non-binding writing by the settlor of a trust that sets forth the manner in which the settlor wishes a trustee to exercise discretion and administer trust terms.

Letters testamentary: A document issued by a probate court that gives the executor or administrator the power to act in a fiduciary manner on behalf of the estate.

Life insurance: A contract between an insurance policy holder and an insurer in which the insurer promises to pay a designated beneficiary a sum of money in exchange for a premium, upon the death of an insured person. There are two main kinds of life insurance: term and whole.

Living will: A legal document that sets forth an individual's personal choices about end-of-life medical treatment. It lays out the procedures or medications that the individual wants—or doesn't want—to prolong life when the person in question is unable to make or communicate such preferences. Also sometimes called an advance medical directive.

Mandatory trust: A trust that gives no discretion to the trustee and requires mandatory distributions to be made according to the trust terms. This is the opposite of a discretionary trust.

Marital child: A child that is born to parents who are married at the time of the child's birth.

Marital property: Property that spouses earn or acquire during the life of a marriage, excluding property that is acquired by gift or bequest. Any other property—property earned or acquired outside of marriage—is separate property. Only marital property is divided and distributed upon divorce.

Material-purpose doctrine: Also known as the Claflin doctrine, this doctrine allows a trustee and beneficiaries, acting together, to modify a trust's terms as long as the modifications further the "material purpose."

Merger: When the sole trustee and the sole beneficiary of a trust are the same person. At this point, true separation between the trustee's legal ownership and the beneficiary's equitable ownership ceases to exist and the trust "merges."

Modern portfolio theory (MPT): A theory of modern investing that requires a trustee to look at an investment's risk and return characteristics not by itself but rather as part of a larger portfolio of investments. MPT also requires a trustee to diversify a trust portfolio in order to minimize firm and industry risk.

Multiparty accounts: Accounts registered in the names of more than one person. Multiparty accounts are nonprobate mechanisms that transfer assets between parties. Joint accounts are types of multiparty accounts, as are payable-on-death accounts. Many types of multiparty accounts (such as payable-on-death accounts) specifically include rights of survivorship, but not all do.

Non-marital child: A child that is born to parents who are unmarried.

Non-probate property: Property that passes outside of the probate process, i.e., through a trust, life insurance policy, or joint tenancy account with survivorship rights.

Omitted child or omitted spouse: A child or spouse that is unintentionally omitted from a will and who may take the omitted share, generally equivalent to the intestate share.

Orphans' court: Another name, used in some jurisdictions, for a probate court.

Parentage: The identity and origins of an individual's parents. Parentage must be proved before a child can inherit from a parent through default rules.

Patent ambiguity: An ambiguity that is apparent from the face of a document such as a will, usually arising from inconsistent or uncertain language. Another type of ambiguity is a latent ambiguity.

Payable on death (POD) account: An account that is a nonprobate mechanism that automatically transfers the account's assets to a designated beneficiary upon the death of the account holder. Also called a "Totten trust."

Per capita: A method for distributing a decedent's estate by which all the living members of the identified group will receive an equal share. This approach differs from the English and modern per stirpes approaches. The current UPC and a handful of jurisdictions have adopted a third method of representation, often called "per capita at each generation."

Per stirpes: A method for distributing a decedent's estate among descendants and collaterals in which each living beneficiary in a certain family branch will receive an equal share. There are several types of per stirpes, including English (or strict) and modern. Under English per stirpes, the property is divided into shares at the generational level closest to the decedent, even if everyone at that generational level predeceases the decedent. Using modern per stirpes, the initial division of the decedent's property is made at the generational level closest to the decedent in which there is one or more individuals who survive the decedent.

Permissible appointees or objects of a power of appointment: A person or persons in whose favor a powerholder may exercise a power of appointment.

Personal property allowance: An allowance given to the surviving spouse at a decedent's death, allowing the surviving spouse to claim a certain amount of personal property.

Personal representative: The executor or administrator for the estate of a deceased person. Personal representatives serve as fiduciaries and must execute the decedent's wishes to the fullest extent possible.

Posthumous child: A child born after the death of one parent. Children can be posthumously born or, through artificial reproductive technology, posthumously conceived. Unlike a posthumous child, who is born after a parent's death but conceived while the parent is alive, a posthumously conceived child is both born and conceived after the death of one or both of the child's genetic parents. A posthumously born child is a marital child, and a posthumously conceived child is a nonmarital child.

Pour over trust: A trust into which the decedent's estate "pours over" at death. Also described as a trust funded by a "pour-over" will.

Power of Appointment: A power given by the property owner to another to choose within certain limits prescribed by the property owner who will receive certain property in the future.

Power of Appointment, general: A general power of appointment is a power exercisable in favor of the holder of the power, the power holder's creditors, the power holder's estate, or the creditors of the power holder's estate. Property over which a decedent has a generally exercisable power of appointment at death is included as part of the decedent's gross estate for estate tax purposes.

Power of Appointment, special or limited or nongeneral: A limited power of appointment is a power exercisable in favor only of those individuals of that class of individuals named by the donor of the power. A limited power of appointment is never exercisable in the donee's favor and for this reason property over which a donee has a limited power of appointment is not included in the donee's gross estate for estate tax purposes.

Power of Attorney, durable: A power of attorney that stays in effect even during the incapacity of the person granting the power. Ordinary, or "nondurable," powers of attorney automatically end if the person who makes them loses mental capacity.

Power of Attorney, springing: A power of attorney that "springs" into action once the person granting the power becomes incapacitated.

Premarital (or prenuptial) agreement: An agreement entered into by prospective spouses or a married couple that governs, most commonly, the characterization and distribution of property at the dissolution of a marriage, including at death.

Pretermitted child: A child who is born after the execution of a will and is not provided for by the will. Many states have statutes that provide for a share of estate property to go to pretermitted children if those children can prove that the disinheritance was unintentional.

Private foundation: A nonprofit organization usually created with funding from one primary donor or set of donors (often family members). The foundation's funds and programs are generally managed by its own board of trustees. A private foundation differs from a public charity in the amount of public donations it receives.

Privity defense: A defense against liability when there is no "privity of contract." States retaining the privity defense prohibit a beneficiary of a decedent's will from bringing any claims of negligence or malpractice against the estate planner, who was only in privity with the decedent.

Probate court: A court with jurisdiction over matters of probate and the administration of estates. In some jurisdictions, such courts may be referred to as Orphans' Courts or Surrogate's Courts.

Probate process: The formal legal process that gives recognition to a will and appoints the executor or personal representative who will administer the estate and distribute assets to the intended beneficiaries. The probate process is also available when a decedent dies intestate.

Probate process, common form: Common form probate requires no notification of heirs with respect to the initiation of the probate process. For that reason, the common form probate procedures do not become binding until a longer period has elapsed from the initial filings.

Probate process, solemn form: Solemn form is a variant of the probate process that requires notification to all heirs.

Probate property: Property in a decedent's estate that transfers to beneficiaries through the probate process.

Proponent: The party who submits the potential will to the probate court for the determination of validity.

Purging statute: A purging statute would remove or "purge" the witness of the interest that he or she would otherwise receive under the terms of the purported will. If the interested witness loses his or her interest (that is the testamentary gift), the witness no longer has an interest in the purported will and can thus testify impartially to the events of the will execution.

Putative spouse: An individual who believed that he or she was lawfully married, but for some technical reason the marriage is not valid. In general, a "putative spouse" will still be able to inherit as a surviving spouse, although statutory variations occur.

Qualified beneficiary: A beneficiary who, on the date on which qualification is determined, is or would be a permissible distribute of trust income or trust principal.

Qualified domestic relations order (QDRO): A type of state court domestic relations order that retirement plans must accept if the order is presented to the plan and satisfies various statutory criteria.

Quitclaim deed: A type of deed that conveys whatever title the grantor has, if anything, to offer and does not provide any warranties or deed covenants.

Real estate investment trust (REIT): A specialized type of trust, modeled after a mutual fund, that pools the capital of multiple investors to purchase, operate, or finance income-generating real estate.

Reformation: The modification of the terms of a will or trust to reflect the donor's intent.

Remedial trust: Also called an implied trust, a remedial trust is a legal fiction that is intended to fix a problem or remedy a fraud. A constructive trust and a resulting trust are examples of remedial trusts.

Representation: Refers to the allocation of shares between and among a multi-generational class of heirs or beneficiaries. The three most common methods of representation are strict per stirpes, modern per stirpes, and per capita at each generation.

Republication: Republication occurs when a testator executes a codicil that changes some part of the will and reaffirms the rest of the will's terms.

Res: Also called corpus or trust property, the asset to be managed by the trustee in accordance with the terms of the trust and the trustee's fiduciary duties.

Residue (residuary): A type of testamentary gift that is the portion of the probate estate not otherwise effectively devised by any provisions in the will.

Retirement account: A contract-based will substitute that is created to provide a source of income when the owner of the account retires. The owner of the account has the ability to designate a beneficiary to receive any amounts remaining in the account when the owner dies.

Revocable trust: Also called a living trust or a revocable lifetime trust, a type of trust that is a popular will substitute because the settlor maintains maximum control with the unilateral right to revoke the trust and yet direct the disposition of any trust property upon the settlor's death.

Rule Against Perpetuities (RAP): A durational limitation that requires interests subject to the rule to vest or fail within a certain timeframe called the perpetuities period.

Satisfaction: Also called ademption by satisfaction, satisfaction applies to a gift that a testator makes during life to "satisfy" a testamentary gift.

Self-dealing: A transaction in which the trustee engages on behalf of the trust but that provides a personal benefit for the trustee.

Self-proving affidavit: A notarized statement signed by the testator and all the witnesses in front of a notary public that recites compliance with the wills act formalities. The self-proving affidavit generally gives rise to a presumption of due execution and may be created at any time when the testator and the attesting witnesses are alive.

Self-settled trust: A type of trust in which the settlor is also a trust beneficiary.

Separate property: Ownership of property during the marriage is determined by reference to the property's title. In a separate property state, spouses within an intact marriage have rights only to that which they have earned or assets titled in their name. Upon dissolution of the marriage or upon death, the separate property is divided between the spouses by reference to equitable distribution or the elective share.

Settlor: Also called a grantor, trustor, or donor, a person who creates a trust.

Slayer rule or Slayer statute: An involuntary bar to inheritance that prevents an heir or beneficiary who intentionally and feloniously killed the decedent from inheriting. Today, most states have codified the slayer rule with so-called slayer statutes.

Special needs trust: A specific type of trust that can be created for a beneficiary who is receiving governmental benefits with the trust property providing supplemental assistance without jeopardizing the beneficiary's eligibility to receive those governmental benefits. Also called a supplemental needs trust.

Specific gift: A type of testamentary gift of a specifically described item of property.

Spendthrift clause: A particular provision that may be included in a variety of trusts to prevent a beneficiary from voluntarily pledging, assigning, selling, or alienating a trust interest and to prevent a beneficiary's creditors from involuntarily attaching an interest in the trust.

Spousal share: Also called a forced share or elective share, the share of the decedent's property that the surviving spouse is entitled to receive.

Stale will: A will in which certain provisions are outdated or fail to take into account changes in circumstances between the date of the will's execution and the testator's date of death.

Stepparent exception: Permits a child who is adopted by the spouse of a genetic parent to inherit from and through both genetic parents and from the adoptive parent, who is the child's stepparent.

Supplemental needs trust: A specific type of trust that can be created for a beneficiary who is receiving governmental benefits with the trust property providing supplemental assistance without jeopardizing the beneficiary's eligibility to receive those governmental benefits. Also called a special needs trust.

Surrogate court: The specific name that some jurisdictions use to identify the probate court. The general name is the probate court, but states use names such as Orphans' Courts, Surrogate's Courts, or Chancery Courts.

Survive: The measure of time in which the heir or beneficiary needs to outlive the decedent in order to inherit the property. The UPC, for example, requires an heir to live more than 120 hours after the decedent's death to be considered to survive.

Survivor account: A type of account that functions as a will substitute because the survivor of the account holders is entitled to all of the account proceeds upon the first account holder's death.

Takers in default, power of appointment: The people or entities who take the property if the power of appointment is not exercised.

Tenancy by the entirety: A special type of joint tenancy with right of survivorship with real estate that is held by two spouses. Upon the death of the first spouse, the surviving spouse receives the property by operation of law as the surviving tenant. Note that tenants in common is a form of concurrent ownership that, in contrast to tenancy by the entirety or joint tenancy with right of survivorship, does not pass automatically to the surviving tenant.

Tenancy in common: A shared tenancy of real estate or other assets (such as accounts) in which each holder has a distinct, separately transferable interest.

Testate: When an individual dies with a valid will that disposes of the individual's probate property.

Testator: A person who creates a valid will.

Tortious interference with inheritance: A tort action in which the plaintiff seeks to recover damages from a third party. Although the requirements vary, the plaintiff typically needs to establish the existence of an expectancy, a reasonable certainty that the expectancy would have been realized but for the interference of the third party, and that interference by the third party was intentional.

Transfer on Death (TOD) account: A common form of will substitute similar to a POD account that permits the account holder to designate a beneficiary who will inherit the account proceeds upon the account holder's death. A TOD account is often used to hold securities.

Transfer on Death (TOD) deed: A will substitute, the TOD deed allows for the designation of a beneficiary to inherit the real property upon the owner's death, but unlike a joint tenancy, the beneficiary has no ownership interest in the real property during the owner's life. The owner continues to have the ability to sell the property, change the beneficiary designation, and revoke the deed.

Trust: A legal device where the property owner (called the settlor) creates a fiduciary relationship by giving property to another (called the trustee) to manage for and distribute to another person (called the beneficiary).

Trust income: Income that is generated by the trust corpus.

Trust principal: The trust corpus or res, including any growth in the value.

Trust protector: A party who is granted authority to exercise certain specified powers over the trust and the trustee. Most commonly, the trust protector is given the power to remove and replace trustees as a form of oversight. A trust protector also may have the power to add beneficiaries or terminate a trust.

Trustee: A fiduciary who manages trust property on behalf of another.

Trustor: Also called the settlor, grantor, or donor, a trustor is the creator of a trust.

Undue influence: A ground for a will contest where the contestant asserts that someone exerted so much inappropriate influence over the testator that the resulting will provision or will expressed the influencer's intent and not the testator's.

Uniform Probate Code (UPC): Developed by the National Conference of Commissioners on Uniform State Laws, the UPC has been highly influential in the adoption, update, and modernization of inheritance law.

Uniform Prudent Investor Act (UPIA): Developed by the National Conference of Commissioners on Uniform State Laws, the UPIA has been highly influential in the adoption, update, and modernization of fiduciary law.

Uniform Trust Code (UTC): Developed by the National Conference of Commissioners on Uniform State Laws, the UTC has been highly influential in the adoption, update, and modernization of trust law.

Unmarried cohabitants: Also called nonmarital partners, individuals who reside together but are unmarried. In general, the surviving unmarried cohabitant does not have the same recognized legal status as married individuals or registered domestic partners.

Will: A testamentary instrument that, if properly created, permits the testator to direct the disposition of the testator's probate property and to nominate fiduciaries.

Will substitute: Also called a nonprobate device, a legal instrument that directs the disposition of property upon the death of the property owner. The legal instrument may be a deed, a contract, or a multi-party bank account. Will substitutes perform the functions of wills but are not subject to the wills act formalities.

Witness, interested: An interested witness is an individual who is identified as a beneficiary or nominated to serve as a fiduciary in the terms of the purported will.

Witness, supernumerary: A supernumerary witness is a third (or even fourth!) individual who signed as an attesting witness but is not needed to testify about the will execution.

APPENDIX

Table of Contents:

1. SAMPLE LIVING WILL

The following is Florida's statutory living will, found in Florida Statutes § 765.303

<u>Living Will</u>

Declaration made this ____ day of ____, (year), I, _____, willfully and voluntarily make known my desire that my dying not be artificially prolonged under the circumstances set forth below, and I do hereby declare that, if at any time I am incapacitated and

___(Initial)___ I have a terminal condition,

Or ___(initial)___ I have an end-stage condition,

Or ___(initial)___ I am in a persistent vegetative state

and if my attending or treating physician and another consulting physician have determined that there is no reasonable medical probability of my recovery from such condition, I direct that life-prolonging procedures be withheld or withdrawn when the application of such procedures would serve only to prolong artificially the process of dying, and that I be permitted to die naturally with only the administration of medication or the performance of any medical procedure deemed necessary to provide me with comfort care or to alleviate pain.

It is my intention that this declaration be honored by my family and physician as the final expression of my legal right to refuse medical or surgical treatment and to accept the consequences for such refusal.

In the event that I have been determined to be unable to provide express and informed consent regarding the withholding, withdrawal, or continuation of life-prolonging procedures, I wish to designate, as my surrogate to carry out the provisions of this declaration:

Name: _____

Address: _____   Zip Code: _____

Phone: _____

I understand the full import of this declaration, and I am emotionally and mentally competent to make this declaration.

Additional Instructions (optional):

(Signed) _____

Witness _____ Address _____ Phone _____

Witness _____ Address _____ Phone _____

2. SAMPLE POWER OF ATTORNEY FOR HEALTH CARE DECISIONMAKING

The following is a statutory form health care power of attorney, found in North Carolina General Statutes, § 32A–25.1.

STATE OF NORTH CAROLINA   HEALTH CARE POWER OF
COUNTY OF _____   ATTORNEY

NOTE: YOU SHOULD USE THIS DOCUMENT TO NAME A PERSON AS YOUR HEALTH CARE AGENT IF YOU ARE COMFORTABLE GIVING THAT PERSON BROAD AND SWEEPING POWERS TO MAKE HEALTH CARE DECISIONS FOR YOU. THERE IS NO LEGAL REQUIREMENT THAT ANYONE EXECUTE A HEALTH CARE POWER OF ATTORNEY.

EXPLANATION: You have the right to name someone to make health care decisions for you when you cannot make or communicate those decisions. This form may be used to create a health care power of attorney, and meets the requirements of North Carolina law. However, you are not required to use this form, and North Carolina law allows the use of other forms that meet certain requirements. If you prepare your own health care power of attorney, you should be very careful to make sure it is consistent with North Carolina law.

*This document gives the person you designate as your health care agent **broad powers** to make health care decisions for you when you cannot make the decision yourself or cannot communicate your decision to other people. You should discuss your wishes concerning life-prolonging measures, mental health treatment, and other health care decisions with your health care agent. Except to the extent that you express specific limitations or restrictions in this form, your health care agent may make any health care decision you could make yourself.*

This form does not impose a duty on your health care agent to exercise granted powers, but when a power is exercised, your health care agent will be obligated to use due care to act in your best interests and in accordance with this document.

This Health Care Power of Attorney form is intended to be valid in any jurisdiction in which it is presented, but places outside North Carolina may impose requirements that this form does not meet.

*If you want to use this form, you must complete it, sign it, and have your signature witnessed by two qualified witnesses and proved by a notary public. Follow the instructions about which choices you can initial very carefully. **Do not sign this form until** two witnesses and a notary public are present to watch you sign it. You then should give a copy to your*

> *health care agent and to any alternates you name. You should consider filing it with the Advance Health Care Directive Registry maintained by the North Carolina Secretary of State.* http://www.sosnc.gov.

1. **Designation of Health Care Agent.**

I, _____, being of sound mind, hereby appoint the following person(s) to serve as my health care agent(s) to act for me and in my name (in any way I could act in person) to make health care decisions for me as authorized in this document. My designated health care agent(s) shall serve alone, in the order named.

A. Name: _____ Home Telephone: _____

Home Address: _____ Work Telephone: _____

_____ Cellular Telephone: _____

B. Name: _____ Home Telephone: _____

Home Address: _____ Work Telephone: _____

C. Name: _____ Home Telephone: _____

Home Address: _____ Work Telephone: _____

Any successor health care agent designated shall be vested with the same power and duties as if originally named as my health care agent, and shall serve any time his or her predecessor is not reasonably available or is unwilling or unable to serve in that capacity.

2. **Effectiveness of Appointment.**

My designation of a health care agent expires only when I revoke it. Absent revocation, the authority granted in this document shall become effective when and if one of the physician(s) listed below determines that I lack capacity to make or communicate decisions relating to my health care, and will continue in effect during that incapacity, or until my death, except if I authorize my health care agent to exercise my rights with respect to anatomical gifts, autopsy, or disposition of my remains, this authority will continue after my death to the extent necessary to exercise that authority.

1. _____ *(Physician)*

2. _____ *(Physician)*

If I have not designated a physician, or no physician(s) named above is reasonably available, the determination that I lack capacity to make or communicate decisions relating to my health care shall be made by my attending physician.

3.   Revocation.

Any time while I am competent, I may revoke this power of attorney in a writing I sign or by communicating my intent to revoke, in any clear and consistent manner, to my health care agent or my health care provider.

4.   General Statement of Authority Granted.

Subject to any restrictions set forth in Section 5 below, I grant to my health care agent full power and authority to make and carry out all health care decisions for me. These decisions include, but are not limited to:

A.   Requesting, reviewing, and receiving any information, verbal or written, regarding my physical or mental health, including, but not limited to, medical and hospital records, and to consent to the disclosure of this information.

B.   Employing or discharging my health care providers.

C.   Consenting to and authorizing my admission to and discharge from a hospital, nursing or convalescent home, hospice, long-term care facility, or other health care facility.

D.   Consenting to and authorizing my admission to and retention in a facility for the care or treatment of mental illness.

E.   Consenting to and authorizing the administration of medications for mental health treatment and electroconvulsive treatment (ECT) commonly referred to as "shock treatment."

F.   Giving consent for, withdrawing consent for, or withholding consent for, X-ray, anesthesia, medication, surgery, and all other diagnostic and treatment procedures ordered by or under the authorization of a licensed physician, dentist, podiatrist, or other health care provider. This authorization specifically includes the power to consent to measures for relief of pain.

G.   Authorizing the withholding or withdrawal of life-prolonging measures.

H.   Providing my medical information at the request of any individual acting as my attorney-in-fact under a durable power of attorney or as a Trustee or successor Trustee under any Trust Agreement of which I am a Grantor or Trustee, or at the request of any other individual whom my health care agent believes should have such information. I desire that such information be provided whenever it would expedite the prompt and proper handling of my affairs or the affairs of any person or entity for which I have some responsibility. In addition, I authorize my health care agent to take any and all legal steps necessary to ensure compliance with my instructions providing access to my protected health information. Such steps shall include resorting to any and all legal procedures in and out of courts as may be necessary to enforce my rights under the law and shall include attempting to recover attorneys' fees against anyone who does not comply with this health care power of attorney.

I. To the extent I have not already made valid and enforceable arrangements during my lifetime that have not been revoked, exercising any right I may have to authorize an autopsy or direct the disposition of my remains.

J. Taking any lawful actions that may be necessary to carry out these decisions, including, but not limited to: (i) signing, executing, delivering, and acknowledging any agreement, release, authorization, or other document that may be necessary, desirable, convenient, or proper in order to exercise and carry out any of these powers; (ii) granting releases of liability to medical providers or others; and (iii) incurring reasonable costs on my behalf related to exercising these powers, provided that this health care power of attorney shall not give my health care agent general authority over my property or financial affairs.

5. Special Provisions and Limitations.

(Notice: The authority granted in this document is intended to be as broad as possible so that your health care agent will have authority to make any decisions you could make to obtain or terminate any type of health care treatment or service. If you wish to limit the scope of your health care agent's powers, you may do so in this section. If none of the following are initialed, there will be no special limitations on your agent's authority.)

	A. Limitations about Artificial Nutrition or Hydration: In exercising the authority to make health care decisions on my behalf, my health care agent:
_____ *(Initial)*	Shall NOT have the authority to withhold artificial nutrition (such as through tubes) OR may exercise that authority only in accordance with the following special provisions:
_____ *(Initial)*	Shall NOT have the authority to withhold artificial hydration (such as through tubes) OR may exercise that authority only in accordance with the following special provisions:
	NOTE: If you initial either block but do not insert any special provisions, your health care agent shall have NO AUTHORITY to withhold artificial nutrition or hydration.
_____ *(Initial)*	B. Limitations Concerning Health Care Decisions. In exercising the authority to make health care decisions on my behalf, the authority of my health care agent is subject to the following special provisions: (Here you may include any specific provisions you deem appropriate such as: your own definition of when life-prolonging measures should be withheld or discontinued, or instructions to refuse any specific types of treatment that are inconsistent with your religious beliefs, or are unacceptable to you for any other reason.).
	NOTE: DO NOT initial unless you insert a limitation.
_____ *(Initial)*	C. Limitations Concerning Mental Health Decisions. In exercising the authority to make mental health decisions on my behalf, the authority of my health care agent is subject to the following special provisions: (Here you may include any specific provisions you deem

	appropriate such as: limiting the grant of authority to make only mental health treatment decisions, your own instructions regarding the administration or withholding of psychotropic medications and electroconvulsive treatment (ECT).).
	NOTE: DO NOT initial unless you insert a limitation.
_____ *(Initial)*	D. <u>Advance Instruction for Mental Health Treatment.</u> (Notice: This health care power of attorney may incorporate or be combined with an advance instruction for mental health treatment, executed in accordance with Part 2 of Chapter 122C of the General Statutes, which you may use to state your instructions regarding mental health treatment in the event you lack capacity to make or communicate mental health treatment decisions. Because your health care agent's decisions must be consistent with any statements you have expressed in an advance instruction, you should indicate here whether you have executed an advance instruction for mental health treatment):
	NOTE: DO NOT initial unless you insert a limitation.
_____ *(Initial)*	E. <u>Autopsy and Disposition of Remains</u>. In exercising the authority to make decisions regarding autopsy and disposition of remains on my behalf, the authority of my health care agent is subject to the following special provisions and limitations. (Here you may include any specific provisions you deem appropriate such as: limiting the grant of authority and the scope of authority, or instructions regarding burial or cremation):

	NOTE: DO NOT initial unless you insert a limitation.

6. Organ Donation

To the extent I have not already made valid and enforceable arrangements during my lifetime that have not been revoked, my health care agent may exercise any right I may have to:

_____ *(Initial)*	donate any needed organs or parts; or
_____ *(Initial)*	donate only the following organs or parts: _____
	NOTE: DO NOT INITIAL BOTH BLOCKS ABOVE
_____ *(Initial)*	donate my body for anatomical study if needed
_____ *(Initial)*	In exercising the authority to make donations, my health care agent is subject to the following special provisions and limitations: (Here you may include any specific limitations you deem appropriate such as: limiting the grant of authority and the scope of authority, or instructions regarding gifts of the body or body parts.)
	NOTE: DO NOT initial unless you insert a limitation.

NOTE: NO AUTHORITY FOR ORGAN DONATION IS GRANTED IN THIS INSTRUMENT WITHOUT YOUR INITIALS.

7. Guardianship Provision.

If it becomes necessary for a court to appoint a guardian of my person, I nominate the persons designated in Section 1, in the order named, to be the guardian of my person, to serve without bond or security. The guardian shall act consistently with G.S. 35A–1201(a)(5).

8. Reliance of Third Parties on Health Care Agent.

A. No person who relies in good faith upon the authority of or any representations by my health care agent shall be liable to me, my estate, my heirs, successors, assigns, or personal representatives, for actions or omissions in reliance on that authority or those representations.

B.   The powers conferred on my health care agent by this document may be exercised by my health care agent alone, and my health care agent's signature or action taken under the authority granted in this document may be accepted by persons as fully authorized by me and with the same force and effect as if I were personally present, competent, and acting on my own behalf. All acts performed in good faith by my health care agent pursuant to this power of attorney are done with my consent and shall have the same validity and effect as if I were present and exercised the powers myself, and shall inure to the benefit of and bind me, my estate, my heirs, successors, assigns, and personal representatives. The authority of my health care agent pursuant to this power of attorney shall be superior to and binding upon my family, relatives, friends, and others.

9.   **Miscellaneous Provisions.**

A.   Revocation of Prior Powers of Attorney. I revoke any prior health care power of attorney. The preceding sentence is not intended to revoke any general powers of attorney, some of the provisions of which may relate to health care; however, this power of attorney shall take precedence over any health care provisions in any valid general power of attorney I have not revoked.

B.   Jurisdiction, Severability, and Durability. This Health Care Power of Attorney is intended to be valid in any jurisdiction in which it is presented. The powers delegated under this power of attorney are severable, so that the invalidity of one or more powers shall not affect any others. This power of attorney shall not be affected or revoked by my incapacity or mental incompetence.

C.   Health Care Agent Not Liable. My health care agent and my health care agent's estate, heirs, successors, and assigns are hereby released and forever discharged by me, my estate, my heirs, successors, assigns, and personal representatives from all liability and from all claims or demands of all kinds arising out of my health care agent's acts or omissions, except for my health care agent's willful misconduct or gross negligence.

D.   No Civil or Criminal Liability. No act or omission of my health care agent, or of any other person, entity, institution, or facility acting in good faith in reliance on the authority of my health care agent pursuant to this Health Care Power of Attorney shall be considered suicide, nor the cause of my death for any civil or criminal purposes, nor shall it be considered unprofessional conduct or as lack of professional competence. Any person, entity, institution, or facility against whom criminal or civil liability is asserted because of conduct authorized by this Health Care Power of Attorney may interpose this document as a defense.

E.   Reimbursement. My health care agent shall be entitled to reimbursement for all reasonable expenses incurred as a result of carrying out any provision of this directive.

By signing here, I indicate that I am mentally alert and competent, fully informed as to the contents of this document, and understand the full import of this grant of powers to my health care agent.

This the ____ day of _____, 20____.

_____ (SEAL)

I hereby state that the principal, _____, being of sound mind, signed (or directed another to sign on the principal's behalf) the foregoing health care power of attorney in my presence, and that I am not related to the principal by blood or marriage, and I would not be entitled to any portion of the estate of the principal under any existing will or codicil of the principal or as an heir under the Intestate Succession Act, if the principal died on this date without a will. I also state that I am not the principal's attending physician, nor a licensed health care provider or mental health treatment provider who is (1) an employee of the principal's attending physician or mental health treatment provider, (2) an employee of the health facility in which the principal is a patient, or (3) an employee of a nursing home or any adult care home where the principal resides. I further state that I do not have any claim against the principal or the estate of the principal.

Date: _____   Witness: _____

Date: _____   Witness: _____

_____ COUNTY, _____ STATE

Sworn to (or affirmed) and subscribed before me this day by

_____

(type/print name of signer)

                               _____

                               (type/print name of witness)

                               _____

                               (type/print name of witness)

Date: _____   _____

        (Official Seal)   *Signature of Notary Public*

                            _____, Notary Public

3. SAMPLE DURABLE FINANCIAL POWER OF ATTORNEY

The following is a durable financial power of attorney, found in Alabama Code, § 26–1A–301.

ALABAMA DURABLE POWER OF ATTORNEY FORM

IMPORTANT INFORMATION

This power of attorney authorizes another person (your agent) to make decisions concerning your property for you (the principal). Your agent will be able to make decisions and act with respect to your property (including your money) whether or not you are able to act for yourself. The meaning of authority over subjects listed on this form is explained in the Alabama Uniform Power of Attorney Act, Chapter 1A, Title 26, Code of Alabama 1975.

This power of attorney does not authorize the agent to make health care decisions for you. Such powers are governed by other applicable law.

You should select someone you trust to serve as your agent. Unless you specify otherwise, generally the agent's authority will continue until you die or revoke the power of attorney or the agent resigns or is unable to act for you.

Your agent is entitled to reimbursement of reasonable expenses and reasonable compensation unless you state otherwise in the Special Instructions.

This form provides for designation of one agent. If you wish to name more than one agent you may name a co-agent in the Special Instructions. Co-agents are not required to act together unless you include that requirement in the Special Instructions.

If your agent is unable or unwilling to act for you, your power of attorney will end unless you have named a successor agent. You may also name a second successor agent.

This power of attorney becomes effective immediately unless you state otherwise in the Special Instructions.

If you have questions about the power of attorney or the authority you are granting to your agent, you should seek legal advice before signing this form.

STATE OF ALABAMA)

_____ COUNTY)

Durable Power of Attorney
Of

_____

KNOW ALL MEN BY THESE PRESENTS that I, _____ of _____ in _____ County, Alabama, do hereby make, constitute and appoint _____of _____, in _____ County, Alabama, phone number _____, as my Attorney-in-Fact, for me and in my name, place and stead, and on my behalf, to do, perform and execute the acts I have authorized, and I grant to him/her every power necessary to carry out the purposes for which this power is granted, including the powers of revocation and substitution, hereby ratifying and affirming that which (s)he or his/her substitute shall lawfully do or cause to be done by virtue of the rights and powers herein granted.

This power of attorney shall not be affected by disability, incompetency, or incapacity of the principal.

GRANT OF GENERAL AUTHORITY

I grant my agent and any successor agent general authority to act for me with respect to the following subjects as defined in the Alabama Uniform Power of Attorney Act, Chapter 1A, Title 26, Code of Alabama 1975:

If you wish to grant general authority over all of the subjects enumerated in this section you may SIGN here:

_____

(Signature of Principal)

OR

If you wish to grant specific authority over less than all subjects enumerated in this section you must INITIAL by each subject you want to include in the agent's authority:

____Real Property as defined in Section 26–1A–204

____Tangible Personal Property as defined in Section 26–1A–205

____Stocks and Bonds as defined in Section 26–1A–206

____Commodities and Options as defined in Section 26–1A–207

____Banks and Other Financial Institutions as defined in Section 26–1A–208

____Operation of Entity or Business as defined in Section 26–1A–209

____Insurance and Annuities as defined in Section 26–1A–210

____Estates, Trusts, and Other Beneficial Interests as defined in Section 26–1A–211

____Claims and Litigation as defined in Section 26–1A–212

____Personal and Family Maintenance as defined in Section 26–1A–213

____Benefits from Governmental Programs or Civil or Military Service as defined in Section 26–1A–214

____Retirement Plans as defined in Section 26–1A–215

____Taxes as defined in Section 26–1A–216

____Gifts as defined in Section 26–1A–217

GRANT OF SPECIFIC AUTHORITY (OPTIONAL)

My agent MAY NOT do any of the following specific acts for me UNLESS I have INITIALED the specific authority listed below:

(CAUTION: Granting any of the following will give your agent the authority to take actions that could significantly reduce your property or change how your property is distributed at your death. INITIAL the specific authority you WANT to give your agent.)

____Create, amend, revoke, or terminate an *inter vivos* trust, by trust or applicable law

____Make a gift to which exceeds the monetary limitations of Section 26–1A–217 of the Alabama Uniform Power of Attorney Act, but subject to any special instructions in this power of attorney

____Create or change rights of survivorship

____Create or change a beneficiary designation

____Authorize another person to exercise the authority granted under this power of attorney

____Waive the principal's right to be a beneficiary of a joint and survivor annuity, including a survivor benefit under a retirement plan

____Exercise fiduciary powers that the principal has authority to delegate

LIMITATIONS ON AGENT'S AUTHORITY

An agent that is not my ancestor, spouse, or descendant MAY NOT use my property to benefit the agent or a person to whom the agent owes an obligation of support unless I have included that authority in the Special Instructions.

Limitation of Power. Except for any special instructions given herein to the agent to make gifts, the following shall apply:

(a)   Any power or authority granted to my Agent herein shall be limited so as to prevent this Power of Attorney from causing any Agent to be taxed on my income or from causing my assets to be subject to a "general power of appointment" by my Agent as defined in 26 U.S.C. § 2041 and 26 U.S.C. § 2514 of the Internal Revenue Code of 1986, as amended.

(b)   My Agent shall have no power or authority whatsoever with respect to any policy of insurance owned by me on the life of my Agent, or any trust created by my Agent as to which I am a trustee.

SPECIAL INSTRUCTIONS (OPTIONAL)

You may give special instructions on the following lines. For your protection, if there are no special instructions write NONE in this section.

NOMINATION OF [CONSERVATOR OR GUARDIAN] (OPTIONAL)

If it becomes necessary for a court to appoint a [conservator or guardian] of my estate or [guardian] of my person, I nominate the following person(s) for appointment:

Name of Nominee for [conservator or guardian] of my estate:

_____

Nominee's Address: _____

Nominee's Telephone Number: _____

Name of Nominee for [guardian] of my person: _____

Nominee's Address: _____

Nominee's Telephone Number: _____

EFFECTIVE DATE

This power of attorney is effective immediately unless I have stated otherwise in the Special Instructions.

RELIANCE ON THIS POWER OF ATTORNEY

Any person, including my agent, may rely upon the validity of this power of attorney or a copy of it unless that person knows it has terminated or is invalid.

SIGNATURE AND ACKNOWLEDGMENT

_____

(Signature of Principal)

Your Signature Date: _____

Your Name Printed: _____

Your Address: _____

Your Telephone Number: _____

STATE OF ALABAMA

_____ COUNTY

I, _____, a Notary Public, in and for the County in this State, hereby certify that _____, whose name is signed to the foregoing document, and who is known to me, acknowledged before me on this day that, being informed of the contents of the document, he or she executed the same voluntarily on the day the same bears date.

Given under my hand this the ____ day of ____, 20____.

_____ (Seal, if any)

Signature of Notary

My commission expires: _____

IMPORTANT INFORMATION FOR AGENT

Agent's Duties

When you accept the authority granted under this power of attorney, a special legal relationship is created between you and the principal. This relationship imposes upon you legal duties that continue until you resign or the power of attorney is terminated or revoked. You must:

(1) do what you know the principal reasonably expects you to do with the principal's property or, if you do not know the principal's expectations, act in the principal's best interest;

(2) act in good faith;

(3) do nothing beyond the authority granted in this power of attorney; and

(4) disclose your identity as an agent whenever you act for the principal by writing or printing the name of the principal and signing your own name as "agent" in the following manner:

(Principal's Name) by (Your Signature) as Agent

Unless the Special Instructions in this power of attorney state otherwise, you must also:

(1) act loyally for the principal's benefit;

(2) avoid conflicts that would impair your ability to act in the principal's best interest;

(3) act with care, competence, and diligence;

(4) keep a record of all receipts, disbursements, and transactions made on behalf of the principal;

(5) cooperate with any person that has authority to make health care decisions for the principal to do what you know the principal reasonably expects or, if you do not know the principal's expectations, to act in the principal's best interest; and

(6) attempt to preserve the principal's estate plan if you know the plan and preserving the plan is consistent with the principal's best interest.

Termination of Agent's Authority

You must stop acting on behalf of the principal if you learn of any event that terminates this power of attorney or your authority under this power of attorney. Events that terminate a power of attorney or your authority to act under a power of attorney include:

(1) death of the principal;

(2) the principal's revocation of the power of attorney or your authority;

(3) the occurrence of a termination event stated in the power of attorney;

(4) the purpose of the power of attorney is fully accomplished; or

(5) if you are married to the principal, a legal action is filed with a court to end your marriage, or for your legal separation, unless the Special Instructions in this power of attorney state that such an action will not terminate your authority.

Liability of Agent

The meaning of the authority granted to you is defined in the Alabama Uniform Power of Attorney Act, Chapter 1A, Title 26, Code of Alabama 1975. If you violate the Alabama Uniform Power of Attorney Act, Chapter 1A, Title 26, Code of Alabama 1975, or act outside the authority granted, you may be liable for any damages caused by your violation.

If there is anything about this document or your duties that you do not understand, you should seek legal advice.

4. ACTEC GENERAL CLIENT CHECKLIST[1]

1. ISSUES A LAWYER SHOULD CONSIDER BEFORE ACCEPTING THE REPRESENTATION

a. Is there any previous or existing client or advisory relationship between/among the lawyer (or his or her firm) and any of the parties, their families or their business or domestic partners? If so, does the lawyer have a conflict in representing any of the parties?

b. If the lawyer (or the lawyer's firm) has represented any of the parties, their families or their business or domestic partners, in what capacity (e.g., individually, as an officer director or manager of an organization, or as a fiduciary or beneficiary of an estate or trust)? What connections do the parties have with each other (e.g., familial, business or personal relationships, fiduciaries or beneficiaries of an estate or trust)?

c. How well does the lawyer know the parties?

d. Are the parties U.S. citizens? Are the parties U.S. residents? What are the domiciles of the parties? If any entity is involved, is the entity duly organized and in good standing in all appropriate jurisdictions? In which jurisdiction or jurisdictions will the entity be organized or authorized to do business? If a trust or estate is involved, in what jurisdiction is it being or will it be administered?

e. Under guidelines issued by the Financial Action Task Force on Money Laundering, before agreeing to represent a person or entity, the best practice consists of:

    1. Confirming the prospective client's identity by examining a government issued identification containing his or her photograph.

    2. Identifying the persons managing and the persons having beneficial interests in business entities and trusts.

    3. Making sure the client's circumstances and businesses are understood.

    4. At a minimum, doing an internet search for suspicious circumstances or activities in which the prospective client is or may be involved. The Task Force also recommends checking the website for the Treasury Department's Office of Foreign Assets

---

[1] Available at http://www.actec.org/assets/1/6/ACTEC_2017_Engagement_Letters.pdf.

Control to see if the prospective client's name appears on its list of with whom U.S. persons are prohibited from dealing.

f.   Do all parties appear to have adequate capacity to enter into the engagement?

g.   What other professionals are involved (e.g., accountants, appraisers, brokers, financial advisors)? Are they known to be competent? What referral relationships exist?

h.   Are the expectations of the parties as to the outcome and timing of the lawyer's work reasonable and obtainable? Do the parties have a common goal and agree on the way to go about achieving it?

i.   What are the fee arrangements?

2. DEFINE THE SCOPE OF THE REPRESENTATION.

a.   Describe with appropriate specificity the objectives of the representation and the means by which those objectives are to be pursued. Define the scope as narrowly as possible (to avoid having clients expect more than you can deliver or that it is cost effective to deliver).

b.   Make it clear that the lawyer (or the firm) will not be obligated to provide services beyond the scope of the engagement described in the original letter absent an updated or separate engagement letter by which the lawyer (or the firm) agrees to render other services.

c.   Describe the nature and consequences of any limitations on the scope of the representation, and obtain the clients' consent to those limitations. For example, if the laws of another jurisdiction come into play in the legal services to be performed and the lawyer is not licensed to practice in that jurisdiction, point out to the client that he or she may have to retain legal counsel in that jurisdiction. Similarly, if due to the nature of estate or trust assets (e.g., intellectual property) or a client's personal circumstances (e.g., a child custody dispute) the lawyer or firm lacks the expertise to attend to all of the client's legal needs, consider pointing out what issues must be addressed by lawyers of different disciplines.

d.   What do the parties expect the "style" of the representation to be (e.g., separate meetings with each party or some parties or are meetings to be attended by all interested parties)? Is one party to be placed in charge of making certain types of decisions?

e. Consider describing the time frame within which the various phases of the engagement will be completed and mentioning any foreseeable delays or periods during which the lawyer may not be available during the engagement. Also consider identifying other attorneys, legal assistants, and support personnel in the lawyer's office who may or should be consulted in the event of the lawyer's absence or unavailability.

f. Describe the extent to which the lawyer will rely upon information furnished by the parties and the extent, if any, to which the lawyer will attempt to verify this information. Describe the circumstances under which the lawyer may be required to verify some or all of the information furnished by the parties in order to comply with the applicable standards of practice (e.g., Circular 230).

3. IDENTIFY THE CLIENT OR CLIENTS.

a. If a prospective client is married, will the lawyer (or firm) represent one spouse or both spouses?

b. If two or more prospective clients are related (personally or professionally) but not married, will the lawyer (or firm) represent one, some or all of the parties affected by the subject matter of the engagement?

c. Are there any doubts about a prospective client's capacity? If so, how will they be resolved? If the doubts cannot be resolved, will the lawyer (or firm) represent the prospective client's legal representative instead?

d. Identify all clients. See the ACTEC Commentaries on Model Rule 1.7 as to who can sign on behalf of an entity (someone other than the represented principal). Consider having the clients represent that their interests are not adversarial.

e. Consider describing how the diminished capacity or death of a client will affect the representation, including those persons who may be given copies of an estate planning client's documents.

4. EXPLAIN THE LAWYER'S DUTY TO AVOID CONFLICTS OF INTEREST AND HOW POTENTIAL OR ACTUAL CONFLICTS OF INTEREST WILL BE RESOLVED.

a. Describe the effect and consequences of any simultaneous representation of multiple clients, including potential conflicts of interest. Note that some jurisdictions may require the lawyer to give examples of conflicts of interest that can arise under the circumstances.

b. Describe how an actual conflict of interest will be resolved, the fact that the firm may have to withdraw from representing some or all parties if an actual conflict arises and the adverse consequences that may result from the firm's withdrawal. (If the lawyer plans to continue to represent some but not all parties if an actual conflict arises, presumably this is because the lawyer has a pre-existing, long-standing relationship with the party or parties whom the lawyer will continue to represent.)

c. Obtain the informed consent of all clients to the specific type of a simultaneous representation of multiple clients (joint or separate). Confirm in the engagement letter that the lawyer discussed the implications of joint versus separate representation with the clients.

d. If appropriate, describe how a prior representation may give rise to a conflict of interest. (See Model Rule of Professional Conduct 1.8 concerning conflicts of interest among current clients and Model Rule 1.9 concerning duties to former clients.)

e. Consider requesting authorization from all of the clients to disclose to all interested parties the actions of any one of the clients constituting fraud, a breach of trust, a violation of the governing documents of any entity involved, or in contravention of a mutual estate plan (if permitted in the jurisdiction in which you practice).

f. If appropriate, describe the possible conflict of interest if the lawyer is to receive an interest in any business as a part of the lawyer's fee.

g. Consider whether each party should be advised to consult independent counsel before consenting to the joint representation.

5. **EXPLAIN THE LAWYER'S DUTY OF CONFIDENTIALITY AND HOW CONFIDENTIAL INFORMATION WILL BE HANDLED.**

a. Describe the lawyer's duty of confidentiality and whether and to what extent confidential information will be shared with the various clients. Obtain the clients' consent to the sharing of information (or refusal to share) in this manner.

b. Describe how electronic communications and the inclusion of non-clients in meetings can compromise confidentiality and the attorney-client privilege.

c. Consider describing how the diminished capacity or death of a client will affect the disclosure of confidential information.

6. **EXPLAIN THE FEE OR THE BASIS FOR THE DETERMINATION OF THE FEE AND THE BILLING ARRANGEMENTS [INCLUDING THE MATERIAL REQUIRED UNDER RULE 1.5 (b)].**

a. If a contingent fee is involved, obtain the client's consent in writing. (Check local rules to determine the extent to which other types of engagements must be agreed to in writing.)

b. Describe factors that might cause the fee to be different from any estimate and how and when changes in standard billing rates may affect the fee.

c. If appropriate, describe how the fee will be shared with other lawyers outside the firm.

d. If someone other than the client will pay the lawyer's fees, then in keeping with Model Rule of Professional Conduct 1.8(f): (i) Make sure that the client gives his or her informed consent to the arrangement; and (ii) consider having the person paying the fees acknowledge in writing that all communications with the client are strictly confidential and that he or she may in no way interfere with the lawyer's relationship with his or her client or with the lawyer's independent professional judgment.

e. Describe who is responsible for paying the lawyer's fees and expenses. If the representation involves multiple clients, describe the extent to which each client is or may be liable for the lawyer's fees and expenses and whether the liability of multiple clients is to be individual or joint and several.

f. Describe the lawyer's billing and collection policies.

g. Verify the client's billing address and contact information.

h. Consider whether you want to ask clients to agree to arbitrate or mediate any fee dispute. (Check local rules on the enforceability of an agreement of this kind.)

7. **FIRM POLICIES OF WHICH CLIENTS SHOULD BE MADE AWARE.**

    a. Retention, destruction and sharing of clients' files and original documents. (Check local rules about the transfer of files on a lawyer's retirement or death.)

    b. Some jurisdictions may require a lawyer who does not carry professional liability insurance to reveal the lack of coverage to clients.

8. **TERMINATION OF THE REPRESENTATION**

    a. Describe the events, dates, or circumstances that will terminate the representation.

    b. Describe the difference between mandatory and permissive withdrawal and any prior Court approval that may be needed before the lawyer (or firm) may cease representing the client(s).

    c. If the representation involves multiple clients, consider describing what information, if any, the lawyer will give to the clients if the lawyer is required to withdraw from the representation.

    d. Describe what will happen when the lawyer withdraws and to whom the records will be sent.

9. **RECOMMENDED PROCEDURES.**

    a. Send an engagement letter to all of the prospective clients prior to the first meeting or telephone conference or immediately following it.

    b. Review the more important terms of the engagement letter with the client.

    c. Require that all clients sign the engagement letter or agreement or otherwise acknowledge the terms of any multiple representation.

Supplemental Checklist for Representation of Spouses

1. **ISSUES THE LAWYER SHOULD CONSIDER BEFORE ACCEPTING THE REPRESENTATION**

    a. Determine what duties, if any, the spouses owe to each other, and how these duties would affect the lawyer's representation and ability to carry out instructions such as those contained in existing pre- or post-marital agreements, contracts to make wills, and rights under pension plans.

b. Determine the obligations of either spouse to third parties (such as child, spousal or parental support) arising, for example, under an agreement, divorce decree, or compensation or retirement plans.

c. Determine what conflicts of interest exist, or may exist, between the two spouses and how they would affect the representation (e.g., knowledge the lawyer has that the plan of one spouse might defeat the plan or adversely affect the interests of the other, that possible future actions by one spouse might defeat the plan or adversely affect the interests of the other, or that a spouse's expectations or understanding of the facts relating to the other spouse or such spouse's intentions are not correct).

2. IDENTIFY THE CLIENT.

a. Will the lawyer represent one spouse or both spouses?

b. If and when an actual conflict of interest arises, it is imperative that another letter be sent to the clients informing them that an actual conflict has arisen which requires the lawyer to withdraw from the representation of either or both of them and indicating who the lawyer will represent going forward (if anyone).

3. EXPLAIN HOW POTENTIAL OR ACTUAL CONFLICTS OF INTEREST WILL BE RESOLVED.

a. If a joint representation fails, the lawyer should address which, if either, of the clients the lawyer may continue to represent in the matter at hand or in related matters. (If the lawyer will continue to represent one spouse, presumably that is due to a long-standing relationship the lawyer had with one of the clients before the lawyer agreed to represent the other spouse.) In the alternative, will the lawyer withdraw from representing either spouse in the matter at hand or in related matters? Describe the possibility of a future prohibition on the lawyer's representation of either one of the spouses in the matter at hand or in related matters.

5.   ACTEC SAMPLE ENGAGEMENT LETTER[2]

Form of an Engagement Letter for the Representation of Both Spouses Jointly in Estate Planning Matters

[*DATE*]

[*NAME(S) and ADDRESS*]

Subject: Representation of Both of You in Estate Planning Matters

Dear [*CLIENTS*]:

Thank you for asking our firm, [*NAME OF FIRM*], to represent you in your estate planning affairs. This will confirm the terms of our agreement to represent you.

<u>Scope of the Engagement</u>. The legal services to be rendered consist of the following: [*DESCRIBE SERVICES TO BE RENDERED*].

<u>Fees for Legal Services and Costs</u>. We will bill for our legal services and costs in the following manner: [*DESCRIBE ARRANGEMENTS PERTAINING TO FEES, COSTS, RETAINERS, BILLING, ETC.*].

[*OPTION—for use in jurisdictions allowing drafting attorneys to be paid their hourly rates for testimony in a Will or Trust Contest.*]

You agree that if a member of or person rendering services to our firm is deposed, called to testify or required to respond to discovery in the context of legal proceedings concerning any aspect of your estate plan, we will be compensated for that person's services at his or her hourly rate to clients at the time of the deposition, other testimony or other discovery. You also agree that we will be entitled to full reimbursement for costs incurred in connection with the production of documents in response to subpoenas and demands for the production of documents issued in any such legal proceedings. This agreement will bind not only you but also anyone managing your financial affairs (before and after your death), your heirs and the beneficiaries under your estate planning documents.

<u>Waiver of Potential Conflicts of Interest</u>. It is common for spouses to employ the same law firm to assist them in planning their estates, as you have requested us to do. Please understand that, because we will represent the two of you jointly, it would be unethical for us to withhold information from either of you that is relevant and material to the subject matter of the engagement. Accordingly, by agreeing to this form of representation, each of you authorizes us to disclose to

---

2   Available at http://www.actec.org/assets/1/6/ACTEC_2017_Engagement_Letters.pdf.

the other information that one of you shares with us or that we acquire from another source which, in our judgment, falls into this category.

We will not take any action or refrain from taking an action (pertaining to the subject matter of our representation of you) that affects one of you without the other's knowledge and consent. Of course, anything either of you discusses with us is privileged from disclosure to third parties, unless you authorize us to disclose the information or disclosure is required or permitted by law or the rules governing our professional conduct.

If a conflict of interest arises between you during the course of your planning or if the two of you have a difference of opinion on any subject, we can point out the pros and cons of your respective positions. However, we cannot advocate one of your positions over the other. Furthermore, we cannot advocate one of your positions over the other if there is a disagreement as to your respective property rights or interests or as to other legal issues. [*NOTE THAT IN SOME JURISDICTIONS, IT MAY BE NECESSARY TO PROVIDE EXAMPLES OF POTENTIAL CONFLICTS.*] By signing this letter, you waive potential conflicts of interest that can arise by virtue of the fact that we represent the two of you together.

[*Pick OPTION 1 or OPTION 2*]

[*Option 1: If an actual conflict arises, lawyer withdraws from representation of either spouse*]

If an actual conflict of interest arises between you that, in our judgment, makes it impossible for us to live up to our ethical obligations to both of you, we will withdraw as your joint attorney and advise each of you to seek other legal counsel.

[*Option 2: If an actual conflict arises, lawyer will continue to represent one spouse but not the other*]

If an actual conflict of interest arises between you that, in our judgment, makes it impossible for us to live up to our ethical obligations to both of you, we will seek to continue to represent [*NAME OF SPOUSE LAWYER WILL CONTINUE TO REPRESENT*], to the extent that we determine that we may appropriately do so, and withdraw as [*NAME OF SPOUSE LAWYER WILL NO LONGER REPRESENT*]'s legal counsel. Your signature below constitutes your consent to our continued future representation of [*NAME OF SPOUSE LAWYER WILL CONTINUE TO REPRESENT*] and each of you agrees not to seek to disqualify us from representing [*HIM/HER*] in the future. Notwithstanding this agreement, we may be required to withdraw or be disqualified from representing [*NAME OF SPOUSE FIRM WISHES TO CONTINUE TO REPRESENT*] after an actual conflict arises.

[OPTION if firm may represent charitable beneficiary or fiduciaries]

Kindly note that we represent several charitable organizations. You may decide to name one or more of these organizations to receive a gift or bequest. We also represent banks and trust companies which serve as professional executors and trustees, as well as lawyers, accountants, business managers and other professional advisors. You may decide to name one or more of these companies or individuals as an Executor or Trustee and may excuse them from being sued for their actions as Trustees or Executors (to the extent permitted by law). In addition, the estate planning documents we prepare for you may allow a professional advisor who serves as an Executor or Trustee to be paid for services rendered in that capacity, in addition to his or her professional services. By signing this letter, you waive any conflict of interest which may arise from these circumstances.

Attorney-Client Communications. Generally, communications made via fax, computer transmission or cellular phone are not as secure from inadvertent disclosure to others as other forms of communication. You acknowledge that by furnishing us with an e-mail address or cell phone or fax number, you authorize us to communicate with you using this mode of communication notwithstanding the inherent confidentiality risks.

With few exceptions under the law, communications among us are protected by the attorney—client privilege. However, if someone else whom we do not represent (such as a family member of yours or financial planner) is included in a meeting or phone call or is copied on correspondence, then the attorney-client privilege may be lost as to things disclosed in that meeting or correspondence. Similarly, if you choose to communicate with us or authorize us to communicate with you using an e-mail address or fax machine to which others have access, the attorney-client privilege may be lost as well. As a result, you or the third party may be forced to disclose the content of a communication in a Court of law or otherwise in the context of litigation. Please keep this in mind when asking us to share information with third parties or when you share information with (or grant access to) others who are not part of our attorney-client relationship.

[OPTION: Firm's Policies on File Storage and Safekeeping of Original Documents. Make sure the definition of "client files" is consistent with local rules.]

Our Policies Concerning Client Files and Original Documents. You agree that we have the right to destroy the client file we create for you *[NUMBER]* years after we cease to actively represent you (i.e., after we last perform legal services for you). Your "client file" consists of all paper and electronic copies of your signed estate planning documents, drafts of any estate planning documents prepared for you which have not yet been signed, documents sent to us by you or third parties (such as recorded deeds, beneficiary designations and business and property agreements), correspondence and other written communications between us and others that pertain to your estate plan. You agree that all other materials pertinent to your estate plan (such as our notes and internal memoranda) are proprietary to us and not part of your client file.

Before destroying your client file, we will attempt to contact you to make arrangements for its delivery to you. If we are unable to contact you at the most recent address contained in our file, subject to applicable law, we may destroy your file without further notice. It will be your responsibility to notify us of any change in your address and other contact information.

[*Pick OPTION 1 or OPTION 2*]

[*Option 1: Firm does not hold clients' original documents*]

We do not hold original estate planning documents for clients. Therefore, you will have to make arrangements to safeguard your own original documents. If you leave original documents with us, we cannot find you, and it has been more than [*NUMBER*] years since our last contact with you, then we have the right to destroy those documents.

[*Option 2: Firm will hold clients' original documents. Be sure to consult applicable state law about firm's safekeeping responsibilities and modify option 2 accordingly.*]

At your request, we will retain your original estate planning documents other than documents associated with your health care. It is important that you place original documents pertaining to your health care in a safe place that is accessible by your health care agents twenty-four hours a day, seven days a week. Original documents retained by us may be requested by you during normal business hours. Kindly request documents at least [NUMBER] days before they are needed.

If you die or someone claims that you are no longer competent and we receive a request for an original document of yours, the document will be released only to the person legally entitled to it in our sole discretion. We reserve the right to petition the Court to determine the person legally entitled to the document. It will be your responsibility to inform the trustees, executors and agents named in your estate planning documents that we hold your original estate planning documents and to instruct them to notify us immediately of your death or inability to continue to manage your financial affairs. We can assume no responsibility for keeping abreast of changes in your personal circumstances.

Following the conclusion (or termination) of our representation of you, if one or both of you request your client file or any original documents in our possession and you are unable to agree on which of you is entitled to these things, we may petition the Court to make that determination. If you agree that your client file or any such original documents will be sent to one of you (or that party's legal counsel) and copies will be sent to the other (or the other's legal counsel), then you agree to reimburse us for the reasonable costs of preparing those copies and delivering them.

No Guarantee of Favorable Outcomes. Although your estate plan may be designed to achieve certain goals such as tax savings or the avoidance of conservatorship or probate proceedings, these and other favorable outcomes cannot be guaranteed. This is because favorable outcomes depend on a variety of factors (such as your diligence in keeping assets titled in the name of the Trustee of a particular trust, the proper management of a trust and changes in the law).

In connection with planning your estate, we will make certain recommendations that it will be up to you to implement (for example, changing beneficiary designations or transferring assets to a trust that may be created as part of your estate plan). Once the recommendations have been made, it is understood and agreed that we will have no responsibility to make sure that you follow our advice.

Conclusion of Representation. Once the following documents are executed, the engagement of this firm will be concluded: [*LIST DOCUMENTS TO BE PREPARED.*] We will be happy to provide additional or continuing legal services. But unless arrangements for such services are made and agreed upon in writing, we will have no further responsibility to either of you with respect to future or ongoing legal issues, nor will we have any duty to notify you of changes in the law or upcoming filing or other deadlines.

[*OPTION for Voluntary Termination*]

You may terminate our representation of you at any time by providing us with written notice of the termination. Upon our receipt of this notice, we will promptly cease providing services to you. Similarly, we may terminate our representation of you at any time by providing you with written notices of the termination. Upon your receipt of this notice, we will promptly cease providing services. However, whether you terminate or we terminate the representation, if we represent you in Court proceedings and prior Court approval is needed in order for us to cease rendering legal services, we will continue to render legal services to you until such time as the Court determines that we may cease rendering services. You will pay for our services rendered to you and costs incurred on your behalf until the cessation of legal services and for any services we must render and costs we must incur thereafter to transfer responsibility for legal affairs we handle to your new counsel.

If you consent to our representation of both of you on these terms, please sign and return the enclosed copy of this letter. If you have any questions about this letter, please let me know. Feel free to consult another lawyer about this letter before signing it.

Sincerely,

[NAME OF ATTORNEY IN CHARGE]

CONSENT

Each of us has read this letter and understands its contents. We consent to *[NAME OF FIRM]*'s representation of both of us on the terms and conditions set forth in it.

Signed:_____, 20____   _____
                                                      (Client 1)

Signed:_____, 20____   _____
                                                      (Client 2)

6. MODEL RULES OF PROFESSIONAL CONDUCT OF SPECIAL RELEVANCE TO INHERITANCE REPRESENTATIONS

Rule 1.2 Scope of Representation and Allocation of Authority Between Client and Lawyer

(a) Subject to paragraphs (c) and (d), a lawyer shall abide by a client's decisions concerning the objectives of representation and, as required by Rule 1.4, shall consult with the client as to the means by which they are to be pursued. A lawyer may take such action on behalf of the client as is impliedly authorized to carry out the representation. A lawyer shall abide by a client's decision whether to settle a matter. In a criminal case, the lawyer shall abide by the client's decision, after consultation with the lawyer, as to a plea to be entered, whether to waive jury trial and whether the client will testify.

(b) A lawyer's representation of a client, including representation by appointment, does not constitute an endorsement of the client's political, economic, social or moral views or activities.

(c) A lawyer may limit the scope of the representation if the limitation is reasonable under the circumstances and the client gives informed consent.

(d) A lawyer shall not counsel a client to engage, or assist a client, in conduct that the lawyer knows is criminal or fraudulent, but a lawyer may discuss the legal consequences of any proposed course of conduct with a client and may counsel or assist a client to make a good faith effort to determine the validity, scope, meaning or application of the law.

Rule 1.4 Communication

(a) A lawyer shall:

(1) promptly inform the client of any decision or circumstance with respect to which the client's informed consent, as defined in Rule 1.0(e), is required by these Rules;

(2) reasonably consult with the client about the means by which the client's objectives are to be accomplished;

(3) keep the client reasonably informed about the status of the matter;

(4) promptly comply with reasonable requests for information; and

(5)   consult with the client about any relevant limitation on the lawyer's conduct when the lawyer knows that the client expects assistance not permitted by the Rules of Professional Conduct or other law.

(b)   A lawyer shall explain a matter to the extent reasonably necessary to permit the client to make informed decisions regarding the representation.

Rule 1.6 Confidentiality of Information

(a)   A lawyer shall not reveal information relating to the representation of a client unless the client gives informed consent, the disclosure is impliedly authorized in order to carry out the representation or the disclosure is permitted by paragraph (b).

(b)   A lawyer may reveal information relating to the representation of a client to the extent the lawyer reasonably believes necessary:

(1)   to prevent reasonably certain death or substantial bodily harm;

(2)   to prevent the client from committing a crime or fraud that is reasonably certain to result in substantial injury to the financial interests or property of another and in furtherance of which the client has used or is using the lawyer's services;

(3)   to prevent, mitigate or rectify substantial injury to the financial interests or property of another that is reasonably certain to result or has resulted from the client's commission of a crime or fraud in furtherance of which the client has used the lawyer's services;

(4)   to secure legal advice about the lawyer's compliance with these Rules;

(5)   to establish a claim or defense on behalf of the lawyer in a controversy between the lawyer and the client, to establish a defense to a criminal charge or civil claim against the lawyer based upon conduct in which the client was involved, or to respond to allegations in any proceeding concerning the lawyer's representation of the client;

(6)   to comply with other law or a court order; or

(7)   to detect and resolve conflicts of interest arising from the lawyer's change of employment or from changes in the composition or ownership of a firm, but only if the revealed information would not compromise the attorney-client privilege or otherwise prejudice the client.

(c)   A lawyer shall make reasonable efforts to prevent the inadvertent or unauthorized disclosure of, or unauthorized access to, information relating to the representation of a client.

Rule 1.7 Conflict of Interest: Current Clients

(a)   Except as provided in paragraph (b), a lawyer shall not represent a client if the representation involves a concurrent conflict of interest. A concurrent conflict of interest exists if:

(1)   the representation of one client will be directly adverse to another client; or

(2)   there is a significant risk that the representation of one or more clients will be materially limited by the lawyer's responsibilities to another client, a former client or a third person or by a personal interest of the lawyer.

(b)   Notwithstanding the existence of a concurrent conflict of interest under paragraph (a), a lawyer may represent a client if:

(1)   the lawyer reasonably believes that the lawyer will be able to provide competent and diligent representation to each affected client;

(2)   the representation is not prohibited by law;

(3)   the representation does not involve the assertion of a claim by one client against another client represented by the lawyer in the same litigation or other proceeding before a tribunal; and

(4)   each affected client gives informed consent, confirmed in writing.

7.   SAMPLE ESTATE PLANNING CLIENT INTAKE QUESTIONNAIRE

Estate Planning Questionnaire

Date _____

Spouse 1 Name _____ Date of Birth _____

Social Security No. _____ Citizenship _____

Spouse 1 Employer _____ Business Tel. No. _____

Business Address _____ E-mail _____

Spouse 2 Name _____ Date of Birth _____

Social Security No. _____ Citizenship _____

Spouse 2 Employer _____ Business Tel. No. _____

Business Address _____ E-mail _____

Home Address _____

Home Tel. No. _____ Date of Marriage _____

Children *(please indicate if adopted or born through artificial reproductive technology):*

Name	Date of Birth	Social Security Number

Parents and Grandchildren *(if living):*

Name	Date of Birth

Special Family Considerations: *(Prior marriages; support obligations beyond immediate family; health problems, etc.)*

Proposed Fiduciaries:

Position	Name	Relationship
Executor(s)		
Health Care Agent(s)		
Financial Agent(s)		
Trustee(s)		

ASSET SUMMARY (Approximate Values)

	Assets in Name of Spouse 1	Assets in Name of Both Spouses	Assets in Name of Spouse 2
Cash, Checking Accounts, Savings Accounts			

Tangible Personal Property			
Residential Real Property Location and Value (Indicate how title is held)			
Investment Real Property— Location and Value			
Securities			
Business Interests (Describe generally; estimate values)			
SUBTOTAL			
Plus (from following pages) Life Insurance Retirement Plans Other Property			
TOTAL			

LIABILITIES

	Owed by Spouse 1	Owed by Both	Owed by Spouse 2
Mortgages			
Other			
TOTAL			

RETIREMENT, DISABILITY AND DEATH BENEFITS

(e.g. pension, profit-sharing, stock bonus, self-employed retirement plan, individual retirement accounts (IRA), deferred compensation plan)

Name of Company & Plan	Current Value	Beneficiary and Payment Options Available

(Note: Please furnish copies of explanatory brochures on each plan.)

OTHER PROPERTY

List and describe here (1) any property of either spouse which is held jointly with persons other than spouse, (2) any property held in "trustee" form for others, (3) any property held in "custodian" form for others, and (4) any community property. Also list any gifts for which federal gift tax returns have been filed and any other gifts over $5,000. Attach copies of gift tax returns or, if no return has been filed, specify names of donees, dates and amounts.

MISCELLANEOUS INFORMATION

Describe any patents, copyright, claims against others or other assets not listed above, including any trusts of which you are a beneficiary or over which you may possess any powers. Describe any significant potential inheritances. Indicate any specific preferences as to anatomical donations, funeral arrangements, etc. which have not already been arranged.

LIFE INSURANCE

Company & Policy	Type	Insured	Owner	Beneficiaries (Primary & Contingent)	Face Value	Cash Value & Loan Balance

8.   STATUTORY WILL (WISCONSIN)

The following is Wisconsin's statutory basic will, found in Wisconsin Statutes Annotated § 853.55.

NOTICE TO THE PERSON WHO SIGNS THIS WILL:

1.   THIS WILL DOES NOT DISPOSE OF PROPERTY WHICH PASSES ON YOUR DEATH TO ANY PERSON BY OPERATION OF LAW OR BY ANY CONTRACT. FOR EXAMPLE, THE WILL DOES NOT DISPOSE OF JOINT TENANCY ASSETS, AND IT DOES NOT NORMALLY APPLY TO PROCEEDS OF LIFE INSURANCE ON YOUR LIFE OR YOUR RETIREMENT PLAN BENEFITS.

2.   THIS WILL IS NOT DESIGNED TO REDUCE TAXES. YOU SHOULD DISCUSS THE TAX RESULTS OF YOUR DECISIONS WITH A COMPETENT TAX ADVISER.

3.   THIS WILL MAY NOT WORK WELL IF YOU HAVE CHILDREN BY A PREVIOUS MARRIAGE OR IF YOU HAVE BUSINESS PROPERTY, PARTICULARLY IF THE BUSINESS IS UNINCORPORATED.

4.   YOU CANNOT CHANGE, DELETE OR ADD WORDS TO THE FACE OF THIS WISCONSIN BASIC WILL. YOU MAY REVOKE THIS WISCONSIN BASIC WILL, AND YOU MAY CHANGE IT BY SIGNING A NEW WILL.

5.   THE FULL TEXT OF THIS WISCONSIN BASIC WILL, THE DEFINITIONS, THE PROPERTY DISPOSITION CLAUSES AND THE MANDATORY CLAUSES FOLLOW THE END OF THIS WILL AND ARE CONTAINED IN THE PROBATE CODE OF WISCONSIN (CHAPTERS 851 TO 882 OF THE WISCONSIN STATUTES).

6.   THE WITNESSES TO THIS WILL SHOULD NOT BE PEOPLE WHO MAY RECEIVE PROPERTY UNDER THIS WILL. YOU SHOULD READ AND CAREFULLY FOLLOW THE WITNESSING PROCEDURE DESCRIBED AT THE END OF THIS WILL.

7.   YOU SHOULD KEEP THIS WILL IN YOUR SAFE-DEPOSIT BOX OR OTHER SAFE PLACE.

8. IF YOU MARRY OR DIVORCE AFTER YOU SIGN THIS WILL, YOU SHOULD MAKE AND SIGN A NEW WILL.

9. THIS WILL TREATS ADOPTED CHILDREN AS IF THEY ARE BIRTH CHILDREN.

10. IF YOU HAVE CHILDREN UNDER 21 YEARS OF AGE, YOU MAY WISH TO USE THE WISCONSIN BASIC WILL WITH TRUST OR ANOTHER TYPE OF WILL.

11. IF THIS WISCONSIN BASIC WILL DOES NOT FIT YOUR NEEDS, YOU MAY WANT TO CONSULT WITH A LAWYER.

[A printed form for a Wisconsin basic will shall set forth the above notice in 10-point boldface type.]

WISCONSIN BASIC WILL OF

(Insert Your Name)

Article 1. Declaration

This is my will and I revoke any prior wills and codicils (additions to prior wills).

Article 2. Disposition of My Property

2.1. PERSONAL, RECREATIONAL AND HOUSEHOLD ITEMS. Except as provided in paragraph 2.2, I give all my furniture, furnishings, household items, recreational equipment, personal automobiles and personal effects to my spouse, if living; otherwise they shall be divided equally among my children who survive me.

2.2. GIFTS TO PERSONS OR CHARITIES. I make the following gifts to the persons or charities in the cash amount stated in words (. . . . Dollars) and figures ($. . . .) or of the property described. I SIGN IN EACH BOX USED. I WRITE THE WORDS "NOT USED" IN THE REMAINING BOXES. If I fail to sign opposite any gift, then no gift is made. If the person mentioned does not survive me or if the charity does not accept the gift, then no gift is made.

FULL NAME OF PERSON OR CHARITY TO RECEIVE GIFT. (Name only one. Please print.)	AMOUNT OF CASH GIFT OR DESCRIPTION OF PROPERTY.	SIGNATURE OF TESTATOR. _____

FULL NAME OF PERSON OR CHARITY TO RECEIVE GIFT. (Name only one. Please print.)	AMOUNT OF CASH GIFT OR DESCRIPTION OF PROPERTY.	SIGNATURE OF TESTATOR. _____
FULL NAME OF PERSON OR CHARITY TO RECEIVE GIFT. (Name only one. Please print.)	AMOUNT OF CASH GIFT OR DESCRIPTION OF PROPERTY.	SIGNATURE OF TESTATOR. _____
FULL NAME OF PERSON OR CHARITY TO RECEIVE GIFT. (Name only one. Please print.)	AMOUNT OF CASH GIFT OR DESCRIPTION OF PROPERTY.	SIGNATURE OF TESTATOR. _____
FULL NAME OF PERSON OR CHARITY TO RECEIVE GIFT. (Name only one. Please print.)	AMOUNT OF CASH GIFT OR DESCRIPTION OF PROPERTY.	SIGNATURE OF TESTATOR. _____

2.3. ALL OTHER ASSETS (MY "RESIDUARY ESTATE"). I adopt only one Property Disposition Clause in this paragraph by writing my signature on the line next to the title of the Property Disposition Clause I wish to adopt. I SIGN ON ONLY ONE LINE. I WRITE THE WORDS "NOT USED" ON THE REMAINING LINE. If I sign on more than one line or if I fail to sign on any line, the property will go under Property Disposition Clause (b) and I realize that means the property will be distributed as if I did not make a will in accordance with Chapter 852 of the Wisconsin Statutes.

PROPERTY DISPOSITION CLAUSES (Select one.)

(a) TO MY SPOUSE IF LIVING; IF NOT LIVING, THEN TO MY CHILDREN AND THE DESCENDANTS OF ANY DECEASED CHILD BY RIGHT OF REPRESENTATION.   . . . .

(b) TO BE DISTRIBUTED AS IF I DID NOT HAVE A WILL.   . . . .

Article 3. Nominations of Personal Representative and Guardian

3.1. PERSONAL REPRESENTATIVE. (Name at least one.)

I nominate the person or institution named in the first box of this paragraph to serve as my personal representative. If that person or institution does not serve, then I nominate the others to serve in the order I list them in the other boxes. I confer upon my personal representative the authority to do and perform any act which he or she determines is in the best interest of the estate, with no limitations. This provision shall be given the broadest possible construction. This authority includes, but is not limited to, the power to borrow money, pledge assets, vote stocks and participate in reorganizations, to sell or exchange real or personal property, and to invest funds and retain securities without any limitation by law for investments by fiduciaries.

FIRST PERSONAL REPRESENTATIVE

SECOND PERSONAL REPRESENTATIVE

THIRD PERSONAL REPRESENTATIVE

3.2. GUARDIAN. (If you have a child under 18 years of age, you should name at least one guardian of the child.)

If my spouse dies before I do or if for any other reason a guardian is needed for any child of mine, then I nominate the person named in the first box of this paragraph to serve as guardian of the person and estate of that child. If the person does not serve, then I nominate the person named in the second box of this paragraph to serve as guardian of that child.

FIRST GUARDIAN

SECOND GUARDIAN

3.3. BOND.

My signature in this box means I request that a bond, as set by law, be required for each individual personal representative or guardian named in this will. IF I DO NOT SIGN IN THIS BOX, I REQUEST THAT A BOND NOT BE REQUIRED FOR ANY OF THOSE PERSONS.

I sign my name to this Wisconsin Basic Will on _____ (date), at _____ (city), _____ (state).

Signature of Testator _____

STATEMENT OF WITNESSES (You must use two witnesses, who should be adults.)

I declare that the testator signed the will in front of me, acknowledged to me that this document was his or her will or acknowledged to me that the signature above is his or her signature. The testator appears to me to be of sound mind and not under undue influence.

Signature _____ Residence Address: _____

Print: _____ Date Signed: _____

I declare that the testator signed the will in front of me, acknowledged to me that this document was his or her will *or* acknowledged to me that the signature above is his or her signature. The testator appears to me to be of sound mind and not under undue influence.

Signature _____ Residence Address: _____

Here: _____ Date Signed: _____

9. LAST WILL AND TESTAMENT OF MICHAEL JOSEPH JACKSON

I, MICHAEL JOSEPH JACKSON, a resident of the State of California, declare this to be my last Will, and do hereby revoke all former wills and codicils made by me.

I

I declare that I am not married. My marriage to DEBORAH JEAN ROWE JACKSON has been dissolved. I have three children now living, PRINCE MICHAEL JACKSON, JR., PARIS MICHAEL KATHERINE JACKSON and PRINCE MICHAEL JOSEPH JACKSON, II. I have no other children, living or deceased.

II

It is my intention by this Will to dispose of all property which I am entitled to dispose of by will. I specifically refrain from exercising all powers of appointment that I may possess at the time of my death.

III

I give my entire estate to the Trustee or Trustees then acting under that certain Amended and Restated Declaration of Trust executed on March 22, 2002 by me as Trustee and Trustor which is called the MICHAEL JACKSON FAMILY TRUST, giving effect to any amendments thereto made prior to my death. All such assets shall be held, managed and distributed as a part of said Trust according to its terms and not as a separate testamentary trust.

If for any reason this gift is not operative or is invalid, or if the aforesaid Trust fails or has been revoked, I give my residuary estate to the Trustee or Trustees named to act in the MICHAEL JACKSON FAMILY TRUST, as Amended and Restated on March 22, 2002, and I direct said Trustee or Trustees to divide, administer, hold and distribute the trust estate pursuant to the provisions of said Trust, as hereinabove referred to as such provisions now exist to the same extent and in the same manner as though that certain Amended and Restated Declaration of Trust, were herein set forth in full, but without giving effect to any subsequent amendments after the date of this Will. The Trustee, Trustees, or any successor Trustee named in such Trust Agreement shall serve without bond.

IV

I direct that all federal estate taxes and state inheritance or succession taxes payable upon or resulting from or by reason of my death (herein "Death Taxes") attributable to property which is part of the trust estate of the MICHAEL JACKSON FAMILY TRUST, including property which passes to said trust from my probate estate shall be paid by the Trustee of said trust in accordance with its terms. Death Taxes attributable to property passing outside this Will, other than property constituting the trust estate of the trust mentioned in the preceding sentence, shall be charged against the taker of said property.

V

I appoint JOHN BRANCA, JOHN McCLAIN and BARRY SIEGEL as co-Executors of this Will. In the event of any of their deaths, resignations, inability, failure or refusal to serve or continue to serve as a co-Executor, the other shall Serve and no replacement need be named. The co-Executors serving at any time after my death may name one or more replacements to serve in the event that none of the three named individuals is willing or able to serve at any time.

The term "my executors" as used in this Will shall include any duly acting personal representative or representatives of my estate. No individual acting as such need post a bond.

I hereby give to my Executors, full power and authority at any time or times to sell, lease, mortgage, pledge, exchange or otherwise dispose of the property, whether real or personal comprising my estate, upon such terms as my Executors shall deem best, to continue any business enterprises, to purchase assets from my estate, to continue in force and pay insurance premiums on any insurance policy, including life insurance, owned by my estate, and for any of the foregoing purposes to make, execute and deliver any and all deeds, contracts, mortgages, bills of sale or other instruments necessary or desirable therefor. In addition, I give to my Executors full power to invest and reinvest the estate funds and assets in any kind of property, real, personal or mixed, and every kind of investment, specifically including, but not by way of limitation, corporate obligations of every kind and stocks, preferred or common, and interests in investment trusts and shares in investment companies, and any common trust fund administered by any corporate executor hereunder, which men of prudent discretion and intelligence acquire for their own account.

VI

Except as otherwise provided in this Will or in the Trust referred to in Article III hereof, I have intentionally omitted to provide for my heirs. I have intentionally omitted to provide for my former wife, DEBORAH JEAN ROWE JACKSON.

VII

If at the time of my death I own or have an interest in property located outside of the State of California requiring ancillary administration, I appoint my domiciliary Executors as ancillary Executors for such property. I give to said domiciliary Executors the following additional powers, rights and privileges to be exercised in their sole and absolute discretion, with reference to such property: to cause such ancillary administration to be commenced, carried on and completed; to determine what assets, if any, are to be sold by the ancillary Executors; to pay directly or to advance funds from the California estate to the ancillary Executors for the payment of all claims, taxes, costs and administration expenses, including compensation of the ancillary Executors and attorneys' fees incurred by reason of the ownership of such property and by such ancillary administration; and upon completion of such ancillary administration, I authorize and direct the ancillary Executors to distribute, transfer and deliver the residue of such property to the domiciliary Executors herein, to be distributed by them under the terms of this Will, it being my intention that my entire estate shall be administered as a unit and that my domiciliary Executors shall supervise and control, so far as permissible by local law, any ancillary administration proceedings deemed necessary in the settlement of my estate.

VIII

If any of my children are minors at the time of my death, I nominate my mother, KATHERINE JACKSON as guardian of the persons and estates of such minor children. If KATHERINE JACKSON fails to survive me, or is unable or unwilling to act as guardian, I nominate DIANA ROSS as guardian of the persons and estates of such minor children.

I subscribe my name to this Will this 7th day of July, 2002

s/ Michael Joseph Jackson

On the date written below, MICHAEL JOSEPH JACKSON, declared to us, the undersigned, that the foregoing instrument consisting of five (5) pages, including the page signed by us as witnesses, was his Will and requested us to act as witnesses to it. He thereupon signed this Will in our presence, all of us being present at the same time. We now, at his request, in his presence and in the presence of each other, subscribe our names as witnesses.

Each of us is now more than eighteen (18) years of age and a competent witness and resides at the address set forth after his name.

Each of us is acquainted with MICHAEL JOSEPH JACKSON. At this time, he is over the age of eighteen (18) years and, to the best of our knowledge, he is of sound mind and is not acting under duress, menace, fraud, misrepresentation or undue influence.

We declare under penalty of perjury that the foregoing is true and correct.

Executed on July 7th, 2002 at 5 p.m., Los Angeles, CA.

_____ Residing At _____

_____ Residing At _____

_____ Residing At _____

10. LAST WILL AND TESTAMENT

of

KATHARINE HEPBURN

I, KATHARINE HEPBURN, of Fenwick, Connecticut, do make, publish and declare this to be my Last Will and Testament, hereby revoking all wills and codicils at any time heretofore made by me.

FIRST: I direct my Executors to make all necessary arrangements for the cremation of my remains and for my ashes to be interred in the family plot at Cedar Hill Cemetery Association, Hartford, Connecticut. I request that there be no funeral or memorial service held for me.

SECOND: A. I give and bequeath the sum of One Hundred Thousand Dollars ($100,000) to NORAH CONSIDINE MOORE, if she survives me.

B.   I give and bequeath the amount of Ten Thousand Dollars ($10,000) to LAURA FRATTI, if she survives me.

C.   I give and bequeath the amount of Fifty Thousand Dollars ($50,000) to ERIK A. HANSON, if he survives me.

D.   I give and bequeath the amount of Ten Thousand Dollars ($10,000) to CYNTHIA A. McFADDEN, if she survives me.

E.   I give and bequeath the amount of Five Thousand Dollars ($5,000) to VALENTINA FRATTI, if she survives me.

F.   I give and bequeath the amount of Five Thousand Dollars ($5,000) to FREYA MANSTON, if she survives me.

G.   I give and bequeath the amount of Two Thousand Five Hundred Dollars ($2,500) to SHARON POWERS, if she survives me.

H.   I give and bequeath the sum of Four Thousand Five Hundred Dollars ($4,500) plus One Thousand Dollars ($1,000) for each full year that he shall have been employed by me since January 1, 1991 to JIMMY LEE DAVIS, if he survives me and is employed by me at the time of my death.

I give and bequeath the amount of Two Thousand Five Hundred Dollars ($2,500) to WEI FUN KOO, if she survives me.

THIRD: A. I give and bequeath the amount of Ten Thousand Dollars ($10,000) to MOTION PICTURE AND TELEVISION FUND located in Woodland Hills, California, for its general purposes, if it is an organization described in Section 2055(a) of the Internal Revenue Code of 1986, as amended, (the "Code") at the time of my death.

B.   I give and bequeath the amount of Ten Thousand Dollars ($10,000) to CHRIST CHURCH, I.U. located on Maryland Route 298, Worton, Maryland, for its general purposes, if it is an organization described in Section 2055(a) of the Code at the time of my death.

C.   I give and bequeath the amount of Ten Thousand Dollars ($10,000) to ACTORS FUND OF AMERICA located in New York, New York, for its general purposes, if it is an organization described in Section 2055(a) of the Code at the time of my death.

FOURTH: A. I release and discharge my nephew TOR HEPBURN, or his estate should he predecease me, from any indebtedness, including interest thereon, which he or his estate may owe to me at the time of my death, and I direct my Executors to cancel any promissory notes or other evidence of his indebtedness to me.

B.   I release and discharge my nephew KUY HEPBURN, or his estate should he predecease me, from any indebtedness, including interest thereon, which he or his estate may owe to me at the time of my death, and I direct my Executors to cancel any promissory notes or other evidence of his indebtedness to me.

FIFTH: A. I give and bequeath all items of tangible personal property owned by me at the time of my death which my individual Executors, in their sale and absolute discretion, determine were given to me during my life by Freya Manston to FREYA MANSTON, if she survives me.

B.   I give and bequeath all costumes and scripts which were used by me in any motion picture or other production in which I appeared, all photographs, letters and awards (including any Oscars received from the Academy of Motion Picture, Arts and Sciences) which relate to my career, my clippings files, and my scrapbooks, to such charitable organization as described in Section 2055(a) of the Code at the time of my death as my individual Executors, in their sole and absolute discretion, shall select. The determination of my Executors regarding what materials constitute my memorabilia shall be binding and conclusive on all persons and organizations interested in my estate.

C.   Except as hereinbefore otherwise effectively bequeathed, I give and bequeath all furniture, furnishings, rugs, pictures, books, silver, plate, linen, china, glassware, objects of art, wearing apparel, jewelry, automobiles and their accessories, and all other tangible personal property owned by me at the time of my death ("my tangible personal property") to and among such of the descendants of my parents, Dr. and Mrs. Thomas Norval Hepburn, my friends, and such one or more charitable organizations which are described in Section 2055(a) of the Code at the time of my death as my Executors, in their sole and absolute discretion, shall select provided, however, that my individual Executors shall be prohibited from participating in any selection or decision to distribute any of my tangible personal property to my individual Executors.

In exercising their discretion to select the recipient or recipients of my tangible personal property, I request, but do not direct, that my Executors be guided by my wishes which I may have made known to them from time to time. In particular, I have indicated my wish that some of my tangible personal property be given to Cynthia A. McFadden and Erik A. Hanson and, accordingly, I authorize my corporate Executor to select and distribute to Cynthia A. McFadden and Erik A. Hanson such items of my tangible personal property which it believes appropriate and which are or would be in accordance with my wishes as expressed from time to time. In exercising their discretion, it is my wish, but not my direction, that my Executors allow my brother, Richard H. Hepburn, if he survives me, to use such articles of tangible personal property owned by me at the time of my death and located on, or customarily used in connection with, my real property at Fenwick, Connecticut which is comprised of approximately 7.17 acres, as my Executors may deem appropriate until such real property is sold.

I authorize my Executors, in their sole and absolute discretion, to sell the balance of my tangible personal property. The net proceeds of sale of any such tangible personal property shall be added to my residuary estate thereafter to be held, administered and disposed of as a part thereof. I authorize my Executors, in their sole and absolute discretion, to determine the manner and time of the sale of any such tangible personal property and, in particular, to sell any of my tangible personal property to any descendant of my parents, Dr. and Mrs. Thomas Norval Hepburn, or my friends as my Executors, in their sole and absolute discretion, may deem appropriate. I wish to grant to my Executors broad latitude in the exercise of their discretion in matters relating to the disposition of my tangible personal property and thus direct that their decisions as to articles to be given to my family and friends and articles to be sold as well as the manner and time of any such sale shall be final and conclusive on all persons interested in my estate.

SIXTH: A. I give and devise that separate parcel of my real property located in the Borough of Fenwick, Town of Old Saybrook, Connecticut, which is located to the East of Mohegan Avenue as set forth on the "Map of New Saybrook, No.2", which is described in the Map of New Saybrook, No.2" as Lots 311, 312, 313, 314, 315, 316, 317, and 318, and which is unimproved (my "East Lot"), including all buildings thereon and all rights and easements appurtenant thereto and all policies of insurance relating thereto, if owned by me at the time of my death, to such one or more of any state or other political subdivision of the United States of America, in all cases for exclusively public purposes, and any corporations transfers to which are deductible for estate tax purposes under the provisions of the Code, as shall be selected by my Executors, in their sole and absolute discretion. Without in any way limiting the sole and absolute nature of the discretion herein given my Executors, I ask, but do not direct, my Executors in selecting such recipient or recipients to be guided by my wish to preserve the afore described lot for the benefit of the general public and to protect the lot from development and, accordingly, to consider as the recipient or recipients of this devise such Federal, state or local body or agency, or environmental or conservation organization as may be best able to realize my wishes.

B.   If my brother Richard H. Hepburn survives me and at my death is residing at my residence located in the Borough of Fenwick, Old Saybrook, Connecticut ("my residence") as his personal residence, I authorize my Executors, in their sole and absolute discretion, to permit him to continue to reside in my residence located in the Borough of Fenwick, Town of Old Saybrook, Connecticut on which is located the main residence and which is located to the West of Mohegan Avenue as set forth on the "Map of New Saybrook, No.2" and which is described in the "Map of New Saybrook, No.2" as Lots 301, 302, 303, 304, 305, 306, 307, 308, 309 and 310, (my "Improved Lot") for a period of time up to four (4) years from the date of my death. During such period of time, if any, that my Executors, in their sale and absolute discretion, permit my brother Richard H. Hepburn to reside in my residence, I also authorize my Executors, in their sole and absolute discretion, to permit my brother Robert H. Hepburn to stay in my residence during the month of July and at such other times as has been his custom during my life. I authorize my Executors to permit my brother Richard H. Hepburn and my brother Robert H. Hepburn to occupy my residence on such terms as my Executors, in their sole and absolute discretion, may determine whether for rent, rent-free, in consideration of the payment of taxes, insurance, maintenance or ordinary repairs, or otherwise as my Executors determine. At the earlier of (i) the date at which my brother Richard H. Hepburn ceases to reside in my residence, (ii) the date on which my brother Richard H. Hepburn dies, (iii) four years from the date of my death or (iv) a determination by my Executors, in their sole and absolute discretion, that my brother Richard H. Hepburn is no longer able to enjoy or derive full benefit from my residence or that it is no longer appropriate for the estate for financial or other reasons to own my residence, I direct that my Improved Lot, including all buildings thereon and all rights and easements appurtenant thereto and all policies of insurance relating thereto, shall be sold and that the net proceeds of sale be added to my residuary estate thereafter to be held, administered and disposed of as a part thereof. In exercising their judgment regarding the length of time to permit my brother Richard H. Hepburn to continue to reside in my residence, I authorize, but do not require, my Executors, in their sole and absolute discretion, to take into consideration whether he is able to enjoy or derive full benefit from my residence. The determinations of my Executors relating to the length of time, if any, of the continued use of my residence by my brother Richard H. Hepburn, the use of my residence by my brother Robert H. Hepburn, and the terms of any such use shall be final and conclusive on all persons interested in my estate.

C. Except as hereinbefore otherwise effectively devised, I direct that all real property owned by me at the time of my death, including all buildings thereon and all rights and easements appurtenant thereto, shall be sold and that the net proceeds of sale be added to my residuary estate thereafter to be held, administered and disposed of as a part thereof.

SEVENTH: A. I direct that (a) all right and interest owned by me at the time of my death in and to any motion picture, television or any other production in which I have appeared or participated, including all rights under any contract with respect to any such motion picture or production, and (b) all rights in any copyright in any literary work created by me which is owned by me at the time of my death, including all royalty or other contract rights with respect to any such literary work, shall be held, administered and disposed of as a part of my residuary estate.

B. Except as hereinbefore otherwise effectively bequeathed, with respect to any manuscripts, letters or other personal papers or records owned by me at the time of my death whether or not created by me (my "literary works"), I authorize my individual Executors to publish my literary works, or any part thereof, if my individual Executors, in their sole and absolute discretion, deem such publication to be appropriate being guided by my wishes which have been imparted to them from time to time. In this regard, I authorize my individual Executors to consult with publishers, editors, literary agents and such other individuals as they deem appropriate in order to make a determination as to the advisability of publishing such literary works or any part thereof.

EIGHTH: If either my nephew Robert Perry or my great niece Fiona Perry survives me, I give and bequeath the amount of One Hundred Thousand Dollars ($100,000) to the Trustees hereinafter named, IN TRUST, NEVERTHELESS, to hold, manage, invest and reinvest the same, to collect the income thereof, and to pay over or apply the net income.

Upon the death of the last to die of my nephew Robert Perry and my great niece Fiona Perry, the principal of the trust, as it is then constituted, shall be divided into a four (4) equal shares, such shares to be disposed of as follows:

A.   One (1) such share shall be transferred, conveyed and paid over to the Trustees of the trust created for the benefit of my brother Richard H. Hepburn and his descendants under paragraph A of Article NINTH of this my Will, thereafter to be held, administered and disposed of as a part thereof or, if no such trust is then in existence, to the descendants of my brother Richard H. Hepburn who are then living, per stirpes or, if no descendant of his is then living, to the descendants of my parents, Dr. and Mrs. Thomas Norval Hepburn, who are then living, per stirpes.

B.   One (1) such share shall be transferred, conveyed and paid over to the Trustees of the trust created for the benefit of my brother Robert H. Hepburn and his descendants under paragraph B of Article NINTH of this my Will, thereafter to be held, administered and disposed of as a part thereof or, if no such trust is then in existence, to the descendants of my brother Robert H. Hepburn who are then living, per stirpes or, if no descendant of his is then living, to the descendants of my parents, Dr. and Mrs. Thomas Norval Hepburn, who are then living, per stripes.

C.   One (1) such share shall be transferred, conveyed and paid over to the Trustees of the trust created for the benefit of the descendants of my sister Marion H. Grant under paragraph C of Article NINTH of this my Will, thereafter to be held, administered and disposed of as a part thereof or, if no such trust is then in existence, to the descendants of my sister Marion H. Grant who are then living, per stirpes or, if no descendant of hers is then living, to the descendants of my parents, Dr. and Mrs. Thomas Norval Hepburn, who are then living, per stripes.

D.   One (1) such share shall be transferred, conveyed and paid over to the Trustees of the trust created for the benefit of my sister Margaret H. Perry and her descendants under paragraph D of Article NINTH of this my Will, thereafter to be held, administered and disposed of as a part thereof or, if no such trust is then in existence, to the descendants of my sister Margaret H. Perry who are then living, per stirpes or, if no descendant of hers is then living, to the descendants of my parents, Dr. and Mrs. Thomas Norval Hepburn, who are then living, per stripes.

NINTH: All the rest, residue and remainder of my property and estate, both real and personal, of whatsoever kind and wheresoever situated, of which I shall die seized or possessed or of which I shall be entitled to dispose at the time of my death (my "residuary estate"), after payment therefrom of all of the taxes directed in Article ELEVENTH of this my Will to be paid from my residuary estate, shall be divided into a four (4) equal shares, such shares to be disposed of as follows:

A. I give, devise and bequeath one (1) such share to the Trustees hereinafter named, IN TRUST, NEVERTHELESS, to hold, manage, invest and reinvest the same, to collect the income thereof, and to pay over or apply the net income, in as nearly equal quarterly installments as may be practicable, to or for the benefit of my brother RICHARD H. HEPBURN, during his life, and after his death, to or for the benefit of his descendants who are living from time to time, per stirpes. I authorize the Trustees, at any time and from time to time,' to pay over to one or more of the class consisting of my brother RICHARD H. HEPBURN and his descendants living from time to time, or to apply for their use, out of the property of the trust, such part or all thereof, as the Trustees, in their sale and absolute discretion, shall determine. In determining the amounts of trust property, if any, to be paid over to or applied for the use of my brother Richard H. Hepburn and his descendants pursuant to the discretionary powers herein granted, I authorize, but do not require, the Trustees, in their sole and absolute discretion, to take into consideration any sources of income available to, or assets owned by or held for the use of, my brother Richard H. Hepburn and his descendants.

Upon the death of the last to die of the children of my brother Richard H. Hepburn, the trust shall terminate and the principal thereof, as it is then constituted, shall be transferred, conveyed and paid over to the descendants of my brother Richard H. Hepburn who are then living, per stirpes or, if no descendant of his is then living, to the descendants of my parents, Dr. and Mrs. Thomas Norval Hepburn, who are then living, per stirpes.

B. I give, devise and bequeath one (1) such share to the Trustees hereinafter named, IN TRUST, NEVERTHELESS, to hold, manage, invest and reinvest the same, to collect the income thereof, and to pay over or apply the net income, in as nearly equal quarterly installments as may be practicable, to or for the benefit of my brother ROBERT H. HEPBURN, during his life, and after his death, to or for the benefit of his descendants who are living from time to time, per stirpes. I authorize the Trustees, at any time and from time to time, to pay over to one or more of the class consisting of my brother ROBERT H. HEPBURN and his descendants living from 'time to time, or to apply for their use, out of the property of the trust, such part or all thereof, as the Trustees, in their sole and absolute discretion, shall determine. In determining the amounts of trust property, if any, to be paid over to or applied for the use of my brother Robert H. Hepburn and his descendants pursuant to the discretionary powers herein granted, I authorize, but do not require, the Trustees, in their sale and absolute discretion, to take into consideration any sources of income available to, or assets owned by or held for the use of, my brother Robert H. Hepburn and his descendants.

Upon the death of the last to die of the children of my brother Robert H. Hepburn, the trust shall terminate and the principal thereof, as it is then constituted, shall be transferred, conveyed and paid over to the descendants of my brother Robert H. Hepburn who are then living, per stirpes or, if no descendant of his is then living, to the descendants of my parents, Dr. and Mrs. Thomas Norval Hepburn, who are then living, per stirpes.

C.   I give, devise and bequeath one (1) such share to the Trustees hereinafter named, IN TRUST, NEVERTHELESS, to hold, manage, invest and reinvest the same, to collect the income thereof, and to pay over or apply the net income, in as nearly equal quarterly installments as may be practicable, to or for the benefit of the descendants of my sister Marion H. Grant who are living from time to time, per stirpes. I authorize the Trustees, at any time and from time to time, to pay over to one or more of the class consisting of the descendants of my sister Marion H. Grant living from time to time, or to apply for their use, out of the property of the trust, such part or all thereof, as the Trustees, in their sale and absolute discretion, shall determine. In determining the amounts of trust property, if any, to be paid over to or applied for the use of the descendants of my sister Marion H. Grant pursuant to the discretionary powers herein granted, I authorize, but do not require, the Trustees, in their sole and absolute discretion, to take into consideration any sources of income available to, or assets owned by or held for the use of, the descendants of my sister Marion H. Grant.

Upon the death of the last to die of the children of my sister Marion H. Grant, the trust shall terminate and the principal thereof, as it is then constituted, shall be transferred, conveyed and paid over to the descendants of my sister Marion H. Grant who are then living, per stirpes or, if no descendant of hers is then living, to the descendants of my parents, Dr. and Mrs. Thomas Norval Hepburn, who are then living, per stirpes.

D. I give, devise and bequeath one (1) such share to the Trustees hereinafter named, IN TRUST, NEVERTHELESS, to hold, manage, invest and reinvest the same, to collect the income thereof, and to pay over or apply the net income, in as nearly equal quarterly installments as may be practicable, to or for the benefit of my sister MARGARET H. PERRY, during her life, and after her death, to or for the benefit of her descendants who are living from time to time, per stirpes. I authorize the Trustees, at any time and from time to time, to pay over to one or more of the class consisting of my sister MARGARET H. PERRY and her descendants living from time to time, or to apply for their use, out of the property of the trust, such part or all thereof, as the Trustees, in their sole and absolute discretion, shall determine. In determining the amounts of trust property, if any, to be paid over to or applied for the use of my sister Margaret H. Perry and her descendants pursuant to the discretionary powers herein granted, I authorize, but do not require, the Trustees, in their sole and absolute discretion, to take into consideration any sources of income available to, or assets owned by or held for the use of, my sister Margaret H. Perry and her descendants.

Upon the death of the last to die of the children of my sister Margaret H. Perry/ the trust shall terminate and the principal thereof, as it is then constituted, shall be transferred, conveyed and paid over to the descendants of my sister Margaret H. Perry who are then living, per stirpes or, if no descendant of hers is then living, to the descendants of my parents, Dr. and Mrs. Thomas Norval Hepburn, who are then living, per stirpes.

TENTH: If any individual under the age of twenty-one (21) years becomes entitled to any property from my estate upon my death or any property from any trust created hereunder upon the termination thereof, such property shall be held by, and I give, devise and bequeath the same to the Trustees hereinafter named, IN TRUST, NEVERTHELESS, for the following uses and purposes: To manage/ invest and reinvest the same, to collect the income and to apply the net income and principal to such extent (including the whole thereof) for such individual's general use and at such time or times as the Trustees, in their sole and absolute discretion, shall determine, until such individual reaches the age of twenty-one (21) years/ and thereupon to transfer, convey and pay over the principal of the trust, as it is then constituted, to such individual. Any net income not so applied shall be accumulated and added to the principal of the trust at least annually and thereafter shall be held, administered and disposed of as a part thereof. Upon the death of such individual before reaching the age of twenty-one (21) years, the Trustees shall transfer, convey and pay over the principal of the trust, as it is then constituted, to such individual's executors or administrators.

If my Executors or the Trustees, as the case may be, in the exercise of their sole and absolute discretion, determine at any time not to transfer in trust or not to continue to hold in trust any part or all of such property/ as the case may be, they shall have full power and authority to transfer and pay over such property, or any part thereof, without bond, to such individual, if an adult under the law of the state of his or her domicile at the time of such payment, or to his or her parent, the guardian of his or her person or property, or to a custodian for such individual under any Uniform Gifts to Minors Act pursuant to which a custodian is acting or may be appointed.

The receipt of such individual, if an adult, or the parent, the guardian or custodian to whom any principal or income is transferred and paid over pursuant to any of the above provisions shall be a full discharge to my Executors or the Trustees, as the case may be, from all liability with respect thereto.

Notwithstanding anything to the contrary contained in this my Will, the Trustees shall not exercise any discretionary power to pay or apply income or principal pursuant to this Article in discharge of any person's duty to support any individual for whom a trust is held hereunder.

ELEVENTH: All estate, inheritance, legacy, succession, transfer or other death taxes (including any interest and penalties thereon) imposed by any domestic or foreign taxing authority with respect to all property owned by me at the time of my death and passing under this my Will (other than any generation-skipping transfer tax imposed by Chapter 13 of the Internal Revenue Code of 1986, or any predecessor or successor section or statute of like import) shall be paid without apportionment out of my residuary estate and without apportionment within my residuary estate, and with no right of reimbursement from any recipient of any such property.

TWELFTH: A.   I appoint CYNTHIA A. McFADDEN, ERIK A. HANSON and FIDUCIARY TRUST COMPANY INTERNATIONAL, its successor or successors by any merger, conversion or consolidation, Executors of this my Last Will and Testament and Trustees of the trusts hereby created.

B.   It is my request, but not my direction, that my brother Robert H. Hepburn, who has been a valued advisor and consultant throughout my life, be consulted by my Executors and Trustees as they deem appropriate in their sole and absolute discretion. I authorize, but do not direct, my Executors and Trustees to compensate Robert H. Hepburn for such counsel, guidance and assistance as he may provide.

C.   If at any time and for any reason there is only one Executor or only one Trustee acting hereunder, I authorize, but do not direct, such Executor or such Trustee to appoint such individual or such bank or trust company as he, she or it in his, her or its sole and absolute discretion, shall select as successor Executor or successor Trustee to act in his, her or its place if he, she or it should cease to act. Any such appointment shall be made by an instrument in writing filed with the clerk of the appropriate court and may be revoked by an individual Executor or individual Trustee during his or her lifetime or by a corporate Executor or corporate Trustee while in office and succeeded by a later appointment, the last such appointment to control.

D.   For its services for acting in any fiduciary capacity under this my Will, Fiduciary Trust Company International shall receive the compensation stipulated in its regularly adopted schedule in effect and applicable at the time such compensation shall become payable, including any stipulated minimum compensation. I acknowledge that I am aware the foregoing compensation may be in excess of that provided for under applicable law, and expressly authorize payment of any excess thereof.

E.   I authorize the individual Trustees (other than any beneficiary of any trust created hereunder should such beneficiary be acting as a Trustee hereunder), in their sale and absolute discretion, to remove any corporate Trustee acting hereunder at any time and, in the event a corporate Trustee is removed, I direct the individual Trustees (other than any beneficiary of any trust created hereunder should such beneficiary be acting as a Trustee hereunder) to appoint such bank or trust company as they, in their sole and absolute discretion, shall select to act in its place. Any such removal and appointment shall be evidenced by an instrument in writing delivered to the corporate Trustee acting hereunder and to the bank or trust company being appointed in its place, and shall be filed with the clerk of the appropriate court.

F.   Any individual Executor or individual Trustee may resign from office without leave of court at any time and for any reason by filing a written instrument of resignation with the clerk of the appropriate court.

G.   Should it be necessary for a representative of my estate to qualify in any jurisdiction wherein the corporate Executor named or appointed herein cannot or may not desire to qualify as such, the individual Executors named or appointed herein shall, without giving any security, act as Executors in such jurisdiction and shall have therein all the rights, powers, privileges, discretions and duties conferred or imposed upon my Executors by the provisions of this my Will, or, if such individual Executors cannot or do not desire to qualify as Executors in such other jurisdiction, or, if at any time and for any reason there shall be no Executor in office in such other jurisdiction, I appoint as Executor therein such person or corporation as may be designated by the corporate Executor. Such substituted Executor shall, without giving any security, have in such other jurisdiction all the rights, powers, privileges, discretions and duties conferred or imposed upon my Executors by the provisions of this my Will.

H.   Whenever the terms "Executors" and "Trustees" are used in this my Will, they shall be deemed to refer to the Executors or Executor and the Trustees or Trustee acting hereunder from time to time.

THIRTEENTH: Except as provided by law, I direct that my Executors shall not be required to file any inventory of my estate and that no Executor or Trustee shall be required to give any bond or file any periodic account. If, notwithstanding the foregoing direction, any bond is required by any law, statute or rule of court, no sureties shall be required thereon.

FOURTEENTH: A. I authorize my Executors to make such elections (other than an election which would cause the disallowance of the Federal estate tax charitable deduction) under the tax laws as they, in their sole and absolute discretion, deem advisable, regardless of the effect thereof on any of the interests under this my Will, and I direct that there shall be no adjustment of such interests by reason of any action taken by my Executors pursuant hereto.

B.   I authorize my Executors to allocate any amount of my GST exemption under Section 2631(a) of the Code to such property of which I am the transferor as they shall select in the exercise of their sole and absolute discretion, whether or not passing under this my Will, including property transferred by me during life whether or not I allocated any GST exemption to such property during my life, and without any duty to favor beneficiaries under this my Will over beneficiaries of property passing outside this my Will.

C.   The Trustees are authorized, in their sale and absolute discretion, to divide any trust being held hereunder that has an inclusion ratio (within the meaning of Section 2642(a) of the Code) of more than zero and less than one into two separate trusts consisting of fractional shares of the original trust, equal respectively to the undivided trust's inclusion ratio and applicable fraction (within the meaning of that Section) at the time of division, so that one trust thereafter will have an inclusion ratio of one and the other of zero.

D. Whenever two trusts under this my Will are directed to be combined into a single trust (for example, because property of one trust is to be added to the other trust), if the trusts have different inclusion ratios with respect to any common transferor in whole or in part for generation-skipping transfer tax purposes, the Trustees are authorized, in their sole and absolute discretion, instead of combining the trusts, to hold them as separate trusts hereunder.

E. I authorize and empower the Trustees, in their sole and absolute discretion, to terminate each trust created under this my Will and to transfer, convey and pay over all of the principal thereof in such amounts and proportions as the Trustees, in their sole and absolute discretion, shall determine to such one or more of the then income beneficiaries of such trust.

FIFTEENTH: A. Any individual Trustee hereunder who shall also be a beneficiary of any trust created hereunder shall be disqualified from participating in all determinations with respect to the payment or application of principal of such trust or the payment, application or accumulation of income thereof. The determinations of the remaining qualified Trustee or Trustees shall be final and binding upon the beneficiaries of such trust.

B. Any individual Trustee hereunder who shall have the legal obligation to support any person eligible to receive a payment or application of principal or income of any trust created hereunder shall be disqualified from participating in all determinations with respect to the payment or application of principal of such trust or the payment, application or accumulation of income thereof. The determinations of the remaining qualified Trustee or Trustees shall be binding upon the beneficiaries of such trust.

SIXTEENTH: A. In addition to, and not by way of limitation of, the powers conferred by law upon fiduciaries, I hereby expressly grant to my Executors with respect to my estate and the Trustees with respect to each of the trust estates herein created, including any accumulated income thereof, the powers hereinafter enumerated, all of such powers so conferred or granted to be exercised by them as they may deem advisable in their sale and absolute discretion:

(1) To purchase or otherwise acquire, and to retain, whether originally a part of my estate or subsequently acquired, any and all stocks, bonds, notes or

other securities, or any variety of real or personal property, including securities of the corporate fiduciary, or any successor or affiliated corporation, interests in common trust funds and securities of or other interests in investment companies and investment trusts, whether or not such investments be of the character permissible for investments by fiduciaries; and to make or retain any such investment without regard to degree of diversification.

(2) To sell, lease, pledge, mortgage, transfer, exchange, convert or otherwise dispose of, or grant options with respect to, any and all property at any time forming a part of my estate or any trust estate, in any manner, at any time or times, for any purpose, for any price and upon any terms, credits and conditions; and to enter into leases which extend beyond the period fixed by statute for leases made by fiduciaries and beyond the duration of any trust.

(3) To borrow money from any lender, including the corporate fiduciary, for any purpose connected with the protection, preservation or improvement of my estate or any trust estate, and as security to mortgage or pledge upon any terms and conditions any real or personal property of which I may die seized or possessed or forming a part of any trust estate.

(4) To vote in person or by general or limited proxy with respect to any shares of stock or other security; directly or through a committee or other agent, to oppose or consent to the reorganization, consolidation, merger, dissolution or liquidation of any corporation, or to the sale, lease, pledge or mortgage of any property by or to any such corporation; and to make any payments and take any steps proper to obtain the benefits of any such transaction.

(5) To the extent permitted by law, to register any security in the name of a nominee with or without the addition of words indicating that such security is held in a fiduciary capacity; and to hold any security in bearer form.

(6) To complete, extend, modify or renew any loans, notes, bonds, mortgages, contracts or any other obligations which I may owe or to which I may be a party or which may be liens or charges against any of my property, or against my estate, although I may not be liable thereon; to pay, compromise, compound, adjust, submit to arbitration, sell or release any claims or demands of my estate or any trust against others or of others against my estate or any trust upon any terms and conditions, including the acceptance of deeds to real property in satisfaction of bonds and mortgages; and to make any payments in connection therewith.

(7) To make distributions in kind (including in satisfaction of pecuniary bequests) and to cause any distribution to be composed of cash, property or

undivided fractional shares in property different in kind from any other distribution without regard to the income tax basis of the property distributed to any beneficiary or any trust.

(8) To appoint, employ and remove, at any time and from time to time, any accountants, attorneys, investment counselors, expert advisors, agents, clerks and employees; and to fix and pay their compensation from income or principal or partially from income and partially from principal.

(9) Whenever permitted by law, to employ a broker-dealer as custodian for all or any part of the securities at any time held by my estate or any trust estate and to register such securities in the name of such broker-dealer.

(10) To execute and deliver any and all instruments to carry out any of the foregoing powers, no party to any such instrument being required to inquire into its validity or to see to the application of any money or other property paid or delivered pursuant to the terms of any such instrument.

B. In exercising any powers conferred by law or in this my Will, my Executors and the Trustees may use the services of any corporation or other organization with or by which any Executor or Trustee is individually affiliated or employed, including (but without limitation) services in connection with the sale and purchase of assets, the borrowing of money, the registration of securities, the maintaining of a custody account and the rendering of investment counsel and accounting services.

SEVENTEENTH: A. As used in this my Will, the terms "child," "children," "descendant" and "descendants" are intended to include adopted persons and the descendants of adopted persons, whether of the blood (legitimate or born out of wedlock) or by adoption and are intended to include persons born out of wedlock and the descendants of persons born out of wedlock, whether of the blood (legitimate or born out of wedlock) or by adoption.

B. A disposition or distribution in this my Will to the descendants of a person per stirpes shall be deemed to require a division into a sufficient number of equal shares to make one share for each child of such person living at the 'time such disposition or distribution becomes effective ad one share for each then deceased child of such person having one or more descendants then living, regardless of whether any child of such person is then living, with the same principle to be applied in any required further division of a share at a more remote generation.

IN WITNESS WHEREOF, I, KATHARINE HEPBURN, have to this my Last Will and Testament subscribed my name and set my seal this [27] day of [January], in the year One Thousand Nine Hundred and Ninety-two.

[s/ *Katharine Hepburn*]

Subscribed and sealed by the Testatrix in the presence of us and of each of us, and at the same time published, declared and acknowledged by her to us to be her Last Will and Testament, and thereupon we, at the request of the said Testatrix, in her presence and in the presence of each other, have hereunto subscribed our names as witnesses this [27] day of [January], 1992.

Subscribed and sealed by the Testatrix in the presence of us and of each of us, and at the same time published, declared and acknowledged by her to us to be her Last Will and Testament, and thereupon we, at the request of the said Testatrix, in her presence and in the presence of each other, have hereunto subscribed our names as witnesses this [27] day of [January], 1992.

_____ residing at _____

_____

_____ residing at _____

_____

_____ residing at _____

_____

11. LAST WILL AND TESTAMENT OF ELVIS PRESLEY

Last Will and Testament of Elvis Presley

I, Elvis A. Presley, a resident and citizen of Shelby County, Tennessee, being of sound mind and disposing memory, do hereby make, publish and declare this instrument to be my last will and testament, hereby revoking any and all wills and codicils by me at any time heretofore made.

Item I

Debts, Expenses and Taxes

I direct my Executor, hereinafter named, to pay all of my matured debts and my funeral expenses, as well as the costs and expenses of the administration of my estate, as soon after my death as practicable. I further direct that all estate, inheritance, transfer and succession taxes which are payable by reason under this will, be paid out of my residuary estate; and I hereby waive on behalf of my estate any right to recover from any person any part of such taxes so paid. My Executor, in his sole discretion, may pay from my domiciliary estate all or any portion of the costs of ancillary administration and similar proceedings in other jurisdictions.

Item II

Instruction Concerning Personal Property: Enjoyment in Specie

I anticipate that included as a part of my property and estate at the time of my death will be tangible personal property of various kinds, characters and values, including trophies and other items accumulated by me during my professional career. I hereby specifically instruct all concerned that my Executor, herein appointed, shall have complete freedom and discretion as to disposal of any and all such property so long as he shall act in good faith and in the best interest of my estate and my beneficiaries, and his discretion so exercised shall not be subject to question by anyone whomsoever.

I hereby expressly authorize my Executor and my Trustee, respectively and successively, to permit any beneficiary of any and all trusts created hereunder to enjoy in specie the use or benefit of any household goods, chattels, or other tangible personal property (exclusive of choses in action, cash, stocks, bonds or other securities) which either my Executor or my Trustees may receive in kind, and my Executor and my Trustees shall not be liable for any consumption, damage, injury to or loss of any tangible property so used, nor shall the beneficiaries of any trusts hereunder or their executors of administrators be liable for any consumption, damage, injury to or loss of any tangible personal property so used.

Item III

Real Estate

If I am the owner of any real estate at the time of my death, I instruct and empower my Executor and my Trustee (as the case may be) to hold such real estate for investment, or to sell same, or any portion thereof, as my Executor or my Trustee (as the case may be) shall in his sole judgment determine to be for the best interest of my estate and the beneficiaries thereof.

Item IV

Residuary Trust

After payment of all debts, expenses and taxes as directed under Item I hereof, I give, devise, and bequeath all the rest, residue, and remainder of my estate, including all lapsed legacies and devices, and any property over which I have a power of appointment, to my Trustee, hereinafter named, in trust for the following purposes:

(a)   The Trustees is directed to take, hold, manage, invest and reinvent the corpus of the trust and to collect the income therefrom in accordance with the rights, powers, duties, authority and discretion hereinafter set forth. The Trustee is directed to pay all the expenses, taxes and costs incurred in the management of the trust estate out of the income thereof.

(b)   After payment of all expenses, taxes and costs incurred in the management of the expenses, taxes and costs incurred in the management of the trust estate, the Trustee is authorizes to accumulate the net income or to pay or apply so much of the net income and such portion of the principal at any time and from time to time to time for health, education, support, comfortable maintenance and welfare of: (1) My daughter, Lisa Marie Presley, and any other lawful issue I might have, (2) my grandmother, Minnie Mae Presley, (3) my father, Vernon E. Presley, and (4) such other relatives of mine living at the time of my death who in the absolute discretion of my Trustees are in need of emergency assistance for any of the above mentioned purposes and the Trustee is able to make such distribution without affecting the ability of the trust to meet the present needs of the first three numbered categories of beneficiaries herein mentioned or to meet the reasonably expected future needs of the first three classes of beneficiaries herein mentioned. Any decision of the Trustee as to whether or not distribution, to any of the persons described hereunder shall be final and conclusive and not subject to question by any legatee or beneficiary hereunder.

(c) Upon the death of my Father, Vernon E. Presley, the Trustee is instructed to make no further distributions to the fourth category of beneficiaries and such beneficiaries shall cease to have any interest whatsoever in this trust.

(d) Upon the death of both my said father and my said grandmother, the Trustee is directed to divide the Residuary Trust into separate and equal trusts, creating one such equal trust for each of my lawful children then surviving and one such equal trust for the living issue collectively, if any, of any deceased child of mine. The share, if any, for the issue of any such deceased child, shall immediately vest in such issue in equal shares but shall be subject to the provisions of Item V herein. Separate books and records shall be kept for each trust, but it shall not be necessary that a physical division of the assets be made as to each trust.

The Trustee may from time to time distribute the whole or any part of the net income or principal from each of the aforesaid trusts as the Trustee, in its uncontrolled discretion, considers necessary or desirable to provide for the comfortable support, education, maintenance, benefit and general welfare of each of my children. Such distributions may be made directly to such beneficiary or to the guardian of the person of such beneficiary and without responsibility on my Trustee to see to the application of any such distributions and in making such distributions, the Trustee shall take into account all other sources of funds known by the Trustee to be available for each respective beneficiary for such purpose.

(e) As each of my respective children attains the age of twenty-five (25) years and provided that both my father and my grandmother are deceased, the trust created hereunder for such child care terminate, and all the remainder of the assets then contained in said trust shall be distributed to such child so attaining the age of twenty-five (25) years outright and free of further trust.

(f) If any of my children for whose benefit a trust has been created hereunder should die before attaining the age of twenty-five (25) years, then the trust created for such a child shall terminate on his death, and all remaining assets then contained in said trust shall be distributed outright and free of further trust and in equal shares to the surviving issue of such deceased child but subject to the provisions of Item V herein; but if there be no such surviving issue, then to the brothers and sisters of such deceased child in equal shares, the issue of any other deceased child being entitled collectively to their deceased parent's share. Nevertheless, if any distribution otherwise becomes payable outright and free of trust under the provisions of this paragraph (f) of the Item IV of my will to a beneficiary for whom the Trustee is then administering a trust for the benefit of such beneficiary under provisions of this last will and testament, such distribution shall not be paid outright to such beneficiary but shall be added to and become a part of the trust so being administered for such beneficiary by the Trustee.

Item V

Distribution to Minor Children

If any share of corpus of any trust established under this will become distributable outright and free of trust to any beneficiary before said beneficiary has attained the age of eighteen (18) years, then said share shall immediately vest in said beneficiary, but the Trustee shall retain possession of such share during the period in which such beneficiary is under the age of eighteen (18) years, and, in the meantime, shall use and expend so much of the income and principal for the care, support, and education of such beneficiary, and any income not so expended with respect to each share so retained all the power and discretion had with respect to such trust generally.

Item VI

Alternate Distributees

In the event that all of my descendants should be deceased at any time prior to the time for the termination of the trusts provided for herein, then in such event all of my estate and all the assets of every trust to be created hereunder (as the case may be) shall then distributed outright in equal shares to my heirs at law per stripes.

Item VII

Unenforceable Provisions

If any provisions of this will are unenforceable, the remaining provisions shall, nevertheless, be carried into effect.

Item VIII

Life Insurance

If my estate is the beneficiary of any life insurance on my life at the time of my death, I direct that the proceeds therefrom will be used by my Executor in payment of the debts, expenses and taxes listed in Item I of this will, to the extent deemed advisable by the Executor. All such proceeds not so used are to be used by my Executor for the purpose of satisfying the devises and bequests contained in Item IV herein.

Item IX

Spendthrift Provision

I direct that the interest of any beneficiary in principal or income of any trust created hereunder shall not be subject to claims of creditors or others, nor to legal process, and may not be voluntarily or involuntarily alienated or encumbered except as herein provided. Any bequests contained herein for any female shall be for her sole and separate use, free from the debts, contracts and control of any husband she may ever have.

Item X

Proceeds from Personal Services

All sums paid after my death (either to my estate or to any of the trusts created hereunder) and resulting from personal services rendered by me during my lifetime, including, but not limited to, royalties of all nature, concerts, motion picture contracts, and personal appearances shall be considered to be income, notwithstanding the provisions of estate and trust law to the contrary.

Item XI

Executor and Trustee

I appoint as executor of this, my last will and testament, and as Trustee of every trust required to be created hereunder, my said father.

I hereby direct that my said father shall be entitled by his last will and testament, duly probated, to appoint a successor Executor of my estate, as well as a successor Trustee or successor Trustees of all the trusts to be created under my last will and testament.

If, for any reason, my said father be unable to serve or to continue to serve as Executor and/or as Trustee, or if he be deceased and shall not have appointed a successor Executor or Trustee, by virtue of his last will and testament as stated above, then I appoint National Bank of Commerce, Memphis, Tennessee, or its successor or the institution with which it may merge, as successor Executor and/or as successor Trustee of all trusts required to be established hereunder.

None of the appointees named hereunder, including any appointment made by virtue of the last will and testament of my said father, shall be required to furnish any bond or security for performance of the respective fiduciary duties required hereunder, notwithstanding any rule of law to the contrary.

Item XII

Powers, Duties, Privileges and Immunities of the Trustee

Except as otherwise stated expressly to the contrary herein, I give and grant to the said Trustee (and to the duly appointed successor Trustee when acting as such) the power to do everything he deems advisable with respect to the administration of each trust required to be established under this, my last will and Testament, even though such powers would not be authorized or appropriate for the Trustee under statutory or other rules of law. By way of illustration and not in limitation of the generality of the foregoing grant of power and authority of the Trustee, I give and grant to him plenary power as follows:

(a)   To exercise all those powers authorized to fiduciaries under the provisions of the Tennessee Code Annotated, Sections 35–616 to 35–618, inclusive, including any amendments thereto in effect at the time of my death, and the same are expressly referred to and incorporated herein by reference.

(b)   Plenary power is granted to the Trustee, not only to relieve him from seeking judicial instruction, but to the extent that the Trustee deems it to be prudent, to encourage determinations freely to be made in favor of persons who are the current income beneficiaries. In such instances the rights of all subsequent beneficiaries are subordinate, and the Trustee shall not be answerable to any subsequent beneficiary for anything done or omitted in favor of a current income beneficiary may compel any such favorable or preferential treatment. Without in anywise minimizing or impairing the scope of this declaration of intent, it includes investment policy, exercise of discretionary power to pay or apply principal and income, and determination principal and income questions;

(c)   It shall be lawful for the Trustee to apply any sum that is payable to or for the benefit of a minor (or any other person who in the Judgment of the Trustee, is incapable of making proper disposition thereof) by payments in discharge of the costs and expenses of educating, maintaining and supporting said beneficiary, or to make payment to anyone with whom said beneficiary resides or who has the care or custody of the beneficiary, temporarily or permanently, all without intervention of any guardian or like fiduciary. The receipt of anyone to whom payment is so authorized to be made shall be a complete discharge of the Trustees without obligation on his part to see to the further application hereto, and without regard to other resource that the beneficiary may have, or the duty of any other person to support the beneficiary;

(d)   In Dealing with the Trustee, no grantee, pledge, vendee, mortgage, lessee or other transference of the trust properties, or any part thereof, shall be bound to inquire with respect to the purpose or necessity of any such disposition or to see to the application of any consideration therefore paid to the Trustee.

Item XIII

Concerning the Trustee and the Executor

(a)   If at any time the Trustee shall have reasonable doubt as to his power, authority or duty in the administration of any trust herein created, it shall be lawful for the Trustee to obtain the advice and counsel of reputable legal counsel without resorting to the courts for instructions; and the Trustee shall be fully absolved from all liability and damage or detriment to the various trust estates of any beneficiary thereunder by reason of anything done, suffered or omitted pursuant to advice of said counsel given and obtained in good faith, provided that nothing contained herein shall be construed to prohibit or prevent the Trustee in all proper cases from applying to a court of competent jurisdiction for instructions in the administration of the trust assets in lieu of obtaining advice of counsel.

(b)   In managing, investing, and controlling the various trust estates, the Trustee shall exercise the judgment and care under the circumstances then prevailing, which men of prudence discretion and judgment exercise in the management of their own affairs, not in regard to speculation, but in regard to the permanent disposition of their funds, considering the probable income as well as the probable safety of their capital, and, in addition, the purchasing power of income distribution to beneficiaries.

(c)   My Trustee (as well as my Executor) shall be entitled to reasonable and adequate and adequate compensation for the fiduciary services rendered by him.

(d)   My Executor and his successor Executor and his successor Executor shall have the same rights, privileges, powers and immunities herein granted to my Trustee wherever appropriate.

(e)   In referring to any fiduciary hereunder, for purposes of construction, masculine pronouns may include a corporate fiduciary and neutral pronouns may include an individual fiduciary.

Item XIV

Law Against Perpetuities

(a)   Having in mind the rule against perpetuities, I direct that (notwithstanding anything contained to the contrary in this last will and testament) each trust created under this will (except such trust created under this will (except such trusts as have heretofore vested in compliance with such rule or law) shall end, unless sooner terminated under other provisions of this will, twenty-one (21) years after the death of the last survivor of such of the beneficiaries hereunder as are living at the time of my death; and thereupon that the property held in trust shall be distributed free of all trust to the persons then entitled to receive the income and/or principal therefrom, in the proportion in proportion in which they are then entitled to receive such income.

(b)   Notwithstanding anything else contained in this will to the contrary, I direct that if any distribution under this will become payable to a person for whom the Trustee is then administering a trust created hereunder for the benefit of such person, such distribution shall be made to such trust and not to the beneficiary outright, and the funds so passing to such trust shall become a part thereof as corpus and be administered and distributed to the same extent and purpose as if such funds had been a part of such a trust at its inception.

Item XV

Payment of Estate and Inheritance Taxes

Notwithstanding the provisions of Item X herein, I authorize my Executor to use such sums received by my estate after my death and resulting from my personal services as identified in Item X as he deem necessary and advisable in order to pay the taxes referred to in Item I of my said will.

In WITNESS WHEREOF, I, the said ELVIS A. PRESLEY, do hereunto set my hand and seal in the presence of two (2) competent witnesses, and in their presence do publish and declare this instrument to be my Last Will and Testament, this 3 day of March, 1977.

[Signed by Elvis A. Presley]

The foregoing instrument, consisting of this and eleven (11) preceding typewritten pages, was signed, sealed, published and declared by ELVIS A. PRESLEY, the Testator, to be his Last Will and Testament, in our presence, and we, at his request and in his presence and in the presence of each other, have hereunto subscribed our names as witnesses, this 3 day of March, 1977, at Memphis, Tennessee.

[Signed by Ginger Alden]

[Signed by Charles F. Hodge]

[Signed by Ann Dewey Smith]

State of Tennessee

County of Shelby

Ginger Alden, Charles F. Hodge, and Ann Dewey Smith, after being first duly sworn, make oath or affirm that the foregoing Last Will and Testament, in the sight and presence of us, the undersigned, who at his request and in his sight and presence, and in the sight and presence of each other, have subscribed our names as attesting witnesses on the 3 day of March, 1977, and we further make oath or affirm that the Testator was of sound mind and disposing memory and not acting under fraud, menace or undue influence of any person, and was more than eighteen (18) years of age; and that each of the attesting witnesses is more than eighteen (18) years of age.

[Signed by Ginger Alden]

[Signed by Charles F. Hodge]

[Signed by Ann Dewey Smith]

Sworn To And Subscribed before me this 3 day of March, 1977.

[signed/sealed by notary public, Drayton Beecker Smith II]

12. LAST WILL AND TESTAMENT
OF WHITNEY HOUSTON

Last Will and Testament of Whitney E. Houston

I, WHITNEY E. HOUSTON, residing in the State of New Jersey, declare this to be my Last Will and Testament and revoke all my prior will is and codicils.

FIRST: I direct that my funeral and cemetery expenses, the expenses of my last illness, all expenses of administration of my estate and all my debts (except mortgage indebtedness and indebtedness secured by any life insurance policy or otherwise secured) that are just and not barred by time be paid by my Executors from my residuary estate.

I give my entire interest in all my household furniture and furnishings and other articles of household use or ornament located at any real estate used by it on a full or part-time basis for my residential purposes, together with all my clothing, personal effects, jewelry, and automobiles, and all insurance policies thereon, if any (hereinafter referred to as my "tangible personal property"), to any children of mine who survive me, in such portions as my Executors, in their sole discretion may deem advisable, or sell the same, or any balance thereof, and add the proceeds to my residuary estate.

If no child of mine survives me:

(1)   I give all jewelry I own at my death to my mother, EMILY CISSY HOUSTON, if she survives me; and

(2)   I give the rest of my tangible personal property (or all of my tangible personal property if my mother does not survive me) to those of my mother, EMILY CISSY HOUSTON, my father, JOHN R. HOUSTON, my husband, ROBERT B. BROWN, my brother, MICHAEL, HOUSTON, and my brother, GARY HOUSTON, as survive me, to be amicably divided among them as they might agree, in shares as nearly equal as possible.

If my mother, my father, my husband and my said brothers cannot agree on the distribution of any property which would otherwise be distributed to them under this Article SECOND, I direct that such property be sold and the proceeds be added to my residuary estate.

THIRD: The balance of my estate, whether real or personal and wherever situate (referred to as my "residuary estate") shall be disposed of as follows:

(A) If any issue of mine survive me, my residuary estate shall be paid to my issue living at my death, per stirpes; provided that any part of my residuary estate passing to a child or more remote descendant of mine who is younger that, thirty (30) years of age at my death shall not be paid to him or her outright, but rather I give the same to my Trustees to hold in a separate trust for his or her benefit pursuant to Article FOURTH.

(B) If I leave no issue at my death, my residuary estate shall be paid, in equal shares, to those of my mother, EMILY CISSY HOUSTON, my father, JOHN R. HOUSTON, my husband, ROBERT B. BROWN, my brother, MICHAEL HOUSTON, and my brother, GARY HOKJSTON, who survive me; provided, however, that as to each of my said brothers (regardless of his age), his share of my residuary estate shall not be paid to him outright, but rather the same shall be paid to my Trustees to hold in a separate trust for the benefit of such brother pursuant to Article FIFTH.

FOURTH: The following are the terms of the separate trusts for the respective benefit of any child or more remote descendant of mine who is younger than thirty (30) years of age, each of whom is hereinafter referred to as the "Beneficiary" of his or her separate trust:

(A) My Trustees may, at any time or from time to time, pay to the Beneficiary, or apply for his or her benefit, upon such occasions as my Trustees in their sole discretion shall deem advisable, so much or all (or none) of the entire net income and so much or all (or more) of the principal of the separate trust held for the Beneficiary as my Trustees may deem desirable. At the end of each trust year, my Trustees shall add to the principal of such separate trust any net income not so paid or applied and thereafter the same shall be dealt with as principal for all purposes. Without limiting my Trustees as to occasions upon which payments may be made and without requiring them to make any payment if they deem it inadvisable, I suggest that purposes for which distributions of income and principal might be made include maintenance, educational requirements, engagement, marriage, acquisition of a home, birth of a child, commencement of a new business enterprise or continuance of an existing one, and medical requirements. In granting discretion to my Trustees to make such payments, it is my desire that such discretion be liberally exercised when the occasion, whether one previously specified or not, is such that the interests of the Beneficiary would, in my Trustees' judgment, be best served thereby.

(B)   My Trustees shall make the following distributions of principal to the Beneficiary from his or her separate trust.

(1)   One-tenth ($^1/_{10}$) of the principal when the Beneficiary reaches the age of twenty-one (21) years;

(2)   One-sixth ($^1/_6$) of the then principal when the Beneficiary reaches the age of twenty-five (25) years; and

(3)   The entire remaining principal, together with all accrued and undistributed income, when the Beneficiary reaches the age of thirty (30) years, whereupon the separate trust held for the Beneficiary shall terminate; provided that if the Beneficiary is at least twenty-one (21) years of age at the time the separate trust is set aside for his or her benefit, one-tenth ($^1/_{10}$) of such separate trust shall then be paid to him or her in lieu of the payment specified in subparagraph "(1)" above; and provided further that if the Beneficiary is at least twenty-five (25) years old at the time the separate trust is set aside for his or her benefit, one-fourth ($^1/_4$) of such separate trust shall then be paid to him or her in lieu of the payment specified in subparagraphs "(1)" and "(2)" above.

(C)   If the Beneficiary dies before reaching the age of thirty (30) years, the separate trust held for him or her shall terminate and my Trustees shall pay the remaining principal, together with all accrued and undistributed income, to my issue then living, per stirpes; provided, however, that any property payable to a child or more remote descendant of mine who is younger than thirty (30) years of age at the Beneficiary's death shall not be paid to him or her outright, but rather the same shall be paid to my Trustees to hold in a separate trust for his or her benefit pursuant. to this Article FOURTH; and provided further that all property payable pursuant to this paragraph to a person who is the Beneficiary of a trust under this Will which is then in existence shall, irrespective of the age of such person, be added in its entirety to the principal thereof to be administered therewith and shall not be paid to him or her outright.

(D)   If there be no issue of mine living at the Beneficiary's death, such property shall be paid, in equal shares, to those of my mother, EMILY CISSY HOUSTON, my father, John R. Houston, my husband,

ROBERT B. BROWN, my brother, MICHAEL HOUSTON, and my brother, GARY HOUSTON, who survive the Beneficiary; provided, however, that as to each of my said brothers (regardless of his age), his share of such property shall not be paid to him outright, but rather the same shall be paid to my Trustees to hold in a separate trust for the benefit of such brother pursuant to Article FIFTH.

(E) Notwithstanding any contrary provision in this Willi, the separate trust held for the Beneficiary shall terminate, to the extent that it shall not have previously terminated, twenty-one (21) years after the death of the last survivor of my father, JOHN R. HOUSTON, as were living at the date of my death. Upon the termination of such separate trust pursuant to this provision, my Trustees shall pay the entire then principal, together with all accrued and undistributed income, to the Beneficiary thereof.

FIFTH: The following are the terms of the separate trusts for the benefit of each of my brothers, MICHAEL HOUSTON and GARY HOUSTON (each of whom shall be referred to in this Article as the "Beneficiary" of his separate trust).

(A) My Trustees may, at any time or from time to time, pay to the Beneficiary, or apply for his benefit, upon such occasions as my Trustees, in their sole discretion shall deem advisable, so much or all (or none) of the net income and so much or all (or none) of the principal of the separate trust held for the Beneficiary as my Trustees may deem desirable. At the end of each trust year, my Trustees shall add to the principal of such separate trust any net income not so paid or applied and thereafter the same shall be dealt with as principal for all purposes. Without limiting my Trustees as to occasions upon which payments may be made and without requiring them to make any payment if they deem it inadvisable, I suggest that purposes for which distributions of income and principal might be made include maintenance, support, care, engagement, marriage, acquisition of a home, birth of a child, commencement of a new business enterprises or continuance of an existing one, medical requirements and vacations. In granting discretion to my Trustees to make such payments of income and principal, it is my desire that such discretion be liberally exercised when the occasion, whether one previously specified or not, is such that the interests of the Beneficiary would, in the judgment of my Trustees, be best served thereby, and that the interests of remaindermen in the principal of the trust shall be disregarded in connection therewith.

(B) Upon the Beneficiary's death, the separate trust held for the Beneficiary shall terminate and my Trustees shall pay the remaining principal, together with all accrued and undistributed income, to the same persons, and in the same proportions, as would have inherited such property from me had Î then died intestate, the absolute owner thereof, and a resident of the State of New Jersey; provided, however, that notwithstanding the foregoing, under no circumstances shall any part of my estate or the property held in trust under this Will be paid to JOHN R. HOUSTON

III.

SIXTH: (A) No assignment, disposition, charge or encumbrance of the income or principal of any trust created herein for the benefit of any beneficiary, or any part thereof, by way of anticipation, alienation or otherwise, shall be waived or in any way binding upon my Trustees and I direct that no beneficiary may assign, transfer, encumber or otherwise dispose of such income or principal, or any part thereof, until the same shall be paid to him or her by my Trustees. No income or principal or any part thereof shall be liable to any claim of any creditor of any beneficiary.

(B) If any beneficiary of this Will dies within thirty (30) days after the date of ray death or after the date of death of any other person upon whose death such beneficiary would, but for this paragraph, become entitled to receive either income or principal under this Will, then I direct that for the purposes of this Will, such beneficiary shall be deemed to have predeceased me or such other person, as the case may be.

(C) whenever used in this Will, the word "issue" shall include, for all purposes, persons attaining that status by formal adoption, it being my intention to expressly include any extension of the line of descent by means of adoption.

SEVENTH: Distribution of any property under this Will to a person who is a minor or who is under some other legal disability may be made by my Executors and Trustees directly to such person or to any one with whom such person resides or, in the sole discretion of my Executors and Trustees, may be made to such person's parent or spouse or Guardian, Conservator or Committee in whatever jurisdiction appointed, or, in the case of any such person who is younger than twenty-one (21) years of age, whether or not a minor, to a Custodian for such person's benefit under the Uniform Gifts to Minors Act or Uniform Transfers to Minors Act of any of the following States: the State in which I am a resident at my death; the State in which such person resides; the State in which any Executor or Trustee serving hereunder resides; or the State in which any ancestor, sibling, uncle or aunt of such person resides. The receipt by the one to whom distribution is made pursuant to this Article shall be a full discharge in respect of any property so distributed ever: though such payee may be a fiduciary hereunder. Reference in this Will to a "minor" shall mean a person younger than twenty-one (21) years of age.

EIGHTH: I direct that there shall be no apportionment of any estate, inheritance, transfer, succession, legacy or other death taxes levied or assessed by reason of my death by any governmental authority, domestic or foreign, with respect to any property passing under this Will, or any Codicil hereto, or in respect of any other property passing apart from this Will which may be subject to such taxes. All such taxes, together with interest and penalties thereon, if any, shall be paid as an administration expense from my residuary estate disposed of in Article THIRD, without apportionment among the beneficiaries of my residuary estate. For purposes of this paragraph, such taxes shall not include any generation skipping transfer taxes which may be payable under Chapter 13 of the Code. I expressly recognize that any reduction in tax attributable to property qualifying for the Federal estate tax marital deduction shall inure to the benefit of all recipients of my residuary estate, and not just to the benefit of the recipient of the property qualifying therefor.

NINTH: I confer upon my Executors and trustees all powers and discretion conferred generally upon fiduciaries by Section 3B: 14–23 of the Statutes of the State of New Jersey, and other provisions of this Will, and in addition, Without limiting the foregoing, my Executors and my Trustees shall have the following powers and discretion with respect to all property of whatever kind at any time held by them, including income held by them until its distribution, which they may exercise as they deem advisable:

(A) To retain, sell (at private or public sale), purchase, exchange, invest and reinvest: in bonds, preferred or common stocks, money market funds, certificates of deposit, mortgages, interests in any kind of investment trust, or other evidences or rights, interests or obligations, secured or unsecured, foreign or domestic, or any other property, real or personal and whether or not in the nature of a wasting asset; and to retain and insure the same for any period If time without liability therefor;

(B) To retain investments, cash or property of which I may die possessed, or which may be received by them, for such length of time as to them may seem proper, without liability by reason of such retention and without limitation as to the length of such time;

(C) To employ and to pay the compensation of such agents, accountants, custodians, experts and counsel, legal or investment (including any firm with which a fiduciary hereunder may be associated), and to delegate discretionary powers to, and rely upon information or advice furnished by, such agents, accountants, custodians, experts or counsel;

(D) To improve, lease (for any term, whether or not beyond the term of the administration of my estate or of any trust created hereunder or the term fixed by any law), partition or otherwise deal with or dispose of any real or personal property or any interest therein; to make alterations in, renovations, and extraordinary improvements to any building now or hereafter located on any such property or to demolish the same; to construct new buildings; and to enter into contracts or grant options (for any period) with respect to any of the foregoing;

(E) To consent to the modification, renewal or extension of any note, whether or not secured, or any bond or mortgage, or any term or provision thereof, or any guarantee thereof, or to the release of such guarantee; to release obligors on bonds secured by mortgages or to refrain from instituting suits or actions against such obligors for deficiencies; to use property held under this Will for the protection of any investment in real property or in any mortgage on real property;

(F) To abandon any property, real or personal, which they shall deem to be worthless or not of sufficient value to warrant keeping or protecting; to abstain from the payment of taxes, water rents, assessments, repairs, maintenance and upkeep of such property; to permit such property to be lost by tax sale or other proceeding, or to convey any such property for nominal or no consideration;

(G) To exercise or dispose of any or all options, privileges or rights appurtenant or incident to the ownership of any property; to vote, assent, subscribe, convert property of any other nature; to become a party to, or deposit securities or other property under, or accept securities issued under, any voting trust agreement;

(H) To oppose, assert, or participate in any reorganization, readjustment, recapitalization, liquidation, partial liquidation, consolidation, merger, dissolution, sale or purchase of assets, lease, mortgage, contract or other action or proceeding by any corporation and, in connection therewith, to subscribe to new securities issued pursuant thereto or exchange any property for any other property or pay any assessments or other expenses; to delegate discretionary powers to any reorganization, protective or similar committee;

(I) To borrow money from any party, including any fiduciary hereunder, whether for the purpose of raising funds to pay taxes, to purchase property, to exercise stock options, or otherwise, and to give or not to give security therefor;

(J) To consent to the election by any corporation to be taxed as an "S" corporation under the Internal Revenue Code as it may from time to time exist (or to continue any such election if such election is in effect at the time of ray death);

(K) To make any loans, either secured or unsecured, in Such amounts, and upon such terms, and at such rates of interest, and to such persons, firms or corporations as in the exercise of their discretion they may determine;

(L) To invest, reinvest, exchange and carry on any business conducted by me or in which I may be interested as a shareholder, partner or otherwise, for any period of time; to sell or liquidate the same; or to incorporate any such business;

(M) To hold property in the name of a nominee or unregistered or in such form as will pass by delivery;

(N) To foreclose any mortgage or mortgages, and to take title to the property or any part thereof affected by such mortgage or, in their discretion, to accept a conveyance of any property in lieu of foreclosure, and to collect the rents and income there from, either through a receiver or directly, and to protect such property against foreclosure under any mortgage that shall be a prior lien on said property, or to redeem from foreclosure under any such mortgage, as well as to protect any such property against nonpayment of taxes, assessments or other liens;

(O) To claim administration and other expenses and losses as deductions either in income tax returns of my estate and/or in any estate tax return, whichever would in their opinion result in the payment of the lowest aggregate Of such taxes, without requiring reimbursement of the principal of my residuary estate because of any increase in the estate tax caused by deducting the same in income tax returns, or without making any other adjustments of income or principal, and regardless of the effect that such action on their part may have on the interest of the various beneficiaries under this Will, although my Executors may make such adjustments if they so determine in their absolute discretion;

(P) To satisfy any legacy hereunder, Whether such legacy be general, pecuniary, residuary or otherwise, with any property, including an undivided interest in property, and to allot any property, including an undivided interest in property, to any separate trust created hereunder whether or not the same kind of property is used in the satisfaction of any other such legacy or as allocated to other trusts created hereunder;

(Q) To allocate any federal exemption from the federal generation-skipping transfer tax to any property with respect to which I am the transferor for purposes of said tax, whether or not such property passes under this Will or outside this Will, including, but not limited to, any property which I have transferred during my life to which I did not make an allocation and any property over which I have a general power of appointment, regardless of whether Í exercise such power of appointment, and to exclude any such property;

(R) My Executors and my Trustees shall he deemed to have acted within the scope of their authority, to have exercised reasonable care, diligence and prudence, and to have acted impartially as to all persons interested including, but not limited to tax elections, unless the contrary be proved by affirmative evidence, and in the absence of such proof shall not be liable for loss arising from depreciation or shrinkage in value of any property herein authorized to be held or acquired.

TENTH: In addition to the powers and discretion conferred upon my fiduciaries by Article NINTH, as to each and any corporation, partnership or other business entity, public or private (including any successor thereto), in which my fiduciaries, as such, hold or acquire any interest (each such corporation, partnership or other business entity being hereafter referred to as the "Entity"), I authorize my fiduciaries to retain the shares thereof or interest therein for as long as they deem it to be in the best interests of my estate or the trusts held under this Will, regardless of the fact that such shares or interest might produce no income, regardless of any duty to diversify investments, and notwithstanding any other fiduciary obligation which might-require them to dispose of such shares or interest, other than the obligation to act with reasonable care.

In addition, I authorize my fiduciaries, to the extent permitted by law, to exercise their rights and powers as holders of such shares or interest to effect the continued operation of the Entity or the sale or other disposition of the Entity or of its assets or business, or, in their sole discretion, to sell, exchange, offer for redemption or otherwise dispose of the shares or interest in the Entity owned by my estate or the trusts held under this Will, or to effect the liquidation or dissolution of the Entity, at such time or times and upon such terms and conditions as shall, in the opinion of my fiduciaries, be in the best interests of my estate or of the trusts held under this Will. So long as my fiduciaries continue to hold any interest in the Entity, I authorize and empower them to participate in the management of the Entity to the extent that their interest therein enables them to do so, without liability or responsibility for any loss resulting from the exercise of the powers hereby granted, or they may delegate their managerial authority to others, whether by means of employment agreements or other arrangements, and they may enter into voting trusts and grant irrevocable proxies, as they deem advisable.

Consequently and to these ends, I expressly authorize my fiduciaries to select, vote for and remove directors of the Entity (if the Entity is a corporation); to take part in the management of the Entity and, to the extent permitted by law, in their managerial capacity to fix, determine or change the policy thereof; to name or change officers, the managing personnel and/or the operating personnel; to employ new management; to reduce, expand, limit or otherwise change the business or type of merchandise dealt in or property invested in and investments held by or product manufactured by or service rendered by the Entity; to require the employees and/or the officers of the Entity to file bonds for the faithful performance of their duties; to determine the amount of bond or bonds to be secured; to select the bonding company; to employ expert outside and disinterested accountants or engineers to make a full and complete survey or appraisal of the Entity's business and its prospects in the trade; to employ investment or legal counsel (including any firm with which a fiduciary hereunder may be associated) whenever my fiduciaries shall deem it advisable; to charge the cost of all such services against the interest in the Entity held by my fiduciaries or to vote or take other action to require the Entity owning said business to pay such expenses; to contribute additional working capital or to subscribe to additional stock as they may see fit; and to take all steps and perform all acts which they shall deem necessary or advisable in connection therewith. Any one or more of my fiduciaries may act as an officer, director, manager or employee of the Entity, and my fiduciaries are specifically authorized to exercise their rights inhering in their ownership, as such fiduciaries, for the election or appointment of any person or persons, including themselves, as directors, officers, managers and the like. Any such fiduciary who may serve as an officer, d3 rector, manager or employee of the Entity shall be entitled to receive compensation for such services notwithstanding that my fiduciaries may themselves (whether individually or as fiduciaries hereunder) be in a position to determine or control the determination of the amount of such compensation, and I direct that no such person shall be required to furnish any bond in connection with any such employment.

In providing as I have, I am aware that conflicts of interest may arise by reason of service hereunder on the part of my fiduciaries and as an officer, director, manager or employee of the Entity. Nevertheless, I have so provided because I have absolute confidence in their business judgment and integrity. It is my intention that any such fiduciary shall, in all respects, be free to exercise the powers and discretion herein conferred as fully and unrestrictedly as if there were no such conflicting interests. With this thought in mind, I expressly exempt my fiduciaries from the adverse operation of any rule of law which might otherwise apply to them in the performance of their fiduciary duties by reason of a conflict of interest. Without limiting the generality of the foregoing, I specifically direct that they shall not have any greater burden of justification in respect of their acts as fiduciaries by reason of a conflict of interest than they would have in the absence of any such conflict.

For purposes of this Will the term "fiduciaries" shall include my Executors, my Trustees, and anyone or more of them and any Successor Executor or Successor.

ELEVENTH: I appoint my attorney, SHELDON PLATT, as Executor of my Will. I appoint my sister-in-law, DONNA HOUSTON, and my attorney, SHELDCN PLATT, as Trustees under this Will. I appoint my husband, ROBERT B. BRÖWN, as Guardian of the person and property of my minor children. If my husband shall fail or cease to act for any reason, I appoint my sister-in-law, DONNA HOUSTON, as Guardian in his place. If ancillary probate of this Will in serving as my Domiciliary fiduciaries. My Ancillary fiduciaries shall have the same powers and discretion, as are conferred upon my Domiciliary fiduciaries.

Except as herein above provided in this Article, the last acting individual sole Trustee for whom no designated successor shall be available to act: for any reason whatsoever may designate pursuant to a written instrument executed by him or her during his or her lifetime, one or more individuals and/or corporate banking institutions as co-Trustee, to serve with such individual or to succeed such individual as Trustee, in the event he or she shall cease to act for any reason whatsoever.

I direct that no fiduciary (including an Ancillary fiduciary) serving hereunder, whether as Executor, Trustee or Guardian, or as Successor thereto, shall be required to file or furnish any bond or other security, any provision of law to the contrary notwithstanding. All references in this Will to my "Executors", "Trustees" and "Guardians" and the pronouns and verbs corresponding thereto, shall be deemed to include all Successors, and shall be deemed to refer to each Executor, Trustee and Guardian serving hereunder at any time and shall be construed in the masculine or feminine and in the singular or plural, whichever construction is consistent with facts prevailing at any given time.

IN WITNESS WHEREOF, I have hereunto set my hand and seal this 3rd day of February, in the year One Thousand Nine Hundred and Ninety-Three.

SUBSCRIBED, PUBLISHED and DECLARED by the above-named Testatrix, WHITNEY E. HOUSTON, as and for her Last Will and Testament in the presence of us, who, at her request, in her presence and in the presence of each other, have hereunto subscribed our names as witnesses, this 3rd day of February in the year One Thousand Nine Hundred and Ninety-Three.

_____ residing at _____

_____ residing at _____

I, WHITNEY E. HOUSTON, as testatrix, sign my name to this instrument this 3rd day of February, 1993, and being first duly sworn, do hereby declare to the undersigned authority that I sign and execute this instrument as my Last Will and Testament and that I sign; it willingly, that I execute it as my free and voluntary act for the purposes therein expressed, and that I am 18 years of age or older, of sound mind, and under no constraint

_____ [signature and date of testator]

And [include names], the witnesses, being first duly sworn, do each hereby declare to the undersigned authority that the testatrix signs and executes this instrument as her Last Will and Testament and that she signs it willingly, and that each of us states that in the presence and hearing of the testatrix he hereby signs this Will as witness to the testatrix's signing, and that to the best of our knowledge the testatrix is 18 years of age or older.

[Witness signatures for self-proving affidavit]

STATE OF NEW JERSEY

COUNTY OF BERGIN

Subscribed, sworn to and acknowledged before me by WHITNEY E. HOUSTON, the testatrix, and subscribed and sworn to before me by _____ and, witnesses this 3rd day of

Jordan S. Weitberg, An Attorney-at-Law of New Jersey

February, 1993.[3]

3　　[Eds.] We have omitted a 2000 codicil, which changed executors and lawyers.

13.   SAMPLE REVOCABLE TRUST AGREEMENT[4]

Trust agreement made *[date of agreement]*, between *[name of trustor]*, of *[address of trustor]* ("trustor"), and *[name of trustee]*, a corporation organized under the laws of *[name of state]*, having its principal office at *[address of trustee]* ("trustee").

In consideration of the terms and conditions set forth in this agreement, the parties agree as follows:

SECTION ONE. TRANSFER IN TRUST

Trustor, concurrently with the execution of this trust agreement, has transferred to trustee the assets set forth in the attached Schedule *[designation of schedule]*, incorporated by this reference and initialed by trustor, trustee, and each of the witnesses to this trust agreement. These assets, together with any assets which may be added to this trust pursuant to the provisions of SECTION SIX, shall be held by trustee on the trust, for the uses and subject to the provisions set forth below.

SECTION TWO. CONTROL OF INVESTMENTS

During trustor's life, unless and until trustor is certified to be incapacitated as provided in this agreement, (a) trustor shall retain the right to approve changes in the investment of the trust assets, (b) trustee shall pay or apply the entire net income from the trust as trustor may from time to time direct in writing, and (c) trustee shall pay to trustor such sums or assets from the principal of the trust as trustor may from time to time request in writing delivered to trustee during trustor's lifetime.

Should trustor at any time during the existence of this trust agreement become so physically or mentally incapacitated as to be unable to attend to business or financial affairs, and that fact is attested to by trustor's regular attending physician, trustee shall pay to or apply directly for the benefit of trustor so much of the net income and principal of the trust as, in the discretion of trustee, is necessary to provide for trustor's maintenance and support in *[his/her]* accustomed manner of living in the payment of *[his/her]* medical, dental, hospital, and nursing care expenses.

---

[4]   Source: Revocable trust agreement—Investment control retained by trustor until trustor's death or incapacity—Division of trust property into separate trusts for trustor's child and grandchildren after trustor's death, 17B AM. JUR. LEGAL FORMS 2d § 251:50, § 251:50. This form is reprinted with permission of Thomson Reuters.

SECTION THREE. DISPOSITION OF TRUST PROPERTY ON TRUSTOR'S DEATH

After trustor's death, trustee shall hold and dispose of the trust property as follows:

A.   Until the trust shall terminate as specified in this agreement, trustee shall pay the entire net income to or for the benefit of trustor's *[son/daughter]*, *[name of child]*.

Trustee is authorized and empowered in the sole discretion of trustee, at any time and from time to time, to disburse the income of the trust estate in such amounts as trustee may deem advisable to provide adequately and properly for the support and maintenance of trustor's *[son/daughter]*, but shall not take from the principal of this trust unless it is necessary for expenses incurred by illness, disability, or education. In determining the amount of principal to be so disbursed, trustee shall take into consideration any other income or property which the party shall have from any other source. Trustee's discretion shall be conclusive as to the advisability of any such disbursement and the same shall not be questioned by anyone. For all sums so disbursed, trustee shall be fully discharged.

B.   On the expiration of *[number of years]* years from the date of the execution of this agreement, or on the death of the *[son/daughter]* of trustor, whichever event first occurs, trustee shall divide the trust property into two separate, equal funds, the first to be distributed outright to the *[son/daughter]* of trustor, *[name of child]*, if living. Trustee shall divide the remaining trust estate, or the entire trust estate if the *[son/daughter]* of trustor shall not then be living, into separate trusts, equal in value, one for each child of the *[son/daughter]* of trustor then-living. Each trust set aside for a living child of the *[son/daughter]* of trustor shall be held and disposed of as follows:

1.   Trustee shall use so much of the income and principal of the trust for the reasonable support and education (including college and professional education) of the child, even to the point of completely exhausting the same.

2.   After the child of the *[son/daughter]* of trustor shall have reached the age of *[age of child at termination]* years, the trust shall terminate as to that child and trustee shall distribute the balance of the child's fund to the child, in fee.

If any child shall have attained the age of *[age of child at termination]* when the trust fund is to be set apart for the child, trustee shall distribute to the child all amounts of the trust fund (instead of holding the same in trust) as are directed to be distributed to the child on attaining such age.

3.   On the death of any child for whom a trust fund has been set apart under this Section, prior to the child's receiving the entire corpus of the child's fund, trustee shall distribute the trust fund equally and in fee to trustor's *[son/daughter]*'s then-living issue, except that the share of any beneficiary for whose primary benefit another trust is then to be held under this instrument shall be added to and commingled with the other trust and held as if it had been an original part of the other trust.

4.   If trustor's *[son/daughter]* and all of *[his/her]* issue shall die prior to the complete distribution of all of the trust created by this agreement, then on the happening of that event trustee shall distribute the trust estate, as then constituted, to trustor's heirs-at-law in accordance with the laws of descent and distribution then in effect in *[name of state]*.

SECTION FOUR. POWERS OF TRUSTEE

[Statement of provisions regarding powers of trustee].

SECTION FIVE. COMPENSATION OF TRUSTEE

As compensation for trustee's services under this agreement, trustee shall receive the fee set forth in trustee's then current Schedule of Trust Fees.

SECTION SIX. REVOCATION AND AMENDMENT OF TRUST

Trustor reserves the right and power to alter, amend, or revoke this agreement at any time. Trustor may do so from time to time, either in whole or in part, without the consent of trustee or any beneficiary under this agreement, by written notice to trustee to that effect. However, the duties, responsibilities, and rate of compensation of trustee shall not be altered or modified without trustee's written consent.

SECTION SEVEN. GOVERNING LAW

This agreement shall be construed and regulated in all respects by the laws of *[name of state]*.

SECTION EIGHT. TRUSTEE'S GENERAL DUTIES INVOLVING ACCOUNTS AND TAXES

Trustee shall be under no duty to examine, verify, question, or audit the books, records, or accounts or transactions of any executor, administrator, or other personal representative of trustor. The trustee shall not have any responsibility for any act or omission of any such executor, administrator, or other personal representative.

In addition to the other provisions of this agreement, and not by way of limitation, trustee may rely conclusively on the written statements of trustor's personal representative with respect to the value of trustor's adjusted gross estate for federal estate tax purposes, the adjusted basis of any property passing to trustee for purposes of gain or loss, and such other information as may be pertinent in making the allocation of the trust property.

SECTION NINE. RESIGNATION OF TRUSTEE

Trustee shall have the right to resign at any time on *[number of days]* days' written notice to trustor, in which event trustee shall deliver all assets held to trustor or in accordance with trustor's written directions.

After trustor's death trustee may resign at any time by giving written notice, specifying the effective date of resignation, to the beneficiary or beneficiaries, at the time of giving notice, of the current income.

SECTION TEN. SUCCESSOR TRUSTEE

Any successor trustee, with the written approval of the person or persons appointing the successor trustee may accept, without examination or review, the accounts rendered and the property delivered by or for a predecessor trustee, without incurring any liability or responsibility for so doing. Any successor trustee shall have all the title, powers, and discretion of trustee succeeded, without the necessity of any conveyance or transfer.

Trustor and trustee have executed this agreement at *[place of execution]* the day and year first above-written.

[Name of trustor]

[Name of trustee]

By:

[Name of officer of trustee]

[Title of officer of trustee]

[Acknowledgments]

[Attachment of schedule]

14. DEED TO TRANSFER REAL PROPERTY TO A TRUST[5]

The Grantor, John Grantor, in consideration of 10 dollars and other valuable considerations received from the Grantee, hereby grants and conveys to the Grantee, Mary Trustee, as trustee of the [Name of Trust], whose mailing address is [Address], all right, title, and interest that the Grantor may have in and to the lands in [County], [State], described below.

[Legal Description]

The Grantee, as trustee, shall have the power and authority to protect, conserve, sell, lease, encumber, or otherwise manage and dispose of the real property described above.

[The trustee named herein has been given the power to appoint a successor trustee in his last will and testament admitted to probate.]

Dated this day of ___, 20.

Signed in the presence of: [Grantor]

Two witnesses

State of

County of

The foregoing instrument was acknowledged before me by Grantor, this day of ___, 20 ___.

Notary Public

15. My commission expires:

16. (Affix notarial seal)

5   Source: *Sample deed from grantor to trustee*, Edward Koren, Estate, Tax and Personal Financial Planning § 19:10 (2017). This form is reprinted with permission of Thomson Reuters.

15. SAMPLE SPECIAL NEEDS TRUST[6]

[Name] IRREVOCABLE TRUST

THIS TRUST is made and entered into by and between the following:

Settlor: *(hereinafter called "Settlor").*

Co-Trustees: and *(hereinafter called "Trustee" or, collectively, "Trustees").*

WITNESSETH:

WHEREAS, the Settlor desires to create a trust to hold such property itemized and described in "Exhibit A" attached hereto and made a part hereof, together with such monies, life insurance, securities, and other assets as the Trustees may hereafter at any time hold or acquire hereunder (all of said property being hereinafter referred to as the "Trust Estate") for the purposes hereinafter set forth.

NOW, THEREFORE, in consideration of the premises and the mutual covenants herein contained, the Settlor agrees to execute such further instruments as shall be necessary to transfer said property to the Trust and the Trustees agree to hold the Trust estate, IN TRUST, NEVERTHELESS, for the following uses and purposes and subject to the terms and conditions hereinafter set forth:

ARTICLE I

DEFINITIONS

A.   ADDITIONS TO CORPUS

The Settlor, or any other person with the consent of the Trustees, may add to the principal of the Trust created herein by donation, deed, will, or otherwise. Such additions shall be covered by the provisions hereof, the same as if originally included herein.

B.   LAWS GOVERNING

This Agreement shall be construed, enforced and regulated in all respects by the laws of the State of Florida and in the Courts of the State of Florida.

C.   BENEFICIARY

(disabled child) is a disabled or disabled person receiving Supplemental Security Income and Medicaid benefits. During her lifetime, she shall be considered the

---

[6]   Source: Irrevocable special needs trust for disabled heir alone, 14 FLA. PRACTICE, ELDER LAW § 11:25 (Jerome Ira Solkoff and Scott M. Solkoff, 2015–2016 ed.).

prime and first beneficiary of this Trust for all purposes and the Trustees shall consider her as the Trustee's primary interest and responsibility. However, all income and principal of the trust estate during the lifetime of *(disabled child)* shall be administered, rearranged, held, applied and/or distributed only in strict conformity with the provisions of Article II-C hereof, as this trust is made expressly to supplement and not replace any governmental assistance available or which may in the future be available to *(disabled child)*.

D.   NAME OF TRUST

This Trust shall, for convenience, be known by the name following and it shall be sufficient that it be referred to as such in any deed, assignment, bequest, or devise by that name, to wit: *[Name]***IRREVOCABLE   TRUST**

E.   EDUCATION

The term "education" shall include all forms of education including but not limited to, public or private schools, primary or secondary, college, advanced college or post-college, commercial, vocational, technical, business or art education; or otherwise.

ARTICLE II

ADMINISTRATION DURING LIFETIME OF SETTLOR

A.   LIFE INSURANCE

The Settlor may, but need not necessarily, name the Trust Estate as beneficiary of life insurance policies. Furthermore, the Settlor may directly maintain life insurance policies, change beneficiaries thereon, borrow against the same, receive dividends thereon, pledge and hypothecate such policies as security for undertakings, exercise any option granted under such policies, and may withdraw such policies from this Trust as the owner of the policies wishes.

B.   RIGHT TO REVOKE AND AMEND THE TRUST

This Trust is irrevocable. The Settlor expressly waives any right to make changes to this Trust agreement other than as described within this subparagraph and state their express intent that this Trust be construed as, and in fact operate as, an irrevocable trust. In no event shall any change to this Trust be effective which would serve to alter the beneficiary designation expressed herein, or which would serve to grant the lifetime beneficiary power over the property of the Trust. The Trustee, however, shall have the power to amend at any time, or from time to time, the administrative provisions of the Trust, by any instrument in writing, signed and acknowledged by the Trustee, to conform with federal or state law or to better effect the purposes of the Trust. For purposes of the foregoing, "administrative provision" refers to any provision of the Trust dealing with the management and administration of the Trust, and in no event shall any such amendment affect, enlarge, or shift any beneficial interests created hereunder. The purpose of this power to amend is to permit the Trustee:

(1)   To cope with tax and/or other circumstantial changes that may affect such trust and/or its beneficiaries;

(2)   To take advantage of changed trust drafting approaches to coping with potential trust problems (or otherwise improve the clarity and administerability of the trust provisions);

(3)   To comply with qualification requirements for public benefit programs, including, but not limited to, Supplemental Security Income, and medical assistance or Medicaid, and further including the changed qualification requirements that may be applicable if *(disabled child)* moves to other states; and/or

(4)   To carry out the expressed intent of the Trust, in the event that changed laws and/or circumstances and/or changes in's *(disabled child)* condition would otherwise cause this trust to fail to carry out such expressed intent.

In exercising this power to amend, the Trustee shall observe the general fiduciary duties of loyalty, good faith, fairness, and due care.

Further, the Trustee or any interested party may seek a judicial amendment of this Trust for the aforementioned purposes upon appropriate motion to a court of competent jurisdiction, however this Trust may not be amended by the Court *sua sponte*, nor may the State seek a judicial amendment of the Trust.

C.   LIFETIME BENEFITS TO OR FOR *(disabled child)*

During the lifetime of *(disabled child)* the Trustee shall manage, invest, and reinvest the portion of the Residuary Trust meant for her, collect the income thereof, and shall, *in the absolute discretion of the Trustee*, pay over or apply all of such part of the income and/or principal thereof as the Trustee deems necessary, wise, or prudent for: (i) *(disabled child)*'s use, care, support, maintenance, or general welfare, or apply the same for any such purposes; and (ii) any taxes of any nature, source or amount levied or assessed against *(disabled child)*, the Trust Estate, this Trust or the income of *(disabled child)*. All undistributed income shall be added to the principal. *(disabled child)*, from time to time, may refuse receipt of any such payment or application and may direct that no payment or application be made in her behalf.

Notwithstanding any provision of this Trust Agreement to the contrary, the whole of *(disabled child)*'s share of income and principal is only to be used for *(disabled child)*'s special needs. A Trustee shall have no discretion to pay or apply income and/or principal to or for the benefit of *(disabled child)* for any purpose other than for the special needs of *(disabled child)*. The term "special needs" refers to the requisites for maintaining *(disabled child)*'s good health, safety, and welfare when, in the discretion of the Trustee, such requisites are not being provided by any public or quasi-public agency, office or department of any state or of the United States. "Special needs" shall include, but not be limited to, medical and dental expenses, insurance therefor, travel, entertainment, programs of training and education, hobby supplies, luxuries, housing, nursing services, psychological and/or psychiatric services, care monitoring and/or management, roommate provision, nurses' aides, podiatry and/or chiropractic services, and/or clothing and other daily necessities. Except to the extent specified above, this Trust is created expressly for *(disabled child)*'s extra and supplemental care, maintenance, support, and education, in addition to and over and above the benefits *(disabled child)* receives or may receive from any local, state, or federal government, or from any private agencies, any of which provide services or benefits to disabled or incapacitated persons. It is the express purpose of this Trust that funds be used solely to supplement other benefits received by *(disabled child)* and not supplant the same. The Trustee shall have no discretion to pay or provide health, food, and home expenses to or for *(disabled child)*.

It is further the intent of this Trust that, except to the extent specified above, no part of the corpus of the trust created herein shall be used to supplant or replace public assistance benefits of any county, state, federal, or governmental agency. For purposes of determining *(disabled child)*'s eligibility for such benefits, except to the extent specified above, no part of the principal or income of the trust estate shall be considered available to *(disabled child)*. In the event the Trustee is requested by any department or agency to release principal or income of the trust to or on behalf of *(disabled child)* to pay for equipment, medication, or services that other organizations or agencies are authorized to provide, or in the event Trustee is requested by any department or agency administering such benefits to petition the court or any other administrative agency for the release of trust principal or income for this purpose, the Trustee shall deny such request and is directed to defend, at the expense of the trust estate, any contest of this Agreement or other attack of any nature. The Trustee shall have complete discretion with regard to the defense of any such claim, including the management of all litigation which may result. Trustee also shall be authorized, in the Trustee's complete discretion, to settle, in whole or in part, or otherwise compromise any such claim or litigation.

The Trustee, when applying funds for the benefit of *(disabled child)*, may apply or give funds to care managers and/ or monitors, social service organizations, and other professionals who provide care management, personal services, or care monitoring services for. Moreover, the Trustee may pay housing expenses and expenses of live-in care management or a live-in monitor for *(disabled child)*.

Should *(disabled child)* abandon a home which may be owned by the Trust for benefit of *(disabled child)*, or should the Trustee believe that it is not economically sound or otherwise feasible for *(disabled child)* to continue to reside in said home, the Trustee may sell the home, after making proper provision for *(disabled child)*'s living arrangements, and apply the net proceeds to the share of *(disabled child)* in the Residuary Trust, to be held pursuant to the provisions of this Agreement.

ARTICLE III

ADMINISTRATION UPON
DEATH OF DISABLED CHILD

A.   COLLECTION OF INSURANCE PROCEEDS

The Trustees shall collect the proceeds of any life insurance policies subject hereto when they, by the terms thereof, become payable to the Trust or to the Trustees in their fiduciary capacity, adding any proceeds thereof to the principal of the Trust Estate. Full authority is given to the Trustees to take legal action to collect all such insurance proceeds and to be reimbursed for the costs thereof and any personal liability they may incur due to such litigation from the Trust Estate. No insurance company shall be required to inquire into or take notice of any of the provisions of this Trust Agreement or to see to the application or distribution of the policy proceeds, and the receipt of the Trustees or any of them to such insurance company shall be effectual to release and discharge the insurance company for any payment so made and shall be binding upon the beneficiaries of this Trust.

B.   EXPENSES AND COST OF ESTATE SETTLEMENT

Upon the death of *(disabled child)*, the Trustees shall comply with all laws regarding Trustees' duties and laws as to creditor claims of her Estate and may pay or settle from the Trust Estate all or part of the just debts, funeral, administrative, and inheritance and/or estate tax expenses of the estate, and Trust administration as the Trustees deem necessary, wise, and/or prudent.

ARTICLE IV

DISTRIBUTION OF TRUST

A. DISTRIBUTIONS

Upon the death of *(disabled child)* the balance of the Trust Estate, after the payments aforesaid, if any, shall be held, managed and distributed as provided in this Article IV and shall be set aside as a separate trust to be designated the "Residuary Trust." The Residuary Trust shall be held, administered, and distributed as follows:

1. Bequests: a) The Trustee shall distribute fifty (50%) percent of the Residuary Trust to or for the benefit of Settlor's child, (name), per stirpes.

b) The Trustee shall distribute the balance of the Residuary Trust, to or for the benefit of the grandchildren of Settlor, then living, in equal shares, per capita. Should no grandchild survive, then all of the Residuary Trust shall be distributed as provided in subparagraph (a) above.

c) Should no child or grandchild of Settlor survive at the time distribution is to be made, then the entire Residuary Trust shall be distributed to (Name of Charity).

2. Payment delays: Any share payment may be delayed as necessary to accommodate maturity dates of time deposits, payments of Trust expenses, and Trust administrative duties.

3. Minors: For purposes of this Agreement a minor is defined as someone under the age of twenty-five (25) years. If a separate share shall be created for someone who is a minor at the time of Settlor's death or who is a minor at the time a payment or application of income and/or principal is to be made to or for the benefit of such minor, such portion shall immediately vest in such minor (except as may otherwise be provided in this Agreement), and the distribution of income and/or principal thereof may be postponed by the Trustees, in the absolute discretion of the Trustees, until such minor attains the age of twenty-five (25) years. In the meantime, however, the Trustees shall pay or apply as much of the net income and/or principal of such portion to or for the benefit of such minor as the Trustees shall deem necessary or proper, in the Trustees' sole discretion, to or for the benefit of such minor.

ARTICLE V

GENERAL PROVISIONS

A. PAYMENTS TO OR FOR BENEFICIARIES

The Trustees have sole and absolute discretion to make payments of principal and/or income to a beneficiary of this Trust in one (1) or more of the following four (4) ways as the Trustees deem best in their opinion: (i) directly to such beneficiary; (ii) to the legally appointed guardian or conservator of such beneficiary; (iii) to some relative or friend of the beneficiary for the care, support, and/or education of such beneficiary; and/or (iv) by the Trustees, using such amounts directly for such beneficiary's care, support, and/or education.

B. SPENDTHRIFT PROVISIONS

No disposition, charge, or encumbrance of either the income or principal of any of the separate shares in trust or any part thereof, by any beneficiary hereunder (including the Settlor as beneficiary) by way of anticipation, shall be of any validity or legal effect or be in anyway regarded by the Trustees, and no such income or principal, or any part, shall in anyway be liable to any claim of any creditor for any such beneficiary, except in those cases where all of the credit extended, liability, claim, and/or the assignment of the beneficiary's interest hereunder as collateral therefor has first been approved unanimously by all Trustees in the absolute discretion of Trustees. In exercising such discretion, the Trustees shall ascertain whether or not it would appear to be in the best interest of the beneficiary or the same would appear to be in the contemplation of Settlor that credit be accepted, the claim or liability be allowed, and collateral given and may, without stated reason, decline to approve such credit, liability, claim, and/or assignment. No beneficiary may, voluntarily or involuntarily, transfer, assign, hypothecate, pledge, or otherwise control any income or principal of his or her share, if any, of the trust without first obtaining the written consent of the Settlors who are then living, or, if the Settlors are deceased, all Trustees then serving. Such consents may be unreasonably denied.

C. PROTECTION AGAINST PERPETUITIES

All distributions required by this Trust Agreement and the final accounting of the Trust must be accomplished and finished as provided in this Agreement and, in any event, no later than twenty-one (21) years after the last to die of the expressly named, individual beneficiaries noted in Article IV hereof, or, if such beneficiaries are all charities, than twenty-one (21) years after the death of the Settlor. No judicial modification of this provision shall be permitted.

ARTICLE VI

POWERS AND DUTIES OF TRUSTEES

A. INVESTMENTS AND DUTIES

The Trustees and each Successor Trustee shall have all powers and authority conferred upon trustees by the laws of the State of Florida, besides such additional powers and authority conferred by the provisions of this Agreement. In exercising such powers, the Trustees shall be bound to do only what a reasonably prudent person would do in like circumstances.

The Trustees of each Trust established hereunder (including any Successor Trustee) shall have the continuing, absolute, discretionary power to deal with any property, real or personal, held in such Trusts. Such power may be exercised independently and without the prior or subsequent approval of any Court or judicial authority, and no person dealing with such Trustees shall be required to inquire into the propriety of any of the actions of such Trustees. The Trustees shall not be limited to the type, amount, and character of investments in which the Trustees may invest the funds of this Trust, so long as the Trustees use reasonable prudence and judgment in the selection of investments. In the event there are Co-Trustees hereof, such Co-Trustees are authorized to arrange that any account with any third party titled in the name of the Trustees or this Trust can be dealt with by less than all of the said Co-Trustees; for example, an account or asset that is titled in the name of all Co-Trustees or this Trust can be established or issued in such manner as to allows for the signature of less than all of the Co-Trustees, including, but not limited to, only one of the Co-Trustees, to act upon such asset or account. The Trustees shall have the following general powers, in addition to, and not by way of limitation of, the powers provided by law:

1.   Retention: To retain any property for any period whether or not the same be of the character permissible for investments by fiduciaries under any applicable law, and without regard to any effect the retention may have upon the diversification of the investments.

2.   Sell: To sell, transfer, exchange, convert, or otherwise dispose of, or grant options with respect to any security or property, real or personal, including homestead property, held as part of the Trust Estate, at public or private sale, with or without security, in such manner, at such time or times, for such purposes, for such prices, and upon such terms, credits, and conditions as the Trustees may deem advisable.

3. Invest: To invest and reinvest all or any part of the Trust Estate in any property and undivided interests in property, wherever located, including bonds, debentures, notes, secured or unsecured, stocks of corporations regardless of class, interests in limited partnerships, real estate or any interest in real estate whether or not productive at the time of investment, interests in trusts, investment trusts, whether of the open and/or closed fund types, and insurance contracts on the life of any beneficiary or annuity contracts for any beneficiary, without being limited by any statute or rule of law concerning investments by fiduciaries.

4. Liquidity: To render liquid the Trust Estate or any trust created hereunder, in whole or in part at any time or from time to time, and hold cash or readily marketable securities of little or no yield for such period as the Trustees may deem advisable.

5. Lease: To lease any such property beyond the period fixed by statutes for leases made by a Trustee and beyond the duration of the Trust Estate or any Trust created hereunder.

6. Securities: To join in or become a party to, or to oppose, any reorganization, readjustment, recapitalization, foreclosure, merger, voting trust, dissolution, consolidation, or exchange, and to deposit any securities with any committee, depository, or trustee, and to pay any and all fees, expenses, and assessments incurred in connection therewith, and to charge the same to the principal, to exercise conversion, subscripting or other rights, and to make any necessary payments in connection therewith, or to sell any such privileges.

7. Vote: To vote in person at any meeting of stock or security holders, or any adjournment of such meetings, or to vote by general or limited proxy with respect to any such shares of stock or other securities held by the Trustees.

8. Nominee: To hold securities in the name of a nominee without indicating the trust character of such holding, or unregistered, or in such form as will pass by delivery.

9. Claims: To pay, compromise, compound, adjust, submit to arbitration, sell, or release any claim or demands of the Trust Estate, or any Trust created hereunder, against others, or of others against the same as the Trustees may deem advisable, including the acceptance of deeds of real property in satisfaction of bonds and mortgages, and to make any payments in connection therewith which the Trustees may deem advisable.

10. Real Property: To possess, manage, sell, insure against loss by fire or other casualties, develop, subdivide, control, partition, mortgage, lease, or otherwise deal with any and all real property, including homestead property; to satisfy and discharge or extend the term of any mortgage thereon; to execute the necessary instruments and covenants to effectuate the foregoing powers, including the giving or granting of options in connection therewith; to make improvements, structural or otherwise, or abandon the same if deemed to be worthless or not of sufficient value to warrant keeping or protecting; to abstain from the payment of taxes, water rents, assessments, repairs, maintenance, or upkeep of the same; to permit to be lost by tax sale or other proceeding or to convey the same for a nominal consideration or without consideration; to set up appropriate reserves out of income for repairs, modernization, and upkeep of buildings, including reserves for depreciation and obsolescence, and to add such reserves to the principal, and, if the income from the property itself should not suffice for such purposes, if allowable in determining the federal estate tax payable by Settlor's estate, to advance any income of the Trust for the amortization of any mortgage on property held in the Trust.

11. Distributions: To make distributions in cash or in kind, or partly in cash and partly in kind and to divide, partition, allocate, or distribute particular assets or undivided interests therein, without any obligation to make proportionate distributions or to distribute to all beneficiaries property having an equivalent income tax basis, and without regard to any provision of law expressing a preference for distribution in kind, and to value such property to the extent permitted by law, and to cause any share to be composed of cash, property, or undivided fractional shares in property different in kind from any other share.

12. Instruments: To execute and deliver any and all instruments in writing which are deemed advisable to carry out any of the foregoing powers. No party to any such instrument in writing signed by the Trustees shall be obliged to inquire into its validity.

13. Trust Funds: To invest any part or all of the principal of the Trust Estate in any common trust fund, legal or discretionary, which may be established and operated by and under the control of the Trustees.

14. Allocations: To determine, irrespective of statute or rule of law, what shall be fairly and equitably charged or credited to income and what to principal, notwithstanding any determination by the courts or by any custom or statute, and whether or not establish depreciation reserves.

15. Possession: To allow temporary possession of, and to make available, personal property for the personal use of any beneficiary hereof; if any item(s) of personal property are held in trust by the Trustees for the benefit of such beneficiary.

16. Employ Experts: To employ legal counsel, accountants, and agents deemed advisable by the Trustee and to pay them reasonable compensation.

17. Distributions: Notwithstanding any provision of F.S.A. § 732.402, subsection 4, to the contrary, a Trustee: (i) may make discretionary distribution of income or principal, to or for the benefit of such Trustee if otherwise provided in this Agreement; and (ii) may make discretionary allocations of receipts or expenses as between principal and income.

B. SHARES

Notwithstanding anything herein to the contrary, the Trustees shall administer any and all Trusts created herein as separate and distinct, but commonly administered shares.

C. COMPENSATION AND ACCOUNTING

1. Compensation: The Trustees shall not be entitled to receive compensation for services rendered hereunder, but shall be reimbursed for all reasonable expenses incurred in the management and protection of the Trust Estate; provided, however, that in the event a bank, trust company, or attorney (who is other than a beneficiary of Settlor) shall be a trustee, he or it shall be entitled to reasonable compensation based upon his or its then standard charge for other trusts of similar size.

2. Accounting: Each Trustee shall render to Settlor and each other Trustee full accounting of such act, payment, distribution, or investment within thirty (30) days of such action. If there are no other trustees and Settlor is deceased or incompetent, the said acting Trustee shall render such full accounting to the beneficiaries named or alluded to in this Trust Agreement's Article IV.

D. DISABILITY OR INCOMPETENCY

1. Definition: Any Trustee shall be automatically and forthwith discharged and removed from authority and duties of a fiduciary or trustee hereunder should he or she be deemed disabled or incompetent as defined herein. A Trustee or Settlor ("the questionable trustee") shall be deemed so disabled or incompetent to act as a trustee if any other Trustee hereunder shall receive in his possession any one of the following: **(a)** a writing from the questionable trustee's physician and a writing from a member of the questionable trustee's immediate family or another Trustee stating that the questionable trustee is too disabled or incompetent to make rational or prudent judgments or handle his personal affairs; **(b)** a court order which he deems jurisdictionally proper and currently applicable holding that the questionable trustee is legally incompetent to act on his own behalf, or appointing a guardian of his person and/or property to act for him; **(c)** duly executed, witnessed, and acknowledged written certificates of two (2) licensed physicians (each of whom represents that he or she is certified by a recognized medical board), each certifying that he has examined the questionable trustee and has concluded that, by reason of accident, physical or mental illness, progressive or intermittent physical or mental deterioration or other similar cause, the questionable person is incompetent or disabled to act rationally and prudently in the questionable trustee's best interests, the interests of the Settlor, or the interest of other beneficiaries hereunder; **(d)** evidence deemed credible and currently applicable that the questionable trustee has disappeared, is unaccountably absent, or is being detained under duress and, thus, unable to effectively and prudently look after his financial interests or that of the Settlor or other beneficiaries hereunder; **(e)** proof that the questionable Trustee is an inmate of or has entered into confinement, residence, or daily care of a skilled or custodial nursing home, mental institution, jail, or prison; or **(f)** proof that the questionable trustee (or someone in his behalf) has applied for, is being considered for, intends to apply for, or is entitled to receive (but for availability of payments or distributions to be made or which may be made under this Agreement) governmental assistance funds based on financial need of such questionable trustee, by reason of the questionable trustee's health, physical or mental condition.

2.   Restoration of Trusteeship Authority: If any of the writings, proofs, certificates, or orders as noted above in this Subparagraph D be negated, changed, canceled, or abrogated to the benefit of the questionable person, the questionable person who was removed from fiduciary authority shall automatically be restored to full fiduciary power and authority and rights of decision or election reserved to him by this Agreement.

ARTICLE VII

APPOINTMENT OF TRUSTEES

A.   APPOINTMENT

Settlor hereby nominates and appoints and, or the survivor of them, as Co-Trustees of this Trust.

B.   APPOINTMENT OF SUCCESSOR

1.   Succession: Upon the death, incompetence, resignation, or discharge of any of the above named as Co-Trustees, the survivor(s) of them shall be the Successor Co-Trustees, even if one (1) alone survives.

2.   Resignation: Any Trustee or Successor Trustee may resign by instrument in writing.

3.   Rights: Any Successor Trustee shall have all the rights, powers, duties, and discretion conferred or imposed on the original Trustee. No Trustee shall be liable for any act or omission unless the same be due to such Trustee's own default. In no event shall a corporate trustee be a corporation owned or controlled by any beneficiary hereof.

4.   Responsibility: Any Successor Trustee shall become responsible for the applicable Trust Estate only when, as, and if the same shall be received by said Trustee and, in determining such estate, such Trustee shall only be responsible to make a reasonable inquiry from the records of the prior Trustee which are available.

5.   New Appointment: If none of the above named Trustees or Successor Trustees shall be serving as such, whether by reason of death, resignation, incompetence, or discharge, the then current income beneficiary or beneficiaries who are of legal age and the guardians of any incompetent or minor current income beneficiary or beneficiaries shall appoint a Successor Trustee. Such Successor Trustee must be one (1) or more of such competent beneficiaries of legal age, a trust company, bank or attorney qualified to act as such, and if a bank or trust company, must possess trust powers, and such Successor Trustee must be approved by all such beneficiaries unanimously. In the event the current income beneficiary or beneficiaries shall fail to so designate promptly a Successor Trustee, the then acting Trustee or any beneficiary shall apply to a court of proper jurisdiction for such appointment and for settlement of account. In no event shall such Successor Trustee be a beneficiary who is to be paid his or her share of income and/or principal over a period of time rather than in one sum, or who is defined as a minor in this Agreement. In no event shall *(disabled child)* be a Trustee.

6.   Signatures and Decisions: Except as noted in Article V-B as to creditor ˉns, all acts, deeds, and transactions, including but not limited to, banking, ˉes, and real estate transactions of any kind, nature, or amount, with regard st Agreement or pursuant thereto, shall require the signature of only ˉe, even though there shall be Co-Trustees available to act.

C.   BOND

It is Settlor's request and direction that no bond or other security shall be required of any Trustee named hereunder.

D.   DISCRETION

Each decision, act, transaction, and deed of a named Trustee herein shall be deemed discretionary and not subject to judicial review in any jurisdiction unless a fraudulent, wanton, criminal, or grossly negligent act of a Trustee is first proven against him. No Trustee shall be liable or responsible for an erroneous act or omission made in good faith.

ARTICLE VIII

MISCELLANEOUS

The paragraph and article headings used herein are for convenience only and shall not be resorted to for interpretation of this Trust. Wherever the context so requires, the masculine gender shall include the feminine and neuter gender (and vice versa) and the singular shall include the plural (and vice versa). Wherever the terms "Settlors" or "Trustees" (plural) are noted they shall also mean "Settlor" or "Trustee" (singular), as the case may be, and vice versa, unless the context would preclude such interpretation. If any portion of this Trust is judicially held to be void or unenforceable, the balance of this Trust shall nevertheless be carried into effect.

IN WITNESS WHEREOF, the parties specified above as Settlor and the Co-Trustees have signed and sealed this Trust Agreement as of the day of ___, 20.

Settlor   Trustee

               Trustee

The foregoing instrument, consisting of typewritten pages and "Exhibit A" attached, was signed, sealed, published, and declared by the Settlor to be their trust agreement, which they understood and agree to, in our presence and the presence of each other, and we, at the Settlor's request and in Settlor's presence and in the presence of each other, have hereunto subscribed our hands as witnesses this day of ___, 20.

Residing at

Residing at

State of Florida

County of

Before me personally appeared as Settlor and Co-Trustees above noted, to me well known and known to me to be the person described in and who executed the foregoing Trust Agreement and who acknowledged to and before me that he executed said instrument in the capacities and for the purposes therein expressed.

WITNESS my hand and official seal this day of ___, 20.

Notary Public

My Commission Expires:

ACCEPTANCE BY TRUSTEE LEGISLATIVELY MANDATED NOTICE TO TRUSTEES

There are rules, statutes, court cases, and other sources of law and guidance which affect a Trustee's duties and responsibilities. While the terms contained in this document are very important to the administration of the trust, the trust language cannot be read without reference to those other sources of law and guidance. The Florida Legislature recognizes that the duties and responsibilities of the Trustee may be unfamiliar to many people. To encourage Trustees to seek professional advice in the administration of trusts, the legislature now requires the following notice to appear in all trust agreements:

The Trustee of a trust may have duties and responsibilities in addition to those described in the instrument creating the trust. If you have questions you should obtain legal advice.

The undersigned hereby accept the trust imposed by the Trust Agreement and agree to serve as Trustees upon the terms and conditions therein set forth.

SIGNED, SEALED, AND DELIVERED

IN THE PRESENCE OF:

Witness #1 Signature   TRUSTEE

Witness #2 Signature

EXHIBIT "A" of the IRREVOCABLE TRUST dated ___, 20 TEN ($10.00) DOLLARS

16. N.Y. STATUTE GOVERNING
SPECIAL NEEDS TRUSTS

E.P.T.L. § 7–1.12 Supplemental needs trusts established for persons with severe and chronic or persistent disabilities

(e)(1) The following language may be used as part of a trust instrument, but is not required, to qualify a trust as a supplemental needs trust:

1. The property shall be held, IN TRUST, for the benefit of (hereinafter the "beneficiary") and shall be held, managed, invested an reinvested by the trustee, who shall collect the income therefrom and, after deducting all charges and expenses properly attributable thereto, shall, at any time and from time to time, apply for the benefit of the beneficiary, so much (even to the extent of the whole) of the net income and/or principal of this trust as the trustee shall deem advisable, in his or her sole and absolute discretion, subject to the limitations set forth below. The trustee shall add to the principal of such trust the balance of net income not so paid or applied.

2. It is the grantor's intent to create a supplemental needs trust which conforms to the provisions of section 7–1.12 of the New York estates, powers and trusts law. The grantor intends that the trust assets be used to supplement, not supplant, impair or diminish, any benefits or assistance of any federal, state, county, city, or other governmental entity for which the beneficiary may otherwise be eligible or which the beneficiary may be receiving. Consistent with that intent, it is the grantor's desire that, before expending any amounts from the net income and/or principal of this trust, the trustee consider the availability of all benefits from government or private assistance programs for which the beneficiary may be eligible and that, where appropriate and to the extent possible, the trustee endeavor to maximize the collection of such benefits and to facilitate the distribution of such benefits for the benefit of the beneficiary.

3. None of the income or principal of this trust shall be applied in such a manner as to supplant, impair or diminish benefits or assistance of any federal, state, county, city, or other governmental entity for which the beneficiary may otherwise be eligible or which the beneficiary may be receiving.

4. The beneficiary does not have the power to assign, encumber, direct, distribute or authorize distributions from this trust.

(2)(i) If the creator elects, the following additional language may be used:

5. Notwithstanding the provisions of paragraphs two and three above, the trustee may make distributions to meet the beneficiary's need for food, clothing,

shelter or health care even if such distributions may result in an impairment or diminution of the beneficiary's receipt or eligibility for government benefits or assistance but only if the trustee determines that (i) the beneficiary's needs will be better met if such distribution is made, and (ii) it is in the beneficiary's best interests to suffer the consequent effect, if any, on the beneficiary's eligibility for or receipt of government benefits or assistance.

(ii)   If the trustee is provided with the authority to make the distributions as described in subparagraph (2)(i), the creator may elect to add the following clause:

provided, however, that if the mere existence of the trustee's authority to make distributions pursuant to this paragraph shall result in the beneficiary's loss of government benefits or assistance, regardless of whether such authority is actually exercised, this paragraph shall be null and void and the trustee's authority to make such distributions shall cease and shall be limited as provided in paragraphs two and three above, without exception.

17.   DEED TO CREATE JOINT TENANCY[7]

DEED

[Name of sole owner] hereby grants to *[name of sole owner]* and to *[name of joint tenant]*, as joint tenants, the real property situated in *[name of county]*, State of California, described as follows: *[description of real property]*.

Dated: *[date of deed]*

[Name of sole owner]

[Acknowledgment]

---

[7]   Source: Jeanne P. Robinson, *Deed—Joint tenancy—Sole owner to self and others*, WEST'S CAL. CODE FORMS, Civil § 683 Form 1 (5th ed. 2015). This form is reprinted with permission of Thomson Reuters.

18. BENEFICIARY DESIGNATION

Fidelity INVESTMENTS **Questions?** Go to fidelity.com/beneficiary or call 1-800-544-6666.

Beneficiaries – Transfer on Death

Use this form to establish or update the beneficiaries on a Transfer on Death (TOD) registration on your non-retirement Fidelity Account or Fidelity Funds Account. Do NOT use for retirement accounts or 529 College Savings Plans. Type on screen or print out and fill in using CAPITAL letters and black ink. If you need more room for information or signatures, use a copy of the relevant page.

Helpful To Know

- **This form preempts any terms in your will concerning the accounts in question.** You may want to review this document with a tax, financial, or legal adviser.
- Tenants-in-common cannot have TOD registrations.

- This form cancels any existing beneficiary information. Be sure this form includes ALL beneficiaries you want on the account(s).
- You can change beneficiaries any time at fidelity.com/beneficiary. To add or change beneficiaries on other types of accounts, go to fidelity.com/forms.

1. Account Owner

Phone numbers will be used if we have questions but will not be used to update your account information. ▶

Name

Evening Phone   Daytime Phone   Extension

2. Accounts Included

For new accounts, attach a copy of account opening form instead of listing account numbers below.

List all accounts you want this form to apply to. To indicate different beneficiaries for different accounts, use copies of this form.

Fidelity Account Number   Fidelity Account Number   Fidelity Account Number

Fidelity Account Number   Fidelity Account Number   Fidelity Account Number

3. Beneficiaries

Primary Beneficiaries

For each beneficiary you list by name, check a beneficiary type and provide all information.

A "non-spouse" is any individual who is not your spouse under federal law.

As an alternative to listing each child by name, you can check "Non-Spouse" and enter "All my children" in the Name box.

If you outlive the beneficiary and you want that beneficiary's share to go to his or her descendants, check "per stirpes."

☐ Spouse
☐ Non-Spouse
☐ Trust
☐ Other Entity

Name If naming spouse as a beneficiary, do so here.

Social Security or Taxpayer ID Number   Date of Birth MM DD YYYY   Share Percentage __%   ☐ Per stirpes

☐ Non-Spouse
☐ Trust
☐ Other Entity

Name

Social Security or Taxpayer ID Number   Date of Birth MM DD YYYY   Share Percentage __%   ☐ Per stirpes

☐ Non-Spouse
☐ Trust
☐ Other Entity

Name

Social Security or Taxpayer ID Number   Date of Birth MM DD YYYY   Share Percentage __%   ☐ Per stirpes

☐ Non-Spouse
☐ Trust
☐ Other Entity

Name

Social Security or Taxpayer ID Number   Date of Birth MM DD YYYY   Share Percentage __%   ☐ Per stirpes

Total must add up to 100%. 0 %

Beneficiaries continues on next page. ▶ ▶

19. 1909 MILTON HERSHEY TRUST[8]

1909 Trust, Hershey Trust Company
Milton S. Hershey, et ux. to Hershey Trust Company.
Hershey Industrial School.

This Indenture Made the Fifteenth day of November, in the year of our Lord One Thousand Nine Hundred and Nine (1909);

Between Milton S. Hershey and Catharine S. Hershey, his wife, of Hershey, Derry Township, Dauphin County, Pennsylvania, parties of the first part, and the Hershey Trust Company of the same place, hereinafter designated as Trustee, party of the second part, and M. S. Hershey, of Hershey, W. H. Lebkicher, and John E. Snyder of Lancaster, John B. Curry and A. W. Stauffer, of Swatara, John A. Landis, of Manada Hill, George M. Hocker, of Union Deposit, Israel Moyer, of Derry Church, and U. G. Risser, of Campbellstown, Pennsylvania, hereinafter designated as Managers, parties of the third part,

Witnesseth: That the parties of the first part, with the purpose of founding and endowing in perpetuity an institution to be known as The Hershey Industrial School; hereinafter designated as the School, to be located in Derry Township, aforesaid, do hereby make, constitute, and appoint M. S. Hershey, W. H. Lebkicher, John B. Curry, John A. Landis, George M. Hocker, A. W. Stauffer, John E. Snyder, Israel Moyer, and U. G. Risser, and their successors, appointed as hereinafter directed, to erect, equip, maintain, direct and manage the school, upon, under, and subject to the trusts and conditions hereinafter declared of and concerning the same, which Managers and their successors shall be known as the Managers of the Hershey Industrial School, and for that purpose, and for other good and lawful considerations, hereby acknowledged, have granted, bargained, sold, aliened, enfeoffed, released, conveyed and confirmed, and by these presents do grant, bargain, sell, alien, enfeoff, release convey, and confirm unto the said party of the second part, its successors and assigns.

All those certain farms situated in the Township of Derry, Dauphin County, Pennsylvania, bounded and described in one tract of land as follows [descriptions of the real property are omitted]

Together with all and singular the stock, implements, tools machinery, apparatus, and all other personal property thereon, the buildings, improvements, woods, ways, rights, liberties, privileges, hereditaments, and appurtenances, to the same belonging, or in any wise appertaining, and the reversion and

---

[8] Available at: http://www.protecthersheychildren.org/resources/Historical/MiltonHershey SchoolDeedofTrustNovember151909Modifications.pdf.

reversions, remainder and remainders, rents, issues and profits thereof, and every part and parcel thereof, and all the estate, right, title, interest, use trust property, possession claim and demand whatsoever, both in law and equity, of the said parties of the first part, of, in, and to the said premises, stock implements, tools, machinery, apparatus and personal property, with the appurtenances, to have and to hold the said premises, stock, implements, tools, machinery, apparatus and personal property, with all and singular, the appurtenances, unto the said party of the second part, its successors and assigns, to the only proper use, benefit and behoof of the said party of the second part, its successors and assigns forever, upon and subject to the trusts and confidences and for the several, uses, intents and purposes herein after mentioned declared of and concerning the same, that is to say: in trust for a permanent institution for the residence and accommodation of poor white male orphans, and the requisite teachers and other persons necessary in and about such an institution, and the maintenance, support, and education, as hereinafter prescribed of such orphans: to collect and receive the rents, revenues, and income therefrom and apply the entire net revenue, income, rents, issues and profits thereof to support and maintain the said institution, and increase the facilities and efficiency thereof according to the directions hereinafter contained; to permit the said Managers, and their agents and employees under their direction, to take charge of, farms and operate the lands hereby conveyed, under such terms and conditions as they think proper, and to use the same in such manner as is in their discretion most advantageous to the purposes of the trust, to keep the said lands and buildings thereon in good repair, to renew and improve the same when necessary by erecting new buildings thereon, to direct and supervise the disposition of the products thereof, the revenues or income derived therefrom to be paid to and received and collected by the Trustee as hereinbefore provided.

1.   If it so happen in the future that gifts, bequests, devises of real or personal property may be made to or for the benefit of the School, the Trustee and the Managers are authorized to accept all such gifts, bequests, devises, whenever the terms, conditions, restrictions, or limitations of such gifts, bequests, devises, are not in the opinion of the Trustee and Managers in contravention of the objects and purposes of this deed, and all such gifts, bequests, devises, whether made to the school by name, or to the Trustee, or to the Managers, or in any manner whatever, shall be paid or transferred by proper conveyance to the Trustee, and be added to and become part of the corpus or principal of the trust estate or of the income, in aid of which the said gifts, bequests, devises, or any of them may have been made; in the absence of any

direction accompanying any such gift, bequest, devise, as to whether the corpus or principal of the trust estate or income is intended to be the recipient of such gift, bequest, devise the Managers shall have the power to determine to which of the funds, or in what proportion to both, such gift, bequest, or devise, shall be paid or transferred, provided however, that if any lands or other real property shall be given conveyed, or devised, to be held, enjoyed or used for the benefit or purposes of the School, the title to the same shall be held by the Trustee under the same trusts as are herein declared of and concerning the lands conveyed to the Trustee, and with the same power to sell and dispose of the said lands or other real property so given, conveyed, or devised, and under the same trusts, as to the proceeds thereof, as are hereinafter declared of and concerning lands which may be sold by the said Trustee and Managers.

2.   The Trustee shall on or before the first day of September in each year make out and deliver to the Managers separate statements of principal and income of the trust estate, showing the revenues, receipts, expenses, and disbursements for the year ending with the thirty-first day of July immediately preceding, showing what investments have been sold, redeemed, or paid and what securities have been bought, acquired, or received, during the year, and a statement showing in detail in what property and securities the trust estate was invested on the preceding thirty-first day of July.

3.   The corpus or principal, and the income of the trust estate shall at all times be kept separate and apart from each other by the Trustee, and separate and true accounts of the corpus or principal and income shall be kept by the Trustee, and at all times during the customary business hours of the Trustee, the Managers shall have access to the said accounts. At least once in every year it shall be the duty of the Trustee to exhibit to the Managers, and the duty of the Managers carefully to examine and count the several securities, and to verify them with the statements and accounts furnished and kept by the Trustee.

4.   The Trustee shall pay from time to time, upon request of the managers, the net income from the premises hereby conveyed and of any future gifts, bequests, and devises, when, and as the same may be required by them, or so much thereof as in the opinion of the Managers may be necessary, to furnish the amount or amounts of money required by the Managers for the purpose of erecting on the premises above mentioned, buildings and improvements for the farms and School, and procuring furniture, stock, materials, machinery, tools, implements, plant, and equipment for the same, for the expenses, support, maintenance, management, renewals, and repairs of the farms and School, its furniture, plant, and equipment, or for the purpose at any time of enlarging,

extending or adding to either or all of said buildings, furniture, plant, and equipment,—the decision of the Managers when expressed in writing and delivered to the Trustee, as to whether the said income, or any part thereof, is or is not required for the purposes mentioned, shall be final and conclusive and binding upon the Trustee, and the receipt of the Managers to the Trustee for all moneys paid to them by the Trustee out of the income, shall be full and sufficient acquittance and discharge of the sums so paid, without any obligation on the part of the Trustee to look to the application of the said moneys.

5.   The funds of the principal of the trust estate and the unexpended income of the property held in trust, not immediately needed for the purposes of the School, shall be invested, and the Trustee at all times by and with the authority and approval of the Managers shall have full power and authority to invest all or any part thereof in any securities which the Trustee and the Managers together may consider safe, whether the said securities or any of them are legal investments for trust funds or not, and neither the Trustee nor the Managers shall be held accountable for the exercise of its and their discretion, exercised in good faith, as to the character of the investments which may be made by the authority and approval of both. No sale of any securities shall at any time be made by the Trustee, without the authority and approval of the Managers, and no investments of any money shall at any time be made by the Trustee except by and with the approval of the Managers.

6.   The Trustee may from time to time, but only with the approval of the managers, sell and convey in fee simple any part or portion of the lands conveyed by this deed, or which may have been bought or otherwise acquired, which in the Judgment of the Managers is not necessary to be kept for the purposes of the School, or which it may be advisable and advantageous to sell, and may execute and deliver a deed, or deeds, or other conveyance for the lands so sold, to the purchaser or purchasers in fee simple, free and discharged of all trusts, and without any obligation on the part of the purchaser or purchasers to look to the application of the purchase money; the purchase money of land so sold shall be held by the Trustee, and invested as herein provided for, and the income therefrom applied to the maintenance of the School. No part of the proceeds of the sale of any land, or of the principal of the trust as it now is, or additions thereto, by gift or otherwise, shall ever be expended for any purpose whatever, except for the purchase of additional land for the purposes of the School.

7.   The Trustee may from time to time, and at any time, but only with the approval of the Managers, purchase any additional land adjoining the School

property, or conveniently near to it, and take title to the same in itself as Trustee under this deed, and hold the same under and subject to the trusts herein set forth, if they consider such land necessary or convenient for the purposes of the School.

8. No part of the corpus or principal of the trust estate, or of the income, or of the proceeds of any real estate sold, arising from the property hereby conveyed, or gifts, bequests, or devises or other accretions thereto, and all moneys and securities arising therefrom, or made with or acquired by the principal or income thereof or accretion thereto, shall at any time be applied to any other purpose or purposes than those herein mentioned and appointed; and in no event shall any part of the corpus or principal of the trust estate ever be used or sold, disposed of or pledged to meet current expenses of the institution for which the current and accumulated income and revenues are exclusively devoted.

9. The Trustee shall receive as its full compensation for the duties required to be performed by it under this deed a commission of five per cent of the income received by it as Trustee, not exceeding however the sum of One Thousand Dollars per annum, and shall make no charge against, and receive no compensation from the corpus or principal of the trust estate. All moneys received by the Managers from the Trustee shall be received, held, and used by the Managers for, upon, and subject to the trusts and confidences, and for the uses and purposes hereinafter declared of and concerning the same, and for none other, that is to say:

10. Out of the moneys received by the Managers from the Trustee, from the revenue or income, to erect suitable buildings, and appurtenances, to lodge, board, and instruct, as many orphans as, in the opinion of the Managers, the revenue and other sources of income, authorized to be expended for the purpose, will provide for to lodge and board as many other persons, such as officers, teachers, agents, workmen, and servants, as in the opinion of the Managers it may be necessary or convenient shall reside upon the premises, for the purpose of fully carrying out the design in view, and of completely establishing and successfully maintaining the School herein intended to be founded; to furnish and fully equip the School with such furniture, materials, machinery, tools, books, equipment, and all things needful to carry into effect the general purpose, as in the judgment of the Managers may be necessary or convenient for the purpose; to pay the insurance, repairs, and renewals of the property, to pay the compensation of officers, agents, teachers, workmen, servants or other employees, materials and supplies, the maintenance, clothing,

and instruction of the orphans, the expense of boarding and lodging such officers and employees whom the Managers may think it proper shall reside at the School, and any other charge or expense contracted or payable by the Managers for, or by reason of the management, maintenance, support, renewal, improvement or repair of the School, its appurtenances, the plant, and equipment thereto belonging and of the lands, buildings, and improvements under their care and management. The decision of the Managers as to what are or may be necessary expenses for the maintenance, support, management, renewal, or repairs of the School, and its appurtenances, the plant and equipment thereto belonging or appertaining, and of the lands, buildings and improvements under their care and management, shall be final and conclusive upon the subject.

11. The institution shall be known as "The Hershey Industrial School; and shall be permanently located in Derry Township, Dauphin County, Pa., upon the land hereby conveyed.

12. The Managers shall employ from time to time, at proper compensation to be fixed and established by them, a competent number of teachers, agents, mechanics, workmen, and servants, necessary to take charge of the said farms and School, and to feed, clothe, educate, and instruct in trades, as hereinafter provided, all orphans admitted to the School, and for other purposes necessary to carry out the objects in view; but no person shall be employed who shall not be of tried skill in his or her proper department, and of established moral character.

13. The institution shall be organized as soon as practicable, and when prepared to receive orphans, the Managers shall from time to time receive and admit to the School as many poor, healthy, white, male orphans of such ages between four and eight years, as may from time to time be determined by the Managers, as in the opinion of the Managers, the extent, capacity, and income of the School will provide for, and shall be adequate to maintain, and from time to time as there may be vacancies, or increased ability from income may warrant, others shall be admitted. The term orphan in this deed designates a child whose father is deceased.

14. On application for admission, an accurate statement shall be taken, in a book prepared for the purpose, of the name, birthplace, age, health, condition as to relatives, and other particulars useful to be known of each orphan.

Those orphans for whose admission application shall first be made, shall be first introduced, and all things concurring, and at all future times, priority of application shall entitle the applicant to preference of admission, all other things concurring, but if there should be at any time more applicants than vacancies, and the applying orphans shall have been born in different places, preference shall be given in the admission: First,—to those born in the Counties of Dauphin, Lancaster, and Lebanon, State of Pennsylvania; Second,—to those born elsewhere in Pennsylvania; Third,—to those born elsewhere in the United States. No orphan who has been properly admitted with reference to the order of preference shall thereafter be displaced to make way for any later or subsequent applicant who may be higher in the order of preference hereinbefore directed to be observed. The decision of the Managers as to the number of orphans to be admitted, and as to the conflicting claims of any or all applicants for admission, shall be final and conclusive.

15. No orphans shall be admitted until the surviving parent, guardian, or other competent authority shall have given by indenture, release, relinquishment, or other lawful acquittance, for such period as the Managers may determine, adequate power to the Managers, or others by them appointed, to enforce, in relation to each orphan, every proper restraint, and to prevent relatives, friends, or others from interfering with, or withdrawing such orphans from the institution.

16. Those orphans who merit it may remain in the School until they shall respectively arrive at eighteen years of age.

17. All orphans admitted to the School shall be fed with plain, wholesome food; plainly, neatly, and comfortably clothed, without distinctive dress, and fitly lodged. Due regard shall be paid to their health; their physical training shall be attended to, and they shall have suitable and proper exercise and recreation. They shall be instructed in the several branches of a sound education, agriculture, horticulture, gardening, such mechanical trades and handicrafts as the Managers may determine, and such natural and physical sciences and practical mathematics as in the opinion of the Managers it may be important for them to acquire, and such other learning and science as the tastes, capacities, and adaptability of the several scholars may merit or warrant, to fit themselves for the trades they are to learn, and a useful occupation in life. No one fixed or established course shall be taken by all scholars, this being in the discretion of the Managers, bearing in mind that the main object in view is to train young men to useful trades and occupations, so that they can earn their own livelihood. Each and every scholar shall be required to learn, and be thoroughly instructed in some occupation or mechanical trade, so that when he leaves the School on the completion of the period for which he is to remain, he may be able to support himself. The Managers shall determine the several kinds of mechanical

trades to be taught, and the determination of the particular one that shall be taught to and acquired by each scholar, the taste, capacity, intelligence, and adaptability of each scholar being ascertained and considered before assigning him to any particular trade; one of the objects of the School being to teach and instruct in agriculture, horticulture, and gardening, each orphan admitted to the School shall at such time or times as may be required, do such work upon the farms as may suit his capacity and ability.

18.   The School shall be non-sectarian, but the moral and religious training of the scholars shall be properly looked after and cared for by the Managers. No favoritism shall be shown by the Managers to any particular sect or creed. Each scholar shall be taught to speak the truth at all times, and each and every scholar shall be thoroughly trained to habits of economy, and industry.

19.   All the advantages and benefits to be derived by the scholars under this deed, shall be in every respect gratuitous, and under no circumstances shall any charge be made to any scholar, or any fees, rewards, or other compensations be accepted by the Managers from or on account of any scholar.

20.   If, in the opinion of the Managers, any orphan admitted to the School should become incompetent to learn, or to master a trade, or from physical ailments it would be inexpedient for him to continue his studies and training, or become insubordinate, to be guilty of vice or crime, or become an unfit companion for the others, or has so conducted himself as not worthy of future and continued support and education, or is so competent to work at his chosen trade, that he is qualified to be self supporting, he may be removed or expelled from the School by the Managers, and all indentures, releases, or other acquittances, shall be so drawn as to permit this to be done. The decision of the Managers as to whether a scholar deserves removal or expulsion, shall be final and conclusive upon the subject. The Managers may cancel the indentures, releases, or acquittances, of any orphan, dismiss him from their care, and remove him from the School, for any reason which in their judgment is good and sufficient.

21.   All orphans shall leave the institution and cease to be the recipients of its benefits on the arrival at the age of eighteen years. The Managers may in their discretion provide for such a system of premiums and rewards dependent upon good behavior, character, proficiency, as shall enable those of the scholars entitled to its benefits to receive from the Managers, when they leave the School at the full expiration of their term, a sum of money not exceeding one hundred dollars to any one scholar, which sum of money shall be paid by the Managers out of any of the moneys received by them as income of the School, or the

Managers may, out of the income, if sufficient for the purpose, before or after the arrival of the scholar at the age of eighteen, provide for or contribute toward the further education of the scholar at some other school, college, or university.

22. All moneys received by the Managers from the sale of products, stock, material, or manufactured articles, or from any source other than those hereinabove described, shall be paid to the Trustee, and expended for the same purposes as are hereinabove prescribed and directed for the expenditure of the income.

23. The Managers shall at all times keep full and accurate statements, in books to be provided by them for the purpose, of all orphans entering, remaining in, and leaving the School, showing their several names, parentage, birthplaces, ages, admission, and departure, and designation of trade learned; and so far as any information upon the subject can readily and without unnecessary expense be obtained, the Managers shall cause a record to be kept and preserved of the residence, occupation, condition, and success in life of all scholars who have fully completed their term, for a period of ten years after their departure from the School.

24. The Managers shall at all times keep books and accounts of the financial condition of the farms and Schools, showing the amount and value of all real and personal property belonging thereto, and exhibiting in detail all receipts and disbursements. In the month of September of each year the Managers shall make a report of the operations of the farms and School for the year ending with the preceding thirty-first day of July, showing the receipts and expenditures of the Managers and the operations of the farms and School during the year. The report must include a statement showing the exact financial condition of the farms, and School at the end of the year, and an inventory and valuation of all the property, stock, implements, machinery, tools, apparatus, and shall be accompanied by other information of the condition of the School, the number of scholars, which the Managers may desire to give, and a copy of said report, signed by the Managers, shall be delivered by the Managers to the Trustee, in the said month of September, and be filed and preserved by the Trustee among the records of its trust.

25. Should any one or more of the individual Managers hereinabove appointed, die, resign, or become incapacitated to act, or decline or refuse to act, his, or their place or places shall be filled by an appointment to be made by the Trustee, from the members of its own Board of Directors, and any vacancy occurring at any time in the number of Managers by any of the above causes, or otherwise howsoever, whether among the Managers herein appointed, or among

those that may be selected to fill a vacancy as herein prescribed, or among their successors to be appointed as aforesaid, shall be filled by an appointment to be made by the Trustee, from the members of its own Board of Directors. The Trustee may at any time hereafter revoke the appointment of any person or persons herein designated as Managers, or of those who become their successors, and remove such person or persons from the Managers and thereafter the person or persons whose appointment is revoked shall no longer exercise the duties of the appointment; the vacancy or vacancies so created shall be filled by an appointment to be made by the Trustee in the Manner herein above described from the members of its own Board of Directors. The Managers and the Trustee may at any times hereafter increase the number of Managers to such a number as they may determine, not greater than the membership of the Board of Directors of the Trustee.

26.   The Managers shall annually elect one of their number as Chairman. The person acting at the time as Treasurer to the Trustee shall be Treasurer of the Board of Managers. They shall appoint a Secretary, and prescribe the duties of the Treasurer and Secretary. The Treasurer shall give bond with good surety in such penal sum as the Managers shall determine, conditioned for the faithful performance of his duties. The offices of Treasurer and Secretary may be filled by one person, and in case of vacancy in the offices of Chairman or Secretary at any time, the Managers shall elect a successor to fill the vacancy. The Managers shall notify the Trustee in writing of their organization, and of the election of Chairman and Secretary, and of any changes in either office as the same may occur. The assent of a Majority of the Managers shall be necessary for the approval of any act.

27.   All and several the trusts herein created and declared shall be held in perpetuity.

28.   If in the opinion of the Managers it may be advantageous and convenient that they should be incorporated, and as a corporation hold and exercise the trusts herein created and directed to be held and exercised by the Managers as individuals, the Managers shall have full power and authority at their option to apply for and obtain and take corporate powers and become a corporation under the laws of the State of Pennsylvania existing at the time of the application for such corporate powers: Always provided however, and subject to the following express conditions, viz:—That the said corporation shall hold its charter in perpetuity, that it shall be called "The Hershey Industrial School", that the Managers holding the trust at the time of the granting of the charter, shall be the sole incorporators and managers of said corporation; that

the rights and powers to fill vacancies in their numbers as such incorporators and managers, be subject to the same restrictions as are hereinabove given and imposed in cases of vacancies among the individual managers, and that the said corporation, under and by virtue of the law or laws of the Commonwealth of Pennsylvania existing at the time of its creation, shall have full and complete legal authority to take and execute the trusts hereinabove created and intended to be exercised and held by the Managers as individuals, to exercise and enjoy as such corporation all the trusts herein created to be exercised and enjoyed by the said individual Managers, with all the powers and authorities, and under and subject to all the conditions, restrictions, and limitations as are herein given, granted, created, prescribed, and declared of and concerning the said trusts to be held and exercised by the said individual Managers; and upon such corporation being formed as aforesaid, it, the said corporation, by name shall thenceforth hold and enjoy all the trusts hereinabove declared and created and intended to be held and exercised by the individual Managers aforesaid, and be and become the successors in the trust of the said Managers. And upon said corporation being formed as aforesaid, the said Managers shall forthwith give notice thereof in writing to the Trustee, and thereafter the said corporation shall be consulted by the Trustee in the matter of the sale and purchase of securities, and have the same power and authority in the matter of the sale and purchase of securities and investments and reinvestments, and in all other matters, as is given to the Managers under this deed; and the said corporation shall thenceforth be entitled to receive from the Trustee, and the Trustee shall pay over to the corporation, all moneys which by this deed are hereinabove directed to be paid by the Trustee to the Managers, and the corporation shall take, receive, and hold the said money subject to all trusts and confidences hereinabove declared of and concerning the same with like effect to all intents and purposes as if the said corporation had been named in this deed instead of the Managers hereinabove named.

20. WILL OF BERNICE PAUAHI BISHOP

Dated October 31, 1883[9]

Pauahi's Will

[The original will is kept by the Hawai'i State Archives and is handwritten on ruled legal stationery that fills approximately 40 pages.]

Know all Men by these Presents, That I, Bernice Pauahi Bishop, the wife of Charles R. Bishop, of Honolulu, Island of Oahu, Hawaiian Islands, being of sound mind and memory, but conscious of the uncertainty of life, do make, publish and declare this my last Will and Testament in manner following, hereby revoking all former wills by me made:

First. I give and bequeath unto my namesakes, E. Bernice Bishop Dunham, niece of my husband, now residing in San Joaquim County, California, Bernice Parke, daughter of W. C. Parke Esq., of Honolulu, Bernice Bishop Barnard, daughter of the late John E. Barnard Esq. of Honolulu, Bernice Bates, daughter of Mr. Dudley C. Bates, of San Francisco, California, Annie Pauahi Cleghorn of Honolulu, Lilah Bernice Wodehouse, daughter of Major J. H. Wodehouse, of Honolulu, and Pauahi Judd the daughter of Col. Charles H. Judd of Honolulu, the sum of Two hundred Dollars ($200.) each.

Second. I give and bequeath unto Mrs. William F. Allen, Mrs. Amoe Haalelea, Mrs. Antone Rosa, and Mrs. Nancy Ellis, the sum of Two Hundred Dollars ($200.) each.

Third. I give and bequeath unto Mrs. Caroline Bush, widow of A .W. Bush, Mrs. Sarah Parmenter, wife of Gilbert Parmenter Mrs. Keomailani Taylor, wife of Mr. Wray Taylor, to their sole and separate use free from the control of their husbands, and to Mrs. Emma Barnard, widow of the late John E Barnard Esq. the sum of Five hundred dollars ($500.) each.

Fourth. I give, devise and bequeath unto H. R. H. Liliuokalani, the wife of Gov. John O. Dominis, all of those tracts of land known as the "Ahupuaa of Lumahai," situated on the Island of Kauai, and the "Ahupuaa of Kealia", situated in South Kona Island of Hawaii; to have and to hold for and during the term of her natural life; and after her decease to my trustees upon the trusts below expressed.

Fifth. I give and bequeath unto Kahakuakoi (w) and Kealohapanole, her husband, and to the survivor of them, the sum of Thirty Dollars ($30.) per

---

9   Available at https://www.ksbe.edu/about_us/about_pauahi/will/.

month, (not $30. each) so long as either of them may live. And I also devise unto them and to their heirs of the body of either, the lot of land called "Mauna Kamala", situated at Kapalama Honolulu; upon default of issue the same to go to my trustees upon the trusts below expressed.

Sixth. I give and bequeath unto Mrs. Kapoli Kamakau, the sum of Forty Dollars ($40.) per month during her life; to my servant woman Kaia the sum of Thirty Dollars ($30.) per month during her life, and to Nakaahiki (w) the sum of Thirty Dollars ($30.) per month during her life.

Seventh. I give, devise and bequeath unto Kapaa (k) the house-lot he now occupies, situated between Merchant and Queen Streets in Honolulu, to have and to hold for and during the term of his natural life; upon his decease to my trustees upon the trusts below expressed.

Eighth. I give, devise and bequeath unto Auhea (w) tile wife of Lokana (k) the house-lot situated on the corner of Richard and Queen Streets, now occupied by G. W. Macfarlane & Co; to have and to hold for and during the term of her natural life; upon her decease to my trustees upon the trusts below expressed.

Ninth. I give, devise and bequeath unto my husband, Charles R. Bishop, all of the various tracts and parcels of land situated upon the Island of Molokai, comprising the "Molokai Ranch", and all of the live-stock and personal property thereon; being the same premises now under the care of R. W. Myer Esq.; and also all of the real property wherever situated, inherited by me from my parents, and also all of that devised to me by my aunt Akahi, except the two lands above devised to H. R. H. Liliuokalani for her life; and also all of my lands at Waikiki, Oahu, situated makai of the government main road leading to Kapiolani Park; to have and to hold together with all tenements, hereditaments, rights, privileges and appurtenances to the game appertaining, for and during the term of his natural life; and upon his decease to my trustees upon the trusts below expressed.

Tenth. I give, devise and bequeath unto Her Majesty Emma Kaleleonalani, Queen Dowager, as a token of my good will, all of the premises situated upon Emma Street in said Honolulu, known as Kaakopua, lately the residence of my cousin Keelikolani; to have and to hold with the appurtenances for and during the term of her natural life; and upon her decease to my trustees upon the trusts below expressed.

Eleventh. I give and bequeath the sum of Five thousand Dollars ($5000.) to be expended by my executors in repairs upon Kawaiahao Church building in Honolulu, or in improvements upon the same-

Twelfth. I give and bequeath the sum of Five thousand Dollars ($5000.) to be expended by my executors for the benefit of the Kawaiahao Family School for Girls (now under charge of Miss Norton) to be expended for additions either to the grounds, buildings or both.

Thirteenth. I give, devise and bequeath all of the rest, residue and remainder of my estate real and personal, wherever situated unto the trustees below named, their heirs and assigns forever, to hold upon the following trusts, namely: to erect and maintain in the Hawaiian Islands two schools, each for boarding and day scholars, one for boys and one for girls, to be known as, and called the Kamehameha Schools.

I direct my trustees to expend such amount as they may deem best, not to exceed however one-half of the fund which may come into their hands, in the purchase of suitable premises, the erection of school buildings, and in furnishing the same with the necessary and appropriate fixtures furniture and apparatus.

I direct my trustees to invest the remainder of my estate in such manner as they may think best, and to expend the annual income in the maintenance of said schools; meaning thereby the salaries of teachers, the repairing buildings and other incidental expenses; and to devote a portion of each years income to the support and education of orphans, and others in indigent circumstances, giving the preference to Hawaiians of pure or part aboriginal blood; the proportion in which said annual income is to be divided among the various objects above mentioned to be determined solely by my said trustees they to have full discretion.

I desire my trustees to provide first and chiefly a good education in the common English branches, and also instruction in morals and in such useful knowledge as may tend to make good and industrious men and women; and I desire instruction in the higher branches to be subsidiary to the foregoing objects.

For the purposes aforesaid I grant unto my said trustees full power to lease or sell any portion of my real estate, and to reinvest the proceeds and the balance of my estate in real estate, or in such other manner as to my said trustees may seem best.

I also give unto my said trustees full power to make all such rules and regulations as they may deem necessary for the government of said schools and to regulate the admission of pupils, and the same to alter, amend and publish upon a vote of a majority of said trustees.

I also direct that my said trustees shall annually make a full and complete report of all receipts and expenditures, and of the condition of said schools to the Chief Justice of the Supreme Court, or other highest judicial officer in this country; and shall also file before him annually an inventory of the property in their hands and how invested, and to publish the same in some Newspaper published in said Honolulu; I also direct my said trustees to keep said school buildings insured in good Companies, and in case of loss to expend the amounts recovered in replacing or repairing said buildings.

I also direct that the teachers of said schools shall forever be persons of the Protestant religion, but I do not intend that the choice should be restricted to persons of any particular sect of Protestants.

Fourteenth. I appoint my husband Charles R. Bishop, Samuel M. Damon, Charles M. Hyde, Charles M. Cooke, and William O. Smith, all of Honolulu, to be my trustees to carry into effect the trusts above specified.

I direct that a majority of my said trustees may act in all cases and may convey real estate and perform all of the duties and powers hereby conferred; but three of them at least must join in all acts.

I further direct that the number of my said trustees shall be kept at five; and that vacancies shall be filled by the choice of a majority of the Justices of the Supreme Court, the selection to be made from persons of the Protestant religion.

Fifteenth. In addition to the above devise to Queen Emma, I also give, devise and bequeath to her (said Emma Kaleleonalani Queen Dowager (sic) the Fish-pond in Kawaa, Honolulu near Oahu Prison, called "Kawa", for and during the term of her natural life; and after her decease to my trustees upon the trusts aforesaid.

Sixteenth. In addition to the above devise to my husband, I also give and bequeath to him, said Charles R. Bishop all of my personal property of every description, including cattle at Molokai; to have and to hold to him, his executors., administrators and assigns forever.

Seventeenth. I hereby nominate and appoint my husband Charles R. Bishop and Samuel M. Damon, executors of this my will.

In witness whereof I, said Bernice Pauahi Bishop, have hereunto set my hand and seal this thirty-first day of October A. D. Eighteen hundred and eighty-three.

BERNICE P. BISHOP (SEAL)

The foregoing instrument, written on eleven pages, was signed, sealed, published and declared by said Bernice Pauahi Bishop, as and for her last will and testament in our presence, who at her request, in her presence, and in the presence of each other, have hereunto set our names as witnesses thereto, this 31st day of October A. D. 1883.

F. W. MACFARLANE

FRANCIS M. HATCH

Index